Mathematical Methods in Data Science

Bridge the gap between theoretical concepts and their practical applications with this rigorous introduction to the mathematics underpinning data science. It covers essential topics in linear algebra, calculus and optimization, and probability and statistics, demonstrating their relevance in the context of data analysis. Key application topics include clustering, regression, classification, dimensionality reduction, network analysis, and neural networks. What sets this text apart is its focus on hands-on learning. Each chapter combines mathematical insights with practical examples, using Python to implement algorithms and solve problems. Self-assessment quizzes, warm-up exercises, and theoretical problems foster both mathematical understanding and computational skills. Designed for advanced undergraduate students and beginning graduate students, this textbook serves as both an invitation to data science for mathematics majors and as a deeper excursion into mathematics for data science students.

Sébastien Roch is a Vilas Distinguished Achievement Professor of Mathematics at the University of Wisconsin–Madison. At UW–Madison, he helped establish the Data Science Major and has developed several courses on the mathematics of data. He is the author of *Modern Discrete Probability: An Essential Toolkit* (2024).

CAMBRIDGE MATHEMATICAL TEXTBOOKS

Cambridge Mathematical Textbooks is a program of undergraduate and beginning graduate-level textbooks for core courses, new courses, and interdisciplinary courses in pure and applied mathematics. These texts provide motivation with plenty of exercises of varying difficulty, interesting examples, modern applications, and unique approaches to the material.

Advisory Board

Paul T. Allen, *Lewis & Clark College*
Melody Chan, *Brown University*
Teena Gerhardt, *Michigan State University*
Illya Hicks, *Rice University*
Greg Lawler, *University of Chicago*
Lawrence Washington, *University of Maryland, College Park*
Talithia Williams, *Harvey Mudd College*

A complete list of books in the series can be found at www.cambridge.org/mathematics

Recent titles include the following:

Chance, Strategy, and Choice: An Introduction to the Mathematics of Games and Elections, S. B. Smith
Set Theory: A First Course, D. W. Cunningham
Chaotic Dynamics: Fractals, Tilings, and Substitutions, G. R. Goodson
A Second Course in Linear Algebra, S. R. Garcia & R. A. Horn
Introduction to Experimental Mathematics, S. Eilers & R. Johansen
Exploring Mathematics: An Engaging Introduction to Proof, J. Meier & D. Smith
A First Course in Analysis, J. B. Conway
Introduction to Probability, D. F. Anderson, T. Seppäläinen & B. Valkó
Linear Algebra, E. S. Meckes & M. W. Meckes
A Short Course in Differential Topology, B. I. Dundas
Abstract Algebra with Applications, A. Terras
Complex Analysis, D. E. Marshall
Abstract Algebra: A Comprehensive Introduction, J. W. Lawrence & F. A. Zorzitto
Algebra: Notes from the Underground, Paolo Aluffi
An Invitation to Combinatorics, S. Shahriari
Modern Mathematical Logic, Joseph Mileti
Matrix Mathematics: A Second Course in Linear Algebra, Stephan Ramon Garcia
Introduction to Proofs and Proof Strategies, Shay Fuchs
Mathematical Methods in Data Science: Bridging Theory and Applications with Python, Sébastien Roch

Mathematical Methods in Data Science

Bridging Theory and Applications with Python

SÉBASTIEN ROCH
University of Wisconsin–Madison

Shaftesbury Road, Cambridge CB2 8EA, United Kingdom

One Liberty Plaza, 20th Floor, New York, NY 10006, USA

477 Williamstown Road, Port Melbourne, VIC 3207, Australia

314–321, 3rd Floor, Plot 3, Splendor Forum, Jasola District Centre, New Delhi – 110025, India

103 Penang Road, #05–06/07, Visioncrest Commercial, Singapore 238467

Cambridge University Press is part of Cambridge University Press & Assessment, a department of the University of Cambridge.

We share the University's mission to contribute to society through the pursuit of education, learning and research at the highest international levels of excellence.

www.cambridge.org
Information on this title: www.cambridge.org/highereducation/isbn/9781009509404

DOI: 10.1017/9781009509435

© Sébastien Roch 2026

This publication is in copyright. Subject to statutory exception and to the provisions of relevant collective licensing agreements, no reproduction of any part may take place without the written permission of Cambridge University Press & Assessment.

When citing this work, please include a reference to the DOI 10.1017/9781009509435

First published 2026

Cover image: Eric Bouchard / iStock / Getty Images Plus

A catalogue record for this publication is available from the British Library

A Cataloging-in-Publication data record for this book is available from the Library of Congress

ISBN 978-1-009-50945-9 Hardback
ISBN 978-1-009-50940-4 Paperback

Additional resources for this publication at www.cambridge.org/Roch

Cambridge University Press & Assessment has no responsibility for the persistence or accuracy of URLs for external or third-party internet websites referred to in this publication and does not guarantee that any content on such websites is, or will remain, accurate or appropriate.

To Ben

"*Mathematical Methods in Data Science* provides a clear and accessible primer on key concepts central to data science and machine learning. Through engaging examples from neural networks, recommender systems, and data visualization, Roch illuminates myriad foundational topics and methods. Designed for readers from a broad range of backgrounds, this text is an indispensable resource for students and professionals."

Professor Rebecca Willett, University of Chicago

"This book is an outstanding introduction to the fundamentals of data science by an expert educator and researcher in the area. Its choice of topics, its use of Python, its plentiful examples and exercises, and its battle-testing in the classroom make it a top choice for students and educators seeking a mathematically rigorous yet practical entrée into data science."

Professor Stephen J Wright, University of Wisconsin

Contents

Preface		*page* xiii
1	**Introduction: A First Data Science Problem**	1
1.1	Motivating Example: Identifying Penguin Species	2
1.2	Background: Quick Refresher on Matrix Algebra, Differential Calculus, and Elementary Probability	5
	1.2.1 Vectors and Matrices	5
	1.2.2 Differential Calculus	14
	1.2.3 Probability	21
1.3	Clustering: An Objective, an Algorithm and a Guarantee	33
	1.3.1 The k-Means Objective	34
	1.3.2 Lloyd's Algorithm and Its Analysis	39
	1.3.3 Matrix Form of K-Means Clustering	47
1.4	Some Observations about High-Dimensional Data	50
	1.4.1 Clustering in High Dimension	50
	1.4.2 Surprising Phenomena in High Dimension	54
1.5	Exercises	58
	1.5.1 Warm-Up Worksheets	58
	1.5.2 Problems	60
2	**Least Squares: Geometric, Algebraic, and Numerical Aspects**	67
2.1	Motivating Example: Predicting Sales	68
2.2	Background: Review of Vector Spaces and Matrix Inverses	71
	2.2.1 Subspaces	71
	2.2.2 Linear Independence and Bases	75
	2.2.3 Inverses	80
2.3	Geometry of Least Squares: The Orthogonal Projection	84
	2.3.1 A Key Concept: Orthogonality	85
	2.3.2 Orthogonal Projection	88
	2.3.3 Orthogonal Complement	93
	2.3.4 Overdetermined Systems	94
2.4	QR Decomposition and Householder Transformations	97
	2.4.1 Matrix Form of Gram–Schmidt	97
	2.4.2 Least Squares via QR	101
	2.4.3 Householder Transformations	104
2.5	Application: Regression Analysis	111
	2.5.1 Linear Regression	112

		2.5.2 Polynomial Regression (and Overfitting)	115
	2.6	Exercises	120
		2.6.1 Warm-Up Worksheets	120
		2.6.2 Problems	123

3 Optimization Theory and Algorithms — 128

- 3.1 Motivating Example: Analyzing Customer Satisfaction — 129
- 3.2 Background: Review of Differentiable Functions of Several Variables — 133
  - 3.2.1 Gradient — 133
  - 3.2.2 Second-Order Derivatives — 137
- 3.3 Optimality Conditions — 140
  - 3.3.1 First-Order Conditions — 140
  - 3.3.2 Second-Order Conditions — 144
  - 3.3.3 Adding Equality Constraints — 150
- 3.4 Convexity — 157
  - 3.4.1 Definitions — 157
  - 3.4.2 Convexity and Unconstrained Optimization — 163
- 3.5 Gradient Descent and Its Convergence Analysis — 169
  - 3.5.1 Gradient Descent — 170
  - 3.5.2 Convergence Analysis — 173
- 3.6 Application: Logistic Regression — 180
  - 3.6.1 Definitions — 180
  - 3.6.2 Implementation — 184
- 3.7 Exercises — 188
  - 3.7.1 Warm-Up Worksheets — 188
  - 3.7.2 Problems — 191

4 Singular Value Decomposition — 200

- 4.1 Motivating Example: Visualizing Viral Evolution — 201
- 4.2 Background: Review of Matrix Rank and Spectral Decomposition — 202
  - 4.2.1 Rank of a Matrix — 202
  - 4.2.2 Eigenvalues and Eigenvectors — 207
- 4.3 Approximating Subspaces and the SVD — 216
  - 4.3.1 An Objective, an Algorithm, and a Guarantee — 216
  - 4.3.2 From Approximating Subspaces to the SVD — 222
- 4.4 Power Iteration — 230
  - 4.4.1 Key Lemma — 230
  - 4.4.2 Computing the Top Singular Vector — 233
- 4.5 Application: Principal Components Analysis — 238
  - 4.5.1 Dimensionality Reduction via Principal Components Analysis (PCA) — 238
- 4.6 Further Applications of the SVD: Low-Rank Approximations and Ridge Regression — 247
  - 4.6.1 Matrix Norms — 247
  - 4.6.2 Low-Rank Approximation — 250
  - 4.6.3 Ridge Regression — 256
- 4.7 Exercises — 259

		4.7.1 Warm-Up Worksheets	259
		4.7.2 Problems	262

5 Spectral Graph Theory   267
   5.1 Motivating Example: Uncovering Social Groups   268
   5.2 Background: Basic Concepts in Graph Theory   269
         5.2.1 Undirected Graphs   269
         5.2.2 Directed Graphs   276
         5.2.3 Matrix Representations of Graphs   279
         5.2.4 Laplacian Matrix   283
   5.3 Variational Characterization of Eigenvalues   285
         5.3.1 Proof of Spectral Theorem   285
         5.3.2 Varational Characterization: Special Cases   289
         5.3.3 General Statement: Courant–Fischer   290
   5.4 Spectral Properties of the Laplacian Matrix   293
         5.4.1 Eigenvalues of the Laplacian Matrix: First Observations   293
         5.4.2 Laplacian Matrix and Connectivity   295
         5.4.3 Variational Characterization of Second Laplacian Eigenvalue   299
   5.5 Application: Graph Partitioning via Spectral Clustering   303
         5.5.1 How to Cut a Graph   303
   5.6 Erdős–Rényi Random Graphs and Stochastic Blockmodels   316
         5.6.1 Inhomogeneous Erdős–Rényi Random Graph   316
         5.6.2 Stochastic Blockmodel   321
   5.7 Exercises   329
         5.7.1 Warm-Up Worksheets   329
         5.7.2 Problems   335

6 Probabilistic Models: From Simple to Complex   341
   6.1 Motivating Example: Tracking Location   342
   6.2 Background: Introduction to Parametric Families and Maximum Likelihood Estimation   343
         6.2.1 Exponential Family   343
         6.2.2 Parameter Estimation   349
         6.2.3 Parameter Estimation for Exponential Families   353
         6.2.4 Generalized Linear Models   356
   6.3 Modeling More Complex Dependencies 1: Using Conditional Independence   361
         6.3.1 Review of Conditioning   362
         6.3.2 The Basic Configurations   365
         6.3.3 Example: Naive Bayes   369
   6.4 Modeling More Complex Dependencies 2: Marginalizing Out an Unobserved Variable   375
         6.4.1 Mixtures   375
         6.4.2 Example: Mixtures of Multivariate Bernoullis and the EM Algorithm   379
         6.4.3 Clustering Handwritten Digits   387
   6.5 Application: Linear-Gaussian Models and Kalman Filtering   395
         6.5.1 Multivariate Gaussians: Marginals and Conditionals   395

		6.5.2	Kalman Filter	401
		6.5.3	Back to Location Tracking	407
	6.6	Exercises		412
		6.6.1	Warm-Up Worksheets	412
		6.6.2	Problems	416

7 Random Walks on Graphs and Markov Chains — 421

	7.1	Motivating Example: Discovering Mathematical Topics		422
	7.2	Background: Elements of Finite Markov Chains		424
		7.2.1	Basic Definitions	425
		7.2.2	Time-Homogeneous Case: Transition Matrix	428
	7.3	Limit Behavior 1: Stationary Distributions		434
		7.3.1	Definitions	434
		7.3.2	Existence	439
	7.4	Limit Behavior 2: Convergence to Equilibrium		445
		7.4.1	Definitions	445
		7.4.2	Convergence Theorems	447
	7.5	Application: Random Walks on Graphs and PageRank		451
		7.5.1	Random Walk on a Graph	451
		7.5.2	PageRank	454
		7.5.3	Personalized PageRank	462
	7.6	Further Applications: Gibbs Sampling and Generating Images		466
		7.6.1	Markov Chain Monte Carlo (MCMC)	466
		7.6.2	Gibbs Sampling	473
	7.7	Exercises		482
		7.7.1	Warm-Up Worksheets	482
		7.7.2	Problems	488

8 Neural Networks, Backpropagation, and Stochastic Gradient Descent — 494

	8.1	Motivating Example: Classifying Natural Images		495
	8.2	Background: Jacobian, Chain Rule, and a Brief Introduction to Automatic Differentiation		496
		8.2.1	More Matrix Algebra: Hadamard and Kronecker Products	497
		8.2.2	Jacobian	499
		8.2.3	Generalization of the Chain Rule	503
		8.2.4	Brief Introduction to Automatic Differentiation in PyTorch	505
	8.3	Building Blocks of AI 1: Backpropagation		510
		8.3.1	Forward vs. Backward	510
		8.3.2	Progressive Functions	516
	8.4	Building Blocks of AI 2: Stochastic Gradient Descent		529
		8.4.1	Algorithm	529
		8.4.2	Example: Multinomial Logistic Regression	533
	8.5	Building Blocks of AI 3: Neural Networks		542
		8.5.1	Multilayer Perceptron	542
		8.5.2	A First Example	544
		8.5.3	Computing the Gradient	547

8.6	Exercises		553
	8.6.1	Warm-Up Worksheets	553
	8.6.2	Problems	556

References 560
Index 561

Preface

This textbook on the mathematics of data has two main intended audiences:

- For students majoring in mathematics or other quantitative fields (physics, economics, engineering, etc.), it is meant as an invitation to data science and artificial intelligence (AI) from a rigorous mathematical perspective.

- For mathematically inclined students in data science–related fields (at the undergraduate or Master's level), it can serve as a mathematical companion to statistics and machine learning courses.

Content-wise it is a second course in linear algebra, multivariable calculus, and probability theory motivated by and illustrated using data science applications. As such, the reader is expected to be familiar with the basics of those areas. That said, extensive review sections are included to allow the book to be used by students with different backgrounds. Rigorous proofs of most results are provided, although many (if not most) can be safely skipped. On the other hand, no knowledge of data science is assumed and the textbook can serve as a tour of some essential techniques that form the foundations of modern data science, including clustering, regression, classification, dimensionality reduction, network analysis, statistical inference, sampling, neural networks, and so on.

Chapter 1 provides a first introduction to the mathematics of data through a concrete example: clustering. It starts by reviewing basic mathematical concepts that will be used throughout the book, especially matrix and vector algebra, differential calculus and optimization, and elementary probability. Chapter 2 introduces the linear least squares problem, in particular emphasizing the various facets of the problem: linear algebraic (normal equations), geometric (orthogonal projection), and numerical (QR decomposition). Chapter 3 looks at more general optimization theory and algorithms. Basic optimality conditions are derived, the concept of convexity is introduced, and gradient descent is analyzed and implemented. Logistic regression serves as a guiding example. Chapter 4 centers on singular value decomposition and applications to dimensionality reduction, including principal components analysis. Chapter 5 considers network data. After reviewing basic graph definitions, it introduces ideas from spectral graph theory, in particular the eigenvalues of the Laplacian and their variational characterization, and applications to graph partitioning. Chapter 6 takes a look at probabilistic models and related statistical problems. It emphasizes the role of conditional independence and marginalization to construct a variety of models. It also describes some standard methods for estimating parameters and hidden states. Applications include Kalman filtering and Gibbs sampling. Chapter 7 continues the analysis of datasets in the form of networks. Through a discussion of PageRank, it shows how the behavior of a random walk provides a powerful way to extract information about the structure of a network. It frames such walks in the more general context of Markov chains and introduces Markov chain Monte Carlo methods. Chapter 8 ends the book with an introduction to the basic mathematical building blocks of modern AI: neural networks, backpropagation, and stochastic gradient descent.

The chapters are meant to be relatively modular. Each one focuses on a specific area of mathematics relevant to data science. Chapters may refer to previous ones on occasion, typically (but not exclusively) to the "background" section included in each chapter.

Each content-based section in the book includes a self-assessment quiz in the form of multiple choice questions testing the basic concepts covered as well as a warm-up worksheet which primarily goes over the fundamental formulas derived in simple settings. Each chapter also includes a series of more challenging problems (typically a few dozen) which focus on theoretical aspects. In the online materials, to be found at https://mmids-textbook.github.io/, students will find an additional, online-only Supplementary Materials section at the end of each chapter that includes a more extensive, interactive version of the former, and partial solutions to the latter.

While the emphasis throughout is on the mathematical concepts and methods, coding is used extensively. In fact, the book is based on a series of Jupyter notebooks that were originally developed as a complement for "MATH 535: Mathematical Methods in Data Science," a popular one-semester advanced undergraduate and Master's level course offered at the University of Wisconsin–Madison every semester for the past five years or so. They eventually grew into a standalone textbook. As a result, mathematical developments, code implementations, and data analyses are tightly integrated, showcasing "mathematics in action" whenever possible. A side effect of this approach is that there is significantly less emphasis on "calculations by hand" than one is perhaps used to seeing in a mathematics textbook at this level; warm-up worksheets for each section – with partial solutions available online – are meant to compensate as well as to provide materials for active learning in the classroom. In terms of programming background, basic familiarity with Python will suffice to follow the coding components. The book itself provides an introduction to some specialized packages, especially NumPy NetworkX, and PyTorch. Python is also used in lieu of pseudocode; indeed the latter becomes somewhat redundant when code is integrated to this extent.

The file mmids.py, which contains all functions defined in the book, is on the GitHub page of the book:

$$\text{https://github.com/MMiDS-textbook/}$$

So are all datasets used. Jupyter notebooks containing (mostly) just the code are also available there; running them in Google Colaboratory is recommended for the curious.

While this book can be read without accessing the datasets, you are invited to do so, especially as indicated by ***bold italic*** type (although you can try code for yourself in other places). Use the GitHub page to navigate to the dataset or code you need.

To run the code in this book, you need to import the following libraries:

```python
import numpy as np
from numpy import linalg as LA
import matplotlib.pyplot as plt
import pandas as pd
import networkx as nx
```

```
import torch
import mmids
```

Throughout the book you will find features headed **TRY IT!**, **CHAT & LEARN**, and **NUMERICAL CORNER**. The end of each NUMERICAL CORNER is indicated by ◁ **NC**.

Over the last year or so, like many, I have been exploring the use of generative AI in teaching, both for developing educational materials and for engaging students with the tool itself. As of this writing (September 2024), I regularly use ChatGPT 4o, Claude 3.5 Sonnet, and Gemini 1.5 Pro – and their usefulness differs significantly between the two main pillars of this book: mathematics vs. coding (and data analysis). These large language models (LLMs) are really quite bad at the former, but at the same time are quite reliable at the latter. In fact, not only are they good coders, but they also in my experience excel at explaining code and can therefore serve as great personal tutors. (I used them myself in that way all the time, and some of the code in the book is indeed written by LLMs.) Hence, I have included CHAT & LEARN activities, which encourage students to explore topics not (or only cursorily) covered in the book using their favorite AI chatbot. These activities mostly concern practical coding or data analysis issues (e.g., data cleaning, cross-validation, more advanced numerical methods, etc.)

On the other hand, LLMs are significantly less reliable when it comes to mathematics, and I warn my own students about using them for this purpose. That said, I have used LLMs myself to produce the self-assessment quizzes and warm-up worksheets in each section, as well as their answers and solutions. But this involves a whole curation process: I feed one section at a time to each of the three AIs mentioned above, give detailed instructions on what type of questions I am looking for and in what style they should be written, ask for a large number of examples, only keep the few best ones, and finally edit and correct them. In my experience, most exercises produced this way are either wrong, at the wrong level, of little relevance or pedagogical value, or downright nonsensical. Hence I would not recommend that students use these AIs to generate practice exams for instance. (This of course may change with the next iterations of these models.) For going deeper into some of the mathematical concepts covered in the book, I do recommend Wikipedia for this particular purpose, and quote from it throughout the book (as well as link to it often in the online version of the book). Note however that Wikipedia articles are frequently edited and updated.

Finally, many figures in the book were made with the help of AI, which produced a first draft of Python or TikZ code based on a word description or sketch of the desired outcome that I then tweaked. However, it was not possible to use figures produced with generative AI systems such as Midjourney or DALL-E because of concerns about copyright infringement.

The textbook was influenced by a number of excellent references on linear algebra, optimization, statistics, machine learning, numerical methods, and so on, especially in the earlier stages where it was merely a series of computational notebooks. These are listed in the References at the end of the book, and many are cited in the text by coding such as [HH] for Holmes and Huber (2019).

Throughout this project, I had the great fortune of being associated with the Institute for Foundations of Data Science (IFDS), funded by the NSF Transdisciplinary Research In Principles Of Data Science (TRIPODS) program. It had a deep influence on this textbook, both through the general transdisciplinary philosophy of the TRIPODS program which is reflected in the attempt to integrate mathematical, computational and statistical aspects, and thanks to the many IFDS colleagues and collaborators I have met, interacted with, and learned from. I am also thankful to my colleagues in the mathematics department at the University of Wisconsin–Madison, especially those who have contributed to our data science offerings, including the "MATH 535: Mathematical Methods in Data Science" course, over the years, as well as to all the students who have taken that course, on which this book is based.

1 Introduction: A First Data Science Problem

This chapter provides a first introduction to the mathematics of data through a concrete example: clustering. This fundamental technique in data analysis and machine learning involves grouping similar data points together based on certain characteristics or features. The goal is to divide a dataset into subsets – or clusters – such that data points within the same subset are more similar to each other than to those in other subsets. We start by reviewing basic mathematical concepts that will be used throughout the book, especially matrix and vector algebra, differential calculus and optimization, and elementary probability. We also highlight some relevant phenomena arising in the context of high-dimensional data. Here is a more detailed overview of the main sections of the chapter.

Background: Quick refresher of matrix algebra, differential calculus, and elementary probability: Section 1.2 reviews key topics such as vectors, matrices, and their operations, as well as important matrix properties like positive semidefiniteness. The section also discusses continuity, differentiability, and optimization, introducing important results like the *Extreme Value Theorem* and the *First-Order Necessary Optimality Condition* for local minimizers. The probability content covers expectation, variance, Chebyshev's inequality, independence, limit theorems like the Weak Law of Large Numbers, random vectors and matrices, covariance matrices, and the normal distribution. Throughout the section, numerical examples using Python and some of its main libraries (especially NumPy and Matplotlib) are provided to illustrate the concepts and their implementation.

Clustering: An objective, an algorithm and a guarantee: Section 1.3 introduces clustering, a fundamental problem in data science where the goal is to partition n data points in d-dimensional space into k clusters. It starts by introducing the k-means objective function, a mathematical formulation to quantify the quality of a clustering solution. An iterative algorithm is derived that alternates between finding optimal cluster representatives (i.e., centroids) for a fixed partition and finding the optimal partition for fixed representatives. One theoretical guarantee is proved: At each step, the algorithm does not deteriorate the objective – but it may not converge to a global minimum. The section also presents a matrix formulation of k-means clustering, showing that minimizing the objective is equivalent to finding a matrix factorization that closely approximates the data in Frobenius norm. The mathematical concepts are illustrated through numerical examples and an application to identifying penguin species.

Some observations about high-dimensional data: Section 1.4 explores the challenges and surprising phenomena that arise when dealing with data in high-dimensional spaces. It begins by demonstrating in numerical simulations how k-means clustering may struggle to distinguish between seemingly well-separated clusters as the dimensionality increases. The section then discusses the counterintuitive properties of high-dimensional spaces, particularly the fact that most of the volume of a high-dimensional cube is concentrated in its corners, making it appear like a "spiky ball." These mathematical insights highlight the "curse of dimensionality" and the need for dimension-reduction techniques when working with high-dimensional data, a topic to which the book returns later on.

1.1 Motivating Example: Identifying Penguin Species

Imagine that you are an evolutionary biologist studying penguins. You have collected measurements on a large number of individual specimens. Your goal is to identify different species within this collection based on those measurements.

We use a *penguin dataset*[1] collected and made available by Dr. Kristen Gorman and the Palmer Station, Antarctica LTER. We upload the data in the form of a data table (similar to a spreadsheet) called `DataFrame` in pandas, where the columns are different measurements (or features) and the rows are different samples. Below, we load the data using `pandas.read_csv` and show the first five lines of the dataset (using `DataFrame.head`). This dataset is a simplified version (i.e., with some columns removed) of the full dataset from Allison Horst's GitHub page.[2]

```
import pandas as pd
data = pd.read_csv('penguins-measurements.csv')
data.head()
```

	bill_length_mm	bill_depth_mm	flipper_length_mm	body_mass_g
0	39.1	18.7	181.0	3750.0
1	39.5	17.4	186.0	3800.0
2	40.3	18.0	195.0	3250.0
3	NaN	NaN	NaN	NaN
4	36.7	19.3	193.0	3450.0

Observe that this dataset has missing values (i.e., the entries NaN above). A common way to deal with this issue is to remove all rows with missing values. This can be done using `pandas.DataFrame.dropna`. This kind of preprocessing is fundamental in data science, but we will not discuss it much in this book. It is however important to be aware of it.

```
data = data.dropna()
data.head()
```

---

[1] You can access datasets and code that you want to **work with yourself** via the GitHub page for this book: https://github.com/MMiDS-textbook/
[2] https://github.com/allisonhorst/palmerpenguins/

	bill_length_mm	bill_depth_mm	flipper_length_mm	body_mass_g
0	39.1	18.7	181.0	3750.0
1	39.5	17.4	186.0	3800.0
2	40.3	18.0	195.0	3250.0
4	36.7	19.3	193.0	3450.0
5	39.3	20.6	190.0	3650.0

There are 342 samples remaining, as can be seen by using pandas.DataFrame.shape which gives the dimensions of the DataFrame as a tuple.

```
data.shape
```

(342, 4)

Let us first extract the columns into a NumPy array using pandas.DataFrame.to_numpy. We will have more to say later on about NumPy, a numerical library for Python that in essence allows us to manipulate vectors and matrices.

```
X = data.to_numpy()
print(X)
```

```
[[  39.1   18.7  181.   3750. ]
 [  39.5   17.4  186.   3800. ]
 [  40.3   18.   195.   3250. ]
 ...
 [  50.4   15.7  222.   5750. ]
 [  45.2   14.8  212.   5200. ]
 [  49.9   16.1  213.   5400. ]]
```

We visualize two measurements in the data, the bill depth and flipper length. (The original dataset used the more precise term culmen depth.) In the figure below, each point is a sample. This is called a scatter plot. Quoting Wikipedia[3]:

> The data are displayed as a collection of points, each having the value of one variable determining the position on the horizontal axis and the value of the other variable determining the position on the vertical axis.

We use matplotlib.pyplot for most of our plotting needs in this book, with a few exceptions. Specifically, here we use the function matplotlib.pyplot.scatter.

---

[3] https://en.wikipedia.org/wiki/Scatter_plot

```
import matplotlib.pyplot as plt
plt.scatter(X[:,1], X[:,2], s=5, c='k')
plt.xlabel('bill_depth_mm'), plt.ylabel('flipper_length_mm')
plt.show()
```

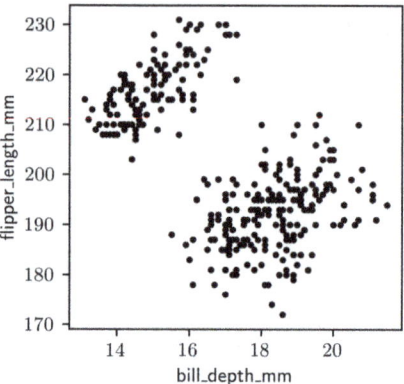

Figure 1.1 Graphical output of code.

We observe what appear to be two fairly well-defined clusters of samples at the top left and bottom right respectively. What is a cluster? Intuitively, it is a group of samples that are close to each other, but far from every other sample. In this case, it may be an indication that these samples come from a separate species.

Now let's look at the full dataset. Visualizing the full four-dimensional data is not straightforward. One way to do this is to consider all pairwise scatter plots. We use the function `seaborn.pairplot` from the library Seaborn.

```
import seaborn as sns
sns.pairplot(data, height=2)
plt.show()
```

Based on the graphical output shown in Figure 1.2, how many species of penguins do you think there are in this dataset?

What would be useful is a method that *automatically* identifies clusters *whatever the dimension of the data*. In this chapter, we will discuss a standard way to do this: k-means clustering. We will come back to the penguins dataset later in the chapter.

But first we need to review some basic concepts about vectors and distances in order to formulate clustering as an appropriate *optimization* problem, a perspective that will be recurring throughout.

CHAT & LEARN Ask your favorite AI chatbot for alternative ways to deal with missing values in a dataset. Implement one of these alternatives on the ***penguins dataset*** (you can ask the chatbot for the code!).

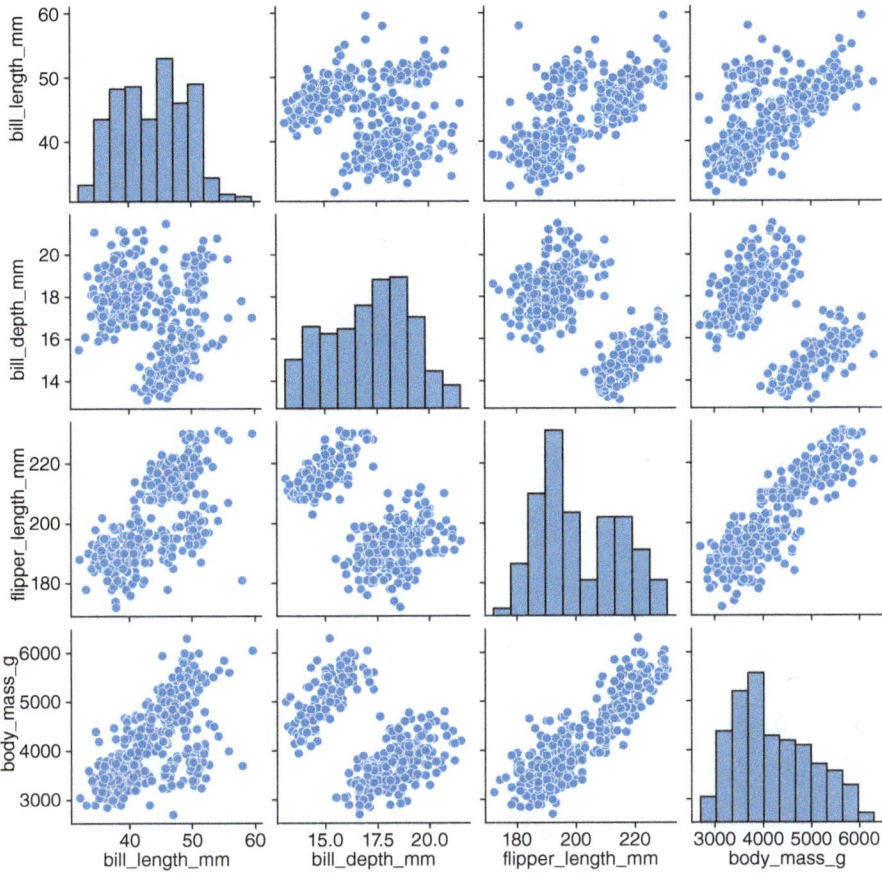

Figure 1.2 Graphical output of code.

1.2 Background: Quick Refresher on Matrix Algebra, Differential Calculus, and Elementary Probability

We first review a few basic mathematical concepts. In this chapter, we focus on vector and matrix algebra, some basic calculus and optimization, and elementary probability. Along the way, we also introduce Python, especially the library NumPy which will be used throughout.

1.2.1 Vectors and Matrices

1.2.1.1 Vectors and Norms

Throughout, $\mathbb{R}$ and $\mathbb{R}_+$ denote respectively the real numbers and positive real numbers. For a vector

$$\mathbf{x} = \begin{bmatrix} x_1 \\ x_2 \\ \vdots \\ x_d \end{bmatrix} \in \mathbb{R}^d$$

the Euclidean norm of **x** is defined as

$$\|\mathbf{x}\|_2 = \sqrt{\sum_{i=1}^{d} x_i^2} = \sqrt{\langle \mathbf{x}, \mathbf{x} \rangle}$$

where

$$\langle \mathbf{u}, \mathbf{v} \rangle = \sum_{i=1}^{d} u_i v_i$$

is the inner product of **u** and **v**. This is also known as the ℓ^2-norm. Throughout we use the simplified notation $\|\mathbf{x}\| = \|\mathbf{x}\|_2$ to indicate the 2-norm of **x** unless specified otherwise. We use x_i and $(\mathbf{x})_i$ to denote the entries of **x**. We also write $\mathbf{x} = (x_1, \ldots, x_d) = (x_i)_{i \in [d]}$, where $[d] := \{1, 2, \ldots, d\}$.

The inner product has the following useful properties (check them!). For one, it is symmetric in the sense that

$$\langle \mathbf{x}, \mathbf{y} \rangle = \langle \mathbf{y}, \mathbf{x} \rangle \qquad \forall \mathbf{x}, \mathbf{y} \in \mathbb{R}^d.$$

Second, it is linear in each input: For any $\mathbf{x}_1, \mathbf{x}_2, \mathbf{x}_3 \in \mathbb{R}^d$ and $\beta \in \mathbb{R}$, it holds that, for the left-hand input,

$$\langle \beta \mathbf{x}_1 + \mathbf{x}_2, \mathbf{x}_3 \rangle = \beta \langle \mathbf{x}_1, \mathbf{x}_3 \rangle + \langle \mathbf{x}_2, \mathbf{x}_3 \rangle$$

and similarly for the right-hand input. Repeated application of the linearity property implies for instance that for any $\mathbf{x}_1, \ldots, \mathbf{x}_m, \mathbf{y}_1, \ldots, \mathbf{y}_\ell \in \mathbb{R}^d$,

$$\left\langle \sum_{i=1}^{m} \mathbf{x}_i, \sum_{j=1}^{\ell} \mathbf{y}_j \right\rangle = \sum_{i=1}^{m} \sum_{j=1}^{\ell} \langle \mathbf{x}_i, \mathbf{y}_j \rangle.$$

The triangle inequality for the ℓ^2-norm follows from the Cauchy–Schwarz inequality, which is useful in proving many facts.

Theorem 1.2.1 *(Cauchy–Schwarz) For all* $\mathbf{u}, \mathbf{v} \in \mathbb{R}^d$

$$|\langle \mathbf{u}, \mathbf{v} \rangle| \leq \|\mathbf{u}\| \, \|\mathbf{v}\|.$$

Given a collection of vectors $\mathbf{u}_1, \ldots, \mathbf{u}_k \in \mathbb{R}^d$ and real numbers $\alpha_1, \ldots, \alpha_k \in \mathbb{R}$, the linear combination of $\mathbf{u}_\ell$'s with coefficients α_ℓ's is the vector

$$\mathbf{z} = \sum_{\ell=1}^{k} \alpha_\ell \mathbf{u}_\ell,$$

whose entries are

$$z_i = \sum_{\ell=1}^{k} \alpha_\ell (\mathbf{u}_\ell)_i, \quad i = 1, \ldots, d.$$

We also use $u_{\ell,i} = (\mathbf{u}_\ell)_i$ to denote the entries of $\mathbf{u}_\ell$.

It will be convenient to introduce special notation for common vectors. The dimension of these vectors will often be clear from the context.

- The all-0 vector in d dimensions is denoted by $\mathbf{0}_d = \mathbf{0}$.

- The all-1 vector in d dimensions is denoted by $\mathbf{1}_d = \mathbf{1}$.

- The standard or canonical basis is denoted by $\mathbf{e}_i$, $i = 1, \ldots, d$, where

$$(\mathbf{e}_i)_j = \begin{cases} 1, & \text{if } j = i, \\ 0, & \text{otherwise.} \end{cases}$$

The Euclidean distance between two vectors $\mathbf{u}$ and $\mathbf{v}$ in $\mathbb{R}^d$ is the 2-norm of their difference,

$$d(\mathbf{u}, \mathbf{v}) = \|\mathbf{u} - \mathbf{v}\|_2.$$

More generally, for $p \geq 1$, the ℓ^p-norm of $\mathbf{x}$ is given by

$$\|\mathbf{x}\|_p = \left(\sum_{i=1}^d |x_i|^p \right)^{1/p}.$$

Finally the ℓ^∞-norm is defined as

$$\|\mathbf{x}\|_\infty = \max_{i=1,\ldots,d} |x_i|.$$

There exist other norms. Formally:

Definition 1.2.2 *(Norm)* *A norm is a function ℓ from $\mathbb{R}^d$ to $\mathbb{R}_+$ that satisfies for all $a \in \mathbb{R}$, $\mathbf{u}, \mathbf{v} \in \mathbb{R}^d$*

- (Absolute homogeneity): $\ell(a\mathbf{u}) = |a|\ell(\mathbf{u})$
- (Triangle inequality): $\ell(\mathbf{u} + \mathbf{v}) \leq \ell(\mathbf{u}) + \ell(\mathbf{v})$
- (Point-separating): $\ell(\mathbf{u}) = 0$ *implies* $\mathbf{u} = 0$.

NUMERICAL CORNER In NumPy, a vector is defined as a 1d array. We first must import the NumPy package, which is often abbreviated by np.

```
import numpy as np
u = np.array([1., 3., 5. ,7.])
print(u)
```

[1. 3. 5. 7.]

We access the entries of u as follows; note that indexing in NumPy starts at 0.

```
print(u[0])
print(u[1])
```

1.0
3.0

To obtain the norm of a vector, we can use the function linalg.norm, which requires the numpy.linalg package (often abbreviated as LA):

```
from numpy import linalg as LA
LA.norm(u)
```

9.16515138991168

which we check next "by hand"

```
np.sqrt(np.sum(u ** 2))
```

9.16515138991168

In NumPy, ** indicates element-wise exponentiation.

◁ **NC**

1.2.1.2 Matrices

For an $n \times m$ matrix $A \in \mathbb{R}^{n \times m}$ with real entries, we denote by $A_{i,j}$ or A_{ij} its entry in row i and column j (unless specified otherwise). We also refer to a matrix as the collection of all of its entries as follows:

$$A = (A_{ij})_{i \in [n], j \in [m]}.$$

We occasionally simplify the notation to $A = (A_{ij})_{i,j}$ when the range of the indices is clear from context. We use the notation

$$A_{i,\cdot} = (A_{i1} \cdots A_{im}),$$

to indicate the i-th row of A – as a row vector, or a matrix with a single row – and similarly

$$A_{\cdot,j} = \begin{pmatrix} A_{1j} \\ \vdots \\ A_{nj} \end{pmatrix},$$

for the j-th column of A – as a column vector, or a matrix with a single column.

Example 1.2.3 *Suppose*

$$A = \begin{bmatrix} 2 & 5 \\ 3 & 6 \\ 1 & 1 \end{bmatrix}.$$

Then the second row and column are respectively

$$A_{2,\cdot} = \begin{bmatrix} 3 & 6 \end{bmatrix} \quad \text{and} \quad A_{\cdot,2} = \begin{bmatrix} 5 \\ 6 \\ 1 \end{bmatrix}.$$

Matrices can be multiplied by scalars: Let $A \in \mathbb{R}^{n \times m} = (A_{ij})_{i \in [n], j \in [m]}$ and $\gamma \in \mathbb{R}$, then $\gamma A = (\gamma A_{ij})_{i \in [n], j \in [m]}$ is the matrix whose entries are multiplied by γ. Matrices can also be added to each other – provided they have the same size: let $A \in \mathbb{R}^{n \times m} = (A_{ij})_{i \in [n], j \in [m]}$ and $B \in \mathbb{R}^{n \times m} = (B_{ij})_{i \in [n], j \in [m]}$, then $C = A + B$ is the matrix $C = (C_{ij})_{i \in [n], j \in [m]}$ where $C_{ij} = A_{ij} + B_{ij}$ for all i, j.

1.2 Matrix Algebra, Differential Calculus, and Elementary Probability

Recall that the transpose A^T of a matrix $A \in \mathbb{R}^{n \times m}$ is defined as the matrix in $\mathbb{R}^{m \times n}$ that switches the row and column indices of A, that is, its entries are

$$[A^T]_{ij} = A_{ji}, \quad i = 1, \ldots, m, j = 1, \ldots, n.$$

Example 1.2.4 *Suppose again*

$$A = \begin{bmatrix} 2 & 5 \\ 3 & 6 \\ 1 & 1 \end{bmatrix}.$$

Then its transpose is

$$A^T = \begin{bmatrix} 2 & 3 & 1 \\ 5 & 6 & 1 \end{bmatrix}.$$

We list some useful properties of the transpose (check them!). For any $\gamma \in \mathbb{R}$ and $A, B \in \mathbb{R}^{n \times m}$:

a) $(A^T)^T = A$
b) $(\gamma A + B)^T = \gamma A^T + B^T$

Definition 1.2.5 *(Symmetric Matrix) A square matrix $B \in \mathbb{R}^{n \times n}$ is symmetric if $B^T = B$.*

The transpose in particular can be used to turn a column vector into a row vector and vice versa. That is, if $\mathbf{b} = (b_1, b_2, \ldots, b_n) \in \mathbb{R}^n$ is a column vector, then $\mathbf{b}^T = \begin{pmatrix} b_1 & b_2 & \cdots & b_n \end{pmatrix}$ is the corresponding row vector. Note the absence of commas in the latter. For instance,

$$\mathbf{b}^T \mathbf{b} = b_1^2 + \cdots + b_n^2 = \sum_{i=1}^n b_i^2 = \|\mathbf{b}\|^2$$

is the squared Euclidean norm of $\mathbf{b}$.

NUMERICAL CORNER We will often work with collections of n vectors $\mathbf{x}_1, \ldots, \mathbf{x}_n$ in $\mathbb{R}^d$ and it will be convenient to stack them up into a matrix

$$X = \begin{bmatrix} \mathbf{x}_1^T \\ \mathbf{x}_2^T \\ \vdots \\ \mathbf{x}_n^T \end{bmatrix} = \begin{bmatrix} x_{11} & x_{12} & \cdots & x_{1d} \\ x_{21} & x_{22} & \cdots & x_{2d} \\ \vdots & \vdots & \ddots & \vdots \\ x_{n1} & x_{n2} & \cdots & x_{nd} \end{bmatrix}.$$

To create a matrix out of two vectors, we use the function numpy.stack.

```
u = np.array([1., 3., 5., 7.])
v = np.array([2., 4., 6., 8.])
X = np.stack((u,v),axis=0)
print(X)
```

```
[[1. 3. 5. 7.]
 [2. 4. 6. 8.]]
```

Quoting the documentation[4]:

---
[4] https://numpy.org/doc/stable/reference/generated/numpy.stack.html

The axis parameter specifies the index of the new axis in the dimensions of the result. For example, if axis=0 it will be the first dimension and if axis=−1 it will be the last dimension.

Alternatively, we can define the same matrix as follows.

```
Y = np.array([[1., 3., 5., 7.],[2., 4., 6., 8.]])
print(Y)
```

```
[[1. 3. 5. 7.]
 [2. 4. 6. 8.]]
```

We access the entries as follows.

```
print(Y[0,0])
print(Y[0,1])
```

```
1.0
3.0
```

◁ **NC**

As for vectors, it will be convenient to introduce a special notation for common matrices. The dimensions are sometimes omitted when clear from context.

- The all-0 matrix of dimension $m \times n$ is denoted by $\mathbf{0}_{m \times n} = \mathbf{0}$.
- The all-1 matrix of dimension $m \times n$ is denoted by $J_{m \times n} = J$.
- A square diagonal matrix $A = (A_{ij}) \in \mathbb{R}^{n \times n}$ is a matrix that satisfies $A_{ij} = 0$ for all $i \neq j$. We denote by $\mathrm{diag}(\lambda_1, \ldots, \lambda_n)$ the diagonal matrix with diagonal entries $\lambda_1, \ldots, \lambda_n$.
- The identity matrix of dimension $n \times n$ is denoted by $I_{n \times n} = I$. Specifically, this the matrix whose i-th column is the standard basis vector $\mathbf{e}_i$, $i = 1, \ldots, n$. Put differently, it is the square diagonal matrix with ones on the diagonal.

1.2.1.3 Matrix–Vector Product

Recall that, for a matrix $A = (A_{ij})_{i \in [n], j \in [m]} \in \mathbb{R}^{n \times m}$ and a column vector $\mathbf{b} = (b_i)_{i \in [m]} \in \mathbb{R}^m$, the matrix–vector product $\mathbf{c} = A\mathbf{b}$ is the vector with entries

$$c_i = (A\mathbf{b})_i = \sum_{j=1}^{m} A_{ij} b_j.$$

In vector form,

$$A\mathbf{b} = \sum_{j=1}^{m} A_{\cdot,j} b_j,$$

that is, $A\mathbf{b}$ is a linear combination of the columns of A where the coefficients are the entries of $\mathbf{b}$. Matrix–vector products are linear in the following sense (check it!): For any $\gamma \in \mathbb{R}$ and $\mathbf{b}_1, \mathbf{b}_2 \in \mathbb{R}^m$

$$A(\gamma \mathbf{b}_1 + \mathbf{b}_2) = \gamma A\mathbf{b}_1 + A\mathbf{b}_2.$$

Example 1.2.6 *(continued from Example 1.2.4) Consider the column vector* $\mathbf{b} = (1, 0)$. *Then*

$$A\mathbf{b} = \begin{bmatrix} 2(1) + 5(0) \\ 3(1) + 6(0) \\ 1(1) + 1(0) \end{bmatrix} = \begin{bmatrix} 2 \\ 3 \\ 1 \end{bmatrix},$$

which can also be written in vector form as

$$(1)\begin{bmatrix} 2 \\ 3 \\ 1 \end{bmatrix} + (0)\begin{bmatrix} 5 \\ 6 \\ 1 \end{bmatrix} = \begin{bmatrix} 2 \\ 3 \\ 1 \end{bmatrix}.$$

1.2.1.4 Matrix–Matrix Product

Recall that, for matrices $A \in \mathbb{R}^{n \times k}$ and $B \in \mathbb{R}^{k \times m}$, their matrix product is defined as the matrix $C = AB \in \mathbb{R}^{n \times m}$ whose entries are

$$C_{i\ell} = (AB)_{i\ell} = \sum_{j=1}^{k} A_{ij} B_{j\ell}.$$

The number of columns of A and the number of rows of B must match. There are many different ways to view this formula that are helpful in interpreting matrix–matrix products in different contexts.

First, we observe that the entry $C_{i\ell}$ is an inner product of the i-th row of A and of the ℓ-th column of B. That is,

$$C_{i\ell} = A_{i,\cdot} B_{\cdot,\ell}.$$

In matrix form,

$$AB = \begin{bmatrix} A_{1,\cdot}B_{\cdot,1} & A_{1,\cdot}B_{\cdot,2} & \cdots & A_{1,\cdot}B_{\cdot,m} \\ A_{2,\cdot}B_{\cdot,1} & A_{2,\cdot}B_{\cdot,2} & \cdots & A_{2,\cdot}B_{\cdot,m} \\ \vdots & \vdots & \ddots & \vdots \\ A_{n,\cdot}B_{\cdot,1} & A_{n,\cdot}B_{\cdot,2} & \cdots & A_{n,\cdot}B_{\cdot,m} \end{bmatrix}.$$

Alternatively,

$$AB = \begin{bmatrix} A(B_{\cdot,1}) & A(B_{\cdot,2}) & \cdots & A(B_{\cdot,m}) \end{bmatrix},$$

where we specify a matrix by the collection of its columns. Put differently, by the matrix–vector product formula, the j-th column of the product AB is a linear combination of the columns of A where the coefficients are the entries in column j of B:

$$(AB)_{\cdot,j} = AB_{\cdot,j} = \sum_{\ell=1}^{k} A_{\cdot,\ell} B_{\ell j}.$$

Similarly, the i-th row of the product AB is a linear combination of the rows of B where the coefficients are the entries in row i of A:

$$(AB)_{i,\cdot} = \sum_{\ell=1}^{k} A_{i\ell} B_{\ell,\cdot}.$$

Example 1.2.7 Recall that if we think of a vector $\mathbf{b} \in \mathbb{R}^n$ as a column vector, then its transpose $\mathbf{b}^T$ is a row vector. We previously showed that $\mathbf{b}^T \mathbf{b} = \sum_{i=1}^{n} b_i^2$ is a scalar, in other words a real number. This time, we compute $\mathbf{b}\mathbf{b}^T$. Let us first make sure that the dimensions fit. Seeing these vectors as matrices, we have $\mathbf{b} \in \mathbb{R}^{n \times 1}$ and $\mathbf{b}^T \in \mathbb{R}^{1 \times n}$. So indeed we can multiply them together since the number of columns of the first matrix matches the number of rows of the second one. What are the dimensions of the final product? Taking the number of rows of the first matrix and the number of columns of the second one, we see that it is $n \times n$.

Finally we get

$$\mathbf{b}\mathbf{b}^T = \begin{bmatrix} b_1 \\ b_2 \\ \vdots \\ b_n \end{bmatrix} \begin{bmatrix} b_1 & b_2 & \cdots & b_n \end{bmatrix} = \begin{bmatrix} b_1 b_1 & b_1 b_2 & \cdots & b_1 b_n \\ b_2 b_1 & b_2 b_2 & \cdots & b_2 b_n \\ \vdots & \vdots & \ddots & \vdots \\ b_n b_1 & b_n b_2 & \cdots & b_n b_n \end{bmatrix}.$$

That is, $(\mathbf{b}\mathbf{b}^T)_{i,j} = b_i b_j$.

We list some useful properties of the matrix–matrix product (check them!). For any $\gamma \in \mathbb{R}$, $A, B \in \mathbb{R}^{n \times m}$ and $C \in \mathbb{R}^{m \times \ell}$:

a) $(\gamma A)B = A(\gamma B) = \gamma AB$

b) $(A + B)C = AC + BC$

c) $(BC)^T = C^T B^T$

1.2.1.5 Block Matrices

It will be convenient to introduce block matrices. First, for a vector $\mathbf{x} \in \mathbb{R}^n$, we write $\mathbf{x} = (\mathbf{x}_1, \mathbf{x}_2)$, where $\mathbf{x}_1 \in \mathbb{R}^{n_1}$ and $\mathbf{x}_2 \in \mathbb{R}^{n_2}$ with $n_1 + n_2 = n$, to indicate that $\mathbf{x}$ is partitioned into two blocks: $\mathbf{x}_1$ corresponds to the first n_1 coordinates of $\mathbf{x}$ while $\mathbf{x}_2$ corresponds to the following n_2 coordinates.

More generally, a block matrix is a partitioning of the rows and columns of a matrix of the form

$$A = \begin{pmatrix} A_{11} & A_{12} \\ A_{21} & A_{22} \end{pmatrix}$$

where $A \in \mathbb{R}^{n \times m}$, $A_{ij} \in \mathbb{R}^{n_i \times m_j}$ for $i, j = 1, 2$ with the conditions $n_1 + n_2 = n$ and $m_1 + m_2 = m$. One can also consider larger numbers of blocks.

Block matrices have a convenient algebra that mimics the usual matrix algebra. Specifically, if $B_{ij} \in \mathbb{R}^{m_i \times p_j}$ for $i, j = 1, 2$, then it holds that

$$\begin{pmatrix} A_{11} & A_{12} \\ A_{21} & A_{22} \end{pmatrix} \begin{pmatrix} B_{11} & B_{12} \\ B_{21} & B_{22} \end{pmatrix} = \begin{pmatrix} A_{11}B_{11} + A_{12}B_{21} & A_{11}B_{12} + A_{12}B_{22} \\ A_{21}B_{11} + A_{22}B_{21} & A_{21}B_{12} + A_{22}B_{22} \end{pmatrix}.$$

Observe that the block sizes of A and B must match for this formula to make sense. You can convince yourself of this identity by trying it on a simple example.

Warning: While the formula is similar to the usual matrix product, the order of multiplication matters because the blocks are matrices and they do not in general commute!

1.2.1.6 Matrix Norms

We will also need notions of matrix norm. A natural way to define a norm for matrices is to notice that an $n \times m$ matrix A can be thought of as an nm vector, with one element for each entry of A. Indeed, addition and scalar multiplication work exactly in the same way. Hence, we can define the 2-norm of a matrix in terms of the sum of its squared entries. (We will encounter other matrix norms later in the course.)

Definition 1.2.8 (*Frobenius Norm*) *The Frobenius norm of an $n \times m$ matrix $A \in \mathbb{R}^{n \times m}$ is defined as*

$$\|A\|_F = \sqrt{\sum_{i=1}^{n} \sum_{j=1}^{m} A_{ij}^2}.$$

Using the row notation, we see that the square of the Frobenius norm can be written as the sum of the squared Euclidean norms of the rows $\|A\|_F^2 = \sum_{i=1}^{n} \|A_{i,\cdot}\|^2$. Similarly in terms of the columns $A_{\cdot,j}$, $j = 1, \ldots, m$, of A we have $\|A\|_F^2 = \sum_{j=1}^{m} \|A_{\cdot,j}\|^2$.

For two matrices $A, B \in \mathbb{R}^{n \times m}$, the Frobenius norm of their difference $\|A - B\|_F$ can be interpreted as a distance between A and B, that is, a measure of how dissimilar they are.

It can be shown using the *Cauchy–Schwarz inequality* (try it!) that for any A, B for which AB is well-defined it holds that

$$\|AB\|_F \leq \|A\|_F \|B\|_F.$$

This applies in particular when B is a column vector, in which case $\|B\|_F$ is its Euclidean norm.

NUMERICAL CORNER In NumPy, the Frobenius norm of a matrix can be computed using the function `numpy.linalg.norm`.

```
A = np.array([[1., 0.],[0., 1.],[0., 0.]])
print(A)
```

```
[[1. 0.]
 [0. 1.]
 [0. 0.]]
```

```
LA.norm(A)
```

```
1.4142135623730951
```

◁ NC

1.2.1.7 Quadratic Forms

Let $B \in \mathbb{R}^{n \times n}$ be a square matrix. The associated quadratic form

$$\langle \mathbf{z}, B\mathbf{z} \rangle = \mathbf{z}^T B \mathbf{z} = \sum_{i=1}^{n} z_i \sum_{j=1}^{n} B_{i,j} z_j = \sum_{i=1}^{n} \sum_{j=1}^{n} z_i B_{i,j} z_j$$

defined for any $\mathbf{z} = (z_1, \ldots, z_n)$, will make many appearances throughout this book.

A form is a homogeneous polynomial $f(\mathbf{z})$, viewed as a function of $\mathbf{z}$. By homogeneous, we mean that for any $\mathbf{z} \in \mathbb{R}^n$ and any scalar $\alpha \in \mathbb{R}$

$$f(\alpha \mathbf{z}) = \alpha^k f(\mathbf{z}),$$

for some integer k that is called the degree of homogeneity. (Note that this is different from the absolute homogeneity of norms.) When $k = 2$, we refer to it as a quadratic form. Let us check that $\langle \mathbf{z}, B\mathbf{z} \rangle$ indeed satisfies these properties. The alternative expression $\sum_{i=1}^{n} \sum_{j=1}^{n} z_i B_{i,j} z_j$ makes it clear that it is a polynomial in the variables $z_1, \ldots, z_n$. Moreover, for any $\alpha \in \mathbb{R}$, by using linearity multiple times,

$$\langle \alpha \mathbf{z}, B(\alpha \mathbf{z}) \rangle = \langle \alpha \mathbf{z}, \alpha B \mathbf{z} \rangle = \alpha \langle \mathbf{z}, \alpha B \mathbf{z} \rangle = \alpha^2 \langle \mathbf{z}, B\mathbf{z} \rangle.$$

In particular, the following property of matrices will play an important role. It is defined in terms of the associated quadratic form.

Definition 1.2.9 *(Positive Semidefinite Matrix) A symmetric matrix $B \in \mathbb{R}^{n \times n}$ is positive semidefinite if*

$$\langle \mathbf{z}, B\mathbf{z} \rangle \geq 0, \quad \forall \mathbf{z} \neq \mathbf{0}.$$

We also write $B \succeq 0$ in that case. If the inequality above is strict, we say that B is positive definite, in which case we write $B \succ 0$.

We will see an important example later in this section.

1.2.2 Differential Calculus

Next, we review some basic concepts from differential calculus. We focus here on definitions and results relevant to optimization theory, which plays a central role in data science.

1.2.2.1 Limits and Continuity

The open r-ball around $\mathbf{x} \in \mathbb{R}^d$ is the set of points within Euclidean distance r of $\mathbf{x}$, that is,

$$B_r(\mathbf{x}) = \{\mathbf{y} \in \mathbb{R}^d : \|\mathbf{y} - \mathbf{x}\| < r\}.$$

A point $\mathbf{x} \in \mathbb{R}^d$ is an interior point of a set $A \subseteq \mathbb{R}^d$ if there exists an $r > 0$ such that $B_r(\mathbf{x}) \subseteq A$. A set A is open if it consists entirely of interior points. A point $\mathbf{x} \in \mathbb{R}^d$ is a limit point of a set $A \subseteq \mathbb{R}^d$ if every open ball around $\mathbf{x}$ contains an element $\mathbf{a}$ of A such that $\mathbf{a} \neq \mathbf{x}$. A set A is closed if every limit point of A belongs to A. Or, put differently, a set is closed if its complement is open. A set $A \subseteq \mathbb{R}^d$ is bounded if there exists an $r > 0$ such that $A \subseteq B_r(\mathbf{0})$, where $\mathbf{0} = (0, \ldots, 0)^T$.

Definition 1.2.10 *(Limits of a Function)* Let $f: D \to \mathbb{R}$ be a real-valued function on $D \subseteq \mathbb{R}^d$. Then f is said to have a limit $L \in \mathbb{R}$ as $\mathbf{x}$ approaches $\mathbf{a}$ if: For any $\varepsilon > 0$, there exists a $\delta > 0$ such that $|f(\mathbf{x}) - L| < \varepsilon$ for all $\mathbf{x} \in D \cap B_\delta(\mathbf{a}) \setminus \{\mathbf{a}\}$. This is written as

$$\lim_{\mathbf{x} \to \mathbf{a}} f(\mathbf{x}) = L.$$

Note that we explicitly exclude $\mathbf{a}$ itself from having to satisfy the condition $|f(\mathbf{x}) - L| < \varepsilon$. In particular, we may have $f(\mathbf{a}) \neq L$. We also do not restrict $\mathbf{a}$ to be in D.

Definition 1.2.11 *(Continuous Function)* Let $f: D \to \mathbb{R}$ be a real-valued function on $D \subseteq \mathbb{R}^d$. Then f is said to be continuous at $\mathbf{a} \in D$ if

$$\lim_{\mathbf{x} \to \mathbf{a}} f(\mathbf{x}) = f(\mathbf{a}).$$

We will not prove the following fundamental analysis result, which will be used repeatedly in this course. (See e.g. Wikipedia[5] for a sketch of the proof.) Suppose $f: D \to \mathbb{R}$ is defined on a set $D \subseteq \mathbb{R}^d$. We say that f attains a maximum value M at $\mathbf{z}^*$ if $f(\mathbf{z}^*) = M$ and $M \geq f(\mathbf{x})$ for all $\mathbf{x} \in D$. Similarly, we say f attains a minimum value m at $\mathbf{z}_*$ if $f(\mathbf{z}_*) = m$ and $m \leq f(\mathbf{x})$ for all $\mathbf{x} \in D$.

Theorem 1.2.12 *(Extreme Value)* Let $f: D \to \mathbb{R}$ be a real-valued, continuous function on a nonempty, closed, bounded set $D \subseteq \mathbb{R}^d$. Then f attains a maximum and a minimum on D.

1.2.2.2 Derivatives

We move on to derivatives. Recall that the derivative of a function of a real variable is the rate of change of the function with respect to the change in the variable. It gives the slope of the tangent line at a point. See Figure 1.3. Formally:

Definition 1.2.13 *(Derivative)* Let $f: D \to \mathbb{R}$ where $D \subseteq \mathbb{R}$ and let $x_0 \in D$ be an interior point of D. The derivative of f at x_0 is

$$f'(x_0) = \frac{\mathrm{d}f(x_0)}{\mathrm{d}x} = \lim_{h \to 0} \frac{f(x_0 + h) - f(x_0)}{h}$$

provided the limit exists.

The following lemma encapsulates a key insight about the derivative of f at x_0: It tells us where to find smaller values.

Lemma 1.2.14 *(Descent Direction)* Let $f: D \to \mathbb{R}$ with $D \subseteq \mathbb{R}$ and let $x_0 \in D$ be an interior point of D where $f'(x_0)$ exists. If $f'(x_0) > 0$, then there is an open ball $B_\delta(x_0) \subseteq D$ around x_0 such that for each x in $B_\delta(x_0)$:

a) $f(x) > f(x_0)$ if $x > x_0$,

b) $f(x) < f(x_0)$ if $x < x_0$.

If instead $f'(x_0) < 0$, the opposite holds.

---

[5] https://en.wikipedia.org/wiki/Extreme_value_theorem

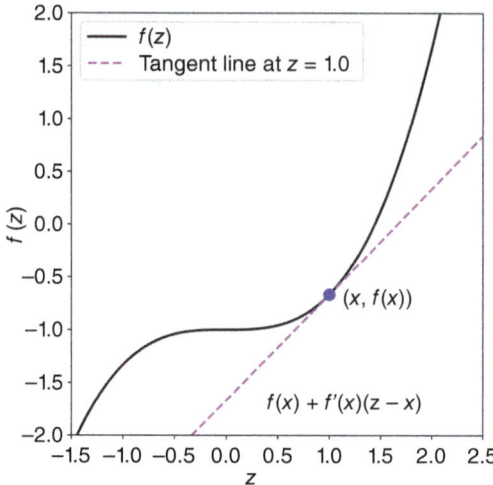

Figure 1.3 The derivative at the blue point is the slope of the line tangent to the curve there.

Proof idea: It follows from the definition of the derivative by taking ε small enough that $f'(x_0) - \varepsilon > 0$.

Proof Take $\varepsilon = f'(x_0)/2$. By definition of the derivative, there is $\delta > 0$ such that
$$f'(x_0) - \frac{f(x_0 + h) - f(x_0)}{h} < \varepsilon$$
for all $0 < h < \delta$. Rearranging gives
$$f(x_0 + h) > f(x_0) + [f'(x_0) - \varepsilon]h > f(x_0)$$
by our choice of ε. The other direction is similar. $\square$

One implication of the *Descent Direction Lemma* is the *Mean Value Theorem* (see Figure 1.4), which will lead us later to *Taylor's Theorem*. First, an important special case:

Theorem 1.2.15 *(Rolle) Let $f: [a, b] \to \mathbb{R}$ be a continuous function and assume that its derivative exists on (a, b). If $f(a) = f(b)$ then there is $a < c < b$ such that $f'(c) = 0$.*

Proof idea: Look at an extremum and use the *Descent Direction Lemma* to get a contradiction.

Proof If $f(x) = f(a)$ for all $x \in (a, b)$, then $f'(x) = 0$ on (a, b) and we are done. So assume there is $y \in (a, b)$ such that $f(y) \neq f(a)$. Assume without loss of generality that $f(y) > f(a)$ (otherwise consider the function $-f$). By the *Extreme Value Theorem*, f attains a maximum value at some $c \in [a, b]$. By our assumption, a and b cannot be the location of the maximum and it must be that $c \in (a, b)$.

We claim that $f'(c) = 0$. We argue by contradiction. Suppose $f'(c) > 0$. By the *Descent Direction Lemma*, there is a $\delta > 0$ such that $f(x) > f(c)$ for some $x \in B_\delta(c)$, a contradiction. A similar argument holds if $f'(c) < 0$. This concludes the proof. $\square$

Theorem 1.2.16 *(Mean Value) Let $f: [a, b] \to \mathbb{R}$ be a continuous function and assume that its derivative exists on (a, b). Then there is $a < c < b$ such that*
$$f(b) = f(a) + (b - a)f'(c),$$

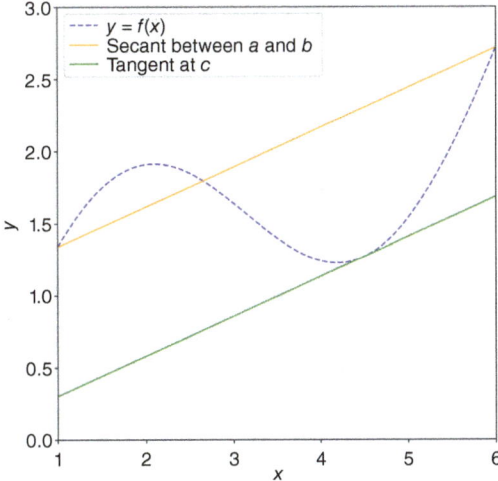

Figure 1.4 Illustration of the *Mean Value Theorem*.

or put differently
$$\frac{f(b) - f(a)}{b - a} = f'(c).$$

Proof idea: Apply *Rolle's Theorem* to
$$\phi(x) = f(x) - \left[f(a) + \frac{f(b) - f(a)}{b - a}(x - a)\right].$$

Proof Let $\phi(x) = f(x) - f(a) - \frac{f(b)-f(a)}{b-a}(x - a)$. Note that $\phi(a) = \phi(b) = 0$ and $\phi'(x) = f'(x) - \frac{f(b)-f(a)}{b-a}$ for all $x \in (a, b)$. Thus, by *Rolle's Theorem*, there is $c \in (a, b)$ such that $\phi'(c) = 0$. That implies $\frac{f(b)-f(a)}{b-a} = \phi'(c)$ and plugging into $\phi(b)$ gives the result. □

We will also use *Taylor's Theorem*, a generalization of the *Mean Value Theorem* that provides a polynomial approximation to a function around a point. We will restrict ourselves to the case of a linear approximation with second-order error term, which will suffice for our purposes.

Theorem 1.2.17 *(Taylor) Let $f: D \to \mathbb{R}$ where $D \subseteq \mathbb{R}$. Suppose f has a continuous derivative on $[a, b]$ and that its second derivative exists on (a, b). Then for any $x \in [a, b]$*
$$f(x) = f(a) + (x - a)f'(a) + \frac{1}{2}(x - a)^2 f''(\xi)$$
for some $a < \xi < x$.

Proof idea: The *Mean Value Theorem* implies that there is $a < \xi < x$ such that
$$f(x) = f(a) + (x - a)f'(\xi).$$

One way to think of the proof of that result is the following: We constructed an affine function that agrees with f at a and x, then used *Rolle's Theorem* to express the coefficient of the linear term using f'. Here we do the same with a polynomial of degree 2. But we now have an extra degree of freedom in choosing this polynomial. Because we are looking for a good approximation close to a, we choose to make the first derivative at a also agree. Applying *Rolle's Theorem* twice gives the claim.

Proof Let

$$P(t) = \alpha_0 + \alpha_1(t-a) + \alpha_2(t-a)^2.$$

We choose the α_i's so that $P(a) = f(a)$, $P'(a) = f'(a)$, and $P(x) = f(x)$. The first two lead to the conditions

$$\alpha_0 = f(a), \quad \alpha_1 = f'(a).$$

Let $\phi(t) = f(t) - P(t)$. By construction $\phi(a) = \phi(x) = 0$. By *Rolle's Theorem*, there is a $\xi' \in (a, x)$ such that $\phi'(\xi') = 0$. Moreover, $\phi'(a) = 0$. Hence we can apply *Rolle's Theorem* again – this time to ϕ' on $[a, \xi']$. It implies that there is $\xi \in (a, \xi')$ such that $\phi''(\xi) = 0$.

The second derivative of ϕ at ξ is

$$0 = \phi''(\xi) = f''(\xi) - P''(\xi) = f''(\xi) - 2\alpha_2$$

so $\alpha_2 = f''(\xi)/2$. Plugging into P and using $\phi(x) = 0$ gives the claim. □

1.2.2.3 Optimization

As we mentioned before, optimization problems play a ubiquitous role in data science. Here we look at unconstrained optimization problems, that is, problems of the form

$$\min_{\mathbf{x} \in \mathbb{R}^d} f(\mathbf{x})$$

where $f : \mathbb{R}^d \to \mathbb{R}$.

Ideally, we would like to find a global minimizer to the optimization problem above.

Definition 1.2.18 *(Global Minimizer)* Let $f : \mathbb{R}^d \to \mathbb{R}$. *The point* $\mathbf{x}^* \in \mathbb{R}^d$ *is a global minimizer of f over $\mathbb{R}^d$ if*

$$f(\mathbf{x}) \geq f(\mathbf{x}^*), \quad \forall \mathbf{x} \in \mathbb{R}^d.$$

Global maximizers are defined similarly.

NUMERICAL CORNER The function $f(x) = x^2$ over $\mathbb{R}$ has a global minimizer at $x^* = 0$. Indeed, we clearly have $f(x) \geq 0$ for all x while $f(0) = 0$. To plot the function, we use the Matplotlib package, and specifically its function `matplotlib.pyplot.plot`. We also use the function `numpy.linspace` to create an array of evenly spaced numbers where we evaluate f.

```
import matplotlib.pyplot as plt

x = np.linspace(-2,2,100)
y = x ** 2

plt.plot(x, y, c='k')
plt.ylim(-0.25,4.25)
plt.show()
```

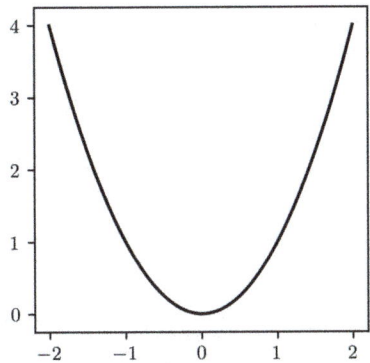

Figure 1.5 Graphical output of code.

The function $f(x) = e^x$ over $\mathbb{R}$ does not have a global minimizer. Indeed, $f(x) > 0$ but no x achieves 0. Also, for any $m > 0$, there is x small enough such that $f(x) < m$. Note that $\mathbb{R}$ is *not* bounded, therefore the *Extreme Value Theorem* does not apply here.

```
x = np.linspace(-2,2,100)
y = np.exp(x)

plt.plot(x, y, c='k')
plt.ylim(-0.25,4.25)
plt.show()
```

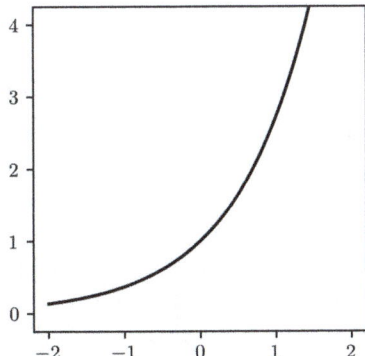

Figure 1.6 Graphical output of code.

The function $f(x) = (x+1)^2(x-1)^2$ over $\mathbb{R}$ has two global minimizers at $x^* = -1$ and $x^{**} = 1$. Indeed, $f(x) \geq 0$ and $f(x) = 0$ if and only $x = x^*$ or $x = x^{**}$.

```
x = np.linspace(-2,2,100)
y = ((x+1)**2) * ((x-1)**2)

plt.plot(x,y,c='k')
```

```
plt.ylim(-0.25,4.25)
plt.show()
```

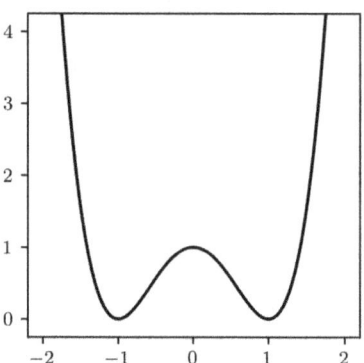

Figure 1.7 Graphical output of code.

In NumPy, ∗ is element-wise multiplication. (For a more careful explanation of how it works, see the broadcasting rules[6] of NumPy.)

◁ **NC**

In general, finding a global minimizer and certifying that one has been found can be difficult unless some special structure is present. Therefore weaker notions of solution have been introduced.

Definition 1.2.19 *(Local Minimizer) Let $f : \mathbb{R}^d \to \mathbb{R}$. The point $\mathbf{x}^* \in \mathbb{R}^d$ is a local minimizer of f over $\mathbb{R}^d$ if there is $\delta > 0$ such that*

$$f(\mathbf{x}) \geq f(\mathbf{x}^*), \quad \forall \mathbf{x} \in B_\delta(\mathbf{x}^*) \setminus \{\mathbf{x}^*\}.$$

If the inequality is strict, we say that $\mathbf{x}^*$ is a strict local minimizer.

In words, $\mathbf{x}^*$ is a local minimizer if there is open ball around $\mathbf{x}^*$ where it attains the minimum value. Local maximizers are defined similarly. In Figure 1.7, $x = 0$ is a local maximizer.

Local minimizers can be characterized in terms of derivatives.

Theorem 1.2.20 *(First-Order Necessary Optimality Condition) Let $f : \mathbb{R} \to \mathbb{R}$ be differentiable (i.e., its derivative exists) on $\mathbb{R}$. If x_0 is a local minimizer, then $f'(x_0) = 0$.*

Proof We argue by contradiction. Suppose that $f'(x_0) \neq 0$. Say $f'(x_0) > 0$ (the other case being similar). By the *Descent Direction Lemma*, there is a $\delta > 0$ such that, for each x in $B_\delta(x_0)$, $f(x) < f(x_0)$ if $x < x_0$. So every open ball around x_0 has a point achieving a smaller value than $f(x_0)$. Thus x_0 is not a local minimizer, a contradiction. So it must be that $f'(x_0) = 0$. □

---

[6] https://numpy.org/doc/stable/user/basics.broadcasting.html

1.2.2.4 Functions of Several Variables

The previous condition generalizes naturally to functions of several variables. The derivative is replaced by the gradient.

Definition 1.2.21 *(Partial Derivative) Let $f: D \to \mathbb{R}$ where $D \subseteq \mathbb{R}^d$ and let $\mathbf{x}_0 = (x_{0,1}, \ldots, x_{0,d}) \in D$ be an interior point of D. The partial derivative of f at $\mathbf{x}_0$ with respect to x_i is*

$$\frac{\partial f(\mathbf{x}_0)}{\partial x_i} = \lim_{h \to 0} \frac{f(\mathbf{x}_0 + h\mathbf{e}_i) - f(\mathbf{x}_0)}{h}$$
$$= \lim_{h \to 0} \frac{f(x_{0,1}, \ldots, x_{0,i-1}, x_{0,i} + h, x_{0,i+1}, \ldots, x_{0,d}) - f(x_{0,1}, \ldots, x_{0,d})}{h}$$

provided the limit exists. If $\frac{\partial f(\mathbf{x}_0)}{\partial x_i}$ exists and is continuous in an open ball around $\mathbf{x}_0$ for all i, then we say that f continuously differentiable at $\mathbf{x}_0$.

Definition 1.2.22 *(Gradient) Let $f: D \to \mathbb{R}$ where $D \subseteq \mathbb{R}^d$ and let $\mathbf{x}_0 \in D$ be an interior point of D. Assume f is continuously differentiable at $\mathbf{x}_0$. The (column) vector*

$$\nabla f(\mathbf{x}_0) = \left(\frac{\partial f(\mathbf{x}_0)}{\partial x_1}, \ldots, \frac{\partial f(\mathbf{x}_0)}{\partial x_d} \right)$$

is called the gradient of f at $\mathbf{x}_0$.

Note that the gradient is itself a function of $\mathbf{x}$. In fact, unlike f, it is a vector-valued function.

We generalize the *Descent Direction Lemma* to the multivariable case. We first need to define what a descent direction is.

Definition 1.2.23 *(Descent Direction) Let $f: \mathbb{R}^d \to \mathbb{R}$. A vector $\mathbf{v}$ is a descent direction for f at $\mathbf{x}_0$ if there is $\alpha^* > 0$ such that*

$$f(\mathbf{x}_0 + \alpha \mathbf{v}) < f(\mathbf{x}_0), \quad \forall \alpha \in (0, \alpha^*).$$

Lemma 1.2.24 *(Descent Direction) Let $f: \mathbb{R}^d \to \mathbb{R}$ be continuously differentiable at $\mathbf{x}_0$ and assume that $\nabla f(\mathbf{x}_0) \neq 0$. Then f has a descent direction at $\mathbf{x}_0$.*

Theorem 1.2.25 *(First-Order Necessary Optimality Condition) Let $f: \mathbb{R}^d \to \mathbb{R}$ be continuously differentiable on $\mathbb{R}^d$. If $\mathbf{x}_0$ is a local minimizer, then $\nabla f(\mathbf{x}_0) = \mathbf{0}$.*

1.2.3 Probability

Finally, we review a few key definitions and results from probability theory.

1.2.3.1 Expectation, Variance, and Chebyshev's Inequality

Recall that the expectation (or mean) of a function h of a discrete random variable X taking values in $\mathcal{X}$ is given by

$$\mathbb{E}[h(X)] = \sum_{x \in \mathcal{X}} h(x) p_X(x)$$

where $p_X(x) = \mathbb{P}[X = x]$ is the probability mass function (PMF) of X. In the continuous case, we have

$$\mathbb{E}[h(X)] = \int h(x) f_X(x) \, \mathrm{d}x$$

where f_X is the probability density function (PDF) of X.

These definitions extend to functions of multiple variables by using instead the joint PMF or PDF.

We sometimes denote the expectation of X by μ_X.

Two key properties of the expectation are:

- *linearity*; that is,
$$\mathbb{E}[\alpha_1 h_1(X) + \alpha_2 h_2(Y) + \beta] = \alpha_1 \mathbb{E}[h_1(X)] + \alpha_2 \mathbb{E}[h_2(Y)] + \beta$$
- *monotonicity*; that is, if $h_1(x) \leq h_2(x)$ for all x then
$$\mathbb{E}[h_1(X)] \leq \mathbb{E}[h_2(X)].$$

The variance of a real-valued random variable X is
$$\mathrm{Var}[X] = \mathbb{E}[(X - \mathbb{E}[X])^2]$$
and its standard deviation is $\sigma_X = \sqrt{\mathrm{Var}[X]}$. The variance does not satisfy linearity, but we have the following property:
$$\mathrm{Var}[\alpha X + \beta] = \alpha^2 \mathrm{Var}[X].$$

The standard deviation is a measure of the typical deviation of X around its mean; that is, of the spread of the distribution.

A quantitative version of this statement is given by *Chebyshev's Inequality*.

Theorem 1.2.26 *(Chebyshev) For a random variable X with finite variance, we have for any $\alpha > 0$*
$$\mathbb{P}[|X - \mathbb{E}[X]| \geq \alpha] \leq \frac{\mathrm{Var}[X]}{\alpha^2}.$$

The intuition is the following: If the expected squared deviation from the mean is small, then the absolute deviation from the mean is unlikely to be large.

To formalize this we prove a more general inequality, *Markov's Inequality*. In words, if a nonnegative random variable has a small expectation then it is unlikely to be large.

Lemma 1.2.27 *(Markov) Let Z be a nonnegative random variable with finite expectation. Then, for any $\beta > 0$,*
$$\mathbb{P}[Z \geq \beta] \leq \frac{\mathbb{E}[Z]}{\beta}.$$

Proof idea: The quantity $\beta \mathbb{P}[Z \geq \beta]$ is a lower bound on the expectation of Z restricted to the range $\{Z \geq \beta\}$, which by nonnegativity is itself lower-bounded by $\mathbb{E}[Z]$.

Proof Formally, let $\mathbf{1}_A$ be the indicator of the event A, that is, it is the random variable that is 1 when A occurs and 0 otherwise. By definition, the expectation of $\mathbf{1}_A$ is
$$\mathbb{E}[\mathbf{1}_A] = 0\,\mathbb{P}[\mathbf{1}_A = 0] + 1\,\mathbb{P}[\mathbf{1}_A = 1] = \mathbb{P}[A]$$
and hence, by linearity and monotonicity,
$$\beta \mathbb{P}[Z \geq \beta] = \beta \mathbb{E}[\mathbf{1}_{Z \geq \beta}] = \mathbb{E}[\beta \mathbf{1}_{Z \geq \beta}] \leq \mathbb{E}[Z].$$
Rearranging gives the claim. $\square$

Finally we return to the proof of *Chebyshev's Inequality*.

Proof idea (Chebyshev): Simply apply *Markov's Inequality* to the squared deviation of X from its mean.

Proof *(Chebyshev)* Let $Z = (X - \mathbb{E}[X])^2$, which is nonnegative by definition. Hence, by *Markov's Inequality*, for any $\beta = \alpha^2 > 0$

$$\begin{aligned}\mathbb{P}[|X - \mathbb{E}[X]| \geq \alpha] &= \mathbb{P}[(X - \mathbb{E}[X])^2 \geq \alpha^2] \\ &= \mathbb{P}[Z \geq \beta] \\ &\leq \frac{\mathbb{E}[Z]}{\beta} \\ &= \frac{\text{Var}[X]}{\alpha^2}\end{aligned}$$

where we used the definition of the variance in the last equality. $\square$

A few important remarks about *Chebyshev's Inequality*:

(1) We sometimes need a one-sided bound of the form

$$\mathbb{P}[X - \mathbb{E}[X] \geq \alpha].$$

Note the absence of absolute values compared to the two-sided form appearing in *Chebyshev's Inequality*. In this case, we can use the fact that the event $\{X - \mathbb{E}[X] \geq \alpha\}$ implies a fortiori that $\{|X - \mathbb{E}[X]| \geq \alpha\}$, so that the probability of the former is smaller than that of the latter by monotonicity, namely,

$$\mathbb{P}[X - \mathbb{E}[X] \geq \alpha] \leq \mathbb{P}[|X - \mathbb{E}[X]| \geq \alpha].$$

We can then use *Chebyshev's Inequality* on the right-hand side to obtain

$$\mathbb{P}[X - \mathbb{E}[X] \geq \alpha] \leq \frac{\text{Var}[X]}{\alpha^2}.$$

Similarly, for the same reasons, we also have

$$\mathbb{P}[X - \mathbb{E}[X] \leq -\alpha] \leq \frac{\text{Var}[X]}{\alpha^2}.$$

(2) In terms of the standard deviation $\sigma_X = \sqrt{\text{Var}[X]}$ of X, the inequality can be rewritten as

$$\mathbb{P}[|X - \mathbb{E}[X]| \geq \alpha] \leq \frac{\text{Var}[X]}{\alpha^2} = \left(\frac{\sigma_X}{\alpha}\right)^2.$$

So to get a small bound on the right-hand side, one needs the deviation α from the mean to be significantly larger than the standard deviation. In words, a random variable is unlikely to be away from its mean by much more than its standard deviation. This observation is consistent with the interpretation of the standard deviation as the typical spread of a random variable.

Chebyshev's Inequality is particularly useful when combined with independence.

1.2.3.2 Independence and Limit Theorems

Recall that discrete random variables X and Y are independent if their joint PMF factorizes, that is

$$p_{X,Y}(x, y) = p_X(x) p_Y(y), \quad \forall x, y$$

where $p_{X,Y}(x,y) = \mathbb{P}[X = x, Y = y]$. Similarly, continuous random variables X and Y are independent if their joint PDF factorizes. One consequence is that expectations of products of single-variable functions factorize as well in this case; that is, for functions g and h we have

$$\mathbb{E}[g(X)h(Y)] = \mathbb{E}[g(X)]\,\mathbb{E}[h(Y)],$$

provided the expectations exist.

An important way to quantify the lack of independence of two random variables is the covariance.

Definition 1.2.28 *(Covariance) The covariance of random variables X and Y with finite means and variances is defined as*

$$\mathrm{Cov}[X, Y] = \mathbb{E}\left[(X - \mathbb{E}[X])(Y - \mathbb{E}[Y])\right].$$

Note that, by definition, the covariance is symmetric: $\mathrm{Cov}[X, Y] = \mathrm{Cov}[Y, X]$.

When X and Y are independent, their covariance is 0:

$$\begin{aligned}
\mathrm{Cov}[X, Y] &= \mathbb{E}\left[(X - \mathbb{E}[X])(Y - \mathbb{E}[Y])\right] \\
&= \mathbb{E}\left[X - \mathbb{E}[X]\right]\mathbb{E}\left[Y - \mathbb{E}[Y]\right] \\
&= (\mathbb{E}[X] - \mathbb{E}[X])\,(\mathbb{E}[Y] - \mathbb{E}[Y]) \\
&= 0,
\end{aligned}$$

where we used independence in the second line and the linearity of expectations in the third one.

A related quantity of interest in data science is the correlation coefficient, which is obtained by dividing the covariance by the product of the standard deviations:

$$\rho_{X,Y} = \frac{\mathrm{Cov}[X, Y]}{\sigma_X \sigma_Y}.$$

By the *Cauchy–Schwarz Inequality*, it lies in $[-1, 1]$ (prove it!).

The covariance leads to a useful identity for the variance of a sum of random variables.

Lemma 1.2.29 *(Variance of a Sum) Let $X_1, \ldots, X_n$ be random variables with finite means and variances. Then we have*

$$\mathrm{Var}[X_1 + \cdots + X_n] = \sum_{i=1}^{n} \mathrm{Var}[X_i] + 2 \sum_{i<j} \mathrm{Cov}[X_i, X_j].$$

Proof By definition of the variance and linearity of expectations,

$$\begin{aligned}
&\mathrm{Var}[X_1 + \cdots + X_n] \\
&= \mathbb{E}\left[(X_1 + \cdots + X_n - \mathbb{E}[X_1 + \cdots + X_n])^2\right] \\
&= \mathbb{E}\left[(X_1 + \cdots + X_n - \mathbb{E}[X_1] - \cdots - \mathbb{E}[X_n])^2\right] \\
&= \mathbb{E}\left[((X_1 - \mathbb{E}[X_1]) + \cdots + (X_n - \mathbb{E}[X_n]))^2\right] \\
&= \sum_{i=1}^{n} \mathbb{E}\left[(X_i - \mathbb{E}[X_i])^2\right] + \sum_{i \neq j} \mathbb{E}\left[(X_i - \mathbb{E}[X_i])(X_j - \mathbb{E}[X_j])\right].
\end{aligned}$$

The claim follows from the definitions of the variance and covariance, and the symmetry of the covariance. $\square$

The previous lemma has the following important implication. If $X_1, \ldots, X_n$ are pairwise-independent real-valued random variables, then

$$\mathrm{Var}[X_1 + \cdots + X_n] = \mathrm{Var}[X_1] + \cdots + \mathrm{Var}[X_n].$$

Notice that, unlike the case of the expectation, this linearity property for the variance requires independence.

Applied to the sample mean of n independent, identically distributed (i.i.d.) random variables $X_1, \ldots, X_n$, we obtain

$$\mathrm{Var}\left[\frac{1}{n}\sum_{i=1}^n X_i\right] = \frac{1}{n^2}\sum_{i=1}^n \mathrm{Var}[X_i]$$
$$= \frac{1}{n^2} n\, \mathrm{Var}[X_1]$$
$$= \frac{\mathrm{Var}[X_1]}{n}.$$

So the variance of the sample mean decreases as n gets large, while its expectation remains the same by linearity:

$$\mathbb{E}\left[\frac{1}{n}\sum_{i=1}^n X_i\right] = \frac{1}{n}\sum_{i=1}^n \mathbb{E}[X_i]$$
$$= \frac{1}{n} n\, \mathbb{E}[X_1]$$
$$= \mathbb{E}[X_1].$$

Together with *Chebyshev's Inequality*, we immediately see that the sample mean approaches its expectation in the following probabilistic sense.

Theorem 1.2.30 *(Weak Law of Large Numbers)* Let $X_1, \ldots, X_n$ be i.i.d. For any $\varepsilon > 0$, as $n \to +\infty$,

$$\mathbb{P}\left[\left|\frac{1}{n}\sum_{i=1}^n X_i - \mathbb{E}[X_1]\right| \geq \varepsilon\right] \to 0.$$

Proof By *Chebyshev's Inequality* and the formulas above,

$$\mathbb{P}\left[\left|\frac{1}{n}\sum_{i=1}^n X_i - \mathbb{E}[X_1]\right| \geq \varepsilon\right] = \mathbb{P}\left[\left|\frac{1}{n}\sum_{i=1}^n X_i - \mathbb{E}\left[\frac{1}{n}\sum_{i=1}^n X_i\right]\right| \geq \varepsilon\right]$$
$$\leq \frac{\mathrm{Var}\left[\frac{1}{n}\sum_{i=1}^n X_i\right]}{\varepsilon^2}$$
$$= \frac{\mathrm{Var}[X_1]}{n\varepsilon^2}$$
$$\to 0$$

as $n \to +\infty$. $\square$

NUMERICAL CORNER We can use simulations to confirm the *Weak Law of Large Numbers*. Recall that a uniform random variable over the interval $[a, b]$ has density

$$f_X(x) = \begin{cases} \frac{1}{b-a} & x \in [a, b] \\ 0 & \text{otherwise.} \end{cases}$$

We write $X \sim U[a, b]$. We can obtain a sample from $U[0, 1]$ by using the function `numpy.random.Generator.uniform`. We must first instantiate a random number generator (RNG) with `numpy.random.default_rng` in NumPy. We provide a seed as an initial state for the RNG. Using the same seed again ensures reproducibility.

```
seed = 535
rng = np.random.default_rng(seed)
rng.uniform()
```

0.9836159914889122

Now we take n samples from $U[0, 1]$ and compute their sample mean. We repeat k times and display the empirical distribution of the sample means using a histogram. We start with $n = 10$.

```
n, k = 10, 1000
sample_mean = [np.mean(rng.random(n)) for i in range(k)]
plt.hist(sample_mean, bins=10, color='lightblue', edgecolor='black')
plt.xlim(0,1)
plt.show()
```

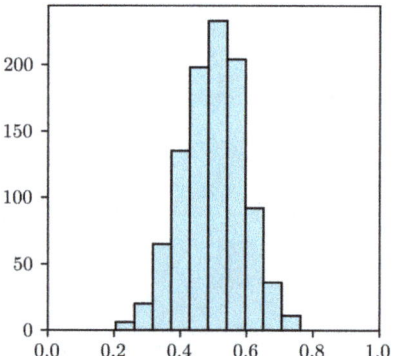

Figure 1.8 Graphical output of code.

Taking n much larger leads to more concentration around the mean.

```
n, k = 100, 1000
sample_mean = [np.mean(rng.random(n)) for i in range(k)]
plt.hist(sample_mean, bins=10, color='lightblue', edgecolor='black')
plt.xlim(0,1)
plt.show()
```

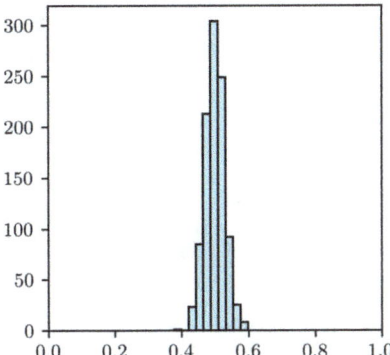

Figure 1.9 Graphical output of code.

TRY IT! Recall that the cumulative distribution function (CDF) of a random variable X is defined as

$$F_X(z) = \mathbb{P}[X \leq z], \quad \forall z \in \mathbb{R}.$$

a) Let $\mathcal{Z}$ be the interval where $F_X(z) \in (0,1)$ and assume that F_X is strictly increasing on $\mathcal{Z}$. Let $U \sim \mathrm{U}[0,1]$. Show that

$$\mathbb{P}[F_X^{-1}(U) \leq z] = F_X(z).$$

b) **Generate a sample** from $\mathrm{U}[a,b]$ for arbitrary a, b using `numpy.random.Generator.uniform` and the observation in a). This is called the inverse transform sampling method. Here is a starter code.

```
a = -1
b = 1
X = rng.uniform()
```

◁ NC

1.2.3.3 Random Vectors and Matrices

A random vector $\mathbf{X} = (X_1, \ldots, X_d)$ in $\mathbb{R}^d$ is a d-dimensional vector whose coordinates $X_1, \ldots, X_d$ are correlated random variables; formally, they live in the same probability space.

The mean $\mu_{\mathbf{X}}$ of a random vector $\mathbf{X}$ is itself a vector, whose coordinates are the means of the coordinates,

$$\mu_{\mathbf{X}} = \mathbb{E}[\mathbf{X}] = \begin{pmatrix} \mathbb{E}[X_1] \\ \vdots \\ \mathbb{E}[X_d] \end{pmatrix}.$$

The linearity of expectation generalizes to (check it!)

$$\mathbb{E}[A\mathbf{X} + \mathbf{b}] = A\,\mathbb{E}[\mathbf{X}] + \mathbf{b}$$

for a deterministic (i.e., nonrandom) matrix $A \in \mathbb{R}^{\ell \times d}$ and vector $\mathbf{b} \in \mathbb{R}^\ell$.

A random matrix $\mathbf{M} = (M_{i,j})_{i,j} \in \mathbb{R}^{\ell \times d}$ is a matrix whose entries are correlated random variables; The expectation of a random matrix is the (deterministic) matrix whose entries are the expectations of the entries of $\mathbf{M}$:

$$\mathbb{E}[\mathbf{M}] = \begin{pmatrix} \mathbb{E}[M_{1,1}] & \cdots & \mathbb{E}[M_{1,d}] \\ \vdots & \ddots & \vdots \\ \mathbb{E}[M_{\ell,1}] & \cdots & \mathbb{E}[M_{\ell,d}] \end{pmatrix}.$$

The linearity of expectation generalizes to (check it!)

$$\mathbb{E}[A\mathbf{M} + B] = A\,\mathbb{E}[\mathbf{M}] + B$$

for a deterministic matrices $A \in \mathbb{R}^{k \times \ell}$ and $B \in \mathbb{R}^{k \times d}$.

The covariance matrix $\Sigma_{\mathbf{X}}$ of a random vector $\mathbf{X}$ (also known as variance matrix or variance-covariance matrix) is the matrix whose (i, j)-entry is the covariance of coordinates i and j,

$$(\Sigma_{\mathbf{X}})_{i,j} = \mathrm{Cov}[X_i, X_j] = \mathbb{E}\left[(X_i - \mathbb{E}[X_i])(X_j - \mathbb{E}[X_j])\right].$$

We will also sometimes denote it as $K_{\mathbf{X},\mathbf{X}} := \Sigma_{\mathbf{X}}$, or simply as $\mathrm{Cov}[\mathbf{X}]$.

Using a previous example, this can be written in a more compact matrix form as

$$\Sigma_{\mathbf{X}} = \mathbb{E}\left[(\mathbf{X} - \mu_{\mathbf{X}})(\mathbf{X} - \mu_{\mathbf{X}})^T\right],$$

where we think of $\mathbf{X}$ as a column vector. Observe that in this calculation, $(\mathbf{X} - \mu_{\mathbf{X}})(\mathbf{X} - \mu_{\mathbf{X}})^T$ is a random matrix.

Covariance matrices have two special properties: they are symmetric and positive semidefinite.

Symmetry comes from the definition of the covariance:

$$\begin{aligned} \mathrm{Cov}[X_i, X_j] &= \mathbb{E}\left[(X_i - \mathbb{E}[X_i])(X_j - \mathbb{E}[X_j])\right] \\ &= \mathbb{E}\left[(X_j - \mathbb{E}[X_j])(X_i - \mathbb{E}[X_i])\right] \\ &= \mathrm{Cov}[X_j, X_i]. \end{aligned}$$

Theorem 1.2.31 *(Positive Semidefiniteness of the Covariance)* *The covariance matrix $\Sigma_{\mathbf{X}}$ of a random vector $\mathbf{X}$ is positive semidefinite.*

Proof idea: The expression $\langle \mathbf{z}, \Sigma_{\mathbf{X}} \mathbf{z} \rangle$ can be rewritten as the variance of a sum of random variables. Variances are always nonnegative.

Proof By definition of the covariance,

$$\begin{aligned} \langle \mathbf{z}, \Sigma_{\mathbf{X}} \mathbf{z} \rangle &= \sum_{i,j} z_i z_j \mathrm{Cov}[X_i, X_j] \\ &= \sum_{i,j} z_i z_j \mathbb{E}\left[(X_i - \mathbb{E}[X_i])(X_j - \mathbb{E}[X_j])\right] \\ &= \sum_{i,j} \mathbb{E}\left[(z_i X_i - \mathbb{E}[z_i X_i])(z_j X_j - \mathbb{E}[z_j X_j])\right] \\ &= \sum_{i,j} \mathrm{Cov}[z_i X_i, z_j X_j]. \end{aligned}$$

Using the fact that $\text{Cov}[X,X] = \text{Var}[X]$ and $\text{Cov}[X,Y] = \text{Cov}[Y,X]$, this last sum can be rearranged as

$$\sum_{i=1}^{d} \text{Var}[z_i X_i] + 2 \sum_{i<j} \text{Cov}[z_i X_i, z_j X_j].$$

We have encountered this expression previously! By the *Variance of a Sum*, this is

$$\text{Var}\left[\sum_{i=1}^{d} z_i X_i\right],$$

which is nonnegative. This concludes the proof. □

Later on, we will the need the covariance matrix of a linear transformation. We first note that the covariance has convenient linearity properties:

$$\begin{aligned}
\text{Cov}[\alpha X + \beta, Y] &= \mathbb{E}\left[(\alpha X + \beta - \mathbb{E}[\alpha X + \beta])(Y - \mathbb{E}[Y])\right] \\
&= \mathbb{E}\left[(\alpha X - \mathbb{E}[\alpha X])(Y - \mathbb{E}[Y])\right] \\
&= \alpha \mathbb{E}\left[(X - \mathbb{E}[X])(Y - \mathbb{E}[Y])\right] \\
&= \alpha \text{Cov}[X, Y].
\end{aligned}$$

Moreover,

$$\begin{aligned}
\text{Cov}[X + Z, Y] &= \mathbb{E}\left[(X + Z - \mathbb{E}[X + Z])(Y - \mathbb{E}[Y])\right] \\
&= \mathbb{E}\left[(X - \mathbb{E}[X] + Z - \mathbb{E}[Z])(Y - \mathbb{E}[Y])\right] \\
&= \mathbb{E}\left[(X - \mathbb{E}[X])(Y - \mathbb{E}[Y])\right] + \mathbb{E}\left[(Z - \mathbb{E}[Z])(Y - \mathbb{E}[Y])\right] \\
&= \text{Cov}[X, Y] + \text{Cov}[Z, Y].
\end{aligned}$$

Lemma 1.2.32 *(Covariance of a Linear Transformation)* Let $\mathbf{X} = (X_1, \ldots, X_d)$ *be a random vector in* $\mathbb{R}^d$ *with finite variances (i.e.,* $\text{Var}[X_i] < +\infty$ *for all i). For a deterministic (i.e., nonrandom)* $A \in \mathbb{R}^{\ell \times d}$, *we have*

$$\text{Cov}[A\mathbf{X}] = A \, \text{Cov}[\mathbf{X}] \, A^T$$

Proof In matrix form, letting $\boldsymbol{\mu}_\mathbf{X}$ and $\boldsymbol{\mu}_\mathbf{Y} = A\boldsymbol{\mu}_\mathbf{X}$ be respectively the means of $\mathbf{X}$ and $\mathbf{Y} = A\mathbf{X}$, we have

$$\begin{aligned}
\text{Cov}[\mathbf{Y}] &= \mathbb{E}\left[(\mathbf{Y} - \boldsymbol{\mu}_\mathbf{Y})(\mathbf{Y} - \boldsymbol{\mu}_\mathbf{Y})^T\right] \\
&= \mathbb{E}\left[(A\mathbf{X} - A\boldsymbol{\mu}_\mathbf{X})(A\mathbf{X} - A\boldsymbol{\mu}_\mathbf{X})^T\right] \\
&= \mathbb{E}\left[A(\mathbf{X} - \boldsymbol{\mu}_\mathbf{X})(\mathbf{X} - \boldsymbol{\mu}_\mathbf{X})^T A^T\right] \\
&= A \, \mathbb{E}\left[(\mathbf{X} - \boldsymbol{\mu}_\mathbf{X})(\mathbf{X} - \boldsymbol{\mu}_\mathbf{X})^T\right] A^T
\end{aligned}$$

where we used linearity of expectation twice. □

For two random vectors $\mathbf{X} \in \mathbb{R}^n$ and $\mathbf{Y} \in \mathbb{R}^m$ defined on the same probability space, we define the cross-covariance matrix as

$$\text{Cov}[\mathbf{X}, \mathbf{Y}] = \mathbb{E}[(\mathbf{X} - \mathbb{E}[\mathbf{X}])(\mathbf{Y} - \mathbb{E}[\mathbf{Y}])^T].$$

This is a matrix of dimension $n \times m$.

The cross-covariance matrix of a random vector with itself is the covariance matrix.

1.2.3.4 Normal Distribution

Recall that a standard Normal variable X has PDF

$$f_X(x) = \frac{1}{\sqrt{2\pi}} \exp\left(-x^2/2\right).$$

Its mean is 0 and its variance is 1.

To construct a d-dimensional version, we take d independent standard Normal variables $X_1, X_2, \ldots, X_d$ and form the vector $\mathbf{X} = (X_1, \ldots, X_d)$. We will say that $\mathbf{X}$ is a standard Normal d-vector. By independence, its joint PDF is given by the product of the PDFs of the X_i's, that is,

$$\begin{aligned} f_{\mathbf{X}}(\mathbf{x}) &= \prod_{i=1}^{d} \frac{1}{\sqrt{2\pi}} \exp\left(-x_i^2/2\right) \\ &= \frac{1}{\prod_{i=1}^{d} \sqrt{2\pi}} \exp\left(-\sum_{i=1}^{d} x_i^2/2\right) \\ &= \frac{1}{(2\pi)^{d/2}} \exp(-\|\mathbf{x}\|^2/2). \end{aligned}$$

We can also shift and scale it.

Definition 1.2.33 *(Spherical Gaussian) Let $\mathbf{Z}$ be a standard Normal d-vector, let $\boldsymbol{\mu} \in \mathbb{R}^d$ and let $\sigma \in \mathbb{R}_+$. Then we will refer to the transformed random variable $\mathbf{X} = \boldsymbol{\mu} + \sigma \mathbf{Z}$ as a spherical Gaussian with mean $\boldsymbol{\mu}$ and variance σ^2. We use the notation $\mathbf{Z} \sim N_d(\boldsymbol{\mu}, \sigma^2 I)$.*

NUMERICAL CORNER The following function generates n data points from a spherical d-dimensional Gaussians with variance σ^2 and mean $\boldsymbol{\mu}$.

Below, `rng.normal(0,1,(n,d))` generates an independent d-dimensional spherical Gaussian with mean **0** (as row vectors).

Throughout, when defining a function that uses a random number generator (RNG), we initialize the RNG outside the function and pass the RNG to it. This allows us to maintain control over the random number generation process at a higher level and ensures consistent results across multiple runs.

```
def spherical_gaussian(rng, d, n, mu, sig):
    return mu + sig * rng.normal(0,1,(n,d))
```

We generate 100 data points in dimension $d = 2$. We take $\sigma^2 = 1$ and $\boldsymbol{\mu} = w \mathbf{e}_1$. Below we use the function `numpy.hstack` to create a vector by concatenating two given vectors. We use `[w]` to create a vector with a single entry `w`. We also use the function `numpy.zeros` to create an all-zero vector.

```
d, n, w, sig = 2, 100, 3., 1.
mu = np.hstack(([w], np.zeros(d-1)))
X = spherical_gaussian(rng, d, n, mu, sig)
plt.scatter(X[:,0], X[:,1], s=5, c='k')
plt.axis([-1, 7, -4, 4])
plt.show()
```

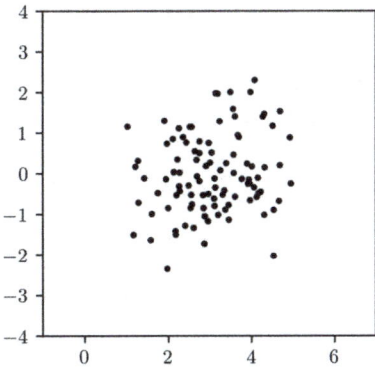

Figure 1.10 Graphical output of code.

◁ **NC**

More generally, we consider mixtures of spherical Gaussians, a special case of the Gaussian mixture model (GMM). To keep things simple, we will restrict ourselves to mixtures of *two* Gaussians, but this can easily be generalized.

This model has a number of parameters. For $i = 0, 1$, we have a mean $\boldsymbol{\mu}_i \in \mathbb{R}^d$ and a positive variance $\sigma_i \in \mathbb{R}_+$. We also have mixture weights $\phi_0, \phi_1 \in (0, 1)$ such that $\phi_0 + \phi_1 = 1$. Suppose we want to generate a total of n samples.

For each sample $j = 1, \ldots, n$, independently from everything else:

1. We first pick a component $i \in \{0, 1\}$ at random according to the mixture weights, that is, $i = 0$ is chosen with probability ϕ_0 and $i = 1$ is chosen with probability ϕ_1.

2. We generate a sample $\mathbf{X}_j = (X_{j,1}, \ldots, X_{j,d})$ according to a spherical Gaussian with mean $\boldsymbol{\mu}_i$ and variance σ_i^2.

NUMERICAL CORNER This is straightforward to implement by using `numpy.random.Generator.choice` to choose the component of each sample.

The code is the following. It returns a d by n array X, where each row is a sample from a two-component spherical Gaussian mixture.

```
def gmm2spherical(rng, d, n, phi0, phi1, mu0, sig0, mu1, sig1):

    phi, mu, sig = np.stack((phi0, phi1)), np.stack((mu0, mu1)),
                   np.stack((sig0,sig1))

    X = np.zeros((n,d))
    component = rng.choice(2, size=n, p=phi)
    for i in range(n):
        X[i,:] = spherical_gaussian(rng, d, 1, mu[component[i],:],
                 sig[component[i]])

    return X
```

Let us try it with the following parameters.

```
d, n, w, sig0, sig1, phi0, phi1 = 2, 1000, 3., 1.5, 0.5, 0.2, 0.8
mu0, mu1 = np.hstack(([w], np.zeros(d-1))), np.hstack(([-w],
        np.zeros(d-1)))
X = gmm2spherical(rng, d, n, phi0, phi1, mu0, sig0, mu1, sig1)
plt.figure(figsize=(6,3))
plt.scatter(X[:,0], X[:,1], s=5, color='k')
plt.axis([-8, 8, -4, 4])
plt.show()
```

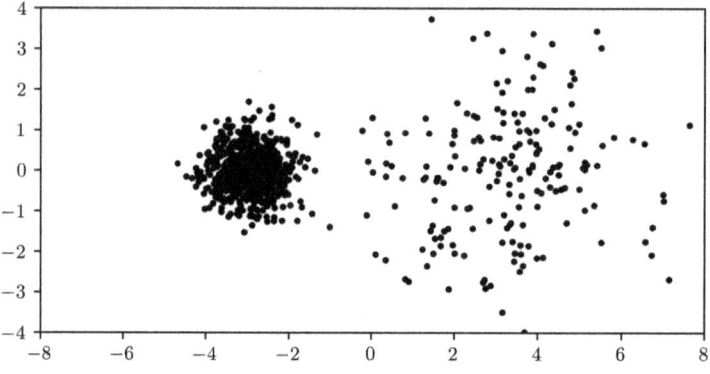

Figure 1.11 Graphical output of code.

As expected, we observe two clusters. The one on the right (component 0) is sparser (i.e., it contains fewer data points) since `phi0` is much smaller than `phi1`. It is also larger as its variance is larger.

◁ **NC**

Self-Assessment Quiz *(with help from Claude, Gemini, and ChatGPT)*

1 Let $A \in \mathbb{R}^{n \times m}$ and $B \in \mathbb{R}^{m \times p}$. What are the dimensions of the matrix product AB?

  a) $n \times m$

  b) $m \times p$

  c) $n \times p$

  d) $p \times n$

2 Which of the following is NOT a property of the transpose of a matrix?

  a) $(A^T)^T = A$

  b) $(\gamma A)^T = \gamma A^T$ for any scalar $\gamma \in \mathbb{R}$

  c) $(A + B)^T = A^T + B^T$

  d) $(AB)^T = A^T B^T$

3. Let $A \in \mathbb{R}^{n \times m}$ be a matrix and $\mathbf{x} \in \mathbb{R}^m$ be a column vector. Which of the following is true about the matrix-vector product $A\mathbf{x}$?
   a) $A\mathbf{x}$ is a linear combination of the rows of A where the coefficients are the entries of $\mathbf{x}$.
   b) $A\mathbf{x}$ is a linear combination of the columns of A where the coefficients are the entries of $\mathbf{x}$.
   c) $A\mathbf{x}$ is a linear combination of the rows of A where the coefficients are the entries of the first row of A.
   d) $A\mathbf{x}$ is a linear combination of the columns of A where the coefficients are the entries of the first column of A.

4. Which of the following is NOT a property of the variance of a random variable?
   a) $\text{Var}[\alpha X + \beta] = \alpha^2 \text{Var}[X]$ for $\alpha, \beta \in \mathbb{R}$
   b) $\text{Var}[X] = \mathbb{E}[(X - \mathbb{E}[X])^2]$
   c) $\text{Var}[X] \geq 0$
   d) $\text{Var}[X + Y] = \text{Var}[X] + \text{Var}[Y]$ for any random variables X and Y

5. If $\mathbf{X}$ is a random vector in $\mathbb{R}^d$ with mean vector $\boldsymbol{\mu}_\mathbf{X}$ and covariance matrix $\Sigma_\mathbf{X}$, which of the following expressions represents the covariance matrix $\Sigma_\mathbf{X}$?
   a) $\mathbb{E}[(\mathbf{X} - \boldsymbol{\mu}_\mathbf{X})^2]$
   b) $\mathbb{E}[(\mathbf{X} - \boldsymbol{\mu}_\mathbf{X})(\mathbf{X} - \boldsymbol{\mu}_\mathbf{X})^T]$
   c) $\mathbb{E}[(\mathbf{X} - \boldsymbol{\mu}_\mathbf{X})^T(\mathbf{X} - \boldsymbol{\mu}_\mathbf{X})]$
   d) $\mathbb{E}[(\mathbf{X} - \boldsymbol{\mu}_\mathbf{X})^T]\mathbb{E}[(\mathbf{X} - \boldsymbol{\mu}_\mathbf{X})]$

Answer for 1: c. Justification: "Taking the number of rows of the first matrix and the number of columns of the second one, we see that [the dimension of AB] is $n \times p$."

Answer for 2: d. Justification: The text states that $(BC)^T = C^T B^T$, not $B^T C^T$.

Answer for 3: b. Justification: The text states, "$A\mathbf{x}$ is a linear combination of the columns of A where the coefficients are the entries of $\mathbf{x}$. In matrix form, $A\mathbf{x} = \sum_{j=1}^m A_{\cdot,j} x_j$."

Answer for 4: d. Justification: The text states that the variance of a sum of random variables is given by $\text{Var}[X_1 + \ldots + X_n] = \sum_{i=1}^n \text{Var}[X_i] + 2\sum_{i<j} \text{Cov}[X_i, X_j]$, which is only equal to $\text{Var}[X] + \text{Var}[Y]$ (in this case) when the covariance term is zero (e.g., when X and Y are independent).

Answer for 5: b. Justification: The covariance matrix $\Sigma_\mathbf{X}$ of a random vector $\mathbf{X}$ is given by $\Sigma_\mathbf{X} = \mathbb{E}[(\mathbf{X} - \boldsymbol{\mu}_\mathbf{X})(\mathbf{X} - \boldsymbol{\mu}_\mathbf{X})^T]$.

1.3 Clustering: An Objective, an Algorithm and a Guarantee

Consider the following fundamental problem in data science.

The input: We are given n vectors $\mathbf{x}_1, \ldots, \mathbf{x}_n$ in $\mathbb{R}^d$.

Our goal is to find a good clustering; loosely speaking, we want to partition these data points into k disjoint subsets – or clusters – with small pairwise distances within clusters and large pairwise distances across clusters. To make this rather vague problem more precise, we consider a specific objective function known as the k-means objective. Our approach here will be typical of how one might approach a mathematical data science problem. We will first formulate the problem as an optimization problem, then derive an algorithm to solve it, and finally provide some rigorous guarantees about the output.

The output: But first, we need to define precisely what we are trying to extract from the data. What is the mathematical structure of the solution sought? Fix a number of clusters k. Formally, we define a clustering as a partition.

Definition 1.3.1 (*Partition*) *A partition of* $[n] = \{1, \ldots, n\}$ *of size k is a collection of nonempty subsets* $C_1, \ldots, C_k \subseteq [n]$ *that*

- *are pairwise disjoint:* $C_i \cap C_j = \emptyset, \forall i \neq j$
- *cover all of* $[n]$, *that is,* $\cup_{i=1}^{k} C_i = [n]$.

Example 1.3.2 *Suppose we are given eight data points in $\mathbb{R}^2$ as follows:*

$$\mathbf{x}_1 = \begin{pmatrix} 1 \\ 0 \end{pmatrix}, \mathbf{x}_2 = \begin{pmatrix} -2 \\ 0 \end{pmatrix}, \mathbf{x}_3 = \begin{pmatrix} -2 \\ 1 \end{pmatrix}, \mathbf{x}_4 = \begin{pmatrix} 1 \\ -3 \end{pmatrix},$$

$$\mathbf{x}_5 = \begin{pmatrix} -10 \\ 10 \end{pmatrix}, \mathbf{x}_6 = \begin{pmatrix} 2 \\ -2 \end{pmatrix}, \mathbf{x}_7 = \begin{pmatrix} -3 \\ 1 \end{pmatrix}, \mathbf{x}_8 = \begin{pmatrix} 3 \\ -1 \end{pmatrix}.$$

So here $n = 8$ and $d = 2$. Assume we look for $k = 3$ clusters. Then a valid clustering would be, for instance,

$$C_1 = \{1, 4, 6, 8\}, C_2 = \{2, 3, 7\}, C_3 = \{5\},$$

which corresponds to assigning data points $\mathbf{x}_1, \mathbf{x}_4, \mathbf{x}_6, \mathbf{x}_8$ *to the first cluster, data points* $\mathbf{x}_2, \mathbf{x}_3, \mathbf{x}_7$ *to the second cluster, and data point* $\mathbf{x}_5$ *to the third cluster. Note in particular that the sets* C_1, C_2, C_3 *satisfy the conditions of a partition: they are disjoint and cover all of* $[8] = \{1, 2, \ldots, 8\}$. *Or put differently, each data point is assigned to one and exactly one cluster.*

We number the clusters $C_1, \ldots, C_k$ for notational convenience, but their order is irrelevant. Two partitions are equivalent if they are the same family of subsets. For instance, in the previous example, $C_1 = \{1, 4, 6, 8\}, C_2 = \{2, 3, 7\}, C_3 = \{5\}$ and $C_1 = \{5\}, C_2 = \{1, 4, 6, 8\}, C_3 = \{2, 3, 7\}$ are equivalent clusterings.

1.3.1 The *k*-Means Objective

Under the k-means objective, the "cost" of $C_1, \ldots, C_k$ is defined as

$$\mathcal{G}(C_1, \ldots, C_k) = \min_{\boldsymbol{\mu}_1, \ldots, \boldsymbol{\mu}_k \in \mathbb{R}^d} \sum_{i=1}^{k} \sum_{j \in C_i} \|\mathbf{x}_j - \boldsymbol{\mu}_i\|^2.$$

Here $\boldsymbol{\mu}_i \in \mathbb{R}^d$ is the representative – or center – of cluster C_i. Note that $\boldsymbol{\mu}_i$ need not be one of the $\mathbf{x}_j$'s.

1.3 Clustering: An Objective, an Algorithm and a Guarantee

Our goal is to find a partition $C_1, \ldots, C_k$ that minimizes $\mathcal{G}(C_1, \ldots, C_k)$, and thus solves the problem

$$\min_{C_1, \ldots, C_k} \mathcal{G}(C_1, \ldots, C_k)$$

over all partitions of $[n]$ of size k. This is a finite optimization problem, as there are only a finite number of such partitions. Note, however, that the objective function itself is an optimization problem over $\mathbb{R}^d \times \cdots \times \mathbb{R}^d$, namely k copies of $\mathbb{R}^d$.

To quote Wikipedia[7]:

> In centroid-based clustering, clusters are represented by a central vector, which may not necessarily be a member of the data set. When the number of clusters is fixed to k, k-means clustering gives a formal definition as an optimization problem: find the k cluster centers and assign the objects to the nearest cluster center, such that the squared distances from the cluster are minimized.

In general, the problem is NP-hard; that is, roughly speaking no "fast" algorithm is expected to exist to solve it. Lloyd's algorithm (also referred to as the k-means algorithm) is a popular heuristic. It is based on the idea that the following two subproblems are easy to solve:

1. finding the optimal representatives for a fixed partition;
2. finding the optimal partition for a fixed set of representatives.

One then alternates between the two (perhaps until progress falls below a tolerance). This is reasonable since our goal, as we pointed out above, is to solve the minimization problem

$$\min_{C_1, \ldots, C_k} \min_{\mu_1, \ldots, \mu_k \in \mathbb{R}^d} \sum_{i=1}^{k} \sum_{j \in C_i} \|\mathbf{x}_j - \boldsymbol{\mu}_i\|^2$$

where $C_1, \ldots, C_k$ ranges over all partitions of $[n]$ of size k. Fixing partition $C_1, \ldots, C_k$ and miniminizing over $\mu_1, \ldots, \mu_k \in \mathbb{R}^d$ corresponds to solving the first problem above, while fixing $\mu_1, \ldots, \mu_k \in \mathbb{R}^d$ and miniminizing over partitions $C_1, \ldots, C_k$ corresponds to solving the second problem.

CHAT & LEARN Ask your favorite AI chatbot about the differences between k-means, k-medians, and k-medoids clustering.

1.3.1.1 Some Useful Optimization Results

To analyze Lloyd's algorithm, we will rely on a few basic observations.

Minimizing a quadratic function: To elaborate on the first step above, we review an elementary fact about quadratic functions. Consider the function

$$q(x) = ax^2 + bx + c.$$

When $a > 0$, q has a unique minimum.

Lemma 1.3.3 *(Minimum of a Quadratic Function)* Let $q(x) = ax^2 + bx + c$ where $a > 0$ and $x \in \mathbb{R}$. The unique global minimum of q is attained at

$$x^* = -\frac{b}{2a}.$$

---

[7] https://en.wikipedia.org/wiki/Cluster_analysis

Proof By the *First-Order Necessary Optimality Condition*, a global minimizer of q (which is necessarily a local minimizer) satisfies the condition

$$\frac{d}{dx}q(x) = 2ax + b = 0,$$

whose unique solution is

$$x^* = -\frac{b}{2a}.$$

To see that x^* is indeed a global minimizer, we rewrite q as

$$\begin{aligned}q(x) &= a\left(x^2 + 2\left[\frac{b}{2a}\right]x\right) + c \\ &= a\left(x^2 + 2\left[\frac{b}{2a}\right]x + \left[\frac{b}{2a}\right]^2\right) - a\left[\frac{b}{2a}\right]^2 + c \\ &= a(x - x^*)^2 + \left[c - \frac{b^2}{4a}\right].\end{aligned}$$

Clearly, any other x gives a higher value for q. The step on the second line above is called completing the square. □

Optimizing an additively separable function: Functions that can be written as the sum of disjoint sets of coordinates arise commonly in optimization and have convenient "separability" properties.

For vectors $\mathbf{x}_i \in \mathbb{R}^{d_i}$, $i \in [\ell]$, with $\sum_{i=1}^{\ell} d_i = d$ their concatenation is denoted as $(\mathbf{x}_1, \ldots, \mathbf{x}_\ell) \in \mathbb{R}^d$. This is the vector obtained by concatenating the coordinates of $\mathbf{x}_1, \ldots, \mathbf{x}_\ell$ into a single vector. A different way to see this is that $(\mathbf{x}_1, \ldots, \mathbf{x}_\ell)$ is a block vector with blocks $\mathbf{x}_1, \ldots, \mathbf{x}_\ell$. For example, if $\mathbf{x}_1 = (1, 2)$ and $\mathbf{x}_2 = (-1, -3, -5)$, then $(\mathbf{x}_1, \mathbf{x}_2) = (1, 2, -1, -3, -5)$.

Lemma 1.3.4 *(Optimizing a Separable Function)* Assume that $\mathbf{z} \in \mathbb{R}^d$ can be broken up into subvectors $\mathbf{x}_i \in \mathbb{R}^{d_i}$, $i \in [\ell]$, with $\sum_{i=1}^{\ell} d_i = d$ as $\mathbf{z} = (\mathbf{x}_1, \ldots, \mathbf{x}_\ell)$. Suppose that the real-valued function $h \colon \mathbb{R}^d \to \mathbb{R}$ can be written in the additively separable form

$$h(\mathbf{z}) = f_1(\mathbf{x}_1) + \cdots + f_\ell(\mathbf{x}_\ell),$$

for a collection of functions $f_i \colon \mathbb{R}^{d_i} \to \mathbb{R}$, $i \in [\ell]$. If, for each $i \in [\ell]$, $\mathbf{x}_i^*$ is a global minimum of f_i, then $\mathbf{z}^* = (\mathbf{x}_1^*, \ldots, \mathbf{x}_\ell^*)$ is a global minimum of h.

Proof idea: Each term in the sum defining h depends on a separate set of coordinates and therefore is unaffected by the choices made in other terms.

Proof Let $\mathbf{z} = (\mathbf{x}_1, \ldots, \mathbf{x}_\ell)$. Since $\mathbf{x}_i^*$ is a global minimum of f_i, it holds that $f_i(\mathbf{x}_i^*) \leq f_i(\mathbf{x}_i)$, for all i. Hence,

$$h(\mathbf{z}^*) = f_1(\mathbf{x}_1^*) + \cdots + f_\ell(\mathbf{x}_\ell^*) \leq f_1(\mathbf{x}_1) + \cdots + f_\ell(\mathbf{x}_\ell) = h(\mathbf{z}).$$

Since $\mathbf{z}$ is arbitrary, we have proved the claim. □

Composing with a nondecreasing function: Recall that a real-valued function f of a single variable is nondecreasing if

$$x \leq y \implies f(x) \leq f(y).$$

Lemma 1.3.5 *(Composing with a Nondecreasing Function) Let $f: \mathbb{R} \to \mathbb{R}$ be nondecreasing, let $g: \mathbb{R}^d \to \mathbb{R}$, and define $h(\mathbf{x}) = f(g(\mathbf{x}))$. If $\mathbf{x}^*$ is a global minimum of g, then it is also a global minimum of h.*

Proof idea: This just follows from applying the definitions.

Proof Let $\mathbf{x} \in \mathbb{R}^d$. Because $\mathbf{x}^*$ is a global minimum of g, $g(\mathbf{x}^*) \leq g(\mathbf{x})$. Further, since f is nondecreasing,

$$h(\mathbf{x}^*) = f(g(\mathbf{x}^*)) \leq f(g(\mathbf{x})) = h(\mathbf{x}).$$

Since $\mathbf{x}$ is arbitrary, we have proved the claim. □

1.3.1.2 Sub-Problem 1: Finding the Optimal Representatives

We denote by $|C_i|$ the number of elements in C_i.

Example 1.3.6 *(continued from Example 1.3.2) Continuing the example above, the sizes of the clusters are respectively $|C_1| = 4, |C_2| = 3, |C_3| = 1$. Note in particular that $|C_1| + |C_2| + |C_3| = 8 = n$, as follows from the fact that C_1, C_2, C_3 is a partition.*

Lemma 1.3.7 *(Optimal Representatives) Fix a partition $C_1, \ldots, C_k$. The optimal representatives under the objective*

$$\mathcal{G}(C_1, \ldots, C_k; \boldsymbol{\mu}_1, \ldots, \boldsymbol{\mu}_k) = \sum_{i=1}^{k} \sum_{j \in C_i} \|\mathbf{x}_j - \boldsymbol{\mu}_i\|^2$$

are the centroids

$$\boldsymbol{\mu}_i^* = \frac{1}{|C_i|} \sum_{j \in C_i} \mathbf{x}_j.$$

Proof idea: The objective $\mathcal{G}$ can be written as a sum, where each term is a quadratic function in one component of one of the $\boldsymbol{\mu}_i$'s. Each of these terms is minimized by the average of the corresponding components of the $\mathbf{x}_j$'s belonging to C_i.

Example 1.3.8 *(continued from Example 1.3.2) Continuing with the previous example, we compute the optimal representatives for the fixed partition C_1, C_2, C_3 above. We get*

$$\boldsymbol{\mu}_1^* = \frac{1}{4}[\mathbf{x}_1 + \mathbf{x}_4 + \mathbf{x}_6 + \mathbf{x}_8]$$
$$= \frac{1}{4}\left[\begin{pmatrix}1\\0\end{pmatrix} + \begin{pmatrix}1\\-3\end{pmatrix} + \begin{pmatrix}2\\-2\end{pmatrix} + \begin{pmatrix}3\\-1\end{pmatrix}\right] = \begin{pmatrix}7/4\\-3/2\end{pmatrix},$$
$$\boldsymbol{\mu}_2^* = \frac{1}{3}[\mathbf{x}_2 + \mathbf{x}_3 + \mathbf{x}_7]$$
$$= \frac{1}{3}\left[\begin{pmatrix}-2\\0\end{pmatrix} + \begin{pmatrix}-2\\1\end{pmatrix} + \begin{pmatrix}-3\\1\end{pmatrix}\right] = \begin{pmatrix}-7/3\\2/3\end{pmatrix},$$
$$\boldsymbol{\mu}_3^* = \frac{1}{1}[\mathbf{x}_5] = \begin{pmatrix}-10\\10\end{pmatrix}.$$

Proof *(Optimal Representatives)* Using the notation $\mathbf{x}_j = (x_{j1}, \ldots, x_{jd})$ and similarly for $\boldsymbol{\mu}_i$, note that we can expand the k-means objective as

$$\sum_{i=1}^{k} \sum_{j \in C_i} \|\mathbf{x}_j - \boldsymbol{\mu}_i\|^2 = \sum_{i=1}^{k} \sum_{j \in C_i} \sum_{m=1}^{d} (x_{jm} - \mu_{im})^2$$

$$= \sum_{i=1}^{k} \sum_{m=1}^{d} \left[\sum_{j \in C_i} (x_{jm} - \mu_{im})^2 \right].$$

The expression in square brackets is a quadratic function in μ_{im},

$$q_{im}(\mu_{im}) = \sum_{j \in C_i} (x_{jm} - \mu_{im})^2$$

$$= \left\{ \sum_{j \in C_i} x_{jm}^2 \right\} + \left\{ -2 \sum_{j \in C_i} x_{jm} \right\} \mu_{im} + \{|C_i|\} \mu_{im}^2.$$

Therefore, by the formula for the *Minimum of a Quadratic Function*, is minimized at

$$\mu_{im}^* = -\frac{-2 \sum_{j \in C_i} x_{jm}}{2|C_i|} = \frac{1}{|C_i|} \sum_{j \in C_i} x_{jm}.$$

Since each term $q_{im}(\mu_{im})$ in the sum over i, m making up the objective function G is minimized at $\boldsymbol{\mu}_1^*, \ldots, \boldsymbol{\mu}_k^*$, so is $\mathcal{G}$ by the *Optimizing a Separable Function Lemma*. □

That the squared norm decomposes into a sum over the coordinates (which the norm itself doesn't because of the square root) is one reason why it is convenient to use here, as was hopefully apparent in this last proof.

1.3.1.3 Sub-Problem 2: Finding the Optimal Partition

Given n vectors $\mathbf{x}_1, \ldots, \mathbf{x}_n$ in $\mathbb{R}^d$ and a partition $C_1, \ldots, C_k \subseteq [n]$, it will be useful to have some notation for the corresponding cluster assignment. We define $c(j) = i$ if $j \in C_i$.

Example 1.3.9 *(continued from Example 1.3.2)* Continuing the example above, the clusters $C_1 = \{1, 4, 6, 8\}, C_2 = \{2, 3, 7\}, C_3 = \{5\}$ *correspond to the assignment*

$$c(1) = 1, c(2) = 2, c(3) = 2, c(4) = 1, c(5) = 3, c(6) = 1, c(7) = (2), c(8) = 1.$$

Lemma 1.3.10 *(Optimal Clustering) Fix the representatives $\boldsymbol{\mu}_1, \ldots, \boldsymbol{\mu}_k$. An optimal partition under the objective*

$$\mathcal{G}(C_1, \ldots, C_k; \boldsymbol{\mu}_1, \ldots, \boldsymbol{\mu}_k) = \sum_{i=1}^{k} \sum_{j \in C_i} \|\mathbf{x}_j - \boldsymbol{\mu}_i\|^2$$

is obtained as follows. For each j, find the $\boldsymbol{\mu}_i$ that minimizes $\|\mathbf{x}_j - \boldsymbol{\mu}_i\|$ (picking one arbitrarily in the case of ties) and assign $\mathbf{x}_j$ to C_i (i.e., add j to C_i).

Proof If c is the cluster assignment associated with $C_1, \ldots, C_k$, then we can rewrite the objective as

$$\sum_{i=1}^{k} \sum_{j \in C_i} \|\mathbf{x}_j - \boldsymbol{\mu}_i\|^2 = \sum_{j=1}^{n} \|\mathbf{x}_j - \boldsymbol{\mu}_{c(j)}\|^2.$$

By definition, when the μ_i's are fixed, each term in the sum on the right-hand side is minimized separately by the assignment in the statement. Hence so is the sum itself by the *Optimizing a Separable Function Lemma*. Note that we used the fact that the square root (and the square) is non-decreasing to conclude that minimizing $\|\mathbf{x}_j - \mu_i\|^2$ or its square root $\|\mathbf{x}_j - \mu_i\|$ are equivalent by the *Composing with a Nondecreasing Function Lemma*. □

Example 1.3.11 *(continued from Example 1.3.2)* *Continuing the example above, suppose that we choose representatives*

$$\mu_1 = \begin{pmatrix} -2 \\ 1 \end{pmatrix}, \mu_2 = \begin{pmatrix} 2 \\ -1 \end{pmatrix}, \mu_3 = \begin{pmatrix} -10 \\ 10 \end{pmatrix}.$$

Then we find the cluster assignment of $\mathbf{x}_1$ *by computing its squared distance to each representative:*

$$\|\mathbf{x}_1 - \mu_1\| = \left\| \begin{pmatrix} 1 \\ 0 \end{pmatrix} - \begin{pmatrix} -2 \\ 1 \end{pmatrix} \right\| = \sqrt{(1-(-2))^2 + (0-1)^2} = \sqrt{10},$$

$$\|\mathbf{x}_1 - \mu_2\| = \left\| \begin{pmatrix} 1 \\ 0 \end{pmatrix} - \begin{pmatrix} 2 \\ -1 \end{pmatrix} \right\| = \sqrt{(1-2)^2 + (0-(-1))^2} = \sqrt{2},$$

$$\|\mathbf{x}_1 - \mu_3\| = \left\| \begin{pmatrix} 1 \\ 0 \end{pmatrix} - \begin{pmatrix} -10 \\ 10 \end{pmatrix} \right\| = \sqrt{(1-(-10))^2 + (0-10)^2} = \sqrt{221}.$$

The minimum is achieved for μ_2 *so we assign* $\mathbf{x}_1$ *to* C_2, *so that* $1 \in C_2$ *and* $c(1) = 2$.

1.3.2 Lloyd's Algorithm and Its Analysis

We are now ready to describe Lloyd's algorithm. We start from a random assignment of clusters. (An alternative initialization strategy is to choose k representatives at random among the data points.) We then alternate between the optimal choices in the lemmas. In lieu of pseudo-code, we write out the algorithm in Python. We will use this approach throughout the book.

The input X is assumed to be a collection of n vectors $\mathbf{x}_1, \ldots, \mathbf{x}_n \in \mathbb{R}^d$ stacked into a matrix, with one row for each data point. The other input, k, is the desired number of clusters. There is an optional input `maxiter` for the maximum number of iterations, which is set to 5 by default.

We first define separate functions for the two main steps. To find the minimum of an array, we use the function `numpy.argmin`. We also use `numpy.linalg.norm` to compute the Euclidean distance.

```
def opt_reps(X, k, assign):
    (n, d) = X.shape
    reps = np.zeros((k, d))
    for i in range(k):
        in_i = [j for j in range(n) if assign[j] == i]
        reps[i,:] = np.sum(X[in_i,:],axis=0) / len(in_i)
    return reps

def opt_clust(X, k, reps):
```

```
    (n, d) = X.shape
    dist = np.zeros(n)
    assign = np.zeros(n, dtype=int)
    for j in range(n):
        dist_to_i = np.array([LA.norm(X[j,:] - reps[i,:]) for i in
                    range(k)])
        assign[j] = np.argmin(dist_to_i)
        dist[j] = dist_to_i[assign[j]]
    G = np.sum(dist ** 2)
    print(G)
    return assign
```

The main function follows. Below, `rng.integers(0,k,n)` is an array of n uniformly chosen integers between 0 and k-1 (inclusive). See the documentation for `random.Generator.integers` for details. Recall that throughout, when defining a function that uses a random number generator (RNG), we initialize the RNG outside the function and pass the RNG to it. This allows us to maintain control over the random number generation process at a higher level and ensures consistent results across multiple runs.

```
def kmeans(rng, X, k, maxiter=5):
    (n, d) = X.shape
    assign = rng.integers(0,k,n)
    reps = np.zeros((k, d), dtype=int)
    for iter in range(maxiter):
        reps = opt_reps(X, k, assign)
        assign = opt_clust(X, k, reps)
    return assign
```

An example is provided in Figure 1.12.

NUMERICAL CORNER We apply our implementation of k-means to Example 1.3.2. We fix k to 3. Here the data matrix X is the following:

```
seed = 535
rng = np.random.default_rng(seed)
X = np.array([[1., 0.],[-2., 0.],[-2.,1.],[1.,-3.],
              [-10.,10.],[2.,-2.],[-3.,1.],[3.,-1.]])
assign = kmeans(rng, X, 3)
```

162.7
74.8611111111111
9.083333333333334
9.083333333333334
9.083333333333334

We vizualize the output by coloring the points according to their cluster assignment.

1.3 Clustering: An Objective, an Algorithm and a Guarantee 41

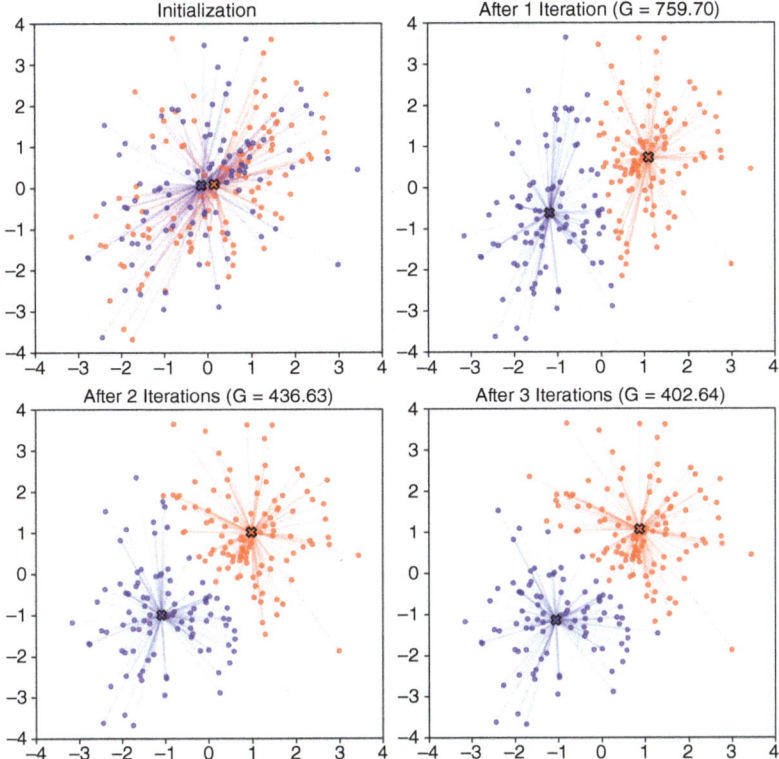

Figure 1.12 Evolution of the assignment for *k*-means clustering on data generated by a mixture of spherical Gaussians with variance 1 and respective means $(-1, -1)$ and $(1, 1)$. The crosses show the cluster representatives. The objective value is shown as G.

```
plt.scatter(X[:,0], X[:,1], s=10, c=assign, cmap='brg')
plt.axis([-11,4,-4,11])
plt.show()
```

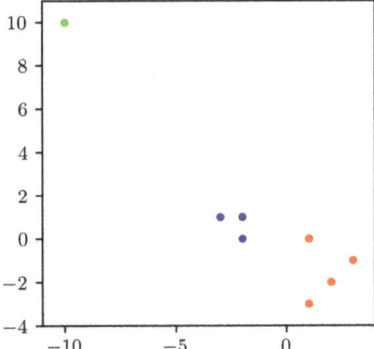

Figure 1.13 Graphical output of code.

We can compute the final representatives (optimal for the final assignment) by using the subroutine opt_reps.

```
print(opt_reps(X, 3, assign))
```

```
[[ -2.33333333   0.66666667]
 [  1.75        -1.5       ]
 [-10.         10.         ]]
```

Each row is the center of the corresponding cluster. Note these match with the ones we previously computed. Indeed, the clustering is the same (although not necessarily in the same order).

TRY IT! *Modify* kmeans to take a tolerance tol as input and stop when the improvement in objective value G falls below the tolerance.

◁ **NC**

Lloyd's algorithm is only a heuristic. In particular, it is not guaranteed to find the global minimum of the k-means objective. However, it is guaranteed to improve the objective at every iteration, or more precisely, not to make it worse.

Theorem 1.3.12 *(Convergence of k-means cost) The sequence of objective function values produced by the k-means algorithm is nonincreasing.*

Proof idea: By the *Optimal Representatives Lemma* and the *Optimal Clustering Lemma*, each step does not increase the objective.

Proof Let $C'_1, \ldots, C'_k$ be the current clusters, with representatives $\mu'_1, \ldots, \mu'_k$. After Step 1, the new representatives are $\mu''_1, \ldots, \mu''_k$. By the *Optimal Representatives Lemma*, they satisfy

$$\sum_{i=1}^{k} \sum_{j \in C'_i} \|\mathbf{x}_j - \mu''_i\|^2 \leq \sum_{i=1}^{k} \sum_{j \in C'_i} \|\mathbf{x}_j - \mu'_i\|^2.$$

After Step 2, the new clusters are $C''_1, \ldots, C''_k$. By the *Optimal Clustering Lemma*, they satisfy

$$\sum_{i=1}^{k} \sum_{j \in C''_i} \|\mathbf{x}_j - \mu''_i\|^2 \leq \sum_{i=1}^{k} \sum_{j \in C'_i} \|\mathbf{x}_j - \mu''_i\|^2.$$

Combining these two inequalities gives

$$\sum_{i=1}^{k} \sum_{j \in C''_i} \|\mathbf{x}_j - \mu''_i\|^2 \leq \sum_{i=1}^{k} \sum_{j \in C'_i} \|\mathbf{x}_j - \mu'_i\|^2,$$

as claimed. □

The sequence of objective values is monotone and bounded from below by 0. Hence it converges. Note that the limit depends on the starting point.

CHAT & LEARN AI chatbots can serve as great personal tutors, especially when it comes to coding, at which they often excel. In particular, they can provide additional information about the code in this book. Just copy-paste a piece of code and ask "What is this code doing?" Don't hesitate to ask follow-up questions.

1.3 Clustering: An Objective, an Algorithm and a Guarantee

Warning: As you probably know, AI chatbots can be wrong so assess what they tell you with a critical mind and/or double-check with other sources (e.g., package documentation).

NUMERICAL CORNER We will test our implementation of *k*-means on the ***penguins dataset*** introduced earlier in the chapter. We first extract the columns and combine them into a data matrix X. As we did previously, we also remove the rows with missing values.

```
data = pd.read_csv('penguins-measurements.csv')
data = data.dropna()
X = data[['bill_length_mm', 'bill_depth_mm',
        'flipper_length_mm', 'body_mass_g']].to_numpy()
```

We visualize a two-dimensional slice of the data.

```
plt.scatter(X[:,1], X[:,3], s=5, c='k')
plt.xlabel('bill_depth_mm'), plt.ylabel('body_mass_g')
plt.show()
```

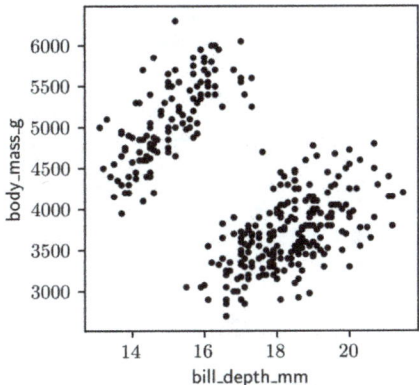

Figure 1.14 Graphical output of code.

Observe that the features have quite different scales (tens versus thousands in the plot above). In such a case, it is common to standardize the data so that each feature has roughly the same scale. For each column of X, we subtract its empirical mean and divide by its empirical standard deviation.

```
mean = np.mean(X, axis=0)
std = np.std(X, axis=0)
X = (X - mean) / std
```

Now we run Lloyd's algorithm with $k = 2$ clusters.

```
assign = kmeans(rng, X, 2)
```

```
1338.2046936914157
820.9361062178352
```

603.8787658966849
575.2587351391593
567.7837494880662

We vizualize the output as we did before, but this time coloring the data points by their cluster assignment.

```
plt.scatter(X[:,1], X[:,3], s=5, c=assign, cmap='brg')
plt.xlabel('bill_depth (standardized)'), plt.ylabel('body_mass
                                                   (standardized)')
plt.show()
```

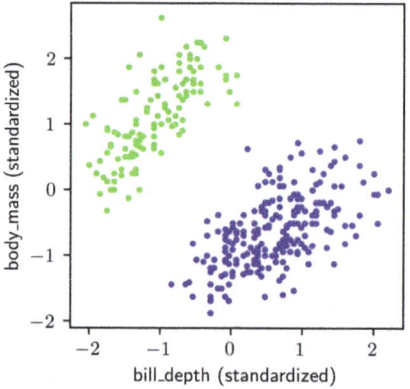

Figure 1.15 Graphical output of code.

This clustering looks quite good. Nevertheless keep in mind that:

1. in this plot we are looking at only two of the four variables while *k*-means uses all of them,
2. we are not guaranteed to find the best solution,
3. our objective function is somewhat arbitrary, and
4. it is not clear what the right choice of *k* is.

In fact, the original dataset contained the correct answer, as provided by biologists. Despite what the figure above may lead us to believe, there are in reality three separate species. So let us try with $k = 3$ clusters.

```
assign = kmeans(rng, X, 3)
```

1312.344945158482
577.1700837839458
428.50397345437966
392.2616692426171
383.3452894259011

The output does not seem quite right.

```
plt.scatter(X[:,1], X[:,3], s=5, c=assign, cmap='brg')
plt.xlabel('bill_depth (standardized)'),
         plt.ylabel('body_mass (standardized)')
plt.show()
```

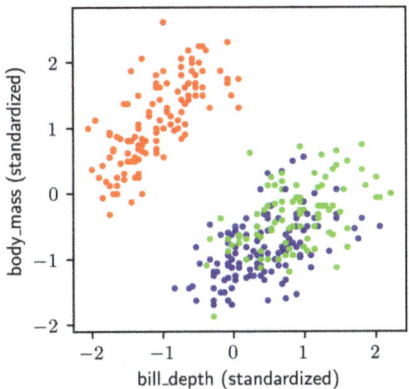

Figure 1.16 Graphical output of code.

However, remembering the warnings mentioned previously, let us look at a different two-dimensional slice.

```
plt.scatter(X[:,0], X[:,3], s=5, c=assign, cmap='brg')
plt.xlabel('bill_length (standardized)'),
         plt.ylabel('body_mass (standardized)')
plt.show()
```

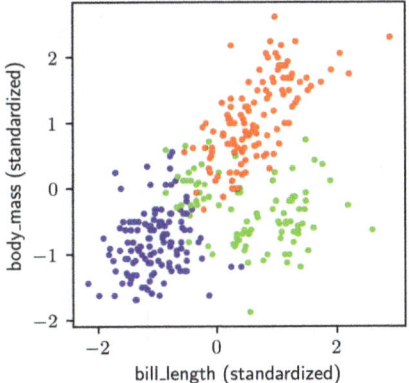

Figure 1.17 Graphical output of code.

Let us load up the truth and compare. We only keep those samples that were not removed because of missing values (see the documentation for `pandas.DataFrame.iloc`).

```
data_truth = pd.read_csv('penguins-species.csv')
data_truth = data_truth.iloc[data.index]
data_truth.head()
```

```
  species
0 Adelie
1 Adelie
2 Adelie
4 Adelie
5 Adelie
```

The species are:

```
species = data_truth['species']
print(species.unique())
```

```
['Adelie' 'Chinstrap' 'Gentoo']
```

To plot the outcome, we color the species blue-green-red using a dictionary.

```
species2color_dict = {'Adelie': 'blue', 'Chinstrap':
                      'lime', 'Gentoo': 'red'}
truth = [species2color_dict[a] for a in species]
```

Finally, we can compare the output to the truth. The match is quite good – but certainly not perfect.

```
f, (ax1, ax2) = plt.subplots(1, 2, sharex=True, sharey=True,
                             figsize=(6.5, 3))
ax1.scatter(X[:,0], X[:,3], s=5, c=truth)
ax1.set_title('truth')
ax2.scatter(X[:,0], X[:,3], s=5, c=assign, cmap='brg')
ax2.set_title('kmeans')
plt.show()
```

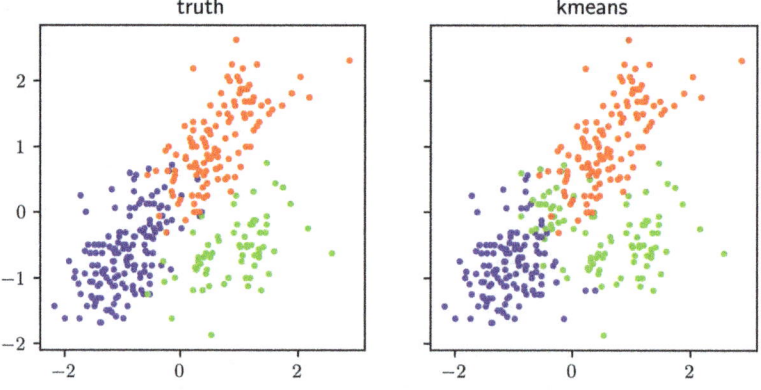

Figure 1.18 Graphical output of code.

Determining the appropriate number of clusters is not a straightforward problem. To quote Wikipedia[8]:

> The correct choice of k is often ambiguous, with interpretations depending on the shape and scale of the distribution of points in a data set and the desired clustering resolution of the user. In addition, increasing k without penalty will always reduce the amount of error in the resulting clustering, to the extreme case of zero error if each data point is considered its own cluster (i.e., when k equals the number of data points, n). Intuitively then, the optimal choice of k will strike a balance between maximum compression of the data using a single cluster, and maximum accuracy by assigning each data point to its own cluster. If an appropriate value of k is not apparent from prior knowledge of the properties of the data set, it must be chosen somehow. There are several categories of methods for making this decision.

In practice, several heuristics are in use. Other approaches to clustering, such as DBSCAN and hierarchical clustering, do not require a number of clusters as input.

TRY IT! *Run the analysis again*, but this time *without the standardization step*. What do you observe? Is one feature more influential on the final output than the others? Why do you think that is?

◁ **NC**

1.3.3 Matrix Form of K-Means Clustering

In this section, we show that the k-means clustering objective can be written in matrix form. We start with some notation and definitions that will be useful throughout.

As we indicated before, for a collection of n data vectors $\mathbf{x}_1, \ldots, \mathbf{x}_n$ in $\mathbb{R}^d$, it is often convenient to stack them up into a matrix

$$X = \begin{bmatrix} \mathbf{x}_1^T \\ \mathbf{x}_2^T \\ \vdots \\ \mathbf{x}_n^T \end{bmatrix} = \begin{bmatrix} x_{11} & x_{12} & \cdots & x_{1d} \\ x_{21} & x_{22} & \cdots & x_{2d} \\ \vdots & \vdots & \ddots & \vdots \\ x_{n1} & x_{n2} & \cdots & x_{nd} \end{bmatrix}.$$

We can do the same with cluster representatives. Given $\boldsymbol{\mu}_1, \ldots, \boldsymbol{\mu}_k$ also in $\mathbb{R}^d$, we form the matrix

$$U = \begin{bmatrix} \boldsymbol{\mu}_1^T \\ \boldsymbol{\mu}_2^T \\ \vdots \\ \boldsymbol{\mu}_k^T \end{bmatrix} = \begin{bmatrix} \mu_{11} & \mu_{12} & \cdots & \mu_{1d} \\ \mu_{21} & \mu_{22} & \cdots & \mu_{2d} \\ \vdots & \vdots & \ddots & \vdots \\ \mu_{k1} & \mu_{k2} & \cdots & \mu_{kd} \end{bmatrix}.$$

Perhaps less obviously, cluster assignments can also be encoded in matrix form. Recall that, given a partition $C_1, \ldots, C_k$ of $[n]$, we define $c(j) = i$ if $j \in C_i$. For $j = 1, \ldots, n$ and $\ell = 1, \ldots, k$, set $Z_{j\ell} = 1$ if $c(j) = \ell$ and 0 otherwise, and let Z be the $n \times k$ matrix with entries $Z = [Z_{j\ell}]_{j,\ell}$. That is, row j has exactly one entry with value 1, corresponding to the assigned cluster $c(j)$ of data point $\mathbf{x}_j$, and all other entries 0.

---

[8] https://en.wikipedia.org/wiki/Determining_the_number_of_clusters_in_a_data_set

With this notation, the representative of the cluster assigned to data point $\mathbf{x}_j$ is obtained through a matrix product

$$\boldsymbol{\mu}_{c(j)}^T = \sum_{\ell=1}^{k} Z_{j\ell} \boldsymbol{\mu}_\ell^T = \sum_{\ell=1}^{k} Z_{j\ell} U_{\ell,\cdot} = (ZU)_{j,\cdot}$$

where we used that the j-th row of a matrix product is a linear combination of the rows of the second matrix, where the coefficients are the entries on the j-th row of the first one.

Example 1.3.13 *(continued from Example 1.3.2)* *Continuing with our previous example, the clusters $C_1 = \{1, 4, 6, 8\}$, $C_2 = \{2, 3, 7\}$, $C_3 = \{5\}$ are encoded as the matrix*

$$Z = \begin{bmatrix} 1 & 0 & 0 \\ 0 & 1 & 0 \\ 0 & 1 & 0 \\ 1 & 0 & 0 \\ 0 & 0 & 1 \\ 1 & 0 & 0 \\ 0 & 1 & 0 \\ 1 & 0 & 0 \end{bmatrix}.$$

Suppose again that the representatives are

$$\boldsymbol{\mu}_1 = \begin{pmatrix} -2 \\ 1 \end{pmatrix}, \boldsymbol{\mu}_2 = \begin{pmatrix} 2 \\ -1 \end{pmatrix}, \boldsymbol{\mu}_3 = \begin{pmatrix} -10 \\ 10 \end{pmatrix}.$$

The corresponding matrix U is then

$$U = \begin{bmatrix} -2 & 1 \\ 2 & -1 \\ -10 & 10 \end{bmatrix}.$$

Hence multiplying Z and U produces a matrix where each row is the representative of the assigned cluster of the corresponding data point:

$$ZU = \begin{bmatrix} 1 & 0 & 0 \\ 0 & 1 & 0 \\ 0 & 1 & 0 \\ 1 & 0 & 0 \\ 0 & 0 & 1 \\ 1 & 0 & 0 \\ 0 & 1 & 0 \\ 1 & 0 & 0 \end{bmatrix} \begin{bmatrix} -2 & 1 \\ 2 & -1 \\ -10 & 10 \end{bmatrix} = \begin{bmatrix} -2 & 1 \\ 2 & -1 \\ 2 & -1 \\ -2 & 1 \\ -10 & 10 \\ -2 & 1 \\ 2 & -1 \\ -2 & 1 \end{bmatrix}.$$

Recall that the Frobenius norm of an $n \times m$ matrix $A \in \mathbb{R}^{n \times m}$ is defined as

$$\|A\|_F = \sqrt{\sum_{i=1}^{n} \sum_{j=1}^{m} A_{ij}^2}.$$

Using the row notation, it can be written as the sum of the squared Euclidean norms of the rows:

$$\|A\|_F^2 = \sum_{i=1}^{n} \|A_{i,\cdot}\|^2.$$

1.3 Clustering: An Objective, an Algorithm and a Guarantee

For two matrices $A, B \in \mathbb{R}^{n \times m}$, the Frobenius norm of their difference $\|A - B\|_F$ can be interpreted as a distance between A and B, that is, a measure of how dissimilar they are.

Finally, we return to the k-means objective. Using the notation introduced in this section and the equivalent formula for the objective $\mathcal{G}$ derived in the proof of the *Optimal Clustering Lemma*, we note that

$$\mathcal{G}(C_1, \ldots, C_k; \boldsymbol{\mu}_1, \ldots, \boldsymbol{\mu}_k) = \sum_{i=1}^{n} \|\mathbf{x}_i - \boldsymbol{\mu}_{c(i)}\|^2$$

$$= \sum_{i=1}^{n} \sum_{\ell=1}^{d} (x_{i\ell} - (ZU)_{i\ell})^2$$

$$= \|X - ZU\|_F^2,$$

where we have used the definition of the Frobenius norm.

In other words, minimizing the k-means objective is equivalent to finding a matrix factorization of the form ZU that is a good fit to the data matrix X in Frobenius norm. This formulation expresses in a more compact form the idea of representing X as a combination of a small number of representatives. Matrix factorization will come back repeatedly in this course.

Self-Assessment Quiz (with help from Claude, Gemini, and ChatGPT)

1 Which of these is NOT a property of a valid partition $C_1, \ldots, C_k$ in the context of k-means?
   a) The subsets are pairwise disjoint.
   b) The subsets cover all data points.
   c) Each subset is nonempty.
   d) Each subset contains an equal number of points.

2 In the k-means objective function, what does the variable $\boldsymbol{\mu}_i$ represent?
   a) The centroid of cluster i
   b) The number of points in cluster i
   c) The distance between clusters i and j
   d) The assignment of point j to a cluster

3 The k-means objective function is a measure of what?
   a) The total number of clusters
   b) The average distance between data points
   c) The sum of squared distances between each data point and its assigned cluster center
   d) The maximum distance between any two cluster centers

4 What is a key property of the sequence of objective function values produced by the k-means algorithm?
   a) It is strictly decreasing.
   b) It is non-increasing.
   c) It is strictly increasing.
   d) It alternates between two values.

5. What is the interpretation of the matrix Z in the matrix formulation of k-means?
   a) It represents the cluster centers.
   b) It represents the distances between data points.
   c) It encodes the cluster assignments of each data point.
   d) It represents the covariance matrix of the data.

Answer for 1: d. Justification: "Formally, we define a clustering as a partition. A partition of $[n] = 1, \ldots, n$ of size k is a collection of nonempty subsets $C_1, \ldots, C_k \subseteq [n]$ that: are pairwise disjoint, $C_i \cap C_j = \emptyset$, $\forall i \neq j$; cover all of $[n]$, $\cup_{i=1}^{k} C_i = [n]$." No requirement for equal-sized subsets is mentioned.

Answer for 2: a. Justification: "Here $\mu_i \in \mathbb{R}^d$ is the representative – or center – of cluster C_i."

Answer for 3: c. Justification: The k-means objective is defined in the text as minimizing the sum of squared distances between data points and their assigned cluster centers.

Answer for 4: b. Justification: "The sequence of objective function values produced by the k-means algorithm is non-increasing."

Answer for 5: c. Justification: The text defines Z as a matrix where "each row has exactly one entry with value 1, corresponding to the assigned cluster of the data point."

1.4 Some Observations about High-Dimensional Data

In this section, we first apply k-means clustering to a high-dimensional example to illustrate the issues that arise in that context. We then discuss some surprising phenomena in high dimensions.

1.4.1 Clustering in High Dimension

In this section, we test our implementation of k-means on a simple simulated dataset in high dimension.

The following function generates n data points from a mixture of two equally likely, spherical d-dimensional Gaussians with variance 1, one with mean $-w\mathbf{e}_1$ and one with mean $w\mathbf{e}_1$. We use gmm2spherical from a previous section. It is found in mmids.py.

```
def two_mixed_clusters(rng, d, n, w):
    mu0 = np.hstack(([w], np.zeros(d-1)))
    mu1 = np.hstack(([-w], np.zeros(d-1)))
    return mmids.gmm2spherical(rng, d, n, 0.5, 0.5, mu0, 1, mu1, 1)
```

1.4 Some Observations about High-Dimensional Data

NUMERICAL CORNER We start with $d = 2$.

```
seed = 535
rng = np.random.default_rng(seed)
d, n, w = 2, 100, 3.
X = two_mixed_clusters(rng, d, n, w)
```

Let's run k-means on this dataset using $k = 2$. We use `kmeans()` from the `mmids.py` file.

```
assign = mmids.kmeans(rng, X, 2)
```

1044.8267883490312
208.5284166285488
204.02397716710018
204.02397716710018
204.02397716710018

Our default of 10 iterations seem to have been enough for the algorithm to converge. We can visualize the result by coloring the points according to the assignment.

```
plt.figure(figsize=(6,3))
plt.scatter(X[:,0], X[:,1], s=10, c=assign, cmap='brg')
plt.axis([-6,6,-3,3])
plt.show()
```

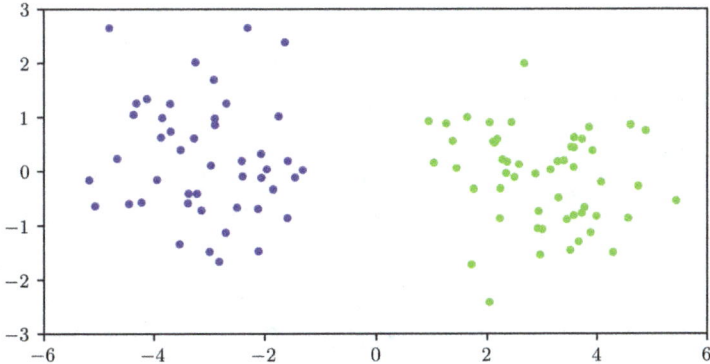

Figure 1.19 Graphical output of code.

Let's see what happens in higher dimension. We repeat our experiment with $d = 1,000$.

```
d, n, w = 1000, 100, 3.
X = two_mixed_clusters(rng, d, n, w)
```

Again, we observe two clearly delineated clusters.

```
plt.figure(figsize=(6,3))
plt.scatter(X[:,0], X[:,1], s=10, c='k')
plt.axis([-6,6,-3,3])
plt.show()
```

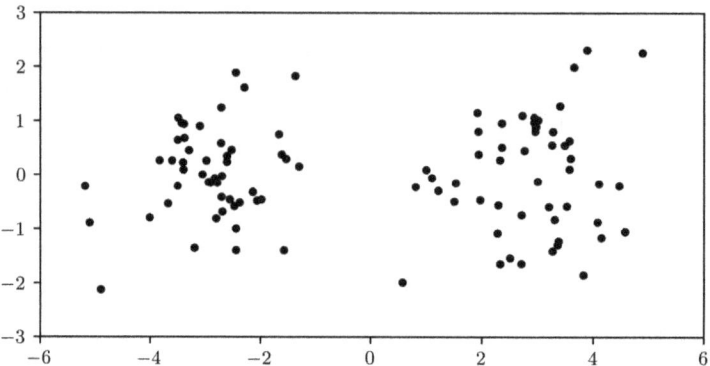

Figure 1.20 Graphical output of code.

This dataset is in 1,000 dimensions, but we've plotted the data in only the first two dimensions. If instead we plot in any two dimensions not including the first one, we see only one cluster.

```
plt.figure(figsize=(6,3))
plt.scatter(X[:,1], X[:,2], s=10, c='k')
plt.axis([-6,6,-3,3])
plt.show()
```

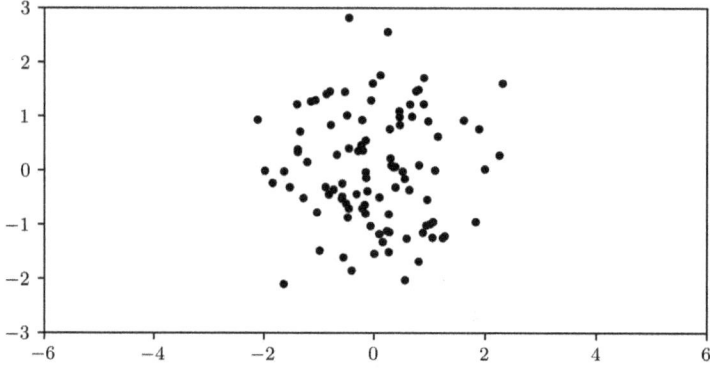

Figure 1.21 Graphical output of code.

Let's see how k-means fares on this dataset.

```
assign = mmids.kmeans(rng, X, 2)
```

```
99518.03165136592
99518.03165136592
99518.03165136592
99518.03165136592
99518.03165136592
```

Our attempt at clustering does not appear to have been successful.

```
plt.figure(figsize=(6,3))
plt.scatter(X[:,0], X[:,1], s=10, c=assign, cmap='brg')
plt.axis([-6,6,-3,3])
plt.show()
```

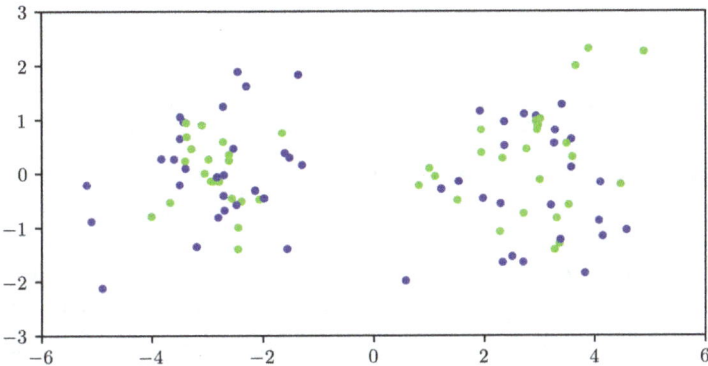

Figure 1.22 Graphical output of code.

◁ **NC**

What happened? While the clusters are easy to tease apart *if we know to look at the first coordinate only*, in the full space the within-cluster and between-cluster distances become harder to distinguish: The noise overwhelms the signal.

As the dimension increases, the distributions of intra- and intercluster distances overlap significantly and become more or less indistinguishable. See Figure 1.23. This provides some insights into why clustering may fail here. Note that we used the same offset for all simulations. On the other hand, if the separation between the clusters is sufficiently large, one would expect clustering to work even in high dimension.

TRY IT! What precedes (and what follows in the next subsection) is not a formal proof that k-means clustering will be unsuccessful here. The behavior of the algorithm is quite complex and depends, in particular, on the initialization and the density of points. Here, increasing the number of data points eventually leads to much better performance. Explore this behavior on your own by *modifying the code*.

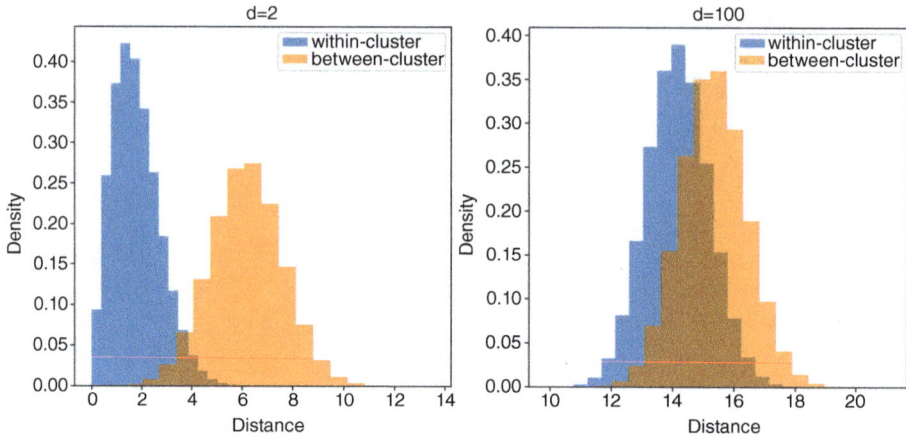

Figure 1.23 Histograms of within-cluster and between-cluster distances for a sample of size $n = 1,000$ in $d = 2$ (left) and $d = 100$ (right) dimensions with a given offset $w = 3$. As d increases, the two distributions become increasingly indistinguishable.

1.4.2 Surprising Phenomena in High Dimension

In the previous section, we saw how the contribution from a large number of "noisy dimensions" can overwhelm the "signal" in the context of clustering. In this section we discuss further properties of high-dimensional space that are relevant to data science problems.

Applying *Chebyshev's Inequality* to sums of independent random variables has useful statistical implications: It shows that, with a large enough number of samples n, the sample mean is close to the population mean. Hence it allows us to infer properties of a population from samples. Interestingly, one can apply a similar argument to a different asymptotic regime: the limit of large dimension d. But as we will see in this section, the statistical implications are quite different.

To start explaining the statement above, we consider a simple experiment. Let $C = [-1/2, 1/2]^d$ be the d-cube with side lengths 1 centered at the origin and let $\mathcal{B} = \{\mathbf{x} \in \mathbb{R}^d : \|\mathbf{x}\| \leq 1/2\}$ be the inscribed d-ball.

Now pick a point $\mathbf{X}$ uniformly at random in C. What is the probability that it falls in $\mathcal{B}$?

To generate $\mathbf{X}$, we pick d independent random variables $X_1, \ldots, X_d \sim U[-1/2, 1/2]$, and form the vector $\mathbf{X} = (X_1, \ldots, X_d)$. Indeed, the PDF of $\mathbf{X}$ is then $f_{\mathbf{X}}(\mathbf{x}) = 1^d = 1$ if $\mathbf{x} \in C$ and 0 otherwise.

The event we are interested in is $A = \{\|\mathbf{X}\| \leq 1/2\}$. The uniform distribution over the set C has the property that $\mathbb{P}[A]$ is the volume of $\mathcal{B}$ divided by the volume of C. In this case, the volume of C is $1^d = 1$ and the volume of $\mathcal{B}$ has an explicit formula.[9]

This leads to the following surprising fact:

Theorem 1.4.1 (High-Dimensional Cube) *Let* $\mathcal{B} = \{\mathbf{x} \in \mathbb{R}^d : \|\mathbf{x}\| \leq 1/2\}$ *and* $C = [-1/2, 1/2]^d$. *Pick* $\mathbf{X} \sim U[C]$. *Then, as* $d \to +\infty$,

$$\mathbb{P}[\mathbf{X} \in \mathcal{B}] \to 0.$$

---

[9] https://en.wikipedia.org/wiki/Volume_of_an_n-ball

1.4 Some Observations about High-Dimensional Data

In words, in high dimension if one picks a point at random from the cube, it is unlikely to be close to the origin. Instead it is likely to be in the corners. A geometric interpretation is that a high-dimensional cube is a bit like a "spiky ball."

We give a proof based on *Chebyshev's Inequality*. It has the advantage of providing some insight into this counter-intuitive phenomenon by linking it to the concentration of sums of independent random variables, in this case the squared norm of **X**.

Proof idea: We think of $\|\mathbf{X}\|^2$ as a sum of independent random variables and apply *Chebyshev's Inequality*. It implies that the norm of **X** is concentrated around its mean, which grows like $\sqrt{d}$. The latter is larger than $1/2$ for d large.

Proof To see the relevance of *Chebyshev's Inequality*, we compute the mean and standard deviation of the norm of **X**. In fact, because of the square root in $\|\mathbf{X}\|$, computing its expectation is difficult. Instead we work with the squared norm

$$\|\mathbf{X}\|^2 = X_1^2 + X_2^2 + \cdots + X_d^2,$$

which has the advantage of being a sum of independent random variables – for which the expectation and variance are much easier to compute. Observe further that the probability of the event of interest $\{\|\mathbf{X}\| \leq 1/2\}$ can be rewritten in terms of $\|\mathbf{X}\|^2$ as follows:

$$\mathbb{P}\left[\|\mathbf{X}\| \leq 1/2\right] = \mathbb{P}\left[\|\mathbf{X}\|^2 \leq 1/4\right].$$

To simplify the notation, we use $\tilde{\mu} = \mathbb{E}[X_1^2]$ and $\tilde{\sigma} = \sqrt{\text{Var}[X_1^2]}$ for the mean and standard deviation of X_1^2 respectively. Using linearity of expectation and the fact that the X_i's are independent, we get

$$\mu_{\|\mathbf{X}\|^2} = \mathbb{E}\left[\|\mathbf{X}\|^2\right] = \sum_{i=1}^{d} \mathbb{E}[X_i^2] = d\,\mathbb{E}[X_1^2] = \tilde{\mu}\,d,$$

and

$$\text{Var}\left[\|\mathbf{X}\|^2\right] = \sum_{i=1}^{d} \text{Var}[X_i^2] = d\,\text{Var}[X_1^2].$$

Taking a square root, we get an expression for the standard deviation of our quantity of interest $\|\mathbf{X}\|^2$ in terms of the standard deviation of X_1^2

$$\sigma_{\|\mathbf{X}\|^2} = \tilde{\sigma}\,\sqrt{d}.$$

(Note that we could compute $\tilde{\mu}$ and $\tilde{\sigma}$ explicitly, but it will not be necessary here.)

We use *Chebyshev's Inequality* to show that $\|\mathbf{X}\|^2$ is highly likely to be close to its mean $\tilde{\mu}\,d$, which is much larger than $1/4$ when d is large, and that therefore $\|\mathbf{X}\|^2$ is highly unlikely to be smaller than $1/4$. We give the details next.

By the one-sided version of *Chebyshev's Inequality* in terms of the standard deviation, we have

$$\mathbb{P}\left[\|\mathbf{X}\|^2 - \mu_{\|\mathbf{X}\|^2} \leq -\alpha\right] \leq \left(\frac{\sigma_{\|\mathbf{X}\|^2}}{\alpha}\right)^2.$$

That is, using the formulas above and rearranging slightly,

$$\mathbb{P}\left[\|\mathbf{X}\|^2 \leq \tilde{\mu}\,d - \alpha\right] \leq \left(\frac{\tilde{\sigma}\,\sqrt{d}}{\alpha}\right)^2.$$

How do we relate this to the probability of interest $\mathbb{P}\left[\|\mathbf{X}\|^2 \leq 1/4\right]$? Recall that we are free to choose α in this inequality. So simply take α such that

$$\tilde{\mu} d - \alpha = \frac{1}{4},$$

that is, $\alpha = \tilde{\mu} d - 1/4$. Observe that, once d is large enough, it holds that $\alpha > 0$.

Finally, replacing this choice of α in the inequality above gives

$$\begin{aligned}
\mathbb{P}\left[\|\mathbf{X}\| \leq 1/2\right] &= \mathbb{P}\left[\|\mathbf{X}\|^2 \leq 1/4\right] \\
&= \mathbb{P}\left[\|\mathbf{X}\|^2 \leq \tilde{\mu} d - \alpha\right] \\
&\leq \left(\frac{\tilde{\sigma}\sqrt{d}}{\alpha}\right)^2 \\
&\leq \left(\frac{\tilde{\sigma}\sqrt{d}}{\tilde{\mu} d - 1/4}\right)^2.
\end{aligned}$$

Critically, $\tilde{\mu}$ and $\tilde{\sigma}$ do not depend on d. So the right-hand side goes to 0 as $d \to +\infty$. Indeed, d is much larger than $\sqrt{d}$ when d is large. This proves the claim. $\square$

We will see later in the course that this high-dimensional phenomenon has implications for data science problems. It is behind what is referred to as the Curse of Dimensionality.

While *Chebyshev's Inequality* correctly implies that $\mathbb{P}[\mathbf{X} \in \mathcal{B}]$ goes to 0, it does not give the correct rate of convergence. In reality, that probability goes to 0 at a much faster rate than $1/d$. Specifically, it can be shown that $\mathbb{P}[\mathbf{X} \in \mathcal{B}]$ goes to 0 roughly as $d^{-d/2}$. We will not derive (or need) this fact here.

NUMERICAL CORNER We can check the theorem in a simulation. Here we pick n points uniformly at random in the d-cube $\mathcal{C}$, for a range of dimensions up to dmax. We then plot the frequency of landing in the inscribed d-ball $\mathcal{B}$ and see that it rapidly converges to 0. Alternatively, we could just plot the formula for the volume of $\mathcal{B}$. But knowing how to do simulations is useful in situations where explicit formulas are unavailable or intractable. We plot the result up to dimension 10.

```
dmax, n = 10, 1000

in_ball = np.zeros(dmax)
for d in range(dmax):
    in_ball[d] = np.mean([(LA.norm(rng.random(d+1) - 1/2) < 1/2) for
                         _ in range(n)])

plt.plot(np.arange(1,dmax+1), in_ball, c='k')
plt.show()
```

1.4 Some Observations about High-Dimensional Data

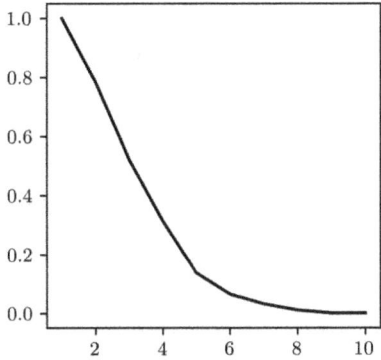

Figure 1.24 Graphical output of code.

◁ NC

Self-Assessment Quiz *(with help from Claude, Gemini, and ChatGPT)*

1. The volume of the d-dimensional cube $C = [-1/2, 1/2]^d$ is
    a) $1/d$
    b) $1/2^d$
    c) 1
    d) 2^d

2. In a high-dimensional cube $C = [-1/2, 1/2]^d$, as the dimension d increases, the probability that a randomly chosen point lies within the inscribed sphere $B = \{x \in \mathbb{R}^d : \|x\| \leq 1/2\}$
    a) approaches 1
    b) approaches 1/2
    c) approaches 0
    d) remains constant

3. Which of the following best describes the appearance of a high-dimensional cube?
    a) A smooth, round ball
    b) A spiky ball with most of its volume concentrated in the corners
    c) A perfect sphere with uniform volume distribution
    d) A flat, pancake-like shape

4. Which inequality is used to prove the theorem about high-dimensional cubes?
    a) Cauchy–Schwarz inequality
    b) Triangle inequality
    c) Markov's inequality
    d) Chebyshev's inequality

5. In the proof of the theorem about high-dimensional cubes, which property of the squared norm $\|X\|^2$ is used?

> a) It is a sum of dependent random variables.
> b) It is a sum of independent random variables.
> c) It is a product of independent random variables.
> d) It is a product of dependent random variables.
>
> Answer for 1: c. Justification: The side length of the cube is 1, and the volume of a d-dimensional cube is the side length raised to the power d.
>
> Answer for 2: c. Justification: This is the statement of the theorem in the text.
>
> Answer for 3: b. Justification: The text mentions that "A geometric interpretation is that a high-dimensional cube is a bit like a 'spiky ball.'"
>
> Answer for 4: d. Justification: The text explicitly states that *Chebyshev's Inequality* is used in the proof.
>
> Answer for 5: b. Justification: The proof states, "we work with the squared norm
> $$\|\mathbf{X}\|^2 = X_1^2 + X_2^2 + \cdots + X_d^2,$$
> which has the advantage of being a sum of independent random variables."

1.5 Exercises

1.5.1 Warm-Up Worksheets
(with help from Claude, Gemini, and ChatGPT)

Section 1.2

E1.2.1 Calculate the Euclidean norm of the vector $\mathbf{x} = (6, 8)$.

E1.2.2 Compute the inner product $\langle \mathbf{u}, \mathbf{v} \rangle$ for vectors $\mathbf{u} = (1, 2, 3)$ and $\mathbf{v} = (4, 5, 6)$.

E1.2.3 Find the transpose of the matrix $A = \begin{pmatrix} 1 & 2 & 3 \\ 4 & 5 & 6 \end{pmatrix}$.

E1.2.4 Compute the Frobenius norm of the matrix $A = \begin{pmatrix} 1 & 2 \\ 3 & 4 \end{pmatrix}$.

E1.2.5 Verify that the matrix $A = \begin{pmatrix} 2 & 0 \\ 0 & 3 \end{pmatrix}$ is symmetric.

E1.2.6 Let $A = \begin{pmatrix} 1 & 2 \\ 3 & 4 \end{pmatrix}$ and $B = \begin{pmatrix} 5 & 6 \\ 7 & 8 \end{pmatrix}$. Compute AB and BA.

E1.2.7 Let $f(x, y) = x^2 + xy + y^2$. Compute the partial derivatives $\frac{\partial f}{\partial x}$ and $\frac{\partial f}{\partial y}$.

E1.2.8 Given the function $g(x, y) = x^2 y + xy^3$, compute its partial derivatives $\frac{\partial g}{\partial x}$ and $\frac{\partial g}{\partial y}$.

E1.2.9 Let $f(x) = x^3 - 3x^2 + 2x$. Use *Taylor's Theorem* to find a linear approximation of f around $a = 1$ with a second-order error term.

E1.2.10 Compute the expectation $\mathbb{E}[X]$ of a discrete random variable X with $\mathbb{P}(X = 1) = 0.2$, $\mathbb{P}(X = 2) = 0.5$, and $\mathbb{P}(X = 3) = 0.3$.

E1.2.11 Calculate the variance $\text{Var}[X]$ of a discrete random variable X with $\mathbb{P}(X = 1) = 0.4$, $\mathbb{P}(X = 2) = 0.6$, and $\mathbb{E}[X] = 1.6$.

1.5 Exercises

E1.2.12 Let X and Y be random variables with $\mathbb{E}[X] = 2$, $\mathbb{E}[Y] = 3$, $\text{Var}[X] = 4$, and $\text{Var}[Y] = 9$. Compute $\mathbb{E}[2X + Y - 1]$ and $\text{Var}[2X + Y - 1]$, assuming X and Y are independent.

E1.2.13 Let X be a random variable with $\mathbb{E}[X] = 3$ and $\text{Var}[X] = 4$. Use *Chebyshev's Inequality* to bound $\mathbb{P}[|X - 3| \geq 4]$.

E1.2.14 A random variable X has mean $\mu = 5$ and variance $\sigma^2 = 4$. Use *Chebyshev's Inequality* to find an upper bound on the probability that X is more than 3 units away from its mean.

E1.2.15 Given the random vector $X = (X_1, X_2)$ where X_1 and X_2 are independent standard normal random variables, what is the covariance matrix of X?

E1.2.16 Let $X = \begin{pmatrix} X_1 \\ X_2 \end{pmatrix}$ be a random vector with $\mathbb{E}[X_1] = 1$, $\mathbb{E}[X_2] = 2$, $\text{Var}[X_1] = 3$, $\text{Var}[X_2] = 4$, and $\text{Cov}[X_1, X_2] = 1$. Write the mean vector μ_X and the covariance matrix Σ_X of X.

E1.2.17 Let $X = \begin{pmatrix} X_1 \\ X_2 \end{pmatrix}$ be a random vector with mean $\mu_X = \begin{pmatrix} 1 \\ 2 \end{pmatrix}$ and covariance matrix $\Sigma_X = \begin{pmatrix} 3 & 1 \\ 1 & 4 \end{pmatrix}$. Let $A = \begin{pmatrix} 1 & 2 \\ 3 & 4 \end{pmatrix}$. Compute $\mathbb{E}[AX]$ and $\text{Cov}[AX]$.

E1.2.18 Let X_1, X_2, X_3 be independent random variables with $\mathbb{E}[X_1] = 1$, $\mathbb{E}[X_2] = 2$, $\mathbb{E}[X_3] = 3$, $\text{Var}[X_1] = 4$, $\text{Var}[X_2] = 5$, and $\text{Var}[X_3] = 6$. Compute $\mathbb{E}[X_1 + X_2 + X_3]$ and $\text{Var}[X_1 + X_2 + X_3]$.

E1.2.19 Let $A = \begin{pmatrix} 2 & -1 \\ -1 & 2 \end{pmatrix}$. Show that A is positive definite.

Section 1.3

E1.3.1 Given the data points $\mathbf{x}_1 = (1, 2)$, $\mathbf{x}_2 = (-1, 1)$, $\mathbf{x}_3 = (0, -1)$, and $\mathbf{x}_4 = (2, 0)$, and the partition $C_1 = \{1, 4\}$, $C_2 = \{2, 3\}$, compute the optimal cluster representatives μ_1^* and μ_2^*.

E1.3.2 For the data points and partition from E1.3.1, compute the k-means objective value $\mathcal{G}(C_1, C_2)$.

E1.3.3 Given the cluster representatives $\mu_1 = (0, 1)$, $\mu_2 = (1, -1)$, and $\mu_3 = (-2, 0)$, and the data points $\mathbf{x}_1 = (1, 1)$, $\mathbf{x}_2 = (-1, -1)$, $\mathbf{x}_3 = (2, -2)$, $\mathbf{x}_4 = (-2, 1)$, and $\mathbf{x}_5 = (0, 0)$, find the optimal partition C_1, C_2, C_3.

E1.3.4 For the data points and cluster representatives from E1.3.3, compute the k-means objective value $\mathcal{G}(C_1, C_2, C_3; \mu_1, \mu_2, \mu_3)$.

E1.3.5 Show that for any two cluster representatives $\mu_1, \mu_2 \in \mathbb{R}^d$ and any data point $\mathbf{x} \in \mathbb{R}^d$, the inequality $\|\mathbf{x} - \mu_1\|^2 \leq \|\mathbf{x} - \mu_2\|^2$ is equivalent to $2(\mu_2 - \mu_1)^T \mathbf{x} \leq \|\mu_2\|^2 - \|\mu_1\|^2$.

E1.3.6 Given the cluster assignment matrix

$$Z = \begin{bmatrix} 1 & 0 & 0 \\ 0 & 1 & 0 \\ 0 & 0 & 1 \\ 1 & 0 & 0 \\ 0 & 1 & 0 \end{bmatrix}$$

and the cluster representative matrix

$$U = \begin{bmatrix} 1 & 2 \\ -1 & 0 \\ 0 & -2 \end{bmatrix},$$

compute the matrix product ZU.

E1.3.7 For any two matrices $A, B \in \mathbb{R}^{n \times m}$, prove that $\|A + B\|_F^2 = \|A\|_F^2 + \|B\|_F^2 + 2 \sum_{i=1}^{n} \sum_{j=1}^{m} A_{ij} B_{ij}$.

E1.3.8 Show that for any matrix $A \in \mathbb{R}^{n \times m}$ and any scalar $c \in \mathbb{R}$, it holds that $\|cA\|_F = |c| \|A\|_F$.

E1.3.9 Complete the square for the quadratic function $q(x) = 3x^2 - 6x + 5$. What is the minimum value of q and where is it attained?

E1.3.10 Let $f_1(x) = x^2 + 1$ and $f_2(y) = 2y^2 - 3$. Define $h(x, y) = f_1(x) + f_2(y)$. Find the global minimum of $h(x, y)$.

E1.3.11 Compute the Frobenius norm of the matrix

$$A = \begin{bmatrix} 2 & -1 \\ 0 & 3 \end{bmatrix}.$$

Section 1.4

E1.4.1 Let $X_1, \ldots, X_d$ be independent random variables uniformly distributed on $[-1/2, 1/2]$. Compute $\mathbb{E}[X_i]$ and $\mathrm{Var}[X_i]$.

E1.4.2 Let $X = (X_1, \ldots, X_d)$ be a d-dimensional vector where each X_i is an independent random variable uniformly distributed on $[-1/2, 1/2]$. Compute $\mathbb{E}[\|X\|^2]$.

E1.4.3 Let $X = (X_1, \ldots, X_d)$ be a d-dimensional vector where each X_i is an independent standard normal random variable. Compute $\mathbb{E}[\|X\|^2]$.

E1.4.4 Let $X_1, X_2, \ldots, X_d$ be independent random variables with $\mathbb{E}[X_i] = \mu$ and $\mathrm{Var}[X_i] = \sigma^2$ for all i. Find $\mathbb{E}[\sum_{i=1}^{d} X_i]$ and $\mathrm{Var}[\sum_{i=1}^{d} X_i]$.

E1.4.5 Given a random variable X with $\mathbb{E}[X] = 1$ and $\mathrm{Var}[X] = 4$, bound $\mathbb{P}[|X - 1| \geq 3]$ using *Chebyshev's Inequality*.

E1.4.6 Let $X = (X_1, \ldots, X_d)$ be a random vector with independent components, each following $U[-\frac{1}{2}, \frac{1}{2}]$. Compute $\mathbb{P}[\|X\| \leq \frac{1}{2}]$ explicitly for $d = 1, 2, 3$. [*Hint*: Use a geometric argument.]

E1.4.7 Given a random variable X with $\mathbb{E}[X] = 0$ and $\mathrm{Var}[X] = 1$, bound $\mathbb{P}[|X| \geq 2\sqrt{d}]$ using *Chebyshev's Inequality* for $d = 1, 10, 100$.

E1.4.8 Let $X = (X_1, \ldots, X_d)$ be a random vector with independent components, each following $U[-\frac{1}{2}, \frac{1}{2}]$. Find an upper bound for $\mathbb{P}[\|X\| \geq \frac{1}{2}]$ using *Chebyshev's Inequality* for $d = 1, 10, 100$.

1.5.2 Problems

1.1 (Adapted from [BV2]) Recall that for two vectors **x** and **y** of the same dimension, their inner product is $\mathbf{x}^T \mathbf{y}$. A vector is said to be nonnegative if *all* of its entries are ≥ 0.

a) Show that the inner product of two nonnegative vectors is necessarily ≥ 0.

b) Suppose the inner product of two nonnegative vectors is *zero*. What can you say about their sparsity patterns – that is, which of their entries are zero or nonzero?

1.2 (Adapted from [BV2]) A Boolean n-vector is one for which all entries are either 0 or 1. Such vectors are used to encode whether each of n conditions holds, with $a_i = 1$ meaning that condition i holds.

a) Another common encoding of the same information uses the two values -1 and 1 for the entries. For example the Boolean vector $(0, 1, 1, 0)$ would be written using this alternative encoding as $(-1, 1, 1, -1)$. Suppose that $\mathbf{x}$ is a Boolean vector, and $\mathbf{y}$ is a vector encoding the same information using the values -1 and 1. Express $\mathbf{y}$ in terms of $\mathbf{x}$ using vector notation. Also, express $\mathbf{x}$ in terms of $\mathbf{y}$ using vector notation.

b) Suppose that $\mathbf{x}$ and $\mathbf{y}$ are Boolean n-vectors. Give a simple word description of their squared Euclidean distance $\|\mathbf{x} - \mathbf{y}\|_2^2$ and justify it mathematically.

1.3 (Adapted from [BV2]) If $\mathbf{a}$ is a vector, then $\mathbf{a}_{r:s}$ is the vector of size $s - r + 1$, with entries $a_r, \ldots, a_s$; that is, $\mathbf{a}_{r:s} = (a_r, \ldots, a_s)$. The vector $\mathbf{a}_{r:s}$ is called a slice. As a more concrete example, if $\mathbf{z}$ is the 4-vector $(1, -1, 2, 0)$, the slice $\mathbf{z}_{2:3} = (-1, 2)$. Suppose the T-vector $\mathbf{x}$ represents a time series or signal. The quantity

$$\mathcal{D}(\mathbf{x}) = (x_1 - x_2)^2 + (x_2 - x_3)^2 + \cdots + (x_{T-1} - x_T)^2,$$

the sum of the differences of adjacent values of the signal, is called the Dirichlet energy of the signal. The Dirichlet energy is a measure of the roughness or wiggliness of the time series.

a) Express $\mathcal{D}(\mathbf{x})$ in vector notation using slicing. [*Hint:* Note the similarity between $\mathcal{D}(\mathbf{x})$ and the squared Euclidean distance between two vectors.]

b) How small can $\mathcal{D}(\mathbf{x})$ be? What signals $\mathbf{x}$ have this minimum value of the Dirichlet energy?

c) Find a signal $\mathbf{x}$ with entries no more than one in absolute value that has the largest possible value of $\mathcal{D}(\mathbf{x})$. Give the value of the Dirichlet energy achieved.

1.4 (Adapted from [BV2]) A vector of length n can represent the number of times each word in a dictionary of n words appears in a document. For example, $(25, 2, 0)$ means that the first dictionary word appears 25 times, the second one twice, and the third one not at all. Suppose the n-vector $\mathbf{w}$ is the word count vector associated with a document and a dictionary of n words. For simplicity we will assume that all words in the document appear in the dictionary.

a) What is $\mathbf{1}^T\mathbf{w}$? Here $\mathbf{1}$ is an all-one vector of the appropriate size.

b) What does $w_{282} = 0$ mean?

c) Let $\mathbf{h}$ be the n-vector that gives the histogram of the word counts; that is, h_i is the fraction of the words in the document that are word i. Use vector notation to express $\mathbf{h}$ in terms of $\mathbf{w}$. (You can assume that the document contains at least one word.)

1.5 (Adapted from [BV2]) Suppose $\mathbf{a}$ and $\mathbf{b}$ are vectors of the same size. The triangle inequality states that $\|\mathbf{a} + \mathbf{b}\|_2 \leq \|\mathbf{a}\|_2 + \|\mathbf{b}\|_2$. Show that we also have $\|\mathbf{a} + \mathbf{b}\|_2 \geq \|\mathbf{a}\|_2 - \|\mathbf{b}\|_2$.

1.6 (Adapted from [BV2]) Verify that the following identities hold for any two vectors $\mathbf{a}$ and $\mathbf{b}$ of the same size.

a) $(\mathbf{a} + \mathbf{b})^T(\mathbf{a} - \mathbf{b}) = \|\mathbf{a}\|_2^2 - \|\mathbf{b}\|_2^2$

b) *The Parallelogram Law:* $\|\mathbf{a} + \mathbf{b}\|_2^2 + \|\mathbf{a} - \mathbf{b}\|_2^2 = 2(\|\mathbf{a}\|_2^2 + \|\mathbf{b}\|_2^2)$

1.7 (Adapted from [BV2]) The root-mean-square (RMS) value of an n-vector $\mathbf{x}$ is defined as

$$\mathrm{rms}(\mathbf{x}) = \sqrt{\frac{x_1^2 + \cdots + x_n^2}{n}} = \frac{\|\mathbf{x}\|_2}{\sqrt{n}}.$$

a) Show that at least one entry of a vector has absolute value at least as large as the RMS value of the vector.

b) For an n-vector $\mathbf{x}$, let $\mathrm{avg}(\mathbf{x}) = \mathbf{1}^T\mathbf{x}/n$ and

$$\mathrm{std}(\mathbf{x}) = \frac{\|\mathbf{x} - \mathrm{avg}(\mathbf{x})\mathbf{1}\|_2}{\sqrt{n}}.$$

Establish the identity

$$\mathrm{rms}(\mathbf{x})^2 = \mathrm{avg}(\mathbf{x})^2 + \mathrm{std}(\mathbf{x})^2.$$

c) Use (b) to show that $|\mathrm{avg}(\mathbf{x})| \leq \mathrm{rms}(\mathbf{x})$.

d) Use (b) to show that $\mathrm{std}(\mathbf{x}) \leq \mathrm{rms}(\mathbf{x})$.

1.8 (Adapted from [BV2]) Suppose that the vectors $\mathbf{x}_1, \ldots, \mathbf{x}_N$ are clustered using k-means, with group representatives $\mathbf{z}_1, \ldots, \mathbf{z}_k$.

a) Suppose the original vectors $\mathbf{x}_i$ are nonnegative, meaning that their entries are nonnegative. Explain why the representatives $\mathbf{z}_j$ are also nonnegative.

b) Suppose the original vectors $\mathbf{x}_i$ represent proportions, meaning that their entries are nonnegative and sum to one. Explain why the representatives $\mathbf{z}_j$ also represent proportions.

c) Suppose the original vectors $\mathbf{x}_i$ are Boolean, so that their entries are either 0 or 1. Give an interpretation of $(\mathbf{z}_j)_i$, the i-th entry of the j-th group representative.

1.9 (Adapted from [BV2]) Clustering a collection of vectors into $k = 2$ groups is called two-way partitioning, since we are partitioning the vectors into 2 groups, with index sets G_1 and G_2. Suppose we run k-means with $k = 2$ on the n-vectors $\mathbf{x}_1, \ldots, \mathbf{x}_N$. Show that there is a nonzero vector $\mathbf{w}$ and a scalar v that satisfy

$$\mathbf{w}^T\mathbf{x}_i + v \geq 0, \forall i \in G_1, \quad \mathbf{w}^T\mathbf{x}_i + v \leq 0, \forall i \in G_2.$$

In other words, the affine function $f(\mathbf{x}) = \mathbf{w}^T\mathbf{x} + v$ is greater than or equal to zero on the first group, and less than or equal to zero on the second group. This is called linear separation of the two groups. [*Hint:* Consider the function $\|\mathbf{x}-\mathbf{z}_1\|_2^2 - \|\mathbf{x}-\mathbf{z}_2\|_2^2$, where $\mathbf{z}_1$ and $\mathbf{z}_2$ are the group representatives.]

1.10 (Adapted from [ASV]) Let $0 < p \leq 1$. A random variable X has the geometric distribution with success parameter p if the possible values of X are $\{1, 2, 3, \ldots\}$ and X satisfies $\mathbb{P}(X = k) = (1-p)^{k-1}p$ for positive integers k. Its mean is $1/p$ and its variance is $(1-p)/p^2$.

Let X be a geometric random variable with parameter $p = 1/6$.

a) Use *Markov's Inequality* to find an upper bound for $\mathbb{P}(X \geq 16)$.

b) Use *Chebyshev's Inequality* to find an upper bound for $\mathbb{P}(X \geq 16)$.

c) Use the sum of a geometric series to compute the probability $\mathbb{P}(X \geq 16)$ explicitly, and compare with the upper bounds you derived.

1.11 (Adapted from [ASV]) Let $0 < \lambda < +\infty$. A random variable X has the exponential distribution with parameter λ if X has density function $f(x) = \lambda e^{-\lambda x}$, for $x \geq 0$ and 0 otherwise. Its mean is $1/\lambda$ and its variance is $1/\lambda^2$.
Let X be an exponential random variable with parameter $\lambda = 1/2$.

a) Use *Markov's Inequality* to find an upper bound for $\mathbb{P}(X > 6)$.

b) Use *Chebyshev's Inequality* to find an upper bound for $\mathbb{P}(X > 6)$.

c) Use an integral to compute the probability $\mathbb{P}(X > 6)$ explicitly, and compare with the upper bounds you derived.

1.12 (Adapted from [ASV]) Suppose that X is a nonnegative random variable with $\mathbb{E}[X] = 10$.

a) Use *Markov's Inequality* to give an upper bound on the probability that X is larger than 15.

b) Suppose that we also know that $\text{Var}(X) = 3$. Use *Chebyshev's Inequality* to give a better upper bound on $\mathbb{P}(X > 15)$ than in part (a).

c) Suppose that $Y_1, Y_2, \ldots, Y_{300}$ are i.i.d. random variables with the same distribution as X, so that, in particular $\mathbb{E}(Y_i) = 10$ and $\text{Var}(Y_i) = 3$. Use *Chebyshev's Inequality* to give an upper bound on the probability that $\sum_{i=1}^{300} Y_i$ is larger than 3060.

1.13 (Adapted from [ASV]) Suppose that we have i.i.d. random variables $X_1, X_2, X_3, \ldots$ with finite mean $\mathbb{E}[X_1] = \mu$ and variance $\text{Var}(X_1) = \sigma^2$. Let $S_n = X_1 + \cdots + X_n$. Prove that for any fixed $\varepsilon > 0$ and $1/2 < \alpha < 1$ we have

$$\lim_{n \to +\infty} \mathbb{P}\left[\left|\frac{S_n - n\mu}{n^\alpha}\right| < \varepsilon\right] = 1.$$

1.14 (Adapted from [ASV]) By mimicking the proof of the *Weak Law of Large Numbers*, prove the following variant. Suppose that we have random variables $X_1, X_2, \ldots$ each with finite mean $\mathbb{E}[X_i] = \mu$ and variance $\text{Var}(X_i) = \sigma^2$. Suppose further that $\text{Cov}(X_i, X_j) = 0$ whenever $|i - j| \geq 2$ and that there is a constant $c > 0$ so that $|\text{Cov}(X_i, X_{i+1})| < c$ for all i. Let $S_n = X_1 + \cdots + X_n$. Then for any fixed $\varepsilon > 0$ we have

$$\lim_{n \to +\infty} \mathbb{P}\left[\left|\frac{S_n}{n} - \mu\right| < \varepsilon\right] = 1.$$

1.15 (Adapted from [ASV]) By mimicking the proof of *Chebyshev's Inequality*, prove the following variant. Let X be a random variable with a finite mean μ and for which $\mathbb{E}[\exp(s(X - \mu))] < +\infty$ for some $s > 0$. Then we have for $c > 0$

$$\mathbb{P}(X \geq \mu + c) \leq \frac{\mathbb{E}[\exp(s(X - \mu))]}{e^{sc}}.$$

Justify your answer carefully.

1.16 (Adapted from [ASV]) Recall that the cumulative distribution function (CDF) of a real-valued random variable Z is the function $F_Z(z) = \mathbb{P}[Z \leq z]$ for all $z \in$

$\mathbb{R}$. Let $X_1, X_2, \ldots, X_n$ be independent random variables with the same cumulative distribution function F. Denote the minimum and the maximum by

$$Z = \min(X_1, X_2, \ldots, X_n) \quad \text{and} \quad W = \max(X_1, X_2, \ldots, X_n).$$

Find the cumulative distribution functions F_Z and F_W of Z and W respectively.

1.17 (Adapted from [ASV]) Suppose that $X_1, X_2, \ldots$ are i.i.d. random variables with exponential distribution with parameter $\lambda = 1$ (see Exercise 1.11 above), and let $M_n = \max(X_1, \ldots, X_n)$. Show that for any $x \in \mathbb{R}$ we have

$$\lim_{n \to +\infty} \mathbb{P}(M_n - \ln n \leq x) = \exp(-e^{-x}).$$

The right-hand side is the cumulative distribution function of the Gumbel distribution, an example of an extreme value distribution. [*Hint:* Use Exercise 1.16 to compute $\mathbb{P}(M_n \leq \ln n + x)$ explicitly, and then evaluate the limit as $n \to +\infty$.]

1.18 (Adapted from [ASV]) Let A and B be two disjoint events. Under what condition are they independent?

1.19 (Adapted from [ASV]) We choose a number from the set $\{10, 11, 12, \ldots, 99\}$ uniformly at random.

a) Let X be the first digit and Y the second digit of the chosen number. Show that X and Y are independent random variables.

b) Let X be the first digit of the chosen number and Z the sum of the two digits. Show that X and Z are not independent.

1.20 (Adapted from [ASV]) Suppose that X and Y have joint probability density function $f(x, y) = 2e^{-(x+2y)}$ for $x > 0, y > 0$ and 0 elsewhere. Show that X and Y are independent random variables and provide their marginal distributions. [*Hint:* Recall the exponential distribution from Problem 1.11.]

1.21 (Adapted from [ASV]) Suppose that X, Y have joint probability density function

$$f(x, y) = c \exp\left[-\frac{x^2}{2} - \frac{(x-y)^2}{2}\right],$$

for $(x, y) \in \mathbb{R}^2$, for some constant $c > 0$.

a) Find the value of the constant c. [*Hint:* The order of integration makes a difference to the ease of calculation. You can do this without doing complicated integrals.] Specifically, recall that for any $\mu \in \mathbb{R}$ and $\sigma > 0$, it holds that

$$\int_{-\infty}^{+\infty} \frac{1}{\sqrt{2\pi\sigma^2}} \exp\left(-\frac{(z-\mu)^2}{2\sigma^2}\right) dz = 1.]$$

b) Find the marginal density functions of X and Y. [*Hint:* You can do this without doing complicated integrals. Complete the square.]

c) Determine whether X and Y are independent. Justify your answer.

1.22 (Adapted from [ASV]) Let $p(x, y)$ be the joint probability mass function of (X, Y). Assume that there are two functions a and b such that $p(x, y) = a(x)b(y)$ for all possible values x of X and y of Y. Show that X and Y are independent. Do *not* assume that a and b are probability mass functions.

1.23 (Adapted from [BHK]) a) Let X and Y be independent random variables with uniform distribution in $[-1/2, 1/2]$. Compute $\mathbb{E}[X]$, $\mathbb{E}[X^2]$, $\text{Var}[X^2]$, $\mathbb{E}[X - Y]$, $\mathbb{E}[XY]$, and $\mathbb{E}[(X - Y)^2]$.

a) What is the expected squared Euclidean distance between two points generated at random inside the unit d-dimensional cube $\mathcal{C} = [-1/2, 1/2]^d$?

1.24 (Adapted from [BHK]) a) For an arbitrary $a > 0$ give a probability distribution for a nonnegative random variable X such that

$$\mathbb{P}[X \geq a] = \frac{\mathbb{E}[X]}{a}.$$

a) Show that for any $c > 0$ there exists a distribution for which *Chebyshev's Inequality* is tight, that is,

$$\mathbb{P}[|X - \mathbb{E}[X]| \geq c] = \frac{\mathrm{Var}[X]}{c^2}.$$

[*Hint:* Choose a distribution symmetric about 0.]

1.25 (Adapted from [BHK]) Let $X_1, X_2, \ldots, X_n$ be i.i.d. random variables with mean μ and variance σ^2. Let

$$\overline{X}_n = \frac{1}{n} \sum_{i=1}^{n} X_i$$

be the sample mean. Suppose one estimates the variance using the sample mean as follows:

$$S_n^2 = \frac{1}{n} \sum_{i=1}^{n} \left(X_i - \overline{X}_n \right)^2.$$

Calculate $\mathbb{E}(S_n^2)$. [*Hint:* Replace $X_i - \overline{X}_n$ with $(X_i - \mu) - (\overline{X}_n - \mu)$.]

1.26 Let f and g have derivatives at x and let α and β be constants. Prove from the definition of the derivative that

$$[\alpha f(x) + \beta g(x)]' = \alpha f'(x) + \beta g'(x).$$

1.27 Let $Z_1 \sim \mathrm{N}(\mu_1, \sigma_1^2)$ and $Z_2 \sim \mathrm{N}(\mu_2, \sigma_2^2)$ be independent Normal variables with mean μ_1, μ_2 and variance σ_1^2 and σ_2^2 respectively. Recall that $Z_1 + Z_2$ is still Normal.

a) What are the mean and variance of $Z_1 + Z_2$?

b) Let $\mathbf{X}_1, \mathbf{X}_2, \mathbf{Y}_1$ be independent spherical d-dimensional Gaussians with mean $-w\mathbf{e}_1$ and variance 1. Let $\mathbf{Y}_2$ be an independent spherical d-dimensional Gaussian with mean $w\mathbf{e}_1$ and variance 1. Compute $\mathbb{E}[\|\mathbf{X}_1 - \mathbf{X}_2\|^2]$ and $\mathbb{E}[\|\mathbf{Y}_1 - \mathbf{Y}_2\|^2]$ explicitly.

1.28 Suppose we are given n vectors $\mathbf{x}_1, \ldots, \mathbf{x}_n$ in $\mathbb{R}^d$ and a partition $C_1, \ldots, C_k \subseteq [n]$. Let $n_i = |C_i|$ be the size of cluster C_i and let

$$\boldsymbol{\mu}_i^* = \frac{1}{n_i} \sum_{j \in C_i} \mathbf{x}_j$$

be the centroid of C_i, for $i = 1, \ldots, k$.

a) Show that

$$\sum_{j \in C_i} \|\mathbf{x}_j - \boldsymbol{\mu}_i^*\|^2 = \left(\sum_{j \in C_i} \|\mathbf{x}_j\|^2 \right) - n_i \|\boldsymbol{\mu}_i^*\|^2.$$

b) Show that
$$\|\boldsymbol{\mu}_i^*\|^2 = \frac{1}{n_i^2}\left(\sum_{j\in C_i}\|\mathbf{x}_j\|^2 + \sum_{\substack{j,\ell\in C_i\\ j\neq \ell}}\mathbf{x}_j^T\mathbf{x}_\ell\right).$$

c) Show that
$$\sum_{\substack{j,\ell\in C_i\\ j\neq \ell}}\|\mathbf{x}_j - \mathbf{x}_\ell\|^2 = 2(n_i - 1)\sum_{j\in C_i}\|\mathbf{x}_j\|^2 - 2\sum_{\substack{j,\ell\in C_i\\ j\neq \ell}}\mathbf{x}_j^T\mathbf{x}_\ell.$$

d) Combine (a), (b), (c) to prove that minimizing the k-means objective $\mathcal{G}(C_1,\ldots,C_k)$ over all partitions $C_1,\ldots,C_k$ of $[n]$ is equivalent to minimizing instead
$$\sum_{i=1}^k \frac{1}{2|C_i|}\sum_{\substack{j,\ell\in C_i}}\|\mathbf{x}_j - \mathbf{x}_\ell\|^2.$$

1.29 Suppose the rows of $A \in \mathbb{R}^{n\times m}$ are given by the transposes of $\mathbf{r}_1,\ldots,\mathbf{r}_n \in \mathbb{R}^m$ and the columns of A are given by $\mathbf{c}_1,\ldots,\mathbf{c}_m \in \mathbb{R}^n$. Give expressions for the elements of $A^T A$ and AA^T in terms of these vectors.

1.30 Give a proof of the *Positive Semidefiniteness of the Covariance* using the matrix form of $\Sigma_\mathbf{X}$.

1.31 Use the *Cauchy–Schwarz Inequality* to prove that the correlation coefficient lies in $[-1, 1]$.

1.32 Let $f(x,y) = g(x) + h(y)$ where $x,y \in \mathbb{R}$ and g,h are real-valued continuously differentiable functions. Compute the gradient of f in terms of the derivatives of g and h.

1.33 Let $A = [a]$ be a 1×1 positive definite matrix. Show that $a > 0$.

1.34 Show that the diagonal elements of a positive definite matrix are necessarily positive.

1.35 Let $A, B \in \mathbb{R}^{n\times m}$ and let $c \in \mathbb{R}$. Show that

a) $(A+B)^T = A^T + B^T$

b) $(cA)^T = cA^T$

2 Least Squares: Geometric, Algebraic, and Numerical Aspects

In this chapter, we introduce the linear least-squares problem, an optimization problem that aims to find the best-fitting linear model for a given set of data points. It is closely connected to regression analysis, one of the most fundamental and widely used statistical techniques. We develop the mathematical concepts at its foundation, emphasizing in particular the various facets of the problem: the algebra, the geometry, and the numerics. Here is a more detailed overview of the main sections of the chapter.

Background: Review of vector spaces and matrix inverses: Section 2.2 reviews fundamental concepts in linear algebra that are essential for data science. It begins by defining linear subspaces and related notions like span, linear independence, and bases. The dimension theorem is stated, establishing that the dimension of a subspace is well-defined. Finally, the section discusses inverses of square matrices, proving that a square matrix is invertible if and only if it is nonsingular, and that the solution to the equation $A\mathbf{x} = \mathbf{b}$ is unique and given by $\mathbf{x} = A^{-1}\mathbf{b}$ when A is nonsingular.

The geometry of least squares: In Section 2.3, the important concept of orthogonality is reviewed, along with key results like Pythagoras' theorem, the Cauchy–Schwarz inequality, and the Gram–Schmidt theorem regarding the existence of orthonormal bases. It then introduces the concept of orthogonal projection, which is the process of finding the closest vector in a linear subspace to a given vector. Finally, these concepts are applied to solve overdetermined systems using the least-squares method, showing that the solution satisfies the normal equations.

QR decomposition and Householder transformations: In Section 2.4, the Gram–Schmidt algorithm is introduced as a way to obtain an orthonormal basis from a set of linearly independent vectors, and its matrix factorization perspective is presented as the QR decomposition. The section then shows how the QR decomposition can be used to solve linear least-squares problems. While the Gram–Schmidt algorithm is geometrically intuitive, it can have numerical issues. Householder reflections, on the other hand, provide a more numerically stable method for computing QR decompositions. These reflections are orthogonal transformations that can be used to introduce zeros below the diagonal of a matrix, ultimately leading to its triangularization.

Application to regression analysis: Section 2.5 applies the least-squares method to regression analysis. It begins by using the method to find the coefficients that best fit a linear model to a given dataset. It then extends this approach to polynomial regression, showing how to fit higher-degree polynomials by adding columns to the data matrix. The section also discusses the concept of overfitting, where a model with too many parameters may fit the noise in the data rather than the underlying relationship.

2.1 Motivating Example: Predicting Sales

The following *advertising dataset*[1] is from the excellent textbook [JWH+]. Quoting [JWH+, Section 2.1]:

> Suppose that we are statistical consultants hired by a client to provide advice on how to improve sales of a particular product. The advertising data set consists of the sales of that product in 200 different markets, along with advertising budgets for the product in each of those markets for three different media: TV, radio, and newspaper. [...] It is not possible for our client to directly increase sales of the product. On the other hand, they can control the advertising expenditure in each of the three media. Therefore, if we determine that there is an association between advertising and sales, then we can instruct our client to adjust advertising budgets, thereby indirectly increasing sales. In other words, our goal is to develop an accurate model that can be used to predict sales on the basis of the three media budgets.

This a regression problem. That is, we want to estimate the relationship between an outcome variable and one or more predictors (or features). We load the data.

```
data = pd.read_csv('advertising.csv')
data.head()
```

	TV	radio	newspaper	sales
0	230.1	37.8	69.2	22.1
1	44.5	39.3	45.1	10.4
2	17.2	45.9	69.3	9.3
3	151.5	41.3	58.5	18.5
4	180.8	10.8	58.4	12.9

We will focus for now on the TV budget.

```
TV = data['TV'].to_numpy()
sales = data['sales'].to_numpy()
```

We make a scatter plot showing the relation between those two quantities.

```
plt.scatter(TV, sales, s=5, c='k')
plt.xlabel('TV'), plt.ylabel('sales')
plt.show()
```

---

[1] You can access the dataset via the GitHub page for this book: https://github.com/MMiDS-textbook/

2.1 Motivating Example: Predicting Sales

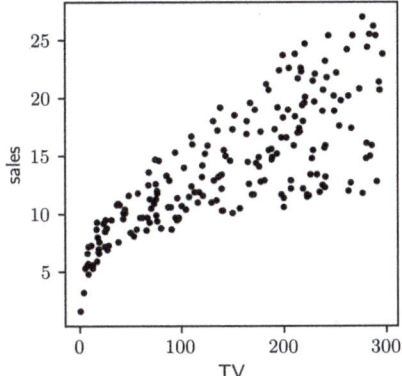

Figure 2.1 Graphical output of code.

There does seem to be a relationship between the two. Roughly, a higher TV budget is linked to higher sales, although the correspondence is not perfect. To express the relationship more quantitatively, we seek a function f such that

$$y \approx f(x)$$

where x denotes a sample TV budget and y is the corresponding observed sales. We might posit for instance that there exists a true f and that each observation is disrupted by some noise ε:

$$y = f(x) + \varepsilon.$$

A natural way to estimate such an f from data is k-nearest-neighbors (k-NN) regression. Let the data be of the form $\{(\mathbf{x}_i, y_i)\}_{i=1}^n$, where $\mathbf{x}_i \in \mathbb{R}^d$ and $y_i \in \mathbb{R}$. In our case $\mathbf{x}_i$ is the TV budget of the i-th sample (with $d = 1$) and y_i is the corresponding sales. For each $\mathbf{x}$ (not necessarily in the data), we do the following:

- find the k nearest $\mathbf{x}_i$'s to $\mathbf{x}$;
- take an average of the corresponding y_i's.

We implement this method in Python. We use the function `numpy.argsort` to sort an array and the function `numpy.absolute` to compute the absolute deviation. Our quick implementation here assumes that the $\mathbf{x}_i$'s are scalars.

```
def knnregression(x,y,k,xnew):
    n = len(x)
    closest = np.argsort([np.absolute(x[i]-xnew) for i in range(n)])
    return np.mean(y[closest[0:k]])
```

For $k = 3$ and a grid of 1000 points, we get the following approximation $\hat{f}$. Here the function `numpy.linspace` creates an array of equally spaced points.

```
k = 3
xgrid = np.linspace(TV.min(), TV.max(), num=1000)
yhat = [knnregression(TV,sales,k,xnew) for xnew in xgrid]
```

```
plt.scatter(TV, sales, s=5, c='b', alpha=0.5)
plt.plot(xgrid, yhat, 'r')
plt.xlabel('TV'), plt.ylabel('sales')
plt.show()
```

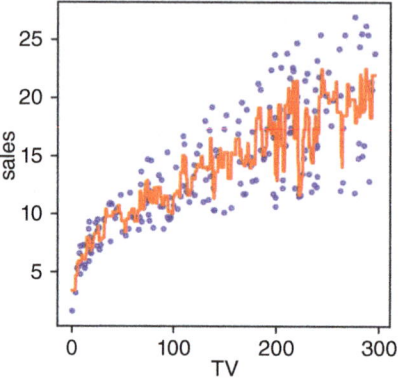

Figure 2.2 Graphical output of code.

One downside of k-NN regression is that it does not give an easily interpretable relationship: If I increase my TV budget by Δ dollars, how is it expected to affect the sales? Another issue arises in high dimension where the counterintuitive phenomena we discussed in Section 1.4 can have a significant impact. Recall in particular the *High-Dimensional Cube Theorem*. If we have d predictors – where d is large – and our data is distributed uniformly in a bounded region, then any given $\mathbf{x}$ will be far from any of our data points. In this case, the y-values of the closest $\mathbf{x}_i$'s may not be predictive. This is referred to as the Curse of Dimensionality.

CHAT & LEARN Ask your favorite AI chatbot for more details on the Curse of Dimensionality and how it arises in data science.

One way out is to make stronger assumptions on the function f. For instance, we can assume that the true relationship is (approximately) affine; that is, $y \approx \beta_0 + \beta_1 x$, or if we have d predictors,

$$y \approx \beta_0 + \sum_{j=1}^{d} \beta_j x_j.$$

How do we estimate appropriate intercept and coefficients? The standard approach is to minimize the sum of the squared errors

$$\sum_{i=1}^{n} \left(y_i - \left\{ \beta_0 + \sum_{j=1}^{d} \beta_j (\mathbf{x}_i)_j \right\} \right)^2$$

where $(\mathbf{x}_i)_j$ is the j-th entry of input vector $\mathbf{x}_i$ and y_i is the corresponding y-value. This is called multiple linear regression.

It is a least-squares problem. We rewrite it in a more convenient matrix form and combine β_0 with the other β_i's by adding a dummy predictor to each sample. Let

$$\mathbf{y} = \begin{pmatrix} y_1 \\ y_2 \\ \vdots \\ y_n \end{pmatrix}, \quad A = \begin{pmatrix} 1 & \mathbf{x}_1^T \\ 1 & \mathbf{x}_2^T \\ \vdots & \vdots \\ 1 & \mathbf{x}_n^T \end{pmatrix}, \quad \text{and} \quad \boldsymbol{\beta} = \begin{pmatrix} \beta_0 \\ \beta_1 \\ \vdots \\ \beta_d \end{pmatrix}.$$

Then observe that

$$\|\mathbf{y} - A\boldsymbol{\beta}\|^2 = \sum_{i=1}^n (y_i - (A\boldsymbol{\beta})_i)^2$$

$$= \sum_{i=1}^n \left(y_i - \left\{ \beta_0 + \sum_{j=1}^d \beta_j (\mathbf{x}_i)_j \right\} \right)^2.$$

The linear least-squares problem is then formulated as

$$\min_{\boldsymbol{\beta}} \|\mathbf{y} - A\boldsymbol{\beta}\|^2.$$

In words, we are looking for a linear combination of the columns of A that is closest to $\mathbf{y}$ in Euclidean distance. Indeed, minimizing the squared Euclidean distance is equivalent to minimizing its square root, as the latter is an increasing function.

One could solve this optimization problem through calculus (and we will come back to this approach later in the book), but understanding the geometric and algebraic structure of the problem turns out to provide powerful insights into its solution – and that of many of problems in data science. It will also be an opportunity to review some basic linear-algebraic concepts along the way.

We will come back to the `advertising` dataset later in the chapter.

2.2 Background: Review of Vector Spaces and Matrix Inverses

In this section, we introduce some basic linear algebra concepts that will be needed throughout this chapter and later on.

2.2.1 Subspaces

We work over the vector space $V = \mathbb{R}^n$. We begin with the concept of a linear subspace.

Definition 2.2.1 *(Linear Subspace) A linear subspace of $\mathbb{R}^n$ is a subset $U \subseteq \mathbb{R}^n$ that is closed under vector addition and scalar multiplication. That is, for all $\mathbf{u}_1, \mathbf{u}_2 \in U$ and $\alpha \in \mathbb{R}$, it holds that*

$$\mathbf{u}_1 + \mathbf{u}_2 \in U \quad \text{and} \quad \alpha \mathbf{u}_1 \in U.$$

It follows from this condition that $\mathbf{0} \in U$.

Alternatively, we can check these conditions by proving that (1) $\mathbf{0} \in U$ and (2) $\mathbf{u}_1, \mathbf{u}_2 \in U$ and $\alpha \in \mathbb{R}$ imply that $\alpha \mathbf{u}_1 + \mathbf{u}_2 \in U$. Indeed, taking $\alpha = 1$ gives the first condition above, while choosing $\mathbf{u}_2 = \mathbf{0}$ gives the second one.

NUMERICAL CORNER The plane P made of all points $(x, y, z) \in \mathbb{R}^3$ that satisfy $z = x + y$ is a linear subspace. Indeed, $0 = 0 + 0$ so $(0, 0, 0) \in P$. And, for any $\mathbf{u}_1 = (x_1, y_1, z_1)$ and $\mathbf{u}_2 = (x_2, y_2, z_2)$ such that $z_1 = x_1 + y_1$ and $z_2 = x_2 + y_2$ and for any $\alpha \in \mathbb{R}$, we have

$$\alpha z_1 + z_2 = \alpha(x_1 + y_1) + (x_2 + y_2) = (\alpha x_1 + x_2) + (\alpha y_1 + y_2).$$

That is, $\alpha \mathbf{u}_1 + \mathbf{u}_2$ satisfies the condition defining P and therefore is itself in P. Note also that P passes through the origin.

In this example, the linear subspace P can be described alternatively as the collection of every vector of the form $(x, y, x + y)$.

We use `plot_surface` to plot it over a grid of points created using `numpy.meshgrid`.

```
x = np.linspace(0,1,num=101)
y = np.linspace(0,1,num=101)
X, Y = np.meshgrid(x, y)
print(X)
```

```
[[0.   0.01 0.02 ... 0.98 0.99 1.  ]
 [0.   0.01 0.02 ... 0.98 0.99 1.  ]
 [0.   0.01 0.02 ... 0.98 0.99 1.  ]
 ...
 [0.   0.01 0.02 ... 0.98 0.99 1.  ]
 [0.   0.01 0.02 ... 0.98 0.99 1.  ]
 [0.   0.01 0.02 ... 0.98 0.99 1.  ]]
```

```
print(Y)
```

```
[[0.   0.   0.   ... 0.   0.   0.  ]
 [0.01 0.01 0.01 ... 0.01 0.01 0.01]
 [0.02 0.02 0.02 ... 0.02 0.02 0.02]
 ...
 [0.98 0.98 0.98 ... 0.98 0.98 0.98]
 [0.99 0.99 0.99 ... 0.99 0.99 0.99]
 [1.   1.   1.   ... 1.   1.   1.  ]]
```

```
Z = X + Y
print(Z)
```

```
[[0.   0.01 0.02 ... 0.98 0.99 1.  ]
 [0.01 0.02 0.03 ... 0.99 1.   1.01]
 [0.02 0.03 0.04 ... 1.   1.01 1.02]
 ...
 [0.98 0.99 1.   ... 1.96 1.97 1.98]
 [0.99 1.   1.01 ... 1.97 1.98 1.99]
 [1.   1.01 1.02 ... 1.98 1.99 2.  ]]
```

```
fig = plt.figure()
ax = fig.add_subplot(111, projection='3d')
ax.plot_surface(X, Y, Z, cmap='viridis')
plt.show()
```

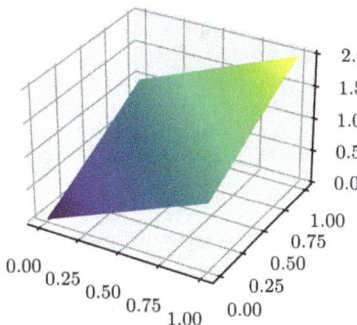

Figure 2.3 Graphical output of code.

◁ **NC**

Here is a key example of a linear subspace.

Definition 2.2.2 (Span) Let $\mathbf{w}_1, \ldots, \mathbf{w}_m \in \mathbb{R}^n$. The span of $\{\mathbf{w}_1, \ldots, \mathbf{w}_m\}$, denoted span$(\mathbf{w}_1, \ldots, \mathbf{w}_m)$, is the set of all linear combinations of the $\mathbf{w}_j$'s. That is,

$$\mathrm{span}(\mathbf{w}_1, \ldots, \mathbf{w}_m) = \left\{ \sum_{j=1}^{m} \alpha_j \mathbf{w}_j : \alpha_1, \ldots, \alpha_m \in \mathbb{R} \right\}.$$

By convention, we declare that the span of the empty list is $\{\mathbf{0}\}$.

Example 2.2.3 *In the example from the previous Numerical Corner, we noted that the plane P is the collection of every vector of the form $(x, y, x+y)$. These can be written as $x\mathbf{w}_1 + y\mathbf{w}_2$ where $\mathbf{w}_1 = (1, 0, 1)$ and $\mathbf{w}_2 = (0, 1, 1)$, and vice versa. Hence $P = \mathrm{span}(\mathbf{w}_1, \mathbf{w}_2)$.*

We check next that a span is indeed a linear subspace.

Lemma 2.2.4 *Let $W = \mathrm{span}(\mathbf{w}_1, \ldots, \mathbf{w}_m)$. Then W is a linear subspace.*

We say that $\mathbf{w}_1, \ldots, \mathbf{w}_m$ span W.

Proof First, $\mathbf{0} = \sum_{j=1}^{m} 0 \mathbf{w}_j \in W$. Second, let $\mathbf{u}_1, \mathbf{u}_2 \in W$ and $\alpha \in \mathbb{R}$. For $i = 1, 2$, because $\mathbf{u}_i$ is in the span of the $\mathbf{w}_j$'s, we can write

$$\mathbf{u}_i = \sum_{j=1}^{m} \beta_{ij} \mathbf{w}_j$$

for some $\beta_{ij} \in \mathbb{R}$ for $j = 1, \ldots, m$.
Therefore

$$\alpha \mathbf{u}_1 + \mathbf{u}_2 = \alpha \sum_{j=1}^{m} \beta_{1j} \mathbf{w}_j + \sum_{j=1}^{m} \beta_{2j} \mathbf{w}_j = \sum_{j=1}^{m} (\alpha \beta_{1j} + \beta_{2j}) \mathbf{w}_j.$$

So $\alpha \mathbf{u}_1 + \mathbf{u}_2 \in W$. □

CHAT & LEARN Consider the following problem:

Prove that if $\{\mathbf{v}_1, \ldots, \mathbf{v}_n\}$ spans U, then so does the list

$$\{\mathbf{v}_1 - \mathbf{v}_2, \mathbf{v}_2 - \mathbf{v}_3, \ldots, \mathbf{v}_{n-1} - \mathbf{v}_n, \mathbf{v}_n\}$$

obtained by subtracting from each vector (except the last one) the next vector in the list.

A popular AI chatbot (which shall remain nameless) provided the following solution:

Suppose that $U = \text{span}(\mathbf{v}_1, \ldots, \mathbf{v}_n)$. Then for any vector $\mathbf{v} \in U$, there exist scalars $a_1, \ldots, a_n \in \mathbb{R}$ such that

$$\mathbf{v} = a_1 \mathbf{v}_1 + a_2 \mathbf{v}_2 + \ldots + a_n \mathbf{v}_n$$

Now let's express each vector in the new list in terms of the given vectors: $\mathbf{v}_1 - \mathbf{v}_2 = a_1(\mathbf{v}_1 - \mathbf{v}_2)$, $\mathbf{v}_2 - \mathbf{v}_3 = (a_1 + a_2)(\mathbf{v}_2 - \mathbf{v}_3)$, $\mathbf{v}_3 - \mathbf{v}_4 = (a_1 + a_2 + a_3)(\mathbf{v}_3 - \mathbf{v}_4)$, $\ldots$, $\mathbf{v}_{n-1} - \mathbf{v}_n = (a_1 + a_2 + \ldots + a_{n-1})(\mathbf{v}_{n-1} - \mathbf{v}_n)$.

Adding up all these expressions, we get:

$$\mathbf{v} = a_1(\mathbf{v}_1 - \mathbf{v}_2) + (a_1 + a_2)(\mathbf{v}_2 - \mathbf{v}_3) + \ldots + (a_1 + a_2 + \ldots + a_{n-1})(\mathbf{v}_{n-1} - \mathbf{v}_n) + a_n \mathbf{v}_n.$$

This shows that $\mathbf{v}$ can be expressed as a linear combination of the vectors in the new list, which means that the new list also spans U. Therefore, the list $\mathbf{v}_1 - \mathbf{v}_2, \mathbf{v}_2 - \mathbf{v}_3, \ldots, \mathbf{v}_{n-1} - \mathbf{v}_n, \mathbf{v}_n$ spans U, completing the proof.

Fix this proof.

In matrix form, we talk about the column space of a (not necessarily square) matrix.

Definition 2.2.5 *(Column Space) Let $A \in \mathbb{R}^{n \times m}$ be an $n \times m$ matrix with columns $\mathbf{a}_1, \ldots, \mathbf{a}_m \in \mathbb{R}^n$. The column space of A, denoted $\text{col}(A)$, is the span of the columns of A, that is, $\text{col}(A) = \text{span}(\mathbf{a}_1, \ldots, \mathbf{a}_m) \subseteq \mathbb{R}^n$.*

When thinking of A as a linear map – the vector-valued function $f(\mathbf{x}) = A\mathbf{x}$ mapping inputs in $\mathbb{R}^m$ to outputs in $\mathbb{R}^n$ – the column space is referred to as the range or image.

We will need another important linear subspace defined in terms of a matrix.

Definition 2.2.6 *(Null Space) Let $B \in \mathbb{R}^{n \times m}$. The null space of B is the linear subspace*

$$\text{null}(B) = \{\mathbf{x} \in \mathbb{R}^m : B\mathbf{x} = \mathbf{0}\}.$$

It can be shown that the null space is a linear subspace. We give a simple example next.

Example 2.2.7 *(continued from Example 2.2.3) Going back to the linear subspace $P = \{(x, y, z)^T \in \mathbb{R}^3 : z = x + y\}$, the condition in the definition can be rewritten as $x + y - z = 0$. Hence $P = \text{null}(B)$ for the single-row matrix $B = \begin{pmatrix} 1 & 1 & -1 \end{pmatrix}$.*

2.2.2 Linear Independence and Bases

It is often desirable to avoid redundancy in the description of a linear subspace. We start with an example.

Example 2.2.8 *Consider the linear subspace* $\mathrm{span}(\mathbf{w}_1, \mathbf{w}_2, \mathbf{w}_3)$, *where* $\mathbf{w}_1 = (1, 0, 1)$, $\mathbf{w}_2 = (0, 1, 1)$, *and* $\mathbf{w}_3 = (1, -1, 0)$. *We claim that*

$$\mathrm{span}(\mathbf{w}_1, \mathbf{w}_2, \mathbf{w}_3) = \mathrm{span}(\mathbf{w}_1, \mathbf{w}_2).$$

Recall that to prove an equality between sets, it suffices to prove inclusion in both directions. First, it is immediate by definition of the span that

$$\mathrm{span}(\mathbf{w}_1, \mathbf{w}_2) \subseteq \mathrm{span}(\mathbf{w}_1, \mathbf{w}_2, \mathbf{w}_3).$$

To prove the other direction, let $\mathbf{u} \in \mathrm{span}(\mathbf{w}_1, \mathbf{w}_2, \mathbf{w}_3)$ *so that*

$$\mathbf{u} = \beta_1 (1, 0, 1) + \beta_2 (0, 1, 1) + \beta_3 (1, -1, 0).$$

Now observe that $(1, -1, 0) = (1, 0, 1) - (0, 1, 1)$. *Put differently,* $\mathbf{w}_3 \in \mathrm{span}(\mathbf{w}_1, \mathbf{w}_2)$. *Replacing above gives*

$$\mathbf{u} = \beta_1 (1, 0, 1) + \beta_2 (0, 1, 1) + \beta_3 [(1, 0, 1) - (0, 1, 1)]$$
$$= (\beta_1 + \beta_3) (1, 0, 1) + (\beta_2 - \beta_3) (0, 1, 1)$$

which shows that $\mathbf{u} \in \mathrm{span}(\mathbf{w}_1, \mathbf{w}_2)$. *In words,* $(1, -1, 0)$ *is redundant. Hence*

$$\mathrm{span}(\mathbf{w}_1, \mathbf{w}_2) \supseteq \mathrm{span}(\mathbf{w}_1, \mathbf{w}_2, \mathbf{w}_3)$$

and that concludes the proof.

Definition 2.2.9 *(Linear Independence) A list of nonzero vectors* $\mathbf{u}_1, \ldots, \mathbf{u}_m$ *is linearly independent if none of them can be written as a linear combination of the others; that is,*

$$\forall i, \ \mathbf{u}_i \notin \mathrm{span}(\{\mathbf{u}_j : j \neq i\}).$$

By convention, we declare the empty list to be linearly independent. A list of vectors is called linearly dependent if it is not linearly independent.

Example 2.2.10 *(continued from Example 2.2.8) In the previous example,* $\mathbf{w}_1, \mathbf{w}_2, \mathbf{w}_3$ *are not linearly independent, because we showed that* $\mathbf{w}_3$ *can be written as a linear combination of* $\mathbf{w}_1, \mathbf{w}_2$. *On the other hand,* $\mathbf{w}_1, \mathbf{w}_2$ *are linearly independent because there is no* $\alpha, \beta \in \mathbb{R}$ *such that* $(1, 0, 1) = \alpha (0, 1, 1)$ *or* $(0, 1, 1) = \beta (1, 0, 1)$. *Indeed, the first equation requires* $1 = \alpha 0$ *(first component) and the second one requires* $1 = \beta 0$ *(second component) – both of which have no solution.*

Example 2.2.11 *Consider the* 2×2 *matrix*

$$A = \begin{pmatrix} a & b \\ c & d \end{pmatrix}.$$

We show that the columns

$$\mathbf{u}_1 = \begin{pmatrix} a \\ c \end{pmatrix} \quad \text{and} \quad \mathbf{u}_2 = \begin{pmatrix} b \\ d \end{pmatrix}$$

are linearly dependent if $ad - bc = 0$. You may recognize the quantity $ad - bc$ as the determinant of A, an important algebraic quantity which nevertheless plays only a small role in this book.

We consider two cases.

Suppose first that all entries of A are non-zero. In that case, $ad = bc$ implies $d/c = b/a =: \gamma$. Multiplying $\mathbf{u}_1$ by γ gives

$$\gamma \mathbf{u}_1 = \gamma \begin{pmatrix} a \\ c \end{pmatrix} = \begin{pmatrix} \gamma a \\ \gamma c \end{pmatrix} = \begin{pmatrix} (b/a)a \\ (d/c)c \end{pmatrix} = \begin{pmatrix} b \\ d \end{pmatrix} = \mathbf{u}_2.$$

Hence $\mathbf{u}_2$ is a multiple of $\mathbf{u}_1$ and these vectors are therefore not linearly independent.

Suppose instead that at least one entry of A is zero. We detail the case $a = 0$, with all other cases being similar. By the condition $ad = bc$, we get that $bc = 0$. That is, either $b = 0$ or $c = 0$. Either way, the second column of A is then a multiple of the first one, establishing the claim.

Lemma 2.2.12 (Equivalent Definition of Linear Independence) *Vectors $\mathbf{u}_1, \ldots, \mathbf{u}_m$ are linearly independent if and only if*

$$\sum_{j=1}^{m} \alpha_j \mathbf{u}_j = \mathbf{0} \implies \alpha_j = 0, \ \forall j.$$

Equivalently, $\mathbf{u}_1, \ldots, \mathbf{u}_m$ are linearly dependent if and only if there exist α_j's, not all zero, such that $\sum_{j=1}^{m} \alpha_j \mathbf{u}_j = \mathbf{0}$.

Proof We prove the second statement.

- Assume $\mathbf{u}_1, \ldots, \mathbf{u}_m$ are linearly dependent. Then $\mathbf{u}_i = \sum_{j \neq i} \alpha_j \mathbf{u}_j$ for some i. Taking $\alpha_i = -1$ gives $\sum_{j=1}^{m} \alpha_j \mathbf{u}_j = \mathbf{0}$.

- Assume $\sum_{j=1}^{m} \alpha_j \mathbf{u}_j = \mathbf{0}$ with α_j's not all zero. In particular $\alpha_i \neq 0$ for some i. Then

$$\mathbf{u}_i = -\frac{1}{\alpha_i} \sum_{j \neq i} \alpha_j \mathbf{u}_j = \sum_{j \neq i} \left(-\frac{\alpha_j}{\alpha_i} \right) \mathbf{u}_j.$$

$\square$

In matrix form: Let $\mathbf{a}_1, \ldots, \mathbf{a}_m \in \mathbb{R}^n$ and form the matrix whose columns are the $\mathbf{a}_i$'s

$$A = \begin{pmatrix} | & & | \\ \mathbf{a}_1 & \cdots & \mathbf{a}_m \\ | & & | \end{pmatrix}.$$

Note that $A\mathbf{x}$ is the following linear combination of the columns of A: $\sum_{j=1}^{m} x_j \mathbf{a}_j$. Hence $\mathbf{a}_1, \ldots, \mathbf{a}_m$ are linearly independent if and only if $A\mathbf{x} = \mathbf{0} \implies \mathbf{x} = \mathbf{0}$. In terms of the null space of A, this last condition translates into $\mathrm{null}(A) = \{\mathbf{0}\}$.

Equivalently, $\mathbf{a}_1, \ldots, \mathbf{a}_m$ are linearly dependent if and only if $\exists \mathbf{x} \neq \mathbf{0}$ such that $A\mathbf{x} = \mathbf{0}$. Put differently, this last condition means that there is a nonzero vector in the null space of A.

In this book, we will typically *not* be interested in checking these types of conditions by hand, but here is a simple example.

Example 2.2.13 (Checking Linear Independence by Hand) *Suppose we have the following vectors*

$$\mathbf{v}_1 = \begin{pmatrix} 1 \\ 2 \\ 3 \end{pmatrix}, \quad \mathbf{v}_2 = \begin{pmatrix} 0 \\ 1 \\ 4 \end{pmatrix}, \quad \mathbf{v}_3 = \begin{pmatrix} 5 \\ 6 \\ 0 \end{pmatrix}.$$

To determine if these vectors are linearly independent, we need to check if the equation

$$\alpha_1 \mathbf{v}_1 + \alpha_2 \mathbf{v}_2 + \alpha_3 \mathbf{v}_3 = \mathbf{0}$$

implies $\alpha_1 = 0$, $\alpha_2 = 0$, and $\alpha_3 = 0$.

Substituting the vectors, we get

$$\alpha_1 \begin{pmatrix} 1 \\ 2 \\ 3 \end{pmatrix} + \alpha_2 \begin{pmatrix} 0 \\ 1 \\ 4 \end{pmatrix} + \alpha_3 \begin{pmatrix} 5 \\ 6 \\ 0 \end{pmatrix} = \begin{pmatrix} 0 \\ 0 \\ 0 \end{pmatrix}.$$

This gives us the following system of equations:

$$\begin{cases} \alpha_1 + 5\alpha_3 = 0, \\ 2\alpha_1 + \alpha_2 + 6\alpha_3 = 0, \\ 3\alpha_1 + 4\alpha_2 = 0. \end{cases}$$

We solve this system step-by-step.

From the first equation, we have

$$\alpha_1 + 5\alpha_3 = 0 \implies \alpha_1 = -5\alpha_3.$$

Substitute $\alpha_1 = -5\alpha_3$ into the second equation:

$$2(-5\alpha_3) + \alpha_2 + 6\alpha_3 = 0 \implies -10\alpha_3 + \alpha_2 + 6\alpha_3 = 0 \implies \alpha_2 - 4\alpha_3 = 0 \implies \alpha_2 = 4\alpha_3.$$

Now, substitute $\alpha_1 = -5\alpha_3$ and $\alpha_2 = 4\alpha_3$ into the third equation:

$$3(-5\alpha_3) + 4(4\alpha_3) = 0 \implies -15\alpha_3 + 16\alpha_3 = 0 \implies \alpha_3 = 0.$$

Since $\alpha_3 = 0$, we also have

$$\alpha_1 = -5\alpha_3 = -5(0) = 0, \alpha_2 = 4\alpha_3 = 4(0) = 0.$$

Thus, $\alpha_1 = 0$, $\alpha_2 = 0$, and $\alpha_3 = 0$.

Since the only solution to the system is the trivial solution where $\alpha_1 = \alpha_2 = \alpha_3 = 0$, the vectors $\mathbf{v}_1, \mathbf{v}_2, \mathbf{v}_3$ are linearly independent.

Bases give a convenient and nonredundant representation of a subspace.

Definition 2.2.14 (Basis) *Let U be a linear subspace of $\mathbb{R}^n$. A basis of U is a list of vectors $\mathbf{u}_1, \ldots, \mathbf{u}_m$ in U that: (1) span U, that is, $U = \text{span}(\mathbf{u}_1, \ldots, \mathbf{u}_m)$; and (2) are linearly independent.*

We denote by $\mathbf{e}_1, \ldots, \mathbf{e}_n$ the standard basis of $\mathbb{R}^n$, where $\mathbf{e}_i$ has a one in coordinate i and zeros in all other coordinates (see the example below). The basis of the linear subspace $\{\mathbf{0}\}$ is the empty list (which, by convention, is independent and has span $\{\mathbf{0}\}$).

Example 2.2.15 *(continued from Example 2.2.10)* The vectors $\mathbf{w}_1, \mathbf{w}_2$ from Example 2.2.8 are a basis of their span $U = \text{span}(\mathbf{w}_1, \mathbf{w}_2)$. Indeed the first condition is trivially satisfied. Plus, we have shown that $\mathbf{w}_1, \mathbf{w}_2$ are linearly independent.

Example 2.2.16 For $i = 1, \ldots, n$, recall that $\mathbf{e}_i \in \mathbb{R}^n$ is the vector with entries

$$(\mathbf{e}_i)_j = \begin{cases} 1, & \text{if } j = i, \\ 0, & \text{otherwise}. \end{cases}$$

Then $\mathbf{e}_1, \ldots, \mathbf{e}_n$ *form a basis of* $\mathbb{R}^n$, *as each vector is in* $\mathbb{R}^n$. *It is known as the standard basis of* $\mathbb{R}^n$. *Indeed, clearly* $\mathrm{span}(\mathbf{e}_1, \ldots, \mathbf{e}_n) \subseteq \mathbb{R}^n$. *Moreover, any vector* $\mathbf{u} = (u_1, \ldots, u_n) \in \mathbb{R}^n$ *can be written as*

$$\mathbf{u} = \sum_{i=1}^{n} u_i \mathbf{e}_i.$$

So $\mathbf{e}_1, \ldots, \mathbf{e}_n$ *spans* $\mathbb{R}^n$. *Furthermore,*

$$\mathbf{e}_i \notin \mathrm{span}(\{\mathbf{e}_j : j \neq i\}), \quad \forall i = 1, \ldots, n,$$

since $\mathbf{e}_i$ *has a nonzero i-th entry while all vectors on the right-hand side have a zero in entry i. Hence the vectors* $\mathbf{e}_1, \ldots, \mathbf{e}_n$ *are linearly independent.*

A key property of a basis is that it provides a *unique* representation of the vectors in the subspace. Indeed, let U be a linear subspace and $\mathbf{u}_1, \ldots, \mathbf{u}_m$ be a basis of U. Suppose that $\mathbf{w} \in U$ can be written as both $\mathbf{w} = \sum_{j=1}^{m} \alpha_j \mathbf{u}_j$ and $\mathbf{w} = \sum_{j=1}^{m} \alpha'_j \mathbf{u}_j$. Then subtracting one equation from the other we arrive at $\sum_{j=1}^{m} (\alpha_j - \alpha'_j) \mathbf{u}_j = \mathbf{0}$. By linear independence, we have $\alpha_j - \alpha'_j = 0$ for each j. That is, there is only one way to express $\mathbf{w}$ as a linear combination of the basis.

The basis itself on the other hand is *not* unique.

A second key property of a basis is that it always has the *same number of elements*, which is called the dimension of the subspace.

Theorem 2.2.17 *(Dimension) Let* $U \neq \{\mathbf{0}\}$ *be a linear subspace of* $\mathbb{R}^n$. *Then all bases of* U *have the same number of elements. We call this number the dimension of* U *and denote it by* $\dim(U)$.

The proof is provided below. It relies on the *Linear Dependence Lemma*. This fundamental lemma has many useful implications, some of which we state now.

A list of linearly independent vectors in a subspace U is referred to as an independent list in U. A list of vectors whose span is U is referred to as a spanning list of U. In the following lemmas, U is a linear subspace of $\mathbb{R}^n$. The first and second lemmas are proved in Section 2.2.2.1. The *Dimension Theorem* immediately follows from the first one (why?).

Lemma 2.2.18 *(Independent is Shorter than Spanning) The length of any independent list in* U *is less than or equal to the length of any spanning list of* U.

Lemma 2.2.19 *(Completing an Independent List) Any independent list in* U *can be completed into a basis of* U.

Lemma 2.2.20 *(Reducing a Spanning List) Any spanning list of* U *can be reduced into a basis of* U.

We mention a few observations implied by the previous lemmas.

Observation D1 Any linear subspace U of $\mathbb{R}^n$ has a basis. To show this, start with the empty list and use the *Completing an Independent List Lemma* to complete it into a basis of U. Observe further that, instead of an empty list, we could have initialized the process with a list containing any vector in U. That is, for any nonzero vector $\mathbf{u} \in U$, we can construct a basis of U that includes $\mathbf{u}$.

Observation D2 The dimension of any linear subspace U of $\mathbb{R}^n$ is less than or equal to n. Indeed, because a basis of U is an independent list in the full space $\mathbb{R}^n$, by the *Completing an Independent List Lemma* it can be completed into a basis of $\mathbb{R}^n$, which has n elements by the *Dimension Theorem* (and the fact that the standard basis has n elements). A similar statement holds more generally for nested linear subspaces $U \subseteq V$, that is, $\dim(U) \leq \dim(V)$.

Observation D3 The dimension of $\text{span}(\mathbf{u}_1, \ldots, \mathbf{u}_m)$ is at most m. Indeed, by the *Reducing a Spanning List Lemma*, the spanning list $\mathbf{u}_1, \ldots, \mathbf{u}_m$ can be reduced into a basis, which therefore necessarily has fewer elements.

When applied to a matrix A, the dimension of the column space of A is called the column rank of A. A matrix A whose columns are linearly independent is said to have full column rank. Similarly the row rank of A is the dimension of its row space.

Definition 2.2.21 (Row Space) *The row space of $A \in \mathbb{R}^{n \times m}$, denoted $\text{row}(A)$, is the span of the rows of A as vectors in $\mathbb{R}^m$.*

Observe that the row space of A is equal to the column space of its transpose A^T. As it turns out, these two notions of rank are the same. Hence, we refer to the row rank and column rank of A simply as the rank, which we denote by $\text{rk}(A)$.

Theorem 2.2.22 (Row Rank Equals Column Rank) *For any $A \in \mathbb{R}^{n \times m}$, the row rank of A equals the column rank of A. Moreover, $\text{rk}(A) \leq \min\{n, m\}$.*

We will come back to the concept of the rank of a matrix, and prove the above theorem, in Section 4.2.1.

2.2.2.1 The Linear Dependence Lemma and Its Implications

We give a proof of the *Dimension Theorem*. The proof relies on a fundamental lemma. It states that we can always remove a vector from a list of linearly dependent ones without changing its span.

Lemma 2.2.23 (Linear Dependence) *Let $\mathbf{u}_1, \ldots, \mathbf{u}_m$ be a list of linearly dependent vectors with $\mathbf{u}_1 \neq \mathbf{0}$. Then there is an i such that 1. $\mathbf{u}_i \in \text{span}(\mathbf{u}_1, \ldots, \mathbf{u}_{i-1})$, 2. $\text{span}(\{\mathbf{u}_j : j \in [m]\}) = \text{span}(\{\mathbf{u}_j : j \in [m], j \neq i\})$.*

Proof idea (Linear Dependence) By linear dependence, $\mathbf{0}$ can be written as a nontrivial linear combination of the $\mathbf{u}_j$'s. Then the index i in property 1. is the largest index with nonzero coefficient.

Proof *(Linear Dependence)* For 1., by linear dependence, $\sum_{j=1}^{m} \alpha_j \mathbf{u}_j = \mathbf{0}$, with α_j's not all zero. Further, because $\mathbf{u}_1 \neq \mathbf{0}$, not all $\alpha_2, \ldots, \alpha_m$ are zero (why?). Take the largest index among the α_j's that are nonzero, say i. Then rearranging the previous equation and using the fact that $\alpha_j = 0$ for $j > i$ gives

$$\mathbf{u}_i = -\sum_{j=1}^{i-1} \frac{\alpha_j}{\alpha_i} \mathbf{u}_j \in \text{span}(\mathbf{u}_1, \ldots, \mathbf{u}_{i-1}).$$

For 2., we note that for any $\mathbf{w} \in \text{span}(\{\mathbf{u}_j : j \in [m]\})$ we can write it as $\mathbf{w} = \sum_{j=1}^{m} \beta_j \mathbf{u}_j$ and we can replace $\mathbf{u}_i$ by the equation above, producing a representation of $\mathbf{w}$ in terms of $\{\mathbf{u}_j : j \in [m], j \neq i\}$. $\square$

We use the *Linear Dependence Lemma* to prove our key claims.

Proof *(Independent is Shorter than Spanning)* Let $\{\mathbf{u}_j : j \in [m]\}$ be an independent list in U and let $\{\mathbf{w}_i : i \in [m']\}$ be a spanning list of U. First consider the new list $\{\mathbf{u}_1, \mathbf{w}_1, \ldots, \mathbf{w}_{m'}\}$. Because the $\mathbf{w}_i$'s are spanning, adding $\mathbf{u}_1 \neq \mathbf{0}$ to them necessarily produces a linearly dependent list. By the *Linear Dependence Lemma*, we can remove one of the $\mathbf{w}_i$'s without changing the span. The new list B has length m' again. Then we add $\mathbf{u}_2$ to B immediately after $\mathbf{u}_1$. By the *Linear Dependence Lemma*, one of the vectors in this list is in the span of the previous ones. It cannot be $\mathbf{u}_2$ as $\{\mathbf{u}_1, \mathbf{u}_2\}$ are linearly independent by assumption. So it must be one of the remaining $\mathbf{w}_i$'s. We remove that one, without changing the span by the *Linear Dependence Lemma* again. This process can be continued until we have added all the $\mathbf{u}_j$'s, as otherwise we would have a contradiction in the argument above. Hence, there must be at least as many $\mathbf{w}_i$'s as there are $\mathbf{u}_j$'s. $\square$

Proof *(Dimension)* Let $\{\mathbf{b}_j : j \in [m]\}$ and $\{\mathbf{b}'_j : j \in [m']\}$ be two bases of U. Because they both form independent and spanning lists, the *Independent is Shorter than Spanning Lemma* implies that each has a length less than or equal to the other. So their lengths must be equal. This proves the claim. $\square$

Proof *(Completing an Independent List)* Let $\{\mathbf{u}_j : j \in [\ell]\}$ be an independent list in U. Let $\{\mathbf{w}_i : i \in [m]\}$ be a spanning list of U, which is guaranteed to exist (prove it!). Add the vectors from the spanning list one by one to the independent list if they are not in the span of the previously constructed list (or discard them otherwise). By the *Linear Dependence Lemma*, the list remains independent at each step. After m steps, the resulting list spans all of the $\mathbf{w}_i$'s. Hence it spans U and is linearly independent – that is, it is a basis of U. $\square$

The *Reducing a Spanning List Lemma* is proved in a similar way (try it!).

2.2.3 Inverses

Recall the following important definition.

Definition 2.2.24 *(Nonsingular Matrix)* A square matrix $A \in \mathbb{R}^{n \times n}$ is nonsingular if it has *full column rank*.

An implication of this is that A is nonsingular if and only if its columns form a basis of $\mathbb{R}^n$. Indeed, suppose the columns of A form a basis of $\mathbb{R}^n$. Then the dimension of col(A) is n. In the other direction, suppose A has full column rank.

1. We first prove a general statement: The columns of $Z \in \mathbb{R}^{k \times m}$ form a basis of col(Z) whenever Z is of full column rank. Indeed, the columns of Z by definition span col(Z). By the *Reducing a Spanning List Lemma*, they can be reduced into a basis of col(Z). If Z has full column rank, then the length of any basis of col(Z) is equal to the number of columns of Z. So the columns of Z must already form a basis.

2. Apply the previous claim to $Z = A$. Then, since the columns of A form an independent list in $\mathbb{R}^n$, by the *Completing an Independent List Lemma* they can be completed into a basis of $\mathbb{R}^n$. But there are already n of them, the dimension of $\mathbb{R}^n$, so they must already form a basis

of $\mathbb{R}^n$. In other words, we have proved another general fact: An independent list of length n in $\mathbb{R}^n$ is a basis of $\mathbb{R}^n$.

Equivalently:

Lemma 2.2.25 *(Invertibility) A square matrix $A \in \mathbb{R}^{n \times n}$ is nonsingular if and only if there exists a unique A^{-1} such that*

$$AA^{-1} = A^{-1}A = I_{n \times n}.$$

The matrix A^{-1} is referred to as the inverse of A. We also say that A is invertible.

Proof idea: We use the nonsingularity of A to write the columns of the identity matrix as unique linear combinations of the columns of A.

Proof Suppose first that A has full column rank. Then its columns are linearly independent and form a basis of $\mathbb{R}^n$. In particular, for any i the standard basis vector $\mathbf{e}_i$ can be written as a unique linear combination of the columns of A, so that there is $\mathbf{b}_i$ such that $A\mathbf{b}_i = \mathbf{e}_i$. Let B be the matrix with columns $\mathbf{b}_i$, $i = 1, \ldots, n$. By construction, $AB = I_{n \times n}$. Applying the same idea to the rows of A (which by the *Row Rank Equals Column Rank Lemma* also form a basis of $\mathbb{R}^n$), there is a unique C such that $CA = I_{n \times n}$. Multiplying both sides by B, we get

$$C = CAB = I_{n \times n}B = B.$$

So we take $A^{-1} = B = C$.

In the other direction, following the same argument, the equation $AA^{-1} = I_{n \times n}$ implies that the standard basis of $\mathbb{R}^n$ is in the column space of A. So the columns of A are a spanning list of all of $\mathbb{R}^n$ and $\text{rk}(A) = n$. This proves the claim. $\square$

Theorem 2.2.26 *(Inverting a Nonsingular System) Let $A \in \mathbb{R}^{n \times n}$ be a nonsingular square matrix. Then for any $\mathbf{b} \in \mathbb{R}^n$, there exists a unique $\mathbf{x} \in \mathbb{R}^n$ such that $A\mathbf{x} = \mathbf{b}$. Moreover $\mathbf{x} = A^{-1}\mathbf{b}$.*

Proof The first claim follows immediately from the fact that the columns of A form a basis of $\mathbb{R}^n$. For the second claim, note that

$$\mathbf{x} = A^{-1}A\mathbf{x} = A^{-1}\mathbf{b}.$$

$\square$

Example 2.2.27 Let $A \in \mathbb{R}^{n \times m}$ with $n \geq m$ have full column rank. We will show that the square matrix $B = A^T A$ is then invertible.

By the first claim following Definition 2.2.24, the columns of A form a basis of its column space. In particular they are linearly independent. We will use this below.

Observe that B is an $m \times m$ matrix. By definition, to show that it is nonsingular, we need to establish that it has full column rank, or put differently that its columns are also linearly independent. By the matrix version of the Equivalent Definition of Linear Independence Lemma, it suffices to show that

$$B\mathbf{x} = \mathbf{0} \implies \mathbf{x} = \mathbf{0}.$$

We establish this next.

Since $B = A^T A$, the equation $B\mathbf{x} = \mathbf{0}$ implies
$$A^T A\mathbf{x} = \mathbf{0}.$$
Now comes the key idea: We multiply both sides by $\mathbf{x}^T$. The left-hand side becomes
$$\mathbf{x}^T(A^T A\mathbf{x}) = (A\mathbf{x})^T(A\mathbf{x}) = \|A\mathbf{x}\|^2,$$
where we used that, for matrices C, D, we have $(CD)^T = D^T C^T$. The right-hand side becomes $\mathbf{x}^T \mathbf{0} = 0$. Hence we have shown that $A^T A\mathbf{x} = \mathbf{0}$ in fact implies $\|A\mathbf{x}\|^2 = 0$.

By the point-separating property of the Euclidean norm, the condition $\|A\mathbf{x}\|^2 = 0$ implies $A\mathbf{x} = \mathbf{0}$. Because A has linearly independent columns, the Equivalent Definition of Linear Independence Lemma *in its matrix form* again implies that $\mathbf{x} = \mathbf{0}$, which is what we needed to prove.

Example 2.2.28 *(Deriving the General Formula for the Inverse of a 2 × 2 Matrix)* Consider a 2×2 matrix A given by
$$A = \begin{pmatrix} a & b \\ c & d \end{pmatrix}.$$
We seek to find its inverse A^{-1} such that $AA^{-1} = I_{2\times 2}$. We guess the form of the inverse A^{-1} to be
$$A^{-1} = \frac{1}{ad - bc} \begin{pmatrix} d & -b \\ -c & a \end{pmatrix},$$
with the condition $ad - bc \neq 0$ being necessary for the existence of the inverse, as we saw in Example 2.2.11.

To check if this form is correct, we multiply A by A^{-1} and see if we get the identity matrix. We perform the matrix multiplication AA^{-1}:
$$\begin{aligned}
AA^{-1} &= \begin{pmatrix} a & b \\ c & d \end{pmatrix} \frac{1}{ad - bc} \begin{pmatrix} d & -b \\ -c & a \end{pmatrix} \\
&= \frac{1}{ad - bc} \begin{pmatrix} a & b \\ c & d \end{pmatrix} \begin{pmatrix} d & -b \\ -c & a \end{pmatrix} \\
&= \frac{1}{ad - bc} \begin{pmatrix} ad - bc & -ab + ab \\ cd - cd & -bc + ad \end{pmatrix} \\
&= \frac{1}{ad - bc} \begin{pmatrix} ad - bc & 0 \\ 0 & ad - bc \end{pmatrix} \\
&= \begin{pmatrix} 1 & 0 \\ 0 & 1 \end{pmatrix}.
\end{aligned}$$

Since the multiplication results in the identity matrix, our guessed form of the inverse is correct under the condition that $ad - bc \neq 0$.

Here is a simple numerical example. Let
$$A = \begin{pmatrix} 2 & 3 \\ 1 & 4 \end{pmatrix}.$$
To find A^{-1}, we calculate
$$ad - bc = 2 \cdot 4 - 3 \cdot 1 = 8 - 3 = 5 \neq 0.$$

2.2 Background: Review of Vector Spaces and Matrix Inverses

Using the formula derived, we have

$$A^{-1} = \frac{1}{5}\begin{pmatrix} 4 & -3 \\ -1 & 2 \end{pmatrix} = \begin{pmatrix} 0.8 & -0.6 \\ -0.2 & 0.4 \end{pmatrix}.$$

We can verify this by checking AA^{-1}:

$$\begin{pmatrix} 2 & 3 \\ 1 & 4 \end{pmatrix}\begin{pmatrix} 0.8 & -0.6 \\ -0.2 & 0.4 \end{pmatrix} = \begin{pmatrix} 2 \cdot 0.8 + 3 \cdot (-0.2) & 2 \cdot (-0.6) + 3 \cdot 0.4 \\ 1 \cdot 0.8 + 4 \cdot (-0.2) & 1 \cdot (-0.6) + 4 \cdot 0.4 \end{pmatrix} = \begin{pmatrix} 1 & 0 \\ 0 & 1 \end{pmatrix}.$$

Finally, here is an example of using this formula to solve a linear system of two equations in two unknowns. Consider the linear system

$$\begin{cases} 2x_1 + 3x_2 = 5, \\ x_1 + 4x_2 = 6. \end{cases}$$

We can represent this system as $A\mathbf{x} = \mathbf{b}$, where

$$A = \begin{pmatrix} 2 & 3 \\ 1 & 4 \end{pmatrix}, \quad \mathbf{x} = \begin{pmatrix} x_1 \\ x_2 \end{pmatrix}, \quad \mathbf{b} = \begin{pmatrix} 5 \\ 6 \end{pmatrix}.$$

To solve for $\mathbf{x}$, we use A^{-1}:

$$\mathbf{x} = A^{-1}\mathbf{b} = \begin{pmatrix} 0.8 & -0.6 \\ -0.2 & 0.4 \end{pmatrix}\begin{pmatrix} 5 \\ 6 \end{pmatrix}.$$

Performing the matrix multiplication, we get

$$\mathbf{x} = \begin{pmatrix} 0.8 \cdot 5 + (-0.6) \cdot 6 \\ -0.2 \cdot 5 + 0.4 \cdot 6 \end{pmatrix} = \begin{pmatrix} 4 - 3.6 \\ -1 + 2.4 \end{pmatrix} = \begin{pmatrix} 0.4 \\ 1.4 \end{pmatrix}.$$

Thus, the solution to the system is $x_1 = 0.4$ and $x_2 = 1.4$.

Self-Assessment Quiz *(with help from Claude, Gemini, and ChatGPT)*

1. What is the span of the vectors $\mathbf{w}_1, \mathbf{w}_2, ..., \mathbf{w}_m \in \mathbb{R}^n$?
   a) The set of all linear combinations of the $\mathbf{w}_j$'s
   b) The set of all vectors orthogonal to the $\mathbf{w}_j$'s
   c) The set of all scalar multiples of the $\mathbf{w}_j$'s
   d) The empty set

2. Which of the following is a necessary condition for a subset U of $\mathbb{R}^n$ to be a linear subspace?
   a) U must contain only nonzero vectors.
   b) U must be closed under vector addition and scalar multiplication.
   c) U must be a finite set.
   d) U must be a proper subset of $\mathbb{R}^n$.

3. If $\mathbf{v}_1, \mathbf{v}_2, \ldots, \mathbf{v}_m$ are linearly independent vectors, which of the following is true?
   a) There exist scalars $\alpha_1, \alpha_2, \ldots, \alpha_m$ such that $\sum_{i=1}^{m} \alpha_i \mathbf{v}_i = 0$ with at least one $\alpha_i \neq 0$.

b) There do not exist scalars $\alpha_1, \alpha_2, \ldots, \alpha_m$ such that $\sum_{i=1}^{m} \alpha_i \mathbf{v}_i = 0$ unless $\alpha_i = 0$ for all i.

c) The vectors $\mathbf{v}_1, \mathbf{v}_2, \ldots, \mathbf{v}_m$ span $\mathbb{R}^n$ for any n.

d) The vectors $\mathbf{v}_1, \mathbf{v}_2, \ldots, \mathbf{v}_m$ are orthogonal.

4 Which of the following matrices has full column rank?

a) $\begin{pmatrix} 1 & 2 \\ 2 & 4 \end{pmatrix}$

b) $\begin{pmatrix} 1 & 0 \\ 1 & 1 \end{pmatrix}$

c) $\begin{pmatrix} 1 & 1 \\ 1 & 1 \end{pmatrix}$

d) $\begin{pmatrix} 1 & 2 & 3 \\ 4 & 5 & 9 \\ 7 & 8 & 15 \end{pmatrix}$

5 What is the dimension of a linear subspace?

a) The number of vectors in any spanning set of the subspace

b) The number of linearly independent vectors in the subspace

c) The number of vectors in any basis of the subspace

d) The number of orthogonal vectors in the subspace

Answer for 1: a. Justification: The text defines the span as "the set of all linear combinations of the $\mathbf{w}_j$'s."

Answer for 2: b. Justification: The text states, "A linear subspace $U \subseteq \mathbb{R}^n$ is a subset that is closed under vector addition and scalar multiplication."

Answer for 3: b. Justification: The text states that a set of vectors is linearly independent if and only if the only solution to $\sum_{i=1}^{m} \alpha_i \mathbf{v}_i = 0$ is $\alpha_i = 0$ for all i.

Answer for 4: b. Justification: The text explains that a matrix has full column rank if its columns are linearly independent, which is true for the matrix $\begin{pmatrix} 1 & 0 \\ 1 & 1 \end{pmatrix}$.

Answer for 5: c. Justification: The text defines the dimension of a linear subspace as "the number of elements" in any basis, and states that "all bases of [a linear subspace] have the same number of elements."

2.3 Geometry of Least Squares: The Orthogonal Projection

We consider the following problem: We are given $A \in \mathbb{R}^{n \times m}$ an $n \times m$ matrix and $\mathbf{b} \in \mathbb{R}^n$ a vector. We are looking to solve the system $A\mathbf{x} \approx \mathbf{b}$. In the special case where A is invertible, a unique exact solution exists. In general, however, a solution may not exist or may not be unique. We focus here on the overdetermined case where the former situation generically occurs. We begin by rewiewing the concept of orthogonality.

2.3.1 A Key Concept: Orthogonality

Orthogonality plays a key role in linear algebra for data science thanks to its computational properties and its connection to the least-squares problem.

Definition 2.3.1 *(Orthogonality) Vectors* $\mathbf{u}$ *and* $\mathbf{v}$ *in* $\mathbb{R}^n$ *(as column vectors) are orthogonal if their inner product is zero:*

$$\langle \mathbf{u}, \mathbf{v} \rangle = \mathbf{u}^T \mathbf{v} = \sum_{i=1}^{n} u_i v_i = 0.$$

Orthogonality has important implications. The following classical result will be useful below. Throughout, we use $\|\mathbf{u}\|$ for the Euclidean norm of $\mathbf{u}$.

Theorem 2.3.2 *(Pythagoras) Let* $\mathbf{u}, \mathbf{v} \in \mathbb{R}^n$ *be orthogonal. Then* $\|\mathbf{u} + \mathbf{v}\|^2 = \|\mathbf{u}\|^2 + \|\mathbf{v}\|^2$.

Proof Using $\|\mathbf{w}\|^2 = \langle \mathbf{w}, \mathbf{w} \rangle$, we get

$$\begin{aligned}\|\mathbf{u} + \mathbf{v}\|^2 &= \langle \mathbf{u} + \mathbf{v}, \mathbf{u} + \mathbf{v} \rangle \\ &= \langle \mathbf{u}, \mathbf{u} \rangle + 2 \langle \mathbf{u}, \mathbf{v} \rangle + \langle \mathbf{v}, \mathbf{v} \rangle \\ &= \|\mathbf{u}\|^2 + \|\mathbf{v}\|^2.\end{aligned}$$

$\square$

An application of *Pythagoras' Theorem* is a proof of the *Cauchy–Schwarz Inequality*.

Proof *(Cauchy–Schwarz)* Let $\mathbf{q} = \frac{\mathbf{v}}{\|\mathbf{v}\|}$ be the unit vector in the direction of $\mathbf{v}$. We want to show $|\langle \mathbf{u}, \mathbf{q} \rangle| \leq \|\mathbf{u}\|$. Decompose $\mathbf{u}$ as follows:

$$\mathbf{u} = \langle \mathbf{u}, \mathbf{q} \rangle \mathbf{q} + \{\mathbf{u} - \langle \mathbf{u}, \mathbf{q} \rangle \mathbf{q}\}.$$

The two terms on the right-hand side are orthogonal:

$$\langle \langle \mathbf{u}, \mathbf{q} \rangle \mathbf{q}, \mathbf{u} - \langle \mathbf{u}, \mathbf{q} \rangle \mathbf{q} \rangle = \langle \mathbf{u}, \mathbf{q} \rangle^2 - \langle \mathbf{u}, \mathbf{q} \rangle^2 \langle \mathbf{q}, \mathbf{q} \rangle = 0.$$

So Pythagoras' Theorem gives

$$\|\mathbf{u}\|^2 = \|\langle \mathbf{u}, \mathbf{q} \rangle \mathbf{q}\|^2 + \|\mathbf{u} - \langle \mathbf{u}, \mathbf{q} \rangle \mathbf{q}\|^2 \geq \|\langle \mathbf{u}, \mathbf{q} \rangle \mathbf{q}\|^2 = \langle \mathbf{u}, \mathbf{q} \rangle^2.$$

Taking a square root gives the claim. $\square$

2.3.1.1 Orthonormal Basis Expansion

To begin to see the power of orthogonality, consider the following. A list of vectors $\{\mathbf{u}_1, \ldots, \mathbf{u}_m\}$ is an orthonormal list if the $\mathbf{u}_i$'s are pairwise orthogonal and each has norm 1; that is, for all i and all $j \neq i$, we have $\|\mathbf{u}_i\| = 1$ and $\langle \mathbf{u}_i, \mathbf{u}_j \rangle = 0$. Alternatively,

$$\langle \mathbf{u}_i, \mathbf{u}_j \rangle = \begin{cases} 1 & \text{if } i = j \\ 0 & \text{if } i \neq j. \end{cases}$$

Lemma 2.3.3 *(Properties of Orthonormal Lists)* Let $\{\mathbf{u}_1, \ldots, \mathbf{u}_m\}$ be an orthonormal list. Then

1. for any $\alpha_j \in \mathbb{R}$, $j = 1, \ldots, m$, we have

$$\left\| \sum_{j=1}^{m} \alpha_j \mathbf{u}_j \right\|^2 = \sum_{j=1}^{m} \alpha_j^2;$$

2. the vectors $\{\mathbf{u}_1, \ldots, \mathbf{u}_m\}$ are linearly independent.

Proof For 1., using that $\|\mathbf{x}\|^2 = \langle \mathbf{x}, \mathbf{x} \rangle$, we have

$$\left\| \sum_{j=1}^{m} \alpha_j \mathbf{u}_j \right\|^2 = \left\langle \sum_{i=1}^{m} \alpha_i \mathbf{u}_i, \sum_{j=1}^{m} \alpha_j \mathbf{u}_j \right\rangle$$

$$= \sum_{i=1}^{m} \alpha_i \left\langle \mathbf{u}_i, \sum_{j=1}^{m} \alpha_j \mathbf{u}_j \right\rangle$$

$$= \sum_{i=1}^{m} \sum_{j=1}^{m} \alpha_i \alpha_j \langle \mathbf{u}_i, \mathbf{u}_j \rangle$$

$$= \sum_{i=1}^{m} \alpha_i^2$$

where we used orthonormality in the last equation: $\langle \mathbf{u}_i, \mathbf{u}_j \rangle$ is 1 if $i = j$ and 0 otherwise.

For 2., suppose $\sum_{i=1}^{m} \beta_i \mathbf{u}_i = \mathbf{0}$, then we must have by 1. that $\sum_{i=1}^{m} \beta_i^2 = 0$. This implies $\beta_i = 0$ for all i. Hence the $\mathbf{u}_i$'s are linearly independent. □

Given a basis $\{\mathbf{u}_1, \ldots, \mathbf{u}_m\}$ of U, we know that for any $\mathbf{w} \in U$, $\mathbf{w} = \sum_{i=1}^{m} \alpha_i \mathbf{u}_i$ for some α_i's. It is not immediately obvious in general how to find the α_i's – one must solve a system of linear equations. In the orthonormal case, however, there is a formula. We say that the basis $\{\mathbf{u}_1, \ldots, \mathbf{u}_m\}$ is orthonormal if it forms an orthonormal list.

Theorem 2.3.4 *(Orthonormal Expansion)* Let $\mathbf{q}_1, \ldots, \mathbf{q}_m$ be an orthonormal basis of U and let $\mathbf{w} \in U$. Then

$$\mathbf{w} = \sum_{j=1}^{m} \langle \mathbf{w}, \mathbf{q}_j \rangle \mathbf{q}_j.$$

Proof Because $\mathbf{w} \in U$, $\mathbf{w} = \sum_{i=1}^{m} \alpha_i \mathbf{q}_i$ for some α_i. Take the inner product with $\mathbf{q}_j$ and use orthonormality:

$$\langle \mathbf{w}, \mathbf{q}_j \rangle = \left\langle \sum_{i=1}^{m} \alpha_i \mathbf{q}_i, \mathbf{q}_j \right\rangle = \sum_{i=1}^{m} \alpha_i \langle \mathbf{q}_i, \mathbf{q}_j \rangle = \alpha_j.$$

Hence, we have determined all α_j's in the basis expansion of $\mathbf{w}$. □

Example 2.3.5 Consider again the linear subspace $W = \text{span}(\mathbf{w}_1, \mathbf{w}_2, \mathbf{w}_3)$, where $\mathbf{w}_1 = (1, 0, 1)$, $\mathbf{w}_2 = (0, 1, 1)$, and $\mathbf{w}_3 = (1, -1, 0)$. We have shown in Example 2.2.8 that in fact

$$\text{span}(\mathbf{w}_1, \mathbf{w}_2, \mathbf{w}_3) = \text{span}(\mathbf{w}_1, \mathbf{w}_2),$$

as $\mathbf{w}_1, \mathbf{w}_2$ form a basis of W. On the other hand,

$$\langle \mathbf{w}_1, \mathbf{w}_2 \rangle = (1)(0) + (0)(1) + (1)(1) = 0 + 0 + 1 = 1 \neq 0$$

so this basis is not orthonormal. Indeed, an orthonormal list is necessarily an independent list, but the opposite may not hold.

To produce an orthonormal basis of W, we can first proceed by normalizing $\mathbf{w}_1$:

$$\mathbf{q}_1 = \frac{\mathbf{w}_1}{\|\mathbf{w}_1\|} = \frac{\mathbf{w}_1}{\sqrt{1^2 + 0^2 + 1^2}} = \frac{1}{\sqrt{2}}\mathbf{w}_1.$$

Then $\|\mathbf{q}_1\| = 1$ since, in general, by absolute homogeneity of the norm

$$\left\|\frac{\mathbf{w}_1}{\|\mathbf{w}_1\|}\right\| = \frac{1}{\|\mathbf{w}_1\|}\|\mathbf{w}_1\| = 1.$$

We then seek a second basis vector. It must satisfy two conditions in this case:

- it must be of unit norm and be orthogonal to $\mathbf{q}_1$; and
- $\mathbf{w}_2$ must be a linear combination of $\mathbf{q}_1$ and $\mathbf{q}_2$.

The latter condition guarantees that $\text{span}(\mathbf{q}_1, \mathbf{q}_2) = \text{span}(\mathbf{w}_1, \mathbf{w}_2)$. (Formally, that would imply only that $\text{span}(\mathbf{w}_1, \mathbf{w}_2) \subseteq \text{span}(\mathbf{q}_1, \mathbf{q}_2)$. In this case, it is easy to see that the containment must go in the opposite direction as well. Why?)

The first condition translates into

$$1 = \|\mathbf{q}_2\|^2 = q_{21}^2 + q_{22}^2 + q_{23}^2,$$

where $\mathbf{q}_2 = (q_{21}, q_{22}, q_{23})$, and

$$0 = \langle \mathbf{q}_1, \mathbf{q}_2 \rangle = \frac{1}{\sqrt{2}}[1 \cdot q_{21} + 0 \cdot q_{22} + 1 \cdot q_{23}] = \frac{1}{\sqrt{2}}[q_{21} + q_{23}].$$

That is, simplifying the second display and plugging into the first, $q_{23} = -q_{21}$ and $q_{22} = \sqrt{1 - 2q_{21}^2}$.

The second condition translates into: There are $\beta_1, \beta_2 \in \mathbb{R}$ such that

$$\mathbf{w}_2 = \begin{pmatrix} 0 \\ 1 \\ 1 \end{pmatrix} = \beta_1 \mathbf{q}_1 + \beta_2 \mathbf{q}_2 = \beta_1 \frac{1}{\sqrt{2}} \begin{pmatrix} 1 \\ 0 \\ 1 \end{pmatrix} + \beta_2 \begin{pmatrix} q_{21} \\ \sqrt{1 - 2q_{21}^2} \\ -q_{21} \end{pmatrix}.$$

The first entry gives $\beta_1/\sqrt{2} + \beta_2 q_{21} = 0$ while the third entry gives $\beta_1/\sqrt{2} - \beta_2 q_{21} = 1$. Adding up the equations gives $\beta_1 = 1/\sqrt{2}$. Plugging back into the first one gives $\beta_2 = -1/(2q_{21})$. Returning to the equation for $\mathbf{w}_2$, we get from the second entry

$$1 = -\frac{1}{2q_{21}}\sqrt{1 - 2q_{21}^2}.$$

Rearranging and taking a square, we need the negative solution to

$$4q_{21}^2 = 1 - 2q_{21}^2,$$

that is, $q_{21} = -1/\sqrt{6}$. Finally, we get $q_{23} = -q_{21} = 1/\sqrt{6}$ and $q_{22} = \sqrt{1 - 2q_{21}^2} = \sqrt{1 - 1/3} = \sqrt{2/3} = 2/\sqrt{6}$.

To summarize, we have

$$\mathbf{q}_1 = \frac{1}{\sqrt{2}}\begin{pmatrix} 1 \\ 0 \\ 1 \end{pmatrix}, \quad \mathbf{q}_2 = \frac{1}{\sqrt{6}}\begin{pmatrix} -1 \\ 2 \\ 1 \end{pmatrix}.$$

We confirm that

$$\langle \mathbf{q}_1, \mathbf{q}_2 \rangle = \frac{1}{\sqrt{2}\sqrt{6}}[(1)(-1) + (0)(2) + (1)(1)] = 0$$

and

$$\|\mathbf{q}_2\|^2 = \left(-\frac{1}{\sqrt{6}}\right)^2 + \left(\frac{2}{\sqrt{6}}\right)^2 + \left(\frac{1}{\sqrt{6}}\right)^2 = \frac{1}{6} + \frac{4}{6} + \frac{1}{6} = 1.$$

We can use the Orthonormal Expansion Theorem *to write* $\mathbf{w}_2$ *as a linear combination of* $\mathbf{q}_1$ *and* $\mathbf{q}_2$. *The inner products are*

$$\langle \mathbf{w}_2, \mathbf{q}_1 \rangle = 0\left(\frac{1}{\sqrt{2}}\right) + 1\left(\frac{0}{\sqrt{2}}\right) + 1\left(\frac{1}{\sqrt{2}}\right) = \frac{1}{\sqrt{2}},$$

$$\langle \mathbf{w}_2, \mathbf{q}_2 \rangle = 0\left(-\frac{1}{\sqrt{6}}\right) + 1\left(\frac{2}{\sqrt{6}}\right) + 1\left(\frac{1}{\sqrt{6}}\right) = \frac{3}{\sqrt{6}}.$$

So

$$\mathbf{w}_2 = \frac{1}{\sqrt{2}}\mathbf{q}_1 + \frac{3}{\sqrt{6}}\mathbf{q}_2.$$

Check it! Try $\mathbf{w}_3$.

2.3.1.2 Gram–Schmidt

We have shown that working with orthonormal bases is desirable. What if we do not have one? We could try to construct one by hand as we did in Example 2.3.5. But there are better ways. We review the Gram–Schmidt algorithm in an upcoming section, which will imply that every linear subspace has an orthonormal basis. That is, we will prove the following theorem.

Theorem 2.3.6 *(Gram–Schmidt) Let* $\mathbf{a}_1, \ldots, \mathbf{a}_m$ *be linearly independent. Then there exists an orthonormal basis* $\mathbf{q}_1, \ldots, \mathbf{q}_m$ *of* $\mathrm{span}(\mathbf{a}_1, \ldots, \mathbf{a}_m)$.

But first, we will need to define the orthogonal projection, which will play a key role in our applications. This is done next.

2.3.2 Orthogonal Projection

To solve the overdetermined case, when $n > m$, we consider the following more general problem first. We have a linear subspace $U \subseteq \mathbb{R}^n$ and a vector $\mathbf{v} \notin U$. We want to find the vector $\mathbf{p}$ in U that is closest to $\mathbf{v}$ in Euclidean norm, that is, we want to solve

$$\min_{\mathbf{p} \in U} \|\mathbf{p} - \mathbf{v}\|.$$

2.3 Geometry of Least Squares: The Orthogonal Projection

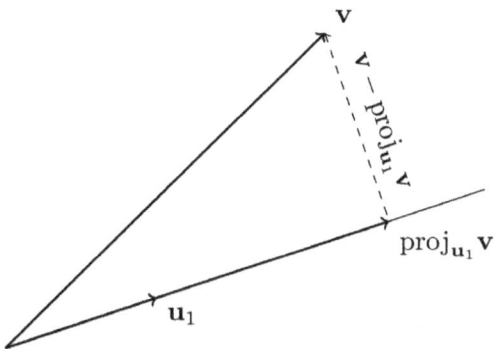

Figure 2.4 Orthogonal projection on a line.

Example 2.3.7 *Consider the two-dimensional case with a one-dimensional subspace, say $U = \mathrm{span}(\mathbf{u}_1)$ with $\|\mathbf{u}_1\| = 1$. The geometrical intuition is illustrated in Figure 2.4. The solution $\mathbf{p} = \mathbf{v}^*$ has the property that the difference $\mathbf{v} - \mathbf{v}^*$ makes a right angle with $\mathbf{u}_1$, that is, it is orthogonal to it.*

Letting $\mathbf{v}^* = \alpha^* \mathbf{u}_1$, the geometrical condition above translates into

$$0 = \langle \mathbf{u}_1, \mathbf{v} - \mathbf{v}^* \rangle = \langle \mathbf{u}_1, \mathbf{v} - \alpha^* \mathbf{u}_1 \rangle = \langle \mathbf{u}_1, \mathbf{v} \rangle - \alpha^* \langle \mathbf{u}_1, \mathbf{u}_1 \rangle = \langle \mathbf{u}_1, \mathbf{v} \rangle - \alpha^*$$

so we have

$$\mathbf{v}^* = \langle \mathbf{u}_1, \mathbf{v} \rangle \mathbf{u}_1.$$

By Pythagoras' Theorem, we then have for any $\alpha \in \mathbb{R}$

$$\begin{aligned} \|\mathbf{v} - \alpha \mathbf{u}_1\|^2 &= \|\mathbf{v} - \mathbf{v}^* + \mathbf{v}^* - \alpha \mathbf{u}_1\|^2 \\ &= \|\mathbf{v} - \mathbf{v}^* + (\alpha^* - \alpha) \mathbf{u}_1\|^2 \\ &= \|\mathbf{v} - \mathbf{v}^*\|^2 + \|(\alpha^* - \alpha) \mathbf{u}_1\|^2 \\ &\geq \|\mathbf{v} - \mathbf{v}^*\|^2, \end{aligned}$$

where we used that $\mathbf{v} - \mathbf{v}^*$ is orthogonal to $\mathbf{u}_1$ (and therefore $(\alpha^* - \alpha)\mathbf{u}_1$) on the third line.

That confirms the optimality of $\mathbf{v}^*$. The argument in this example carries through in higher dimension, as we show next.

Definition 2.3.8 *(Orthogonal Projection on an Orthonormal List)* Let $\mathbf{q}_1, \ldots, \mathbf{q}_m$ *be an orthonormal list. The orthogonal projection of $\mathbf{v} \in \mathbb{R}^n$ on $\{\mathbf{q}_i\}_{i=1}^m$ is defined as*

$$\mathrm{proj}_{\{\mathbf{q}_i\}_{i=1}^m} \mathbf{v} = \sum_{j=1}^m \langle \mathbf{v}, \mathbf{q}_j \rangle \mathbf{q}_j.$$

Theorem 2.3.9 *(Orthogonal Projection)* Let $U \subseteq V$ *be a linear subspace and let $\mathbf{v} \in \mathbb{R}^n$. Then*

a) There exists a unique solution $\mathbf{p}^*$ to

$$\min_{\mathbf{p} \in U} \|\mathbf{p} - \mathbf{v}\|.$$

We denote it by $\mathbf{p}^* = \mathrm{proj}_U \mathbf{v}$ and refer to it as the orthogonal projection of $\mathbf{v}$ onto U.

b) *The solution* $\mathbf{p}^*$ *is characterized geometrically by*

$$(*) \qquad \langle \mathbf{v} - \mathbf{p}^*, \mathbf{u} \rangle = 0, \quad \forall \mathbf{u} \in U.$$

c) *For any orthonormal basis* $\mathbf{q}_1, \ldots, \mathbf{q}_m$ *of* U,

$$\mathrm{proj}_U \mathbf{v} = \mathrm{proj}_{\{\mathbf{q}_i\}_{i=1}^m} \mathbf{v}.$$

Proof Let $\mathbf{p}^*$ be any vector in U satisfying $(*)$. We show first that it necessarily satisfies

$$(**) \qquad \|\mathbf{p}^* - \mathbf{v}\| \leq \|\mathbf{p} - \mathbf{v}\|, \quad \forall \mathbf{p} \in U.$$

Note that for any $\mathbf{p} \in U$ the vector $\mathbf{u} = \mathbf{p} - \mathbf{p}^*$ is also in U. Hence by $(*)$ and Pythagoras' Theorem,

$$\begin{aligned}\|\mathbf{p} - \mathbf{v}\|^2 &= \|\mathbf{p} - \mathbf{p}^* + \mathbf{p}^* - \mathbf{v}\|^2 \\ &= \|\mathbf{p} - \mathbf{p}^*\|^2 + \|\mathbf{p}^* - \mathbf{v}\|^2 \\ &\geq \|\mathbf{p}^* - \mathbf{v}\|^2.\end{aligned}$$

Furthermore, equality holds only if $\|\mathbf{p} - \mathbf{p}^*\|^2 = 0$ which holds only if $\mathbf{p} = \mathbf{p}^*$ by the point-separating property of the Euclidean norm. Hence, if such a vector $\mathbf{p}^*$ exists, it is unique. Vice versa, any minimizer must satisfy $(*)$ (prove it!).

It remains to show that there is at least one vector in U satisfying $(*)$. By the *Gram–Schmidt Theorem*, the linear subspace U has an orthonormal basis $\mathbf{q}_1, \ldots, \mathbf{q}_m$. By definition, $\mathrm{proj}_{\{\mathbf{q}_i\}_{i=1}^m} \mathbf{v} \in \mathrm{span}(\{\mathbf{q}_i\}_{i=1}^m) = U$. We show that $\mathrm{proj}_{\{\mathbf{q}_i\}_{i=1}^m} \mathbf{v}$ satisfies $(*)$. We can write any $\mathbf{u} \in U$ as $\sum_{i=1}^m \alpha_i \mathbf{q}_i$ with $\alpha_i = \langle \mathbf{u}, \mathbf{q}_i \rangle$. So, using this representation, we get

$$\begin{aligned}\left\langle \mathbf{v} - \sum_{j=1}^m \langle \mathbf{v}, \mathbf{q}_j \rangle \mathbf{q}_j, \sum_{i=1}^m \alpha_i \mathbf{q}_i \right\rangle &= \sum_{j=1}^m \langle \mathbf{v}, \mathbf{q}_j \rangle \alpha_j - \sum_{j=1}^m \sum_{i=1}^m \alpha_i \langle \mathbf{v}, \mathbf{q}_j \rangle \langle \mathbf{q}_j, \mathbf{q}_i \rangle \\ &= \sum_{j=1}^m \langle \mathbf{v}, \mathbf{q}_j \rangle \alpha_j - \sum_{j=1}^m \alpha_j \langle \mathbf{v}, \mathbf{q}_j \rangle \\ &= 0,\end{aligned}$$

where we used the orthonormality of the $\mathbf{q}_j$'s on the second line. $\square$

Example 2.3.10 *(continued from Example 2.3.5)* Consider again the linear subspace $W = \mathrm{span}(\mathbf{w}_1, \mathbf{w}_2, \mathbf{w}_3)$, where $\mathbf{w}_1 = (1, 0, 1)$, $\mathbf{w}_2 = (0, 1, 1)$, and $\mathbf{w}_3 = (1, -1, 0)$. We have shown that

$$\mathbf{q}_1 = \frac{1}{\sqrt{2}} \begin{pmatrix} 1 \\ 0 \\ 1 \end{pmatrix}, \quad \mathbf{q}_2 = \frac{1}{\sqrt{6}} \begin{pmatrix} -1 \\ 2 \\ 1 \end{pmatrix}$$

is an orthonormal basis. Let $\mathbf{w}_4 = (0, 0, 2)$. It is immediate that $\mathbf{w}_4 \notin \mathrm{span}(\mathbf{w}_1, \mathbf{w}_2)$ since vectors in that span are of the form $(x, y, x + y)$ for some $x, y \in \mathbb{R}$.

We can however compute the orthogonal projection $\mathbf{w}_4$ onto W. The inner products are

$$\langle \mathbf{w}_4, \mathbf{q}_1 \rangle = 0 \left(\frac{1}{\sqrt{2}} \right) + 0 \left(\frac{0}{\sqrt{2}} \right) + 2 \left(\frac{1}{\sqrt{2}} \right) = \frac{2}{\sqrt{2}},$$

$$\langle \mathbf{w}_4, \mathbf{q}_2 \rangle = 0 \left(-\frac{1}{\sqrt{6}} \right) + 0 \left(\frac{2}{\sqrt{6}} \right) + 2 \left(\frac{1}{\sqrt{6}} \right) = \frac{2}{\sqrt{6}}.$$

So
$$\operatorname{proj}_W \mathbf{w}_4 = \frac{2}{\sqrt{2}} \mathbf{q}_1 + \frac{2}{\sqrt{6}} \mathbf{q}_2 = \begin{pmatrix} 2/3 \\ 2/3 \\ 4/3 \end{pmatrix}.$$

As a sanity check, note that $\mathbf{w}_4 \in W$ since its third entry is equal to the sum of its first two entries.

The map proj_U is linear: $\operatorname{proj}_U(\alpha \mathbf{x} + \mathbf{y}) = \alpha \operatorname{proj}_U \mathbf{x} + \operatorname{proj}_U \mathbf{y}$ for all $\alpha \in \mathbb{R}$ and $\mathbf{x}, \mathbf{y} \in \mathbb{R}^n$. Indeed,

$$\operatorname{proj}_U(\alpha \mathbf{x} + \mathbf{y}) = \sum_{j=1}^{m} \langle \alpha \mathbf{x} + \mathbf{y}, \mathbf{q}_j \rangle \mathbf{q}_j$$

$$= \sum_{j=1}^{m} \{\alpha \langle \mathbf{x}, \mathbf{q}_j \rangle + \langle \mathbf{y}, \mathbf{q}_j \rangle\} \mathbf{q}_j$$

$$= \alpha \operatorname{proj}_U \mathbf{x} + \operatorname{proj}_U \mathbf{y}.$$

Any linear map from $\mathbb{R}^n$ to $\mathbb{R}^n$ can be encoded as an $n \times n$ matrix P.

Let
$$Q = \begin{pmatrix} | & & | \\ \mathbf{q}_1 & \cdots & \mathbf{q}_m \\ | & & | \end{pmatrix}$$

and note that computing

$$Q^T \mathbf{v} = \begin{pmatrix} \langle \mathbf{v}, \mathbf{q}_1 \rangle \\ \cdots \\ \langle \mathbf{v}, \mathbf{q}_m \rangle \end{pmatrix}$$

lists the coefficients in the expansion of $\operatorname{proj}_U \mathbf{v}$ over the basis $\mathbf{q}_1, \ldots, \mathbf{q}_m$.

Hence we see that
$$P = QQ^T.$$

Indeed, for any vector $\mathbf{v}$,
$$P\mathbf{v} = QQ^T \mathbf{v} = Q[Q^T \mathbf{v}].$$

So the output is a linear combination of the columns of Q (i.e., the $\mathbf{q}_i$'s) where the coefficients are the entries of the vector in square brackets $Q^T \mathbf{v}$.

Example 2.3.11 *(continued from Example 2.3.10) Consider again the linear subspace $W = \operatorname{span}(\mathbf{w}_1, \mathbf{w}_2, \mathbf{w}_3)$, where $\mathbf{w}_1 = (1, 0, 1)$, $\mathbf{w}_2 = (0, 1, 1)$, and $\mathbf{w}_3 = (1, -1, 0)$, with orthonormal basis*

$$\mathbf{q}_1 = \frac{1}{\sqrt{2}} \begin{pmatrix} 1 \\ 0 \\ 1 \end{pmatrix}, \quad \mathbf{q}_2 = \frac{1}{\sqrt{6}} \begin{pmatrix} -1 \\ 2 \\ 1 \end{pmatrix}.$$

Then orthogonal projection onto W can be written in matrix form as follows. The matrix Q is

$$Q = \begin{pmatrix} 1/\sqrt{2} & -1/\sqrt{6} \\ 0 & 2/\sqrt{6} \\ 1/\sqrt{2} & 1/\sqrt{6} \end{pmatrix}.$$

Then

$$QQ^T = \begin{pmatrix} 1/\sqrt{2} & -1/\sqrt{6} \\ 0 & 2/\sqrt{6} \\ 1/\sqrt{2} & 1/\sqrt{6} \end{pmatrix} \begin{pmatrix} 1/\sqrt{2} & 0 & 1/\sqrt{2} \\ -1/\sqrt{6} & 2/\sqrt{6} & 1/\sqrt{6} \end{pmatrix}$$

$$= \begin{pmatrix} 2/3 & -1/3 & 1/3 \\ -1/3 & 2/3 & 1/3 \\ 1/3 & 1/3 & 2/3 \end{pmatrix}.$$

So the projection of $\mathbf{w}_4 = (0, 0, 2)$ *is*

$$\begin{pmatrix} 2/3 & -1/3 & 1/3 \\ -1/3 & 2/3 & 1/3 \\ 1/3 & 1/3 & 2/3 \end{pmatrix} \begin{pmatrix} 0 \\ 0 \\ 2 \end{pmatrix} = \begin{pmatrix} 2/3 \\ 2/3 \\ 4/3 \end{pmatrix},$$

as previously computed.

The matrix $P = QQ^T$ is not to be confused with

$$Q^T Q = \begin{pmatrix} \langle \mathbf{q}_1, \mathbf{q}_1 \rangle & \cdots & \langle \mathbf{q}_1, \mathbf{q}_m \rangle \\ \langle \mathbf{q}_2, \mathbf{q}_1 \rangle & \cdots & \langle \mathbf{q}_2, \mathbf{q}_m \rangle \\ \vdots & \ddots & \vdots \\ \langle \mathbf{q}_m, \mathbf{q}_1 \rangle & \cdots & \langle \mathbf{q}_m, \mathbf{q}_m \rangle \end{pmatrix} = I_{m \times m}$$

where $I_{m \times m}$ denotes the $m \times m$ identity matrix. This follows from the fact that the $\mathbf{q}_i$'s are orthonormal.

Example 2.3.12 *Let* $\mathbf{q}_1, \ldots, \mathbf{q}_n$ *be an orthonormal basis of* $\mathbb{R}^n$ *and form the matrix*

$$Q = \begin{pmatrix} | & & | \\ \mathbf{q}_1 & \cdots & \mathbf{q}_n \\ | & & | \end{pmatrix}.$$

We show that $Q^{-1} = Q^T$.

We use that

$$Q^T Q = \begin{pmatrix} \langle \mathbf{q}_1, \mathbf{q}_1 \rangle & \cdots & \langle \mathbf{q}_1, \mathbf{q}_n \rangle \\ \langle \mathbf{q}_2, \mathbf{q}_1 \rangle & \cdots & \langle \mathbf{q}_2, \mathbf{q}_n \rangle \\ \vdots & \ddots & \vdots \\ \langle \mathbf{q}_n, \mathbf{q}_1 \rangle & \cdots & \langle \mathbf{q}_n, \mathbf{q}_n \rangle \end{pmatrix} = I_{n \times n}$$

where $I_{n \times n}$ denotes the $n \times n$ identity matrix.

In the other direction, we claim that $QQ^T = I_{n \times n}$ as well. Indeed the matrix QQ^T is the orthogonal projection on the span of the $\mathbf{q}_i$'s, that is, $\mathbb{R}^n$. By the Orthogonal Projection Theorem, the orthogonal projection $QQ^T\mathbf{v}$ finds the closest vector to $\mathbf{v}$ in the span of the $\mathbf{q}_i$'s. But that span contains all vectors, including $\mathbf{v}$, so we must have $QQ^T\mathbf{v} = \mathbf{v}$. Since this holds for all $\mathbf{v} \in \mathbb{R}^n$, the matrix QQ^T is the identity map and we have proved the claim.

Matrices that satisfy

$$Q^T Q = QQ^T = I_{n \times n}$$

are called orthogonal matrices.

Definition 2.3.13 *(Orthogonal Matrix)* *A square matrix $Q \in \mathbb{R}^{m \times m}$ is orthogonal if $Q^T Q = QQ^T = I_{m \times m}$.*

2.3.3 Orthogonal Complement

Before returning to overdetermined systems, we take a little detour to derive a consequence of the orthogonal projection that will be useful later. The *Orthogonal Projection Theorem* implies that any $\mathbf{v} \in \mathbb{R}^n$ can be decomposed into its orthogonal projection onto U and a vector orthogonal to it.

Definition 2.3.14 *(Orthogonal Complement)* *Let $U \subseteq \mathbb{R}^n$ be a linear subspace. The orthogonal complement of U, denoted $U^\perp$, is defined as*

$$U^\perp = \{\mathbf{w} \in \mathbb{R}^n : \langle \mathbf{w}, \mathbf{u} \rangle = 0, \forall \mathbf{u} \in U\}.$$

Example 2.3.15 *(continued from Example 2.3.5)* *Continuing a previous example, we compute the orthogonal complement of the linear subspace $W = \mathrm{span}(\mathbf{w}_1, \mathbf{w}_2, \mathbf{w}_3)$, where $\mathbf{w}_1 = (1, 0, 1)$, $\mathbf{w}_2 = (0, 1, 1)$, and $\mathbf{w}_3 = (1, -1, 0)$. One way to proceed is to find all vectors that are orthogonal to the orthonormal basis*

$$\mathbf{q}_1 = \frac{1}{\sqrt{2}} \begin{pmatrix} 1 \\ 0 \\ 1 \end{pmatrix}, \quad \mathbf{q}_2 = \frac{1}{\sqrt{6}} \begin{pmatrix} -1 \\ 2 \\ 1 \end{pmatrix}.$$

We require

$$0 = \langle \mathbf{u}, \mathbf{q}_1 \rangle = u_1 \left(\frac{1}{\sqrt{2}} \right) + u_2 \left(\frac{0}{\sqrt{2}} \right) + u_3 \left(\frac{1}{\sqrt{2}} \right) = \frac{u_1 + u_3}{\sqrt{2}},$$

$$0 = \langle \mathbf{u}, \mathbf{q}_2 \rangle = u_1 \left(-\frac{1}{\sqrt{6}} \right) + u_2 \left(\frac{2}{\sqrt{6}} \right) + u_3 \left(\frac{1}{\sqrt{6}} \right) = \frac{-u_1 + 2u_2 + u_3}{\sqrt{6}}.$$

The first equation implies $u_3 = -u_1$, which after replacing into the second equation and rearranging gives $u_2 = u_1$.

So all vectors of the form $(u_1, u_1, -u_1)$ for some $u_1 \in \mathbb{R}$ are orthogonal to all of W. This is a one-dimensional linear subspace. We can choose an orthonormal basis by finding a solution to

$$1 = (u_1)^2 + (u_1)^2 + (-u_1)^2 = 3u_1^2,$$

Take $u_1 = 1/\sqrt{3}$, that is, let

$$\mathbf{q}_3 = \frac{1}{\sqrt{3}} \begin{pmatrix} 1 \\ 1 \\ -1 \end{pmatrix}.$$

Then we have

$$W^\perp = \mathrm{span}(\mathbf{q}_3).$$

Lemma 2.3.16 *(Orthogonal Decomposition)* *Let $U \subseteq \mathbb{R}^n$ be a linear subspace and let $\mathbf{v} \in \mathbb{R}^n$. Then $\mathbf{v}$ can be decomposed as $\mathrm{proj}_U \mathbf{v} + (\mathbf{v} - \mathrm{proj}_U \mathbf{v})$ where $\mathrm{proj}_U \mathbf{v} \in U$ and $(\mathbf{v} - \mathrm{proj}_U \mathbf{v}) \in U^\perp$. Moreover, this decomposition is unique in the following sense: if $\mathbf{v} = \mathbf{u} + \mathbf{u}^\perp$ with $\mathbf{u} \in U$ and $\mathbf{u}^\perp \in U^\perp$, then $\mathbf{u} = \mathrm{proj}_U \mathbf{v}$ and $\mathbf{u}^\perp = \mathbf{v} - \mathrm{proj}_U \mathbf{v}$.*

Proof The first part is an immediate consequence of the *Orthogonal Projection Theorem*. For the second part, assume $\mathbf{v} = \mathbf{u} + \mathbf{u}^\perp$ with $\mathbf{u} \in U$ and $\mathbf{u}^\perp \in U^\perp$. Subtracting $\mathbf{v} = \text{proj}_U \mathbf{v} + (\mathbf{v} - \text{proj}_U \mathbf{v})$, we see that

$$(*) \quad \mathbf{0} = \mathbf{w}_1 + \mathbf{w}_2$$

with

$$\mathbf{w}_1 = \mathbf{u} - \text{proj}_U \mathbf{v} \in U, \quad \mathbf{w}_2 = \mathbf{u}^\perp - (\mathbf{v} - \text{proj}_U \mathbf{v}) \in U^\perp.$$

If $\mathbf{w}_1 = \mathbf{w}_2 = \mathbf{0}$, we are done. Otherwise, they must both be nonzero by $(*)$. Further, by the *Properties of Orthonormal Lists Lemma*, $\mathbf{w}_1$ and $\mathbf{w}_2$ must be linearly independent. But this is contradicted by the fact that $\mathbf{w}_2 = -\mathbf{w}_1$ by $(*)$. □

Formally, the *Orthogonal Decomposition Lemma* states that $\mathbb{R}^n$ is a direct sum of any linear subspace U and of its orthogonal complement $U^\perp$: that is, any vector $\mathbf{v} \in \mathbb{R}^n$ can be written uniquely as $\mathbf{v} = \mathbf{u} + \mathbf{u}^\perp$ with $\mathbf{u} \in U$ and $\mathbf{u}^\perp \in U^\perp$. This is denoted $\mathbb{R}^n = U \oplus U^\perp$.

Let $\mathbf{a}_1, \ldots, \mathbf{a}_\ell$ be an orthonormal basis of U and $\mathbf{b}_1, \ldots, \mathbf{b}_k$ be an orthonormal basis of $U^\perp$. By definition of the orthogonal complement, the list

$$\mathcal{L} = \{\mathbf{a}_1, \ldots, \mathbf{a}_\ell, \mathbf{b}_1, \ldots, \mathbf{b}_k\}$$

is orthonormal, so it forms a basis of its span. Because any vector in $\mathbb{R}^n$ can be written as a sum of a vector from U and a vector from $U^\perp$, all of $\mathbb{R}^n$ is in the span of $\mathcal{L}$. It follows from the *Dimension Theorem* that $n = \ell + k$, that is,

$$\dim(U) + \dim(U^\perp) = n.$$

2.3.4 Overdetermined Systems

In this section, we discuss the least-squares problem. Let again $A \in \mathbb{R}^{n \times m}$ be an $n \times m$ matrix with linearly independent columns and let $\mathbf{b} \in \mathbb{R}^n$ be a vector. We are looking to solve the system

$$A\mathbf{x} \approx \mathbf{b}.$$

If $n = m$, we can use the matrix inverse to solve the (provided A is nonsingular). But we are interested in the overdetermined case, when $n > m$: There are more equations than variables. We cannot use the matrix inverse then. Indeed, because the columns do not span all of $\mathbb{R}^n$, there is a vector $\mathbf{b} \in \mathbb{R}^n$ that is not in the column space of A.

A natural way to make sense of the overdetermined problem is to cast it as the linear least-squares problem

$$\min_{\mathbf{x} \in \mathbb{R}^m} \|A\mathbf{x} - \mathbf{b}\|^2.$$

In words, we look for the best-fitting solution under the Euclidean norm. Equivalently, writing

$$A = \begin{pmatrix} | & & | \\ \mathbf{a}_1 & \cdots & \mathbf{a}_m \\ | & & | \end{pmatrix} = \begin{pmatrix} a_{11} & \cdots & a_{1m} \\ a_{21} & \cdots & a_{2m} \\ \vdots & \ddots & \vdots \\ a_{n1} & \cdots & a_{nm} \end{pmatrix} \quad \text{and} \quad \mathbf{b} = \begin{pmatrix} b_1 \\ \vdots \\ b_n \end{pmatrix}$$

we seek a linear combination of the columns of A that minimizes the objective

$$\left\| \sum_{j=1}^{m} x_j \mathbf{a}_j - \mathbf{b} \right\|^2 = \sum_{i=1}^{n} \left(\sum_{j=1}^{m} a_{ij} x_j - b_i \right)^2.$$

We have already solved a closely related problem when we introduced the orthogonal projection. We make the connection explicit next.

Theorem 2.3.17 (Normal Equations) *Let $A \in \mathbb{R}^{n \times m}$ be an $n \times m$ matrix with $n \geq m$ and let $\mathbf{b} \in \mathbb{R}^n$ be a vector. A solution $\mathbf{x}^*$ to the linear least-squares problem*

$$\min_{\mathbf{x} \in \mathbb{R}^m} \|A\mathbf{x} - \mathbf{b}\|^2$$

satisfies the normal equations

$$A^T A \mathbf{x}^* = A^T \mathbf{b}.$$

If further the columns of A are linearly independent, then there exists a unique solution $\mathbf{x}^*$.

Proof idea: Apply our characterization of the orthogonal projection onto the column space of A.

Proof Let $U = \text{col}(A) = \text{span}(\mathbf{a}_1, \ldots, \mathbf{a}_m)$. By the *Orthogonal Projection Theorem*, the orthogonal projection $\mathbf{p}^* = \text{proj}_U \mathbf{b}$ of $\mathbf{b}$ onto U is the unique closest vector to $\mathbf{b}$ in U; that is,

$$\mathbf{p}^* = \arg\min_{\mathbf{p} \in U} \|\mathbf{p} - \mathbf{b}\|.$$

Because $\mathbf{p}^*$ is in $U = \text{col}(A)$, it must be of the form $\mathbf{p}^* = A\mathbf{x}^*$. This establishes that $\mathbf{x}^*$ is a solution to the linear least-squares problem in the statement (why can we ignore the square?).

By the *Orthogonal Projection Theorem*, it must satisfy $\langle \mathbf{b} - A\mathbf{x}^*, \mathbf{u} \rangle = 0$ for all $\mathbf{u} \in U$. Because the columns $\mathbf{a}_i$ are in U, that implies that

$$0 = \langle \mathbf{b} - A\mathbf{x}^*, \mathbf{a}_i \rangle = \mathbf{a}_i^T (\mathbf{b} - A\mathbf{x}^*), \qquad \forall i \in [m].$$

Stacking up these equations gives in matrix form

$$A^T (\mathbf{b} - A\mathbf{x}^*) = \mathbf{0},$$

as claimed (after rearranging).

Important observation: While we have shown that $\mathbf{p}^*$ is unique (by the *Orthogonal Projection Theorem*), it is not clear at all that $\mathbf{x}^*$ (i.e., the linear combination of columns of A corresponding to $\mathbf{p}^*$) is unique.

We have seen in Example 2.2.27 that, when A has full column rank, the matrix $A^T A$ is invertible. This implies the uniqueness claim. $\square$

NUMERICAL CORNER To solve a linear system in NumPy, use `numpy.linalg.solve`. As an example, we consider the overdetermined system with

$$A = \begin{pmatrix} 1 & 0 \\ 0 & 1 \\ 1 & 1 \end{pmatrix} \quad \text{and} \quad \mathbf{b} = \begin{pmatrix} 0 \\ 0 \\ 2 \end{pmatrix}.$$

We use `numpy.ndarray.T` for the transpose and `@` for matrix-matrix or matrix-vector product.

```
w1 = np.array([1., 0., 1.])
w2 = np.array([0., 1., 1.])
A = np.stack((w1, w2),axis=-1)
b = np.array([0., 0., 2.])
x = LA.solve(A.T @ A, A.T @ b)
print(x)
```

[0.66666667 0.66666667]

We can also use numpy.linalg.lstsq directly on the overdetermined system to compute the least-square solution.

```
x = LA.lstsq(A, b, rcond=None)[0]
print(x)
```

[0.66666667 0.66666667]

◁ NC

> ***Self-Assessment Quiz*** *(with help from Claude, Gemini, and ChatGPT)*
>
> 1. Let $\mathbf{q}_1, \ldots, \mathbf{q}_m$ be an orthonormal list of vectors in $\mathbb{R}^n$. Which of the following is the orthogonal projection of a vector $\mathbf{v} \in \mathbb{R}^n$ onto $\mathrm{span}(\mathbf{q}_1, \ldots, \mathbf{q}_m)$?
>   a) $\sum_{i=1}^{m} \mathbf{q}_i$
>   b) $\sum_{i=1}^{m} \langle \mathbf{v}, \mathbf{q}_i \rangle$
>   c) $\sum_{i=1}^{m} \langle \mathbf{v}, \mathbf{q}_i \rangle \mathbf{q}_i$
>   d) $\sum_{i=1}^{m} \langle \mathbf{q}_i, \mathbf{q}_i \rangle \mathbf{v}$
>
> 2. According to the *Normal Equations Theorem*, what condition must a solution $\mathbf{x}^*$ to the linear least-squares problem satisfy?
>   a) $A^T A \mathbf{x}^* = \mathbf{b}$
>   b) $A^T A \mathbf{x}^* = A^T \mathbf{b}$
>   c) $A \mathbf{x}^* = A^T \mathbf{b}$
>   d) $A \mathbf{x}^* = \mathbf{b}$
>
> 3. Which property characterizes the orthogonal projection $\mathrm{proj}_U \mathbf{v}$ of a vector $\mathbf{v}$ onto a subspace U?
>   a) $\mathbf{v} - \mathrm{proj}_U \mathbf{v}$ is a scalar multiple of $\mathbf{v}$.
>   b) $\mathbf{v} - \mathrm{proj}_U \mathbf{v}$ is orthogonal to $\mathbf{v}$.
>   c) $\mathbf{v} - \mathrm{proj}_U \mathbf{v}$ is orthogonal to U.
>   d) $\mathrm{proj}_U \mathbf{v}$ is always the zero vector.
>
> 4. What is the interpretation of the linear least-squares problem $A\mathbf{x} \approx \mathbf{b}$ in terms of the column space of A?
>   a) Finding the exact solution $\mathbf{x}$ such that $A\mathbf{x} = \mathbf{b}$

b) Finding the vector **x** that makes the linear combination $A\mathbf{x}$ of the columns of A as close as possible to **b** in Euclidean norm

c) Finding the orthogonal projection of **b** onto the column space of A

d) Finding the orthogonal complement of the column space of A

5 Which matrix equation must hold true for a matrix Q to be orthogonal?
   a) $QQ^T = 0$
   b) $QQ^T = I$
   c) $Q^T Q = 0$
   d) $Q^T = Q$

Answer for 1: c. Justification: This is the definition of the orthogonal projection onto an orthonormal list given in the text.

Answer for 2: b. Justification: The *Normal Equations Theorem* states that a solution $\mathbf{x}^*$ to the linear least-squares problem satisfies $A^T A \mathbf{x}^* = A^T \mathbf{b}$.

Answer for 3: c. Justification: The text states that the orthogonal projection $\text{proj}_U \mathbf{v}$ has the property that "the difference $\mathbf{v} - \text{proj}_U \mathbf{v}$ is orthogonal to U."

Answer for 4: b. Justification: The text defines the linear least-squares problem as seeking a linear combination of the columns of A that minimizes the distance to **b** in Euclidean norm.

Answer for 5: b. Justification: The text states thats an orthogonal matrix Q must satisfy $QQ^T = I$.

2.4 QR Decomposition and Householder Transformations

We have some business left over from previous sections: constructing orthonormal bases. We go over the Gram–Schimdt algorithm below. Through a matrix factorization perspective, we give an alternative way to solve the linear least-squares problem.

2.4.1 Matrix Form of Gram–Schmidt

In this subsection, we prove the *Gram–Schmidt Theorem* and introduce a fruitful matrix perspective.

2.4.1.1 Gram–Schmidt Algorithm

Let $\mathbf{a}_1, \ldots, \mathbf{a}_m$ be linearly independent. We use the Gram–Schmidt algorithm to obtain an orthonormal basis of $\text{span}(\mathbf{a}_1, \ldots, \mathbf{a}_m)$. The process takes advantage of the properties of the orthogonal projection derived above. In essence we add the vectors $\mathbf{a}_i$ one by one, but only after taking out their orthogonal projection on the previously included vectors. The outcome spans the same subspace and the *Orthogonal Projection Theorem* ensures orthogonality.

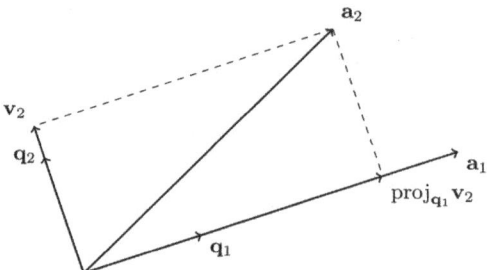

Figure 2.5 Gram–Schmidt process.

Proof idea: (Gram–Schmidt) Suppose first that $m = 1$. In that case, all that needs to be done is to divide $\mathbf{a}_1$ by its norm to obtain a unit vector whose span is the same as $\mathbf{a}_1$, that is, we set $\mathbf{q}_1 = \frac{\mathbf{a}_1}{\|\mathbf{a}_1\|}$.

Suppose now that $m = 2$. We first let $\mathbf{q}_1 = \frac{\mathbf{a}_1}{\|\mathbf{a}_1\|}$ as in the previous case. Then we subtract from $\mathbf{a}_2$ its projection on $\mathbf{q}_1$, that is, we set $\mathbf{v}_2 = \mathbf{a}_2 - \langle \mathbf{q}_1, \mathbf{a}_2 \rangle \mathbf{q}_1$. It is easily checked that $\mathbf{v}_2$ is orthogonal to $\mathbf{q}_1$ (see the proof of the *Orthogonal Projection Theorem* for a similar calculation). Moreover, because $\mathbf{a}_2$ is a linear combination of $\mathbf{q}_1$ and $\mathbf{v}_2$, we have $\mathrm{span}(\mathbf{q}_1, \mathbf{v}_2) = \mathrm{span}(\mathbf{a}_1, \mathbf{a}_2)$. It remains to divide by the norm of the resulting vector: $\mathbf{q}_2 = \frac{\mathbf{v}_2}{\|\mathbf{v}_2\|}$. See Figure 2.5.

For general m, we proceed similarly but project onto the subspace spanned by the previously added vectors at each step.

Proof *(Gram–Schmidt)* The first step of the induction is described above. Then the general inductive step is the following. Assume that we have constructed orthonormal vectors $\mathbf{q}_1, \ldots, \mathbf{q}_{j-1}$ such that

$$U_{j-1} := \mathrm{span}(\mathbf{q}_1, \ldots, \mathbf{q}_{j-1}) = \mathrm{span}(\mathbf{a}_1, \ldots, \mathbf{a}_{j-1}).$$

Constructing $\mathbf{q}_j$: By the *Properties of Orthonormal Lists Lemma*, $\{\mathbf{q}\}_{i=1}^{j-1}$ is an independent list and therefore forms an orthonormal basis for U_{j-1}. So we can compute the orthogonal projection of $\mathbf{a}_j$ on U_{j-1} as

$$\mathrm{proj}_{U_{j-1}} \mathbf{a}_j = \sum_{i=1}^{j-1} r_{ij} \mathbf{q}_i,$$

where we define $r_{ij} = \langle \mathbf{q}_i, \mathbf{a}_j \rangle$. And we set

$$\mathbf{v}_j = \mathbf{a}_j - \mathrm{proj}_{U_{j-1}} \mathbf{a}_j = \mathbf{a}_j - \sum_{i=1}^{j-1} r_{ij} \mathbf{q}_i \quad \text{and} \quad \mathbf{q}_j = \frac{\mathbf{v}_j}{\|\mathbf{v}_j\|}.$$

The last step is possible because:

Lemma 2.4.1 $\|\mathbf{v}_j\| > 0$.

Proof Indeed otherwise $\mathbf{a}_j$ would be equal to its projection $\mathrm{proj}_{U_{j-1}} \mathbf{a}_j \in \mathrm{span}(\mathbf{a}_1, \ldots, \mathbf{a}_{j-1})$ which would contradict linear independence of the $\mathbf{a}_k$'s. □

The vector $\mathbf{q}_j$ is of unit norm by construction. It is also orthogonal to $\mathrm{span}(\mathbf{q}_1, \ldots, \mathbf{q}_{j-1})$ by the definition of $\mathbf{v}_j$ and the *Orthogonal Projection Theorem*. So $\mathbf{q}_1, \ldots, \mathbf{q}_j$ form an orthonormal list.

2.4 QR Decomposition and Householder Transformations

Pushing the induction through: It remains to prove that $\text{span}(\mathbf{q}_1, \ldots, \mathbf{q}_j) = \text{span}(\mathbf{a}_1, \ldots, \mathbf{a}_j)$. Because by induction $\text{span}(\mathbf{q}_1, \ldots, \mathbf{q}_{j-1}) = \text{span}(\mathbf{a}_1, \ldots, \mathbf{a}_{j-1})$, all we have to prove are the following two claims.

Lemma 2.4.2 $\mathbf{q}_j \in \text{span}(\mathbf{a}_1, \ldots, \mathbf{a}_j)$.

Proof By construction,

$$\mathbf{q}_j = \frac{1}{\|\mathbf{v}_j\|} \left\{ \mathbf{a}_j - \text{proj}_{U_{j-1}} \mathbf{a}_j \right\} = \frac{1}{\|\mathbf{v}_j\|} \mathbf{a}_j + \frac{1}{\|\mathbf{v}_j\|} \text{proj}_{U_{j-1}} \mathbf{a}_j.$$

By definition of the orthogonal projection,

$$\text{proj}_{U_{j-1}} \mathbf{a}_j \in U_{j-1} = \text{span}(\mathbf{a}_1, \ldots, \mathbf{a}_{j-1}) \subseteq \text{span}(\mathbf{a}_1, \ldots, \mathbf{a}_j).$$

Hence we have written $\mathbf{q}_j$ as a linear combination of vectors in $\text{span}(\mathbf{a}_1, \ldots, \mathbf{a}_j)$. This proves the claim. □

Lemma 2.4.3 $\mathbf{a}_j \in \text{span}(\mathbf{q}_1, \ldots, \mathbf{q}_j)$.

Proof Unrolling the calculations above, $\mathbf{a}_j$ can be rewritten as the following linear combination of $\mathbf{q}_1, \ldots, \mathbf{q}_j$:

$$\begin{aligned}
\mathbf{a}_j &= \text{proj}_{U_{j-1}} \mathbf{a}_j + \mathbf{v}_j \\
&= \text{proj}_{U_{j-1}} \mathbf{a}_j + \|\mathbf{v}_j\| \mathbf{q}_j \\
&= \text{proj}_{U_{j-1}} \mathbf{a}_j + \|\mathbf{a}_j - \text{proj}_{U_{j-1}} \mathbf{a}_j\| \mathbf{q}_j \\
&= \sum_{i=1}^{j-1} r_{ij} \mathbf{q}_i + \left\| \mathbf{a}_j - \sum_{i=1}^{j-1} r_{ij} \mathbf{q}_i \right\| \mathbf{q}_j \\
&= \sum_{i=1}^{j-1} r_{ij} \mathbf{q}_i + r_{jj} \mathbf{q}_j,
\end{aligned}$$

where we defined $r_{jj} = \left\| \mathbf{a}_j - \sum_{i=1}^{j-1} r_{ij} \mathbf{q}_i \right\| = \|\mathbf{v}_j\|$. □

Hence $\mathbf{q}_1, \ldots, \mathbf{q}_j$ forms an orthonormal list with $\text{span}(\mathbf{a}_1, \ldots, \mathbf{a}_j)$. So induction goes through. That concludes the proof of the theorem. □

We implement the Gram–Schmidt algorithm in Python. For reasons that will become clear in the next subsection, we output both the $\mathbf{q}_j$'s and r_{ij}'s, each in matrix form. Here we use numpy.dot to compute inner products.

```
def gramschmidt(A):
    (n,m) = A.shape
    Q = np.zeros((n,m))
    R = np.zeros((m,m))
    for j in range(m):
        v = np.copy(A[:,j])
        for i in range(j):
            R[i,j] = np.dot(Q[:,i], A[:,j])
            v -= R[i,j]*Q[:,i]
        R[j,j] = LA.norm(v)
```

```
    Q[:,j] = v/R[j,j]
return Q, R
```

NUMERICAL CORNER Let's try a simple example.

```
w1 = np.array([1., 0., 1.])
w2 = np.array([0., 1., 1.])
A = np.stack((w1, w2),axis=-1)
print(A)
```

```
[[1. 0.]
 [0. 1.]
 [1. 1.]]
```

```
Q, R = gramschmidt(A)
print(Q)
```

```
[[ 0.70710678 -0.40824829]
 [ 0.         0.81649658]
 [ 0.70710678  0.40824829]]
```

```
print(R)
```

```
[[1.41421356 0.70710678]
 [0.         1.22474487]]
```

◁ **NC**

2.4.1.2 Matrix Form

Let $\mathbf{a}_1, \ldots, \mathbf{a}_m \in \mathbb{R}^n$ be linearly independent. Above, we presented the Gram–Schmidt algorithm to obtain an orthonormal basis of span$(\mathbf{a}_1, \ldots, \mathbf{a}_m)$. We revisit it in matrix form.

Let

$$A = \begin{pmatrix} | & & | \\ \mathbf{a}_1 & \cdots & \mathbf{a}_m \\ | & & | \end{pmatrix} \quad \text{and} \quad Q = \begin{pmatrix} | & & | \\ \mathbf{q}_1 & \cdots & \mathbf{q}_m \\ | & & | \end{pmatrix}.$$

Recalling that, for all j,

$$\mathbf{a}_j = \sum_{i=1}^{j-1} r_{ij}\, \mathbf{q}_i + r_{jj}\, \mathbf{q}_j,$$

the output of the Gram–Schmidt algorithm can be written in the following compact form, known as a QR decomposition:

$$A = QR$$

where column i of the $m \times m$ matrix R contains the coefficients of the linear combination of the $\mathbf{q}_j$'s that produce $\mathbf{a}_i$.

By the proof of the *Gram–Schmidt Theorem*, $\mathbf{a}_i \in \text{span}(\mathbf{q}_1, \ldots, \mathbf{q}_i)$. So column i of R has only zeros below the diagonal. Hence R has a special structure we have previously encountered: It is upper triangular. The proof also established that the diagonal elements of R are strictly positive.

Definition 2.4.4 (Triangular matrix) *A matrix $R = (r_{ij})_{i,j} \in \mathbb{R}^{n \times m}$ is upper triangular if all entries below the diagonal are zero; that is, if $i > j$ implies $r_{ij} = 0$. Similarly, a lower-triangular matrix has zeros above the diagonal.*

An upper-triangular matrix looks like this:

$$R = \begin{bmatrix} r_{1,1} & r_{1,2} & r_{1,3} & \cdots & r_{1,n} \\ 0 & r_{2,2} & r_{2,3} & \cdots & r_{2,n} \\ & & 0 & \ddots & \ddots & \vdots \\ & & & \ddots & \ddots & r_{n-1,n} \\ 0 & & & & 0 & r_{n,n} \end{bmatrix}.$$

Remarks:

a) If the input vectors $\mathbf{a}_1, \ldots, \mathbf{a}_m$ are not linearly independent (in which case we say that the matrix A is rank-deficient), the Gram–Schmidt algorithm will fail. Indeed, at some point we will have that $\mathbf{a}_j \in U_{j-1}$ and the normalization of $\mathbf{v}_j$ will not be possible. In that case, one can instead use a technique called column pivoting, which we will not describe.

b) The QR decomposition we have derived here is technically called a reduced QR decomposition. In a full QR decomposition, the matrix Q is square and orthogonal. In other words, the columns of such a Q form an orthonormal basis of the full space $\mathbb{R}^n$. Let $A = Q_1 R_1$ be a reduced QR decomposition, as obtained through the Gram–Schmidt algorithm. Then the columns of Q_1 form an orthonormal basis of $\text{col}(A)$ and can be completed into an orthonormal basis of $\mathbb{R}^n$ by adding further vectors $\mathbf{q}_{m+1}, \ldots, \mathbf{q}_n$. Let Q_2 be the matrix with columns $\mathbf{q}_{m+1}, \ldots, \mathbf{q}_n$. Then a full QR decomposition of A is

$$Q = \begin{pmatrix} Q_1 & Q_2 \end{pmatrix} \quad R = \begin{pmatrix} R_1 \\ \mathbf{0}_{(n-m) \times m} \end{pmatrix}$$

where $\mathbf{0}_{(n-m) \times m}$ is the all-zero matrix of size $(n-m) \times m$. A numerical method for computing a full QR decomposition is presented in subsection 2.4.3.

c) The Gram–Schmidt algorithm is appealing geometrically, but it is known to have numerical issues. Other methods exist for computing QR decompositions with better numerical properties. We discuss such a method in subsection 2.4.3. (See that same subsection for an example where the $\mathbf{q}_j$'s produced by Gram–Schmidt are far from orthogonal.)

2.4.2 Least Squares via QR

Let $A \in \mathbb{R}^{n \times m}$ be an $n \times m$ matrix with linearly independent columns and let $\mathbf{b} \in \mathbb{R}^n$ be a vector. Recall that a solution $\mathbf{x}^*$ to the linear least-squares problem

$$\min_{\mathbf{x} \in \mathbb{R}^m} \|A\mathbf{x} - \mathbf{b}\|^2$$

satisfies the normal equations

$$A^T A \mathbf{x}^* = A^T \mathbf{b}.$$

2.4.2.1 Solving the Normal Equations

In a first linear algebra course, one learns how to solve linear systems such as the normal equations. For this task a common approach is Gaussian elimination, or row reduction. Quoting Wikipedia[2]:

> To perform row reduction on a matrix, one uses a sequence of elementary row operations to modify the matrix until the lower left-hand corner of the matrix is filled with zeros, as much as possible. [...] Once all of the leading coefficients (the leftmost nonzero entry in each row) are 1, and every column containing a leading coefficient has zeros elsewhere, the matrix is said to be in reduced row echelon form. [...] The process of row reduction [...] can be divided into two parts. The first part (sometimes called forward elimination) reduces a given system to row echelon form, from which one can tell whether there are no solutions, a unique solution, or infinitely many solutions. The second part (sometimes called back substitution) continues to use row operations until the solution is found; in other words, it puts the matrix into reduced row echelon form.

We will not go over Gaussian elimination here. In this subsection, we develop an alternative approach to solving the normal equations using the QR decomposition. We will need one component of Gaussian elimination, back substitution. It is based on the observation that triangular systems of equations are straightforward to solve. We start with an example.

Example 2.4.5 *Here is a concrete example of back substitution. Consider the system $R\mathbf{x} = \mathbf{b}$ with*

$$R = \begin{pmatrix} 2 & -1 & 2 \\ 0 & 1 & 1 \\ 0 & 0 & 2 \end{pmatrix} \quad \mathbf{b} = \begin{pmatrix} 0 \\ -2 \\ 0 \end{pmatrix}.$$

This corresponds to the linear equations

$$2x_1 - x_2 + 2x_3 = 0$$
$$x_2 + x_3 = -2$$
$$2x_3 = 0.$$

The third equation gives $x_3 = 0/2 = 0$. Plugging into the second one, we get $x_2 = -2 - x_3 = -2$. Plugging into the first one, we finally have $x_1 = (x_2 - 2x_3)/2 = -1$. So the solution is $\mathbf{x} = (-1, -2, 0)$.

In general, solving a triangular system of equations works as follows. Let $R = (r_{i,j})_{i,j} \in \mathbb{R}^{m \times m}$ be upper triangular and let $\mathbf{b} \in \mathbb{R}^m$ be the left-hand vector; that is, we want to solve the system

$$R\mathbf{x} = \mathbf{b}.$$

[2] https://en.wikipedia.org/wiki/Gaussian_elimination

2.4 QR Decomposition and Householder Transformations

Starting from the last row of the system, $r_{m,m}x_m = b_m$ or $x_m = b_m/r_{m,m}$, assuming that $r_{m,m} \neq 0$. Moving to the second-to-last row, $r_{m-1,m-1}x_{m-1} + r_{m-1,m}x_m = b_{m-1}$ or $x_{m-1} = (b_{m-1} - r_{m-1,m}x_m)/r_{m-1,m-1}$, assuming that $r_{m-1,m-1} \neq 0$. And so on. This procedure is known as back substitution.

Analogously, in the lower-triangular case $L \in \mathbb{R}^{m \times m}$, we have forward substitution. These procedures implicitly define inverses for R and L *when the diagonal elements are all nonzero*. We will not write them down explicitly here.

We implement back substitution in Python. In our naive implementation, we assume that the diagonal entries are not zero, which will suffice for our purposes.

```
def backsubs(R,b):
    m = b.shape[0]
    x = np.zeros(m)
    for i in reversed(range(m)):
        x[i] = (b[i] - np.dot(R[i,i+1:m],x[i+1:m]))/R[i,i]
    return x
```

Forward substitution is implemented similarly.

```
def forwardsubs(L,b):
    m = b.shape[0]
    x = np.zeros(m)
    for i in range(m):
        x[i] = (b[i] - np.dot(L[i,0:i],x[0:i]))/L[i,i]
    return x
```

2.4.2.2 Using QR

We show how to solve the normal equations via the QR decomposition.

1. Construct an orthonormal basis of col(A) through a QR decomposition

$$A = QR.$$

2. Form the orthogonal projection matrix

$$P = QQ^T.$$

3. Apply the projection to **b** and observe that, by the proof of the *Normal Equations Theorem*, **x*** satisfies

$$A\mathbf{x}^* = QQ^T\mathbf{b}.$$

4. Plug in the QR decomposition for A to get

$$QR\mathbf{x}^* = QQ^T\mathbf{b}.$$

5. Multiply both sides by Q^T and use $Q^TQ = I_{m \times m}$:

$$R\mathbf{x}^* = Q^T\mathbf{b}.$$

6. Solving this system for **x*** is straightforward via back substitution because R is upper triangular.

Theorem 2.4.6 (*Least Squares via QR*) *Let $A \in \mathbb{R}^{n \times m}$ be an $n \times m$ matrix with linearly independent columns, let $\mathbf{b} \in \mathbb{R}^n$ be a vector, and let $A = QR$ be a QR decomposition of A. The solution to the linear least-squares problem*

$$\min_{\mathbf{x} \in \mathbb{R}^m} \|A\mathbf{x} - \mathbf{b}\|^2$$

satisfies

$$R\mathbf{x}^* = Q^T \mathbf{b}.$$

Note that, in reality, we do not need to form the matrix QQ^T.

We implement the QR approach to least squares.

```
def ls_by_qr(A, b):
    Q, R = gramschmidt(A)
    return backsubs(R, Q.T @ b)
```

NUMERICAL CORNER We return to our simple overdetermined system example.

```
w1 = np.array([1., 0., 1.])
w2 = np.array([0., 1., 1.])
A = np.stack((w1, w2),axis=-1)
b = np.array([0., 0., 2.])

x = ls_by_qr(A, b)
print(x)
```

[0.66666667 0.66666667]

◁ **NC**

2.4.3 Householder Transformations

While the Gram–Schmidt algorithm gives a natural way to compute a (reduced) QR decomposition, there are many other numerical algorithms for this purpose. Some have better numerical behavior, specifically in terms of how they handle roundoff error. Quoting Wikipedia[3]:

> A roundoff error, also called rounding error, is the difference between the result produced by a given algorithm using exact arithmetic and the result produced by the same algorithm using finite-precision, rounded arithmetic. Rounding errors are due to inexactness in the representation of real numbers and the arithmetic operations done with them. [...] When a sequence of calculations with an input involving roundoff error are made, errors may accumulate, sometimes dominating the calculation.

We will not prove this here, but the following method based on Householder reflections is numerically more stable.

---

[3] https://en.wikipedia.org/wiki/Round-off_error

2.4 QR Decomposition and Householder Transformations

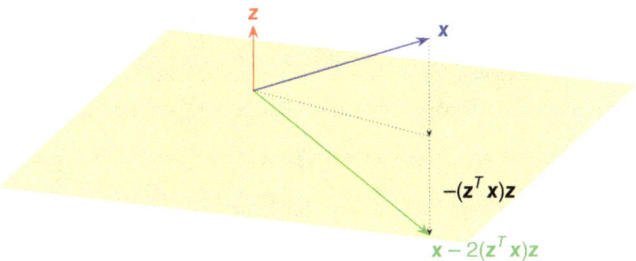

Figure 2.6 Householder reflection.

Recall that a square matrix $Q \in \mathbb{R}^{m \times m}$ is orthogonal if $Q^T Q = Q Q^T = I_{m \times m}$. In words, the matrix inverse of Q is its transpose. This is equivalent to the columns of Q forming an orthonormal basis of $\mathbb{R}^m$ (why?).

It can be shown that the product of two orthogonal matrices Q_1 and Q_2 is also orthogonal. (Try it!)

An important property of orthogonal matrices is that they preserve inner products: If $Q \in \mathbb{R}^{m \times m}$ is orthogonal, then for any $\mathbf{x}, \mathbf{y} \in \mathbb{R}^m$

$$\langle Q\mathbf{x}, Q\mathbf{y} \rangle = (Q\mathbf{x})^T Q\mathbf{y} = \mathbf{x}^T Q^T Q \mathbf{y} = \mathbf{x}^T \mathbf{y} = \langle \mathbf{x}, \mathbf{y} \rangle.$$

In particular, orthogonal matrices preserve norms and angles.

2.4.3.1 Reflections

One such family of transformations are reflections.

Definition 2.4.7 *(Hyperplane)* *A hyperplane W is a linear subspace of $\mathbb{R}^m$ of dimension $m-1$.*

Definition 2.4.8 *(Householder Reflection)* *Let $\mathbf{z} \in \mathbb{R}^m$ be a unit vector and let W be the hyperplane orthogonal to it. The reflection across W is given by*

$$H = I_{m \times m} - 2\mathbf{z}\mathbf{z}^T.$$

This is referred to as a Householder reflection.

In words, we subtract twice the projection onto $\mathbf{z}$, as depicted in Figure 2.6.

Lemma 2.4.9 *Let $H = I_{m \times m} - 2\mathbf{z}\mathbf{z}^T$ be a Householder reflection. Then H is an orthogonal matrix.*

Proof We check the definition:

$$\begin{aligned} H^T H &= (I_{m \times m} - 2\mathbf{z}\mathbf{z}^T)^T (I_{m \times m} - 2\mathbf{z}\mathbf{z}^T) \\ &= (I_{m \times m} - 2\mathbf{z}\mathbf{z}^T)(I_{m \times m} - 2\mathbf{z}\mathbf{z}^T) \\ &= I_{m \times m} - 2\mathbf{z}\mathbf{z}^T - 2\mathbf{z}\mathbf{z}^T + 4\mathbf{z}\mathbf{z}^T \mathbf{z}\mathbf{z}^T \\ &= I_{m \times m} - 2\mathbf{z}\mathbf{z}^T - 2\mathbf{z}\mathbf{z}^T + 4\mathbf{z}\mathbf{z}^T \end{aligned}$$

which is equal to $I_{m \times m}$. The calculation for HH^T is the same. □

2.4.3.2 QR Decomposition by Introducing Zeros

We return to QR decompositions. One way to construct a (full) QR decomposition of a matrix $A \in \mathbb{R}^{n \times m}$ is to find a sequence of orthogonal matrices $H_1, \ldots, H_m$ that triangularize A:

$$H_m \cdots H_2 H_1 A = R$$

for an upper-triangular matrix R. Indeed, by the properties of orthogonal matrices, we then have

$$A = H_1^T H_2^T \cdots H_m^T H_m \cdots H_2 H_1 A = H_1^T H_2^T \cdots H_m^T R$$

where $Q = H_1^T H_2^T \cdots H_m^T$ is itself orthogonal as a product of orthogonal matrices. So to proceed we need to identify orthogonal matrices that have the effect of introducing zeros below the diagonal:

$$H_2 H_1 A = \begin{pmatrix} \times & \times & \times & \times & \times \\ 0 & \times & \times & \times & \times \\ 0 & 0 & \times & \times & \times \\ 0 & 0 & \boxed{\times} & \times & \times \\ 0 & 0 & \boxed{\times} & \times & \times \\ 0 & 0 & \boxed{\times} & \times & \times \end{pmatrix}.$$

It turns out that a well-chosen Householder reflection does the trick. Let $\mathbf{y}_1$ be the first column of A and take

$$\mathbf{z}_1 = \frac{\|\mathbf{y}_1\| \mathbf{e}_1^{(n)} - \mathbf{y}_1}{\|\|\mathbf{y}_1\| \mathbf{e}_1^{(n)} - \mathbf{y}_1\|} \quad \text{and} \quad H_1 = I_{n \times n} - 2\mathbf{z}_1 \mathbf{z}_1^T$$

where $\mathbf{e}_1^{(n)}$ is the first vector in the canonical basis of $\mathbb{R}^n$. As depicted in Figure 2.7, this choice sends $\mathbf{y}_1$ to

$$\|\mathbf{y}_1\| \mathbf{e}_1^{(n)} = \begin{pmatrix} \|\mathbf{y}_1\| \\ 0 \\ \vdots \\ 0 \end{pmatrix}.$$

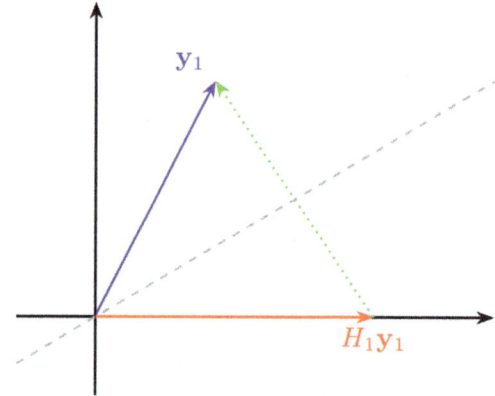

Figure 2.7 Introducing zeros by Householder reflection.

(It is clear that if $H_1\mathbf{y}_1$ is proportional to $\mathbf{e}_1^{(n)}$, than it can only be $\|\mathbf{y}_1\|\mathbf{e}_1^{(n)}$ or $-\|\mathbf{y}_1\|\mathbf{e}_1^{(n)}$. Prove it!)

Lemma 2.4.10 *(Householder)* Let $\mathbf{y}_1$, $\mathbf{z}_1$, and H_1 be as above. Then
$$H_1\mathbf{y}_1 = \|\mathbf{y}_1\|\mathbf{e}_1^{(n)}.$$

Proof idea: The proof by picture is in Figure 2.7.

Proof Note that
$$\|\|\mathbf{y}_1\|\mathbf{e}_1^{(n)} - \mathbf{y}_1\|^2 = (\|\mathbf{y}_1\| - y_{1,1})^2 + \sum_{j=2}^{n} y_{1,j}^2$$
$$= \|\mathbf{y}_1\|^2 - 2\|\mathbf{y}_1\|y_{1,1} + y_{1,1}^2 + \sum_{j=2}^{n} y_{1,j}^2$$
$$= 2(\|\mathbf{y}_1\|^2 - \|\mathbf{y}_1\|y_{1,1})$$

and
$$2\mathbf{z}_1\mathbf{z}_1^T\mathbf{y}_1 = 2\mathbf{z}_1\frac{\|\mathbf{y}_1\|(\mathbf{e}_1^{(n)})^T\mathbf{y}_1 - \mathbf{y}_1^T\mathbf{y}_1}{\|\|\mathbf{y}_1\|\mathbf{e}_1^{(n)} - \mathbf{y}_1\|}$$
$$= 2\frac{\|\mathbf{y}_1\|y_{1,1} - \|\mathbf{y}_1\|^2}{\|\|\mathbf{y}_1\|\mathbf{e}_1^{(n)} - \mathbf{y}_1\|^2}(\|\mathbf{y}_1\|\mathbf{e}_1^{(n)} - \mathbf{y}_1)$$
$$= -(\|\mathbf{y}_1\|\mathbf{e}_1^{(n)} - \mathbf{y}_1)$$

where we used the previous equation. Hence
$$H_1\mathbf{y}_1 = (I_{n\times n} - 2\mathbf{z}_1\mathbf{z}_1^T)\mathbf{y}_1 = \mathbf{y}_1 + (\|\mathbf{y}_1\|\mathbf{e}_1^{(n)} - \mathbf{y}_1) = \|\mathbf{y}_1\|\mathbf{e}_1^{(n)}.$$

This establishes the claim. □

The upshot is that multiplying A by H_1 introduces zeros below the diagonal in the first column. To see this, recall that one interpretation of the matrix–matrix product is that each column of the second matrix gets multiplied by the first one. By the *Householder Lemma*, applying H_1 to A gives
$$H_1 A = \begin{pmatrix} H_1\mathbf{y}_1 & H_1 A_{\cdot,2} & \cdots & H_1 A_{\cdot,m} \end{pmatrix} = \begin{pmatrix} \|\mathbf{y}_1\|\mathbf{e}_1^{(n)} & H_1 A_{\cdot,2} & \cdots & H_1 A_{\cdot,m} \end{pmatrix}$$
so the first column is now proportional to $\mathbf{e}_1$, which has zeros in all but the first element. (What should we do if $\mathbf{y}_1$ is already equal to $\|\mathbf{y}_1\|\mathbf{e}_1^{(n)}$?)

2.4.3.3 Putting Everything Together

We have shown how to introduce zeros below the diagonal in the first column of a matrix. To introduce zeros in the second column below the diagonal we use a block matrix. Recall that if $A_{ij} \in \mathbb{R}^{n_i \times m_j}$ and $B_{ij} \in \mathbb{R}^{m_i \times p_j}$ for $i, j = 1, 2$, then we have the following formula:
$$\begin{pmatrix} A_{11} & A_{12} \\ A_{21} & A_{22} \end{pmatrix} \begin{pmatrix} B_{11} & B_{12} \\ B_{21} & B_{22} \end{pmatrix} = \begin{pmatrix} A_{11}B_{11} + A_{12}B_{21} & A_{11}B_{12} + A_{12}B_{22} \\ A_{21}B_{11} + A_{22}B_{21} & A_{21}B_{12} + A_{22}B_{22} \end{pmatrix}.$$

Now consider the block matrix
$$H_2 = \begin{pmatrix} 1 & \mathbf{0} \\ \mathbf{0} & F_2 \end{pmatrix}$$

where F_2 is the following Householder reflection. Write the second column of $H_1 A$ as $(y^{(2)}, \mathbf{y}_2)$. That is, $\mathbf{y}_2$ comprises the entries $2, \ldots, n$ of that column. Define

$$F_2 = I_{(n-1) \times (n-1)} - 2\mathbf{z}_2 \mathbf{z}_2^T \quad \text{with} \quad \mathbf{z}_2 = \frac{\|\mathbf{y}_2\| \mathbf{e}_1^{(n-1)} - \mathbf{y}_2}{\|\|\mathbf{y}_2\| \mathbf{e}_1^{(n-1)} - \mathbf{y}_2\|}$$

where now $\mathbf{e}_1^{(n-1)} \in \mathbb{R}^{n-1}$. By the *Householder Lemma*, we have $F_2 \mathbf{y}_2 = \|\mathbf{y}_2\| \mathbf{e}_1^{(n-1)}$. It can be shown that $\mathbf{y}_2 \neq \mathbf{0}$ when the columns of A are linearly independent. (Try it!)

Applying H_2 to $H_1 A$ preserves the first row and column, and introduces zeros under the diagonal in the second column. To see this, first rewrite $H_1 A$ in block form:

$$H_1 A = \begin{pmatrix} \|\mathbf{y}_1\| & \mathbf{g}_2^T \\ \mathbf{0} & G_2 \end{pmatrix}$$

where we used our previous observation about the first column of $H_1 A$ and where $\mathbf{g}_2 \in \mathbb{R}^{m-1}$, $G_2 \in \mathbb{R}^{(n-1) \times (m-1)}$. One important point to note: The first column of G_2 is equal to $\mathbf{y}_2$. Now multiply by H_2 to get

$$H_2 H_1 A = \begin{pmatrix} 1 & \mathbf{0} \\ \mathbf{0} & F_2 \end{pmatrix} \begin{pmatrix} \|\mathbf{y}_1\| & \mathbf{g}_2^T \\ \mathbf{0} & G_2 \end{pmatrix} = \begin{pmatrix} \|\mathbf{y}_1\| & \mathbf{g}_2^T \\ \mathbf{0} & F_2 G_2 \end{pmatrix}.$$

Computing the block $F_2 G_2$ column by column we get

$$F_2 G_2 = \begin{pmatrix} F_2 \mathbf{y}_2 & F_2 (G_2)_{\cdot,2} & \cdots & F_2 (G_2)_{\cdot,m-1} \end{pmatrix}$$
$$= \begin{pmatrix} \|\mathbf{y}_2\| \mathbf{e}_1^{(n-1)} & F_2 (G_2)_{\cdot,2} & \cdots & F_2 (G_2)_{\cdot,m-1} \end{pmatrix}$$

where $(G_2)_{\cdot,j}$ is the j-th column of G_2. So the second column of $H_2 H_1 A$ has zeros in all but the first two elements.

And so on. At Step k, we split the k-th column of $H_{k-1} \cdots H_1 A$ into its first $k-1$ and last $n-k+1$ entries $(\mathbf{y}^{(k)}, \mathbf{y}_k)$ and form the matrix

$$H_k = \begin{pmatrix} I_{(k-1) \times (k-1)} & \mathbf{0} \\ \mathbf{0} & F_k \end{pmatrix}$$

where

$$F_k = I_{(n-k+1) \times (n-k+1)} - 2\mathbf{z}_k \mathbf{z}_k^T \quad \text{with} \quad \mathbf{z}_k = \frac{\|\mathbf{y}_k\| \mathbf{e}_1^{(n-k+1)} - \mathbf{y}_k}{\|\|\mathbf{y}_k\| \mathbf{e}_1^{(n-k+1)} - \mathbf{y}_k\|}.$$

This time the first $k-1$ rows and columns are preserved, while zeros are introduced under the diagonal of the k-th column. We omit the details (try it!).

We implement the procedure above in Python. We will need the following function. For $\alpha \in \mathbb{R}$, let the sign of α be

$$\text{sign}(\alpha) = \begin{cases} 1 & \text{if } \alpha > 0 \\ 0 & \text{if } \alpha = 0 \\ -1 & \text{if } \alpha < 0. \end{cases}$$

In Python, this is done using the function `numpy.sign`.

The following function constructs the upper-triangular matrix R by iteratively modifying the relevant block of A. On the other hand, computing the matrix Q actually requires extra computational work that is often not needed. We saw that, in the context of the least-squares

2.4 QR Decomposition and Householder Transformations

problem, we really only need to compute $Q^T \mathbf{b}$ for some input vector $\mathbf{b}$. This can be done at the same time that R is constructed, as follows. The key point to note is that $Q^T \mathbf{b} = H_m \cdots H_1 \mathbf{b}$.

We use numpy.outer to compute $\mathbf{zz}^T$, which is referred to as an outer product. See the documentation for an explanation of numpy.copy.

```
def householder(A, b):
    n, m = A.shape
    R = np.copy(A)
    Qtb = np.copy(b)
    for k in range(m):
        
        y = R[k:n,k]
        e1 = np.zeros(n-k)
        e1[0] = 1
        z = np.sign(y[0]) * LA.norm(y) * e1 + y
        z = z / LA.norm(z)
        
        R[k:n,k:m] = R[k:n,k:m] - 2 * np.outer(z, z) @ R[k:n,k:m]
        Qtb[k:n] = Qtb[k:n] - 2 * np.outer(z, z) @ Qtb[k:n]
        
    return R[0:m,0:m], Qtb[0:m]
```

In Problem 2.21, it is shown that there is another Householder reflection $\tilde{H}_1$ such that $\tilde{H}_1 \mathbf{y}_1 = -\|\mathbf{y}_1\| \mathbf{e}_1^{(n)}$. In householder, we use both reflections. We will not prove this here, but the particular choice made has good numerical properties. Quoting [TB, Lecture 10] (where H^+ refers to the hyperplane used for the reflection when $z = 1$):

> Mathematically, either choice of sign is satisfactory. However, this is a case where numerical stability – insensitivity to rounding errors – dictates that one choice should be taken rather than the other. For numerical stability, it is desirable to reflect $\mathbf{x}$ to the vector $z\|\mathbf{x}\|\mathbf{e}_1$ that is not too close to $\mathbf{x}$ itself. [...] Suppose that [in the figure above] the angle between H^+ and the $\mathbf{e}_1$ axis is very small. Then the vector $\mathbf{v} = \|\mathbf{x}\|\mathbf{e}_1 - \mathbf{x}$ is much smaller than $\mathbf{x}$ or $\|\mathbf{x}\|\mathbf{e}_1$. Thus the calculation of $\mathbf{v}$ represents a subtraction of nearby quantities and will tend to suffer from cancellation errors.

NUMERICAL CORNER We return to our overdetermined system example.

```
w1 = np.array([1., 0., 1.])
w2 = np.array([0., 1., 1.])
A = np.stack((w1, w2),axis=-1)
b = np.array([0., 0., 2.])
R, Qtb = householder(A, b)
x = backsubs(R, Qtb)
print(x)
```

```
[0.66666667 0.66666667]
```

One advantage of the Householder approach is that it produces a matrix Q with very good orthogonality, namely $Q^T Q \approx I$. We give a quick example below comparing Gram–Schmidt and Householder. (The choice of matrix A will become clearer when we discuss the singular value decomposition in Chapter 4.)

```
seed = 535
rng = np.random.default_rng(seed)

n = 50
U, W = LA.qr(rng.normal(0,1,(n,n)))
V, W = LA.qr(rng.normal(0,1,(n,n)))
S = np.diag((1/2) ** np.arange(1,n+1))
A = U @ S @ V.T

Qgs, Rgs = gramschmidt(A)
print(LA.norm(A - Qgs @ Rgs))
print(LA.norm(Qgs.T @ Qgs - np.identity(n)))
```

1.4369568046009742e-16
19.745599060592102

As you can see above, the Q and R factors produced by the Gram–Schmidt algorithm do have the property that $QR \approx A$. However, Q is far from orthogonal. (Recall that `LA.norm` computes the Frobenius norm introduced previously.)

On the other hand, Householder reflections perform much better in that respect as we show next. Here we use the implementation of Householder transformations in `numpy.linalg.qr`.

```
Qhh, Rhh = LA.qr(A)
print(LA.norm(A - Qhh @ Rhh))
print(LA.norm(Qhh.T @ Qhh - np.identity(n)))
```

4.739138228891714e-16
5.33506987519293e-15

◁ **NC**

Self-Assessment Quiz (with help from Claude, Gemini, and ChatGPT)

1 Which of the following matrices is upper triangular?

a) $\begin{pmatrix} 1 & 2 \\ 0 & 3 \end{pmatrix}$

b) $\begin{pmatrix} 1 & 0 \\ 2 & 3 \end{pmatrix}$

c) $\begin{pmatrix} 0 & 1 \\ 1 & 0 \end{pmatrix}$

d) $\begin{pmatrix} 1 & 2 \\ 3 & 4 \end{pmatrix}$

2. What is the output of the Gram–Schmidt algorithm when applied to a set of linearly independent vectors?

   a) An orthogonal basis for the subspace spanned by the vectors
   b) An orthonormal basis for the subspace spanned by the vectors
   c) A set of linearly dependent vectors
   d) A single vector that is orthogonal to all the input vectors

3. What is the dimension of a hyperplane in $\mathbb{R}^m$?

   a) m
   b) $m - 1$
   c) $m - 2$
   d) 1

4. Which of the following is true about a Householder reflection?

   a) It is a reflection across a hyperplane orthogonal to a unit vector.
   b) It is a reflection across a unit vector.
   c) It is a rotation around a hyperplane orthogonal to a unit vector.
   d) It is a rotation around a unit vector.

5. How can a sequence of Householder reflections be used to compute a QR decomposition of a matrix A?

   a) By iteratively introducing zeros above the diagonal of A
   b) By iteratively introducing zeros below the diagonal of A
   c) By iteratively introducing zeros on the diagonal of A
   d) By iteratively introducing zeros in the entire matrix A

Answer for 1: a. Justification: The text defines an upper triangular matrix as one with all entries below the diagonal equal to zero.

Answer for 2: b. Justification: The text states that the Gram–Schmidt algorithm "produces an orthonormal basis of span$(a_1, \ldots, a_m)$."

Answer for 3: b. Justification: The text defines a hyperplane as a linear subspace of $\mathbb{R}^m$ of dimension $m - 1$.

Answer for 4: a. Justification: The text defines a Householder reflection as follows: "Let $\mathbf{z} \in \mathbb{R}^m$ be a unit vector and let W be the hyperplane orthogonal to it. The reflection across W is given by $H = I_{m \times m} - 2\mathbf{z}\mathbf{z}^T$."

Answer for 5: b. Justification: The text states, "One way to construct a (full) QR decomposition of a matrix $A \in \mathbb{R}^{n \times m}$ is to find a sequence of orthogonal matrices $H_1, \ldots, H_m$ that triangularize A: $H_m \cdots H_2 H_1 A = R$ for an upper-triangular matrix R."

2.5 Application: Regression Analysis

We return to our motivating example, the regression problem, and apply the least-squares approach.

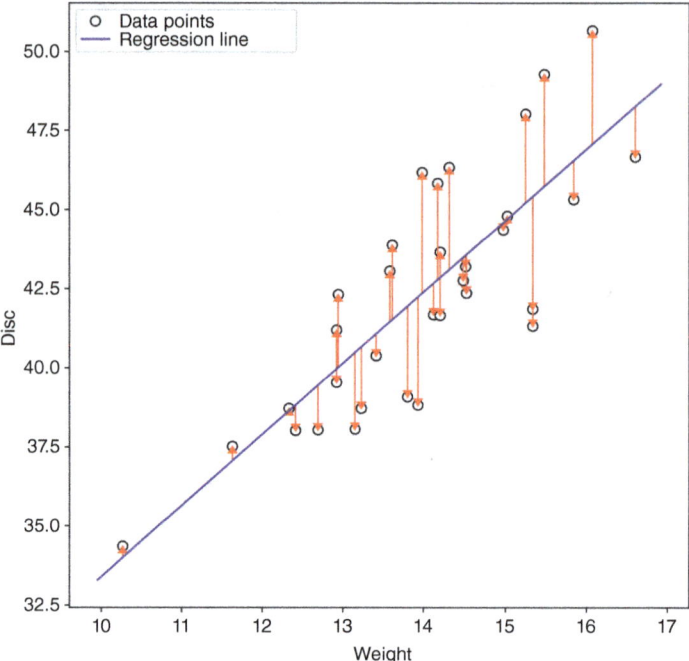

Figure 2.8 A regression line.

2.5.1 Linear Regression

Linear Regression We seek an affine function to fit input data points $\{(\mathbf{x}_i, y_i)\}_{i=1}^n$. The common approach involves finding coefficients β_j's that minimize the criterion

$$\sum_{i=1}^{n}\left(y_i - \left\{\beta_0 + \sum_{j=1}^{d}\beta_j x_{i,j}\right\}\right)^2.$$

This is indeed a linear least-squares problem. See Figure 2.8.[4]

In matrix form, let

$$\mathbf{y} = \begin{pmatrix} y_1 \\ y_2 \\ \vdots \\ y_n \end{pmatrix}, \qquad A = \begin{pmatrix} 1 & \mathbf{x}_1^T \\ 1 & \mathbf{x}_2^T \\ \vdots & \vdots \\ 1 & \mathbf{x}_n^T \end{pmatrix}, \quad \text{and} \quad \boldsymbol{\beta} = \begin{pmatrix} \beta_0 \\ \beta_1 \\ \vdots \\ \beta_d \end{pmatrix}.$$

Then the problem is

$$\min_{\boldsymbol{\beta}} \|\mathbf{y} - A\boldsymbol{\beta}\|^2.$$

We assume that the columns of A are linearly independent, which is often the case with real data (unless there is an algebraic relationship between some columns). The normal equations are then

$$A^T A \boldsymbol{\beta} = A^T \mathbf{y}.$$

---

[4] Code converted by ChatGPT from [HH]. See https://web.stanford.edu/class/bios221/book/07-chap.html

2.5 Application: Regression Analysis

Let $\hat{\boldsymbol{\beta}} = (\hat{\beta}_0, \ldots, \hat{\beta}_d)$ be the unique solution of the system. It gives the vector of coefficients in our fitted model. We refer to

$$\hat{y}_i = \hat{\beta}_0 + \sum_{j=1}^{d} \hat{\beta}_j x_{i,j}, \quad i = 1, \ldots, n$$

as the fitted values and to

$$r_i = y_i - \hat{y}_i, \quad i = 1, \ldots, n$$

as the residuals. In vector form, we obtain $\hat{\mathbf{y}} = (\hat{y}_1, \ldots, \hat{y}_n)$ and $\mathbf{r} = (r_1, \ldots, r_n)$ as

$$\hat{\mathbf{y}} = A\hat{\boldsymbol{\beta}} \quad \text{and} \quad \mathbf{r} = \mathbf{y} - \hat{\mathbf{y}}.$$

The residual sum of squares (RSS) is given by

$$\sum_{i=1}^{n} r_i^2 = \sum_{i=1}^{n} \left(y_i - \left\{ \hat{\beta}_0 + \sum_{j=1}^{d} \hat{\beta}_j x_{i,j} \right\} \right)^2$$

or, in vector form,

$$\|\mathbf{r}\|^2 = \|\mathbf{y} - \hat{\mathbf{y}}\|^2 = \|\mathbf{y} - A\hat{\boldsymbol{\beta}}\|^2.$$

NUMERICAL CORNER We test our least-squares method on simulated data. This has the advantage that we know the truth.

Suppose the truth is a linear function of one variable.

```
n, b0, b1 = 100, -1, 1
x = np.linspace(0,10,num=n)
y = b0 + b1*x

plt.scatter(x, y, s=3, c='k')
plt.show()
```

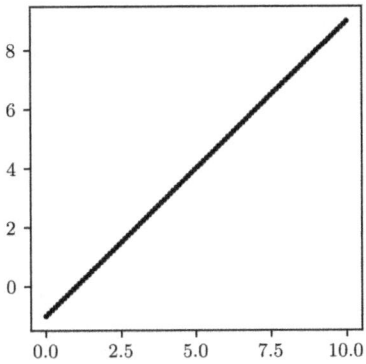

Figure 2.9 Graphical output of code.

A perfect straight line is little too easy. So let's add some noise. That is, to each y_i we add an independent random variable ε_i with a standard Normal distribution (mean 0, variance 1).

```
seed = 535
rng = np.random.default_rng(seed)

y += rng.normal(0,1,n)

plt.scatter(x, y, s=5, c='k')
plt.show()
```

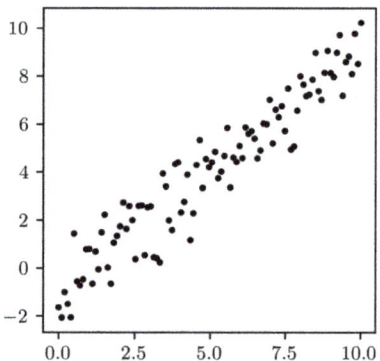

Figure 2.10 Graphical output of code.

We form the matrix A and use our least-squares code to solve for $\hat{\beta}$. The function ls_by_qr, which we implemented previously, is in mmids.py, which is available on the GitHub of the book.[5]

```
A = np.stack((np.ones(n),x),axis=-1)
coeff = mmids.ls_by_qr(A,y)
print(coeff)
```

```
[-1.03381171  1.01808039]
```

```
plt.scatter(x, y, s=5, c='b', alpha=0.5)
plt.plot(x, coeff[0]+coeff[1]*x, 'r')
plt.show()
```

---

[5] See https://github.com/MMiDS-textbook/MMiDS-textbook.github.io/tree/main

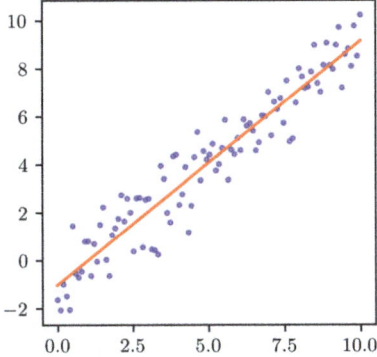

Figure 2.11 Graphical output of code.

◁ NC

2.5.2 Polynomial Regression (and Overfitting)

2.5.2.1 Beyond Linearity

The linear assumption is not as restrictive as it may first appear. The same approach can be extended straightforwardly to fit polynomials or more complicated combination of functions. For instance, suppose $d = 1$. To fit a second-degree polynomial to the data $\{(x_i, y_i)\}_{i=1}^n$, we add a column to the A matrix with the squares of the x_i's. That is, we let

$$A = \begin{pmatrix} 1 & x_1 & x_1^2 \\ 1 & x_2 & x_2^2 \\ \vdots & \vdots & \vdots \\ 1 & x_n & x_n^2 \end{pmatrix}.$$

Then, we are indeed fitting a degree-two polynomial as follows:

$$(A\boldsymbol{\beta})_i = \beta_0 + \beta_1 x_i + \beta_2 x_i^2.$$

The solution otherwise remains the same.

This idea of adding columns can also be used to model interactions between predictors. Suppose $d = 2$. Then we can consider the following A matrix, where the last column combines both predictors into their product,

$$A = \begin{pmatrix} 1 & x_{11} & x_{12} & x_{11}x_{12} \\ 1 & x_{21} & x_{22} & x_{21}x_{22} \\ \vdots & \vdots & \vdots & \vdots \\ 1 & x_{n1} & x_{n2} & x_{n1}x_{n2} \end{pmatrix}.$$

NUMERICAL CORNER Suppose the truth is in fact a degree-two polynomial of one variable with Gaussian noise.

```
n, b0, b1, b2 = 100, 0, 0, 1
x = np.linspace(0,10,num=n)
y = b0 + b1 * x + b2 * x**2 + 10*rng.normal(0,1,n)
```

```
plt.scatter(x, y, s=5, c='k')
plt.show()
```

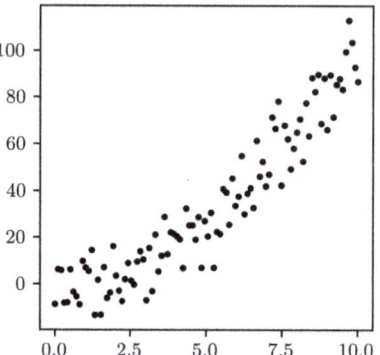

Figure 2.12 Graphical output of code.

We form the matrix A and use our least-squares code to solve for $\hat{\beta}$.

```
A = np.stack((np.ones(n), x, x**2), axis=-1)
coeff = mmids.ls_by_qr(A,y)
print(coeff)
```

[-2.76266982 1.01627798 0.93554204]

```
plt.scatter(x, y, s=5, c='b', alpha=0.5)
plt.plot(x, coeff[0] + coeff[1] * x + coeff[2] * x**2, 'r')
plt.show()
```

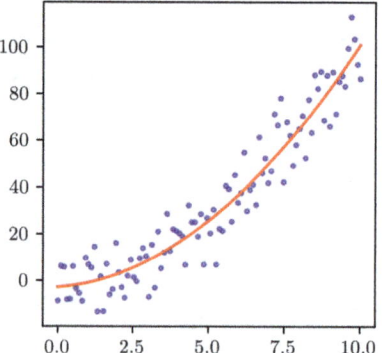

Figure 2.13 Graphical output of code.

◁ NC

2.5 Application: Regression Analysis

2.5.2.2 Overfitting in Polynomial Regression

In adding more parameters, one must worry about overfitting. To quote Wikipedia[6]:

> In statistics, overfitting is "the production of an analysis that corresponds too closely or exactly to a particular set of data, and may therefore fail to fit additional data or predict future observations reliably." An overfitted model is a statistical model that contains more parameters than can be justified by the data. The essence of overfitting is to have unknowingly extracted some of the residual variation (i.e. the noise) as if that variation represented underlying model structure.

We briefly illustrate this issue on the `Advertising` dataset.

NUMERICAL CORNER We return to the `Advertising` dataset from [JWH+]. We load the dataset again.

```
data = pd.read_csv('advertising.csv')
```

We will focus for now on the TV budget. We form the matrix A and use our least-squares code to solve for β.

```
TV = data['TV'].to_numpy()
sales = data['sales'].to_numpy()
n = np.size(TV)
A = np.stack((np.ones(n),TV),axis=-1)
coeff = mmids.ls_by_qr(A,sales)
print(coeff)
```

```
[7.03259355 0.04753664]
```

```
TVgrid = np.linspace(TV.min(), TV.max(), num=100)
plt.scatter(TV, sales, s=5, c='b', alpha=0.5)
plt.plot(TVgrid, coeff[0]+coeff[1]*TVgrid, 'r')
plt.show()
```

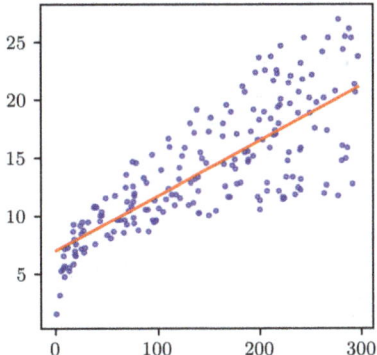

Figure 2.14 Graphical output of code.

---

[6] https://en.wikipedia.org/wiki/Overfitting

A degree-two polynomial might be a better fit.

```
A = np.stack((np.ones(n), TV, TV**2), axis=-1)
coeff = mmids.ls_by_qr(A,sales)
print(coeff)
```

```
[ 6.11412013e+00  6.72659270e-02 -6.84693373e-05]
```

```
plt.scatter(TV, sales, s=5, c='b', alpha=0.5)
plt.plot(TVgrid,
    coeff[0] + coeff[1] * TVgrid + coeff[2]* TVgrid**2, 'r')
plt.show()
```

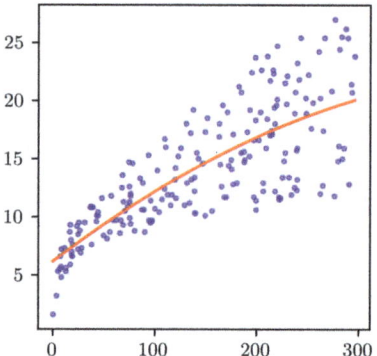

Figure 2.15 Graphical output of code.

The fit looks slightly better than the linear one. This is not entirely surprising though, given that the linear model is a subset of the quadratic one. But as we mentioned earlier, when adding more parameters we must now worry about overfitting the data. To illustrate, let's see what happens with a degree-20 polynomial fit.

```
deg = 20
A = np.stack([TV**i for i in range(deg+1)], axis=-1)
coeff = mmids.ls_by_qr(A,sales)
print(coeff)
```

```
[ 1.06538698e+00  6.72896471e-01 -1.53138969e-02 -2.74088516e-04
  1.83651714e-05 -3.40080020e-07  3.17915742e-09 -1.64042005e-11
  4.43633296e-14 -4.25654490e-17 -5.28727398e-20  1.11822932e-22
 -3.47096893e-27 -2.44665112e-30 -2.79435976e-33 -4.05263859e-36
 -6.83137511e-39 -1.27993830e-41 -2.59569760e-44 -5.59960687e-47
 -1.26949578e-49]
```

```
saleshat = np.sum([coeff[i] * TVgrid**i for i in range(deg+1)],
            axis=0)
```

2.5 Application: Regression Analysis

```
plt.scatter(TV, sales, s=5, c='b', alpha=0.5)
plt.plot(TVgrid, saleshat, 'r')
plt.show()
```

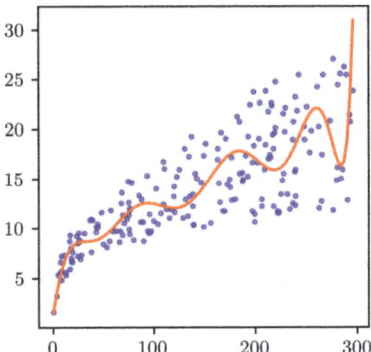

Figure 2.16 Graphical output of code.

The outcome now seems to vary wildly, seemingly driven by the randomness of the data.

◁ NC

CHAT & LEARN Ask your favorite AI chatbot about using cross-validation to choose a suitable degree. Ask for code and *apply it to this dataset*.

Self-Assessment Quiz (with help from Claude, Gemini, and ChatGPT)

1. In linear regression, the goal is to find coefficients β_j's that minimize which of the following criteria?
   a) $\sum_{i=1}^{n}(y_i - \beta_0 - \sum_{j=1}^{d} \beta_j x_{ij})$
   b) $\sum_{i=1}^{n}(y_i - \beta_0 - \sum_{j=1}^{d} \beta_j x_{ij})^2$
   c) $\sum_{i=1}^{n}(y_i - \{\beta_0 + \sum_{j=1}^{d} \beta_j x_{ij}\}^2)$
   d) $\sum_{i=1}^{n}|y_i - \beta_0 - \sum_{j=1}^{d} \beta_j x_{ij}|$

2. The normal equations for linear regression are:
   a) $A^T A \beta = A^T y$
   b) $A A^T \beta = A y$
   c) $A^T A \beta = A y$
   d) $A A^T \beta = A^T y$

3. In the numerical example with a degree-20 polynomial fit, the fitted curve
   a) fits the data perfectly.
   b) fails to capture the overall trend in the data.
   c) captures the noise in the data as if it were the underlying structure.
   d) is a straight line.

4 What is the primary advantage of using simulated data to test the least-squares method?

  a) Simulated data eliminates the need for real-world data.
  b) Simulated data provides a perfect fit without noise.
  c) Simulated data allows us to know the ground truth.
  d) Simulated data reduces computational complexity.

5 Which of the following best describes overfitting?

  a) The model fits the training data well but generalizes poorly to new data.
  b) The model fits both the training data and new data well.
  c) The model fits the training data poorly but generalizes well to new data.
  d) The model ignores random noise in the training data.

Answer for 1: b. Justification: The text states that in linear regression, we seek to find coefficients β_j's that minimize the criterion $\sum_{i=1}^{n}(y_i - \beta_0 - \sum_{j=1}^{d}\beta_j x_{ij})^2$.

Answer for 2: a. Justification: The text states, "The normal equations are then $A^T A \beta = A^T y$."

Answer for 3: c. Justification: The text states that "The essence of overfitting is to have unknowingly extracted some of the residual variation (i.e., the noise) as if that variation represented underlying model structure."

Answer for 4: c. Justification: The text notes, "This has the advantage that we know the truth."

Answer for 5: a. Justification: The text quotes Wikipedia: "An overfitted model is a statistical model that contains more parameters than can be justified by the data."

2.6 Exercises

2.6.1 Warm-Up Worksheets
(with help from Claude, Gemini, and ChatGPT)

Section 2.2

E2.2.1 Determine whether the set $U = \{(x, y, z) \in \mathbb{R}^3 : x + 2y - z = 0\}$ is a linear subspace of $\mathbb{R}^3$.

E2.2.2 Determine whether the vectors $\mathbf{u}_1 = (1, 1, 1)$, $\mathbf{u}_2 = (1, 0, -1)$, and $\mathbf{u}_3 = (2, 1, 0)$ are linearly independent.

E2.2.3 Find a basis for the subspace $U = \{(x, y, z) \in \mathbb{R}^3 : x - y + z = 0\}$.

E2.2.4 Find the dimension of the subspace $U = \{(x, y, z, w) \in \mathbb{R}^4 : x + y = 0, z = w\}$.

E2.2.5 Verify whether the vectors $\mathbf{u}_1 = (1/\sqrt{2}, 1/\sqrt{2})$, $\mathbf{u}_2 = (1/\sqrt{2}, -1/\sqrt{2})$ form an orthonormal list.

E2.2.6 Given the orthonormal basis $\mathbf{q}_1 = (1/\sqrt{2}, 1/\sqrt{2})$, $\mathbf{q}_2 = (1/\sqrt{2}, -1/\sqrt{2})$, find the orthonormal expansion of $\mathbf{w} = (1, 0)$.

E2.2.7 Determine if the matrix $A = \begin{pmatrix} 1 & 2 \\ 3 & 4 \end{pmatrix}$ is nonsingular.

E2.2.8 Solve the system of equations $A\mathbf{x} = \mathbf{b}$, where $A = \begin{pmatrix} 1 & 2 \\ 3 & 4 \end{pmatrix}$ and $\mathbf{b} = (5, 11)$.

E2.2.9 Given the vectors $\mathbf{w}_1 = (1, 0, 1)$ and $\mathbf{w}_2 = (0, 1, 1)$, express the vector $\mathbf{v} = (2, 3, 5)$ as a linear combination of $\mathbf{w}_1$ and $\mathbf{w}_2$.

E2.2.10 Verify if the vectors $\mathbf{u} = (1, 2, 3)$ and $\mathbf{v} = (4, -2, 1)$ are orthogonal.

E2.2.11 Find the null space of the matrix $B = \begin{pmatrix} 1 & 2 & 3 \\ 4 & 5 & 6 \end{pmatrix}$.

E2.2.12 Given the basis $\{\mathbf{e}_1, \mathbf{e}_2, \mathbf{e}_3\}$ for $\mathbb{R}^3$, express the vector $\mathbf{v} = (4, 5, 6)$ as a linear combination of the basis vectors.

E2.2.13 Determine whether the vectors $\mathbf{u}_1 = (1, 2, 3)$, $\mathbf{u}_2 = (2, -1, 0)$, and $\mathbf{u}_3 = (1, 8, 6)$ are linearly independent.

E2.2.14 Verify the *Cauchy–Schwarz Inequality* for the vectors $\mathbf{u} = (2, 1)$ and $\mathbf{v} = (1, -3)$.

E2.2.15 Solve the system of equations $2x + y = 3$ and $x - y = 1$ using matrix inversion.

Section 2.3

E2.3.1 Let $Q = \begin{pmatrix} \frac{1}{\sqrt{2}} & \frac{-1}{\sqrt{6}} \\ 0 & \frac{2}{\sqrt{6}} \\ \frac{1}{\sqrt{2}} & \frac{1}{\sqrt{6}} \end{pmatrix}$. Is Q an orthogonal matrix?

E2.3.2 True or False: The orthogonal projection of a vector onto a subspace is always strictly shorter than the original vector.

E2.3.3 For the vector $\mathbf{v} = (2, 3)$ and the linear subspace U made from the line spanned by $\mathbf{u} = (1, 1)$, find the orthogonal projection $\text{proj}_U \mathbf{v}$.

E2.3.4 Let $U = \text{span}((1, 1, 0))$ and $\mathbf{v} = (1, 2, 3)$. Compute $\|\mathbf{v}\|^2$ and $\|\text{proj}_U \mathbf{v}\|^2$.

E2.3.5 Find the orthogonal projection of $\mathbf{v} = (1, 2, 1)$ onto the subspace spanned by $\mathbf{u} = (1, 1, 0)$.

E2.3.6 Let $U = \text{span}((1, 0, 1), (0, 1, 1))$. Find a basis for $U^\perp$.

E2.3.7 Let $\mathbf{v} = (1, 2, 3)$ and $U = \text{span}((1, 0, 1), (0, 1, 1))$. Compute $\text{proj}_U \mathbf{v}$.

E2.3.8 Let $\mathbf{v} = (1, 2, 3)$ and $U = \text{span}((1, 0, 1), (0, 1, 1))$. Decompose $\mathbf{v}$ into its orthogonal projection onto U and a vector in $U^\perp$.

E2.3.9 Let $\mathbf{v} = (1, 2, 3)$ and $U = \text{span}((1, 0, 1), (0, 1, 1))$. Verify *Pythagoras' Theorem*: $\|\mathbf{v}\|^2 = \|\text{proj}_U \mathbf{v}\|^2 + \|\mathbf{v} - \text{proj}_U \mathbf{v}\|^2$.

E2.3.10 Let $A = \begin{pmatrix} 1 & 0 \\ 0 & 1 \\ 1 & 1 \end{pmatrix}$. Is $P = AA^T$ an orthogonal projection matrix?

E2.3.11 Let $\mathbf{u}_1 = \begin{pmatrix} 2 \\ 1 \\ -2 \end{pmatrix}$ and $\mathbf{u}_2 = \begin{pmatrix} 1 \\ 1 \\ 1 \end{pmatrix}$. Compute $\text{proj}_{\mathbf{u}_1} \mathbf{u}_2$.

E2.3.12 Find the orthogonal complement of the subspace spanned by $\mathbf{u} = (1, 1, 0)$ in $\mathbb{R}^3$.

E2.3.13 Let $W = \text{span}((1, 1, 0))$. Find a basis for $W^\perp$.

E2.3.14 Let $A = \begin{pmatrix} 1 & 2 \\ 0 & 1 \\ 1 & 0 \end{pmatrix}$ and $\mathbf{b} = \begin{pmatrix} 3 \\ 1 \\ 2 \end{pmatrix}$. Set up the normal equations to solve the linear least-squares problem $A\mathbf{x} \approx \mathbf{b}$.

E2.3.15 Solve the normal equation $A^T A \mathbf{x} = A^T \mathbf{b}$ for $A = \begin{pmatrix} 1 & 1 \\ 1 & -1 \end{pmatrix}$ and $\mathbf{b} = \begin{pmatrix} 3 \\ 1 \end{pmatrix}$.

E2.3.16 Let $\mathbf{a} = (1, 2, 1)$ and $\mathbf{b} = (1, 0, -1)$. Find the orthogonal projection of $\mathbf{a}$ onto span($\mathbf{b}$).

Section 2.4

E2.4.1 Let $\mathbf{a}_1 = (1, 0)$ and $\mathbf{a}_2 = (1, 1)$. Apply the Gram–Schmidt algorithm to find an orthonormal basis for span($\mathbf{a}_1, \mathbf{a}_2$).

E2.4.2 Determine the QR decomposition of the matrix $A = \begin{pmatrix} 1 & 1 \\ 0 & 1 \end{pmatrix}$ using the Gram–Schmidt algorithm.

E2.4.3 Apply the Gram–Schmidt algorithm to transform the basis $\{(1, 1), (1, 0)\}$ into an orthonormal basis.

E2.4.4 Given the vectors $\mathbf{a}_1 = (1, 1, 1)$, $\mathbf{a}_2 = (1, 0, -1)$, apply the Gram–Schmidt algorithm to obtain an orthonormal basis for span($\mathbf{a}_1, \mathbf{a}_2$).

E2.4.5 For the vectors $\mathbf{a}_1$ and $\mathbf{a}_2$ from E2.4.4, find the QR decomposition of the matrix $A = [\mathbf{a}_1 \ \mathbf{a}_2]$.

E2.4.6 Solve the system $R\mathbf{x} = \begin{pmatrix} 1 & 1 \\ 0 & 2 \end{pmatrix} \mathbf{x} = \begin{pmatrix} 1 \\ 2 \end{pmatrix}$ using back substitution.

E2.4.7 Let $R = \begin{pmatrix} 2 & -1 \\ 0 & 3 \end{pmatrix}$ and $\mathbf{b} = (4, 3)$. Solve the system of equations $R\mathbf{x} = \mathbf{b}$ using back substitution.

E2.4.8 Given the matrix $A = \begin{pmatrix} 1 & 1 \\ 0 & 1 \end{pmatrix}$ and the vector $\mathbf{b} = (1, 2)$, solve the least-squares problem $\min_{\mathbf{x} \in \mathbb{R}^2} \|A\mathbf{x} - \mathbf{b}\|$ using the QR decomposition.

E2.4.9 Let $\mathbf{z} = (1, -1, 0)$. Find the Householder reflection matrix H that reflects across the hyperplane orthogonal to $\mathbf{z}$.

E2.4.10 Find the Householder reflection matrix that introduces zeros below the diagonal in the first column of the matrix $A = \begin{pmatrix} 1 & 2 \\ 3 & 4 \end{pmatrix}$.

E2.4.11 Verify that the Householder reflection matrix H_1 from E2.4.10 is orthogonal and symmetric.

E2.4.12 Apply the Householder reflection matrix H_1 from E2.4.10 to the matrix A from E2.4.10 and verify that it introduces zeros below the diagonal in the first column.

E2.4.13 Using the Householder reflection matrix H_1 from E2.4.10, find the QR decomposition of the matrix A from E2.4.10.

E2.4.14 Verify that the QR decomposition from E2.4.13 satisfies $A = QR$ and that Q is orthogonal.

E2.4.15 Let $A = \begin{pmatrix} 3 & 1 \\ 4 & 2 \end{pmatrix}$. Find a Householder reflection matrix H_1 such that the first column of $H_1 A$ has a zero in the second entry.

E2.4.16 Let $A = \begin{pmatrix} 1 & 1 \\ 1 & -1 \\ 0 & 1 \end{pmatrix}$ and $\mathbf{b} = (2, 0, 1)$. Set up the normal equations $A^T A \mathbf{x} = A^T \mathbf{b}$ for the linear least squares problem associated with A and $\mathbf{b}$.

E2.4.17 Use the QR decomposition to solve the linear least-squares problem $Ax = b$ for $A = \begin{pmatrix} 1 & 1 \\ 1 & -1 \end{pmatrix}$ and $b = \begin{pmatrix} 2 \\ 0 \end{pmatrix}$.

Section 2.5

E2.5.1 Given the data points $(x_1, y_1) = (1, 2)$, $(x_2, y_2) = (2, 4)$, $(x_3, y_3) = (3, 5)$, and $(x_4, y_4) = (4, 7)$, find the coefficients β_0 and β_1 that minimize the least-squares criterion $\sum_{i=1}^{4} (y_i - \beta_0 - \beta_1 x_i)^2$.

E2.5.2 For the data points in E2.5.1, compute the fitted values and residuals for the linear regression model.

E2.5.3 Given the data points $(x_1, y_1) = (1, 3)$, $(x_2, y_2) = (2, 5)$, and $(x_3, y_3) = (3, 8)$, construct the needed A and y for finding the least-squares line.

E2.5.4 For the data in E2.5.3, compute the normal equations $A^T A \beta = A^T y$.

E2.5.5 Solve the normal equations from E2.5.4 to find the coefficients β_0 and β_1 of the least-squares line.

E2.5.6 Using the data from E2.5.3 and the fitted line from E2.5.5, calculate the residuals for each data point.

E2.5.7 Given the data points $(x_1, y_1) = (-1, 2)$, $(x_2, y_2) = (0, 1)$, and $(x_3, y_3) = (1, 3)$, construct the matrix A for fitting a quadratic polynomial (degree 2).

E2.5.8 Suppose we have a sample of $n = 100$ observations and we perform bootstrapping by resampling with replacement.[7] What is the probability that a specific observation is included in a given bootstrap sample?

E2.5.9 Given the matrix $A = \begin{pmatrix} 1 & 1 \\ 1 & 2 \\ 1 & 3 \end{pmatrix}$ and the vector $y = \begin{pmatrix} 1 \\ 2 \\ 3 \end{pmatrix}$, solve for the coefficients β in the least-squares problem.

E2.5.10 For the polynomial regression problem $y = \beta_0 + \beta_1 x + \beta_2 x^2$ with points $(0, 1)$, $(1, 2)$, $(2, 5)$, form the matrix A.

E2.5.11 What is the residual sum of squares (RSS) for the linear fit $y = 2x + 1$ on the data points $(1, 3), (2, 5), (3, 7)$?

E2.5.12 For the polynomial regression $y = \beta_0 + \beta_1 x + \beta_2 x^2$ on points $(1, 1), (2, 4), (3, 9)$, find the normal equations.

2.6.2 Problems

2.1 Show that **0** is an element of any (non-empty) linear subspace.

2.2 Prove that $\text{null}(B)$ is a linear subspace.

2.3 Let $\beta_j \neq 0$ for all $j \in [m]$. Show that $\text{span}(\beta_1 w_1, \ldots, \beta_m w_m) = \text{span}(w_1, \ldots, w_m)$.

2.4 (Adapted from [Sol]) Suppose that U_1 and U_2 are linear subspaces of vector space V. Show that $U_1 \cap U_2$ is a linear subspace of V. Is $U_1 \cup U_2$ always a linear subspace of V?

2.5 Let $\mathcal{U}, \mathcal{V}$ be linear subspaces of V such that $\mathcal{U} \subseteq \mathcal{V}$. Show that $\dim(\mathcal{U}) \leq \dim(\mathcal{V})$. [*Hint:* Complete the basis.]

---

[7] For more information on bootstrapping, see: https://mmids-textbook.github.io/chap02_ls/supp/roch-mmids-ls-supp.html

2.6 (Adapted from [Axl]) Prove that if $\{\mathbf{v}_1, \ldots, \mathbf{v}_n\}$ spans U, then so does the list

$$\{\mathbf{v}_1 - \mathbf{v}_2, \mathbf{v}_2 - \mathbf{v}_3, \ldots, \mathbf{v}_{n-1} - \mathbf{v}_n, \mathbf{v}_n\}$$

obtained by subtracting from each vector (except the last one) the following vector.

2.7 (Adapted from [Axl]) Prove that if $\{\mathbf{v}_1, \ldots, \mathbf{v}_n\}$ is linearly independent, then so is the list

$$\{\mathbf{v}_1 - \mathbf{v}_2, \mathbf{v}_2 - \mathbf{v}_3, \ldots, \mathbf{v}_{n-1} - \mathbf{v}_n, \mathbf{v}_n\}$$

obtained by subtracting from each vector (except the last one) the following vector.

2.8 (Adapted from [Axl]) Suppose $\{\mathbf{v}_1, \ldots, \mathbf{v}_n\}$ are linearly independent in U and $\mathbf{w} \in U$. Prove that if $\{\mathbf{v}_1 + \mathbf{w}, \ldots, \mathbf{v}_n + \mathbf{w}\}$ are linearly dependent, then $\mathbf{w} \in \text{span}(\mathbf{v}_1, \ldots, \mathbf{v}_n)$.

2.9 Establish that $U^\perp$ is a linear subspace.

2.10 Let $U \subseteq V$ be a linear subspace and let $\mathbf{v} \in U$. Show that $\text{proj}_U \mathbf{v} = \mathbf{v}$.

2.11 Let $A \in \mathbb{R}^{n \times n}$ be a square matrix. Show that, if for any $\mathbf{b} \in \mathbb{R}^n$ there exists a unique $\mathbf{x} \in \mathbb{R}^n$ such that $A\mathbf{x} = \mathbf{b}$, then A is nonsingular. [*Hint*: Consider $\mathbf{b} = \mathbf{0}$.]

2.12 Show that, if $B \in \mathbb{R}^{n \times m}$ and $C \in \mathbb{R}^{m \times p}$, then $(BC)^T = C^T B^T$. [*Hint*: Check that the entries match.]

2.13 Let $A \in \mathbb{R}^{n \times m}$ be an $n \times m$ matrix with linearly independent columns. Show that $m \leq n$.

2.14 Is the vector $\mathbf{v} = (0, 0, 1)$ in the span of

$$\mathbf{q}_1 = \frac{1}{\sqrt{2}} \begin{pmatrix} 1 \\ 0 \\ 1 \end{pmatrix}, \quad \mathbf{q}_2 = \frac{1}{\sqrt{3}} \begin{pmatrix} -1 \\ 1 \\ 1 \end{pmatrix}$$

2.15 Given a vector $\mathbf{v} = (1, 2, 3)$ and a plane spanned by $\mathbf{u}_1 = (1, 0, 0)$ and $\mathbf{u}_2 = (0, 1, 0)$, find the orthogonal projection of $\mathbf{v}$ onto this plane.

2.16 Given the orthonormal basis $\{(1/\sqrt{2}, 1/\sqrt{2}), (-1/\sqrt{2}, 1/\sqrt{2})\}$, find the projection of the vector $\mathbf{v} = (3, 3)$ onto the subspace spanned by this basis.

2.17 Find the orthogonal projection of the vector $\mathbf{v} = (4, 3, 0)$ onto the line spanned by $\mathbf{u} = (1, 1, 1)$ in $\mathbb{R}^3$.

2.18 Let $Q, W \in \mathbb{R}^{n \times n}$ be invertible. Show that $(QW)^{-1} = W^{-1} Q^{-1}$ and $(Q^T)^{-1} = (Q^{-1})^T$.

2.19 Prove the *Reducing a Spanning List Lemma*.

2.20 Show that for any $\mathbf{x}_1, \mathbf{x}_2, \mathbf{x}_3 \in \mathbb{R}^n$ and $\beta \in \mathbb{R}$:

a) $\langle \mathbf{x}_1, \mathbf{x}_2 \rangle = \langle \mathbf{x}_2, \mathbf{x}_1 \rangle$

b) $\langle \beta \mathbf{x}_1 + \mathbf{x}_2, \mathbf{x}_3 \rangle = \beta \langle \mathbf{x}_1, \mathbf{x}_3 \rangle + \langle \mathbf{x}_2, \mathbf{x}_3 \rangle$

c) $\|\mathbf{x}_1\|^2 = \langle \mathbf{x}_1, \mathbf{x}_1 \rangle$

2.21 Using the notation introduced for Householder reflections, define

$$\tilde{\mathbf{z}}_1 = \frac{\|\mathbf{y}_1\| \mathbf{e}_1^{(n)} + \mathbf{y}_1}{\|\|\mathbf{y}_1\| \mathbf{e}_1^{(n)} + \mathbf{y}_1\|} \quad \text{and} \quad \tilde{H}_1 = I_{n \times n} - 2\tilde{\mathbf{z}}_1 \tilde{\mathbf{z}}_1^T.$$

a) Show that $\tilde{H}_1 \mathbf{y}_1 = -\|\mathbf{y}_1\| \mathbf{e}_1^{(n)}$.

b) Compute the matrix $\tilde{H}_1$ in the case $\mathbf{y}_1 = \|\mathbf{y}_1\| \mathbf{e}_1^{(n)}$.

2.22 Show that the product of two orthogonal matrices Q_1 and Q_2 is also orthogonal.

2.23 Establish that $(U^\perp)^\perp = U$.

2.24 Compute $U^\perp \cap U$ and justify your answer.

2.25 (Adapted from [Sol]) If $\mathbf{x}, \mathbf{y} \in \mathbb{R}^m$ with $\|\mathbf{x}\| = \|\mathbf{y}\|$, write an algorithm for finding an orthogonal matrix Q such that $Q\mathbf{x} = \mathbf{y}$.

2.26 (Adapted from [Sol]) Suppose $A \in \mathbb{R}^{m \times n}$ has rank m, with $m \leq n$. Let

$$A^T = QR$$

be the QR decomposition of A^T obtained by the Gram–Schmidt algorithm. Provide a solution $\mathbf{x}$ to the underdetermined system $A\mathbf{x} = \mathbf{b}$ in terms of Q and R. [*Hint:* Try the square case first. Then guess and check the solution to the general case by adding 0's.]

2.27 (Adapted from [Sol]) Let $A \in \mathbb{R}^{m \times m}$ have full column rank and suppose $L \in \mathbb{R}^{m \times m}$ is a lower-triangular matrix with positive diagonal entries such that $A^T A = LL^T$ (this is called a Cholesky decomposition).

a) Prove that L^T is invertible by showing that its columns are linearly independent.

b) Define $Q = A(L^T)^{-1}$. Show that the columns of Q form an orthonormal list.

c) Give a QR decomposition of A using the matrix Q in (b). Make sure to show that R has the desired structure.

2.28 (Adapted from [Sol]) Suppose $A \in \mathbb{R}^{m \times n}$ has full column rank and $A = QR$ is a QR decomposition obtained by the Gram–Schmidt algorithm. Show that $P_0 = I_{m \times m} - QQ^T$ is the projection matrix onto the null space of A^T. [*Hint:* Check the geometric characterization in the *Orthogonal Projection Theorem*.]

2.29 Suppose we consider $\mathbf{a} \in \mathbb{R}^n$ as an $n \times 1$ matrix. Write out its QR decomposition explicitly.

2.30 (Adapted from [Sol]) Show that a matrix $A \in \mathbb{R}^{m \times n}$ with linearly independent columns can be factored into $A = QL$, where L is lower triangular. [*Hint:* Modify our procedure for obtaining the QR decomposition.]

2.31 (Adapted from [Sol]) Suppose $A \in \mathbb{R}^{n \times p}$, $B \in \mathbb{R}^{m \times p}$, $\mathbf{a} \in \mathbb{R}^n$, and $\mathbf{b} \in \mathbb{R}^m$. Find a linear system of equations satisfied by any $\mathbf{x}$ minimizing $\|A\mathbf{x} - \mathbf{a}\|^2 + \|B\mathbf{x} - \mathbf{b}\|^2$. [*Hint:* Rewrite the problem as a linear least-squares problem.]

2.32 Let P be a projection matrix. Show that

a) $P^2 = P$

b) $P^T = P$

c) Check the above two claims for the projection onto the span of $\mathbf{u} = (1, 0, 1)$ in $\mathbb{R}^3$.

2.33 Show that for any $\mathbf{x}_1, \ldots, \mathbf{x}_m, \mathbf{y}_1, \ldots, \mathbf{y}_\ell, \in \mathbb{R}^n$,

$$\left\langle \sum_{i=1}^m \mathbf{x}_i, \sum_{j=1}^\ell \mathbf{y}_j \right\rangle = \sum_{i=1}^m \sum_{j=1}^\ell \langle \mathbf{x}_i, \mathbf{y}_j \rangle.$$

2.34 Let $A \in \mathbb{R}^{n \times m}$ be an $n \times m$ matrix with $n \geq m$ and let $\mathbf{b} \in \mathbb{R}^n$ be a vector. Let

$$\mathbf{p}^* = \arg\min_{\mathbf{p} \in U} \|\mathbf{p} - \mathbf{b}\|,$$

and let $\mathbf{x}^*$ be such that $\mathbf{p}^* = A\mathbf{x}^*$. Construct an A and a $\mathbf{b}$ such that $\mathbf{x}^*$ is *not* unique.

2.35 Let $H_k \in \mathbb{R}^{n \times n}$ be a matrix of the form

$$H_k = \begin{pmatrix} I_{(k-1) \times (k-1)} & 0 \\ 0 & F_k \end{pmatrix}$$

where

$$F_k = I_{(n-k+1) \times (n-k+1)} - 2\mathbf{z}_k \mathbf{z}_k^T$$

for some unit vector $\mathbf{z}_k \in \mathbb{R}^{n-k+1}$. Show that H_k is an orthogonal matrix.

2.36 Using the notation for Householder reflections, let A have linearly independent columns.
  a) Assuming that $\mathbf{z}_1 \neq \mathbf{0}$, show that $\mathbf{y}_2 \neq \mathbf{0}$.
  b) Assuming that $\mathbf{z}_1, \mathbf{z}_2 \neq \mathbf{0}$, show that $\mathbf{y}_3 \neq \mathbf{0}$.

2.37 Let $R \in \mathbb{R}^{n \times m}$, with $n \geq m$, be upper triangular with nonzero entries on the diagonal. Show that the columns of R are linearly independent.

2.38 Consider the linear regression problem on input data $\{(\mathbf{x}_i, y_i)\}_{i=1}^n$.
  a) Show that the problem has a unique solution if there are $d+1$ vectors of the form

$$\begin{pmatrix} 1 \\ \mathbf{x}_i \end{pmatrix}$$

  that form an independent list.

  b) Simplify the previous condition in the case $d = 1$, namely when the x_i's are real-valued.

2.39 Let U be a linear subspace of $\mathbb{R}^n$ and assume that $\mathbf{q}_1, \ldots, \mathbf{q}_k$ is an orthonormal basis of U. Let $\mathbf{v} \in \mathbb{R}^n$.
  a) Show that the orthogonal projection of $\mathbf{v}$ onto the subspace $U^\perp$ (i.e., the orthogonal complement of U) is $\mathbf{v} - \text{proj}_U \mathbf{v}$. [*Hint:* Use the geometric characterization of the projection.]
  b) Let Q be the matrix with columns $\mathbf{q}_1, \ldots, \mathbf{q}_k$. Write the projection matrix onto the subspace $U^\perp$ in terms of Q. [*Hint:* Use a).]

2.40 Prove the following claim, which is known as the *Subspace Intersection Lemma*. Let $\mathcal{S}_1$ and $\mathcal{S}_2$ be linear subspaces of $\mathbb{R}^d$ and let

$$\mathcal{S}_1 + \mathcal{S}_2 = \{\mathbf{x}_1 + \mathbf{x}_2 : \forall \mathbf{x}_1 \in \mathcal{S}_1, \mathbf{x}_2 \in \mathcal{S}_2\}.$$

Then it holds that

$$\dim(\mathcal{S}_1 + \mathcal{S}_2) = \dim(\mathcal{S}_1) + \dim(\mathcal{S}_2) - \dim(\mathcal{S}_1 \cap \mathcal{S}_2).$$

[*Hint:* Consider a basis of $\mathcal{S}_1 \cap \mathcal{S}_2$ and complete into bases of $\mathcal{S}_1$ and $\mathcal{S}_2$. Show that the resulting list of vectors is linearly independent.]

2.41 Let $\mathcal{U}, \mathcal{V} \subseteq \mathbb{R}^d$ be subspaces such that $\dim(\mathcal{U}) + \dim(\mathcal{V}) > d$. Use Problem 2.40 to show there exists a nonzero vector in the intersection $\mathcal{U} \cap \mathcal{V}$.

2.42 Show that, for any linear subspaces $\mathcal{S}_1, \ldots, \mathcal{S}_m$ of $\mathcal{V} = \mathbb{R}^d$, it holds that

$$\dim \left(\bigcap_{k=1}^m \mathcal{S}_k \right) \geq \sum_{k=1}^m \dim(\mathcal{S}_k) - (m-1) \dim(\mathcal{V}).$$

[*Hint:* Use the *Subspace Intersection Lemma* in Problem 2.40 and induction.]

2.43 Let $\mathcal{W}$ be a linear subspace of $\mathbb{R}^d$ and let $\mathbf{w}_1, \ldots, \mathbf{w}_k$ be an orthonormal basis of $\mathcal{W}$. Show that there exists an orthonormal basis of $\mathbb{R}^d$ that includes the $\mathbf{w}_i$'s.

2.44 Let $\mathcal{U}, \mathcal{V}$ be linear subspaces of V such that $\mathcal{U} \subseteq \mathcal{V}$. Show that if $\dim(\mathcal{U}) = \dim(\mathcal{V})$ then $\mathcal{U} = \mathcal{V}$. [*Hint:* Complete the basis.]

2.45 Let $\mathcal{U}, \mathcal{V}$ be linear subspaces of V such that $\mathcal{U} \subseteq \mathcal{V}$. Show that if $\dim(\mathcal{U}) < \dim(\mathcal{V})$ then there is a $\mathbf{u} \in \mathcal{V}$ such that $\mathbf{u} \notin \mathcal{U}$. [*Hint:* Complete the basis.]

2.46 Let $\mathcal{Z} \subseteq \mathcal{W}$ be linear subspaces such that $\dim(\mathcal{Z}) < \dim(\mathcal{W})$. Show that there exists a unit vector $\mathbf{w} \in \mathcal{W}$ that is orthogonal to $\mathcal{Z}$.

2.47 Let $\mathcal{W} = \text{span}(\mathbf{w}_1, \ldots, \mathbf{w}_\ell)$ and consider $\mathbf{z} \in \mathcal{W}$ of unit norm. Show that there exists an orthonormal basis of $\mathcal{W}$ that includes $\mathbf{z}$.

2.48 Let $\{\mathbf{u}_1, \ldots, \mathbf{u}_m\}$ be an independent list. Show that for any nonzero $\beta_1, \ldots, \beta_m \in \mathbb{R}$, the list $\{\beta_1 \mathbf{u}_1, \ldots, \beta_m \mathbf{u}_m\}$ is also independent.

2.49 Let $\mathcal{Z}$ be a linear subspace of $\mathbb{R}^n$ and let $\mathbf{v} \in \mathbb{R}^n$. Show that $\|\text{proj}_\mathcal{Z} \mathbf{v}\|_2 \leq \|\mathbf{v}\|_2$.

3 Optimization Theory and Algorithms

In this chapter, we turn to optimization theory and algorithms, which lie at the core of modern data science and AI. We derive basic optimality conditions, including in the presence of convexity. We then introduce a fundamental optimization algorithm, the gradient descent method, and detail a theoretical analysis of its convergence under different assumptions. We illustrate these concepts on an important supervised learning problem. Here is a more detailed overview of the main sections of the chapter.

Background: Review of differentiable functions of several variables: Section 3.2 reviews the fundamental concepts of differentiable functions of several variables. The gradient is defined as a vector of partial derivatives, generalizing the concept of the derivative for functions of a single variable. The section also introduces the Hessian matrix, which contains second-order partial derivatives. The *Chain Rule* for functions of several variables is presented and used to prove a multivariable version of the *Mean Value Theorem*. Finally, the section provides examples of calculating gradients and Hessians for various functions, including affine and quadratic functions.

Optimality conditions: Section 3.3 focuses on deriving optimality conditions for unconstrained continuous optimization problems. It introduces the concept of a global minimizer, which is a point where a function attains its minimum value over its entire domain. Recognizing the difficulty of finding global minimizers, the section also defines local minimizers, points where a function takes its minimum value within a neighborhood. It introduces the concepts of first-order conditions based on the gradient and second-order conditions based on the Hessian matrix. The section explains that while the first-order necessary condition of the gradient being zero at a point is not sufficient for a local minimizer, the second-order sufficient condition involving the positive definiteness of the Hessian at a point satisfying the first-order condition guarantees a strict local minimizer. The section concludes by extending the discussion to optimization problems with equality constraints, presenting the method of Lagrange multipliers.

Convexity: Section 3.4 introduces the concept of convexity, which plays a crucial role in optimization problems. It defines convex sets and functions, and provides examples and properties of each. A set is convex if the line segment connecting any two points in the set lies entirely within the set. Convex functions are defined similarly, with the additional requirement that the function's value at any point on the line segment is less than or equal to the corresponding weighted average of the function's values at the endpoints. The section then establishes the connection between convexity and optimization, showing that for convex functions, any local minimizer is also a global minimizer. It also presents conditions for convexity based on the gradient and Hessian. The section concludes by introducing the notion of strong convexity, which guarantees the existence and uniqueness of global minimizers, and provides examples of strongly convex functions, such as least-squares objectives.

Gradient descent and its convergence analysis: Section 3.5 discusses gradient descent, a numerical optimization method for finding the minimum of a continuously differentiable function. The method iteratively takes steps in the direction of the negative gradient, which is proven to be the steepest descent direction. The convergence of gradient descent is analyzed under different assumptions on the function being minimized. For smooth functions, gradient descent with an appropriate step size is shown to produce a sequence of points whose objective values decrease and whose gradients vanish in the limit. When the function is both smooth and strongly convex, a faster convergence rate is obtained, with the function values converging exponentially to the global minimum. The section also includes examples and Python implementations to illustrate the concepts.

Application: Logistic regression: Section 3.6 applies gradient descent to logistic regression, a method for modeling the probability of a binary outcome based on input features. It derives the gradient and Hessian of the logistic regression objective function, proves the objective is convex and smooth, and provides Python code to implement gradient descent for logistic regression. The method is applied to example datasets.

3.1 Motivating Example: Analyzing Customer Satisfaction

We now turn to classification. Quoting Wikipedia[1]:

> In machine learning and statistics, classification is the problem of identifying to which of a set of categories (sub-populations) a new observation belongs, on the basis of a training set of data containing observations (or instances) whose category membership is known. Examples are assigning a given email to the "spam" or "non-spam" class, and assigning a diagnosis to a given patient based on observed characteristics of the patient (sex, blood pressure, presence or absence of certain symptoms, etc.). Classification is an example of pattern recognition. In the terminology of machine learning, classification is considered an instance of supervised learning, i.e., learning where a training set of correctly identified observations is available.

We will illustrate this problem on an ***airline customer satisfaction dataset***[2] available on Kaggle, an excellent source of data and community contributed analyses. The background is the following[3]:

> The dataset consists of the details of customers who have already flown with them. The feedback of the customers on various context and their flight data has been consolidated. The main purpose of this dataset is to predict whether a future customer would be satisfied with their service given the details of the other parameters' values.

We first load the data and convert it to an appropriate matrix representation. We (or, more precisely, ChatGPT) preprocessed the original file to remove rows with missing data or 0 ratings, convert categorical variables into one-hot encodings, and keep only a subset of the rows and columns.

---

[1] https://en.wikipedia.org/wiki/Statistical_classification
[2] You can access datasets and code that you want to **work with yourself** via the GitHub page for this book: https://github.com/MMiDS-textbook
[3] https://www.kaggle.com/datasets/sjleshrac/airlines-customer-satisfaction

```
data = pd.read_csv('customer_airline_satisfaction.csv')
```

This is a large dataset. Here are the first five rows and first six columns.

```
print(data.iloc[:5, :6])
```

```
   Satisfied  Age  Class_Business  Class_Eco  Class_Eco Plus  Business travel
0          0   63               1          0               0                1
1          0   34               1          0               0                1
2          0   52               0          1               0                0
3          0   40               0          1               0                1
4          1   46               0          1               0                1
```

It has 100,000 rows and 24 columns.

```
data.shape
```

(100000, 24)

The column names are:

```
print(data.columns.tolist())
```

['Satisfied', 'Age', 'Class_Business', 'Class_Eco', 'Class_Eco Plus', 'Business travel', 'Loyal customer', 'Flight Distance', 'Departure Delay in Minutes', 'Arrival Delay in Minutes', 'Seat comfort', 'Departure/Arrival time convenient', 'Food and drink', 'Gate location', 'Inflight wifi service', 'Inflight entertainment', 'Online support', 'Ease of Online booking', 'On-board service', 'Leg room service', 'Baggage handling', 'Checkin service', 'Cleanliness', 'Online boarding']

The first column indicates whether a customer was satisfied (with 1 meaning satisfied). The next six columns give some information about the customers, for instance, their age or whether they are members of a loyalty program with the airline. The following three columns give information about the flight, with names that should be self-explanatory: `Flight Distance`, `Departure Delay in Minutes`, and `Arrival Delay in Minutes`. The remaining columns give the customers' ratings, between 1 and 5, of various features, such as `Baggage handling`, `Checkin service`.

Our goal will be to predict the first column, `Satisfied`, from the rest of the columns. For this, we transform our data into NumPy arrays.

```
y = data['Satisfied'].to_numpy()
X = data.drop(columns=['Satisfied']).to_numpy()
print(y)
```

[0 0 0 ... 0 1 0]

```
print(X)
```

```
[[63  1  0  ...  3  3  4]
 [34  1  0  ...  2  3  4]
 [52  0  1  ...  4  3  4]
 ...
 [39  0  1  ...  4  1  1]
 [25  0  0  ...  5  3  1]
 [44  1  0  ...  1  2  2]]
```

Some features may affect satisfication more than others. Let us look at age for instance. The following code extracts the `Age` column from X (i.e., column 0) and computes the fraction of satisfied customers in several age bins.

Explanation by ChatGPT (who wrote the code):

1. `numpy.digitize` bins the age data into the specified age bins. The -1 adjustment is to match zero-based indexing.

2. `numpy.bincount` counts the occurrences of each bin index. The `minlength` parameter ensures that the resulting array length matches the number of age bins (`age_labels`). This is important if some bins have zero counts, ensuring the counts array covers all bins.

3. `freq_satisfied = counts_satisfied / counts_all` calculates the satisfaction frequency for each age group by dividing the counts of satisfied customers by the total counts in each age group.

```python
age_col_index = 0
age_data = X[:, age_col_index]
age_bins = [0, 18, 25, 35, 45, 55, 65, 100]
age_labels = ['0-17', '18-24', '25-34', '35-44', '45-54', '55-64',
              '65+']
age_bin_indices = np.digitize(age_data, bins=age_bins) - 1
counts_all = np.bincount(age_bin_indices, minlength=len(age_labels))
counts_satisfied = np.bincount(age_bin_indices[y == 1],
                   minlength=len(age_labels))
freq_satisfied = counts_satisfied / counts_all
age_group_labels = np.array(age_labels)
```

The results are plotted using matplotlib's `matplotlib.pyplot.bar` function. We see in particular that younger people tend to be more dissatisfied. Of course, this might be because they cannot afford the most expensive services.

```python
plt.figure(figsize=(4, 4))
plt.bar(age_group_labels, freq_satisfied, color='lightblue',
        edgecolor='black')
plt.xlabel('Age Group'), plt.ylabel('Frequency of Satisfied
           Customers')
plt.show()
```

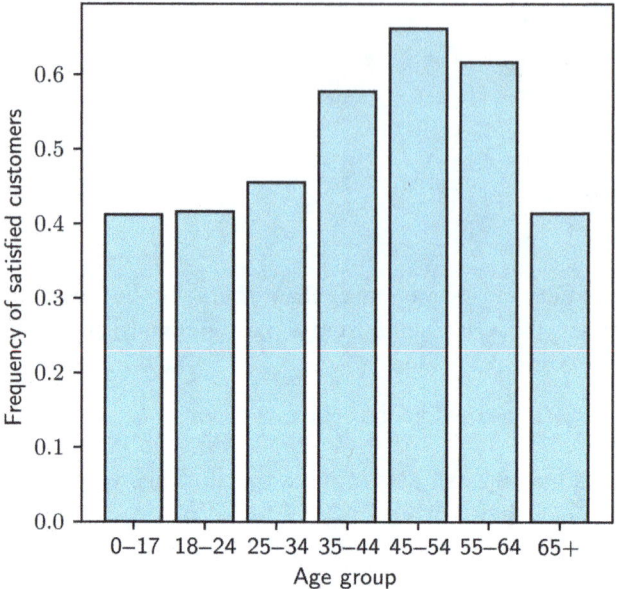

Figure 3.1 Graphical output of code.

The input data is now of the form $\{(\mathbf{x}_i, y_i): i = 1, \ldots, n\}$ where $\mathbf{x}_i \in \mathbb{R}^d$ are the features and $y_i \in \{0, 1\}$ is the label. Above we use the matrix representation $X \in \mathbb{R}^{n \times d}$ with rows $\mathbf{x}_i^T$, $i = 1, \ldots, n$ and $\mathbf{y} = (y_1, \ldots, y_n) \in \{0, 1\}^n$.

Our goal:

> learn a classifier from the examples $\{(\mathbf{x}_i, y_i): i = 1, \ldots, n\}$, namely a function $\hat{f} \colon \mathbb{R}^d \to \mathbb{R}$ such that $\hat{f}(\mathbf{x}_i) \approx y_i$.

We may want to enforce that the output is in $\{0, 1\}$ as well. This problem is referred to as binary classification.

A natural approach to this type of supervised learning problem is to define two objects:

1. **Family of classifiers:** a class $\widehat{\mathcal{F}}$ of classifiers from which to pick $\hat{f}$.
2. **Loss function:** a loss function $\ell(\hat{f}, (\mathbf{x}, y))$ which quantifies how good of a fit $\hat{f}(\mathbf{x})$ is to y.

Our goal is then to solve

$$\min_{\hat{f} \in \widehat{\mathcal{F}}} \frac{1}{n} \sum_{i=1}^{n} \ell(\hat{f}, (\mathbf{x}_i, y_i));$$

that is, we seek to find a classifier among $\widehat{\mathcal{F}}$ that minimizes the average loss over the examples.

For instance, in logistic regression, we consider linear classifiers of the form

$$\hat{f}(\mathbf{x}) = \sigma(\mathbf{x}^T \boldsymbol{\theta}) \quad \text{with} \quad \sigma(t) = \frac{1}{1 + e^{-t}}$$

where $\boldsymbol{\theta} \in \mathbb{R}^d$ is a parameter vector. And we use the cross-entropy loss

$$\ell(\hat{f}, (\mathbf{x}, y)) = -y \log(\sigma(\mathbf{x}^T \boldsymbol{\theta})) - (1 - y) \log(1 - \sigma(\mathbf{x}^T \boldsymbol{\theta})).$$

In parametric form, the problem boils down to

$$\min_{\theta \in \mathbb{R}^d} -\frac{1}{n}\sum_{i=1}^n y_i \log(\sigma(\mathbf{x}_i^T \boldsymbol{\theta})) - \frac{1}{n}\sum_{i=1}^n (1-y_i)\log(1-\sigma(\mathbf{x}_i^T\boldsymbol{\theta})).$$

To obtain a prediction in $\{0, 1\}$ here, we could cutoff $\hat{f}(\mathbf{x})$ at a threshold $\tau \in [0, 1]$; that is, return $\mathbf{1}\{\hat{f}(\mathbf{x}) > \tau\}$.

We will explain in Chapter 6 where this choice comes from.

The purpose of this chapter is to develop some of the mathematical theory and algorithms needed to solve this type of optimization formulation.

CHAT & LEARN Ask your favorite AI chatbot to help you explore the following hypothesis about the ***airline customer satisfaction dataset***:

> Younger people tend to be more dissatisfied because they cannot afford the best services.

For example, consider the relationship between age, satisfaction, and class (e.g., economy, business, etc.). Specifically:

1. Compare the distribution of class types among different age groups.
2. Compare the satisfaction levels within each class type for different age groups.

3.2 Background: Review of Differentiable Functions of Several Variables

We review the differential calculus of several variables. We highlight a few key results that will play an important role: the *Chain Rule* and the *Mean Value Theorem*.

3.2.1 Gradient

Recall the definition of the gradient.

Definition 3.2.1 *(Gradient) Let $f : D \to \mathbb{R}$ where $D \subseteq \mathbb{R}^d$ and let $\mathbf{x}_0 \in D$ be an interior point of D. Assume f is continuously differentiable at $\mathbf{x}_0$. The (column) vector*

$$\nabla f(\mathbf{x}_0) = \left(\frac{\partial f(\mathbf{x}_0)}{\partial x_1}, \ldots, \frac{\partial f(\mathbf{x}_0)}{\partial x_d}\right)$$

is called the gradient of f at $\mathbf{x}_0$.

Note that the gradient is itself a function of $\mathbf{x}$. In fact, unlike f, it is a vector-valued function. See Figure 3.2.[4]

Example 3.2.2 *Consider the affine function*

$$f(\mathbf{x}) = \mathbf{q}^T \mathbf{x} + r$$

where $\mathbf{x} = (x_1, \ldots, x_d), \mathbf{q} = (q_1, \ldots, q_d) \in \mathbb{R}^d$. The partial derivatives of the linear term are given by

$$\frac{\partial}{\partial x_i}[\mathbf{q}^T \mathbf{x}] = \frac{\partial}{\partial x_i}\left[\sum_{j=1}^d q_j x_j\right] = \frac{\partial}{\partial x_i}[q_i x_i] = q_i.$$

---

[4] Code by ChatGPT converted from https://commons.wikimedia.org/wiki/File:3d-gradient-cos.svg

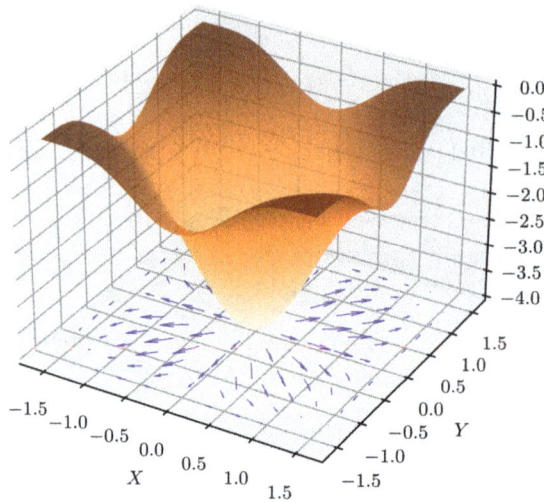

Figure 3.2 Gradient as a function.

So the gradient of f is

$$\nabla f(\mathbf{x}) = \mathbf{q}.$$

Example 3.2.3 *Consider the quadratic function*

$$f(\mathbf{x}) = \frac{1}{2}\mathbf{x}^T P \mathbf{x} + \mathbf{q}^T \mathbf{x} + r,$$

where $\mathbf{x} = (x_1, \ldots, x_d)$, $\mathbf{q} = (q_1, \ldots, q_d) \in \mathbb{R}^d$, *and* $P \in \mathbb{R}^{d \times d}$. *The partial derivatives of the quadratic term are given by*

$$\frac{\partial}{\partial x_i}[\mathbf{x}^T P \mathbf{x}] = \frac{\partial}{\partial x_i}\left[\sum_{j,k=1}^{d} P_{jk} x_j x_k\right]$$

$$= \frac{\partial}{\partial x_i}\left[P_{ii} x_i^2 + \sum_{j=1, j \neq i}^{d} P_{ji} x_j x_i + \sum_{k=1, k \neq i}^{d} P_{ik} x_i x_k\right],$$

where we used the fact that all terms not including x_i *have partial derivative 0.*

This last expression is

$$= 2 P_{ii} x_i + \sum_{j=1, j \neq i}^{d} P_{ji} x_j + \sum_{k=1, k \neq i}^{d} P_{ik} x_k$$

$$= \sum_{j=1}^{d} [P^T]_{ij} x_j + \sum_{k=1}^{d} [P]_{ik} x_k$$

$$= ([P + P^T]\mathbf{x})_i.$$

So the gradient of f is

$$\nabla f(\mathbf{x}) = \frac{1}{2}[P + P^T]\mathbf{x} + \mathbf{q}.$$

If P is symmetric, this further simplifies to $\nabla f(\mathbf{x}) = P\mathbf{x} + \mathbf{q}$.

It will be useful to compute the derivative of a function $f(\mathbf{x})$ of several variables along a parametric curve $\mathbf{g}(t) = (g_1(t), \ldots, g_d(t)) \in \mathbb{R}^d$ for t in some closed interval of $\mathbb{R}$. The following result is a special case of an important fact. We will use the notation $\mathbf{g}'(t) = (g'_1(t), \ldots, g'_m(t))$, where g'_i is the derivative of g_i. We say that $\mathbf{g}(t)$ is continuously differentiable at $t = t_0$ if each of its components is.

Example 3.2.4 *(Parametric Line)* The straight line between $\mathbf{x}_0 = (x_{0,1}, \ldots, x_{0,d})$ and $\mathbf{x}_1 = (x_{1,1}, \ldots, x_{1,d})$ in $\mathbb{R}^d$ can be parametrized as

$$\mathbf{g}(t) = \mathbf{x}_0 + t(\mathbf{x}_1 - \mathbf{x}_0),$$

where t goes from 0 (at which $\mathbf{g}(0) = \mathbf{x}_0$) to 1 (at which $\mathbf{g}(1) = \mathbf{x}_1$).
Then

$$g'_i(t) = \frac{d}{dt}[x_{0,i} + t(x_{1,i} - x_{0,i})] = x_{1,i} - x_{0,i},$$

so that

$$\mathbf{g}'(t) = \mathbf{x}_1 - \mathbf{x}_0.$$

Recall the *Chain Rule* in the single-variable case. Quoting Wikipedia[5]:

> The simplest form of the chain rule is for real-valued functions of one real variable. It states that if g is a function that is differentiable at a point c (i.e. the derivative $g'(c)$ exists) and f is a function that is differentiable at $g(c)$, then the composite function $f \circ g$ is differentiable at c, and the derivative is $(f \circ g)'(c) = f'(g(c)) \cdot g'(c)$.

Here is a straightforward generalization of the *Chain Rule*.

Theorem 3.2.5 *(Chain Rule)* Let $f: D_1 \to \mathbb{R}$, where $D_1 \subseteq \mathbb{R}$, and let $g: D_2 \to \mathbb{R}$, where $D_2 \subseteq \mathbb{R}^d$. Assume that f is continuously differentiable at $g(\mathbf{x}_0)$, an interior point of D_1, and that g is continuously differentiable at $\mathbf{x}_0$, an interior point of D_2. Then

$$\nabla(f \circ g)(\mathbf{x}_0) = f'(g(\mathbf{x}_0))\nabla g(\mathbf{x}_0).$$

Proof We apply the *Chain Rule* for functions of one variable to the partial derivatives. For all i,

$$\frac{\partial}{\partial x_i} f(g(\mathbf{x}_0)) = f'(g(\mathbf{x}_0))\frac{\partial}{\partial x_i} g(\mathbf{x}_0).$$

Collecting the partial derivatives in a vector gives the claim. $\square$

Here is a different generalization of the *Chain Rule*. Again the composition $f \circ \mathbf{g}$ denotes the function $f \circ \mathbf{g}(t) = f(\mathbf{g}(t))$.

Theorem 3.2.6 *(Chain Rule)* Let $f: D_1 \to \mathbb{R}$, where $D_1 \subseteq \mathbb{R}^d$, and let $\mathbf{g}: D_2 \to \mathbb{R}^d$, where $D_2 \subseteq \mathbb{R}$. Assume that f is continuously differentiable at $\mathbf{g}(t_0)$, an interior point of D_1, and that $\mathbf{g}$ is continuously differentiable at t_0, an interior point of D_2. Then

$$(f \circ \mathbf{g})'(t_0) = \nabla f(\mathbf{g}(t_0))^T \mathbf{g}'(t_0).$$

---

[5] https://en.wikipedia.org/wiki/Chain_rule

Proof To simplify the notation, suppose that f is a real-valued function of $\mathbf{x} = (x_1,\ldots,x_d)$ whose components are themselves functions of $t \in \mathbb{R}$. Assume f is continuously differentiable at $\mathbf{x}(t)$. To compute the total derivative $\frac{df(t)}{dt}$, let $\Delta x_k = x_k(t+\Delta t) - x_k(t)$, $x_k = x_k(t)$ and

$$\Delta f = f(x_1 + \Delta x_1,\ldots,x_d + \Delta x_d) - f(x_1,\ldots,x_d).$$

We seek to compute the limit $\lim_{\Delta t \to 0} \frac{\Delta f}{\Delta t}$. To relate this limit to partial derivatives of f, we rewrite Δf as a telescoping sum where each term involves variation of a single variable x_k. That is,

$$\Delta f = [f(x_1 + \Delta x_1,\ldots,x_d + \Delta x_d) - f(x_1, x_2 + \Delta x_2,\ldots, x_d + \Delta x_d)]$$
$$+ [f(x_1, x_2 + \Delta x_2,\ldots,x_d + \Delta x_d) - f(x_1, x_2, x_3 + \Delta x_3,\ldots,x_d + \Delta x_d)]$$
$$+ \cdots + [f(x_1,\cdots,x_{d-1},x_d + \Delta x_d) - f(x_1,\ldots,x_d)].$$

Applying the *Mean Value Theorem* to each term gives

$$\Delta f = \Delta x_1 \frac{\partial f(x_1 + \theta_1 \Delta x_1, x_2 + \Delta x_2,\ldots,x_d + \Delta x_d)}{\partial x_1}$$
$$+ \Delta x_2 \frac{\partial f(x_1, x_2 + \theta_2 \Delta x_2, x_3 + \Delta x_3,\ldots,x_d + \Delta x_d)}{\partial x_2}$$
$$+ \cdots + \Delta x_d \frac{\partial f(x_1,\cdots,x_{d-1},x_d + \theta_d \Delta x_d)}{\partial x_d}$$

where $0 < \theta_k < 1$ for $k = 1,\ldots,d$. Dividing by Δt, taking the limit $\Delta t \to 0$, and using the fact that f is continuously differentiable, we get

$$\frac{df(t)}{dt} = \sum_{k=1}^{d} \frac{\partial f(\mathbf{x}(t))}{\partial x_k} \frac{dx_k(t)}{dt}. \qquad \square$$

As a first application of the *Chain Rule*, we generalize the *Mean Value Theorem* to the case of several variables. We will use this result later to prove a multivariable Taylor expansion result that will play a central role in this chapter.

Theorem 3.2.7 *(Mean Value)* Let $f: D \to \mathbb{R}$ where $D \subseteq \mathbb{R}^d$. Let $\mathbf{x}_0 \in D$ and $\delta > 0$ be such that $B_\delta(\mathbf{x}_0) \subseteq D$. If f is continuously differentiable on $B_\delta(\mathbf{x}_0)$, then for any $\mathbf{x} \in B_\delta(\mathbf{x}_0)$

$$f(\mathbf{x}) = f(\mathbf{x}_0) + \nabla f(\mathbf{x}_0 + \xi \mathbf{p})^T \mathbf{p}$$

for some $\xi \in (0,1)$, where $\mathbf{p} = \mathbf{x} - \mathbf{x}_0$.

One way to think of the *Mean Value Theorem* is as a 0-th order Taylor expansion. It says that, when $\mathbf{x}$ is close to $\mathbf{x}_0$, the value $f(\mathbf{x})$ is close to $f(\mathbf{x}_0)$ in a way that can be controlled in terms of the gradient in the neighborhood of $\mathbf{x}_0$. From this point of view, the term $\nabla f(\mathbf{x}_0 + \xi \mathbf{p})^T \mathbf{p}$ is called the Lagrange remainder.

Proof idea: We apply the single-variable result and the *Chain Rule*.

Proof Let $\phi(t) = f(\alpha(t))$ where $\alpha(t) = \mathbf{x}_0 + t\mathbf{p}$. Observe that $\phi(0) = f(\mathbf{x}_0)$ and $\phi(1) = f(\mathbf{x})$. By the *Chain Rule* and the parametric line example,

$$\phi'(t) = \nabla f(\alpha(t))^T \alpha'(t) = \nabla f(\alpha(t))^T \mathbf{p} = \nabla f(\mathbf{x}_0 + t\mathbf{p})^T \mathbf{p}.$$

In particular, ϕ has a continuous first derivative on $[0,1]$. By the *Mean Value Theorem* in the single-variable case

$$\phi(t) = \phi(0) + t\phi'(\xi)$$

for some $\xi \in (0, t)$. Plugging in the expressions for $\phi(0)$ and $\phi'(\xi)$ and taking $t = 1$ gives the claim. □

3.2.2 Second-Order Derivatives

One can also define higher-order derivatives. We start with the single-variable case, where $f: D \to \mathbb{R}$ with $D \subseteq \mathbb{R}$ and $x_0 \in D$ is an interior point of D. Note that, if f' exists in D, then it is itself a function of x. Then the second derivative at x_0 is

$$f''(x_0) = \frac{d^2 f(x_0)}{dx^2} = \lim_{h \to 0} \frac{f'(x_0 + h) - f'(x_0)}{h}$$

provided the limit exists.

In the several-variable case, we have the following:

Definition 3.2.8 *(Second Partial Derivatives and Hessian)* Let $f: D \to \mathbb{R}$ where $D \subseteq \mathbb{R}^d$ and let $\mathbf{x}_0 \in D$ be an interior point of D. Assume that f is continuously differentiable in an open ball around $\mathbf{x}_0$. Then $\partial f(\mathbf{x})/\partial x_i$ is itself a function of $\mathbf{x}$ and its partial derivative with respect to x_j, if it exists, is denoted by

$$\frac{\partial^2 f(\mathbf{x}_0)}{\partial x_j \partial x_i} = \lim_{h \to 0} \frac{\frac{\partial f}{\partial x_i}(\mathbf{x}_0 + h\mathbf{e}_j) - \frac{\partial f}{\partial x_i}(\mathbf{x}_0)}{h}.$$

To simplify the notation, we write this as $\partial^2 f(\mathbf{x}_0)/\partial x_i^2$ when $j = i$. If $\partial^2 f(\mathbf{x})/\partial x_j \partial x_i$ and $\partial^2 f(\mathbf{x})/\partial x_i^2$ exist and are continuous in an open ball around $\mathbf{x}_0$ for all i, j, we say that f is twice continuously differentiable at $\mathbf{x}_0$.

The matrix of second derivatives is called the Hessian and is denoted by

$$\mathbf{H}_f(\mathbf{x}_0) = \begin{pmatrix} \frac{\partial^2 f(\mathbf{x}_0)}{\partial x_1^2} & \cdots & \frac{\partial^2 f(\mathbf{x}_0)}{\partial x_d \partial x_1} \\ \vdots & \ddots & \vdots \\ \frac{\partial^2 f(\mathbf{x}_0)}{\partial x_1 \partial x_d} & \cdots & \frac{\partial^2 f(\mathbf{x}_0)}{\partial x_d^2} \end{pmatrix}.$$

Like f and the gradient ∇f, the Hessian $\mathbf{H}_f$ is a function of $\mathbf{x}$. It is a matrix-valued function, however.

When f is twice continuously differentiable at $\mathbf{x}_0$, its Hessian is a symmetric matrix.

Theorem 3.2.9 *(Symmetry of the Hessian)* Let $f: D \to \mathbb{R}$ where $D \subseteq \mathbb{R}^d$ and let $\mathbf{x}_0 \in D$ be an interior point of D. Assume that f is twice continuously differentiable at $\mathbf{x}_0$. Then for all $i \neq j$

$$\frac{\partial^2 f(\mathbf{x}_0)}{\partial x_j \partial x_i} = \frac{\partial^2 f(\mathbf{x}_0)}{\partial x_i \partial x_j}.$$

Proof idea: Two applications of the *Mean Value Theorem* show that the limits can be interchanged.

Proof By definition of the partial derivative,

$$\frac{\partial^2 f(\mathbf{x}_0)}{\partial x_j \partial x_i} = \lim_{h_j \to 0} \frac{\frac{\partial f}{\partial x_i}(\mathbf{x}_0 + h_j \mathbf{e}_j) - \frac{\partial f}{\partial x_i}(\mathbf{x}_0)}{h_j}$$

$$= \lim_{h_j \to 0} \lim_{h_i \to 0} \frac{1}{h_j h_i} \left\{ [f(\mathbf{x}_0 + h_j \mathbf{e}_j + h_i \mathbf{e}_i) - f(\mathbf{x}_0 + h_j \mathbf{e}_j)] - [f(\mathbf{x}_0 + h_i \mathbf{e}_i) - f(\mathbf{x}_0)] \right\}$$

$$= \lim_{h_j \to 0} \lim_{h_i \to 0} \frac{1}{h_i} \left\{ \frac{[f(\mathbf{x}_0 + h_i \mathbf{e}_i + h_j \mathbf{e}_j) - f(\mathbf{x}_0 + h_i \mathbf{e}_i)] - [f(\mathbf{x}_0 + h_j \mathbf{e}_j) - f(\mathbf{x}_0)]}{h_j} \right\}$$

$$= \lim_{h_j \to 0} \lim_{h_i \to 0} \frac{1}{h_i} \left\{ \frac{\partial}{\partial x_j} [f(\mathbf{x}_0 + h_i \mathbf{e}_i + \theta_j h_j \mathbf{e}_j) - f(\mathbf{x}_0 + \theta_j h_j \mathbf{e}_j)] \right\}$$

$$= \lim_{h_j \to 0} \lim_{h_i \to 0} \frac{1}{h_i} \left\{ \frac{\partial f}{\partial x_j}(\mathbf{x}_0 + h_i \mathbf{e}_i + \theta_j h_j \mathbf{e}_j) - \frac{\partial f}{\partial x_j}(\mathbf{x}_0 + \theta_j h_j \mathbf{e}_j) \right\}$$

for some $\theta_j \in (0, 1)$. Note that, in the third line, we rearranged the terms and, in the fourth line, we applied the *Mean Value Theorem* to $f(\mathbf{x}_0 + h_i \mathbf{e}_i + h_j \mathbf{e}_j) - f(\mathbf{x}_0 + h_j \mathbf{e}_j)$ as a continuously differentiable function of h_j.

Because $\partial f / \partial x_j$ is continuously differentiable in an open ball around $\mathbf{x}_0$, a second application of the *Mean Value Theorem* gives for some $\theta_i \in (0, 1)$

$$\lim_{h_j \to 0} \lim_{h_i \to 0} \frac{1}{h_i} \left\{ \frac{\partial f}{\partial x_j}(\mathbf{x}_0 + h_i \mathbf{e}_i + \theta_j h_j \mathbf{e}_j) - \frac{\partial f}{\partial x_j}(\mathbf{x}_0 + \theta_j h_j \mathbf{e}_j) \right\}$$

$$= \lim_{h_j \to 0} \lim_{h_i \to 0} \frac{\partial}{\partial x_i} \left[\frac{\partial f}{\partial x_j}(\mathbf{x}_0 + \theta_j h_j \mathbf{e}_j + \theta_i h_i \mathbf{e}_i) \right]$$

$$= \lim_{h_j \to 0} \lim_{h_i \to 0} \frac{\partial^2 f(\mathbf{x}_0 + \theta_j h_j \mathbf{e}_j + \theta_i h_i \mathbf{e}_i)}{\partial x_i \partial x_j}.$$

The claim then follows from the continuity of $\partial^2 f / \partial x_i \partial x_j$. □

Example 3.2.10 *Consider the quadratic function*

$$f(\mathbf{x}) = \frac{1}{2} \mathbf{x}^T P \mathbf{x} + \mathbf{q}^T \mathbf{x} + r.$$

Recall that the gradient of f is

$$\nabla f(\mathbf{x}) = \frac{1}{2} [P + P^T] \mathbf{x} + \mathbf{q}.$$

To simplify the calculation, let $B = \frac{1}{2}[P + P^T]$ and denote the rows of B by $\mathbf{b}_1^T, \ldots, \mathbf{b}_d^T$.

Each component of ∇f is an affine function of $\mathbf{x}$, specifically,

$$\frac{\partial f(\mathbf{x})}{\partial x_i} = \mathbf{b}_i^T \mathbf{x} + q_i.$$

Row i of the Hessian is simply the gradient transposed of $\frac{\partial f(\mathbf{x})}{\partial x_i}$ which, by our previous results, is

$$\left(\nabla \frac{\partial f(\mathbf{x})}{\partial x_i} \right)^T = \mathbf{b}_i^T.$$

Putting this together we get

$$\mathbf{H}_f(\mathbf{x}) = \frac{1}{2}[P + P^T].$$

Observe that this is indeed a symmetric matrix.

3.2 Review of Differentiable Functions of Several Variables

Self-Assessment Quiz (with help from Claude, Gemini, and ChatGPT)

1. What does it mean for a function f to be continuously differentiable at $\mathbf{x}_0$?
   a) f is continuous at $\mathbf{x}_0$.
   b) All partial derivatives of f exist at $\mathbf{x}_0$.
   c) All partial derivatives of f exist and are continuous in an open ball around $\mathbf{x}_0$.
   d) The gradient of f is zero at $\mathbf{x}_0$.

2. What is the gradient of a function $f: D \to \mathbb{R}$, where $D \subseteq \mathbb{R}^d$, at a point $\mathbf{x}_0 \in D$?
   a) The rate of change of f with respect to $\mathbf{x}$ at $\mathbf{x}_0$
   b) The vector of all second partial derivatives of f at $\mathbf{x}_0$
   c) The vector of all first partial derivatives of f at $\mathbf{x}_0$
   d) The matrix of all second partial derivatives of f at $\mathbf{x}_0$

3. Which of the following statements is true about the Hessian matrix of a twice continuously differentiable function?
   a) It is always a diagonal matrix.
   b) It is always a symmetric matrix.
   c) It is always an invertible matrix.
   d) It is always a positive definite matrix.

4. Let $f(x, y, z) = x^2 + y^2 - z^2$. What is the Hessian matrix of f?
   a) $\begin{pmatrix} 2 & 0 & 0 \\ 0 & 2 & 0 \\ 0 & 0 & -2 \end{pmatrix}$
   b) $\begin{pmatrix} 2x & 2y & -2z \end{pmatrix}$
   c) $\begin{pmatrix} 2 & 0 \\ 0 & 2 \end{pmatrix}$
   d) $\begin{pmatrix} 0 & 0 & 0 \\ 0 & 0 & 0 \\ 0 & 0 & 0 \end{pmatrix}$

5. What is the Hessian matrix of the quadratic function $f(\mathbf{x}) = \frac{1}{2}\mathbf{x}^T P \mathbf{x} + \mathbf{q}^T \mathbf{x} + \mathbf{r}$, where $P \in \mathbb{R}^{d \times d}$ and $\mathbf{q} \in \mathbb{R}^d$?
   a) $\mathbf{H}_f(\mathbf{x}) = P$
   b) $\mathbf{H}_f(\mathbf{x}) = P^T$
   c) $\mathbf{H}_f(\mathbf{x}) = \frac{1}{2}[P + P^T]$
   d) $\mathbf{H}_f(\mathbf{x}) = [P + P^T]$

Answer for 1: c. Justification: The text states, "If f exists and is continuous in an open ball around $\mathbf{x}_0$ for all i, then we say that f is continuously differentiable at $\mathbf{x}_0$."

Answer for 2: c. Justification: From the text: "The (column) vector $\nabla f(\mathbf{x}_0) = (\frac{\partial f(\mathbf{x}_0)}{\partial \mathbf{x}_1}, \ldots, \frac{\partial f(\mathbf{x}_0)}{\partial \mathbf{x}_d})$ is called the gradient of f at $\mathbf{x}_0$."

Answer for 3: b. Justification: The text states: "When f is twice continuously differentiable at $\mathbf{x}_0$, its Hessian is a symmetric matrix."

Answer for 4: a. Justification: The Hessian is the matrix of second partial derivatives:

$$\begin{pmatrix} \frac{\partial^2 f}{\partial x^2} & \frac{\partial^2 f}{\partial x \partial y} & \frac{\partial^2 f}{\partial x \partial z} \\ \frac{\partial^2 f}{\partial y \partial x} & \frac{\partial^2 f}{\partial y^2} & \frac{\partial^2 f}{\partial y \partial z} \\ \frac{\partial^2 f}{\partial z \partial x} & \frac{\partial^2 f}{\partial z \partial y} & \frac{\partial^2 f}{\partial z^2} \end{pmatrix} = \begin{pmatrix} 2 & 0 & 0 \\ 0 & 2 & 0 \\ 0 & 0 & -2 \end{pmatrix}$$

Answer for 5: c. Justification: The text shows that the Hessian of the quadratic function is $\mathbf{H}_f(\mathbf{x}) = \frac{1}{2}[P + P^T]$.

3.3 Optimality Conditions

In this section, we derive optimality conditions for unconstrained continuous optimization problems.

We will be interested in unconstrained optimization of the form

$$\min_{\mathbf{x} \in \mathbb{R}^d} f(\mathbf{x})$$

where $f \colon \mathbb{R}^d \to \mathbb{R}$. In this subsection, we define several notions of solution and derive characterizations.

We have observed before that, in general, finding a global minimizer and certifying that one has been found can be difficult unless some special structure is present. Therefore weaker notions of solution are needed. We previously introduced the concept of a local minimizer. In words, $\mathbf{x}^*$ is a local minimizer if there is an open ball around $\mathbf{x}^*$ where it attains the minimum value. The difference between global and local minimizers is illustrated in the next figure.

3.3.1 First-Order Conditions

Local minimizers can be characterized in terms of the gradient. We first define the concept of directional derivative.

3.3.1.1 Directional Derivative

Partial derivatives measure the rate of change of a function along the axes. More generally:

Definition 3.3.1 (*Directional Derivative*) Let $f \colon D \to \mathbb{R}$ where $D \subseteq \mathbb{R}^d$, let $\mathbf{x}_0 = (x_{0,1}, \ldots, x_{0,d}) \in D$ be an interior point of D, and let $\mathbf{v} = (v_1, \ldots, v_d) \in \mathbb{R}^d$ be a nonzero vector. The directional derivative of f at $\mathbf{x}_0$ in the direction $\mathbf{v}$ is

$$\begin{aligned}\frac{\partial f(\mathbf{x}_0)}{\partial \mathbf{v}} &= \lim_{h \to 0} \frac{f(\mathbf{x}_0 + h\mathbf{v}) - f(\mathbf{x}_0)}{h} \\ &= \lim_{h \to 0} \frac{f(x_{0,1} + h v_1, \ldots, x_{0,d} + h v_d) - f(x_{0,1}, \ldots, x_{0,d})}{h}\end{aligned}$$

provided the limit exists.

Typically, $\mathbf{v}$ is a unit vector.

3.3 Optimality Conditions

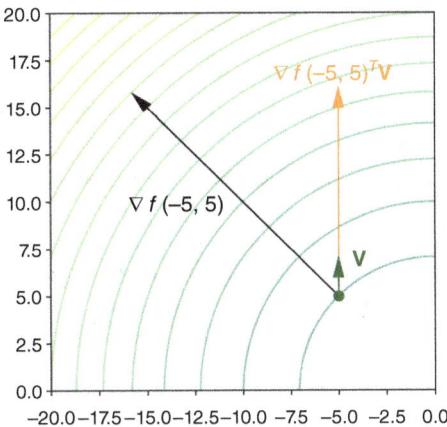

Figure 3.3 Contour plot of the function $f(x, y) = x^2 + y^2$. At the point $(-5, 5)$, the gradient and a directional derivative are shown.

Note that taking $\mathbf{v} = \mathbf{e}_i$ recovers the i-th partial derivative

$$\frac{\partial f(\mathbf{x}_0)}{\partial \mathbf{e}_i} = \lim_{h \to 0} \frac{f(\mathbf{x}_0 + h\mathbf{e}_i) - f(\mathbf{x}_0)}{h} = \frac{\partial f(\mathbf{x}_0)}{\partial x_i}.$$

Conversely, a general directional derivative can be expressed in terms of the partial derivatives.

Theorem 3.3.2 (Directional Derivative and Gradient) *Let $f : D \to \mathbb{R}$ where $D \subseteq \mathbb{R}^d$, let $\mathbf{x}_0 \in D$ be an interior point of D and let $\mathbf{v} \in \mathbb{R}^d$ be a vector. Assume that f is continuously differentiable at $\mathbf{x}_0$. Then the directional derivative of f at $\mathbf{x}_0$ in the direction $\mathbf{v}$ is given by*

$$\frac{\partial f(\mathbf{x}_0)}{\partial \mathbf{v}} = \nabla f(\mathbf{x}_0)^T \mathbf{v}.$$

Put differently, when $\mathbf{v}$ is a unit vector, the directional derivative is the length of the orthogonal projection of the gradient onto $\mathbf{v}$. See Figure 3.3.[6]

Proof idea: To bring out the partial derivatives, we rewrite the directional derivative as the derivative of a composition of f with an affine function. We then use the *Chain Rule*.

Proof Consider the composition $\beta(h) = f(\alpha(h))$ where $\alpha(h) = \mathbf{x}_0 + h\mathbf{v}$. Observe that $\alpha(0) = \mathbf{x}_0$ and $\beta(0) = f(\mathbf{x}_0)$. Then, by definition of the derivative,

$$\frac{d\beta(0)}{dh} = \lim_{h \to 0} \frac{\beta(h) - \beta(0)}{h} = \lim_{h \to 0} \frac{f(\mathbf{x}_0 + h\mathbf{v}) - f(\mathbf{x}_0)}{h} = \frac{\partial f(\mathbf{x}_0)}{\partial \mathbf{v}}.$$

Applying the *Chain Rule* and Example 3.2.4 from the previous section, we arrive at

$$\frac{d\beta(0)}{dh} = \nabla f(\alpha(0))^T \alpha'(0) = \nabla f(\mathbf{x}_0)^T \mathbf{v}. \qquad \square$$

---

[6] Code by ChatGPT converted from https://commons.wikimedia.org/wiki/File:Directional_derivative_contour_plot.svg

3.3.1.2 Descent Direction

Earlier in the book, we proved a key insight about the derivative of a single-variable function f at a point x_0: It tells us where to find smaller values. We generalize the *Descent Direction Lemma* to the multivariable case.

First, we observe that in the continuously differentiable case the directional derivative gives a criterion for descent directions.

Lemma 3.3.3 *(Descent Direction and Directional Derivative)* Let $f: \mathbb{R}^d \to \mathbb{R}$ be continuously differentiable at $\mathbf{x}_0$. A vector $\mathbf{v}$ is a descent direction[7] for f at $\mathbf{x}_0$ if

$$\frac{\partial f(\mathbf{x}_0)}{\partial \mathbf{v}} = \nabla f(\mathbf{x}_0)^T \mathbf{v} < 0;$$

that is, if the directional derivative of f at $\mathbf{x}_0$ in the direction $\mathbf{v}$ is negative.

Proof idea: In anticipation of the proof of the second-order condition, we use the *Mean Value Theorem* to show that f takes smaller values in direction $\mathbf{v}$. A simpler proof based on the definition of the directional derivative is also possible (try it!).

Proof Suppose there is $\mathbf{v} \in \mathbb{R}^d$ such that $\nabla f(\mathbf{x}_0)^T \mathbf{v} = -\eta < 0$. For $\alpha > 0$, the *Mean Value Theorem* implies that there is $\xi_\alpha \in (0,1)$ such that

$$f(\mathbf{x}_0 + \alpha \mathbf{v}) = f(\mathbf{x}_0) + \nabla f(\mathbf{x}_0 + \xi_\alpha \alpha \mathbf{v})^T (\alpha \mathbf{v}) = f(\mathbf{x}_0) + \alpha \nabla f(\mathbf{x}_0 + \xi_\alpha \alpha \mathbf{v})^T \mathbf{v}.$$

We want to show that the second term on the right-hand side is negative. We cannot immediately apply our condition on $\mathbf{v}$ as the gradient in the previous equation is taken at $\mathbf{x}_0 + \xi_\alpha \alpha \mathbf{v}$, not $\mathbf{x}_0$.

The gradient is continuous (in the sense that all its components are continuous). In particular, the function $\nabla f(\mathbf{x})^T \mathbf{v}$ is continuous as a linear combination of continuous functions. By the definition of continuity, for any $\epsilon > 0$ – say $\epsilon = \eta/2$ – there is $\delta > 0$ small enough such that all $\mathbf{x} \in B_\delta(\mathbf{x}_0)$ satisfy

$$\left| \nabla f(\mathbf{x})^T \mathbf{v} - \nabla f(\mathbf{x}_0)^T \mathbf{v} \right| < \epsilon = \eta/2.$$

Take $\alpha^* > 0$ small enough that $\mathbf{x}_0 + \alpha^* \mathbf{v} \in B_\delta(\mathbf{x}_0)$. Then, for all $\alpha \in (0, \alpha^*)$, whatever $\xi_\alpha \in (0,1)$ is, it holds that $\mathbf{x}_0 + \xi_\alpha \alpha \mathbf{v} \in B_\delta(\mathbf{x}_0)$. Hence,

$$\begin{aligned}
\nabla f(\mathbf{x}_0 + \xi_\alpha \alpha \mathbf{v})^T \mathbf{v} &= \nabla f(\mathbf{x}_0)^T \mathbf{v} + (\nabla f(\mathbf{x}_0 + \xi_\alpha \alpha \mathbf{v})^T \mathbf{v} - \nabla f(\mathbf{x}_0)^T \mathbf{v}) \\
&\leq \nabla f(\mathbf{x}_0)^T \mathbf{v} + \left| \nabla f(\mathbf{x}_0 + \xi_\alpha \alpha \mathbf{v})^T \mathbf{v} - \nabla f(\mathbf{x}_0)^T \mathbf{v} \right| \\
&< -\eta + \eta/2 \\
&= -\eta/2 < 0.
\end{aligned}$$

by definition of η. That implies

$$f(\mathbf{x}_0 + \alpha \mathbf{v}) < f(\mathbf{x}_0) - \alpha \eta/2 < f(\mathbf{x}_0), \quad \forall \alpha \in (0, \alpha^*)$$

and proves the claim. $\square$

Lemma 3.3.4 *(Descent Direction)* Let $f: \mathbb{R}^d \to \mathbb{R}$ be continuously differentiable at $\mathbf{x}_0$ and assume that $\nabla f(\mathbf{x}_0) \neq 0$. Then f has a descent direction at $\mathbf{x}_0$.

---

[7] See Definition 1.2.23.

Proof Take $\mathbf{v} = -\nabla f(\mathbf{x}_0)$. Then $\nabla f(\mathbf{x}_0)^T \mathbf{v} = -\|\nabla f(\mathbf{x}_0)\|^2 < 0$ since $\nabla f(\mathbf{x}_0) \neq \mathbf{0}$. □

This leads to the following fundamental result.

Theorem 3.3.5 *(First-Order Necessary Optimality Condition) Let $f : \mathbb{R}^d \to \mathbb{R}$ be continuously differentiable on $\mathbb{R}^d$. If $\mathbf{x}_0$ is a local minimizer, then $\nabla f(\mathbf{x}_0) = \mathbf{0}$.*

Proof idea: In a descent direction, f decreases; hence there cannot be one at a local minimizer.

Proof We argue by contradiction. Suppose that $\nabla f(\mathbf{x}_0) \neq \mathbf{0}$. By the *Descent Direction Lemma*, there is a descent direction $\mathbf{v} \in \mathbb{R}^d$ at $\mathbf{x}_0$. That implies

$$f(\mathbf{x}_0 + \alpha \mathbf{v}) < f(\mathbf{x}_0), \quad \forall \alpha \in (0, \alpha^*)$$

for some $\alpha^* > 0$. So every open ball around $\mathbf{x}_0$ has a point achieving a smaller value than $f(\mathbf{x}_0)$. Thus $\mathbf{x}_0$ is not a local minimizer, a contradiction. So it must be that $\nabla f(\mathbf{x}_0) = \mathbf{0}$. □

A point satisfying the first-order necessary conditions is called a stationary point.

Definition 3.3.6 *(Stationary Point) Let $f : D \to \mathbb{R}$ be continuously differentiable on an open set $D \subseteq \mathbb{R}^d$. If $\nabla f(\mathbf{x}_0) = \mathbf{0}$, we say that $\mathbf{x}_0 \in D$ is a stationary point of f.*

Example 3.3.7 *(Rayleigh Quotient) Let $A \in \mathbb{R}^{d \times d}$ be a symmetric matrix. The associated Rayleigh quotient is*

$$\mathcal{R}_A(\mathbf{u}) = \frac{\langle \mathbf{u}, A\mathbf{u} \rangle}{\langle \mathbf{u}, \mathbf{u} \rangle}$$

which is defined for any $\mathbf{u} = (u_1, \ldots, u_d) \neq \mathbf{0}$ in $\mathbb{R}^d$. As a function from $\mathbb{R}^d \setminus \{\mathbf{0}\}$ to $\mathbb{R}$, $\mathcal{R}_A(\mathbf{u})$ is continuously differentiable. We find its stationary points.

We use the quotient rule and our previous results on the gradient of quadratic functions. Specifically, note that (using that A is symmetric)

$$\begin{aligned}
\frac{\partial}{\partial u_i} \mathcal{R}_A(\mathbf{u}) &= \frac{\left(\frac{\partial}{\partial u_i} \langle \mathbf{u}, A\mathbf{u} \rangle\right) \langle \mathbf{u}, \mathbf{u} \rangle - \langle \mathbf{u}, A\mathbf{u} \rangle \left(\frac{\partial}{\partial u_i} \langle \mathbf{u}, \mathbf{u} \rangle\right)}{\langle \mathbf{u}, \mathbf{u} \rangle^2} \\
&= \frac{2\left(\frac{\partial}{\partial u_i} \frac{1}{2} \mathbf{u}^T A \mathbf{u}\right) \|\mathbf{u}\|^2 - \mathbf{u}^T A \mathbf{u} \left(\frac{\partial}{\partial u_i} \sum_{j=1}^d u_j^2\right)}{\|\mathbf{u}\|^4} \\
&= \frac{2(A\mathbf{u})_i \|\mathbf{u}\|^2 - \mathbf{u}^T A \mathbf{u} (2u_i)}{\|\mathbf{u}\|^4} \\
&= \frac{2}{\|\mathbf{u}\|^2} \{(A\mathbf{u})_i - \mathcal{R}_A(\mathbf{u}) u_i\}.
\end{aligned}$$

In vector form this is

$$\nabla \mathcal{R}_A(\mathbf{u}) = \frac{2}{\|\mathbf{u}\|^2} \{A\mathbf{u} - \mathcal{R}_A(\mathbf{u}) \mathbf{u}\}.$$

The stationary points satisfy $\nabla \mathcal{R}_A(\mathbf{u}) = \mathbf{0}$, or after getting rid of the denominator and rearranging,

$$A\mathbf{u} = \mathcal{R}_A(\mathbf{u}) \mathbf{u}.$$

The solutions to this system are eigenvectors of A, that is, they satisfy $A\mathbf{u} = \lambda\mathbf{u}$ for some eigenvalue λ. If $\mathbf{q}_i$ is a unit eigenvector of A with eigenvalue λ_i, then we have that $\mathcal{R}_A(\mathbf{q}_i) = \lambda_i$ (check it!) and

$$A\mathbf{q}_i = \mathcal{R}_A(\mathbf{q}_i)\mathbf{q}_i = \lambda_i \mathbf{q}_i.$$

The eigenvectors of A are not in general local minimizers of its Rayleigh quotient. In fact one of them – the largest one – is a global maximizer!

3.3.2 Second-Order Conditions

Local minimizers can also be characterized in terms of the Hessian.

We will make use of *Taylor's Theorem*, a generalization of the *Mean Value Theorem* that provides polynomial approximations to a function around a point. We restrict ourselves to the case of a linear approximation with second-order error term, which will suffice for our purposes.

3.3.2.1 Taylor's Theorem

We begin by reviewing the single-variable case, which we will use to prove the general verison.

Theorem 3.3.8 *(Taylor) Let $f : D \to \mathbb{R}$ where $D \subseteq \mathbb{R}$. Suppose f has a continuous derivative on $[a, b]$ and that its second derivative exists on (a, b). Then for any $x \in [a, b]$*

$$f(x) = f(a) + (x-a)f'(a) + \frac{1}{2}(x-a)^2 f''(\xi)$$

for some $a < \xi < x$.

The third term on the right-hand side of *Taylor's Theorem* is called the Lagrange remainder. It can be seen as an error term between $f(x)$ and the linear approximation $f(a) + (x-a)f'(a)$. There are other forms for the remainder. The form we stated here is useful when one has a bound on the second derivative. Here is an example.

NUMERICAL CORNER Consider $f(x) = e^x$. Then $f'(x) = f''(x) = e^x$. Suppose we are interested in approximating f in the interval $[0, 1]$. We take $a = 0$ and $b = 1$ in *Taylor's Theorem*. The linear term is

$$f(a) + (x-a)f'(a) = 1 + xe^0 = 1 + x.$$

Then for any $x \in [0, 1]$

$$f(x) = 1 + x + \frac{1}{2}x^2 e^{\xi_x}$$

where $\xi_x \in (0, 1)$ depends on x. We get a uniform bound on the error over $[0, 1]$ by replacing ξ_x with its worst possible value over $[0, 1]$:

$$|f(x) - (1+x)| \leq \frac{1}{2}x^2 e^{\xi_x} \leq \frac{e}{2}x^2.$$

3.3 Optimality Conditions

```
x = np.linspace(0,1,100)
y = np.exp(x)
taylor = 1 + x
err = (np.exp(1)/2) * x**2
```

If we plot the upper and lower bounds, we see that f indeed falls within them.

```
plt.plot(x,y,label='f')
plt.plot(x,taylor,label='taylor')
plt.plot(x,taylor-err,linestyle=':',color='green',label='lower')
plt.plot(x,taylor+err,linestyle='--',color='green',label='upper')
plt.legend()
plt.show()
```

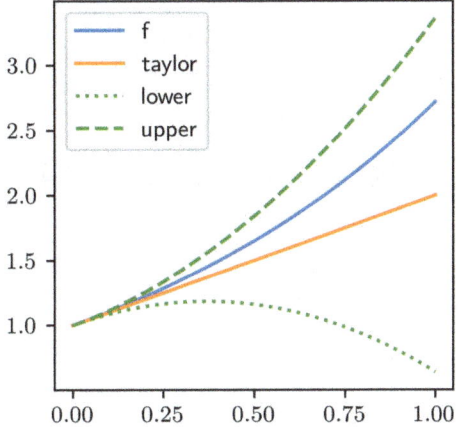

Figure 3.4 Graphical output of code.

◁ **NC**

In the case of several variables, we again restrict ourselves to the second order.

Theorem 3.3.9 *(Taylor) Let $f: D \to \mathbb{R}$ where $D \subseteq \mathbb{R}^d$. Let $\mathbf{x}_0 \in D$ and $\delta > 0$ be such that $B_\delta(\mathbf{x}_0) \subseteq D$. If f is twice continuously differentiable on $B_\delta(\mathbf{x}_0)$, then for any $\mathbf{x} \in B_\delta(\mathbf{x}_0)$*

$$f(\mathbf{x}) = f(\mathbf{x}_0) + \nabla f(\mathbf{x}_0)^T(\mathbf{x} - \mathbf{x}_0) + \frac{1}{2}(\mathbf{x} - \mathbf{x}_0)^T \mathbf{H}_f(\mathbf{x}_0 + \xi(\mathbf{x} - \mathbf{x}_0))(\mathbf{x} - \mathbf{x}_0),$$

for some $\xi \in (0, 1)$.

As in the single-variable case, we think of $f(\mathbf{x}_0) + \nabla f(\mathbf{x}_0)^T(\mathbf{x}-\mathbf{x}_0)$ for fixed $\mathbf{x}_0$ as a linear – or more accurately affine – approximation to f at $\mathbf{x}_0$. The third term on the right-hand side above quantifies the error of this approximation.

Proof idea: We apply the single-variable result to $\phi(t) = f(\alpha(t))$. We use the *Chain Rule* to compute the needed derivatives.

Proof Let $\mathbf{p} = \mathbf{x} - \mathbf{x}_0$ and $\phi(t) = f(\alpha(t))$ where $\alpha(t) = \mathbf{x}_0 + t\mathbf{p}$. Observe that $\phi(0) = f(\mathbf{x}_0)$ and $\phi(1) = f(\mathbf{x})$. As observed in the proof of the *Mean Value Theorem*, $\phi'(t) = \nabla f(\alpha(t))^T \mathbf{p}$. By the *Chain Rule* and Example 3.2.4,

$$\phi''(t) = \frac{d}{dt}\left[\sum_{i=1}^{d} \frac{\partial f(\alpha(t))}{\partial x_i} p_i\right]$$

$$= \sum_{i=1}^{d} \left(\nabla \frac{\partial f(\alpha(t))}{\partial x_i}\right)^T \alpha'(t) p_i$$

$$= \sum_{i=1}^{d} \sum_{j=1}^{d} \frac{\partial^2 f(\alpha(t))}{\partial x_j \partial x_i} p_j p_i$$

$$= \mathbf{p}^T \mathbf{H}_f(\mathbf{x}_0 + t\mathbf{p})\,\mathbf{p}.$$

In particular, ϕ has continuous first and second derivatives on $[0, 1]$.

By *Taylor's Theorem* in the single-variable case,

$$\phi(t) = \phi(0) + t\phi'(0) + \frac{1}{2}t^2 \phi''(\xi)$$

for some $\xi \in (0, t)$. Plugging in the expressions for $\phi(0)$, $\phi'(0)$, and $\phi''(\xi)$ and taking $t = 1$ gives the claim. $\square$

Example 3.3.10 *Consider the function* $f(x_1, x_2) = x_1 x_2 + x_1^2 + e^{x_1} \cos x_2$. *We apply* Taylor's Theorem *with* $\mathbf{x}_0 = (0, 0)$ *and* $\mathbf{x} = (x_1, x_2)$. *The gradient is*

$$\nabla f(x_1, x_2) = (x_2 + 2x_1 + e^{x_1} \cos x_2, x_1 - e^{x_1} \sin x_2)$$

and the Hessian is

$$\mathbf{H}_f(x_1, x_2) = \begin{pmatrix} 2 + e^{x_1} \cos x_2 & 1 - e^{x_1} \sin x_2 \\ 1 - e^{x_1} \sin x_2 & -e^{x_1} \cos x_2 \end{pmatrix}.$$

So $f(0, 0) = 1$ *and* $\nabla f(0, 0) = (1, 0)$. *Thus, by* Taylor's Theorem, *there is* $\xi \in (0, 1)$ *such that*

$$f(x_1, x_2) = 1 + x_1 + \frac{1}{2}[2x_1^2 + 2x_1 x_2 + (x_1^2 - x_2^2) e^{\xi x_1} \cos(\xi x_2) - 2x_1 x_2 e^{\xi x_1} \sin(\xi x_2)].$$

3.3.2.2 Second Directional Derivative

To control the error term in *Taylor's Theorem*, it will be convenient to introduce a notion of second directional derivative.

Definition 3.3.11 *(Second Directional Derivative)* Let $f: D \to \mathbb{R}$ where $D \subseteq \mathbb{R}^d$, let $\mathbf{x}_0 \in D$ be an interior point of D and let $\mathbf{v} \in \mathbb{R}^d$ be a nonzero vector. The second directional derivative of f at $\mathbf{x}_0$ in the direction $\mathbf{v}$ is

$$\frac{\partial^2 f(\mathbf{x}_0)}{\partial \mathbf{v}^2} = \lim_{h \to 0} \frac{1}{h}\left[\frac{\partial f(\mathbf{x}_0 + h\mathbf{v})}{\partial \mathbf{v}} - \frac{\partial f(\mathbf{x}_0)}{\partial \mathbf{v}}\right]$$

provided the limit exists.

Typically, $\mathbf{v}$ is a unit vector.

Theorem 3.3.12 *(Second Directional Derivative and Hessian)* Let $f: D \to \mathbb{R}$ where $D \subseteq \mathbb{R}^d$, let $\mathbf{x}_0 \in D$ be an interior point of D, and let $\mathbf{v} \in \mathbb{R}^d$ be a vector. Assume that f is *twice continuously differentiable at* $\mathbf{x}_0$. *Then the second directional derivative of f at* $\mathbf{x}_0$ *in the direction* $\mathbf{v}$ *is given by*

$$\frac{\partial^2 f(\mathbf{x}_0)}{\partial \mathbf{v}^2} = \mathbf{v}^T \mathbf{H}_f(\mathbf{x}_0) \mathbf{v}.$$

Note the similarity to the quadratic term in *Taylor's Theorem*.

Proof idea: We have already done this calculation in the proof of *Taylor's Theorem*.

Proof By definition of the derivative,

$$\lim_{h \to 0} \frac{1}{h} \left[\frac{\partial f(\mathbf{x}_0 + h\mathbf{v})}{\partial \mathbf{v}} - \frac{\partial f(\mathbf{x}_0)}{\partial \mathbf{v}} \right] = \lim_{h \to 0} \frac{1}{h} \left[\nabla f(\mathbf{x}_0 + h\mathbf{v})^T \mathbf{v} - \nabla f(\mathbf{x}_0)^T \mathbf{v} \right]$$

$$= \lim_{h \to 0} \frac{1}{h} \sum_{i=1}^{n} v_i \left[\frac{\partial f(\mathbf{x}_0 + h\mathbf{v})}{\partial x_i} - \frac{\partial f(\mathbf{x}_0)}{\partial x_i} \right]$$

$$= \sum_{i=1}^{n} v_i \lim_{h \to 0} \frac{1}{h} \left[\frac{\partial f(\mathbf{x}_0 + h\mathbf{v})}{\partial x_i} - \frac{\partial f(\mathbf{x}_0)}{\partial x_i} \right]$$

$$= \sum_{i=1}^{n} v_i \frac{\partial g_i(\mathbf{x}_0)}{\partial \mathbf{v}},$$

where $g_i(\mathbf{x}_0) = \frac{\partial f(\mathbf{x}_0)}{\partial x_i}$. So

$$\frac{\partial g_i(\mathbf{x}_0)}{\partial \mathbf{v}} = \nabla g_i(\mathbf{x}_0)^T \mathbf{v} = \sum_{j=1}^{n} v_j \frac{\partial^2 f(\mathbf{x}_0)}{\partial x_i \partial x_j}$$

by the *Directional Derivative and Gradient Theorem*. Plugging back above we get

$$\frac{\partial^2 f(\mathbf{x}_0)}{\partial \mathbf{v}^2} = \sum_{i=1}^{n} v_i \sum_{j=1}^{n} v_j \frac{\partial^2 f(\mathbf{x}_0)}{\partial x_i \partial x_j} = \mathbf{v}^T \mathbf{H}_f(\mathbf{x}_0) \mathbf{v}.$$

□

So going back to *Taylor's Theorem*,

$$f(\mathbf{x}) = f(\mathbf{x}_0) + \nabla f(\mathbf{x}_0)^T (\mathbf{x} - \mathbf{x}_0) + \frac{1}{2} (\mathbf{x} - \mathbf{x}_0)^T \mathbf{H}_f(\mathbf{x}_0 + \xi(\mathbf{x} - \mathbf{x}_0))(\mathbf{x} - \mathbf{x}_0),$$

we see that the second term on the right-hand side is the directional derivative at $\mathbf{x}_0$ in the direction $\mathbf{x} - \mathbf{x}_0$ and that the third term is half of the second directional derivative at $\mathbf{x}_0 + \xi(\mathbf{x} - \mathbf{x}_0)$ in the same direction.

3.3.2.3 Necessary Condition

When f is twice continuously differentiable, we get a necessary condition based on the Hessian.

Theorem 3.3.13 (Second-Order Necessary Optimality Condition) *Let* $f: \mathbb{R}^d \to \mathbb{R}$ *be twice continuously differentiable on* $\mathbb{R}^d$. *If* $\mathbf{x}_0$ *is a local minimizer, then* $\nabla f(\mathbf{x}_0) = \mathbf{0}$ *and* $\mathbf{H}_f(\mathbf{x}_0)$ *is positive semidefinite.*[8]

Proof idea: By *Taylor's Theorem* and the *First-Order Necessary Optimality Condition*,

$$f(\mathbf{x}_0 + \alpha \mathbf{v}) = f(\mathbf{x}_0) + \nabla f(\mathbf{x}_0)^T (\alpha \mathbf{v}) + \frac{1}{2} (\alpha \mathbf{v})^T \mathbf{H}_f(\mathbf{x}_0 + \xi_\alpha \alpha \mathbf{v})(\alpha \mathbf{v})$$

$$= f(\mathbf{x}_0) + \frac{1}{2} \alpha^2 \mathbf{v}^T \mathbf{H}_f(\mathbf{x}_0 + \xi_\alpha \alpha \mathbf{v}) \mathbf{v}.$$

---

[8] See Definition 1.2.9.

If $\mathbf{H}_f$ is positive semidefinite in a neighborhood around $\mathbf{x}_0$, then the second term on the right-hand side is nonnegative, which is necessary for $\mathbf{x}_0$ to be a local minimizer. Formally we argue by contradiction: Indeed, if $\mathbf{H}_f$ is not positive semidefinite, then there must exist a direction in which the second directional derivative is negative; since the gradient is $\mathbf{0}$ at $\mathbf{x}_0$, intuitively the directional derivative must become negative in that direction as well and the function must decrease.

Proof We argue by contradiction. Suppose that $\mathbf{H}_f(\mathbf{x}_0)$ is not positive semidefinite. By definition, there must be a unit vector $\mathbf{v}$ such that

$$\langle \mathbf{v}, \mathbf{H}_f(\mathbf{x}_0)\mathbf{v}\rangle = -\eta < 0.$$

That is, $\mathbf{v}$ is a direction in which the second directional derivative is negative.

For $\alpha > 0$, *Taylor's Theorem* implies that there is $\xi_\alpha \in (0, 1)$ such that

$$f(\mathbf{x}_0 + \alpha\mathbf{v}) = f(\mathbf{x}_0) + \nabla f(\mathbf{x}_0)^T(\alpha\mathbf{v}) + \frac{1}{2}(\alpha\mathbf{v})^T\mathbf{H}_f(\mathbf{x}_0 + \xi_\alpha\alpha\mathbf{v})(\alpha\mathbf{v})$$

$$= f(\mathbf{x}_0) + \frac{1}{2}\alpha^2\mathbf{v}^T\mathbf{H}_f(\mathbf{x}_0 + \xi_\alpha\alpha\mathbf{v})\mathbf{v}$$

where we used $\nabla f(\mathbf{x}_0) = \mathbf{0}$ by the *First-Order Necessary Optimality Condition*. We want to show that the second term on the right-hand side is negative.

The Hessian is continuous (in the sense that all its entries are continuous functions of $\mathbf{x}$). In particular, the second directional derivative $\mathbf{v}^T\mathbf{H}_f(\mathbf{x})\mathbf{v}$ is continuous as a linear combination of continuous functions. So, by definition of continuity, for any $\epsilon > 0$ – say $\epsilon = \eta/2$ – there is $\delta > 0$ small enough that

$$\left|\mathbf{v}^T\mathbf{H}_f(\mathbf{x})\mathbf{v} - \mathbf{v}^T\mathbf{H}_f(\mathbf{x}_0)\mathbf{v}\right| < \eta/2$$

for all $\mathbf{x} \in B_\delta(\mathbf{x}_0)$.

Take $\alpha^* > 0$ small enough that $\mathbf{x}_0 + \alpha^*\mathbf{v} \in B_\delta(\mathbf{x}_0)$. Then, for all $\alpha \in (0, \alpha^*)$, whatever $\xi_\alpha \in (0, 1)$ is, it holds that $\mathbf{x}_0 + \xi_\alpha\alpha\mathbf{v} \in B_\delta(\mathbf{x}_0)$. Hence,

$$\mathbf{v}^T\mathbf{H}_f(\mathbf{x}_0 + \xi_\alpha\alpha\mathbf{v})\mathbf{v} = \mathbf{v}^T\mathbf{H}_f(\mathbf{x}_0)\mathbf{v} + (\mathbf{v}^T\mathbf{H}_f(\mathbf{x}_0 + \xi_\alpha\alpha\mathbf{v})\mathbf{v} - \mathbf{v}^T\mathbf{H}_f(\mathbf{x}_0)\mathbf{v})$$

$$\leq \mathbf{v}^T\mathbf{H}_f(\mathbf{x}_0)\mathbf{v} + |\mathbf{v}^T\mathbf{H}_f(\mathbf{x}_0 + \xi_\alpha\alpha\mathbf{v})\mathbf{v} - \mathbf{v}^T\mathbf{H}_f(\mathbf{x}_0)\mathbf{v}|$$

$$< -\eta + \eta/2$$

$$< -\eta/2 < 0$$

by definition of η. That implies

$$f(\mathbf{x}_0 + \alpha\mathbf{v}) < f(\mathbf{x}_0) - \alpha^2\eta/4 < f(\mathbf{x}_0).$$

Since this holds for all sufficiently small α, every open ball around $\mathbf{x}_0$ has a point achieving a lower value than $f(\mathbf{x}_0)$. Thus $\mathbf{x}_0$ is not a local minimizer, a contradiction. So it must be that $\mathbf{H}_f(\mathbf{x}_0) \succeq \mathbf{0}$. $\square$

3.3.2.4 Sufficient Condition

The necessary condition above is not in general sufficient, as the following example shows.

NUMERICAL CORNER Let $f(x) = x^3$. Then $f'(x) = 3x^2$ and $f''(x) = 6x$ so that $f'(0) = 0$ and $f''(0) \geq 0$. Hence $x = 0$ is a stationary point. But $x = 0$ is not a local minimizer. Indeed $f(0) = 0$ but, for any $\delta > 0$, $f(-\delta) < 0$.

3.3 Optimality Conditions

```
x = np.linspace(-2,2,100)
y = x**3

plt.plot(x,y, c='k')
plt.ylim(-5,5)
plt.show()
```

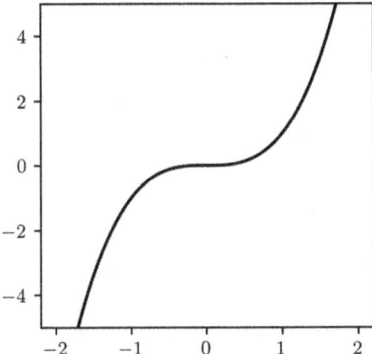

Figure 3.5 Graphical output of code.

◁ **NC**

We give sufficient conditions for a point to be a local minimizer.

Theorem 3.3.14 (*Second-Order Sufficient Optimality Condition*) *Let $f: \mathbb{R}^d \to \mathbb{R}$ be twice continuously differentiable on $\mathbb{R}^d$. If $\nabla f(\mathbf{x}_0) = \mathbf{0}$ and $\mathbf{H}_f(\mathbf{x}_0)$ is positive definite,[9] then $\mathbf{x}_0$ is a strict local minimizer.*

Proof idea: We use *Taylor's Theorem* again. This time we use the positive definiteness of the Hessian to bound the value of the function from below.

We will need a lemma.[10]

Lemma 3.3.15 (*Quadratic Form and Frobenius Norm*) *Let $A = (a_{i,j})_{i,j}$ and $B = (b_{i,j})_{i,j}$ be matrices in $\mathbb{R}^{n \times m}$. For any unit vectors $\mathbf{u} \in \mathbb{R}^n$ and $\mathbf{v} \in \mathbb{R}^m$*

$$\left|\mathbf{u}^T A \mathbf{v} - \mathbf{u}^T B \mathbf{v}\right| \leq \|A - B\|_F.$$

Proof By the *Cauchy–Schwarz inequality*,

$$\left|\mathbf{u}^T A \mathbf{v} - \mathbf{u}^T B \mathbf{v}\right| = \left|\sum_{i=1}^n \sum_{j=1}^m u_i v_j (a_{i,j} - b_{i,j})\right|$$

$$\leq \sqrt{\sum_{i=1}^n \sum_{j=1}^m u_i^2 v_j^2} \sqrt{\sum_{i=1}^n \sum_{j=1}^m (a_{i,j} - b_{i,j})^2}$$

$$= \|A - B\|_F,$$

where we used the fact that $\mathbf{u}$ and $\mathbf{v}$ have unit norm on the last line. □

---

[9] See Definition 1.2.9.
[10] Recall the Frobenius norm of a matrix from Definition 1.2.8.

Proof *(Second-Order Sufficient Optimality Condition)* By *Taylor's Theorem*, for all unit vectors $\mathbf{v} \in \mathbb{R}^d$ and $\alpha \in \mathbb{R}$, there is $\xi_\alpha \in (0, 1)$ such that

$$f(\mathbf{x}_0 + \alpha \mathbf{v}) = f(\mathbf{x}_0) + \nabla f(\mathbf{x}_0)^T (\alpha \mathbf{v}) + \frac{1}{2}(\alpha \mathbf{v})^T \mathbf{H}_f(\mathbf{x}_0 + \xi_\alpha \alpha \mathbf{v})(\alpha \mathbf{v})$$

$$= f(\mathbf{x}_0) + \frac{1}{2}\alpha^2 \mathbf{v}^T \mathbf{H}_f(\mathbf{x}_0 + \xi_\alpha \alpha \mathbf{v}) \mathbf{v},$$

where we used the fact that $\nabla f(\mathbf{x}_0) = \mathbf{0}$. The second term on the last line is 0 at $\mathbf{v} = \mathbf{0}$. Our goal is to show that it is strictly positive (except at $\mathbf{0}$) in a neighborhood of $\mathbf{0}$.

The set $\mathbb{S}^{d-1}$ of unit vectors in $\mathbb{R}^d$ is closed and bounded. The expression $\mathbf{v}^T \mathbf{H}_f(\mathbf{x}_0) \mathbf{v}$, viewed as a function of $\mathbf{v}$, is continuous since it is a polynomial. Hence, by the *Extreme Value Theorem*, it attains its minimum on $\mathbb{S}^{d-1}$. By our assumption that $\mathbf{H}_f(\mathbf{x}_0)$ is positive definite, that minimum must be strictly positive, say $\mu > 0$.

By the *Quadratic Form and Frobenius Norm Lemma* (ignoring the absolute value),

$$\mathbf{v}^T \mathbf{H}_f(\mathbf{x}_0) \mathbf{v} - \mathbf{v}^T \mathbf{H}_f(\mathbf{x}_0 + \mathbf{w}) \mathbf{v} \leq \|\mathbf{H}_f(\mathbf{x}_0) - \mathbf{H}_f(\mathbf{x}_0 + \mathbf{w})\|_F.$$

The Frobenius norm above is continuous in $\mathbf{w}$ as a composition of continuous functions. Moreover, we have at $\mathbf{w} = \mathbf{0}$ that this Frobenius norm is 0. Hence, by definition of continuity, for any $\epsilon > 0$, say $\epsilon := \mu/2$, there is $\delta > 0$ such that $\mathbf{w} \in B_\delta(\mathbf{0})$ implies $\|\mathbf{H}_f(\mathbf{x}_0) - \mathbf{H}_f(\mathbf{x}_0 + \mathbf{w})\|_F < \epsilon = \mu/2$.

Since $\mathbf{v}^T \mathbf{H}_f(\mathbf{x}_0) \mathbf{v} > \mu$, the inequality in the previous display implies that

$$\mathbf{v}^T \mathbf{H}_f(\mathbf{x}_0 + \mathbf{w}) \mathbf{v} \geq \mathbf{v}^T \mathbf{H}_f(\mathbf{x}_0) \mathbf{v} - \|\mathbf{H}_f(\mathbf{x}_0) - \mathbf{H}_f(\mathbf{x}_0 + \mathbf{w})\|_F > \frac{\mu}{2}.$$

This holds for any unit vector $\mathbf{v}$ and any $\mathbf{w} \in B_\delta(\mathbf{0})$.

Going back to our Taylor expansion, for $\alpha > 0$ small enough (not depending on $\mathbf{v}$), it holds that $\mathbf{w} = \xi_\alpha \alpha \mathbf{v} \in B_\delta(\mathbf{0})$ so that we get from the previous inequality

$$f(\mathbf{x}_0 + \alpha \mathbf{v}) = f(\mathbf{x}_0) + \frac{1}{2}\alpha^2 \mathbf{v}^T \mathbf{H}_f(\mathbf{x}_0 + \xi_\alpha \alpha \mathbf{v}) \mathbf{v}$$

$$> f(\mathbf{x}_0) + \frac{1}{4}\alpha^2 \mu$$

$$> f(\mathbf{x}_0).$$

Therefore $\mathbf{x}_0$ is a strict local minimizer. $\square$

3.3.3 Adding Equality Constraints

Until now, we have considered *unconstrained* optimization problems, in which, the variable $\mathbf{x}$ can take any value in $\mathbb{R}^d$. However, it is common to impose conditions on $\mathbf{x}$. Hence, we consider the *constrained* minimization problem

$$\min_{\mathbf{x} \in \mathcal{X}} f(\mathbf{x})$$

where $\mathcal{X} \subset \mathbb{R}^d$.

Example 3.3.16 *For instance, the entries of $\mathbf{x}$ may have to satisfy certain bounds. In that case, we would have*

$$\mathcal{X} = \{\mathbf{x} = (x_1, \ldots, x_d) \in \mathbb{R}^d : x_i \in [a_i, b_i], \forall i\}$$

for some constants $a_i < b_i$, $i = 1, \ldots, d$.

3.3 Optimality Conditions

In this more general problem, the notion of global and local minimizer can be adapted straightforwardly. Note that, for simplicity, we will assume that f is defined over all of $\mathbb{R}^d$. When $\mathbf{x} \in \mathcal{X}$, it is said to be feasible.

Definition 3.3.17 *(Global Minimizer) Let $f : \mathbb{R}^d \to \mathbb{R}$. The point $\mathbf{x}^* \in \mathcal{X}$ is a global minimizer of f over $\mathcal{X}$ if*

$$f(\mathbf{x}) \geq f(\mathbf{x}^*), \quad \forall \mathbf{x} \in \mathcal{X}.$$

Definition 3.3.18 *(Local Minimizer) Let $f : \mathbb{R}^d \to \mathbb{R}$. The point $\mathbf{x}^* \in \mathcal{X}$ is a local minimizer of f over $\mathcal{X}$ if there is $\delta > 0$ such that*

$$f(\mathbf{x}) \geq f(\mathbf{x}^*), \quad \forall \mathbf{x} \in (B_\delta(\mathbf{x}^*) \setminus \{\mathbf{x}^*\}) \cap \mathcal{X}.$$

If the inequality is strict, we say that $\mathbf{x}^*$ is a strict local minimizer.

In this subsection, we restrict ourselves to one important class of constraints: equality constraints. That is, we consider the minimization problem

$$\min f(\mathbf{x})$$
$$\text{s.t. } h_i(\mathbf{x}) = 0, \ \forall i \in [\ell]$$

where s.t. stands for "subject to." In other words, we only allow those $\mathbf{x}$'s such that $h_i(\mathbf{x}) = 0$ for all i. Here $f : \mathbb{R}^d \to \mathbb{R}$ and $h_i : \mathbb{R}^d \to \mathbb{R}$, $i \in [\ell]$. We will sometimes use the notation $\mathbf{h} : \mathbb{R}^d \to \mathbb{R}^\ell$, where $\mathbf{h}(\mathbf{x}) = (h_1(\mathbf{x}), \ldots, h_\ell(\mathbf{x}))$.

Example 3.3.19 *If we want to minimize $2x_1^2 + 3x_2^2$ over all two-dimensional unit vectors $\mathbf{x} = (x_1, x_2)$, then we can let*

$$f(\mathbf{x}) = 2x_1^2 + 3x_2^2$$

and

$$h_1(\mathbf{x}) = 1 - x_1^2 - x_2^2 = 1 - \|\mathbf{x}\|^2.$$

Observe that we could have chosen a different equality constraint to express the same minimization problem.

The following theorem generalizes the *First-Order Necessary Optimality Condition*. The proof is omitted.

Theorem 3.3.20 *(Lagrange Multipliers) Assume $f : \mathbb{R}^d \to \mathbb{R}$ and $h_i : \mathbb{R}^d \to \mathbb{R}$, $i \in [\ell]$, are continuously differentiable. Let $\mathbf{x}^*$ be a local minimizer of f s.t. $\mathbf{h}(\mathbf{x}) = \mathbf{0}$. Assume further that the vectors $\nabla h_i(\mathbf{x}^*)$, $i \in [\ell]$, are linearly independent. Then there exists a unique vector*

$$\boldsymbol{\lambda}^* = (\lambda_1^*, \ldots, \lambda_\ell^*)$$

satisfying

$$\nabla f(\mathbf{x}^*) + \sum_{i=1}^{\ell} \lambda_i^* \nabla h_i(\mathbf{x}^*) = \mathbf{0}.$$

The quantities $\lambda_1^*, \ldots, \lambda_\ell^*$ are called Lagrange multipliers.

Example 3.3.21 *(continued from Example 3.3.19) Returning to the previous example,*

$$\nabla f(\mathbf{x}) = \left(\frac{\partial f(\mathbf{x})}{\partial x_1}, \frac{\partial f(\mathbf{x})}{\partial x_2}\right) = (4x_1, 6x_2)$$

and

$$\nabla h_1(\mathbf{x}) = \left(\frac{\partial h_1(\mathbf{x})}{\partial x_1}, \frac{\partial h_1(\mathbf{x})}{\partial x_2}\right) = (-2x_1, -2x_2).$$

The conditions in the Lagrange Multipliers Theorem *read*

$$4x_1 - 2\lambda_1 x_1 = 0$$
$$6x_2 - 2\lambda_1 x_2 = 0.$$

The constraint $x_1^2 + x_2^2 = 1$ must also be satisfied. Observe that the linear independence condition is automatically satisfied since there is only one constraint.

There are several cases to consider.

1. *If neither x_1 nor x_2 is 0, then the first equation gives $\lambda_1 = 2$ while the second one gives $\lambda_1 = 3$. So that case cannot happen.*

2. *If $x_1 = 0$, then $x_2 = 1$ or $x_2 = -1$ by the constraint and the second equation gives $\lambda_1 = 3$ in either case.*

3. *If $x_2 = 0$, then $x_1 = 1$ or $x_1 = -1$ by the constraint and the first equation gives $\lambda_1 = 2$ in either case.*

Do any of these last four solutions, namely $(x_1, x_2, \lambda_1) = (0, 1, 3)$, $(x_1, x_2, \lambda_1) = (0, -1, 3)$, $(x_1, x_2, \lambda_1) = (1, 0, 2)$, and $(x_1, x_2, \lambda_1) = (-1, 0, 2)$, actually correspond to a local minimizer?

This problem can be solved manually. Indeed, substitute $x_2^2 = 1 - x_1^2$ into the objective function to obtain

$$2x_1^2 + 3(1 - x_1^2) = -x_1^2 + 3.$$

This is minimized for the largest value that x_1^2 can take, namely when $x_1 = 1$ or $x_1 = -1$. Indeed, we must have $0 \leq x_1^2 \leq x_1^2 + x_2^2 = 1$. So both $(x_1, x_2) = (1, 0)$ and $(x_1, x_2) = (-1, 0)$ are global minimizers. A fortiori, they must be local minimizers.

What about $(x_1, x_2) = (0, 1)$ and $(x_1, x_2) = (0, -1)$? Arguing as above, they in fact correspond to global maximizers of the objective function.

Assume $\mathbf{x}$ is feasible, that is, $\mathbf{h}(\mathbf{x}) = \mathbf{0}$. We let

$$\mathscr{F}_\mathbf{h}(\mathbf{x}) = \left\{ \mathbf{v} \in \mathbb{R}^d : \nabla h_i(\mathbf{x})^T \mathbf{v} = 0, \ \forall i \in [\ell] \right\}$$

be the linear subspace of first-order feasible directions at $\mathbf{x}$. To explain the name, note that by a first-order Taylor expansion, if $\mathbf{v} \in \mathscr{F}_\mathbf{h}(\mathbf{x})$ then it holds that

$$h_i(\mathbf{x} + \delta \mathbf{v}) \approx h_i(\mathbf{x}) + \delta \nabla h_i(\mathbf{x})^T \mathbf{v} = 0$$

for all i.

The theorem says that, if $\mathbf{x}^*$ is a local minimizer, then the gradient of f is orthogonal to the set of first-order feasible directions at $\mathbf{x}^*$. Indeed by the *Lagrange Multipliers Theorem* any $\mathbf{v} \in \mathscr{F}_\mathbf{h}(\mathbf{x}^*)$ satisfies

3.3 Optimality Conditions

$$\nabla f(\mathbf{x}^*)^T \mathbf{v} = \left(-\sum_{i=1}^{\ell} \lambda_i^* \nabla h_i(\mathbf{x}^*)\right)^T \mathbf{v} = -\sum_{i=1}^{\ell} \lambda_i^* \nabla h_i(\mathbf{x}^*)^T \mathbf{v} = 0.$$

Intuitively, following a first-order feasible direction does not alter the objective function value up to second-order error:

$$f(\mathbf{x}^* + \alpha \mathbf{v}) \approx f(\mathbf{x}^*) + \alpha \nabla f(\mathbf{x}^*)^T \mathbf{v} = f(\mathbf{x}^*).$$

NUMERICAL CORNER Returning to Example 3.3.21, the points satisfying $h_1(\mathbf{x}) = 0$ sit on the circle of radius 1 around the origin. We have already seen that

$$\nabla h_1(\mathbf{x}) = \left(\frac{\partial h_1(\mathbf{x})}{\partial x_1}, \frac{\partial h_1(\mathbf{x})}{\partial x_2}\right) = (-2x_1, -2x_2).$$

Here is code illustrating the theorem (with help from ChatGPT). We first compute the function h_1 at a grid of points using `numpy.meshgrid`.

```
def h1(x1, x2):
    return 1 - x1**2 - x2**2

x1, x2 = np.linspace(-1.5, 1.5, 400), np.linspace(-1.5, 1.5, 400)
X1, X2 = np.meshgrid(x1, x2)
H1 = h1(X1, X2)
```

We use `matplotlib.pyplot.contour` to plot the constraint set as a contour line (for the constant value 0) of h_1. Gradients of h_1 are plotted at a collection of `points` with the `matplotlib.pyplot.quiver` function, which is used for plotting vectors as arrows. We see that the directions of first-order feasible directions are orthogonal to the arrows, and therefore are tangent to the constraint set.

At those same `points`, we also plot the gradient of f, which recall is

$$\nabla f(\mathbf{x}) = \left(\frac{\partial f(\mathbf{x})}{\partial x_1}, \frac{\partial f(\mathbf{x})}{\partial x_2}\right) = (4x_1, 6x_2).$$

We make all gradients into unit vectors.

```
plt.figure(figsize=(4, 4))
plt.contour(X1, X2, H1, levels=[0], colors='b')
points = [(0.5, np.sqrt(3)/2), (-0.5, np.sqrt(3)/2),
    (0.5, -np.sqrt(3)/2),
    (-0.5, -np.sqrt(3)/2), (1, 0), (-1, 0), (0, 1), (0, -1)]
for x1, x2 in points:
    plt.quiver(x1, x2, -x1/np.sqrt(x1**2 + x2**2),
            -x2/np.sqrt(x1**2 + x2**2),
            scale=10, color='r')
    plt.quiver(x1, x2, 4*x1/np.sqrt(16 * x1**2 + 36 * x2**2),
            6*x2/np.sqrt(16 * x1**2 + 36 * x2**2),
            scale=10, color='lime')
```

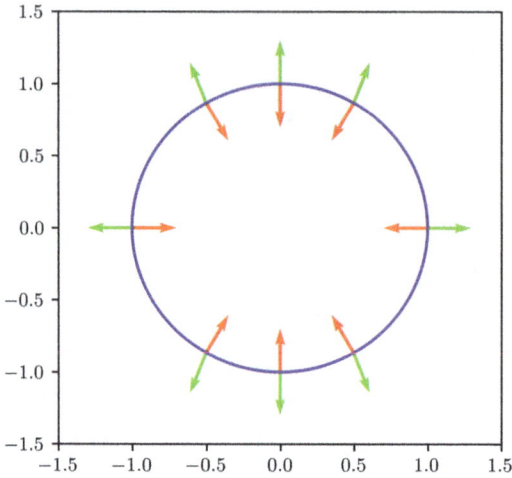

Figure 3.6 Graphical output of code.

We see that, at $(-1, 0)$ and $(1, 0)$, the gradient is indeed orthogonal to the first-order feasible directions.

◁ **NC**

A feasible vector $\mathbf{x}$ is said to be *regular* if the vectors $\nabla h_i(\mathbf{x}^*)$, $i \in [\ell]$, are linearly independent. We reformulate the previous theorem in terms of the Lagrangian function, which is defined as

$$L(\mathbf{x}, \lambda) = f(\mathbf{x}) + \sum_{i=1}^{\ell} \lambda_i h_i(\mathbf{x}),$$

where $\lambda = (\lambda_1, \ldots, \lambda_\ell)$. Then, by the *Lagrange Multipliers Theorem*, a regular local minimizer satisfies

$$\nabla_{\mathbf{x}} L(\mathbf{x}, \lambda) = \mathbf{0}$$
$$\nabla_{\lambda} L(\mathbf{x}, \lambda) = \mathbf{0}.$$

Here the notation $\nabla_{\mathbf{x}}$ (respectively ∇_{λ}) indicates that we are taking the vector of partial derivatives with respect to only the variables in $\mathbf{x}$ (respectively λ).

To see that these equations hold, note that

$$\nabla_{\mathbf{x}} L(\mathbf{x}, \lambda) = \nabla f(\mathbf{x}) + \sum_{i=1}^{\ell} \lambda_i \nabla h_i(\mathbf{x})$$

and

$$\nabla_{\lambda} L(\mathbf{x}, \lambda) = \mathbf{h}(\mathbf{x}).$$

So $\nabla_{\mathbf{x}} L(\mathbf{x}, \lambda) = \mathbf{0}$ is a restatement of the Lagrange multipliers condition and $\nabla_{\lambda} L(\mathbf{x}, \lambda) = \mathbf{0}$ is a restatement of feasibility. Together, they form a system of $d + \ell$ equations in $d + \ell$ variables.

Example 3.3.22 *Consider the constrained minimization problem on $\mathbb{R}^3$ where the objective function is*

$$f(\mathbf{x}) = \frac{1}{2}(x_1^2 + x_2^2 + x_3^2)$$

and the only constraint function is

$$h_1(\mathbf{x}) = 3 - x_1 - x_2 - x_3.$$

The gradients are

$$\nabla f(\mathbf{x}) = (x_1, x_2, x_3)$$

and

$$\nabla h_1(\mathbf{x}) = (-1, -1, -1).$$

In particular, regularity is always satisfied since there is only one nonzero vector to consider. So we are looking for solutions to the system of equations

$$x_1 - \lambda_1 = 0$$
$$x_2 - \lambda_1 = 0$$
$$x_3 - \lambda_1 = 0$$
$$3 - x_1 - x_2 - x_3 = 0.$$

The first three equations imply that $x_1 = x_2 = x_3 = \lambda_1$. Substituting in the fourth equation gives $3 - 3\lambda_1 = 0$ so $\lambda_1 = 1$. Hence, $x_1 = x_2 = x_3 = 1$ and this is the only solution.

So the only local minimizer, if it exists, must be the vector $(1, 1, 1)$ with Lagrange multiplier 1. How can we know for sure whether this is the case?

As in the unconstrained case, there are *sufficient* conditions. Also as in that case, they involve second-order derivatives. We give one such theorem next without proof.

Theorem 3.3.23 Assume $f: \mathbb{R}^d \to \mathbb{R}$ and $h_i: \mathbb{R}^d \to \mathbb{R}$, $i \in [\ell]$, are twice continuously differentiable. Let $\mathbf{x}^* \in \mathbb{R}^d$ and $\lambda^* \in \mathbb{R}^\ell$ satisfy

$$\nabla f(\mathbf{x}^*) + \sum_{i=1}^{\ell} \lambda_i^* \nabla h_i(\mathbf{x}^*) = \mathbf{0}$$

$$\mathbf{h}(\mathbf{x}^*) = \mathbf{0}$$

and

$$\mathbf{v}^T \left(\mathbf{H}_f(\mathbf{x}^*) + \sum_{i=1}^{\ell} \lambda_i^* \mathbf{H}_{h_i}(\mathbf{x}^*) \right) \mathbf{v} > 0$$

for all $\mathbf{v} \in \mathscr{F}_{\mathbf{h}}(\mathbf{x})$.

Then $\mathbf{x}^*$ is a strict local minimizer of f s.t. $\mathbf{h}(\mathbf{x}) = \mathbf{0}$.

Example 3.3.24 (*continued from Example 3.3.22*) We return to the previous example. We found a unique solution

$$(x_1^*, x_2^*, x_3^*, \lambda_1^*) = (1, 1, 1, 1)$$

to the system

$$\nabla f(\mathbf{x}^*) + \sum_{i=1}^{\ell} \lambda_i^* \nabla h_i(\mathbf{x}^*) = \mathbf{0}$$

$$\mathbf{h}(\mathbf{x}^*) = \mathbf{0}.$$

To check the second-order condition, we need the Hessians. It is straightforward to compute the second-order partial derivatives, which do not depend on **x**. We obtain

$$\mathbf{H}_f(\mathbf{x}) = I_{3\times 3}$$

and

$$\mathbf{H}_{h_1}(\mathbf{x}) = \mathbf{0}_{3\times 3}.$$

So

$$\mathbf{H}_f(\mathbf{x}^*) + \sum_{i=1}^{\ell} \lambda_i^* \mathbf{H}_{h_i}(\mathbf{x}^*) = I_{3\times 3}$$

and it follows that

$$\mathbf{v}^T \left(\mathbf{H}_f(\mathbf{x}^*) + \sum_{i=1}^{\ell} \lambda_i^* \mathbf{H}_{h_i}(\mathbf{x}^*) \right) \mathbf{v} = \mathbf{v}^T I_{3\times 3} \mathbf{v} = \|\mathbf{v}\|^2 > 0$$

for any nonzero vector, including those in $\mathscr{F}_\mathbf{h}(\mathbf{x})$.

It follows from the previous theorem that $\mathbf{x}^*$ is a strict local minimizer of the constrained problem.

Self-Assessment Quiz *(with help from Claude, Gemini, and ChatGPT)*

1. Which of the following is the correct definition of a global minimizer $\mathbf{x}^*$ of a function $f: \mathbb{R}^d \to \mathbb{R}$?

   a) $f(\mathbf{x}) \geq f(\mathbf{x}^*)$ for all $\mathbf{x}$ in some open ball around $\mathbf{x}^*$.
   b) $f(\mathbf{x}) \geq f(\mathbf{x}^*)$ for all $\mathbf{x} \in \mathbb{R}^d$.
   c) $\nabla f(\mathbf{x}^*) = \mathbf{0}$.
   d) $\mathbf{v}^T \mathbf{H}_f(\mathbf{x}^*) \mathbf{v} > 0$ for all $\mathbf{v} \in \mathbb{R}^d$.

2. Let $f: \mathbb{R}^d \to \mathbb{R}$ be continuously differentiable at $\mathbf{x}_0$. The directional derivative of f at $\mathbf{x}_0$ in the direction $\mathbf{v} \in \mathbb{R}^d$ is NOT given by

   a) $\frac{\partial f(\mathbf{x}_0)}{\partial \mathbf{v}} = \nabla f(\mathbf{x}_0)^T \mathbf{v}$.
   b) $\frac{\partial f(\mathbf{x}_0)}{\partial \mathbf{v}} = \mathbf{v}^T \nabla f(\mathbf{x}_0)$.
   c) $\frac{\partial f(\mathbf{x}_0)}{\partial \mathbf{v}} = \mathbf{v}^T \mathbf{H}_f(\mathbf{x}_0) \mathbf{v}$.
   d) $\frac{\partial f(\mathbf{x}_0)}{\partial \mathbf{v}} = \lim_{h \to 0} \frac{f(\mathbf{x}_0 + h\mathbf{v}) - f(\mathbf{x}_0)}{h}$.

3. Let $f: \mathbb{R}^d \to \mathbb{R}$ be twice continuously differentiable. If $\nabla f(\mathbf{x}_0) = \mathbf{0}$ and $\mathbf{H}_f(\mathbf{x}_0)$ is positive definite, then $\mathbf{x}_0$ is

   a) a global minimizer of f.
   b) a local minimizer of f, but not necessarily a strict local minimizer.
   c) a strict local minimizer of f.
   d) a saddle point of f.

4. Consider the optimization problem $\min_\mathbf{x} f(\mathbf{x})$ subject to $\mathbf{h}(\mathbf{x}) = \mathbf{0}$, where $f: \mathbb{R}^d \to \mathbb{R}$ and $\mathbf{h}: \mathbb{R}^d \to \mathbb{R}^\ell$ are continuously differentiable. Let $\mathbf{x}^*$ be a local minimizer and assume that the vectors $\nabla h_i(\mathbf{x}^*), i \in [\ell]$, are linearly independent. According to the *Lagrange Multipliers Theorem*, which of the following must be true?

a) $\nabla f(\mathbf{x}^*) = \mathbf{0}$.
b) $\nabla f(\mathbf{x}^*) + \sum_{i=1}^{\ell} \lambda_i^* \nabla h_i(\mathbf{x}^*) = \mathbf{0}$ for some $\lambda^* \in \mathbb{R}^\ell$.
c) $\mathbf{h}(\mathbf{x}^*) = \mathbf{0}$.
d) Both b) and c).

5 Which of the following is a correct statement of *Taylor's theorem* (to second order) for a twice continuously differentiable function $f : D \to \mathbb{R}$, where $D \subseteq \mathbb{R}^d$, at an interior point $\mathbf{x}_0 \in D$?

a) For any $\mathbf{x} \in B_\delta(\mathbf{x}_0)$, $f(\mathbf{x}) = f(\mathbf{x}_0) + \nabla f(\mathbf{x}_0)^T(\mathbf{x} - \mathbf{x}_0) + \frac{1}{2}(\mathbf{x} - \mathbf{x}_0)^T \mathbf{H} f(\mathbf{x}_0 + \xi(\mathbf{x} - \mathbf{x}_0))(\mathbf{x} - \mathbf{x}_0)$ for some $\xi \in (0, 1)$.
b) For any $\mathbf{x} \in B_\delta(\mathbf{x}_0)$, $f(\mathbf{x}) = f(\mathbf{x}_0) + \nabla f(\mathbf{x}_0 + \xi(\mathbf{x} - \mathbf{x}_0))^T(\mathbf{x} - \mathbf{x}_0) + \frac{1}{2}(\mathbf{x} - \mathbf{x}_0)^T \mathbf{H} f(\mathbf{x}_0 + \xi(\mathbf{x} - \mathbf{x}_0))(\mathbf{x} - \mathbf{x}_0)$.
c) For any $\mathbf{x} \in B_\delta(\mathbf{x}_0)$, $f(\mathbf{x}) = f(\mathbf{x}_0) + \nabla f(\mathbf{x}_0 + \xi(\mathbf{x} - \mathbf{x}_0))^T(\mathbf{x} - \mathbf{x}_0)$.
d) For any $\mathbf{x} \in B_\delta(\mathbf{x}_0)$, $f(\mathbf{x}) = f(\mathbf{x}_0) + \frac{1}{2}(\mathbf{x}_0 + \xi(\mathbf{x} - \mathbf{x}_0))^T \mathbf{H} f(\mathbf{x}_0)(\mathbf{x}_0 + \xi(\mathbf{x} - \mathbf{x}_0))$.

Answer for 1: b. Justification: The text states that "The point $\mathbf{x}^* \in \mathbb{R}^d$ is a global minimizer of f over $\mathbb{R}^d$ if $f(\mathbf{x}) \geq f(\mathbf{x}^*), \forall \mathbf{x} \in \mathbb{R}^d$."

Answer for 2: c. Justification: The text states the *Directional Derivative from Gradient Theorem*: "Assume that f is continuously differentiable at $\mathbf{x}_0$. Then the directional derivative of f at $\mathbf{x}_0$ in the direction $\mathbf{v}$ is given by $\frac{\partial f(\mathbf{x}_0)}{\partial \mathbf{v}} = \nabla f(\mathbf{x}_0)^T \mathbf{v}$."

Answer for 3: c. Justification: The text states the *Second-Order Sufficient Condition Theorem*: "If $\nabla f(\mathbf{x}_0) = \mathbf{0}$ and $\mathbf{H}_f(\mathbf{x}_0)$ is positive definite, then $\mathbf{x}_0$ is a strict local minimizer."

Answer for 4: d. Justification: The *Lagrange Multipliers Theorem* states that under the given conditions, there exists a unique vector $\lambda^* = (\lambda_1^*, \ldots, \lambda_\ell^*)$ satisfying $\nabla f(\mathbf{x}^*) + \sum_{i=1}^{\ell} \lambda_i^* \nabla h_i(\mathbf{x}^*) = 0$ and $\mathbf{h}(\mathbf{x}^*) = \mathbf{0}$.

Answer for 5: a. Justification: This is the statement of *Taylor's Theorem* as presented in the text.

3.4 Convexity

Our optimality conditions have only concerned local minimizers. Indeed, in the absence of global structure, local information such as gradients and Hessians can only inform us about the immediate neighborhood of points. Here we introduce convexity, a commonly encountered condition under which local minimizers become global minimizers.

3.4.1 Definitions

3.4.1.1 Convex Sets

We start with convex sets.

Definition 3.4.1 *(Convex Set)* A set $D \subseteq \mathbb{R}^d$ is convex if for all $\mathbf{x}, \mathbf{y} \in D$ and all $\alpha \in (0, 1)$

$$(1 - \alpha)\mathbf{x} + \alpha \mathbf{y} \in D.$$

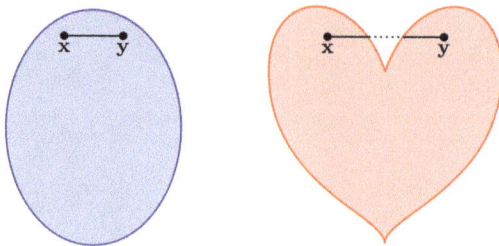

Figure 3.7 Left: A convex set. Right: A set that is not convex.

Note that, as α goes from 0 to 1,

$$(1-\alpha)\mathbf{x} + \alpha\mathbf{y} = \mathbf{x} + \alpha(\mathbf{y}-\mathbf{x})$$

traces a line joining $\mathbf{x}$ and $\mathbf{y}$. In words, a set is convex if all segments between pairs of points in the set also lie in it. See Figure 3.7.

Example 3.4.2 *An open ball in $\mathbb{R}^d$ is convex.* Indeed, let $\delta > 0$ and $\mathbf{x}_0 \in \mathbb{R}^d$. For any $\mathbf{x}, \mathbf{y} \in B_\delta(\mathbf{x}_0)$ and any $\alpha \in [0,1]$, we have

$$\begin{aligned}
\|[(1-\alpha)\mathbf{x} + \alpha\mathbf{y}] - \mathbf{x}_0\|_2 &= \|(1-\alpha)(\mathbf{x}-\mathbf{x}_0) + \alpha(\mathbf{y}-\mathbf{x}_0)\|_2 \\
&\leq \|(1-\alpha)(\mathbf{x}-\mathbf{x}_0)\|_2 + \|\alpha(\mathbf{y}-\mathbf{x}_0)\|_2 \\
&= (1-\alpha)\|\mathbf{x}-\mathbf{x}_0\|_2 + \alpha\|\mathbf{y}-\mathbf{x}_0\|_2 \\
&< (1-\alpha)\delta + \alpha\delta \\
&= \delta
\end{aligned}$$

where we used the triangle inequality in the second line. Hence we have established that $(1-\alpha)\mathbf{x} + \alpha\mathbf{y} \in B_\delta(\mathbf{x}_0)$.

One remark. All we used in this argument is that the Euclidean norm is homogeneous and satisfies the triangle inequality. That is true of every norm. So we conclude that an open ball under any norm is convex. Also, the open nature of the set played no role. The same holds for closed balls in any norm.

Example 3.4.3 *Here is an important generalization.* Think of the space of $n \times n$ symmetric matrices

$$\mathbf{S}^n = \{X \in \mathbb{R}^{n \times n} : X = X^T\},$$

as a linear subspace of $\mathbb{R}^{n^2}$ (how?). The dimension of $\mathbf{S}^n$ is $\binom{n}{2} + n$, the number of free parameters under the symmetry assumption. Consider now the set of all positive semidefinite matrices in $\mathbf{S}^n$,

$$\mathbf{S}^n_+ = \{X \in \mathbf{S}^n : X \succeq \mathbf{0}\}.$$

(Observe that $\mathbf{S}^n_+$ is not the same as the set of symmetric matrices with nonnegative elements.)

We claim that the set $\mathbf{S}^n_+$ is convex. Indeed let $X, Y \in \mathbf{S}^n_+$ and $\alpha \in [0,1]$. Then by positive semidefiniteness of X and Y, for any $\mathbf{v} \in \mathbb{R}^n$

$$\langle \mathbf{v}, [(1-\alpha)X + \alpha Y]\mathbf{v} \rangle = (1-\alpha)\langle \mathbf{v}, X\mathbf{v} \rangle + \alpha\langle \mathbf{v}, Y\mathbf{v} \rangle \geq 0.$$

This shows that $(1-\alpha)X + \alpha Y \succeq \mathbf{0}$ and hence that $\mathbf{S}^n_+$ is convex.

A number of operations preserve convexity. In an abuse of notation, we think of a pair of vectors $(\mathbf{x}_1, \mathbf{x}_2) \in \mathbb{R}^d \times \mathbb{R}^f$ as a vector in $\mathbb{R}^{d+f}$. Put differently, $(\mathbf{x}_1, \mathbf{x}_2)$ is the vertical concatenation of column vectors $\mathbf{x}_1$ and $\mathbf{x}_2$. This is not to be confused with $\begin{pmatrix} \mathbf{x}_1 & \mathbf{x}_2 \end{pmatrix}$ which is the $d \times 2$ matrix with columns $\mathbf{x}_1$ and $\mathbf{x}_2$ – provided $f = d$ (otherwise it is not a well-defined matrix).

Lemma 3.4.4 *(Operations that Preserve Convexity)* Let $S_1, S_2 \subseteq \mathbb{R}^d$, $S_3 \subseteq \mathbb{R}^f$, and $S_4 \subseteq \mathbb{R}^{d+f}$ *be convex sets. Let* $\beta \in \mathbb{R}$ *and* $\mathbf{b} \in \mathbb{R}^d$. *The following sets are also convex:*

a) *Scaling:* $\beta S_1 = \{\beta \mathbf{x} \colon \mathbf{x} \in S_1\}$

b) *Translation:* $S_1 + \mathbf{b} = \{\mathbf{x} + \mathbf{b} \colon \mathbf{x} \in S_1\}$

c) *Sum:* $S_1 + S_2 = \{\mathbf{x}_1 + \mathbf{x}_2 \colon \mathbf{x}_1 \in S_1 \text{ and } \mathbf{x}_2 \in S_2\}$

d) *Cartesian product:* $S_1 \times S_3 = \{(\mathbf{x}_1, \mathbf{x}_2) \colon \mathbf{x}_1 \in S_1 \text{ and } \mathbf{x}_2 \in S_3\}$

e) *Projection:* $T = \{\mathbf{x}_1 \in \mathbb{R}^d \colon (\mathbf{x}_1, \mathbf{x}_2) \in S_4 \text{ for some } \mathbf{x}_2 \in \mathbb{R}^f\}$

f) *Intersection:* $S_1 \cap S_2$

Proof We only prove f). The other statements are left as an exercise (see Problem 3.10). Suppose $\mathbf{x}, \mathbf{y} \in S_1 \cap S_2$ and $\alpha \in [0, 1]$. Then, by the convexity of S_1, $(1 - \alpha)\mathbf{x} + \alpha \mathbf{y} \in S_1$ and, by the convexity of S_2, $(1 - \alpha)\mathbf{x} + \alpha \mathbf{y} \in S_2$. Hence

$$(1 - \alpha)\mathbf{x} + \alpha \mathbf{y} \in S_1 \cap S_2.$$

This property can be extended to an intersection of an arbitrary number of convex sets. $\square$

3.4.1.2 Convex Functions

Our main interest is in convex functions. Here is the definition.

Definition 3.4.5 *(Convex Function) A function* $f \colon \mathbb{R}^d \to \mathbb{R}$ *is convex if, for all* $\mathbf{x}, \mathbf{y} \in \mathbb{R}^d$ *and all* $\alpha \in (0, 1)$,

$$f((1 - \alpha)\mathbf{x} + \alpha \mathbf{y}) \leq (1 - \alpha)f(\mathbf{x}) + \alpha f(\mathbf{y}).$$

More generally, a function $f \colon D \to \mathbb{R}$ *with a convex domain* $D \subseteq \mathbb{R}^d$ *is said to be convex over* D *if the definition above holds over all* $\mathbf{x}, \mathbf{y} \in D$. *A function is said to be strictly convex if a strict inequality holds. If* $-f$ *is convex (respectively, strictly convex), then* f *is said to be concave (respectively, strictly concave).*

The definition above is sometimes referred to as the secant line definition. See Figure 3.8.

Lemma 3.4.6 *(Affine Functions are Convex) Let* $\mathbf{w} \in \mathbb{R}^d$ *and* $b \in \mathbb{R}$. *The function* $f(\mathbf{x}) = \mathbf{w}^T \mathbf{x} + b$ *is convex.*

Proof For any $\mathbf{x}, \mathbf{y} \in \mathbb{R}^d$ and $\alpha \in [0, 1]$,

$$f((1 - \alpha)\mathbf{x} + \alpha \mathbf{y}) = \mathbf{w}^T[(1 - \alpha)\mathbf{x} + \alpha \mathbf{y}] + b = (1 - \alpha)[\mathbf{w}^T \mathbf{x} + b] + \alpha[\mathbf{w}^T \mathbf{y} + b]$$

which proves the claim. $\square$

Here is a less straightforward example. A concrete application is given below.

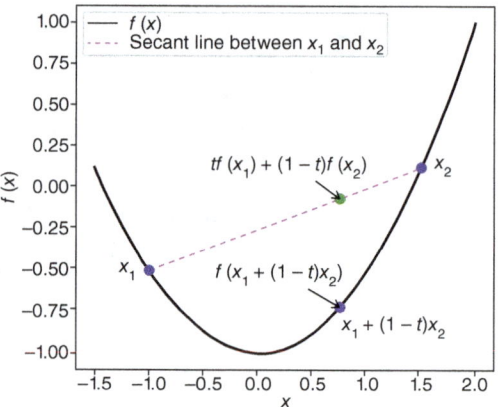

Figure 3.8 A convex function.

Lemma 3.4.7 *(Infimum over a Convex Set)* Let $f: \mathbb{R}^{d+f} \to \mathbb{R}$ be a convex function and let $C \subseteq \mathbb{R}^f$ be a convex set. The function

$$g(\mathbf{x}) = \inf_{\mathbf{y} \in C} f(\mathbf{x}, \mathbf{y})$$

is convex provided $g(\mathbf{x}) > -\infty$ *for all* $\mathbf{x} \in \mathbb{R}^d$.

Proof Let $\mathbf{x}_1, \mathbf{x}_2 \in \mathbb{R}^d$ and $\alpha \in [0, 1]$. For $i = 1, 2$, by definition of g, for any $\epsilon > 0$ there is $\mathbf{y}_i \in C$ such that $f(\mathbf{x}_i, \mathbf{y}_i) \leq g(\mathbf{x}_i) + \epsilon$.

By the convexity of C, $\alpha \mathbf{y}_1 + (1 - \alpha)\mathbf{y}_2 \in C$. So because g is an infimum over points $\mathbf{y}$ in C, we have

$$g(\alpha \mathbf{x}_1 + (1 - \alpha)\mathbf{x}_2) \leq f(\alpha \mathbf{x}_1 + (1 - \alpha)\mathbf{x}_2, \alpha \mathbf{y}_1 + (1 - \alpha)\mathbf{y}_2)$$
$$= f(\alpha(\mathbf{x}_1, \mathbf{y}_1) + (1 - \alpha)(\mathbf{x}_2, \mathbf{y}_2))$$
$$\leq \alpha f(\mathbf{x}_1, \mathbf{y}_1) + (1 - \alpha)f(\mathbf{x}_2, \mathbf{y}_2)$$
$$\leq \alpha[g(\mathbf{x}_1) + \epsilon] + (1 - \alpha)[g(\mathbf{x}_2) + \epsilon]$$
$$\leq \alpha g(\mathbf{x}_1) + (1 - \alpha)g(\mathbf{x}_2) + \epsilon,$$

where we used the convexity of f on the second line. Because $\epsilon > 0$ is arbitrary, the claim follows. □

Example 3.4.8 *(Distance to a Convex Set)* Let C be a convex set in $\mathbb{R}^d$. We show that the distance to C,

$$g(\mathbf{x}) = \inf_{\mathbf{y} \in C} \|\mathbf{x} - \mathbf{y}\|_2,$$

is convex.

To apply the **Infimum over a Convex Set Lemma**, we first need to show that $f(\mathbf{x}, \mathbf{y}) := \|\mathbf{x} - \mathbf{y}\|_2$ is convex as a function of $(\mathbf{x}, \mathbf{y})$. Let $\mathbf{x}_1, \mathbf{x}_2 \in \mathbb{R}^d$, $\mathbf{y}_1, \mathbf{y}_2 \in C$, and $\alpha \in [0, 1]$. We want to show that f evaluated at the convex combination

$$\alpha(\mathbf{x}_1, \mathbf{y}_1) + (1 - \alpha)(\mathbf{x}_2, \mathbf{y}_2) = (\alpha \mathbf{x}_1 + (1 - \alpha)\mathbf{x}_2, \alpha \mathbf{y}_1 + (1 - \alpha)\mathbf{y}_2)$$

is bounded above by the same convex combination of the values of f at $(\mathbf{x}_1, \mathbf{y}_1)$ and $(\mathbf{x}_2, \mathbf{y}_2)$.

By the triangle inequality and the absolute homogeneity of the norm,

$$\begin{aligned}
&f(\alpha \mathbf{x}_1 + (1-\alpha)\mathbf{x}_2, \alpha \mathbf{y}_1 + (1-\alpha)\mathbf{y}_2) \\
&= \|[\alpha \mathbf{x}_1 + (1-\alpha)\mathbf{x}_2] - [\alpha \mathbf{y}_1 + (1-\alpha)\mathbf{y}_2]\|_2 \\
&= \|\alpha(\mathbf{x}_1 - \mathbf{y}_1) + (1-\alpha)(\mathbf{x}_2 - \mathbf{y}_2)\|_2 \\
&\leq \alpha \|\mathbf{x}_1 - \mathbf{y}_1\|_2 + (1-\alpha)\|\mathbf{x}_2 - \mathbf{y}_2\|_2 \\
&= \alpha f(\mathbf{x}_1, \mathbf{y}_1) + (1-\alpha) f(\mathbf{x}_2, \mathbf{y}_2).
\end{aligned}$$

It remains to show that $g(\mathbf{x}) > -\infty$ for all $\mathbf{x}$. But this is immediate since $\|\mathbf{x} - \mathbf{y}\|_2 \geq 0$. Hence the previous lemma gives the claim.

3.4.1.3 Conditions Based on the Gradient and Hessian

A common way to prove that a function is convex is to look at its Hessian (or second derivative in the single-variable case). We start with a first-order characterization of convexity.

Throughout, when we say that a function $f: D \to \mathbb{R}$ is continuously differentiable, we implicitly assume that D is open or that D is contained in an open set where f is continuously differentiable. The same applies for twice continuously differentiable functions.

Lemma 3.4.9 *(First-Order Convexity Condition)* Let $f: D \to \mathbb{R}$ *be continuously differentiable, where $D \subseteq \mathbb{R}^d$ is convex. Then f is convex over D if and only if*

$$f(\mathbf{y}) \geq f(\mathbf{x}) + \nabla f(\mathbf{x})^T (\mathbf{y} - \mathbf{x}), \qquad \forall \mathbf{x}, \mathbf{y} \in D.$$

On the right-hand side above, you should recognize the linear approximation to f at $\mathbf{x}$ from *Taylor's Theorem* without the remainder. See Figure 3.9.

Proof *(First-Order Convexity Condition)* Suppose first that $f(\mathbf{z}_2) \geq f(\mathbf{z}_1) + \nabla f(\mathbf{z}_1)^T (\mathbf{z}_2 - \mathbf{z}_1)$ for all $\mathbf{z}_1, \mathbf{z}_2 \in D$. For any $\mathbf{x}, \mathbf{y} \in D$ and $\alpha \in [0, 1]$, let $\mathbf{w} = (1-\alpha)\mathbf{x} + \alpha \mathbf{y}$ (which is in D by convexity). Then taking $\mathbf{z}_1 = \mathbf{w}$ and $\mathbf{z}_2 = \mathbf{x}$ gives

$$f(\mathbf{x}) \geq f(\mathbf{w}) + \nabla f(\mathbf{w})^T (\mathbf{x} - \mathbf{w})$$

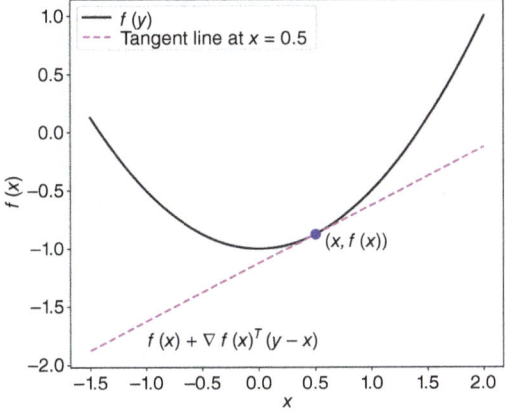

Figure 3.9 Illustration of the first-order convexity condition.

and taking $\mathbf{z}_1 = \mathbf{w}$ and $\mathbf{z}_2 = \mathbf{y}$ gives
$$f(\mathbf{y}) \geq f(\mathbf{w}) + \nabla f(\mathbf{w})^T (\mathbf{y} - \mathbf{w}).$$
Multiplying the first inequality by $(1 - \alpha)$ and the second one by α, and adding them up gives
$$(1 - \alpha) f(\mathbf{x}) + \alpha f(\mathbf{y}) \geq f(\mathbf{w}) + \nabla f(\mathbf{w})^T ([(1 - \alpha)\mathbf{x} + \alpha \mathbf{y}] - \mathbf{w}) = f(\mathbf{w})$$
proving convexity.

For the other direction, assume that f is convex over D. For any $\mathbf{x}, \mathbf{y} \in D$ and $\alpha \in (0, 1)$, by the *Mean Value Theorem*, for some $\xi_\alpha \in (0, 1)$ it holds that
$$f(\mathbf{w}) = f(\mathbf{x} + \alpha(\mathbf{y} - \mathbf{x})) = f(\mathbf{x}) + \alpha(\mathbf{y} - \mathbf{x})^T \nabla f(\mathbf{x} + \xi_\alpha \alpha (\mathbf{y} - \mathbf{x}))$$
while convexity implies
$$f(\mathbf{w}) \leq (1 - \alpha) f(\mathbf{x}) + \alpha f(\mathbf{y}).$$
Combining, rearranging, and dividing by α gives
$$(\mathbf{y} - \mathbf{x})^T \nabla f(\mathbf{x} + \xi_\alpha \alpha (\mathbf{y} - \mathbf{x})) \leq f(\mathbf{y}) - f(\mathbf{x}).$$
Taking $\alpha \to 0$ gives the claim. $\square$

We move on to second-order conditions. We start with the case $D = \mathbb{R}^d$.

Lemma 3.4.10 *(Second-Order Convexity Condition)* Let $f: \mathbb{R}^d \to \mathbb{R}$ *be twice continuously differentiable. Then f is convex (over $\mathbb{R}^d$) if and only if $\mathbf{H}_f(\mathbf{x})$ is positive semidefinite for all $\mathbf{x} \in \mathbb{R}^d$.*

Proof Suppose first that $\mathbf{H}_f(\mathbf{z}_1) \geq 0$ for all $\mathbf{z}_1$. For any $\mathbf{x}, \mathbf{y}$, by *Taylor's Theorem*, there is $\xi \in (0, 1)$ such that
$$f(\mathbf{y}) = f(\mathbf{x}) + \nabla f(\mathbf{x})^T (\mathbf{y} - \mathbf{x}) + (\mathbf{y} - \mathbf{x})^T \mathbf{H}_f (\mathbf{x} + \xi(\mathbf{y} - \mathbf{x})) (\mathbf{y} - \mathbf{x})$$
$$\geq f(\mathbf{x}) + \nabla f(\mathbf{x})^T (\mathbf{y} - \mathbf{x})$$
where we used the positive semidefiniteness of the Hessian. By the *First-Order Convexity Condition*, this implies that f is convex.

For the other direction, assume that f is convex. For any $\mathbf{x}, \mathbf{w}$ and $\alpha \in (0, 1)$, by *Taylor's Theorem* again, for some $\xi_\alpha \in (0, 1)$ it holds that
$$f(\mathbf{x} + \alpha \mathbf{w}) = f(\mathbf{x}) + \alpha \mathbf{w}^T \nabla f(\mathbf{x}) + \alpha^2 \mathbf{w}^T \mathbf{H}_f (\mathbf{x} + \xi_\alpha \alpha \mathbf{w}) \mathbf{w}$$
while the *First-Order Convexity Condition* implies
$$f(\mathbf{x} + \alpha \mathbf{w}) \geq f(\mathbf{x}) + \alpha \mathbf{w}^T \nabla f(\mathbf{x}).$$
Combining, rearranging, and dividing by α^2 gives
$$\mathbf{w}^T \mathbf{H}_f (\mathbf{x} + \xi_\alpha \alpha \mathbf{w}) \mathbf{w} \geq 0.$$
Taking $\alpha \to 0$ and using the continuity of the Hessian shows that $\mathbf{w}^T \mathbf{H}_f(\mathbf{x}) \mathbf{w} \geq 0$. Since $\mathbf{w}$ is arbitrary, this implies that the Hessian is positive semidefinite at $\mathbf{x}$. This holds for any $\mathbf{x}$, which proves the claim. $\square$

Example 3.4.11 *Consider the quadratic function*
$$f(\mathbf{x}) = \frac{1}{2} \mathbf{x}^T P \mathbf{x} + \mathbf{q}^T \mathbf{x} + r,$$

where P is a symmetric matrix. We showed previously that the Hessian is

$$\mathbf{H}_f(\mathbf{x}) = \frac{1}{2}[P + P^T] = P.$$

So f is convex if and only if the matrix P is positive semidefinite.

In the more general case over a convex set, we have the following statement. The proof is essentially unchanged.

Lemma 3.4.12 *(Second-Order Convexity Condition) Let $f: D \to \mathbb{R}$ be twice continuously differentiable, wherere $D \subseteq \mathbb{R}^d$ is convex. If $\mathbf{H}_f(\mathbf{x})$ is positive semidefinite (respectively positive definite) for all $\mathbf{x} \in D$, then f is convex (respectively strictly convex) over D.*

The following example shows what can go wrong in the other direction.

Example 3.4.13 *Consider the function*

$$f(\mathbf{x}) = x_1^2 - x_2^2$$

on the convex set

$$D = \{\mathbf{x}: x_2 = 0\}.$$

On D, the function reduces to x_1^2 which is convex. The Hessian is

$$\mathbf{H}_f(\mathbf{x}) = \begin{pmatrix} 1 & 0 \\ 0 & -1 \end{pmatrix}$$

which is not positive semidefinite (why?).

3.4.2 Convexity and Unconstrained Optimization

Now comes the key property of convex functions (at least as far as we are concerned).

3.4.2.1 Global Minimization in the Convex Case

In the convex case, global minimization reduces to local minimization.

Theorem 3.4.14 *(Global Minimizers of a Convex Function) Let $f: D \to \mathbb{R}$ be a convex function, where $D \subseteq \mathbb{R}^d$ is convex. Then any local minimizer of f over D is also a global minimizer over D.*

Proof By contradiction, suppose $\mathbf{x}_0$ is a local minimizer, but not a global minimizer. Then there is $\mathbf{y} \in D$ such that

$$f(\mathbf{y}) < f(\mathbf{x}_0).$$

By convexity of f and D, for any $\alpha \in (0, 1)$

$$f(\mathbf{x}_0 + \alpha(\mathbf{y} - \mathbf{x}_0)) \le (1 - \alpha)f(\mathbf{x}_0) + \alpha f(\mathbf{y}) < f(\mathbf{x}_0).$$

But that implies that every open ball around $\mathbf{x}_0$ contains a point taking a smaller value than $f(\mathbf{x}_0)$, a contradiction. □

When f is strictly convex, the global minimizer is unique (if it exists). (Why?)

For our purposes, we will need a uniform version of strict convexity known as strong convexity which we define in the next subsection.

In the continuously differentiable case over $\mathbb{R}^d$, we get in addition that a vanishing gradient at $\mathbf{x}_0$ is now a sufficient condition for $\mathbf{x}_0$ to be a local – and therefore global – minimizer.

Theorem 3.4.15 *(First-Order Optimality Condition for Unconstrained Convex Functions)* *Let $f : \mathbb{R}^d \to \mathbb{R}$ be a continuously differentiable, convex function. Then $\mathbf{x}_0$ is a local minimizer – and therefore a global minimizer – if and only if $\nabla f(\mathbf{x}_0) = \mathbf{0}$.*

Proof Assume $\nabla f(\mathbf{x}_0) = \mathbf{0}$. By the *First-Order Convexity Condition*, for any $\mathbf{y}$

$$f(\mathbf{y}) - f(\mathbf{x}_0) \geq \nabla f(\mathbf{x}_0)^T (\mathbf{y} - \mathbf{x}_0) = 0.$$

So $\mathbf{x}_0$ is a global minimizer.

The other direction follows immediately from the *First-Order Necessary Optimality Condition*. □

Example 3.4.16 *(Quadratic Function)* Consider the quadratic function

$$f(\mathbf{x}) = \frac{1}{2}\mathbf{x}^T P \mathbf{x} + \mathbf{q}^T \mathbf{x} + r$$

where P is symmetric and positive semidefinite. The Hessian is then

$$\mathbf{H}_f(\mathbf{x}) = \frac{1}{2}[P + P^T] = P$$

for any $\mathbf{x}$. So f is convex. Further the gradient is

$$\nabla f(\mathbf{x}) = P\mathbf{x} + \mathbf{q}$$

for all $\mathbf{x}$. Any $\mathbf{x}$ satisfying

$$P\mathbf{x} = -\mathbf{q}$$

is a global minimizer.

More generally, we have the following.

Theorem 3.4.17 *(First-Order Optimality Condition for Convex Functions on Convex Sets)* *Let $f: D \to \mathbb{R}$ be a continuously differentiable, convex function, where $D \subseteq \mathbb{R}^d$ is convex. Then $\mathbf{x}_0$ is a local minimizer – and therefore a global minimizer – if and only if for any $\mathbf{y} \in D$*

$$\nabla f(\mathbf{x}_0)^T (\mathbf{y} - \mathbf{x}_0) \geq 0.$$

Proof idea: Put differently the condition above says that, in any direction $\mathbf{v}$ of the form $\mathbf{y} - \mathbf{x}_0$ for some $\mathbf{y} \in D$, the directional derivative $\frac{\partial f(\mathbf{x}_0)}{\partial \mathbf{v}}$ is nonnegative. Indeed, otherwise $\mathbf{v}$ would be a descent direction and we could find points in D arbitrarily close to $\mathbf{x}_0$ taking a smaller f value.

Proof Assume the condition holds. By the *First-Order Convexity Condition*, for any $\mathbf{y} \in D$

$$f(\mathbf{y}) - f(\mathbf{x}_0) \geq \nabla f(\mathbf{x}_0)^T (\mathbf{y} - \mathbf{x}_0) \geq 0.$$

So $\mathbf{x}_0$ is a global minimizer.

For the other direction, assume that there is $\mathbf{y} \in D$ such that

$$\nabla f(\mathbf{x}_0)^T (\mathbf{y} - \mathbf{x}_0) < 0.$$

For any $\alpha \in (0, 1)$, by the *Mean Value Theorem*, for some $\xi_\alpha \in (0, 1)$ it holds that

$$f(\mathbf{x}_0 + \alpha(\mathbf{y} - \mathbf{x}_0)) = f(\mathbf{x}_0) + \alpha(\mathbf{y} - \mathbf{x}_0)^T \nabla f(\mathbf{x}_0 + \xi_\alpha \alpha(\mathbf{y} - \mathbf{x}_0)).$$

By continuity of the gradient, for α small enough, we have by the assumption above that

$$(\mathbf{y} - \mathbf{x}_0)^T \nabla f(\mathbf{x}_0 + \xi_\alpha \alpha(\mathbf{y} - \mathbf{x}_0)) < 0.$$

Plugging this back above, it follows that for all such α

$$f(\mathbf{x}_0 + \alpha(\mathbf{y} - \mathbf{x}_0)) < f(\mathbf{x}_0),$$

contradicting the fact that $\mathbf{x}_0$ is a local minimizer. $\square$

Example 3.4.18 *Consider the function $f(x) = \frac{1}{2}x^2$ for $x \in D = \{x \colon x \geq 1\}$. The function f is convex for any x since $f''(x) = 1 > 0$.*

Over D, the global minimizer is $x^* = 1$, yet the derivative is $f'(1) = 1 \neq 0$. Indeed, because x^* is on the boundary of the domain D, it does not matter that the function decreases when moving to the left from x^*. We only care about directions that take us into the domain D, in this case the right direction at x^*.

The condition in the theorem reads

$$f'(1)(y - 1) \geq 0, \qquad \forall y \geq 1.$$

This is equivalent to $f'(1) \geq 0$, which is indeed satisfied here.

If $x > 1$, then the condition is

$$f'(x)(y - x) \geq 0.$$

Taking $y = x + 1$, we get $f'(x) \geq 0$ while taking $y = \frac{1}{2}(1 + x)$ gives $f'(x)\frac{1}{2}(1 - x) \geq 0$ which implies $f'(x) \leq 0$ (why?). Combining the two gives $f'(x) = 0$. No $x > 1$ satisfies this condition.

3.4.2.2 Strong Convexity

With stronger assumptions, we obtain stronger guarantees. One such assumption is strong convexity, which we define next in the special case of twice continuously differentiable functions. It generalizes the single-variable condition of requiring that the second derivative $f''(x) > m > 0$ for all $x \in \mathbb{R}$. Specifically we require that the second derivative "in every direction" is bounded from below. For this purpose, we use the second directional derivative.

A strongly convex function is one where the second directional derivative along all unit vector directions is uniformly bounded below away from 0. That is, there is $m > 0$ such that

$$\frac{\partial^2 f(\mathbf{x})}{\partial \mathbf{v}^2} = \mathbf{v}^T \mathbf{H}_f(\mathbf{x}) \mathbf{v} \geq m$$

for all $\mathbf{x} \in \mathbb{R}^d$ and all unit vectors $\mathbf{v} \in \mathbb{R}^d$.

We will use the following notation to state it formally. Let $A, B \in \mathbb{R}^{d \times d}$ be symmetric matrices. Recall that $A \succeq 0$ means that A is positive semidefinite. We write $A \preceq B$ (respectively $A \succeq B$) to indicate that $B - A \succeq 0$ (respectively $A - B \succeq 0$). A different, useful way to put this is the following. Recall that $B - A \succeq 0$ means $\mathbf{z}^T B \mathbf{z} - \mathbf{z}^T A \mathbf{z} \geq 0$ for all $\mathbf{z} \in \mathbb{R}^d$. Hence, rearranging,

$$A \preceq B \iff \mathbf{z}^T A \mathbf{z} \leq \mathbf{z}^T B \mathbf{z}, \qquad \forall \mathbf{z} \in \mathbb{R}^d.$$

Similarly,
$$A \succeq B \iff \mathbf{z}^T A \mathbf{z} \geq \mathbf{z}^T B \mathbf{z}, \quad \forall \mathbf{z} \in \mathbb{R}^d.$$

Definition 3.4.19 (Strongly Convex Function) *Let $f: \mathbb{R}^d \to \mathbb{R}$ be twice continuously differentiable and let $m > 0$. We say that f is m-strongly convex if*
$$\mathbf{H}_f(\mathbf{x}) \succeq m I_{d \times d}, \quad \forall \mathbf{x} \in \mathbb{R}^d.$$

By the observation above, noting that $\mathbf{z}^T I \mathbf{z} = \|\mathbf{z}\|^2$, we get that the condition above is equivalent to
$$\mathbf{z}^T \mathbf{H}_f(\mathbf{x}) \mathbf{z} \geq m \|\mathbf{z}\|^2, \quad \forall \mathbf{x}, \mathbf{z} \in \mathbb{R}^d.$$

In particular, for a unit vector $\mathbf{v}$ we get $\mathbf{v}^T \mathbf{H}_f(\mathbf{x}) \mathbf{v} \geq m$. Vice versa, if $\mathbf{v}^T \mathbf{H}_f(\mathbf{x}) \mathbf{v} \geq m$ for all $\mathbf{x} \in \mathbb{R}^d$ and all unit vectors $\mathbf{v} \in \mathbb{R}^d$, then it holds that for any nonzero vector $\mathbf{z} \in \mathbb{R}^d$
$$\left(\frac{\mathbf{z}}{\|\mathbf{z}\|}\right)^T \mathbf{H}_f(\mathbf{x}) \left(\frac{\mathbf{z}}{\|\mathbf{z}\|}\right) \geq m,$$

which after rearranging gives $\mathbf{z}^T \mathbf{H}_f(\mathbf{x}) \mathbf{z} \geq m \|\mathbf{z}\|^2$.

Combined with *Taylor's Theorem*, this immediately gives the following. The proof is left as an exercise (see Problem 3.18).

Lemma 3.4.20 (Quadratic Bound for Strongly Convex Functions) *Let $f: \mathbb{R}^d \to \mathbb{R}$ be twice continuously differentiable. Then f is m-strongly convex if and only if*
$$f(\mathbf{y}) \geq f(\mathbf{x}) + \nabla f(\mathbf{x})^T (\mathbf{y} - \mathbf{x}) + \frac{m}{2} \|\mathbf{y} - \mathbf{x}\|^2, \quad \forall \mathbf{x}, \mathbf{y} \in \mathbb{R}^d.$$

This lemma immediately leads to the following fundamental result.

Theorem 3.4.21 (Global Minimizer of a Strongly Convex Function) *Let $f: \mathbb{R}^d \to \mathbb{R}$ be twice continuously differentiable and m-strongly convex with $m > 0$. If $\nabla f(\mathbf{x}^*) = \mathbf{0}$, then $\mathbf{x}^*$ is a unique global minimizer of f.*

Proof If $\nabla f(\mathbf{x}^*) = \mathbf{0}$, by the *Quadratic Bound for Strongly Convex Functions*,
$$f(\mathbf{y}) \geq f(\mathbf{x}^*) + \frac{m}{2} \|\mathbf{y} - \mathbf{x}^*\|^2 > f(\mathbf{x}^*)$$

for all $\mathbf{y} \neq \mathbf{x}^*$, which proves the claim. $\square$

Example 3.4.22 (continued from Example 3.4.16) Consider again the quadratic function
$$f(\mathbf{x}) = \frac{1}{2} \mathbf{x}^T P \mathbf{x} + \mathbf{q}^T \mathbf{x} + r$$

where P is symmetric and, this time, positive definite. Again, for any $\mathbf{x}$, the Hessian is
$$\mathbf{H}_f(\mathbf{x}) = \frac{1}{2} [P + P^T] = P.$$

The expression $\mathbf{v}^T P \mathbf{v}$, viewed as a function of $\mathbf{v}$ is continuous, attaining its minimum on $\mathbb{S}^{d-1}$ by the Extreme Value Theorem, where $\mathbb{S}^{d-1} = \{\mathbf{v} \in \mathbb{R}^d : \|\mathbf{v}\| = 1\}$ are the unit vectors in $\mathbb{R}^d$. By our assumption that P is positive definite, that minimum must be strictly positive, say $\mu > 0$. Then f is μ-strongly convex. The Global Minimizer of a Strongly Convex Function Theorem *then indicates that there is a unique global minimizer in that case. Using a previous calculation, it is obtained by computing* $\mathbf{x}^* = -P^{-1} \mathbf{q}$. *(Why is P invertible?)*

3.4 Convexity

Example 3.4.23 *Consider the least-squares objective function*

$$f(\mathbf{x}) = \|A\mathbf{x} - \mathbf{b}\|^2$$

where $A \in \mathbb{R}^{n \times d}$ has full column rank and $\mathbf{b} \in \mathbb{R}^n$. This objective function can be rewritten as a quadratic function:

$$\begin{aligned} f(\mathbf{x}) &= \|A\mathbf{x} - \mathbf{b}\|^2 \\ &= (A\mathbf{x} - \mathbf{b})^T (A\mathbf{x} - \mathbf{b}) \\ &= \mathbf{x}^T A^T A \mathbf{x} - 2\mathbf{b}^T A \mathbf{x} + \mathbf{b}^T \mathbf{b} \\ &= \frac{1}{2}\mathbf{x}^T P \mathbf{x} + \mathbf{q}^T \mathbf{x} + r \end{aligned}$$

where $P = 2A^T A$ is symmetric, $\mathbf{q} = -2A^T \mathbf{b}$, and $r = \mathbf{b}^T \mathbf{b} = \|\mathbf{b}\|^2$.

The Hessian of f is

$$\mathbf{H}_f(\mathbf{x}) = 2A^T A.$$

This Hessian is positive definite. Indeed we have proved previously that, for any $\mathbf{z} \in \mathbb{R}^d$,

$$\langle \mathbf{z}, 2A^T A \mathbf{z} \rangle = 2(A\mathbf{z})^T (A\mathbf{z}) = 2\|A\mathbf{z}\|^2 > 0,$$

since $A\mathbf{z} = \mathbf{0}$ implies $\mathbf{z} = \mathbf{0}$ by the full column rank assumption.

By the previous example, f is μ-strongly convex for some $\mu > 0$. The Global Minimizer of a Strongly Convex Function Theorem *then indicates that there is a unique global minimizer to the least-squares objective in that case.*

Example 3.4.24 *Let $D \subseteq \mathbb{R}^d$ be a nonempty, closed, convex set. For $\mathbf{x} \in \mathbb{R}^d$ we define the projection of $\mathbf{x}$ onto D as*

$$\mathrm{proj}_D(\mathbf{x}) = \arg\min \{\|\mathbf{x} - \mathbf{z}\| : \mathbf{z} \in D\}.$$

Let $\mathbf{w} \in D$. By the Extreme Value Theorem *applied to $\|\mathbf{x} - \mathbf{z}\|$ on the closed, bounded set $\{\mathbf{z} \in D : \|\mathbf{x} - \mathbf{z}\| \leq \|\mathbf{x} - \mathbf{w}\|\}$, there is a global minimizer for this problem. Moreover, the problem is equivalent to minimizing the* squared *norm $\|\mathbf{x} - \mathbf{z}\|^2$ which is strongly convex as a function of $\mathbf{z}$ since*

$$\|\mathbf{x} - \mathbf{z}\|^2 = \mathbf{z}^T \mathbf{z} - 2\mathbf{x}^T \mathbf{z} + \|\mathbf{x}\|^2.$$

As a result, the minimizer is unique.

We use the First-Order Optimality Conditions for Convex Functions on Convex Sets *to characterize it. The gradient of $\|\mathbf{x} - \mathbf{z}\|^2$ as a function of $\mathbf{z}$ is $2\mathbf{z} - 2\mathbf{x}$ by our previous formula for quadratic functions (see Example 3.2.3). So the optimality condition reads (after simplifying the factor of 2)*

$$(\mathrm{proj}_D(\mathbf{x}) - \mathbf{x})^T (\mathbf{y} - \mathrm{proj}_D(\mathbf{x})) \geq 0, \qquad \forall \mathbf{y} \in D.$$

This formula generalizes the Orthogonal Projection Theorem *beyond the case of linear subspaces.*

Self-Assessment Quiz (with help from Claude, Gemini, and ChatGPT)

1. Which of the following is NOT an operation that preserves the convexity of sets?
   a) Scaling a convex set by a real number
   b) Translating a convex set by a vector
   c) Taking the union of two convex sets
   d) Taking the intersection of two convex sets

2. Let $f: \mathbb{R}^d \to \mathbb{R}$ be twice continuously differentiable. Which of the following conditions is sufficient for f to be convex?
   a) $\nabla^2 f(\mathbf{x}) \prec \mathbf{0}$, for all $\mathbf{x} \in \mathbb{R}^d$
   b) $\nabla^2 f(\mathbf{x}) \preceq \mathbf{0}$, for all $\mathbf{x} \in \mathbb{R}^d$
   c) $\nabla^2 f(\mathbf{x}) \succeq \mathbf{0}$, for all $\mathbf{x} \in \mathbb{R}^d$
   d) $\nabla^2 f(\mathbf{x}) \succ \mathbf{0}$, for all $\mathbf{x} \in \mathbb{R}^d$

3. Let $f: \mathbb{R}^d \to \mathbb{R}$ be a continuously differentiable, convex function. Which of the following is a necessary and sufficient condition for $\mathbf{x}_0$ to be a global minimizer of f?
   a) $\nabla f(\mathbf{x}_0) \neq \mathbf{0}$
   b) $\nabla f(\mathbf{x}_0) = \mathbf{0}$
   c) $\nabla^2 f(\mathbf{x}_0) \succeq \mathbf{0}$
   d) $\nabla^2 f(\mathbf{x}_0) \succ \mathbf{0}$

4. A function $f: \mathbb{R}^d \to \mathbb{R}$ is m-strongly convex if
   a) $\nabla^2 f(\mathbf{x}) \succeq m I_{d \times d}$, for all $\mathbf{x} \in \mathbb{R}^d$ and some $m > 0$.
   b) $\nabla^2 f(\mathbf{x}) \preceq m I_{d \times d}$, for all $\mathbf{x} \in \mathbb{R}^d$ and some $m > 0$.
   c) $\nabla^2 f(\mathbf{x}) \succeq -m I_{d \times d}$, for all $\mathbf{x} \in \mathbb{R}^d$ and some $m > 0$.
   d) $\nabla^2 f(\mathbf{x}) \preceq -m I_{d \times d}$, for all $\mathbf{x} \in \mathbb{R}^d$ and some $m > 0$.

5. Which of the following statements is true about the least-squares objective function $f(\mathbf{x}) = \|A\mathbf{x} - \mathbf{b}\|_2^2$, where $A \in \mathbb{R}^{n \times d}$ has full column rank and $\mathbf{b} \in \mathbb{R}^n$?
   a) $f(\mathbf{x})$ is convex but not necessarily strongly convex.
   b) $f(\mathbf{x})$ is strongly convex.
   c) $f(\mathbf{x})$ is convex if and only if $\mathbf{b} = \mathbf{0}$.
   d) $f(\mathbf{x})$ is strongly convex if and only if $\mathbf{b} = \mathbf{0}$.

Answer for 1: c. Justification: The text states that scaling, translation, addition, Cartesian product, projection, and intersection preserve convexity. It does not mention the union. In fact, the union of two convex sets is not necessarily convex (e.g., take the union of two distinct points).

Answer for 2: c. Justification: The text states the second-order convexity condition: If $f: \mathbb{R}^d \to \mathbb{R}$ is twice continuously differentiable, then f is convex if and only if $\nabla^2 f(\mathbf{x}) \succeq \mathbf{0}$, for all $\mathbf{x} \in \mathbb{R}^d$.

Answer for 3: b. Justification: The text states and proves the first-order optimality condition for convex functions on $\mathbb{R}^d$: If $f: \mathbb{R}^d \to \mathbb{R}$ is a continuously differentiable, convex function, then $\mathbf{x}_0$ is a global minimizer if and only if $\nabla f(\mathbf{x}_0) = \mathbf{0}$.

> Answer for 4: a. Justification: The text defines an m-strongly convex function $f \colon \mathbb{R}^d \to \mathbb{R}$ as one satisfying $\nabla^2 f(\mathbf{x}) \succeq m I_{d \times d}$, for all $\mathbf{x} \in \mathbb{R}^d$ and some $m > 0$.
>
> Answer for 5: b. Justification: The text shows that the Hessian of the least-squares objective function is $2A^T A$, which is positive definite when A has full column rank. Therefore, the least-squares objective function is strongly convex.

3.5 Gradient Descent and Its Convergence Analysis

We consider a natural approach for solving optimization problems numerically: a class of algorithms known as descent methods.

Let $f \colon \mathbb{R}^d \to \mathbb{R}$ be continuously differentiable. We restrict ourselves to unconstrained minimization problems of the form

$$\min_{\mathbf{x} \in \mathbb{R}^d} f(\mathbf{x}).$$

Ideally one would like to identify a global minimizer of f. A naive approach might be to evaluate f at a large number of points $\mathbf{x}$, say on a dense grid. However, even if we were satisfied with an approximate solution and limited ourselves to a bounded subset of the domain of f, this type of exhaustive search is wasteful and impractical in large dimension d, as the number of points interrogated grows exponentially with d.

A less naive approach might be to find all stationary points of f – that is, those $\mathbf{x}$ such that $\nabla f(\mathbf{x}) = \mathbf{0}$ – and then choose an $\mathbf{x}$ among them that produces the smallest value of $f(\mathbf{x})$. This indeed works in many problems, like the following example we have encountered previously.

Example 3.5.1 *(Least Squares) Consider again the least-squares problem*

$$\min_{\mathbf{x} \in \mathbb{R}^d} \|A\mathbf{x} - \mathbf{b}\|^2$$

where $A \in \mathbb{R}^{n \times d}$ has full column rank and $\mathbf{b} \in \mathbb{R}^n$. In particular, $d \leq n$. We saw in a previous example that the objective function is a quadratic function

$$f(\mathbf{x}) = \frac{1}{2} \mathbf{x}^T P \mathbf{x} + \mathbf{q}^T \mathbf{x} + r,$$

where $P = 2A^T A$ is symmetric, $\mathbf{q} = -2A^T \mathbf{b}$, and $r = \mathbf{b}^T \mathbf{b} = \|\mathbf{b}\|^2$. We also showed that f is μ-strongly convex. So there is a unique global minimizer.

By a previous calculation (see Example 3.4.23),

$$\nabla f(\mathbf{x}) = P\mathbf{x} + \mathbf{q} = 2A^T A \mathbf{x} - 2A^T \mathbf{b}.$$

So the stationary points satisfy

$$A^T A \mathbf{x} = A^T \mathbf{b}$$

which you may recognize as the normal equations for the least-squares problem.

Unfortunately, identifying stationary points often leads to systems of nonlinear equations that do not have explicit solutions. Hence we resort to a different approach.

3.5.1 Gradient Descent

In gradient descent, we attempt to find smaller values of f by successively following directions in which f decreases locally. As we have seen in the proof of the *First-Order Necessary Optimality Condition*, $-\nabla f$ provides such a direction. In fact, it is the direction of steepest descent in the following sense.

Recall from the *Descent Direction and Directional Derivative Lemma* that $\mathbf{v}$ is a descent direction at $\mathbf{x}_0$ if the directional derivative of f at $\mathbf{x}_0$ in the direction $\mathbf{v}$ is negative.

Lemma 3.5.2 *(Steepest Descent)* Let $f: \mathbb{R}^d \to \mathbb{R}$ be continuously differentiable at $\mathbf{x}_0$. For any unit vector $\mathbf{v} \in \mathbb{R}^d$,

$$\frac{\partial f(\mathbf{x}_0)}{\partial \mathbf{v}} \geq \frac{\partial f(\mathbf{x}_0)}{\partial \mathbf{v}^*}$$

where

$$\mathbf{v}^* = -\frac{\nabla f(\mathbf{x}_0)}{\|\nabla f(\mathbf{x}_0)\|}.$$

Proof idea: This is an immediate application of the *Cauchy–Schwarz Inequality*.

Proof By the *Cauchy–Schwarz Inequality*, since $\mathbf{v}$ has unit norm,

$$\left|\frac{\partial f(\mathbf{x}_0)}{\partial \mathbf{v}}\right| = \left|\nabla f(\mathbf{x}_0)^T \mathbf{v}\right|$$
$$\leq \|\nabla f(\mathbf{x}_0)\| \|\mathbf{v}\|$$
$$= \|\nabla f(\mathbf{x}_0)\|.$$

Or, put differently,

$$-\|\nabla f(\mathbf{x}_0)\| \leq \frac{\partial f(\mathbf{x}_0)}{\partial \mathbf{v}} \leq \|\nabla f(\mathbf{x}_0)\|.$$

On the other hand, by the choice of $\mathbf{v}^*$,

$$\frac{\partial f(\mathbf{x}_0)}{\partial \mathbf{v}^*} = \nabla f(\mathbf{x}_0)^T \left(-\frac{\nabla f(\mathbf{x}_0)}{\|\nabla f(\mathbf{x}_0)\|}\right)$$
$$= -\left(\frac{\nabla f(\mathbf{x}_0)^T \nabla f(\mathbf{x}_0)}{\|\nabla f(\mathbf{x}_0)\|}\right)$$
$$= -\left(\frac{\|\nabla f(\mathbf{x}_0)\|^2}{\|\nabla f(\mathbf{x}_0)\|}\right)$$
$$= -\|\nabla f(\mathbf{x}_0)\|.$$

The last two displays combined give the result. □

At each iteration of gradient descent, we take a step in the direction of the negative of the gradient; that is,

$$\mathbf{x}^{t+1} = \mathbf{x}^t - \alpha_t \nabla f(\mathbf{x}^t), \quad t = 0, 1, 2, \ldots$$

for a sequence of step sizes $\alpha_t > 0$. Choosing the right step size (also known as steplength or learning rate) is a large subject in itself. We will only consider the case of fixed step size here.

CHAT & LEARN Ask your favorite AI chatbot about the different approaches for selecting a step size in gradient descent methods.

In general, we will not be able to guarantee that a global minimizer is reached in the limit, even if one exists. Our goal for now is more modest: to find a point where the gradient of f approximately vanishes.

We implement gradient descent in Python. We assume that a function `f` and its gradient `grad_f` are provided. We first code the basic steepest descent step with a step size α = `alpha`.

```python
def desc_update(grad_f, x, alpha):
    return x - alpha*grad_f(x)

def gd(f, grad_f, x0, alpha=1e-3, niters=int(1e6)):

    xk = x0
    for _ in range(niters):
        xk = desc_update(grad_f, xk, alpha)

    return xk, f(xk)
```

NUMERICAL CORNER We illustrate using a simple example.

```python
def f(x):
    return (x-1)**2 + 10

def grad_f(x):
    return 2*(x-1)

xgrid = np.linspace(-5,5,100)
plt.plot(xgrid, f(xgrid), label='f')
plt.plot(xgrid, grad_f(xgrid), label='grad_f')
plt.ylim((-20,50)), plt.legend()
plt.show()
```

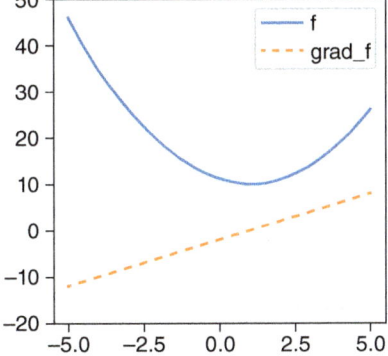

Figure 3.10 Graphical output of code.

```
gd(f, grad_f, 0)
```

```
(0.9999999999999722, 10.0)
```

We found a global minmizer in this case.

The next example shows that a different local minimizer may be reached depending on the starting point.

```
def f(x):
    return 4 * (x-1)**2 * (x+1)**2 - 2*(x-1)

def grad_f(x):
    return 8 * (x-1) * (x+1)**2 + 8 * (x-1)**2 * (x+1) - 2

xgrid = np.linspace(-2,2,100)
plt.plot(xgrid, f(xgrid), label='f')
plt.plot(xgrid, grad_f(xgrid), label='grad_f')
plt.ylim((-10,10)), plt.legend()
plt.show()
```

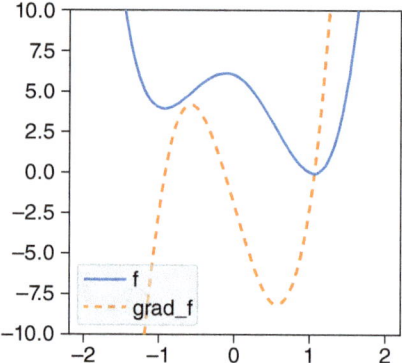

Figure 3.11 Graphical output of code.

```
gd(f, grad_f, 0)
```

```
(1.057453770738375, -0.0590145651028224)
```

```
gd(f, grad_f, -2)
```

```
(-0.9304029265558538, 3.933005966859003)
```

TRY IT! In this last example, *does changing the step size* affect the outcome?

In the final example, we end up at a stationary point that is not a local minimizer. Here both the first and second derivatives are zero. This is known as a saddle point.

3.5 Gradient Descent and Its Convergence Analysis

```
def f(x):
    return x**3

def grad_f(x):
    return 3 * x**2

xgrid = np.linspace(-2,2,100)
plt.plot(xgrid, f(xgrid), label='f')
plt.plot(xgrid, grad_f(xgrid), label='grad_f')
plt.ylim((-10,10)), plt.legend()
plt.show()
```

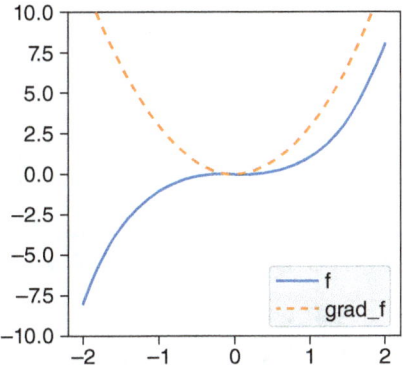

Figure 3.12 Graphical output of code.

```
gd(f, grad_f, 2)
```

(0.00033327488712690107, 3.701755838398568e-11)

```
gd(f, grad_f, -2, niters=100)
```

(-4.93350410883896, -120.0788396909241)

◁ **NC**

3.5.2 Convergence Analysis

In this section, we prove some results about the convergence of gradient descent. We start with the smooth case.

3.5.2.1 Smooth Case

Informally, a function is smooth if its gradient does not change too fast. The formal definition we will use here follows. We restrict ourselves to the twice continuously differentiable case.

Definition 3.5.3 (*Smooth Function*) Let $f: \mathbb{R}^d \to \mathbb{R}$ be twice continuously differentiable. We say that f is *L-smooth* if

$$-LI_{d \times d} \preceq \mathbf{H}_f(\mathbf{x}) \preceq LI_{d \times d}, \quad \forall \mathbf{x} \in \mathbb{R}^d.$$

In the single-variable case, this reduces to $-L \leq f''(x) \leq L$ for all $x \in \mathbb{R}$. More generally, recall that

$$A \preceq B \iff \mathbf{z}^T A \mathbf{z} \leq \mathbf{z}^T B \mathbf{z}, \quad \forall \mathbf{z} \in \mathbb{R}^d.$$

So the condition above is equivalent to

$$-L\|\mathbf{z}\|^2 \leq \mathbf{z}^T \mathbf{H}_f(\mathbf{x}) \mathbf{z} \leq L\|\mathbf{z}\|^2, \quad \forall \mathbf{x}, \mathbf{z} \in \mathbb{R}^d.$$

A different way to put this is that the second directional derivative satisfies

$$-L \leq \frac{\partial^2 f(\mathbf{x})}{\partial \mathbf{v}^2} \leq L$$

for all $\mathbf{x} \in \mathbb{R}^d$ and all unit vectors $\mathbf{v} \in \mathbb{R}^d$.

Combined with *Taylor's Theorem*, this immediately gives the following.

Lemma 3.5.4 (*Quadratic Bound for Smooth Functions*) Let $f: \mathbb{R}^d \to \mathbb{R}$ be twice continuously differentiable. Then f is *L-smooth* if and only if for all $\mathbf{x}, \mathbf{y} \in \mathbb{R}^d$ it holds that

$$\left|f(\mathbf{y}) - \{f(\mathbf{x}) + \nabla f(\mathbf{x})^T (\mathbf{y} - \mathbf{x})\}\right| \leq \frac{L}{2} \|\mathbf{y} - \mathbf{x}\|^2.$$

Proof idea: We apply *Taylor's Theorem*, then bound the second-order term.

Proof By *Taylor's Theorem*, for any $\alpha > 0$ there is $\xi_\alpha \in (0, 1)$ such that

$$f(\mathbf{x} + \alpha \mathbf{p}) = f(\mathbf{x}) + \alpha \nabla f(\mathbf{x})^T \mathbf{p} + \frac{1}{2} \alpha^2 \mathbf{p}^T \mathbf{H}_f(\mathbf{x} + \xi_\alpha \alpha \mathbf{p}) \mathbf{p}$$

where $\mathbf{p} = \mathbf{y} - \mathbf{x}$.

If f is *L-smooth*, then at $\alpha = 1$ by the observation after Definition 3.5.3,

$$-L\|\mathbf{p}\|^2 \leq \mathbf{p}^T \mathbf{H}_f(\mathbf{x} + \xi_1 \mathbf{p}) \mathbf{p} \leq L\|\mathbf{p}\|^2.$$

This implies the inequality in the statement.

On the other hand, if that inequality holds, by combining with the Taylor expansion above we get

$$\left|\frac{1}{2}\alpha^2 \mathbf{p}^T \mathbf{H}_f(\mathbf{x} + \xi_\alpha \alpha \mathbf{p}) \mathbf{p}\right| \leq \frac{L}{2}\alpha^2 \|\mathbf{p}\|^2$$

where we used that $\|\alpha \mathbf{p}\| = \alpha \|\mathbf{p}\|$ by absolute homogeneity of the norm. Dividing by $\alpha^2/2$, then taking $\alpha \to 0$ and using the continuity of the Hessian gives

$$\left|\mathbf{p}^T \mathbf{H}_f(\mathbf{x}) \mathbf{p}\right| \leq L\|\mathbf{p}\|^2.$$

By the observation after Definition 3.5.3 again, this implies that f is *L-smooth*. $\square$

3.5 Gradient Descent and Its Convergence Analysis

We show next that, in the smooth case, steepest descent with an appropriately chosen step size produces a sequence of points whose objective values decrease (or stay the same) and whose gradients vanish in the limit. We also give a quantitative convergence rate. Note that this result does not imply convergence to a local (or global) minimizer.

Theorem 3.5.5 (Convergence of Gradient Descent in the Smooth Case) *Suppose that $f \colon \mathbb{R}^d \to \mathbb{R}$ is L-smooth and bounded from below; that is, there is $\bar{f} > -\infty$ such that $f(\mathbf{x}) \geq \bar{f}$, $\forall \mathbf{x} \in \mathbb{R}^d$. Then gradient descent with step size $\alpha_t = \alpha := 1/L$ started from any $\mathbf{x}^0$ produces a sequence $\mathbf{x}^t$, $t = 1, 2, \ldots$ such that*

$$f(\mathbf{x}^{t+1}) \leq f(\mathbf{x}^t), \quad \forall t$$

and

$$\lim_{t \to +\infty} \|\nabla f(\mathbf{x}^t)\| = 0.$$

Moreover, after S steps, there is a t in $\{0, \ldots, S\}$ such that

$$\|\nabla f(\mathbf{x}^t)\| \leq \sqrt{\frac{2L\left[f(\mathbf{x}^0) - \bar{f}\right]}{S}}.$$

The assumption that a lower bound on f is known may seem far-fetched. But there are in fact many settings where this is natural. For instance, in the case of the least-squares problem, the objective function f is nonnegative by definition and therefore we can take $\bar{f} = 0$.

A different way to put the claim above regarding the convergence rate is the following. Take any $\epsilon > 0$. If our goal is to find a point $\mathbf{x}$ such that $\|\nabla f(\mathbf{x})\| \leq \epsilon$, then we are guaranteed to find one if we perform S steps such that

$$\min_{t=0,\ldots,S-1} \|\nabla f(\mathbf{x}^t)\| \leq \sqrt{\frac{2L\left[f(\mathbf{x}^0) - \bar{f}\right]}{S}} \leq \epsilon,$$

that is, after rearranging,

$$S \geq \frac{2L[f(\mathbf{x}^0) - \bar{f}]}{\epsilon^2}.$$

The heart of the proof is the following fundamental inequality. It also informs the choice of step size.

Lemma 3.5.6 (Descent Guarantee in the Smooth Case) *Suppose that $f \colon \mathbb{R}^d \to \mathbb{R}$ is L-smooth. For any $\mathbf{x} \in \mathbb{R}^d$,*

$$f\left(\mathbf{x} - \frac{1}{L}\nabla f(\mathbf{x})\right) \leq f(\mathbf{x}) - \frac{1}{2L}\|\nabla f(\mathbf{x})\|^2.$$

Proof idea: Intuitively, the *Quadratic Bound for Smooth Functions Lemma* shows that f is well approximated by a quadratic function in a neighborhood of $\mathbf{x}$ whose size depends on the smoothness parameter L. Choosing a step size that minimizes this approximation leads to a guaranteed improvement. The approach taken here is a special case of what is referred to as Majorize-Minimization (MM).

Proof By the *Quadratic Bound for Smooth Functions Lemma*, letting $\mathbf{p} = -\nabla f(\mathbf{x})$,

$$f(\mathbf{x} + \alpha \mathbf{p}) \leq f(\mathbf{x}) + \nabla f(\mathbf{x})^T (\alpha \mathbf{p}) + \frac{L}{2} \|\alpha \mathbf{p}\|^2$$

$$= f(\mathbf{x}) - \alpha \|\nabla f(\mathbf{x})\|^2 + \alpha^2 \frac{L}{2} \|\nabla f(\mathbf{x})\|^2$$

$$= f(\mathbf{x}) + \left(-\alpha + \alpha^2 \frac{L}{2}\right) \|\nabla f(\mathbf{x})\|^2.$$

The quadratic function in parentheses is convex and minimized at the stationary point α satisfying

$$\frac{d}{d\alpha}\left(-\alpha + \alpha^2 \frac{L}{2}\right) = -1 + \alpha L = 0.$$

Taking $\alpha = 1/L$, where $-\alpha + \alpha^2 \frac{L}{2} = -\frac{1}{2L}$, and replacing in the inequality above gives

$$f\left(\mathbf{x} - \frac{1}{L}\nabla f(\mathbf{x})\right) \leq f(\mathbf{x}) - \frac{1}{2L}\|\nabla f(\mathbf{x})\|^2,$$

as claimed. □

We return to the proof of the theorem.

Proof idea (Convergence of Gradient Descent in the Smooth Case): We use a telescoping argument to write $f(\mathbf{x}^S)$ as a sum of stepwise increments, each of which can be bounded by Lemma 3.5.6. Because $f(\mathbf{x}^S)$ is bounded from below, it then follows that the gradients must vanish in the limit.

Proof *(Convergence of Gradient Descent in the Smooth Case)* By the *Descent Guarantee in the Smooth Case Lemma*,

$$f(\mathbf{x}^{t+1}) \leq f(\mathbf{x}^t) - \frac{1}{2L}\|\nabla f(\mathbf{x}^t)\|^2 \leq f(\mathbf{x}^t), \quad \forall t.$$

Furthermore, using a telescoping sum, we get

$$f(\mathbf{x}^S) = f(\mathbf{x}^0) + \sum_{t=0}^{S-1}[f(\mathbf{x}^{t+1}) - f(\mathbf{x}^t)]$$

$$\leq f(\mathbf{x}^0) - \frac{1}{2L}\sum_{t=0}^{S-1}\|\nabla f(\mathbf{x}^t)\|^2.$$

Rearranging and using $f(\mathbf{x}^S) \geq \bar{f}$ leads to

$$\sum_{t=0}^{S-1}\|\nabla f(\mathbf{x}^t)\|^2 \leq 2L[f(\mathbf{x}^0) - \bar{f}].$$

We get the quantitative bound

$$\min_{t=0,\ldots,S-1} \|\nabla f(\mathbf{x}^t)\|^2 \leq \frac{1}{S}\sum_{t=0}^{S-1}\|\nabla f(\mathbf{x}^t)\|^2$$

$$\leq \frac{2L[f(\mathbf{x}^0) - \bar{f}]}{S}$$

as the minimum is necessarily less than or equal to the average. Moreover, as $S \to +\infty$, we must have $\|\nabla f(\mathbf{x}^S)\|^2 \to 0$ by standard analytical arguments. This proves the claim. □

3.5.2.2 Smooth and Strongly Convex Case

With stronger assumptions, we obtain stronger convergence results. One such assumption is strong convexity, which we defined in Section 3.4.2.2 for twice continuously differentiable functions.

We prove a convergence result for smooth, strongly convex functions. We show something stronger this time. We control the value of f itself and obtain a much faster rate of convergence. If f is m-strongly convex and has a global minimizer $\mathbf{x}^*$, then the global minimizer is unique and characterized by $\nabla f(\mathbf{x}^*) = \mathbf{0}$. Strong convexity allows us to relate the value of the function at a point $\mathbf{x}$ and the gradient of f at that point. This is proved in the following lemma, which is key to our convergence result.

Lemma 3.5.7 *(Relating a function and its gradient)* Let $f: \mathbb{R}^d \to \mathbb{R}$ be twice continuously differentiable, m-strongly convex with a global minimizer at $\mathbf{x}^*$. Then for any $\mathbf{x} \in \mathbb{R}^d$

$$f(\mathbf{x}) - f(\mathbf{x}^*) \leq \frac{\|\nabla f(\mathbf{x})\|^2}{2m}.$$

Proof By the *Quadratic Bound for Strongly Convex Functions Lemma*,

$$f(\mathbf{x}^*) \geq f(\mathbf{x}) + \nabla f(\mathbf{x})^T(\mathbf{x}^* - \mathbf{x}) + \frac{m}{2}\|\mathbf{x}^* - \mathbf{x}\|^2$$

$$= f(\mathbf{x}) + \nabla f(\mathbf{x})^T \mathbf{w} + \frac{1}{2}\mathbf{w}^T (mI_{d \times d}) \mathbf{w}$$

$$=: r + \mathbf{q}^T \mathbf{w} + \frac{1}{2}\mathbf{w}^T P \mathbf{w}$$

where in the second line we defined $\mathbf{w} = \mathbf{x}^* - \mathbf{x}$. The right-hand side is a quadratic function in $\mathbf{w}$ (for $\mathbf{x}$ fixed), and in the third line we used our previous notation P, $\mathbf{q}$, and r for such a function (see Example 3.2.3). So the inequality is still valid if we replace $\mathbf{w}$ with the global minimizer $\mathbf{w}^*$ of that quadratic function.

The matrix $P = mI_{d \times d}$ is positive definite. By Example 3.4.16, we know that the minimizer is achieved when the gradient $\frac{1}{2}[P + P^T]\mathbf{w}^* + \mathbf{q} = \mathbf{0}$, which is equivalent to

$$\mathbf{w}^* = -(mI_{d \times d})^{-1}\nabla f(\mathbf{x}) = -(m^{-1}I_{d \times d})\nabla f(\mathbf{x}) = -\frac{1}{m}\nabla f(\mathbf{x}).$$

So, replacing $\mathbf{w}$ with $\mathbf{w}^*$, we have the inequality

$$f(\mathbf{x}^*) \geq f(\mathbf{x}) + \nabla f(\mathbf{x})^T \left\{-\frac{1}{m}\nabla f(\mathbf{x})\right\}$$

$$+ \frac{1}{2}\left\{-\frac{1}{m}\nabla f(\mathbf{x})\right\}^T (mI_{d \times d}) \left\{-\frac{1}{m}\nabla f(\mathbf{x})\right\}$$

$$= f(\mathbf{x}) - \frac{1}{2m}\|\nabla f(\mathbf{x})\|^2.$$

Rearranging gives the claim. □

We can now state our convergence result.

Theorem 3.5.8 *(Convergence of Gradient Descent in the Strongly Convex Case)* Suppose that $f: \mathbb{R}^d \to \mathbb{R}$ is L-smooth and m-strongly convex with a global minimizer at $\mathbf{x}^*$. Then gradient descent with step size $\alpha = 1/L$ started from any $\mathbf{x}^0$ produces a sequence $\mathbf{x}^t$, $t = 1, 2, \ldots$ such that

$$\lim_{t \to +\infty} f(\mathbf{x}^t) = f(\mathbf{x}^*).$$

Moreover, after S steps, we have

$$f(\mathbf{x}^S) - f(\mathbf{x}^*) \leq \left(1 - \frac{m}{L}\right)^S [f(\mathbf{x}^0) - f(\mathbf{x}^*)].$$

Observe that $f(\mathbf{x}^S) - f(\mathbf{x}^*)$ decreases exponentially fast in S. A related bound can be proved for $\|\mathbf{x}^S - \mathbf{x}^*\|$.

Put differently, fix any $\epsilon > 0$. If our goal is to find a point $\mathbf{x}$ such that $f(\mathbf{x}) - f(\mathbf{x}^*) \leq \epsilon$, then we are guaranteed to find one if we perform S steps such that

$$f(\mathbf{x}^S) - f(\mathbf{x}^*) \leq \left(1 - \frac{m}{L}\right)^S [f(\mathbf{x}^0) - f(\mathbf{x}^*)] \leq \epsilon,$$

that is, after rearranging,

$$S \geq \frac{\log \epsilon^{-1} + \log(f(\mathbf{x}^0) - \bar{f})}{\log\left(1 - \frac{m}{L}\right)^{-1}}.$$

Proof idea (Convergence of Gradient Descent in the Strongly Convex Case): We apply the *Descent Guarantee for Smooth Functions Lemma* together with Lemma 3.5.7.

Proof *(Convergence of Gradient Descent in the Strongly Convex Case)* By the *Descent Guarantee for Smooth Functions Lemma* together with Lemma 3.5.7, we have for all t

$$f(\mathbf{x}^{t+1}) \leq f(\mathbf{x}^t) - \frac{1}{2L}\|\nabla f(\mathbf{x}^t)\|^2 \leq f(\mathbf{x}^t) - \frac{m}{L}[f(\mathbf{x}^t) - f(\mathbf{x}^*)].$$

Subtracting $f(\mathbf{x}^*)$ on both sides gives

$$f(\mathbf{x}^{t+1}) - f(\mathbf{x}^*) \leq \left(1 - \frac{m}{L}\right)[f(\mathbf{x}^t) - f(\mathbf{x}^*)].$$

Recursing, this is

$$\leq \left(1 - \frac{m}{L}\right)^2 [f(\mathbf{x}^{t-1}) - f(\mathbf{x}^*)],$$

and so on. That gives the claim. $\square$

NUMERICAL CORNER We revisit our first simple single-variable example.

```
def f(x):
    return (x-1)**2 + 10

def grad_f(x):
    return 2*(x-1)
```

The second derivative is $f''(x) = 2$. Hence, this f is L-smooth and m-strongly convex with $L = m = 2$. The theory we developed suggests taking step size $\alpha_t = \alpha = 1/L = 1/2$. It also implies that

$$f(x^1) - f(x^*) \leq \left(1 - \frac{m}{L}\right)[f(x^0) - f(x^*)] = 0.$$

We converge in one step! And that holds for any starting point x^0.

Let's try this!

```
gd(f, grad_f, 0, alpha=0.5, niters=1)
```

(1.0, 10.0)

Let's try a different starting point.

```
gd(f, grad_f, 100, alpha=0.5, niters=1)
```

(1.0, 10.0)

◁ NC

> *Self-Assessment Quiz* (with help from Claude, Gemini, and ChatGPT)
>
> 1. In the gradient descent update rule $\mathbf{x}^{t+1} = \mathbf{x}^t - \alpha_t \nabla f(\mathbf{x}^t)$, what does α_t represent?
>   a) The gradient of f at $\mathbf{x}^t$
>   b) The step size or learning rate
>   c) The direction of steepest ascent
>   d) The Hessian matrix of f at $\mathbf{x}^t$
>
> 2. A function $f: \mathbb{R}^d \to \mathbb{R}$ is said to be L-smooth if
>   a) $\|\nabla f(\mathbf{x})\| \le L$ for all $\mathbf{x} \in \mathbb{R}^d$.
>   b) $-LI_{d \times d} \preceq \mathbf{H}_f(\mathbf{x}) \preceq LI_{d \times d}$ for all $\mathbf{x} \in \mathbb{R}^d$.
>   c) $f(\mathbf{y}) \le f(\mathbf{x}) + \nabla f(\mathbf{x})^T(\mathbf{y}-\mathbf{x}) + \frac{L}{2}\|\mathbf{y}-\mathbf{x}\|^2$ for all $\mathbf{x}, \mathbf{y} \in \mathbb{R}^d$.
>   d) both b) and c) hold.
>
> 3. Suppose $f: \mathbb{R}^d \to \mathbb{R}$ is L-smooth and bounded from below. According to Theorem 3.5.5, gradient descent with step size $\alpha_t = 1/L$ started from any $\mathbf{x}^0$ produces a sequence $\{\mathbf{x}^t\}$ such that
>   a) $\lim_{t \to +\infty} f(\mathbf{x}^t) = 0$.
>   b) $\lim_{t \to +\infty} \|\nabla f(\mathbf{x}^t)\| = 0$.
>   c) $\min_{t=0,\ldots,S-1} \|\nabla f(\mathbf{x}^t)\| \le \sqrt{\frac{2L[f(\mathbf{x}^0) - \bar{f}]}{S}}$ after S steps.
>   d) both b) and c).
>
> 4. Suppose $f: \mathbb{R}^d \to \mathbb{R}$ is L-smooth and m-strongly convex with a global minimizer at $\mathbf{x}^*$. According to Theorem 3.5.8, gradient descent with step size $\alpha = 1/L$ started from any $\mathbf{x}^0$ produces a sequence $\{\mathbf{x}^t\}$ such that after S steps,
>   a) $f(\mathbf{x}^S) - f(\mathbf{x}^*) \le (1 - \frac{m}{L})^S [f(\mathbf{x}^0) - f(\mathbf{x}^*)]$.
>   b) $f(\mathbf{x}^S) - f(\mathbf{x}^*) \ge (1 - \frac{m}{L})^S [f(\mathbf{x}^0) - f(\mathbf{x}^*)]$.
>   c) $f(\mathbf{x}^S) - f(\mathbf{x}^*) \le (1 + \frac{m}{L})^S [f(\mathbf{x}^0) - f(\mathbf{x}^*)]$.
>   d) $f(\mathbf{x}^S) - f(\mathbf{x}^*) \ge (1 + \frac{m}{L})^S [f(\mathbf{x}^0) - f(\mathbf{x}^*)]$.
>
> 5. If a function f is m-strongly convex, what can we say about its global minimizer?
>   a) It may not exist.
>   b) It exists and is unique.
>   c) It exists but may not be unique.
>   d) It always occurs at the origin.

> Answer for 1: b. Justification: The text states "At each iteration of gradient descent, we take a step in the direction of the negative of the gradient, that is, $\mathbf{x}^{t+1} = \mathbf{x}^t - \alpha_t \nabla f(\mathbf{x}^t), t = 0, 1, 2, \ldots$ for a sequence of step sizes $\alpha_t > 0$."
>
> Answer for 2: d. Justification: The text provides both the definition in terms of the Hessian matrix (option b) and the equivalent characterization in terms of the quadratic bound (option c).
>
> Answer for 3: d. Justification: The theorem states both the asymptotic convergence of the gradients to zero (option b) and the quantitative bound on the minimum gradient norm after S steps (option c).
>
> Answer for 4: a. Justification: This is the convergence rate stated in the theorem.
>
> Answer for 5: b. Justification: The text states that if f is m-strongly convex, then "the global minimizer is unique."

3.6 Application: Logistic Regression

We return to logistic regression, to which we alluded in the motivating example of this chapter. The input data is of the form $\{(\boldsymbol{\alpha}_i, b_i) : i = 1, \ldots, n\}$ where $\boldsymbol{\alpha}_i = (\alpha_{i,1}, \ldots, \alpha_{i,d}) \in \mathbb{R}^d$ are the features and $b_i \in \{0, 1\}$ is the label. As before we use a matrix representation: $A \in \mathbb{R}^{n \times d}$ has rows $\boldsymbol{\alpha}_i^T, i = 1, \ldots, n$ and $\mathbf{b} = (b_1, \ldots, b_n) \in \{0, 1\}^n$.

3.6.1 Definitions

We summarize the logistic regression approach. Our goal is to find a function of the features that approximates the probability of the label 1. For this purpose, we model the log-odds (or logit function) of the probability of label 1 as a linear function of the features $\boldsymbol{\alpha} \in \mathbb{R}^d$:

$$\log \frac{p(\mathbf{x}; \boldsymbol{\alpha})}{1 - p(\mathbf{x}; \boldsymbol{\alpha})} = \boldsymbol{\alpha}^T \mathbf{x}$$

where $\mathbf{x} \in \mathbb{R}^d$ is the vector of coefficients (i.e., parameters). Inverting this expression gives

$$p(\mathbf{x}; \boldsymbol{\alpha}) = \sigma(\boldsymbol{\alpha}^T \mathbf{x})$$

where the sigmoid function is

$$\sigma(z) = \frac{1}{1 + e^{-z}}$$

for $z \in \mathbb{R}$.

NUMERICAL CORNER We plot the sigmoid function.

```
def sigmoid(z):
    return 1/(1+np.exp(-z))


grid = np.linspace(-5, 5, 100)
plt.plot(grid, sigmoid(grid), c='k')
plt.show()
```

3.6 Application: Logistic Regression

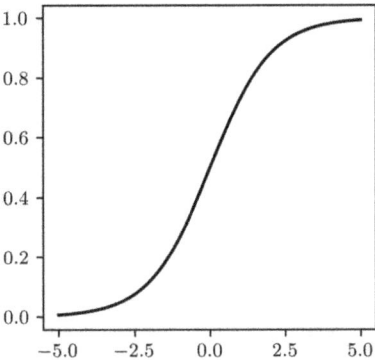

Figure 3.13 Graphical output of code.

◁ **NC**

We seek to maximize the probability of observing the data, also known as the likelihood function, assuming the labels are independent given the features (see Section 6.2.4 for more details). The likelihood function is given by

$$\mathcal{L}(\mathbf{x}; A, \mathbf{b}) = \prod_{i=1}^{n} p(\boldsymbol{\alpha}_i; \mathbf{x})^{b_i} (1 - p(\boldsymbol{\alpha}_i; \mathbf{x}))^{1-b_i}.$$

Taking a logarithm, multiplying by $-1/n$ and substituting the sigmoid function, we want to minimize the cross-entropy loss

$$\ell(\mathbf{x}; A, \mathbf{b}) = \frac{1}{n} \sum_{i=1}^{n} \left\{ -b_i \log(\sigma(\boldsymbol{\alpha}_i^T \mathbf{x})) - (1 - b_i) \log(1 - \sigma(\boldsymbol{\alpha}_i^T \mathbf{x})) \right\}.$$

We used standard properties of the logarithm: For $x, y > 0$, $\log(xy) = \log x + \log y$ and $\log(x^y) = y \log x$.

Hence, we want to solve the minimization problem

$$\min_{\mathbf{x} \in \mathbb{R}^d} \ell(\mathbf{x}; A, \mathbf{b}).$$

We are implicitly using here the fact that the logarithm is a strictly increasing function and therefore does not change the global optimum of a function; multiplying by $-1/n$ changed the global maximum into a global minimum.

To use gradient descent, we need the gradient of ℓ. We use the *Chain Rule* and first compute the derivative of σ, which is

$$\sigma'(z) = \frac{e^{-z}}{(1 + e^{-z})^2} = \frac{1}{1 + e^{-z}} \left(1 - \frac{1}{1 + e^{-z}}\right) = \sigma(z)(1 - \sigma(z)).$$

The latter expression is known as the logistic differential equation. It arises in a variety of applications, including the modeling of population dynamics. Here it will be a convenient way to compute the gradient.

Observe that, for $\boldsymbol{\alpha} = (\alpha_1, \ldots, \alpha_d) \in \mathbb{R}^d$, by the *Chain Rule*:

$$\nabla \sigma(\boldsymbol{\alpha}^T \mathbf{x}) = \sigma'(\boldsymbol{\alpha}^T \mathbf{x}) \nabla(\boldsymbol{\alpha}^T \mathbf{x}) = \sigma'(\boldsymbol{\alpha}^T \mathbf{x}) \boldsymbol{\alpha}$$

where, throughout, the gradient is with respect to $\mathbf{x}$.

Alternatively, we can obtain the same formula by applying the single-variable *Chain Rule*:

$$\frac{\partial}{\partial x_j}\sigma(\boldsymbol{\alpha}^T\mathbf{x}) = \sigma'(\boldsymbol{\alpha}^T\mathbf{x})\frac{\partial}{\partial x_j}(\boldsymbol{\alpha}^T\mathbf{x})$$

$$= \sigma'(\boldsymbol{\alpha}^T\mathbf{x})\frac{\partial}{\partial x_j}\left(\alpha_j x_j + \sum_{\ell=1,\ell\neq j}^{d}\alpha_\ell x_\ell\right)$$

$$= \sigma(\boldsymbol{\alpha}^T\mathbf{x})(1-\sigma(\boldsymbol{\alpha}^T\mathbf{x}))\,\alpha_j$$

so that

$$\nabla\sigma(\boldsymbol{\alpha}^T\mathbf{x}) = \left(\sigma(\boldsymbol{\alpha}^T\mathbf{x})(1-\sigma(\boldsymbol{\alpha}^T\mathbf{x}))\,\alpha_1,\ldots,\sigma(\boldsymbol{\alpha}^T\mathbf{x})(1-\sigma(\boldsymbol{\alpha}^T\mathbf{x}))\,\alpha_d\right)$$

$$= \sigma(\boldsymbol{\alpha}^T\mathbf{x})(1-\sigma(\boldsymbol{\alpha}^T\mathbf{x}))\,(\alpha_1,\ldots,\alpha_d)$$

$$= \sigma(\boldsymbol{\alpha}^T\mathbf{x})(1-\sigma(\boldsymbol{\alpha}^T\mathbf{x}))\,\boldsymbol{\alpha}.$$

By another application of the *Chain Rule*, since $\frac{d}{dz}\log z = \frac{1}{z}$,

$$\nabla\ell(\mathbf{x};A,\mathbf{b}) = \nabla\left[\frac{1}{n}\sum_{i=1}^{n}\left\{-b_i\log(\sigma(\boldsymbol{\alpha}_i^T\mathbf{x})) - (1-b_i)\log(1-\sigma(\boldsymbol{\alpha}_i^T\mathbf{x}))\right\}\right]$$

$$= -\frac{1}{n}\sum_{i=1}^{n}\frac{b_i}{\sigma(\boldsymbol{\alpha}_i^T\mathbf{x})}\nabla\sigma(\boldsymbol{\alpha}_i^T\mathbf{x}) - \frac{1}{n}\sum_{i=1}^{n}\frac{1-b_i}{1-\sigma(\boldsymbol{\alpha}_i^T\mathbf{x})}\nabla(1-\sigma(\boldsymbol{\alpha}_i^T\mathbf{x}))$$

$$= -\frac{1}{n}\sum_{i=1}^{n}\frac{b_i}{\sigma(\boldsymbol{\alpha}_i^T\mathbf{x})}\nabla\sigma(\boldsymbol{\alpha}_i^T\mathbf{x}) + \frac{1}{n}\sum_{i=1}^{n}\frac{1-b_i}{1-\sigma(\boldsymbol{\alpha}_i^T\mathbf{x})}\nabla\sigma(\boldsymbol{\alpha}_i^T\mathbf{x}).$$

Using the expression for the gradient of the sigmoid functions, this is equal to

$$-\frac{1}{n}\sum_{i=1}^{n}\frac{b_i}{\sigma(\boldsymbol{\alpha}_i^T\mathbf{x})}\sigma(\boldsymbol{\alpha}_i^T\mathbf{x})(1-\sigma(\boldsymbol{\alpha}_i^T\mathbf{x}))\,\boldsymbol{\alpha}_i$$

$$+\frac{1}{n}\sum_{i=1}^{n}\frac{1-b_i}{1-\sigma(\boldsymbol{\alpha}_i^T\mathbf{x})}\sigma(\boldsymbol{\alpha}_i^T\mathbf{x})(1-\sigma(\boldsymbol{\alpha}_i^T\mathbf{x}))\,\boldsymbol{\alpha}_i$$

$$= -\frac{1}{n}\sum_{i=1}^{n}\left(b_i(1-\sigma(\boldsymbol{\alpha}_i^T\mathbf{x})) - (1-b_i)\sigma(\boldsymbol{\alpha}_i^T\mathbf{x})\right)\boldsymbol{\alpha}_i$$

$$= -\frac{1}{n}\sum_{i=1}^{n}(b_i - \sigma(\boldsymbol{\alpha}_i^T\mathbf{x}))\,\boldsymbol{\alpha}_i.$$

To implement this formula, it will be useful to rewrite it in terms of the matrix representation $A \in \mathbb{R}^{n\times d}$ (which has rows $\boldsymbol{\alpha}_i^T$, $i = 1,\ldots,n$) and $\mathbf{b} = (b_1,\ldots,b_n) \in \{0,1\}^n$. Let $\boldsymbol{\sigma}\colon \mathbb{R}^n \to \mathbb{R}$ be the vector-valued function that applies the sigmoid σ entry-wise; that is, $\boldsymbol{\sigma}(\mathbf{z}) = (\sigma(z_1),\ldots,\sigma(z_n))$ where $\mathbf{z} = (z_1,\ldots,z_n)$. Thinking of $\sum_{i=1}^{n}(b_i - \sigma(\boldsymbol{\alpha}_i^T\mathbf{x}))\,\boldsymbol{\alpha}_i$ as a linear combination of the columns of A^T with coefficients being the entries of the vector $\mathbf{b} - \boldsymbol{\sigma}(A\mathbf{x})$, we see that

$$\nabla\ell(\mathbf{x};A,\mathbf{b}) = -\frac{1}{n}\sum_{i=1}^{n}(b_i - \sigma(\boldsymbol{\alpha}_i^T\mathbf{x}))\,\boldsymbol{\alpha}_i = -\frac{1}{n}A^T[\mathbf{b} - \boldsymbol{\sigma}(A\mathbf{x})].$$

We turn to the Hessian. By symmetry, we can think of the j-th column of the Hessian as the gradient of the partial derivative with respect to x_j. Hence we start by computing the gradient of the j-th entry of the summands in the gradient of ℓ. We note that, for $\boldsymbol{\alpha} = (\alpha_1,\ldots,\alpha_d) \in \mathbb{R}^d$,

$$\nabla[(b - \sigma(\boldsymbol{\alpha}^T\mathbf{x}))\,\alpha_j] = -\nabla[\sigma(\boldsymbol{\alpha}^T\mathbf{x})]\,\alpha_j = -\sigma(\boldsymbol{\alpha}^T\mathbf{x})(1-\sigma(\boldsymbol{\alpha}^T\mathbf{x}))\,\boldsymbol{\alpha}\alpha_j.$$

Thus, using the fact that $\alpha\alpha_j$ is the j-th column of the matrix $\alpha\alpha^T$, we get

$$\mathbf{H}_\ell(\mathbf{x}; A, \mathbf{b}) = \frac{1}{n} \sum_{i=1}^{n} \sigma(\alpha_i^T \mathbf{x})(1 - \sigma(\alpha_i^T \mathbf{x})) \, \alpha_i \alpha_i^T$$

where $\mathbf{H}_\ell(\mathbf{x}; A, \mathbf{b})$ indicates the Hessian with respect to the $\mathbf{x}$ variables, for fixed $A, \mathbf{b}$.

Lemma 3.6.1 *(Convexity of logistic regression)* *The function $\ell(\mathbf{x}; A, \mathbf{b})$ is convex as a function of $\mathbf{x} \in \mathbb{R}^d$.*

Proof Indeed, the Hessian is positive semidefinite: For any $\mathbf{z} \in \mathbb{R}^d$

$$\mathbf{z}^T \mathbf{H}_\ell(\mathbf{x}; A, \mathbf{b}) \mathbf{z} = \frac{1}{n} \sum_{i=1}^{n} \sigma(\alpha_i^T \mathbf{x})(1 - \sigma(\alpha_i^T \mathbf{x})) \, \mathbf{z}^T \alpha_i \alpha_i^T \mathbf{z}$$

$$= \frac{1}{n} \sum_{i=1}^{n} \sigma(\alpha_i^T \mathbf{x})(1 - \sigma(\alpha_i^T \mathbf{x})) \, (\mathbf{z}^T \alpha_i)^2$$

$$\geq 0$$

since $\sigma(t) \in [0, 1]$ for all t. □

Convexity is one reason for working with the cross-entropy loss (rather than the mean squared error for instance).

Lemma 3.6.2 *(Smoothness of logistic regression)* *The function $\ell(\mathbf{x}; A, \mathbf{b})$ is L-smooth for*

$$L = \frac{1}{4n} \sum_{i=1}^{n} \|\alpha_i\|^2 = \frac{1}{4n} \|A\|_F^2.$$

Proof We use convexity and the expression for the Hessian to derive that, for any unit vector $\mathbf{z} \in \mathbb{R}^d$,

$$0 \leq \mathbf{z}^T H_\ell(\mathbf{x}; A, \mathbf{b}) \mathbf{z} = \frac{1}{n} \sum_{i=1}^{n} \sigma(\alpha_i^T \mathbf{x})(1 - \sigma(\alpha_i^T \mathbf{x})) \, (\mathbf{z}^T \alpha_i)^2.$$

We need to find the maximum value that the factor $\sigma(\alpha_i^T \mathbf{x})(1 - \sigma(\alpha_i^T \mathbf{x}))$ can take. Note that $\sigma(t) \in [0, 1]$ for all t and $\sigma(t) + (1 - \sigma(t)) = 1$. Taking the derivatives of the function $f(w) = w(1 - w) = w - w^2$ we get $f'(w) = 1 - 2w$ and $f''(w) = -2$. So f is concave and achieve its maximum at $w^* = 1/2$ where it takes the value $f(1/2) = 1/4$. We have proved that

$$\sigma(\alpha_i^T \mathbf{x})(1 - \sigma(\alpha_i^T \mathbf{x})) \leq 1/4$$

for any $\mathbf{z}$.

Going back to the upper bound on $\mathbf{z}^T \mathbf{H}_\ell(\mathbf{x}; A, \mathbf{b}) \mathbf{z}$ we get

$$\mathbf{z}^T \mathbf{H}_\ell(\mathbf{x}; A, \mathbf{b}) \mathbf{z} = \frac{1}{n} \sum_{i=1}^{n} \sigma(\alpha_i^T \mathbf{x})(1 - \sigma(\alpha_i^T \mathbf{x})) \, (\mathbf{z}^T \alpha_i)^2$$

$$\leq \frac{1}{4n} \sum_{i=1}^{n} (\mathbf{z}^T \alpha_i)^2$$

$$\leq \frac{1}{4n} \sum_{i=1}^{n} \|\mathbf{z}\|^2 \|\alpha_i\|^2$$

$$\leq \frac{1}{4n} \sum_{i=1}^{n} \|\alpha_i\|^2,$$

where we used the *Cauchy–Schwarz Inequality* in the third line and the fact that **z** is a unit vector in the fourth one.

This implies L-smoothness. □

For step size β, one step of gradient descent is therefore

$$\mathbf{x}^{t+1} = \mathbf{x}^t + \beta \frac{1}{n} \sum_{i=1}^{n} (b_i - \sigma(\boldsymbol{\alpha}_i^T \mathbf{x}^t)) \, \boldsymbol{\alpha}_i.$$

3.6.2 Implementation

We modify our implementation of gradient descent to take a dataset as input. Recall that to run gradient descent, we first implement a function computing a descent update. It takes as input a function `grad_fn` computing the gradient itself, as well as a current iterate and a step size. We now also feed a dataset as additional input.

```
def desc_update_for_logreg(grad_fn, A, b, curr_x, beta):
    gradient = grad_fn(curr_x, A, b)
    return curr_x - beta*gradient
```

We are ready to implement gradient descent. Our function takes as input a function `loss_fn` computing the objective, a function `grad_fn` computing the gradient, the dataset A and b, and an initial guess `init_x`. Optional parameters are the step size and the number of iterations.

```
def gd_for_logreg(loss_fn, grad_fn, A, b, init_x, beta=1e-3,
    niters=int(1e5)):
    curr_x = init_x

    for iter in range(niters):
        curr_x = desc_update_for_logreg(grad_fn, A, b, curr_x, beta)

    return curr_x
```

To implement `loss_fn` and `grad_fn`, we define the sigmoid as above. Below, `pred_fn` is $\sigma(A\mathbf{x})$. Here we write the loss function as

$$\ell(\mathbf{x}; A, \mathbf{b}) = \frac{1}{n} \sum_{i=1}^{n} \left\{ -b_i \log(\sigma(\boldsymbol{\alpha}_i^T \mathbf{x})) - (1 - b_i) \log(1 - \sigma(\boldsymbol{\alpha}_i^T \mathbf{x})) \right\}$$

$$= \text{mean}\left(-\mathbf{b} \odot \log(\sigma(A\mathbf{x})) - (\mathbf{1} - \mathbf{b}) \odot \log(\mathbf{1} - \sigma(A\mathbf{x}))\right),$$

where $\odot$ is the Hadamard product, or element-wise product (e.g., $\mathbf{u} \odot \mathbf{v} = (u_1 v_1, \ldots, u_n v_n)$), the logarithm (denoted in bold) is applied element-wise, and mean(**z**) is the mean of the entries of **z** (i.e., mean(**z**) $= n^{-1} \sum_{i=1}^{n} z_i$).

3.6 Application: Logistic Regression

```python
def pred_fn(x, A):
    return sigmoid(A @ x)

def loss_fn(x, A, b):
    return np.mean(-b*np.log(pred_fn(x, A)) -
                   (1 - b)*np.log(1 - pred_fn(x, A)))

def grad_fn(x, A, b):
    return -A.T @ (b - pred_fn(x, A))/len(b)
```

We can choose a step size based on the smoothness of the objective as above. Recall that `numpy.linalg.norm` computes the Frobenius norm by default.

```python
def stepsize_for_logreg(A, b):
    L = LA.norm(A)**2 / (4 * len(b))
    return 1/L
```

NUMERICAL CORNER We return to our original motivation, the airline customer satisfaction dataset. We first load the dataset. We will need the column names later.

```python
data = pd.read_csv('customer_airline_satisfaction.csv')
column_names = data.columns.tolist()
print(column_names)
```

```
['Satisfied', 'Age', 'Class_Business', 'Class_Eco', 'Class_Eco Plus',
 'Business travel', 'Loyal customer', 'Flight Distance', 'Departure
 Delay in Minutes', 'Arrival Delay in Minutes', 'Seat comfort',
 'Departure/Arrival time convenient', 'Food and drink', 'Gate location',
 'Inflight wifi service', 'Inflight entertainment', 'Online support',
 'Ease of Online booking', 'On-board service', 'Leg room service',
 'Baggage handling', 'Checkin service', 'Cleanliness',
 'Online boarding']
```

Our goal will be to predict the first column, `Satisfied`, from the rest of the columns. For this, we transform our data into NumPy arrays. We also standardize the columns by subtracting their mean and dividing by their standard deviation. This will allow us to compare the influence of different features on the prediction. We add a column of 1s to account for the intercept.

```python
y = data['Satisfied'].to_numpy()
X = data.drop(columns=['Satisfied']).to_numpy()

means = np.mean(X, axis=0)
stds = np.std(X, axis=0)
X_standardized = (X - means) / stds

A = np.concatenate((np.ones((len(y),1)), X_standardized), axis=1)
b = y
```

We use the functions `loss_fn` and `grad_fn` which were written for general logistic regression problems.

```
init_x = np.zeros(A.shape[1])
best_x = gd_for_logreg(loss_fn, grad_fn, A, b, init_x,
        beta=1e-3, niters=int(1e3))
print(best_x)
```

```
[ 0.03622497  0.04123861  0.10020177 -0.08786108 -0.02485893  0.0420605
  0.11995567 -0.01799992 -0.02399636 -0.02653084  0.1176043  -0.02382631
  0.05909378 -0.01161711  0.06553672  0.21313777  0.12883519  0.14631027
  0.12239595  0.11282894  0.08556647  0.08954403  0.08447245  0.108043  ]
```

To interpret the results, we plot the coefficients in decreasing order.

```
coefficients, features = best_x[1:], column_names[1:]

sorted_indices = np.argsort(coefficients)
sorted_coefficients = coefficients[sorted_indices]
sorted_features = np.array(features)[sorted_indices]

plt.figure(figsize=(6, 5))
plt.barh(sorted_features, sorted_coefficients,
    color='lightblue', edgecolor='black')
plt.xlabel('Coefficient Value'),
plt.title('Logistic Regression Coefficients')
plt.show()
```

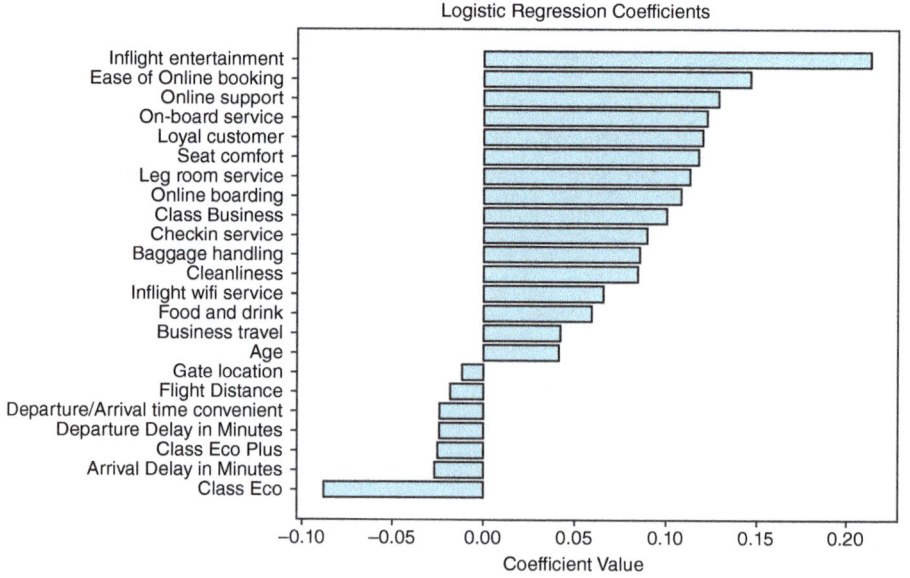

Figure 3.14 Graphical output of code.

3.6 Application: Logistic Regression

We see from the first ten bars or so that, as might be expected, higher ratings on various aspects of the flight generally contribute to a higher predicted likelihood of satisfaction (with one exception being `Gate location` whose coefficient is negative but may not be statistically significant). `Inflight entertainment` seems particularly influential. Age also shows the same pattern, something we had noticed in the introductory section through a different analysis. On the other hand, `Departure Delay in Minutes` and `Arrival Delay in Minutes` contribute to a lower predicted likelihood of satisfaction, again an expected pattern. The most negative influence however appears to come from `Class_Eco`.

CHAT & LEARN There are faster methods for logistic regression. Ask your favorite AI chatbot for an explanation and implementation of the iteratively reweighted least-squares method. ***Try it on this dataset.***

TRY IT! One can attempt to predict whether a new customer, whose feature vector is α, will be satisfied by using the prediction function $p(\mathbf{x}; \alpha) = \sigma(\alpha^T \mathbf{x})$, where $\mathbf{x}$ is the fitted coefficients. Say a customer is predicted to be satisfied if $\sigma(\alpha^T \mathbf{x}) > 0.5$. ***Implement this predictor*** and compute its accuracy on this dataset.

CHAT & LEARN Because of the issue of overfitting, computing the accuracy of a predictor on a dataset used to estimate the coefficients is problematic. Ask your favorite AI chatbot about scikit-learn's `train_test_split` function and how it helps resolve this issue. ***Implement it on this dataset.***

◁ NC

Self-Assessment Quiz (with help from Claude, Gemini, and ChatGPT)

1. What is the primary goal of logistic regression?
    a) To predict a continuous outcome variable.
    b) To classify data points into multiple categories.
    c) To model the probability of a binary outcome.
    d) To find the optimal linear combination of features.

2. What is the relationship between maximizing the likelihood function and minimizing the cross-entropy loss in logistic regression?
    a) They are unrelated concepts.
    b) Maximizing the likelihood is equivalent to minimizing the cross-entropy loss.
    c) Minimizing the cross-entropy loss is a first step toward maximizing the likelihood.
    d) Maximizing the likelihood is a special case of minimizing the cross-entropy loss.

3. Which of the following is the correct formula for the logistic regression objective function (cross-entropy loss)?
    a) $\ell(\mathbf{x}; A, \mathbf{b}) = \frac{1}{n} \sum_{i=1}^{n} \log(1 + \exp(-b_i \alpha_i^T \mathbf{x}))$
    b) $\ell(\mathbf{x}; A, \mathbf{b}) = \frac{1}{n} \sum_{i=1}^{n} (b_i - \sigma(\alpha_i^T \mathbf{x}))^2$
    c) $\ell(\mathbf{x}; A, \mathbf{b}) = \frac{1}{n} \sum_{i=1}^{n} \{-b_i \log(\sigma(\alpha_i^T \mathbf{x})) - (1 - b_i) \log(1 - \sigma(\alpha_i^T \mathbf{x}))\}$
    d) $\ell(\mathbf{x}; A, \mathbf{b}) = \frac{1}{n} \sum_{i=1}^{n} b_i \alpha_i^T \mathbf{x}$

4. What is the purpose of standardizing the input features in the airline customer satisfaction dataset example?
   a) To ensure the objective function is convex.
   b) To speed up the convergence of gradient descent.
   c) To allow comparison of the influence of different features on the prediction.
   d) To handle missing data in the dataset.

5. Which of the following is a valid reason for adding a column of 1's to the feature matrix in logistic regression?
   a) To ensure the objective function is convex.
   b) To allow for an intercept term in the model.
   c) To standardize the input features.
   d) To handle missing data in the dataset.

Answer for 1: c. Justification: The text states that the goal of logistic regression is to "find a function of the features that approximates the probability of the label."

Answer for 2: b. Justification: The text states: "We seek to maximize the probability of observing the data … which is given by …. Taking a logarithm, multiplying by $-1/n$ and substituting the sigmoid function, we want to minimize the cross-entropy loss."

Answer for 3: c. Justification: The text states: "Hence, we want to solve the minimization problem $\min_{\mathbf{x} \in \mathbb{R}^d} \ell(\mathbf{x}; A, \mathbf{b})$," where $\ell(\mathbf{x}; A, \mathbf{b}) = \frac{1}{n}\sum_{i=1}^{n}\{-b_i \log(\sigma(\boldsymbol{\alpha}_i^T \mathbf{x})) - (1 - b_i)\log(1 - \sigma(\boldsymbol{\alpha}_i^T \mathbf{x}))\}$.

Answer for 4: c. Justification: The text states: "We also standardize the columns by subtracting their mean and dividing by their standard deviation. This will allow us to compare the influence of different features on the prediction."

Answer for 5: b. Justification: The text states: "To allow an affine function of the features, we add a column of 1's as we have done before."

3.7 Exercises

3.7.1 Warm-Up Worksheets
(with help from Claude, Gemini, and ChatGPT)

Section 3.2

E3.2.1 Calculate the gradient of the function $f(x_1, x_2) = 3x_1^2 - 2x_1x_2 + 4x_2^2 - 5x_1 + 2x_2$ at the point $(1, -1)$.

E3.2.2 Find the Hessian matrix of the function $f(x_1, x_2, x_3) = 2x_1x_2 + 3x_2x_3 - x_1^2 - 4x_3^2$.

E3.2.3 Compute the partial derivatives $\frac{\partial f}{\partial x_1}$ and $\frac{\partial f}{\partial x_2}$ for the function $f(x_1, x_2) = \sin(x_1)\cos(x_2)$ at the point $(\frac{\pi}{4}, \frac{\pi}{3})$.

E3.2.4 Let $f(x_1, x_2) = e^{x_1} + x_1x_2 - x_2^2$ and $\mathbf{g}(t) = (t^2, t)$. Calculate $(f \circ \mathbf{g})'(1)$ using the Chain Rule.

E3.2.5 Verify the *Symmetry of the Hessian* for the function $f(x_1, x_2) = x_1^3 + 3x_1x_2^2 - 2x_2^3$ at the point $(1, 2)$.

E3.2.6 Find the gradient of the function $f(x_1, x_2, x_3) = 2x_1 - 3x_2 + 4x_3$ at the point $(1, -2, 3)$.

E3.2.7 Calculate the second-order partial derivatives of the function $f(x_1, x_2) = x_1^2 \sin(x_2)$.

E3.2.8 Compute the gradient of the quadratic function $f(x_1, x_2) = 3x_1^2 + 2x_1x_2 - x_2^2 + 4x_1 - 2x_2$ at the point $(1, -1)$.

E3.2.9 Find the Hessian matrix of the function $f(x_1, x_2, x_3) = x_1^2 + 2x_2^2 + 3x_3^2 - 2x_1x_2 + 4x_1x_3 - 6x_2x_3$.

E3.2.10 Apply the multivariable *Mean Value Theorem* to the function $f(x_1, x_2) = x_1^2 + x_2^2$ on the line segment joining the points $(0, 0)$ and $(1, 2)$.

E3.2.11 Find the partial derivatives $\frac{\partial f}{\partial x}$ and $\frac{\partial f}{\partial y}$ of the function $f(x, y) = x^3 y^2 - 2xy^3 + y^4$.

E3.2.12 Compute the gradient $\nabla f(x, y)$ of the function $f(x, y) = \ln(x^2 + 2y^2)$ at the point $(1, 2)$.

E3.2.13 Find the Hessian matrix of the function $g(x, y) = \sin(x)\cos(y)$.

E3.2.14 If $p(x, y, z) = x^2 yz + 3xyz^2$, find all second partial derivatives of p.

E3.2.15 Verify that the function $q(x, y) = x^3 - 3xy^2$ satisfies Laplace's equation: $\frac{\partial^2 q}{\partial x^2} + \frac{\partial^2 q}{\partial y^2} = 0$.

E3.2.16 Consider the function $s(x, y) = x^2 + 4xy + 5y^2$. Use the *Mean Value Theorem* (with $\xi = 0$) to approximate $s(1.1, 0.9)$ using the point $(1, 1)$.

E3.2.17 A particle moves along a path given by $\mathbf{c}(t) = (t^2, t^3)$. The temperature at a point (x, y) is given by $u(x, y) = e^{-x^2 - y^2}$. Find the rate of change of the temperature experienced by the particle at time $t = 1$.

E3.2.18 Apply the *Chain Rule* to find $\frac{d}{dt} f(\mathbf{g}(t))$ for $f(x, y) = x^2 + y^2$ and $\mathbf{g}(t) = (t, \sin t)$.

E3.2.19 Use the *Chain Rule* to find $\frac{d}{dt} f(\mathbf{g}(t))$ for $f(x, y) = xy$ and $\mathbf{g}(t) = (t^2, \cos t)$.

Section 3.3

E3.3.1 Consider the function $f(x_1, x_2) = x_1^2 + 2x_2^2$. Find all points (x_1, x_2) where $\nabla f(x_1, x_2) = 0$.

E3.3.2 Let $f(x_1, x_2) = x_1^2 - x_2^2$. Find the directional derivative of f at the point $(1, 1)$ in the direction $\mathbf{v} = (\frac{1}{\sqrt{2}}, \frac{1}{\sqrt{2}})$.

E3.3.3 Consider the function $f(x_1, x_2) = x_1^2 + 2x_1x_2 + x_2^2$. Find the second directional derivative of f at the point $(1, 1)$ in the direction $\mathbf{v} = (\frac{1}{\sqrt{2}}, \frac{1}{\sqrt{2}})$.

E3.3.4 Consider the optimization problem $\min_{x_1, x_2} x_1^2 + x_2^2$ subject to $x_1 + x_2 = 1$. Write down the Lagrangian function $L(x_1, x_2, \lambda)$.

E3.3.5 For the optimization problem in E3.3.4, find all points (x_1, x_2, λ) satisfying the first-order necessary conditions.

E3.3.6 For the optimization problem in E3.3.4, check the second-order sufficient conditions at the point $(\frac{1}{2}, \frac{1}{2}, -1)$.

E3.3.7 Consider the function $f(x_1, x_2, x_3) = x_1^2 + x_2^2 + x_3^2$. Find all points (x_1, x_2, x_3) satisfying the first-order necessary conditions for the optimization problem $\min_{x_1, x_2, x_3} f(x_1, x_2, x_3)$ subject to $x_1 + 2x_2 + 3x_3 = 6$.

E3.3.8 For the optimization problem in E3.3.7, check the second-order sufficient conditions at the point $(\frac{1}{2}, 1, \frac{3}{2}, -1)$.

E3.3.9 Let $f: \mathbb{R}^2 \to \mathbb{R}$ be defined by $f(x_1, x_2) = x_1^3 - 3x_1 x_2^2$. Determine whether the vector $v = (1, 1)$ is a descent direction for f at the point $(1, 0)$.

E3.3.10 Let $f: \mathbb{R}^2 \to \mathbb{R}$ be defined by $f(x_1, x_2) = x_1^2 + x_2^2 - 2x_1 - 4x_2 + 5$. Find the Hessian matrix of f.

E3.3.11 Let $f: \mathbb{R}^2 \to \mathbb{R}$ be defined by $f(x_1, x_2) = -x_1^2 - x_2^2$. Compute the second directional derivative of f at the point $(0, 0)$ in the direction $\mathbf{v} = (1, 0)$.

E3.3.12 Calculate the directional derivative of $f(x,y) = x^2 + y^2$ at the point $(1,1)$ in the direction of $\mathbf{v} = (1,1)$.

E3.3.13 Determine the Hessian matrix of $f(x,y) = x^3 + y^3 - 3xy$ at the point $(1,1)$.

Section 3.4

E3.4.1 Find the convex combination of points $(2,3)$ and $(4,5)$ with $\alpha = 0.3$.

E3.4.2 Determine whether the following set is convex:
$$S = \{(x_1, x_2) \in \mathbb{R}^2 : x_1^2 + x_2^2 \leq 1\}.$$

E3.4.3 Let $S_1 = \{x \in \mathbb{R}^2 : x_1 + x_2 \leq 1\}$ and $S_2 = \{x \in \mathbb{R}^2 : x_1 - x_2 \leq 1\}$. Show directly that $S_1 \cap S_2$ is a convex set.

E3.4.4 Verify that the function $f(\mathbf{x}) = \log(e^{x_1} + e^{x_2})$ is convex using the Hessian matrix.

E3.4.5 Find the global minimizer of the function $f(x) = x^2 + 2x + 1$.

E3.4.6 Consider the function $f(x) = |x|$. Show that f is convex but not differentiable at $x = 0$.

E3.4.7 Verify that the function $f(x,y) = x^2 + 2y^2$ is strongly convex with $m = 2$.

E3.4.8 Find the projection of the point $x = (1,2)$ onto the set $D = \{(x_1, x_2) \in \mathbb{R}^2 : x_1 + x_2 = 1\}$.

E3.4.9 Let $f(x) = x^4 - 2x^2 + 1$. Determine whether f is convex.

E3.4.10 Let $f(x) = e^x$. Determine whether f is log-concave, i.e., $\log f$ is concave.

E3.4.11 Let $f(x) = x^2 - 2x + 2$. Determine whether f is strongly convex.

E3.4.12 Let $A = \begin{pmatrix} 1 & 2 \\ 2 & 5 \end{pmatrix}$ and $\mathbf{b} = \begin{pmatrix} 1 \\ 0 \end{pmatrix}$. Find the vector $\mathbf{x}$ that minimizes $\|A\mathbf{x} - \mathbf{b}\|_2^2$.

E3.4.13 Given the set $D = \{(x,y) \in \mathbb{R}^2 : x^2 + y^2 < 4\}$, determine if D is convex.

E3.4.14 Determine if the set $D = \{(x,y) \in \mathbb{R}^2 : x + y \leq 1\}$ is convex.

E3.4.15 Determine if the set $D = \{(x,y) \in \mathbb{R}^2 : x^2 - y^2 \leq 1\}$ is convex.

Section 3.5

E3.5.1 Given the function $f(x,y) = x^2 + 4y^2$, find the direction of steepest descent at the point $(1,1)$.

E3.5.2 Consider the function $f(x) = x^2 + 4x + 5$. Compute the derivative $f'(x)$ and find the direction of steepest descent at $x_0 = 1$.

E3.5.3 Given the function $f(x) = x^3 - 6x^2 + 9x + 2$, perform two iterations of gradient descent starting from $x_0 = 0$ with a step size of $\alpha = 0.1$.

E3.5.4 Let $f(x) = x^2$. Show that f is L-smooth for some $L > 0$.

E3.5.5 Let $f(x) = x^2$. Perform one step of gradient descent starting from $x_0 = 2$ with step size $\alpha = 0.1$.

E3.5.6 Consider the 2-smooth function $f(x) = x^2$. Starting from $x_0 = 3$, compute the point x_1 obtained after one iteration of gradient descent with step size $\alpha = \frac{1}{2}$.

E3.5.7 Verify that the function $f(x) = 2x^2 + 1$ is 4-strongly convex.

E3.5.8 For the 4-strongly convex function $f(x) = 2x^2 + 1$ with global minimizer $x^* = 0$, compute $\frac{1}{2m}|f'(1)|^2$ and compare it with $f(1) - f(x^*)$.

E3.5.9 Let $f(x) = x^4$. Is f L-smooth for some $L > 0$? Justify your answer.

E3.5.10 Let $f(x) = x^3$. Is f m-strongly convex for some $m > 0$? Justify your answer.

E3.5.11 Let $f(x) = x^2 + 2x + 1$. Show that f is m-strongly convex for some $m > 0$.

E3.5.12 Let $f(x) = x^2 + 2x + 1$. Perform one step of gradient descent starting from $x_0 = -3$ with step size $\alpha = 0.2$.

E3.5.13 Given the function $f(x,y) = x^2 + y^2$, perform two steps of gradient descent starting at $(1, 1)$ with a step size $\alpha = 0.1$.

E3.5.14 For a quadratic function $f(x) = ax^2 + bx + c$ with $a > 0$, derive the value of α under which gradient descent will converge to the minimum in one step.

Section 3.6

E3.6.1 Compute the log-odds of an event with probability $p = 0.25$.

E3.6.2 Given the features $\mathbf{x} = (2, -1)$ and the coefficients $\alpha = (0.5, -0.3)$, compute the linear combination $\alpha^T \mathbf{x}$.

E3.6.3 For the data point $\mathbf{x} = (1, 3)$ with the label $b = 1$ and the coefficients $\alpha = (-0.2, 0.4)$, calculate the probability $p(\mathbf{x}; \alpha)$ using the sigmoid function.

E3.6.4 Compute the cross-entropy loss for a single data point $\mathbf{x} = (1, 2)$ with label $b = 0$, given $\alpha = (0.3, -0.4)$.

E3.6.5 Prove that the logistic function $\sigma(z) = \frac{1}{1+e^{-z}}$ satisfies $\sigma'(z) = \sigma(z)(1 - \sigma(z))$.

E3.6.6 Given the feature vectors $\alpha_1 = (1, 2)$, $\alpha_2 = (-1, 1)$, $\alpha_3 = (0, -1)$, and the corresponding labels $b_1 = 1$, $b_2 = 0$, $b_3 = 1$, compute the logistic regression objective function $\ell(\mathbf{x}; A, \mathbf{b})$ for $\mathbf{x} = (1, 1)$.

E3.6.7 For the same data as in E3.6.6, compute the gradient of the logistic regression objective function $\nabla \ell(\mathbf{x}; A, \mathbf{b})$ at $\mathbf{x} = (1, 1)$.

E3.6.8 For the same data as in E3.6.6, compute the Hessian $\mathbf{H}_\ell(\mathbf{x}; A, \mathbf{b})$ of the logistic regression objective function at $\mathbf{x} = (1, 1)$.

E3.6.9 For the same data as in E3.6.6, perform one step of gradient descent with step size $\beta = 0.1$ starting from $\mathbf{x}^0 = (0, 0)$.

E3.6.10 For the same data as in E3.6.6, compute the smoothness parameter L of the logistic regression objective function.

3.7.2 Problems

3.1 Let $f: \mathbb{R} \to \mathbb{R}$ be twice continuously differentiable, let $\mathbf{a}_1, \mathbf{a}_2$ be vectors in $\mathbb{R}^d$, and let $b_1, b_2 \in \mathbb{R}$. Consider the following real-valued function of $\mathbf{x} \in \mathbb{R}^d$:

$$g(\mathbf{x}) = \frac{1}{2} f(\mathbf{a}_1^T \mathbf{x} + b_1) + \frac{1}{2} f(\mathbf{a}_2^T \mathbf{x} + b_2).$$

a) Compute the gradient of g **in vector form** in terms of the derivative f' of f. (By vector form, we mean that it is not enough to write down each element of $\nabla g(\mathbf{x})$ separately.)

b) Compute the Hessian of g **in matrix form** in terms of the first derivative f' and second derivative f'' of f. (By matrix form, we mean that it is not enough to write down each element of $\mathbf{H}_g(\mathbf{x})$ or each of its columns separately.)

3.2 Give an alternative proof of the *Descent Direction and Directional Derivative Lemma* using the definition of the directional derivative. [*Hint:* Mimic the proof of the single-variable case.]

3.3 (Adapted from [BV1]) Show that if S_1 and S_2 are convex sets in $\mathbb{R}^{m+n}$, then so is their partial sum
$$S = \{(\mathbf{x}, \mathbf{y}_1 + \mathbf{y}_2) : \mathbf{x} \in \mathbb{R}^m, \mathbf{y}_1, \mathbf{y}_2 \in \mathbb{R}^n, (\mathbf{x}, \mathbf{y}_1) \in S_1, (\mathbf{x}, \mathbf{y}_2) \in S_2\}.$$

3.4 A convex combination of $\mathbf{z}_1, \ldots, \mathbf{z}_m \in \mathbb{R}^d$ is a linear combination of the form
$$\mathbf{w} = \sum_{i=1}^{m} \alpha_i \mathbf{z}_i$$
where $\alpha_i \geq 0$ for all i and $\sum_{i=1}^{m} \alpha_i = 1$. Show that a set is convex if and only if it contains all convex combinations of its elements. [*Hint:* Use induction on m.]

3.5 A set $C \subseteq \mathbb{R}^d$ is a cone if, for all $\mathbf{x} \in C$ and all $\alpha \geq 0$, $\alpha \mathbf{x} \in C$. A conic combination of $\mathbf{z}_1, \ldots, \mathbf{z}_m \in \mathbb{R}^d$ is a linear combination of the form
$$\mathbf{w} = \sum_{i=1}^{m} \alpha_i \mathbf{z}_i$$
where $\alpha_i \geq 0$ for all i. Show that a set C is a convex cone if and only if it contains all conic combinations of its elements.

3.6 Show that any linear subspace of $\mathbb{R}^d$ is convex.

3.7 Show that the set
$$\mathbb{R}_+^d = \{\mathbf{x} \in \mathbb{R}^d : \mathbf{x} \geq \mathbf{0}\}$$
is convex.

3.8 Let $f : \mathbb{R}^d \to \mathbb{R}$ be a strictly convex function. Assume further that there is a global minimizer $\mathbf{x}^*$. Show that it is unique.

3.9 Show that $\mathbf{S}_+^n$ is a convex cone.

3.10 Prove (a)–(e) from the *Operations that Preserve Convexity Lemma*.

3.11 Let $f : \mathbb{R}^d \to \mathbb{R}$ be a function. The epigraph of f is the set
$$\mathbf{epi}\, f = \{(\mathbf{x}, y) : \mathbf{x} \in \mathbb{R}^d, y \geq f(\mathbf{x})\}.$$
Show that f is convex if and only if $\mathbf{epi}\, f$ is a convex set.

3.12 Let $f_1, \ldots, f_m : \mathbb{R}^d \to \mathbb{R}$ be convex functions and let $\beta_1, \ldots, \beta_m \geq 0$. Show that
$$f(\mathbf{x}) = \sum_{i=1}^{m} \beta_i f_i(\mathbf{x})$$
is convex.

3.13 Let $f_1, f_2 : \mathbb{R}^d \to \mathbb{R}$ be convex functions. Show that the pointwise maximum function
$$f(\mathbf{x}) = \max\{f_1(\mathbf{x}), f_2(\mathbf{x})\}$$
is convex. [*Hint:* First show that $\max\{\alpha + \beta, \eta + \phi\} \leq \max\{\alpha, \eta\} + \max\{\beta, \phi\}$.]

3.14 Prove the following composition theorem: If $f : \mathbb{R}^d \to \mathbb{R}$ is convex and $g : \mathbb{R} \to \mathbb{R}$ is convex and nondecreasing, then the composition $h = g \circ f$ is convex.

3.15 Show that $f(x) = e^{\beta x}$, where $x, \beta \in \mathbb{R}$, is convex.

3.16 Let $f : \mathbb{R} \to \mathbb{R}$ be twice continuously differentiable. Show that f is L-smooth if $|f''(x)| \leq L$ for all $x \in \mathbb{R}$.

3.17 For $a \in [-1, 1]$ and $b \in \{0, 1\}$, let $\hat{f}(x, a) = \sigma(xa)$ where
$$\sigma(t) = \frac{1}{1 + e^{-t}}$$

is a classifier parametrized by $x \in \mathbb{R}$. For a dataset $a_i \in [-1, 1]$ and $b_i \in \{0, 1\}$, $i = 1, \ldots, n$, let the cross-entropy loss be

$$\mathcal{L}(x, \{(a_i, b_i)\}_{i=1}^n) = \frac{1}{n} \sum_{i=1}^n \ell(x, a_i, b_i)$$

where

$$\ell(x, a, b) = -b \log(\hat{f}(x, a)) - (1 - b) \log(1 - \hat{f}(x, a)).$$

a) Show that $\sigma'(t) = \sigma(t)(1 - \sigma(t))$ for all $t \in \mathbb{R}$.

b) Use (a) to show that

$$\frac{\partial}{\partial x} \mathcal{L}(x, \{(a_i, b_i)\}_{i=1}^n) = -\frac{1}{n} \sum_{i=1}^n (b_i - \hat{f}(x, a_i)) a_i.$$

c) Use (b) to show that

$$\frac{\partial^2}{\partial x^2} \mathcal{L}(x, \{(a_i, b_i)\}_{i=1}^n) = \frac{1}{n} \sum_{i=1}^n \hat{f}(x, a_i)(1 - \hat{f}(x, a_i)) a_i^2.$$

d) Use (c) to show that, for any dataset $\{(a_i, b_i)\}_{i=1}^n$, $\mathcal{L}$ is convex and 1-smooth as a function of x.

3.18 Prove the *Quadratic Bound for Strongly Convex Functions Lemma*. [*Hint:* Adapt the proof of the *Quadratic Bound for Smooth Functions Lemma*.]

3.19 Show that $\log x \leq x - 1$ for all $x > 0$. [*Hint:* Compute the derivative of $s(x) = x - 1 - \log x$ and the value $s(1)$.]

3.20 Consider the affine function

$$f(\mathbf{x}) = \mathbf{q}^T \mathbf{x} + r$$

where $\mathbf{x} = (x_1, \ldots, x_d), \mathbf{q} = (q_1, \ldots, q_d) \in \mathbb{R}^d$, and $r \in \mathbb{R}$. Fix a value $c \in \mathbb{R}$. Assume that

$$f(\mathbf{x}_0) = f(\mathbf{x}_1) = c.$$

Show that

$$\nabla f(\mathbf{x}_0)^T (\mathbf{x}_1 - \mathbf{x}_0) = 0.$$

3.21 Let $f: D_1 \to \mathbb{R}$, where $D_1 \subseteq \mathbb{R}^d$, and let $\mathbf{g}: D_2 \to \mathbb{R}^d$, where $D_2 \subseteq \mathbb{R}$. Assume that f is continuously differentiable at $\mathbf{g}(t_0)$, an interior point of D_1, and that $\mathbf{g}$ is continuously differentiable at t_0, an interior point of D_2. Assume further that there is a value $c \in \mathbb{R}$ such that

$$f \circ \mathbf{g}(t) = c, \qquad \forall t \in D_2.$$

Show that $\mathbf{g}'(t_0)$ is orthogonal to $\nabla f(\mathbf{g}(t_0))$.

3.22 Fix a partition $C_1, \ldots, C_k$ of $[n]$. Under the k-means objective, its cost is

$$\mathcal{G}(C_1, \ldots, C_k) = \min_{\boldsymbol{\mu}_1, \ldots, \boldsymbol{\mu}_k \in \mathbb{R}^d} G(C_1, \ldots, C_k; \boldsymbol{\mu}_1, \ldots, \boldsymbol{\mu}_k)$$

where
$$G(C_1,\ldots,C_k;\mu_1,\ldots,\mu_k) = \sum_{i=1}^{k}\sum_{j\in C_i}\|\mathbf{x}_j-\mu_i\|^2 = \sum_{j=1}^{n}\|\mathbf{x}_j-\mu_{c(j)}\|^2,$$
with $\mu_i \in \mathbb{R}^d$, the center of cluster C_i.

a) Suppose μ_i^* is a global minimizer of
$$F_i(\mu_i) = \sum_{j\in C_i}\|\mathbf{x}_j-\mu_i\|^2$$
for each i. Show that $\mu_1^*,\ldots,\mu_k^*$ is a global minimizer of $G(C_1,\ldots,C_k;\mu_1,\ldots,\mu_k)$.

b) Compute the gradient of $F_i(\mu_i)$.

c) Find the stationary points of $F_i(\mu_i)$.

d) Compute the Hessian of $F_i(\mu_i)$.

e) Show that $F_i(\mu_i)$ is convex.

f) Compute the global minimizer of $G(C_1,\ldots,C_k;\mu_1,\ldots,\mu_k)$. Justify your answer.

3.23 Consider the quadratic function
$$f(\mathbf{x}) = \frac{1}{2}\mathbf{x}^T P\mathbf{x} + \mathbf{q}^T\mathbf{x} + r$$
where P is symmetric. Show that, if P is positive definite, then f is strongly convex.

3.24 A closed halfspace is a set of the form
$$K = \{\mathbf{x}\in\mathbb{R}^d : \mathbf{a}^T\mathbf{x} \le b\},$$
for some $\mathbf{a}\in\mathbb{R}^d$ and $b\in\mathbb{R}$.

a) Show that K is convex.

b) Show that there exists $\mathbf{x}_0 \in \mathbb{R}^d$ such that
$$K = \{\mathbf{x}\in\mathbb{R}^d : \mathbf{a}^T(\mathbf{x}-\mathbf{x}_0) \le 0\}.$$

3.25 A hyperplane is a set of the form
$$H = \{\mathbf{x}\in\mathbb{R}^d : \mathbf{a}^T\mathbf{x} = b\},$$
for some $\mathbf{a}\in\mathbb{R}^d$ and $b\in\mathbb{R}$.

a) Show that H is convex.

b) Assume $b = 0$. Compute $H^\perp$ and justify your answer.

3.26 Recall that the ℓ^1-norm is defined as
$$\|\mathbf{x}\|_1 = \sum_{i=1}^{d}|x_i|.$$

a) Show that the ℓ^1-norm satisfies the triangle inequality.

b) Show that the closed ℓ^1 ball
$$\{\mathbf{x}\in\mathbb{R}^d : \|\mathbf{x}\|_1 \le r\},$$
for some $r > 0$, is convex.

3.27 The Lorentz cone is the set
$$C = \{(\mathbf{x}, t) \in \mathbb{R}^d \times \mathbb{R}: \|\mathbf{x}\|_2 \leq t\}.$$
Show that C is convex.

3.28 A polyhedron is a set of the form
$$K = \{\mathbf{x} \in \mathbb{R}^d: \mathbf{a}_i^T \mathbf{x} \leq b_i, i = 1, \ldots, m, \text{ and } \mathbf{c}_j^T \mathbf{x} = d_j, j = 1, \ldots, n\},$$
for some $\mathbf{a}_i \in \mathbb{R}^d$, $b_i \in \mathbb{R}$, $i = 1, \ldots, m$, and $\mathbf{c}_j \in \mathbb{R}^d$, $d_j \in \mathbb{R}$, $j = 1, \ldots, n$. Show that K is convex.

3.29 The probability simplex in $\mathbb{R}^d$ is the set
$$\Delta = \{\mathbf{x} \in \mathbb{R}^d: \mathbf{x} \geq \mathbf{0} \text{ and } \mathbf{x}^T \mathbf{1} = 1\}.$$
Show that Δ is convex.

3.30 Consider the function
$$f^*(\mathbf{y}) = \sup_{\mathbf{x} \in \mathbb{R}^d} \{\mathbf{y}^T \mathbf{x} - \|\mathbf{x}\|_2\}.$$

a) Show that if $\|\mathbf{y}\|_2 \leq 1$ then $f^*(\mathbf{y}) = 0$.

b) Show that if $\|\mathbf{y}\|_2 > 1$ then $f^*(\mathbf{y}) = +\infty$.

3.31 Let $f, g: D \to \mathbb{R}$ for some $D \subseteq \mathbb{R}^d$ and let $\mathbf{x}_0$ be an interior point of D. Assume f and g are continuously differentiable at $\mathbf{x}_0$. Let $h(\mathbf{x}) = f(\mathbf{x})g(\mathbf{x})$ for all $\mathbf{x}$ in D. Compute $\nabla h(\mathbf{x}_0)$. [*Hint:* You can make use of the corresponding single-variable result.]

3.32 Let $f: D \to \mathbb{R}$ for some $D \subseteq \mathbb{R}^d$ and let $\mathbf{x}_0$ be an interior point of D where $f(\mathbf{x}_0) \neq 0$. Assume f is continuously differentiable at $\mathbf{x}_0$. Compute $\nabla(1/f)$. [*Hint:* You can make use of the corresponding single-variable result without proof.]

3.33 Let $f, g: D \to \mathbb{R}$ for some $D \subseteq \mathbb{R}^d$ and let $\mathbf{x}_0$ be an interior point of D. Assume f and g are twice continuously differentiable at $\mathbf{x}_0$. Let $h(\mathbf{x}) = f(\mathbf{x})g(\mathbf{x})$ for all $\mathbf{x}$ in D. Compute $\mathbf{H}_h(\mathbf{x}_0)$.

3.34 (Adapted from [Rud]) Let $f: D \to \mathbb{R}$ for some convex open set $D \subseteq \mathbb{R}^d$. Assume that f is continuously differentiable everywhere on D and that further $\frac{\partial f}{\partial x_1}(\mathbf{x}_0) = 0$ for all $\mathbf{x}_0 \in D$. Show that f depends only on $x_2, \ldots, x_d$.

3.35 (Adapted from [Rud]) Let $\mathbf{g}: D \to \mathbb{R}^d$ for some open set $D \subseteq \mathbb{R}$. Assume that $\mathbf{g}$ is continuously differentiable everywhere on D and that further
$$\|\mathbf{g}(t)\|^2 = 1, \qquad \forall t \in D.$$
Show that $\mathbf{g}'(t)^T \mathbf{g}(t) = 0$ for all $t \in D$. [*Hint:* Use composition.]

3.36 (Adapted from [Khu]) Let $f: D \to \mathbb{R}$ for some open set $D \subseteq \mathbb{R}^d$. Assume that f is continuously differentiable everywhere on D and that further
$$f(t\mathbf{x}) = t^n f(\mathbf{x}),$$
for any $\mathbf{x} \in D$ and any scalar t such that $t\mathbf{x} \in D$. In that case, f is said to be homogeneous of degree n. Prove that for all $\mathbf{x} \in D$ we have
$$\mathbf{x}^T \nabla f(\mathbf{x}) = n f(\mathbf{x}).$$

3.37 (Adapted from [Khu]) Apply *Taylor's Theorem* in the neighborhood of **0** to the function
$$f(x_1, x_2) = \exp(x_2 \sin x_1).$$
[*Hint:* You can use standard formulas for the derivatives of single-variable functions without proof.]

3.38 (Adapted from [Khu]) Apply *Taylor's Theorem* in the neighborhood of **0** to the function
$$f(x_1, x_2) = \cos(x_1 x_2).$$
[*Hint:* You can use standard formulas for the derivatives of single-variable functions without proof.]

3.39 (Adapted from [Khu]) Apply *Taylor's Theorem* in the neighborhood of **0** to the function
$$f(x_1, x_2, x_3) = \sin(e^{x_1} + x_2^2 + x_3^3).$$
[*Hint:* You can use standard formulas for the derivatives of single-variable functions without proof.]

3.40 (Adapted from [Khu]) Consider the function
$$f(x_1, x_2) = (x_2 - x_1^2)(x_2 - 2x_1^2).$$

a) Compute the gradient and Hessian of f at $(0,0)$.

b) Show that $(0,0)$ is not a strict local minimizer of f. [*Hint:* Consider a parametric curve of the form $x_1 = t^\alpha$ and $x_2 = t^\beta$.]

c) Let $\mathbf{g}(t) = \mathbf{a}t$ for some nonzero vector $\mathbf{a} = (a_1, a_2) \in \mathbb{R}^2$. Show that $t = 0$ is a strict local minimizer of $h(t) = f(\mathbf{g}(t))$.

3.41 Suppose $f: \mathbb{R}^d \to \mathbb{R}$ is convex. Let $A \in \mathbb{R}^{d \times m}$ and $\mathbf{b} \in \mathbb{R}^d$. Show that
$$g(\mathbf{x}) = f(A\mathbf{x} + \mathbf{b})$$
is convex over $\mathbb{R}^m$.

3.42 (Adapted from [BV1]) For $\mathbf{x} = (x_1, \ldots, x_n) \in \mathbb{R}^n$, let
$$x_{[1]} \geq x_{[2]} \geq \cdots \geq x_{[n]},$$
be the coordinates of $\mathbf{x}$ in nonincreasing order. Let $1 \leq r \leq n$ be an integer and $w_1 \geq w_2 \geq \cdots \geq w_r \geq 0$. Show that
$$f(\mathbf{x}) = \sum_{i=1}^{r} w_i x_{[i]},$$
is convex.

3.43 For a fixed $\mathbf{z} \in \mathbb{R}^d$, let
$$f(\mathbf{x}) = \|\mathbf{x} - \mathbf{z}\|_2^2.$$

a) Compute the gradient and Hessian of f.

b) Show that f is strongly convex.

c) For a finite set $Z \subseteq \mathbb{R}^d$, let

$$g(\mathbf{x}) = \max_{\mathbf{z} \in Z} \|\mathbf{x} - \mathbf{z}\|_2^2.$$

Use *Problem 3.13* to show that g is convex.

3.44 Let $S_i, i \in I$, be a collection of convex subsets of $\mathbb{R}^d$. Here I can be infinite. Show that

$$\bigcap_{i \in I} S_i,$$

is convex.

3.45 a) Let $f_i, i \in I$, be a collection of convex real-valued functions over $\mathbb{R}^d$. Use *Problems 3.11, 3.44* to show that

$$g(\mathbf{x}) = \sup_{i \in I} f_i(\mathbf{x})$$

is convex.

b) Let $f: \mathbb{R}^{d+f} \to \mathbb{R}$ be a convex function and let $S \subseteq \mathbb{R}^f$ be a (not necessarily convex) set. Use (a) to show that the function

$$g(\mathbf{x}) = \sup_{\mathbf{y} \in S} f(\mathbf{x}, \mathbf{y}),$$

is convex. You can assume that $g(\mathbf{x}) < +\infty$ for all $\mathbf{x} \in \mathbb{R}^d$.

3.46 Use *Problem 3.45* to show that the largest eigenvalue of a matrix is a convex function over the set of all symmetric matrices. [*Hint:* See Example 3.3.7. First show that $\langle \mathbf{x}, A\mathbf{x} \rangle$ is a linear function of A.]

3.47 Let $f: \mathbb{R}^d \to \mathbb{R}$ be a convex function. Show that the set of global minimizers is convex.

3.48 Consider the set of symmetric $n \times n$ matrices

$$\mathbf{S}^n = \left\{ X \in \mathbb{R}^{n \times n} : X = X^T \right\}.$$

a) Show that $\mathbf{S}^n$ is a linear subspace of the vector space of $n \times n$ matrices in the sense that for all $X_1, X_2 \in \mathbf{S}^n$ and $\alpha \in \mathbb{R}$,

$$X_1 + X_2 \in \mathbf{S}^n$$

and

$$\alpha X_1 \in \mathbf{S}^n.$$

b) Show that there exists a collection of symmetric matrices $X_1, \ldots, X_d \in \mathbf{S}^n$, where $d = \binom{n}{2} + n$, such that any matrix $Y \in \mathbf{S}^n$ can be written as a linear combination

$$Y = \sum_{i=1}^{d} \alpha_i X_i,$$

for some $\alpha_1, \ldots, \alpha_d \in \mathbb{R}$.

c) Check that the matrices $X_1, \ldots, X_d \in \mathbf{S}^n$ you constructed in b) are linearly independent in the sense that

$$\sum_{i=1}^{d} \alpha_i X_i = \mathbf{0}_{n \times n} \quad \Longrightarrow \quad \alpha_1 = \cdots = \alpha_d = 0.$$

3.49 Let $f: D \to \mathbb{R}$ be a convex function over the set

$$D = \{\mathbf{x} = (x_1, \ldots, x_d) \in \mathbb{R}^d : x_i \geq 0, \forall i\}.$$

a) Show that D is convex.

b) Show that the *First-Order Optimality Conditions for a Convex Functions on Convex Sets Theorem* reduces to

$$\frac{\partial f(\mathbf{x}^0)}{\partial x_i} \geq 0, \quad \forall i \in [d]$$

and

$$\frac{\partial f(\mathbf{x}^0)}{\partial x_i} = 0, \quad \text{if } x_i^0 > 0.$$

[*Hint:* Choose the right $\mathbf{y}$ in the condition of the theorem.]

3.50 Let $f: \mathbb{R}^d \to \mathbb{R}$ be twice continuously differentiable and m-strongly convex with $m > 0$.

a) Show that

$$f(\mathbf{y}_n) \to +\infty$$

along any sequence $(\mathbf{y}_n)$ such that $\|\mathbf{y}_n\| \to +\infty$ as $n \to +\infty$.

b) Show that, for any $\mathbf{x}^0$, the set

$$C = \{\mathbf{x} \in \mathbb{R}^d : f(\mathbf{x}) \leq f(\mathbf{x}^0)\},$$

is closed and bounded.

c) Show that there exists a unique global minimizer $\mathbf{x}^*$ of f.

3.51 Suppose that $f: \mathbb{R}^d \to \mathbb{R}$ is L-smooth and m-strongly convex with a global minimizer at $\mathbf{x}^*$. Apply gradient descent with step size $\alpha = 1/L$ started from an arbitrary point $\mathbf{x}^0$.

a) Show that $\mathbf{x}^t \to \mathbf{x}^*$ as $t \to +\infty$. [*Hint:* Use the *Quadratic Bound for Strongly Convex Functions Lemma* at $\mathbf{x}^*$.]

b) Give a bound on $\|\mathbf{x}^t - \mathbf{x}^*\|$ depending on $t, m, L, f(\mathbf{x}^0)$, and $f(\mathbf{x}^*)$.

3.52 Let $f: \mathbb{R}^d \to \mathbb{R}$ be twice continuously differentiable.

a) Show that

$$\nabla f(\mathbf{y}) = \nabla f(\mathbf{x}) + \int_0^1 \mathbf{H}_f(\mathbf{x} + \xi \mathbf{p}) \, \mathbf{p} \, d\xi,$$

where $\mathbf{p} = \mathbf{y} - \mathbf{x}$. Here the integral of a vector-valued function is performed entry-wise. [*Hint:* Let $g_i(\xi) = \frac{\partial}{\partial x_i} f(\mathbf{x} + \xi \mathbf{p})$. The fundamental theorem of calculus implies that $g_i(1) - g_i(0) = \int_0^1 g_i'(\xi) \, d\xi$.]

b) Assume f is L-smooth. Use (a) to show that the gradient of f is L-Lipschitz in the sense that
$$\|\nabla f(\mathbf{y}) - \nabla f(\mathbf{x})\|_2 \leq L \|\mathbf{y} - \mathbf{x}\|_2, \qquad \forall \mathbf{x}, \mathbf{y} \in \mathbb{R}^d.$$

3.53 Consider the quadratic function
$$f(\mathbf{x}) = \frac{1}{2} \mathbf{x}^T P \mathbf{x} + \mathbf{q}^T \mathbf{x} + r,$$
where P is a symmetric matrix. Use the *First-Order Convexity Condition Lemma* to show that f is convex if and only P is positive semidefinite.

3.54 Let
$$\ell(\mathbf{x}; A, \mathbf{b}) = \frac{1}{n} \sum_{i=1}^n \left\{ -b_i \log(\sigma(\boldsymbol{\alpha}_i^T \mathbf{x})) - (1 - b_i) \log(1 - \sigma(\boldsymbol{\alpha}_i^T \mathbf{x})) \right\}.$$
be the loss function in logistic regression, where $A \in \mathbb{R}^{n \times d}$ has rows $\boldsymbol{\alpha}_i^T$. Show that
$$H_\ell(\mathbf{x}; A, \mathbf{b}) \preceq \frac{1}{4n} A^T A.$$

[*Hint:* Read the proof of the *Smoothness of Logistic Regression Lemma*.]

4 Singular Value Decomposition

In this chapter, we introduce the singular value decomposition (SVD), a fundamental concept in linear algebra. It is related to the spectral decomposition, but exists for any matrix including rectangular ones. The SVD has many applications in data science, including principle components analysis, low-rank approximation, pseudoinverses, and more. Here is a more detailed overview of the main sections of the chapter.

Background: Review of matrix rank and spectral decomposition: Section 4.2 covers two key linear algebra concepts: matrix rank and the spectral theorem. The rank of a matrix is defined as the dimension of its column or row space. Properties of the rank are discussed, including the *Rank-Nullity Theorem* relating the rank and the dimension of the null space. The spectral theorem states that a real symmetric matrix has an orthonormal basis of eigenvectors with real eigenvalues, allowing for a spectral decomposition of the matrix. The section also characterizes positive semidefinite and positive definite matrices in terms of their eigenvalues.

Approximating subspaces and the SVD: Section 4.3 introduces the SVD as a matrix factorization that can be used to find the best low-dimensional approximating subspace to a set of data points. The section shows that this problem can be solved greedily by finding the best one-dimensional subspace, then the best one-dimensional subspace orthogonal to the first, and so on. It then formally defines the SVD and proves its existence for any matrix. It also discusses the relationship between the SVD and the spectral decomposition of a matrix. The section also discusses some important properties and relations satisfied by the SVD.

Power iteration: Section 4.4 discusses the power iteration method for computing the (truncated) SVD of a matrix. The key lemma for power iteration states in essence that repeated multiplication of $A^T A$ with a random vector will converge to the top right singular vector $\mathbf{v}_1$ of A. The section also covers how to compute the corresponding singular value and left singular vector using the converged $\mathbf{v}_1$.

Application: Principal components analysis: Section 4.5 discusses principal components analysis (PCA) as a dimensionality reduction technique. It explains that PCA finds linear combinations of features, called principal components, that capture the maximum variance in the data. The first principal component $t_{i1} = \sum_{j=1}^{p} \phi_{j1} x_{ij}$ is obtained by solving $\max \{\frac{1}{n-1} \|X\boldsymbol{\phi}_1\|^2 : \|\boldsymbol{\phi}_1\|^2 = 1\}$, where X is the centered data matrix. Subsequent principal components are obtained by imposing additional constraints, in particular uncorrelatedness with previous components. The section establishes a connection between PCA and the SVD.

Further applications of the SVD: Low-rank approximations and ridge regression: Section 4.6 first defines matrix norms, in particular the induced 2-norm, and relates them to the singular values. The section then considers low-rank matrix approximations, highlighting the Eckart–Young theorem, which states that the best low-rank approximation of a matrix in both Frobenius and induced 2-norms is achieved by truncating the SVD. Finally, the section discusses ridge regression, a regularization technique that addresses multicollinearity in overdetermined systems by balancing data fitting with minimizing the solution's norm.

4.1 Motivating Example: Visualizing Viral Evolution

We consider an application of dimensionality reduction in biology. We will look at *single-nucleotide polymorphism (SNP) data*[1] from viruses. A little background first. From Wikipedia[2]:

> A single-nucleotide polymorphism (SNP) is a substitution of a single nucleotide that occurs at a specific position in the genome, where each variation is present at a level of more than 1% in the population. For example, at a specific base position in the human genome, the C nucleotide may appear in most individuals, but in a minority of individuals, the position is occupied by an A. This means that there is a SNP at this specific position, and the two possible nucleotide variations – C or A – are said to be the alleles for this specific position.

Quoting Jombart et al., BMC Genetics (2010),[3] we analyze:

> [...] the population structure of seasonal influenza A/H3N2 viruses using hemagglutinin (HA) sequences. Changes in the HA gene are largely responsible for immune escape of the virus (antigenic shift), and allow seasonal influenza to persist by mounting yearly epidemics peaking in winter. These genetic changes also force influenza vaccines to be updated on a yearly basis. [...] Assessing the genetic evolution of a pathogen through successive epidemics is of considerable epidemiological interest. In the case of seasonal influenza, we would like to ascertain how genetic changes accumulate among strains from one winter epidemic to the next. [...] For this purpose, we retrieved all sequences of H3N2 hemagglutinin (HA) collected between 2001 and 2007 available from Genbank. Only sequences for which a location (country) and a date (year and month) were available were retained, which allowed us to classify strains into yearly winter epidemics.

We load a subset of the strains from the dataset mentioned above.

```
data = pd.read_csv('h3n2-snp.csv')
```

This is a large dataset. Here are the first five rows and first 10 columns.

```
print(data.iloc[:5, :10])
```

	strain	s6a	s6c	s6g	s17a	s17g	s17t	s39a	s39c	s39g
0	AB434107	1.0	0.0	0.0	1.0	0.0	0.0	0.0	0.0	1.0
1	AB434108	1.0	0.0	0.0	1.0	0.0	0.0	0.0	0.0	1.0
2	CY000113	1.0	0.0	0.0	1.0	0.0	0.0	0.0	0.0	1.0
3	CY000209	1.0	0.0	0.0	1.0	0.0	0.0	0.0	0.0	1.0
4	CY000217	1.0	0.0	0.0	1.0	0.0	0.0	0.0	0.0	1.0

---

[1] You can access datasets and code that you want to *work with yourself* via the GitHub page for this book: https://github.com/MMiDS-textbook
[2] https://en.wikipedia.org/wiki/Single-nucleotide_polymorphism
[3] https://bmcgenet.biomedcentral.com/articles/10.1186/1471-2156-11-94

For positions 6, 17, 39, and so on, the corresponding columns indicate which nucleotide (a, c, g, t) is present in the strain with a 1.0. For example, strain AB434107 has an a at position 6 and 17, and a g at position 39.

Overall it contains 1642 strains (whose names are listed in the first colum). The data lives in a 317-dimensional space (not counting the name of strain, i.e., the first column).

```
data.shape
```

(1642, 318)

Obviously, vizualizing this data is not straightforward. How can we make sense of it? More specifically, how can we explore any underlying structure it might have? Quoting Wikipedia[4]:

> In statistics, exploratory data analysis (EDA) is an approach of analyzing data sets to summarize their main characteristics, often using statistical graphics and other data visualization methods. [...] Exploratory data analysis has been promoted by John Tukey since 1970 to encourage statisticians to explore the data, and possibly formulate hypotheses that could lead to new data collection and experiments.

In this chapter we will encounter an important mathematical technique for dimension reduction, which allow us to explore this data – and find interesting structure – in *two* (rather than 317!) dimensions.

4.2 Background: Review of Matrix Rank and Spectral Decomposition

We will need two additional concepts from linear algebra, the rank of a matrix and the spectral theorem.

4.2.1 Rank of a Matrix

Recall that the dimension of the column space of A is called the column rank of A. Similarly the row rank of A is the dimension of its row space. As it turns out, these two notions of rank are the same by the *Row Rank Equals Column Rank Theorem*. We give a proof of that theorem next. We refer to the row rank and column rank of A simply as the rank, which we denote by $\text{rk}(A)$.

Proof idea: (Row Rank Equals Column Rank) Write A as a matrix factorization BC where the columns of B form a basis of $\text{col}(A)$. Then the rows of C necessarily form a spanning set of $\text{row}(A)$. So, because the number of columns of B and the number of rows of C match, we conclude that the row rank is less than or equal to the column rank. Applying the same argument to the transpose gives the claim.

---

[4] https://en.wikipedia.org/wiki/Exploratory_data_analysis

4.2 Review of Matrix Rank and Spectral Decomposition

Recall the following observation from Section 2.2.2.

Observation D1: Any linear subspace U of $\mathbb{R}^n$ has a basis.

Observation D2: If U and V are linear subspaces such that $U \subseteq V$, then $\dim(U) \leq \dim(V)$.

Observation D3: The dimension of $\text{span}(\mathbf{u}_1, \ldots, \mathbf{u}_m)$ is at most m.

Proof *(Row Rank Equals Column Rank)* Assume that A has column rank r. Then there exists a basis $\mathbf{b}_1, \ldots, \mathbf{b}_r \in \mathbb{R}^n$ of $\text{col}(A)$ by *Observation D1* above, and we know that $r \leq n$ by *Observation D2*. That is, for each j, letting $\mathbf{a}_j = A_{\cdot, j}$ be the j-th column of A we can write

$$\mathbf{a}_j = \sum_{\ell=1}^{r} \mathbf{b}_\ell c_{\ell j}$$

for some $c_{\ell j}$'s. Let B be the matrix whose columns are $\mathbf{b}_1, \ldots, \mathbf{b}_r$ and let C be the matrix with entries $(C)_{\ell j} = c_{\ell j}$, $\ell = 1, \ldots, r$, $j = 1, \ldots, m$. Then the equation above can be rewritten as the matrix factorization $A = BC$. Indeed, by our previous observations about matrix–matrix products, the columns of A are linear combinations of the columns of B with coefficients taken from the corresponding column of C.

The key point is the following: C necessarily has r rows. Let $\boldsymbol{\alpha}_i^T = A_{i, \cdot}$ be the i-th row of A and $\mathbf{c}_\ell^T = C_{\ell, \cdot}$ be the ℓ-th row of C. Using our alternative representation of matrix–matrix product in terms of rows (see Section 1.2.1), the decomposition is equivalent to

$$\boldsymbol{\alpha}_i^T = \sum_{\ell=1}^{r} b_{i\ell} \mathbf{c}_\ell^T, \quad i = 1, \ldots, n,$$

where $b_{i\ell} = (\mathbf{b}_i)_\ell = (B)_{i\ell}$ is the i-th entry of the ℓ-th column of B. In words, the rows of A are linear combinations of the rows of C with coefficients taken from the corresponding row of B. In particular, $\mathcal{C} = \{\mathbf{c}_j : j = 1, \ldots, r\}$ is a spanning list of the row space of A; that is, each row of A can be written as a linear combination of $\mathcal{C}$. Put differently, $\text{row}(A) \subseteq \text{span}(\mathcal{C})$.

So the row rank of A is at most r, the column rank of A, by *Observation D2*.

Applying the same argument to A^T, which switches the role of the columns and the rows, gives that the column rank of A (i.e., the row rank of A^T) is at most the row rank of A (i.e., the column rank of A^T). Hence the two notions of rank must be equal. (We also deduce $r \leq m$ by *Observation D2* again.) $\square$

Example 4.2.1 *(continued from Example 2.2.15) We illustrate the proof of the theorem. Continuing a previous example, let A be the matrix with columns $\mathbf{w}_1 = (1, 0, 1)$, $\mathbf{w}_2 = (0, 1, 1)$, and $\mathbf{w}_3 = (1, -1, 0)$*

$$A = \begin{pmatrix} 1 & 0 & 1 \\ 0 & 1 & -1 \\ 1 & 1 & 0 \end{pmatrix}.$$

We know that $\mathbf{w}_1$ and $\mathbf{w}_2$ form a basis of $\text{col}(A)$. We use them to construct our matrix B

$$B = \begin{pmatrix} 1 & 0 \\ 0 & 1 \\ 1 & 1 \end{pmatrix}.$$

Recall that $\mathbf{w}_3 = \mathbf{w}_1 - \mathbf{w}_2$. Hence the matrix C is

$$C = \begin{pmatrix} 1 & 0 & 1 \\ 0 & 1 & -1 \end{pmatrix}.$$

Indeed, column j of C gives the coefficients in the linear combination of the columns of B that produces column j of A. Check that A = BC.

NUMERICAL CORNER In NumPy, one can compute the rank of a matrix using the function `numpy.linalg.matrix_rank`. We will see later in the chapter how to compute it using the singular value decomposition (which is how `LA.matrix_rank` does it). Let's try the example above.

```
w1 = np.array([1., 0., 1.])
w2 = np.array([0., 1., 1.])
w3 = np.array([1., -1., 0.])
A = np.stack((w1, w2, w3), axis=-1)
print(A)
```

```
[[ 1.  0.  1.]
 [ 0.  1. -1.]
 [ 1.  1.  0.]]
```

We compute the rank of A.

```
LA.matrix_rank(A)
```

2

We take only the first two columns of A this time to form B.

```
B = np.stack((w1, w2),axis=-1)
print(B)
```

```
[[1. 0.]
 [0. 1.]
 [1. 1.]]
```

```
LA.matrix_rank(B)
```

2

Recall that, in NumPy, @ is used for matrix product.

```
C = np.array([[1., 0., 1.],[0., 1., -1.]])
print(C)
```

```
[[ 1.  0.  1.]
 [ 0.  1. -1.]]
```

```
LA.matrix_rank(C)
```

2

```
print(B @ C)
```
```
[[ 1.  0.  1.]
 [ 0.  1. -1.]
 [ 1.  1.  0.]]
```

◁ **NC**

Example 4.2.2 *Let $A \in \mathbb{R}^{n \times k}$ and $B \in \mathbb{R}^{k \times m}$. Then we claim that*

$$\mathrm{rk}(AB) \leq \mathrm{rk}(A).$$

Indeed, the columns of AB are linear combinations of the columns of A. Hence $\mathrm{col}(AB) \subseteq \mathrm{col}(A)$. *The claim follows by* Observation D2.

Example 4.2.3 *Let $A \in \mathbb{R}^{n \times k}$ and $B \in \mathbb{R}^{n \times m}$. Then we claim that*

$$\mathrm{rk}(A + B) \leq \mathrm{rk}(A) + \mathrm{rk}(B).$$

Indeed, the columns of $A + B$ are linear combinations of the columns of A and of B. Let $\mathbf{u}_1, \ldots, \mathbf{u}_h$ be a basis of $\mathrm{col}(A)$ and let $\mathbf{v}_1, \ldots, \mathbf{v}_\ell$ be a basis of $\mathrm{col}(B)$ by Observation D1. Then, we deduce

$$\mathrm{col}(A + B) \subseteq \mathrm{span}(\mathbf{u}_1, \ldots, \mathbf{u}_h, \mathbf{v}_1, \ldots, \mathbf{v}_\ell).$$

By Observation D2, it follows that

$$\mathrm{rk}(A + B) \leq \dim(\mathrm{span}(\mathbf{u}_1, \ldots, \mathbf{u}_h, \mathbf{v}_1, \ldots, \mathbf{v}_\ell)).$$

By Observation D3, the right-hand side is at most the length of the spanning list, $h + \ell$. But by construction $\mathrm{rk}(A) = h$ and $\mathrm{rk}(B) = \ell$, so we are done.

Example 4.2.4 *(A Proof of the Rank-Nullity Theorem) Let $A \in \mathbb{R}^{n \times m}$. Recall that the column space of A, $\mathrm{col}(A) \subseteq \mathbb{R}^n$, is the span of its columns. We compute its othogonal complement. By definition, the columns of A, which we denote by $\mathbf{a}_1, \ldots, \mathbf{a}_m$, form a spanning list of $\mathrm{col}(A)$. So $\mathbf{u} \in \mathrm{col}(A)^\perp \subseteq \mathbb{R}^n$ if and only if*

$$\mathbf{a}_i^T \mathbf{u} = \langle \mathbf{u}, \mathbf{a}_i \rangle = 0, i = 1, \ldots, m.$$

Indeed that then implies that for any $\mathbf{v} \in \mathrm{col}(A)$, say $\mathbf{v} = \beta_1 \mathbf{a}_1 + \cdots + \beta_m \mathbf{a}_m$, we have

$$\left\langle \mathbf{u}, \sum_{i=1}^{m} \beta_i \mathbf{a}_i \right\rangle = \sum_{i=1}^{m} \beta_i \langle \mathbf{u}, \mathbf{a}_i \rangle = 0.$$

The m conditions above can be written in matrix form as

$$A^T \mathbf{u} = \mathbf{0}.$$

That is, the orthogonal complement of the column space of A is the null space of A^T,

$$\mathrm{col}(A)^\perp = \mathrm{null}(A^T).$$

Applying the same argument to the column space of A^T, it follows that

$$\mathrm{col}(A^T)^\perp = \mathrm{null}(A),$$

where note that $\text{null}(A) \subseteq \mathbb{R}^m$. *The four linear subspaces* $\text{col}(A)$, $\text{col}(A^T)$, $\text{null}(A)$, *and* $\text{null}(A^T)$ *are referred to as the fundamental subspaces of A.* We have shown

$$\text{col}(A) \oplus \text{null}(A^T) = \mathbb{R}^n \quad \text{and} \quad \text{col}(A^T) \oplus \text{null}(A) = \mathbb{R}^m.$$

By the Row Rank Equals Column Rank Theorem, $\dim(\text{col}(A)) = \dim(\text{col}(A^T))$. *Moreover, by our previous observation about the dimensions of direct sums (see Section 2.3.3), we have*

$$n = \dim(\text{col}(A)) + \dim(\text{null}(A^T)) = \dim(\text{col}(A^T)) + \dim(\text{null}(A^T))$$

and

$$m = \dim(\text{col}(A^T)) + \dim(\text{null}(A)) = \dim(\text{col}(A)) + \dim(\text{null}(A)).$$

So we deduce that

$$\dim(\text{null}(A)) = m - \text{rk}(A)$$

and

$$\dim(\text{null}(A^T)) = n - \text{rk}(A).$$

These formulas are referred to the Rank-Nullity Theorem. *The dimension of the null space is called the nullity.*

4.2.1.1 Outer Products and Rank-One Matrices

Let $\mathbf{u} = (u_1, \ldots, u_n) \in \mathbb{R}^n$ and $\mathbf{v} = (v_1, \ldots, v_m) \in \mathbb{R}^m$ be two column vectors. Their outer product is defined as the matrix

$$\mathbf{u}\mathbf{v}^T = \begin{pmatrix} u_1 v_1 & u_1 v_2 & \cdots & u_1 v_m \\ u_2 v_1 & u_2 v_2 & \cdots & u_2 v_m \\ \vdots & \vdots & \ddots & \vdots \\ u_n v_1 & u_n v_2 & \cdots & u_n v_m \end{pmatrix} = \begin{pmatrix} | & & | \\ v_1 \mathbf{u} & \cdots & v_m \mathbf{u} \\ | & & | \end{pmatrix}.$$

This is not to be confused with the inner product $\mathbf{u}^T \mathbf{v}$, which requires $n = m$ and produces a scalar.

If $\mathbf{u}$ and $\mathbf{v}$ are nonzero, the matrix $\mathbf{u}\mathbf{v}^T$ has rank one. Indeed, its columns are all a multiple of the same vector $\mathbf{u}$. So the column space spanned by the columns of $\mathbf{u}\mathbf{v}^T$ is one-dimensional. Vice versa, any rank-one matrix can be written in this form by definition of the rank.

We have seen many different interpretations of matrix–matrix products. Here is yet another one. Let $A = (a_{ij})_{i,j} \in \mathbb{R}^{n \times k}$ and $B = (b_{ij})_{i,j} \in \mathbb{R}^{k \times m}$. Denote by $\mathbf{a}_1, \ldots, \mathbf{a}_k$ the columns of A and denote by $\mathbf{b}_1^T, \ldots, \mathbf{b}_k^T$ the rows of B.
Then

$$AB = \begin{pmatrix} \sum_{j=1}^k a_{1j} b_{j1} & \sum_{j=1}^k a_{1j} b_{j2} & \cdots & \sum_{j=1}^k a_{1j} b_{jm} \\ \sum_{j=1}^k a_{2j} b_{j1} & \sum_{j=1}^k a_{2j} b_{j2} & \cdots & \sum_{j=1}^k a_{2j} b_{jm} \\ \vdots & \vdots & \ddots & \vdots \\ \sum_{j=1}^k a_{nj} b_{j1} & \sum_{j=1}^k a_{nj} b_{j2} & \cdots & \sum_{j=1}^k a_{nj} b_{jm} \end{pmatrix}$$

$$= \sum_{j=1}^{k} \begin{pmatrix} a_{1j}b_{j1} & a_{1j}b_{j2} & \cdots & a_{1j}b_{jm} \\ a_{2j}b_{j1} & a_{2j}b_{j2} & \cdots & a_{2j}b_{jm} \\ \vdots & \vdots & \ddots & \vdots \\ a_{nj}b_{j1} & a_{nj}b_{j2} & \cdots & a_{nj}b_{jm} \end{pmatrix}$$

$$= \sum_{j=1}^{k} \mathbf{a}_j \mathbf{b}_j^T.$$

In words, the matrix product AB can be interpreted as a sum of k rank-one matrices, each of which is the outer product of a column of A with the corresponding row of B.

Because the rank of a sum is at most the sum of the ranks (as shown in Example 4.2.3), it follows that the rank of AB is at most k. This is consistent with the fact that the rank of a product is at most the minimum of the ranks (shown in Example 4.2.2).

4.2.2 Eigenvalues and Eigenvectors

Recall the concepts of eigenvalues and eigenvectors. We work on $\mathbb{R}^d$.

Definition 4.2.5 (*Eigenvalues and Eigenvectors*) Let $A \in \mathbb{R}^{d \times d}$ be a square matrix. Then $\lambda \in \mathbb{R}$ is an eigenvalue of A if there exists a nonzero vector $\mathbf{x} \neq \mathbf{0}$ such that

$$A\mathbf{x} = \lambda \mathbf{x}.$$

The vector $\mathbf{x}$ is referred to as an eigenvector.

As the next example shows, not every matrix has a (real) eigenvalue.

Example 4.2.6 (*No Real Eigenvalues*) Set $d = 2$ and let

$$A = \begin{pmatrix} 0 & -1 \\ 1 & 0 \end{pmatrix}.$$

For λ to be an eigenvalue, there must be a nonzero eigenvector $\mathbf{x} = (x_1, x_2)$ such that

$$A\mathbf{x} = \lambda \mathbf{x}$$

or put differently $-x_2 = \lambda x_1$ and $x_1 = \lambda x_2$. Substituting these equations into each other, it must be that $-x_2 = \lambda^2 x_2$ and $x_1 = -\lambda^2 x_1$. Because x_1, x_2 cannot both be 0, λ must satisfy the equation $\lambda^2 = -1$ for which there is no real solution.

In general, $A \in \mathbb{R}^{d \times d}$ has at most d distinct eigenvalues.

Lemma 4.2.7 (*Number of Eigenvalues*) Let $A \in \mathbb{R}^{d \times d}$ and let $\lambda_1, \ldots, \lambda_m$ be distinct eigenvalues of A with corresponding eigenvectors $\mathbf{x}_1, \ldots, \mathbf{x}_m$. Then $\mathbf{x}_1, \ldots, \mathbf{x}_m$ are linearly independent. In particular, $m \leq d$.

Proof Assume by contradiction that $\mathbf{x}_1, \ldots, \mathbf{x}_m$ are linearly dependent. By the *Linear Dependence Lemma*, there is $k \leq m$ such that

$$\mathbf{x}_k \in \text{span}(\mathbf{x}_1, \ldots, \mathbf{x}_{k-1})$$

where $\mathbf{x}_1, \ldots, \mathbf{x}_{k-1}$ are linearly independent. In particular, there are $a_1, \ldots, a_{k-1}$ such that

$$\mathbf{x}_k = a_1 \mathbf{x}_1 + \cdots + a_{k-1} \mathbf{x}_{k-1}.$$

Transform the equation above in two ways: (1) multiply both sides by λ_k and (2) apply A. Then subtract the resulting equations. That leads to

$$\mathbf{0} = a_1(\lambda_k - \lambda_1)\mathbf{x}_1 + \cdots + a_{k-1}(\lambda_k - \lambda_{k-1})\mathbf{x}_{k-1}.$$

Because the λ_i's are distinct and $\mathbf{x}_1, \ldots, \mathbf{x}_{k-1}$ are linearly independent, we must have $a_1 = \cdots = a_{k-1} = 0$. But that implies that $\mathbf{x}_k = \mathbf{0}$, a contradiction.

For the second claim, if there were more than d distinct eigenvalues, then there would be more than d corresponding linearly independent eigenvectors by the first claim, a contradiction. □

Example 4.2.8 *(Diagonal (and Similar) Matrices)* *Recall that we use the notation* $\text{diag}(\lambda_1, \ldots, \lambda_d)$ *for the diagonal matrix with diagonal entries* $\lambda_1, \ldots, \lambda_d$. *The upper bound in the* Number of Eigenvalues Lemma *can be achieved, for instance, by diagonal matrices with distinct diagonal entries* $A = \text{diag}(\lambda_1, \ldots, \lambda_d)$. *Each standard basis vector* $\mathbf{e}_i$ *is then an eigenvector:*

$$A\mathbf{e}_i = \lambda_i \mathbf{e}_i.$$

More generally, let A be similar to a matrix $D = \text{diag}(\lambda_1, \ldots, \lambda_d)$ with distinct diagonal entries; that is, there exists a nonsingular matrix P such that

$$A = PDP^{-1}.$$

Let $\mathbf{p}_1, \ldots, \mathbf{p}_d$ be the columns of P. Note that, because the columns of P form a basis of $\mathbb{R}^d$, the entries of the vector $\mathbf{c} = P^{-1}\mathbf{x}$ are the coefficients of the unique linear combination of the $\mathbf{p}_i$'s equal to $\mathbf{x}$. Indeed, $P\mathbf{c} = \mathbf{x}$. Hence, $A\mathbf{x}$ is can be thought of as: (1) expressing $\mathbf{x}$ in the basis $\mathbf{p}_1, \ldots, \mathbf{p}_d$ and (2) scaling the $\mathbf{p}_i$'s by the corresponding λ_i's. In particular, the $\mathbf{p}_i$'s are eigenvectors of A since, by the above, $P^{-1}\mathbf{p}_i = \mathbf{e}_i$ and so

$$A\mathbf{p}_i = PDP^{-1}\mathbf{p}_i = PD\mathbf{e}_i = P(\lambda_i \mathbf{e}_i) = \lambda_i \mathbf{p}_i.$$

NUMERICAL CORNER In NumPy, the eigenvalues and eigenvectors of a matrix can be computed using `numpy.linalg.eig`.

```
A = np.array([[2.5, -0.5], [-0.5, 2.5]])
```

```
w, v = LA.eig(A)
print(w)
print(v)
```

```
[3. 2.]
[[ 0.70710678  0.70710678]
 [-0.70710678  0.70710678]]
```

Above, `w` are the eigenvalues in an array, whereas the columns of `v` are the corresponding eigenvectors.

◁ **NC**

4.2.2.1 Some Matrix Algebra

We will need a few useful observations about matrices.

A (not necessarily square) matrix $D \in \mathbb{R}^{k \times r}$ is diagonal if its nondiagonal entries are zero. That is, $i \neq j$ implies that $D_{ij} = 0$. Note that a diagonal matrix is not necessarily square and that the diagonal element are allowed to be zero.

Multiplying a matrix by a diagonal one has a very specific effect. Let $A \in \mathbb{R}^{n \times k}$ and $B \in \mathbb{R}^{r \times m}$. We focus here on the case $k \geq r$. The matrix product AD produces a matrix whose columns are linear combinations of the columns of A where the coefficients are taken from the corresponding column of D. But the columns of D have at most one nonzero element, the diagonal one. So the columns of AD are in fact multiples of the columns of A,

$$AD = \begin{pmatrix} | & & | \\ d_{11}\mathbf{a}_1 & \cdots & d_{rr}\mathbf{a}_r \\ | & & | \end{pmatrix}$$

where $\mathbf{a}_1, \ldots, \mathbf{a}_k$ are the columns of A and $d_{11}, \ldots, d_{rr}$ are the diagonal elements of D.

Similarly, the rows of DB are linear combinations of the rows of B where the coefficients are taken from the corresponding row of D. The rows of D have at most one nonzero element, the diagonal one. In the case $k \geq r$, rows $r+1, \ldots, k$ necessarily have only zero entries since there is no diagonal entry there. Hence the first r rows of DB are multiples of the rows of B and the next $k - r$ are $\mathbf{0}$,

$$DB = \begin{pmatrix} - & d_{11}\mathbf{b}_1^T & - \\ & \vdots & \\ - & d_{rr}\mathbf{b}_r^T & - \\ - & \mathbf{0} & - \\ & \vdots & \\ - & \mathbf{0} & - \end{pmatrix}$$

where $\mathbf{b}_1^T, \ldots, \mathbf{b}_r^T$ are the rows of B.

Example 4.2.9 *The following special case will be useful later in this chapter. Suppose $D, F \in \mathbb{R}^{n \times n}$ are both square diagonal matrices. Then DF is the matrix whose diagonal elements are $d_{11}f_{11}, \ldots, d_{nn}f_{nn}$.*

4.2.2.2 Spectral Theorem

When A is symmetric, a remarkable result is that there exists an orthonormal basis of $\mathbb{R}^d$ made of eigenvectors of A. We will prove this result in Section 5.3.1.

Before stating the result formally, we make a few observations. Let $A \in \mathbb{R}^{d \times d}$ be symmetric. Suppose that $\mathbf{v}_i$ and $\mathbf{v}_j$ are eigenvectors corresponding respectively to distinct eigenvalues λ_i and λ_j. Then the following quantity can be written in two ways:

$$\langle \mathbf{v}_i, A\mathbf{v}_j \rangle = \langle \mathbf{v}_i, \lambda_j \mathbf{v}_j \rangle = \lambda_j \langle \mathbf{v}_i, \mathbf{v}_j \rangle$$

and, by symmetry of A,

$$\langle \mathbf{v}_i, A\mathbf{v}_j \rangle = \mathbf{v}_i^T A \mathbf{v}_j = \mathbf{v}_i^T A^T \mathbf{v}_j = (A\mathbf{v}_i)^T \mathbf{v}_j = \langle A\mathbf{v}_i, \mathbf{v}_j \rangle = \langle \lambda_i \mathbf{v}_i, \mathbf{v}_j \rangle = \lambda_i \langle \mathbf{v}_i, \mathbf{v}_j \rangle.$$

Subtracting the two,
$$(\lambda_j - \lambda_i)\langle \mathbf{v}_i, \mathbf{v}_j \rangle = 0$$
and using that $\lambda_i \neq \lambda_j$
$$\langle \mathbf{v}_i, \mathbf{v}_j \rangle = 0.$$
That is, $\mathbf{v}_i$ and $\mathbf{v}_j$ are necessarily orthogonal.

We proved:

Lemma 4.2.10 *Let $A \in \mathbb{R}^{d \times d}$ be symmetric. Suppose that $\mathbf{v}_i$ and $\mathbf{v}_j$ are eigenvectors corresponding to distinct eigenvalues. Then $\mathbf{v}_i$ and $\mathbf{v}_j$ are orthogonal.*

This lemma gives a different proof – in the symmetric case – that the number of eigenvalues is at most d since a list of pairwise orthogonal vectors are linearly independent.

In fact:

Theorem 4.2.11 (Spectral Theorem) *Let $A \in \mathbb{R}^{d \times d}$ be a symmetric matrix; that is, $A^T = A$. Then A has d orthonormal eigenvectors $\mathbf{q}_1, \ldots, \mathbf{q}_d$ with corresponding (not necessarily distinct) real eigenvalues $\lambda_1 \geq \lambda_2 \geq \cdots \geq \lambda_d$. Moreover, A can be written as the matrix factorization*
$$A = Q \Lambda Q^T = \sum_{i=1}^{d} \lambda_i \mathbf{q}_i \mathbf{q}_i^T$$
where Q has columns $\mathbf{q}_1, \ldots, \mathbf{q}_d$ and $\Lambda = \mathrm{diag}(\lambda_1, \ldots, \lambda_d)$.

We refer to this factorization as a spectral decomposition of A.

Note that this decomposition indeed produces the eigenvectors of A. For any j, we have
$$A\mathbf{q}_j = \sum_{i=1}^{d} \lambda_i \mathbf{q}_i \mathbf{q}_i^T \mathbf{q}_j = \lambda_j \mathbf{q}_j,$$
where we used that, by orthonormality, $\mathbf{q}_i^T \mathbf{q}_j = 0$ if $i \neq j$ and $\mathbf{q}_i^T \mathbf{q}_j = 1$ if $i = j$. The equation above says precisely that $\mathbf{q}_j$ is an eigenvector of A with corresponding eigenvalue λ_j. Since we have found d eigenvalues (possibly with repetition), we have found all of them.

Let $\lambda_1, \lambda_2, \ldots, \lambda_d$ be the eigenvalues whose existence is guaranteed by the *Spectral Theorem*. We first argue that there is no other eigenvalue. Indeed, assume $\mu \neq \lambda_1, \lambda_2, \ldots, \lambda_d$ is an eigenvalue with corresponding eigenvector $\mathbf{p}$. We have seen that $\mathbf{p}$ is orthogonal to the eigenvectors $\mathbf{q}_1, \ldots, \mathbf{q}_d$. Since the latter list forms an orthonormal basis of $\mathbb{R}^d$, this cannot be the case and we have a contradiction.

Some of the eigenvalues $\lambda_1, \lambda_2, \ldots, \lambda_d$ can be repeated, however; that is, there can be i, j such that $\lambda_i = \lambda_j$. For instance, if $A = I_{d \times d}$ is the identity matrix, then the eigenvalues are $\lambda_i = 1$ for all $i \in [d]$.

For a fixed eigenvalue λ of A, the set of eigenvectors with eigenvalue λ satisfy
$$A\mathbf{v} = \lambda \mathbf{v} = \lambda I_{d \times d} \mathbf{v}$$
or, rearranging,
$$(A - \lambda I_{d \times d})\mathbf{v} = \mathbf{0}.$$

Put differently, it is the set $\text{null}(A - \lambda I_{d \times d})$.

The eigenvectors in the *Spectral Theorem* corresponding the same eigenvalue λ can be replaced by any orthonormal basis of the subspace $\text{null}(A - \lambda I_{d \times d})$. But, beyond this freedom, we have the following characterization: Let $\mu_1, \ldots, \mu_f$ be the unique values in $\lambda_1, \lambda_2, \ldots, \lambda_d$. Then

$$\mathbb{R}^d = \text{null}(A - \mu_1 I_{d \times d}) \oplus \text{null}(A - \mu_2 I_{d \times d}) \oplus \cdots \oplus \text{null}(A - \mu_f I_{d \times d}),$$

where we used the fact that for any $\mathbf{u} \in \text{null}(A - \mu_i I_{d \times d})$ and $\mathbf{v} \in \text{null}(A - \mu_j I_{d \times d})$ with $i \neq j$, we have that $\mathbf{u}$ is orthogonal to $\mathbf{v}$.

We have shown in particular that the sequence of eigenvalues in the *Spectral Theorem* is unique (counting repeats).

Two matrices $B, D \in \mathbb{R}^{d \times d}$ are similar if there is an invertible matrix P such that $B = P^{-1}DP$. It can be shown that B and D correspond to the same linear map, but expressed in different bases. When $P = Q$ is an orthogonal matrix, the transformation simplifies to $B = Q^T D Q$.

Hence, a different way to think about a spectral decomposition is that it expresses the fact that any symmetric matrix is similar to a diagonal matrix through an orthogonal transformation. The basis in which the corresponding linear map is represented by a diagonal matrix is the basis of eigenvectors.

Example 4.2.12 *(Eigendecomposition of 2×2 Symmetric Matrix) The simplest nontrivial case is the 2×2 symmetric matrix*

$$A = \begin{pmatrix} a & b \\ b & d \end{pmatrix}.$$

We derive a step-by-step recipe to compute its eigenvalues and eigenvectors.

As shown previously, an eigenvalue λ corresponds to a nonempty $\text{null}(A - \lambda I_{2 \times 2})$ and the corresponding eigenvector solves

$$\mathbf{0} = (A - \lambda I_{2 \times 2})\mathbf{v} = \begin{pmatrix} a - \lambda & b \\ b & d - \lambda \end{pmatrix} \mathbf{v}.$$

Put differently, the matrix $\begin{pmatrix} a - \lambda & b \\ b & d - \lambda \end{pmatrix}$ has linearly dependent columns. We have seen that one way to check this is to compute the determinant, which in the 2×2 case is simply

$$\det \left[\begin{pmatrix} a - \lambda & b \\ b & d - \lambda \end{pmatrix} \right] = (a - \lambda)(d - \lambda) - b^2.$$

This is a polynomial of degree 2 in λ, called the characteristic polynomial of the matrix A.

The roots of the characteristic polynomial, namely the solutions of

$$0 = (a - \lambda)(d - \lambda) - b^2 = \lambda^2 - (a + d)\lambda + (ad - b^2),$$

are

$$\lambda_1 = \frac{(a + d) + \sqrt{(a + d)^2 - 4(ad - b^2)}}{2}$$

and

$$\lambda_2 = \frac{(a + d) - \sqrt{(a + d)^2 - 4(ad - b^2)}}{2}.$$

Expanding the expression in the square root,

$$(a+d)^2 - 4(ad - b^2) = a^2 + d^2 - 2ad + 4b^2 = (a-d)^2 + 4b^2,$$

we see that the square root is well-defined (i.e., produces a real value) for any a, b, d.

It remains to find the corresponding eigenvectors $\mathbf{v}_1 = (v_{1,1}, v_{1,2})$ and $\mathbf{v}_2 = (v_{2,1}, v_{2,2})$ by solving the 2×2 systems of linear equations

$$\begin{pmatrix} a - \lambda_i & b \\ b & d - \lambda_i \end{pmatrix} \begin{pmatrix} v_{i,1} \\ v_{i,2} \end{pmatrix} = \begin{pmatrix} 0 \\ 0 \end{pmatrix}$$

which are guaranteed to have solutions. When $\lambda_1 = \lambda_2$, one needs to find two linearly independent solutions.

Here is a numerical example. Consider the matrix

$$A = \begin{pmatrix} 3 & 1 \\ 1 & 3 \end{pmatrix}.$$

The characteristic polynomial equation is

$$\lambda^2 - 6\lambda + 8 = 0.$$

The eigenvalues are

$$\lambda_1, \lambda_2 = \frac{6 \pm \sqrt{36 - 4(9 - 1)}}{2} = \frac{6 \pm \sqrt{4}}{2} = 4, 2.$$

We then solve for the eigenvectors. For $\lambda_1 = 4$

$$\begin{pmatrix} 3 - \lambda_1 & 1 \\ 1 & 3 - \lambda_1 \end{pmatrix} \begin{pmatrix} v_{1,1} \\ v_{1,2} \end{pmatrix} = \begin{pmatrix} 0 \\ 0 \end{pmatrix} \Leftrightarrow \begin{cases} -v_{1,1} + v_{1,2} = 0 \\ v_{1,1} - v_{1,2} = 0 \end{cases}$$

so, after normalizing, we take

$$\mathbf{v}_1 = \frac{1}{\sqrt{2}} \begin{pmatrix} 1 \\ 1 \end{pmatrix}.$$

For $\lambda_2 = 2$

$$\begin{pmatrix} 3 - \lambda_2 & 1 \\ 1 & 3 - \lambda_2 \end{pmatrix} \begin{pmatrix} v_{2,1} \\ v_{2,2} \end{pmatrix} = \begin{pmatrix} 0 \\ 0 \end{pmatrix} \Leftrightarrow \begin{cases} v_{1,1} + v_{1,2} = 0 \\ v_{1,1} + v_{1,2} = 0 \end{cases}$$

so, after normalizing, we take

$$\mathbf{v}_2 = \frac{1}{\sqrt{2}} \begin{pmatrix} 1 \\ -1 \end{pmatrix}.$$

The fact that these are the eigenvectors can be checked by hand (try it!).

More generally, for any matrix $A \in \mathbb{R}^{d\times d}$, the roots of the characteristic polynomial $\det(A - \lambda I_{d\times d})$ are eigenvalues of A. We will derive a more efficient numerical approach to compute them in Section 4.4.1.

4.2.2.3 The Case of Positive Semidefinite Matrices

The eigenvalues of a symmetric matrix – while real – may be negative. There is however an important special case where the eigenvalues are nonnegative: positive semidefinite matrices.

Theorem 4.2.13 *(Characterization of Positive Semidefiniteness)* Let $A \in \mathbb{R}^{d\times d}$ be a symmetric matrix and let $A = Q\Lambda Q^T$ be a spectral decomposition of A with $\Lambda = \mathrm{diag}(\lambda_1, \ldots, \lambda_d)$. Then $A \succeq 0$ if and only if its eigenvalues $\lambda_1, \ldots, \lambda_d$ are nonnegative.

Proof Assume $A \succeq 0$. Let $\mathbf{q}_i$ be an eigenvector of A with corresponding eigenvalue λ_i. Then

$$\langle \mathbf{q}_i, A\mathbf{q}_i \rangle = \langle \mathbf{q}_i, \lambda_i \mathbf{q}_i \rangle = \lambda_i$$

which must be nonnegative by definition of a positive semidefinite matrix.

In the other direction, assume $\lambda_1, \ldots, \lambda_d \geq 0$. Then, by the spectral decomposition in outer-product form

$$\langle \mathbf{x}, A\mathbf{x} \rangle = \mathbf{x}^T \left(\sum_{i=1}^d \lambda_i \mathbf{q}_i \mathbf{q}_i^T \right) \mathbf{x} = \sum_{i=1}^d \lambda_i \mathbf{x}^T \mathbf{q}_i \mathbf{q}_i^T \mathbf{x} = \sum_{i=1}^d \lambda_i \langle \mathbf{q}_i, \mathbf{x} \rangle^2$$

which is necessarily nonnegative. $\square$

Similarly, a symmetric matrix is positive definite if and only if all its eigenvalues are strictly positive. The proof is essentially the same.

Recall that an important application of positive semidefiniteness is as a characterization of convexity. Here are some examples.

Example 4.2.14 *(Convexity via Eigenvalues of Hessian)* Consider the function

$$f(x,y) = \frac{3}{2}x^2 + xy + \frac{3}{2}y^2 + 5x - 2y + 1.$$

To show it is convex, we compute its Hessian

$$\mathbf{H}_f(x,y) = \begin{pmatrix} 3 & 1 \\ 1 & 3 \end{pmatrix}$$

for all x, y. By Example 4.2.12, its eigenvalues are 2 and 4, both of which are strictly positive. That proves the claim by the Second-Order Convexity Condition Lemma.

Example 4.2.15 *(Log-Concavity) A function $f : \mathbb{R}^d \to \mathbb{R}$ is said to be log-concave if $-\log f$ is convex. Put differently, we require for all $\mathbf{x}, \mathbf{y} \in \mathbb{R}^d$ and $\alpha \in (0,1)$*

$$-\log f((1-\alpha)\mathbf{x} + \alpha \mathbf{y}) \leq -(1-\alpha)\log f(\mathbf{x}) - \alpha \log f(\mathbf{y}).$$

This is equivalent to

$$\log f((1-\alpha)\mathbf{x} + \alpha \mathbf{y}) \geq (1-\alpha)\log f(\mathbf{x}) + \alpha \log f(\mathbf{y}),$$

or, because $a \log b = \log b^a$ and the logarithm is strictly increasing,

$$f((1-\alpha)\mathbf{x} + \alpha \mathbf{y}) \geq f(\mathbf{x})^{1-\alpha} f(\mathbf{y})^\alpha.$$

We will see in Section 6.2.1 that a multivariate Gaussian vector $\mathbf{X}$ on $\mathbb{R}^d$ with mean $\boldsymbol{\mu} \in \mathbb{R}^d$ and positive definite covariance matrix $\boldsymbol{\Sigma} \in \mathbb{R}^{d \times d}$ has probability density function (PDF)

$$f_{\boldsymbol{\mu}, \boldsymbol{\Sigma}}(\mathbf{x}) = \frac{1}{(2\pi)^{d/2} |\boldsymbol{\Sigma}|^{1/2}} \exp\left(-\frac{1}{2}(\mathbf{x} - \boldsymbol{\mu})^T \boldsymbol{\Sigma}^{-1} (\mathbf{x} - \boldsymbol{\mu})\right)$$

where $|A|$ is the determinant of A, which in the case of a symmetric matrix is simply the product of its eigenvalues (with repeats). We claim that this PDF is log-concave.

From the definition,

$$-\log f_{\boldsymbol{\mu}, \boldsymbol{\Sigma}}(\mathbf{x})$$
$$= \frac{1}{2}(\mathbf{x} - \boldsymbol{\mu})^T \boldsymbol{\Sigma}^{-1} (\mathbf{x} - \boldsymbol{\mu}) + \log(2\pi)^{d/2} |\boldsymbol{\Sigma}|^{1/2}$$
$$= \frac{1}{2}\mathbf{x}^T \boldsymbol{\Sigma}^{-1} \mathbf{x} - \boldsymbol{\mu}^T \boldsymbol{\Sigma}^{-1} \mathbf{x} + \left[\frac{1}{2}\boldsymbol{\mu}^T \boldsymbol{\Sigma}^{-1} \boldsymbol{\mu} + \log(2\pi)^{d/2} |\boldsymbol{\Sigma}|^{1/2}\right].$$

Let $P = \boldsymbol{\Sigma}^{-1}$, $\mathbf{q} = -\boldsymbol{\mu}^T \boldsymbol{\Sigma}^{-1}$, and $r = \frac{1}{2}\boldsymbol{\mu}^T \boldsymbol{\Sigma}^{-1} \boldsymbol{\mu} + \log(2\pi)^{d/2} |\boldsymbol{\Sigma}|^{1/2}$.

Example 3.4.11 then implies that the PDF is log-concave if $\boldsymbol{\Sigma}^{-1}$ is positive semidefinite. Since $\boldsymbol{\Sigma}$ is positive definite by assumption, $\boldsymbol{\Sigma} = Q \Lambda Q^T$ has a spectral decomposition where all diagonal entries of Λ are stricly positive. Then $\boldsymbol{\Sigma}^{-1} = Q \Lambda^{-1} Q^T$ where the diagonal entries of Λ^{-1} are the inverses of those of Λ, and hence strictly positive as well. In particular, $\boldsymbol{\Sigma}^{-1}$ is positive semidefinite.

NUMERICAL CORNER Hence, we can check whether a matrix is positive semidefinite by computing its eigenvalues using `numpy.linalg.eig`.

```
A = np.array([[1, -1], [-1, 1]])
```

```
w, v = LA.eig(A)
print(w)
```

```
[2. 0.]
```

```
B = np.array([[1, -2], [-2, 1]])
```

```
z, u = LA.eig(B)
print(z)
```

```
[ 3. -1.]
```

◁ NC

> *Self-Assessment Quiz* (with help from Claude, Gemini, and ChatGPT)
>
> 1 What is the rank of a matrix $A \in \mathbb{R}^{n \times m}$?
>   a) The number of nonzero entries in A
>   b) The dimension of the row space of A

4.2 Review of Matrix Rank and Spectral Decomposition

    c) The dimension of the null space of A

    d) The trace of A

2. Which of the following is true about the rank of a matrix $A \in \mathbb{R}^{n \times m}$?

    a) $\text{rk}(A) \leq \min\{n, m\}$

    b) $\text{rk}(A) \geq \max\{n, m\}$

    c) $\text{rk}(A) = \text{rk}(A^T)$ only if A is symmetric

    d) $\text{rk}(A) = \text{rk}(A^T)$ only if A is square

3. Let $A \in \mathbb{R}^{n \times k}$ and $B \in \mathbb{R}^{k \times m}$. Which of the following is true in general?

    a) $\text{rk}(AB) \leq \text{rk}(A)$

    b) $\text{rk}(AB) \geq \text{rk}(A)$

    c) $\text{rk}(AB) = \text{rk}(A)$

    d) $\text{rk}(AB) = \text{rk}(B)$

4. Let $A \in \mathbb{R}^{d \times d}$ be symmetric. Which of the following is true according to the *Spectral Theorem*?

    a) A has at most d distinct eigenvalues

    b) A has exactly d distinct eigenvalues

    c) A has at least d distinct eigenvalues

    d) The number of distinct eigenvalues of A is unrelated to d

5. Which of the following is true about the outer product of two vectors **u** and **v**?

    a) It is a scalar.

    b) It is a vector.

    c) It is a matrix of rank one.

    d) It is a matrix of rank zero.

Answer for 1: b. Justification: The text states "the row rank and column rank of A [are] simply [...] the rank, which we denote by $\text{rk}(A)$."

Answer for 2: a. Justification: The text states in the *Row Rank Equals Column Rank Theorem* that "the row rank of A equals the column rank of A. Moreover, $\text{rk}(A) \leq \min\{n, m\}$."

Answer for 3: a. Justification: The text shows that "the columns of AB are linear combinations of the columns of A. Hence $\text{col}(AB) \subseteq \text{col}(A)$. The claim follows by *Observation D2*."

Answer for 4: a. Justification: The *Spectral Theorem* states that "A symmetric matrix A has d orthonormal eigenvectors $\mathbf{q}_1, \ldots, \mathbf{q}_d$ with corresponding (not necessarily distinct) real eigenvalues $\lambda_1 \geq \lambda_2 \geq \cdots \geq \lambda_d$."

Answer for 5: c. Justification: The text defines the outer product and states that "If **u** and **v** are nonzero, the matrix $\mathbf{u}\mathbf{v}^T$ has rank one."

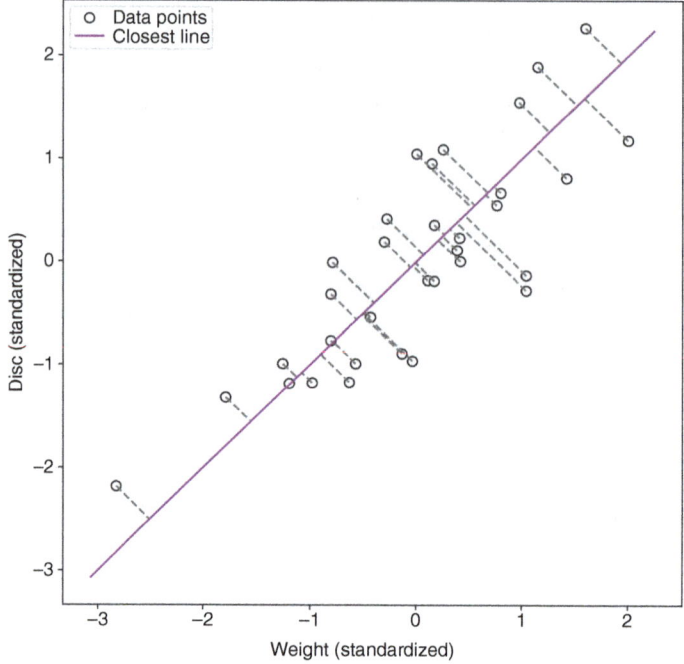

Figure 4.1 The closest line to some data points.

4.3 Approximating Subspaces and the SVD

In this section, we introduce the singular value decomposition. We motivate it via the problem of finding a best approximating subspace to a collection of data points – although it has applications far beyond.

4.3.1 An Objective, an Algorithm, and a Guarantee

Let $\alpha_1, \ldots, \alpha_n$ be a collection of n data points in $\mathbb{R}^m$. A natural way to extract low-dimensional structure in this dataset is to find a low-dimensional linear subspace $\mathcal{Z}$ of $\mathbb{R}^m$ such that the α_i's are "close to it." See Figure 4.1.[5]

4.3.1.1 Mathematical Formulation of the Problem

Again the squared Euclidean norm turns out to be computationally convenient. So we look for a linear subspace $\mathcal{Z}$ that minimizes

$$\sum_{i=1}^{n} \|\alpha_i - \text{proj}_{\mathcal{Z}}(\alpha_i)\|^2$$

---

[5] Code by ChatGPT converted from [HH]. See https://web.stanford.edu/class/bios221/book/07-chap.html

over all linear subspaces of $\mathbb{R}^m$ of dimension k. To solve this problem, which we refer to as the best approximating subspace problem, we make a series of observations.

The first observation gives a related, useful characterization of the optimal solution.

Lemma 4.3.1 *(Best Subspace as Maximimization) Let α_i, $i = 1\ldots,n$, be vectors in $\mathbb{R}^m$. A linear subspace $\mathcal{Z}$ of $\mathbb{R}^m$ that minimizes*

$$\sum_{i=1}^{n} \|\alpha_i - \mathrm{proj}_{\mathcal{Z}}(\alpha_i)\|^2$$

over all linear subspaces of dimension at most k also maximizes

$$\sum_{i=1}^{n} \|\mathrm{proj}_{\mathcal{Z}}(\alpha_i)\|^2$$

over the same linear subspaces. And vice versa.

Proof idea: This is a straightforward application of the triangle inequality.

Proof By *Pythagoras' Theorem*,

$$\|\alpha_i - \mathrm{proj}_{\mathcal{Z}}(\alpha_i)\|^2 + \|\mathrm{proj}_{\mathcal{Z}}(\alpha_i)\|^2 = \|\alpha_i\|^2$$

since, by the *Orthogonal Projection Theorem*, $\mathrm{proj}_{\mathcal{Z}}(\alpha_i)$ is orthogonal to $\alpha_i - \mathrm{proj}_{\mathcal{Z}}(\alpha_i)$. Rearranging,

$$\|\alpha_i - \mathrm{proj}_{\mathcal{Z}}(\alpha_i)\|^2 = \|\alpha_i\|^2 - \|\mathrm{proj}_{\mathcal{Z}}(\alpha_i)\|^2.$$

The result follows from the fact that the first term on the right-hand side does not depend on the choice of $\mathcal{Z}$. More specifically, optimizing over linear subspaces $\mathcal{Z}$ of dimension k,

$$\begin{aligned}
\min_{\mathcal{Z}} \sum_{i=1}^{n} \|\alpha_i - \mathrm{proj}_{\mathcal{Z}}(\alpha_i)\|^2 &= \min_{\mathcal{Z}} \sum_{i=1}^{n} \left\{ \|\alpha_i\|^2 - \|\mathrm{proj}_{\mathcal{Z}}(\alpha_i)\|^2 \right\} \\
&= \sum_{i=1}^{n} \|\alpha_i\|^2 + \min_{\mathcal{Z}} \left\{ -\sum_{i=1}^{n} \|\mathrm{proj}_{\mathcal{Z}}(\alpha_i)\|^2 \right\} \\
&= \sum_{i=1}^{n} \|\alpha_i\|^2 - \max_{\mathcal{Z}} \sum_{i=1}^{n} \|\mathrm{proj}_{\mathcal{Z}}(\alpha_i)\|^2.
\end{aligned}$$

$\square$

How do we specify a k-dimensional linear subspace? Through a basis of it, or – even better – an orthonormal basis. In the latter case, we also have an explicit formula for the orthogonal projection. And the dimension of the linear subspace is captured by the number of elements in the basis, by the *Dimension Theorem*. In other words, the best approximating subspace can be obtained by solving the problem

$$\max_{\mathbf{w}_1,\ldots,\mathbf{w}_k} \sum_{i=1}^{n} \left\| \sum_{j=1}^{k} \langle \alpha_i, \mathbf{w}_j \rangle \mathbf{w}_j \right\|^2$$

over all orthonormal lists $\mathbf{w}_1, \ldots, \mathbf{w}_k$ of length k. Our next observation rewrites the problem in matrix form.

Lemma 4.3.2 (Best Subpace in Matrix Form) *Consider the matrix $A \in \mathbb{R}^{n \times m}$ with rows $\boldsymbol{\alpha}_i^T$. A solution to the best approximating subspace problem is obtained by solving*

$$\max_{\mathbf{w}_1,\ldots,\mathbf{w}_k} \sum_{j=1}^{k} \|A\mathbf{w}_j\|^2$$

over all orthonormal lists $\mathbf{w}_1, \ldots, \mathbf{w}_k$ of length k.

Proof idea: We start with the one-dimensional case. A one-dimensional space $\mathcal{Z}$ is determined by a unit vector $\mathbf{w}_1$. The projection $\boldsymbol{\alpha}_i$ onto the span of $\mathbf{w}_1$ is given by the inner product formula $\langle \boldsymbol{\alpha}_i, \mathbf{w}_1 \rangle \mathbf{w}_1$. So

$$\sum_{i=1}^{n} \|\langle \boldsymbol{\alpha}_i, \mathbf{w}_1 \rangle \mathbf{w}_1\|^2 = \sum_{i=1}^{n} \langle \boldsymbol{\alpha}_i, \mathbf{w}_1 \rangle^2$$
$$= \sum_{i=1}^{n} (\boldsymbol{\alpha}_i^T \mathbf{w}_1)^2$$
$$= \|A\mathbf{w}_1\|^2$$

where, again, A is the matrix with rows $\boldsymbol{\alpha}_i^T$, $i = 1, \ldots, n$. Hence the solution to the one-dimensional problem is

$$\mathbf{v}_1 \in \arg\max\{\|A\mathbf{w}_1\|^2 : \|\mathbf{w}_1\| = 1\}.$$

Here arg max means that $\mathbf{v}_1$ is a vector $\mathbf{w}_1$ that achieves the maximum. Note that there could be more than one such $\mathbf{w}_1$, so the right-hand side is a set containing all such solutions. By the *Extreme Value Theorem* (since the set $\{\mathbf{w}_1 : \|\mathbf{w}_1\| = 1\}$ is closed and bounded, and since furthermore the function $\|A\mathbf{w}_1\|^2$ is continuous in $\mathbf{w}_1$), there is at least one solution.

Proof For general k, we are looking for an orthonormal list $\mathbf{w}_1, \ldots, \mathbf{w}_k$ of length k that maximizes

$$\sum_{i=1}^{n} \left\| \sum_{j=1}^{k} \langle \boldsymbol{\alpha}_i, \mathbf{w}_j \rangle \mathbf{w}_j \right\|^2 = \sum_{i=1}^{n} \sum_{j=1}^{k} \langle \boldsymbol{\alpha}_i, \mathbf{w}_j \rangle^2$$
$$= \sum_{j=1}^{k} \left(\sum_{i=1}^{n} (\boldsymbol{\alpha}_i^T \mathbf{w}_j)^2 \right)$$
$$= \sum_{j=1}^{k} \|A\mathbf{w}_j\|^2$$

where $\mathcal{Z}$ is the subspace spanned by $\mathbf{w}_1, \ldots, \mathbf{w}_k$. On the second line, we used the *Properties of Orthonormal Lists Lemma*. That proves the claim. □

We show next that a simple algorithm solves this problem.

4.3.1.2 A Greedy Algorithm

Remarkably, the problem admits a greedy solution. Before discussing this solution, we take a small detour and give a classical example. Indeed, greedy approaches are a standard algorithmic tool for optimization problems. This is how Wikipedia describes them[6]:

---

[6] https://en.wikipedia.org/wiki/Greedy_algorithm

4.3 Approximating Subspaces and the SVD

A greedy algorithm is any algorithm that follows the problem-solving heuristic of making the locally optimal choice at each stage. In many problems, a greedy strategy does not produce an optimal solution, but a greedy heuristic can yield locally optimal solutions that approximate a globally optimal solution in a reasonable amount of time.

Example 4.3.3 *Suppose you are a thief and you broke into an antique shop at night.*[7] *You cannot steal every item in the store. You have estimated that you can carry 10 lb worth of merchandise, and still run fast enough to get away. Suppose that there are four items of interest with the following weights and values:*

Table 4.1 Data for Example 4.3.3.

Item	Weight (lb)	Value ($)
1	8	1,600
2	6	1,100
3	4	700
4	1	100

There is exactly one of each item. Which items do you take? The siren is blaring, and you cannot try every combination. A quick scheme is to first pick the item of greatest value, namely Item 1. Now your bag has 8 lb of merchandise in it. Then you consider the remaining items and choose whichever has highest value among those that still fit, namely those that are 2 lb or lighter. That leaves only one choice, Item 4. Then you go – with a total value of $1,700.

This is called a greedy or myopic strategy, because you chose the first item to maximize your profit without worrying about the constraints it imposes on future choice. Indeed, in this case, there is a better combination: You could have picked Items 2 and 3 with a total value of $1,800.

Other greedy schemes are possible here. A slightly more clever approach is to choose items of high value per unit weight, rather than considering value alone. But that would not make a difference in this particular example (try it!).

Going back to the approximating subspace problem, we derive a greedy solution for it. Recall that we are looking for a solution to

$$\max_{\mathbf{w}_1,\ldots,\mathbf{w}_k} \|A\mathbf{w}_1\|^2 + \|A\mathbf{w}_2\|^2 + \cdots + \|A\mathbf{w}_k\|^2$$

over all orthonormal lists $\mathbf{w}_1, \ldots, \mathbf{w}_k$ of length k.

In a greedy approach, we first solve for $\mathbf{w}_1$ by itself, without worrying about constraints it will impose on the next steps. That is, we compute

$$\mathbf{v}_1 \in \arg\max\{\|A\mathbf{w}_1\|^2 : \|\mathbf{w}_1\| = 1\}.$$

As indicated before, by the *Extreme Value Theorem*, such a $\mathbf{v}_1$ exists, but may not be unique (in which case we pick an arbitrary one). Then, fixing $\mathbf{w}_1 = \mathbf{v}_1$, we consider all unit vectors $\mathbf{w}_2$ orthogonal to $\mathbf{v}_1$ and maximize the contribution of $\mathbf{w}_2$ to the objective function. That is, we solve

$$\mathbf{v}_2 \in \arg\max\{\|A\mathbf{w}_2\|^2 : \|\mathbf{w}_2\| = 1, \langle \mathbf{w}_2, \mathbf{v}_1 \rangle = 0\}.$$

---

[7] The author would like to clarify that this example is for educational purposes only. Please optimize your life choices more carefully than our hypothetical thief.

Again, such a $\mathbf{v}_2$ exists by the *Extreme Value Theorem*. Then proceeding by induction, for each $i = 3, \ldots, k$, we compute

$$\mathbf{v}_i \in \arg\max\{\|A\mathbf{w}_i\|^2 : \|\mathbf{w}_i\| = 1, \langle \mathbf{w}_i, \mathbf{v}_j \rangle = 0, \forall j \leq i-1\}.$$

A different way to write the constraint is

$$\mathbf{v}_i \in \arg\max\{\|A\mathbf{w}_i\|^2 : \|\mathbf{w}_i\| = 1, \mathbf{w}_i \in \text{span}(\mathbf{v}_1, \ldots, \mathbf{v}_{i-1})^\perp\}.$$

While it is clear that, after k steps, this procedure constructs an orthonormal set of size k, it is far from obvious that it maximizes $\sum_{j=1}^{k} \|A\mathbf{v}_j\|^2$ over all such sets. Remarkably it does. The claim – which requires a proof – is that the best k-dimensional approximating subspace is obtained by finding the best 1-dimensional subspace, then the best 1-dimensional subspace orthogonal to the first one, and so on. This follows from the next theorem.

Theorem 4.3.4 (*Greedy Finds Best Subspace*) *Let $A \in \mathbb{R}^{n \times m}$ be a matrix with rows $\boldsymbol{\alpha}_i^T$, $i = 1, \ldots, n$. For any $k \leq m$, let $\mathbf{v}_1, \ldots, \mathbf{v}_k$ be a greedy sequence as constructed above. Then $\mathcal{Z}^* = \text{span}(\mathbf{v}_1, \ldots, \mathbf{v}_k)$ is a solution to the minimization problem*

$$\min\left\{\sum_{i=1}^{n} \|\boldsymbol{\alpha}_i - \text{proj}_{\mathcal{Z}}(\boldsymbol{\alpha}_i)\|^2 : \mathcal{Z} \text{ is a linear subspace of dimension } k\right\}.$$

Beyond the potential computational advantage of solving several lower-dimensional problems rather one larger-dimensional one, a greedy sequence has a more subtle property that is powerful. It allows us to solve the problem for all choices k of target dimension *simultaneously*. To explain, note that the largest k value, $k = m$, leads to a trivial problem. Indeed, the data points $\boldsymbol{\alpha}_i$, $i = 1, \ldots, n$, already lie in an m-dimensional linear subspace, $\mathbb{R}^m$ itself. So we can take $\mathcal{Z} = \mathbb{R}^m$, and we have an objective value of

$$\sum_{i=1}^{n} \|\boldsymbol{\alpha}_i - \text{proj}_{\mathcal{Z}}(\boldsymbol{\alpha}_i)\|^2 = \sum_{i=1}^{n} \|\boldsymbol{\alpha}_i - \boldsymbol{\alpha}_i\|^2 = 0,$$

which clearly cannot be improved. So any orthonormal basis of $\mathbb{R}^m$ will do. Say $\mathbf{e}_1, \ldots, \mathbf{e}_m$.

On the other hand, a greedy sequence $\mathbf{v}_1, \ldots, \mathbf{v}_m$ has a very special property. For any $k \leq m$, the *truncation* $\mathbf{v}_1, \ldots, \mathbf{v}_k$ solves the approximating subspace problem in k dimensions. That follows immediately from the *Greedy Finds Best Subspace Theorem*. The basis $\mathbf{e}_1, \ldots, \mathbf{e}_m$ (or any old basis of $\mathbb{R}^m$ for that matter) does *not* have this property. The idea of truncation is very useful and plays an important role in many data science applications; we will come back to it later in this section and the next one.

We sketch the proof of a weaker claim via the *Spectral Theorem*, an approach which reveals additional structure in the solution.

We rewrite the objective function as

$$\sum_{j=1}^{k} \|A\mathbf{w}_j\|^2 = \sum_{j=1}^{k} \mathbf{w}_j^T A^T A \mathbf{w}_j$$

and we observe that $A^T A \in \mathbb{R}^{m \times m}$ is a square, symmetric matrix (why?). It is also positive, semidefinite (why?). Hence, by the *Spectral Theorem*, the matrix $A^T A$ has m orthonormal eigenvectors $\mathbf{q}_1, \ldots, \mathbf{q}_m \in \mathbb{R}^m$ with corresponding real eigenvalues $\lambda_1 \geq \lambda_2 \geq \cdots \geq \lambda_m \geq 0$. This ordering of the eigenvalues will play a critical role. Moreover

$$A^T A = \sum_{i=1}^{m} \lambda_i \mathbf{q}_i \mathbf{q}_i^T.$$

Plugging this in the objective we get

$$\sum_{j=1}^{k} \|A\mathbf{w}_j\|^2 = \sum_{j=1}^{k} \mathbf{w}_j^T \left(\sum_{i=1}^{m} \lambda_i \mathbf{q}_i \mathbf{q}_i^T \right) \mathbf{w}_j = \sum_{j=1}^{k} \sum_{i=1}^{m} \lambda_i (\mathbf{w}_j^T \mathbf{q}_i)^2.$$

Here is the claim. While a greedy sequence $\mathbf{v}_1, \ldots, \mathbf{v}_k$ is not in general unique, one can always choose $\mathbf{v}_i = \mathbf{q}_i$ for all i. Moreover that particular choice indeed solves the k-dimensional best approximating subspace problem. We restrict ourselves to the case $k = 2$.

4.3.1.3 Eigenvectors Form a Greedy Sequence

We claim that eigenvectors form a greedy sequence. Recall that $\mathbf{v}_1$ maximizes $\|A\mathbf{w}_1\|$ over all unit vectors $\mathbf{w}_1$. Now note that, expanding over the eigenvectors (which form an orthonormal basis), we have

$$\|A\mathbf{w}_1\|^2 = \sum_{i=1}^{m} \lambda_i (\mathbf{w}_1^T \mathbf{q}_i)^2$$

and

$$\|\mathbf{w}_1\|^2 = \sum_{i=1}^{m} (\mathbf{w}_1^T \mathbf{q}_i)^2 = 1.$$

Writing $x_i = (\mathbf{w}_1^T \mathbf{q}_i)^2$, this boils down to maximizing $\sum_{i=1}^{m} \lambda_i x_i$ subject to the constraints $\sum_{i=1}^{m} x_i = 1$ and $x_i \geq 0$ for all i. But, under the constraints and the assumption on the ordering of the eigenvalues,

$$\sum_{i=1}^{m} \lambda_i x_i \leq \lambda_1 \sum_{i=1}^{m} x_i = \lambda_1.$$

Formally, we have shown that $\|A\mathbf{w}_1\|^2 \leq \lambda_1$, for any unit vector $\mathbf{w}_1$. Now, note that this upper bound is actually achieved by taking $\mathbf{v}_1 = \mathbf{w}_1 = \mathbf{q}_1$, which corresponds to $\mathbf{x} = (x_1, \ldots, x_m) = \mathbf{e}_1$.

Given that choice, the vector $\mathbf{v}_2$ maximizes $\|A\mathbf{w}_2\|$ over all unit vectors $\mathbf{w}_2$ such that further $\mathbf{w}_2^T \mathbf{v}_1 = \mathbf{w}_2^T \mathbf{q}_1 = 0$, where this time

$$\|A\mathbf{w}_2\|^2 = \sum_{i=1}^{m} \lambda_i (\mathbf{w}_2^T \mathbf{q}_i)^2 = \sum_{i=2}^{m} \lambda_i (\mathbf{w}_2^T \mathbf{q}_i)^2$$

and

$$\|\mathbf{w}_2\|^2 = \sum_{i=1}^{m} (\mathbf{w}_2^T \mathbf{q}_i)^2 = \sum_{i=2}^{m} (\mathbf{w}_2^T \mathbf{q}_i)^2 = 1.$$

In both equations above, we used the orthogonality constraint. This reduces to the previous problem without the term depending on $\mathbf{q}_1$. The solution is otherwise the same: The optimal objective is λ_2 and is achieved by taking $\mathbf{v}_2 = \mathbf{w}_2 = \mathbf{q}_2$.

4.3.1.4 Eigenvectors Solve the Approximating Subspace Problem

We claim that eigenvectors solve the approximating subspace problem. The approximating subspace problem for $k = 2$ involves maximizing

$$\|A\mathbf{w}_1\|^2 + \|A\mathbf{w}_2\|^2 = \sum_{i=1}^{m} \lambda_i(\mathbf{w}_1^T\mathbf{q}_i)^2 + \sum_{i=1}^{m} \lambda_i(\mathbf{w}_2^T\mathbf{q}_i)^2$$

over orthonormal lists $\mathbf{w}_1, \mathbf{w}_2$. In particular, we require

$$\|\mathbf{w}_1\|^2 = \sum_{i=1}^{m}(\mathbf{w}_1^T\mathbf{q}_i)^2 = 1$$

and

$$\|\mathbf{w}_2\|^2 = \sum_{i=1}^{m}(\mathbf{w}_2^T\mathbf{q}_i)^2 = 1.$$

Moreover, for each i, by definition of the orthogonal projection on the subspace $\mathcal{W} = \text{span}(\mathbf{w}_1, \mathbf{w}_2)$ and the *Properties of Orthonormal Lists Lemma*

$$(\mathbf{w}_1^T\mathbf{q}_i)^2 + (\mathbf{w}_2^T\mathbf{q}_i)^2 = \|\text{proj}_{\mathcal{W}}\mathbf{q}_i\|^2 \leq \|\mathbf{q}_i\|^2 = 1.$$

(Prove the inequality!) Write $x_i = (\mathbf{w}_1^T\mathbf{q}_i)^2$ and $y_i = (\mathbf{w}_2^T\mathbf{q}_i)^2$. The objective function can be written as $\sum_{i=1}^{m} \lambda_i(x_i + y_i)$ and the constraints we have derived are $\sum_{i=1}^{m} x_i = \sum_{i=1}^{m} y_i = 1$ and $x_i + y_i \leq 1$ for all i. Also clearly $x_i, y_i \geq 0$ for all i. So

$$\sum_{i=1}^{m} \lambda_i(x_i + y_i) = \lambda_1(x_1 + y_1) + \lambda_2(x_2 + y_2) + \sum_{i=3}^{m} \lambda_i(x_i + y_i)$$

$$\leq \lambda_1(x_1 + y_1) + \lambda_2(x_2 + y_2) + \lambda_2 \sum_{i=3}^{m}(x_i + y_i)$$

$$= \lambda_1(x_1 + y_1) + \lambda_2(x_2 + y_2) + \lambda_2([1 - x_1 - x_2] + [1 - y_1 - y_2])$$

$$= (\lambda_1 - \lambda_2)(x_1 + y_1) + (\lambda_2 - \lambda_2)(x_2 + y_2) + 2\lambda_2$$

$$\leq \lambda_1 - \lambda_2 + 2\lambda_2$$

$$= \lambda_1 + \lambda_2.$$

Formally, we have shown that $\|A\mathbf{w}_1\|^2 + \|A\mathbf{w}_2\|^2 \leq \lambda_1 + \lambda_2$ for any orthonormal list $\mathbf{w}_1, \mathbf{w}_2$. That upper bound is achieved by taking $\mathbf{w}_1 = \mathbf{q}_1$ and $\mathbf{w}_2 = \mathbf{q}_2$, proving the claim.

Note that we have not entirely solved the best approximating subspace problem from a computational point of view, as we have not given an explicit procedure to construct a solution to the lower-dimensional subproblems; that is, to construct the eigenvectors. We have only shown that the solutions exist and have the right properties. We will take care of computational issues Section 4.4.

4.3.2 From Approximating Subspaces to the SVD

While solving the approximating subspace problem in the previous subsection, we derived the building blocks of a matrix factorization that has found many applications, the singular value decomposition (SVD). In this section, we define the SVD formally. We describe a simple method to compute it in the next section, where we also return to the application to dimensionality reduction.

4.3.2.1 Definition and Existence of the SVD

We now come to our main definition.

Definition 4.3.5 *(Singular Value Decomposition) Let $A \in \mathbb{R}^{n \times m}$ be a matrix. A singular value decomposition of A is a matrix factorization*

$$A = U\Sigma V^T = \sum_{j=1}^{r} \sigma_j \mathbf{u}_j \mathbf{v}_j^T$$

where the columns of $U \in \mathbb{R}^{n \times r}$ and those of $V \in \mathbb{R}^{m \times r}$ are orthonormal, and $\Sigma \in \mathbb{R}^{r \times r}$ is a diagonal matrix. Here the $\mathbf{u}_j$'s are the columns of U and are referred to as left singular vectors. Similarly the $\mathbf{v}_j$'s are the columns of V and are referred to as right singular vectors. The σ_j's, which are positive and in non-increasing order,

$$\sigma_1 \geq \sigma_2 \geq \cdots \geq \sigma_r > 0,$$

are the diagonal elements of Σ and are referred to as singular values.

To see where the equality $U\Sigma V^T = \sum_{j=1}^{r} \sigma_j \mathbf{u}_j \mathbf{v}_j^T$ comes from, we break it up into two steps.

1. First note that the matrix product $U\Sigma$ has columns $\sigma_1 \mathbf{u}_1, \ldots, \sigma_r \mathbf{u}_r$, and that the rows of V^T are the columns of V as row vectors.

2. In terms of outer products, the matrix product $U\Sigma V^T = (U\Sigma)V^T$ is the sum of the outer products of the columns of $U\Sigma$ and of the rows of V^T (i.e., the columns of V as row vectors).

That proves the equality.

Remarkably, any matrix has an SVD.

Theorem 4.3.6 *(Existence of an SVD) Any matrix $A \in \mathbb{R}^{n \times m}$ has a singular value decomposition.*

We give a proof via the *Spectral Theorem*.

The construction: Let $A \in \mathbb{R}^{n \times m}$ and recall that $A^T A$ is symmetric and positive semidefinite. Hence the latter has a spectral decomposition

$$A^T A = Q \Lambda Q^T.$$

Order the eigenvalues in non-increasing order $\lambda_1 \geq \cdots \geq \lambda_m \geq 0$. Assume that the eigenvalues $\lambda_1, \ldots, \lambda_r$ are nonzero while $\lambda_{r+1} = \cdots = \lambda_m = 0$. Let $\mathbf{q}_1, \ldots, \mathbf{q}_n$ be corresponding eigenvectors. Let $Q_1 \in \mathbb{R}^{m \times r}$ be the matrix whose columns are $\mathbf{q}_1, \ldots, \mathbf{q}_r$ and $\Lambda_1 \in \mathbb{R}^{r \times r}$ be the diagonal matrix with $\lambda_1, \ldots, \lambda_r$ on its diagonal. Similarly, let $Q_2 \in \mathbb{R}^{m \times (m-r)}$ be the matrix whose columns are $\mathbf{q}_{r+1}, \ldots, \mathbf{q}_m$ and $\Lambda_2 = \mathbf{0} \in \mathbb{R}^{(m-r) \times (m-r)}$.

The matrix $A^T A$, which is comprised of all inner products of the data points, is known as a Gram matrix.

We are now ready for our main claim. For a diagonal matrix D with nonnegative diagonal entries, we let $D^{1/2}$ denote the diagonal matrix obtained by taking the square root of each diagonal entry. Similarly, when D has positive diagonal entries, we define $D^{-1/2}$ as the diagonal matrix whose diagonal entries are the reciprocals of the square roots of the corresponding diagonal entries of D.

Theorem 4.3.7 *(SVD via Spectral Decomposition)* Let $A \in \mathbb{R}^{n \times m}$ and let Q_1, Λ_1 be as above. Define

$$U = AQ_1\Lambda_1^{-1/2} \quad \text{and} \quad \Sigma = \Lambda_1^{1/2} \quad \text{and} \quad V = Q_1.$$

Then $A = U\Sigma V^T$ is a singular value decomposition of A.

Proof idea: Check by hand that all properties of the SVD are satisfied by the construction above.

Proof By construction, the columns of $V = Q_1$ are orthonormal. The matrix $\Sigma = \Lambda_1^{1/2}$ is diagonal and, because A^TA is positive semidefinite, the eigenvalues are nonnegative. So it remains to prove two things: that the columns of U are orthonormal and, finally, that $A = U\Sigma V^T$.

Lemma 4.3.8 *(Step 1)* The columns of U are orthonormal.

Proof By direct computation,

$$U^T U = (AQ_1\Lambda_1^{-1/2})^T AQ_1\Lambda_1^{-1/2} = \Lambda_1^{-1/2}Q_1^T A^T AQ_1\Lambda_1^{-1/2}.$$

Because the columns of Q_1 are eigenvectors of A^TA, we have that $A^TAQ_1 = Q_1\Lambda_1$. Further those eigenvectors are orthonormal so that $Q_1^T Q_1 = I_{r \times r}$. Substituting and simplifying gives

$$\Lambda_1^{-1/2}Q_1^T A^T AQ_1\Lambda_1^{-1/2} = \Lambda_1^{-1/2}Q_1^T Q_1\Lambda_1\Lambda_1^{-1/2} = \Lambda_1^{-1/2}I_{r \times r}\Lambda_1\Lambda_1^{-1/2} = I_{r \times r},$$

as claimed. □

Lemma 4.3.9 *(Step 2)* It holds that $A = U\Sigma V^T$.

Proof By direct computation, we have

$$U\Sigma V^T = AQ_1\Lambda_1^{-1/2}\Lambda_1^{1/2}Q_1^T = AQ_1Q_1^T.$$

The matrix $Q_1Q_1^T$ is an orthogonal projection onto the subspace spanned by the vectors $\mathbf{q}_1, \ldots, \mathbf{q}_r$. Similarly, the matrix $Q_2Q_2^T$ is an orthogonal projection on the orthogonal complement (spanned by $\mathbf{q}_{r+1}, \ldots, \mathbf{q}_m$). Hence $Q_1Q_1^T + Q_2Q_2^T = I_{m \times m}$. Replacing above we get

$$U\Sigma V^T = A(I_{n \times n} - Q_2Q_2^T) = A - AQ_2Q_2^T.$$

Now note that for any $\mathbf{q}_i$, $i = r+1, \ldots, m$, we have $A^TA\mathbf{q}_i = \mathbf{0}$, so that $\mathbf{q}_i^T A^T A \mathbf{q}_i = \|A\mathbf{q}_i\|^2 = 0$. That implies that $A\mathbf{q}_i = \mathbf{0}$ and further $AQ_2 = \mathbf{0}$. Substituting above concludes the proof. □

This concludes the proof of the theorem. □

We record the following important consequence.

Lemma 4.3.10 *(SVD and Rank)* Let $A \in \mathbb{R}^{n \times m}$ have singular value decomposition $A = U\Sigma V^T$ with $U \in \mathbb{R}^{n \times r}$ and $V \in \mathbb{R}^{m \times r}$. Then the columns of U form an orthonormal basis of $\mathrm{col}(A)$ and the columns of V form an orthonormal basis of $\mathrm{row}(A)$. In particular, the rank of A is r.

Proof idea: We use the SVD to show that the span of the columns of U is $\mathrm{col}(A)$, and similarly for V.

Proof We first prove that any column of A can be written as a linear combination of the columns of U. Indeed, this follows immediately from the SVD by noting that for any canonical basis vector $\mathbf{e}_i \in \mathbb{R}^m$ (which produces column i of A with $A\mathbf{e}_i$)

$$A\mathbf{e}_i = \left(\sum_{j=1}^r \sigma_j \mathbf{u}_j \mathbf{v}_j^T\right)\mathbf{e}_i = \sum_{j=1}^r (\sigma_j \mathbf{v}_j^T \mathbf{e}_i)\mathbf{u}_j.$$

Vice versa, any column of U can be written as a linear combination of the columns of A. To see this, we use the orthonormality of the $\mathbf{v}_j$'s and the positivity of the singular values to obtain

$$A(\sigma_i^{-1}\mathbf{v}_i) = \sigma_i^{-1}\left(\sum_{j=1}^r \sigma_j \mathbf{u}_j \mathbf{v}_j^T\right)\mathbf{v}_i = \sigma_i^{-1}\sum_{j=1}^r (\sigma_j \mathbf{v}_j^T \mathbf{v}_i)\mathbf{u}_j = \sigma_i^{-1}(\sigma_i \mathbf{v}_i^T \mathbf{v}_i)\mathbf{u}_i = \mathbf{u}_i.$$

That is, $\mathrm{col}(U) = \mathrm{col}(A)$. We have already shown that the columns of U are orthonormal. Since their span is $\mathrm{col}(A)$, they form an orthonormal basis of it. Applying the same argument to A^T gives the claim for V (try it!). $\square$

Example 4.3.11 *Let*

$$A = \begin{pmatrix} 1 & 0 \\ -1 & 0 \end{pmatrix}.$$

We compute its SVD. In this case it can be done (or guessed) using what we know about the SVD. Note first that A is not invertible. Indeed, its rows are a multiple of one another. In particular, they are not linearly independent. In fact, that tells us that the rank of A is 1, the dimension of its row space. In the rank one case, computing the SVD boils down to writing the matrix A in outer product form

$$A = \sigma_1 \mathbf{u}_1 \mathbf{v}_1^T$$

where we require that $\sigma_1 > 0$ and that $\mathbf{u}_1, \mathbf{v}_1$ are of unit norm.

Recall that an outer product has columns that are all multiples of the same vector. Here because the second column of A is $\mathbf{0}$, it must be that the second component of $\mathbf{v}_1$ is 0. To be of unit norm, its first component must be 1 or -1. (The choice here does not matter because multiplying all left and right singular vectors by -1 produces another SVD.) We choose 1; that is, we let

$$\mathbf{v}_1 = \begin{pmatrix} 1 \\ 0 \end{pmatrix}.$$

This vector is indeed an orthonormal basis of the row space of A. Then we need

$$\sigma_1 \mathbf{u}_1 = \begin{pmatrix} 1 \\ -1 \end{pmatrix}.$$

For $\mathbf{u}_1$ to be of unit norm, we must have

$$\mathbf{u}_1 = \begin{pmatrix} 1/\sqrt{2} \\ -1/\sqrt{2} \end{pmatrix} \quad \text{and} \quad \sigma_1 = \sqrt{2}.$$

Observe that $\mathbf{u}_1$ is indeed an orthonormal basis of the column space of A.

One might hope that the SVD of a symmetric matrix generates identical left and right singular vectors. However this is not the case.

Example 4.3.12 *An SVD of $A = (-1)$ is $A = (1)(1)(-1)$. That is, $\mathbf{u}_1 = (1)$ and $\mathbf{v} = (-1)$.*

We collect in the next lemma some relationships between the singular vectors and singular values that will be used repeatedly. It also further clarifies the connection between the SVD of A and the spectral decomposition of $A^T A$ and $A A^T$.

Lemma 4.3.13 *(SVD Relations) Let $A = \sum_{j=1}^{r} \sigma_j \mathbf{u}_j \mathbf{v}_j^T$ be an SVD of $A \in \mathbb{R}^{n \times m}$ with $\sigma_1 \geq \sigma_2 \geq \cdots \geq \sigma_r > 0$. Then, for $i = 1, \ldots, r$,*

$$A\mathbf{v}_i = \sigma_i \mathbf{u}_i, \qquad A^T \mathbf{u}_i = \sigma_i \mathbf{v}_i, \qquad \|A\mathbf{v}_i\| = \sigma_i, \qquad \|A^T \mathbf{u}_i\| = \sigma_i.$$

A fortiori

$$A^T A \mathbf{v}_i = \sigma_i^2 \mathbf{v}_i, \qquad A A^T \mathbf{u}_i = \sigma_i^2 \mathbf{u}_i.$$

and, for $j \neq i$,

$$\langle A\mathbf{v}_i, A\mathbf{v}_j \rangle = 0, \qquad \langle A^T \mathbf{u}_i, A^T \mathbf{u}_j \rangle = 0.$$

We previously established the existence of an SVD via the spectral decomposition of $A^T A$. The above lemma shows that in fact, in any SVD, the $\mathbf{v}_i$'s are orthonormal eigenvectors of $A^T A$. They do not form an orthonormal basis of the full space $\mathbb{R}^m$ however, as the rank r can be strictly smaller than m. But observe that any vector $\mathbf{w}$ orthogonal to $\text{span}(\mathbf{v}_1, \ldots, \mathbf{v}_r)$ is such that

$$A\mathbf{w} = \sum_{j=1}^{r} \sigma_j \mathbf{u}_j \mathbf{v}_j^T \mathbf{w} = \mathbf{0}$$

and, a fortiori,

$$A^T A \mathbf{w} = \mathbf{0}.$$

So $\mathbf{w}$ is in fact an eigenvector of $A^T A$ with eigenvalue 0. Let $\mathbf{v}_{r+1}, \ldots, \mathbf{v}_m$ be any orthonormal basis of $\text{span}(\mathbf{v}_1, \ldots, \mathbf{v}_r)^\perp$. Then $\mathbf{v}_1, \ldots, \mathbf{v}_m$ is an orthonormal basis of eigenvectors of $A^T A$.

The lemma also shows that the $\mathbf{u}_i$'s are orthonormal eigenvectors of $A A^T$!

4.3.2.2 Full vs. Compact SVD

What we have introduced above is in fact referred to as a compact SVD. In contrast, in a full SVD, the matrices U and V are square and orthogonal, and the matrix Σ is diagonal, but may not be square and may have zeros on the diagonal. In particular, in that case, the columns of $U \in \mathbb{R}^{n \times n}$ form an orthonormal basis of $\mathbb{R}^n$ and the columns of $V \in \mathbb{R}^{m \times m}$ form an orthonormal basis of $\mathbb{R}^m$.

Let $A = U_1 \Sigma_1 V_1^T$ be a compact SVD. Complete the columns of U_1 into an orthonormal basis of $\mathbb{R}^n$ and let U_2 be the matrix whose columns are the additional basis vectors. Similary, complete the columns of V_1 into an orthonormal basis of $\mathbb{R}^m$ and let V_2 be the matrix whose columns are the additional basis vectors. Then a full SVD is given by

$$U = \begin{pmatrix} U_1 & U_2 \end{pmatrix}, \quad V = \begin{pmatrix} V_1 & V_2, \end{pmatrix}, \quad \Sigma = \begin{pmatrix} \Sigma_1 & \mathbf{0}_{r \times (m-r)} \\ \mathbf{0}_{(n-r) \times r} & \mathbf{0}_{(n-r) \times (m-r)} \end{pmatrix}.$$

By the *SVD and Rank Lemma*, the columns of U_1 form an orthonormal basis of $\text{col}(A)$. Because $\text{col}(A)^\perp = \text{null}(A^T)$, the columns of U_2 form an orthonormal basis of $\text{null}(A^T)$. Similarly, the columns of V_1 form an orthonormal basis of $\text{col}(A^T)$. Because $\text{col}(A^T)^\perp = \text{null}(A)$, the columns of V_2 form an orthonormal basis of null(A). Hence, a full SVD provides an orthonormal basis for all four fundamental subspaces of A.

Vice versa, given a full SVD $A = U\Sigma V^T$, the compact SVD can be obtained by keeping only the square submatrix of Σ with stricly positive diagonal entries, together with the corresponding columns of U and V.

Example 4.3.14 *(continued from Example 4.3.11) Let again*
$$A = \begin{pmatrix} 1 & 0 \\ -1 & 0 \end{pmatrix}.$$
We previously computed its compact SVD,
$$A = \sigma_1 \mathbf{u}_1 \mathbf{v}_1^T$$
where
$$\mathbf{u}_1 = \begin{pmatrix} 1/\sqrt{2} \\ -1/\sqrt{2} \end{pmatrix}, \quad \mathbf{v}_1 = \begin{pmatrix} 1 \\ 0 \end{pmatrix}, \quad \text{and} \quad \sigma_1 = \sqrt{2}.$$
We now compute a full SVD. For this, we need to complete the bases. We can choose (why?)
$$\mathbf{u}_2 = \begin{pmatrix} 1/\sqrt{2} \\ 1/\sqrt{2} \end{pmatrix}, \quad \mathbf{v}_2 = \begin{pmatrix} 0 \\ 1 \end{pmatrix}, \quad \text{and} \quad \sigma_2 = 0.$$
Then, a full SVD is given by
$$U = \begin{pmatrix} 1/\sqrt{2} & 1/\sqrt{2} \\ -1/\sqrt{2} & 1/\sqrt{2} \end{pmatrix}, \quad V = \begin{pmatrix} 1 & 0 \\ 0 & 1 \end{pmatrix}, \quad \text{and} \quad \Sigma = \begin{pmatrix} \sqrt{2} & 0 \\ 0 & 0 \end{pmatrix}.$$
Indeed, $A = U\Sigma V^T$ (check it!).

The full SVD also has a natural geometric interpretation. To quote [Sol, p. 133]:

> The SVD provides a complete geometric characterization of the action of A. Since U and V are orthogonal, they have no effect on lengths and angles; as a diagonal matrix, Σ scales individual coordinate axes. Since the SVD always exists, all matrices $A \in \mathbb{R}^{n \times m}$ are a composition of an isometry, a scale in each coordinate, and a second isometry.

4.3.2.3 Coming Full Circle: Solving the Approximating Subspace Problem via the SVD

Think of the rows $\boldsymbol{\alpha}_i^T$ of a matrix $A \in \mathbb{R}^{n \times m}$ as a collection of n data points in $\mathbb{R}^m$. Let
$$A = \sum_{j=1}^{r} \sigma_j \mathbf{u}_j \mathbf{v}_j^T$$
be a (compact) SVD of A. Fix $k \leq \text{rk}(A)$. We are looking for a linear subspace $\mathcal{Z}$ that minimizes
$$\sum_{i=1}^{n} \|\boldsymbol{\alpha}_i - \text{proj}_{\mathcal{Z}}(\boldsymbol{\alpha}_i)\|^2$$
over all linear subspaces of $\mathbb{R}^m$ of dimension at most k. By the observations in Section 4.3.1, a solution is given by
$$\mathcal{Z} = \text{span}(\mathbf{v}_1, \ldots, \mathbf{v}_k).$$

By the proofs of the *Best Subspace as Maximization* and *Best Subspace in Matrix Form* lemmas, the objective value achieved is

$$\sum_{i=1}^{n} \|\alpha_i - \operatorname{proj}_{\mathcal{Z}}(\alpha_i)\|^2 = \sum_{i=1}^{n} \|\alpha_i\|^2 - \sum_{j=1}^{k} \|A\mathbf{v}_j\|^2$$

$$= \sum_{i=1}^{n} \|\alpha_i\|^2 - \sum_{j=1}^{k} \sigma_j^2.$$

So the singular value σ_j associated with the right singular vector $\mathbf{v}_j$ captures its contribution to the fit of the approximating subspace. The larger the singular value, the larger the contribution.

To obtain a low-dimensional embedding of our original datasets, we compute $\mathbf{z}_i := \operatorname{proj}_{\mathcal{Z}}(\alpha_i)$ for each i as follows (in row form):

$$\mathbf{z}_i^T = \sum_{j=1}^{k} \langle \alpha_i, \mathbf{v}_j \rangle \mathbf{v}_j^T$$

$$= \sum_{j=1}^{k} \alpha_i^T \mathbf{v}_j \mathbf{v}_j^T$$

$$= A_{i,\cdot} V_{(k)} V_{(k)}^T,$$

where $V_{(k)}$ is the matrix with the first k columns of V. Let Z be the matrix with rows $\mathbf{z}_i^T$. Then we have

$$Z = A V_{(k)} V_{(k)}^T = U_{(k)} \Sigma_{(k)} V_{(k)}^T = \sum_{j=1}^{k} \sigma_j \mathbf{u}_j \mathbf{v}_j^T,$$

where $U_{(k)}$ is the matrix with the first k columns of U, and $\Sigma_{(k)}$ is the matrix with the first k rows and columns of Σ. Indeed, recall that $A\mathbf{v}_j = \sigma_j \mathbf{u}_j$, or in matrix form $AV_{(k)} = U_{(k)} \Sigma_{(k)}$. The rightmost expression for Z reveals that it is in fact a truncated SVD. We can interpret the rows of $U_{(k)} \Sigma_{(k)}$ as the coefficients of each data point in the basis $\mathbf{v}_1, \ldots, \mathbf{v}_k$. Those coefficients provide the desired low-dimensional representation.

We can rewrite the objective function in a more compact matrix form by using the Frobenius norm as follows

$$\sum_{i=1}^{n} \|\alpha_i - \operatorname{proj}_{\mathcal{Z}}(\alpha_i)\|^2 = \sum_{i=1}^{n} \|\alpha_i - \mathbf{z}_i\|^2 = \sum_{i=1}^{n} \|\alpha_i^T - \mathbf{z}_i^T\|^2 = \|A - Z\|_F^2.$$

We note that the matrix Z has rank less than or equal to k. Indeed, all of its rows lie in the optimal subspace $\mathcal{Z}$, which has dimension k by construction. We will see in Section 4.6.2 that Z is the best approximation to A among all rank-k matrices under the Frobenius norm; that is,

$$\|A - Z\|_F \leq \|A - B\|_F$$

for any matrix B of rank at most k.

4.3 Approximating Subspaces and the SVD

Self-Assessment Quiz (with help from Claude, Gemini, and ChatGPT)

1. Let $\alpha_1, \ldots, \alpha_n$ be data points in $\mathbb{R}^m$. What is the objective of the best approximating subspace problem?
   a) To find a linear subspace $\mathcal{Z}$ of $\mathbb{R}^m$ that minimizes the sum of the distances between the α_i's and $\mathcal{Z}$.
   b) To find a linear subspace $\mathcal{Z}$ of $\mathbb{R}^m$ that minimizes the sum of the squared distances between the α_i's and their orthogonal projections onto $\mathcal{Z}$.
   c) To find a linear subspace $\mathcal{Z}$ of $\mathbb{R}^m$ that maximizes the sum of the squared norms of the orthogonal projections of the α_i's onto $\mathcal{Z}$.
   d) Both b and c.

2. Consider the data points $\alpha_1 = (-2, 2)$ and $\alpha_2 = (3, -3)$. For $k = 1$, what is the solution of the best approximating subspace problem?
   a) $\mathcal{Z} = \{(x, y) \in \mathbb{R}^2 : y = x\}$
   b) $\mathcal{Z} = \{(x, y) \in \mathbb{R}^2 : y = -x\}$
   c) $\mathcal{Z} = \{(x, y) \in \mathbb{R}^2 : y = x + 1\}$
   d) $\mathcal{Z} = \{(x, y) \in \mathbb{R}^2 : y = x - 1\}$

3. Which of the following is true about the SVD of a matrix A?
   a) The SVD of A is unique.
   b) The right singular vectors of A are the eigenvectors of $A^T A$.
   c) The left singular vectors of A are the eigenvectors of $A A^T$.
   d) Both b and c.

4. Let $A = U \Sigma V^T$ be an SVD of A. Which of the following is true?
   a) $A \mathbf{v}_i = \sigma_i \mathbf{u}_i$ for all i.
   b) $A^T \mathbf{u}_i = \sigma_i \mathbf{v}_i$ for all i.
   c) $\|A \mathbf{v}_i\| = \sigma_i$ for all i.
   d) All of the above.

5. The columns of U in the compact SVD form an orthonormal basis for which subspace?
   a) col(A)
   b) row(A)
   c) null(A)
   d) null(A^T)

Answer for 1: d. Justification: The text defines the best approximating subspace problem as minimizing the sum of squared distances between the data points and their projections onto the subspace, and it also states a lemma that this problem is equivalent to maximizing the sum of squared norms of the projections.

Answer for 2: b. Justification: By symmetry, the best approximating line must pass through the origin and bisect the angle between the two points. This is the line $y = -x$.

Answer for 3: d. Justification: The SVD is not unique in general. The other two statements are true and are mentioned in the text.

Answer for 4: d. Justification: This is a lemma stated in the text.

Answer for 5: a. Justification: The text states in the *SVD and Rank Lemma:* "the columns of U form an orthonormal basis of col(A)."

4.4 Power Iteration

There is in general no exact method for computing SVDs. Instead we must rely on iterative methods; that is, methods that progressively approach the solution. We describe in this section the power iteration method. This method is behind an effective numerical approach for computing SVDs.

The focus here is on numerical methods and we will not spend much time computing SVDs by hand. But note that the connection between the SVD and the spectral decomposition of $A^T A$ can be used for this purpose on small examples.

4.4.1 Key Lemma

We now derive the main idea behind an algorithm to compute singular vectors. Let $U\Sigma V^T$ be a (compact) SVD of A. Because of the orthogonality of U and V, the powers of $A^T A$ have a simple representation. Indeed

$$B = A^T A = (U\Sigma V^T)^T (U\Sigma V^T) = V\Sigma^T U^T U\Sigma V^T = V\Sigma^T \Sigma V^T.$$

Note that this formula is closely related to our previously uncovered connection between the SVD and the spectral decomposition of $A^T A$ – although it is not quite a spectral decomposition of $A^T A$ since V is not orthogonal.

Iterating,

$$B^2 = (V\Sigma^T \Sigma V^T)(V\Sigma^T \Sigma V^T) = V(\Sigma^T \Sigma)^2 V^T,$$

and, for general k,

$$B^k = V(\Sigma^T \Sigma)^k V^T.$$

Hence, defining

$$\widetilde{\Sigma} = \Sigma^T \Sigma = \begin{pmatrix} \sigma_1^2 & 0 & \cdots & 0 \\ 0 & \sigma_2^2 & \cdots & 0 \\ \vdots & \vdots & \ddots & \vdots \\ 0 & 0 & \cdots & \sigma_r^2 \end{pmatrix},$$

we see that

$$\widetilde{\Sigma}^k = \begin{pmatrix} \sigma_1^{2k} & 0 & \cdots & 0 \\ 0 & \sigma_2^{2k} & \cdots & 0 \\ \vdots & \vdots & \ddots & \vdots \\ 0 & 0 & \cdots & \sigma_r^{2k} \end{pmatrix}.$$

When $\sigma_1 > \sigma_2, \ldots, \sigma_r$, which is typically the case with real datasets, we get that $\sigma_1^{2k} \gg \sigma_2^{2k}, \ldots, \sigma_r^{2k}$ when k is large. Then, we get the approximation

$$B^k = \sum_{j=1}^{r} \sigma_j^{2k} \mathbf{v}_j \mathbf{v}_j^T \approx \sigma_1^{2k} \mathbf{v}_1 \mathbf{v}_1^T.$$

Finally, we arrive at:

Lemma 4.4.1 *(Power Iteration)* *Let $A \in \mathbb{R}^{n \times m}$ be a matrix and let $U \Sigma V^T$ be a (compact) SVD of A such that $\sigma_1 > \sigma_2 > 0$. Define $B = A^T A$ and assume that $\mathbf{x} \in \mathbb{R}^m$ is a vector satisfying $\langle \mathbf{v}_1, \mathbf{x} \rangle > 0$. Then*

$$\frac{B^k \mathbf{x}}{\|B^k \mathbf{x}\|} \to \mathbf{v}_1$$

as $k \to +\infty$. If instead $\langle \mathbf{v}_1, \mathbf{x} \rangle < 0$, then the limit is $-\mathbf{v}_1$.

Proof idea: We use the approximation above and divide by the norm to get a unit norm vector in the direction of $\mathbf{v}_1$.

Proof We have

$$B^k \mathbf{x} = \sum_{j=1}^{r} \sigma_j^{2k} \mathbf{v}_j \mathbf{v}_j^T \mathbf{x}.$$

So

$$\frac{B^k \mathbf{x}}{\|B^k \mathbf{x}\|} = \sum_{j=1}^{r} \mathbf{v}_j \frac{\sigma_j^{2k} (\mathbf{v}_j^T \mathbf{x})}{\|B^k \mathbf{x}\|}$$

$$= \mathbf{v}_1 \left\{ \frac{\sigma_1^{2k} (\mathbf{v}_1^T \mathbf{x})}{\|B^k \mathbf{x}\|} \right\} + \sum_{j=2}^{r} \mathbf{v}_j \left\{ \frac{\sigma_j^{2k} (\mathbf{v}_j^T \mathbf{x})}{\|B^k \mathbf{x}\|} \right\}.$$

This goes to $\mathbf{v}_1$ as $k \to +\infty$ if the expression in the first curly brackets goes to 1 and the one in the second curly brackets goes to 0. We prove this in the next claim.

Lemma 4.4.2 *As $k \to +\infty$,*

$$\frac{\sigma_1^{2k} (\mathbf{v}_1^T \mathbf{x})}{\|B^k \mathbf{x}\|} \to 1 \quad \text{and} \quad \frac{\sigma_j^{2k} (\mathbf{v}_j^T \mathbf{x})}{\|B^k \mathbf{x}\|} \to 0, \; j = 2, \ldots, r.$$

Proof Because the $\mathbf{v}_j$'s are an orthonormal basis,

$$\|B^k \mathbf{x}\|^2 = \sum_{j=1}^{r} \left[\sigma_j^{2k} (\mathbf{v}_j^T \mathbf{x}) \right]^2 = \sum_{j=1}^{r} \sigma_j^{4k} (\mathbf{v}_j^T \mathbf{x})^2.$$

So, as $k \to +\infty$, using the fact that $\langle \mathbf{v}_1, \mathbf{x} \rangle \neq 0$ by assumption,

$$\frac{\|B^k \mathbf{x}\|^2}{\sigma_1^{4k} (\mathbf{v}_1^T \mathbf{x})^2} = 1 + \sum_{j=2}^{r} \frac{\sigma_j^{4k} (\mathbf{v}_j^T \mathbf{x})^2}{\sigma_1^{4k} (\mathbf{v}_1^T \mathbf{x})^2}$$

$$= 1 + \sum_{j=2}^{r} \left(\frac{\sigma_j}{\sigma_1} \right)^{4k} \frac{(\mathbf{v}_j^T \mathbf{x})^2}{(\mathbf{v}_1^T \mathbf{x})^2}$$

$$\to 1,$$

since $\sigma_j < \sigma_1$ for all $j = 2, \ldots, r$. That implies the first part of the claim by taking a square root and using $\langle \mathbf{v}_1, \mathbf{x} \rangle > 0$. The second part of the claim follows essentially from the same argument. $\square$

$\square$

Example 4.4.3 *(continued from Example 4.3.11)* *We revisit the example*

$$A = \begin{pmatrix} 1 & 0 \\ -1 & 0 \end{pmatrix}.$$

We previously computed its SVD and found that

$$\mathbf{v}_1 = \begin{pmatrix} 1 \\ 0 \end{pmatrix}.$$

This time we use the Power Iteration Lemma. *Here*

$$B = A^T A = \begin{pmatrix} 2 & 0 \\ 0 & 0 \end{pmatrix}.$$

Taking powers of this matrix is easy:

$$B^k = \begin{pmatrix} 2^k & 0 \\ 0 & 0 \end{pmatrix}.$$

Let's choose an arbitrary initial vector $\mathbf{x}$, *say* $(-1, 2)$. *Then*

$$B^k \mathbf{x} = \begin{pmatrix} -2^k \\ 0 \end{pmatrix} \quad \text{and} \quad \|B^k \mathbf{x}\| = 2^k.$$

So

$$\frac{B^k \mathbf{x}}{\|B^k \mathbf{x}\|} \to \begin{pmatrix} -1 \\ 0 \end{pmatrix} = -\mathbf{v}_1,$$

as $k \to +\infty$. *In fact, in this case, convergence occurs after one step.*

The argument leading to the *Power Iteration Lemma* also holds more generally for the eigenvectors of positive semidefinite matrices. Let A be a symmetric, positive semidefinite matrix in $\mathbb{R}^{d \times d}$. By the *Spectral Theorem*, it has an eigenvector decomposition

$$A = Q \Lambda Q^T = \sum_{i=1}^{d} \lambda_i \mathbf{q}_i \mathbf{q}_i^T$$

where further $0 \leq \lambda_d \leq \cdots \leq \lambda_1$ by the *Characterization of Positive Semidefiniteness*. Because of the orthogonality of Q, the powers of A have a simple representation. The square gives

$$A^2 = (Q \Lambda Q^T)(Q \Lambda Q^T) = Q \Lambda^2 Q^T.$$

Repeating, we obtain

$$A^k = Q \Lambda^k Q^T.$$

This leads to the following version of the *Power Iteration Lemma* for the positive semidefinite case:

Lemma 4.4.4 *(Power Iteration) Let A be a symmetric, positive semidefinite matrix in $\mathbb{R}^{d \times d}$ with eigenvector decomposition $A = Q \Lambda Q^T$ where the eigenvalues satisfy $0 \le \lambda_d \le \cdots \le \lambda_2 < \lambda_1$. Assume that $\mathbf{x} \in \mathbb{R}^d$ is a vector such that $\langle \mathbf{q}_1, \mathbf{x} \rangle > 0$. Then*

$$\frac{A^k \mathbf{x}}{\|A^k \mathbf{x}\|} \to \mathbf{q}_1$$

as $k \to +\infty$. If instead $\langle \mathbf{q}_1, \mathbf{x} \rangle < 0$, then the limit is $-\mathbf{q}_1$.

The proof is similar to the case of singular vectors.

4.4.2 Computing the Top Singular Vector

Power iteration gives us a way to compute $\mathbf{v}_1$ – at least approximately if we use a large enough k. But how do we find an appropriate vector $\mathbf{x}$, as required by the *Power Iteration Lemma*? It turns out that a random vector will do. For instance, let $\mathbf{X}$ be an m-dimensional spherical Gaussian with mean 0 and variance 1. Then, $\mathbb{P}[\langle \mathbf{v}_1, \mathbf{X} \rangle = 0] = 0$.

We implement the algorithm suggested by the *Power Iteration Lemma*. That is, we compute $B^k \mathbf{x}$, then normalize it. To obtain the corresponding singular value and left singular vector, we use that $\sigma_1 = \|A \mathbf{v}_1\|$ and $\mathbf{u}_1 = A \mathbf{v}_1 / \sigma_1$.

```
def topsing(rng, A, maxiter=10):
    x = rng.normal(0,1,np.shape(A)[1])
    B = A.T @ A
    for _ in range(maxiter):
        x = B @ x
    v = x / LA.norm(x)
    s = LA.norm(A @ v)
    u = A @ v / s
    return u, s, v
```

NUMERICAL CORNER We will apply it to our previous two-cluster example. The necessary functions are in mmids.py, which is available on the GitHub for the book.[8]

```
seed = 42
rng = np.random.default_rng(seed)
d, n, w = 10, 100, 3.
X = mmids.two_mixed_clusters(rng, d, n, w)
plt.figure(figsize=(6,3))
plt.scatter(X[:,0], X[:,1], s=10, c='k')
plt.axis([-6,6,-3,3])
plt.show()
```

---

[8] Specifically, at https://github.com/MMiDS-textbook/

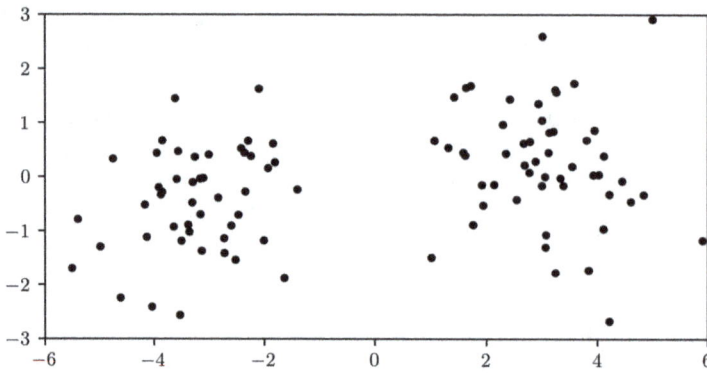

Figure 4.2 Graphical output of code.

Let's compute the top singular vector.

```
u, s, v = topsing(rng, X)
print(v)
```

```
[ 0.99257882  0.10164805  0.01581003  0.03202184  0.02075852  0.02798115
 -0.02920916 -0.028189   -0.0166094  -0.00648726]
```

This is approximately $-\mathbf{e}_1$. We get roughly the same answer (possibly up to sign) from Python's numpy.linalg.svd function.

```
u, s, vh = LA.svd(X)
print(vh.T[:,0])
```

```
[ 0.99257882  0.10164803  0.01581003  0.03202184  0.02075851  0.02798112
 -0.02920917 -0.028189   -0.01660938 -0.00648724]
```

Recall that, when we applied k-means clustering to this example with $d = 1000$ dimension, we obtained a very poor clustering.

```
d, n, w = 1000, 100, 3.
X = mmids.two_mixed_clusters(rng, d, n, w)

assign = mmids.kmeans(rng, X, 2)
```

99423.42794703908
99423.42794703908
99423.42794703908
99423.42794703908
99423.42794703908

```
plt.figure(figsize=(6,3))
plt.scatter(X[:,0], X[:,1], s=10, c=assign, cmap='brg')
```

```
plt.axis([-6,6,-3,3])
plt.show()
```

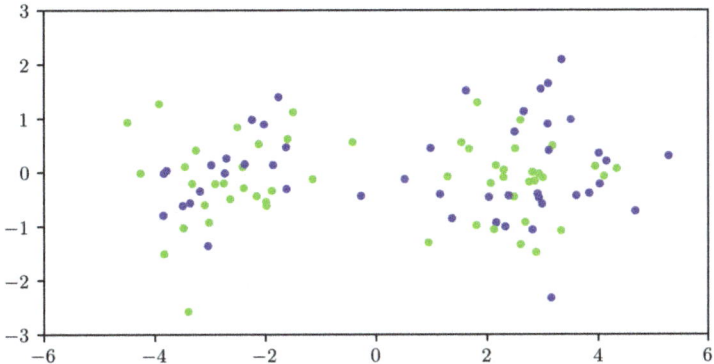

Figure 4.3 Graphical output of code.

Let's try again, but after projecting on the top singular vector. Recall that this corresponds to finding the best one-dimensional approximating subspace. The projection can be computed using the truncated SVD $Z = U_{(1)}\Sigma_{(1)}V_{(1)}^T$. We can interpret the rows of $U_{(1)}\Sigma_{(1)}$ as the coefficients of each data point in the basis $\mathbf{v}_1$. We will work in that basis. We need one small hack: Because our implementation of k-means clustering expects data points in at least two dimensions, we add a column of 0's.

```
u, s, v = topsing(rng, X)
Xproj = np.stack((u*s, np.zeros(np.shape(X)[0])), axis=-1)
fig = plt.figure()
ax = fig.add_subplot(111, aspect='equal')
ax.scatter(Xproj[:,0], Xproj[:,1], s=10, c='b', alpha=0.25)
plt.ylim([-3,3])
plt.show()
```

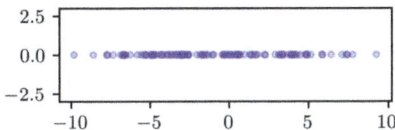

Figure 4.4 Graphical output of code.

There is a small – yet noticeable – gap around 0. We run k-means clustering on the projected data.

```
assign = mmids.kmeans(rng, Xproj, 2)
```

1779.020119584778
514.1899426112672

```
514.1899426112672
514.1899426112672
514.1899426112672
```

```
plt.figure(figsize=(6,3))
plt.scatter(X[:,0], X[:,1], s=10, c=assign, cmap='brg')
plt.axis([-6,6,-3,3])
plt.show()
```

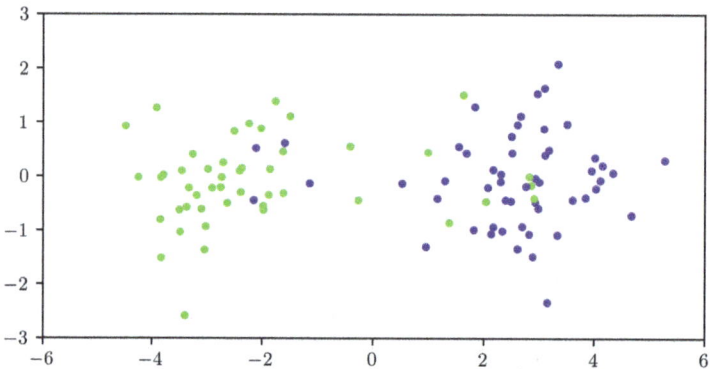

Figure 4.5 Graphical output of code.

Much better. We give a more formal explanation of this outcome in Section 4.6.2. In essence, quoting [BHK, Section 7.5.1]:

> [...] let's understand the central advantage of doing the projection to [the top k right singular vectors]. It is simply that for any reasonable (unknown) clustering of data points, the projection brings data points closer to their cluster centers.

Finally, looking at the top right singular vector (or its first ten entries for lack of space), we see that it does align quite well (but not perfectly) with the first dimension.

```
print(v[:10])
```

```
[-0.55564563 -0.02433674  0.02193487 -0.0333936  -0.00445505 -0.00243003
  0.02576056  0.02523275 -0.00682153  0.02524646]
```

◁ **NC**

CHAT & LEARN There are other methods to compute the SVD. Ask your favorite AI chatbot about randomized algorithms for the SVD. What are their advantages in terms of computational efficiency for large matrices?

Self-Assessment Quiz (with help from Claude, Gemini, and ChatGPT)

1. In the *Power Iteration Lemma* for the positive semidefinite case, what happens when the initial vector $\mathbf{x}$ satisfies $\langle \mathbf{q}_1, \mathbf{x} \rangle < 0$?
    a) The iteration converges to $\mathbf{q}_1$.
    b) The iteration converges to $-\mathbf{q}_1$.
    c) The iteration does not converge.
    d) The iteration converges to a random eigenvector.

2. In the *Power Iteration Lemma* for the SVD case, what is the convergence result for a random vector $\mathbf{x}$?
    a) $B^k\mathbf{x}/\|B^k\mathbf{x}\|$ converges to $\mathbf{u}_1$.
    b) $B^k\mathbf{x}/\|B^k\mathbf{x}\|$ converges to $\mathbf{v}_1$ or $-\mathbf{v}_1$.
    c) $B^k\mathbf{x}/\|B^k\mathbf{x}\|$ converges to σ_1.
    d) $B^k\mathbf{x}/\|B^k\mathbf{x}\|$ does not converge.

3. Suppose you apply the power iteration method to a matrix A and obtain a vector $\mathbf{v}$. How can you compute the corresponding singular value σ and left singular vector $\mathbf{u}$?
    a) $\sigma = \|A\mathbf{v}\|$ and $\mathbf{u} = A\mathbf{v}/\sigma$
    b) $\sigma = \|A^T\mathbf{v}\|$ and $\mathbf{u} = A^T\mathbf{v}/\sigma$
    c) $\sigma = \|\mathbf{v}\|$ and $\mathbf{u} = \mathbf{v}/\sigma$
    d) $\sigma = 1$ and $\mathbf{u} = A\mathbf{v}$

4. What is required for the initial vector $\mathbf{x}$ in the power iteration method to ensure convergence to the top eigenvector?
    a) $\mathbf{x}$ must be a zero vector.
    b) $\mathbf{x}$ must be orthogonal to the top eigenvector.
    c) $\langle \mathbf{q}_1, \mathbf{x} \rangle \neq 0$.
    d) $\mathbf{x}$ must be the top eigenvector itself.

5. What does the truncated SVD $Z = U_{(2)}\Sigma_{(2)}V_{(2)}^T$ correspond to?
    a) The best one-dimensional approximating subspace
    b) The best two-dimensional approximating subspace
    c) The projection of the data onto the top singular vector
    d) The projection of the data onto the top two singular vectors

Answer for 1: b. Justification: The lemma states that if $\langle \mathbf{q}_1, \mathbf{x} \rangle < 0$, then the limit of $A^k\mathbf{x}/\|A^k\mathbf{x}\|$ is $-\mathbf{q}_1$.

Answer for 2: b. Justification: The lemma states that if $\langle \mathbf{v}_1, \mathbf{x} \rangle > 0$, then $B^k\mathbf{x}/\|B^k\mathbf{x}\|$ converges to $\mathbf{v}_1$, and if $\langle \mathbf{v}_1, \mathbf{x} \rangle < 0$, then the limit is $-\mathbf{v}_1$.

Answer for 3: a. Justification: The text provides these formulas in the "Numerical Corner" section.

Answer for 4: c. Justification: The key lemma states that convergence is ensured if $\mathbf{x}$ is such that $\langle \mathbf{q}_1, \mathbf{x} \rangle \neq 0$.

> Answer for 5: d. Justification: The text states that "projecting on the top two singular vectors ... corresponds to finding the best two-dimensional approximating subspace. The projection can be computed using the truncated SVD $Z = U_{(2)}\Sigma_{(2)}V_{(2)}^T$."

4.5 Application: Principal Components Analysis

We discuss an application to principal components analysis and revisit our genetic dataset from ealier in the chapter.

4.5.1 Dimensionality Reduction via Principal Components Analysis (PCA)

Principal components analysis (PCA) is a commonly used dimensionality reduction approach that is closely related to what we described in the previous sections. We formalize the connection.

The data matrix: In PCA we are given n data points $\mathbf{x}_1, \ldots, \mathbf{x}_n \in \mathbb{R}^p$ with p features (i.e., coordinates). We denote the components of $\mathbf{x}_i$ as $(x_{i1}, \ldots, x_{ip})$. As usual, we stack them up into a matrix X whose i-th row is $\mathbf{x}_i^T$.

The first step of PCA is to center the data; that is, we assume that

$$\frac{1}{n}\sum_{i=1}^n x_{ij} = 0, \qquad j = 1, \ldots, p.$$

Put differently, the empirical mean of each column is 0. Quoting Wikipedia (and this will become clearer below)[9]:

> Mean subtraction (a.k.a. "mean centering") is necessary for performing classical PCA to ensure that the first principal component describes the direction of maximum variance. If mean subtraction is not performed, the first principal component might instead correspond more or less to the mean of the data. A mean of zero is needed for finding a basis that minimizes the mean square error of the approximation of the data.

An optional step is to divide each column by the square root of its sample variance, equivalent to assuming that

$$\frac{1}{n-1}\sum_{i=1}^n x_{ij}^2 = 1, \qquad j = 1, \ldots, p.$$

As we mentioned in Section 3.6.2, this is particularly important when the features are measured in different units to ensure that their variability can be meaningfully compared.

The first principal component: The first principal component is the linear combination of the features

$$t_{i1} = \phi_{11}x_{i1} + \cdots + \phi_{p1}x_{ip}$$

---

[9] https://en.wikipedia.org/wiki/Principal_component_analysis

with largest sample variance. For this to make sense, we need to constrain the ϕ_{j1}'s. Specifically, we require

$$\sum_{j=1}^{p} \phi_{j1}^2 = 1.$$

The ϕ_{j1}'s are referred to as the *loadings* and the t_{i1}'s are referred to as the *scores*.

Formally, we seek to solve

$$\max\left\{\frac{1}{n-1}\sum_{i=1}^{n}\left(\sum_{j=1}^{p}\phi_{j1}x_{ij}\right)^2 : \sum_{j=1}^{p}\phi_{j1}^2 = 1\right\},$$

where we used the fact that the t_{i1}'s are centered,

$$\frac{1}{n}\sum_{i=1}^{n} t_{i1} = \frac{1}{n}\sum_{i=1}^{n}[\phi_{11}x_{i1} + \cdots + \phi_{p1}x_{ip}]$$

$$= \phi_{11}\frac{1}{n}\sum_{i=1}^{n} x_{i1} + \cdots + \phi_{p1}\frac{1}{n}\sum_{i=1}^{n} x_{ip}$$

$$= 0,$$

to compute their sample variance as the mean of their square:

$$\frac{1}{n-1}\sum_{i=1}^{n} t_{i1}^2 = \frac{1}{n-1}\sum_{i=1}^{n}\left(\sum_{j=1}^{p}\phi_{j1}x_{ij}\right)^2.$$

Let $\boldsymbol{\phi}_1 = (\phi_{11}, \ldots, \phi_{p1})$ and $\mathbf{t}_1 = (t_{11}, \ldots, t_{n1})$. Then for all i

$$t_{i1} = \mathbf{x}_i^T \boldsymbol{\phi}_1,$$

or in vector form

$$\mathbf{t}_1 = X\boldsymbol{\phi}_1.$$

Also

$$\frac{1}{n-1}\sum_{i=1}^{n} t_{i1}^2 = \frac{1}{n-1}\|\mathbf{t}_1\|^2 = \frac{1}{n-1}\|X\boldsymbol{\phi}_1\|^2.$$

Rewriting the maximization problem above in vector form,

$$\max\left\{\frac{1}{n-1}\|X\boldsymbol{\phi}_1\|^2 : \|\boldsymbol{\phi}_1\|^2 = 1\right\},$$

we see that we have already encountered this problem (up to the factor of $1/(n-1)$ which does not affect the solution). The solution is to take $\boldsymbol{\phi}_1$ to be the top right singular vector of $\frac{1}{\sqrt{n-1}}X$ (or simply X). As we know, this is equivalent to computing the top eigenvector of the matrix $\frac{1}{n-1}X^TX$, which is the sample covariance matrix of the data (accounting for the fact that the data is already centered).

The second principal component: The second principal component is the linear combination of the features

$$t_{i2} = \phi_{12} x_{i1} + \cdots + \phi_{p2} x_{ip}$$

with largest sample variance that is also uncorrelated with the first principal component, in the sense that

$$\frac{1}{n-1} \sum_{i=1}^{n} t_{i1} t_{i2} = 0.$$

The next lemma shows how to deal with this condition. Again, we also require

$$\sum_{j=1}^{p} \phi_{j2}^2 = 1.$$

As before, let $\boldsymbol{\phi}_2 = (\phi_{12}, \ldots, \phi_{p2})$ and $\mathbf{t}_2 = (t_{12}, \ldots, t_{n2})$.

Lemma 4.5.1 *(Uncorrelated Principal Components)* Assume $X \neq 0$. Let t_{i1}, t_{i2}, $\boldsymbol{\phi}_1$, $\boldsymbol{\phi}_2$ be as above (where, in particular, $\boldsymbol{\phi}_1$ is a top right singular vector of X). Then

$$\frac{1}{n-1} \sum_{i=1}^{n} t_{i1} t_{i2} = 0$$

holds if and only if

$$\langle \boldsymbol{\phi}_1, \boldsymbol{\phi}_2 \rangle = 0.$$

Proof The condition

$$\frac{1}{n-1} \sum_{i=1}^{n} t_{i1} t_{i2} = 0$$

is equivalent to

$$\langle \mathbf{t}_1, \mathbf{t}_2 \rangle = 0,$$

where we dropped the $1/(n-1)$ factor as it does not play any role. Using the fact that $\mathbf{t}_1 = X\boldsymbol{\phi}_1$, and similarly $\mathbf{t}_2 = X\boldsymbol{\phi}_2$, this is in turn equivalent to

$$\langle X\boldsymbol{\phi}_1, X\boldsymbol{\phi}_2 \rangle = 0.$$

Because $\boldsymbol{\phi}_1$ can be chosen as a top right singular vector in an SVD of X, it follows from the *SVD Relations Lemma* that $X^T X \boldsymbol{\phi}_1 = \sigma_1^2 \boldsymbol{\phi}_1$, where σ_1 is the singular value associated with $\boldsymbol{\phi}_1$. Since $X \neq 0$, $\sigma_1 > 0$. Plugging this in the inner product on the left-hand side above, we get

$$\begin{aligned}
\langle X\boldsymbol{\phi}_1, X\boldsymbol{\phi}_2 \rangle &= \langle X\boldsymbol{\phi}_2, X\boldsymbol{\phi}_1 \rangle \\
&= (X\boldsymbol{\phi}_2)^T (X\boldsymbol{\phi}_1) \\
&= \boldsymbol{\phi}_2^T X^T X \boldsymbol{\phi}_1 \\
&= \boldsymbol{\phi}_2^T (\sigma_1^2 \boldsymbol{\phi}_1) \\
&= \langle \boldsymbol{\phi}_2, \sigma_1^2 \boldsymbol{\phi}_1 \rangle \\
&= \sigma_1^2 \langle \boldsymbol{\phi}_1, \boldsymbol{\phi}_2 \rangle.
\end{aligned}$$

Because $\sigma_1 \neq 0$, this is 0 if and only if $\langle \boldsymbol{\phi}_1, \boldsymbol{\phi}_2 \rangle = 0$. □

4.5 Application: Principal Components Analysis

As a result, we can write the maximization problem for the second principal component in matrix form as

$$\max \left\{ \frac{1}{n-1} \|X\phi_2\|^2 : \|\phi_2\|^2 = 1, \langle \phi_1, \phi_2 \rangle = 0 \right\}.$$

Again, we see that we have encountered this problem before. The solution is to take ϕ_2 to be a second right singular vector in an SVD of $\frac{1}{\sqrt{n-1}}X$ (or simply X). Again, this is equivalent to computing the second eigenvector of the sample covariance matrix $\frac{1}{n-1}X^TX$.

Further principal components: We can proceed in a similar fashion and define further principal components.

To quote Wikipedia[10]:

> PCA essentially rotates the set of points around their mean in order to align with the principal components. This moves as much of the variance as possible (using an orthogonal transformation) into the first few dimensions. The values in the remaining dimensions, therefore, tend to be small and may be dropped with minimal loss of information [...] PCA is often used in this manner for dimensionality reduction. PCA has the distinction of being the optimal orthogonal transformation for keeping the subspace that has largest "variance" [...]

Formally, let

$$X = U\Sigma V^T$$

be the SVD of the data matrix X. The principal component transformation, truncated at the ℓ-th component, is

$$T = XV_{(\ell)},$$

where T is the matrix whose columns are the vectors $\mathbf{t}_1, \ldots, \mathbf{t}_\ell$. Recall that $V_{(\ell)}$ is the matrix made of the first k columns of V.

Then, using the orthonormality of the right singular vectors,

$$T = U\Sigma V^T V_{(\ell)} = U\Sigma \begin{bmatrix} I_{\ell \times \ell} \\ \mathbf{0}_{(p-\ell) \times \ell} \end{bmatrix} = U \begin{bmatrix} \Sigma_{(\ell)} \\ \mathbf{0}_{(p-\ell) \times \ell} \end{bmatrix} = U_{(\ell)} \Sigma_{(\ell)}.$$

Put differently, the vector $\mathbf{t}_i$ is the left singular vector $\mathbf{u}_i$ scaled by the corresponding singular value σ_i.

Having established a formal connection between PCA and SVD, we implement PCA using the SVD algorithm numpy.linalg.svd. We perform mean centering (now is the time to read that quote about the importance of mean centering again), but not the optional standardization. We use the fact that, in NumPy, subtracting a matrix by a vector whose dimension matches the number of columns performs row-wise subtraction.

```
def pca(X, l):
    mean = np.mean(X, axis=0)
    Y = X - mean
    U, S, Vt = LA.svd(Y, full_matrices=False)
    return U[:, :l] @ np.diag(S[:l])
```

---

[10] https://en.wikipedia.org/wiki/Principal_component_analysis

NUMERICAL CORNER We apply PCA to the Gaussian mixture model.

```
seed = 535
rng = np.random.default_rng(seed)
d, n, w = 1000, 100, 3.
X = mmids.two_mixed_clusters(rng, d, n, w)
T = pca(X, 2)
```

Plotting the result, we see that PCA does succeed in finding the main direction of variation. Note the gap in the middle.

```
fig = plt.figure()
ax = fig.add_subplot(111,aspect='equal')
ax.scatter(T[:,0], T[:,1], s=5, c='k')
plt.show()
```

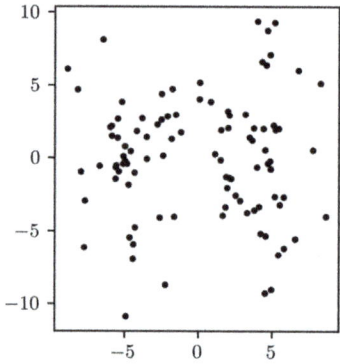

Figure 4.6 Graphical output of code.

Note however that the first two principal components in fact "capture more noise" than what can be seen in the orginal first two coordinates, a form of overfitting.

TRY IT! *Compute the first two right singular vectors* v_1 *and* v_2 *of X after mean centering.* Do they align well with the first and second standard basis vectors e_1 and e_2? Why or why not?

◁ NC

We return to our motivating example. We apply PCA to our genetic dataset.

NUMERICAL CORNER We load the dataset again. Recall that it contains 1642 strains and lives in a 317-dimensional space.

4.5 Application: Principal Components Analysis

```
data = pd.read_csv('h3n2-snp.csv')
```

Our goal is to find a "good" low-dimensional representation of the data. We work with 10 dimensions using PCA.

```
A = data[[data.columns[i] for i in range(1,len(data.columns))]].
        to_numpy()
n_dims = 10
T = pca(A, n_dims)
```

We plot the first two principal components, and see what appears to be some potential structure.

```
plt.figure(figsize=(5,3))
plt.scatter(T[:,0], T[:,1], s=10, c='k')
plt.axis([-3,6,-3,3])
plt.show()
```

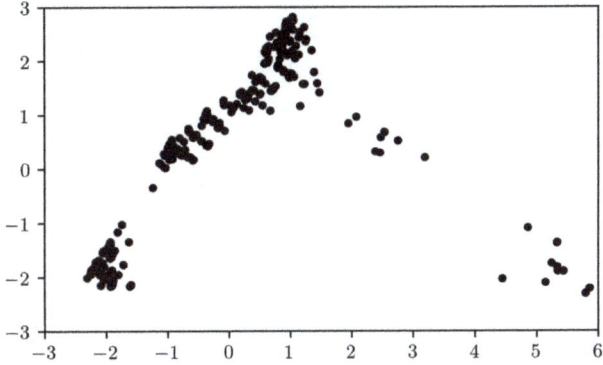

Figure 4.7 Graphical output of code.

There seem to be some reasonably well-defined clusters in this projection. We use k-means to identiy clusters. We take advantage of the implementation in scikit-learn, sklearn.cluster.KMeans. By default, it finds eight clusters. The clusters can be extracted from the attribute labels_.

```
from sklearn.cluster import KMeans

n_clusters = 8
kmeans = KMeans(n_clusters=n_clusters, init='k-means++',
                random_state=seed, n_init=10).fit(T)
assign = kmeans.labels_
```

To further reveal the structure, we look at our the clusters spread out over the years. That information is in a separate file.

```
data_oth = pd.read_csv('h3n2-other.csv')
data_oth.head()
```

	strain	length	country	year	lon	lat	date
0	AB434107	1701	Japan	2002	137.215474	35.584176	2002/02/25
1	AB434108	1701	Japan	2002	137.215474	35.584176	2002/03/01
2	CY000113	1762	USA	2002	-73.940000	40.670000	2002/01/29
3	CY000209	1760	USA	2002	-73.940000	40.670000	2002/01/17
4	CY000217	1760	USA	2002	-73.940000	40.670000	2002/02/26

```
year = data_oth['year'].to_numpy()
```

For each cluster, we plot how many of its data points come from a specific year. Each cluster has a different color.

```
fig, ax = plt.subplots(figsize=(6,4))

for i in range(n_clusters):
    unique, counts = np.unique(year[assign == i], return_counts=True)
    ax.bar(unique, counts, label=i)

ax.set(xlim=(2001, 2007), xticks=np.arange(2002, 2007))
ax.legend()
plt.show()
```

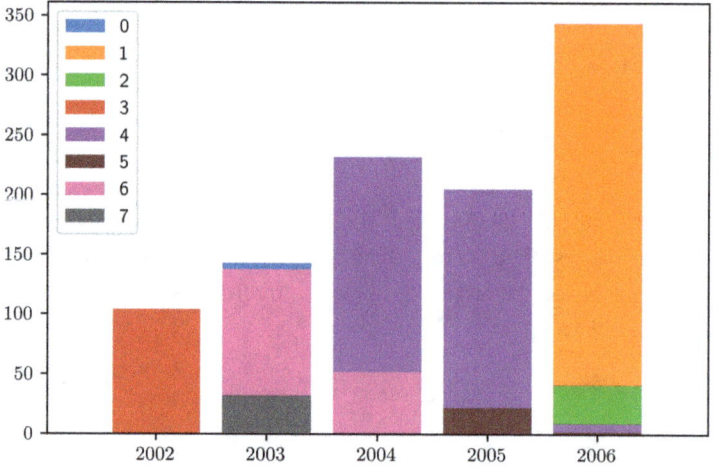

Figure 4.8 Graphical output of code.

Remarkably, we see that each cluster comes mostly from one year or two consecutive ones. In other words, the clustering in this low-dimensional projection captures some true underlying structure that is not explicitly in the genetic data on which it is computed.

4.5 Application: Principal Components Analysis

Going back to the first two principal components, we color the points on the scatter plot by year. (We use `legend_elements` for automatic legend creation.)

```
fig = plt.figure(figsize=(5,3))
ax = fig.add_subplot(111, aspect='equal')
scatter = ax.scatter(T[:,0], T[:,1], s=10, c=year, label=year)
plt.legend(*scatter.legend_elements())
plt.show()
```

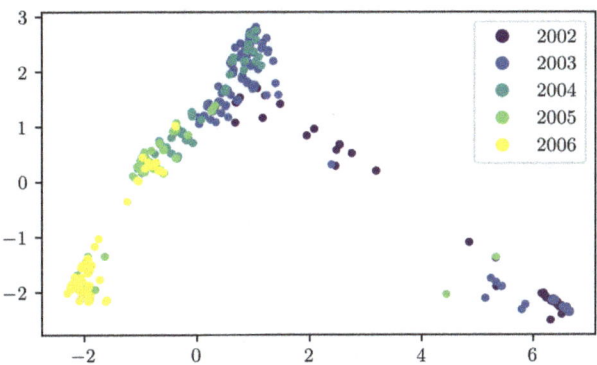

Figure 4.9 Graphical output of code.

To some extent, one can "see" the virus evolving from year to year. The x-axis in particular seems to correlate strongly with the year, in the sense that samples from later years tend to be toward one side of the plot.

To further quantify this observation, we use `numpy.corrcoef` to compute the correlation coefficients between the year and the first 10 principal components.

```
corr = np.zeros(n_dims)
for i in range(n_dims):
    corr[i] = np.corrcoef(np.stack((T[:,i], year)))[0,1]

print(corr)
```

[-0.7905001 -0.42806325 0.0870437 -0.16839491 0.05757342 -0.06046913
 -0.07920042 0.01436618 -0.02544749 0.04314641]

Indeed, we see that the first three or four principal components correlate well with the year.

Using related techniques, one can also identify which mutations distinguish different epidemics (i.e., years).

◁ **NC**

CHAT & LEARN Ask your favorite AI chatbot about the difference between principal components analysis (PCA) and linear discriminant analysis (LDA).

Self-Assessment Quiz (with help from Claude, Gemini, and ChatGPT)

1. What is the goal of principal components analysis (PCA)?
   a) To find clusters in the data
   b) To find a low-dimensional representation of the data that captures the maximum variance
   c) To find the mean of each feature in the data
   d) To find the correlation between features in the data

2. Formally, the first principal component is the linear combination of features $t_{i1} = \sum_{j=1}^{p} \phi_{j1} x_{ij}$ that solves which optimization problem?
   a) $\max \left\{ \frac{1}{n-1} \|X\phi_1\|^2 : \|\phi_1\|^2 = 1 \right\}$
   b) $\min \left\{ \frac{1}{n-1} \|X\phi_1\|^2 : \|\phi_1\|^2 = 1 \right\}$
   c) $\max \left\{ \frac{1}{n-1} \|X\phi_1\|^2 : \|\phi_1\|^2 \leq 1 \right\}$
   d) $\min \left\{ \frac{1}{n-1} \|X\phi_1\|^2 : \|\phi_1\|^2 \leq 1 \right\}$

3. What is the relationship between the loadings in PCA and the singular vectors of the data matrix?
   a) The loadings are the left singular vectors.
   b) The loadings are the right singular vectors.
   c) The loadings are the singular values.
   d) There is no direct relationship between loadings and singular vectors.

4. What is the dimensionality of the matrix T in the principal component transformation $T = XV^{(l)}$?
   a) $n \times p$
   b) $n \times l$
   c) $l \times p$
   d) $p \times l$

5. What is the purpose of centering the data in PCA?
   a) To make the calculations easier
   b) To ensure the first principal component describes the direction of maximum variance
   c) To normalize the data
   d) To remove outliers

Answer for 1: b. Justification: The text states that "Principal components analysis (PCA) is a commonly used dimensionality reduction approach" and that "The first principal component is the linear combination of the features ... with largest sample variance."

Answer for 2: a. Justification: The text states that "Formally, we seek to solve $\max \left\{ \frac{1}{n-1} \|X\phi_1\|^2 : \|\phi_1\|^2 = 1 \right\}$."

Answer for 3: b. Justification: The text explains that the solution to the PCA optimization problem is to take the loadings to be the top right singular vector of the data matrix.

Answer for 4: b. Justification: The matrix T contains the scores of the data points on the first l principal components. Since there are n data points and l principal components, the dimensionality of T is $n \times l$.

Answer for 5: b. Justification: The text mentions that "Mean subtraction (a.k.a. 'mean centering') is necessary for performing classical PCA to ensure that the first principal component describes the direction of maximum variance."

4.6 Further Applications of the SVD: Low-Rank Approximations and Ridge Regression

In this section, we discuss further properties of the SVD. We first introduce an additional matrix norm.

4.6.1 Matrix Norms

Recall that the Frobenius norm of an $n \times m$ matrix $A = (a_{i,j})_{i,j} \in \mathbb{R}^{n \times m}$ is defined as

$$\|A\|_F = \sqrt{\sum_{i=1}^{n} \sum_{j=1}^{m} a_{i,j}^2}.$$

Here we introduce a different notion of matrix norm that has many uses in data science (and beyond).

4.6.1.1 Induced Norm

The Frobenius norm does not directly relate to A as a representation of a linear map. In particular, it is desirable in many contexts to quantify how two matrices differ in terms of how they act on vectors. For instance, one is often interested in bounding quantities of the following form. Let $B, B' \in \mathbb{R}^{n \times m}$ and let $\mathbf{x} \in \mathbb{R}^m$ be of unit norm. What can be said about $\|B\mathbf{x} - B'\mathbf{x}\|$? Intuitively, what we would like is this: If the norm of $B - B'$ is small then B is close to B' as a linear map; that is, the vector norm $\|B\mathbf{x} - B'\mathbf{x}\|$ is small for any unit vector $\mathbf{x}$. The following definition provides us with such a notion. Define the unit sphere $\mathbb{S}^{m-1} = \{\mathbf{x} \in \mathbb{R}^m : \|\mathbf{x}\| = 1\}$ in m dimensions.

Definition 4.6.1 (*2-Norm*) *The 2-norm of a matrix* $A \in \mathbb{R}^{n \times m}$ *is*

$$\|A\|_2 := \max_{\mathbf{0} \neq \mathbf{x} \in \mathbb{R}^m} \frac{\|A\mathbf{x}\|}{\|\mathbf{x}\|} = \max_{\mathbf{x} \in \mathbb{S}^{m-1}} \|A\mathbf{x}\|.$$

The equality in the definition uses the absolute homogeneity of the vector norm. Also the definition implicitly uses the *Extreme Value Theorem*. In this case, we use the fact that the function $f(\mathbf{x}) = \|A\mathbf{x}\|$ is continuous and the set $\mathbb{S}^{m-1}$ is closed and bounded to conclude that there exists $\mathbf{x}^* \in \mathbb{S}^{m-1}$ such that $f(\mathbf{x}^*) \geq f(\mathbf{x})$ for all $\mathbf{x} \in \mathbb{S}^{m-1}$.

The 2-norm of a matrix has many other useful properties. The first four below are what makes it a norm.

Lemma 4.6.2 *(Properties of the 2-Norm) Let $A, B \in \mathbb{R}^{n \times m}$ and $\alpha \in \mathbb{R}$. The following hold:*

a) $\|A\|_2 \geq 0$

b) $\|A\|_2 = 0$ *if and only if* $A = 0$

c) $\|\alpha A\|_2 = |\alpha| \|A\|_2$

d) $\|A + B\|_2 \leq \|A\|_2 + \|B\|_2$

e) $\|AB\|_2 \leq \|A\|_2 \|B\|_2$

f) $\|A\mathbf{x}\| \leq \|A\|_2 \|\mathbf{x}\|$, $\forall \mathbf{0} \neq \mathbf{x} \in \mathbb{R}^m$

Proof These properties all follow from the definition of the 2-norm and the corresponding properties for the vector norm:

- Claims a) and f) are immediate from the definition.
- For b) note that $\|A\|_2 = 0$ implies $\|A\mathbf{x}\|_2 = 0, \forall \mathbf{x} \in \mathbb{S}^{m-1}$, so that $A\mathbf{x} = \mathbf{0}, \forall \mathbf{x} \in \mathbb{S}^{m-1}$. In particular, $a_{ij} = \mathbf{e}_i^T A \mathbf{e}_j = 0, \forall i, j$.
- For c), d), e), observe that for all $\mathbf{x} \in \mathbb{S}^{m-1}$

$$\|\alpha A \mathbf{x}\| = |\alpha| \|A\mathbf{x}\|,$$

$$\|(A + B)\mathbf{x}\| = \|A\mathbf{x} + B\mathbf{x}\| \leq \|A\mathbf{x}\| + \|B\mathbf{x}\| \leq \|A\|_2 + \|B\|_2$$

$$\|(AB)\mathbf{x}\| = \|A(B\mathbf{x})\| \leq \|A\|_2 \|B\mathbf{x}\| \leq \|A\|_2 \|B\|_2.$$

Then apply the definition of 2-norm. For example, for (c),

$$\begin{aligned}\|\alpha A\|_2 &= \max_{\mathbf{x} \in \mathbb{S}^{m-1}} \|\alpha A \mathbf{x}\| \\ &= \max_{\mathbf{x} \in \mathbb{S}^{m-1}} |\alpha| \|A\mathbf{x}\| \\ &= |\alpha| \max_{\mathbf{x} \in \mathbb{S}^{m-1}} \|A\mathbf{x}\| \\ &= |\alpha| \|A\|_2,\end{aligned}$$

where we used the fact that $|\alpha|$ does not depend on $\mathbf{x}$. $\square$

NUMERICAL CORNER In NumPy, the Frobenius norm of a matrix can be computed using the default of the function `numpy.linalg.norm` while the induced norm can be computed using the same function with `ord` parameter set to 2.

```
A = np.array([[1., 0.],[0., 1.],[0., 0.]])
print(A)
```

```
[[1. 0.]
 [0. 1.]
 [0. 0.]]
```

```
LA.norm(A)
```

1.4142135623730951

```
LA.norm(A, 2)
```

1.0

◁ **NC**

4.6.1.2 Matrix Norms and SVD

As it turns out, the two notions of matrix norms we have introduced admit simple expressions in terms of the singular values of the matrix.

Lemma 4.6.3 *(Matrix Norms and Singular Values)* Let $A \in \mathbb{R}^{n \times m}$ be a matrix with compact SVD

$$A = \sum_{\ell=1}^{r} \sigma_\ell \mathbf{u}_\ell \mathbf{v}_\ell^T$$

where recall that $\sigma_1 \geq \sigma_2 \geq \cdots \sigma_r > 0$. Then

$$\|A\|_F^2 = \sum_{\ell=1}^{r} \sigma_\ell^2$$

and

$$\|A\|_2^2 = \sigma_1^2.$$

Proof We will use the notation $\mathbf{v}_\ell = (v_{\ell,1}, \ldots, v_{\ell,m})$. Using the fact that the squared Frobenius norm of A is the sum of the squared norms of its columns, we have

$$\|A\|_F^2 = \left\|\sum_{\ell=1}^{r} \sigma_\ell \mathbf{u}_\ell \mathbf{v}_\ell^T\right\|_F^2 = \sum_{j=1}^{m} \left\|\sum_{\ell=1}^{r} \sigma_\ell v_{\ell,j} \mathbf{u}_\ell\right\|^2.$$

Because the $\mathbf{u}_\ell$'s are orthonormal, this is

$$\sum_{j=1}^{m} \sum_{\ell=1}^{r} \sigma_\ell^2 v_{\ell,j}^2 = \sum_{\ell=1}^{r} \sigma_\ell^2 \left(\sum_{j=1}^{m} v_{\ell,j}^2\right) = \sum_{\ell=1}^{r} \sigma_\ell^2 \|\mathbf{v}_\ell\|^2 = \sum_{\ell=1}^{r} \sigma_\ell^2,$$

where we used the fact that the $\mathbf{v}_\ell$'s are also orthonormal.

For the second claim, recall that the 2-norm is defined as

$$\|A\|_2^2 = \max_{\mathbf{x} \in \mathbb{S}^{m-1}} \|A\mathbf{x}\|^2.$$

We have shown previously that $\mathbf{v}_1$ solves this problem. Hence $\|A\|_2^2 = \|A\mathbf{v}_1\|^2 = \sigma_1^2$. □

4.6.2 Low-Rank Approximation

Now that we have defined a notion of distance between matrices, we will consider the problem of finding a good approximation to a matrix A among all matrices of rank at most k. We will start with the Frobenius norm, which is easier to work with, and we will show later on that the solution is the same under the induced norm. The solution to this problem will be familiar. In essence, we will reinterpret our solution to the best approximating subspace as a low-rank approximation.

4.6.2.1 Low-Rank Approximation in the Frobenius Norm

From the proof of the *Row Rank Equals Column Rank Lemma*, it follows that a rank-r matrix A can be written as a sum of r rank-1 matrices,

$$A = \sum_{i=1}^{r} \mathbf{b}_i \mathbf{c}_i^T.$$

We will now consider the problem of finding a "simpler" approximation to A,

$$A \approx \sum_{i=1}^{k} \mathbf{b}_i' (\mathbf{c}_i')^T$$

where $k < r$. Here we measure the quality of this approximation using a matrix norm.

We are ready to state our key observation. In words, the best rank-k approximation to A in Frobenius norm is obtained by projecting the rows of A onto a linear subspace of dimension k. We will come back to how one finds the best such subspace below. (*Hint:* We have already solved this problem.)

Lemma 4.6.4 (*Projection and Rank-k Approximation*) Let $A = (a_{i,j})_{i,j} \in \mathbb{R}^{n \times m}$. For any matrix $B = (b_{i,j})_{i,j} \in \mathbb{R}^{n \times m}$ of rank $k \leq \min\{n, m\}$,

$$\|A - B_\perp\|_F \leq \|A - B\|_F$$

where $B_\perp \in \mathbb{R}^{n \times m}$ is the matrix of rank at most k obtained as follows. Denote row i of A, B, and $B_\perp$ respectively by $\boldsymbol{\alpha}_i^T$, $\mathbf{b}_i^T$, and $\mathbf{b}_{\perp,i}^T$, $i = 1, \ldots, n$. Set $\mathbf{b}_{\perp,i}$ to be the orthogonal projection of $\boldsymbol{\alpha}_i$ onto $\mathcal{Z} = \text{span}(\mathbf{b}_1, \ldots, \mathbf{b}_n)$.

Proof idea: The square of the Frobenius norm decomposes as a sum of squared row norms. Each term in the sum is minimized by the orthogonal projection.

Proof By definition of the Frobenius norm, we note that

$$\|A - B\|_F^2 = \sum_{i=1}^{n} \sum_{j=1}^{m} (a_{i,j} - b_{i,j})^2 = \sum_{i=1}^{n} \|\boldsymbol{\alpha}_i - \mathbf{b}_i\|^2$$

and similarly for $\|A - B_\perp\|_F$. We make two observations:

1. Because the orthogonal projection of $\boldsymbol{\alpha}_i$ onto $\mathcal{Z}$ minimizes the distance to $\mathcal{Z}$, it follows that term by term $\|\boldsymbol{\alpha}_i - \mathbf{b}_{\perp,i}\| \leq \|\boldsymbol{\alpha}_i - \mathbf{b}_i\|$, so that

$$\|A - B_\perp\|_F^2 = \sum_{i=1}^{n} \|\boldsymbol{\alpha}_i - \mathbf{b}_{\perp,i}\|^2 \leq \sum_{i=1}^{n} \|\boldsymbol{\alpha}_i - \mathbf{b}_i\|^2 = \|A - B\|_F^2.$$

2. Moreover, because the projections satisfy $\mathbf{b}_{\perp,i} \in \mathcal{Z}$ for all i, $\text{row}(B_\perp) \subseteq \text{row}(B)$ and, hence, the rank of $B_\perp$ is at most the rank of B.

That concludes the proof. □

Recall the approximating subspace problem. That is, think of the rows $\boldsymbol{\alpha}_i^T$ of $A \in \mathbb{R}^{n \times m}$ as a collection of n data points in $\mathbb{R}^m$. We are looking for a linear subspace $\mathcal{Z}$ that minimizes $\sum_{i=1}^n \|\boldsymbol{\alpha}_i - \text{proj}_\mathcal{Z}(\boldsymbol{\alpha}_i)\|^2$ over all linear subspaces of $\mathbb{R}^m$ of dimension at most k. By the *Projection and Rank-k Approximation Lemma*, this problem is equivalent to finding a matrix B that minimizes $\|A - B\|_F$ among all matrices in $\mathbb{R}^{n \times m}$ of rank at most k. Of course we have solved this problem before.

Let $A \in \mathbb{R}^{n \times m}$ be a matrix with SVD $A = \sum_{j=1}^r \sigma_j \mathbf{u}_j \mathbf{v}_j^T$. For $k < r$, truncate the sum at the k-th term $A_k = \sum_{j=1}^k \sigma_j \mathbf{u}_j \mathbf{v}_j^T$. The rank of A_k is exactly k. Indeed, by construction,

1. the vectors $\{\mathbf{u}_j : j = 1, \ldots, k\}$ are orthonormal, and
2. since $\sigma_j > 0$ for $j = 1, \ldots, k$ and the vectors $\{\mathbf{v}_j : j = 1, \ldots, k\}$ are orthonormal, $\{\mathbf{u}_j : j = 1, \ldots, k\}$ spans the column space of A_k.

We have shown before that A_k is the best approximation to A among matrices of rank at most k in Frobenius norm. Specifically, the *Greedy Finds Best Fit Theorem* implies that, for any matrix $B \in \mathbb{R}^{n \times m}$ of rank at most k,

$$\|A - A_k\|_F \leq \|A - B\|_F.$$

This result is known as the *Eckart–Young Theorem*. It also holds in the induced 2-norm, as we show next.

4.6.2.2 Low-Rank Approximation in the Induced Norm

We show in this section that the *Eckart–Young Theorem* holds in the induced norm. First, some observations.

Lemma 4.6.5 *(Matrix Norms and Singular Values: Truncation)* *Let $A \in \mathbb{R}^{n \times m}$ be a matrix with SVD*

$$A = \sum_{j=1}^r \sigma_j \mathbf{u}_j \mathbf{v}_j^T$$

where recall that $\sigma_1 \geq \sigma_2 \geq \cdots \sigma_r > 0$ and let A_k be the truncation defined above. Then

$$\|A - A_k\|_F^2 = \sum_{j=k+1}^r \sigma_j^2$$

and

$$\|A - A_k\|_2^2 = \sigma_{k+1}^2.$$

Proof For the first claim, by definition, summing over the columns of $A - A_k$,

$$\|A - A_k\|_F^2 = \left\| \sum_{j=k+1}^r \sigma_j \mathbf{u}_j \mathbf{v}_j^T \right\|_F^2 = \sum_{i=1}^m \left\| \sum_{j=k+1}^r \sigma_j v_{j,i} \mathbf{u}_j \right\|^2.$$

Because the $\mathbf{u}_j$'s are orthonormal, this is

$$\sum_{i=1}^{m} \sum_{j=k+1}^{r} \sigma_j^2 v_{j,i}^2 = \sum_{j=k+1}^{r} \sigma_j^2 \left(\sum_{i=1}^{m} v_{j,i}^2 \right) = \sum_{j=k+1}^{r} \sigma_j^2$$

where we used that the $\mathbf{v}_j$'s are also orthonormal.

For the second claim, recall that the induced norm is defined as

$$\|B\|_2 = \max_{\mathbf{x} \in \mathbb{S}^{m-1}} \|B\mathbf{x}\|.$$

For any $\mathbf{x} \in \mathbb{S}^{m-1}$,

$$\|(A - A_k)\mathbf{x}\|^2 = \left\| \sum_{j=k+1}^{r} \sigma_j \mathbf{u}_j (\mathbf{v}_j^T \mathbf{x}) \right\|^2 = \sum_{j=k+1}^{r} \sigma_j^2 \langle \mathbf{v}_j, \mathbf{x} \rangle^2.$$

Because the σ_j's are in decreasing order, this is maximized when $\langle \mathbf{v}_j, \mathbf{x} \rangle = 1$ if $j = k+1$ and 0 otherwise. That is, we take $\mathbf{x} = \mathbf{v}_{k+1}$ and the norm is then σ_{k+1}^2, as claimed. $\square$

Theorem 4.6.6 *(Low-Rank Approximation in the Induced Norm)* Let $A \in \mathbb{R}^{n \times m}$ be a matrix with SVD

$$A = \sum_{j=1}^{r} \sigma_j \mathbf{u}_j \mathbf{v}_j^T$$

and let A_k be the truncation defined above with $k < r$. For any matrix $B \in \mathbb{R}^{n \times m}$ of rank at most k,

$$\|A - A_k\|_2 \leq \|A - B\|_2.$$

Proof idea: We know that $\|A - A_k\|_2^2 = \sigma_{k+1}^2$. So we want to lower-bound $\|A - B\|_2^2$ by σ_{k+1}^2. For that, we have to find an appropriate $\mathbf{z}$ for any given B of rank at most k. The idea is to take a vector $\mathbf{z}$ in the intersection of the null space of B and the span of the singular vectors $\mathbf{v}_1, \ldots, \mathbf{v}_{k+1}$. By the former, the squared norm of $(A - B)\mathbf{z}$ is equal to the squared norm of $A\mathbf{z}$, which lower-bounds $\|A\|_2^2$. By the latter, $\|A\mathbf{z}\|^2$ is at least σ_{k+1}^2.

Proof By the *Rank-Nullity Theorem*, the dimension of null(B) is at least $m - k$ so there is a unit vector $\mathbf{z}$ in the intersection

$$\mathbf{z} \in \text{null}(B) \cap \text{span}(\mathbf{v}_1, \ldots, \mathbf{v}_{k+1}).$$

(Prove it!) Then $(A - B)\mathbf{z} = A\mathbf{z}$ since $\mathbf{z} \in \text{null}(B)$. Also since $\mathbf{z} \in \text{span}(\mathbf{v}_1, \ldots, \mathbf{v}_{k+1})$, and therefore orthogonal to $\mathbf{v}_{k+2}, \ldots, \mathbf{v}_r$, we have

$$\|(A - B)\mathbf{z}\|^2 = \|A\mathbf{z}\|^2$$

$$= \left\| \sum_{j=1}^{r} \sigma_j \mathbf{u}_j \mathbf{v}_j^T \mathbf{z} \right\|^2$$

$$= \left\| \sum_{j=1}^{k+1} \sigma_j \mathbf{u}_j \mathbf{v}_j^T \mathbf{z} \right\|^2$$

$$= \sum_{j=1}^{k+1} \sigma_j^2 \langle \mathbf{v}_j, \mathbf{z} \rangle^2$$

$$\geq \sigma_{k+1}^2 \sum_{j=1}^{k+1} \langle \mathbf{v}_j, \mathbf{z} \rangle^2$$

$$= \sigma_{k+1}^2.$$

By Lemma 4.6.5, $\sigma_{k+1}^2 = \|A - A_k\|_2$ and we are done. □

4.6.2.3 An Application: Why Project?

We return to k-means clustering and the question of why projecting to a lower-dimensional subspace can produce better results. We prove a simple inequality that provides some insight. Quoting [BHK, Section 7.5.1]:

> [...] let's understand the central advantage of doing the projection to [the top k right singular vectors]. It is simply that for any reasonable (unknown) clustering of data points, the projection brings data points closer to their cluster centers.

To elaborate, suppose we have n data points in d dimensions in the form of the rows α_i^T, $i = 1 \ldots, n$, of matrix $A \in \mathbb{A}^{n \times d}$, where we assume that $n > d$ and that A has full column rank. Imagine these data points come from an unknown ground-truth k-clustering assignment $g(i) \in [k]$, $i = 1, \ldots, n$, with corresponding unknown centers $\mathbf{c}_j$, $j = 1, \ldots, k$. Let $C \in \mathbb{R}^{n \times d}$ be the corresponding matrix; that is, row i of C is $\mathbf{c}_j^T$ if $g(i) = j$. The k-means objective of the true clustering is then

$$\sum_{j \in [k]} \sum_{i:\ g(i)=j} \|\alpha_i - \mathbf{c}_j\|^2 = \sum_{j \in [k]} \sum_{i:\ g(i)=j} \sum_{\ell=1}^{d} (a_{i,\ell} - c_{j,\ell})^2$$

$$= \sum_{i=1}^{n} \sum_{\ell=1}^{d} (a_{i,\ell} - c_{g(i),\ell})^2$$

$$= \|A - C\|_F^2.$$

The matrix A has an SVD $A = \sum_{j=1}^{r} \sigma_j \mathbf{u}_j \mathbf{v}_j^T$ and for $k < r$ we have the truncation $A_k = \sum_{j=1}^{k} \sigma_j \mathbf{u}_j \mathbf{v}_j^T$, which corresponds to projecting each row of A onto the linear subspace spanned by the first k right singular vectors $\mathbf{v}_1, \ldots, \mathbf{v}_k$. To see this, note that the i-th row of A is $\alpha_i^T = \sum_{j=1}^{r} \sigma_j u_{j,i} \mathbf{v}_j^T$ and that, because the $\mathbf{v}_j$'s are linearly independent and in particular $\mathbf{v}_1, \ldots, \mathbf{v}_k$ is an orthonormal basis of its span, the projection of α_i onto $\text{span}(\mathbf{v}_1, \ldots, \mathbf{v}_k)$ is

$$\sum_{\ell=1}^{k} \mathbf{v}_\ell \left\langle \sum_{j=1}^{r} \sigma_j u_{j,i} \mathbf{v}_j, \mathbf{v}_\ell \right\rangle = \sum_{\ell=1}^{k} \sigma_\ell u_{\ell,i} \mathbf{v}_\ell$$

which is the i-th row of A_k. The k-means objective of A_k with respect to the ground-truth centers $\mathbf{c}_j$, $j = 1, \ldots, k$, is $\|A_k - C\|_F^2$.

One more observation: The rank of C is at most k. Indeed, there are k different rows in C so its row rank is k if these different rows are linearly independent and less than k otherwise.

Theorem 4.6.7 *(Why Project)* Let $A \in \mathbb{A}^{n \times d}$ be a matrix and let A_k be the truncation above. For any matrix $C \in \mathbb{R}^{n \times d}$ of rank $\leq k$,

$$\|A_k - C\|_F^2 \leq 8k\|A - C\|_2^2.$$

Observe that we used different matrix norms on the different sides of the inequality. The content of this inequality is the following. The quantity $\|A_k - C\|_F^2$ is the k-means objective of the projection A_k with respect to the true centers; that is, the sum of the squared distances to the centers. By the *Matrix Norms and Singular Values Lemma*, the inequality above gives that

$$\|A_k - C\|_F^2 \leq 8k\sigma_1(A - C)^2,$$

where $\sigma_j(A - C)$ is the j-th singular value of $A - C$. On the other hand, by the same lemma, the k-means objective of the unprojected data is

$$\|A - C\|_F^2 = \sum_{j=1}^{\text{rk}(A-C)} \sigma_j(A - C)^2.$$

If the rank of $A - C$ is much larger than k and the singular values of $A - C$ decay slowly, then the latter quantity may be much larger. In other words, projecting may bring the data points closer to their true centers, potentially making it easier to cluster them.

Proof *(Why Project)* We have shown previously that, for any matrices $A, B \in \mathbb{R}^{n \times m}$, the rank of their sum is less than or equal to the sum of their ranks, that is, $\text{rk}(A + B) \leq \text{rk}(A) + \text{rk}(B)$. So the rank of the difference $A_k - C$ is at most the sum of the ranks

$$\text{rk}(A_k - C) \leq \text{rk}(A_k) + \text{rk}(-C) \leq 2k$$

where we used the fact that the rank of A_k is k and the rank of C is $\leq k$ since it has k distinct rows. By the *Matrix Norms and Singular Values Lemma*,

$$\|A_k - C\|_F^2 \leq 2k\|A_k - C\|_2^2.$$

By the triangle inequality for matrix norms,

$$\|A_k - C\|_2 \leq \|A_k - A\|_2 + \|A - C\|_2.$$

By the *Low-Rank Approximation in the Induced Norm Theorem*,

$$\|A - A_k\|_2 \leq \|A - C\|_2$$

since C has rank at most k. Putting these three inequalities together,

$$\|A_k - C\|_F^2 \leq 2k(2\|A - C\|_2)^2 = 8k\|A - C\|_2^2. \qquad \square$$

NUMERICAL CORNER We return to our example with the two Gaussian clusters. We use a function producing two separate clusters.

```
def two_separate_clusters(rng, d, n, w):

    mu0 = np.concatenate(([w], np.zeros(d-1)))
    mu1 = np.concatenate(([-w], np.zeros(d-1)))

    X0 = mmids.spherical_gaussian(rng, d, n, mu0, 1)
```

4.6 Further Applications of the SVD

```
    X1 = mmids.spherical_gaussian(rng, d, n, mu1, 1)

    return X0, X1
```

We first generate the data.

```
seed = 535
rng = np.random.default_rng(seed)
d, n, w = 1000, 100, 3.
X1, X2 = two_separate_clusters(rng, d, n, w)
X = np.vstack((X1, X2))
```

In reality, we cannot compute the matrix norms of $X - C$ and $X_k - C$ as the true centers are not known. But, because this is simulated data, we happen to know the truth and we can check the validity of our results in this case. The centers are:

```
C1 = np.stack([np.concatenate(([w], np.zeros(d-1)))
               for _ in range(n)])
C2 = np.stack([np.concatenate(([-w], np.zeros(d-1)))
               for _ in range(n)])
C = np.vstack((C1, C2))
```

We use numpy.linalg.svd function to compute the norms from the formulas in the *Matrix Norms and Singular Values Lemma*. First, we observe that the singular values of $X - C$ are decaying slowly.

```
uc, sc, vhc = LA.svd(X-C)
plt.plot(sc, c='k')
plt.show()
```

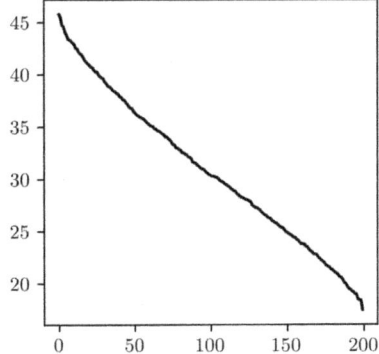

Figure 4.10 Graphical output of code.

The k-means objective with respect to the true centers under the full-dimensional data is:

```
print(np.sum(sc**2))
```

200925.669068181

while the square of the top singular value of $X - C$ is only:

```
print(sc[0]**2)
```

2095.357155856167

Finally, we compute the k-means objective with respect to the true centers under the projected one-dimensional data:

```
u, s, vh = LA.svd(X)
print(np.sum((s[0] * np.outer(u[:,0],vh[:,0]) - C)**2))
```

1614.2173799824254

◁ NC

CHAT & LEARN Ask your favorite AI chatbot about the applications of SVD in recommendation systems. How is it used to predict user preferences?

CHAT & LEARN Ask your favorite AI chatbot about nonnegative matrix factorization (NMF) and how it compares to SVD. What are the key differences in their constraints and applications? How does NMF handle interpretability in topics like text analysis or image processing? Explore some algorithms used to compute NMF.

4.6.3 Ridge Regression

Here we consider what is called Tikhonov regularization, an idea that turns out to be useful in overdetermined linear systems, particularly when the columns of the matrix A are linearly dependent or close to linearly dependent (which is sometimes referred to as multicollinearity in statistics). It trades off minimizing the fit to the data versus minimizing the norm of the solution. More precisely, for a parameter $\lambda > 0$ to be chosen, we solve

$$\min_{\mathbf{x} \in \mathbb{R}^m} \|A\mathbf{x} - \mathbf{b}\|_2^2 + \lambda \|\mathbf{x}\|_2^2.$$

The second term is referred to as an L_2-regularizer. Here $A \in \mathbb{R}^{n \times m}$ with $n \geq m$ and $\mathbf{b} \in \mathbb{R}^n$.

To solve this optimization problem, we show that the objective function is strongly convex. We then find its unique stationary point. Rewriting the objective in quadratic function form,

$$\begin{aligned} f(\mathbf{x}) &= \|A\mathbf{x} - \mathbf{b}\|_2^2 + \lambda \|\mathbf{x}\|_2^2 \\ &= \mathbf{x}^T A^T A \mathbf{x} - 2\mathbf{b}^T A \mathbf{x} + \mathbf{b}^T \mathbf{b} + \lambda \mathbf{x}^T \mathbf{x} \\ &= \mathbf{x}^T (A^T A + \lambda I_{m \times m}) \mathbf{x} - 2\mathbf{b}^T A \mathbf{x} + \mathbf{b}^T \mathbf{b} \\ &= \frac{1}{2} \mathbf{x}^T P \mathbf{x} + \mathbf{q}^T \mathbf{x} + r, \end{aligned}$$

where $P = 2(A^T A + \lambda I_{m \times m})$ is symmetric, $\mathbf{q} = -2A^T \mathbf{b}$, and $r = \mathbf{b}^T \mathbf{b} = \|\mathbf{b}\|^2$.

As we previously computed in Example 3.2.10, the Hessian of f is $\mathbf{H}_f(\mathbf{x}) = P$. Now comes a key observation. The matrix P is positive definite whenever $\lambda > 0$. Indeed, for any $\mathbf{z} \in \mathbb{R}^m$,

$$\mathbf{z}^T[2(A^TA + \lambda I_{m \times m})]\mathbf{z} = 2\|A\mathbf{z}\|_2^2 + 2\lambda\|\mathbf{z}\|_2^2 > 0.$$

Let $\mu = 2\lambda > 0$. Then f is μ-strongly convex. This holds whether or not the columns of A are linearly independent.

The stationary points are easily characterized. Recall from Example 3.2.3 that the gradient is $\nabla f(\mathbf{x}) = P\mathbf{x} + \mathbf{q}$. Equating to $\mathbf{0}$ leads to the system

$$2(A^TA + \lambda I_{m \times m})\mathbf{x} - 2A^T\mathbf{b} = \mathbf{0},$$

that is

$$\mathbf{x}^{**} = (A^TA + \lambda I_{m \times m})^{-1}A^T\mathbf{b}.$$

The matrix in parenthesis is invertible as it is $1/2$ of the Hessian, which is positive definite.

4.6.3.1 Connection to SVD

Expressing the solution in terms of a compact SVD $A = U\Sigma V^T = \sum_{j=1}^r \sigma_j \mathbf{u}_j \mathbf{v}_j^T$ provides some insights into how ridge regression works. Suppose that A has full column rank. This implies that $VV^T = I_{m \times m}$. Then observe that

$$\begin{aligned}
(A^TA + \lambda I_{m \times m})^{-1} &= (V\Sigma^T U^T U\Sigma V^T + \lambda I_{m \times m})^{-1} \\
&= (V\Sigma^2 V^T + \lambda I_{m \times m})^{-1} \\
&= (V\Sigma^2 V^T + V\lambda I_{m \times m} V^T)^{-1} \\
&= (V[\Sigma^2 + \lambda I_{m \times m}]V^T)^{-1} \\
&= V(\Sigma^2 + \lambda I_{m \times m})^{-1} V^T.
\end{aligned}$$

Hence

$$\mathbf{x}^{**} = (A^TA + \lambda I_{m \times m})^{-1}A^T\mathbf{b} = V(\Sigma^2 + \lambda I_{m \times m})^{-1}V^T V\Sigma U^T\mathbf{b} = V(\Sigma^2 + \lambda I_{m \times m})^{-1}\Sigma U^T\mathbf{b}.$$

Our predictions are

$$\begin{aligned}
A\mathbf{x}^{**} &= U\Sigma V^T V(\Sigma^2 + \lambda I_{m \times m})^{-1}\Sigma U^T\mathbf{b} \\
&= U\Sigma(\Sigma^2 + \lambda I_{m \times m})^{-1}\Sigma U^T\mathbf{b} \\
&= \sum_{j=1}^r \mathbf{u}_j \left\{\frac{\sigma_j^2}{\sigma_j^2 + \lambda}\right\} \mathbf{u}_j^T\mathbf{b}.
\end{aligned}$$

Note that the terms in curly brackets are < 1 when $\lambda > 0$.

Compare this to the unregularized least-squares solution, which is obtained simply by setting $\lambda = 0$ above,

$$A\mathbf{x}^* = \sum_{j=1}^r \mathbf{u}_j \mathbf{u}_j^T\mathbf{b}.$$

The difference is that the regularized solution reduces the contributions from the left singular vectors corresponding to small singular values.

Self-Assessment Quiz *(with help from Claude, Gemini, and ChatGPT)*

1. Which of the following best describes the Frobenius norm of a matrix $A \in \mathbb{R}^{n \times m}$?
   a) The maximum singular value of A
   b) The square root of the sum of the squares of all entries in A
   c) The maximum absolute row sum of A
   d) The maximum absolute column sum of A

2. Let $A \in \mathbb{R}^{n \times m}$ be a matrix with SVD $A = \sum_{j=1}^{r} \sigma_j \mathbf{u}_j \mathbf{v}_j^T$ and let $A_k = \sum_{j=1}^{k} \sigma_j \mathbf{u}_j \mathbf{v}_j^T$ be the truncated SVD with $k < r$. Which of the following is true about the Frobenius norm of $A - A_k$?
   a) $\|A - A_k\|_F^2 = \sum_{j=1}^{k} \sigma_j^2$
   b) $\|A - A_k\|_F^2 = \sum_{j=k+1}^{r} \sigma_j^2$
   c) $\|A - A_k\|_F^2 = \sigma_k^2$
   d) $\|A - A_k\|_F^2 = \sigma_{k+1}^2$

3. The ridge regression problem is formulated as $\min_{\mathbf{x} \in \mathbb{R}^m} \|A\mathbf{x} - \mathbf{b}\|_2^2 + \lambda \|\mathbf{x}\|_2^2$. What is the role of the parameter λ?
   a) It controls the trade-off between fitting the data and minimizing the norm of the solution.
   b) It determines the rank of the matrix A.
   c) It is the smallest singular value of A.
   d) It is the largest singular value of A.

4. Let A be an $n \times m$ matrix with compact SVD $A = \sum_{j=1}^{r} \sigma_j \mathbf{u}_j \mathbf{v}_j^T$. How does the ridge regression solution $\mathbf{x}^{**}$ compare to the least-squares solution $\mathbf{x}^*$?
   a) $\mathbf{x}^{**}$ has larger components along the left singular vectors corresponding to small singular values.
   b) $\mathbf{x}^{**}$ has smaller components along the left singular vectors corresponding to small singular values.
   c) $\mathbf{x}^{**}$ is identical to $\mathbf{x}^*$.
   d) None of the above.

5. Let $A \in \mathbb{R}^{n \times n}$ be a square nonsingular matrix with compact SVD $A = \sum_{j=1}^{n} \sigma_j \mathbf{u}_j \mathbf{v}_j^T$. Which of the following is true about the induced 2-norm of the inverse A^{-1}?
   a) $\|A^{-1}\|_2 = \sigma_1$
   b) $\|A^{-1}\|_2 = \sigma_n$
   c) $\|A^{-1}\|_2 = \sigma_1^{-1}$
   d) $\|A^{-1}\|_2 = \sigma_n^{-1}$

Answer for 1: b. Justification: The text defines the Frobenius norm of an $n \times m$ matrix A as $\|A\|_F = \sqrt{\sum_{i=1}^{n} \sum_{j=1}^{m} a_{ij}^2}$.

Answer for 2: b. Justification: The text proves that $\|A - A_k\|_F^2 = \sum_{j=k+1}^{r} \sigma_j^2$ in the *Matrix Norms and Singular Values: Truncation Lemma*.

Answer for 3: a. Justification: The text explains that ridge regression "trades off minimizing the fit to the data versus minimizing the norm of the solution," and λ is the parameter that controls this trade-off.

Answer for 4: b. Justification: The text notes that the ridge regression solution "reduces the contributions from the left singular vectors corresponding to small singular values."

Answer for 5: d. Justification: For a square nonsingular matrix A, $\|A^{-1}\|_2 = \sigma_n^{-1}$, where σ_n is the smallest singular value of A.[11]

4.7 Exercises

4.7.1 Warm-Up Worksheets
(with help from Claude, Gemini, and ChatGPT)

Section 4.2

E4.2.1 Compute the rank of the matrix $A = \begin{pmatrix} 1 & 2 & 3 \\ 0 & 1 & 1 \\ 1 & 3 & 4 \end{pmatrix}$.

E4.2.2 Let $A = \begin{pmatrix} 1 & 2 \\ 3 & 4 \end{pmatrix}$ and $B = \begin{pmatrix} 1 & 0 \\ 0 & 1 \end{pmatrix}$. Compute $\text{rk}(A)$, $\text{rk}(B)$, and $\text{rk}(A+B)$.

E4.2.3 Find the eigenvalues and corresponding eigenvectors of the matrix $A = \begin{pmatrix} 3 & 1 \\ 1 & 3 \end{pmatrix}$.

E4.2.4 Verify that the eigenvectors from E4.2.3 are orthogonal.

E4.2.5 Write the spectral decomposition of the matrix A from E4.2.3.

E4.2.6 Determine whether the matrix $A = \begin{pmatrix} 2 & -1 \\ -1 & 2 \end{pmatrix}$ is positive definite, positive semidefinite, or neither.

E4.2.7 Compute the outer product $\mathbf{uv}$ for $\mathbf{u} = (1, 2, 3)$ and $\mathbf{v} = (4, 5)$.

E4.2.8 Write the matrix $A = \begin{pmatrix} 1 & 2 & 3 \\ 2 & 4 & 6 \\ 3 & 6 & 9 \end{pmatrix}$ as a sum of rank-one matrices.

E4.2.9 Let $A = \begin{pmatrix} 1 & 2 \\ 3 & 6 \end{pmatrix}$. What is the rank of A?

E4.2.10 Let $\mathbf{u} = \begin{pmatrix} 1 \\ 2 \end{pmatrix}$ and $\mathbf{v} = \begin{pmatrix} 3 \\ 4 \end{pmatrix}$. Compute the outer product $\mathbf{uv}^T$.

E4.2.11 Let $A = \begin{pmatrix} 2 & 1 \\ 1 & 2 \end{pmatrix}$. Find the eigenvalues and eigenvectors of A.

E4.2.12 Let $A = \begin{pmatrix} 1 & 2 \\ 2 & 1 \end{pmatrix}$. Verify that $\mathbf{v} = \begin{pmatrix} 1 \\ 1 \end{pmatrix}$ is an eigenvector of A and find the corresponding eigenvalue.

E4.2.13 Let $A = \begin{pmatrix} 1 & 2 \\ 2 & 4 \end{pmatrix}$. Find a basis for the column space of A.

---

[11] Refer to the online supplementary materials: `https://mmids-textbook.github.io/chap04_svd/supp/roch-mmids-svd-supp.html`

E4.2.14 Let $A = \begin{pmatrix} 1 & 2 \\ 2 & 4 \end{pmatrix}$. Find a basis for the null space of A.

E4.2.15 Let $A = \begin{pmatrix} 1 & 2 \\ 2 & 1 \end{pmatrix}$. Is A positive semidefinite?

E4.2.16 Determine if the function $f(x,y) = x^2 + y^2 + xy$ is convex.

E4.2.17 Is the function $f(x,y) = x^2 - y^2$ convex?

E4.2.18 Check the convexity of the function $f(x,y) = e^{x+y}$.

E4.2.19 Check the convexity of the function $f(x,y) = \log(x^2 + y^2 + 1)$.

E4.2.20 Is the function $f(x,y) = xy$ convex?

Section 4.3

E4.3.1 Let $\boldsymbol{\alpha}_1 = (1,2)$ and $\boldsymbol{\alpha}_2 = (-2,1)$. Find a unit vector $\mathbf{w}_1$ in $\mathbb{R}^2$ that maximizes $\|A\mathbf{w}_1\|^2$, where A is the matrix with rows $\boldsymbol{\alpha}_1^T$ and $\boldsymbol{\alpha}_2^T$.

E4.3.2 Let $\mathbf{u} = (1/\sqrt{2}, 1/\sqrt{2})$ and $\mathbf{v} = (1/\sqrt{2}, -1/\sqrt{2})$. Compute the outer product $\mathbf{u}\mathbf{v}^T$.

E4.3.3 Let $A = \begin{pmatrix} 3 & 0 \\ 0 & 2 \end{pmatrix}$. Find an SVD of A.

E4.3.4 Let $A = \begin{pmatrix} 1 & 1 \\ 1 & 1 \end{pmatrix}$. Find a compact SVD of A.

E4.3.5 Let $A = \begin{pmatrix} 1 & 2 \\ 2 & 4 \end{pmatrix}$. Find the eigenvalues and eigenvectors of $A^T A$.

E4.3.6 Let $A = \begin{pmatrix} 1 & 2 \\ 2 & 4 \end{pmatrix}$ as in E4.3.5. Find the eigenvalues and eigenvectors of AA^T.

E4.3.7 Let $A = \begin{pmatrix} 1 & 2 \\ 2 & 4 \end{pmatrix}$ as in E4.3.5. Find a compact SVD of A.

E4.3.8 Let $A = \begin{pmatrix} 1 & 2 \\ 2 & 4 \end{pmatrix}$ as in E4.3.5. Find a full SVD of A.

E4.3.9 Let $A = \begin{pmatrix} 1 & 2 \\ 2 & 4 \end{pmatrix}$ as in E4.3.5. Find an orthonormal basis for each of the four fundamental subspaces of A.

E4.3.10 Given the data points $\boldsymbol{\alpha}_1 = (1,2)$, $\boldsymbol{\alpha}_2 = (2,1)$, $\boldsymbol{\alpha}_3 = (-1,1)$, and $\boldsymbol{\alpha}_4 = (3,-1)$, compute the matrix A and the matrices $A^T A$ and AA^T.

E4.3.11 Find the eigenvalues and eigenvectors of the matrix $A^T A$ from E4.3.10.

E4.3.12 Compute a compact SVD of the matrix A from E4.3.10.

E4.3.13 Compute the matrix $U_1 \Sigma_1 V_1^T$ from E4.3.12 and verify that it is equal to A from E4.3.10.

E4.3.14 Based on E4.3.12, verify the relations $A^T \mathbf{u}_i = \sigma_i \mathbf{v}_i$ for $i = 1, 2$.

E4.3.15 Based on E4.3.12, verify the relations $A^T A \mathbf{v}_i = \sigma_i^2 \mathbf{v}_i$ and $AA^T \mathbf{u}_i = \sigma_i^2 \mathbf{u}_i$ for $i = 1, 2$.

E4.3.16 Based on E4.3.12, find the best approximating subspace of dimension $k = 2$ and compute the sum of squared distances to this subspace.

E4.3.17 Based on E4.3.12, find the best approximating subspace of dimension $k = 1$ and compute the sum of squared distances to this subspace.

E4.3.18 Based on E4.3.17, compute the matrix Z obtained from the truncated SVD with $k = 1$.

Section 4.4

E4.4.1 Let $A = \begin{pmatrix} 3 & 0 \\ 0 & 1 \end{pmatrix}$. Compute A^2, A^3, and A^4. What pattern do you observe?

E4.4.2 Let $B = \begin{pmatrix} 2 & 1 \\ 1 & 2 \end{pmatrix}$. Compute B^2 and B^3. If you were to continue computing higher powers of B, what would you expect to happen to the entries?

E4.4.3 Given the symmetric matrix $A = \begin{pmatrix} 2 & 1 \\ 1 & 2 \end{pmatrix}$ and the vector $\mathbf{x} = \begin{pmatrix} 1 \\ 0 \end{pmatrix}$, compute $A^k\mathbf{x}$ for $k = 1, 2, 3$ and $\frac{A^k\mathbf{x}}{\|A^k\mathbf{x}\|}$.

E4.4.4 Given the symmetric matrix $A = \begin{pmatrix} 2 & 1 \\ 1 & 2 \end{pmatrix}$ and the vector $\mathbf{x} = \begin{pmatrix} 0 \\ 1 \end{pmatrix}$, compute $A^k\mathbf{x}$ for $k = 1, 2, 3$ and $\frac{A^k\mathbf{x}}{\|A^k\mathbf{x}\|}$.

E4.4.5 Given the matrix $A = \begin{pmatrix} 2 & 0 \\ 0 & 1 \end{pmatrix}$ and the vector $\mathbf{x} = \begin{pmatrix} 1 \\ 1 \end{pmatrix}$, compute $A^k\mathbf{x}$ for $k = 1, 2, 3$.

E4.4.6 Let $A = \begin{pmatrix} 4 & 1 \\ 1 & 4 \end{pmatrix}$. Find the eigenvalues and eigenvectors of A.

E4.4.7 Let A be as in E4.4.6. Compute A^2 and A^3 using the spectral decomposition of A.

E4.4.8 Let A be as in E4.4.6. Let $\mathbf{x} = \begin{pmatrix} 2 \\ 1 \end{pmatrix}$. Compute $A^2\mathbf{x}$ and $A^3\mathbf{x}$. What do you notice about the direction of these vectors as the power increases?

E4.4.9 Let $A = \begin{pmatrix} 1 & 2 \\ 0 & 1 \end{pmatrix}$. Compute A^TA. Determine whether A^TA is positive semidefinite by computing its eigenvalues.

Section 4.5

E4.5.1 Given a loading vector $\boldsymbol{\phi}_1 = \left(\frac{1}{\sqrt{2}}, \frac{1}{\sqrt{2}}\right)$, verify that it satisfies the unit norm constraint.

E4.5.2 Given two loading vectors $\boldsymbol{\phi}_1 = \left(\frac{1}{\sqrt{2}}, \frac{1}{\sqrt{2}}\right)$ and $\boldsymbol{\phi}_2 = \left(\frac{1}{\sqrt{2}}, -\frac{1}{\sqrt{2}}\right)$, verify that they are orthogonal.

E4.5.3 Given a centered data matrix $\tilde{X} = \begin{pmatrix} -1 & 1 \\ 1 & -1 \end{pmatrix}$ and a loading vector $\boldsymbol{\phi}_1 = \left(\frac{1}{\sqrt{2}}, \frac{1}{\sqrt{2}}\right)$, compute the first principal component scores t_{i1}.

E4.5.4 Given a centered data matrix $\tilde{X} = \begin{pmatrix} -1 & 1 \\ 1 & -1 \end{pmatrix}$ and two loading vectors $\boldsymbol{\phi}_1 = \left(\frac{1}{\sqrt{2}}, \frac{1}{\sqrt{2}}\right)$ and $\boldsymbol{\phi}_2 = \left(\frac{1}{\sqrt{2}}, -\frac{1}{\sqrt{2}}\right)$, compute the first and second principal component scores t_{i1} and t_{i2}.

E4.5.5 Given the first and second principal component scores from E4.5.4, verify that they are uncorrelated.

E4.5.6 Given a data matrix $X = \begin{pmatrix} 1 & 3 \\ -1 & -3 \end{pmatrix}$, compute the centered data matrix $\tilde{X}$.

E4.5.7 Given the data matrix
$$X = \begin{pmatrix} 1 & 2 \\ 3 & 4 \\ 5 & 6 \end{pmatrix},$$
compute the mean-centered data matrix.

E4.5.8 Given the SVD of the centered data matrix from E4.5.7, extract the first principal component loading vector $\boldsymbol{\phi}_1$.

E4.5.9 Given the centered data matrix $\tilde{X}$ and the first principal component loading vector ϕ_1 from E4.5.7 and E4.5.8, compute the first principal component scores t_{i1}.

E4.5.10 Given a data matrix X with centered columns, show that the sample covariance matrix of X can be expressed as $\frac{1}{n-1} X^T X$.

E4.5.11 Given the loading vector $\varphi_1 = (0.8, 0.6)$ for the first principal component, find a loading vector φ_2 for the second principal component.

E4.5.12 Given the data points $\mathbf{x}_1 = (1, 0)$, $\mathbf{x}_2 = (0, 1)$, and $\mathbf{x}_3 = (-1, 0)$, compute the first principal component vector.

Section 4.6

E4.6.1 Compute the Frobenius norm of the matrix $A = \begin{pmatrix} 1 & 2 \\ 3 & 4 \\ 5 & 6 \end{pmatrix}$.

E4.6.2 Compute the SVD of $A = \begin{pmatrix} 1 & 2 \\ 2 & 4 \end{pmatrix}$.

E4.6.3 Let $A = \begin{pmatrix} 1 & 2 \\ 2 & 4 \end{pmatrix}$. Compute the Frobenius norm $\|A\|_F$.

E4.6.4 Let $A = \begin{pmatrix} 1 & 2 \\ 2 & 4 \end{pmatrix}$. Compute the induced 2-norm $\|A\|_2$.

E4.6.5 Let $A = \begin{pmatrix} 1 & 2 \\ 2 & 4 \end{pmatrix}$ and $B = \begin{pmatrix} 1 & 1 \\ 1 & 1 \end{pmatrix}$. Compute $\|A - B\|_F$.

E4.6.6 Let $A = \begin{pmatrix} 1 & 2 \\ 2 & 4 \end{pmatrix}$ and let $A_1 = \sigma_1 \mathbf{u}_1 \mathbf{v}_1^T$ be the rank-1 truncated SVD of A. Compute $\|A - A_1\|_F$.

E4.6.7 Let $A = \begin{pmatrix} 1 & 2 \\ 2 & 4 \end{pmatrix}$ and let $A_1 = \sigma_1 \mathbf{u}_1 \mathbf{v}_1^T$ be the rank-1 truncated SVD of A. Compute $\|A - A_1\|_2$.

E4.6.8 Let $A = \begin{pmatrix} 1 & 2 \\ 2 & 4 \end{pmatrix}$, $\mathbf{b} = \begin{pmatrix} 5 \\ 10 \end{pmatrix}$, and $\lambda = 1$. Compute the ridge regression solution $\mathbf{x}^{**}$ to $\min_{\mathbf{x} \in \mathbb{R}^2} \|A\mathbf{x} - \mathbf{b}\|_2^2 + \lambda \|\mathbf{x}\|_2^2$.

E4.6.9 Let $A = \begin{pmatrix} 1 & 2 \\ 2 & 4 \end{pmatrix}$. Compute $\|A^{-1}\|_2$.

E4.6.10 Compute the ridge regression solution for $A = \begin{pmatrix} 1 & 1 \\ 1 & 2 \\ 1 & 3 \end{pmatrix}$, $\mathbf{b} = \begin{pmatrix} 1 \\ 2 \\ 2 \end{pmatrix}$, and $\lambda = 1$.

4.7.2 Problems

4.1 Let $Q \in \mathbb{R}^{n \times n}$ be an orthogonal matrix. Use the *SVD via Spectral Decomposition Theorem* to compute an SVD of Q. Is there a difference between the compact and full SVD in this case?

4.2 Let $W \subseteq \mathbb{R}^m$ be a hyperplane. Show that there exists a unit vector $\mathbf{z} \in \mathbb{R}^m$ such that

$$\mathbf{w} \in W \iff \langle \mathbf{z}, \mathbf{w} \rangle = 0.$$

4.3 Construct a matrix $A \in \mathbb{R}^{n \times n}$ for which there exist multiple solutions to the maximization problem

4.7 Exercises

$$\mathbf{v}_1 \in \arg\max\{\|A\mathbf{v}\| : \|\mathbf{v}\| = 1\}.$$

4.4 Prove an analogue of the *Characterization of Positive Semidefiniteness Theorem* for positive definite matrices.

4.5 (Adapted from [Sol]) Show that $\|A\|_2 = \|\Sigma\|_2$, where $A = U\Sigma V^T$ is a singular value decomposition of A.

4.6 Let A, $U\Sigma V^T$, B be as in the *Power Iteration Lemma*. Assume further that $\sigma_2 > \sigma_3$ and that $\mathbf{y} \in \mathbb{R}^m$ satisfies both $\langle \mathbf{v}_1, \mathbf{y} \rangle = 0$ and $\langle \mathbf{v}_2, \mathbf{y} \rangle > 0$. Show that $\frac{B^k \mathbf{y}}{\|B^k \mathbf{y}\|} \to \mathbf{v}_2$ as $k \to +\infty$. How would you find such a $\mathbf{y}$?

4.7 Let $A \in \mathbb{R}^{n \times m}$. Use the *Cauchy–Schwarz Inequality* to show that

$$\|A\|_2 = \max\left\{ \mathbf{x}^T A \mathbf{y} : \|\mathbf{x}\| = \|\mathbf{y}\| = 1 \right\}.$$

4.8 Let $A \in \mathbb{R}^{n \times m}$.

a) Show that $\|A\|_F^2 = \sum_{j=1}^m \|A\mathbf{e}_j\|^2$.

b) Use a) and the *Cauchy–Schwarz Inequality* to show that $\|A\|_2 \le \|A\|_F$.

c) Give an example such that $\|A\|_F = \sqrt{n}\|A\|_2$.

4.9 Use the *Cauchy–Schwarz Inequality* to show that for any A, B for which AB is well-defined it holds that

$$\|AB\|_F \le \|A\|_F \|B\|_F.$$

4.10 (*Note*: Refers to the online supplementary materials.[12]) Let $A \in \mathbb{R}^{n \times n}$ be nonsingular with SVD $A = U\Sigma V^T$ where the singular values satisfy $\sigma_1 \ge \cdots \ge \sigma_n > 0$. Show that

$$\min_{\mathbf{x} \ne 0} \frac{\|A\mathbf{x}\|}{\|\mathbf{x}\|} = \min_{\mathbf{y} \ne 0} \frac{\|\mathbf{y}\|}{\|A^{-1}\mathbf{y}\|} = \sigma_n = 1/\|A^+\|_2.$$

4.11 Let $X \in \mathbb{R}^{n \times d}$ be a matrix with rows $\mathbf{x}_1^T, \ldots, \mathbf{x}_n^T$. Write the following sum in matrix form in terms of X:

$$\frac{1}{n} \sum_{i=1}^n \mathbf{x}_i \mathbf{x}_i^T.$$

Justify your answer.

4.12 Let $A \in \mathbb{R}^{d \times d}$ be a symmetric matrix. Show that $A \preceq M I_{d \times d}$ if and only if the eigenvalues of A are at most M. Similarly, $m I_{d \times d} \preceq A$ if and only if the eigenvalues of A are at least m. [*Hint*: Observe that the eigenvectors of A are also eigenvectors of the identity matrix $I_{d \times d}$.]

4.13 Prove the *Power Iteration in the Positive Semidefinite Case Lemma*.

4.14 Recall that the trace tr(A) of matrix $A = (a_{i,j})_{i,j} \in \mathbb{R}^n$ is the sum of its diagonal entries: $\mathrm{tr}(A) = \sum_{i=1}^n a_{i,i}$.

a) Show that, for any $A \in \mathbb{R}^{n \times m}$ and $B \in \mathbb{R}^{m \times n}$, it holds that $\mathrm{tr}(AB) = \mathrm{tr}(BA)$.

b) Use a) to show that, if a symmetric matrix A has spectral decomposition $\sum_{i=1}^n \lambda_i \mathbf{q}_i \mathbf{q}_i^T$, then

$$\mathrm{tr}(A) = \sum_{i=1}^n \lambda_i.$$

---

[12] https://mmids-textbook.github.io/chap04_svd/supp/roch-mmids-svd-supp.html

4.15 (Adapted from [Sol]) Suppose $A \in \mathbb{R}^{m \times n}$ and $B \in \mathbb{R}^{n \times m}$. Show $\|A\|_F^2 = \text{tr}(A^T A)$ and $\text{tr}(AB) = \text{tr}(BA)$, where recall that the trace of a matrix C, denoted $\text{tr}(C)$, is the sum of the diagonal elements of C.

4.16 (Adapted from [Str]) Let $A \in \mathbb{R}^{n \times k}$ and $B \in \mathbb{R}^{k \times m}$. Show that the null space of AB contains the null space of B.

4.17 (Adapted from [Str]) Let $A \in \mathbb{R}^{n \times m}$. Show that $A^T A$ has the same null space as A.

4.18 (Adapted from [Str]) Let $A \in \mathbb{R}^{m \times r}$ and $B \in \mathbb{R}^{r \times n}$, both of rank r.

  a) Show that $A^T A$, BB^T, and $A^T A B B^T$ are all invertible.

  b) Show that $r = \text{rk}(A^T A B B^T) \leq \text{rk}(AB)$.

  c) Conclude that $\text{rk}(AB) = r$.

4.19 For any $n \geq 1$, give an example of a matrix $A \in \mathbb{R}^{n \times n}$ with $A \neq I_{n \times n}$ such that $A^2 = I_{n \times n}$.

4.20 Let $A \in \mathbb{R}^{n \times k}$ and $B \in \mathbb{R}^{r \times m}$, and let $D \in \mathbb{R}^{k \times r}$ be a diagonal matrix. Assume $k < r$. Compute the columns of AD and the rows of DB.

4.21 Compute an SVD of $A = [-1]$.

4.22 We show in this exercise that a matrix can have many distinct SVDs. Let $Q, W \in \mathbb{R}^{n \times n}$ be orthogonal matrices. Give four different SVDs for Q, one where $V = I$, one where $V = Q$, one where $V = Q^T$ and one where $V = W$. Make sure to check all requirements of the SVD. Do the singular values change?

4.23 (Adapted from [Sol]) Show that adding a row to a matrix cannot decrease its largest singular value.

4.24 Let $\mathbf{v}_1, \ldots, \mathbf{v}_n \in \mathbb{R}^n$ be an orthonormal basis. Fix $1 \leq k < n$. Let Q_1 be the matrix with columns $\mathbf{v}_1, \ldots, \mathbf{v}_k$ and let Q_2 be the matrix with columns $\mathbf{v}_{k+1}, \ldots, \mathbf{v}_n$. Show that

$$Q_1 Q_1^T + Q_2 Q_2^T = I_{n \times n}.$$

[*Hint:* Multiply both sides by $\mathbf{e}_i$.]

4.25 (*Note*: Refers to the online supplementary materials.[13]) Let $Q \in \mathbb{R}^{n \times n}$ be an orthogonal matrix. Compute its condition number

$$\kappa_2(Q) = \|Q\|_2 \|Q^{-1}\|_2.$$

4.26 Prove the *SVD Relations Lemma*.

4.27 Let $A = \sum_{j=1}^r \sigma_j \mathbf{u}_j \mathbf{v}_j^T$ be an SVD of $A \in \mathbb{R}^{n \times m}$ with $\sigma_1 \geq \sigma_2 \geq \cdots \geq \sigma_r > 0$. Define

$$B = A - \sigma_1 \mathbf{u}_1 \mathbf{v}_1^T.$$

Show that

$$\mathbf{v}_2 \in \arg\max\{\|B\mathbf{v}\| : \|\mathbf{v}\| = 1\}.$$

4.28 (Adapted from [Sol]) The stable rank of $A \in \mathbb{R}^{n \times n}$ is defined as

$$\text{StableRk}(A) = \frac{\|A\|_F^2}{\|A\|_2^2}.$$

---

[13] https://mmids-textbook.github.io/chap04_svd/supp/roch-mmids-svd-supp.html

a) Show that, if all columns of A are the same nonzero vector $\mathbf{v} \in \mathbb{R}^n$, then StableRk$(A) = 1$.

b) Show that, when the columns of A are orthonormal, then StableRk$(A) = n$.

c) Is StableRk(A) always an integer? Justify your answer.

d) More generally, show that

$$1 \leq \text{StableRk}(A) \leq n.$$

e) Show that, in general, it holds that

$$\text{StableRk}(A) \leq \text{Rk}(A).$$

[*Hint:* Use the *Matrix Norms and Singular Values Lemma*.]

4.29 Let $A \in \mathbb{R}^{n \times n}$ be a square matrix with full SVD $A = U\Sigma V^T$.

a) Justify the formula

$$A = (UV^T)(V\Sigma V^T).$$

b) Let

$$Q = UV^T, \qquad S = V\Sigma V^T.$$

Show that Q is orthogonal and that S is positive semidefinite. A factorization of the form $A = QS$ is called a polar decomposition.

4.30 Let $A \in \mathbb{R}^{n \times m}$ be a matrix with full SVD $A = U\Sigma V^T$ where the singular values satisfy $\sigma_1 \geq \cdots \geq \sigma_m \geq 0$. Define the unit sphere in m dimensions $\mathbb{S}^{m-1} = \{\mathbf{x} \in \mathbb{R}^m : \|\mathbf{x}\| = 1\}$. Show that

$$\sigma_m^2 = \min_{\mathbf{x} \in \mathbb{S}^{m-1}} \|A\mathbf{x}\|^2.$$

4.31 Let $A \in \mathbb{R}^{n \times m}$ be a matrix with columns $\mathbf{a}_1, \ldots, \mathbf{a}_m$. Show that for all i

$$\|\mathbf{a}_i\|_2 \leq \|A\|_2.$$

4.32 Let (U_i, V_i), $i = 1, \ldots, n$, be i.i.d. random vectors taking values in $\mathbb{R}^2$. Assume that $\mathbb{E}[U_1^2], \mathbb{E}[V_1^2] < +\infty$.

a) Show that

$$\mathbb{E}\left[\frac{1}{n}\sum_{i=1}^n U_i\right] = \mathbb{E}[U_1].$$

b) Show that

$$\mathbb{E}\left[\frac{1}{n-1}\sum_{i=1}^n \left(U_i - \frac{1}{n}\sum_{j=1}^n U_j\right)^2\right] = \text{Var}[U_1].$$

c) Show that

$$\mathbb{E}\left[\frac{1}{n-1}\sum_{i=1}^n \left(U_i - \frac{1}{n}\sum_{j=1}^n U_j\right)\left(V_i - \frac{1}{n}\sum_{k=1}^n V_k\right)\right] = \text{Cov}[U_1, V_1].$$

In words, the left-hand side of each equation above (inside the expectation) is a so-called unbiased estimator of the right-hand side. Those estimators are called respectively the sample mean, the sample variance, and the sample covariance.

4.33 Give an equivalent matrix representation of the best k-dimensional approximating subspace in terms of the data matrix $A \in \mathbb{R}^{n \times m}$ and a matrix W whose columns are orthonormal. [*Hint:* Use the Frobenius norm.]

4.34 Let $\mathbf{q}_1, \ldots, \mathbf{q}_m$ be an orthonormal list in $\mathbb{R}^n$ and consider the matrix

$$M = \sum_{i=1}^{m} \mathbf{q}_i \mathbf{q}_i^T.$$

a) Suppose $m = n$. Show that $M = I_{n \times n}$ by computing $\mathbf{e}_i^T M \mathbf{e}_j$ for all i, j.

b) Suppose $m \leq n$. What is the geometric interpretation of M? Based on your answer, give a second proof of (a).

4.35 Let $A \in \mathbb{R}^{n \times m}$ be a matrix with compact SVD $A = U \Sigma V^T$. Let $A^+ = V \Sigma^{-1} U^T$ (known as a pseudoinverse). Show that $AA^+A = A$ and $A^+AA^+ = A^+$.

4.36 Let $A \in \mathbb{R}^{n \times n}$ be a symmetric matrix with orthonormal eigenvectors $\mathbf{q}_1, \ldots, \mathbf{q}_n$ and corresponding eigenvalues $\lambda_1 \geq \cdots \geq \lambda_n$.

a) Compute an spectral decomposition of $A^T A$.

b) Use a) to compute $\|A\|_2$ in terms of two of the eigenvalues of A.

5 Spectral Graph Theory

In this chapter, we look at network data. We begin by defining basic graph concepts. We then introduce ideas from spectral graph theory, in particular the eigenvalues of the Laplacian and their variational characterization. We discuss and implement some applications, including community detection. Here is a more detailed overview of the main sections of the chapter.

Background: Basic concepts in graph theory: Section 5.2 provides an introduction to the basic concepts of graph theory, covering both undirected and directed graphs. It introduces key definitions such as vertices, edges, paths, connectivity, and various special types of graphs like cliques, trees, and directed acyclic graphs. The section also discusses different matrix representations. It discusses the Laplacian matrix, emphasizing its role in understanding graph connectivity. Finally, the section underscores the practical use of these concepts with the NetworkX Python package for graph manipulation and visualization.

Variational characterization of eigenvalues: Section 5.3 explores a variational characterization of eigenvalues, offering a different perspective on understanding these important mathematical objects. It begins by presenting a proof of the *Spectral Theorem*, showcasing how orthogonal transformations can be employed to diagonalize a symmetric matrix. This proof serves as a foundation for the subsequent exploration of variational characterizations, which involve expressing eigenvalues as solutions to optimization problems. The section details specific cases, demonstrating how the largest and smallest eigenvalues can be determined through optimization procedures involving the Rayleigh quotient. Finally, it presents the *Courant–Fischer Theorem*.

Spectral properties of the Laplacian matrix: Section 5.4 discusses the spectral properties of the Laplacian matrix of a graph. It begins by observing that the Laplacian matrix is symmetric and positive semidefinite, and that the constant unit vector is always an eigenvector with eigenvalue 0. The section then explores the connection between the Laplacian matrix and graph connectivity, proving that a graph is connected if and only if the second smallest eigenvalue (i.e., the algebraic connectivity) is strictly positive. Finally, the section presents a variational characterization of the second smallest eigenvalue, which minimizes the sum of squared differences of values assigned to adjacent vertices, subject to a centering and normalization constraint. This characterization is used to explain why eigenvectors of the Laplacian matrix are useful for graph drawing and revealing the underlying geometry of the graph.

Application: Graph partitioning via spectral clustering: Section 5.5 explores graph partitioning, the division of a graph into two sets of nodes with minimal connections between them. It introduces a measure of a cut's quality, balancing the minimization of edges between sets against the need for balanced set sizes, as well as the related concept of the isoperimetric number (or Cheeger constant) of a graph. *Cheeger's Inequalities* are presented, linking the isoperimetric number to the second smallest Laplacian eigenvalue, demonstrating the relationship between spectral graph theory and graph partitioning. The section outlines a graph-cutting algorithm leveraging Laplacian eigenvectors, offering a heuristic approach to finding good cuts with provable guarantees, and discusses the computational challenges of finding optimal cuts. It concludes by revisiting community detection, applying spectral properties to identify sub-communities within a graph.

Erdős–Rényi random graphs and stochastic blockmodels: Section 5.6 discusses random graph models, focusing on the inhomogeneous Erdős–Rényi (ER) random graph and the stochastic blockmodel (SBM). The inhomogeneous ER random graph is a versatile model for generating random graphs, where each edge is included independently with a specified probability. A special case is the ER random graph, where all edges between distinct vertices have the same probability of being present. The SBM extends this concept by partitioning vertices into blocks and assigning different probabilities for connections within and between blocks, enabling to capture in particular the tendency of nodes within the same group to connect more frequently.

5.1 Motivating Example: Uncovering Social Groups

In this chapter, we analyze datasets in the form of networks. As motivation, we first look at the Karate Club dataset.

From Wikipedia[1]:

> A social network of a karate club was studied by Wayne W. Zachary for a period of three years from 1970 to 1972. The network captures 34 members of a karate club, documenting links between pairs of members who interacted outside the club. During the study a conflict arose between the administrator "John A" and instructor "Mr. Hi" (pseudonyms), which led to the split of the club into two. Half of the members formed a new club around Mr. Hi; members from the other part found a new instructor or gave up karate. Based on collected data Zachary correctly assigned all but one member of the club to the groups they actually joined after the split.

We use the `NetworkX` package to load the data and visualize it (with help from Claude, who really likes the number 42). We will say more about it later in this chapter.

```
import networkx as nx
G = nx.karate_club_graph()

plt.figure(figsize=(6,6))
pos = nx.spring_layout(G, k=0.7, iterations=50, seed=42)
nx.draw_networkx(G, pos=pos, node_size=300, node_color='black',
    font_color='white')
plt.axis('off')
plt.show()
```

---

[1] https://en.wikipedia.org/wiki/Zachary%27s_karate_club

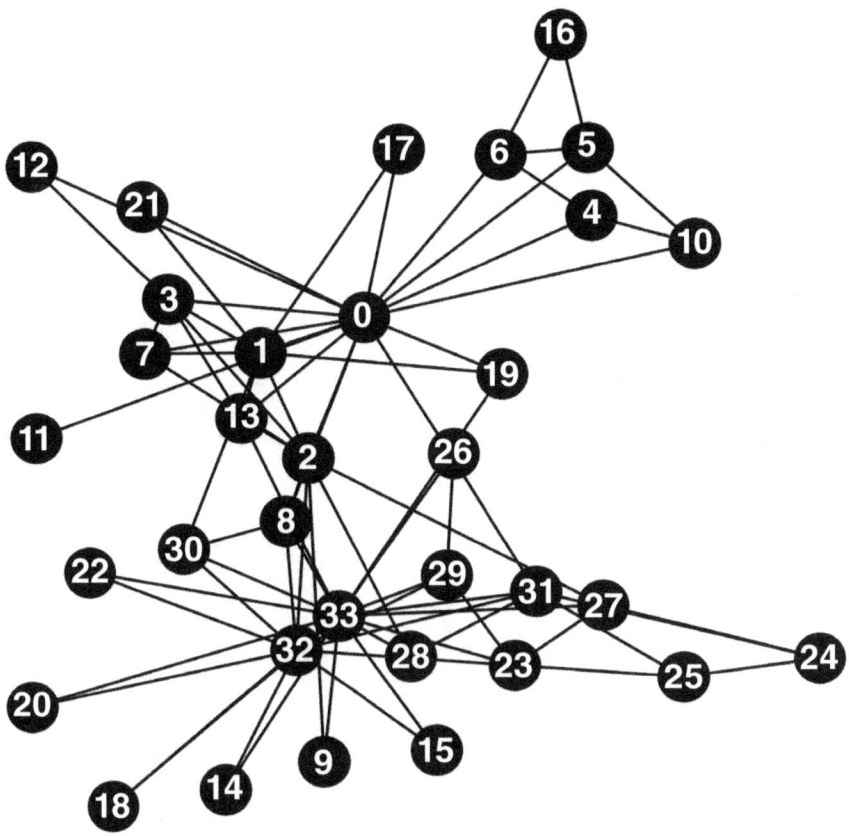

Figure 5.1 Graphical output of code.

Our goal:

Identify natural subgroups in the network.

That is, we want to find groups of nodes that have many links between them, but relatively few with the other nodes.

It will turn out that the eigenvectors of the Laplacian matrix, a matrix naturally associated with the graph, contain useful information about such communities.

CHAT & LEARN Ask your favorite AI chatbot why it likes the number 42 so much.

5.2 Background: Basic Concepts in Graph Theory

In this section, we cover the basics of graph theory. We also introduce the `NetworkX` package.

5.2.1 Undirected Graphs

We start with undirected graphs.

Definition 5.2.1 *(Undirected Graph)* *An undirected graph (or graph for short) is a pair* $G = (V, E)$ *where V is the set of vertices (or nodes) and*

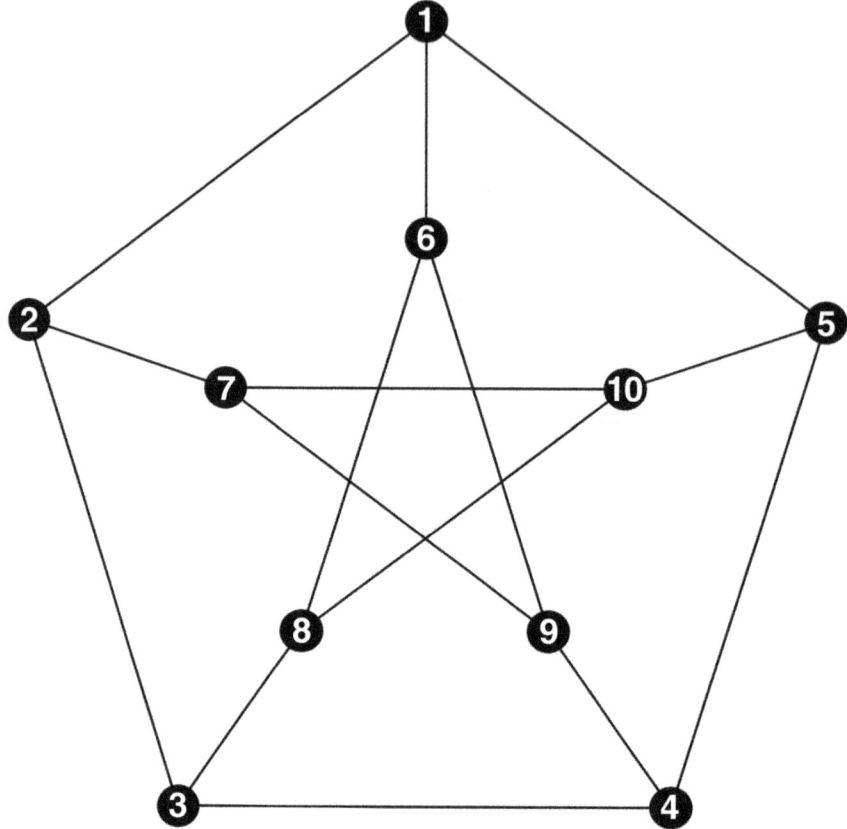

Figure 5.2 The Petersen graph.

$$E \subseteq \{\{u,v\} : u,v \in V, u \neq v\}$$

is the set of edges.

Note that, unless otherwise stated, we typically do not allow self-loops, namely edges that connect a vertex to itself.

We occasionally write $V(G)$ and $E(G)$ for the vertices and edges of the graph G. In our case, the set of vertices V is always finite.

Definition 5.2.2 *(Incidence and Adjacency) A vertex $v \in V$ is incident with an edge $e \in E$ if $v \in e$. The incident vertices of an edge are called its endvertices. Two vertices $u, v \in V$ are adjacent (or neighbors), which we denote by $u \sim v$, if $\{u,v\} \in E$.*

Definition 5.2.3 *(Neighborhood and Degree) The set of adjacent vertices of v, denoted by $N(v)$, is called the neighborhood of v and its size, $\delta(v) := |N(v)|$, is the degree of v. A vertex v with $\delta(v) = 0$ is called isolated. A graph is called d-regular if all its degrees are d.*

A well-known result, sometimes referred to as the Handshaking Lemma, says that the sum of all degrees is twice the number of edges (prove it!).

Example 5.2.4 *(Petersen Graph) The Petersen graph is shown in Figure 5.2. All its vertices have degree 3; that is, it is 3-regular. In particular there is no isolated vertex.*

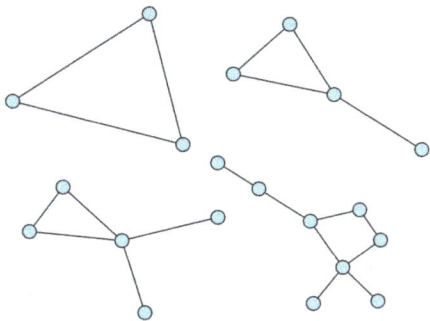

Figure 5.3 Connected components.

Definition 5.2.5 *(Path)* *A path in G is a sequence of (not necessarily distinct) vertices $x_0 \sim x_1 \sim \cdots \sim x_k$ with each consecutive pair being adjacent. The number of edges, k, is called the length of the path. If the endvertices x_0, x_k coincide, that is, $x_0 = x_k$, we call the path a cycle. If the vertices are all distinct (except possibly for the endvertices), we say that the path (or cycle) is self-avoiding. The length of the shortest self-avoiding path connecting two distinct vertices u, v is called the graph distance between u and v, denoted by $\rho(u, v)$.*

Definition 5.2.6 *(Connected)* *We write $u \leftrightarrow v$ if there is a path between u and v. (By convention $u \leftrightarrow u$.) A graph is connected if there is a path between any two of its vertices; that is, if $u \leftrightarrow v$ for all $u, v \in V$.*

Example 5.2.7 *(continued from Example 5.2.4)* *The Petersen graph is connected.*

Lemma 5.2.8 *The relation $\leftrightarrow$ is an equivalence relation; that is, $u \leftrightarrow u$ for all u (reflexivity), $u \leftrightarrow v$ if and only if $v \leftrightarrow u$ (symmetry), and $u \leftrightarrow v$ and $v \leftrightarrow w$ implies $u \leftrightarrow w$ (transitivity).*

Proof The first property is immediate from the definition. The second one is obtained by noting that we can reverse the path between u and v to construct a path between v and u. The third one is obtained by noting that we can add a path between v and w to a path between u and v to construct a path between u and w. □

Definition 5.2.9 *(Connected Components)* *The equivalence class $C[u] = \{v \in V : u \leftrightarrow v\}$, namely the set of all vertices reachable from u through a path, is called a connected component. A graph is connected if and only if it has only one connected component.*

See Figure 5.3. We show next that the (distinct) connected components form a partition of V. This holds more generally for the equivalence classes of any equivalence relation.

Lemma 5.2.10 *The following statements are equivalent:*

a) $u \leftrightarrow v$

b) $C[u] = C[v]$

c) $C[u] \cap C[v] \neq \varnothing$

As a consequence, either $C[u] = C[v]$ or $C[u] \cap C[v] = \varnothing$.

Proof a) $\Longrightarrow$ b): Let $w \in C[u]$. So $u \leftrightarrow w$. Symmetry and transitivity imply that $v \leftrightarrow w$, which proves the claim.

b) $\Longrightarrow$ c): Since $u \in C[u]$ by reflexivity, we have $\varnothing \neq C[u] = C[v] = C[u] \cap C[v]$.

c) $\Longrightarrow$ a): Let $w \in C[u] \cap C[v]$. Then $u \leftrightarrow w$ and $v \leftrightarrow w$. Symmetry and transitivity imply that $u \leftrightarrow v$. $\square$

Subgraphs and special graphs: In network analysis, one is often interested in finding or counting interesting motifs or subgraphs within a much larger graph. We will not cover this important problem in network analysis much here, but see the *Exercises* section for this chapter.

Definition 5.2.11 *(Subgraph) A subgraph of $G = (V, E)$ is a graph $G' = (V', E')$ with $V' \subseteq V$ and $E' \subseteq E$. Implicit in this definition is the fact that the edges in E' are incident only to V'. The subgraph G' is said to be induced if*

$$E' = \{\{x, y\} : x, y \in V', \{x, y\} \in E\},$$

that is, if it contains all edges of G between the vertices of V'. In that case the notation $G' := G[V']$ is used.

Definition 5.2.12 *(Spanning Subgraph) A subgraph is said to be spanning if $V' = V$.*

Definition 5.2.13 *(Clique) A subgraph containing all possible edges between its vertices is called a complete subgraph or clique.*

Example 5.2.14 *(continued from Example 5.2.4) The Petersen graph contains no triangle (i.e., a complete subgraph with three vertices), induced or otherwise.*

Definition 5.2.15 *(Tree and Forest) A forest is a graph with no self-avoiding cycle. A tree is a connected forest. Vertices of degree 1 are called leaves. A spanning tree of G is a subgraph that is a tree and is also spanning.*

NUMERICAL CORNER In Python, the `NetworkX` package provides many functionalities for defining, modifying and plotting graphs. For instance, many standard graphs can be defined conveniently. The `networkx.petersen_graph` function defines the Petersen graph.

```
G = nx.petersen_graph()
```

The graph can be plotted using the function `networkx.draw_networkx`. Recall that in NumPy array indices start at 0. Consistently, NetworkX also names vertices starting at 0. Note, however, that this conflicts with our mathematical conventions.

```
nx.draw_networkx(G, node_color='black', font_color='white',
    node_size=200)
plt.axis('off')
plt.show()
```

5.2 Basic Concepts in Graph Theory

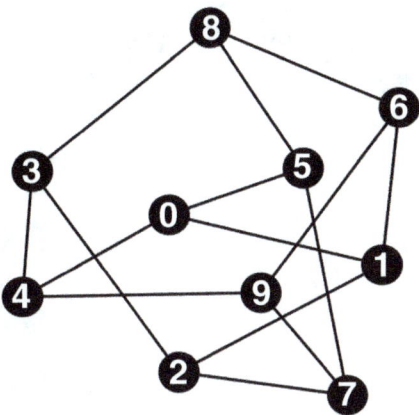

Figure 5.4 Graphical output of code.

Other standard graphs can be generated with special functions, for example complete graphs using `networkx.complete_graph`.

```
G = nx.complete_graph(3)

nx.draw_networkx(G, node_color='black', font_color='white')
plt.axis('off')
plt.show()
```

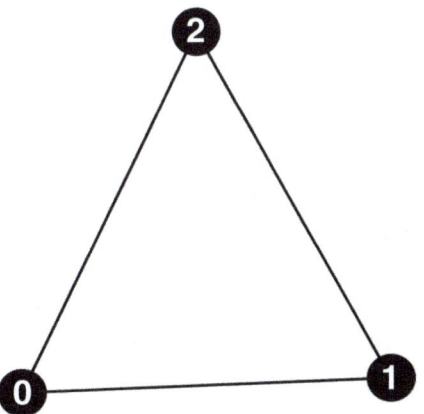

Figure 5.5 Graphical output of code.

Here are a few examples of functions to access various properties of a graph:

```
G = nx.path_graph(10)

nx.draw_networkx(G, node_color='black', font_color='white')
plt.axis('off')
plt.show()
```

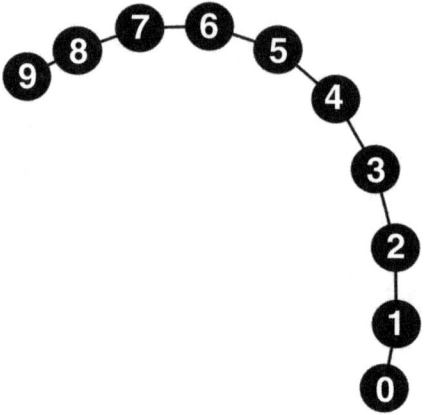

Figure 5.6 Graphical output of code.

```
G.number_of_nodes()  # number of nodes
```

10

```
G.number_of_edges()  # number of edges
```

9

```
G.has_node(7)  # checks whether the graph has a particular vertex
```

True

```
G.has_node(10)
```

False

```
G.has_edge(0, 1)  # checks whether the graph has a particular edge
```

True

```
G.has_edge(0, 2)
```

False

```
[n for n in G.neighbors(2)]  # returns a list of neighbors of the
    specified vertex
```

[1, 3]

```
nx.is_connected(G)  # checks whether the graph is connected
```

True

5.2 Basic Concepts in Graph Theory

```
[cc for cc in nx.connected_components(G)]  # returns the connected
  components
```

`[{0, 1, 2, 3, 4, 5, 6, 7, 8, 9}]`

```
for e in G.edges():
    print(e)
```

(0, 1)
(1, 2)
(2, 3)
(3, 4)
(4, 5)
(5, 6)
(6, 7)
(7, 8)
(8, 9)

Another way of specifying a graph is to start with an empty graph with a given number of vertices and then add edges one by one. The following command creates a graph with four vertices and no edge (see `networkx.empty_graph`).

```
G = nx.empty_graph(4)
G.add_edge(0, 1)
G.add_edge(2, 3)
G.add_edge(0, 3)
G.add_edge(3, 0)

nx.draw_networkx(G, node_color='black', font_color='white')
plt.axis('off')
plt.show()
```

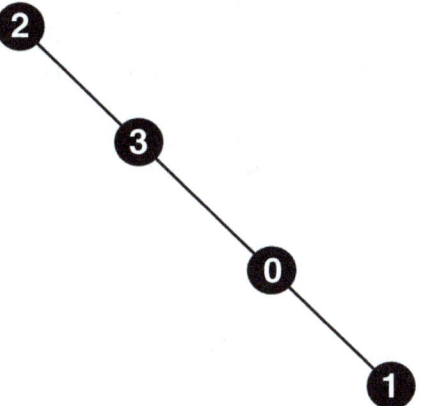

Figure 5.7 Graphical output of code.

◁ **NC**

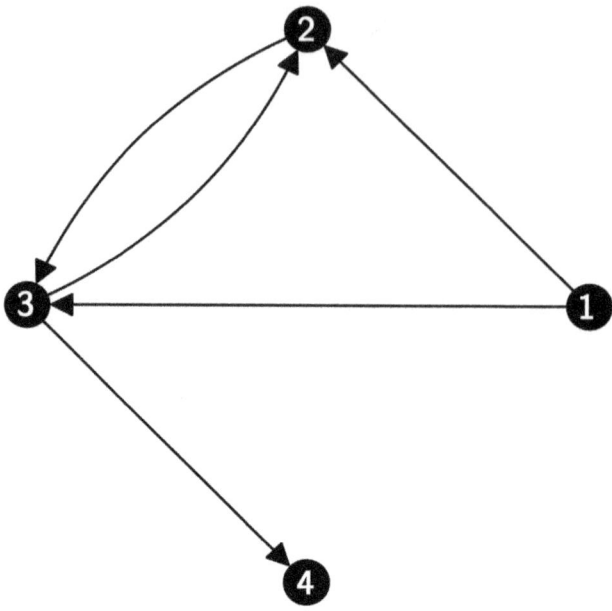

Figure 5.8 A directed graph.

5.2.2 Directed Graphs

We will also need directed graphs.

Definition 5.2.16 *(Directed Graph) A directed graph (or digraph for short) is a pair $G = (V, E)$ where V is a set of vertices (or nodes) and*

$$E \subseteq V^2 = \{(u, v) : u, v \in V\}$$

is a set of directed edges (or arcs).

See Figure 5.8. Note that, in the directed case, we explicitly allow self-loops, namely edges of the form (u, u) that connect a vertex to itself.

Note that, unlike the undirected case, in a digraph the edges are ordered pairs – which is taken to mean that they have an orientation. If $e = (i, j) \in E$ is an edge in a digraph $G = (V, E)$, then i is called the source of e and j is the destination.

The definitions discussed in the undirected case can be adapted to the directed case.

In the directed case, one distinguishes between the out-degree and the in-degree.

Definition 5.2.17 *(Out-Degree and In-Degree) Let $G = (V, E)$ be a digraph. The out-degree of $v \in V$, denoted by $\delta^+(v)$, is the number of edges with source v. The in-degree of v, denoted by $\delta^-(v)$, is the number of edges with destination v.*

Paths and connectivity are also generalized naturally.

Definition 5.2.18 *(Directed Path) A directed path is a sequence of vertices $x_0, \ldots, x_k$ with $(x_{i-1}, x_i) \in E$ for all $i = 1, \ldots, k$. We write $u \to v$ if there is such a path with $x_0 = u$ and $x_k = v$. If the endvertices x_0, x_k coincide, that is, $x_0 = x_k$, we call it a directed cycle.*

5.2 Basic Concepts in Graph Theory

Definition 5.2.19 *(Communication)* We say that $u, v \in V$ communicate, which we denote by $u \leftrightarrow v$, if $u \to v$ and $v \to u$. The $\leftrightarrow$ relation is again an equivalence relation, with the convention that $u \leftrightarrow u$. The equivalence classes of $\leftrightarrow$ are called the strongly connected components of G.

Definition 5.2.20 *(Strongly Connected)* A digraph is strongly connected if any two of its vertices communicate, that is, if $u \leftrightarrow v$ for all $u, v \in V$, or put differently, if there is only one strongly connected component.

Definition 5.2.21 *(Directed Acyclic Graph)* A digraph is said to be a directed acyclic graph (DAG) if it contains no directed cycle.

NUMERICAL CORNER The package `NetworkX` also supports digraphs.

```
G = nx.DiGraph()
nx.add_star(G, [0, 1, 2, 3, 4])

nx.draw_networkx(G, node_color='black', font_color='white')
plt.axis('off')
plt.show()
```

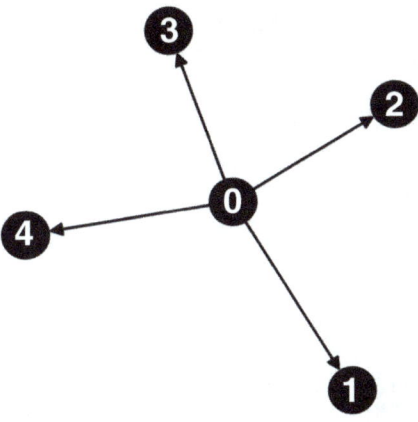

Figure 5.9 Graphical output of code.

Another way of specifying a digraph is to start with an empty graph with a given number of vertices and then add edges one by one (compare to the undirected case above).

```
G = nx.DiGraph()
G.add_edge(0, 1)
G.add_edge(2, 3)
G.add_edge(0, 3)
G.add_edge(3, 0)
G.add_edge(1, 1)

nx.draw_networkx(G, node_color='black', font_color='white')
```

```
plt.axis('off')
plt.show()
```

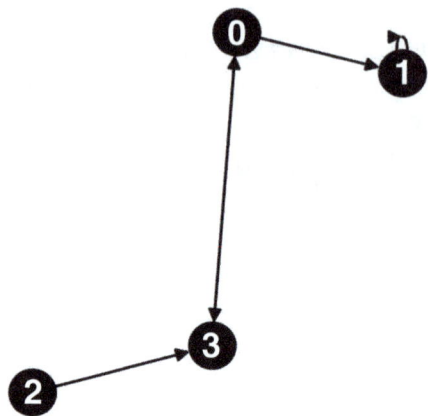

Figure 5.10 Graphical output of code.

Note that edges in both directions are depicted here with a double-arrow. Also the self-loop is hard to see. We can use networkx.draw_networkx_edges (together with networkx.draw_networkx_nodes and networkx.draw_networkx_labels) to have more control over the drawing of the edges.

```
pos = nx.spring_layout(G, seed=42)
nx.draw_networkx_nodes(G, pos, node_color='black')
nx.draw_networkx_labels(G, pos, font_color='white')
nx.draw_networkx_edges(G, pos, connectionstyle="arc3,rad=0.3")
plt.axis('off')
plt.show()
```

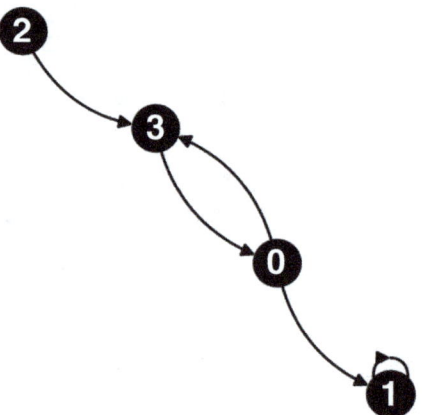

Figure 5.11 Graphical output of code.

◁ NC

5.2.3 Matrix Representations of Graphs

A convenient and useful way of specifying a graph is through a matrix representation. There are many such representations.

We start with the adjacency matrix.

Definition 5.2.22 (Adjacency Matrix) *Assume the (undirected) graph $G = (V, E)$ has $n = |V|$ vertices numbered $1, \ldots, n$. The adjacency matrix A of G is the $n \times n$ symmetric matrix defined as*

$$A_{xy} = \begin{cases} 1 & \text{if } \{x, y\} \in E \\ 0 & \text{otherwise.} \end{cases}$$

Example 5.2.23 *The adjancency matrix of the graph in Figure 5.12 is*

$$A = \begin{pmatrix} 0 & 1 & 1 & 1 \\ 1 & 0 & 0 & 0 \\ 1 & 0 & 0 & 1 \\ 1 & 0 & 1 & 0 \end{pmatrix}.$$

Note that it is indeed symmetric.

Another useful matrix associated with a graph is its incidence matrix. For convenience, we assume again that the vertices of $G = (V, E)$ are numbered $1, \ldots, n$, where n is the number of vertices. We assume further that the edges are labeled $e_1, \ldots, e_m$, where m is the number of edges.

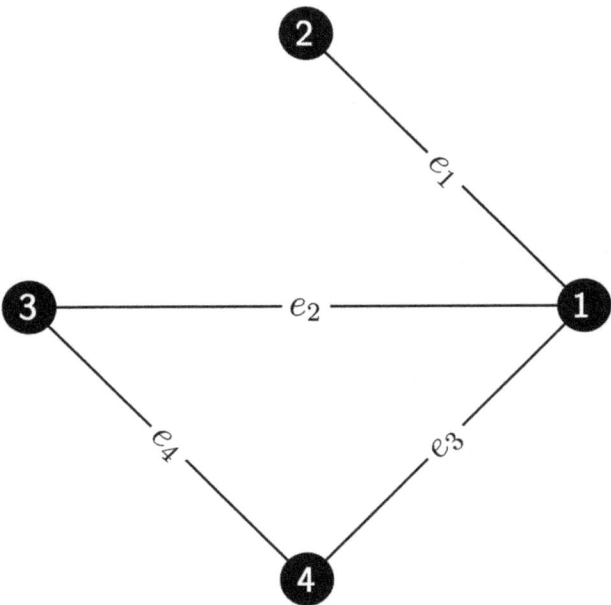

Figure 5.12 A graph with four edges.

Definition 5.2.24 *(Incidence Matrix)* The incidence matrix of an undirected graph $G = (V, E)$ is the $n \times m$ matrix B, where $n = |V|$ and $m = |E|$ are the numbers of vertices and edges respectively, such that $B_{ij} = 1$ if the vertex i and edge e_j are incident and 0 otherwise.

Example 5.2.25 *(continued from Example 5.2.23)* The incidence matrix of the graph from the previous example is given by

$$B = \begin{pmatrix} 1 & 1 & 1 & 0 \\ 1 & 0 & 0 & 0 \\ 0 & 1 & 0 & 1 \\ 0 & 0 & 1 & 1 \end{pmatrix}.$$

This matrix is not symmetric. In fact, in general, it is not even square.

NUMERICAL CORNER Using NetworkX, the adjacency matrix of a graph can be obtained with `networkx.adjacency_matrix`. By default, it returns a SciPy sparse matrix. Alternatively, one can get a regular array with `toarray`.

```
G = nx.complete_graph(4)
```

```
A = nx.adjacency_matrix(G)
print(A)
```

```
  (0, 1)    1
  (0, 2)    1
  (0, 3)    1
  (1, 0)    1
  (1, 2)    1
  (1, 3)    1
  (2, 0)    1
  (2, 1)    1
  (2, 3)    1
  (3, 0)    1
  (3, 1)    1
  (3, 2)    1
```

```
A = nx.adjacency_matrix(G).toarray()
print(A)
```

```
[[0 1 1 1]
 [1 0 1 1]
 [1 1 0 1]
 [1 1 1 0]]
```

The incidence matrix is obtained with `networkx.incidence_matrix` – again as a sparse array.

```
B = nx.incidence_matrix(G)
print(B)
```

```
(0, 0)      1.0
(1, 0)      1.0
(0, 1)      1.0
(2, 1)      1.0
(0, 2)      1.0
(3, 2)      1.0
(1, 3)      1.0
(2, 3)      1.0
(1, 4)      1.0
(3, 4)      1.0
(2, 5)      1.0
(3, 5)      1.0
```

```
B = nx.incidence_matrix(G).toarray()
print(B)
```

```
[[1. 1. 1. 0. 0. 0.]
 [1. 0. 0. 1. 1. 0.]
 [0. 1. 0. 1. 0. 1.]
 [0. 0. 1. 0. 1. 1.]]
```

◁ **NC**

In the digraph case, the definitions are adapted as follows. The adjacency matrix A of a digraph $G = (V, E)$ is the matrix defined as

$$A_{xy} = \begin{cases} 1 & \text{if } (x, y) \in E \\ 0 & \text{otherwise.} \end{cases}$$

The incidence matrix of a digraph G with vertices $1, \ldots, n$ and edges $e_1, \ldots, e_m$ is the matrix B such that $B_{ij} = -1$ if egde e_j leaves vertex i, $B_{ij} = 1$ if egde e_j enters vertex i, and 0 otherwise.

Returning to undirected graphs, an orientation of an (undirected) graph $G = (V, E)$ is a choice of direction for each of its edges, turning it into a digraph. See Figure 5.13.

Definition 5.2.26 *(Oriented Incidence Matrix)* An oriented incidence matrix of an undirected graph $G = (V, E)$ is the incidence matrix of an orientation of G.

NUMERICAL CORNER We revisit an earlier directed graph.

```
G = nx.DiGraph()
G.add_edge(0, 1)
G.add_edge(2, 3)
G.add_edge(0, 3)
G.add_edge(3, 0)
G.add_edge(1,1)
```

We compute the adjacency and incidence matrices. For the incidence matrix, one must specify `oriented=True` for the oriented version.

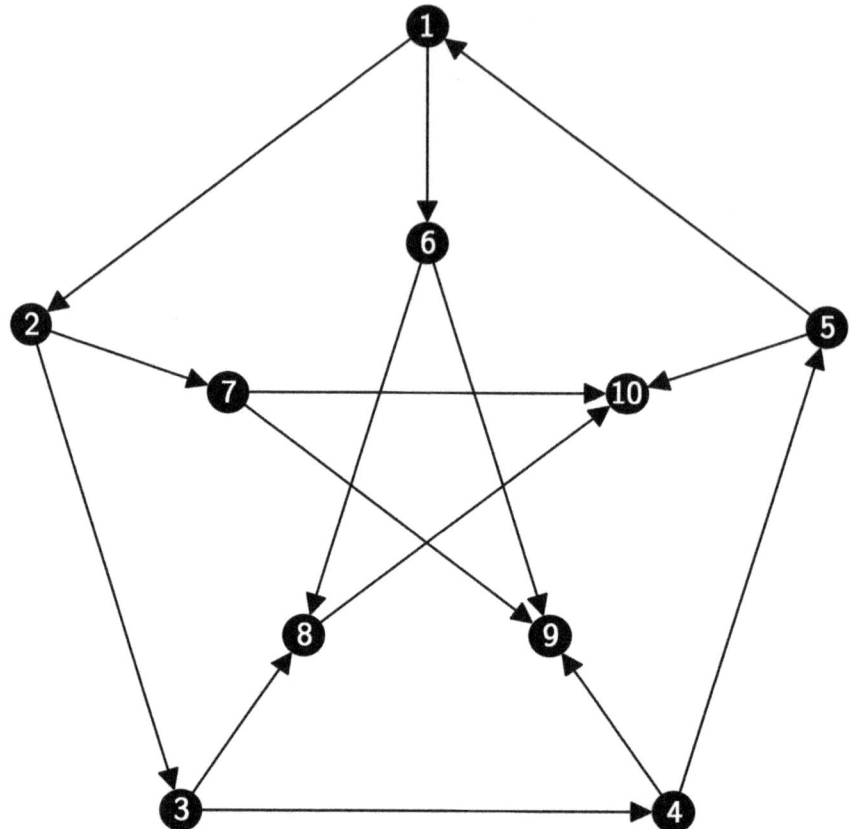

Figure 5.13 An orientation of the Petersen graph.

```
A = nx.adjacency_matrix(G).toarray()
print(A)
```

```
[[0 1 0 1]
 [0 1 0 0]
 [0 0 0 1]
 [1 0 0 0]]
```

```
B = nx.incidence_matrix(G, oriented=True).toarray()
print(B)
```

```
[[-1. -1.  0.  0.  1.]
 [ 1.  0.  0.  0.  0.]
 [ 0.  0.  0. -1.  0.]
 [ 0.  1.  0.  1. -1.]]
```

Revisiting an earlier undirected graph, we note that `networkx.incidence_matrix` can also produce an arbitrary oriented incidence matrix by using the `oriented=True` option.

```
G = nx.empty_graph(4)
G.add_edge(0, 1)
G.add_edge(2, 3)
G.add_edge(0, 3)
G.add_edge(3, 0)

B = nx.incidence_matrix(G, oriented=True).toarray()
print(B)
```

```
[[-1. -1.  0.]
 [ 1.  0.  0.]
 [ 0.  0. -1.]
 [ 0.  1.  1.]]
```

⊲ NC

5.2.4 Laplacian Matrix

A main matrix of interest for us will be the Laplacian matrix. It is a graph analog of the Laplace–Beltrami operator in differential geometry. We will show in particular that it contains useful information about the connectedness of the graph and we will describe an application to graph partitioning in Section 5.5. But first some theory.

Recall that, given a graph $G = (V, E)$, the quantity $\delta(v)$ denotes the degree of $v \in V$.

Definition 5.2.27 (Degree Matrix) *Let $G = (V, E)$ be a graph with vertices $V = \{1, \ldots, n\}$. The degree matrix is the diagonal matrix with the degrees on the diagonal, $D =$ diag $(\delta(1), \ldots, \delta(n))$.*

The key definition is the following.

Definition 5.2.28 (Laplacian Matrix) *Let $G = (V, E)$ be a graph with vertices $V = \{1, \ldots, n\}$, adjacency matrix $A \in \mathbb{R}^{n \times n}$, and degree matrix $D =$ diag$(\delta(1), \ldots, \delta(n))$. The Laplacian matrix associated with G is defined as $L = D - A$. Its entries are*

$$l_{ij} = \begin{cases} \delta(i) & \text{if } i = j \\ -1 & \text{if } \{i, j\} \in E \\ 0 & \text{otherwise.} \end{cases}$$

Like the adjacency matrix, the Laplacian matrix is symmetric. Unlike the adjacency matrix, however, it is also positive semidefinite.

Theorem 5.2.29 (Properties of the Laplacian) *For any graph G, the Laplacian matrix is symmetric and positive semidefinite.*

Proof Observe that the Laplacian matrix L of a graph G is indeed symmetric:

$$L^T = (D - A)^T = D^T - A^T = D - A$$

using the fact that both D and A are themselves symmetric.

To prove the second claim, we need a lemma.

Lemma 5.2.30 *(Laplacian and Incidence)* Let L be the Laplacian matrix of a graph G. Let B be any oriented incidence matrix of G. Then
$$L = BB^T.$$

Proof idea: We just check the claim entry by entry.

Proof Enumerate the edges $e_1, \ldots, e_m$. Let b_{ik} be entry (i,k) of B. For $i \neq j$, entry (i,j) of BB^T is
$$(BB^T)_{ij} = \sum_{k=1}^{m} b_{ik} b_{jk}.$$

Note that $b_{ik} b_{jk}$ is equal to (a) 0 if i or j (or both) are not incident with e_k or (b) -1 if both i and j are incident with e_k (since one of i or j has a 1 in the column of B corresponding to e_k and the other one has a -1). So $(BB^T)_{ij} = -1$ when $\{i,j\} \in E$ and is otherwise 0. So it coincides with the corresponding entry of the Laplacian matrix there.

For $i = j$,
$$(BB^T)_{ii} = \sum_{k=1}^{m} b_{ik}^2 = \sum_{e=\{x,y\}\in E:\, i\in e} b_{xy}^2 = \sum_{e=\{x,y\}\in E:\, i\in e} 1 = \delta(i),$$

where we used the fact that $b_{xy}^2 = 1$ because $b_{xy} \in \{-1, 1\}$ when $\{x, y\} \in E$. Again this coincides with the corresponding entry of the Laplacian matrix. □

We return to the proof of the theorem. By the previous lemma, for any $\mathbf{x} \in \mathbb{R}^n$,
$$\mathbf{x}^T L \mathbf{x} = \mathbf{x}^T BB^T \mathbf{x} = \|B^T \mathbf{x}\|^2 \geq 0.$$

This proves positive semidefiniteness. □

Self-Assessment Quiz (with help from Claude, Gemini, and ChatGPT)

1. Which of the following is NOT a valid definition of an undirected graph?
   a) A pair $G = (V, E)$, where V is the set of vertices and E is a set of unordered pairs of vertices
   b) A collection of nodes connected by edges, where the edges have no direction
   c) A pair $G = (V, E)$, where V is the set of vertices and E is a set of ordered pairs of vertices
   d) A mathematical structure used to model pairwise relations between objects

2. In a graph, what does the equivalence relation $\leftrightarrow$ signify?
   a) Two vertices are in the same connected component.
   b) Two vertices have the same degree.
   c) Two vertices are adjacent.
   d) Two vertices are part of a cycle.

3. In a directed graph, what is the relationship between the in-degree and out-degree of a vertex?
   a) The in-degree is always greater than or equal to the out-degree.
   b) The out-degree is always greater than or equal to the in-degree.

c) The in-degree and out-degree are always equal.

d) There is no fixed relationship between the in-degree and out-degree.

4 Which of the following is NOT a property of the Laplacian matrix of a graph?

   a) It is symmetric.
   b) It is positive semidefinite.
   c) It is always invertible.
   d) Its entries sum to zero in each row and column.

5 Which matrix representation of a graph is typically symmetric?

   a) Adjacency matrix of an undirected graph
   b) Incidence matrix of an undirected graph
   c) Adjacency matrix of a directed graph
   d) All of the above

Answer for 1: c. Justification: The text defines an undirected graph as a pair $G = (V, E)$, where E is a set of unordered pairs of vertices, not ordered pairs.

Answer for 2: a. Justification: The text defines the relation $\leftrightarrow$ as an equivalence relation that indicates two vertices are in the same connected component.

Answer for 3: d. Justification: The in-degree and out-degree of a vertex in a directed graph depend on the number of edges entering and leaving the vertex, respectively, and there is no fixed relationship between them.

Answer for 4: c. Justification: The text proves that the Laplacian matrix is symmetric and positive semidefinite, but does not claim that it is always invertible.

Answer for 5: a. Justification: The text states that the adjacency matrix of an undirected graph is symmetric.

5.3 Variational Characterization of Eigenvalues

In this section, we characterize eigenvalues in terms of certain optimization problems, an idea we have already encountered in the closely related context of the SVD. Such variational characterizations are very useful in applications, as we will see later in the chapter. We first give a proof of the *Spectral Theorem* where this idea is used explicitly.

5.3.1 Proof of Spectral Theorem

We will need the following block matrix formula. Suppose

$$A = \begin{pmatrix} A_{11} \\ A_{21} \end{pmatrix} \quad \text{and} \quad B = \begin{pmatrix} B_{11} & B_{12} \end{pmatrix}$$

where $A_{11} \in \mathbb{R}^{n_1 \times p}$, $A_{21} \in \mathbb{R}^{n_2 \times p}$, $B_{11} \in \mathbb{R}^{p \times n_1}$, $B_{12} \in \mathbb{R}^{p \times n_2}$; then

$$AB = \begin{pmatrix} A_{11}B_{11} & A_{11}B_{12} \\ A_{21}B_{11} & A_{21}B_{12} \end{pmatrix}.$$

Indeed this is just a special case of the 2×2 block matrix product formula we have encountered previously in Section 1.2.1.5, with empty blocks $A_{12}, A_{22}, B_{21}, B_{22}$.
We restate the *Spectral Theorem* here.

Theorem 5.3.1 *(Spectral Theorem)* *Let $A \in \mathbb{R}^{d \times d}$ be a symmetric matrix; that is, $A^T = A$. Then A has d orthonormal eigenvectors $\mathbf{q}_1, \ldots, \mathbf{q}_d$ with corresponding (not necessarily distinct) real eigenvalues $\lambda_1 \geq \lambda_2 \geq \cdots \geq \lambda_d$. Moreover, A can be written as the matrix factorization*

$$A = Q \Lambda Q^T = \sum_{i=1}^{d} \lambda_i \mathbf{q}_i \mathbf{q}_i^T$$

where Q has columns $\mathbf{q}_1, \ldots, \mathbf{q}_d$ and $\Lambda = \mathrm{diag}(\lambda_1, \ldots, \lambda_d)$.

Proof idea (Spectral Theorem): Similarly to how we used Householder transformations to "add zeros under the diagonal," here we will use a sequence of orthogonal transformations to add zeros both below and above the diagonal. Recall that two matrices $C, D \in \mathbb{R}^{d \times d}$ are similar if there is an invertible matrix P such that $C = P^{-1}DP$, and that, when $P = W$ is an orthogonal matrix, the transformation simplifies to $C = W^T D W$.

We construct a sequence of orthogonal matrices $\hat{W}_1, \ldots, \hat{W}_d$ and progressively compute $W_1^T A W_1$, $W_2^T W_1^T A W_1 W_2$, and so on in such a way that

$$\Lambda = W_d^T \cdots W_2^T W_1^T A W_1 W_2 \cdots W_d$$

is diagonal. Then the matrix Q is simply $W_1 W_2 \cdots W_d$ (check it!).

To define these matrices, we use a greedy sequence maximizing the quadratic form $\langle \mathbf{v}, A\mathbf{v} \rangle$. How is this quadratic form related to eigenvalues? Recall that, for a unit eigenvector $\mathbf{v}$ with eigenvalue λ, we have $\langle \mathbf{v}, A\mathbf{v} \rangle = \langle \mathbf{v}, \lambda \mathbf{v} \rangle = \lambda$.

Proof *(Spectral Theorem)* We proceed by induction. We have already encountered the idea that eigenvectors are stationary points of an optimization problem (see Example 3.3.7). The proof in fact uses that idea.

A first eigenvector: Let $A_1 = A$. Define

$$\mathbf{v}_1 \in \arg\max\{\langle \mathbf{v}, A_1 \mathbf{v} \rangle : \|\mathbf{v}\| = 1\}$$

which exists by the *Extreme Value Theorem*, and further define

$$\lambda_1 = \max\{\langle \mathbf{v}, A_1 \mathbf{v} \rangle : \|\mathbf{v}\| = 1\}.$$

Complete $\mathbf{v}_1$ into an orthonormal basis of $\mathbb{R}^d$, $\mathbf{v}_1, \hat{\mathbf{v}}_2, \ldots, \hat{\mathbf{v}}_d$, and form the block matrix

$$\hat{W}_1 = \begin{pmatrix} \mathbf{v}_1 & \hat{V}_1 \end{pmatrix}$$

where the columns of $\hat{V}_1$ are $\hat{\mathbf{v}}_2, \ldots, \hat{\mathbf{v}}_d$. Note that $\hat{W}_1$ is orthogonal by construction.

5.3 Variational Characterization of Eigenvalues

Getting one step closer to diagonalization: We show next that $\hat{W}_1$ gets us one step closer to a diagonal matrix by similarity transformation. Note first that

$$\hat{W}_1^T A_1 \hat{W}_1 = \begin{pmatrix} \mathbf{v}_1^T \\ \hat{V}_1^T \end{pmatrix} A_1 \begin{pmatrix} \mathbf{v}_1 & \hat{V}_1 \end{pmatrix}$$

$$= \begin{pmatrix} \mathbf{v}_1^T \\ \hat{V}_1^T \end{pmatrix} \begin{pmatrix} A_1 \mathbf{v}_1 & A_1 \hat{V}_1 \end{pmatrix}$$

$$= \begin{pmatrix} \mathbf{v}_1^T A_1 \mathbf{v}_1 & \mathbf{v}_1^T A_1 \hat{V}_1 \\ \hat{V}_1^T A_1 \mathbf{v}_1 & \hat{V}_1^T A_1 \hat{V}_1 \end{pmatrix}$$

$$= \begin{pmatrix} \lambda_1 & \mathbf{w}_1^T \\ \mathbf{w}_1 & A_2 \end{pmatrix}$$

where $\mathbf{w}_1 = \hat{V}_1^T A_1 \mathbf{v}_1$ and $A_2 = \hat{V}_1^T A_1 \hat{V}_1$.

The key claim is that $\mathbf{w}_1 = \mathbf{0}$. This follows from a contradiction argument. Indeed, suppose $\mathbf{w}_1 \neq \mathbf{0}$ and consider the unit vector (check that $\|\mathbf{z}\| = 1$)

$$\mathbf{z} = \hat{W}_1 \frac{1}{\sqrt{1 + \delta^2 \|\mathbf{w}_1\|^2}} \begin{pmatrix} 1 \\ \delta \mathbf{w}_1 \end{pmatrix}$$

which achieves the objective value (see Problem 5.4):

$$\mathbf{z}^T A_1 \mathbf{z} = \frac{1}{1 + \delta^2 \|\mathbf{w}_1\|^2} \begin{pmatrix} 1 \\ \delta \mathbf{w}_1 \end{pmatrix}^T \begin{pmatrix} \lambda_1 & \mathbf{w}_1^T \\ \mathbf{w}_1 & A_2 \end{pmatrix} \begin{pmatrix} 1 \\ \delta \mathbf{w}_1 \end{pmatrix}$$

$$= \frac{1}{1 + \delta^2 \|\mathbf{w}_1\|^2} \left(\lambda_1 + 2\delta \|\mathbf{w}_1\|^2 + \delta^2 \mathbf{w}_1^T A_2 \mathbf{w}_1 \right).$$

By the sum of a geometric series, for $\varepsilon \in (0, 1)$,

$$\frac{1}{1 + \varepsilon^2} = 1 - \varepsilon^2 + \varepsilon^4 + \cdots .$$

So, for $\delta > 0$ small enough,

$$\mathbf{z}^T A_1 \mathbf{z} \approx (\lambda_1 + 2\delta \|\mathbf{w}_1\|^2 + \delta^2 \mathbf{w}_1^T A_2 \mathbf{w}_1)(1 - \delta^2 \|\mathbf{w}_1\|^2)$$

$$\approx \lambda_1 + 2\delta \|\mathbf{w}_1\|^2 + C\delta^2$$

$$> \lambda_1$$

where $C \in \mathbb{R}$ depends on $\mathbf{w}_1$ and A_2, and where we ignored the "higher-order" terms involving $\delta^3, \delta^4, \delta^5, \ldots$ whose overall contribution is negligible when δ is small (why?). That gives the desired contradiction – that is, it would imply the existence of a vector achieving a strictly better objective value than the optimal $\mathbf{v}_1$.

So, letting $W_1 = \hat{W}_1$,

$$W_1^T A_1 W_1 = \begin{pmatrix} \lambda_1 & \mathbf{0} \\ \mathbf{0} & A_2 \end{pmatrix}.$$

Finally note that $A_2 = \hat{V}_1^T A_1 \hat{V}_1$ is symmetric:

$$A_2^T = (\hat{V}_1^T A_1 \hat{V}_1)^T = \hat{V}_1^T A_1^T \hat{V}_1 = \hat{V}_1^T A_1 \hat{V}_1 = A_2$$

by the symmetry of A_1 itself.

Next step of the induction: Apply the same argument to the symmetric matrix $A_2 \in \mathbb{R}^{(d-1)\times(d-1)}$, let $\hat{W}_2 = (\mathbf{v}_2 \ \hat{V}_2) \in \mathbb{R}^{(d-1)\times(d-1)}$ be the corresponding orthogonal matrix, and define λ_2 and A_3 by the equation

$$\hat{W}_2^T A_2 \hat{W}_2 = \begin{pmatrix} \lambda_2 & \mathbf{0} \\ \mathbf{0} & A_3 \end{pmatrix}.$$

Now define the block matrix

$$W_2 = \begin{pmatrix} 1 & \mathbf{0} \\ \mathbf{0} & \hat{W}_2 \end{pmatrix}.$$

Observe that (check it!)

$$W_2^T W_1^T A_1 W_1 W_2 = W_2^T \begin{pmatrix} \lambda_1 & \mathbf{0} \\ \mathbf{0} & A_2 \end{pmatrix} W_2 = \begin{pmatrix} \lambda_1 & \mathbf{0} \\ \mathbf{0} & \hat{W}_2^T A_2 \hat{W}_2 \end{pmatrix} = \begin{pmatrix} \lambda_1 & 0 & \mathbf{0} \\ 0 & \lambda_2 & \mathbf{0} \\ \mathbf{0} & \mathbf{0} & A_3 \end{pmatrix}.$$

Proceeding similarly by induction gives the claim. □

A couple of remarks about the proof:

First, the fact that $\mathbf{w}_1 = \mathbf{0}$ is perhaps more intuitively understood through vector calculus by using the method of Lagrangian multipliers on $\max\{\langle \mathbf{v}, A_1 \mathbf{v}\rangle : \|\mathbf{v}\| = 1\}$ to see that $A_1 \mathbf{v}_1$ must be proportional to $\mathbf{v}_1$. Hence $\mathbf{w}_1 = \hat{V}_1^T A_1 \mathbf{v}_1 = \mathbf{0}$ by construction of $\hat{V}_1^T$. Indeed, define the Lagrangian function

$$L(\mathbf{v}, \lambda) = \langle \mathbf{v}, A_1 \mathbf{v}\rangle - \lambda(\|\mathbf{v}\|^2 - 1).$$

The first-order necessary conditions for a local maximizer $\mathbf{v}_1$ are (check it!)

$$\nabla_\mathbf{v} L(\mathbf{v}_1, \lambda_1) = 2A_1 \mathbf{v}_1 - 2\lambda_1 \mathbf{v}_1 = \mathbf{0}$$

$$\nabla_\lambda L(\mathbf{v}_1, \lambda_1) = \|\mathbf{v}_1\|^2 - 1 = 0.$$

From the first condition, we have

$$A_1 \mathbf{v}_1 = \lambda_1 \mathbf{v}_1.$$

This shows that $A_1 \mathbf{v}_1$ is proportional to $\mathbf{v}_1$ as claimed.

Second, by construction, the vector $\mathbf{v}_2$ (i.e., the first column of $\hat{W}_2$) is the solution to

$$\mathbf{v}_2 \in \arg\max\{\langle \mathbf{v}, A_2 \mathbf{v}\rangle : \|\mathbf{v}\| = 1\}.$$

Note that, by definition of A_2 (and the fact that $A_1 = A$),

$$\mathbf{v}^T A_2 \mathbf{v} = \mathbf{v}^T \hat{V}_1^T A_1 \hat{V}_1 \mathbf{v} = (\hat{V}_1 \mathbf{v})^T A (\hat{V}_1 \mathbf{v}).$$

So we can think of the solution $\mathbf{v}_2$ as specifying an optimal linear combination of the columns of $\hat{V}_1$ – which form a basis of the space $\text{span}(\mathbf{v}_1)^\perp$ of vectors orthogonal to $\mathbf{v}_1$. In essence $\mathbf{v}_2$ solves the same problem as $\mathbf{v}_1$, *but restricted to* $\text{span}(\mathbf{v}_1)^\perp$. We will come back to this below.

5.3.2 Varational Characterization: Special Cases

We begin with a definition.

Definition 5.3.2 *(Rayleigh Quotient)* *Let $A \in \mathbb{R}^{d \times d}$ be a symmetric matrix. The Rayleigh quotient is defined as*

$$\mathcal{R}_A(\mathbf{u}) = \frac{\langle \mathbf{u}, A\mathbf{u}\rangle}{\langle \mathbf{u}, \mathbf{u}\rangle}$$

which is defined for any $\mathbf{u} \neq \mathbf{0}$ in $\mathbb{R}^d$.

To start seeing the connection to the spectral decomposition, let $\mathbf{v}$ be a (not necessarily unit) eigenvector of A with eigenvalue λ. One can show that $\mathcal{R}_A(\mathbf{v}) = \lambda$. (Try it!) In fact, recall that we have previously shown that eigenvectors of A are stationary points of $\mathcal{R}_A$ (see Example 3.3.7).

Before stating a general variational characterization, we prove a few special cases. Throughout, let $A \in \mathbb{R}^{d \times d}$ be a symmetric matrix with spectral decomposition $A = \sum_{i=1}^{d} \lambda_i \mathbf{v}_i \mathbf{v}_i^T$ where $\lambda_1 \geq \cdots \geq \lambda_d$.

The largest eigenvalue: Since $\mathbf{v}_1, \ldots, \mathbf{v}_d$ forms an orthonormal basis of $\mathbb{R}^d$, any nonzero vector $\mathbf{u}$ can be written as $\mathbf{u} = \sum_{i=1}^{d} \langle \mathbf{u}, \mathbf{v}_i\rangle \mathbf{v}_i$ and it follows that, by the *Properties of Orthonormal Lists Lemma* and the bilinearity of the inner product,

$$\langle \mathbf{u}, \mathbf{u}\rangle = \|\mathbf{u}\|^2 = \left\|\sum_{i=1}^{d} \langle \mathbf{u}, \mathbf{v}_i\rangle \mathbf{v}_i\right\|^2 = \sum_{i=1}^{d} \langle \mathbf{u}, \mathbf{v}_i\rangle^2$$

$$\langle \mathbf{u}, A\mathbf{u}\rangle = \left\langle \mathbf{u}, \sum_{i=1}^{d} \langle \mathbf{u}, \mathbf{v}_i\rangle A\mathbf{v}_i\right\rangle = \left\langle \mathbf{u}, \sum_{i=1}^{d} \langle \mathbf{u}, \mathbf{v}_i\rangle \lambda_i \mathbf{v}_i\right\rangle = \sum_{i=1}^{d} \lambda_i \langle \mathbf{u}, \mathbf{v}_i\rangle^2.$$

Thus,

$$\mathcal{R}_A(\mathbf{u}) = \frac{\langle \mathbf{u}, A\mathbf{u}\rangle}{\langle \mathbf{u}, \mathbf{u}\rangle} = \frac{\sum_{i=1}^{d} \lambda_i \langle \mathbf{u}, \mathbf{v}_i\rangle^2}{\sum_{i=1}^{d} \langle \mathbf{u}, \mathbf{v}_i\rangle^2} \leq \lambda_1 \frac{\sum_{i=1}^{d} \langle \mathbf{u}, \mathbf{v}_i\rangle^2}{\sum_{i=1}^{d} \langle \mathbf{u}, \mathbf{v}_i\rangle^2} = \lambda_1,$$

where we used $\lambda_1 \geq \cdots \geq \lambda_d$ and the fact that $\langle \mathbf{u}, \mathbf{v}_i\rangle^2 \geq 0$. Moreover $\mathcal{R}_A(\mathbf{v}_1) = \lambda_1$. So we have established

$$\lambda_1 = \max_{\mathbf{u} \neq \mathbf{0}} \mathcal{R}_A(\mathbf{u}).$$

The smallest eigenvalue: Arguing in the opposite direction, we get a characterization of the smallest eigenvalue. Using the same notation as before, we have

$$\mathcal{R}_A(\mathbf{u}) = \frac{\langle \mathbf{u}, A\mathbf{u}\rangle}{\langle \mathbf{u}, \mathbf{u}\rangle} = \frac{\sum_{i=1}^{d} \lambda_i \langle \mathbf{u}, \mathbf{v}_i\rangle^2}{\sum_{i=1}^{d} \langle \mathbf{u}, \mathbf{v}_i\rangle^2} \geq \lambda_d \frac{\sum_{i=1}^{d} \langle \mathbf{u}, \mathbf{v}_i\rangle^2}{\sum_{i=1}^{d} \langle \mathbf{u}, \mathbf{v}_i\rangle^2} = \lambda_d,$$

where, again, we used $\lambda_1 \geq \cdots \geq \lambda_d$ and the fact that $\langle \mathbf{u}, \mathbf{v}_i\rangle^2 \geq 0$. Moreover $\mathcal{R}_A(\mathbf{v}_d) = \lambda_d$. So we have established

$$\lambda_d = \min_{\mathbf{u} \neq \mathbf{0}} \mathcal{R}_A(\mathbf{u}).$$

The second smallest eigenvalue: To pick out the second smallest eigenvalue, we argue as above but restrict the optimization to the space $\mathcal{V}_{d-1} = \text{span}(\mathbf{v}_1, \ldots, \mathbf{v}_{d-1})$. Indeed, if $\mathbf{u}$ is in the linear subspace $\mathcal{V}_{d-1}$, it can be written as $\mathbf{u} = \sum_{i=1}^{d-1} \langle \mathbf{u}, \mathbf{v}_i \rangle \mathbf{v}_i$ (since $\mathbf{v}_1, \ldots, \mathbf{v}_{d-1}$ forms an orthonormal basis of it; why?) and it follows that

$$\langle \mathbf{u}, \mathbf{u} \rangle = \sum_{i=1}^{d-1} \langle \mathbf{u}, \mathbf{v}_i \rangle^2$$

$$\langle \mathbf{u}, A\mathbf{u} \rangle = \left\langle \mathbf{u}, \sum_{i=1}^{d-1} \langle \mathbf{u}, \mathbf{v}_i \rangle \lambda_i \mathbf{v}_i \right\rangle = \sum_{i=1}^{d-1} \lambda_i \langle \mathbf{u}, \mathbf{v}_i \rangle^2.$$

Thus,

$$\mathcal{R}_A(\mathbf{u}) = \frac{\langle \mathbf{u}, A\mathbf{u} \rangle}{\langle \mathbf{u}, \mathbf{u} \rangle} = \frac{\sum_{i=1}^{d-1} \lambda_i \langle \mathbf{u}, \mathbf{v}_i \rangle^2}{\sum_{i=1}^{d-1} \langle \mathbf{u}, \mathbf{v}_i \rangle^2} \geq \lambda_{d-1} \frac{\sum_{i=1}^{d-1} \langle \mathbf{u}, \mathbf{v}_i \rangle^2}{\sum_{i=1}^{d-1} \langle \mathbf{u}, \mathbf{v}_i \rangle^2} = \lambda_{d-1},$$

where we used $\lambda_1 \geq \cdots \geq \lambda_{d-1}$ and the fact that $\langle \mathbf{u}, \mathbf{v}_i \rangle^2 \geq 0$. Moreover $\mathcal{R}_A(\mathbf{v}_{d-1}) = \lambda_{d-1}$ and of course $\mathbf{v}_{d-1} \in \mathcal{V}_{d-1}$. So we have established

$$\lambda_{d-1} = \min_{\mathbf{0} \neq \mathbf{u} \in \mathcal{V}_{d-1}} \mathcal{R}_A(\mathbf{u}).$$

Now what is $\mathcal{V}_{d-1}$? It is spanned by the orthonormal list $\mathbf{v}_1, \ldots, \mathbf{v}_{d-1}$, each of which is orthogonal to $\mathbf{v}_d$. So (why?)

$$\mathcal{V}_{d-1} = \text{span}(\mathbf{v}_d)^\perp.$$

So, equivalently,

$$\lambda_{d-1} = \min \{\mathcal{R}_A(\mathbf{u}): \mathbf{u} \neq \mathbf{0}, \langle \mathbf{u}, \mathbf{v}_d \rangle = 0\}.$$

In fact, for any $\mathbf{u} \neq \mathbf{0}$, we can normalize it by defining $\mathbf{z} = \mathbf{u}/\|\mathbf{u}\|$ and we note that

$$\mathcal{R}_A(\mathbf{u}) = \frac{\langle \mathbf{u}, A\mathbf{u} \rangle}{\langle \mathbf{u}, \mathbf{u} \rangle} = \frac{\langle \mathbf{u}, A\mathbf{u} \rangle}{\|\mathbf{u}\|^2} = \left\langle \frac{\mathbf{u}}{\|\mathbf{u}\|}, A \frac{\mathbf{u}}{\|\mathbf{u}\|} \right\rangle = \langle \mathbf{z}, A\mathbf{z} \rangle.$$

So,

$$\lambda_{d-1} = \min \{\langle \mathbf{z}, A\mathbf{z} \rangle: \|\mathbf{z}\| = 1, \langle \mathbf{z}, \mathbf{v}_d \rangle = 0\}.$$

5.3.3 General Statement: Courant–Fischer

Before stating a general result, we give one more example.

The second smallest eigenvalue (take two): Interestingly, there is a second characterization of the second smallest eigenvalue. Indeed, suppose we restrict the optimization to the space $\mathcal{W}_2 = \text{span}(\mathbf{v}_{d-1}, \mathbf{v}_d)$ instead. If $\mathbf{u}$ is in the linear subspace $\mathcal{W}_2$, it can be written as $\mathbf{u} = \sum_{i=d-1}^{d} \langle \mathbf{u}, \mathbf{v}_i \rangle \mathbf{v}_i$ (since $\mathbf{v}_{d-1}, \mathbf{v}_d$ forms an orthonormal basis of it) and it follows that

$$\langle \mathbf{u}, \mathbf{u} \rangle = \sum_{i=d-1}^{d} \langle \mathbf{u}, \mathbf{v}_i \rangle^2$$

$$\langle \mathbf{u}, A\mathbf{u} \rangle = \left\langle \mathbf{u}, \sum_{i=d-1}^{d} \langle \mathbf{u}, \mathbf{v}_i \rangle \lambda_i \mathbf{v}_i \right\rangle = \sum_{i=d-1}^{d} \lambda_i \langle \mathbf{u}, \mathbf{v}_i \rangle^2.$$

Thus,
$$\mathcal{R}_A(\mathbf{u}) = \frac{\langle \mathbf{u}, A\mathbf{u} \rangle}{\langle \mathbf{u}, \mathbf{u} \rangle} = \frac{\sum_{i=d-1}^{d} \lambda_i \langle \mathbf{u}, \mathbf{v}_i \rangle^2}{\sum_{i=d-1}^{d} \langle \mathbf{u}, \mathbf{v}_i \rangle^2} \leq \lambda_{d-1} \frac{\sum_{i=d-1}^{d} \langle \mathbf{u}, \mathbf{v}_i \rangle^2}{\sum_{i=d-1}^{d} \langle \mathbf{u}, \mathbf{v}_i \rangle^2} = \lambda_{d-1},$$

where we used $\lambda_{d-1} \geq \lambda_d$ and the fact that $\langle \mathbf{u}, \mathbf{v}_i \rangle^2 \geq 0$. Moreover $\mathcal{R}_A(\mathbf{v}_{d-1}) = \lambda_{d-1}$. So we have established

$$\lambda_{d-1} = \max_{\mathbf{0} \neq \mathbf{u} \in \mathcal{W}_2} \mathcal{R}_A(\mathbf{u}).$$

Theorem 5.3.3 (Courant–Fischer) *Let $A \in \mathbb{R}^{d \times d}$ be a symmetric matrix with spectral decomposition $A = \sum_{i=1}^{d} \lambda_i \mathbf{v}_i \mathbf{v}_i^T$ where $\lambda_1 \geq \cdots \geq \lambda_d$. For each $k = 1, \ldots, d$, define the subspace*

$$\mathcal{V}_k = \mathrm{span}(\mathbf{v}_1, \ldots, \mathbf{v}_k) \quad \text{and} \quad \mathcal{W}_{d-k+1} = \mathrm{span}(\mathbf{v}_k, \ldots, \mathbf{v}_d).$$

Then, for all $k = 1, \ldots, d$,

$$\lambda_k = \min_{\mathbf{u} \in \mathcal{V}_k} \mathcal{R}_A(\mathbf{u}) = \max_{\mathbf{u} \in \mathcal{W}_{d-k+1}} \mathcal{R}_A(\mathbf{u}),$$

which are referred to as the local formulas. Furthermore we have the following min-max (or global) formulas, which do not depend on the choice of a spectral decomposition: For all $k = 1, \ldots, d$,

$$\lambda_k = \max_{\dim(\mathcal{V})=k} \min_{\mathbf{u} \in \mathcal{V}} \mathcal{R}_A(\mathbf{u}) = \min_{\dim(\mathcal{W})=d-k+1} \max_{\mathbf{u} \in \mathcal{W}} \mathcal{R}_A(\mathbf{u}).$$

Proof idea: For the local formula, we expand a vector in $\mathcal{V}_k$ into the basis $\mathbf{v}_1, \ldots, \mathbf{v}_k$ and use the facts that $\mathcal{R}_A(\mathbf{v}_i) = \lambda_i$ and the eigenvalues are in nonincreasing order. The global formulas follow from a dimension argument.

Example 5.3.4 (Third Smallest Eigenvalue) *The* Courant–Fischer Theorem *can be used to recover the special cases of the previous subsection. One also gets new cases of interest. We give a characterization of the third smallest eigenvalue next. Let $A \in \mathbb{R}^{d \times d}$ be a symmetric matrix with spectral decomposition $A = \sum_{i=1}^{d} \lambda_i \mathbf{v}_i \mathbf{v}_i^T$ where $\lambda_1 \geq \cdots \geq \lambda_d$. Using $k = d - 2$ in the* Courant–Fischer Theorem *gives*

$$\lambda_{d-2} = \min_{\mathbf{u} \in \mathcal{V}_{d-2}} \mathcal{R}_A(\mathbf{u}),$$

where

$$\mathcal{V}_{d-2} = \mathrm{span}(\mathbf{v}_1, \ldots, \mathbf{v}_{d-2}).$$

It can be seen that

$$\mathrm{span}(\mathbf{v}_1, \ldots, \mathbf{v}_{d-2}) = \mathrm{span}(\mathbf{v}_{d-1}, \mathbf{v}_d)^\perp.$$

So we finally arrive at the following characterization of the third smallest eigenvalue:

$$\lambda_{d-2} = \min\{\mathcal{R}_A(\mathbf{u}) : \mathbf{0} \neq \mathbf{u}, \langle \mathbf{u}, \mathbf{v}_d \rangle = 0, \langle \mathbf{u}, \mathbf{v}_{d-1} \rangle = 0\}.$$

Using the same argument as we used for λ_{d-1}, we get also

$$\lambda_{d-2} = \min\{\langle \mathbf{z}, A\mathbf{z} \rangle : \|\mathbf{z}\| = 1, \langle \mathbf{z}, \mathbf{v}_d \rangle = 0, \langle \mathbf{z}, \mathbf{v}_{d-1} \rangle = 0\}.$$

We now give a proof of the *Courant–Fischer Theorem*. The local formulas follow from the same argument used to derive the special cases above so we omit the general proof (but try to prove it!). The global formulas require a new idea.

Proof *(Courant–Fischer)* Since $\mathcal{V}_k$ has dimension k, it follows from the local formula that
$$\lambda_k = \min_{\mathbf{u} \in \mathcal{V}_k} \mathcal{R}_A(\mathbf{u}) \leq \max_{\dim(\mathcal{V})=k} \min_{\mathbf{u} \in \mathcal{V}} \mathcal{R}_A(\mathbf{u}).$$
Let $\mathcal{V}$ be any subspace with dimension k. Because $\mathcal{W}_{d-k+1}$ has dimension $d - k + 1$, we have that $\dim(\mathcal{V}) + \dim(\mathcal{W}_{d-k+1}) > d$ and there must be a nonzero vector $\mathbf{u}_0$ in the intersection $\mathcal{V} \cap \mathcal{W}_{d-k+1}$ (prove it!).

We then have by the other local formula that
$$\lambda_k = \max_{\mathbf{u} \in \mathcal{W}_{d-k+1}} \mathcal{R}_A(\mathbf{u}) \geq \mathcal{R}_A(\mathbf{u}_0) \geq \min_{\mathbf{u} \in \mathcal{V}} \mathcal{R}_A(\mathbf{u}).$$
Since this inequality holds for any subspace of dimension k, we have
$$\lambda_k \geq \max_{\dim(\mathcal{V})=k} \min_{\mathbf{u} \in \mathcal{V}} \mathcal{R}_A(\mathbf{u}).$$
Combining with the inequality in the other direction above gives the claim. The other global formula is proved similarly. □

Self-Assessment Quiz (with help from Claude, Gemini, and ChatGPT)

1. According to the variational characterization of the largest eigenvalue λ_1 of a symmetric matrix A, which of the following is true?
   a) $\lambda_1 = \min_{\mathbf{u} \neq 0} \mathcal{R}_A(\mathbf{u})$
   b) $\lambda_1 = \max_{\mathbf{u} \neq 0} \mathcal{R}_A(\mathbf{u})$
   c) $\lambda_1 = \min_{\|\mathbf{u}\|=0} \mathcal{R}_A(\mathbf{u})$
   d) $\lambda_1 = \max_{\|\mathbf{u}\|=0} \mathcal{R}_A(\mathbf{u})$

2. Let $\mathcal{V}_{d-1} = \text{span}(\mathbf{v}_1, \ldots, \mathbf{v}_{d-1})$, where $\mathbf{v}_1, \ldots, \mathbf{v}_d$ are the eigenvectors of a symmetric matrix A with eigenvalues $\lambda_1 \geq \cdots \geq \lambda_d$. Which of the following characterizes the second smallest eigenvalue λ_{d-1}?
   a) $\lambda_{d-1} = \min_{0 \neq \mathbf{u} \in \mathcal{V}_{d-1}} \mathcal{R}_A(\mathbf{u})$
   b) $\lambda_{d-1} = \max_{0 \neq \mathbf{u} \in \mathcal{V}_{d-1}} \mathcal{R}_A(\mathbf{u})$
   c) $\lambda_{d-1} = \min_{\|\mathbf{u}\|=0, \mathbf{u} \in \mathcal{V}_{d-1}} \mathcal{R}_A(\mathbf{u})$
   d) $\lambda_{d-1} = \max_{\|\mathbf{u}\|=0, \mathbf{u} \in \mathcal{V}_{d-1}} \mathcal{R}_A(\mathbf{u})$

3. Let $\mathcal{W}_2 = \text{span}(\mathbf{v}_{d-1}, \mathbf{v}_d)$, where $\mathbf{v}_1, \ldots, \mathbf{v}_d$ are the eigenvectors of a symmetric matrix A with eigenvalues $\lambda_1 \geq \cdots \geq \lambda_d$. Which of the following characterizes the second smallest eigenvalue λ_{d-1}?
   a) $\lambda_{d-1} = \min_{0 \neq \mathbf{u} \in \mathcal{W}_2} \mathcal{R}_A(\mathbf{u})$
   b) $\lambda_{d-1} = \max_{0 \neq \mathbf{u} \in \mathcal{W}_2} \mathcal{R}_A(\mathbf{u})$
   c) $\lambda_{d-1} = \min_{\|\mathbf{u}\|=0, \mathbf{u} \in \mathcal{W}_2} \mathcal{R}_A(\mathbf{u})$
   d) $\lambda_{d-1} = \max_{\|\mathbf{u}\|=0, \mathbf{u} \in \mathcal{W}_2} \mathcal{R}_A(\mathbf{u})$

4. According to the *Courant–Fischer Theorem*, which of the following is the global formula for the k-th eigenvalue λ_k of a symmetric matrix A?

a) $\lambda_k = \min_{\mathbf{u} \in \mathcal{V}_k} R_A(\mathbf{u}) = \max_{\mathbf{u} \in \mathcal{W}_{d-k+1}} R_A(\mathbf{u})$
b) $\lambda_k = \max_{\mathbf{u} \in \mathcal{V}_k} R_A(u) = \min_{u \in \mathcal{W}_{d-k+1}} R_A(u)$
c) $\lambda_k = \max_{\dim(\mathcal{V})=k} \min_{\mathbf{u} \in \mathcal{V}} R_A(\mathbf{u}) = \min_{\dim(\mathcal{W})=d-k+1} \max_{\mathbf{u} \in \mathcal{W}} R_A(\mathbf{u})$
d) $\lambda_k = \max_{\dim(\mathcal{V})=k} \max_{\mathbf{u} \in \mathcal{V}} R_A(\mathbf{u}) = \min_{\dim(\mathcal{W})=d-k+1} \min_{\mathbf{u} \in \mathcal{W}} R_A(\mathbf{u})$

5 What is the main difference between the local and global formulas in the *Courant–Fischer Theorem*?
   a) The local formulas are easier to compute than the global formulas.
   b) The local formulas depend on a specific choice of eigenvectors, while the global formulas do not.
   c) The local formulas apply only to symmetric matrices, while the global formulas apply to any matrix.
   d) The local formulas provide upper bounds on the eigenvalues, while the global formulas provide lower bounds.

Answer for 1: b. Justification: The text establishes that $\lambda_1 = \max_{\mathbf{u} \neq 0} R_A(\mathbf{u})$.

Answer for 2: a. Justification: The text establishes that $\lambda_{d-1} = \min_{0 \neq \mathbf{u} \in \mathcal{V}_{d-1}} R_A(\mathbf{u})$.

Answer for 3: b. Justification: The text establishes that $\lambda_{d-1} = \max_{0 \neq \mathbf{u} \in \mathcal{W}_2} R_A(\mathbf{u})$.

Answer for 4: c. Justification: The *Courant–Fischer Theorem* states that the global formula for the *k*-th eigenvalue is $\lambda_k = \max_{\dim(\mathcal{V})=k} \min_{\mathbf{u} \in \mathcal{V}} R_A(\mathbf{u}) = \min_{\dim(\mathcal{W})=d-k+1} \max_{\mathbf{u} \in \mathcal{W}} R_A(\mathbf{u})$.

Answer for 5: b. Justification: The text highlights that the global formulas "do not depend on the choice of spectral decomposition," unlike the local formulas, which rely on a specific set of eigenvectors.

5.4 Spectral Properties of the Laplacian Matrix

In this section, we look at the spectral properties of the Laplacian of a graph.

5.4.1 Eigenvalues of the Laplacian Matrix: First Observations

Let $G = (V, E)$ be a graph with $n = |V|$ vertices. Two observations:

First, since the Laplacian matrix L of G is symmetric, by the *Spectral Theorem* it has a spectral decomposition

$$L = \sum_{i=1}^{n} \mu_i \mathbf{y}_i \mathbf{y}_i^T$$

where the $\mathbf{y}_i$'s form an orthonormal basis of $\mathbb{R}^n$.

Second, because L is positive semidefinite, the eigenvalues are nonnegative. By convention, we assume

$$0 \leq \mu_1 \leq \mu_2 \leq \cdots \leq \mu_n.$$

Another observation:

Lemma 5.4.1 *Let $G = (V, E)$ be a graph with $n = |V|$ vertices and Laplacian matrix L. The constant unit vector*

$$\mathbf{y}_1 = \frac{1}{\sqrt{n}}(1, \ldots, 1)$$

is an eigenvector of L with eigenvalue 0.

Proof Let B be an oriented incidence matrix of G and recall that $L = BB^T$. By construction $B^T \mathbf{y}_1 = \mathbf{0}$ since each column of B has exactly one 1 and one -1. So $L\mathbf{y}_1 = BB^T \mathbf{y}_1 = \mathbf{0}$ as claimed. $\square$

In general, the constant vector may not be the only eigenvector with eigenvalue one.

NUMERICAL CORNER One use of the spectral decomposition of the Laplacian matrix is in graph drawing. We illustrate this next. Given a graph $G = (V, E)$, it is not clear a priori how to draw it in the plane since the only information available consists of adjacencies of vertices. One approach is just to position the vertices at random. The function `networkx.draw` or `networkx.draw_networkx` can take as input different graph layout functions that return an x- and y-coordinate for each vertex.

We will test this on a grid graph. We use `networkx.grid_2d_graph` to construct such a graph.

```
G = nx.grid_2d_graph(4,7)
```

One layout approach is to choose random locations for the nodes. Specifically, for every node, a position is generated by choosing each coordinate uniformly at random on the interval $[0, 1]$.

```
nx.draw_networkx(G, pos=nx.random_layout(G, seed=535),
                 with_labels=False,
                 node_size=50, node_color='black', width=0.5)
plt.axis('off')
plt.show()
```

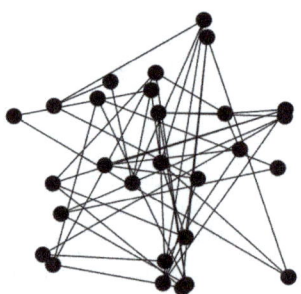

Figure 5.14 Graphical output of code.

Clearly, this is hard to read.

5.4 Spectral Properties of the Laplacian Matrix

Another approach is to map the vertices to two eigenvectors, similarly to what we did for dimensionality reduction. The eigenvector associated with μ_1 is constant and therefore not useful for drawing. We try the next two. We use the Laplacian matrix. This is done using `networkx.spectral_layout`.

```
nx.draw_networkx(G, pos=nx.spectral_layout(G), with_labels=False,
                 node_size=50, node_color='black', width=0.5)
plt.axis('off')
plt.show()
```

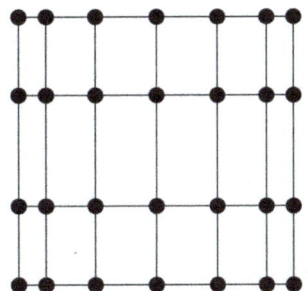

Figure 5.15 Graphical output of code.

Interestingly, the outcome is a much more natural drawing of the graph, revealing its underlying structure as a grid. We will come back later to try to explain this, after we have developed further understanding of the spectral properties of the Laplacian matrix.

◁ **NC**

5.4.2 Laplacian Matrix and Connectivity

As we indicated before, the Laplacian matrix contains information about the connectedness of G. We elaborate on a first concrete connection here. But first we will need a useful form of the Laplacian quadratic form $\mathbf{x}^T L \mathbf{x}$, one which enters in the variational characterization of the eigenvalues.

Lemma 5.4.2 *(Laplacian Quadratic Form) Let $G = (V, E)$ be a graph with $n = |V|$ vertices and Laplacian matrix L. We have the following formula for the Laplacian quadratic form:*

$$\mathbf{x} L \mathbf{x} = \sum_{e=\{i,j\} \in E} (x_i - x_j)^2$$

for any $\mathbf{x} = (x_1, \ldots, x_n) \in \mathbb{R}^n$.

Here is an intuitive way of interpreting this lemma. If one thinks of $\mathbf{x} = (x_1, \ldots, x_n) \in \mathbb{R}^n$ as a real-valued function over the vertices (i.e., it associates a real value x_i to vertex i for each i), then the Laplacian quadratic form measures how "smooth" the function is over the graph in the following sense: A small value of $\mathbf{x}^T L \mathbf{x}$ indicates that adjacent vertices tend to get assigned close values.

Proof Let B be an oriented incidence matrix of G. We have that $L = BB^T$. Thus, for any $\mathbf{x}$, we have $(B^T\mathbf{x})_k = x_v - x_u$ if the edge $e_k = \{u, v\}$ is oriented as (u, v) under B. That implies

$$\mathbf{x}^T L \mathbf{x} = \mathbf{x}^T B B^T \mathbf{x} = \|B^T \mathbf{x}\|^2 = \sum_{e=\{i,j\} \in E} (x_i - x_j)^2.$$

Since the latter is always nonnegative, it also implies that L is positive semidefinite. $\square$

We are now ready to derive connectivity consequences. Recall that, for any graph G, the Laplacian eigenvalue $\mu_1 = 0$.

Lemma 5.4.3 *(Laplacian and Connectivity) If G is connected, then the Laplacian eigenvalue $\mu_2 > 0$.*

Proof Let $G = (V, E)$ with $n = |V|$ and let $L = \sum_{i=1}^n \mu_i \mathbf{y}_i \mathbf{y}_i^T$ be a spectral decomposition of its Laplacian L with $0 = \mu_1 \leq \cdots \leq \mu_n$. Suppose by way of contradiction that $\mu_2 = 0$. Any eigenvector $\mathbf{y} = (y_1, \ldots, y_n)$ with 0 eigenvalue satisfies $L\mathbf{y} = \mathbf{0}$ by definition. By the *Laplacian Quadratic Form Lemma*,

$$0 = \mathbf{y}^T L \mathbf{y} = \sum_{e=\{i,j\} \in E} (y_i - y_j)^2.$$

First, in order for this to hold, it must be that any two adjacent vertices i and j have $y_i = y_j$. That is, $\{i, j\} \in E$ implies $y_i = y_j$.

Second, because G is connected, between any two of its vertices u and v – adjacent or not – there is a path $u = w_0 \sim \cdots \sim w_k = v$ along which the y_w's must be the same. Thus $\mathbf{y}$ is a constant vector.

But that is a contradiction since the eigenvectors $\mathbf{y}_1, \ldots, \mathbf{y}_n$ are in fact linearly independent, so that $\mathbf{y}_1$ and $\mathbf{y}_2$ cannot both be a constant vector. $\square$

The quantity μ_2 is sometimes referred to as the algebraic connectivity of the graph. The corresponding eigenvector, $\mathbf{y}_2$, is known as the Fiedler vector.

We state the following (more general) converse result without proof.

Lemma 5.4.4 *If μ_{k+1} is the smallest nonzero Laplacian eigenvalue of G, then G has k connected components.*

We will be interested in more quantitative results of this type. Before proceeding, we start with a simple observation. By our proof of the *Spectral Theorem*, the largest eigenvalue μ_n of the Laplacian matrix L is the solution to the optimization problem

$$\mu_n = \max\{\langle \mathbf{x}, L\mathbf{x}\rangle : \|\mathbf{x}\| = 1\}.$$

Such extremal characterization is useful in order to bound the eigenvalue μ_n, since any choice of $\mathbf{x}$ with $\|\mathbf{x}\| = 1$ gives a lower bound through the quantity $\langle \mathbf{x}, L\mathbf{x}\rangle$. That perspective will be key to our application to graph partitioning.

For now, we give a simple consequence.

Lemma 5.4.5 *(Laplacian and Maximum Degree) Let $G = (V, E)$ be a graph with maximum degree $\bar{\delta}$. Let μ_n be the largest eigenvalue of its Laplacian matrix L. Then*

$$\bar{\delta} + 1 \leq \mu_n \leq 2\bar{\delta}.$$

Proof idea: As explained before the statement of the lemma, for the lower bound it suffices to find a good test unit vector $\mathbf{x}$ to plug into $\langle \mathbf{x}, L\mathbf{x}\rangle$. A clever choice does the trick.

Proof We start with the lower bound. Let $u \in V$ be a vertex with degree $\bar{\delta}$. Let $\mathbf{z}$ be the vector with entries

$$z_i = \begin{cases} \bar{\delta} & \text{if } i = u \\ -1 & \text{if } \{i, u\} \in E \\ 0 & \text{otherwise} \end{cases}$$

and let $\mathbf{x}$ be the unit vector $\mathbf{z}/\|\mathbf{z}\|$. By definition of the degree of u, $\|\mathbf{z}\|^2 = \bar{\delta}^2 + \bar{\delta}(-1)^2 = \bar{\delta}(\bar{\delta} + 1)$. Using the *Laplacian Quadratic Form Lemma*,

$$\langle \mathbf{z}, L\mathbf{z} \rangle = \sum_{e=\{i,j\} \in E} (z_i - z_j)^2 \geq \sum_{i: \{i,u\} \in E} (z_i - z_u)^2 = \sum_{i: \{i,u\} \in E} (-1 - \bar{\delta})^2 = \bar{\delta}(\bar{\delta} + 1)^2$$

where we restricted the sum to those edges incident with u and used the fact that all terms in the sum are nonnegative. Finally

$$\langle \mathbf{x}, L\mathbf{x} \rangle = \left\langle \frac{\mathbf{z}}{\|\mathbf{z}\|}, L\frac{\mathbf{z}}{\|\mathbf{z}\|} \right\rangle = \frac{1}{\|\mathbf{z}\|^2} \langle \mathbf{z}, L\mathbf{z} \rangle = \frac{\bar{\delta}(\bar{\delta}+1)^2}{\bar{\delta}(\bar{\delta}+1)} = \bar{\delta} + 1$$

so that

$$\mu_n = \max\{\langle \mathbf{x}', L\mathbf{x}' \rangle : \|\mathbf{x}'\| = 1\} \geq \langle \mathbf{x}, L\mathbf{x} \rangle = \bar{\delta} + 1$$

as claimed.

We proceed with the upper bound. For any unit vector $\mathbf{x}$,

$$\langle \mathbf{x}, L\mathbf{x} \rangle = \sum_{i,j} L_{ij} x_i x_j$$

$$\leq \sum_{i,j} |L_{ij}| |x_i| |x_j|$$

$$= \sum_{i,j} (D_{ij} + A_{ij}) |x_i| |x_j|$$

$$= \sum_i \delta(i) x_i^2 + \sum_{i,j} A_{ij} |x_i| |x_j|.$$

By the *Cauchy–Schwarz Inequality*, this is

$$\leq \bar{\delta} + \left(\sum_{i,j} A_{ij} x_i^2 \right)^{1/2} \left(\sum_{i,j} A_{ij} x_j^2 \right)^{1/2}$$

$$\leq \bar{\delta} + \left(\bar{\delta} \sum_i x_i^2 \right)^{1/2} \left(\bar{\delta} \sum_j x_j^2 \right)^{1/2}$$

$$\leq 2\bar{\delta}.$$

□

NUMERICAL CORNER We construct a graph with two connected components and check the results above. We work directly with the adjacency matrix.

```
A = np.array([[0, 1, 1, 0, 0],
              [1, 0, 1, 0, 0],
              [1, 1, 0, 0, 0],
```

```
                [0, 0, 0, 0, 1],
                [0, 0, 0, 1, 0]])
print(A)
```

```
[[0 1 1 0 0]
 [1 0 1 0 0]
 [1 1 0 0 0]
 [0 0 0 0 1]
 [0 0 0 1 0]]
```

Note the block structure.

The degrees can be obtained by summing the rows of the adjacency matrix.

```
degrees = A.sum(axis=1)
print(degrees)
```

```
[2 2 2 1 1]
```

```
D = np.diag(degrees)
print(D)
```

```
[[2 0 0 0 0]
 [0 2 0 0 0]
 [0 0 2 0 0]
 [0 0 0 1 0]
 [0 0 0 0 1]]
```

```
L = D - A
print(L)
```

```
[[ 2 -1 -1  0  0]
 [-1  2 -1  0  0]
 [-1 -1  2  0  0]
 [ 0  0  0  1 -1]
 [ 0  0  0 -1  1]]
```

```
print(LA.eigvals(L))
```

```
[ 3.00000000e+00 -3.77809194e-16  3.00000000e+00  2.00000000e+00
  0.00000000e+00]
```

Observe that (up to numerical error) there are two 0 eigenvalues and that the largest eigenvalue is greater than or equal to the maximum degree plus one.

To compute the Laplacian matrix, one can also use the function `networkx.laplacian_matrix`. For example, the Laplacian of the Petersen graph is the following:

```
G = nx.petersen_graph()
L = nx.laplacian_matrix(G).toarray()
print(L)
```

```
[[ 3 -1  0  0 -1 -1  0  0  0  0]
 [-1  3 -1  0  0  0 -1  0  0  0]
 [ 0 -1  3 -1  0  0  0 -1  0  0]
 [ 0  0 -1  3 -1  0  0  0 -1  0]
 [-1  0  0 -1  3  0  0  0  0 -1]
 [-1  0  0  0  0  3  0 -1 -1  0]
 [ 0 -1  0  0  0  0  3  0 -1 -1]
 [ 0  0 -1  0  0 -1  0  3  0 -1]
 [ 0  0  0 -1  0 -1 -1  0  3  0]
 [ 0  0  0  0 -1  0 -1 -1  0  3]]
```

```
print(LA.eigvals(L))
```

```
[ 5.00000000e+00  2.00000000e+00 -2.80861083e-17  5.00000000e+00
  5.00000000e+00  2.00000000e+00  2.00000000e+00  5.00000000e+00
  2.00000000e+00  2.00000000e+00]
```

◁ NC

5.4.3 Variational Characterization of Second Laplacian Eigenvalue

The definition $A\mathbf{x} = \lambda \mathbf{x}$ is perhaps not the best way to understand why the eigenvectors of the Laplacian matrix are useful. Instead the following application of the *Courant–Fischer Theorem* provides much insight, as we will see in the rest of this chapter.

Theorem 5.4.6 *(Variational Characterization of μ_2)* Let $G = (V, E)$ be a graph with $n = |V|$ vertices. Assume the Laplacian L of G has spectral decomposition $L = \sum_{i=1}^{n} \mu_i \mathbf{y}_i \mathbf{y}_i^T$ with $0 = \mu_1 \leq \mu_2 \leq \cdots \leq \mu_n$ and $\mathbf{y}_1 = \frac{1}{\sqrt{n}}(1, \ldots, 1)$. Then

$$\mu_2 = \min\left\{ \sum_{\{i,j\} \in E} (x_i - x_j)^2 : \mathbf{x} = (x_1, \ldots, x_n) \in \mathbb{R}^n, \sum_{i=1}^{n} x_i = 0, \sum_{j=1}^{n} x_j^2 = 1 \right\}.$$

Taking $\mathbf{x} = \mathbf{y}_2$ achieves this minimum.

Proof By the *Courant–Fischer Theorem*,

$$\mu_2 = \min_{\mathbf{0} \neq \mathbf{u} \in \mathcal{V}_{n-1}} \mathcal{R}_L(\mathbf{u}),$$

where $\mathcal{V}_{n-1} = \text{span}(\mathbf{y}_2, \ldots, \mathbf{y}_n) = \text{span}(\mathbf{y}_1)^{\perp}$. Observe that, because we reverse the order of the eigenvalues compared to the convention used in the *Courant–Fischer Theorem*, we must adapt the definition of $\mathcal{V}_{n-1}$ slightly. Moreover we know that $\mathcal{R}_L(\mathbf{y}_2) = \mu_2$. We make a simple transformation of the problem.

We claim that

$$\mu_2 = \min\{\langle \mathbf{x}, L\mathbf{x} \rangle : \|\mathbf{x}\| = 1, \langle \mathbf{x}, \mathbf{y}_1 \rangle = 0\}. \quad (*)$$

Indeed, if $\mathbf{u} \in \text{span}(\mathbf{y}_1)^\perp$ has unit norm, $\|\mathbf{u}\| = 1$, then

$$\mathcal{R}_L(\mathbf{u}) = \frac{\langle \mathbf{u}, L\mathbf{u} \rangle}{\langle \mathbf{u}, \mathbf{u} \rangle} = \frac{\langle \mathbf{u}, L\mathbf{u} \rangle}{\|\mathbf{u}\|^2} = \langle \mathbf{u}, L\mathbf{u} \rangle.$$

In other words, we shown that

$$\min_{\mathbf{0} \neq \mathbf{u} \in \mathcal{V}_{n-1}} \mathcal{R}_L(\mathbf{u}) \leq \min \{\langle \mathbf{x}, L\mathbf{x} \rangle : \|\mathbf{x}\| = 1, \langle \mathbf{x}, \mathbf{y}_1 \rangle = 0\}.$$

To prove the other direction, for any $\mathbf{u} \neq \mathbf{0}$, we can normalize it by defining $\mathbf{x} = \mathbf{u}/\|\mathbf{u}\|$ and we note that

$$\mathcal{R}_L(\mathbf{u}) = \frac{\langle \mathbf{u}, L\mathbf{u} \rangle}{\langle \mathbf{u}, \mathbf{u} \rangle} = \frac{\langle \mathbf{u}, L\mathbf{u} \rangle}{\|\mathbf{u}\|^2} = \left\langle \frac{\mathbf{u}}{\|\mathbf{u}\|}, L\frac{\mathbf{u}}{\|\mathbf{u}\|} \right\rangle = \langle \mathbf{x}, L\mathbf{x} \rangle.$$

Moreover $\langle \mathbf{u}, \mathbf{y}_1 \rangle = 0$ if only if $\langle \mathbf{x}, \mathbf{y}_1 \rangle = 0$. This establishes $(*)$, since any objective value achieved in the original formulation can be achieved in the new one.

Using the fact that $\mathbf{y}_1 = \frac{1}{\sqrt{n}}(1, \ldots, 1)$, the condition $\langle \mathbf{x}, \mathbf{y}_1 \rangle = 0$ or $\sum_{i=1}^{n}(x_i/\sqrt{n}) = 0$, is equivalent to $\sum_{i=1}^{n} x_i = 0$. Similary, the condition $\|\mathbf{x}\| = 1$ is equivalent, after squaring each side, to $\sum_{j=1}^{n} x_j^2 = 1$.

Finally, the claim follows from the *Laplacian Quadratic Form Lemma.* □

One application of this extremal characterization is the graph drawing heuristic we described previously. Consider the entries of the second Laplacian eigenvector $\mathbf{y}_2$. Its entries are centered around 0 by the condition $\langle \mathbf{y}_1, \mathbf{y}_2 \rangle = 0$. Because it minimizes the following quantity over all centered unit vectors,

$$\sum_{\{i,j\} \in E} (x_i - x_j)^2,$$

the eigenvector $\mathbf{y}_2$ tends to assign similar coordinates to adjacent vertices. A similar reasoning applies to the third Laplacian eigenvector, which in addition is orthogonal to the second one. So coordinates based on the second and third Laplacian eigenvectors should be expected to position adjacent vertices close by and hence minimizing the need for long-range edges in the visualization. In particular, it reveals some of the underlying Euclidean geometry of the graph, as the next example shows.

NUMERICAL CORNER This is perhaps easiest to see on a path graph. Recall that NetworkX numbers vertices $0, \ldots, n - 1$.

```
G = nx.path_graph(10)
```

We plot the second Laplacian eigenvector (i.e., the eigenvector of the Laplacian matrix corresponding to the second smallest eigenvalue). We use `numpy.argsort` to find the index of the second smallest eigenvalue. Because indices start at 0, we want entry 1 of the output.

```
L = nx.laplacian_matrix(G).toarray()
w, v = LA.eigh(L)
y2 = v[:,np.argsort(w)[1]]

plt.plot(y2, c='k')
plt.show()
```

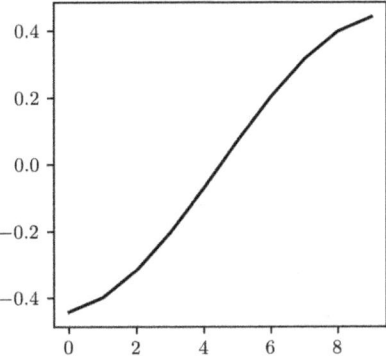

Figure 5.16 Graphical output of code.

◁ NC

Example 5.4.7 *(Two-Component Graph) Let $G = (V, E)$ be a graph with two connected components $\varnothing \neq V_1, V_2 \subseteq V$. By the properties of connected components, we have $V_1 \cap V_2 = \varnothing$ and $V_1 \cup V_2 = V$. Assume the Laplacian L of G has spectral decomposition $L = \sum_{i=1}^{n} \mu_i \mathbf{y}_i \mathbf{y}_i^T$ with $0 = \mu_1 \leq \mu_2 \leq \cdots \leq \mu_n$ and $\mathbf{y}_1 = \frac{1}{\sqrt{n}}(1, \ldots, 1)$. We claimed earlier that for such a graph $\mu_2 = 0$. We prove this here using the* Variational Characterization of μ_2 *Theorem:*

$$\mu_2 = \min\left\{ \sum_{\{u,v\} \in E} (x_u - x_v)^2 : \mathbf{x} = (x_1, \ldots, x_n) \in \mathbb{R}^n, \sum_{u=1}^{n} x_u = 0, \sum_{u=1}^{n} x_u^2 = 1 \right\}.$$

Based on this characterization, it suffices to find a vector $\mathbf{x}$ satisfying $\sum_{u=1}^{n} x_u = 0$ and $\sum_{u=1}^{n} x_u^2 = 1$ such that $\sum_{\{u,v\} \in E}(x_u - x_v)^2 = 0$. Indeed, since $\mu_2 \geq 0$ and any such $\mathbf{x}$ gives an upper bound on μ_2, we then necessarily have that $\mu_2 = 0$.

For $\sum_{\{u,v\} \in E}(x_u - x_v)^2$ to be 0, one might be tempted to take a constant vector $\mathbf{x}$. But then we could not satisfy $\sum_{u=1}^{n} x_u = 0$ and $\sum_{u=1}^{n} x_u^2 = 1$ simultaneously. Instead, we modify this guess slightly. Because the graph has two connected components, there is no edge between V_1 and V_2. Hence we can assign a different value to each component and still get $\sum_{\{u,v\} \in E}(x_u - x_v)^2 = 0$. So we look for a vector $\mathbf{x} = (x_1, \ldots, x_n)$ of the form

$$x_u = \begin{cases} \alpha, & \text{if } u \in V_1, \\ \beta, & \text{if } u \in V_2. \end{cases}$$

To satisfy the constraints on $\mathbf{x}$, we require

$$\sum_{u=1}^{n} x_u = \sum_{u \in V_1} \alpha + \sum_{u \in V_2} \beta = |V_1|\alpha + |V_2|\beta = 0$$

and

$$\sum_{u=1}^{n} x_u^2 = \sum_{u \in V_1} \alpha^2 + \sum_{u \in V_2} \beta^2 = |V_1|\alpha^2 + |V_2|\beta^2 = 1.$$

Substituting the first equation in the second one, we get

$$|V_1|\left(\frac{-|V_2|\beta}{|V_1|}\right)^2 + |V_2|\beta^2 = \frac{|V_2|^2\beta^2}{|V_1|} + |V_2|\beta^2 = 1,$$

or

$$\beta^2 = \frac{|V_1|}{|V_2|(|V_2|+|V_1|)} = \frac{|V_1|}{n|V_2|}.$$

Take

$$\beta = -\sqrt{\frac{|V_1|}{n|V_2|}}, \qquad \alpha = \frac{-|V_2|\beta}{|V_1|} = \sqrt{\frac{|V_2|}{n|V_1|}}.$$

The vector $\mathbf{x}$ we constructed is in fact an eigenvector of L. Indeed, let B be an oriented incidence matrix of G. Then, for $e_k = \{u, v\}$, $(B^T\mathbf{x})_k$ is either $x_u - x_v$ or $x_v - x_u$. In both cases, that is 0. So $L\mathbf{x} = BB^T\mathbf{x} = \mathbf{0}$; that is, $\mathbf{x}$ is an eigenvector of L with eigenvalue 0.

We have shown that $\mu_2 = 0$ when G has two connected components. A slight modification of this argument shows that $\mu_2 = 0$ whenever G is not connected.

Self-Assessment Quiz *(with help from Claude, Gemini, and ChatGPT)*

1. Which of the following is NOT a property of the Laplacian matrix L of a graph G?
   a) L is symmetric.
   b) L is positive semidefinite.
   c) The constant unit vector $\frac{1}{\sqrt{n}}(1, \ldots, 1)$ is an eigenvector of L with eigenvalue 0.
   d) L is positive definite.

2. Which vector is known as the Fiedler vector?
   a) The eigenvector corresponding to the largest eigenvalue of the Laplacian matrix
   b) The eigenvector corresponding to the smallest eigenvalue of the Laplacian matrix
   c) The eigenvector corresponding to the second smallest eigenvalue of the Laplacian matrix
   d) The eigenvector corresponding to the average of all eigenvalues of the Laplacian matrix

3. For a connected graph G, which of the following statements about the second smallest eigenvalue μ_2 of its Laplacian matrix is true?
   a) $\mu_2 = 0$
   b) $\mu_2 < 0$
   c) $\mu_2 > 0$
   d) The value of μ_2 cannot be determined without additional information.

4. The Laplacian quadratic form $\mathbf{x}^T L \mathbf{x}$ for a graph G with Laplacian matrix L can be written as

$$\mathbf{x}^T L \mathbf{x} = \sum_{\{i,j\} \in E} (x_i - x_j)^2.$$

   What does this quadratic form measure?
   a) The average distance between vertices in the graph

b) The number of connected components in the graph

c) The "smoothness" of the function **x** over the graph

d) The degree of each vertex in the graph

5. The Laplacian matrix L of a graph G can be decomposed as $L = BB^T$, where B is an oriented incidence matrix. What does this decomposition imply about L?

a) L is positive definite.

b) L is symmetric and positive semidefinite.

c) L is antisymmetric.

d) L is a diagonal matrix.

Answer for 1: d. Justification: The text states that "because L is positive semidefinite, the eigenvalues are nonnegative," but it does not claim that L is positive definite.

Answer for 2: c. Justification: The text refers to the eigenvector corresponding to μ_2 (the second smallest eigenvalue) as the Fiedler vector.

Answer for 3: c. Justification: The text proves that "If G is connected, then the Laplacian eigenvalue $\mu_2 > 0$."

Answer for 4: c. Justification: The text states that "the Laplacian quadratic form measures how 'smooth' the function **x** is over the graph in the following sense. A small value of $\mathbf{x}^T L \mathbf{x}$ indicates that adjacent vertices tend to get assigned close values."

Answer for 5: b. Justification: The text states, "Let B be an oriented incidence matrix of G. By construction, $L = BB^T$. This implies that L is symmetric and positive semidefinite."

5.5 Application: Graph Partitioning via Spectral Clustering

In this section, we use the spectral properties of the Laplacian of a graph to identify "good" cuts.

5.5.1 How to Cut a Graph

Let $G = (V, E)$ be a graph. Imagine that we are interested in finding a good cut. That is, roughly speaking, we seek to divide it into two disjoint subsets of vertices to achieve two goals simultaneously:

1. The two sets have relatively few edges between them.

2. Neither set is too small.

We will show that the Laplacian eigenvectors provide useful information in order to perform this kind of graph cutting. First we formulate the problem formally.

5.5.1.1 Cut Ratio

One way to make the graph cutting more precise is to consider the following combinatorial quantity.

Definition 5.5.1 *(Isoperimetric Number)* Let $G = (V, E)$ be a graph. A cut is a bipartition (S, S^c) of the vertices of G, where S and $S^c = V \setminus S$ are nonempty subsets of V. The corresponding cutset is the set of edges between S and S^c

$$E(S, S^c) = \{\{i, j\} \in E : i \in S, j \in S^c\}.$$

This is also known as the edge boundary of S (denoted ∂S). The size of the cutset is then $|E(S, S^c)|$, the number of edges between S and S^c. The cut ratio of (S, S^c) is defined as

$$\phi(S) = \frac{|E(S, S^c)|}{\min\{|S|, |S^c|\}}$$

and the isoperimetric number (or Cheeger constant) of G is the smallest value this quantity can take on G; that is,

$$\phi_G = \min_{\emptyset \neq S \subset V} \phi(S).$$

In words: The cut ratio is attempting to minimize the number of edges across a cut, while penalizing cuts with a small number of vertices on either side. These correspond to the goals above and we will use this criterion to assess the quality of graph cuts.

Why do we need the denominator? If we were to minimize only the numerator $|E(S, S^c)|$ over all cuts (without the deonominator in $\phi(S)$), we would get what is known as the minimum cut (or min-cut) problem. That problem is easier to solve. In particular, it can be solved using a beautiful randomized algorithm. However, it tends to produce unbalanced cuts, where one side is much smaller than the other. This is not what we want here.

Example 5.5.2 *(A Random Tree)* We illustrate the definitions above on a tree, that is, a connected graph with no cycle. The function `networkx.random_tree` can produce a random one. As before we use a seed for reproducibility. Again, we use $0, \ldots, n-1$ for the vertex set.

```
G_tree = nx.random_tree(n=6, seed=111)

nx.draw_networkx(G_tree, pos=nx.circular_layout(G_tree),
                 node_color='black', font_color='white')
plt.axis('off')
plt.show()
```

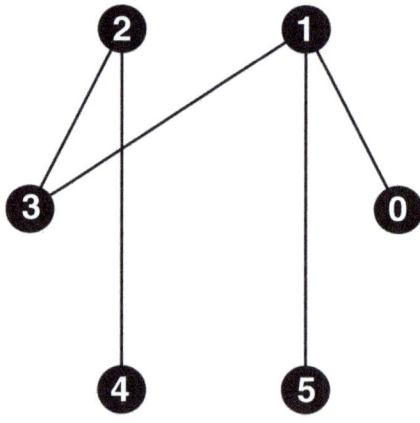

Figure 5.17 Graphical output of code.

Suppose we take $S = \{0, 1, 2, 3\}$. Then $S^c = \{4, 5\}$ and

$$E(S, S^c) = \{\{1, 5\}, \{2, 4\}\}.$$

The cut ratio is then

$$\phi(S) = \frac{|E(S, S^c)|}{\min\{|S|, |S^c|\}} = \frac{2}{2} = 1.$$

A better cut is given by $S = \{0, 1, 5\}$. In that case $S^c = \{2, 3, 4\}$,

$$E(S, S^c) = \{\{1, 3\}\},$$

and

$$\phi(S) = \frac{|E(S, S^c)|}{\min\{|S|, |S^c|\}} = \frac{1}{3}.$$

This is also equal to ϕ_G. Indeed, in a connected graph with n vertices, the numerator is at least 1 and the denominator is at most $n/2$, which is achieved here.

5.5.1.2 Cheeger's Inequalities

A key result of spectral graph theory establishes a quantitative relation between the isoperimetric number and the second smallest Laplacian eigenvalue.

Theorem 5.5.3 *(Cheeger)* Let $G = (V, E)$ be a graph with $n = |V|$ vertices and maximum degree $\bar{\delta}$. Let $0 = \mu_1 \leq \mu_2 \leq \cdots \leq \mu_n$ be its Laplacian eigenvalues. Then

$$\frac{\phi_G^2}{2\bar{\delta}} \leq \mu_2 \leq 2\phi_G.$$

We only prove the easy direction, $\mu_2 \leq 2\phi_G$, which shows explicitly how the connection between μ_2 and ϕ_G comes about.

Proof idea: To show that $\mu_2 \leq 2\phi_G$, we find an appropriate test vector to plug into the extremal characterization of μ_2 and link it to ϕ_G.

Proof Recall that, from the *Variational Characterization of μ_2 Theorem*, we have

$$\mu_2 = \min \left\{ \sum_{\{u,v\} \in E} (x_u - x_v)^2 : \mathbf{x} = (x_1, \ldots, x_n) \in \mathbb{R}^n, \sum_{u=1}^n x_u = 0, \sum_{u=1}^n x_u^2 = 1 \right\}.$$

Constructing a good test vector: We construct an $\mathbf{x}$ that provides a good upper bound. Let $\emptyset \neq S \subset V$ be a proper, nonempty subset of V such that $0 < |S| \leq \frac{1}{2}|V|$. We choose a vector that takes one value on S and a different value on S^c. Taking a cue from the two-component example above (see Example 5.4.7) we consider the vector with entries

$$x_i = \begin{cases} \sqrt{\frac{|S^c|}{n|S|}} & \text{if } i \in S \\ -\sqrt{\frac{|S|}{n|S^c|}} & \text{if } i \in S^c. \end{cases}$$

This choice ensures that

$$\sum_{i=1}^{n} x_i = \sum_{i \in S} \sqrt{\frac{|S^c|}{n|S|}} + \sum_{i \in S^c} \left(-\sqrt{\frac{|S|}{n|S^c|}}\right)$$

$$= |S|\sqrt{\frac{|S^c|}{n|S|}} - |S^c|\sqrt{\frac{|S|}{n|S^c|}}$$

$$= \sqrt{\frac{|S||S^c|}{n}} - \sqrt{\frac{|S||S^c|}{n}}$$

$$= 0$$

and also

$$\sum_{i=1}^{n} x_i^2 = \sum_{i \in S} \left(\sqrt{\frac{|S^c|}{n|S|}}\right)^2 + \sum_{i \in S^c} \left(-\sqrt{\frac{|S|}{n|S^c|}}\right)^2$$

$$= |S|\frac{|S^c|}{n|S|} + |S^c|\frac{|S|}{n|S^c|}$$

$$= \frac{|S^c| + |S|}{n}$$

$$= 1.$$

To evaluate the Laplacian quadratic form, we note that $\mathbf{x}$ takes the same value everywhere on S (and on S^c). Hence the sum over edges reduces to

$$\sum_{\{i,j\} \in E} (x_i - x_j)^2 = \sum_{\substack{\{i,j\} \in E \\ x_i \neq x_j}} \left(\sqrt{\frac{|S^c|}{n|S|}} + \sqrt{\frac{|S|}{n|S^c|}}\right)^2$$

$$= \sum_{\substack{\{i,j\} \in E \\ x_i \neq x_j}} \left(\frac{|S^c| + |S|}{\sqrt{n|S||S^c|}}\right)^2$$

$$= |E(S, S^c)| \frac{n}{|S||S^c|},$$

where we used the fact that, for each edge $\{i, j\} \in E$ where $x_i \neq x_j$, one endvertex is in S and one endvertex is in S^c.

Using the definition of the isoperimetric number: So for this choice of $\mathbf{x}$ we have

$$\mu_2 \leq \sum_{\{i,j\} \in E} (x_i - x_j)^2 = \frac{n|E(S, S^c)|}{|S^c||S|} = \frac{|E(S, S^c)|}{(|S^c|/n)|S|} \leq 2\frac{|E(S, S^c)|}{|S|}$$

where we used that $|S^c| \geq n/2$. This inequality holds for any S such that $0 < |S| \leq \frac{1}{2}|V|$. In particular, it holds for the S producing the smallest value. Hence, by the definition of the isoperimetric number, we get

$$\mu_2 \leq 2\phi_G$$

as claimed. $\square$

5.5 Application: Graph Partitioning via Spectral Clustering

NUMERICAL CORNER We return to the random tree example above. We claimed that $\phi_G = 1/3$. The maximum degree is $\bar{\delta} = 3$. We now compute μ_2. We first compute the Laplacian matrix.

```
phi_G = 1/3
max_deg = 3
```

We now compute μ_2. We first compute the Laplacian matrix.

```
L_tree = nx.laplacian_matrix(G_tree).toarray()
print(L_tree)
```

```
[[ 1 -1  0  0  0  0]
 [-1  3  0 -1  0 -1]
 [ 0  0  2 -1 -1  0]
 [ 0 -1 -1  2  0  0]
 [ 0  0 -1  0  1  0]
 [ 0 -1  0  0  0  1]]
```

```
w, v = LA.eigh(L_tree)
mu_2 = np.sort(w)[1]
print(mu_2)
```

0.32486912943335317

We check *Cheeger's Inequalities*. The left-hand side is:

```
(phi_G ** 2) / (2 * max_deg)
```

0.018518518518518517

The right-hand side is:

```
2 * phi_G
```

0.6666666666666666

◁ **NC**

5.5.1.3 A Graph-Cutting Algorithm

We only proved the easy direction of *Cheeger's Inequalities*. It is however useful to sketch the other direction (the actual Cheeger's inequality in the graph context), as it contains an important algorithmic idea.

An algorithm: The input is the graph $G = (V, E)$. Let $\mathbf{y}_2 \in \mathbb{R}^n$ be the unit-norm eigenvector of the Laplacian matrix L associated with its second smallest eigenvalue μ_2; that is, $\mathbf{y}_2$ is the Fiedler vector. There is one entry of $\mathbf{y}_2 = (y_{2,1}, \ldots, y_{2,n})$ for each vertex of G. We use these entries to embed the graph G in $\mathbb{R}$; vertex i is mapped to $y_{2,i}$. Now order the entries $y_{2,\pi(1)}, \ldots, y_{2,\pi(n)}$, where π is a permutation, namely a reordering of $1, \ldots, n$. Specifically, $\pi(1)$ is the vertex corresponding to the smallest entry of $\mathbf{y}_2$, $\pi(2)$ is the second smallest, and so on. We consider only cuts of the form

$$S_k = \{\pi(1), \ldots, \pi(k)\}$$

and we output the cut (S_k, S_k^c) that minimizes the cut ratio

$$\phi(S_k) = \frac{|E(S_k, S_k^c)|}{\min\{k, n-k\}}$$

for $k \leq n-1$.

What can be proved rigorously (but we will not do this here) is that there exists some $k^* \in \{1, \ldots, n-1\}$ such that

$$\mu_2 = \sum_{\{u,v\} \in E} (y_{2,u} - y_{2,v})^2 \geq \frac{\phi(S_{k^*})^2}{2\bar{\delta}} \geq \frac{\phi_G^2}{2\bar{\delta}},$$

which implies the lower bound in *Cheeger's Inequalities*. The leftmost inequality is the nontrivial one.

Since $\mu_2 \leq 2\phi_G$, this implies that

$$\phi(S_{k^*}) \leq \sqrt{4\bar{\delta}\phi_G}.$$

So $\phi(S_{k^*})$ may not achieve ϕ_G, but we do get some guarantee on the quality of the cut produced by this algorithm.

The above provides a heuristic to find a cut with provable guarantees. We implement it next. In contrast, the problem of finding a cut which minimizes the cut ratio is known to be NP-hard, that is, roughly speaking it is computationally intractable.

We now implement in Python the heuristic for the graph cutting algorithm above. We first write an auxiliary function that takes as input an adjacency matrix, an ordering of the vertices, and a value k. It returns the cut ratio for the first k vertices in the order.

```
def cut_ratio(A, order, k):

    n = A.shape[0]
    edge_boundary = 0
    for i in range(k+1):
        for j in range(k+1,n):
            edge_boundary += A[order[i],order[j]]

    denominator = np.minimum(k+1, n-k-1)

    return edge_boundary/denominator
```

5.5 Application: Graph Partitioning via Spectral Clustering

Using the `cut_ratio` function, we first compute the Laplacian to find the second eigenvector and corresponding order of vertices. Then we compute the cut ratio for every k. Finally we output the cut (both S_k and S_k^c) corresponding to the minimum, as a tuple of arrays.

```python
def spectral_cut2(A):
    n = A.shape[0]
    
    degrees = A.sum(axis=1)
    D = np.diag(degrees)
    L = D - A
    w, v = LA.eigh(L)
    order = np.argsort(v[:,np.argsort(w)[1]])
    
    phi = np.zeros(n-1)
    for k in range(n-1):
        phi[k] = cut_ratio(A, order, k)
    imin = np.argmin(phi)
    
    return order[0:imin+1], order[imin+1:n]
```

Finally, to help visualize the output, we write a function coloring the vertices according to which side of the cut they are on.

```python
def viz_cut(G, s, pos, node_size=100, with_labels=False):
    n = G.number_of_nodes()
    assign = np.zeros(n)
    assign[s] = 1
    nx.draw(G, node_color=assign, pos=pos, with_labels=with_labels,
            cmap='spring', node_size=node_size, font_color='k')
    plt.show()
```

NUMERICAL CORNER We will illustrate this on the path graph.

```python
n = 10
G = nx.path_graph(n)

nx.draw_networkx(G, pos=nx.spectral_layout(G),
                 node_color='black', font_color='white')
plt.axis('off')
plt.show()
```

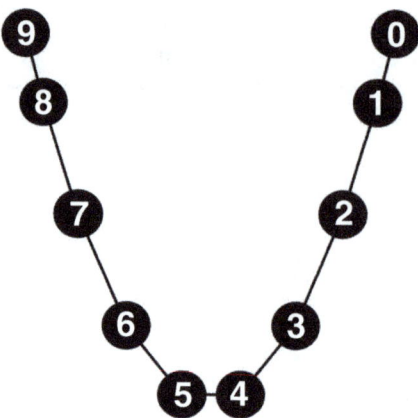

Figure 5.18 Graphical output of code.

We apply our spectral-based cutting algorithm.

```
A = nx.adjacency_matrix(G).toarray()
s, sc = spectral_cut2(A)
print(s)
print(sc)
```

[0 1 2 3 4]
[5 6 7 8 9]

```
pos = nx.spectral_layout(G)
viz_cut(G, s, pos)
```

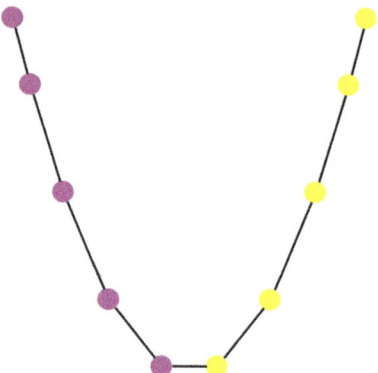

Figure 5.19 Graphical output of code.

Let's try it on the grid graph. Can you guess what the cut will be?

```
G = nx.grid_2d_graph(4,7)
A = nx.adjacency_matrix(G).toarray()
s, sc = spectral_cut2(A)
```

```
pos = nx.spectral_layout(G)
viz_cut(G, s, pos)
```

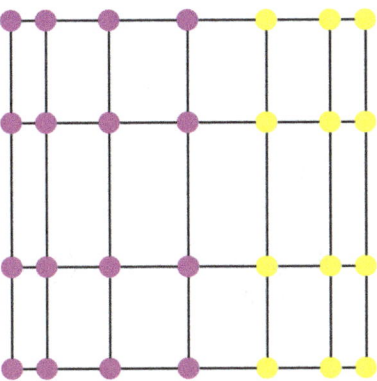

Figure 5.20 Graphical output of code.

◁ NC

5.5.1.4 How to Compute the Second Smallest Eigenvalue?

There is one last piece of business to take care of. How do we compute the Fiedler vector? Previously, we have seen an iterative approach based on taking powers of the matrix to compute *the largest eigenvalue and corresponding eigenvector* of a positive semidefinite matrix. We show here how to adapt this approach to our task at hand. The details are left as a series of exercises.

First, we modify the Laplacian matrix to invert the order of the eigenvalues without changing the eigenvectors themselves. This way the smallest eigenvalues will become the largest ones. By the *Laplacian and Maximum Degree Lemma*, $\mu_i \leq 2\bar{\delta}$ for all $i = 1, \ldots, n$, where recall that $\bar{\delta}$ is the largest degree of the graph.

Lemma 5.5.4 (*Inverting the Order of Eigenvalues*) *For $i = 1, \ldots, n$, let $\lambda_i = 2\bar{\delta} - \mu_i$. The matrix $M = 2\bar{\delta}I_{n\times n} - L$ is positive semidefinite and has eigenvector decomposition*

$$M = \sum_{i=1}^{n} \lambda_i \mathbf{y}_i \mathbf{y}_i^T.$$

Second, our goal is now to compute the second largest eigenvalue of M – not the largest one. But we already know the largest one. It is $\lambda_1 = 2\bar{\delta} - \mu_1 = 2\bar{\delta}$ and its associated eigenvector is $\mathbf{y}_1 = \frac{1}{\sqrt{n}}(1, \ldots, 1)$. It turns out that we can simply apply power iteration with a starting vector that is orthogonal to $\mathbf{y}_1$. Such a vector can be constructed by taking a random vector and subtracting its orthogonal projection on $\mathbf{y}_1$.

Lemma 5.5.5 (*Power Iteration for the Second Largest Eigenvalue*) *Assume that $\mu_1 < \mu_2 < \mu_3$. Let $\mathbf{x} \in \mathbb{R}^n$ be a vector such that $\langle \mathbf{y}_1, \mathbf{x} \rangle = 0$ and $\langle \mathbf{y}_2, \mathbf{x} \rangle > 0$. Then*

$$\frac{M^k \mathbf{x}}{\|M^k \mathbf{x}\|} \to \mathbf{y}_2$$

as $k \to +\infty$. If instead $\langle \mathbf{y}_2, \mathbf{x} \rangle < 0$, then the limit is $-\mathbf{y}_2$.

5.5.1.5 The Relaxation Perspective

Here is another intuitive way to shed light on the effectiveness of spectral partitioning. Assume we have a graph $G = (V, E)$ with an even number $n = |V|$ of vertices. Suppose we are looking for the best balanced cut (S, S^c) in the sense that it minimizes the number of edges $|E(S, S^c)|$ across it over all cuts with $|S| = |S^c| = n/2$. This is known as the minimum bisection problem.

Mathematically, we can formulate this as the following discrete optimization problem:

$$\min\left\{\frac{1}{4}\sum_{\{i,j\}\in E}(x_i - x_j)^2 : \mathbf{x} = (x_1,\ldots,x_n) \in \{-1,+1\}^n, \sum_{i=1}^n x_i = 0\right\}.$$

The condition $\mathbf{x} \in \{-1, +1\}^n$ implicitly assigns each vertex i to S (if $x_i = -1$) or S^c (if $x_i = +1$). The condition $\sum_{i=1}^n x_i = 0$ then ensures that the cut (S, S^c) is balanced, that is, that $|S| = |S^c|$. Under this interpretation, the term $(x_i - x_j)^2$ is either 0 if i and j are on the same side of the cut, or 4 if they are on opposite sides.

This is a hard computational problem. One way to approach such a discrete optimization problem is to relax it; that is, to turn it into an optimization problem with continuous variables. Specifically here we consider instead

$$\min\left\{\frac{1}{4}\sum_{\{i,j\}\in E}(x_i - x_j)^2 : \mathbf{x} = (x_1,\ldots,x_n) \in \mathbb{R}^n, \sum_{i=1}^n x_i = 0, \sum_{i=1}^n x_i^2 = n\right\}.$$

The optimal objective value of this relaxed problem is necessarily less than or equal to the original one. Indeed any solution to the original problem satisfies the constraints of the relaxation. Up to a scaling factor, this last problem is equivalent to the variational characterization of μ_2. Indeed, one can prove that the minimum achieved is $\frac{\mu_2 n}{4}$ (try it!).

NUMERICAL CORNER We return to the Karate Club dataset.

```
G = nx.karate_club_graph()
n = G.number_of_nodes()
A = nx.adjacency_matrix(G).toarray()
```

We seek to find natural sub-communities. We use the spectral properties of the Laplacian. Specifically, we use our `spectral_cut2` and `viz_cut` functions to compute a good cut and vizualize it.

```
s, sc = spectral_cut2(A)
print(s)
print(sc)
```

```
[18 26 20 14 29 22 24 15 23 25 32 27  9 33 31 28 30  8]
[ 2 13  1 19  7  3 12  0 21 17 11  4 10  6  5 16]
```

```
plt.figure(figsize=(6,6))
pos = nx.spring_layout(G, k=0.7, iterations=50, seed=42)
viz_cut(G, s, pos, node_size=300, with_labels=True)
```

5.5 Application: Graph Partitioning via Spectral Clustering

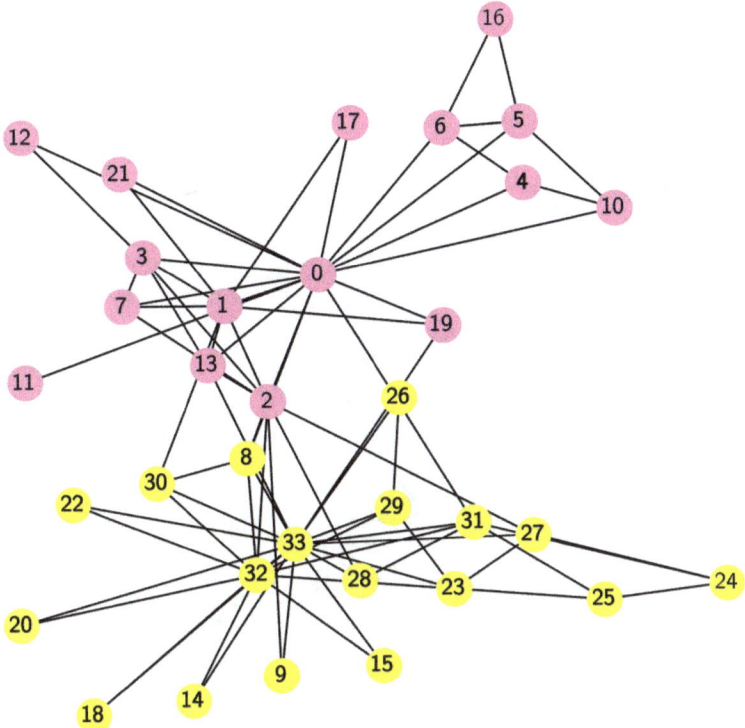

Figure 5.21 Graphical output of code.

It is not trivial to assess the quality of the resulting cut. But this particular example has a known ground-truth community structure as we saw from the Wikipedia quotation at the start of Section 5.1 (which partly explains its widespread use).

This ground truth is the following. We use numpy.nonzero to convert it into a cut.

```
truth = np.array([0, 0, 0, 0, 0, 0, 0, 0, 1, 1, 0, 0, 0, 0, 1, 1, 0,
                  0, 1, 0, 1, 0, 1, 1, 1, 1, 1, 1, 1, 1, 1, 1, 1, 1])
s_truth = np.nonzero(truth)
plt.figure(figsize=(6,6))
viz_cut(G, s_truth, pos, node_size=300, with_labels=True)
```

The output is in Figure 5.22. You can check that our cut perfectly matches the ground truth.

CHAT & LEARN Investigate alternative graph partitioning algorithms, such as the Kernighan–Lin algorithm. Ask your favorite AI chatbot to explain how it works and *compare its performance to spectral clustering* on this dataset.

◁ NC

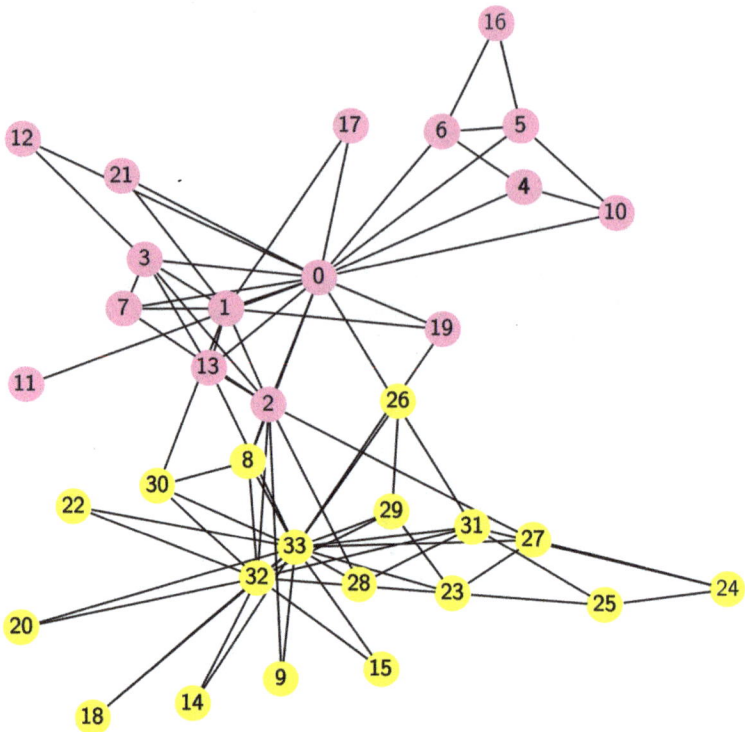

Figure 5.22 Graphical output of code; compare with previous figure.

Self-Assessment Quiz *(with help from Claude, Gemini, and ChatGPT)*

1. Which of the following best describes the "cut ratio" of a graph cut (S, S^c)?
   a) The ratio of the number of edges between S and S^c to the total number of edges in the graph
   b) The ratio of the number of edges between S and S^c to the size of the smaller set, $\min\{|S|, |S^c|\}$
   c) The ratio of the number of edges within S to the number of edges within S^c
   d) The ratio of the total number of edges in the graph to the number of edges between S and S^c

2. What is the isoperimetric number (or Cheeger constant) of a graph G?
   a) The largest value of the cut ratio over all possible cuts
   b) The smallest value of the cut ratio over all possible cuts
   c) The average value of the cut ratio over all possible cuts
   d) The median value of the cut ratio over all possible cuts

3. What do *Cheeger's Inequalities* establish?
   a) A relationship between the isoperimetric number and the largest Laplacian eigenvalue

b) A relationship between the isoperimetric number and the second largest Laplacian eigenvalue

c) A relationship between the isoperimetric number and the smallest Laplacian eigenvalue

d) A relationship between the isoperimetric number and the second smallest Laplacian eigenvalue

4 In the context of spectral graph theory, what is the Fiedler vector?

a) The eigenvector associated with the largest eigenvalue of the Laplacian matrix

b) The eigenvector associated with the smallest eigenvalue of the Laplacian matrix

c) The eigenvector associated with the second smallest eigenvalue of the Laplacian matrix

d) The eigenvector associated with the second largest eigenvalue of the Laplacian matrix

5 Which of the following is the relaxation of the minimum bisection problem presented in the text?

a)
$$\min \frac{1}{4}\left\{\sum_{\{i,j\}\in E}(x_i-x_j)^2 : \mathbf{x}=(x_1,...,x_n)\in\mathbb{R}^n, \sum_{i=1}^n x_i=0, \sum_{i=1}^n x_i^2=n\right\}$$

b)
$$\min \frac{1}{4}\left\{\sum_{\{i,j\}\in E}|x_i-x_j| : \mathbf{x}=(x_1,...,x_n)\in\mathbb{R}^n, \sum_{i=1}^n x_i=0, \sum_{i=1}^n x_i^2=n\right\}$$

c)
$$\max \frac{1}{4}\left\{\sum_{\{i,j\}\in E}(x_i-x_j)^2 : \mathbf{x}=(x_1,...,x_n)\in\mathbb{R}^n, \sum_{i=1}^n x_i=0, \sum_{i=1}^n x_i^2=n\right\}$$

d)
$$\max \frac{1}{4}\left\{\sum_{\{i,j\}\in E}|x_i-x_j| : \mathbf{x}=(x_1,...,x_n)\in\mathbb{R}^n, \sum_{i=1}^n x_i=0, \sum_{i=1}^n x_i^2=n\right\}$$

Answer for 1: b. Justification: The text defines the cut ratio as $\phi(S) = \frac{|E(S,S^c)|}{\min\{|S|,|S^c|\}}$, where $|E(S,S^c)|$ is the number of edges between S and S^c.

Answer for 2: b. Justification: The text defines the isoperimetric number as "the smallest value [the cut ratio] can take on G, that is, $\phi_G = \min_{\emptyset \neq S \subset V} \phi(S)$."

Answer for 3: d. Justification: The text states that "A key result of spectral graph theory establishes a quantitative relation between the isoperimetric number and the second smallest Laplacian eigenvalue."

Answer for 4: c. Justification: The text refers to the eigenvector associated with the second smallest eigenvalue of the Laplacian matrix as the Fiedler vector.

Answer for 5: a. Justification: The text replaces the constraint $\mathbf{x} = (x_1, ..., x_n) \in \{-1, +1\}^n$ with $\mathbf{x} = (x_1, ..., x_n) \in \mathbb{R}^n$ and adds the constraint $\sum_{i=1}^{n} x_i^2 = n$ to maintain the balanced cut property.

5.6 Erdős–Rényi Random Graphs and Stochastic Blockmodels

A natural way to test an algorithm is by running it on a simulated dataset whose "ground truth" is known. We encountered this idea for instance in clustering, where we used a mixture of Gaussians; there, the ground truth was the mixture component from which a data point was generated. What is an appropriate stochastic model in the context of network analysis?

In fact there are many models of random graphs; that is, graphs whose edges are picked at random. Which one to use depends on the task at hand. For graph partitioning, one requires a graph with a "planted partition." The stochastic blockmodel is a canonical example of such a model. We begin with a more general setting.

5.6.1 Inhomogeneous Erdős–Rényi Random Graph

A simple approach to generating a random graph is to include each edge *independently*. More precisely, let $V = [n]$ be a set of n vertices. Consider a symmetric matrix $M = (m_{i,j}) \in [0, 1]^{n \times n}$ with arbitrary entries in $[0, 1]$. The entry $m_{i,j} = m_{j,i}$ is the probability that edge $\{i, j\}$ is present (i.e., that $\{i, j\} \in E$), independently of all other edges. The outcome is a random graph $G = (V, E)$ with random adjacency matrix $A = (A_{i,j}) \in \{0, 1\}^{n \times n}$. This model is known as an inhomogeneous Erdős–Rényi (ER) random graph.

Observe that

$$\mathbb{E}[A_{i,j}] = 1 \cdot m_{i,j} + 0 \cdot (1 - m_{i,j}) = m_{i,j}.$$

Indeed each entry $A_{i,j}$ is a Bernoulli random variable with success probability $m_{i,j}$. In other words, in matrix form, we have

$$\mathbb{E}[A] = M,$$

that is, M is the expected adjacency matrix. Note in particular that M is deterministic while A is random (which is why we use lowercase entries for M but uppercase entries for A).

An important special case is obtained when $m_{i,j} = m_{j,i} = p \in (0, 1)$ for all $i \neq j$ and $m_{k,k} = 0$ for all k. That is, each possible edge between two distinct vertices is present with the same probability p. This model is known simply as an Erdős–Rényi (ER) random graph. Put differently,

$$\mathbb{E}[A] = M = p(J - I_{n \times n}),$$

where $J \in \mathbb{R}^{n \times n}$ is the all-one matrix. In this calculation, we subtract the identity matrix to account for the fact that the diagonal is 0.

The properties of this model are very well studied. We give a couple of examples next. For an event $\mathcal{F}$, the indicator random variable $\mathbf{1}_{\mathcal{F}}$ is 1 if $\mathcal{F}$ occurs, and 0 otherwise.

Example 5.6.1 *Let $G = (V, E)$ be an ER graph with n vertices. The parameter p can be interpreted as an edge density. Indeed, let's compute the expected number of edges G. By summing over all pairs and using linearity of expectation, we have*

$$\mathbb{E}[|E|] = \mathbb{E}\left[\sum_{i<j} \mathbf{1}_{\{i,j\}\in E}\right]$$
$$= \sum_{i<j} \mathbb{E}\left[\mathbf{1}_{\{i,j\}\in E}\right]$$
$$= \binom{n}{2}p.$$

Or, put differently, we have shown that the expected edge density $\mathbb{E}\left[|E|/\binom{n}{2}\right]$ is p.

A similar calculation gives the expected number of triangles. Denote by T_3 the number of triangles in G; that is, the number of triples i, j, k of distinct vertices such that $\{i, j\}, \{j, k\}, \{i, k\} \in E$ (i.e., all edges between them are present). Then

$$\mathbb{E}[|T_3|] = \mathbb{E}\left[\sum_{i<j<k} \mathbf{1}_{\{i,j\},\{j,k\},\{i,k\}\in E}\right]$$
$$= \mathbb{E}\left[\sum_{i<j<k} \mathbf{1}_{\{i,j\}\in E}\mathbf{1}_{\{j,k\}\in E}\mathbf{1}_{\{i,k\}\in E}\right]$$
$$= \sum_{i<j<k} \mathbb{E}\left[\mathbf{1}_{\{i,j\}\in E}\right] \mathbb{E}\left[\mathbf{1}_{\{j,k\}\in E}\right] \mathbb{E}\left[\mathbf{1}_{\{i,k\}\in E}\right]$$
$$= \binom{n}{3}p^3.$$

We used the independence of the edges in the third line. Or, put differently, we have shown that the expected triangle density $\mathbb{E}\left[|T_3|/\binom{n}{3}\right]$ is p^3.

We implement the generation of an inhomogeneous ER graph using NetworkX. We first initialize a pseudorandom number generator rng. To determine whether an edge is present between i and j, we generate a uniform random variable rng.random() (see numpy.random.Generator.random) and add the edge with G.add_edge(i, j) if the random variable is < M[i, j] – an event which indeed occurs with the desired probability (check it!).

```
def inhomogeneous_er_random_graph(rng, n, M):

    G = nx.Graph()
    G.add_nodes_from(range(n))
    for i in range(n):
        for j in range(i + 1, n):
            if rng.random() < M[i, j]:
                G.add_edge(i, j)

    return G
```

NUMERICAL CORNER Here is an example usage. We generate probabilities $m_{i,j}$ uniformly at random between 0 and 1.

```
seed = 535
rng = np.random.default_rng(seed)

n = 20
M = rng.random([n, n])
M = (M + M.T) / 2 # ensures symmetry of M

G = inhomogeneous_er_random_graph(rng, n, M)
```

We draw the resulting graph.

```
nx.draw_networkx(G, node_color='black', font_color='white')
plt.axis('off')
plt.show()
```

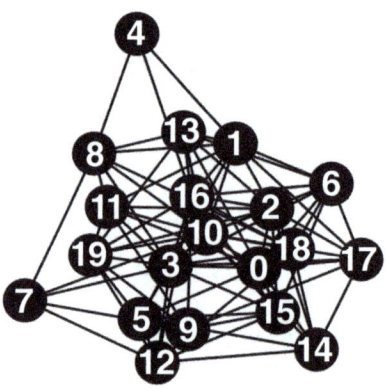

Figure 5.23 Graphical output of code.

◁ **NC**

The following subroutine generates an ER graph.

```
def er_random_graph(rng, n, p):
    M = p * (np.ones((n, n)) - np.eye(n))
    return inhomogeneous_er_random_graph(rng, n, M)
```

To confirm our previous calculations, below is the implementation of a routine to estimate the edge density for an ER graph with a fixed parameter p. Recall that the edge density is defined as the number of edges present divided by the number of possible edges (i.e., the number

5.6 Erdős–Rényi Random Graphs and Stochastic Blockmodels

of pairs of distinct vertices). The routine takes advantage of the *Law of Large Numbers* by generating a large number of sample graphs, computing their edge density, and then taking the mean.

```
def estimate_edge_density(rng, n, p, num_samples=100):

    total_edges = 0
    total_possible_edges = n * (n - 1) / 2

    for _ in range(num_samples):
        G = er_random_graph(rng, n, p)
        total_edges += G.number_of_edges()

    average_edges = total_edges / num_samples
    edge_density = average_edges / total_possible_edges
    return edge_density
```

NUMERICAL CORNER On a small example, we indeed get that the edge density is roughly p.

```
n = 10
p = 0.3
num_samples = 1000

estimated_density = estimate_edge_density(rng, n, p, num_samples)
print(f"Estimated edge density for an ER graph with n={n}
       and p={p}: {estimated_density}")
```

Estimated edge density for an ER graph with n=10 and p=0.3:
  0.3004888888888889

TRY IT! *Modify the code above* to estimate the density of triangles.

◁ NC

When n, the number of vertices, is large, random graphs tend to exhibit large-scale emergent behavior. One classical example involves the probability of being connected in an ER graph. To illustrate, below is code to estimate that probability over a range of edge densities p (with help from Claude and ChatGPT).

```
def estimate_connected_probability(rng, n, p, num_samples=100):

    connected_count = 0

    for _ in range(num_samples):
        G = er_random_graph(rng, n, p)
```

```
        if nx.is_connected(G):
            connected_count += 1

    connected_probability = connected_count / num_samples
    return connected_probability

def plot_connected_probability(rng, n, p_values, num_samples=100):

    probabilities = []
    for p in p_values:
        prob = estimate_connected_probability(rng, n, p, num_samples)
        probabilities.append(prob)

    plt.figure(figsize=(6, 4))
    plt.plot(p_values, probabilities, marker='o', color='black')
    plt.xlabel('$p$'), plt.ylabel('Estimated probability of being
                connected')
    plt.show()
```

NUMERICAL CORNER We run the code for n equal to 100. What do you observe?

```
n = 100
p_values = np.linspace(0, 0.1, 50)
num_samples = 250
plot_connected_probability(rng, n, p_values, num_samples)
```

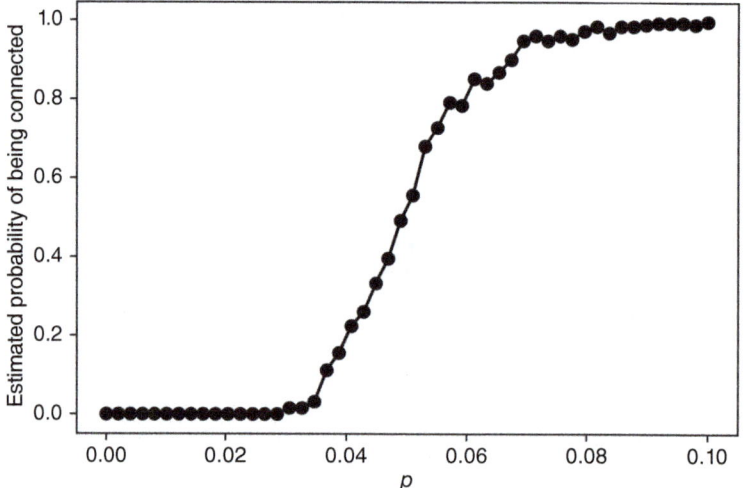

Figure 5.24 Graphical output of code.

5.6 Erdős–Rényi Random Graphs and Stochastic Blockmodels

The probability of being connected starts out at 0 when p is small, which is not surprising since it implies that the graph has a relatively small number of edges. But then that probability increases – rapidly – to 1 as p crosses a threshold. This is referred to as the phase transition of the ER graph.

It can be shown rigorously that the transition occurs at roughly $p = \log n/n$. That is:

```
np.log(n)/n
```

0.04605170185988092

which is consistent with the plot.

TRY IT! Taking a larger n would produce a sharper transition. *Try it for yourself*. Also try drawing one random sample for increasing values of p around the threshold. What do you observe?

TRY IT! Many other properties exhibit such sharp threshold behavior. *Modify the code* to estimate the probability that a clique of size 4 exists in the graph.

◁ NC

5.6.2 Stochastic Blockmodel

We return to our original motivation. How can we create a random graph with a planted partition? The stochastic blockmodel (SBM) is such a model. Here we imagine that $[n]$ is partitioned into two disjoint sets C_1 and C_2, referred to as blocks. We set $z(i) = j$ if vertex i is in block C_j. We also encode the block assignment with a matrix $Z \in \{0, 1\}^{n \times 2}$ where row i is $\mathbf{e}_j^T$ if vertex i is assigned to block C_j.

Let $b_{i,j} \in [0, 1]$ be the probability that a vertex in block C_i and a vertex in block C_j are connected by an edge, independently of all other edges. We enforce $b_{1,2} = b_{2,1}$. We collect these probabilities in the matrix

$$B = \begin{pmatrix} b_{1,1} & b_{1,2} \\ b_{2,1} & b_{2,2} \end{pmatrix}.$$

By our assumption, the matrix B is symmetric.

We typically take

$$\min\{b_{1,1}, b_{2,2}\} > b_{1,2},$$

that is, edges are more likely between vertices in the same block than between vertices in different blocks. This corresponds to the intuition that, in social networks or other types of networks, members of the same group (i.e., block) tend to interact more frequently with each other than with members of different groups. For instance, friends within the same social circle are more likely to be connected than with people outside their circle. That is related to the concept of homophily which describes the tendency of individuals to associate and bond with similar others.

This is a special case of the inhomogeneous ER graph model. What is the corresponding M matrix? Note that, for each pair of vertices $1 \leq i < j \leq n$, edge $\{i, j\}$ is present in E with probability

$$m_{i,j} := b_{z(i),z(j)} = Z_{i,\cdot} B Z_{j,\cdot}^T.$$

where recall that $Z_{i,\cdot}$ is row i of matrix Z.

In matrix form, this is saying that

$$M = ZBZ^T.$$

So, given B and Z, we can generate an SBM as a special case of an inhomogeneous ER graph.

We implement the SBM model. We use blocks numbered 0 and 1.

```
def sbm_random_graph(rng, n, block_assignments, B):

    num_blocks = B.shape[0]
    Z = np.zeros((n, num_blocks))
    for i in range(n):
        Z[i, block_assignments[i]] = 1
    M = Z @ B @ Z.T

    return inhomogeneous_er_random_graph(rng, n, M)
```

NUMERICAL CORNER Here is an example usage. We first pick a block assignment at random. Specifically, blocks are assigned randomly with `numpy.random.Generator.choice`. It produces two blocks by assigning each vertex with equal probability to either block, independently of all other choices.

```
n = 50
block_assignments = rng.choice(2, n)

B = np.array([[0.8, 0.1], [0.1, 0.8]])

G = sbm_random_graph(rng, n, block_assignments, B)
```

We draw the graph with colored nodes based on block assignments. The "good" cut is clearly visible in this layout.

```
plt.figure(figsize=(6,6))
pos = nx.spring_layout(G)
nx.draw(G, pos, with_labels=True, node_color=block_assignments,
        cmap='rainbow',
        node_size=200, font_size=10, font_color='white')
plt.show()
```

5.6 Erdős–Rényi Random Graphs and Stochastic Blockmodels

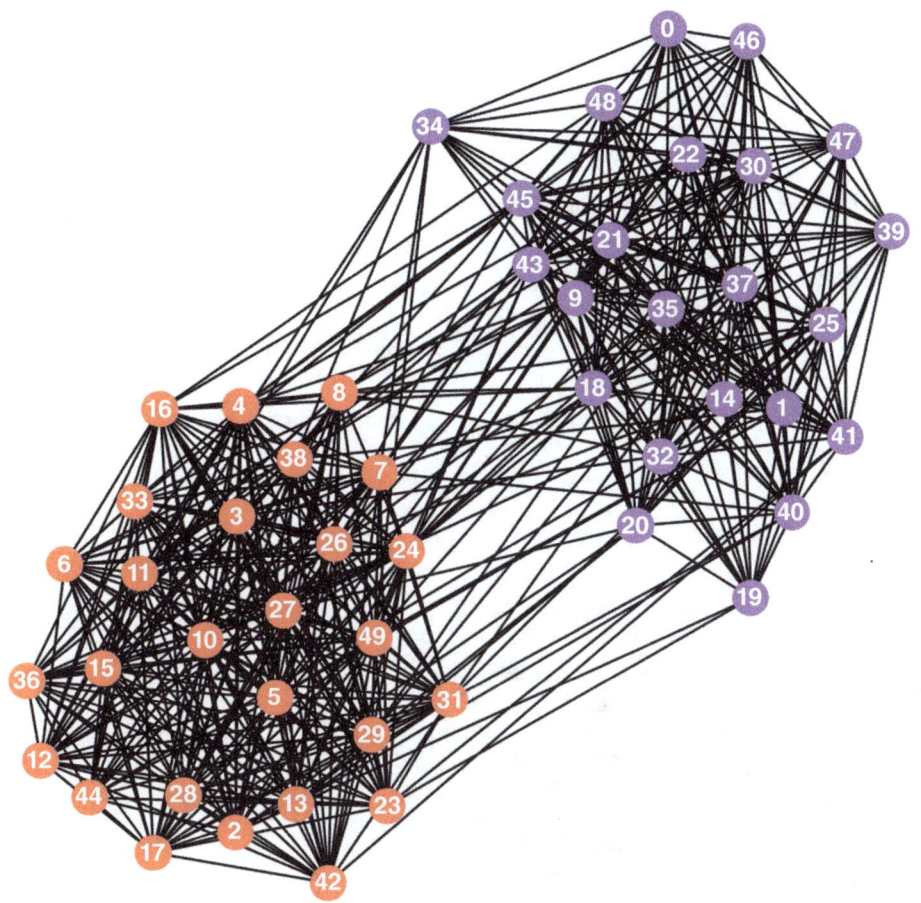

Figure 5.25 Graphical output of code.

◁ **NC**

We introduce a subroutine which assigns blocks at random as follows. Let $\beta_1, \beta_2 \in [0, 1]$ with $\beta_1 + \beta_2 = 1$ be the probabilities that a vertex belongs respectively to block 1 or block 2. We collect these probabilities in the vector

$$\boldsymbol{\beta} = (\beta_1, \beta_2).$$

We pick block $z(i) \in \{1, 2\}$ for each vertex $1 \leq i \leq n$ according to the distribution $\boldsymbol{\beta}$, independently of all other vertices $\neq i$.

```
def generate_block_assignments(rng, n, beta):
    return rng.choice(len(beta), size=n, p=beta)
```

NUMERICAL CORNER Here is an example usage.

```
n = 50
beta = [0.33, 0.67]
```

```
B = np.array([[0.5, 0.03], [0.03, 0.4]])

block_assignments = generate_block_assignments(rng, n, beta)
G = sbm_random_graph(rng, n, block_assignments, B)
```

Observe that the blocks are more unbalanced this time.

```
plt.figure(figsize=(6,6))
pos = nx.spring_layout(G)
nx.draw(G, pos, with_labels=True, node_color=block_assignments,
        cmap=plt.cm.rainbow,
        node_size=200, font_size=10, font_color='white')
plt.show()
```

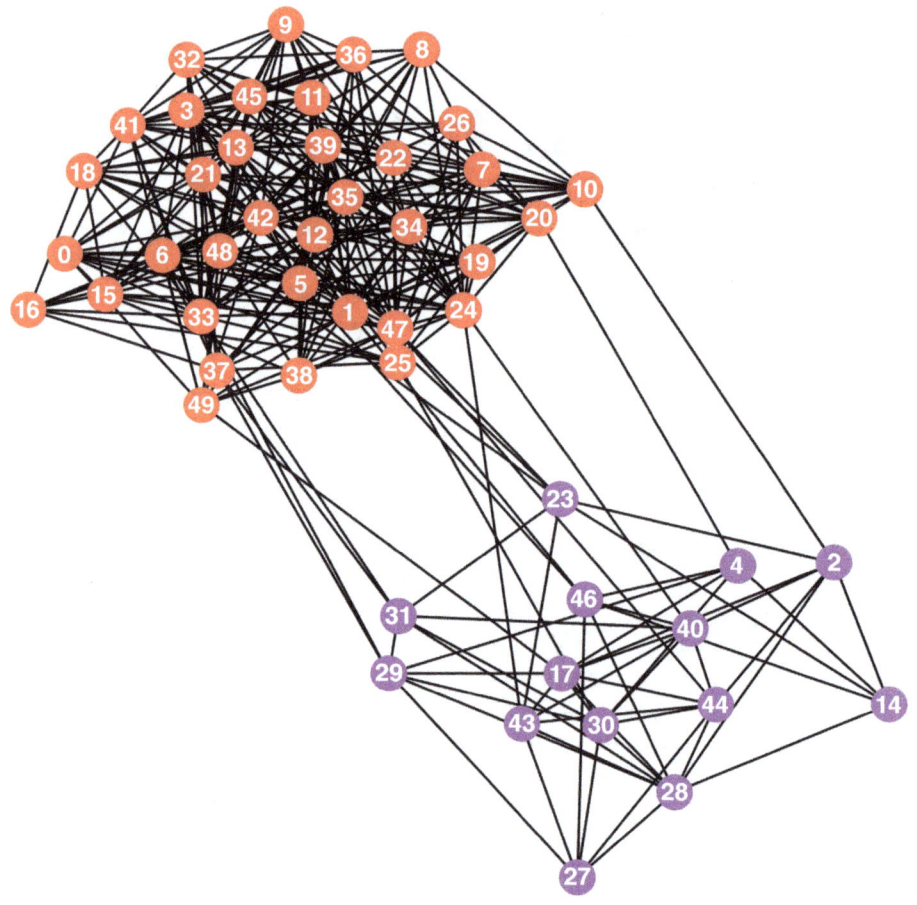

Figure 5.26 Graphical output of code.

To test our spectral partitioning algorithm, we run `spectral_cut2`, which indeed recovers the ground truth.

5.6 Erdős–Rényi Random Graphs and Stochastic Blockmodels

```
A = nx.adjacency_matrix(G).toarray()
s, sc = mmids.spectral_cut2(A)

plt.figure(figsize=(6,6))
mmids.viz_cut(G, s, pos, node_size=200, with_labels=True)
```

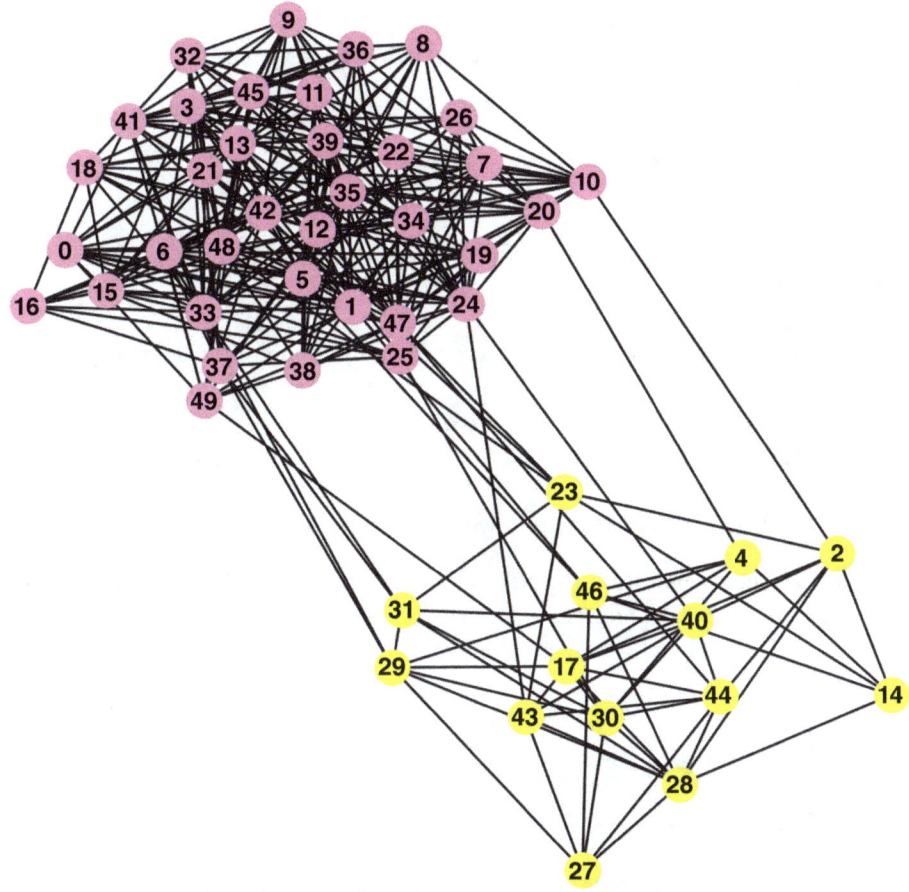

Figure 5.27 Graphical output of code.

◁ **NC**

The following code computes the fraction of incorrectly assigned vertices. Note that it considers *two* assignments corresponding to swapping the labels 0 and 1, which cannot be inferred.

```
def calculate_incorrect_fraction(block_assignments, inferred_s,
                                 inferred_sc):

    n = len(block_assignments)
```

```
            inferred_assignments = np.zeros(n)
            for i in inferred_s:
                inferred_assignments[i] = 0
            for i in inferred_sc:
                inferred_assignments[i] = 1

            incorrect_assignments_1 = np.sum(block_assignments
            != inferred_assignments)/n
            incorrect_assignments_2 = np.sum(block_assignments
            == inferred_assignments)/n

            return np.minimum(incorrect_assignments_1,
            incorrect_assignments_2)
```

NUMERICAL CORNER We confirm on our previous example that the ground truth was perfectly recovered.

```
fraction_incorrect = calculate_incorrect_fraction(block_assignments,
                s, sc)
print(f"Fraction of incorrectly assigned vertices:
    {fraction_incorrect}")
```

Fraction of incorrectly assigned vertices: 0.0

One expects that the ground truth is harder to recover if the probability of an edge between blocks is close to that within blocks, which makes the community structure more murky. To test this hypothesis, we modify our previous example by significantly increasing the inter-block probability.

```
n = 100
beta = [0.55, 0.45]
B = np.array([[0.55, 0.25], [0.25, 0.45]])

block_assignments = generate_block_assignments(rng, n, beta)
G = sbm_random_graph(rng, n, block_assignments, B)
```

We run `spectral_cut2`. It recovers the ground truth only partially this time.

```
A = nx.adjacency_matrix(G).toarray()
s, sc = mmids.spectral_cut2(A)
fraction_incorrect = calculate_incorrect_fraction(block_assignments,
    s, sc)
print(f"Fraction of incorrectly assigned vertices:
    {fraction_incorrect}")
```

Fraction of incorrectly assigned vertices: 0.22

◁ **NC**

5.6 Erdős–Rényi Random Graphs and Stochastic Blockmodels

Self-Assessment Quiz (*with help from Claude, Gemini, and ChatGPT*)

1. In a stochastic blockmodel (SBM), what does $b_{i,j}$ represent?
   a) The probability that vertex i is assigned to block j
   b) The probability that there is an edge between any two vertices
   c) The probability that there is an edge between a vertex in block C_i and a vertex in block C_j
   d) The weight of the edge between vertex i and vertex j

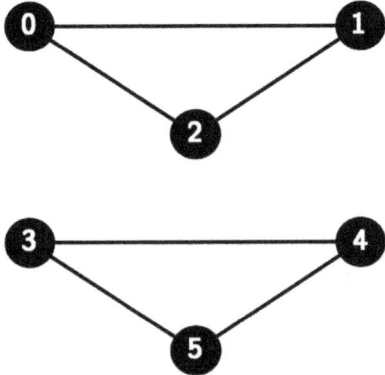

Figure 5.28 Graph for self-assessment quiz 2.

2. Consider the graph in Figure 5.28 generated using NetworkX in Python. Which of the following models could have produced this graph?
   a) An Erdős–Rényi (ER) random graph
   b) A stochastic blockmodel (SBM) with two communities
   c) A symmetric stochastic blockmodel (SSBM) with two equal-sized communities (i.e., where in addition $b_{1,1} = b_{2,2}$)
   d) All of the above

3. Consider an Erdős–Rényi (ER) random graph with n vertices and edge probability p. What is the expected number of edges in the graph?
   a) $n^2 p$
   b) $\binom{n}{2} p$
   c) np
   d) $n(n-1)p$

4. Consider the following Python code snippet:

```
n, p = 5, 0.4
rng = np.random.default_rng(123)
```

```
G = nx.Graph()
G.add_nodes_from(range(n))
for i in range(n):
    for j in range(i + 1, n):
        if rng.random() < p:
            G.add_edge(i, j)
```

Which of the following best describes the graph generated by this code?

a) An Erdős–Rényi (ER) random graph with $n = 5$ vertices and edge probability $p = 0.4$

b) A stochastic blockmodel (SBM) with $n = 5$ vertices and intra-block probability $p = 0.4$

c) A symmetric stochastic blockmodel (SSBM) with $n = 5$ vertices and inter-block probability $p = 0.4$

d) An inhomogeneous Erdős–Rényi (ER) random graph with $n = 5$ vertices and edge probabilities given by a matrix M

5 In the stochastic blockmodel, what happens to the difficulty of recovering the community structure if the inter-block connection probability $b_{1,2}$ is close to the intra-block connection probability $b_{1,1}$?

a) It becomes easier.

b) It remains unchanged.

c) It becomes harder.

d) None of the above.

Answer for 1: c. Justification: The text defines $b_{i,j}$ as "the probability that a vertex in block C_i and a vertex in block C_j are connected by an edge."

Answer for 2: d. Justification: The graph consists of two cliques (complete subgraphs) of size 3 each, one with vertices 0, 1, and 2 and another with vertices 3, 4, and 5. There are no edges between the two cliques. It has a positive probability of occurring under any ER, SBM, or SSBM random graph model where all edge probabilities are in $(0, 1)$.

Answer for 3: b. Justification: The text states: "Let's compute the expected number of edges G. By summing over all pairs and using linearity of expectation, we have $\mathbb{E}[|E|] = \mathbb{E}[\sum_{i<j} \mathbf{1}_{\{i,j\} \in E}] = \sum_{i<j} \mathbb{E}[\mathbf{1}_{\{i,j\} \in E}] = \binom{n}{2} p$."

Answer for 4: a. Justification: The code generates an ER random graph with $n = 5$ vertices, where each edge is included independently with probability $p = 0.4$. This is evident from the nested loop structure and the condition `if rng.random() < p` for adding edges.

Answer for 5: c. Justification: When the inter-block connection probability $b_{1,2}$ is close to the intra-block connection probability $b_{1,1}$, the community structure becomes harder to recover because the distinction between the blocks is less clear.

5.7 Exercises

5.7.1 Warm-Up Worksheets
(with help from Claude, Gemini, and ChatGPT)

Section 5.2

E5.2.1 For the graph in Figure 5.29, write down the set of vertices V and the set of edges E.

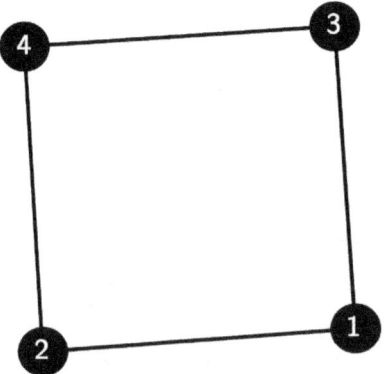

Figure 5.29 Graph for E5.2.1.

E5.2.2 For the graph in E5.2.1, write down the neighborhood $N(1)$ and the degree $\delta(1)$ of vertex 1.

E5.2.3 For the graph in E5.2.1, find a path between vertices 1 and 4, and compute its length.

E5.2.4 For the directed graph in Figure 5.30, write down the adjacency matrix A.

Figure 5.30 Directed graph for E5.2.4.

E5.2.5 For the directed graph in E5.2.4, write down the in-degree $\delta^-(2)$ and the out-degree $\delta^+(2)$ of vertex 2.

E5.2.6 Consider an undirected graph G with vertices $V = \{1, 2, 3, 4\}$ and edges $E = \{\{1, 2\}, \{2, 3\}, \{3, 4\}, \{4, 1\}\}$. Compute the degree of each vertex.

E5.2.7 Determine if the undirected graph G with vertices $V = \{1, 2, 3, 4\}$ and edges $E = \{\{1, 2\}, \{2, 3\}, \{3, 4\}\}$ is connected.

E5.2.8 Write the Laplacian matrix L for the undirected graph G with vertices $V = \{1, 2, 3\}$ and edges $E = \{\{1, 2\}, \{2, 3\}, \{1, 3\}\}$.

E5.2.9 Given an undirected graph G with vertices $V = \{1, 2, 3, 4\}$ and edges $E = \{\{1, 2\}, \{2, 3\}, \{3, 4\}, \{4, 1\}\}$, compute the number of connected components.

E5.2.10 Consider the graph in Figure 5.31.

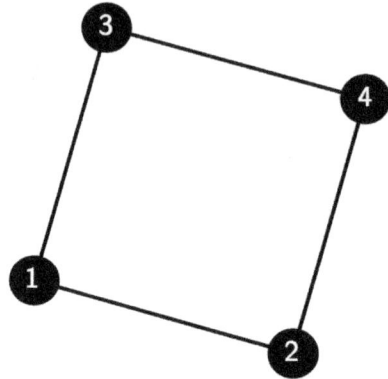

Figure 5.31 Graph for E5.2.10.

Give the adjacency matrix A of this graph.

E5.2.11 Consider the same graph as in E5.2.10. Give its incidence matrix B.

E5.2.12 Consider the directed graph in Figure 5.32.

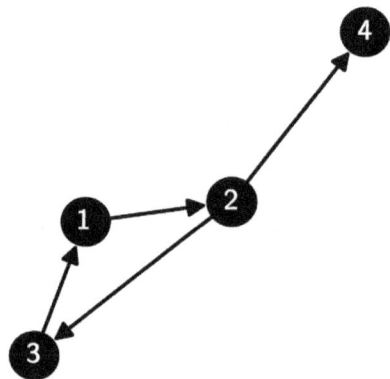

Figure 5.32 Directed graph for E5.2.12.

Give the adjacency matrix A of this graph.

E5.2.13 Consider the same directed graph as in E5.2.12. Give its incidence matrix B.

E5.2.14 Given the directed graph G with vertices $V = \{1, 2, 3\}$ and directed edges $E = \{(1, 2), (2, 3), (3, 1)\}$, compute the out-degree and in-degree of each vertex.

E5.2.15 A graph is said to be d-regular if all its vertices have degree d. For which value of d is the Petersen graph d-regular?

Section 5.3

E5.3.1 Let $A = \begin{pmatrix} 5 & 3 \\ 3 & 5 \end{pmatrix}$. Find a matrix W whose columns form an orthonormal basis of $\mathbb{R}^2$ and such that $W^T A W$ is diagonal.

E5.3.2 Let $A = \begin{pmatrix} 3 & 1 \\ 1 & 3 \end{pmatrix}$. Find the quadratic form $\langle \mathbf{u}, A\mathbf{u} \rangle$ for $\mathbf{u} = \begin{pmatrix} 1 \\ 2 \end{pmatrix}$.

E5.3.3 Given a symmetric matrix $A = \begin{pmatrix} 3 & 1 \\ 1 & 2 \end{pmatrix}$ and a vector $\mathbf{u} = \begin{pmatrix} \frac{\sqrt{3}}{2} \\ \frac{1}{2} \end{pmatrix}$, compute the Rayleigh quotient $\mathcal{R}_A(\mathbf{u})$.

E5.3.4 Let $A = \begin{pmatrix} 3 & 1 \\ 1 & 3 \end{pmatrix}$. Compute the Rayleigh quotient $\mathcal{R}_A(\mathbf{u})$ for $\mathbf{u} = \begin{pmatrix} 1 \\ 1 \end{pmatrix}$.

E5.3.5 Given a symmetric matrix $A = \begin{pmatrix} 2 & -1 \\ -1 & 2 \end{pmatrix}$, find the eigenvalues and eigenvectors of A, and verify that the largest eigenvalue λ_1 satisfies the variational characterization $\lambda_1 = \max_{\mathbf{u} \neq 0} \mathcal{R}_A(\mathbf{u})$.

E5.3.6 Given a symmetric matrix $A = \begin{pmatrix} 4 & 2 \\ 2 & 1 \end{pmatrix}$, find the eigenvalues and eigenvectors of A, and verify that the smallest eigenvalue λ_2 satisfies the variational characterization $\lambda_2 = \min_{\mathbf{u} \neq 0} \mathcal{R}_A(\mathbf{u})$.

E5.3.7 Given a symmetric matrix $A = \begin{pmatrix} 1 & 2 & 0 \\ 2 & 1 & 0 \\ 0 & 0 & 3 \end{pmatrix}$ and its eigenvectors $\mathbf{v}_1 = \frac{1}{\sqrt{2}}\begin{pmatrix} 1 \\ 1 \\ 0 \end{pmatrix}$, $\mathbf{v}_2 = \frac{1}{\sqrt{2}}\begin{pmatrix} -1 \\ 1 \\ 0 \end{pmatrix}$, $\mathbf{v}_3 = \begin{pmatrix} 0 \\ 0 \\ 1 \end{pmatrix}$, verify that the second smallest eigenvalue λ_2 satisfies the variational characterization $\lambda_2 = \min_{0 \neq \mathbf{u} \in V_2} \mathcal{R}_A(\mathbf{u})$, where $V_2 = \text{span}(\mathbf{v}_1, \mathbf{v}_2)$.

E5.3.8 Let $A = \begin{pmatrix} 1 & 0 & 0 \\ 0 & 2 & 0 \\ 0 & 0 & 3 \end{pmatrix}$. Find the subspaces V_2 and W_2 as defined in the Courant–Fischer Theorem.

Section 5.4

E5.4.1 Given the graph G with adjacency matrix

$$A = \begin{pmatrix} 0 & 1 & 0 & 0 \\ 1 & 0 & 1 & 1 \\ 0 & 1 & 0 & 1 \\ 0 & 1 & 1 & 0 \end{pmatrix},$$

find the degree matrix D and the Laplacian matrix L.

E5.4.2 Given the adjacency matrix of a graph G with five vertices,

$$A = \begin{pmatrix} 0 & 1 & 0 & 1 & 0 \\ 1 & 0 & 1 & 0 & 0 \\ 0 & 1 & 0 & 1 & 1 \\ 1 & 0 & 1 & 0 & 0 \\ 0 & 0 & 1 & 0 & 0 \end{pmatrix},$$

compute the degree matrix D and the Laplacian matrix $L = D - A$.

E5.4.3 For the Laplacian matrix L from E5.4.2, verify that the constant unit vector $\mathbf{y}_1 = \frac{1}{\sqrt{5}}(1, 1, 1, 1, 1)$ is an eigenvector of L with eigenvalue 0.

E5.4.4 Consider the path graph P_4 with four vertices. Compute its Laplacian matrix L.

E5.4.5 For the Laplacian matrix L of P_4 from E5.4.4, verify that the following vectors are eigenvectors of L:

$$\mathbf{y}_1 = \frac{1}{2}(1, 1, 1, 1), \quad \mathbf{y}_2 = \frac{1}{2}(1, \frac{1}{\sqrt{2}}, -\frac{1}{\sqrt{2}}, -1).$$

E5.4.6 For the path graph P_4, compute the Laplacian quadratic form $\mathbf{y}^T L \mathbf{y}$ for the vector $\mathbf{y} = (1, -1, 1, -1)$.

E5.4.7 For the complete graph K_4, find a lower and an upper bound for the largest eigenvalue μ_4 of its Laplacian matrix using the maximum degree $\bar{\delta}$ of the graph.

E5.4.8 Consider the graph G with adjacency matrix

$$A = \begin{pmatrix} 0 & 1 & 1 & 0 & 0 & 0 \\ 1 & 0 & 1 & 0 & 0 & 0 \\ 1 & 1 & 0 & 0 & 0 & 0 \\ 0 & 0 & 0 & 0 & 1 & 1 \\ 0 & 0 & 0 & 1 & 0 & 1 \\ 0 & 0 & 0 & 1 & 1 & 0 \end{pmatrix}.$$

Find a vector $\mathbf{x} = (x_1, \ldots, x_6)$ that is an eigenvector of the Laplacian matrix of G with eigenvalue 0, such that $\mathbf{x}$ is not a constant vector.

E5.4.9 Let G be a graph with n vertices. Show that the sum of the entries in each row of the Laplacian matrix L_G is zero.

E5.4.10 Let G be a graph with n vertices and m edges. Compute the trace of the Laplacian matrix L_G.

E5.4.11 Let G be a graph with n vertices. Is the Laplacian matrix L_G always positive semidefinite?

E5.4.12 Let G be a graph with maximum degree $\bar{\delta} = 3$. What is the best upper bound on the largest eigenvalue μ_n of L_G that you can obtain from the inequality in the text?

E5.4.13 Let G be a complete graph with n vertices. Compute the eigenvalues of L_G.

E5.4.14 Let G be a graph with n vertices. Show that if L_G has rank $n-1$, then G is connected.

Section 5.5

E5.5.1 Given a graph with five vertices and the adjacency matrix

$$A = \begin{pmatrix} 0 & 1 & 0 & 0 & 1 \\ 1 & 0 & 1 & 0 & 0 \\ 0 & 1 & 0 & 1 & 0 \\ 0 & 0 & 1 & 0 & 1 \\ 1 & 0 & 0 & 1 & 0 \end{pmatrix},$$

compute the cut ratio for the cut $S = \{2\}$, $S^c = \{1, 3, 4, 5\}$.

E5.5.2 For the graph in E5.5.1, find a cut with a smaller cut ratio than the one given in E5.5.1.

E5.5.3 For a graph with six vertices, what is the smallest possible value of the isoperimetric number (Cheeger constant)?

E5.5.4 Given a graph with Laplacian eigenvalues $\mu_1 = 0$, $\mu_2 = 0.5$, and maximum degree $\bar{\delta} = 4$, find a lower bound for the isoperimetric number using *Cheeger's Inequalities*.

E5.5.5 For the graph in E5.5.4, find an upper bound for the isoperimetric number using *Cheeger's Inequality*.

E5.5.6 Given a graph with adjacency matrix

$$A = \begin{pmatrix} 0 & 1 & 0 & 1 \\ 1 & 0 & 1 & 0 \\ 0 & 1 & 0 & 1 \\ 1 & 0 & 1 & 0 \end{pmatrix},$$

compute the degree matrix D and the Laplacian matrix L.

E5.5.7 For the graph in E5.5.6, verify that the eigenvectors of the Laplacian matrix are $(1, 1, 1, 1)/2$, $(-1, -1, 1, 1)/2$, $(1, -1, -1, 1)/2$, and $(1, -1, 1, -1)/2$, and find their corresponding eigenvalues.

E5.5.8 Among the eigenvectors in E5.5.7, identify the Fiedler vector (the eigenvector associated with the second smallest eigenvalue of the Laplacian matrix).

E5.5.9 Using one of the Fiedler vectors from E5.5.8, order the vertices of the graph in E5.5.6 according to the graph-cutting algorithm based on the Fiedler vector.

E5.5.10 For the ordering in E5.5.9, compute the cut ratios for all possible cuts of the form $S_k = \{\pi(1), \ldots, \pi(k)\}$, $k \leq n - 1$, and find the one with the smallest cut ratio.

E5.5.11 Find the isoperimetric number (Cheeger constant) of the graph in E5.5.6 and compare it to the results obtained in E5.5.8 and E5.5.10, as well as to the bounds given by *Cheeger's Inequalities*.

E5.5.12 Given a graph G with vertices $V = \{1, 2, 3, 4, 5\}$ and edges $E = \{\{1,2\}, \{1,3\}, \{2,3\}, \{2,4\}, \{3,5\}\}$, compute the adjacency matrix A of G.

E5.5.13 Compute the degree matrix D for the graph G in E5.5.12.

E5.5.14 Compute the Laplacian matrix L for the graph G in E5.5.12 using $L = D - A$.

E5.5.15 Find the cutset and cut ratio for the cut $S = \{1, 2\}$ and $S^c = \{3, 4, 5\}$ in the graph G from E5.5.12.

E5.5.16 Given the Fiedler vector $\mathbf{y}_2 \approx (0, -0.205, 0.205, -0.677, 0.677)$ corresponding to $\mu_2 \approx 0.697$ for the graph G from E5.5.12, sort the vertices based on $\mathbf{y}_2$ values and suggest a cut.

E5.5.17 Draw the graph G from E5.5.12 and highlight the cut $S = \{1, 2\}$ and $S^c = \{3, 4, 5\}$ using NetworkX in Python.

Section 5.6

E5.6.1 Consider an Erdős–Rényi (ER) random graph with $n = 6$ vertices and edge probability $p = 0.4$. Compute the expected number of edges in the graph.

E5.6.2 Consider an ER random graph with $n = 8$ vertices. If the expected number of edges is 14, find the edge probability p.

E5.6.3 Consider an ER random graph with $n = 10$ vertices and edge probability $p = 0.3$. Compute the expected triangle density, $\mathbb{E}[|T_3|/\binom{n}{3}]$, where $|T_3|$ is the number of triangles in the graph.

E5.6.4 Consider a stochastic blockmodel (SBM) with $n = 6$ vertices, two blocks of equal size $\{1, 2, 3\}$ and $\{4, 5, 6\}$, intra-block probability $p = 0.8$, and inter-block probability $q = 0.2$. Write down the matrix $M = \mathbb{E}[A]$, where A is the adjacency matrix of the graph.

E5.6.5 Consider an SBM with $n = 8$ vertices, two blocks of equal size $\{1, 2, 3, 4\}$ and $\{5, 6, 7, 8\}$, and block probability matrix $B = \begin{pmatrix} 0.6 & 0.3 \\ 0.3 & 0.7 \end{pmatrix}$. Write down the block assignment matrix Z.

E5.6.6 Consider the SBM from E5.6.5. Compute the matrix $M = \mathbb{E}[A]$, where A is the adjacency matrix of the graph.

E5.6.7 Compute the degree distribution of a vertex in an ER random graph with $n = 4$ and $p = 0.5$.

E5.6.8 In a stochastic blockmodel with $n_1 = 3$ and $n_2 = 3$, $B = \begin{pmatrix} 0.5 & 0.1 \\ 0.1 & 0.6 \end{pmatrix}$, calculate the expected degree of a vertex in block 1.

E5.6.9 For an ER random graph with $n = 3$ and $p = 0.5$, compute the variance of the number of edges.

E5.6.10 Consider an inhomogeneous ER random graph with probability matrix

$$M = \begin{pmatrix} 0 & 1/2 & 1/4 \\ 1/2 & 0 & 1/3 \\ 1/4 & 1/3 & 0 \end{pmatrix}.$$

What is the probability that the graph is a triangle?

E5.6.11 Consider a stochastic blockmodel with two blocks, $C_1 = \{1, 2\}$ and $C_2 = \{3, 4\}$, and connection probability matrix

$$B = \begin{pmatrix} 3/4 & 1/4 \\ 1/4 & 1/2 \end{pmatrix}.$$

What is the probability that there is an edge between vertices 2 and 4?

E5.6.12 Consider a stochastic blockmodel with block assignment matrix

$$Z = \begin{pmatrix} 1 & 0 \\ 1 & 0 \\ 0 & 1 \\ 0 & 1 \end{pmatrix}$$

and connection probability matrix

$$B = \begin{pmatrix} 1/2 & 1/3 \\ 1/3 & 1/4 \end{pmatrix}.$$

What is the expected adjacency matrix $\mathbb{E}[A]$?

E5.6.13 (Refers to Online Supplementary Materials.[2]) In a symmetric stochastic blockmodel (SSBM) with $n = 8$, $p = 3/4$, and $q = 1/4$, what is the expected degree of each vertex?

E5.6.14 (Refers to Online Supplementary Materials.) In a symmetric stochastic blockmodel (SSBM) with $n = 12$, $p = 5/6$, $q = 1/6$, and blocks $\{1, \ldots, 6\}$ and $\{7, \ldots, 12\}$, what is the expected Laplacian matrix L?

---

[2] https://mmids-textbook.github.io/chap05_specgraph/supp/roch-mmids-specgraph-supp.html#

E5.6.15 Consider an inhomogeneous ER random graph with probability matrix

$$M = \begin{pmatrix} 0 & 1/2 & 1/4 \\ 1/2 & 0 & 1/2 \\ 1/4 & 1/2 & 0 \end{pmatrix}.$$

What is the variance of the number of edges present in the graph?

5.7.2 Problems

5.1 Let $A \in \mathbb{R}^{d \times d}$ be a symmetric matrix. Let $\mathbf{v}$ be a (not necessarily unit) eigenvector of A with eigenvalue λ. Show that $\mathcal{R}_A(\mathbf{v}) = \lambda$.

5.2 A graph $G = (V, E)$ is bipartite if there is a bipartition of the vertices V_1, V_2 (i.e., $V_1 \cap V_2 = \emptyset$ and $V_1 \cup V_2 = V$) such that all edges are between V_1 and V_2; that is, for any edge $e = \{u, v\} \in E$ we have that $e \cap V_1 \neq \emptyset$ and $e \cap V_2 \neq \emptyset$. A graph is δ-regular if all its vertices have degree δ. Show that if G is a δ-regular, bipartite graph, then its adjacency matrix has an eigenvalue $-\delta$. [*Hint*: Try a vector that takes different values on V_1 and V_2.]

5.3 In the first step of the proof of the *Spectral Theorem*,

a) prove that $\mathbf{z}$ is a unit vector;

b) justify formally that $\mathbf{w}_1 \neq \mathbf{0}$ implies that $\mathbf{z}^T A_1 \mathbf{z} > \lambda_1$ for $\delta > 0$ small enough.

5.4 Consider the block matrices

$$\begin{pmatrix} \mathbf{y} \\ \mathbf{z} \end{pmatrix} \quad \text{and} \quad \begin{pmatrix} A & B \\ C & D \end{pmatrix}$$

where $\mathbf{y} \in \mathbb{R}^{d_1}$, $\mathbf{z} \in \mathbb{R}^{d_2}$, $A \in \mathbb{R}^{d_1 \times d_1}$, $B \in \mathbb{R}^{d_1 \times d_2}$, $C \in \mathbb{R}^{d_2 \times d_1}$, and $D \in \mathbb{R}^{d_2 \times d_2}$. Show that

$$\begin{pmatrix} \mathbf{y} \\ \mathbf{z} \end{pmatrix}^T \begin{pmatrix} A & B \\ C & D \end{pmatrix} \begin{pmatrix} \mathbf{y} \\ \mathbf{z} \end{pmatrix} = \mathbf{y}^T A \mathbf{y} + \mathbf{y}^T B \mathbf{z} + \mathbf{z}^T C \mathbf{y} + \mathbf{z}^T D \mathbf{z}.$$

5.5 The *trace* of a square matrix $A \in \mathbb{R}^{n \times n}$, denoted $\mathrm{tr}(A)$, is the sum of its diagonal elements. That is,

$$\mathrm{tr}(A) = \sum_{i=1}^{n} A_{ii}.$$

a) Show by direct computation that, for any two matrices $A \in \mathbb{R}^{n \times m}, B \in \mathbb{R}^{m \times n}$,

$$\mathrm{tr}(AB) = \mathrm{tr}(BA).$$

b) Use a) to show that, for any three matrices $A, B, C \in \mathbb{R}^{n \times n}$,

$$\mathrm{tr}(ABC) = \mathrm{tr}(CAB).$$

c) Use b) and the *Spectral Theorem* to show that, for any symmetric matrix A, the trace of A is the sum of its eigenvalues.

5.6 Let A^n be the n-th matrix power of the adjacency matrix A of a graph $G = (V, E)$. Prove that the (i, j)-th entry a_{ij}^n is the number of paths of length exactly n between vertices i and j in G. [*Hint*: Use induction on n.]

5.7 Let A^n be the n-th matrix power of the adjacency matrix A of a graph $G = (V, E)$.
  a) What does $\text{tr}(A^n)$ count? [*Hint:* Use the two previous exercises.]
  b) Show that
  $$|E| = \frac{1}{2}\text{tr}(A^2).$$
  c) Let T_3 be the set of triangles (as subgraphs) in G. Show that
  $$|T_3| = \frac{1}{6}\text{tr}(A^3).$$

5.8 Let G be a graph with two connected components. Show that its Laplacian L has at least two linearly independent unit eigenvectors with eigenvalue zero. [*Hint:* Write L as a block matrix and use the fact that $\mu_1 = 0$.]

5.9 Construct a graph whose adjacency matrix is *not* positive semidefinite.

5.10 Show that the isoperimetric number of G is equal to
$$\phi_G = \min\left\{\frac{|\partial S|}{|S|} : S \subseteq V, 0 < |S| \leq \frac{1}{2}|V|\right\}.$$

5.11 Construct a symmetric matrix A whose eigenvector decomposition $Q\Lambda Q^T$ is not unique. What is special about the eigenvalues of your example? (*Hint:* A small, simple matrix will do.)

5.12 Consider the graph G in Figure 5.33.

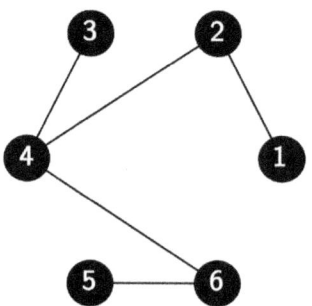

Figure 5.33 Graph for Problem 5.12.

  a) Compute the adjacency matrix of G.
  b) Compute an oriented incidence matrix of G.
  c) Compute the degree matrix of G.
  d) Compute the Laplacian matrix of G.

5.13 Prove the local formulas in the *Courant–Fischer Theorem*.

5.14 Let L be the Laplacian matrix of a graph $G = (V, E)$ with $V = \{1, \ldots, n\}$. Show that for any $\mathbf{x} \in \mathbb{R}^n$
$$(L\mathbf{x})_i = \sum_{j:\ \{i,j\} \in E} (x_i - x_j).$$

[*Hint:* Use the representation in terms of an oriented incidence matrix.]

5.15 Let $G = (V, E)$ be a path graph with $n = 6$ vertices denoted $1, \ldots, 6$; that is, a graph like the one in Figure 5.34.

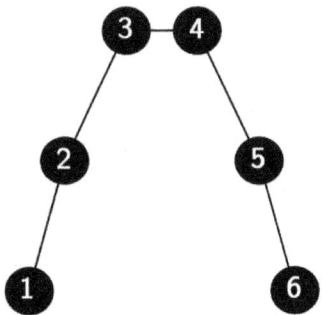

Figure 5.34 Graph for Problem 5.15.

For $\mathbf{x} \in \mathbb{R}^n$, compute $L\mathbf{x}$. [*Hint:* Do Problem 5.14 first.]

5.16 Let $G = (V, E)$ be a $(3,3)$ grid graph; that is, a graph like the one in Figure 5.35.

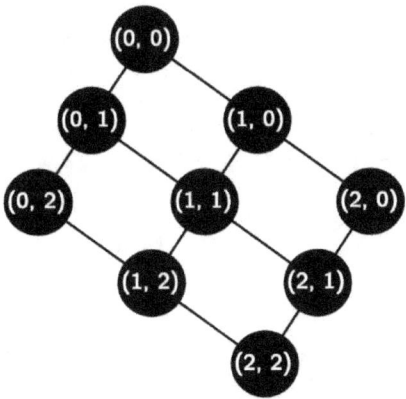

Figure 5.35 Graph for Problem 5.16.

For $\mathbf{x} \in \mathbb{R}^n$, compute $(L\mathbf{x})_\mathbf{v}$, where $\mathbf{v}$ is the central vertex denoted $(1, 1)$ above. [*Hint:* Do Problem 5.14 first.]

5.17 Let $\mathbf{v}_1, \ldots, \mathbf{v}_d$ be an orthonormal list in $\mathbb{R}^d$. Show that

$$\mathrm{span}(\mathbf{v}_1, \ldots, \mathbf{v}_\ell)^\perp = \mathrm{span}(\mathbf{v}_{\ell+1}, \ldots, \mathbf{v}_d)$$

for any $\ell = 1, \ldots, d$.

5.18 Let $G = (V, E)$ be an undirected, unweighted graph. Show that

$$\sum_{i \in V} \delta(i) = 2|E|.$$

5.19 Let $G = (V, E)$ be a graph with vertices $[n]$. Recall that $\delta(i)$ is the degree of i. Let P_2 be the set of paths of length 2 (as subgraphs) in G. Show that

$$|P_2| = \sum_{i=1}^{n} \binom{\delta(i)}{2}.$$

5.20 Recall that in an Erdős–Rényi random graph G on n vertices with parameter $p \in (0,1)$, each possible edge $\{i,j\}$ is present (i.e., $\{i,j\} \in E$) with probability p, independently of all other possible edges. Let T_3 be the set of triangles (as subgraphs) in G. Compute $\mathrm{Var}[|T_3|]$. [*Hint:* Most pairs of triangles are independent, but not all of them.]

5.21 Let $G = (V, E)$ be a graph. Let $\emptyset \neq S \subset V$ be a proper, nonempty subset of V such that $0 < |S| \leq \frac{1}{2}|V|$. Assume further that $n = |V|$ is odd. Show that
$$\phi(S) \leq |S^c|.$$
Conclude that
$$\phi_G \leq \frac{n+1}{2}.$$

5.22 Let $G = (V, E)$ be a connected graph with $V = [n]$ and Laplacian matrix L. Show that
$$\dim(\mathrm{null}(L)) = 1, \qquad \dim(\mathrm{col}(L)) = n - 1.$$

5.23 Show that
$$\min\left\{\frac{1}{4}\sum_{\{i,j\}\in E}(x_i - x_j)^2 : \mathbf{x} = (x_1, \ldots, x_n)^T \in \mathbb{R}^n, \sum_{i=1}^n x_i = 0, \sum_{i=1}^n x_i^2 = n\right\} = \frac{\mu_2 n}{4}.$$

5.24 Let $G = (V, E)$ be a connected graph with n vertices.

a) Show that $|E(S, S^c)| \geq 1$ for any cut (S, S^c).

b) Show that
$$\phi_G \geq \frac{2}{n}.$$

5.25 Let $G = (V, E)$ be the n-dimensional Boolean hypercube; that is,
$$V = \{0,1\}^n := \{\mathbf{x} = (x_1, \ldots, x_n) : x_i \in \{0,1\}, \forall i\},$$
and
$$E = \{\{\mathbf{x}, \mathbf{y}\} : \mathbf{x}, \mathbf{y} \in V, \|\mathbf{x} - \mathbf{y}\|_1 = 1\},$$
where recall that $\|\mathbf{z}\|_1 = \sum_{i=1}^n |z_i|$. In words, the edges of G are all pairs of vectors in $\{0,1\}^n$ that differ by exactly one coordinate.

a) For $i \in \{1, \ldots, n\}$, consider the cut (S, S^c) where
$$S = \{\mathbf{x} = (x_1, \ldots, x_n) \in V : x_i = 0\}.$$
Compute $\phi(S)$.

b) Use a) to give an upper bound on μ_2, the second smallest eigenvalue of the Laplacian matrix of G.

5.26 Let $G = (V, E)$ be the n-cycle graph; that is, $V = [n]$ and E contains all edges of the form $\{i, i+1\}$ for $i = 1, \ldots, n-1$ plus the edge $\{n, 1\}$.

a) For $k = 1, \ldots, n-1$, consider the cut (S_k, S_k^c) with $S_k = \{1, \ldots, k\}$. Compute $\phi(S_k)$. [*Hint:* You may want to try a concrete example with small n first.]

b) Use a) to give an upper bound on μ_2, the second smallest eigenvalue of the Laplacian matrix of G.

5.27 Prove the *Inverting the Order of Eigenvalues Lemma*.

5.28 Prove the *Power Iteration for the Second Largest Eigenvalue Lemma*.

5.29 Let $\mathbf{v}_1, \ldots, \mathbf{v}_k \in \mathbb{R}^n$ be a list of vectors. Show that

$$\operatorname{span}(\mathbf{v}_1, \ldots, \mathbf{v}_k)^\perp = \{\mathbf{z} \in \mathbb{R}^n : \langle \mathbf{z}, \mathbf{v}_i \rangle = 0, \forall i \in [k]\}.$$

5.30 A weighted graph is a triple $G = (V, E, w)$ where (V, E) is a graph and $w: E \to \mathbb{R}_+$ is a function that assigns positive real weights to the edges. We write $w_e = w_{ij}$ for the weight of edge $e = \{i, j\}$. The degree of a vertex i is $\delta(i) = \sum_{j: \{i,j\} \in E} w_{ij}$ and we let $D = \operatorname{diag}(\delta(1), \ldots, \delta(n))$ be the weighted degree matrix. The adjacency matrix A of G has entries

$$A_{ij} = \begin{cases} w_{ij} & \text{if } \{i, j\} \in E \\ 0 & \text{otherwise.} \end{cases}$$

The weighted Laplacian matrix associated with G is defined as $L = D - A$. Prove the formula

$$\langle \mathbf{x}, L\mathbf{x} \rangle = \sum_{\{i,j\} \in E} w_{ij}(x_i - x_j)^2$$

for $\mathbf{x} = (x_1, \ldots, x_n) \in \mathbb{R}^n$. [*Hint:* For an orientation $G^\sigma = (V, E^\sigma)$ of G (i.e., give an arbitrary direction to each edge to turn it into a digraph), consider the matrix $B^\sigma \in \mathbb{R}^{n \times m}$ where the column corresponding to arc (i, j) has $-\sqrt{w_{ij}}$ in row i and $\sqrt{w_{ij}}$ in row j, and every other entry is 0.]

5.31 Using the notation from Problem 5.30, let $G = (V, E, w)$ be a weighted graph with weighted Laplacian L. Denote the eigenvalues of L by $0 = \mu_1 \leq \mu_2 \leq \cdots \leq \mu_n$. Prove that

$$\mu_2 = \min\left\{ \sum_{\{u,v\} \in E} w_{uv}(x_u - x_v)^2 : \mathbf{x} = (x_1, \ldots, x_n) \in \mathbb{R}^n, \sum_{u=1}^n x_u = 0, \sum_{u=1}^n x_u^2 = 1 \right\}.$$

5.32 Using the notation from Problems 5.30 and 5.31, let $G = (V, E, w)$ be a weighted graph with weighted Laplacian L, whose eigenvalues are $0 = \mu_1 \leq \mu_2 \leq \cdots \leq \mu_n$. Define

$$\phi(S) = \frac{\sum_{i \in S, j \in S^c} w_{ij}}{\min\{|S|, |S^c|\}}$$

for $\emptyset \neq S \subset V$ and let

$$\phi_G = \min\{\phi(S) : \emptyset \neq S \subset V\}.$$

Prove the inequality $\mu_2 \leq 2\phi_G$ in this weighted graph case. [*Hint:* Adapt the proof for the unweighted case.]

5.33 Using the notation from Problem 5.30, let $G = (V, E, w)$ be a weighted graph with adjacency matrix A and degree matrix D. The normalized Laplacian of G is defined as

$$\mathcal{L} = I - D^{-1/2} A D^{-1/2}.$$

a) Show that
$$\mathcal{L} = D^{-1/2} L D^{-1/2},$$
where the weighted Laplacian L was defined in Problem 5.30.

b) Show that $\mathcal{L}$ is symmetric and positive semidefinite.

c) Let $0 \le \eta_1 \le \eta_2 \le \cdots \le \eta_n$ be the eigenvalues of $\mathcal{L}$. Show that $\eta_1 = 0$.

d) Show that
$$\mathbf{x}^T \mathcal{L} \mathbf{x} = \sum_{\{i,j\} \in E} w_{ij} \left(\frac{x_i}{\sqrt{\delta(i)}} - \frac{x_j}{\sqrt{\delta(j)}} \right)^2$$
for $\mathbf{x} = (x_1, \ldots, x_n) \in \mathbb{R}^n$.

5.34 Using the notation from Problems 5.30 and 5.33, let $G = (V, E, w)$ be a weighted graph with normalized Laplacian matrix $\mathcal{L}$, whose eigenvalues are $0 = \eta_1 \le \eta_2 \le \cdots \le \eta_n$. Show that
$$\eta_2 = \min \left\{ \sum_{\{u,v\} \in E} w_{uv}(y_u - y_v)^2 : \mathbf{y} = (y_1, \ldots, y_n) \in \mathbb{R}^n, \sum_{u=1}^n \delta(u) y_u = 0, \sum_{u=1}^n \delta(u) y_u^2 = 1 \right\}.$$

[*Hint:* Make the change of variables $y_i = \frac{x_i}{\sqrt{\delta(i)}}$.]

5.35 Using the notation from Problems 5.30 and 5.33, let $G = (V, E, w)$ be a weighted graph with normalized Laplacian matrix $\mathcal{L} = \sum_{i=1}^n \eta_i \mathbf{z}_i \mathbf{z}_i^T$. For a subset of vertices $S \subseteq V$, let
$$|S|_w = \sum_{i \in S} \delta(i),$$
which we call the volume of S. Define
$$\phi^N(S) = \frac{\sum_{i \in S, j \in S^c} w_{ij}}{\min\{|S|_w, |S^c|_w\}}$$
for $\emptyset \ne S \subset V$ and let
$$\phi_G^N = \min \{ \phi^N(S) : \emptyset \ne S \subset V \}.$$

Show that
$$\eta_2 \le 2\phi_G^N.$$

[*Hint:* Follow the proof in the unweighted case but replace cardinalities of sets with their volumes.]

6 Probabilistic Models: From Simple to Complex

In this chapter, we take a deeper look at probabilistic models, which we have already encountered throughout this book. We show how to construct a variety of models, in particular by using the notion of conditional independence. We also describe some standard methods for estimating parameters and hidden states. Finally, we discuss and implement some applications, including Kalman filtering. We discuss sampling in Chapter 7. Here is a more detailed overview of the main sections of the chapter.

Background: Introduction to parametric families and maximum likelihood estimation: Section 6.2 introduces parametric families of probability distributions, focusing on exponential families, which include many common distributions such as Bernoulli, categorical, multinomial, multivariate Gaussian, and Dirichlet distributions. It then discusses parameter estimation, specifically maximum likelihood estimation, which chooses the parameter that maximizes the probability of observing the data, and derives the maximum likelihood estimator for exponential families. The section proves that, under certain conditions, the maximum likelihood estimator is guaranteed to converge to the true parameter as the number of samples grows, a property known as statistical consistency. Finally, it presents generalized linear models, which provide an important generalization of linear regression using exponential families, and revisits linear and logistic regression from this perspective.

Modeling more complex dependencies 1: Using conditional independence: Section 6.3 discusses techniques for constructing joint probability distributions from simpler building blocks, focusing on imposing conditional independence relations. It introduces the basic configurations of conditional independence for three random variables: the fork ($Y \leftarrow X \rightarrow Z$), the chain ($X \rightarrow Y \rightarrow Z$), and the collider ($X \rightarrow Z \leftarrow Y$). The section then presents the naive Bayes model as an example of applying conditional independence to document classification, where the presence or absence of words in a document is assumed to be conditionally independent given the document's topic. Finally, it demonstrates fitting a naive Bayes model using maximum likelihood estimation.

Modeling more complex dependencies 2: Marginalizing out an unobserved variable: Section 6.4 discusses modeling dependencies in joint distributions by marginalizing out an unobserved random variable. It introduces the concept of mixtures as convex combinations of distributions. The section then considers the specific case of mixtures of multivariate Bernoullis and the Expectation-Maximization (EM) algorithm for parameter estimation in this context, leveraging the more general principle of majorization-minimization. Finally, the mixture of multivariate Bernoullis model is applied to clustering handwritten digits from the MNIST dataset.

Application: Linear-Gaussian models and Kalman filtering: Section 6.5 discusses the application of linear-Gaussian models and Kalman filtering for object tracking. It begins by presenting the properties of block matrices and the Schur complement, which are used to derive the marginal and conditional distributions of multivariate Gaussians. The section then introduces the Kalman filter, a recursive algorithm for inferring unobserved states in a linear-Gaussian system, where the state evolves according to a linear-Gaussian model and noisy observations are made at each time step. The section concludes by applying the Kalman filter to a location tracking example, which consists in estimating the true path of an object from noisy observations.

6.1 Motivating Example: Tracking Location

Suppose we let loose a cyborg corgi in a large park. We would like to know where it is at all time. For this purpose, it has an implanted location device that sends a signal to a tracking app.

Figure 6.1 provides an example of the data we might have, through a simulation we will explain later on in this chapter. The dots are recorded locations at regular time intervals. The dotted line helps keep track of the time order of the recordings.

By convention, we start at $(0,0)$. Notice how squiggly the trajectory is. One issue might be that the times at which the location is recorded are too far between. But, in fact, there is another issue: The tracking device is *inaccurate*.

To get a better estimate of the true trajectory, it is natural to try to model the noise in the measurement as well as the dynamics itself. Probabilistic models are perfectly suited for this.

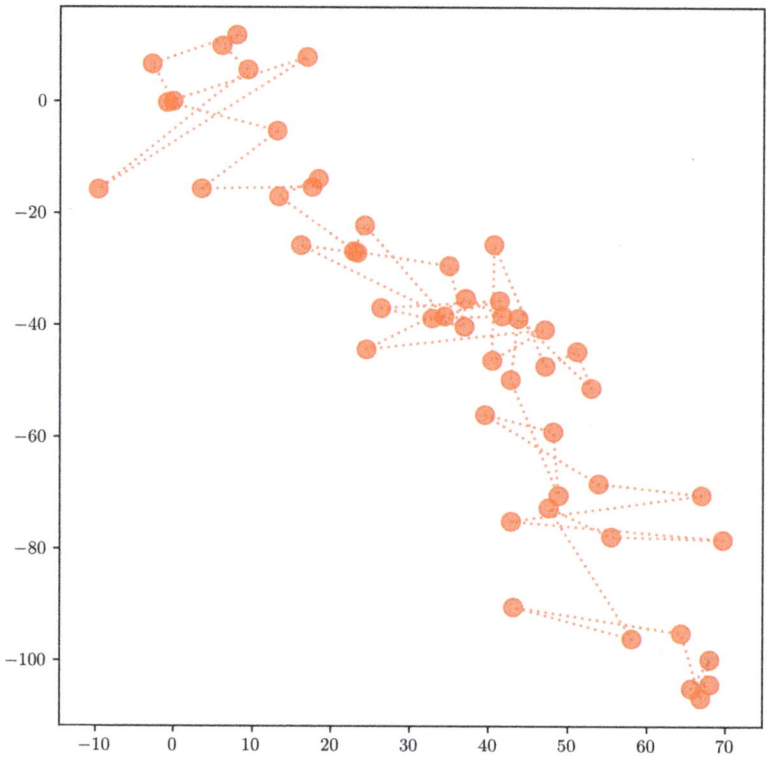

Figure 6.1 Recorded locations.

In this chapter, we will encounter a variety of such models and show how to take advantage of them to estimate unknown states (or parameters). In particular, conditional independence will play a key role.

We will come back to location tracking later in the chapter.

6.2 Background: Introduction to Parametric Families and Maximum Likelihood Estimation

In this section, we introduce some fundamental concepts used to construct probabilistic models for statistical purposes. We also define a common family of distributions, the exponential family.

Throughout this topic, all formal proofs are done under the assumption of a discrete distribution with finite support to avoid unnecessary technicalities and focus on the concepts. But everything we discuss can be adapted to continuous distributions.

Parametric families of probability distributions serve as basic building blocks for more complex models. By a parametric family, we mean a collection $\{p_\theta : \theta \in \Theta\}$, where p_θ is a probability distribution over a set S_θ and θ is a vector-valued parameter.

Example 6.2.1 *(Bernoulli)* *The random variable X is Bernoulli with parameter $q \in [0, 1]$, denoted $X \sim \text{Ber}(q)$, if it takes values in $S_X = \{0, 1\}$ and $\mathbb{P}[X = 1] = q$. Varying q produces the family of Bernoulli distributions.*

Here we focus on exponential families, which include many common distributions (including the Bernoulli distribution).

6.2.1 Exponential Family

One particularly useful class of probability distributions in data science is the exponential family, which includes many well-known cases.

Definition 6.2.2 *(Exponential Family: Discrete Case)* *A parametric collection of probability distributions $\{p_\theta : \theta \in \Theta\}$ over a discrete space S is an exponential family if it can be written in the form*

$$p_\theta(\mathbf{x}) = \frac{1}{Z(\theta)} h(\mathbf{x}) \exp\left(\theta^T \phi(\mathbf{x})\right)$$

where $\theta \in \mathbb{R}^m$ are the canonical parameters, $\phi : S \to \mathbb{R}^m$ are the sufficient statistics, and $Z(\theta)$ is the partition function. It is often convenient to introduce the log-partition function $A(\theta) = \log Z(\theta)$ and rewrite

$$p_\theta(\mathbf{x}) = h(\mathbf{x}) \exp\left(\theta^T \phi(\mathbf{x}) - A(\theta)\right).$$

Example 6.2.3 *(continued from Example 6.2.1)* *For $x \in \{0, 1\}$, the $\text{Ber}(q)$ distribution for $0 < q < 1$ can be written as*

$$q^x (1-q)^{1-x} = (1-q) \left(\frac{q}{1-q}\right)^x$$

$$= (1-q) \exp\left[x \log\left(\frac{q}{1-q}\right)\right]$$

$$= \frac{1}{Z(\theta)} h(x) \exp(\theta \, \phi(x))$$

where we define $h(x) \equiv 1$, $\phi(x) = x$, $\theta = \log\left(\frac{q}{1-q}\right)$ and, since $Z(\theta)$ serves as the normalization constant in p_θ,

$$Z(\theta) = \sum_{x \in \{0,1\}} h(x) \exp(\theta\,\phi(x)) = 1 + e^\theta.$$

The following is an important generalization. Recall that i.i.d. is the abbreviation for independent and identically distributed. We use the convention $0! = 1$.

Example 6.2.4 *(Categorical and Multinomial)* A categorical variable $\mathbf{Y}$ takes $K \geq 2$ possible values. A standard choice is to use one-hot encoding defined as $\mathcal{S} = \{\mathbf{e}_i : i = 1, \ldots, K\}$ where $\mathbf{e}_i$ is the i-th canonical basis in $\mathbb{R}^K$. The distribution is specified by setting the probabilities $\boldsymbol{\pi} = (\pi_1, \ldots, \pi_K)$:

$$\pi_i = \mathbb{P}[\mathbf{Y} = \mathbf{e}_i].$$

We denote this $\mathbf{Y} \sim \mathrm{Cat}(\boldsymbol{\pi})$ and we assume $\pi_i > 0$ for all i.

To see that this is an exponential family, write the probability mass function at $\mathbf{x} = (x_1, \ldots, x_K)$ as

$$\prod_{i=1}^K \pi_i^{x_i} = \exp\left(\sum_{i=1}^K x_i \log \pi_i\right).$$

So we can take $h(\mathbf{x}) \equiv 1$, $\boldsymbol{\theta} = (\log \pi_i)_{i=1}^K$, $\boldsymbol{\phi}(\mathbf{x}) = (x_i)_{i=1}^K$, and $Z(\boldsymbol{\theta}) \equiv 1$.

The multinomial distribution arises as a sum of independent categorical variables. Let $n \geq 1$ be the number of trials (or samples) and let $\mathbf{Y}_1, \ldots, \mathbf{Y}_n$ be i.i.d. $\mathrm{Cat}(\boldsymbol{\pi})$. Define $\mathbf{X} = \sum_{i=1}^n \mathbf{Y}_i$. The probability mass function of $\mathbf{X}$ at

$$\mathbf{x} = (x_1, \ldots, x_K) \in \left\{\mathbf{x} \in \{0, 1, \ldots, n\}^K : \sum_{i=1}^K x_i = n\right\} =: \mathcal{S}$$

is

$$\frac{n!}{x_1! \cdots x_K!} \prod_{i=1}^K \pi_i^{x_i} = \frac{n!}{x_1! \cdots x_K!} \exp\left(\sum_{i=1}^K x_i \log \pi_i\right)$$

and we can take $h(\mathbf{x}) = \frac{n!}{x_1! \cdots x_K!}$, $\boldsymbol{\theta} = (\log \pi_i)_{i=1}^K$, $\boldsymbol{\phi}(\mathbf{x}) = (x_i)_{i=1}^K$, and $Z(\boldsymbol{\theta}) \equiv 1$. This is an exponential family if we think of n as fixed.

We use the notation $\mathbf{X} \sim \mathrm{Mult}(n, \boldsymbol{\pi})$.

While we have focused so far on discrete distributions, one can adapt the definitions above by replacing mass functions with density functions. We give two important examples.

We need some definitions for our first example.

The trace of a square matrix $A \in \mathbb{R}^{d \times d}$, denoted $\mathrm{tr}(A)$, is the sum of its diagonal entries. We will need the following trace identity whose proof we leave as an exercise: $\mathrm{tr}(ABC) = \mathrm{tr}(CAB) = \mathrm{tr}(BCA)$ for any matrices A, B, C for which AB, BC, and CA are well-defined.

The determinant of a square matrix A is denoted by $|A|$. For our purposes, it will be enough to consider symmetric, positive semidefinite matrices, for which the determinant is the product of the eigenvalues (with repeats). Recall that we proved that the sequence of eigenvalues (with repeats) of a symmetric matrix is unique (in the sense that any two spectral decompositions have the same sequence of eigenvalues).

A symmetric, positive definite matrix $A \in \mathbb{R}^{d \times d}$ is necessarily invertible. Indeed, it has a spectral decomposition

$$A = Q \Lambda Q^T = \sum_{i=1}^{d} \lambda_i \mathbf{q}_i \mathbf{q}_i^T$$

where $\lambda_1 \geq \cdots \geq \lambda_d > 0$ and $\mathbf{q}_1, \ldots, \mathbf{q}_d$ are orthonormal. Then

$$A^{-1} = Q \Lambda^{-1} Q^T.$$

To see this, note that

$$AA^{-1} = Q \Lambda Q^T Q \Lambda^{-1} Q^T = QQ^T = I_{d \times d}.$$

The last equality follows from the fact that QQ^T is the orthogonal projection on the orthonormal basis $\mathbf{q}_1, \ldots, \mathbf{q}_d$. Similarly, $A^{-1}A = I_{d \times d}$.

Example 6.2.5 (*Multivariate Gaussian*) *A multivariate Gaussian vector* $\mathbf{X} = (X_1, \ldots, X_d)$ *on $\mathbb{R}^d$ with mean $\boldsymbol{\mu} \in \mathbb{R}^d$ and positive definite covariance matrix $\boldsymbol{\Sigma} \in \mathbb{R}^{d \times d}$ has probability density function*

$$f_{\boldsymbol{\mu}, \boldsymbol{\Sigma}}(\mathbf{x}) = \frac{1}{(2\pi)^{d/2} |\boldsymbol{\Sigma}|^{1/2}} \exp\left(-\frac{1}{2}(\mathbf{x} - \boldsymbol{\mu})^T \boldsymbol{\Sigma}^{-1} (\mathbf{x} - \boldsymbol{\mu})\right).$$

We use the notation $\mathbf{X} \sim N_d(\boldsymbol{\mu}, \boldsymbol{\Sigma})$.

It can be shown that indeed the mean is

$$\mathbb{E}[\mathbf{X}] = \boldsymbol{\mu}$$

and the covariance matrix is

$$\mathbb{E}[(\mathbf{X} - \boldsymbol{\mu})(\mathbf{X} - \boldsymbol{\mu})^T] = \mathbb{E}[\mathbf{X}\mathbf{X}^T] - \boldsymbol{\mu}\boldsymbol{\mu}^T = \boldsymbol{\Sigma}.$$

In the bivariate case (i.e., when $d = 2$), the covariance matrix reduces to

$$\boldsymbol{\Sigma} = \begin{bmatrix} \sigma_1^2 & \rho \sigma_1 \sigma_2 \\ \rho \sigma_1 \sigma_2 & \sigma_2^2 \end{bmatrix}$$

where σ_1^2 and σ_2^2 are the respective variances of X_1 and X_2, and

$$\rho = \frac{\mathrm{Cov}[X_1, X_2]}{\sigma_1 \sigma_2}$$

is the correlation coefficient. Recall that, by the **Cauchy–Schwarz Inequality**, *it lies in* $[-1, 1]$.

We can rewrite the density as

$$f_{\boldsymbol{\mu}, \boldsymbol{\Sigma}}(\mathbf{x}) = \frac{e^{-(1/2)\boldsymbol{\mu}^T \boldsymbol{\Sigma}^{-1} \boldsymbol{\mu}}}{(2\pi)^{d/2} |\boldsymbol{\Sigma}|^{1/2}} \exp\left(-\mathbf{x}^T \boldsymbol{\Sigma}^{-1} \boldsymbol{\mu} - \frac{1}{2} \mathrm{tr}\left(\mathbf{x}\mathbf{x}^T \boldsymbol{\Sigma}^{-1}\right)\right)$$

where we used the symmetric nature of $\boldsymbol{\Sigma}^{-1}$ in the first term of the exponential and the previous trace identity in the second term. The expression in parentheses is linear in the entries of $\mathbf{x}$ and $\mathbf{x}\mathbf{x}^T$, which can then be taken as sufficient statistics (formally, using vectorization). Indeed note that

$$\mathbf{x}^T \boldsymbol{\Sigma}^{-1} \boldsymbol{\mu} = \sum_{i=1}^{d} x_i (\boldsymbol{\Sigma}^{-1} \boldsymbol{\mu})_i$$

and

$$\operatorname{tr}\left(\mathbf{x}\mathbf{x}^T \boldsymbol{\Sigma}^{-1}\right) = \sum_{i=1}^{d}\left(\sum_{j=1}^{d}(\mathbf{x}\mathbf{x}^T)_{i,j}(\boldsymbol{\Sigma}^{-1})_{j,i}\right) = \sum_{i=1}^{d}\sum_{j=1}^{d} x_i x_j (\boldsymbol{\Sigma}^{-1})_{j,i}.$$

So we can take

$$\boldsymbol{\phi}(\mathbf{x}) = (x_1, \ldots, x_d, x_1 x_1, \ldots, x_d x_1, x_1 x_2, \ldots, x_d x_2, \ldots, x_1 x_d, \ldots, x_d x_d)$$

$$\boldsymbol{\theta} = \bigg(-(\boldsymbol{\Sigma}^{-1}\boldsymbol{\mu})_1, \ldots, -(\boldsymbol{\Sigma}^{-1}\boldsymbol{\mu})_d,$$
$$-\frac{1}{2}(\boldsymbol{\Sigma}^{-1})_{1,1}, \ldots, -\frac{1}{2}(\boldsymbol{\Sigma}^{-1})_{1,d},$$
$$-\frac{1}{2}(\boldsymbol{\Sigma}^{-1})_{2,1}, \ldots, -\frac{1}{2}(\boldsymbol{\Sigma}^{-1})_{2,d},$$
$$\ldots, -\frac{1}{2}(\boldsymbol{\Sigma}^{-1})_{d,1}, \ldots, -\frac{1}{2}(\boldsymbol{\Sigma}^{-1})_{d,d}\bigg)$$

and $h(\mathbf{x}) \equiv 1$. Expressing $Z(\boldsymbol{\theta})$ explicitly is not straightforward. But note that $\boldsymbol{\theta}$ includes all entries of $\boldsymbol{\Sigma}^{-1}$, from which $\boldsymbol{\Sigma}$ can be computed (e.g., from Cramer's rule), and in turn from which $\boldsymbol{\mu}$ can be extracted out of the entries of $\boldsymbol{\Sigma}^{-1}\boldsymbol{\mu}$ in $\boldsymbol{\theta}$. So the normalizing factor $\frac{(2\pi)^{d/2}|\boldsymbol{\Sigma}|^{1/2}}{e^{-(1/2)\boldsymbol{\mu}^T\boldsymbol{\Sigma}^{-1}\boldsymbol{\mu}}}$ can in principle be expressed in terms of $\boldsymbol{\theta}$.

This shows that the multivariate normal is an exponential family.

The matrix $\boldsymbol{\Lambda} = \boldsymbol{\Sigma}^{-1}$ is also known as the precision matrix.

Alternatively, let $\mathbf{Z}$ be a standard normal d-vector, let $\boldsymbol{\mu} \in \mathbb{R}^d$, and let $\boldsymbol{\Sigma} \in \mathbb{R}^{d \times d}$ be positive definite. Then the transformed random variable $\mathbf{X} = \boldsymbol{\mu} + \boldsymbol{\Sigma}\mathbf{Z}$ is a multivariate Gaussian with mean $\boldsymbol{\mu}$ and covariance matrix $\boldsymbol{\Sigma}$. This can be proved using the change of variables formula (try it!).

NUMERICAL CORNER The following code, which plots the density in the bivariate case, was adapted from [Mur2][1] by ChatGPT.

CHAT & LEARN Ask your favorite AI chatbot to explain the code! ***Try different covariance matrices.***

```
from scipy.stats import multivariate_normal

def gaussian_pdf(X, Y, mean, cov):
    xy = np.stack([X.flatten(), Y.flatten()], axis=-1)
    return multivariate_normal.pdf(
        xy, mean=mean, cov=cov).reshape(X.shape)

def make_surface_plot(X, Y, Z):
    fig = plt.figure()
    ax = fig.add_subplot(111, projection='3d')
    surf = ax.plot_surface(
        X, Y, Z, cmap=plt.cm.viridis, antialiased=False)
    plt.show()
```

[1] https://github.com/probml/pyprobml/blob/master/notebooks/book1/03/gauss_plot_2d.ipynb

6.2 Parametric Families and Maximum Likelihood Estimation

We plot the density for mean $(0, 0)$ with two different covariance matrices:

$$\Sigma_1 = \begin{bmatrix} 1.0 & 0 \\ 0 & 1.0 \end{bmatrix} \quad \text{and} \quad \Sigma_2 = \begin{bmatrix} \sigma_1^2 & \rho\sigma_1\sigma_2 \\ \rho\sigma_1\sigma_2 & \sigma_2^2 \end{bmatrix}$$

where $\sigma_1 = 1.5$, $\sigma_2 = 0.5$, and $\rho = -0.75$.

```
start_point = 5
stop_point = 5
num_samples = 100
points = np.linspace(-start_point, stop_point, num_samples)
X, Y = np.meshgrid(points, points)

mean = np.array([0., 0.])
cov = np.array([[1., 0.], [0., 1.]])
make_surface_plot(X, Y, gaussian_pdf(X, Y, mean, cov))
```

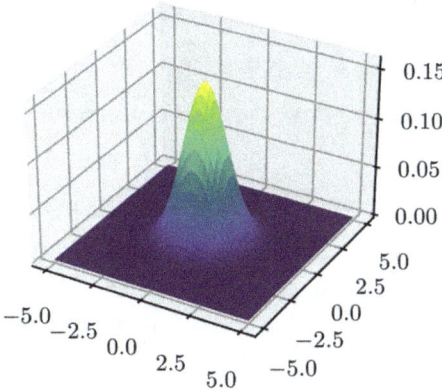

Figure 6.2 Graphical output of code.

```
mean = np.array([0., 0.])
cov = np.array([[1.5 ** 2., -0.75 * 1.5 * 0.5],
                [-0.75 * 1.5 * 0.5, 0.5 ** 2.]])
make_surface_plot(X, Y, gaussian_pdf(X, Y, mean, cov))
```

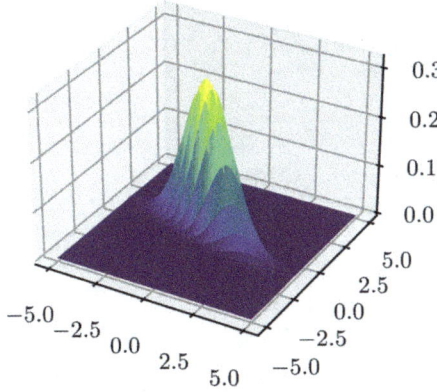

Figure 6.3 Graphical output of code.

◁ NC

The Dirichlet distribution, which we describe next, is a natural probability distribution over probability distributions. In particular, it is used in Bayesian data analysis as a prior on the parameters of categorical and multinomial distribution, largely because of a property known as conjugacy. We will not describe Bayesian approaches here.

Example 6.2.6 *(Dirichlet) The Dirichlet distribution is a distribution over the $(K-1)$-simplex*

$$\mathcal{S} = \Delta_K := \left\{ \mathbf{x} = (x_1, \ldots, x_K) : \mathbf{x} \geq \mathbf{0}, \sum_{i=1}^{K} x_i = 1 \right\}.$$

Its parameters are $\alpha = (\alpha_1, \ldots, \alpha_K) \in \mathbb{R}$ and the density is

$$f_\alpha(\mathbf{x}) = \frac{1}{B(\alpha)} \prod_{i=1}^{K} x_i^{\alpha_i - 1}, \quad \mathbf{x} \in \Delta_K$$

where the normalizing constant $B(\alpha)$ is the multivariate Beta function.

Rewriting the density as

$$\frac{1}{B(\alpha)} \prod_{i=1}^{K} x_i^{\alpha_i - 1} = \frac{1}{B(\alpha)} \frac{1}{\prod_{i=1}^{K} x_i} \exp\left(\sum_{i=1}^{K} \alpha_i \log x_i \right)$$

shows that this is an exponential family with the canonical parameters α and sufficient statistics $(\log x_i)_{i=1}^{K}$.

See Wikipedia[2] for many more examples. Observe, in particular, that the same distribution can have several representations as an exponential family.

NUMERICAL CORNER In NumPy, as we have seen before, the module numpy.random provides a way to sample from a variety of standard distributions. We first initialize the pseudorandom number generator with a random seed. Recall that it allows the results to be reproducible: Using the same seed produces the same results again.

```
seed = 535
rng = np.random.default_rng(seed)
```

Here is the case of the Binomial distribution.[3]

```
p = 0.1
N = 5
print(rng.binomial(1, p, size=N))
```

[1 0 0 0 0]

Here are a few other examples.

```
p = [0.1, 0.2, 0.7]
n = 100
print(rng.multinomial(n, p, size=N))
```

---

[2] https://en.wikipedia.org/wiki/Exponential_family#Table_of_distributions
[3] There are lists of probability distributions available at https://numpy.org/doc/stable/reference/random/generator.html#distributions

```
[[ 9 12 79]
 [ 5 20 75]
 [13 18 69]
 [ 8 18 74]
 [ 8 24 68]]
```

```
mu = np.array([0.1, -0.3])
sig = np.array([[2., 0.],[0., 3.]])
print(rng.multivariate_normal(mu, sig, size=N))
```

```
[[-0.7275232   2.66555155]
 [ 0.45641186 -2.65834344]
 [ 1.13188325  0.43920735]
 [ 0.69846716  2.49891659]
 [ 0.91725117  1.89618733]]
```

◁ NC

6.2.2 Parameter Estimation

When modeling data via a parametric family of distributions, the parameters must be determined from the data itself. In a typical setting, we assume that the data comprises n independent samples $\mathbf{X}_1, \ldots, \mathbf{X}_n$ from a parametric family p_θ with unknown $\theta \in \Theta$. Many methods exist for estimating θ, depending on the context. Here we focus on maximum likelihood estimation. It has many good theoretical properties which we will not describe here, as well as drawbacks.

The idea behind maximum likelihood estimation is simple and intuitive: We choose the parameter that maximizes the probability of observing the data.

Definition 6.2.7 (*Maximum Likelihood Estimator*) *Assume that* $\mathbf{X}_1, \ldots, \mathbf{X}_n$ *are n independent samples from a parametric family p_{θ^*} with unknown $\theta^* \in \Theta$. The maximum likelihood estimator of θ is defined as*

$$\hat{\theta}_{\mathrm{MLE}} \in \arg\max \left\{ \prod_{i=1}^{n} p_\theta(\mathbf{X}_i) : \theta \in \Theta \right\}.$$

It is often useful to work with the negative log-likelihood (NLL)

$$L_n(\theta; \{\mathbf{X}_i\}_{i=1}^n) = - \sum_{i=1}^{n} \log p_\theta(\mathbf{X}_i),$$

in which case we are minimizing.

Example 6.2.8 (*Biased Coin*) *Suppose we observe n coin flips $X_1, \ldots, X_n \in \{0, 1\}$ from a biased coin with an unknown probability θ^* of producing 1. We assume the flips are independent. We compute the MLE of the parameter θ.*

The definition is

$$\hat{\theta}_{\mathrm{MLE}} \in \arg\min \left\{ L_n(\theta; \{X_i\}_{i=1}^n) : \theta \in \Theta = [0, 1] \right\}$$

where, using our previous Bernoulli example (see Example 6.2.3), the NLL is

$$L_n(\theta; \{X_i\}_{i=1}^n) = -\sum_{i=1}^n \log p_\theta(X_i)$$

$$= -\sum_{i=1}^n \log\left[\theta^{X_i}(1-\theta)^{1-X_i}\right]$$

$$= -\sum_{i=1}^n \left[X_i \log \theta + (1-X_i)\log(1-\theta)\right].$$

We compute the first and second derivatives of $L_n(\theta; \{X_i\}_{i=1}^n)$ as a function of θ:

$$\frac{d}{d\theta} L_n(\theta; \{X_i\}_{i=1}^n) = -\sum_{i=1}^n \left[\frac{X_i}{\theta} - \frac{1-X_i}{1-\theta}\right]$$

$$= -\frac{\sum_{i=1}^n X_i}{\theta} + \frac{n - \sum_{i=1}^n X_i}{1-\theta}$$

and

$$\frac{d^2}{d\theta^2} L_n(\theta; \{X_i\}_{i=1}^n) = \frac{\sum_{i=1}^n X_i}{\theta^2} + \frac{n - \sum_{i=1}^n X_i}{(1-\theta)^2}.$$

The second derivative is nonnegative and therefore the NLL is convex. To find a global minimizer, it suffices to find a stationary point.

We make the derivative of the NLL equal to 0 :

$$0 = -\frac{\sum_{i=1}^n X_i}{\theta} + \frac{n - \sum_{i=1}^n X_i}{1-\theta}$$

$$\iff \frac{\sum_{i=1}^n X_i}{\theta} = \frac{n - \sum_{i=1}^n X_i}{1-\theta}$$

$$\iff (1-\theta)\sum_{i=1}^n X_i = \theta\left(n - \sum_{i=1}^n X_i\right)$$

$$\iff \sum_{i=1}^n X_i = \theta n.$$

So

$$\hat{\theta}_{\text{MLE}} = \frac{\sum_{i=1}^n X_i}{n}.$$

This is in fact a natural estimator: the empirical frequency of 1's.

We give an alternative perspective on the maximum likelihood estimator. Assume that p_θ is supported on a fixed finite set $\mathcal{X}$ for all $\theta \in \Theta$. Given samples $\mathbf{X}_1, \ldots, \mathbf{X}_n$, for each $\mathbf{x} \in \mathcal{X}$, let

$$N_\mathbf{x} = \sum_{i=1}^n \mathbf{1}_{\{\mathbf{X}_i = \mathbf{x}\}}$$

count the number of times $\mathbf{x}$ is observed in the data, and let

$$\hat{\mu}_n(\mathbf{x}) = \frac{N_\mathbf{x}}{n}$$

be the empirical frequency of $\mathbf{x}$ in the sample. Observe that $\hat{\mu}_n$ is a probability distribution over $\mathcal{X}$.

The following theorem characterizes the maximum likelihood estimator in terms of the Kullback–Liebler divergence.

For two probability distributions

$$\mathbf{p}, \mathbf{q} \in \Delta_K := \left\{ (p_1, \ldots, p_K) \in [0,1]^K : \sum_{k=1}^K p_k = 1 \right\},$$

it is defined as

$$\mathrm{KL}(\mathbf{p} \| \mathbf{q}) = \sum_{i=1}^K p_i \log \frac{p_i}{q_i}$$

where it will suffice to restrict ourselves to the case $\mathbf{q} > \mathbf{0}$ and where we use the convention $0 \log 0 = 0$ (so that terms with $p_i = 0$ contribute 0 to the sum).

Notice that $\mathbf{p} = \mathbf{q}$ implies $\mathrm{KL}(\mathbf{p}\|\mathbf{q}) = 0$. We show that $\mathrm{KL}(\mathbf{p}\|\mathbf{q}) \geq 0$, a result known as *Gibbs' Inequality*.

Theorem 6.2.9 *(Gibbs)* For any $\mathbf{p}, \mathbf{q} \in \Delta_K$ with $\mathbf{q} > \mathbf{0}$,

$$\mathrm{KL}(\mathbf{p}\|\mathbf{q}) \geq 0.$$

Proof Let I be the set of indices i such that $p_i > 0$. Hence

$$\mathrm{KL}(\mathbf{p}\|\mathbf{q}) = \sum_{i \in I} p_i \log \frac{p_i}{q_i}.$$

It can be proved that $\log x \leq x - 1$ for all $x > 0$ (try it!). So

$$\mathrm{KL}(\mathbf{p}\|\mathbf{q}) = -\sum_{i \in I} p_i \log \frac{q_i}{p_i}$$
$$\geq -\sum_{i \in I} p_i \left(\frac{q_i}{p_i} - 1 \right)$$
$$= -\sum_{i \in I} q_i + \sum_{i \in I} p_i$$
$$= -\sum_{i \in I} q_i + 1$$
$$\geq 0$$

where we used the facts that $\log z^{-1} = -\log z$ in the first line and $p_i = 0$ for all $i \notin I$ in the fourth line. □

Theorem 6.2.10 *(MLE via KL)* Assume that, for all $\theta \in \Theta$, p_θ is supported on a fixed finite set $\mathcal{X}$, and that $p_\theta(\mathbf{x}) > 0$ for all $\mathbf{x} \in \mathcal{X}$. Given samples $\mathbf{X}_1, \ldots, \mathbf{X}_n$ from p_{θ^*}, let $\{\hat{\mu}_n(\mathbf{x})\}_{\mathbf{x} \in \mathcal{X}}$ be the corresponding empirical frequencies. Then the maximum likelihood estimator $\hat{\theta}_{\mathrm{MLE}}$ of θ is also a solution to

$$\hat{\theta}_{\mathrm{MLE}} \in \arg\min \{\mathrm{KL}(\hat{\mu}_n \| p_\theta) : \theta \in \Theta\}.$$

Proof idea: Manipulate the negative log-likelihood to bring out its relationship to the Kullback–Liebler divergence.

Proof We can rewrite the negative log-likelihood as

$$L_n(\theta; \{\mathbf{X}_i\}_{i=1}^n) = -\sum_{i=1}^n \log p_\theta(\mathbf{X}_i) = -\sum_{\mathbf{x} \in \mathcal{X}} N_\mathbf{x} \log p_\theta(\mathbf{x}).$$

To bring out the Kullback–Liebler divergence, we further transform the previous equation into

$$\frac{1}{n}L_n(\theta; \{\mathbf{X}_i\}_{i=1}^n) = -\frac{1}{n}\sum_{\mathbf{x}\in\mathcal{X}} N_\mathbf{x} \log p_\theta(\mathbf{x})$$

$$= \sum_{\mathbf{x}\in\mathcal{X}} (N_\mathbf{x}/n) \log \frac{N_\mathbf{x}/n}{p_\theta(\mathbf{x})} - \sum_{\mathbf{x}\in\mathcal{X}} (N_\mathbf{x}/n) \log(N_\mathbf{x}/n)$$

$$= \sum_{\mathbf{x}\in\mathcal{X}} \hat{\mu}_n(\mathbf{x}) \log \frac{\hat{\mu}_n(\mathbf{x})}{p_\theta(\mathbf{x})} - \sum_{\mathbf{x}\in\mathcal{X}} \hat{\mu}_n(\mathbf{x}) \log \hat{\mu}_n(\mathbf{x})$$

$$= \mathrm{KL}(\hat{\mu}_n \| p_\theta) + \mathrm{H}(\hat{\mu}_n),$$

where the second term is referred to as the entropy of $\hat{\mu}_n$.

Because $\mathrm{H}(\hat{\mu}_n)$ does not depend on θ, minimizing $L_n(\theta; \{\mathbf{X}_i\}_{i=1}^n)$ is equivalent to minimizing $\mathrm{KL}(\hat{\mu}_n \| p_\theta)$ as claimed. □

In words, the maximum likelihood estimator chooses the parametric distribution that is closest to $\hat{\mu}_n$ in Kullback–Liebler divergence. One can think of this as "projecting" $\hat{\mu}_n$ onto the space $\{p_\theta : \theta \in \Theta\}$ under the Kullback–Liebler notion of distance.

Example 6.2.11 (*Special Case*) *One special case is where $\mathcal{X}$ is finite, $\theta = (\theta_\mathbf{x})_{\mathbf{x}\in\mathcal{X}}$ is a probability distribution over $\mathcal{X}$, and $p_\theta = \theta$. That is, we consider the class of all probability distributions over $\mathcal{X}$. Given samples $\mathbf{X}_1, \ldots, \mathbf{X}_n$ from p_{θ^*}, in this case we have*

$$\mathrm{KL}(\hat{\mu}_n \| p_\theta) = \sum_{\mathbf{x}\in\mathcal{X}} \hat{\mu}_n(\mathbf{x}) \log \frac{\hat{\mu}_n(\mathbf{x})}{p_\theta(\mathbf{x})} = \sum_{\mathbf{x}\in\mathcal{X}} \hat{\mu}_n(\mathbf{x}) \log \frac{\hat{\mu}_n(\mathbf{x})}{\theta_\mathbf{x}},$$

where recall that, by convention, if $\hat{\mu}_n(\mathbf{x}) = 0$ then $\hat{\mu}_n(\mathbf{x}) \log \frac{\hat{\mu}_n(\mathbf{x})}{\theta_\mathbf{x}} = 0$ for any $\theta_\mathbf{x}$. So, letting $\mathbb{X}_n = \{\mathbf{X}_1, \ldots, \mathbf{X}_n\}$ be the set of distinct values encountered in the sample (ignoring repetitions), we have

$$\mathrm{KL}(\hat{\mu}_n \| p_\theta) = \sum_{\mathbf{x}\in\mathbb{X}_n} \hat{\mu}_n(\mathbf{x}) \log \frac{\hat{\mu}_n(\mathbf{x})}{\theta_\mathbf{x}}.$$

Note that $\sum_{\mathbf{x}\in\mathbb{X}_n} \hat{\mu}_n(\mathbf{x}) = 1$.

We have previously established Gibbs' Inequality, which says that for any $\mathbf{p}, \mathbf{q} \in \Delta_K$ with $\mathbf{q} > \mathbf{0}$, it holds that $\mathrm{KL}(\mathbf{p}\|\mathbf{q}) \geq 0$.

The minimum $\mathrm{KL}(\hat{\mu}_n \| p_\theta) = 0$ can be achieved by setting $\theta_\mathbf{x} = \hat{\mu}_n(\mathbf{x})$ for all $\mathbf{x} \in \mathbb{X}_n$ and $\theta_\mathbf{x} = 0$ for all $\mathbf{x} \notin \mathbb{X}_n$. The condition

$$\sum_{\mathbf{x}\in\mathcal{X}} \theta_\mathbf{x} = \sum_{\mathbf{x}\in\mathbb{X}_n} \theta_\mathbf{x} + \sum_{\mathbf{x}\notin\mathbb{X}_n} \theta_\mathbf{x} = \sum_{\mathbf{x}\in\mathbb{X}_n} \hat{\mu}_n(\mathbf{x}) = 1$$

is then satisfied.

So in this case $\hat{\mu}_n$ is a maximum likelihood estimator.

A special case of this is the biased coin *example (see Example 6.2.8).*

CHAT & LEARN Explore the concept of Bayesian parameter estimation. Ask your favorite AI chatbot how Bayesian parameter estimation differs from maximum likelihood estimation and discuss their relative strengths and weaknesses. Here are some possible follow-ups. (1) Get an example implementation using a simple dataset. (2) The categorical and multinomial distributions are related to the Dirichlet distribution. Ask about their relationship and how the Dirichlet distribution is used in Bayesian inference for these distributions.

6.2.3 Parameter Estimation for Exponential Families

For exponential families, maximum likelihood estimation takes a particularly natural form. We provide details in the discrete case.

Theorem 6.2.12 *(Maximum Likelihood Estimator for Exponential Families) Assume that p_θ takes the exponential family form*

$$p_\theta(\mathbf{x}) = h(\mathbf{x}) \exp\left(\boldsymbol{\theta}^T \boldsymbol{\phi}(\mathbf{x}) - A(\boldsymbol{\theta})\right),$$

that the support S is finite, and that A is twice continuously differentiable over the open set Θ. Let $\mathbf{X}_1, \ldots, \mathbf{X}_n$ be n independent samples from a parametric family $p_{\boldsymbol{\theta}^*}$ with unknown $\boldsymbol{\theta}^* \in \Theta$. Then $L_n(\boldsymbol{\theta}; \{\mathbf{X}_i\}_{i=1}^n)$, as a function of $\boldsymbol{\theta}$, is convex and the maximum likelihood estimator of $\boldsymbol{\theta}$ – if it exists – solves the system of moment-matching equations

$$\mathbb{E}[\boldsymbol{\phi}(\mathbf{X})] = \frac{1}{n} \sum_{i=1}^n \boldsymbol{\phi}(\mathbf{X}_i),$$

where $\mathbf{X} \sim p_{\hat{\boldsymbol{\theta}}_{\mathrm{MLE}}}$.

Recall that the covariance matrix of a random vector $\mathbf{Z}$ taking values in $\mathbb{R}^m$ whose components have finite variances is defined as $K_{\mathbf{Z},\mathbf{Z}} = \mathbb{E}[(\mathbf{Z} - \mathbb{E}[\mathbf{Z}])(\mathbf{Z} - \mathbb{E}[\mathbf{Z}])^T]$ and is a positive semidefinite matrix. It is also sometimes denoted as $\Sigma_{\mathbf{Z}}$.

The function A has properties worth highlighting that will be used in the proof.

Lemma 6.2.13 *(Derivatives of A) Assume that p_θ takes the exponential family form*

$$p_\theta(\mathbf{x}) = h(\mathbf{x}) \exp\left(\boldsymbol{\theta}^T \boldsymbol{\phi}(\mathbf{x}) - A(\boldsymbol{\theta})\right),$$

that the support S is finite, and that A is twice continuously differentiable over the open set Θ. Then

$$\nabla A(\boldsymbol{\theta}) = \mathbb{E}[\boldsymbol{\phi}(\mathbf{X})] \quad \text{and} \quad \mathbf{H}_A(\boldsymbol{\theta}) = K_{\boldsymbol{\phi}(\mathbf{X}),\boldsymbol{\phi}(\mathbf{X})},$$

where $\mathbf{X} \sim p_\theta$.

Proof idea: Follows from a direct calculation.

Proof We observe first that

$$A(\boldsymbol{\theta}) = \log Z(\boldsymbol{\theta}) = \log\left(\sum_{\mathbf{x} \in S} h(\mathbf{x}) \exp(\boldsymbol{\theta}^T \boldsymbol{\phi}(\mathbf{x}))\right),$$

where we used the fact that, by definition, $Z(\boldsymbol{\theta})$ is the normalization constant of p_θ. In particular, as the logarithm of a finite, weighted sum of exponentials, the function $A(\boldsymbol{\theta})$ is continuously differentiable. Hence so is $p_\theta(\mathbf{x})$ as a function of $\boldsymbol{\theta}$.

From the formula above and the basic rules of calculus,

$$\frac{\partial}{\partial \theta_j} A(\boldsymbol{\theta}) = \frac{\partial}{\partial \theta_j} \log \left(\sum_{\mathbf{x} \in \mathcal{S}} h(\mathbf{x}) \exp(\boldsymbol{\theta}^T \boldsymbol{\phi}(\mathbf{x})) \right)$$

$$= \frac{\sum_{\mathbf{x} \in \mathcal{S}} h(\mathbf{x}) \phi_j(\mathbf{x}) \exp(\boldsymbol{\theta}^T \boldsymbol{\phi}(\mathbf{x}))}{\sum_{\mathbf{x} \in \mathcal{S}} h(\mathbf{x}) \exp(\boldsymbol{\theta}^T \boldsymbol{\phi}(\mathbf{x}))}$$

$$= \sum_{\mathbf{x} \in \mathcal{S}} \phi_j(\mathbf{x}) \frac{1}{Z(\boldsymbol{\theta})} h(\mathbf{x}) \exp(\boldsymbol{\theta}^T \boldsymbol{\phi}(\mathbf{x}))$$

$$= \sum_{\mathbf{x} \in \mathcal{S}} \phi_j(\mathbf{x}) h(\mathbf{x}) \exp(\boldsymbol{\theta}^T \boldsymbol{\phi}(\mathbf{x}) - A(\boldsymbol{\theta}))$$

$$= \mathbb{E}[\phi_j(\mathbf{X})],$$

where $\mathbf{X} \sim p_{\boldsymbol{\theta}}$.

Differentiating again, this time with respect to θ_i, we obtain

$$\frac{\partial^2}{\partial \theta_i \partial \theta_j} A(\boldsymbol{\theta}) = \frac{\partial}{\partial \theta_i} \left\{ \sum_{\mathbf{x} \in \mathcal{S}} \phi_j(\mathbf{x}) h(\mathbf{x}) \exp(\boldsymbol{\theta}^T \boldsymbol{\phi}(\mathbf{x}) - A(\boldsymbol{\theta})) \right\}$$

$$= \sum_{\mathbf{x} \in \mathcal{S}} \phi_j(\mathbf{x}) h(\mathbf{x}) \exp(\boldsymbol{\theta}^T \boldsymbol{\phi}(\mathbf{x}) - A(\boldsymbol{\theta})) \left\{ \phi_i(\mathbf{x}) - \frac{\partial}{\partial \theta_i} A(\boldsymbol{\theta}) \right\}$$

$$= \sum_{\mathbf{x} \in \mathcal{S}} \phi_i(\mathbf{x}) \phi_j(\mathbf{x}) h(\mathbf{x}) \exp(\boldsymbol{\theta}^T \boldsymbol{\phi}(\mathbf{x}) - A(\boldsymbol{\theta}))$$

$$- \left(\sum_{\mathbf{x} \in \mathcal{S}} \phi_i(\mathbf{x}) h(\mathbf{x}) \exp(\boldsymbol{\theta}^T \boldsymbol{\phi}(\mathbf{x}) - A(\boldsymbol{\theta})) \right)$$

$$\times \left(\sum_{\mathbf{x} \in \mathcal{S}} \phi_j(\mathbf{x}) h(\mathbf{x}) \exp(\boldsymbol{\theta}^T \boldsymbol{\phi}(\mathbf{x}) - A(\boldsymbol{\theta})) \right)$$

$$= \mathbb{E}[\phi_i(\mathbf{X}) \phi_j(\mathbf{X})] - \mathbb{E}[\phi_i(\mathbf{X})] \mathbb{E}[\phi_j(\mathbf{X})],$$

where again $\mathbf{X} \sim p_{\boldsymbol{\theta}}$. This concludes the proof. □

We are now ready to the prove the main theorem.

Proof *(Maximum Likelihood Estimator for Exponential Families)* We begin by computing the stationary points of the negative log-likelihood, for which we need the gradient with respect to $\boldsymbol{\theta} \in \mathbb{R}^m$. We will also need the second-order derivatives to establish convexity. We have

$$\frac{\partial}{\partial \theta_j} \{-\log p_{\boldsymbol{\theta}}(\mathbf{x})\} = \frac{\partial}{\partial \theta_j} \{-\log h(\mathbf{x}) - \boldsymbol{\theta}^T \boldsymbol{\phi}(\mathbf{x}) + A(\boldsymbol{\theta})\}$$

$$= -\phi_j(\mathbf{x}) + \frac{\partial}{\partial \theta_j} A(\boldsymbol{\theta})$$

and

$$\frac{\partial^2}{\partial \theta_i \partial \theta_j} \{-\log p_{\boldsymbol{\theta}}(\mathbf{x})\} = \frac{\partial}{\partial \theta_i} \left\{ -\phi_j(\mathbf{x}) + \frac{\partial}{\partial \theta_j} A(\boldsymbol{\theta}) \right\}$$

$$= \frac{\partial^2}{\partial \theta_i \partial \theta_j} A(\boldsymbol{\theta}).$$

We use the expressions for the derivatives of A obtained above.

Plugging into the formula for the negative log-likelihood (as a function of θ), we get for the gradient with respect to θ

$$\nabla_\theta L_n(\theta; \{\mathbf{X}_i\}_{i=1}^n) = -\sum_{i=1}^n \nabla_\theta \log p_\theta(\mathbf{X}_i)$$

$$= \sum_{i=1}^n \{-\boldsymbol{\phi}(\mathbf{X}_i) + \nabla_\theta A(\boldsymbol{\theta})\}$$

$$= \sum_{i=1}^n \{-\boldsymbol{\phi}(\mathbf{X}_i) + \mathbb{E}[\boldsymbol{\phi}(\mathbf{X})]\}.$$

This is also known in statistics as the score.

For the Hessian with respect to θ, we get

$$\mathbf{H}_{L_n}(\boldsymbol{\theta}; \{\mathbf{X}_i\}_{i=1}^n) = \sum_{i=1}^n \mathbf{H}_A(\boldsymbol{\theta}) = n\, \mathbf{K}_{\boldsymbol{\phi}(\mathbf{X}), \boldsymbol{\phi}(\mathbf{X})}.$$

This is also known in statistics as the observed information. (In fact, in this case, it reduces to the Fisher information.) Since $\mathbf{K}_{\boldsymbol{\phi}(\mathbf{X}),\boldsymbol{\phi}(\mathbf{X})}$ is positive semidefinite, so is $\mathbf{H}_{L_n}(\boldsymbol{\theta}; \{\mathbf{X}_i\}_{i=1}^n)$.

Hence, a stationary point $\hat{\boldsymbol{\theta}}_{\text{MLE}}$ must satisfy

$$\mathbf{0} = \nabla L_n(\boldsymbol{\theta}; \{\mathbf{X}_i\}_{i=1}^n) = \sum_{i=1}^n \{-\boldsymbol{\phi}(\mathbf{X}_i) + \mathbb{E}[\boldsymbol{\phi}(\mathbf{X})]\},$$

where $\mathbf{X} \sim p_{\hat{\boldsymbol{\theta}}_{\text{MLE}}}$ or, after rearranging,

$$\mathbb{E}[\boldsymbol{\phi}(\mathbf{X})] = \frac{1}{n} \sum_{i=1}^n \boldsymbol{\phi}(\mathbf{X}_i).$$

Because L_n is convex, a stationary point – if it exists – is necessarily a global minimum (and vice versa). $\square$

Example 6.2.14 (Bernoulli/Biased Coin, continued from Example 6.2.3) *For $x \in \{0, 1\}$, recall that the* Ber(q) *distribution can be written as*

$$p_\theta(x) = \frac{1}{Z(\theta)} h(x) \exp(\theta\, \phi(x))$$

where we define $h(x) \equiv 1$, $\phi(x) = x$, $\theta = \log\left(\frac{q}{1-q}\right)$, and $Z(\theta) = 1 + e^\theta$. Let $X_1, \ldots, X_n$ be independent samples from p_{θ^*}.

For $X \sim p_{\hat{\theta}_{\text{MLE}}}$, the moment-matching equations reduce to

$$\hat{q}_{\text{MLE}} := \mathbb{E}[X] = \mathbb{E}[\phi(X)] = \frac{1}{n}\sum_{i=1}^n \phi(X_i) = \frac{1}{n}\sum_{i=1}^n X_i.$$

To compute the left-hand side in terms of $\hat{\theta}_{\text{MLE}}$ we use the relationship $\theta = \log\left(\frac{q}{1-q}\right)$; that is,

$$\hat{\theta}_{\text{MLE}} = \log\left(\frac{\frac{1}{n}\sum_{i=1}^n X_i}{1 - \frac{1}{n}\sum_{i=1}^n X_i}\right).$$

Hence, $\hat{\theta}_{\text{MLE}}$ is well-defined when $\frac{1}{n}\sum_{i=1}^n X_i \neq 0, 1$.

Define q^* as the solution to

$$\theta^* = \log\left(\frac{q^*}{1-q^*}\right)$$

so that

$$q^* = \frac{e^{\theta^*}}{1 + e^{\theta^*}} = \frac{1}{1 + e^{-\theta^*}} = \sigma(\theta^*),$$

where σ is the sigmoid function.

By the law of large numbers, as $n \to +\infty$ we get the convergence

$$\frac{1}{n} \sum_{i=1}^{n} X_i \to q^*,$$

with probability one.

Because the function $\log\left(\frac{q}{1-q}\right)$ is continuous for $q \in (0, 1)$, we have furthermore

$$\hat{\theta}_{\text{MLE}} = \log\left(\frac{\frac{1}{n}\sum_{i=1}^{n} X_i}{1 - \frac{1}{n}\sum_{i=1}^{n} X_i}\right) \to \log\left(\frac{q^*}{1 - q^*}\right) = \theta^*.$$

In words, the maximum likelihood estimator $\hat{\theta}_{\text{MLE}}$ is guaranteed to converge to the true parameter θ^* when the number of samples grows. This fundamental property is known as statistical consistency.

Statistical consistency holds more generally for the maximum likelihood estimator under exponential families provided certain technical conditions hold. We will not provide further details here.

Unlike Example 6.2.14, one does not always have an explicit formula for the maximum likelihood estimator under exponential families. Instead, optimization methods, are used in such cases.

Example 6.2.15 *(Multivariate Gaussian)* We established the theorem for finite $\mathcal{S}$, but it holds more generally. Consider the multivariate Gaussian case. Here the sufficient statistics are

$$\boldsymbol{\phi}(\mathbf{x}) = (x_1, \ldots, x_d, x_1 x_1, \ldots, x_d x_1, x_1 x_2, \ldots, x_d x_2, \ldots, x_1 x_d, \ldots, x_d x_d)$$

which is simply the vector $\mathbf{x}$ itself stacked with the vectorized form of the matrix $\mathbf{x}\mathbf{x}^T$. So the moment-matching equations boil down to

$$\mathbb{E}[\mathbf{X}] = \frac{1}{n} \sum_{i=1}^{n} \mathbf{X}_i$$

and

$$\mathbb{E}[\mathbf{X}\mathbf{X}^T] = \frac{1}{n} \sum_{i=1}^{n} \mathbf{X}_i \mathbf{X}_i^T.$$

The first equation says to choose $\boldsymbol{\mu} = \frac{1}{n}\sum_{i=1}^{n} \mathbf{X}_i$. The second one says to take

$$\boldsymbol{\Sigma} = \mathbb{E}[\mathbf{X}\mathbf{X}^T] - \mathbb{E}[\mathbf{X}]\mathbb{E}[\mathbf{X}]^T = \frac{1}{n}\sum_{i=1}^{n} \mathbf{X}_i \mathbf{X}_i^T - \left(\frac{1}{n}\sum_{i=1}^{n} \mathbf{X}_i\right)\left(\frac{1}{n}\sum_{i=1}^{n} \mathbf{X}_i^T\right).$$

6.2.4 Generalized Linear Models

Generalized linear models (GLM) provide a broad generalization of linear regression using exponential families. Quoting from Wikipedia,[4] the context in which they arise is the following:

[4] https://en.wikipedia.org/wiki/Generalized_linear_model

6.2 Parametric Families and Maximum Likelihood Estimation

Ordinary linear regression predicts the expected value of a given unknown quantity (the response variable, a random variable) as a linear combination of a set of observed values (predictors). This implies that a constant change in a predictor leads to a constant change in the response variable (i.e. a linear-response model). This is appropriate when the response variable can vary, to a good approximation, indefinitely in either direction, or more generally for any quantity that only varies by a relatively small amount compared to the variation in the predictive variables, e.g. human heights. However, these assumptions are inappropriate for some types of response variables. For example, in cases where the response variable is expected to be always positive and varying over a wide range, constant input changes lead to geometrically (i.e. exponentially) varying, rather than constantly varying, output changes. [...] Similarly, a model that predicts a probability of making a yes/no choice (a Bernoulli variable) is even less suitable as a linear-response model, since probabilities are bounded on both ends (they must be between 0 and 1). [...] Generalized linear models cover all these situations by allowing for response variables that have arbitrary distributions (rather than simply normal distributions), and for an arbitrary function of the response variable (the link function) to vary linearly with the predicted values (rather than assuming that the response itself must vary linearly).

In its simplest form, a generalized linear model assumes that an outcome variable $y \in \mathbb{R}$ is generated from an exponential family p_θ, where $\theta \in \mathbb{R}$ is a linear combination of the predictor variables $\mathbf{x} \in \mathbb{R}^d$. That is, we assume that $\theta = \mathbf{w}^T \mathbf{x}$ for unknown $\mathbf{w} \in \mathbb{R}^d$ and the probability distribution of y is of the form

$$p_{\mathbf{w}^T \mathbf{x}}(y) = h(y) \exp\left((\mathbf{w}^T \mathbf{x}) \phi(y) - A(\mathbf{w}^T \mathbf{x})\right)$$

for some sufficient statistic $\phi(y)$. We further assume that A is twice continuously differentiable over $\mathbb{R}$.

Given data points $(\mathbf{x}_i, y_i)_{i=1}^n$, the model is fitted using maximum likelihood as follows. Under independence of the samples, the likelihood of the data is $\prod_{i=1}^n p_{\mathbf{w}^T \mathbf{x}_i}(y_i)$, which we seek to maximize over $\mathbf{w}$ (which is different from maximizing over θ!). As before, we work with the negative log-likelihood, which we denote as (with a slight abuse of notation)

$$L_n(\mathbf{w}; \{(\mathbf{x}_i, y_i)_{i=1}^n\}) = -\sum_{i=1}^n \log p_{\mathbf{w}^T \mathbf{x}_i}(y_i).$$

The gradient with respect to $\mathbf{w}$ is given by

$$\nabla_\mathbf{w} L_n(\mathbf{w}; \{(\mathbf{x}_i, y_i)_{i=1}^n\}) = -\sum_{i=1}^n \nabla_\mathbf{w} \log\left[h(y_i) \exp\left(\mathbf{w}^T \mathbf{x}_i \phi(y_i) - A(\mathbf{w}^T \mathbf{x}_i)\right)\right]$$

$$= -\sum_{i=1}^n \nabla_\mathbf{w} \left[\log h(y_i) + \mathbf{w}^T \mathbf{x}_i \phi(y_i) - A(\mathbf{w}^T \mathbf{x}_i)\right]$$

$$= -\sum_{i=1}^n \left[\mathbf{x}_i \phi(y_i) - \nabla_\mathbf{w} A(\mathbf{w}^T \mathbf{x}_i)\right].$$

By the *Chain Rule* and our previous formulas (see Lemma 6.2.13),

$$\nabla_\mathbf{w} A(\mathbf{w}^T \mathbf{x}_i) = A'(\mathbf{w}^T \mathbf{x}_i) \mathbf{x}_i = \mu(\mathbf{w}; \mathbf{x}_i) \mathbf{x}_i$$

where $\mu(\mathbf{w}; \mathbf{x}_i) = \mathbb{E}[\phi(Y_i)]$ with $Y_i \sim p_{\mathbf{w}^T \mathbf{x}_i}$. That is,

$$\nabla_{\mathbf{w}} L_n(\mathbf{w}; \{(\mathbf{x}_i, y_i)_{i=1}^n\}) = -\sum_{i=1}^n \mathbf{x}_i(\phi(y_i) - \mu(\mathbf{w}; \mathbf{x}_i)).$$

The Hessian of $A(\mathbf{w}^T \mathbf{x}_i)$, again by the *Chain Rule* and our previous formulas, is

$$A''(\mathbf{w}^T \mathbf{x}_i) \mathbf{x}_i \mathbf{x}_i^T = \sigma^2(\mathbf{w}; \mathbf{x}_i) \mathbf{x}_i \mathbf{x}_i^T$$

where $\sigma^2(\mathbf{w}; \mathbf{x}_i) = K_{\phi(Y_i), \phi(Y_i)} = \text{Var}[\phi(Y_i)]$ with $Y_i \sim p_{\mathbf{w}^T \mathbf{x}_i}$. So the Hessian of the negative log-likelihood is

$$\mathbf{H}_{L_n}(\mathbf{w}) = \sum_{i=1}^n \sigma^2(\mathbf{w}; \mathbf{x}_i) \mathbf{x}_i \mathbf{x}_i^T$$

which is positive semidefinite (prove it!).

As a result, the negative log-likelihood is convex and the maximum likelihood estimator $\hat{\mathbf{w}}_{\text{MLE}}$ solves the equation $\nabla_{\mathbf{w}} L_n(\mathbf{w}; \{(\mathbf{x}_i, y_i)_{i=1}^n\}) = \mathbf{0}$; that is,

$$\sum_{i=1}^n \mathbf{x}_i \mu(\mathbf{w}; \mathbf{x}_i) = \sum_{i=1}^n \mathbf{x}_i \phi(y_i).$$

We revisit linear and logistic regression next.

Example 6.2.16 *(Linear Regression) Consider the case where p_θ is a univariate Gaussian with mean θ and fixed variance 1. That is,*

$$\begin{aligned} p_\theta(y) &= \frac{1}{\sqrt{2\pi}} \exp\left(-\frac{(y-\theta)^2}{2}\right) \\ &= \frac{1}{\sqrt{2\pi}} \exp\left(-\frac{1}{2}[y^2 - 2y\theta + \theta^2]\right) \\ &= \frac{1}{\sqrt{2\pi}} \exp\left(-\frac{y^2}{2}\right) \exp\left(\theta y - \frac{\theta^2}{2}\right) \\ &= h(y) \exp(\theta \phi(y) - A(\theta)), \end{aligned}$$

where $\phi(y) = y$ and $A(\theta) = \theta^2/2$. We now assume that $\theta = \mathbf{x}^T \mathbf{w}$ to obtain the corresponding generalized linear model.

Given data points $(\mathbf{x}_i, y_i)_{i=1}^n$, recall that the maximum likelihood estimator $\hat{\mathbf{w}}_{\text{MLE}}$ solves the equation

$$\sum_{i=1}^n \mathbf{x}_i \mu(\mathbf{w}; \mathbf{x}_i) = \sum_{i=1}^n \mathbf{x}_i \phi(y_i)$$

where $\mu(\mathbf{w}; \mathbf{x}_i) = \mathbb{E}[\phi(Y_i)]$ with $Y_i \sim p_{\mathbf{x}_i^T \mathbf{w}}$. Here $\mathbb{E}[\phi(Y_i)] = \mathbb{E}[Y_i] = \mathbf{x}_i^T \mathbf{w}$. So the equation reduces to

$$\sum_{i=1}^n \mathbf{x}_i \mathbf{x}_i^T \mathbf{w} = \sum_{i=1}^n \mathbf{x}_i y_i.$$

You may not recognize this equation, but we have encountered it before in a different form. Let A be the matrix with row i equal to $\mathbf{x}_i$ and let $\mathbf{y}$ be the vector with i-th entry equal to y_i. Then

$$\sum_{i=1}^n \mathbf{x}_i \mathbf{x}_i^T = A^T A \quad \text{and} \quad \sum_{i=1}^n \mathbf{x}_i y_i = A^T \mathbf{y}$$

as can be checked entry by entry or by using our previous characterizations of matrix–matrix products (in outer-product form) and matrix–vector products (as linear combinations of columns). Therefore, the equation above is equivalent to $A^T A \mathbf{w} = A^T \mathbf{y}$ – the normal equations of linear regression.

To make sense of this finding, we look back at the negative log-likelihood

$$\begin{aligned} L_n(\mathbf{w}; \{(\mathbf{x}_i, y_i)_{i=1}^n\}) &= -\sum_{i=1}^n \log p_{\mathbf{x}_i^T \mathbf{w}}(y_i) \\ &= -\sum_{i=1}^n \log\left(\frac{1}{\sqrt{2\pi}} \exp\left(-\frac{(y_i - \mathbf{x}_i^T \mathbf{w})^2}{2}\right)\right) \\ &= -\log(\sqrt{2\pi}) + \frac{1}{2} \sum_{i=1}^n (y_i - \mathbf{x}_i^T \mathbf{w})^2. \end{aligned}$$

Observe that minimizing this expression over $\mathbf{w}$ is equivalent to solving the least-squares problem, as the first term does not depend on $\mathbf{w}$ and the factor of $1/2$ does not affect the optimum.

While we have rederived the least squares problem from a probabilistic model, it should be noted that the Gaussian assumption is not in fact required for linear regression to be warranted. Rather, it gives a different perspective on the same problem.

Example 6.2.17 *(Logistic Regression)* Consider the case where p_θ is a Bernoulli distribution. That is, for $y \in \{0, 1\}$,

$$p_\theta(y) = h(y) \exp(\theta \, \phi(y) - A(\theta)),$$

where $h(y) \equiv 1$, $\phi(y) = y$, and $A(\theta) = \log(1 + e^\theta)$. We assume that $\theta = \mathbf{x}^T \mathbf{w}$ to obtain the corresponding generalized linear model. Given data points $(\mathbf{x}_i, y_i)_{i=1}^n$, the maximum likelihood estimator $\hat{\mathbf{w}}_{\text{MLE}}$ solves the equation

$$\sum_{i=1}^n \mathbf{x}_i \mu(\mathbf{w}; \mathbf{x}_i) = \sum_{i=1}^n \mathbf{x}_i \phi(y_i)$$

where $\mu(\mathbf{w}; \mathbf{x}_i) = \mathbb{E}[\phi(Y_i)]$ with $Y_i \sim p_{\mathbf{x}_i^T \mathbf{w}}$. Here, by our formula for the gradient of A,

$$\mathbb{E}[\phi(Y_i)] = \mathbb{E}[Y_i] = A'(\mathbf{x}_i^T \mathbf{w}) = \frac{e^{\mathbf{x}_i^T \mathbf{w}}}{1 + e^{\mathbf{x}_i^T \mathbf{w}}} = \sigma(\mathbf{x}_i^T \mathbf{w}),$$

where σ is the sigmoid function. So the equation reduces to

$$\sum_{i=1}^n \mathbf{x}_i \sigma(\mathbf{x}_i^T \mathbf{w}) = \sum_{i=1}^n \mathbf{x}_i y_i.$$

The equation in this case cannot be solved explicitly. Instead we can use gradient descent, or a variant, to minimize the negative log-likelihood directly. The latter is

$$L_n(\mathbf{w}; \{(\mathbf{x}_i, y_i)_{i=1}^n\}) = -\sum_{i=1}^n \log p_{\mathbf{x}_i^T \mathbf{w}}(y_i)$$
$$= -\sum_{i=1}^n \log\left(\exp((\mathbf{x}_i^T \mathbf{w})y_i - \log(1 + e^{\mathbf{x}_i^T \mathbf{w}}))\right)$$
$$= -\sum_{i=1}^n \left[(\mathbf{x}_i^T \mathbf{w})y_i - \log(1 + e^{\mathbf{x}_i^T \mathbf{w}})\right]$$
$$= -\sum_{i=1}^n \left[y_i \log(e^{\mathbf{x}_i^T \mathbf{w}}) - (y_i + (1 - y_i)) \log(1 + e^{\mathbf{x}_i^T \mathbf{w}})\right]$$
$$= -\sum_{i=1}^n \left[y_i \log(\sigma(\mathbf{x}_i^T \mathbf{w})) + (1 - y_i) \log(1 - \sigma(\mathbf{x}_i^T \mathbf{w}))\right].$$

Minimizing $L_n(\mathbf{w}; \{(\mathbf{x}_i, y_i)_{i=1}^n\})$ is equivalent to logistic regression.

To use gradient descent, we compute

$$\nabla_{\mathbf{w}} L_n(\mathbf{w}; \{(\mathbf{x}_i, y_i)_{i=1}^n\}) = -\sum_{i=1}^n \mathbf{x}_i(\phi(y_i) - \mu(\mathbf{w}; \mathbf{x}_i))$$
$$= -\sum_{i=1}^n \mathbf{x}_i(y_i - \sigma(\mathbf{x}_i^T \mathbf{w})).$$

This expression is indeed consistent with what we previously derived for logistic regression (see Section 3.6).

CHAT & LEARN Generalized linear models can be extended to handle more complex data structures. Ask your favorite AI chatbot to explain what generalized additive models (GAMs) are and how they differ from generalized linear models. Also, ask about some common applications of GAMs.

Self-Assessment Quiz (with help from Claude, Gemini, and ChatGPT)

1. Which of the following is NOT an example of an exponential family of distributions?
   a) Bernoulli
   b) Categorical
   c) Uniform
   d) Multivariate Gaussian

2. In the exponential family form $p_\theta(\mathbf{x}) = h(\mathbf{x}) \exp(\theta^T \phi(x) - A(\theta))$, what does $A(\theta)$ represent?
   a) The sufficient statistic
   b) The log-partition function
   c) The canonical parameter
   d) The base measure

3. Given n independent samples $X_1, \ldots, X_n$ from a parametric family p_{θ^*} with unknown $\theta^* \in \Theta$, the maximum likelihood estimator $\hat{\theta}_{\text{MLE}}$ is defined as:

   a) $\hat{\theta}_{\text{MLE}} \in \arg\max \left\{ \prod_{i=1}^n p_\theta(X_i) : \theta \in \Theta \right\}$
   b) $\hat{\theta}_{\text{MLE}} \in \arg\min \left\{ \prod_{i=1}^n p_\theta(X_i) : \theta \in \Theta \right\}$
   c) $\hat{\theta}_{\text{MLE}} \in \arg\max \left\{ \sum_{i=1}^n p_\theta(X_i) : \theta \in \Theta \right\}$
   d) $\hat{\theta}_{\text{MLE}} \in \arg\min \left\{ \sum_{i=1}^n p_\theta(X_i) : \theta \in \Theta \right\}$

4. In a generalized linear model, the maximum likelihood estimator $\hat{\mathbf{w}}_{\text{MLE}}$ solves the equation:

   a) $\sum_{i=1}^n \mathbf{x}_i \mu(\mathbf{w}; \mathbf{x}_i) = \sum_{i=1}^n \mathbf{x}_i \phi(\mathbf{y}_i)$
   b) $\sum_{i=1}^n \mathbf{x}_i \mu(\mathbf{w}; \mathbf{x}_i) = \sum_{i=1}^n \mathbf{y}_i \phi(\mathbf{x}_i)$
   c) $\sum_{i=1}^n \mu(\mathbf{w}; \mathbf{x}_i) = \sum_{i=1}^n \phi(\mathbf{y}_i)$
   d) $\sum_{i=1}^n \mu(\mathbf{w}; \mathbf{x}_i) = \sum_{i=1}^n \mathbf{y}_i$

5. In logistic regression, which distribution is used for the outcome variable?

   a) Normal distribution
   b) Poisson distribution
   c) Bernoulli distribution
   d) Exponential distribution

Answer for 1: c. Justification: The text provides examples of Bernoulli, categorical, and multivariate Gaussian distributions as members of the exponential family. The uniform distribution, however, does not fit the exponential family form.

Answer for 2: b. Justification: The text states that $A(\theta) = \log Z(\theta)$, where $Z(\theta)$ is referred to as the partition function.

Answer for 3: a. Justification: The text provides the definition of the maximum likelihood estimator as $\hat{\theta}_{\text{MLE}} \in \arg\max \left\{ \prod_{i=1}^n p_\theta(X_i) : \theta \in \Theta \right\}$.

Answer for 4: a. Justification: The text derives the equation $\sum_{i=1}^n \mathbf{x}_i \mu(\mathbf{w}; \mathbf{x}_i) = \sum_{i=1}^n \mathbf{x}_i \phi(\mathbf{y}_i)$ as the one that the maximum likelihood estimator solves in a generalized linear model.

Answer for 5: c. Justification: The text describes logistic regression as a GLM where the outcome variable is assumed to follow a Bernoulli distribution.

6.3 Modeling More Complex Dependencies 1: Using Conditional Independence

In this section, we discuss the first of two standard techniques for constructing joint distributions from simpler building blocks: (1) imposing conditional independence relations and (2) marginalizing out an unobserved random variable. Combining them produces a large class of models known as probabilistic graphical models, which we do not discuss in generality. As before, we make our rigorous derivations in the finite support case, but these can be adapted to the continuous or hybrid cases.

6.3.1 Review of Conditioning

We first review the concept of conditioning, which generally plays a key role in probabilistic modeling and reasoning.

6.3.1.1 Conditional Probability

We start with events. Throughout, we work on a fixed probability space $(\Omega, \mathcal{F}, \mathbb{P})$, which we assume is discrete; that is, the number of elements in Ω is countable.

Definition 6.3.1 *(Conditional Probability) Let A and B be two events with $\mathbb{P}[B] > 0$. The conditional probability of A given B is defined as*

$$\mathbb{P}[A|B] = \frac{\mathbb{P}[A \cap B]}{\mathbb{P}[B]}.$$

The intuitive interpretation goes something like this: Knowing that event B has occurred, the updated probability of observing A is the probability of its restriction to B, properly normalized to reflect that outcomes outside B have updated probability 0.

Conditional probabilities generally behave like "unconditional" probabilities. (See for instance Problems 6.8, 7.1, and 7.9.)

Independence can be characterized in terms of conditional probability. In words, A and B are independent if conditioning on one of them having taken place does not change the probability of the other occurring.

Lemma 6.3.2 *Let A and B be two events of positive probability. Then A and B are independent, which we will denote as $A \perp\!\!\!\perp B$, if and only if $\mathbb{P}[A|B] = \mathbb{P}[A]$ and $\mathbb{P}[B|A] = \mathbb{P}[B]$.*

Proof If A and B are independent, then $\mathbb{P}[A \cap B] = \mathbb{P}[A]\mathbb{P}[B]$, which implies

$$\mathbb{P}[A|B] = \frac{\mathbb{P}[A \cap B]}{\mathbb{P}[B]} = \frac{\mathbb{P}[A]\mathbb{P}[B]}{\mathbb{P}[B]} = \mathbb{P}[A].$$

In the other direction,

$$\mathbb{P}[A] = \mathbb{P}[A|B] = \frac{\mathbb{P}[A \cap B]}{\mathbb{P}[B]}$$

implies $\mathbb{P}[A \cap B] = \mathbb{P}[A]\mathbb{P}[B]$ after rearranging. $\square$

The conditional probability is often used in three fundamental ways, which we recall next. Proofs can be found in most probability textbooks.

- **Multiplication Rule:** For any collection of events $A_1, \ldots, A_r$,

$$\mathbb{P}\left[\cap_{i=1}^{r} A_i\right] = \prod_{i=1}^{r} \mathbb{P}\left[A_i \,\Big|\, \cap_{j=1}^{i-1} A_j\right].$$

- **Law of Total Probability:** For any event B and any partition $A_1, \ldots, A_r$ of Ω,

$$\mathbb{P}[B] = \sum_{i=1}^{r} \mathbb{P}[B|A_i]\mathbb{P}[A_i].$$

- **Bayes' Rule:** For any events A and B with positive probability,

$$\mathbb{P}[A|B] = \frac{\mathbb{P}[B|A]\mathbb{P}[A]}{\mathbb{P}[B]}.$$

6.3 Using Conditional Independence

It is implicit that all formulas above hold provided all conditional probabilities are well-defined.

6.3.1.2 Conditioning on a Random Variable

Conditional probabilities extend naturally to random variables. If X is a discrete random variable, we let p_X be its probability mass function and $\mathcal{S}_X$ be its support, namely the set of values where it has positive probability. Then we can for instance condition on the event $\{X = x\}$ for any $x \in \mathcal{S}_X$.

We define next the conditional probability mass function.

Definition 6.3.3 *(Conditional Probability Mass Function) Let X and Y be discrete random variables with joint probability mass function $p_{X,Y}$ and marginals p_X and p_Y. The conditional probability mass function of X given Y is defined as*

$$p_{X|Y}(x|y) := P[X = x | Y = y] = \frac{p_{X,Y}(x,y)}{p_Y(y)}$$

which is defined for all $x \in \mathcal{S}_X$ and $y \in \mathcal{S}_Y$.

The conditional expectation can then be defined in a natural way as the expectation over the conditional probability mass function.

Definition 6.3.4 *(Conditional Expectation) Let X and Y be discrete random variables where X takes real values and has a finite mean. The conditional expectation of X given $Y = y$ is given by*

$$\mathbb{E}[X|Y=y] = \sum_{x \in \mathcal{S}_X} x\, p_{X|Y}(x|y).$$

More generally, for a function f over the range of X, we can define

$$\mathbb{E}[f(X)|Y=y] = \sum_{x \in \mathcal{S}_X} f(x)\, p_{X|Y}(x|y).$$

We mention one useful formula: the *Law of Total Expectation*, the expectation version of the *Law of Total Probability*. It reads

$$\mathbb{E}[f(X)] = \sum_{y \in \mathcal{S}_Y} \mathbb{E}[f(X)|Y=y]\, p_Y(y).$$

6.3.1.3 Conditional Expectation as Least-Squares Estimator

Thinking of $\mathbb{E}[X|Y = y]$ as a function of y leads to a fundamental characterization of the conditional expectation.

Theorem 6.3.5 *Let X and Y be discrete random variables where X takes real values and has a finite variance. Then the conditional expectation $h(y) = \mathbb{E}[X|Y = y]$ minimizes the least-squares criterion*

$$\min_{h} \mathbb{E}\left[(X - h(Y))^2\right]$$

where the minimum is over all real-valued functions of y.

Proof Think of $h(y)$ as a vector $\mathbf{h} = (h_y)_{y \in S_Y}$, indexed by S_Y (which is countable by assumption), with $h_y = h(y) \in \mathbb{R}$. Then

$$\mathcal{L}(\mathbf{h}) = \mathbb{E}\left[(X - h(Y))^2\right]$$
$$= \sum_{x \in S_X} \sum_{y \in S_Y} (x - h_y)^2 p_{X,Y}(x, y)$$
$$= \sum_{y \in S_Y} \left[\sum_{x \in S_X} (x - h_y)^2 p_{X,Y}(x, y)\right].$$

Expanding the sum in the square brackets (which we denote by q_y and think of as a function of h_y) gives

$$q_y(h_y) := \sum_{x \in S_X} (x - h_y)^2 p_{X,Y}(x, y)$$
$$= \sum_{x \in S_X} [x^2 - 2xh_y + h_y^2] p_{X,Y}(x, y)$$
$$= \left\{\sum_{x \in S_X} x^2 p_{X,Y}(x, y)\right\} + \left\{-2 \sum_{x \in S_X} x p_{X,Y}(x, y)\right\} h_y + \{p_Y(y)\} h_y^2.$$

By the *Minimizing a Quadratic Function Lemma*, the unique global minimum of $q_y(h_y)$ — provided $p_Y(y) > 0$ — is attained at

$$h_y = -\frac{-2 \sum_{x \in S_X} x p_{X,Y}(x, y)}{2 p_Y(y)}.$$

After rearranging, we get

$$h_y = \sum_{x \in S_X} x \frac{p_{X,Y}(x, y)}{p_Y(y)} = \sum_{x \in S_X} x p_{X|Y}(x|y) = \mathbb{E}[X|Y = y]$$

as claimed. □

6.3.1.4 Conditional Independence

Next, we discuss conditional independence. We begin with the formal definition.

Definition 6.3.6 *(Conditional Independence) Let A, B, C be events such that $\mathbb{P}[C] > 0$. Then A and B are conditionally independent given C, denoted $A \perp\!\!\!\perp B | C$, if*

$$\mathbb{P}[A \cap B | C] = \mathbb{P}[A | C] \mathbb{P}[B | C].$$

In words, quoting Wikipedia[5]:

> A and B are conditionally independent given C if and only if, given knowledge that C occurs, knowledge of whether A occurs provides no information on the likelihood of B occurring, and knowledge of whether B occurs provides no information on the likelihood of A occurring.

In general, conditionally independent events are not (unconditionally) independent.

Example 6.3.7 *Imagine I have two six-sided dice. Die 1 has faces $\{1, 3, 5, 7, 9, 11\}$ and die 2 has faces $\{2, 4, 6, 8, 10, 12\}$. Suppose I perform the following experiment: I pick one of the two*

---
[5] https://en.wikipedia.org/wiki/Conditional_independence

dice uniformly at random, and then I roll that die twice. Let X_1 and X_2 be the outcomes of the rolls. Consider the events $A = \{X_1 = 1\}$, $B = \{X_2 = 2\}$, and $C = \{die\ 1\ is\ picked\}$. The events A and B are clearly dependent: If A occurs, then I know that die 1 was picked, and hence B cannot occur. Knowledge of one event provides information about the likelihood of the other event occurring. Formally, by the law of total probability,

$$\mathbb{P}[A] = \mathbb{P}[A|C]\mathbb{P}[C] + \mathbb{P}[A|C^c]\mathbb{P}[C^c] = \frac{1}{6}\frac{1}{2} + 0\frac{1}{2} = \frac{1}{12}.$$

Similarly $\mathbb{P}[B] = \frac{1}{12}$. Yet $\mathbb{P}[A \cap B] = 0 \neq \frac{1}{12}\frac{1}{12}$.

On the other hand, we claim that A and B are conditionally independent given C. Again this is intuitively clear: Once I pick a die, the two rolls are independent. For a given die choice, knowledge of one roll provides no information about the likelihood of the other roll. Note that the phrase "for a given die choice" is critical in the last statement. Formally, by our experiment, we have $\mathbb{P}[A|C] = 1/6$, $\mathbb{P}[B|C] = 0$ and $\mathbb{P}[A \cap B|C] = 0$. So indeed

$$\mathbb{P}[A \cap B|C] = \mathbb{P}[A|C]\,\mathbb{P}[B|C]$$

as claimed.

Conditional independence is naturally extended to random vectors.

Definition 6.3.8 (Conditional Independence of Random Vectors) *Let $\mathbf{X}, \mathbf{Y}, \mathbf{W}$ be discrete random vectors. Then $\mathbf{X}$ and $\mathbf{Y}$ are said to be conditionally independent given $\mathbf{W}$, denoted $\mathbf{X} \perp\!\!\!\perp \mathbf{Y}|\mathbf{W}$, if for all $\mathbf{x} \in \mathcal{S}_{\mathbf{X}}$, $\mathbf{y} \in \mathcal{S}_{\mathbf{Y}}$, and $\mathbf{w} \in \mathcal{S}_{\mathbf{W}}$*

$$\mathbb{P}[\mathbf{X} = \mathbf{x}, \mathbf{Y} = \mathbf{y}|\mathbf{W} = \mathbf{w}] = \mathbb{P}[\mathbf{X} = \mathbf{x}|\mathbf{W} = \mathbf{w}]\,\mathbb{P}[\mathbf{Y} = \mathbf{y}|\mathbf{W} = \mathbf{w}].$$

An important consequence is that we can drop the conditioning by the independent variable.

Lemma 6.3.9 (Role of Independence) *Let $\mathbf{X}, \mathbf{Y}, \mathbf{W}$ be discrete random vectors such that $\mathbf{X} \perp\!\!\!\perp \mathbf{Y}|\mathbf{W}$. For all $\mathbf{x} \in \mathcal{S}_{\mathbf{X}}$, $\mathbf{y} \in \mathcal{S}_{\mathbf{Y}}$, and $\mathbf{w} \in \mathcal{S}_{\mathbf{W}}$,*

$$\mathbb{P}[\mathbf{X} = \mathbf{x}|\mathbf{Y} = \mathbf{y}, \mathbf{W} = \mathbf{w}] = \mathbb{P}[\mathbf{X} = \mathbf{x}|\mathbf{W} = \mathbf{w}].$$

Proof Problem 6.10 will show that $A \perp\!\!\!\perp B|C$ implies $\mathbb{P}[A|B \cap C] = \mathbb{P}[A|C]$. That implies the claim. $\square$

CHAT & LEARN The concept of conditional independence is closely related to the concept of d-separation in probabilistic graphical models. Ask your favorite AI chatbot to explain d-separation.

6.3.2 The Basic Configurations

A powerful approach for constructing complex probability distributions is the use of conditional independence. The case of three random variables exemplifies key probabilistic relationships. By the product rule, we can write

$$\mathbb{P}[X = x, Y = y, Z = z] = \mathbb{P}[X = x]\,\mathbb{P}[Y = y|X = x]\,\mathbb{P}[Z = z|X = x, Y = y].$$

This is conveniently represented through a digraph where the vertices are the variables. Recall that an arrow (i, j), from i to j, indicates that i is a parent of j and that j is a child of i. Let

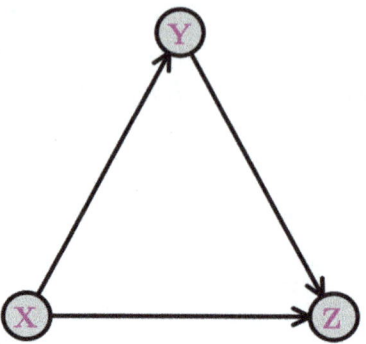

Figure 6.4 The full case.

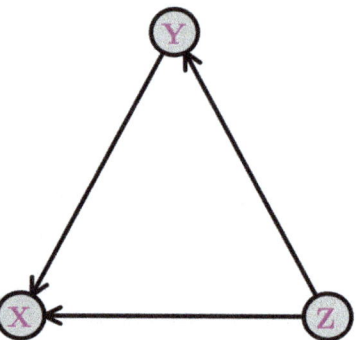

Figure 6.5 Another full case.

pa(i) be the set of parents of i. The digraph $G = (V, E)$ in Figure 6.4 encodes the following sampling scheme, known as ancestral sampling.

1. We pick X according to its marginal $\mathbb{P}[X = x]$. Note that X has no parent in G.
2. We pick Y according to the conditional probability distribution (CPD) $\mathbb{P}[Y = y|X = x]$. Note that X is the only parent of Y.
3. Finally we pick Z according to the CPD $\mathbb{P}[Z = z|X = x, Y = y]$. Note that the parents of Z are X and Y.

The graph above is acyclic; that is, it has no directed cycle. The variables X, Y, Z are in topological order, that is, all edges (i, j) are such that i comes before j in that order.

The same joint distribution can be represented by a different digraph if the product rule is used in a different order. For instance,

$$\mathbb{P}[X = x, Y = y, Z = z] = \mathbb{P}[Z = z]\,\mathbb{P}[Y = y|Z = z]\,\mathbb{P}[X = x|Z = z, Y = y]$$

is represented by the digraph in Figure 6.5. A topological order this time is Z, Y, X.

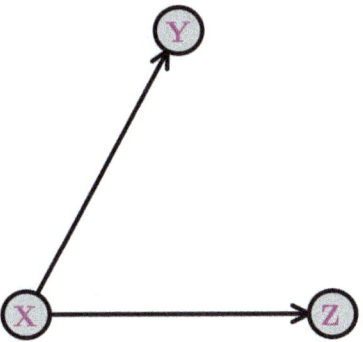

Figure 6.6 The fork.

6.3.2.1 The Fork

Removing edges in the first graph above encodes conditional independence relations. For instance, removing the edge from Y to Z gives the graph in Figure 6.6, known as a fork. We denote this configuration as $Y \leftarrow X \rightarrow Z$.

The joint distribution simplifies as follows:

$$\mathbb{P}[X = x, Y = y, Z = z] = \mathbb{P}[X = x]\,\mathbb{P}[Y = y|X = x]\,\mathbb{P}[Z = z|X = x].$$

So, in this case, what has changed is that the CPD of Z does not depend on the value of Y. From the *Role of Independence Lemma*, this corresponds to assuming the conditional independence $Z \perp\!\!\!\perp Y|X$. Indeed, we can check that claim directly from the joint distribution

$$\begin{aligned}
\mathbb{P}[Y = y, Z = z|X = x] &= \frac{\mathbb{P}[X = x, Y = y, Z = z]}{\mathbb{P}[X = x]} \\
&= \frac{\mathbb{P}[X = x]\,\mathbb{P}[Y = y|X = x]\,\mathbb{P}[Z = z|X = x]}{\mathbb{P}[X = x]} \\
&= \mathbb{P}[Y = y|X = x]\,\mathbb{P}[Z = z|X = x]
\end{aligned}$$

as claimed.

6.3.2.2 The Chain

Removing the edge from X to Z gives the graph in Figure 6.7, known as a chain (or pipe). We denote this configuration as $X \rightarrow Y \rightarrow Z$.

The joint distribution simplifies as follows:

$$\mathbb{P}[X = x, Y = y, Z = z] = \mathbb{P}[X = x]\,\mathbb{P}[Y = y|X = x]\,\mathbb{P}[Z = z|Y = y].$$

In this case, what has changed is that the CPD of Z does not depend on the value of X. Compare this to the fork. The corresponding conditional independence relation is $Z \perp\!\!\!\perp X|Y$. Indeed, we can check that claim directly:

$$\begin{aligned}
\mathbb{P}[X = x, Z = z|Y = y] &= \frac{\mathbb{P}[X = x, Y = y, Z = z]}{\mathbb{P}[Y = y]} \\
&= \frac{\mathbb{P}[X = x]\,\mathbb{P}[Y = y|X = x]\,\mathbb{P}[Z = z|Y = y]}{\mathbb{P}[Y = y]}.
\end{aligned}$$

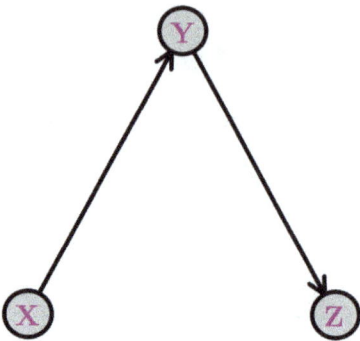

Figure 6.7 The chain.

Now we have to use *Bayes' Rule* to get

$$= \frac{\mathbb{P}[X=x]\,\mathbb{P}[Y=y|X=x]\,\mathbb{P}[Z=z|Y=y]}{\mathbb{P}[Y=y]}$$
$$= \frac{\mathbb{P}[Y=y|X=x]\,\mathbb{P}[X=x]}{\mathbb{P}[Y=y]}\mathbb{P}[Z=z|Y=y]$$
$$= \mathbb{P}[X=x|Y=y]\,\mathbb{P}[Z=z|Y=y]$$

as claimed.

For any x, y, z where the joint probability is positive, we can rewrite

$$\mathbb{P}[X=x, Y=y, Z=z]$$
$$= \mathbb{P}[X=x]\,\mathbb{P}[Y=y|X=x]\,\mathbb{P}[Z=z|Y=y]$$
$$= \mathbb{P}[Y=y]\,\mathbb{P}[X=x|Y=y]\,\mathbb{P}[Z=z|Y=y],$$

where we used that

$$\mathbb{P}[X=x, Y=y] = \mathbb{P}[X=x]\,\mathbb{P}[Y=y|X=x] = \mathbb{P}[Y=y]\,\mathbb{P}[X=x|Y=y]$$

by definition of the conditional probability. In other words, we have shown that the chain $X \to Y \to Z$ is in fact equivalent to the fork $X \leftarrow Y \to Z$. In particular, they both correspond to assuming the conditional independence relation $Z \perp\!\!\!\perp X|Y$, although they capture a different way to sample the joint distribution.

6.3.2.3 The Collider

Removing the edge from X to Y gives the graph in Figure 6.8, known as a collider. We denote this configuration as $X \to Z \leftarrow Y$.

The joint distribution simplifies as follows:

$$\mathbb{P}[X=x, Y=y, Z=z] = \mathbb{P}[X=x]\,\mathbb{P}[Y=y]\,\mathbb{P}[Z=z|X=x, Y=y].$$

In this case, what has changed is that the CPD of Y does not depend on the value of X. Compare this to the fork and the chain. This time we have $X \perp\!\!\!\perp Y$. Indeed, we can check that claim directly:

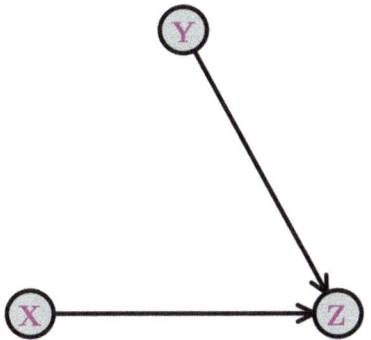

Figure 6.8 The collider.

$$\mathbb{P}[X = x, Y = y] = \sum_{z \in \mathcal{S}_z} \mathbb{P}[X = x, Y = y, Z = z]$$
$$= \sum_{z \in \mathcal{S}_z} \mathbb{P}[X = x]\, \mathbb{P}[Y = y]\, \mathbb{P}[Z = z | X = x, Y = y]$$
$$= \mathbb{P}[X = x]\, \mathbb{P}[Y = y]$$

as claimed. In particular, the collider cannot be reframed as a chain or fork as its underlying assumption is stronger.

Perhaps counterintuitively, conditioning on Z makes X and Y dependent in general. This is known as explaining away or Berkson's Paradox.

6.3.3 Example: Naive Bayes

The model-based justification we gave for logistic regression in Section 6.2.4 used a so-called discriminative approach, where the conditional distribution of the target y given the features $\mathbf{x}$ is specified – but not the full distribution of the data $(\mathbf{x}, y)$. Here we give an example of the generative approach, which models the full distribution.

The naive Bayes model is a simple discrete model for supervised learning. It is useful for document classification for instance, and we will use that terminology here to be concrete. We assume that a document has a single topic C from a list $\mathcal{C} = \{1, \ldots, K\}$ with probability distribution $\pi_k = \mathbb{P}[C = k]$. There is a vocabulary of size M and we record the presence or absence of a word m in the document with a Bernoulli variable $X_m \in \{0, 1\}$, where $p_{k,m} = \mathbb{P}[X_m = 1 | C = k]$. We denote by $\mathbf{X} = (X_1, \ldots, X_M)$ the corresponding vector.

The conditional independence assumption comes next: We assume that, given a topic C, the word occurrences are independent. That is,

$$\mathbb{P}[\mathbf{X} = \mathbf{x} | C = k] = \prod_{m=1}^{M} \mathbb{P}[X_m = x_m | C = k]$$
$$= \prod_{m=1}^{M} p_{k,m}^{x_m} (1 - p_{k,m})^{1-x_m}.$$

Figure 6.9 Naive Bayes.

Finally, the joint distribution is

$$\mathbb{P}[C = k, \mathbf{X} = \mathbf{x}] = \mathbb{P}[\mathbf{X} = \mathbf{x}|C = k]\,\mathbb{P}[C = k]$$
$$= \pi_k \prod_{m=1}^{M} p_{k,m}^{x_m}(1 - p_{k,m})^{1-x_m}.$$

Graphically, this is similar to a fork with C at its center and M prongs for the X_m's. This is represented using the so-called plate notation. The box with the M in the corner in Figure 6.9 indicates that X_m is repeated M times, all copies being conditionally independent given C.

6.3.3.1 Model Fitting

Before using the model for prediction, one must first fit the model from training data $\{\mathbf{x}_i, c_i\}_{i=1}^{n}$. In this case, it means estimating the unknown parameters π and $\{\mathbf{p}_k\}_{k=1}^{K}$, where $\mathbf{p}_k = (p_{k,1}, \ldots, p_{k,M})$. For each k, m let

$$N_{k,m} = \sum_{i=1}^{n} \mathbf{1}_{\{c_i=k\}} x_{i,m}, \quad N_k = \sum_{i=1}^{n} \mathbf{1}_{\{c_i=k\}}.$$

We use maximum likelihood estimation which, recall, entails finding the parameters that maximize the probability of observing the data,

$$\mathcal{L}(\pi, \{\mathbf{p}_k\}; \{\mathbf{x}_i, c_i\}) = \prod_{i=1}^{n} \pi_{c_i} \prod_{m=1}^{M} p_{c_i,m}^{x_{i,m}}(1 - p_{c_i,m})^{1-x_{i,m}}.$$

Here, as usual, we assume that the samples are independent and identically distributed. We take a logarithm to turn the products into sums and consider the negative log-likelihood (NLL)

$$L_n(\pi, \{\mathbf{p}_k\}; \{\mathbf{x}_i, c_i\})$$
$$= -\sum_{i=1}^{n} \log \pi_{c_i} - \sum_{i=1}^{n} \sum_{m=1}^{M} [x_{i,m} \log p_{c_i,m} + (1 - x_{i,m}) \log(1 - p_{c_i,m})]$$
$$= -\sum_{k=1}^{K} N_k \log \pi_k - \sum_{k=1}^{K} \sum_{m=1}^{M} [N_{k,m} \log p_{k,m} + (N_k - N_{k,m}) \log(1 - p_{k,m})].$$

The NLL can be broken up naturally into several terms that depend on different sets of parameters – and therefore can be optimized separately. First, there is a term that depends only on the π_k's:

$$J_0(\pi; \{\mathbf{x}_i, c_i\}) = -\sum_{k=1}^{K} N_k \log \pi_k.$$

The rest of the sum can be further split into KM terms, each depending only on $p_{k,m}$ for a fixed k and m:

$$J_{k,m}(p_{k,m}; \{\mathbf{x}_i, c_i\}) = -N_{k,m} \log p_{k,m} - (N_k - N_{k,m}) \log(1 - p_{k,m}).$$

So
$$L_n(\pmb{\pi}, \{\mathbf{p}_k\}; \{\mathbf{x}_i, c_i\}) = J_0(\pmb{\pi}; \{\mathbf{x}_i, c_i\}) + \sum_{k=1}^{K} \sum_{m=1}^{M} J_{k,m}(p_{k,m}; \{\mathbf{x}_i, c_i\}).$$

We minimize these terms separately. We assume that $N_k > 0$ for all k.

We use a special case of maximum likelihood estimation, which we previously worked out in Example 6.2.11, where we consider the space of all probability distributions over a finite set. The maximum likelihood estimator in that case is given by the empirical frequencies. Notice that minimizing $J_0(\pmb{\pi}; \{\mathbf{x}_i, c_i\})$ is precisely of this form: We observe N_k samples from class k) and we seek the maximum likelihood estimator of π_k, the probability of observing k. Hence the solution is simply

$$\hat{\pi}_k = \frac{N_k}{N},$$

for all k. Similarly, for each k, m, $J_{k,m}$ is of that form as well. Here the states correspond to word m being present or absent in a document of class k, and we observe $N_{k,m}$ documents of type k where the word m is present. So the solution is

$$\hat{p}_{k,m} = \frac{N_{k,m}}{N_k}$$

for all k, m.

6.3.3.2 Prediction

To predict the class of a new document, it is natural to maximize over k the probability that $\{C = k\}$ given $\{\mathbf{X} = \mathbf{x}\}$. By Bayes' rule,

$$\mathbb{P}[C = k | \mathbf{X} = \mathbf{x}] = \frac{\mathbb{P}[C = k, \mathbf{X} = \mathbf{x}]}{\mathbb{P}[\mathbf{X} = \mathbf{x}]}$$
$$= \frac{\pi_k \prod_{m=1}^{M} p_{k,m}^{x_m} (1 - p_{k,m})^{1-x_m}}{\sum_{k'=1}^{K} \pi_{k'} \prod_{m=1}^{M} p_{k',m}^{x_m} (1 - p_{k',m})^{1-x_m}}.$$

As the denominator does not in fact depend on k, maximizing $\mathbb{P}[C = k | \mathbf{X} = \mathbf{x}]$ boils down to maximizing the numerator $\pi_k \prod_{m=1}^{M} p_{k,m}^{x_m} (1 - p_{k,m})^{1-x_m}$, which is straightforward to compute. As we did previously, we take a negative logarithm – which has some numerical advantages – and we refer to it as the *score*. Since the parameters are unknown, we use $\hat{\pi}_k$ and $\hat{p}_{k,m}$ in place of π_k and $p_{k,m}$.

$$-\log \left(\pi_k \prod_{m=1}^{M} p_{k,m}^{x_m} (1 - p_{k,m})^{1-x_m} \right)$$
$$= -\log \pi_k - \sum_{m=1}^{M} [x_m \log p_{k,m} + (1 - x_m) \log(1 - p_{k,m})].$$

More specifically, taking a negative logarithm turns out to be a good idea here because computing a product of probabilities can produce very small numbers that, when they fall beneath machine precision, are approximated by zero. This is called underflow. By taking a negative logarithm, these probabilities are transformed into positive numbers of reasonable magnitude and the product becomes the sum of these. Moreover, because this transformation is monotone, we can use the transformed values directly to compute the optimal score, which is our ultimate goal in the prediction step.

CHAT & LEARN Ask your favorite AI chatbot for more information on the issue of underflow, and its cousin overflow, in particular in the context of multiypling probabilities.

While maximum likehood estimation has desirable theoretical properties, it does suffer from overfitting. If for instance a particular word m does not occur in any training document, then the probability of observing a new document that happens to contain that word is estimated to be 0 for any class (i.e., $\hat{p}_{k,m} = 0$ for all k so that $\hat{\pi}_k \prod_{m=1}^{M} \hat{p}_{k,m}^{x_m} (1 - \hat{p}_{k,m})^{1-x_m} = 0$ for all k) and the maximization problem above is not well-defined.

One approach to deal with this is Laplace smoothing:

$$\bar{\pi}_k = \frac{N_k + \alpha}{N + K\alpha}, \quad \bar{p}_{k,m} = \frac{N_{k,m} + \beta}{N_k + 2\beta}$$

where $\alpha, \beta > 0$, which can be justified using a Bayesian or regularization perspective.

We implement the naive Bayes model with Laplace smoothing.

We encode the data into a table, where the rows are the classes and the columns are the features. The entries are the corresponding $N_{k,m}$'s. In addition we provide the vector $(N_k)_k$. Using N_k[:, np.newaxis] below reshapes the one-dimensional array N_k into a two-dimensional column vector, ensuring that each element in a row of N_km is divided by the corresponding value in N_k through broadcasting.

```
def nb_fit_table(N_km,N_k, alpha=1., beta=1.):

    K, M = N_km.shape
    N = np.sum(N_k)
    pi_k = (N_k+alpha) / (N+K*alpha)
    p_km = (N_km+beta) / (N_k[:,np.newaxis]+2*beta)

    return pi_k, p_km
```

The next function computes the negative logarithm of $\pi_k \prod_{m=1}^{M} p_{k,m}^{x_m} (1 - p_{k,m})^{1-x_m}$, that is, the score of k, and outputs a k achieving the minimum score.

```
def nb_predict(pi_k, p_km, x, label_set):

    K = len(pi_k)

    score_k = np.zeros(K)
    for k in range(K):

        score_k[k] -= np.log(pi_k[k])
        score_k[k] -= np.sum(x * np.log(p_km[k,:])
                            + (1 - x)*np.log(1 - p_km[k,:]))

    return label_set[np.argmin(score_k, axis=0)]
```

NUMERICAL CORNER We use a simple example from Stack Overflow[6]:

---
[6] https://stackoverflow.com/questions/10059594/

6.3 Using Conditional Independence

Example: Let's say we have data on 1000 pieces of fruit. They happen to be Banana, Orange or some Other Fruit. We know 3 characteristics about each fruit: whether it is long, whether it is sweet, and if its color is yellow[, as displayed in Table 6.1 below].

Table 6.1 Fruit data.

Fruit	Long	Sweet	Yellow	Total
Banana	400	350	450	500
Orange	0	150	300	300
Other	100	150	50	200
Total	500	650	800	1,000

```
N_km = np.array([[400., 350., 450.],
                 [0., 150., 300.],
                 [100., 150., 50.]])
N_k = np.array([500., 300., 200.])
```

We run `nb_fit_table` on our simple dataset.

```
pi_k, p_km = nb_fit_table(N_km,N_k)
```

```
print(pi_k)
```

[0.4995015 0.3000997 0.2003988]

```
print(p_km)
```

[[0.79880478 0.69920319 0.89840637]
 [0.00331126 0.5   0.99668874]
 [0.5   0.74752475 0.0.25247525]]

Continuing on with our previous example:

Let's say that we are given the properties of an unknown fruit, and asked to classify it. We are told that the fruit is Long, Sweet and Yellow. Is it a Banana? Is it an Orange? Or Is it some Other Fruit?

We run `nb_predict` on our dataset with the additional fruit from the quote above.

```
label_set = ['Banana', 'Orange', 'Other']
x = np.array([1., 1., 1.])
nb_predict(pi_k, p_km, x, label_set)
```

'Banana'

◁ NC

CHAT & LEARN Laplace smoothing is a special case of a more general technique known as Bayesian parameter estimation. Ask your favorite AI chatbot to explain Bayesian parameter estimation and how it relates to maximum likelihood estimation and Laplace smoothing.

Self-Assessment Quiz (with help from Claude, Gemini, and ChatGPT)

1 Which of the following statements is NOT true about conditional probabilities?
   a) $P[A|B] = \frac{P[A \cap B]}{P[B]}$ for events A and B with $P[B] > 0$.
   b) If A and B are independent, then $P[A|B] = P[A]$.
   c) Conditional probabilities can be used to express the multiplication rule and the law of total probability.
   d) $P[A|B] = P[B|A]$ for any events A and B.

2 Which of the following is the correct mathematical expression for the conditional independence of events A and B given event C, denoted as $A \perp\!\!\!\perp B \mid C$?
   a) $P[A \cap B \mid C] = P[A \mid C] + P[B \mid C]$
   b) $P[A \cup B \mid C] = P[A \mid C]P[B \mid C]$
   c) $P[A \cap B \mid C] = P[A \mid C]P[B \mid C]$
   d) $P[A \mid B \cap C] = P[A \mid C]$

3 In the fork configuration $Y \leftarrow X \rightarrow Z$, which of the following conditional independence relations always holds?
   a) $X \perp\!\!\!\perp Y \mid Z$
   b) $Y \perp\!\!\!\perp Z \mid X$
   c) $X \perp\!\!\!\perp Z \mid Y$
   d) $Y \perp\!\!\!\perp Z$

4 In the collider configuration $X \rightarrow Z \leftarrow Y$, which of the following conditional independence relations always holds?
   a) $X \perp\!\!\!\perp Y \mid Z$
   b) $Y \perp\!\!\!\perp Z \mid X$
   c) $X \perp\!\!\!\perp Z \mid Y$
   d) $X \perp\!\!\!\perp Y$

5 Which of the following best describes the graphical representation of the naive Bayes model for document classification?
   a) A chain with the topic variable at the center and word variables as the links.
   b) A collider with the topic variable at the center and word variables as the parents.
   c) A fork with the topic variable at the center and word variables as the prongs.
   d) A complete graph with edges between all pairs of variables.

Answer for 1: d. Justification: In general, $P[A|B] \neq P[B|A]$. Bayes' rule provides the correct relationship between these two conditional probabilities.

Answer for 2: c. Justification: The text states, "Then A and B are conditionally independent given C, denoted $A \perp\!\!\!\perp B \mid C$, if $P[A \cap B \mid C] = P[A \mid C]P[B \mid C]$."

Answer for 3: b. Justification: The text states, "Removing the edge from Y to Z gives the following graph, known as a fork. We denote this configuration as $Y \leftarrow X \rightarrow Z$. [...] The corresponding conditional independence relation is $Z \perp\!\!\!\perp Y \mid X$."

Answer for 4: d. Justification: The text states, "Removing the edge from X to Y gives the following graph, known as a collider. We denote this configuration as $X \rightarrow Z \leftarrow Y$. [...] This time we have $X \perp\!\!\!\perp Y$."

Answer for 5: c. Justification: The text states, "Graphically, this is similar to a fork with C at its center and M prongs for the X_m's."

6.4 Modeling More Complex Dependencies 2: Marginalizing Out an Unobserved Variable

In this section, we move on to the second technique for constructing joint distributions from simpler building blocks: marginalizing out an unobserved random variable.

6.4.1 Mixtures

Mixtures are a natural way to define probability distributions. The basic idea is to consider a pair of random vectors $(\mathbf{X}, \mathbf{Y})$ and assume that $\mathbf{Y}$ is unobserved. The effect on the observed vector $\mathbf{X}$ is that $\mathbf{Y}$ is marginalized out. Indeed, by the law of total probability, for any $\mathbf{x} \in \mathcal{S}_\mathbf{X}$

$$\begin{aligned} p_\mathbf{X}(\mathbf{x}) &= \mathbb{P}[\mathbf{X} = \mathbf{x}] \\ &= \sum_{\mathbf{y} \in \mathcal{S}_\mathbf{Y}} \mathbb{P}[\mathbf{X} = \mathbf{x} \mid \mathbf{Y} = \mathbf{y}] \, \mathbb{P}[\mathbf{Y} = \mathbf{y}] \\ &= \sum_{\mathbf{y} \in \mathcal{S}_\mathbf{Y}} p_{\mathbf{X} \mid \mathbf{Y}}(\mathbf{x} \mid \mathbf{y}) \, p_\mathbf{Y}(\mathbf{y}) \end{aligned}$$

where we used the fact that the events $\{\mathbf{Y} = \mathbf{y}\}$, $\mathbf{y} \in \mathcal{S}_\mathbf{Y}$, form a partition of the probability space. We interpret this equation as defining $p_\mathbf{X}(\mathbf{x})$ as a convex combination – a mixture – of the distributions $p_{\mathbf{X} \mid \mathbf{Y}}(\mathbf{x} \mid \mathbf{y})$, $\mathbf{y} \in \mathcal{S}_\mathbf{Y}$, with mixing weights $p_\mathbf{Y}(\mathbf{y})$. In general, we need to specify the full conditional probability distribution (CPD): $p_{\mathbf{X} \mid \mathbf{Y}}(\mathbf{x} \mid \mathbf{y}), \forall \mathbf{x} \in \mathcal{S}_\mathbf{X}, \mathbf{y} \in \mathcal{S}_\mathbf{Y}$. But assuming that the mixing weights and/or CPD come from parametric families can help reduce the complexity of the model.

This can be represented in a digraph with a directed edge from a vertex for $\mathbf{Y}$ to a vertex for $\mathbf{X}$. Further, we let the vertex for $\mathbf{X}$ be shaded to indicate that it is observed, while the vertex for $\mathbf{Y}$ is not shaded to indicate that it is not. Mathematically, this corresponds to applying the law of total probability as we did previously. See Figure 6.10.

In the parametric context, this gives rise to a fruitful approach to expanding distribution families. Suppose $\{p_\theta : \theta \in \Theta\}$ is a parametric family of distributions. Let $K \geq 2, \theta_1, \ldots, \theta_K \in \Theta$,

Figure 6.10 A mixture.

and $\boldsymbol{\pi} = (\pi_1, \ldots, \pi_K) \in \Delta_K$. Suppose $Y \sim \text{Cat}(\boldsymbol{\pi})$ and that the conditional distributions satisfy

$$p_{\mathbf{X}|Y}(\mathbf{x}|i) = p_{\boldsymbol{\theta}_i}(\mathbf{x}).$$

We write this as $\mathbf{X}|\{Y = i\} \sim p_{\boldsymbol{\theta}_i}$. Then we obtain the mixture model

$$p_{\mathbf{X}}(\mathbf{x}) = \sum_{i=1}^{K} p_{\mathbf{X}|Y}(\mathbf{x}|i) \, p_Y(i) = \sum_{i=1}^{K} \pi_i p_{\boldsymbol{\theta}_i}(\mathbf{x}).$$

Example 6.4.1 *(Mixture of Multinomials)* Let $n, m, K \geq 1$, $\boldsymbol{\pi} \in \Delta_K$, and, for $i = 1, \ldots, K$, $\mathbf{p}_i = (p_{i1}, \ldots, p_{im}) \in \Delta_m$. Suppose that $Y \sim \text{Cat}(\boldsymbol{\pi})$ and that the conditional distributions are

$$\mathbf{X}|\{Y = i\} \sim \text{Mult}(n, \mathbf{p}_i).$$

Then $\mathbf{X}$ is a mixture of multinomials. Its distribution is then

$$p_{\mathbf{X}}(\mathbf{x}) = \sum_{i=1}^{K} \pi_i \frac{n!}{x_1! \cdots x_m!} \prod_{j=1}^{m} p_{ij}^{x_j}.$$

Next is an important continuous example.

Example 6.4.2 *(Gaussian Mixture Model)* For $i = 1, \ldots, K$, let $\boldsymbol{\mu}_i$ and $\boldsymbol{\Sigma}_i$ be the mean and covariance matrix of a multivariate Gaussian. Let $\boldsymbol{\pi} \in \Delta_K$. A Gaussian mixture model (GMM) is obtained as follows: Take $Y \sim \text{Cat}(\boldsymbol{\pi})$ and

$$\mathbf{X}|\{Y = i\} \sim N_d(\boldsymbol{\mu}_i, \boldsymbol{\Sigma}_i).$$

Its probability density function (PDF) takes the form

$$f_{\mathbf{X}}(\mathbf{x}) = \sum_{i=1}^{K} \pi_i \frac{1}{(2\pi)^{d/2} |\boldsymbol{\Sigma}_i|^{1/2}} \exp\left(-\frac{1}{2}(\mathbf{x} - \boldsymbol{\mu}_i)^T \boldsymbol{\Sigma}_i^{-1} (\mathbf{x} - \boldsymbol{\mu}_i)\right).$$

NUMERICAL CORNER We plot the density for means $\boldsymbol{\mu}_1 = (-2, -2)$ and $\boldsymbol{\mu}_2 = (2, 2)$ and covariance matrices

$$\boldsymbol{\Sigma}_1 = \begin{bmatrix} 1.0 & 0 \\ 0 & 1.0 \end{bmatrix} \quad \text{and} \quad \boldsymbol{\Sigma}_2 = \begin{bmatrix} \sigma_1^2 & \rho \sigma_1 \sigma_2 \\ \rho \sigma_1 \sigma_2 & \sigma_2^2 \end{bmatrix}$$

where $\sigma_1 = 1.5$, $\sigma_2 = 0.5$, and $\rho = -0.75$. The mixing weights are $\pi_1 = 0.25$ and $\pi_2 = 0.75$.

```
from scipy.stats import multivariate_normal

def gmm2_pdf(X, Y, mean1, cov1, pi1, mean2, cov2, pi2):
    xy = np.stack([X.flatten(), Y.flatten()], axis=-1)
    Z1 = multivariate_normal.pdf(
        xy, mean=mean1, cov=cov1).reshape(X.shape)
    Z2 = multivariate_normal.pdf(
```

```
        xy, mean=mean2, cov=cov2).reshape(X.shape)
    return pi1 * Z1 + pi2 * Z2
```

```
start_point = 6
stop_point = 6
num_samples = 100
points = np.linspace(-start_point, stop_point, num_samples)
X, Y = np.meshgrid(points, points)

mean1 = np.array([-2., -2.])
cov1 = np.array([[1., 0.], [0., 1.]])
pi1 = 0.5
mean2 = np.array([2., 2.])
cov2 = np.array([[1.5 ** 2., -0.75 * 1.5 * 0.5],
                 [-0.75 * 1.5 * 0.5, 0.5 ** 2.]])
pi2 = 0.5
Z = gmm2_pdf(X, Y, mean1, cov1, pi1, mean2, cov2, pi2)
mmids.make_surface_plot(X, Y, Z)
```

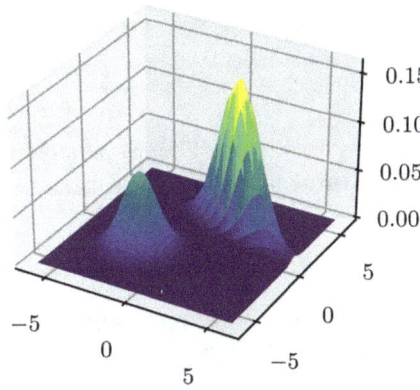

Figure 6.11 Graphical output of code.

◁ **NC**

In NumPy, as we have seen before, the module numpy.random also provides a way to sample from mixture models by using numpy.random.Generator.choice.

For instance, we consider mixtures of multivariate Gaussians. We change the notation slightly to track Python's indexing. For $i = 0, 1$, we have a mean $\mu_i \in \mathbb{R}^d$ and a positive definite covariance matrix $\Sigma_i \in \mathbb{R}^{d \times d}$. We also have mixture weights $\phi_0, \phi_1 \in (0, 1)$ such that $\phi_0 + \phi_1 = 1$. Suppose we want to generate a total of n samples.

For each sample $j = 1, \ldots, n$, independently from everything else:

1. We first pick a component $i \in \{0, 1\}$ at random according to the mixture weights; that is, $i = 0$ is chosen with probability ϕ_0 and $i = 1$ is chosen with probability ϕ_1.

2. We generate a sample $\mathbf{X}_j = (X_{j,1}, \ldots, X_{j,d})$ according to a multivariate Gaussian with mean μ_i and covariance Σ_i.

This is straightforward to implement by using again `numpy.random.Generator.choice` to choose the component of each sample and `numpy.random.Generator.multivariate_normal` to generate multivariate Gaussians. For convenience, we will stack the means and covariances into one array with a new dimension. So, for instance, the covariance matrices will now be in a 3d-array, that is, an array with three indices. The first index corresponds to the component (here 0 or 1).

The code is the following. It returns a d by n array X, where each row is a sample from a 2-component Gaussian mixture.

```python
def gmm2(rng, d, n, phi0, phi1, mu0, sigma0, mu1, sigma1):

    phi = np.stack((phi0, phi1))
    mu = np.stack((mu0, mu1))
    sigma = np.stack((sigma0,sigma1))

    X = np.zeros((n,d))
    component = rng.choice(2, size=n, p=phi)
    for i in range(n):
        X[i,:] = rng.multivariate_normal(
            mu[component[i],:],
            sigma[component[i],:,:])

    return X
```

NUMERICAL CORNER Let us try it with following parameters. We first define the covariance matrices and show what happens when they are stacked into a 3d-array (as is done within gmm2).

```python
d = 2
sigma0 = np.outer(np.array([2., 2.]), np.array([2., 2.]))
sigma0 += np.outer(np.array([-0.5, 0.5]), np.array([-0.5, 0.5]))
sigma1 = 2 * np.identity(d)
sigma = np.stack((sigma0,sigma1))
print(sigma[0,:,:])
```

```
[[4.25 3.75]
 [3.75 4.25]]
```

```python
print(sigma[1,:,:])
```

```
[[2. 0.]
 [0. 2.]]
```

Then we define the rest of the parameters.

```python
seed = 535
rng = np.random.default_rng(seed)
```

6.4 Marginalizing Out an Unobserved Variable

```
n, w = 200, 5.
phi0 = 0.8
phi1 = 0.2
mu0 = np.concatenate(([w], np.zeros(d-1)))
mu1 = np.concatenate(([-w], np.zeros(d-1)))
X = gmm2(rng, d, n, phi0, phi1, mu0, sigma0, mu1, sigma1)

plt.scatter(X[:,0], X[:,1], s=5, marker='o', c='k')
plt.axis('equal')
plt.show()
```

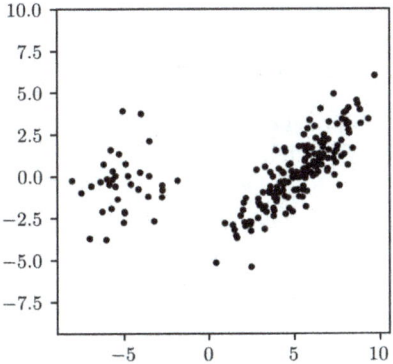

Figure 6.12 Graphical output of code.

◁ NC

6.4.2 Example: Mixtures of Multivariate Bernoullis and the EM Algorithm

Let $\mathcal{C} = \{1, \ldots, K\}$ be a collection of classes. Let C be a random variable taking values in $\mathcal{C}$ and, for $m = 1, \ldots, M$, let X_i take values in $\{0, 1\}$. Define $\pi_k = \mathbb{P}[C = k]$ and $p_{k,m} = \mathbb{P}[X_m = 1 | C = k]$ for $m = 1, \ldots, M$. We denote by $\mathbf{X} = (X_1, \ldots, X_M)$ the corresponding vector of X_i's and assume that the entries are conditionally independent given C.

However, we assume this time that C itself is *not observed*. So the resulting joint distribution is the mixture

$$\mathbb{P}[\mathbf{X} = \mathbf{x}] = \sum_{k=1}^{K} \mathbb{P}[C = k, \mathbf{X} = \mathbf{x}]$$

$$= \sum_{k=1}^{K} \mathbb{P}[\mathbf{X} = \mathbf{x} | C = k] \, \mathbb{P}[C = k]$$

$$= \sum_{k=1}^{K} \pi_k \prod_{m=1}^{M} p_{k,m}^{x_m} (1 - p_{k,m})^{1-x_m}.$$

Figure 6.13 Mixture of multivariate Bernoullis.

Graphically, this is the same are the naive Bayes model, except that C is not observed and therefore is not shaded. See Figure 6.13.

This type of model is useful in particular for clustering tasks, where the c_k's can be thought of as different clusters. Similarly to what we did in Section 6.3.3, our goal is to infer the parameters from samples and then predict the class of an old or new sample given its features. The main – substantial – difference is that the true labels of the samples are not observed. As we will see, that complicates the task considerably.

6.4.2.1 Model Fitting

We first fit the model from training data $\{\mathbf{x}_i\}_{i=1}^n$. Recall that the corresponding class labels c_i's are not observed. In this type of model, they are referred to as hidden or latent variables and we will come back to their inference below.

We would like to use maximum likelihood estimation; that is, maximize the probability of observing the data:

$$\mathcal{L}(\boldsymbol{\pi}, \{\mathbf{p}_k\}; \{\mathbf{x}_i\}) = \prod_{i=1}^n \left(\sum_{k=1}^K \pi_k \prod_{m=1}^M p_{k,m}^{x_{i,m}} (1 - p_{k,m})^{1-x_{i,m}} \right).$$

As usual, we assume that the samples are independent and identically distributed. Consider the negative log-likelihood (NLL)

$$L_n(\boldsymbol{\pi}, \{\mathbf{p}_k\}; \{\mathbf{x}_i\}) = -\sum_{i=1}^n \log \left(\sum_{k=1}^K \pi_k \prod_{m=1}^M p_{k,m}^{x_{i,m}} (1 - p_{k,m})^{1-x_{i,m}} \right).$$

Already, we see that things are potentially more difficult than they were in the supervised (or fully observed) case. The NLL does not decompose into a sum of terms depending on different sets of parameters.

At this point, one could fall back on the field of optimization and use a gradient-based method to minimize the NLL. Indeed that is an option, although note that one must be careful to account for the constrained nature of the problem (i.e., the parameters sum to one). There is a vast array of constrained optimization techniques suited for this task.

Instead a more popular approach in this context, the EM algorithm, is based on the general principle of majorization-minimization, which we have encountered implicitly in the k-means algorithm and the convergence proof of gradient descent in the smooth case. We detail this important principle next, before returning to model fitting in mixtures.

6.4.2.2 Majorization-Minimization

Here is a deceptively simple, yet powerful observation. Suppose we want to minimize a function $f: \mathbb{R}^d \to \mathbb{R}$. Finding a local minimum of f may not be easy. But imagine that

6.4 Marginalizing Out an Unobserved Variable

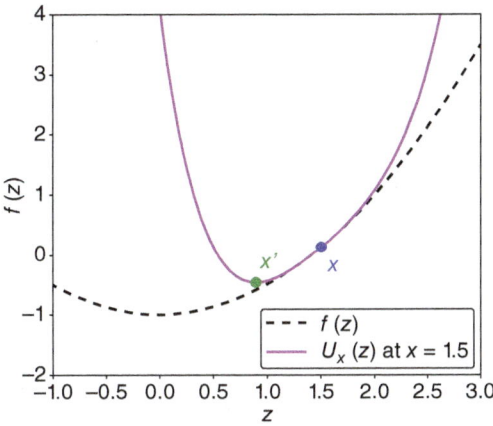

Figure 6.14 A majorizing function.

for each $\mathbf{x} \in \mathbb{R}^d$ we have a surrogate function $U_\mathbf{x} \colon \mathbb{R}^d \to \mathbb{R}$ that (1) dominates f in the following sense:

$$U_\mathbf{x}(\mathbf{z}) \geq f(\mathbf{z}), \quad \forall \mathbf{z} \in \mathbb{R}^d$$

and (2) equals f at $\mathbf{x}$:

$$U_\mathbf{x}(\mathbf{x}) = f(\mathbf{x}).$$

We say that $U_\mathbf{x}$ majorizes f at $\mathbf{x}$. Then we prove in the next lemma that $U_\mathbf{x}$ can be used to make progress toward minimizing f, that is, find a point $\mathbf{x}'$ such that $f(\mathbf{x}') \leq f(\mathbf{x})$. If in addition $U_\mathbf{x}$ is easier to minimize than f itself, say because an explicit minimum can be computed, then this observation naturally leads to an iterative algorithm. See Figure 6.14.

Lemma 6.4.3 *(Majorization-Minimization)* Let $f \colon \mathbb{R}^d \to \mathbb{R}$ and suppose $U_\mathbf{x}$ majorizes f at $\mathbf{x}$. Let $\mathbf{x}'$ be a global minimum of $U_\mathbf{x}$. Then

$$f(\mathbf{x}') \leq f(\mathbf{x}).$$

Proof Indeed

$$f(\mathbf{x}') \leq U_\mathbf{x}(\mathbf{x}') \leq U_\mathbf{x}(\mathbf{x}) = f(\mathbf{x}),$$

where the first inequality follows from the domination property of $U_\mathbf{x}$, the second inequality follows from the fact that $\mathbf{x}'$ is a global minimum of $U_\mathbf{x}$ and the equality follows from the fact that $U_\mathbf{x}$ equals f at $\mathbf{x}$. □

We have already encountered this idea.

Example 6.4.4 *(Minimizing a Smooth Function)* Let $f \colon \mathbb{R}^d \to \mathbb{R}$ be L-smooth. By the Quadratic Bound for Smooth Functions Lemma, for all $\mathbf{x}, \mathbf{z} \in \mathbb{R}^d$ it holds that

$$f(\mathbf{z}) \leq U_\mathbf{x}(\mathbf{z}) := f(\mathbf{x}) + \nabla f(\mathbf{x})^T(\mathbf{z} - \mathbf{x}) + \frac{L}{2}\|\mathbf{z} - \mathbf{x}\|^2.$$

By showing that $U_\mathbf{x}$ is minimized at $\mathbf{z} = \mathbf{x} - (1/L)\nabla f(\mathbf{x})$, we previously obtained the descent guarantee

$$f(\mathbf{x} - (1/L)\nabla f(\mathbf{x})) \leq f(\mathbf{x}) - \frac{1}{2L}\|\nabla f(\mathbf{x})\|^2$$

for gradient descent, which played a central role in the analysis of its convergence.

Example 6.4.5 *(k-Means)* Let $\mathbf{x}_1, \ldots, \mathbf{x}_n$ be n vectors in $\mathbb{R}^d$. One way to formulate the k-means clustering problem is as the minimization of

$$f(\boldsymbol{\mu}_1, \ldots, \boldsymbol{\mu}_K) = \sum_{i=1}^n \min_{j \in [K]} \|\mathbf{x}_i - \boldsymbol{\mu}_j\|^2$$

over the centers $\boldsymbol{\mu}_1, \ldots, \boldsymbol{\mu}_K$, where recall that $[K] = \{1, \ldots, K\}$. For fixed $\boldsymbol{\mu}_1, \ldots, \boldsymbol{\mu}_K$ and $\mathbf{m} = (\boldsymbol{\mu}_1, \ldots, \boldsymbol{\mu}_K)$, define

$$c_{\mathbf{m}}(i) \in \arg\min \left\{ \|\mathbf{x}_i - \boldsymbol{\mu}_j\|^2 : j \in [K] \right\}, \quad i = 1, \ldots, n$$

and

$$U_{\mathbf{m}}(\boldsymbol{\lambda}_1, \ldots, \boldsymbol{\lambda}_K) = \sum_{i=1}^n \|\mathbf{x}_i - \boldsymbol{\lambda}_{c_{\mathbf{m}}(i)}\|^2$$

for $\boldsymbol{\lambda}_1, \ldots, \boldsymbol{\lambda}_K \in \mathbb{R}^d$. That is, we fix the optimal cluster assignments under $\boldsymbol{\mu}_1, \ldots, \boldsymbol{\mu}_K$ and then vary the centers.

We claim that $U_{\mathbf{m}}$ is majorizing f at $\boldsymbol{\mu}_1, \ldots, \boldsymbol{\mu}_K$. Indeed

$$f(\boldsymbol{\lambda}_1, \ldots, \boldsymbol{\lambda}_K) = \sum_{i=1}^n \min_{j \in [K]} \|\mathbf{x}_i - \boldsymbol{\lambda}_j\|^2 \le \sum_{i=1}^n \|\mathbf{x}_i - \boldsymbol{\lambda}_{c_{\mathbf{m}}(i)}\|^2 = U_{\mathbf{m}}(\boldsymbol{\lambda}_1, \ldots, \boldsymbol{\lambda}_K)$$

and

$$f(\boldsymbol{\mu}_1, \ldots, \boldsymbol{\mu}_K) = \sum_{i=1}^n \min_{j \in [K]} \|\mathbf{x}_i - \boldsymbol{\mu}_j\|^2 = \sum_{i=1}^n \|\mathbf{x}_i - \boldsymbol{\mu}_{c_{\mathbf{m}}(i)}\|^2 = U_{\mathbf{m}}(\boldsymbol{\mu}_1, \ldots, \boldsymbol{\mu}_K).$$

Moreover $U_{\mathbf{m}}(\boldsymbol{\lambda}_1, \ldots, \boldsymbol{\lambda}_K)$ is easy to minimize. We showed previously that the optimal representatives are

$$\boldsymbol{\mu}'_j = \frac{1}{|C_j|} \sum_{i \in C_j} \mathbf{x}_i$$

where $C_j = \{i : c_{\mathbf{m}}(i) = j\}$.

The Majorization-Minimization Lemma *implies that*

$$f(\boldsymbol{\mu}'_1, \ldots, \boldsymbol{\mu}'_K) \le f(\boldsymbol{\mu}_1, \ldots, \boldsymbol{\mu}_K).$$

This argument is equivalent to our previous analysis of the k-means algorithm.

CHAT & LEARN The mixture of multivariate Bernoullis model assumes a fixed number of clusters. Ask your favorite AI chatbot to discuss Bayesian nonparametric extensions of this model, such as the Dirichlet process mixture model, which can automatically infer the number of clusters from the data.

6.4.2.3 EM algorithm

The Expectation-Maximization (EM) algorithm is an instantiation of the majorization-minimization principle that applies widely to parameter estimation of mixtures. Here we focus on the mixture of multivariate Bernoullis.

Recall that the objective to be minimized is

$$L_n(\boldsymbol{\pi}, \{\mathbf{p}_k\}; \{\mathbf{x}_i\}) = -\sum_{i=1}^n \log \left(\sum_{k=1}^K \pi_k \prod_{m=1}^M p_{k,m}^{x_{i,m}} (1 - p_{k,m})^{1-x_{i,m}} \right).$$

To simplify the notation and highlight the general idea, we let $\theta = (\boldsymbol{\pi}, \{\mathbf{p}_k\})$, denote by Θ the set of allowed values for θ, and use $\mathbb{P}_\theta$ to indicate that probabilities are computed under the parameters θ. We also return to the description of the model in terms of the unobserved latent variables $\{C_i\}$. That is, we write the NLL as

$$L_n(\theta) = -\sum_{i=1}^n \log\left(\sum_{k=1}^K \mathbb{P}_\theta[\mathbf{X}_i = \mathbf{x}_i | C_i = k]\,\mathbb{P}_\theta[C_i = k]\right)$$

$$= -\sum_{i=1}^n \log\left(\sum_{k=1}^K \mathbb{P}_\theta[\mathbf{X}_i = \mathbf{x}_i, C_i = k]\right).$$

To derive a majorizing function, we use the convexity of the negative logarithm. Indeed

$$\frac{\partial}{\partial z}[-\log z] = -\frac{1}{z} \quad \text{and} \quad \frac{\partial^2}{\partial^2 z}[-\log z] = \frac{1}{z^2} > 0, \quad \forall z > 0.$$

The first step of the construction is not obvious – it just works. For each $i = 1, \ldots, n$, we let $r^\theta_{k,i}$, $k = 1, \ldots, K$, be a strictly positive probability distribution over $[K]$. In other words, it defines a convex combination for every i. Then we use convexity to obtain the upper bound

$$L_n(\tilde{\theta}) = -\sum_{i=1}^n \log\left(\sum_{k=1}^K r^\theta_{k,i} \frac{\mathbb{P}_{\tilde{\theta}}[\mathbf{X}_i = \mathbf{x}_i, C_i = k]}{r^\theta_{k,i}}\right)$$

$$\leq -\sum_{i=1}^n \sum_{k=1}^K r^\theta_{k,i} \log\left(\frac{\mathbb{P}_{\tilde{\theta}}[\mathbf{X}_i = \mathbf{x}_i, C_i = k]}{r^\theta_{k,i}}\right),$$

which holds for any $\tilde{\theta} = (\tilde{\boldsymbol{\pi}}, \{\tilde{\mathbf{p}}_k\}) \in \Theta$.

We choose

$$r^\theta_{k,i} = \mathbb{P}_\theta[C_i = k | \mathbf{X}_i = \mathbf{x}_i]$$

(which for the time being we assume is strictly positive) and we denote the right-hand side of the inequality by $Q_n(\tilde{\theta}|\theta)$ (as a function of $\tilde{\theta}$).

We make two observations.

1. *Dominating property*: For any $\tilde{\theta} \in \Theta$, the inequality above implies immediately that $L_n(\tilde{\theta}) \leq Q_n(\tilde{\theta}|\theta)$.

2. *Equality at θ*: At $\tilde{\theta} = \theta$,

$$Q_n(\theta|\theta) = -\sum_{i=1}^n \sum_{k=1}^K r^\theta_{k,i} \log\left(\frac{\mathbb{P}_\theta[\mathbf{X}_i = \mathbf{x}_i, C_i = k]}{r^\theta_{k,i}}\right)$$

$$= -\sum_{i=1}^n \sum_{k=1}^K r^\theta_{k,i} \log\left(\frac{\mathbb{P}_\theta[C_i = k | \mathbf{X}_i = \mathbf{x}_i]\mathbb{P}_\theta[\mathbf{X}_i = \mathbf{x}_i]}{r^\theta_{k,i}}\right)$$

$$= -\sum_{i=1}^n \sum_{k=1}^K r^\theta_{k,i} \log \mathbb{P}_\theta[\mathbf{X}_i = \mathbf{x}_i]$$

$$= -\sum_{i=1}^n \log \mathbb{P}_\theta[\mathbf{X}_i = \mathbf{x}_i]$$

$$= L_n(\theta).$$

The two properties above show that $Q_n(\tilde{\theta}|\theta)$, as a function of $\tilde{\theta}$, majorizes L_n at θ.

Lemma 6.4.6 *(EM Guarantee) Let θ^* be a global minimizer of $Q_n(\tilde{\theta}|\theta)$ as a function of $\tilde{\theta}$, provided it exists. Then*

$$L_n(\theta^*) \leq L_n(\theta).$$

Proof The result follows directly from the *Majorization-Minimization Lemma*. □

What have we gained from this? As we mentioned before, using the *Majorization-Minimization Lemma* makes sense if Q_n is easier to minimize than L_n itself. Let us see why that is the case here.

E Step: The function Q_n naturally decomposes into two terms:

$$Q_n(\tilde{\theta}|\theta) = -\sum_{i=1}^{n}\sum_{k=1}^{K} r_{k,i}^{\theta} \log\left(\frac{\mathbb{P}_{\tilde{\theta}}[\mathbf{X}_i = \mathbf{x}_i, C_i = k]}{r_{k,i}^{\theta}}\right)$$

$$= -\sum_{i=1}^{n}\sum_{k=1}^{K} r_{k,i}^{\theta} \log \mathbb{P}_{\tilde{\theta}}[\mathbf{X}_i = \mathbf{x}_i, C_i = k] + \sum_{i=1}^{n}\sum_{k=1}^{K} r_{k,i}^{\theta} \log r_{k,i}^{\theta}.$$

Because $r_{k,i}^{\theta}$ depends on θ but not $\tilde{\theta}$, the second term is irrelevant to the opimization with respect to $\tilde{\theta}$.

The first term above can be written as

$$-\sum_{i=1}^{n}\sum_{k=1}^{K} r_{k,i}^{\theta} \log \mathbb{P}_{\tilde{\theta}}[\mathbf{X}_i = \mathbf{x}_i, C_i = k]$$

$$= -\sum_{i=1}^{n}\sum_{k=1}^{K} r_{k,i}^{\theta} \log \left(\tilde{\pi}_k \prod_{m=1}^{M} \tilde{p}_{k,m}^{x_{i,m}} (1 - \tilde{p}_{k,m})^{1-x_{i,m}}\right)$$

$$= -\sum_{k=1}^{K} \eta_k^{\theta} \log \tilde{\pi}_k - \sum_{k=1}^{K}\sum_{m=1}^{M} [\eta_{k,m}^{\theta} \log \tilde{p}_{k,m} + (\eta_k^{\theta} - \eta_{k,m}^{\theta}) \log(1 - \tilde{p}_{k,m})],$$

where we defined, for $k = 1, \ldots, K$,

$$\eta_{k,m}^{\theta} = \sum_{i=1}^{n} x_{i,m} r_{k,i}^{\theta} \quad \text{and} \quad \eta_k^{\theta} = \sum_{i=1}^{n} r_{k,i}^{\theta}.$$

Here comes the key observation: This last expression is essentially the same as the NLL for the fully observed naive Bayes model, except that the terms $\mathbf{1}_{\{c_i=k\}}$ are replaced by $r_{k,i}^{\theta}$. If θ is our current estimate of the parameters, then the quantity $r_{k,i}^{\theta} = \mathbb{P}_{\theta}[C_i = k | \mathbf{X}_i = \mathbf{x}_i]$ is our estimate – under the current parameter θ – of the probability that the sample $\mathbf{x}_i$ comes from cluster k. We have previously computed $r_{k,i}^{\theta}$ for prediction under the naive Bayes model. We showed there that

$$r_{k,i}^{\theta} = \frac{\pi_k \prod_{m=1}^{M} p_{k,m}^{x_{i,m}} (1 - p_{k,m})^{1-x_{i,m}}}{\sum_{k'=1}^{K} \pi_{k'} \prod_{m=1}^{M} p_{k',m}^{x_{i,m}} (1 - p_{k',m})^{1-x_{i,m}}},$$

which in this new context is referred to as the responsibility that cluster k takes for data point i. So we can interpret the expression above as follows: The variables $\mathbf{1}_{\{c_i=k\}}$ are not observed here, but we have estimated their conditional probability distribution given the observed data $\{\mathbf{x}_i\}$, and we are taking an expectation with respect to that distribution instead.

The "E" in E Step (and EM) stands for "expectation," which refers to using a surrogate function that is essentially an expected NLL.

6.4 Marginalizing Out an Unobserved Variable

M Step: In any case, from a practical point of view, minimizing $Q_n(\tilde{\theta}|\theta)$ over $\tilde{\theta}$ turns out to be a variant of fitting a naive Bayes model – and the upshot to all this is that there is a straightforward formula for that! Recall that this happens because the NLL in the naive Bayes model decomposes: It naturally breaks up into terms that depend on separate sets of parameters, each of which can be optimized with a closed-form expression. The same happens with Q_n as should be clear from the derivation.

Adapting our previous calculations for fitting a naive Bayes model, we get that $Q_n(\tilde{\theta}|\theta)$ is minimized at

$$\pi_k^* = \frac{\eta_k^\theta}{n} \quad \text{and} \quad p_{k,m}^* = \frac{\eta_{k,m}^\theta}{\eta_k^\theta} \quad \forall k \in [K], m \in [M].$$

We used the fact that

$$\sum_{k=1}^{K} \eta_k^\theta = \sum_{k=1}^{K} \sum_{i=1}^{n} r_{k,i}^\theta$$

$$= \sum_{i=1}^{n} \sum_{k=1}^{K} \mathbb{P}_\theta[C_i = k | \mathbf{X}_i = \mathbf{x}_i]$$

$$= \sum_{i=1}^{n} 1$$

$$= n,$$

since the conditional probability $\mathbb{P}_\theta[C_i = k | \mathbf{X}_i = \mathbf{x}_i]$ adds up to one when summed over k.

The "M" in M Step (and EM) stands for maximization, which here turns into minimization because of the use of the NLL.

To summarize, the EM algorithm works as follows in this case. Assume we have data points $\{\mathbf{x}_i\}_{i=1}^n$, that we have fixed K, and that we have some initial parameter estimate $\theta^0 = (\boldsymbol{\pi}^0, \{\mathbf{p}_k^0\}) \in \Theta$ with strictly positive π_k^0's and $p_{k,m}^0$'s. For $t = 0, 1, \ldots, T-1$ we compute for all $i \in [n]$, $k \in [K]$, and $m \in [M]$

$$r_{k,i}^t = \frac{\pi_k^t \prod_{m=1}^{M}(p_{k,m}^t)^{x_{i,m}}(1-p_{k,m}^t)^{1-x_{i,m}}}{\sum_{k'=1}^{K} \pi_{k'}^t \prod_{m=1}^{M}(p_{k',m}^t)^{x_{i,m}}(1-p_{k',m}^t)^{1-x_{i,m}}}, \quad \text{(E Step)}$$

$$\eta_{k,m}^t = \sum_{i=1}^{n} x_{i,m} r_{k,i}^t \quad \text{and} \quad \eta_k^t = \sum_{i=1}^{n} r_{k,i}^t,$$

and

$$\pi_k^{t+1} = \frac{\eta_k^t}{n} \quad \text{and} \quad p_{k,m}^{t+1} = \frac{\eta_{k,m}^t}{\eta_k^t}. \quad \text{(M Step)}$$

Provided $\sum_{i=1}^{n} x_{i,m} > 0$ for all m, the $\eta_{k,m}^t$'s and η_k^t's remain positive for all t and the algorithm is well-defined. The *EM Guarantee* Lemma stipulates that the NLL cannot deteriorate, although note that it does not guarantee convergence to a global minimum.

We implement the EM algorithm for mixtures of multivariate Bernoullis. For this purpose, we adapt our previous naive Bayes routines. We also allow for the possibility of using Laplace smoothing.

```python
def responsibility(pi_k, p_km, x):

    K = len(pi_k)
    score_k = np.zeros(K)
    for k in range(K):

        score_k[k] -= np.log(pi_k[k])
        score_k[k] -= np.sum(x * np.log(p_km[k,:])
                            + (1 - x) * np.log(1 - p_km[k,:]))
    r_k = np.exp(-score_k)/(np.sum(np.exp(-score_k)))

    return r_k

def update_parameters(eta_km, eta_k, eta, alpha, beta):

    K = len(eta_k)
    pi_k = (eta_k+alpha) / (eta+K*alpha)
    p_km = (eta_km+beta) / (eta_k[:,np.newaxis]+2*beta)

    return pi_k, p_km
```

We implement the E and M Step next.

```python
def em_bern(X, K, pi_0, p_0, maxiters = 10, alpha=0., beta=0.):

    n, M = X.shape
    pi_k = pi_0
    p_km = p_0

    for _ in range(maxiters):

        # E Step
        r_ki = np.zeros((K,n))
        for i in range(n):
            r_ki[:,i] = responsibility(pi_k, p_km, X[i,:])

        # M Step
        eta_km = np.zeros((K,M))
        eta_k = np.sum(r_ki, axis=-1)
        eta = np.sum(eta_k)
        for k in range(K):
            for m in range(M):
                eta_km[k,m] = np.sum(X[:,m] * r_ki[k,:])
        pi_k, p_km = update_parameters(
```

```
            eta_km, eta_k, eta, alpha, beta)

    return pi_k, p_km
```

NUMERICAL CORNER We test the algorithm on a very simple dataset.

```
X = np.array([[1., 1., 1.],[1., 1., 1.],[1., 1., 1.],[1., 0., 1.],
              [0., 1., 1.],[0., 0., 0.],[0., 0., 0.],[0., 0., 1.]])
n, M = X.shape
K = 2
pi_0 = np.ones(K)/K
p_0 = rng.random((K,M))

pi_k, p_km = em_bern(
    X, K, pi_0, p_0, maxiters=100, alpha=0.01, beta=0.01)

print(pi_k)
```

```
[0.66500949 0.33499051]
```

```
print(p_km)
```

```
[[0.74982646 0.74982646 0.99800266]
 [0.00496739 0.00496739 0.25487292]]
```

We compute the probability that the vector $(0, 0, 1)$ is in each cluster.

```
x_test = np.array([0., 0., 1.])
print(responsibility(pi_k, p_km, x_test))
```

```
[0.32947702 0.67052298]
```

CHAT & LEARN The EM algorithm can sometimes get stuck in local optima. Ask your favorite AI chatbot to discuss strategies for initializing the EM algorithm to avoid this issue, such as using multiple random restarts or using the *k*-means algorithm for initialization.

◁ NC

6.4.3 Clustering Handwritten Digits

To give a more involved example, we use the MNIST dataset.
Quoting Wikipedia[7] again:

> The MNIST database (Modified National Institute of Standards and Technology database) is a large database of handwritten digits that is commonly used for training various image processing systems. The database is also widely used for training and testing in the field of

---
[7] https://en.wikipedia.org/wiki/MNIST_database

machine learning. It was created by "re-mixing" the samples from NIST's original datasets. The creators felt that since NIST's training dataset was taken from American Census Bureau employees, while the testing dataset was taken from American high school students, it was not well-suited for machine learning experiments. Furthermore, the black and white images from NIST were normalized to fit into a 28x28 pixel bounding box and anti-aliased, which introduced grayscale levels. The MNIST database contains 60,000 training images and 10,000 testing images. Half of the training set and half of the test set were taken from NIST's training dataset, while the other half of the training set and the other half of the test set were taken from NIST's testing dataset.

NUMERICAL CORNER We load it from PyTorch. The data can be accessed with `torchvision.datasets.MNIST`.[8] The `squeeze` command below removes the color dimension in the image, which is grayscale. The `numpy` command converts the PyTorch tensors into NumPy arrays. See `torch.utils.data.DataLoader`[9] for details on the data loading. We will say more about PyTorch in Chapter 8.

```
from torchvision import datasets, transforms
from torch.utils.data import DataLoader

mnist = datasets.MNIST(root='./data', train=True,
                       download=True, transform=transforms.
                       ToTensor())
train_loader = DataLoader(mnist, batch_size=len(mnist),
                          shuffle=False)

imgs, labels = next(iter(train_loader))
imgs = imgs.squeeze().numpy()
labels = labels.numpy()
```

We turn the grayscale images into black-and-white images by rounding the pixels:

```
imgs = np.round(imgs)
```

There are two common ways to write a 2. Let's see if a mixture of multivariate Bernoullis can find them. We extract the images labelled 2.

```
mask = labels == 2
imgs2 = imgs[mask]
labels2 = labels[mask]
```

---

[8] https://pytorch.org/vision/stable/generated/torchvision.datasets.MNIST.html
[9] https://pytorch.org/docs/stable/data.html#torch.utils.data.DataLoader

The first image is the following.

```
plt.imshow(imgs2[0], cmap='gray_r')
plt.show()
```

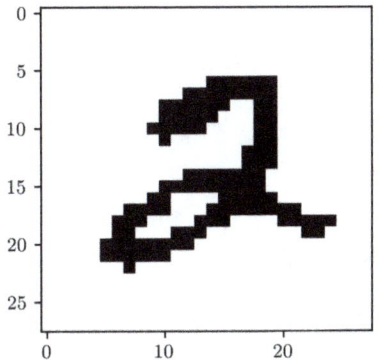

Figure 6.15 Graphical output of code.

Next, we transform the images into vectors.

```
X = imgs2.reshape(len(imgs2), -1)
```

We run the algorithm with two clusters.

```
n, M = X.shape
K = 2
pi_0 = np.ones(K)/K
p_0 = rng.random((K,M))

pi_k, p_km = em_bern(
    X, K, pi_0, p_0, maxiters=10, alpha=1., beta=1.)

print(pi_k)
```

[nan nan]

Something went wrong. We encountered a numerical issue, underflow, which we discussed briefly previously. To confirm this, we run the code again but ask Python to warn us about it using `numpy.seterr`. (By default, warnings are turned off in the book, but they can be reactivated using `warnings.resetwarnings`.)

```
warnings.resetwarnings()
old_settings = np.seterr(all='warn')

pi_k, p_km = em_bern(
    X, K, pi_0, p_0, maxiters=10, alpha=1., beta=1.)
```

```
/var/folders/k0/7k0fxl7j54q4k8dyqnrc6sz00000gr/T/ipykernel_74869/
  2844323350.py:1
0: RuntimeWarning: underflow encountered in exp
  r_k = np.exp(-score_k)/(np.sum(np.exp(-score_k)))
/var/folders/k0/7k0fxl7j54q4k8dyqnrc6sz00000gr/T/ipykernel_74869/
  2844323350.py:1
0: RuntimeWarning: invalid value encountered in divide
  r_k = np.exp(-score_k)/(np.sum(np.exp(-score_k)))
```

◁ **NC**

When we compute the responsibilities

$$r_{k,i}^t = \frac{\pi_k^t \prod_{m=1}^M (p_{k,m}^t)^{x_{i,m}} (1 - p_{k,m}^t)^{1-x_{i,m}}}{\sum_{k'=1}^K \pi_{k'}^t \prod_{m=1}^M (p_{k',m}^t)^{x_{i,m}} (1 - p_{k',m}^t)^{1-x_{i,m}}},$$

we first compute the negative logarithm of each term in the numerator as we did in the naive Bayes case. But then we apply the function e^{-x}, because this time we are not simply computing an optimal score. When all scores are high, this last step may result in underflow; that is, it produces numbers so small that they get rounded down to zero by NumPy. Then the ratio defining r_k is not well-defined.

To deal with this, we introduce a technique called the log-sum-exp trick. Consider the computation of a function of $\mathbf{a} = (a_1, \ldots, a_n)$ of the form

$$h(\mathbf{a}) = \log\left(\sum_{i=1}^n e^{-a_i}\right).$$

When the a_i values are large positive numbers, the terms e^{-a_i} can be so small that they underflow to zero. To counter this, the log-sum-exp trick involves a shift to bring these terms into a more favorable numerical range.

It proceeds as follows:

1. Identify the minimum value M among the a_i's:

$$M = \min\{a_1, a_2, \ldots, a_n\}.$$

2. Subtract M from each a_i before exponentiation:

$$\log\left(\sum_{i=1}^n e^{-a_i}\right) = \log\left(e^{-M} \sum_{i=1}^n e^{-(a_i - M)}\right).$$

3. Rewrite using log properties:

$$= -M + \log\left(\sum_{i=1}^n e^{-(a_i - M)}\right).$$

Why does this help with underflow? By subtracting M, the smallest value in the set, from each a_i, (i) the largest term in $\{e^{-(a_i-M)} : i = 1, \ldots, n\}$ becomes $e^0 = 1$; and (ii) all other terms are between 0 and 1, as they are exponentiations of negative numbers or zero. This manipulation avoids terms underflowing to zero because even very large values, when shifted by M, are less likely to hit the underflow threshold.

Here is an example. Imagine you have $\mathbf{a} = (1000, 1001, 1002)$.

- Direct computation: e^{-1000}, e^{-1001}, and e^{-1002} might all underflow to zero.
- With the log-sum-exp trick: Subtract $M = 1000$, leading to e^0, e^{-1}, and e^{-2}, all meaningful, nonzero results that accurately contribute to the sum.

We implement in NumPy.

```
def log_sum_exp_trick(a):
    min_val = np.min(a)
    return - min_val + np.log(np.sum(np.exp(- a + min_val)))
```

NUMERICAL CORNER We try it on a simple example.

```
a = np.array([1000, 1001, 1002])
```

We first attempt a direct computation.

```
np.log(np.sum(np.exp(-a)))
```

```
/var/folders/k0/7k0fxl7j54q4k8dyqnrc6sz00000gr/T/ipykernel_74869/
    214275762.py:1:
RuntimeWarning: underflow encountered in exp
    np.log(np.sum(np.exp(-a)))
/var/folders/k0/7k0fxl7j54q4k8dyqnrc6sz00000gr/T/ipykernel_74869/
    214275762.py:1:
RuntimeWarning: divide by zero encountered in log
    np.log(np.sum(np.exp(-a)))
```

```
-inf
```

Predictably, we get an underflow error and a useless output.

Next, we try the log-sum-exp trick.

```
log_sum_exp_trick(a)
```

```
-999.5923940355556
```

This time we get an output which seems reasonable, something slightly larger than -1000 as expected (why?).

◁ **NC**

After this long – but important! – parenthesis, we return to the EM algorithm. We modify it by implementing the log-sum-exp trick in the subroutine `responsibility`.

```
def responsibility(pi_k, p_km, x):

    K = len(pi_k)
    score_k = np.zeros(K)
    for k in range(K):

        score_k[k] -= np.log(pi_k[k])
        score_k[k] -= np.sum(x * np.log(p_km[k,:])
                            + (1 - x) * np.log(1 - p_km[k,:]))
    r_k = np.exp(-score_k - log_sum_exp_trick(score_k))

    return r_k
```

NUMERICAL CORNER We go back to the MNIST example with only the 2s.

```
pi_k, p_km = em_bern(X, K, pi_0, p_0, maxiters=10, alpha=1., beta=1.)
```

Here are the parameters of one cluster.

```
plt.figure()
plt.imshow(p_km[0,:].reshape((28,28)))
plt.show()
```

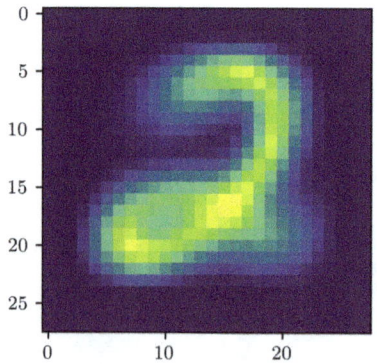

Figure 6.16 Graphical output of code.

Here is the other one.

```
plt.figure()
plt.imshow(p_km[1,:].reshape((28,28)))
plt.show()
```

6.4 Marginalizing Out an Unobserved Variable

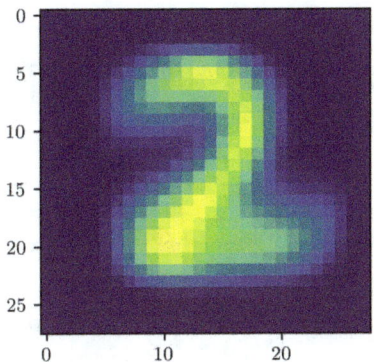

Figure 6.17 Graphical output of code.

Now that the model is trained, we compute the probability that an example image is in each cluster. We use the first image in the dataset that we plotted earlier.

```
responsibility(pi_k, p_km, X[0,:])
```

```
array([1.00000000e+00, 5.09357087e-17])
```

It indeed identifies the second cluster as significantly more likely.

TRY IT! In the MNIST example, as we have seen, the probabilities involved are extremely small and the responsibilities are close to 0 or 1. Implement a variant of EM, called hard EM, which replaces responsibilities with the one-hot encoding of the largest responsibility. ***Test it on the MNIST example*** again.

◁ NC

CHAT & LEARN The mixture of multivariate Bernoullis model is a simple example of a latent variable model. Ask your favorite AI chatbot to discuss more complex latent variable models, such as the variational autoencoder or the Gaussian process latent variable model, and their applications in unsupervised learning.

> *Self-Assessment Quiz (with help from Claude, Gemini, and ChatGPT)*
>
> 1 In the mixture of multivariate Bernoullis model, the joint distribution is given by:
>   a) $P[\mathbf{X} = \mathbf{x}] = \prod_{k=1}^{K} P[C = k, \mathbf{X} = \mathbf{x}]$
>   b) $P[\mathbf{X} = \mathbf{x}] = \sum_{k=1}^{K} P[\mathbf{X} = \mathbf{x} | C = k] P[C = k]$
>   c) $P[\mathbf{X} = \mathbf{x}] = \prod_{k=1}^{K} P[\mathbf{X} = \mathbf{x} | C = k] P[C = k]$
>   d) $P[\mathbf{X} = \mathbf{x}] = \sum_{\mathbf{x}} P[C = k, \mathbf{X} = \mathbf{x}]$
>
> 2 The majorization-minimization principle states that:
>   a) If $U_{\mathbf{x}}$ majorizes f at $\mathbf{x}$, then a global minimum $\mathbf{x}'$ of $U_{\mathbf{x}}$ satisfies $f(\mathbf{x}') \geq f(\mathbf{x})$.
>   b) If $U_{\mathbf{x}}$ majorizes f at $\mathbf{x}$, then a global minimum $\mathbf{x}'$ of $U_{\mathbf{x}}$ satisfies $f(\mathbf{x}') \leq f(\mathbf{x})$.

c) If $U_{\mathbf{x}}$ minorizes f at $\mathbf{x}$, then a global minimum $\mathbf{x}'$ of $U_{\mathbf{x}}$ satisfies $f(\mathbf{x}') \geq f(\mathbf{x})$.

d) If $U_{\mathbf{x}}$ minorizes f at $\mathbf{x}$, then a global minimum $\mathbf{x}'$ of $U_{\mathbf{x}}$ satisfies $f(\mathbf{x}') \leq f(\mathbf{x})$.

3. In the EM algorithm for mixtures of multivariate Bernoullis, the M-step involves:
    a) Updating the parameters π_k and $p_{k,m}$
    b) Computing the responsibilities $r_{k,i}^t$
    c) Minimizing the negative log-likelihood
    d) Applying the log-sum-exp trick

4. The mixture of multivariate Bernoullis model is represented by the following graphical model:

    a)
    ```
    G = nx.DiGraph()
    G.add_node("X", shape="circle", style="filled", fillcolor="gray")
    G.add_node("C", shape="circle", style="filled", fillcolor="white")
    G.add_edge("C", "X")
    ```

    b)
    ```
    G = nx.DiGraph()
    G.add_node("X", shape="circle", style="filled", fillcolor="white")
    G.add_node("C", shape="circle", style="filled", fillcolor="gray")
    G.add_edge("C", "X")
    ```

    c)
    ```
    G = nx.DiGraph()
    G.add_node("X", shape="circle", style="filled", fillcolor="gray")
    G.add_node("C", shape="circle", style="filled", fillcolor="gray")
    G.add_edge("C", "X")
    ```

    d)
    ```
    G = nx.DiGraph()
    G.add_node("X", shape="circle", style="filled", fillcolor="white")
    G.add_node("C", shape="circle", style="filled", fillcolor="white")
    G.add_edge("C", "X")
    ```

5. In the context of clustering, what is the interpretation of the responsibilities computed in the E-step of the EM algorithm?
    a) They represent the distance of each data point to the cluster centers.
    b) They indicate the probability of each data point belonging to each cluster.
    c) They determine the optimal number of clusters.
    d) They are used to initialize the cluster centers in the M-step.

Answer for 1: b. Justification: The text states, "$P[\mathbf{X} = \mathbf{x}] = \sum_{k=1}^{K} P[C = k, \mathbf{X} = \mathbf{x}] = \sum_{k=1}^{K} P[\mathbf{X} = \mathbf{x}|C = k]P[C = k]$."

Answer for 2: b. Justification: "Let $f: \mathbb{R}^d \to \mathbb{R}$ and suppose $U_\mathbf{x}$ majorizes f at $\mathbf{x}$. Let $\mathbf{x}'$ be a global minimizer of $U_\mathbf{x}(\mathbf{z})$ as a function of $\mathbf{z}$, provided it exists. Then $f(\mathbf{x}') \le f(\mathbf{x})$."

Answer for 3: a. Justification: In the summary of the EM algorithm, the M-step is described as updating the parameters: "$\pi_k^{t+1} = \frac{n_k^t}{n}$ and $p_{k,m}^{t+1} = \frac{n_{k,m}^t}{n_k^t}$.", which require the responsibilities.

Answer for 4: b. Justification: The text states, "Mathematically, this corresponds to applying the law of total probability as we did previously. Further, we let the vertex for X be shaded to indicate that it is observed, while the vertex for Y is not shaded to indicate that it is not."

Answer for 5: b. Justification: The text refers to responsibilities as "our estimate – under the current parameter – of the probability that the sample comes from cluster k."

6.5 Application: Linear-Gaussian Models and Kalman Filtering

In this section, we illustrate the use of linear-Gaussian models for object tracking. We first give some background.

6.5.1 Multivariate Gaussians: Marginals and Conditionals

We will need the marginal and conditional densities of a multivariate Gaussian. For this purpose, we require various formulas and results about block matrices.

6.5.1.1 Properties of Block Matrices

Recall from Section 1.2.1 that block matrices have a convenient algebra that mimics the usual matrix algebra.

Consider a square block matrix with the same partitioning of the rows and columns,

$$A = \begin{pmatrix} A_{11} & A_{12} \\ A_{21} & A_{22} \end{pmatrix}$$

where $A \in \mathbb{R}^{n \times n_j}$, $A_{ij} \in \mathbb{R}^{n_i \times n_j}$ for $i, j = 1, 2$ with the condition $n_1 + n_2 = n$. Then it is straightforward to check (try it!) that the transpose can be written as

$$A^T = \begin{pmatrix} A_{11}^T & A_{21}^T \\ A_{12}^T & A_{22}^T \end{pmatrix}.$$

In particular, if A is symmetric then $A_{11} = A_{11}^T$, $A_{22} = A_{22}^T$, and $A_{21} = A_{12}^T$.

Example 6.5.1 *For instance, consider* $\mathbf{z} = (\mathbf{z}_1, \mathbf{z}_2)$, *where* $\mathbf{z}_1 \in \mathbb{R}^{n_1}$ *and* $\mathbf{z}_2 \in \mathbb{R}^{n_2}$. *We want to compute the quadratic form*

$$\mathbf{z}^T \begin{pmatrix} A_{11} & A_{12} \\ A_{12}^T & A_{22} \end{pmatrix} \mathbf{z}$$

where $A_{ij} \in \mathbb{R}^{n_i \times n_j}$ *for* $i, j = 1, 2$ *with the conditions* $n_1 + n_2 = n$, *and* $A_{11}^T = A_{11}$ *and* $A_{22}^T = A_{22}$.

We apply the block matrix product formula twice to get

$$(\mathbf{z}_1, \mathbf{z}_2)^T \begin{pmatrix} A_{11} & A_{12} \\ A_{12}^T & A_{22} \end{pmatrix} (\mathbf{z}_1, \mathbf{z}_2)$$
$$= (\mathbf{z}_1, \mathbf{z}_2)^T \begin{pmatrix} A_{11}\mathbf{z}_1 + A_{12}\mathbf{z}_2 \\ A_{12}^T \mathbf{z}_1 + A_{22}\mathbf{z}_2 \end{pmatrix}$$
$$= \mathbf{z}_1^T A_{11} \mathbf{z}_1 + \mathbf{z}_1^T A_{12} \mathbf{z}_2 + \mathbf{z}_2^T A_{12}^T \mathbf{z}_1 + \mathbf{z}_2^T A_{22} \mathbf{z}_2$$
$$= \mathbf{z}_1^T A_{11} \mathbf{z}_1 + 2\mathbf{z}_1^T A_{12} \mathbf{z}_2 + \mathbf{z}_2^T A_{22} \mathbf{z}_2.$$

Example 6.5.2 Let $A_{ii} \in \mathbb{R}^{n_i \times n_i}$ for $i = 1, 2$ be invertible. We claim that

$$\begin{pmatrix} A_{11} & 0 \\ 0 & A_{22} \end{pmatrix}^{-1} = \begin{pmatrix} A_{11}^{-1} & 0 \\ 0 & A_{22}^{-1} \end{pmatrix}.$$

The matrix on the right-hand side is well-defined by the invertibility of A_{11} and A_{22}. We check the claim using the formula for matrix products of block matrices. The matrices above are block diagonal.

Indeed, we obtain

$$\begin{pmatrix} A_{11} & 0 \\ 0 & A_{22} \end{pmatrix} \begin{pmatrix} A_{11}^{-1} & 0 \\ 0 & A_{22}^{-1} \end{pmatrix}$$
$$= \begin{pmatrix} A_{11} A_{11}^{-1} + 0 & 0 + 0 \\ 0 + 0 & 0 + A_{22} A_{22}^{-1} \end{pmatrix} = \begin{pmatrix} I_{n_1 \times n_1} & 0 \\ 0 & I_{n_2 \times n_2} \end{pmatrix} = I_{n \times n}$$

and similarly for the other way round.

Example 6.5.3 Let $A_{21} \in \mathbb{R}^{n_2 \times n_1}$. Then we claim that

$$\begin{pmatrix} I_{n_1 \times n_1} & 0 \\ A_{21} & I_{n_2 \times n_2} \end{pmatrix}^{-1} = \begin{pmatrix} I_{n_1 \times n_1} & 0 \\ -A_{21} & I_{n_2 \times n_2} \end{pmatrix}.$$

A similar formula holds for the block upper triangular case. In particular, such matrices are invertible (which can be proved in other ways, for instance through determinants).

It suffices to check:

$$\begin{pmatrix} I_{n_1 \times n_1} & 0 \\ A_{21} & I_{n_2 \times n_2} \end{pmatrix} \begin{pmatrix} I_{n_1 \times n_1} & 0 \\ -A_{21} & I_{n_2 \times n_2} \end{pmatrix}$$
$$= \begin{pmatrix} I_{n_1 \times n_1} I_{n_1 \times n_1} + 0 & 0 + 0 \\ A_{21} I_{n_1 \times n_1} + (-A_{21}) I_{n_1 \times n_1} & 0 + I_{n_2 \times n_2} I_{n_2 \times n_2} \end{pmatrix} = \begin{pmatrix} I_{n_1 \times n_1} & 0 \\ 0 & I_{n_2 \times n_2} \end{pmatrix} = I_{n \times n}$$

Taking a transpose gives a similar formula for the block upper triangular case.

6.5.1.2 Inverting a Block Matrix

We will need a classical formula for inverting a block matrix. We start with the concept of a Schur complement.

Definition 6.5.4 *(Schur Complement)* Consider the matrix $B \in \mathbb{R}^{n \times n}$ in block form

$$B = \begin{pmatrix} B_{11} & B_{12} \\ B_{21} & B_{22} \end{pmatrix}$$

where $B_{11} \in \mathbb{R}^{n_1 \times n_1}$, $B_{22} \in \mathbb{R}^{n-n_1 \times n-n_1}$, $B_{12} \in \mathbb{R}^{n_1 \times n-n_1}$, and $B_{21} \in \mathbb{R}^{n-n_1 \times n_1}$. Then, provided B_{22} is invertible, the Schur complement of the block B_{22} is defined as the matrix

$$B/B_{22} := B_{11} - B_{12} B_{22}^{-1} B_{21}.$$

Similarly, provided B_{11} is invertible,

$$B/B_{11} := B_{22} - B_{21} B_{11}^{-1} B_{12}.$$

Lemma 6.5.5 *(Inverting a Block Matrix)* Consider the matrix $B \in \mathbb{R}^{n \times n}$ in block form as

$$B = \begin{pmatrix} B_{11} & B_{12} \\ B_{21} & B_{22} \end{pmatrix}$$

where $B_{11} \in \mathbb{R}^{n_1 \times n_1}$, $B_{22} \in \mathbb{R}^{n-n_1 \times n-n_1}$, $B_{12} \in \mathbb{R}^{n_1 \times n-n_1}$, and $B_{21} \in \mathbb{R}^{n-n_1 \times n_1}$. Then, provided B_{22} is invertible,

$$B^{-1} = \begin{pmatrix} (B/B_{22})^{-1} & -(B/B_{22})^{-1} B_{12} B_{22}^{-1} \\ -B_{22}^{-1} B_{21} (B/B_{22})^{-1} & B_{22}^{-1} B_{21} (B/B_{22})^{-1} B_{12} B_{22}^{-1} + B_{22}^{-1} \end{pmatrix}.$$

Alternatively, provided B_{11} is invertible,

$$B^{-1} = \begin{pmatrix} B_{11}^{-1} B_{12} (B/B_{11})^{-1} B_{21} B_{11}^{-1} + B_{11}^{-1} & -B_{11}^{-1} B_{12} (B/B_{11})^{-1} \\ -(B/B_{11})^{-1} B_{21} B_{11}^{-1} & (B/B_{11})^{-1} \end{pmatrix}.$$

Proof idea: One way to prove this is to multiply B and B^{-1} and check that the identity matrix comes out (try it!). We give a longer proof that provides more insight into where the formula is coming from.

The trick is to multiply B on the left and right by carefully chosen block triangular matrices with identity matrices on the diagonal (which we know are invertible by Example 6.5.3) to produce a block diagonal matrix with invertible matrices on the diagonal (which we know how to invert by Example 6.5.2).

Proof We only prove the first formula. The proof is a calculation based on the formula for matrix products of block matrices. We will need that, if C, D, and E are invertible and of the same size, then $(CDE)^{-1} = E^{-1} D^{-1} C^{-1}$ (check it!).

We make a series of observations.

1. Our first step is to get a zero block in the upper right corner using an invertible matrix. Note that (recall that the order of multiplication matters here!)

$$\begin{pmatrix} I_{n_1 \times n_1} & -B_{12} B_{22}^{-1} \\ 0 & I_{n_2 \times n_2} \end{pmatrix} \begin{pmatrix} B_{11} & B_{12} \\ B_{21} & B_{22} \end{pmatrix}$$
$$= \begin{pmatrix} B_{11} - B_{12} B_{22}^{-1} B_{21} & B_{12} - B_{12} B_{22}^{-1} B_{22} \\ 0 + B_{21} & 0 + B_{22} \end{pmatrix} = \begin{pmatrix} B/B_{22} & 0 \\ B_{21} & B_{22} \end{pmatrix}.$$

2. Next we get a zero block in the bottom left corner. Starting from the final matrix in the last display,

$$\begin{pmatrix} B/B_{22} & 0 \\ B_{21} & B_{22} \end{pmatrix} \begin{pmatrix} I_{n_1 \times n_1} & 0 \\ -B_{22}^{-1} B_{21} & I_{n_2 \times n_2} \end{pmatrix}$$
$$= \begin{pmatrix} B/B_{22} + 0 & 0 + 0 \\ B_{21} - B_{22} B_{22}^{-1} B_{21} & 0 + B_{22} \end{pmatrix} = \begin{pmatrix} B/B_{22} & 0 \\ 0 & B_{22} \end{pmatrix}.$$

3. Combining the last two steps, we have shown that
$$\begin{pmatrix} I_{n_1 \times n_1} & -B_{12}B_{22}^{-1} \\ 0 & I_{n_2 \times n_2} \end{pmatrix} \begin{pmatrix} B_{11} & B_{12} \\ B_{21} & B_{22} \end{pmatrix} \begin{pmatrix} I_{n_1 \times n_1} & 0 \\ -B_{22}^{-1}B_{21} & I_{n_2 \times n_2} \end{pmatrix} = \begin{pmatrix} B/B_{22} & 0 \\ 0 & B_{22} \end{pmatrix}.$$

Using the formula for the inverse of a product of three invertible matrices, we obtain
$$\begin{pmatrix} I_{n_1 \times n_1} & 0 \\ -B_{22}^{-1}B_{21} & I_{n_2 \times n_2} \end{pmatrix}^{-1} \begin{pmatrix} B_{11} & B_{12} \\ B_{21} & B_{22} \end{pmatrix}^{-1} \begin{pmatrix} I_{n_1 \times n_1} & -B_{12}B_{22}^{-1} \\ 0 & I_{n_2 \times n_2} \end{pmatrix}^{-1}$$
$$= \begin{pmatrix} B/B_{22} & 0 \\ 0 & B_{22} \end{pmatrix}^{-1}.$$

4. Rearranging and using the formula for the inverse of a block diagonal matrix, we finally get

$$\begin{pmatrix} B_{11} & B_{12} \\ B_{21} & B_{22} \end{pmatrix}^{-1}$$
$$= \begin{pmatrix} I_{n_1 \times n_1} & 0 \\ -B_{22}^{-1}B_{21} & I_{n_2 \times n_2} \end{pmatrix} \begin{pmatrix} B/B_{22} & 0 \\ 0 & B_{22} \end{pmatrix}^{-1} \begin{pmatrix} I_{n_1 \times n_1} & -B_{12}B_{22}^{-1} \\ 0 & I_{n_2 \times n_2} \end{pmatrix}$$
$$= \begin{pmatrix} I_{n_1 \times n_1} & 0 \\ -B_{22}^{-1}B_{21} & I_{n_2 \times n_2} \end{pmatrix} \begin{pmatrix} (B/B_{22})^{-1} & 0 \\ 0 & B_{22}^{-1} \end{pmatrix} \begin{pmatrix} I_{n_1 \times n_1} & -B_{12}B_{22}^{-1} \\ 0 & I_{n_2 \times n_2} \end{pmatrix}$$
$$= \begin{pmatrix} I_{n_1 \times n_1} & 0 \\ -B_{22}^{-1}B_{21} & I_{n_2 \times n_2} \end{pmatrix} \begin{pmatrix} (B/B_{22})^{-1} + 0 & -(B/B_{22})^{-1}B_{12}B_{22}^{-1} + 0 \\ 0 + 0 & 0 + B_{22}^{-1} \end{pmatrix}$$
$$= \begin{pmatrix} I_{n_1 \times n_1} & 0 \\ -B_{22}^{-1}B_{21} & I_{n_2 \times n_2} \end{pmatrix} \begin{pmatrix} (B/B_{22})^{-1} & -(B/B_{22})^{-1}B_{12}B_{22}^{-1} \\ 0 & B_{22}^{-1} \end{pmatrix}$$
$$= \begin{pmatrix} (B/B_{22})^{-1} & -(B/B_{22})^{-1}B_{12}B_{22}^{-1} \\ -B_{22}^{-1}B_{21}(B/B_{22})^{-1} & B_{22}^{-1}B_{21}(B/B_{22})^{-1}B_{12}B_{22}^{-1} + B_{22}^{-1} \end{pmatrix},$$

as claimed. $\square$

6.5.1.3 The Positive Definite Case

In applying the inversion formula, it will be enough to restrict ourselves to the positive definite case, where the lemmas that follow guarantee the required invertibility conditions.

First,

Lemma 6.5.6 (Invertibility of Positive Definite Matrices) *Let $B \in \mathbb{R}^{n \times n}$ be symmetric, positive definite. Then B is invertible.*

Proof For any $\mathbf{x} \neq \mathbf{0}$, it holds by positive definiteness that $\mathbf{x}^T B \mathbf{x} > 0$. In particular, it must be that $\mathbf{x}^T B \mathbf{x} \neq 0$ and therefore, by contradiction, $B\mathbf{x} \neq \mathbf{0}$ (since for any $\mathbf{z}$, it holds that $\mathbf{z}^T \mathbf{0} = 0$). The claim follows from the *Equivalent Definition of Linear Independence Lemma*. $\square$

A principal submatrix is a square submatrix obtained by removing some rows and columns. Moreover we require that the set of row indices that remain is the same as the set of column indices that remain.

Lemma 6.5.7 (Principal Submatrices) *Let $B \in \mathbb{R}^{n \times n}$ be positive definite and let $Z \in \mathbb{R}^{n \times p}$ have full column rank. Then $Z^T B Z$ is positive definite. In particular all principal submatrices of positive definite matrices are positive definite.*

Proof If $\mathbf{x} \neq \mathbf{0}$, then $\mathbf{x}^T(Z^T B Z)\mathbf{x} = \mathbf{y}^T B \mathbf{y}$, where we defined $\mathbf{y} = Z\mathbf{x}$. Because Z has full column rank and $\mathbf{x} \neq \mathbf{0}$, it follows that $\mathbf{y} \neq \mathbf{0}$ by the *Equivalent Definition of Linear Independence Lemma*. Hence, since $B > 0$, we have $\mathbf{y}^T B \mathbf{y} > 0$ which proves the first claim. For the second claim, take Z of the form $(\mathbf{e}_{m_1}\ \mathbf{e}_{m_2}\ \ldots\ \mathbf{e}_{m_p})$, where the indices $m_1, \ldots, m_p$ are distinct and increasing. The columns of Z are then linearly independent since they are distinct basis vectors. $\square$

To better understand the last claim in the proof, note that

$$(Z^T B Z)_{i,j} = (Z^T)_{i,\cdot} B Z_{\cdot,j} = (Z_{\cdot,i})^T B Z_{\cdot,j} = \sum_{k=1}^n \sum_{\ell=1}^n Z_{k,i} B_{k,\ell} Z_{\ell,j}.$$

So if the i-th column of Z is $\mathbf{e}_{m_i}$ and the j-th column of Z is $\mathbf{e}_{m_j}$, then the rightmost summation picks up only one element, B_{m_i, m_j}. In other words, $Z^T B Z$ is the principal submatrix of B corresponding to rows and columns $m_1, \ldots, m_p$.

Lemma 6.5.8 *(Schur Complement)* Let $B \in \mathbb{R}^{n \times n}$ be positive definite and write it in block form as

$$B = \begin{pmatrix} B_{11} & B_{12} \\ B_{12}^T & B_{22} \end{pmatrix}$$

where $B_{11} \in \mathbb{R}^{n_1 \times n_1}$ and $B_{22} \in \mathbb{R}^{n-n_1 \times n-n_1}$ are symmetric, and $B_{12} \in \mathbb{R}^{n_1 \times n-n_1}$. Then the Schur complement of the block B_{11}, namely, the matrix $B/B_{11} := B_{22} - B_{12}^T B_{11}^{-1} B_{12}$, is well-defined, symmetric, and positive definite. The same holds for $B/B_{22} := B_{11} - B_{12} B_{22}^{-1} B_{12}^T$.

Proof By the *Principal Submatrices Lemma*, B_{11} is positive definite. By the *Invertibility of Positive Definite Matrices Lemma*, B_{11} is therefore invertible. Hence the Schur complement is well defined. Moreover, it is symmetric since

$$(B/B_{11})^T = B_{22}^T - (B_{12}^T B_{11}^{-1} B_{12})^T = B_{22} - B_{12}^T B_{11}^{-1} B_{12} = B/B_{11},$$

by the symmetry of B_{11}, B_{22}, and B_{11}^{-1} (prove that last one!).

For a nonzero $\mathbf{x} \in \mathbb{R}^{n_2}$, let

$$\mathbf{z} = \begin{pmatrix} \mathbf{z}_1 \\ \mathbf{z}_2 \end{pmatrix} = \begin{pmatrix} B_{11}^{-1} B_{12} \mathbf{x} \\ -\mathbf{x} \end{pmatrix}.$$

The result then follows from the observation that

$$\mathbf{z}^T \begin{pmatrix} B_{11} & B_{12} \\ B_{12}^T & B_{22} \end{pmatrix} \mathbf{z}$$
$$= \mathbf{z}_1^T B_{11} \mathbf{z}_1 + 2\mathbf{z}_1^T B_{12} \mathbf{z}_2 + \mathbf{z}_2^T B_{22} \mathbf{z}_2$$
$$= (B_{11}^{-1} B_{12} \mathbf{x})^T B_{11} B_{11}^{-1} B_{12} \mathbf{x} + 2(B_{11}^{-1} B_{12} \mathbf{x})^T B_{12}(-\mathbf{x}) + (-\mathbf{x})^T B_{22}(-\mathbf{x})$$
$$= \mathbf{x}^T B_{12}^T B_{11}^{-1} B_{12} \mathbf{x} - 2\mathbf{x}^T B_{12}^T B_{11}^{-1} B_{12} \mathbf{x} + \mathbf{x}^T B_{22} \mathbf{x}$$
$$= \mathbf{x}^T (B_{22} - B_{12}^T B_{11}^{-1} B_{12}) \mathbf{x}.$$
$\square$

6.5.1.4 Marginals and Conditionals

We are now ready to derive the distribution of marginals and conditionals of multivariate Gaussians. Recall that a multivariate Gaussian vector $\mathbf{X} = (X_1, \ldots, X_d)$ on $\mathbb{R}^d$ with mean $\boldsymbol{\mu} \in \mathbb{R}^d$ and positive definite covariance matrix $\boldsymbol{\Sigma} \in \mathbb{R}^{d \times d}$ has probability density function

$$f_{\boldsymbol{\mu}, \boldsymbol{\Sigma}}(\mathbf{x}) = \frac{1}{(2\pi)^{d/2} |\boldsymbol{\Sigma}|^{1/2}} \exp\left(-\frac{1}{2}(\mathbf{x} - \boldsymbol{\mu})^T \boldsymbol{\Sigma}^{-1} (\mathbf{x} - \boldsymbol{\mu})\right).$$

Recall that one way to compute $|\Sigma|$ is as the product of all eigenvalues of Σ (with repeats). The matrix $\Lambda = \Sigma^{-1}$ is called the precision matrix.

Partition $\mathbf{X}$ as the column vector $(\mathbf{X}_1, \mathbf{X}_2)$ where $\mathbf{X}_i \in \mathbb{R}^{d_i}$, $i = 1, 2$, with $d_1 + d_2 = d$. Similarly, consider the corresponding block vectors and matrices

$$\mu = \begin{pmatrix} \mu_1 \\ \mu_2 \end{pmatrix} \qquad \Sigma = \begin{pmatrix} \Sigma_{11} & \Sigma_{12} \\ \Sigma_{21} & \Sigma_{22} \end{pmatrix} \qquad \Lambda = \begin{pmatrix} \Lambda_{11} & \Lambda_{12} \\ \Lambda_{21} & \Lambda_{22} \end{pmatrix}.$$

Note that by the symmetry of Σ, we have $\Sigma_{21} = \Sigma_{12}^T$. Furthemore, it can be proved that a symmetric, invertible matrix has a symmetric inverse (try it!) so that $\Lambda_{21} = \Lambda_{12}^T$.

We seek to compute the marginals $f_{\mathbf{X}_1}(\mathbf{x}_1)$ and $f_{\mathbf{X}_2}(\mathbf{x}_2)$, as well as the conditional density of $\mathbf{X}_1$ given $\mathbf{X}_2$, which we denote as $f_{\mathbf{X}_1|\mathbf{X}_2}(\mathbf{x}_1|\mathbf{x}_2)$, and similarly $f_{\mathbf{X}_2|\mathbf{X}_1}(\mathbf{x}_2|\mathbf{x}_1)$.

By the multiplication rule, the joint density $f_{\mathbf{X}_1,\mathbf{X}_2}(\mathbf{x}_1, \mathbf{x}_2)$ can be decomposed as

$$f_{\mathbf{X}_1,\mathbf{X}_2}(\mathbf{x}_1, \mathbf{x}_2) = f_{\mathbf{X}_1|\mathbf{X}_2}(\mathbf{x}_1|\mathbf{x}_2) f_{\mathbf{X}_2}(\mathbf{x}_2).$$

We use the *Inverting a Block Matrix Lemma* to rewrite $f_{\mathbf{X}_1,\mathbf{X}_2}(\mathbf{x}_1, \mathbf{x}_2)$ in this form and "reveal" the marginal and conditional involved. Indeed, once the joint density is in this form, by integrating over $\mathbf{x}_1$ we obtain that the marginal density of $\mathbf{X}_2$ is $f_{\mathbf{X}_2}$ and the conditional density of $\mathbf{X}_1$ given $\mathbf{X}_2$ is obtained by taking the ratio of the joint and the marginal.

In fact, it will be easier to work with an expression derived in the proof of that lemma, specifically

$$\begin{pmatrix} \Sigma_{11} & \Sigma_{12} \\ \Sigma_{21} & \Sigma_{22} \end{pmatrix}^{-1}$$
$$= \begin{pmatrix} I_{d_1 \times d_1} & 0 \\ -\Sigma_{22}^{-1}\Sigma_{12}^T & I_{d_2 \times d_2} \end{pmatrix} \begin{pmatrix} (\Sigma/\Sigma_{22})^{-1} & 0 \\ 0 & \Sigma_{22}^{-1} \end{pmatrix} \begin{pmatrix} I_{d_1 \times d_1} & -\Sigma_{12}\Sigma_{22}^{-1} \\ 0 & I_{d_2 \times d_2} \end{pmatrix}.$$

We will use the fact that the first matrix on the last line is the transpose of the third one (check it!).

To evaluate the joint density, we need to expand the quadratic function $(\mathbf{x} - \mu)^T \Sigma^{-1}(\mathbf{x} - \mu)$ appearing in the exponential. We break this up in a few steps.

1. Note first that

$$\begin{pmatrix} I_{d_1 \times d_1} & -\Sigma_{12}\Sigma_{22}^{-1} \\ 0 & I_{d_2 \times d_2} \end{pmatrix} \begin{pmatrix} \mathbf{x}_1 - \mu_1 \\ \mathbf{x}_2 - \mu_2 \end{pmatrix} = \begin{pmatrix} (\mathbf{x}_1 - \mu_1) - \Sigma_{12}\Sigma_{22}^{-1}(\mathbf{x}_2 - \mu_2) \\ \mathbf{x}_2 - \mu_2 \end{pmatrix}$$

and similarly for its transpose. We define

$$\mu_{1|2}(\mathbf{x}_2) := \mu_1 + \Sigma_{12}\Sigma_{22}^{-1}(\mathbf{x}_2 - \mu_2).$$

2. Plugging this back in the quadratic function, we get

$$(\mathbf{x} - \mu)^T \Sigma^{-1}(\mathbf{x} - \mu)$$
$$= \begin{pmatrix} \mathbf{x}_1 - \mu_{1|2}(\mathbf{x}_2) \\ \mathbf{x}_2 - \mu_2 \end{pmatrix}^T \begin{pmatrix} (\Sigma/\Sigma_{22})^{-1} & 0 \\ 0 & \Sigma_{22}^{-1} \end{pmatrix} \begin{pmatrix} \mathbf{x}_1 - \mu_{1|2}(\mathbf{x}_2) \\ \mathbf{x}_2 - \mu_2 \end{pmatrix}$$
$$= (\mathbf{x}_1 - \mu_{1|2}(\mathbf{x}_2))^T (\Sigma/\Sigma_{22})^{-1} (\mathbf{x}_1 - \mu_{1|2}(\mathbf{x}_2)) + (\mathbf{x}_2 - \mu_2)^T \Sigma_{22}^{-1}(\mathbf{x}_2 - \mu_2).$$

Note that both terms have the same form as the original quadratic function.

3. Going back to the density, we use $\propto$ to indicate that the expression holds up to a constant not depending on $\mathbf{x}$. Using that the exponential of a sum is the product of exponentials, we obtain

$$f_{\mathbf{X}_1,\mathbf{X}_2}(\mathbf{x}_1,\mathbf{x}_2)$$
$$\propto \exp\left(-\frac{1}{2}(\mathbf{x}-\boldsymbol{\mu})^T \boldsymbol{\Sigma}^{-1}(\mathbf{x}-\boldsymbol{\mu})\right)$$
$$\propto \exp\left(-\frac{1}{2}(\mathbf{x}_1-\boldsymbol{\mu}_{1|2}(\mathbf{x}_2))^T (\boldsymbol{\Sigma}/\boldsymbol{\Sigma}_{22})^{-1}(\mathbf{x}_1-\boldsymbol{\mu}_{1|2}(\mathbf{x}_2))\right)$$
$$\times \exp\left(-\frac{1}{2}(\mathbf{x}_2-\boldsymbol{\mu}_2)^T \boldsymbol{\Sigma}_{22}^{-1}(\mathbf{x}_2-\boldsymbol{\mu}_2)\right).$$

We have shown that

$$f_{\mathbf{X}_1|\mathbf{X}_2}(\mathbf{x}_1|\mathbf{x}_2) \propto \exp\left(-\frac{1}{2}(\mathbf{x}_1-\boldsymbol{\mu}_{1|2}(\mathbf{x}_2))^T (\boldsymbol{\Sigma}/\boldsymbol{\Sigma}_{22})^{-1}(\mathbf{x}_1-\boldsymbol{\mu}_{1|2}(\mathbf{x}_2))\right)$$

and

$$f_{\mathbf{X}_2}(\mathbf{x}_2) \propto \exp\left(-\frac{1}{2}(\mathbf{x}_2-\boldsymbol{\mu}_2)^T \boldsymbol{\Sigma}_{22}^{-1}(\mathbf{x}_2-\boldsymbol{\mu}_2)\right).$$

In other words, the marginal density of $\mathbf{X}_2$ is multivariate Gaussian with mean $\boldsymbol{\mu}_2$ and covariance $\boldsymbol{\Sigma}_{22}$. The conditional density of $\mathbf{X}_1$ given $\mathbf{X}_2$ is multivariate Gaussian with mean $\boldsymbol{\mu}_{1|2}(\mathbf{X}_2)$ and covariance $\boldsymbol{\Sigma}/\boldsymbol{\Sigma}_{22} = \boldsymbol{\Sigma}_{11} - \boldsymbol{\Sigma}_{12}\boldsymbol{\Sigma}_{22}^{-1}\boldsymbol{\Sigma}_{12}^T$. We write this as

$$\mathbf{X}_1|\mathbf{X}_2 \sim N_{d_1}(\boldsymbol{\mu}_{1|2}(\mathbf{X}_2), \boldsymbol{\Sigma}/\boldsymbol{\Sigma}_{22})$$

and

$$\mathbf{X}_2 \sim N_{d_2}(\boldsymbol{\mu}_2, \boldsymbol{\Sigma}_{22}).$$

Similarly, by exchanging the roles of $\mathbf{X}_1$ and $\mathbf{X}_2$, we see that the marginal density of $\mathbf{X}_1$ is multivariate Gaussian with mean $\boldsymbol{\mu}_1$ and covariance $\boldsymbol{\Sigma}_{11}$. The conditional density of $\mathbf{X}_2$ given $\mathbf{X}_1$ is multivariate Gaussian with mean $\boldsymbol{\mu}_{2|1}(\mathbf{X}_1) = \boldsymbol{\mu}_2 + \boldsymbol{\Sigma}_{21}\boldsymbol{\Sigma}_{11}^{-1}(\mathbf{X}_1 - \boldsymbol{\mu}_1)$ and covariance $\boldsymbol{\Sigma}/\boldsymbol{\Sigma}_{11} = \boldsymbol{\Sigma}_{22} - \boldsymbol{\Sigma}_{12}^T \boldsymbol{\Sigma}_{11}^{-1}\boldsymbol{\Sigma}_{12}$.

6.5.2 Kalman Filter

We consider a stochastic process $\{\mathbf{X}_t\}_{t=0}^T$ (i.e., a collection of random vectors – often indexed by time) with state space $\mathcal{S} = \mathbb{R}^{d_0}$ of the following form

$$\mathbf{X}_{t+1} = F\mathbf{X}_t + \mathbf{W}_t$$

where the $\mathbf{W}_t$'s are i.i.d. $N_{d_0}(\mathbf{0}, Q)$ and F and Q are known $d_0 \times d_0$ matrices. We denote the initial state by $\mathbf{X}_0 \sim N_{d_0}(\boldsymbol{\mu}_0, \boldsymbol{\Sigma}_0)$. We assume that the process $\{\mathbf{X}_t\}_{t=1}^T$ is not observed, but rather that an auxiliary observed process $\{\mathbf{Y}_t\}_{t=1}^T$ with state space $\mathcal{S} = \mathbb{R}^d$ satisfies

$$\mathbf{Y}_t = H\mathbf{X}_t + \mathbf{V}_t$$

where the $\mathbf{V}_t$'s are i.i.d. $N_d(\mathbf{0}, R)$ and $H \in \mathbb{R}^{d \times d_0}$ and $R \in \mathbb{R}^{d \times d}$ are known matrices. This is an example of a linear-Gaussian system (also known as linear-Gaussian state space model).

Our goal is to infer the unobserved states given the observed process. Specifically, we look at the filtering problem. Quoting Wikipedia[10]:

> The task is to compute, given the model's parameters and a sequence of observations, the distribution over hidden states of the last latent variable at the end of the sequence, i.e. to compute $P(x(t)|y(1),\ldots,y(t))$. This task is normally used when the sequence of latent variables is thought of as the underlying states that a process moves through at a sequence of points of time, with corresponding observations at each point in time. Then, it is natural to ask about the state of the process at the end.

6.5.2.1 Key Lemma

Given the structure of the linear-Gaussian model, the following lemma will play a key role.

Lemma 6.5.9 (Linear-Gaussian System) *Let* $\mathbf{W} \sim N_d(\boldsymbol{\mu}, \boldsymbol{\Sigma})$ *and* $\mathbf{W}'|\mathbf{W} \sim N_{d'}(A\mathbf{W}, \boldsymbol{\Sigma}')$ *where* $A \in \mathbb{R}^{d' \times d}$ *is a deterministic matrix, and* $\boldsymbol{\Sigma} \in \mathbb{R}^{d \times d}$ *and* $\boldsymbol{\Sigma}' \in \mathbb{R}^{d' \times d'}$ *are positive definite. Then* $(\mathbf{W}, \mathbf{W}')$ *is multivariate Gaussian with mean vector*

$$\boldsymbol{\mu}'' = \begin{pmatrix} \boldsymbol{\mu} \\ A\boldsymbol{\mu} \end{pmatrix}$$

and positive definite covariance matrix

$$\boldsymbol{\Sigma}'' = \begin{pmatrix} \boldsymbol{\Sigma} & \boldsymbol{\Sigma} A^T \\ A\boldsymbol{\Sigma} & A\boldsymbol{\Sigma} A^T + \boldsymbol{\Sigma}' \end{pmatrix}.$$

Proof We have

$$f_{\mathbf{W},\mathbf{W}'}(\mathbf{w}, \mathbf{w}')$$
$$= f_{\mathbf{W}}(\mathbf{w}) f_{\mathbf{W}'|\mathbf{W}}(\mathbf{w}'|\mathbf{w})$$
$$\propto \exp\left(-\frac{1}{2}(\mathbf{w} - \boldsymbol{\mu})^T \boldsymbol{\Sigma}^{-1}(\mathbf{w} - \boldsymbol{\mu})\right)$$
$$\times \exp\left(-\frac{1}{2}(\mathbf{w}' - A\mathbf{w})^T (\boldsymbol{\Sigma}')^{-1}(\mathbf{w}' - A\mathbf{w})\right)$$
$$\propto \exp\left(-\frac{1}{2}\left[(\mathbf{w} - \boldsymbol{\mu})^T \boldsymbol{\Sigma}^{-1}(\mathbf{w} - \boldsymbol{\mu}) + (\mathbf{w}' - A\mathbf{w})^T (\boldsymbol{\Sigma}')^{-1}(\mathbf{w}' - A\mathbf{w})\right]\right).$$

We rewrite the quadratic function in square brackets in the exponent as follows:

$$(\mathbf{w} - \boldsymbol{\mu})^T \boldsymbol{\Sigma}^{-1}(\mathbf{w} - \boldsymbol{\mu}) + (\mathbf{w}' - A\mathbf{w})^T (\boldsymbol{\Sigma}')^{-1}(\mathbf{w}' - A\mathbf{w})$$
$$= (\mathbf{w} - \boldsymbol{\mu})^T \boldsymbol{\Sigma}^{-1}(\mathbf{w} - \boldsymbol{\mu})$$
$$\quad + ([\mathbf{w}' - A\boldsymbol{\mu}] - A[\mathbf{w} - \boldsymbol{\mu}])^T (\boldsymbol{\Sigma}')^{-1}([\mathbf{w}' - A\boldsymbol{\mu}] - A[\mathbf{w} - \boldsymbol{\mu}])$$
$$= (\mathbf{w} - \boldsymbol{\mu})^T (A^T (\boldsymbol{\Sigma}')^{-1} A + \boldsymbol{\Sigma}^{-1})(\mathbf{w} - \boldsymbol{\mu})$$
$$\quad - 2(\mathbf{w} - \boldsymbol{\mu})^T A^T (\boldsymbol{\Sigma}')^{-1}(\mathbf{w}' - A\boldsymbol{\mu}) + (\mathbf{w}' - A\boldsymbol{\mu})^T (\boldsymbol{\Sigma}')^{-1}(\mathbf{w}' - A\boldsymbol{\mu})$$
$$= \begin{pmatrix} \mathbf{w} - \boldsymbol{\mu} \\ \mathbf{w}' - A\boldsymbol{\mu} \end{pmatrix}^T \begin{pmatrix} A^T (\boldsymbol{\Sigma}')^{-1} A + \boldsymbol{\Sigma}^{-1} & -A^T (\boldsymbol{\Sigma}')^{-1} \\ -(\boldsymbol{\Sigma}')^{-1} A & (\boldsymbol{\Sigma}')^{-1} \end{pmatrix} \begin{pmatrix} \mathbf{w} - \boldsymbol{\mu} \\ \mathbf{w}' - A\boldsymbol{\mu} \end{pmatrix}$$
$$= \begin{pmatrix} \mathbf{w} - \boldsymbol{\mu} \\ \mathbf{w}' - A\boldsymbol{\mu} \end{pmatrix}^T \Lambda'' \begin{pmatrix} \mathbf{w} - \boldsymbol{\mu} \\ \mathbf{w}' - A\boldsymbol{\mu} \end{pmatrix},$$

---

[10] https://en.wikipedia.org/wiki/Hidden_Markov_model

where the last line defines Λ'' and the second line shows that it is positive definite (why?). We have shown that $(\mathbf{W}, \mathbf{W}')$ is multivariate Gaussian with mean $(\mu, A\mu)$.

We use the *Inverting a Block Matrix Lemma* to invert Λ'' and reveal the covariance matrix. (One could also compute the covariance directly; try it!) We break up Λ'' into blocks:

$$\Lambda'' = \begin{pmatrix} \Lambda''_{11} & \Lambda''_{12} \\ (\Lambda''_{12})^T & \Lambda''_{22} \end{pmatrix}$$

where $\Lambda''_{11} \in \mathbb{R}^{d \times d}$, $\Lambda''_{22} \in \mathbb{R}^{d' \times d'}$, and $\Lambda''_{12} \in \mathbb{R}^{d \times d'}$. Recall that the inverse is

$$B^{-1} = \begin{pmatrix} (B/B_{22})^{-1} & -(B/B_{22})^{-1} B_{12} B_{22}^{-1} \\ -B_{22}^{-1} B_{12}^T (B/B_{22})^{-1} & B_{22}^{-1} B_{12}^T (B/B_{22})^{-1} B_{12} B_{22}^{-1} + B_{22}^{-1} \end{pmatrix}$$

where here $B = \Lambda''$.

The Schur complement is

$$\begin{aligned}
\Lambda''/\Lambda''_{22} &= \Lambda''_{11} - \Lambda''_{12}(\Lambda''_{22})^{-1}(\Lambda''_{12})^T \\
&= A^T(\Sigma')^{-1}A + \Sigma^{-1} - (-A^T(\Sigma')^{-1})((\Sigma')^{-1})^{-1}(-A^T(\Sigma')^{-1})^T \\
&= A^T(\Sigma')^{-1}A + \Sigma^{-1} - A^T(\Sigma')^{-1}\Sigma'(\Sigma')^{-1}A \\
&= A^T(\Sigma')^{-1}A + \Sigma^{-1} - A^T(\Sigma')^{-1}A \\
&= \Sigma^{-1}.
\end{aligned}$$

Hence $(\Lambda''/\Lambda''_{22})^{-1} = \Sigma$.

Moreover,

$$\begin{aligned}
-(\Lambda''/\Lambda''_{22})^{-1}\Lambda''_{12}(\Lambda''_{22})^{-1} &= -\Sigma(-A^T(\Sigma')^{-1})((\Sigma')^{-1})^{-1} \\
&= \Sigma A^T(\Sigma')^{-1}\Sigma' \\
&= \Sigma A^T
\end{aligned}$$

and

$$\begin{aligned}
(\Lambda''_{22})^{-1}(\Lambda''_{12})^T(\Lambda''/\Lambda''_{22})^{-1}\Lambda''_{12}(\Lambda''_{22})^{-1} + (\Lambda''_{22})^{-1} &= ((\Sigma')^{-1})^{-1}(-A^T(\Sigma')^{-1})^T\Sigma(-A^T(\Sigma')^{-1})((\Sigma')^{-1})^{-1} + ((\Sigma')^{-1})^{-1} \\
&= \Sigma'(\Sigma')^{-1}A\Sigma A^T(\Sigma')^{-1}\Sigma' + \Sigma' \\
&= A\Sigma A^T + \Sigma'.
\end{aligned}$$

Plugging back into the formula for the inverse of a block matrix completes the proof. $\square$

6.5.2.2 Joint Distribution

We extend our previous notation as follows: For two disjoint, finite collections of random vectors $\{\mathbf{U}_i\}_i$ and $\{\mathbf{W}_j\}_j$ defined on the same probability space, we let $f_{\{\mathbf{U}_i\}_i,\{\mathbf{W}_j\}_j}$ be their joint density, $f_{\{\mathbf{U}_i\}_i|\{\mathbf{W}_j\}_j}$ be the conditional density of $\{\mathbf{U}_i\}_i$ given $\{\mathbf{W}_j\}_j$, and $f_{\{\mathbf{U}_i\}_i}$ be the marginal density of $\{\mathbf{U}_i\}_i$. Formally, our goal is to compute

$$f_{\mathbf{X}_t|\mathbf{Y}_{1:t}} := f_{\{\mathbf{X}_t\}|\{\mathbf{Y}_1,\ldots,\mathbf{Y}_t\}}$$

recursively in t, where we define $\mathbf{Y}_{1:t} = \{\mathbf{Y}_1, \ldots, \mathbf{Y}_t\}$. We will see that all densities appearing in this calculation are multivariate Gaussians, and therefore keeping track of the means and covariances will suffice.

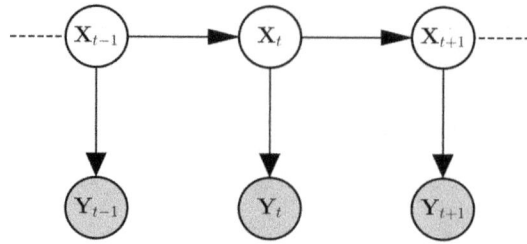

Figure 6.18 Graphical representation of linear-Gaussian system.

Formally, we posit that the density of the full process (with both observed and unobserved parts) is

$$f_{\mathbf{X}_0}(\mathbf{x}_0) \prod_{t=1}^{T} f_{\mathbf{X}_t|\mathbf{X}_{t-1}}(\mathbf{x}_t|\mathbf{x}_{t-1}) f_{\mathbf{Y}_t|\mathbf{X}_t}(\mathbf{y}_t|\mathbf{x}_t)$$

where the description of the model stipulates that

$$\mathbf{X}_t|\mathbf{X}_{t-1} \sim N_{d_0}(F\mathbf{X}_{t-1}, Q)$$

and

$$\mathbf{Y}_t|\mathbf{X}_t \sim N_d(H\mathbf{X}_t, R)$$

for all $t \geq 1$ and $\mathbf{X}_0 \sim N_{d_0}(\boldsymbol{\mu}_0, \boldsymbol{\Sigma}_0)$. We assume that $\boldsymbol{\mu}_0$ and $\boldsymbol{\Sigma}_0$ are known. Applying the *Linear-Gaussian System Lemma* inductively shows that the full process $(\mathbf{X}_{0:T}, \mathbf{Y}_{1:T})$ is jointly multivariate Gaussian (try it!). In particular, all marginals and conditionals are multivariate Gaussians.

Graphically, it can be represented as in Figure 6.18, where as before each variable is a node and its conditional distribution depends only on its parent nodes.

6.5.2.3 Conditional Independence

The stipulated form of the joint density of the full process implies many conditional independence relations. We will need the following two:

1. $\mathbf{X}_t$ is conditionally independent of $\mathbf{Y}_{1:t-1}$ given $\mathbf{X}_{t-1}$,
2. $\mathbf{Y}_t$ is conditionally independent of $\mathbf{Y}_{1:t-1}$ given $\mathbf{X}_t$.

We prove the first one and leave the second one as an exercise (see Problem 6.20). In fact, we prove something stronger: $\mathbf{X}_t$ is conditionally independent of $\mathbf{X}_{0:t-2}, \mathbf{Y}_{1:t-1}$ given $\mathbf{X}_{t-1}$.

First, by integrating over $\mathbf{y}_T$, then $\mathbf{x}_T$, then $\mathbf{y}_{T-1}$, then $\mathbf{x}_{T-1}$, ..., then $\mathbf{y}_t$, we see that the joint density of $(\mathbf{X}_{0:t}, \mathbf{Y}_{1:t-1})$ is

$$f_{\mathbf{X}_0}(\mathbf{x}_0) \left(\prod_{s=1}^{t-1} f_{\mathbf{X}_s|\mathbf{X}_{s-1}}(\mathbf{x}_s|\mathbf{x}_{s-1}) f_{\mathbf{Y}_s|\mathbf{X}_s}(\mathbf{y}_s|\mathbf{x}_s) \right) f_{\mathbf{X}_t|\mathbf{X}_{t-1}}(\mathbf{x}_t|\mathbf{x}_{t-1}).$$

Similarly, the joint density of $(\mathbf{X}_{0:t-1}, \mathbf{Y}_{1:t-1})$ is

$$f_{\mathbf{X}_0}(\mathbf{x}_0) \left(\prod_{s=1}^{t-1} f_{\mathbf{X}_s|\mathbf{X}_{s-1}}(\mathbf{x}_s|\mathbf{x}_{s-1}) f_{\mathbf{Y}_s|\mathbf{X}_s}(\mathbf{y}_s|\mathbf{x}_s) \right).$$

The conditional density given $\mathbf{X}_{t-1}$ is then obtained by dividing the first expression by the marginal density of $\mathbf{X}_{t-1}$:

$$\frac{f_{\mathbf{X}_0}(\mathbf{x}_0)\left(\prod_{s=1}^{t-1} f_{\mathbf{X}_s|\mathbf{X}_{s-1}}(\mathbf{x}_s|\mathbf{x}_{s-1}) f_{\mathbf{Y}_s|\mathbf{X}_s}(\mathbf{y}_s|\mathbf{x}_s)\right) f_{\mathbf{X}_t|\mathbf{X}_{t-1}}(\mathbf{x}_t|\mathbf{x}_{t-1})}{f_{\mathbf{X}_{t-1}}(\mathbf{x}_{t-1})}$$

$$= \frac{f_{\mathbf{X}_0}(\mathbf{x}_0)\left(\prod_{s=1}^{t-1} f_{\mathbf{X}_s|\mathbf{X}_{s-1}}(\mathbf{x}_s|\mathbf{x}_{s-1}) f_{\mathbf{Y}_s|\mathbf{X}_s}(\mathbf{y}_s|\mathbf{x}_s)\right) f_{\mathbf{X}_t|\mathbf{X}_{t-1}}(\mathbf{x}_t|\mathbf{x}_{t-1})}{f_{\mathbf{X}_{t-1}}(\mathbf{x}_{t-1})}$$

$$= \frac{f_{\mathbf{X}_0}(\mathbf{x}_0)\left(\prod_{s=1}^{t-1} f_{\mathbf{X}_s|\mathbf{X}_{s-1}}(\mathbf{x}_s|\mathbf{x}_{s-1}) f_{\mathbf{Y}_s|\mathbf{X}_s}(\mathbf{y}_s|\mathbf{x}_s)\right)}{f_{\mathbf{X}_{t-1}}(\mathbf{x}_{t-1})} f_{\mathbf{X}_t|\mathbf{X}_{t-1}}(\mathbf{x}_t|\mathbf{x}_{t-1})$$

$$= f_{\mathbf{X}_{0:t-2},\mathbf{Y}_{1:t-1}|\mathbf{X}_{t-1}}(\mathbf{x}_{0:t-2},\mathbf{y}_{1:t-1}|\mathbf{x}_{t-1}) f_{\mathbf{X}_t|\mathbf{X}_{t-1}}(\mathbf{x}_t|\mathbf{x}_{t-1})$$

as claimed.

6.5.2.4 Algorithm for Solving the Filtering Problem

We give a recursive algorithm for solving the filtering problem; that is, for computing the mean vector and covariance matrix of the conditional density $f_{\mathbf{X}_t|\mathbf{Y}_{1:t}}$.

Initial step: We first compute $f_{\mathbf{X}_1|\mathbf{Y}_1}$. We do this through a series of observations, which will generalize straightforwardly.

First, note that we have $\mathbf{X}_0 \sim N_{d_0}(\boldsymbol{\mu}_0, \boldsymbol{\Sigma}_0)$ and $\mathbf{X}_1|\mathbf{X}_0 \sim N_{d_0}(F\mathbf{X}_0, Q)$. So, by the *Linear-Gaussian System Lemma*, the joint vector $(\mathbf{X}_0, \mathbf{X}_1)$ is multivariate Gaussian with mean vector $(\boldsymbol{\mu}_0, F\boldsymbol{\mu}_0)$ and covariance matrix

$$\begin{pmatrix} \boldsymbol{\Sigma}_0 & \boldsymbol{\Sigma}_0 F^T \\ F\boldsymbol{\Sigma}_0 & F\boldsymbol{\Sigma}_0 F^T + Q \end{pmatrix}.$$

Hence the marginal density of $\mathbf{X}_1$ is multivariate Gaussian with mean vector $F\boldsymbol{\mu}_0$ and covariance matrix

$$P_0 := F\boldsymbol{\Sigma}_0 F^T + Q.$$

Second, combining the previous observation about the marginal density of $\mathbf{X}_1$ with the fact that $\mathbf{Y}_1|\mathbf{X}_1 \sim N_d(H\mathbf{X}_1, R)$, the *Linear-Gaussian System Lemma* says that $(\mathbf{X}_1, \mathbf{Y}_1)$ is multivariate Gaussian with mean vector $(F\boldsymbol{\mu}_0, HF\boldsymbol{\mu}_0)$ and covariance matrix

$$\begin{pmatrix} P_0 & P_0 H^T \\ HP_0 & HP_0 H^T + R \end{pmatrix}.$$

Finally, define $K_1 := P_0 H^T (HP_0 H^T + R)^{-1}$. This new observation and the conditional density formula give that

$$\mathbf{X}_1|\mathbf{Y}_1 \sim N_d(\boldsymbol{\mu}_1, \boldsymbol{\Sigma}_1)$$

where we define

$$\boldsymbol{\mu}_1 := F\boldsymbol{\mu}_0 + P_0 H^T (HP_0 H^T + R)^{-1}(\mathbf{Y}_1 - HF\boldsymbol{\mu}_0)$$
$$= F\boldsymbol{\mu}_0 + K_1(\mathbf{Y}_1 - HF\boldsymbol{\mu}_0)$$

and
$$\Sigma_1 := P_0 - P_0 H^T (H P_0 H^T + R)^{-1} H P_0$$
$$= (I_{d_0 \times d_0} - K_1 H) P_0.$$

General step: Assuming by induction that $\mathbf{X}_{t-1} | \mathbf{Y}_{1:t-1} \sim N_{d_0}(\boldsymbol{\mu}_{t-1}, \Sigma_{t-1})$ where $\boldsymbol{\mu}_{t-1}$ depends implicitly on $\mathbf{Y}_{1:t-1}$ (but Σ_{t-1} does not), we deduce the next step. It mimics closely the initial step.

Predict: We first "predict" $\mathbf{X}_t$ given $\mathbf{Y}_{1:t-1}$. We use the fact that $\mathbf{X}_{t-1}|\mathbf{Y}_{1:t-1} \sim N_{d_0}(\boldsymbol{\mu}_{t-1}, \Sigma_{t-1})$. Moreover, we have that $\mathbf{X}_t | \mathbf{X}_{t-1} \sim N_{d_0}(F\mathbf{X}_{t-1}, Q)$ and that $\mathbf{X}_t$ is conditionally independent of $\mathbf{Y}_{1:t-1}$ given $\mathbf{X}_{t-1}$. So, $\mathbf{X}_t | \{\mathbf{X}_{t-1}, \mathbf{Y}_{1:t-1}\} \sim N_{d_0}(F\mathbf{X}_{t-1}, Q)$ by the *Role of Independence Lemma*. By the *Linear-Gaussian System Lemma*, the joint vector $(\mathbf{X}_{t-1}, \mathbf{X}_t)$ conditioned on $\mathbf{Y}_{1:t-1}$ is multivariate Gaussian with mean vector $(\boldsymbol{\mu}_{t-1}, F\boldsymbol{\mu}_{t-1})$ and covariance matrix

$$\begin{pmatrix} \Sigma_{t-1} & \Sigma_{t-1} F^T \\ F\Sigma_{t-1} & F\Sigma_{t-1}F^T + Q \end{pmatrix}.$$

As a consequence, the conditional marginal density of $\mathbf{X}_t$ given $\mathbf{Y}_{1:t-1}$ is multivariate Gaussian with mean vector $F\boldsymbol{\mu}_{t-1}$ and covariance matrix

$$P_{t-1} := F\Sigma_{t-1}F^T + Q.$$

Update: Next we "update" our prediction of $\mathbf{X}_t$ using the new observation $\mathbf{Y}_t$. We have that $\mathbf{Y}_t | \mathbf{X}_t \sim N_d(H\mathbf{X}_t, R)$ and that $\mathbf{Y}_t$ is conditionally independent of $\mathbf{Y}_{1:t-1}$ given $\mathbf{X}_t$. So $\mathbf{Y}_t | \{\mathbf{X}_t, \mathbf{Y}_{1:t-1}\} \sim N_d(H\mathbf{X}_t, R)$ by the *Role of Independence Lemma*. Combining this with the previous observation, the *Linear-Gaussian System Lemma* says that $(\mathbf{X}_t, \mathbf{Y}_t)$ given $\mathbf{Y}_{1:t-1}$ is multivariate Gaussian with mean vector $(F\boldsymbol{\mu}_{t-1}, HF\boldsymbol{\mu}_{t-1})$ and covariance matrix

$$\begin{pmatrix} P_{t-1} & P_{t-1} H^T \\ H P_{t-1} & H P_{t-1} H^T + R \end{pmatrix}.$$

Finally, define $K_t := P_{t-1} H^T (H P_{t-1} H^T + R)^{-1}$. This new observation and the conditional density formula give

$$\mathbf{X}_t | \{\mathbf{Y}_t, \mathbf{Y}_{1:t-1}\} = \mathbf{X}_t | \mathbf{Y}_{1:t} \sim N_d(\boldsymbol{\mu}_t, \Sigma_t)$$

where we define

$$\boldsymbol{\mu}_t := F\boldsymbol{\mu}_{t-1} + K_t(\mathbf{Y}_t - HF\boldsymbol{\mu}_{t-1})$$

and

$$\Sigma_t := (I_{d_0 \times d_0} - K_t H) P_{t-1}.$$

Summary: Let $\boldsymbol{\mu}_t$ and Σ_t be the mean and covariance matrix of $\mathbf{X}_t$ conditioned on $\mathbf{Y}_{1:t}$. The recursions for these quantities are the following:

$$\boldsymbol{\mu}_t = F\boldsymbol{\mu}_{t-1} + K_t(\mathbf{Y}_t - HF\boldsymbol{\mu}_{t-1})$$
$$\Sigma_t = (I_{d_0 \times d_0} - K_t H) P_{t-1}$$

where

$$P_{t-1} = F \Sigma_{t-1} F^T + Q$$
$$K_t = P_{t-1} H^T (H P_{t-1} H^T + R)^{-1}.$$

This last matrix is known as the Kalman gain matrix. The vector $\mathbf{Y}_t - HF\mu_{t-1}$ is referred to as innovation; it compares the new observation $\mathbf{Y}_t$ to its predicted expectation $HF\mu_{t-1}$ based on the previous observations. Hence, in some sense, the Kalman gain matrix represents the "weight" given to the observation at time t when updating the state estimate μ_t. The solution above is known as Kalman filtering.

6.5.3 Back to Location Tracking

We apply Kalman filtering to location tracking. Returning to our cyborg corgi example, we imagine that we get noisy observations about its successive positions in a park. (Think of GPS measurements.) We seek to get a better estimate of its location using the method above.

We model the true location as a linear-Gaussian system over the 2d position $(z_{1,t}, z_{2,t})_t$ and velocity $(\dot{z}_{1,t}, \dot{z}_{2,t})_t$ sampled at Δ intervals of time. Formally,

$$\mathbf{X}_t = (z_{1,t}, z_{2,t}, \dot{z}_{1,t}, \dot{z}_{2,t}), \quad F = \begin{pmatrix} 1 & 0 & \Delta & 0 \\ 0 & 1 & 0 & \Delta \\ 0 & 0 & 1 & 0 \\ 0 & 0 & 0 & 1 \end{pmatrix},$$

so the unobserved dynamics are

$$\begin{pmatrix} z_{1,t+1} \\ z_{2,t+1} \\ \dot{z}_{1,t+1} \\ \dot{z}_{2,t+1} \end{pmatrix} = \mathbf{X}_{t+1} = F\mathbf{X}_t + \mathbf{W}_t = \begin{pmatrix} z_{1,t} + \Delta \dot{z}_{1,t} + W_{1,t} \\ z_{2,t} + \Delta \dot{z}_{2,t} + W_{2,t} \\ \dot{z}_{1,t} + \dot{W}_{1,t} \\ \dot{z}_{2,t} + \dot{W}_{2,t} \end{pmatrix}$$

where the $\mathbf{W}_t = (W_{1,t}, W_{2,t}, \dot{W}_{1,t}, \dot{W}_{2,t}) \sim N_{d_0}(\mathbf{0}, Q)$ with Q known.

In words, the velocity is unchanged, up to Gaussian perturbation. The position changes proportionally to the velocity in the corresponding dimension, again up to Gaussian perturbation. The observations $(\tilde{z}_{1,t}, \tilde{z}_{2,t})_t$ are modeled as

$$\mathbf{Y}_t = (\tilde{z}_{1,t}, \tilde{z}_{2,t}), \quad H = \begin{pmatrix} 1 & 0 & 0 & 0 \\ 0 & 1 & 0 & 0 \end{pmatrix}$$

so the observed process satisfies

$$\begin{pmatrix} \tilde{z}_{1,t} \\ \tilde{z}_{2,t} \end{pmatrix} = \mathbf{Y}_t = H\mathbf{X}_t + \mathbf{V}_t = \begin{pmatrix} z_{1,t} + \tilde{V}_{1,t} \\ z_{2,t} + \tilde{V}_{2,t} \end{pmatrix}$$

where the $\mathbf{V}_t = (\tilde{V}_{1,t}, \tilde{V}_{2,t}) \sim N_d(\mathbf{0}, R)$ with R known.

In words, we only observe the positions, up to Gaussian noise.

6.5.3.1 Implementing the Kalman Filter

We implement the Kalman filter as described above with known covariance matrices. We take $\Delta = 1$ for simplicity. The code is adapted from [Mur1].[11]

---

[11] https://github.com/probml/pmtk3/blob/master/demos/kalmanTrackingDemo.m

We will test Kalman filtering on a simulated path drawn from the linear-Gaussian model above. The following function creates such a path and its noisy observations.

```python
def lgSamplePath(rng, ss, os, F, H, Q, R, init_mu, init_Sig, T):
    x = np.zeros((ss,T))
    y = np.zeros((os,T))
    
    x[:,0] = rng.multivariate_normal(init_mu, init_Sig)
    for t in range(1,T):
        x[:,t] = rng.multivariate_normal(F @ x[:,t-1],Q)
        y[:,t] = rng.multivariate_normal(H @ x[:,t],R)
    
    return x, y
```

NUMERICAL CORNER Here is an example.

```python
seed = 535
rng = np.random.default_rng(seed)
ss = 4 # state size
os = 2 # observation size
F = np.array([[1., 0., 1., 0.],
              [0., 1., 0., 1.],
              [0., 0., 1., 0.],
              [0., 0., 0., 1.]])
H = np.array([[1., 0., 0., 0.],
              [0., 1, 0., 0.]])
Q = 0.1 * np.diag(np.ones(ss))
R = 10 * np.diag(np.ones(os))
init_mu = np.array([0., 0., 1., 1.])
init_Sig = 1 * np.diag(np.ones(ss))
T = 50
x, y = lgSamplePath(rng, ss, os, F, H, Q, R, init_mu, init_Sig, T)
```

In the next plot (and throughout this section), the dots are the noisy observations. The unobserved true path is also shown as a dotted line.

```python
plt.scatter(y[0,:], y[1,:], s=5, c='r', alpha=0.5)
plt.plot(x[0,:], x[1,:], c='g', linestyle='dotted')
plt.xlim((np.min(y[0,:])-5, np.max(y[0,:])+5))
plt.ylim((np.min(y[1,:])-5, np.max(y[1,:])+5))
plt.show()
```

6.5 Application: Linear-Gaussian Models and Kalman Filtering

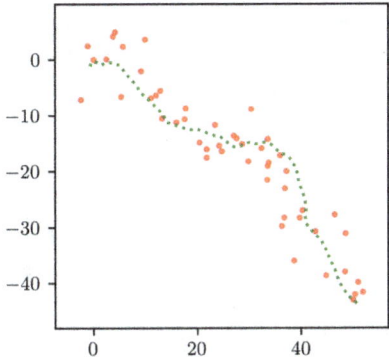

Figure 6.19 Graphical output of code.

◁ **NC**

The following function implements the Kalman filter. The full recursion is broken up into several steps. We use `numpy.linalg.inv` to compute the Kalman gain matrix. Below, `mu_pred` is $F\mu_{t-1}$ and `Sig_pred` is $P_{t-1} = F\Sigma_{t-1}F^T + Q$, which are the mean vector and covariance matrix of $\mathbf{X}_t$ given $\mathbf{Y}_{1:t-1}$ as computed in the *Predict* step.

```
def kalmanUpdate(ss, F, H, Q, R, y_t, mu_prev, Sig_prev):

    mu_pred = F @ mu_prev
    Sig_pred = F @ Sig_prev @ F.T + Q

    e_t = y_t - H @ mu_pred
    S = H @ Sig_pred @ H.T + R
    Sinv = LA.inv(S)
    K = Sig_pred @ H.T @ Sinv

    mu_new = mu_pred + K @ e_t
    Sig_new = (np.diag(np.ones(ss)) - K @ H) @ Sig_pred

    return mu_new, Sig_new
```

```
def kalmanFilter(ss, os, y, F, H, Q, R, init_mu, init_Sig, T):

    mu = np.zeros((ss, T))
    Sig = np.zeros((ss, ss, T))
    mu[:,0] = init_mu
    Sig[:,:,0] = init_Sig
    for t in range(1,T):
        mu[:,t], Sig[:,:,t] = kalmanUpdate(ss, F, H, Q, R, y[:,t],
            mu[:,t-1], Sig[:,:,t-1])

    return mu, Sig
```

NUMERICAL CORNER We apply this to the location tracking example. The inferred states, or more precisely their estimated mean, are in blue. Note that we also inferred the velocity at each time point, but we are not plotting that information.

```
init_mu = np.array([0., 0., 1., 1.])
init_Sig = 1 * np.diag(np.ones(ss))
mu, Sig = kalmanFilter(ss, os, y, F, H, Q, R, init_mu, init_Sig, T)
plt.plot(mu[0,:], mu[1,:], c='b', marker='s', markersize=2,
         linewidth=1)
plt.scatter(y[0,:], y[1,:], s=5, c='r', alpha=0.5)
plt.plot(x[0,:], x[1,:], c='g', linestyle='dotted', alpha=0.5)
plt.xlim((np.min(y[0,:])-5, np.max(y[0,:])+5))
plt.ylim((np.min(y[1,:])-5, np.max(y[1,:])+5))
plt.show()
```

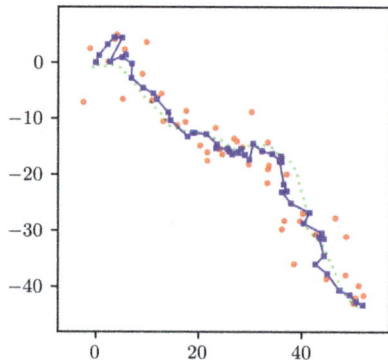

Figure 6.20 Graphical output of code.

To quantify the improvement in the inferred means compared to the observations, we compute the mean squared error in both cases.

```
dobs = x[0:1,:] - y[0:1,:]
mse_obs = np.sqrt(np.sum(dobs**2))
print(mse_obs)
```

22.891982252201856

```
dfilt = x[0:1,:] - mu[0:1,:]
mse_filt = np.sqrt(np.sum(dfilt**2))
print(mse_filt)
```

9.778610100463018

We indeed observe a substantial reduction.

6.5 Application: Linear-Gaussian Models and Kalman Filtering

CHAT & LEARN Explore the concept of sequential Monte Carlo methods, also known as particle filters, as an alternative to the Kalman filter. Ask your favorite AI chatbot for an explanation and implementation of a particle filter. ***Try it on this dataset***.

◁ NC

CHAT & LEARN The Kalman filter assumes that the parameters of the state evolution and observation models are known. Ask your favorite AI chatbot about methods for estimating these parameters from data, such as the expectation-maximization algorithm or the variational Bayes approach.

Self-Assessment Quiz (with help from Claude, Gemini, and ChatGPT)

1. Which of the following is the Schur complement of the block B_{11} in the positive definite matrix $B = \begin{pmatrix} B_{11} & B_{12} \\ B_{12}^T & B_{22} \end{pmatrix}$?

   a) $B_{22} - B_{12}^T B_{11}^{-1} B_{12}$
   b) $B_{11} - B_{12} B_{22}^{-1} B_{12}^T$
   c) B_{22}
   d) B_{11}

2. Which of the following is true about the Schur complement B/B_{11} of the block B_{11} in a positive definite matrix B?

   a) It is always symmetric.
   b) It is always positive definite.
   c) Both a and b.
   d) Neither a nor b.

3. What is the conditional distribution of X_1 given X_2 in a multivariate Gaussian distribution?

   a) $X_1|X_2 \sim N_{d_1}(\mu_1 + \Sigma_{12}\Sigma_{22}^{-1}(X_2 - \mu_2), \Sigma_{11} - \Sigma_{12}\Sigma_{22}^{-1}\Sigma_{12}^T)$
   b) $X_1|X_2 \sim N_{d_1}(\mu_1 - \Sigma_{12}\Sigma_{22}^{-1}(X_2 - \mu_2), \Sigma_{11} + \Sigma_{12}\Sigma_{22}^{-1}\Sigma_{12}^T)$
   c) $X_1|X_2 \sim N_{d_1}(\mu_1 + \Sigma_{12}\Sigma_{22}^{-1}(X_2 - \mu_2), \Sigma_{11} + \Sigma_{12}\Sigma_{22}^{-1}\Sigma_{12}^T)$
   d) $X_1|X_2 \sim N_{d_1}(\mu_1 - \Sigma_{12}\Sigma_{22}^{-1}(X_2 - \mu_2), \Sigma_{11} - \Sigma_{12}\Sigma_{22}^{-1}\Sigma_{12}^T)$

4. In a linear-Gaussian system, which of the following is true about the conditional independence relationships?

   a) X_t is conditionally independent of $Y_{1:t-1}$ given X_{t-1}.
   b) Y_t is conditionally independent of $Y_{1:t-1}$ given X_t.
   c) X_t is conditionally independent of X_{t-2} given X_{t-1}.
   d) All of the above.

5. In the Kalman filter, what does the Kalman gain matrix K_t represent?

   a) The covariance matrix of the state estimate at time t
   b) The covariance matrix of the observation at time t
   c) The weight given to the observation at time t when updating the state estimate

d) The weight given to the previous state estimate when predicting the current state

Answer for 1: a. Justification: The text defines the Schur complement of B_{11} as $B/B_{11} := B_{22} - B_{12}^T B_{11}^{-1} B_{12}$.

Answer for 2: c. Justification: The text states "the Schur complement of the block B_{11}, namely the matrix $B/B_{11} := B_{22} - B_{12}^T B_{11}^{-1} B_{12}$, is symmetric and positive definite."

Answer for 3: a. Justification: The conditional distribution of $\mathbf{X}_1$ given $\mathbf{X}_2$ is derived in the text as $\mathbf{X}_1|\mathbf{X}_2 \sim N_{d_1}(\boldsymbol{\mu}_1 + \Sigma_{12}\Sigma_{22}^{-1}(\mathbf{X}_2 - \boldsymbol{\mu}_2), \Sigma_{11} - \Sigma_{12}\Sigma_{22}^{-1}\Sigma_{12}^T)$.

Answer for 4: d. Justification: The text explicitly states these conditional independence relationships.

Answer for 5: c. Justification: The text defines $K_t := P_{t-1}H^T(HP_{t-1}H^T + R)^{-1}$ as the Kalman gain matrix, which is used to update the state estimate as $\boldsymbol{\mu}_t := F\boldsymbol{\mu}_{t-1} + K_t(\mathbf{Y}_t - HF\boldsymbol{\mu}_{t-1})$, where K_t weighs the innovation $(\mathbf{Y}_t - HF\boldsymbol{\mu}_{t-1})$.

6.6 Exercises

6.6.1 Warm-Up Worksheets
(with help from Claude, Gemini, and ChatGPT)

Section 6.2

E6.2.1 For a categorical variable $\mathbf{Y}$ with $K = 3$ categories and probabilities $\pi_1 = 0.2$, $\pi_2 = 0.5$, and $\pi_3 = 0.3$, compute the probability $\mathbb{P}(\mathbf{Y} = \mathbf{e}_2)$.

E6.2.2 Given a dataset of 10 coin flips $(1, 0, 1, 1, 0, 0, 1, 1, 0, 1)$, find the maximum likelihood estimate of the parameter q of a Bernoulli distribution.

E6.2.3 Prove that the maximum likelihood estimator for the parameter of a Bernoulli distribution is statistically consistent.

E6.2.4 Given a dataset $\{(x_i, y_i)\}_{i=1}^n$ with $x_i \in \mathbb{R}$ and $y_i \in \{0, 1\}$, write down the negative log-likelihood for logistic regression and compute its gradient.

E6.2.5 For the dataset $\{(1, 1), (2, 0), (3, 1), (4, 0)\}$, perform one step of gradient descent for logistic regression with learning rate $\eta = 0.1$ and initial parameter $w = 0$.

E6.2.6 Compute the gradient and Hessian of the negative log-likelihood for a generalized linear model with a Poisson distribution with mean λ.

E6.2.7 A discrete random variable X has probability mass function given by

$$P(X = x) = \frac{1}{Z(\theta)} h(x) \exp(\theta x),$$

where $x \in \{-1, 0, 1\}$. Find the value of $Z(\theta)$.

E6.2.8 Let X be a random variable with probability mass function given by

$$P(X = x) = \frac{1}{Z(\theta)} \exp(\theta x^2),$$

where $x \in \{-1, 0, 1\}$. Find the partition function $Z(\theta)$.

E6.2.9 Given the sample $\{X_1 = 1, X_2 = 2, X_3 = 2, X_4 = 3\}$ from a multinomial distribution with $n = 4$ trials and $K = 3$ categories, compute the empirical frequency for each category.

E6.2.10 Compute the determinant of the covariance matrix $\Sigma = \begin{pmatrix} 4 & 2 \\ 2 & 3 \end{pmatrix}$.

E6.2.11 For a multivariate Gaussian vector $X \in \mathbb{R}^2$ with mean $\mu = \begin{pmatrix} 1 \\ 2 \end{pmatrix}$ and covariance matrix $\Sigma = \begin{pmatrix} 2 & 1 \\ 1 & 2 \end{pmatrix}$, compute the log-likelihood of observing $\mathbf{X} = \begin{pmatrix} 1 \\ 3 \end{pmatrix}$.

Section 6.3

E6.3.1 Given the events A and B with $P(A) = 0.4$, $P(B) = 0.5$, and $P(A \cap B) = 0.2$, compute the conditional probability $P(A|B)$.

E6.3.2 Given the random variables X and Y with joint probability mass function $p_{X,Y}(x,y) = \frac{1}{4}$ for $x, y \in \{0, 1\}$, find $P(Y = 1|X = 0)$.

E6.3.3 Calculate the conditional expectation $\mathbb{E}[X|Y = y]$ for a discrete random variable X with $\mathbb{P}(X = 1|Y = y) = 0.3$ and $\mathbb{P}(X = 2|Y = y) = 0.7$.

E6.3.4 For the events A and B with $P(A|B) = 0.6$ and $P(B) = 0.5$, calculate $P(A \cap B)$.

E6.3.5 Given events A, B, and C with $P[A] = 0.6$, $P[B] = 0.5$, $P[C] = 0.4$, $P[A \cap B] = 0.3$, $P[A \cap C] = 0.2$, $P[B \cap C] = 0.1$, and $P[A \cap B \cap C] = 0.05$, compute $P[A \mid B \cap C]$.

E6.3.6 Given events A, B, and C with $P[A] = 0.7$, $P[B \mid A] = 0.6$, and $P[C \mid A \cap B] = 0.4$, compute $P[A \cap B \cap C]$.

E6.3.7 Given events A, B, and C with $P[A] = 0.8$, $P[B] = 0.6$, and $P[C] = 0.5$, and assuming that A, B, and C are pairwise independent, compute $P[A \cap B \cap C]$.

E6.3.8 Let X, Y, Z be random variables taking values in $\{0, 1\}$. Given a fork configuration $Y \leftarrow X \rightarrow Z$ with $(P[X = x])_x = (0.2, 0.8)$, $P([Y = y \mid X = x])_{x,y} = \begin{pmatrix} 0.6 & 0.4 \\ 0.3 & 0.7 \end{pmatrix}$, and $(P[Z = z \mid X = x])_{x,z} = \begin{pmatrix} 0.8 & 0.2 \\ 0.1 & 0.9 \end{pmatrix}$, compute $(P[Y = y, Z = z])_{y,z}$.

E6.3.9 Let X, Y, Z be random variables taking values in $\{0, 1\}$. Given a chain configuration $X \rightarrow Y \rightarrow Z$ with $(P[X = x])_x = (0.3, 0.7)$, $(P[Y = y \mid X = x])_{x,y} = \begin{pmatrix} 0.2 & 0.8 \\ 0.6 & 0.4 \end{pmatrix}$, and $(P[Z = z \mid Y = y])_{y,z} = \begin{pmatrix} 0.5 & 0.5 \\ 0.1 & 0.9 \end{pmatrix}$, compute $(P[X = x, Z = z])_{x,z}$.

E6.3.10 Consider a document classification problem with a vocabulary of four words and two topics. Given $\pi = (0.5, 0.5)$, $p_1 = (0.1, 0.5, 0.1, 0.5)$, and $p_2 = (0.5, 0.5, 0.1, 0.1)$, compute $P[C = 1, X = (1, 0, 1, 0)]$.

E6.3.11 Consider a document classification problem with a vocabulary of three words and two topics. Given a training dataset with $N_{1,1} = 10$, $N_{1,2} = 20$, $N_{1,3} = 20$, $N_{2,1} = 40$, $N_{2,2} = 30$, $N_{2,3} = 30$, $N_1 = 50$, and $N_2 = 100$, compute the maximum likelihood estimates of π_1, $p_{1,1}$, and $p_{2,1}$.

E6.3.12 Suppose A, B, and C are events such that $P[C] > 0$ and $A \perp\!\!\!\perp B|C$. If $P[A|C] = 0.3$ and $P[B|C] = 0.6$, calculate $P[A \cap B|C]$.

E6.3.13 Consider the following graphical model:

```
G = nx.DiGraph()
G.add_edges_from([("X", "Y"), ("X", "Z")])
```

Write down the joint probability distribution $P[X = x, Y = y, Z = z]$ using the chain rule of probability.

E6.3.14 In the naive Bayes model, if a document contains the words "love" and "great," but no other word in the vocabulary, and the model parameters are $p_{1,love} = 0.8$, $p_{1,great} = 0.7$, $p_{2,love} = 0.2$, and $p_{2,great} = 0.3$, which equally likely class (1 or 2) is the document more likely to belong to?

Section 6.4

E6.4.1 Let X be a random variable that follows a mixture of two Bernoulli distributions with parameters $p_1 = 0.3$ and $p_2 = 0.8$, and mixing weights $\pi_1 = 0.6$ and $\pi_2 = 0.4$. Compute $P(X = 1)$.

E6.4.2 In a Gaussian mixture model (GMM) with two components, suppose $\mu_1 = (1, 2)$, $\mu_2 = (-1, -1)$, $\Sigma_1 = \Sigma_2 = I_{2\times 2}$, and $\pi_1 = \pi_2 = 0.5$. Write down the probability density function of this GMM.

E6.4.3 Given a mixture of two multivariate Bernoulli distributions with parameters $\pi_1 = 0.4$, $\pi_2 = 0.6$, $p_{1,1} = 0.7$, $p_{1,2} = 0.3$, $p_{2,1} = 0.2$, and $p_{2,2} = 0.8$, compute the probability of observing the data point $\mathbf{x} = (1, 0)$.

E6.4.4 Given a mixture of two univariate Gaussian distributions with parameters $\pi_1 = 0.3$, $\pi_2 = 0.7$, $\mu_1 = 1$, $\mu_2 = 4$, $\sigma_1^2 = 1$, and $\sigma_2^2 = 2$, compute the probability density function at $x = 2$.

E6.4.5 Given a mixture of two multivariate Bernoulli distributions with parameters $\pi_1 = 0.5$, $\pi_2 = 0.5$, $p_{1,1} = 0.8$, $p_{1,2} = 0.2$, $p_{2,1} = 0.1$, and $p_{2,2} = 0.9$, compute the responsibilities $r_{1,i}$ and $r_{2,i}$ for the data point $\mathbf{x}_i = (1, 1)$.

E6.4.6 Given a mixture of two multivariate Bernoulli distributions with parameters $\pi_1 = 0.4$, $\pi_2 = 0.6$, $p_{1,1} = 0.7$, $p_{1,2} = 0.1$, $p_{2,1} = 0.2$, and $p_{2,2} = 0.3$, compute the responsibilities $r_{1,i}$ and $r_{2,i}$ for the data point $\mathbf{x}_i = (0, 1)$.

E6.4.7 Given a mixture of two multivariate Bernoulli distributions with parameters $\pi_1 = 0.6$, $\pi_2 = 0.4$, and responsibilities $r_{1,1} = 0.8$ and $r_{2,2} = 0.2$ for data points $\mathbf{x}_1 = (1, 0)$ and $\mathbf{x}_2 = (0, 1)$, update the parameters π_1 and π_2 using the M-step of the EM algorithm.

E6.4.8 Given a mixture of two multivariate Bernoulli distributions with parameters $\pi_1 = 0.5$, $\pi_2 = 0.5$, responsibilities $r_{1,1} = 0.7$, $r_{1,2} = 0.3$, and data points $\mathbf{x}_1 = (1, 1)$ and $\mathbf{x}_2 = (0, 0)$, update the parameters π_1 and π_2 using the M-step of the EM algorithm.

E6.4.9 In the EM algorithm for mixtures of multivariate Bernoullis, suppose you have three data points: $\mathbf{x}_1 = (1, 0, 1)$, $\mathbf{x}_2 = (0, 1, 0)$, and $\mathbf{x}_3 = (1, 1, 1)$. If the current parameter estimates are $\pi_1 = 0.4$, $\pi_2 = 0.6$, $p_{1,1} = 0.2$, $p_{1,2} = 0.7$, $p_{1,3} = 0.9$, $p_{2,1} = 0.8$, $p_{2,2} = 0.3$, and $p_{2,3} = 0.5$, compute the responsibility $r_{1,2}$ (the responsibility that cluster 1 takes for data point 2).

E6.4.10 Let $f(x) = x^2$. Find a function $U_x(z)$ that majorizes f at $x = 2$.

E6.4.11 For a Gaussian mixture model with component means $\mu_1 = -1$, $\mu_2 = 3$, and mixing weights $\pi_1 = 0.5$, $\pi_2 = 0.5$, compute the expected value $\mathbb{E}[X]$.

E6.4.12 Given the mixture weights $\pi_1 = 0.3$, $\pi_2 = 0.7$, and component densities $p_{\theta_1}(x) = 0.25$, $p_{\theta_2}(x) = 0.75$, compute the log-likelihood $\log(p_X(x))$.

E6.4.13 For a Gaussian mixture model with two components, $\pi_1 = 0.4$, $\pi_2 = 0.6$, $\mu_1 = 0$, $\mu_2 = 4$, and $\sigma_1^2 = 1$, $\sigma_2^2 = 2$, compute $\text{Var}(X)$.

Section 6.5

E6.5.1 Given a positive definite matrix $B = \begin{pmatrix} 2 & 1 \\ 1 & 3 \end{pmatrix}$, compute the Schur complement B/B_{11}.

E6.5.2 Given the block matrix
$$A = \begin{pmatrix} 1 & 2 & 0 \\ 3 & 4 & 5 \\ 0 & 6 & 7 \end{pmatrix},$$
partition A into four blocks where A_{11} is formed from the first two rows and columns.

E6.5.3 Compute the Schur complement of the block A_{11} in the matrix A given in E6.5.2.

E6.5.4 Given a multivariate Gaussian vector $\mathbf{X} = (X_1, X_2)$ with mean $\boldsymbol{\mu} = (1, 2)$ and covariance matrix $\Sigma = \begin{pmatrix} 2 & 1 \\ 1 & 3 \end{pmatrix}$, compute the marginal mean and variance of X_1.

E6.5.5 Given a multivariate Gaussian vector $\mathbf{X} = (X_1, X_2)$ with mean $\boldsymbol{\mu} = (1, 2)$ and covariance matrix $\Sigma = \begin{pmatrix} 2 & 1 \\ 1 & 3 \end{pmatrix}$, compute the conditional mean of X_1 given $X_2 = 3$.

E6.5.6 Given the multivariate Gaussian vector $\mathbf{X} = (X_1, X_2) \sim N_2\left(\begin{pmatrix} 0 \\ 0 \end{pmatrix}, \begin{pmatrix} 2 & 1 \\ 1 & 2 \end{pmatrix}\right)$, compute $\mathbb{E}[X_1 | X_2 = 1]$.

E6.5.7 Let $\mathbf{X} = (X_1, X_2)$ be a multivariate Gaussian random variable with mean vector $\boldsymbol{\mu} = (0, 0)$ and covariance matrix $\Sigma = \begin{pmatrix} 4 & 1 \\ 1 & 2 \end{pmatrix}$. Find the conditional distribution of X_1 given $X_2 = 1$.

E6.5.8 Let $\mathbf{X} = (X_1, X_2, X_3)$ be a multivariate Gaussian random variable with mean vector $\boldsymbol{\mu} = (1, -1, 0)$ and covariance matrix $\Sigma = \begin{pmatrix} 3 & 1 & 0 \\ 1 & 2 & -1 \\ 0 & -1 & 1 \end{pmatrix}$. Write down the marginal distribution of (X_1, X_3).

E6.5.9 Let $\mathbf{X}$ be a multivariate Gaussian random variable with mean vector $\begin{pmatrix} 1 \\ -2 \end{pmatrix}$ and covariance matrix $\begin{pmatrix} 3 & 1 \\ 1 & 2 \end{pmatrix}$. Find the distribution of the linear transformation $\mathbf{Y} = A\mathbf{X}$, where $A = \begin{pmatrix} 1 & 2 \\ -1 & 1 \end{pmatrix}$.

E6.5.10 Given a linear-Gaussian system with state evolution $\mathbf{X}_{t+1} = \begin{pmatrix} 1 & 1 \\ 0 & 1 \end{pmatrix} \mathbf{X}_t + \mathbf{W}_t$, where $\mathbf{W}_t \stackrel{iid}{\sim} N_2(0, I_2)$, and initial state distribution $\mathbf{X}_0 \sim N_2((1, 1), I_2)$, compute the mean and covariance matrix of X_1.

E6.5.11 Given a linear-Gaussian system with observation model $Y_t = \begin{pmatrix} 1 & 0 \end{pmatrix} \mathbf{X}_t + V_t$, where $V_t \stackrel{iid}{\sim} N_1(0, 1)$, and state distribution $\mathbf{X}_t \sim N_2((1, 2), I_2)$, compute the mean and variance of Y_t.

E6.5.12 Given a linear-Gaussian system with state evolution $\mathbf{X}_{t+1} = \begin{pmatrix} 1 & 1 \\ 0 & 1 \end{pmatrix} \mathbf{X}_t + \mathbf{W}_t$, where $\mathbf{W}_t \stackrel{iid}{\sim} N_2(0, I_2)$, observation model $Y_t = \begin{pmatrix} 1 & 0 \end{pmatrix} \mathbf{X}_t + V_t$, where $V_t \stackrel{iid}{\sim} N_1(0, 1)$, and initial state distribution $\mathbf{X}_0 \sim N_2((1, 1), I_2)$, compute the Kalman gain matrix K_1.

E6.5.13 Given the measurement model $Y_t = H\mathbf{X}_t + V_t$ with $H = \begin{pmatrix} 1 & 0 \end{pmatrix}$ and $V_t \sim N_1(0, 0.1)$, compute the innovation $e_t = Y_t - H\boldsymbol{\mu}_{\text{pred}}$ given $Y_t = 3$ and $\boldsymbol{\mu}_{\text{pred}} = \begin{pmatrix} 3 \\ 1 \end{pmatrix}$.

E6.5.14 Determine the Kalman gain matrix $K_t == \Sigma_{pred} H^T (H \Sigma_{pred} H^T + R)^{-1}$ for the model in E6.5.13, with $\Sigma_{pred} = \begin{pmatrix} 0.2 & 0.1 \\ 0.1 & 0.2 \end{pmatrix}$ and $R = 0.1$.

E6.5.15 Using the Kalman gain matrix K_t from E6.5.14, update the state estimate μ_t given $\mu_{pred} = \begin{pmatrix} 3 \\ 1 \end{pmatrix}$ and $e_t = 0$.

E6.5.16 Compute the updated covariance matrix $\Sigma_t = (I - K_t H) \Sigma_{pred}$ using the Kalman gain matrix K_t from E6.5.14 and $\Sigma_{pred} = \begin{pmatrix} 0.2 & 0.1 \\ 0.1 & 0.2 \end{pmatrix}$.

6.6.2 Problems

6.1 Show using a spectral decomposition that if $A \in \mathbb{R}^{n \times n}$ is positive definite, then it is invertible.

6.2 Let $\mathbf{X} = (X_1, \ldots, X_n) \in \mathbb{R}^d$ be a random vector and assume that $\mathbb{E}[X_i^2] < +\infty$ for all $i = 1, \ldots, n$. Recall that the covariance matrix $C \in \mathbb{R}^{n \times n}$ has entries

$$C_{ij} = \text{Cov}[X_i, X_j] = \mathbb{E}[(X_i - \mathbb{E}[X_i])(X_j - \mathbb{E}[X_j])].$$

  a) Show that C is symmetric.

  b) Show that C is positive semidefinite. $\left[\textit{Hint:} \text{ Compute } \mathbb{E}\left[\{\mathbf{z}^T(\mathbf{X} - \mathbb{E}[\mathbf{X}])\}^2\right].\right]$

6.3 Show that

$$K_{\mathbf{Z},\mathbf{Z}} = \mathbb{E}[\mathbf{Z}\mathbf{Z}^T] - \mathbb{E}[\mathbf{Z}]\mathbb{E}[\mathbf{Z}]^T.$$

6.4 Show that $H_{L_n}(\mathbf{w})$ is positive semidefinite, where L_n is the negative log-likelihood in the generalized linear model.

6.5 Assume that, for each i, p_{θ_i} is a univariate Gaussian with mean $\theta_i = \mathbf{x}_i^T \mathbf{w}$ and known variance σ_i^2. Show that the maximum likelihood estimator of $\mathbf{w}$ solves a variant of the least-squares problem.

6.6 a) Show that the exponential family form of the Poisson distribution with mean λ has sufficient statistic $\phi(y) = y$ and natural parameter $\theta = \log \lambda$.

  b) In Poisson regression, we assume that $p_\theta(y)$ is Poisson with $\theta = \mathbf{x}^T \mathbf{w}$. Compute the gradient and Hessian of the negative log-likelihood in this case.

6.7 For $i = 1, \ldots, K$, let p_i be a probability mass function over the set $\mathcal{S}_i \subseteq \mathbb{R}$ with mean μ_i and variance σ_i^2. Let $\boldsymbol{\pi} = (\pi_1, \ldots, \pi_K) \in \Delta_K$. Suppose X is drawn from the mixture distribution

$$p_X(x) = \sum_{i=1}^K \pi_i p_i(x).$$

Establish the following formulas:

  a) $\mu := \mathbb{E}[X] = \sum_{i=1}^K \pi_i \mu_i$

  b) $\text{Var}[X] = \sum_{i=1}^K \pi_i (\sigma_i^2 + \mu_i^2 - \mu^2)$.

6.8 Let A, B, and C be events. Use the product rule to show that

$$\mathbb{P}[A \cap B | C] = \mathbb{P}[A | B \cap C] \, \mathbb{P}[B | C].$$

In words, conditional probabilities satisfy the product rule.

6.9 Let A, B, C be events such that $\mathbb{P}[C] > 0$ and $A \perp\!\!\!\perp B|C$. Show that $A \perp\!\!\!\perp B^c|C$.

6.10 Let A, B, C be events such that $\mathbb{P}[B \cap C], \mathbb{P}[A \cap C] > 0$. Show that $A \perp\!\!\!\perp B|C$ if and only if

$$\mathbb{P}[A|B \cap C] = \mathbb{P}[A|C] \quad \text{and} \quad \mathbb{P}[B|A \cap C] = \mathbb{P}[B|C].$$

6.11 Let A, B, C be events such that $\mathbb{P}[B \cap C] > 0$.

a) First show that

$$\mathbb{P}[A|B \cap C] = \frac{\mathbb{P}[C|A \cap B]\,\mathbb{P}[A|B]}{\mathbb{P}[C|A \cap B]\,\mathbb{P}[A|B] + \mathbb{P}[C|A^c \cap B]\,\mathbb{P}[A^c|B]}.$$

b) Now suppose $\mathbf{1}_B \perp\!\!\!\perp \mathbf{1}_C | \mathbf{1}_A$. Show that

$$\mathbb{P}[A|B \cap C] = \frac{\mathbb{P}[C|A]\,\mathbb{P}[A|B]}{\mathbb{P}[C|A]\,\mathbb{P}[A|B] + \mathbb{P}[C|A^c]\,\mathbb{P}[A^c|B]}.$$

6.12 Let $\mathbf{X}, \mathbf{Y}, \mathbf{Z}, \mathbf{W}$ be discrete random vectors. Show that $\mathbf{X} \perp\!\!\!\perp (\mathbf{Y}, \mathbf{Z})|\mathbf{W}$ implies that $\mathbf{X} \perp\!\!\!\perp \mathbf{Y}|\mathbf{W}$ and $\mathbf{X} \perp\!\!\!\perp \mathbf{Z}|\mathbf{W}$.

6.13 Let $\mathbf{X}, \mathbf{Y}, \mathbf{Z}$ be discrete random vectors. Suppose that $\mathbf{X} \perp\!\!\!\perp \mathbf{Y}|\mathbf{Z}$ and $\mathbf{X} \perp\!\!\!\perp \mathbf{Z}$. Show that $\mathbf{X} \perp\!\!\!\perp (\mathbf{Y}, \mathbf{Z})$.

6.14 Let $A \in \mathbb{R}^{n \times n}$ be an invertible matrix.

a) Show that $(A^T)^{-1} = (A^{-1})^T$. [*Hint:* Use the definition of an inverse.]

b) Suppose furthermore that A is symmetric. Show that A^{-1} is symmetric.

6.15 A random matrix $\mathbf{M} = (M_{i,j})_{i,j} \in \mathbb{R}^{\ell \times d}$ is a matrix whose entries are correlated random variables; that is, they live in the same probability space. The expectation of a random matrix is the (deterministic) matrix whose entries are the expectations of the entries of $\mathbf{M}$,

$$\mathbb{E}[\mathbf{M}] = \begin{pmatrix} \mathbb{E}[M_{1,1}] & \cdots & \mathbb{E}[M_{1,d}] \\ \vdots & \ddots & \vdots \\ \mathbb{E}[M_{\ell,1}] & \cdots & \mathbb{E}[M_{\ell,d}] \end{pmatrix}.$$

Prove that the linearity of expectation for random variables generalizes to

$$\mathbb{E}[A\mathbf{M} + B] = A\,\mathbb{E}[\mathbf{M}] + B$$

for a deterministic matrix $A \in \mathbb{R}^{k \times \ell}$ and matrix $B \in \mathbb{R}^{k \times d}$.

6.16 Recall that the trace of a square matrix A, denoted $\mathrm{tr}(A)$, is the sum of its diagonal entries. For a matrix $A = (a_{i,j})_{i,j} \in \mathbb{R}^{n \times m}$, the vectorization of A is the following vector:

$$\mathrm{vec}(A) = (a_{1,1}, \ldots, a_{n,1}, a_{1,2}, \ldots, a_{n,2}, \ldots, a_{1,m}, \ldots, a_{n,m});$$

that is, it is obtained by stacking the columns of the matrix on top of one another. Show that, for any $A, B \in \mathbb{R}^{n \times n}$, it holds that $\mathrm{tr}(A^T B) = \mathrm{vec}(A)^T \mathrm{vec}(B)$.

6.17 Let $\mathbf{X}_1, \ldots, \mathbf{X}_n$ be random vectors in $\mathbb{R}^d$. Show that

$$\frac{1}{n}\sum_{i=1}^n \mathbf{X}_i \mathbf{X}_i^T - \left(\frac{1}{n}\sum_{i=1}^n \mathbf{X}_i\right)\left(\frac{1}{n}\sum_{i=1}^n \mathbf{X}_i^T\right)$$
$$= \frac{1}{n}\sum_{i=1}^n \left[\mathbf{X}_i - \left(\frac{1}{n}\sum_{i=1}^n \mathbf{X}_i\right)\right]\left[\mathbf{X}_i^T - \left(\frac{1}{n}\sum_{i=1}^n \mathbf{X}_i^T\right)\right].$$

6.18 Recall that a categorical variable $\mathbf{Y}$ takes $K \geq 2$ possible values. We assume it takes values in the set $\mathcal{S}_\mathbf{Y} = \{\mathbf{e}_i : i = 1, \ldots, K\}$ where $\mathbf{e}_i$ is the i-th standard basis in $\mathbb{R}^K$. The distribution is specified by setting the probabilities $\boldsymbol{\pi} = (\pi_1, \ldots, \pi_K)$ with $\pi_i = \mathbb{P}[\mathbf{Y} = \mathbf{e}_i]$. We denote this by $\mathbf{Y} \sim \text{Cat}(\boldsymbol{\pi})$ and we assume $\pi_i > 0$ for all i. The multinomial distribution arises as a sum of independent categorical variables. Let $n \geq 1$ be the number of trials and let $\mathbf{Y}_1, \ldots, \mathbf{Y}_n$ be i.i.d. $\text{Cat}(\boldsymbol{\pi})$. Define $\mathbf{X} = \sum_{i=1}^n \mathbf{Y}_i$. The probability mass function of $\mathbf{X}$ at

$$\mathbf{x} = (x_1, \ldots, x_K) \in \left\{ \mathbf{x} \in \{0, 1, \ldots, n\}^K : \sum_{i=1}^K x_i = n \right\} =: \mathcal{S}_\mathbf{X}$$

is

$$p_\mathbf{X}(\mathbf{x}) = \frac{n!}{x_1! \cdots x_K!} \prod_{i=1}^K \pi_i^{x_i}.$$

We write $\mathbf{X} \sim \text{Mult}(n, \boldsymbol{\pi})$. Let $\boldsymbol{\mu}_\mathbf{X}$ and $\boldsymbol{\Sigma}_\mathbf{X}$ be its mean vector and covariance matrix.

a) Show that the multinomial distribution is an exponential family by specifying h, ϕ, and A. Justify your answer.

b) Show that $\boldsymbol{\mu}_\mathbf{X} = n\boldsymbol{\pi}$.

c) Show that $\boldsymbol{\Sigma}_\mathbf{X} = n[\text{Diag}(\boldsymbol{\pi}) - \boldsymbol{\pi}\boldsymbol{\pi}^T]$.

6.19 Let $\mathbf{X} \in \mathbb{R}^d$ be a random vector with mean $\boldsymbol{\mu}$ and covariance $\boldsymbol{\Sigma}$ and let $B \in \mathbb{R}^{\ell \times d}$ be a deterministic matrix. Define the random vector $\mathbf{Y} = B\mathbf{X}$.

a) Compute $\mathbb{E}[\mathbf{Y}]$.

b) Compute $\text{Cov}[\mathbf{X}, \mathbf{Y}]$.

c) Compute $\text{Cov}[\mathbf{Y}, \mathbf{Y}]$.

6.20 Let the process $(\mathbf{X}_{0:T}, \mathbf{Y}_{1:T})$ have a joint density of the form

$$f_{\mathbf{X}_0}(\mathbf{x}_0) \prod_{t=1}^T f_{\mathbf{X}_t | \mathbf{X}_{t-1}}(\mathbf{x}_t | \mathbf{x}_{t-1}) f_{\mathbf{Y}_t | \mathbf{X}_t}(\mathbf{y}_t | \mathbf{x}_t).$$

Show that, for any $t = 1, \ldots, T$, $\mathbf{Y}_t$ is conditionally independent of $\mathbf{Y}_{1:t-1}$ given $\mathbf{X}_t$.

6.21 Consider a square block matrix with the same partitioning of the rows and columns; that is,

$$A = \begin{pmatrix} A_{11} & A_{12} \\ A_{21} & A_{22} \end{pmatrix}$$

where $A \in \mathbb{R}^{n \times n}$, $A_{ij} \in \mathbb{R}^{n_i \times n_j}$ for $i, j = 1, 2$ with the condition $n_1 + n_2 = n$. Show that the transpose can be written as

$$A^T = \begin{pmatrix} A_{11}^T & A_{21}^T \\ A_{12}^T & A_{22}^T \end{pmatrix}$$

by writing down the entries $(A^T)_{i,j}$ in terms of the blocks of A. Make sure to consider carefully all cases (e.g., $i \leq n_1$ and $j > n_1$, etc.).

6.22 Prove the *Inverting a Block Matrix Lemma* by directly computing BB^{-1} and $B^{-1}B$ using the formula for the product of block matrices.

6.23 Let $A, B \in \mathbb{R}^{n \times n}$ be invertible matrices. Which ones of the following matrices are also invertible? Specify the inverse or provide a counterexample.

a) $A + B$

b) $\begin{pmatrix} A & 0 \\ 0 & B \end{pmatrix}$

c) $\begin{pmatrix} A & A+B \\ 0 & B \end{pmatrix}$

d) ABA

6.24 In the derivation of the EM algorithm, justify rigorously the formulas

$$\pi_k^* = \frac{\eta_k^\theta}{n} \quad \text{and} \quad p_{k,m}^* = \frac{\eta_{k,m}^\theta}{\eta_k^\theta} \quad \forall k \in [K], m \in [M]$$

by adapting the argument for the naive Bayes model step–by–step.

6.25 Consider the graphical representation of a linear-Gaussian system in Figure 6.21.

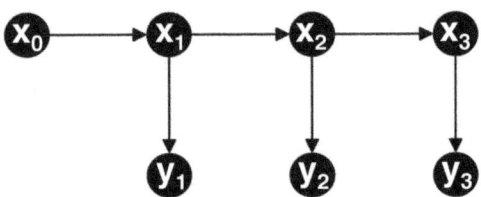

Figure 6.21 Graph for Problem 6.26.

Prove the following statements:

a) Y_3 is conditionally independent of X_1 given X_2.

b) Y_3 is conditionally independent of Y_1 given X_2.

c) X_3 is conditionally independent of X_1 given X_2.

6.26 Redo the calculations in the proof of the *Schur Complement Lemma* for B/B_{22}.

6.27 Let $\mathbf{X} = (X_1, X_2, X_3)$ be distributed as $N_3(\boldsymbol{\mu}, \boldsymbol{\Sigma})$ where

$$\boldsymbol{\mu} = \begin{pmatrix} 2 \\ -1 \\ 3 \end{pmatrix} \quad \boldsymbol{\Sigma} = \begin{pmatrix} 4 & 1 & 0 \\ 1 & 2 & 1 \\ 0 & 1 & 3 \end{pmatrix}.$$

a) Compute $f_{X_1, X_2 | X_3}$, the conditional density of (X_1, X_2) given X_3.

b) What is the correlation coefficient between X_1 and X_2 under the marginal density f_{X_1, X_2}?

6.28 Consider the block matrix

$$\begin{pmatrix} C & B & 0 \\ B^T & 0 & D \\ 0 & 0 & BB^T \end{pmatrix}.$$

Suppose that $B \in \mathbb{R}^{2\times 5}$. What are the dimensions of the blocks C and D? Justify your answer.

6.29 a) Let $A_{11} \in \mathbb{R}^{n\times n}$ and $A_{22} \in \mathbb{R}^{m\times m}$ be invertible. Let $A_{12} \in \mathbb{R}^{n\times m}$. Find the inverse of the block matrix

$$A = \begin{pmatrix} A_{11} & A_{12} \\ 0 & A_{22} \end{pmatrix}.$$

[*Hint:* You may want to guess what the solution is by considering the case when the blocks are scalars.]

b) Let $\mathbf{b} \in \mathbb{R}^n$ be a nonzero vector. Show that the block matrix

$$B = \begin{pmatrix} I_{n\times n} & \mathbf{b} \\ \mathbf{b}^T & 0 \end{pmatrix}$$

is invertible by establishing that $B\mathbf{z} = \mathbf{0}$ implies $\mathbf{z} = \mathbf{0}$.

7 Random Walks on Graphs and Markov Chains

In this chapter, we continue to analyze datasets in the form of networks. A powerful way to extract information about the structure of a network is to analyze the behavior of a random walk "diffusing" on it. We will frame such walks in the more general context of Markov chains, a class of stochastic processes with many applications in data science, including Markov chain Monte Carlo and PageRank. Here is a more detailed overview of the main sections of the chapter.

Background: Elements of finite Markov chains: Section 7.2 introduces the concept of discrete-time Markov chains on a finite state space, focusing on the time-homogeneous case. It defines the transition matrix P, which encodes the probabilities of transitioning from one state to another. The section also introduces the concept of the transition graph, a directed graph representation of the Markov chain. It emphasizes the role of the *Markov Property*, which states that the past and future are independent given the present. In particular, the distribution of a sample path is derived using the *Multiplication Rule* and *Markov Property*. It then derives the formula for the time marginals, showing that the marginal distribution of X_s is given by a matrix power of P. The section concludes with a numerical example demonstrating how to simulate a Markov chain.

Limit behavior 1: Stationary distributions: Section 7.3 discusses the concept of a stationary distribution for finite-space, discrete-time, time-homogeneous Markov chains. It defines a stationary distribution as a probability distribution over the state space that remains unchanged after a transition step. The existence of a stationary distribution implies a form of equilibrium for the Markov chain. The section then introduces the notion of irreducibility, which means that every state can be reached from every other state, and proves that a finite irreducible Markov chain has a unique stationary distribution with all entries being strictly positive. Finally, the section provides numerical methods for computing the stationary distribution.

Limit behavior 2: Convergence to equilibrium: Section 7.4 discusses notions of convergence for finite-space discrete-time Markov chains. After introducing the concept of aperiodicity, two key theorems are presented: the *Convergence to Equilibrium Theorem*, which establishes convergence of the distribution at time t to the stationary distribution for irreducible and aperiodic chains, and the *Ergodic Theorem*, which applies to irreducible chains and states that the frequency of visits to any state converges to the stationary distribution. The section also provides numerical examples.

Application: Random walks on graphs and PageRank: Section 7.5 explores random walks on graphs, a powerful tool for understanding network structures. It begins by defining random walks on directed and undirected graphs, discussing their transition matrices, stationary distributions, and the concept of reversibility. The section then introduces PageRank as a way to identify central nodes in a directed graph, modeling the behavior of a random surfer clicking through web pages. The PageRank vector is computed as the stationary distribution of a modified random walk that incorporates a damping factor to ensure irreducibility. The section also discusses degree centrality for undirected graphs and introduces Personalized PageRank, which tailors the result to specific interests by modifying the teleportation distribution.

Further applications: Gibbs sampling and generating images: Section 7.6 discusses Markov chain Monte Carlo (MCMC) methods, focusing on the Metropolis–Hastings algorithm and Gibbs sampling, which are used to generate samples from complex probability distributions. The Metropolis–Hastings algorithm constructs a Markov chain with the desired stationary distribution by using a proposal distribution and an acceptance probability that depends on the target distribution. Gibbs sampling is a special case of the Metropolis–Hastings algorithm that exploits the conditional independence structure of the target distribution, making it particularly useful for high-dimensional problems. The section illustrates the application of Gibbs sampling to generate natural-looking images of handwritten digits using a restricted Boltzmann machine (RBM) trained on the MNIST dataset.

7.1 Motivating Example: Discovering Mathematical Topics

A common task in network analysis is to identify "central" vertices in a graph. Centrality is a vague concept. It can be defined in many different ways depending on the context and the type of network. Quoting from Wikipedia[1]:

> In graph theory and network analysis, indicators of centrality assign numbers or rankings to nodes within a graph corresponding to their network position. Applications include identifying the most influential person(s) in a social network, key infrastructure nodes in the Internet or urban networks, super-spreaders of disease, and brain networks. [...] Centrality indices are answers to the question "What characterizes an important vertex?" The answer is given in terms of a real-valued function on the vertices of a graph, where the values produced are expected to provide a ranking which identifies the most important nodes. The word "importance" has a wide number of meanings, leading to many different definitions of centrality.

In an undirected graph, a natural approach is to look at the degree of a vertex as a measure of its importance (also referred to as degree centrality). But it is hardly the only one. One could for instance look at the average distance to all other nodes (its reciprocal is the closeness centrality) or at the number of shortest paths between pairs of vertices going through the vertex (known as betweenness centrality).

What if the graph is directed? Things are somewhat more complicated there. For instance, there is now the in-degree as well as the out-degree.

Let us look at a particular example of practical importance, the World Wide Web (from now on, the Web). In this case, the vertices are webpages and a directed edge from u to v indicates a hyperlink from page u to page v. The Web is much too large to analyze here. Instead, we will consider a tiny (but still interesting!) subset of it, the pages of Wolfram's MathWorld, a wonderful mathematics resource.

---

[1] https://en.wikipedia.org/wiki/Centrality

7.1 Motivating Example: Discovering Mathematical Topics

Each page of MathWorld concerns a particular mathematical concept, such as scale-free network. A definition and notable properties are described. Importantly for us, in a section entitled "SEE ALSO," other related mathematical concepts are listed with a link to their MathWorld page. In the case of scale-free networks, the small world network topic is referenced, among others.

The resulting directed graph is available through the NetSet datasets.[2] We load it now. For convenience, we have reformatted it into the files `mathworld-adjacency.csv` and `mathworld-titles.csv`, which are available on the GitHub of the book.[3]

```
data_edges = pd.read_csv('mathworld-adjacency.csv')
data_edges.head()
```

	from	to
0	0	2
1	1	47
2	1	404
3	1	2721
4	2	0

It consists of a list of directed edges. For example, the first one is an edge from vertex 0 to vertex 2, the second one is from 1 to 47, and so on.

There is a total of 49,069 edges.

```
data_edges.shape[0]
```

49069

The second file contains the titles of the pages.

```
data_titles = pd.read_csv('mathworld-titles.csv')
data_titles.head()
```

	title
0	Alexander's Horned Sphere
1	Exotic Sphere
2	Antoine's Horned Sphere
3	Flat
4	Poincaré Manifold

So the first edge above is from `Alexander's Horned Sphere` to `Antoine's Horned Sphere`. That is, the latter is listed in the "SEE ALSO" section of the former.

There are 12,362 topics.

```
n = data_titles.shape[0]
print(n)
```

---

[2] https://netset.telecom-paris.fr/pages/mathworld.html
[3] https://github.com/MMiDS-textbook

12362

We construct the graph by adding the edges one by one. We first convert df_edges into a NumPy array.

```
edgelist = data_edges[['from','to']].to_numpy()
print(edgelist)
```

```
[[    0     2]
 [    1    47]
 [    1   404]
 ...
 [12361 12306]
 [12361 12310]
 [12361 12360]]
```

```
G = nx.empty_graph(n, create_using=nx.DiGraph)
for i in range(edgelist.shape[0]):
    G.add_edge(edgelist[i,0], edgelist[i,1])
```

Returning to the question of centrality, we can now try to measure the importance of different nodes. For instance, the in-degree of Alexander's Horned Sphere is:

```
G.in_degree(0)
```

5

while that of Antoine's Horned Sphere is:

```
G.in_degree(2)
```

1

suggesting that the former is more central than the latter, at least in the sense that it is referenced more often.

But is that the right measure? Consider the following: Antoine's Horned Sphere receives only one reference, but it is from a seemingly relatively important vertex, Alexander's Horned Sphere. How can one take this into account in quantifying its importance in the network?

We will come back to this question later in this chapter. To hint at things to come, it will turn out that "exploring the graph at random" provides a powerful perspective on centrality.

7.2 Background: Elements of Finite Markov Chains

As we mentioned, we are interested in analyzing the behavior of a random walk "diffusing" on a graph. Before we develop such techniques, it will be worthwhile to cast them in the more general framework of discrete-time Markov chains on a finite state space. Indeed Markov chains have many more applications in data science.

7.2.1 Basic Definitions

A discrete-time Markov chain is a stochastic process, namely a collection of random variables in this case indexed by time. We assume that the random variables take values in a common finite state space $\mathcal{S}$. What makes it "Markovian" is that "it forgets the past" in the sense that "its future only depends on its present state." More formally:

Definition 7.2.1 *(Discrete-Time Markov Chain) The sequence of random variables $(X_t)_{t \geq 0} = (X_0, X_1, X_2, \ldots)$ taking values in the finite state space $\mathcal{S}$ is a Markov chain if for all $t \geq 1$ and all $x_0, x_1, \ldots, x_t \in \mathcal{S}$*

$$(*) \quad \mathbb{P}[X_t = x_t \mid X_{t-1} = x_{t-1}, X_{t-2} = x_{t-2}, \ldots, X_0 = x_0] = \mathbb{P}[X_t = x_t \mid X_{t-1} = x_{t-1}]$$

provided the conditional probabilities are well-defined.

To be clear, the event in the conditioning is

$$\{X_{t-1} = x_{t-1}, X_{t-2} = x_{t-2}, \ldots, X_0 = x_0\} = \{X_{t-1} = x_{t-1}\} \cap \{X_{t-2} = x_{t-2}\} \cap \cdots \cap \{X_0 = x_0\}.$$

It will sometimes be convenient to assume that the common state space $\mathcal{S}$ is of the form $[m] = \{1, \ldots, m\}$.

Example 7.2.2 *(Weather Model) Here is a simple weather model. Every day is either Dry or Wet. We model the transitions as Markovian; intuitively, we assume that tomorrow's weather only depends – in a random fashion independent of the past – on today's weather. Say the weather changes with 25% chance. More formally, let $X_t \in \mathcal{S}$ be the weather on day t with $\mathcal{S} = \{\text{Dry}, \text{Wet}\}$. Assume that $X_0 = \text{Dry}$ and let $(Z_t)_{t \geq 0}$ be an i.i.d. (i.e., independent, identically distributed) sequence of random variables taking values in $\{\text{Same}, \text{Change}\}$ satisfying*

$$\mathbb{P}[Z_t = \text{Same}] = 1 - \mathbb{P}[Z_t = \text{Change}] = 3/4.$$

Then define for all $t \geq 0$

$$X_{t+1} = f(X_t, Z_t) = \begin{cases} X_t & \text{if } Z_t = \text{Same}, \\ \text{Wet} & \text{if } X_t = \text{Dry and } Z_t = \text{Change}, \\ \text{Dry} & \text{if } X_t = \text{Wet and } Z_t = \text{Change}. \end{cases}$$

We claim that $(X_t)_{t \geq 0}$ is a Markov chain. We use two observations:

1. By composition,

$$X_1 = f(X_0, Z_0),$$

$$X_2 = f(X_1, Z_1) = f(f(X_0, Z_0), Z_1),$$

$$X_3 = f(X_2, Z_2) = f(f(X_1, Z_1), Z_2) = f(f(f(X_0, Z_0), Z_1), Z_2),$$

and, more generally,

$$X_t = f(X_{t-1}, Z_{t-1}) = f(f(X_{t-2}, Z_{t-2}), Z_{t-1}) = f(f(\cdots f(f(X_0, Z_0), Z_1), \cdots), Z_{t-1})$$

is a deterministic function of $X_0 = $ Dry and $Z_0, \ldots, Z_{t-1}$.

2. For any $x_1, \ldots, x_t \in \mathcal{S}$, there is precisely one value of $z \in \{\text{Same}, \text{Change}\}$ such that $x_t = f(x_{t-1}, z)$: If $x_t = x_{t-1}$ we must have $z = $ Same and if $x_t \neq x_{t-1}$ we must have $z = $ Change.

Fix $x_0 = $ Dry. For any $x_1, \ldots, x_t \in \mathcal{S}$, letting z be as in Observation 2,

$$\begin{aligned}
&\mathbb{P}[X_t = x_t \mid X_{t-1} = x_{t-1}, X_{t-2} = x_{t-2}, \ldots, X_0 = x_0] \\
&= \mathbb{P}[f(X_{t-1}, Z_{t-1}) = x_t \mid X_{t-1} = x_{t-1}, X_{t-2} = x_{t-2}, \ldots, X_0 = x_0] \\
&= \mathbb{P}[f(x_{t-1}, Z_{t-1}) = x_t \mid X_{t-1} = x_{t-1}, X_{t-2} = x_{t-2}, \ldots, X_0 = x_0] \\
&= \mathbb{P}[Z_{t-1} = z \mid X_{t-1} = x_{t-1}, X_{t-2} = x_{t-2}, \ldots, X_0 = x_0] \\
&= \mathbb{P}[Z_{t-1} = z],
\end{aligned}$$

where we used that Z_{t-1} is independent of $Z_{t-2}, \ldots, Z_0$ and X_0 (which is deterministic), and therefore is independent of $X_{t-1}, \ldots, X_0$ by Observation 1. The same argument shows that

$$\mathbb{P}[X_t = x_t \mid X_{t-1} = x_{t-1}] = \mathbb{P}[Z_{t-1} = z],$$

and that proves the claim.

More generally, one can pick X_0 according to an initial distribution, independently from the sequence $(Z_t)_{t \geq 0}$. The argument above can be adapted to this case.

Example 7.2.3 *(Random Walk on the Petersen Graph)* Let $G = (V, E)$ be the Petersen graph. Each vertex i has degree 3, that is, it has three neighbors which we denote $v_{i,1}, v_{i,2}, v_{i,3}$ in some arbitrary order. For instance, denoting the vertices by $1, \ldots, 10$ as in Chapter 5, Figure 5.2, vertex 9 has neighbors $v_{9,1} = 4, v_{9,2} = 6, v_{9,3} = 7$.

We consider the following random walk on G. We start at $X_0 = 1$. Then, for each $t \geq 0$, we let X_{t+1} be a neighbor of X_t chosen uniformly at random, independently of the previous history. That is, we jump at random from neighbor to neighbor. Formally, fix $X_0 = 1$ and let $(Z_t)_{t \geq 0}$ be an i.i.d. sequence of random variables taking values in $\{1, 2, 3\}$ and satisfying

$$\mathbb{P}[Z_t = 1] = \mathbb{P}[Z_t = 2] = \mathbb{P}[Z_t = 3] = 1/3.$$

Then define, for all $t \geq 0$, $X_{t+1} = f(X_t, Z_t) = v_{i, Z_t}$ if $X_t = v_i$.

By an argument similar to the previous example, $(X_t)_{t \geq 0}$ is a Markov chain. Also as in the previous example, one can pick X_0 according to an initial distribution, independently from the sequence $(Z_t)_{t \geq 0}$.

There are various useful generalizations of the condition $(*)$ in the definition of a Markov chain. These are all special cases of the *Markov Property*, which can be summarized as: The past and the future are independent given the present. We record a version general enough for us here. Let $(X_t)_{t \geq 0}$ be a Markov chain on the state space $\mathcal{S}$. For any integer $h \geq 0$, $x_{t-1} \in \mathcal{S}$, and subsets $\mathcal{P} \subseteq \mathcal{S}^{t-1}$, $\mathcal{F} \subseteq \mathcal{S}^{h+1}$ of state sequences of length $t-1$ and $h+1$ respectively, it holds that

$$\begin{aligned}
&\mathbb{P}[(X_t, \ldots, X_{t+h}) \in \mathcal{F} \mid X_{t-1} = x_{t-1}, (X_0, \ldots, X_{t-2}) \in \mathcal{P}] \\
&= \mathbb{P}[(X_t, \ldots, X_{t+h}) \in \mathcal{F} \mid X_{t-1} = x_{t-1}].
\end{aligned}$$

One important implication of the *Markov Property* is that the distribution of a sample path, namely an event of the form $\{X_0 = x_0, X_1 = x_1, \ldots, X_T = x_T\}$, simplifies considerably.

Theorem 7.2.4 *(Distribution of a Sample Path)* For any $x_0, x_1, \ldots, x_T \in \mathcal{S}$,

$$\mathbb{P}[X_0 = x_0, X_1 = x_1, \ldots, X_T = x_T] = \mathbb{P}[X_0 = x_0] \prod_{t=1}^{T} \mathbb{P}[X_t = x_t \mid X_{t-1} = x_{t-1}].$$

Proof idea: We use the *Multiplication Rule* and the *Markov Property*.

Proof We first apply the *Multiplication Rule*

$$\mathbb{P}\left[\cap_{i=1}^{r} A_i\right] = \prod_{i=1}^{r} \mathbb{P}\left[A_i \mid \cap_{j=1}^{i-1} A_j\right]$$

with $A_i = \{X_{i-1} = x_{i-1}\}$ and $r = T + 1$. That gives

$$\mathbb{P}[X_0 = x_0, X_1 = x_1, \ldots, X_T = x_T]$$
$$= \mathbb{P}[X_0 = x_0] \prod_{t=1}^{T} \mathbb{P}[X_t = x_t \mid X_{t-1} = x_{t-1}, \ldots, X_0 = x_0].$$

Then we use the *Markov Property* to simplify each term in the product. □

Example 7.2.5 *(Weather Model, continued from Example 7.2.2)* Going back to the weather model, fix $x_0 =$ Dry and $x_1, \ldots, x_t \in \mathcal{S}$. Then, by the Distribution of a Sample Path Theorem,

$$\mathbb{P}[X_0 = x_0, X_1 = x_1, \ldots, X_T = x_T] = \mathbb{P}[X_0 = x_0] \prod_{t=1}^{T} \mathbb{P}[X_t = x_t \mid X_{t-1} = x_{t-1}].$$

By assumption $\mathbb{P}[X_0 = x_0] = 1$. Moreover, we have previously shown that

$$\mathbb{P}[X_t = x_t \mid X_{t-1} = x_{t-1}] = \mathbb{P}[Z_{t-1} = z_{t-1}],$$

where $z_{t-1} =$ Same if $x_t = x_{t-1}$ and $z_{t-1} =$ Change if $x_t \neq x_{t-1}$.

Hence, using the distribution of Z_t,

$$\mathbb{P}[X_t = x_t \mid X_{t-1} = x_{t-1}] = \begin{cases} 3/4 & \text{if } x_t = x_{t-1}, \\ 1/4 & \text{if } x_t \neq x_{t-1}. \end{cases}$$

Let $n_T = |\{0 < t \leq T : x_t = x_{t-1}\}|$ be the number of transitions without change. Then,

$$\mathbb{P}[X_0 = x_0, X_1 = x_1, \ldots, X_T = x_T] = \mathbb{P}[X_0 = x_0] \prod_{t=1}^{T} \mathbb{P}[X_t = x_t \mid X_{t-1} = x_{t-1}]$$
$$= \prod_{t=1}^{T} \mathbb{P}[Z_{t-1} = z_{t-1}]$$
$$= (3/4)^{n_T} (1/4)^{T-n_T}.$$

It will be useful later on to observe that the *Distribution of a Sample Path Theorem* generalizes to

$$\mathbb{P}[X_{s+1} = x_{s+1}, X_{s+2} = x_{s+2}, \ldots, X_T = x_T \mid X_s = x_s] = \prod_{t=s+1}^{T} \mathbb{P}[X_t = x_t \mid X_{t-1} = x_{t-1}].$$

Based on the *Distribution of a Sample Path Theorem*, in order to specify the distribution of the process it suffices to specify

1. the *initial distribution* $\mu_x := \mathbb{P}[X_0 = x]$ for all x; and
2. the *transition probabilities* $\mathbb{P}[X_{t+1} = x \mid X_t = x']$ for all t, x, x'.

7.2.2 Time-Homogeneous Case: Transition Matrix

It is common to further assume that the process is *time-homogeneous*, which means that the transition probabilities do not depend on t:

$$\mathbb{P}[X_{t+1} = x \mid X_t = x'] = \mathbb{P}[X_1 = x \mid X_0 = x'] =: p_{x',x}, \quad \text{for } t = 1, \ldots$$

where the last equality is a definition. We can then collect the transition probabilities into a matrix.

Definition 7.2.6 *(Transition Matrix)* The matrix

$$P = (p_{x',x})_{x,x' \in \mathcal{S}}$$

is called the transition matrix of the chain.

We also let $\mu_x = \mathbb{P}[X_0 = x]$ and we think of $\mu = (\mu_x)_{x \in \mathcal{S}}$ as a vector. The convention in Markov chain theory is to think of probability distributions such as μ as *row vectors*. We will see later why it simplifies the notation somewhat.

Example 7.2.7 *(continued from Example 7.2.2) Going back to the weather model, let us number the states as follows:* $1 = $ *Dry and* $2 = $ *Wet. Then the transition matrix is*

$$P = \begin{pmatrix} 3/4 & 1/4 \\ 1/4 & 3/4 \end{pmatrix}.$$

Example 7.2.8 *(continued from Example 7.2.3) Consider again the random walk on the Petersen graph* $G = (V, E)$. *We number the vertices* $1, 2, \ldots, 10$. *To compute the transition matrix, we list for each vertex its neighbors and put the value* $1/3$ *in the corresponding columns. For instance, vertex 1 has neighbors 2, 5, and 6, so row 1 has* $1/3$ *in columns 2, 5, and 6. And so on.*

We get:

$$P = \begin{pmatrix} 0 & 1/3 & 0 & 0 & 1/3 & 1/3 & 0 & 0 & 0 & 0 \\ 1/3 & 0 & 1/3 & 0 & 0 & 0 & 1/3 & 0 & 0 & 0 \\ 0 & 1/3 & 0 & 1/3 & 0 & 0 & 0 & 1/3 & 0 & 0 \\ 0 & 0 & 1/3 & 0 & 1/3 & 0 & 0 & 0 & 1/3 & 0 \\ 1/3 & 0 & 0 & 1/3 & 0 & 0 & 0 & 0 & 0 & 1/3 \\ 1/3 & 0 & 0 & 0 & 0 & 0 & 0 & 1/3 & 1/3 & 0 \\ 0 & 1/3 & 0 & 0 & 0 & 0 & 0 & 0 & 1/3 & 1/3 \\ 0 & 0 & 1/3 & 0 & 0 & 1/3 & 0 & 0 & 0 & 1/3 \\ 0 & 0 & 0 & 1/3 & 0 & 1/3 & 1/3 & 0 & 0 & 0 \\ 0 & 0 & 0 & 0 & 1/3 & 0 & 1/3 & 1/3 & 0 & 0 \end{pmatrix}$$

We have already encountered a matrix that encodes the neighbors of each vertex, the adjacency matrix. Here we can recover the transition matrix by multiplying the adjacency matrix by $1/3$.

Transition matrices have a very special structure.

Theorem 7.2.9 *(Transition Matrix is Stochastic) The transition matrix* P *is a stochastic matrix; that is, all its entries are nonnegative and all its rows sum to one.*

7.2 Background: Elements of Finite Markov Chains

Proof Indeed,

$$\sum_{x \in S} p_{x',x} = \sum_{x \in S} \mathbb{P}[X_1 = x \mid X_0 = x'] = \mathbb{P}[X_1 \in S \mid X_0 = x'] = 1$$

by the properties of conditional probability. □

In matrix form, the condition can be stated as $P\mathbf{1} = \mathbf{1}$, where $\mathbf{1}$ is an all-one vector of the appropriate size.

We have seen that any transition matrix is stochastic. Conversely, any stochastic matrix is the transition matrix of a Markov chain. That is, we can specify a Markov chain by choosing the number of states n, an initial distribution over $S = [n]$ and a stochastic matrix $P \in \mathbb{R}^{n \times n}$. Row i of P stipulates the probability distribution of the next state given that we are currently at state i.

Example 7.2.10 *(Robot Vacuum) Suppose a robot vacuum roams around a large mansion with the following rooms: 1 = Study, 2 = Hall, 3 = Lounge, 4 = Library, 5 = Billiard Room, 6 = Dining Room, 7 = Conservatory, 8 = Ball Room, 9 = Kitchen.*

Once it is done cleaning a room, it moves to another one nearby according to the following stochastic matrix (check it is stochastic!):

$$P = \begin{pmatrix} 0 & 0.8 & 0 & 0.2 & 0 & 0 & 0 & 0 & 0 \\ 0.3 & 0 & 0.2 & 0 & 0 & 0.5 & 0 & 0 & 0 \\ 0 & 0.6 & 0 & 0 & 0 & 0.4 & 0 & 0 & 0 \\ 0.1 & 0.1 & 0 & 0 & 0.8 & 0 & 0 & 0 & 0 \\ 0 & 0 & 0 & 0.25 & 0 & 0 & 0.75 & 0 & 0 \\ 0 & 0.15 & 0.15 & 0 & 0 & 0 & 0 & 0.35 & 0.35 \\ 0 & 0 & 0 & 0 & 0 & 0 & 0 & 1 & 0 \\ 0 & 0 & 0 & 0 & 0.3 & 0.4 & 0.2 & 0 & 0.1 \\ 0 & 0 & 0 & 0 & 0 & 1 & 0 & 0 & 0 \end{pmatrix}$$

Suppose the initial distribution μ is uniform over the state space and let X_t be the room the vacuum is in at iteration t. Then $(X_t)_{t \geq 0}$ is a Markov chain. Unlike our previous examples, P is not symmetric. In particular, its rows sum to 1 but its columns do not. (Check it!)

When both rows and columns sum to 1, we say that P is *doubly stochastic*.

With the notation just introduced, the distribution of a sample path simplifies further to

$$\mathbb{P}[X_0 = x_0, X_1 = x_1, \ldots, X_T = x_T] = \mu_{x_0} \prod_{t=1}^{T} p_{x_{t-1}, x_t}.$$

This formula has a remarkable consequence. The marginal distribution of X_s is a matrix power of P. As usual, we denote by P^s the s-th matrix power of P. Recall also that μ is a row vector.

Theorem 7.2.11 *(Time Marginals) For any $s \geq 1$ and $x_s \in S$*

$$\mathbb{P}[X_s = x_s] = (\mu P^s)_{x_s}.$$

Proof idea: The idea is to think of $\mathbb{P}[X_s = x_s]$ as the time s marginal over all trajectories up to time s – quantities for which we know how to compute the probabilities. Then we use the *Distribution of a Sample Path Theorem* and "push the sums in." This is easier seen on a simple case. We do the case $s = 2$ first.

Summing over all trajectories up to time 2,

$$\mathbb{P}[X_2 = x_2]$$
$$= \sum_{x_0 \in S} \sum_{x_1 \in S} \mathbb{P}[X_0 = x_0, X_1 = x_1, X_2 = x_2]$$
$$= \sum_{x_0 \in S} \sum_{x_1 \in S} \mu_{x_0} p_{x_0, x_1} p_{x_1, x_2},$$

where we used the *Distribution of a Sample Path Theorem*.

Pushing the sum over x_1 in, this becomes

$$= \sum_{x_0 \in S} \mu_{x_0} \sum_{x_1 \in S} p_{x_0, x_1} p_{x_1, x_2}$$
$$= \sum_{x_0 \in S} \mu_{x_0} (P^2)_{x_0, x_2},$$

where we recognized the definition of a matrix product – here P^2. The result then follows.

Proof For any s, by definition of a marginal,

$$\mathbb{P}[X_s = x_s] = \sum_{x_0, \ldots, x_{s-1} \in S} \mathbb{P}[X_0 = x_0, X_1 = x_1, \ldots, X_{s-1} = x_{s-1}, X_s = x_s].$$

Using the *Distribution of a Sample Path Theorem* in the time-homogeneous case, this evaluates to

$$\mathbb{P}[X_s = x_s] = \sum_{x_0, \ldots, x_{s-1} \in S} \mu_{x_0} \prod_{t=1}^{s} p_{x_{t-1}, x_t}.$$

The sum can be simplified by pushing the individual sums as far into the summand as possible

$$\sum_{x_0, \ldots, x_{s-1} \in S} \mu_{x_0} \prod_{t=1}^{s} p_{x_{t-1}, x_t}$$
$$= \sum_{x_0 \in S} \mu_{x_0} \sum_{x_1 \in S} p_{x_0, x_1} \cdots \sum_{x_{s-2} \in S} p_{x_{s-3}, x_{s-2}} \sum_{x_{s-1} \in S} p_{x_{s-2}, x_{s-1}} p_{x_{s-1}, x_s}$$
$$= \sum_{x_0 \in S} \mu_{x_0} \sum_{x_1 \in S} p_{x_0, x_1} \cdots \sum_{x_{s-2} \in S} p_{x_{s-3}, x_{s-2}} (P^2)_{x_{s-2}, x_s}$$
$$= \sum_{x_0 \in S} \mu_{x_0} \sum_{x_1 \in S} p_{x_0, x_1} \cdots \sum_{x_{s-3} \in S} p_{x_{s-4}, x_{s-3}} (P^3)_{x_{s-3}, x_s}$$
$$= \cdots$$
$$= (\mu P^s)_{x_s}$$

where in the second line we recognized the innermost sum as a matrix product, then proceeded similarly. □

The special case $\mu = \mathbf{e}_x^T$ gives that for any $x, y \in [n]$

$$\mathbb{P}[X_s = y \mid X_0 = x] = (\mu P^s)_y = (\mathbf{e}_x^T P^s)_y = (P^s)_{x,y}.$$

Example 7.2.12 *(continued from Example 7.2.2)* Suppose day 0 is Dry; that is, the initial distribution is $\mu = (1, 0)^T$. What is the probability that it is Wet on day 2? We apply the formula above to get $\mathbb{P}[X_2 = 2] = (\mu P^2)_2$. Note that

7.2 Background: Elements of Finite Markov Chains

$$\mu P^2 = (1,0)^T \begin{pmatrix} 3/4 & 1/4 \\ 1/4 & 3/4 \end{pmatrix} \begin{pmatrix} 3/4 & 1/4 \\ 1/4 & 3/4 \end{pmatrix}$$

$$= (3/4, 1/4)^T \begin{pmatrix} 3/4 & 1/4 \\ 1/4 & 3/4 \end{pmatrix}$$

$$= (10/16, 6/16)^T$$

$$= (5/8, 3/8)^T.$$

So the answer is 3/8.

It will be useful later on to observe that the *Time Marginals Theorem* generalizes to

$$\mathbb{P}[X_t = x_t \,|\, X_s = x_s] = (P^{t-s})_{x_s, x_t},$$

for $s \leq t$.

In the time-homogeneous case, an alternative way to represent a transition matrix is with a directed graph showing all possible transitions.

Definition 7.2.13 *(Transition Graph)* Let $(X_t)_{t \geq 0}$ be a Markov chain over the state space $S = [n]$ with transition matrix $P = (p_{i,j})_{i,j=1}^n$. The transition graph (or state transition diagram) of $(X_t)_{t \geq 0}$ is a directed graph with vertices $[n]$ and a directed edge from i to j if and only if $p_{i,j} > 0$. We often associate a weight $p_{i,j}$ to that edge.

NUMERICAL CORNER Returning to our *Robot Vacuum Example* from Example 7.2.10, the transition graph of the chain can be obtained by thinking of P as the weighted adjacency matrix of the transition graph.

```
P_robot = np.array([[0, 0.8, 0, 0.2, 0, 0, 0, 0, 0],
                    [0.3, 0, 0.2, 0, 0, 0.5, 0, 0, 0],
                    [0, 0.6, 0, 0, 0, 0.4, 0, 0, 0],
                    [0.1, 0.1, 0, 0, 0.8, 0, 0, 0, 0],
                    [0, 0, 0, 0.25, 0, 0, 0.75, 0, 0],
                    [0, 0.15, 0.15, 0, 0, 0, 0.35, 0.35],
                    [0, 0, 0, 0, 0, 0, 0, 1, 0],
                    [0, 0, 0, 0, 0.3, 0.4, 0.2, 0, 0.1],
                    [0, 0, 0, 0, 0, 1, 0, 0, 0]])
```

We define a graph from its adjacency matrix. See the documentation for networkx.from_numpy_array.

```
G_robot = nx.from_numpy_array(P_robot, create_using=nx.DiGraph)
```

Drawing edge weights on a directed graph in a readable fashion is not straightforward. We will not do this here.

```
n_robot = P_robot.shape[0]
nx.draw_networkx(G_robot, pos=nx.circular_layout(G_robot),
            labels={i: i+1 for i in range(n_robot)},
            node_color='black', font_color='white',
            connectionstyle='arc3, rad = 0.2')
```

```
plt.axis('off')
plt.show()
```

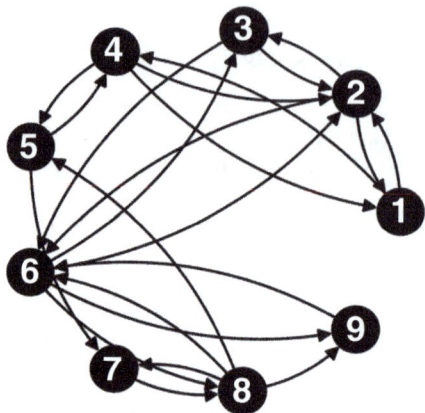

Figure 7.1 Graphical output of code.

◁ **NC**

Once we have specified a transition matrix (and an initial distribution), we can simulate the corresponding Markov chain. This is useful to compute (approximately) probabilities of complex events through the law of large numbers. Here is some code to generate one sample path up to some given time T. We assume that the state space is $[n]$. We use `rng.choice` to generate each transition.

```
def SamplePath(rng, mu, P, T):

    n = mu.shape[0]
    X = np.zeros(T+1)
    for i in range(T+1):
        if i == 0:
            X[i] = rng.choice(a=np.arange(start=1,stop=n+1),p=mu)
        else:
            X[i] = rng.choice(a=np.arange(start=1,stop=n+1),
                              p=P[int(X[i-1]-1),:])

    return X
```

NUMERICAL CORNER Let's try with our *Robot Vacuum*. We take the initial distribution to be the uniform distribution.

```
seed = 535
rng = np.random.default_rng(seed)
```

7.2 Background: Elements of Finite Markov Chains

```
mu = np.ones(n_robot) / n_robot
print(SamplePath(rng, mu, P_robot, 10))
```

[9. 6. 3. 6. 8. 6. 2. 1. 2. 6. 8.]

For example, we can use a simulation to approximate the expected number of times that room 9 is visited up to time 10. To do this, we run the simulation a large number of times (say 1,000) and count the average number of visits to 9.

```
z = 9
N_samples = 1000
visits_to_z = np.zeros(N_samples)

for i in range(N_samples):
    visits_to_z[i] = np.count_nonzero(SamplePath(rng, mu, P_robot,
                                                 10) == z)

print(np.mean(visits_to_z))
```

1.193

◁ NC

CHAT & LEARN Markov decision processes (MDPs) are a framework for modeling decision making in situations where outcomes are partly random and partly under the control of a decision maker. Ask your favorite AI chatbot to explain the basic components of an MDP and how they relate to Markov chains. Discuss some applications of MDPs, such as in robotics or game theory.

Self-assessment quiz (with help from Claude, Gemini, and ChatGPT)

1. Which of the following is true about the transition matrix P of a Markov chain?
   a) All entries of P are nonnegative, and all columns sum to one.
   b) All entries of P are nonnegative, and all rows sum to one.
   c) All entries of P are nonnegative, and both rows and columns sum to one.
   d) All entries of P are nonnegative, and either rows or columns sum to one, but not both.

2. What is the *Markov Property*?
   a) The past and future are independent.
   b) The past and future are independent given the present.
   c) The present and future are independent given the past.
   d) The past, present, and future are all independent.

3. Consider a Markov chain $(X_t)_{t \geq 0}$ on state space S. Which of the following equations is a direct consequence of the *Markov Property*?
   a) $\mathbb{P}[X_{t+1} = x_{t+1} | X_t = x_t] = \mathbb{P}[X_{t+1} = x_{t+1}]$

b) $\mathbb{P}[X_{t+1} = x_{t+1} | X_t = x_t, X_{t-1} = x_{t-1}] = \mathbb{P}[X_{t+1} = x_{t+1} | X_t = x_t]$
c) $\mathbb{P}[X_{t+1} = x_{t+1} | X_t = x_t] = \mathbb{P}[X_{t+1} = x_{t+1} | X_0 = x_0]$
d) $\mathbb{P}[X_{t+1} = x_{t+1} | X_t = x_t, X_{t-1} = x_{t-1}] = \mathbb{P}[X_{t+1} = x_{t+1}]$

4 Consider a Markov chain $(X_t)_{t \geq 0}$ with transition matrix $P = (p_{i,j})_{i,j}$ and initial distribution μ. Which of the following is true about the distribution of a sample path $(X_0, X_1, \ldots, X_T)$?
   a) $\mathbb{P}[X_0 = x_0, X_1 = x_1, \ldots, X_T = x_T] = \mu_{x_0} \prod_{t=1}^{T} p_{x_{t-1}, x_t}$
   b) $\mathbb{P}[X_0 = x_0, X_1 = x_1, \ldots, X_T = x_T] = \mu_{x_0} \sum_{t=1}^{T} p_{x_{t-1}, x_t}$
   c) $\mathbb{P}[X_0 = x_0, X_1 = x_1, \ldots, X_T = x_T] = \prod_{t=0}^{T} \mu_{x_t}$
   d) $\mathbb{P}[X_0 = x_0, X_1 = x_1, \ldots, X_T = x_T] = \sum_{t=0}^{T} \mu_{x_t}$

5 In the random walk on the Petersen graph example, if the current state is vertex 9, what is the probability of transitioning to vertex 4 in the next step?
   a) 0
   b) 1/10
   c) 1/3
   d) 1

Answer for 1: b. Justification: The text states that "the transition matrix P is a stochastic matrix; that is, all its entries are nonnegative and all its rows sum to one."

Answer for 2: b. Justification: The text summarizes the *Markov Property* as "the past and the future are independent given the present."

Answer for 3: b. Justification: This is a direct statement of the *Markov Property*, where the future state X_{t+1} depends only on the present state X_t and not on the past state X_{t-1}.

Answer for 4: a. Justification: The text states the *Distribution of a Sample Path Theorem*:

$$\mathbb{P}[X_0 = x_0, X_1 = x_1, \ldots, X_T = x_T] = \mu_{x_0} \prod_{t=1}^{T} p_{x_{t-1}, x_t}.$$

Answer for 5: c. Justification: In the Petersen graph, each vertex has three neighbors, and the random walk chooses one uniformly at random.

7.3 Limit Behavior 1: Stationary Distributions

We continue our exploration of basic Markov chain theory. In this section, we begin our study of the long-term behavior of a chain. As we did in the previous section, we restrict ourselves to finite-space discrete-time Markov chains that are also time-homogeneous.

7.3.1 Definitions

An important property of Markov chains is that, when run for long enough, they converge to a sort of "equilibrium." We develop parts of this theory here. What do we mean by "equilibrium"? Here is the key definition.

7.3 Limit Behavior 1: Stationary Distributions

Definition 7.3.1 (Stationary Distribution) *Let $(X_t)_{t \geq 0}$ be a Markov chain on $\mathcal{S} = [n]$ with transition matrix $P = (p_{i,j})_{i,j=1}^n$. A probability distribution $\boldsymbol{\pi} = (\pi_i)_{i=1}^n$ over $[n]$ is a stationary distribution of $(X_t)_{t \geq 0}$ (or of P) if*

$$\sum_{i=1}^n \pi_i p_{i,j} = \pi_j, \qquad \forall j \in \mathcal{S}.$$

In matrix form, this condition can be stated as

$$\boldsymbol{\pi} P = \boldsymbol{\pi},$$

where recall that we think of $\boldsymbol{\pi}$ as a row vector. One way to put this is that $\boldsymbol{\pi}$ is a fixed point of P (through multiplication from the left). Another way to put it is that $\boldsymbol{\pi}$ is a left (row) eigenvector of P with eigenvalue 1.

To see why a stationary distribution is indeed an equilibrium, we note the following.

Lemma 7.3.2 (Stationarity) *Let $\mathbf{z} \in \mathbb{R}^n$ be a left eigenvector of transition matrix $P \in \mathbb{R}^{n \times n}$ with eigenvalue 1. Then $\mathbf{z}P^s = \mathbf{z}$ for all integers $s \geq 0$.*

Proof Indeed,

$$\mathbf{z}P^s = (\mathbf{z}P)P^{s-1} = \mathbf{z}P^{s-1} = (\mathbf{z}P)P^{s-2} = \mathbf{z}P^{s-2} = \cdots = \mathbf{z}. \qquad \square$$

Suppose the initial distribution is equal to a stationary distribution $\boldsymbol{\pi}$. Then, from the *Time Marginals Theorem* and the *Stationarity Lemma*, the distribution at *any time* $s \geq 1$ is

$$\boldsymbol{\pi} P^s = \boldsymbol{\pi}.$$

That is, the distribution at all times indeed remains stationary.

In the next section we will derive a remarkable fact: Under certain conditions, a Markov chain started from an arbitrary initial distribution converges in the limit of $t \to +\infty$ to a stationary distribution.

Example 7.3.3 (continued from Example 7.2.2) Going back to the weather model, we compute a stationary distribution. We need $\boldsymbol{\pi} = (\pi_1, \pi_2)^T$ to satisfy

$$(\pi_1, \pi_2)^T \begin{pmatrix} 3/4 & 1/4 \\ 1/4 & 3/4 \end{pmatrix} = (\pi_1, \pi_2)^T;$$

that is,

$$\frac{3}{4}\pi_1 + \frac{1}{4}\pi_2 = \pi_1$$
$$\frac{1}{4}\pi_1 + \frac{3}{4}\pi_2 = \pi_2.$$

You can check that, after rearranging, these two equations are in fact the same one.

Note, however, that we have some further restrictions: $\boldsymbol{\pi}$ is a probability distribution. So $\pi_1, \pi_2 \geq 0$ and $\pi_1 + \pi_2 = 1$. Replacing the latter in the first equation we get

$$\frac{3}{4}\pi_1 + \frac{1}{4}(1 - \pi_1) = \pi_1$$

so that we require

$$\pi_1 = \frac{1/4}{1/2} = \frac{1}{2}.$$

We then have $\pi_2 = 1 - \pi_1 = 1/2$. The second equation above is also automatically satisfied.

The previous example is quite special. It generalizes to all doubly stochastic matrices (including the *Random Walk on the Petersen Graph* Example for instance). Indeed, we claim that the uniform distribution is always a stationary distribution in the doubly stochastic case. Let $P = (p_{i,j})_{i,j=1}^n$ be doubly stochastic over $[n]$ and let $\boldsymbol{\pi} = (\pi_i)_{i=1}^n$ be the uniform distribution on $[n]$. Then for all $j \in [n]$

$$\sum_{i=1}^n \pi_i p_{i,j} = \sum_{i=1}^n \frac{1}{n} p_{i,j} = \frac{1}{n} \sum_{i=1}^n p_{i,j} = \frac{1}{n} = \pi_j$$

because the columns sum to 1. This proves the claim.

Is a stationary distribution guaranteed to exist? Is it unique? To answer these questions, we first need some graph-theoretic concepts relevant to the long-term behavior of the chain.

Definition 7.3.4 *($x \to y$) A state $x \in \mathcal{S}$ is said to communicate with a state $y \in \mathcal{S}$ if there exists a sequence of states $z_0 = x, z_1, z_2, \ldots, z_{r-1}, z_r = y$ such that for all $\ell = 1, \ldots, r$*

$$p_{z_{\ell-1}, z_\ell} > 0.$$

We denote this property as $x \to y$.

In terms of the transition graph of the chain, the condition $x \to y$ says that there exists a directed path from x to y. It is important to see the difference between (1) the existence of a direct edge from x to y (which implies $x \to y$ but is not necessary) and (2) the existence of a directed path from x to y. See the next example.

Example 7.3.5 *(continued from Example 7.2.10)* Going back to the Robot Vacuum Example, *recall the transition graph. While there is no direct edge from 4 to 3, we do have $4 \to 3$ through the path $(4, 2), (2, 3)$. Do we have $3 \to 4$?*

Here is an important consequence of this graph-theoretic notion on the long-term behavior of the chain.

Lemma 7.3.6 *(Communication) If $x \to y$, then there is an integer $r \geq 1$ such that*

$$\mathbb{P}[X_r = y \mid X_0 = x] = (\mathbf{e}_x^T P^r)_y = (P^r)_{x,y} > 0.$$

Proof idea: We lower bound the probability in the statement with the probability of visiting the particular sequence of states in the definition of $x \to y$.

Proof By definition of $x \to y$, there exists a sequence of states $z_0 = x, z_1, z_2, \ldots, z_{r-1}, z_r = y$ such that, for $\ell = 1, \ldots, r, p_{z_{\ell-1}, z_\ell} > 0$. Hence,

$$\mathbb{P}[X_r = y \mid X_0 = x]$$
$$\geq \mathbb{P}[X_1 = z_1, X_2 = z_2, \ldots, X_{r-1} = z_{r-1}, X_r = y \mid X_0 = x]$$
$$= \prod_{\ell=1}^r \mathbb{P}[X_\ell = z_\ell \mid X_{\ell-1} = z_{\ell-1}]$$
$$= \prod_{\ell=1}^r p_{z_{\ell-1}, z_\ell} > 0,$$

as claimed. □

The following example shows that the probability in the lemma is positive, but may not be 1. It also gives some insights about the question of the uniqueness of the stationary distribution.

7.3 Limit Behavior 1: Stationary Distributions

NUMERICAL CORNER Consider random walk on the following digraph, which we refer to as the *Two Sinks Example* (why do you think?).

```
G_sinks = nx.DiGraph()
n_sinks = 5

for i in range(n_sinks):
    G_sinks.add_node(i)

G_sinks.add_edge(0, 0, weight=1/3)
G_sinks.add_edge(0, 1, weight=1/3)
G_sinks.add_edge(1, 1, weight=1/3)
G_sinks.add_edge(1, 2, weight=1/3)
G_sinks.add_edge(2, 2, weight=1)
G_sinks.add_edge(3, 3, weight=1)
G_sinks.add_edge(0, 4, weight=1/3)
G_sinks.add_edge(1, 4, weight=1/3)
G_sinks.add_edge(4, 3, weight=1)

nx.draw_networkx(G_sinks, pos=nx.circular_layout(G_sinks),
                 labels={i: i+1 for i in range(n_sinks)},
                 node_color='black', font_color='white',
                 connectionstyle='arc3, rad = -0.2')
plt.axis('off')
plt.show()
```

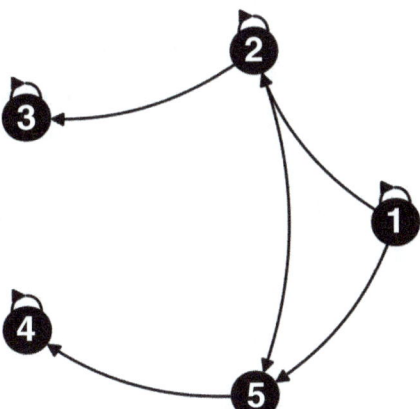

Figure 7.2 Graphical output of code.

Here we have $1 \to 4$ (why?). The *Communication Lemma* implies that, when started at 1, $(X_t)_{t \geq 0}$ visits 4 with positive probability. But that probability is not one. Indeed we also have $1 \to 3$ (why?), so there is a positive probability of visiting 3 as well. But if we do so before visiting 4, we stay at 3 forever and hence cannot subsequently reach 4.

In fact, intuitively, if we run this chain long enough we will either get stuck at 3 or get stuck at 4. These give rise to different stationary distributions. The transition matrix is the following.

```
P_sinks = nx.adjacency_matrix(G_sinks).toarray()
print(P_sinks)
```

```
[[0.33333333 0.33333333 0.         0.         0.33333333]
 [0.         0.33333333 0.33333333 0.         0.33333333]
 [0.         0.         1.         0.         0.        ]
 [0.         0.         0.         1.         0.        ]
 [0.         0.         0.         1.         0.        ]]
```

It is easy to check that $\pi = (0, 0, 1, 0, 0)^T$ and $\pi' = (0, 0, 0, 1, 0)^T$ are both stationary distributions.

```
pi = np.array([0.,0.,1.,0.,0.])
pi_prime = np.array([0.,0.,0.,1.,0.])
```

```
pi@P_sinks
```

```
array([0., 0., 1., 0., 0.])
```

```
pi_prime @ P_sinks
```

```
array([0., 0., 0., 1., 0.])
```

In fact, there are infinitely many stationary distributions in this case.

◁ NC

To avoid the behavior in the previous example, we introduce the following assumption.

Definition 7.3.7 *(Irreducibility) A Markov chain on $\mathcal{S}$ is irreducible if for all $x, y \in \mathcal{S}$ with $x \neq y$ we have $x \to y$ and $y \to x$. We also refer to the transition matrix as irreducible in that case.*

In graphical terms, a Markov chain is irreducible if and only if its transition graph is strongly connected.

NUMERICAL CORNER Because irreducibility is ultimately a graph-theoretic property, it is easy to check using NetworkX. For this, we use the function `is_strongly_connected`. Revisiting the *Robot Vacuum Example*:

```
P_robot = np.array([[0, 0.8, 0, 0.2, 0, 0, 0, 0, 0],
                    [0.3, 0, 0.2, 0, 0, 0.5, 0, 0, 0],
                    [0, 0.6, 0, 0, 0, 0.4, 0, 0, 0],
                    [0.1, 0.1, 0, 0, 0.8, 0, 0, 0, 0],
                    [0, 0, 0, 0.25, 0, 0, 0.75, 0, 0],
                    [0, 0.15, 0.15, 0, 0, 0, 0, 0.35, 0.35],
                    [0, 0, 0, 0, 0, 0, 0, 1, 0],
```

```
                     [0, 0, 0, 0, 0.3, 0.4, 0.2, 0, 0.1],
                     [0, 0, 0, 0, 0, 1, 0, 0, 0]])
```

```
G_robot = nx.from_numpy_array(P_robot, create_using=nx.DiGraph)
```

```
print(nx.is_strongly_connected(G_robot))
```

True

Consider again the *Two Sinks Example*. It turns out not to be irreducible:

```
print(nx.is_strongly_connected(G_sinks))
```

False

◁ **NC**

7.3.2 Existence

In the irreducible case, it turns out that a stationary distribution always exists – and is in fact unique. (The presence of a single strongly connected component suffices for uniqueness to hold in this case, but we will not derive this here. Also, in the finite case, a stationary distribution always exists, but again we will not prove this here.)

Theorem 7.3.8 *(Existence of Stationary Distribution) Let P be an irreducible transition matrix on $[n]$. Then there exists a unique stationary distribution π. Further, all entries of π are strictly positive.*

Proof The proof is not straightforward. We make a series of claims to establish existence.

Lemma 7.3.9 *(Step 1) There is a nonzero row vector $\mathbf{z} \in \mathbb{R}^n$ such that $\mathbf{z}P = \mathbf{z}$.*

Lemma 7.3.10 *(Step 2) Let $\mathbf{z} \in \mathbb{R}^n$ be a nonzero row vector with $\mathbf{z}P = \mathbf{z}$. Then*

$$\pi = \frac{\mathbf{z}}{\sum_x z_x}$$

is a strictly positive stationary distribution of P.

Lemma 7.3.11 *(Step 3) Let π_1 and π_2 be stationary distributions of P. Then $\pi_1 = \pi_2$.*

Proof *(Lemma (Step 1))* Because P is stochastic, we have by definition that $P\mathbf{1} = \mathbf{1}$, where $\mathbf{1}$ is the column all-one vector of dimension n. Put differently,

$$(P - I)\mathbf{1} = \mathbf{0};$$

that is, the columns of $P - I$ are linearly dependent. In particular $\text{rk}(P - I) < n$. That in turn implies that the rows of $P - I$ are linearly dependent by the *Row Rank Equals Column Rank Theorem*. So there exists a nonzero row vector $\mathbf{z} \in \mathbb{R}^n$ such that $\mathbf{z}(P - I) = \mathbf{0}$, or after rearranging,

$$\mathbf{z}P = \mathbf{z}.$$

This proves the claim. □

Proof *(Lemma (Step 2))* We break up the proof into several claims.

To take advantage of irreducibility, we first construct a positive stochastic matrix with **z** as a left eigenvector of eigenvalue 1. We then show that all entries of **z** have the same sign. Finally, we normalize **z**.

Lemma 7.3.12 *(Step 2a) There exists a nonnegative integer h such that*

$$R = \frac{1}{h+1}[I + P + P^2 + \cdots + P^h]$$

has only strictly positive entries and satisfies $\mathbf{z}R = \mathbf{z}$.

Lemma 7.3.13 *(Step 2b) The entries of* **z** *are either all nonnegative or all nonpositive.*

Lemma 7.3.14 *(Step 2c) Let* $\pi = \frac{\mathbf{z}}{\mathbf{z}\mathbf{1}}$. *Then* π *is a strictly positive stationary distribution.*

We prove the claims next.

Proof *(Lemma (Step 2a))* By irreducibility and the *Communication Lemma*, for any $x, y \in [n]$ there is $h_{x,y}$ such that $(P^{h_{x,y}})_{x,y} > 0$. Now define

$$h = \max_{x,y \in [n]} h_{x,y}.$$

It can be shown (try it!) that P^s (as a product of stochastic matrices) is itself a stochastic matrix for all s. In particular, it has nonnegative entries. Hence, for each x, y,

$$R_{x,y} = \frac{1}{h+1}[I_{x,y} + P_{x,y} + (P^2)_{x,y} + \cdots + (P^h)_{x,y}] \geq \frac{1}{h+1}(P^{h_{x,y}})_{x,y} > 0.$$

It can be shown (try it!) that R (as a convex combination of stochastic matrices) is itself a stochastic matrix.

Moreover, by the *Stationarity Lemma*, since $\mathbf{z}P = \mathbf{z}$ it follows that $\mathbf{z}P^s = \mathbf{z}$ for all s. Therefore,

$$\mathbf{z}R = \frac{1}{h+1}[\mathbf{z}I + \mathbf{z}P + \mathbf{z}P^2 + \cdots + \mathbf{z}P^h] = \frac{1}{h+1}[\mathbf{z} + \mathbf{z} + \mathbf{z} + \cdots + \mathbf{z}] = \mathbf{z}.$$

That concludes the proof. □

Proof *(Lemma (Step 2b))* We argue by contradiction. Suppose that two entries of $\mathbf{z} = (z_x)_{x \in [n]}$ have different signs. Say $z_i > 0$ while $z_j < 0$. Let $R = (r_{x,y})_{x,y=1}^n$. By *Step 2a*,

$$|z_y| = \left| \sum_x z_x r_{x,y} \right| = \left| \sum_{x: z_x \geq 0} z_x r_{x,y} + \sum_{x: z_x < 0} z_x r_{x,y} \right|.$$

Because $r_{x,y} > 0$ for all x, y, the first term in the rightmost expression is strictly positive (since it is at least $z_i r_{i,y} > 0$) while the second term is strictly negative (since it is at most $z_j r_{j,y} < 0$). Hence, because of cancellations, this expression is strictly smaller than the sum of the absolute values:

$$|z_y| < \sum_x |z_x| r_{x,y}.$$

Since R is stochastic by the proof of the previous claim, we deduce after summing over y

$$\sum_y |z_y| < \sum_y \sum_x |z_x| r_{x,y} = \sum_x |z_x| \sum_y r_{x,y} = \sum_x |z_x|,$$

a contradiction, proving the claim. □

7.3 Limit Behavior 1: Stationary Distributions

Proof *(Lemma (Step 2c))* Now define $\boldsymbol{\pi} = (\pi_x)_{x \in [n]}$ as

$$\pi_x = \frac{z_x}{\sum_i z_i} = \frac{|z_x|}{\sum_i |z_i|} \geq 0,$$

where the second equality comes from *Step 2b*. We also used the fact that $\mathbf{z} \neq \mathbf{0}$. For all y,

$$\sum_x \pi_x p_{x,y} = \sum_x \frac{z_x}{\sum_i z_i} p_{x,y} = \frac{1}{\sum_i z_i} \sum_x z_x p_{x,y} = \frac{z_y}{\sum_i z_i} = \pi_y.$$

The same holds with $p_{x,y}$ replaced with $r_{x,y}$ by *Step 2a*. Since $r_{x,y} > 0$ and $\mathbf{z} \neq \mathbf{0}$ it follows that $\pi_y > 0$ for all y. This proves the claim. □

That concludes the proof of *Lemma (Step 2)*. □

It remains to prove uniqueness.

Suppose there are two distinct stationary distributions $\boldsymbol{\pi}_1$ and $\boldsymbol{\pi}_2$. Since they are distinct, they are not multiples of each other and therefore are linearly independent. Apply the Gram–Schmidt algorithm:

$$\mathbf{q}_1 = \frac{\boldsymbol{\pi}_1}{\|\boldsymbol{\pi}_1\|} \quad \text{and} \quad \mathbf{q}_2 = \frac{\boldsymbol{\pi}_2 - \langle \boldsymbol{\pi}_2, \mathbf{q}_1 \rangle \mathbf{q}_1}{\|\boldsymbol{\pi}_2 - \langle \boldsymbol{\pi}_2, \mathbf{q}_1 \rangle \mathbf{q}_1\|}.$$

Then

$$\mathbf{q}_1 P = \frac{\boldsymbol{\pi}_1}{\|\boldsymbol{\pi}_1\|} P = \frac{\boldsymbol{\pi}_1 P}{\|\boldsymbol{\pi}_1\|} = \frac{\boldsymbol{\pi}_1}{\|\boldsymbol{\pi}_1\|} = \mathbf{q}_1$$

and all entries of $\mathbf{q}_1$ are strictly positive.

Similarly,

$$\begin{aligned}
\mathbf{q}_2 P &= \frac{\boldsymbol{\pi}_2 - \langle \boldsymbol{\pi}_2, \mathbf{q}_1 \rangle \mathbf{q}_1}{\|\boldsymbol{\pi}_2 - \langle \boldsymbol{\pi}_2, \mathbf{q}_1 \rangle \mathbf{q}_1\|} P \\
&= \frac{\boldsymbol{\pi}_2 P - \langle \boldsymbol{\pi}_2, \mathbf{q}_1 \rangle \mathbf{q}_1 P}{\|\boldsymbol{\pi}_2 - \langle \boldsymbol{\pi}_2, \mathbf{q}_1 \rangle \mathbf{q}_1\|} \\
&= \frac{\boldsymbol{\pi}_2 - \langle \boldsymbol{\pi}_2, \mathbf{q}_1 \rangle \mathbf{q}_1}{\|\boldsymbol{\pi}_2 - \langle \boldsymbol{\pi}_2, \mathbf{q}_1 \rangle \mathbf{q}_1\|} \\
&= \mathbf{q}_2.
\end{aligned}$$

By *Steps 2a-2c*, there is a multiple of $\mathbf{q}_2$, say $\mathbf{q}_2' = \alpha \mathbf{q}_2$ with $\alpha \neq 0$, such that $\mathbf{q}_2' P = \mathbf{q}_2'$ and all entries of $\mathbf{q}_2'$ are strictly positive.

By the properties of the Gram–Schmidt algorithm,

$$\langle \mathbf{q}_1, \mathbf{q}_2' \rangle = \langle \mathbf{q}_1, \alpha \mathbf{q}_2 \rangle = \alpha \langle \mathbf{q}_1, \mathbf{q}_2 \rangle = 0.$$

But this is a contradiction – both vectors are strictly positive. That concludes the proof. □

A few more observations about the eigenvalues of P.

1. Whenever λ is a left eigenvalue of P (i.e., $\mathbf{z}P = \lambda \mathbf{z}$ for some $\mathbf{z} \in \mathbb{R}^n$ as a row vector), it is also a right eigenvalue of P (i.e., $P\mathbf{y} = \lambda \mathbf{y}$ for some $\mathbf{y} \in \mathbb{R}^n$). One way to see this using our previous results is to note that $\mathbf{z}P = \lambda \mathbf{z}$ is equivalent to $P^T \mathbf{z}^T = \lambda \mathbf{z}^T$, or put differently $(P^T - \lambda I)\mathbf{z}^T = \mathbf{0}$, so that

$$\mathbf{z}^T \in \text{null}(P^T - \lambda I).$$

Similarly, $P\mathbf{y} = \lambda \mathbf{y}$ is equivalent to

$$\mathbf{y} \in \text{null}(P - \lambda I).$$

By the *Rank-Nullity Theorem*, these two null spaces have the same dimension since $(P - \lambda I)^T = P^T - \lambda I^T = P^T - \lambda I$. In particular, when one of them has dimension greater than 0 (i.e., it contains nonzero vectors), so does the other.

That is not to say that they are the same space – only their dimension match! In other words, the left and right eigenvalues are the same, but the left and right eigenvectors *are not*.

2. What we have shown in the previous theorem is that, if P is irreducible then it has a unique (up to scaling) left eigenvector with eigenvalue 1. By the first observation, $\mathbf{1}$ is also the unique right eigenvector of P with eigenvalue 1 in this case. That is, the geometric multiplicity of 1 is 1.

3. What about the other eigenvalues? Suppose that $\mathbf{z}P = \lambda \mathbf{z}$ for a nonzero row vector $\mathbf{z}$, then taking the ℓ_1-norm of the left-hand side we get

$$\|\mathbf{z}P\|_1 = \sum_{j=1}^{n} \left| \sum_{i=1}^{n} z_i p_{i,j} \right| \le \sum_{j=1}^{n} \sum_{i=1}^{n} |z_i| p_{i,j} = \sum_{i=1}^{n} |z_i| \sum_{j=1}^{n} p_{i,j} = \sum_{i=1}^{n} |z_i| = \|\mathbf{z}\|_1,$$

where we used that P is stochastic.

The ℓ_1-norm of the leftmost expression is $\|\lambda \mathbf{z}\|_1 = |\lambda| \|\mathbf{z}\|_1$. Hence $|\lambda| \|\mathbf{z}\|_1 \le \|\mathbf{z}\|_1$, which after simplifying implies $|\lambda| \le 1$.

4. So all left and right eigenvalues of P are less than or equal to 1 in absolute value. In the irreducible case, we know that 1 is achieved and has geometric multiplicity 1. What about -1? Suppose $\mathbf{z}P = -\mathbf{z}$. Then applying P again to both sides we get

$$\mathbf{z}P^2 = -\mathbf{z}P = \mathbf{z}.$$

So *if P^2* (which is stochastic) is irreducible, then there is a unique such $\mathbf{z}$.

But we already know of one. Indeed, the unique stationary distribution π of P satisfies

$$\pi P^2 = \pi P = \pi.$$

But it does not satisfy $\pi P = -\pi$. Hence there is no eigenvector with eigenvalue -1 in this case.

NUMERICAL CORNER In general, computing stationary distributions is not as straightforward as in Example 7.3.3. We conclude this subsection with some numerical recipes.

Going back to the *Robot Vacuum Example*, finding a solution to $\pi P = \pi$ in this case is not obvious. One way to do this is to note that, taking transposes, this condition is equivalent to $P^T \pi^T = \pi^T$. That is, π^T is an eigenvector of P^T with eigenvalue 1. (Or, as we noted previously, the row vector π is a left eigenvector of P with eigenvalue 1.) It must also satisfy $\pi \ge 0$ with at least one nonzero entry. Here, we use NumPy.

```
w, v = LA.eig(P_robot.T)
```

The first eigenvalue is approximately 1, as seen below.

```
print(w)
```

```
[ 1.          +0.j          0.67955052+0.j          0.50519638+0.j
 -0.70014828+0.j         -0.59989603+0.j         -0.47710224+0.32524037j
 -0.47710224-0.32524037j  0.03475095+0.04000569j  0.03475095-0.04000569j]
```

The corresponding eigenvector is approximately nonnegative.

```
print(v[:,0])
```

```
[0.08933591+0.j 0.27513917+0.j 0.15744007+0.j 0.06794162+0.j
 0.20029774+0.j 0.68274825+0.j 0.24751961+0.j 0.48648149+0.j
 0.28761004+0.j]
```

To obtain a stationary distribution, we remove the imaginary part and normalize it to sum to 1.

```
pi_robot = np.real(v[:,0]) / np.sum(np.real(v[:,0]))
print(pi_robot)
```

```
[0.03581295 0.11029771 0.06311453 0.02723642 0.0802953  0.27369992
 0.09922559 0.19502056 0.11529703]
```

Alternatively, we can solve the linear system

$$\sum_{i=1}^{n} \pi_i p_{i,j} = \pi_j, \qquad \forall j \in [n].$$

It turns out that the last equation is a linear combination over the other equations (see Problem 7.21), so we remove it and replace it instead with the condition $\sum_{i=1}^{n} \pi_i = 1$.

The left-hand side of the resulting linear system is (after taking the transpose to work with column vectors):

```
n_robot = P_robot.shape[0]
A = np.copy(P_robot.T) - np.diag(np.ones(n_robot))
A[n_robot-1,:] = np.ones(n_robot)
print(A)
```

```
[[-1.    0.3   0.    0.1   0.    0.    0.    0.    0.  ]
 [ 0.8  -1.    0.6   0.1   0.    0.15  0.    0.    0.  ]
 [ 0.    0.2  -1.    0.    0.    0.15  0.    0.    0.  ]
 [ 0.2   0.    0.   -1.    0.25  0.    0.    0.    0.  ]
 [ 0.    0.    0.    0.8  -1.    0.    0.    0.3   0.  ]
 [ 0.    0.5   0.4   0.    0.   -1.    0.    0.4   1.  ]
 [ 0.    0.    0.    0.    0.75  0.   -1.    0.2   0.  ]
 [ 0.    0.    0.    0.    0.    0.35  1.   -1.    0.  ]
 [ 1.    1.    1.    1.    1.    1.    1.    1.    1.  ]]
```

The right-hand side of the resulting linear system is:

```
b = np.concatenate((np.zeros(n_robot-1),[1.]))
print(b)
```

```
[0. 0. 0. 0. 0. 0. 0. 0. 1.]
```

We solve the linear system using `numpy.linalg.solve`.

```
pi_robot_solve = LA.solve(A,b)
print(pi_robot_solve)
```

```
[0.03581295 0.11029771 0.06311453 0.02723642 0.0802953  0.27369992
 0.09922559 0.19502056 0.11529703]
```

This last approach is known as "Replace an Equation."

◁ **NC**

CHAT & LEARN The Perron–Frobenius theorem is a powerful result about the eigenvalues and eigenvectors of certain types of matrices, including irreducible stochastic matrices. Ask your favorite AI chatbot to explain the Perron–Frobenius theorem and how it relates to the material in this section.

Self-assessment quiz (with help from Claude, Gemini, and ChatGPT)

1. Which of the following is the correct condition for a probability distribution $\pi = (\pi_i)_{i=1}^n$ to be a stationary distribution of a Markov chain with transition matrix $P = (p_{i,j})_{i,j=1}^n$?
   a) $\sum_{j=1}^n \pi_i p_{i,j} = \pi_j$ for all $i \in [n]$
   b) $\sum_{i=1}^n \pi_i p_{i,j} = \pi_j$ for all $j \in [n]$
   c) $\sum_{j=1}^n \pi_i p_{i,j} = \pi_i$ for all $i \in [n]$
   d) $\sum_{i=1}^n \pi_i p_{i,j} = \pi_i$ for all $j \in [n]$

2. Which of the following is the matrix form of the condition for a probability distribution π to be a stationary distribution of a Markov chain with transition matrix P?
   a) $\pi P = \pi$
   b) $P\pi = \pi$
   c) $\pi P^T = \pi^T$
   d) $P^T \pi^T = \pi$

3. A Markov chain is irreducible if
   a) every state communicates with every other state.
   b) there exists a state that communicates with every other state.
   c) the transition graph of the chain is strongly connected.
   d) Both a and c.

4. Consider the following transition graph of a Markov chain:

   ```
   G = nx.DiGraph()
   G.add_edges_from([(1, 2), (2, 1), (2, 3), (3, 3)])
   ```

   Is this Markov chain irreducible?

a) Yes

b) No

5. In an irreducible Markov chain, the left and right eigenvectors corresponding to eigenvalue 1 are

   a) the same up to scaling.
   b) always different.
   c) transposes of each other.
   d) not necessarily related to each other.

Answer for 1: b. Justification: The text states that a probability distribution $\pi = (\pi_i)_{i=1}^n$ over $[n]$ is a stationary distribution of a Markov chain with transition matrix $P = (p_{i,j})_{i,j=1}^n$ if $\sum_{i=1}^n \pi_i p_{i,j} = \pi_j$ for all $j \in [n]$.

Answer for 2: a. Justification: The text states that the condition for a probability distribution π to be a stationary distribution of a Markov chain with transition matrix P can be written in matrix form as $\pi P = \pi$, where π is thought of as a row vector.

Answer for 3: d. Justification: The text states that a Markov chain on S is irreducible if for all $x, y \in S$ with $x \neq y$, we have $x \to y$ and $y \to x$. It also mentions that a Markov chain is irreducible if and only if its transition graph is strongly connected.

Answer for 4: b. Justification: The Markov chain is not irreducible because there is no way to get back to state 1 from state 3.

Answer for 5: d. Justification: The text states that for an irreducible Markov chain, the left and right eigenvalues are the same, but the left and right eigenvectors are not necessarily the same. It also mentions that the geometric multiplicity of eigenvalue 1 is 1, implying that the left and right eigenvectors corresponding to eigenvalue 1 are unique up to scaling, but they are not necessarily related to each other.

7.4 Limit Behavior 2: Convergence to Equilibrium

We continue our study of the long-term behavior of a chain. Again, we restrict ourselves to finite-space discrete-time Markov chains that are also time-homogeneous.

7.4.1 Definitions

Now that we have established the existence and uniqueness of a stationary distribution (at least in the irreducible case), it remains to justify its relevance. As we indicated before, the fixed-point nature of the stationary distribution definition suggests that it arises as a limit of repeatedly applying P. Indeed it can be shown that, starting from any distribution, the state distribution at time t converges to the stationary distribution as $t \to +\infty$ – under an additional assumption.

The additional assumption involves issues of periodicity. The following example will suffice to illustrate.

Example 7.4.1 *(A Periodic Chain) Consider a two-state Markov chain with transition matrix*

$$P = \begin{pmatrix} 0 & 1 \\ 1 & 0 \end{pmatrix}.$$

Note that this chain is irreducible. Its unique stationary distribution is $\pi = (1/2, 1/2)^T$ since indeed

$$\pi P = (1/2, 1/2)^T \begin{pmatrix} 0 & 1 \\ 1 & 0 \end{pmatrix} = (1/2, 1/2)^T = \pi.$$

We compute the distribution at time t, started from state 1. That is,

$$\mu = (1, 0)^T.$$

Then

$$\mu P = (0, 1)^T,$$

$$\mu P^2 = (1, 0)^T,$$

$$\mu P^3 = (0, 1)^T,$$

and so on.

In general, by induction,

$$\mu P^k = \begin{cases} (1, 0)^T & \text{if } k \text{ is even} \\ (0, 1)^T & \text{if } k \text{ is odd.} \end{cases}$$

Clearly the distribution is not converging. Note however that the time average does:

$$\lim_{t \to +\infty} \frac{1}{t} \sum_{k \leq t} \mu P^k = (1/2, 1/2)^T = \pi.$$

We will need the following definition.

Definition 7.4.2 *(Aperiodic) Let $(X_t)_{t \geq 0}$ be a Markov chain over a finite state space $\mathcal{S}$. We say that state $i \in \mathcal{S}$ is aperiodic if*

$$\mathbb{P}[X_t = i \mid X_0 = i] > 0,$$

for all sufficiently large t. A chain is aperiodic if all its states are.

Example 7.4.3 *(continued from Example 7.4.1) Going back to the two-state chain above, we note that neither state is aperiodic. For state 1, we have shown that*

$$\mathbb{P}[X_t = 1 \mid X_0 = 1] = 0$$

for all t odd.

We will not need to explore this definition in great details here. Instead we give a simple *sufficient* condition that is typically good enough for data science applications.

Definition 7.4.4 *(Lazy)* *We say that a Markov chain $(X_t)_{t \geq 0}$ is lazy if every state i satisfies*

$$\mathbb{P}[X_1 = i \mid X_0 = i] > 0.$$

Put differently, all entries on the diagonal of the transition matrix are strictly positive.

Graphically, the chain has self-loops on each vertex. This terminology (which is not entirely standard) emphasizes the idea that the chain can "lazily" stay in its current state rather than always transitioning to a different one.

We check that a lazy chain is necessarily aperiodic. For any state $i \in \mathcal{S}$ and any t,

$$\mathbb{P}[X_t = i \mid X_0 = i] \geq \prod_{s=1}^{t} \mathbb{P}[X_s = i \mid X_{s-1} = i] = (\mathbb{P}[X_1 = i \mid X_0 = i])^t > 0,$$

by assumption. In words, the probability of being at i at time t given that we started at i is at least the probability that we never left.

Example 7.4.5 *Any Markov chain can be modified to be lazy by adding self-loops to all vertices. Specifically, let $P = (p_{i,j})_{i,j} \in \mathbb{R}^{n \times n}$ be the transition matrix of a Markov chain on $[n]$. Consider the modified transition matrix $Q = (q_{i,j})_{i,j}$ defined as*

$$Q = \frac{1}{2}(I_{n \times n} + P).$$

We check that this is indeed a stochastic matrix. For each $i, j \in [n]$, we have

$$q_{i,j} = \frac{1}{2}\mathbf{1}_{i=j} + \frac{1}{2}p_{i,j} \geq \frac{1}{2}p_{i,j} \geq 0$$

and

$$\sum_{\ell=1}^{n} q_{i,\ell} = \sum_{\ell=1}^{n}\left[\frac{1}{2}\mathbf{1}_{i=\ell} + \frac{1}{2}p_{i,\ell}\right] = \frac{1}{2}\sum_{\ell=1}^{n}\mathbf{1}_{i=\ell} + \frac{1}{2}\sum_{\ell=1}^{n}p_{i,\ell} = \frac{1}{2} + \frac{1}{2} = 1.$$

Finally, we note that Q is lazy since

$$q_{i,i} = \frac{1}{2}\mathbf{1}_{i=i} + \frac{1}{2}p_{i,i} = \frac{1}{2} + \frac{1}{2}p_{i,i} \geq \frac{1}{2} > 0.$$

The chain Q is often referred to as the "lazy version" of P.

7.4.2 Convergence Theorems

We are ready to state two key theorems.

First, the *Convergence to Equilibrium Theorem* applies to irreducible and aperiodic chains. Such chains have a unique stationary distribution. The theorem says that, started from any initial distribution, the distribution at time t converges to the stationary distribution as $t \to +\infty$.

Theorem 7.4.6 *(Convergence to Equilibrium)* *Let $(X_t)_{t \geq 0}$ be a finite irreducible and aperiodic Markov chain with unique stationary distribution π. Then for any initial distribution μ and any state i*

$$\mathbb{P}[X_t = i] \to \pi_i$$

as $t \to +\infty$.

Put differently, this theorem should look familiar. Using the formula $(\mu P^t)_i$ for the probability that the state is i at time t, we can rephrase the theorem in matrix form as

$$\mu P^t \to \pi$$

as $t \to +\infty$. This is highly reminiscent of the *Power Iteration Lemma*. Here repeated multiplication by P starting from an arbitrary distribution converges to π, which recall is a left eigenvector of P with eigenvalue 1. Unlike the *Power Iteration Lemma*, there is no need to normalize here. This is because we implicitly work with the ℓ_1-norm and P is stochastic, thereby preserving the norm.

Second, the *Ergodic Theorem* applies to irreducible (but not necessarily aperiodic) chains. Again such chains have a unique stationary distribution. The theorem says that, starting from any initial distribution, the frequency of visits to any state i converges to the stationary distribution. Below, we use the notation $\mathbf{1}[X_s = i]$ which is 1 when $X_s = i$ and 0 otherwise.

Theorem 7.4.7 (Ergodic Theorem) *Let* $(X_t)_{t \geq 0}$ *be a finite irreducible Markov chain with unique stationary distribution* π. *Then for any initial distribution* μ *and any state* i

$$\frac{1}{t} \sum_{s=0}^{t} \mathbf{1}[X_s = i] \to \pi_i$$

as $t \to +\infty$.

Above, $\sum_{s=0}^{t} \mathbf{1}[X_s = i]$ is the number of visits to i up to time t.

Note that neither of these two theorems immediately implies the other. They are both useful in their own way.

NUMERICAL CORNER The *Convergence to Equilibrium Theorem* implies that we can use power iteration to compute the unique stationary distribution in the irreducible case. We revisit the *Robot Vaccum Example*. We initialize with the uniform distribution, then repeatedly multiply by P.

```
P_robot = np.array([[0, 0.8, 0, 0.2, 0, 0, 0, 0, 0],
                    [0.3, 0, 0.2, 0, 0, 0.5, 0, 0, 0],
                    [0, 0.6, 0, 0, 0, 0.4, 0, 0, 0],
                    [0.1, 0.1, 0, 0, 0.8, 0, 0, 0, 0],
                    [0, 0, 0, 0.25, 0, 0, 0.75, 0, 0],
                    [0, 0.15, 0.15, 0, 0, 0, 0, 0.35, 0.35],
                    [0, 0, 0, 0, 0, 0, 0, 1, 0],
                    [0, 0, 0, 0, 0.3, 0.4, 0.2, 0, 0.1],
                    [0, 0, 0, 0, 0, 1, 0, 0, 0]])
n_robot = P_robot.shape[0]
mu = np.ones(n_robot)/n_robot
print(mu)
```

```
[0.11111111 0.11111111 0.11111111 0.11111111 0.11111111 0.11111111
 0.11111111 0.11111111 0.11111111]
```

```
mu = mu @ P_robot
print(mu)
```

```
[0.04444444 0.18333333 0.03888889 0.05       0.12222222 0.25555556
 0.10555556 0.15       0.05       ]
```

```python
mu = mu @ P_robot
print(mu)
```

```
[0.06       0.10222222 0.075      0.03944444 0.085      0.21722222
 0.12166667 0.195      0.10444444]
```

We repeat, say, 10 more times and compare to the truth `pi_robot`.

```python
for _ in range(10):
    mu = mu @ P_robot
print(mu)
```

```
[0.0358112  0.10982018 0.06297235 0.02721311 0.08055026 0.27393441
 0.09944157 0.19521946 0.11503747]
```

```python
w, v = LA.eig(P_robot.T)
pi_robot = np.real(v[:,0]) / np.sum(np.real(v[:,0]))
print(pi_robot)
```

```
[0.03581295 0.11029771 0.06311453 0.02723642 0.0802953  0.27369992
 0.09922559 0.19502056 0.11529703]
```

We see that a small number of iterations sufficed to get an accurate answer. In general, the speed of convergence depends on the eigenvalues of P that are strictly smaller than 1 in absolute value.

We can also check the *Ergodic Theorem* through simulation. We generate a long sample path and compare the state visit frequencies to `pi_robot`.

```python
seed = 535
rng = np.random.default_rng(seed)

mu = np.ones(n_robot) / n_robot
path_length = 50000
visit_freq = np.zeros(n_robot)

path = mmids.SamplePath(rng, mu, P_robot, path_length)
for i in range(n_robot):
    visit_freq[i] = np.count_nonzero(path == i+1)/(path_length+1)

print(visit_freq)
```

```
[0.03627927 0.10927781 0.0601788  0.02645947 0.08045839 0.27359453
 0.10119798 0.19693606 0.11561769]
```

```
print(pi_robot)
```

[0.03581295 0.11029771 0.06311453 0.02723642 0.0802953 0.27369992
 0.09922559 0.19502056 0.11529703]

◁ NC

CHAT & LEARN The mixing time is an important quantity in the study of Markov chains. Ask your favorite AI chatbot to define this concept and discuss its relevance to the convergence of Markov chains. Explore some bounds on the mixing time for specific classes of Markov chains.

> *Self-assessment quiz* (with help from Claude, Gemini, and ChatGPT)
>
> 1 Which of the following is a sufficient condition for a Markov chain to be aperiodic?
>   a) The chain is irreducible.
>   b) The chain has a unique stationary distribution.
>   c) The chain is lazy.
>   d) The chain has a finite state space.
>
> 2 In a Markov chain with state space S and transition matrix P, what does it mean if the chain is lazy?
>   a) $\mathbb{E}[X_t] = 0$ for all t.
>   b) $P_{ii} > 0$ for all $i \in S$.
>   c) $P_{ij} = 0$ for all $i \neq j$.
>   d) $\text{Var}(X_t) = 1$ for all t.
>
> 3 The *Convergence to Equilibrium Theorem* applies to which type of Markov chains?
>   a) Irreducible and aperiodic chains
>   b) Irreducible and periodic chains
>   c) Reducible and aperiodic chains
>   d) Reducible and periodic chains
>
> 4 The *Ergodic Theorem* applies to which type of Markov chains?
>   a) Irreducible chains
>   b) Aperiodic chains
>   c) Reducible chains
>   d) Periodic chains
>
> 5 Which of the following describes a key difference between the *Convergence to Equilibrium Theorem* and the *Ergodic Theorem*?
>   a) The *Convergence to Equilibrium Theorem* applies to periodic chains, while the *Ergodic Theorem* applies to aperiodic chains.
>   b) The *Convergence to Equilibrium Theorem* concerns the state distribution, while the *Ergodic Theorem* concerns the frequency of state visits.

c) The *Convergence to Equilibrium Theorem* requires a diagonal transition matrix, while the *Ergodic Theorem* does not.

d) The *Convergence to Equilibrium Theorem* is applicable only to finite Markov chains, while the *Ergodic Theorem* is not.

Answer for 1: c. Justification: The text states, "We check that a lazy chain is necessarily aperiodic."

Answer for 2: b. Justification: A weakly lazy Markov chain is defined as having all diagonal entries of the transition matrix strictly positive: $P_{ii} > 0$ for all $i \in S$.

Answer for 3: a. Justification: The text states, "First, the *Convergence to Equilibrium Theorem* applies to irreducible and aperiodic chains."

Answer for 4: a. Justification: The text states, "Second, the *Ergodic Theorem* applies to irreducible (but not necessarily aperiodic) chains."

Answer for 5: b. Justification: The *Convergence to Equilibrium Theorem* addresses the convergence of the state distribution to the stationary distribution, while the *Ergodic Theorem* focuses on the frequency of visits to any state converging to the stationary distribution.

7.5 Application: Random Walks on Graphs and PageRank

As we mentioned earlier in this chapter, a powerful way to extract information about the structure of a network is to analyze the behavior of a walker randomly "diffusing" on it.

7.5.1 Random Walk on a Graph

We first specialize the theory of the previous section to random walks on graphs. We start with the case of digraphs. The undirected case leads to useful simplifications.

7.5.1.1 Directed Case

We first define a random walk on a digraph.

Definition 7.5.1 (*Random Walk on a Digraph*) *Let $G = (V, E)$ be a directed graph. If a vertex does not have an outgoing edge (i.e., an edge with it as its source), add a self-loop to it. A random walk on G is a time-homogeneous Markov chain $(X_t)_{t \geq 0}$ with state space $S = V$ and transition probabilities*

$$p_{i,j} = \mathbb{P}[X_{t+1} = j \mid X_t = i] = \frac{1}{\delta^+(i)}, \qquad \forall i \in V, j \in N^+(i),$$

where $\delta^+(i)$ is the out-degree of i, meaning the number of outgoing edges, and $N^+(i) = \{j \in V : (i, j) \in E\}$.

In words, at each step, we choose an outgoing edge from the current state uniformly at random. Choosing a self-loop (i.e., an edge of the form (i, i)) means staying where we are.

Let $G = (V, E)$ be a digraph with $n = |V|$ vertices. Without loss of generality, we let the vertex set be $[n] = \{1, \ldots, n\}$. The adjacency matrix of G is denoted as $A = (a_{i,j})_{i,j}$. We define the out-degree matrix D as the diagonal matrix with diagonal entries $\delta^+(i)$, $i = 1, \ldots, n$. That is,

$$D = \text{diag}(A\mathbf{1}).$$

Lemma 7.5.2 *(Transition Matrix in Terms of Adjacency)* The transition matrix of a random walk on G satisfying the conditions of the definition above is

$$P = D^{-1}A.$$

Proof The formula follows immediately from the definition. □

We specialize irreducibility to the case of a random walk on a digraph.

Lemma 7.5.3 *(Irreducibility)* Let $G = (V, E)$ be a digraph. A random walk on G is irreducible if and only if G is strongly connected.

Proof Simply note that the transition graph of the walk is G itself. We have seen previously that irreducibility is equivalent to the transition graph being strongly connected. □

In the undirected case, more structure emerges, as we detail next.

7.5.1.2 Undirected Case

Specializing the previous definitions and observations to undirected graphs, we get the following. It will be convenient to allow self-loops, meaning that entry $a_{i,i}$ of the adjacency matrix can be 1 for some i.

Definition 7.5.4 *(Random Walk on a Graph)* Let $G = (V, E)$ be a graph. If a vertex is isolated, add a self-loop to it. A random walk on G is a time-homogeneous Markov chain $(X_t)_{t \geq 0}$ with state space $\mathcal{S} = V$ and transition probabilities

$$p_{i,j} = \mathbb{P}[X_{t+1} = j \mid X_t = i] = \frac{1}{\delta(i)}, \qquad \forall i \in V, j \in N(i)$$

where $\delta(i)$ is the degree of i and $N(i) = \{j \in V : \{i, j\} \in E\}$.

As we have seen previously, the transition matrix of a random walk on G satisfying the conditions of the definition above is $P = D^{-1}A$, where $D = \text{diag}(A\mathbf{1})$ is the degree matrix. For instance, we have previously derived the transition matrix for a random walk on the Petersen graph (see Example 7.2.8).

We specialize irreducibility to the case of a random walk on a graph.

Lemma 7.5.5 *(Irreducibility)* Let $G = (V, E)$ be a graph. A random walk on G is irreducible if and only if G is connected.

Proof We only prove one direction. Suppose G is connected. Then between any two vertices i and j there is a sequence of vertices $z_0 = i, z_1, \ldots, z_r = j$ such that $\{z_{\ell-1}, z_\ell\} \in E$ for all $\ell = 1, \ldots, r$. In particular, $a_{z_{\ell-1}, z_\ell} > 0$ which implies $p_{z_{\ell-1}, z_\ell} > 0$. This proves irreducibility. □

By the previous lemma and the *Existence of a Stationary Distribution Theorem*, provided G is connected, it has a unique stationary distribution. It turns out to be straightforward to compute it as we see in the next subsection.

7.5.1.3 Reversible Chains

A Markov chain is said to be reversible if it satisfies the so-called detailed balance conditions.

Definition 7.5.6 (*Reversibility*) *A transition matrix* $P = (p_{i,j})_{i,j=1}^n$ *is reversible with respect to a probability distribution* $\pi = (\pi_i)_{i=1}^n$ *if it satisfies the detailed balance conditions*

$$\pi_i p_{i,j} = \pi_j p_{j,i}, \qquad \forall i,j.$$

The next theorem explains why this definition is useful to us.

Theorem 7.5.7 (*Reversibility and Stationarity*) *Let* $P = (p_{i,j})_{i,j=1}^n$ *be a transition matrix reversible with respect to a probability distribution* $\pi = (\pi_i)_{i=1}^n$. *Then* π *is a stationary distribution of P.*

Proof idea: Just check the definition.

Proof For any j, by the definition of reversibility,

$$\sum_i \pi_i p_{i,j} = \sum_i \pi_j p_{j,i} = \pi_j \sum_i p_{j,i} = \pi_j,$$

where we used the fact that P is stochastic in the last equality. □

We return to a random walk on a weighted graph. We show that it is reversible and derive the stationary dsitribution.

Theorem 7.5.8 (*Stationary Distribution on a Graph*) *Let* $G = (V, E)$ *be a graph. Assume further that G is connected. Then the unique stationary distribution of a random walk on G is given by*

$$\pi_i = \frac{\delta(i)}{\sum_{i \in V} \delta(i)}, \qquad \forall i \in V.$$

Proof idea: We prove this in two parts. We first argue that $\pi = (\pi_i)_{i \in V}$ is indeed a probability distribution. Then we show that the transition matrix P is reversible with respect to π.

Proof We first show that $\pi = (\pi_v)_{v \in V}$ is a probability distribution. Its entries are nonnegative by definition. Further

$$\sum_{i \in V} \pi_i = \sum_{i \in V} \frac{\delta(i)}{\sum_{i \in V} \delta(i)} = \frac{\sum_{i \in V} \delta(i)}{\sum_{i \in V} \delta(i)} = 1.$$

It remains to establish reversibility. For any i, j, by definition,

$$\pi_i p_{i,j} = \frac{\delta(i)}{\sum_{i \in V} \delta(i)} \frac{a_{i,j}}{\sum_k a_{i,k}}$$

$$= \frac{\delta(i)}{\sum_{i \in V} \delta(i)} \frac{a_{i,j}}{\delta(i)}$$

$$= \frac{1}{\sum_{i \in V} \delta(i)} a_{i,j}.$$

Changing the roles of i and j gives the same expression since $a_{j,i} = a_{i,j}$. □

7.5.2 PageRank

One is often interested in identifying central nodes in a network. Intuitively, they should correspond to entities (e.g., individuals or webpages depending on the network) that are particularly influential or authoritative. There are many ways of uncovering such nodes. Formally one defines a notion of node centrality, which ranks nodes by importance. Here we focus on one important such notion, PageRank. We will see that it is closely related to random walks on graphs.

7.5.2.1 A Notion of Centrality for Directed Graphs

We start with the directed case.

Let $G = (V, E)$ be a digraph on n vertices. We seek to associate a measure of importance to each vertex. We will denote this (row) vector by

$$\mathbf{PR} = (\text{PR}_1, \ldots, \text{PR}_n)^T,$$

where PR stands for PageRank.

We posit that each vertex has a certain amount of influence associated with it and that it distributes that influence equally among the neighbors it points to. We seek a (row) vector $\mathbf{z} = (z_1, \ldots, z_n)^T$ that satisfies an equation of the form

$$z_i = \sum_{j \in N^-(i)} z_j \frac{1}{\delta^+(j)},$$

where $\delta^+(j) = |N^+(j)|$ is the out-degree of j and $N^-(i)$ is the set of vertices j with an edge (j, i). Observe that we explicitly take into account the direction of the edges. We think of an edge (j, i) as an indication that j values i.

- On the Web for instance, a link toward a page indicates that the destination page has information of value. Quoting Wikipedia[4]:

  PageRank works by counting the number and quality of links to a page to determine a rough estimate of how important the website is. The underlying assumption is that more important websites are likely to receive more links from other websites.

- On X (formerly known as Twitter), following an account is an indication that the latter is of interest.

We have already encountered this set of equations. Consider a random walk on the directed graph G (where a self-loop is added to each vertex without an outgoing edge). That is, at every step, we pick an outgoing edge of the current state uniformly at random. Then the transition matrix is

$$P = D^{-1}A,$$

where D is the diagonal matrix with the out-degrees on its diagonal.

A stationary distribution $\boldsymbol{\pi} = (\pi_1, \ldots, \pi_n)^T$ is a row vector satisfying in this case

$$\pi_i = \sum_{j=1}^n \pi_j p_{j,i} = \sum_{j \in N^-(i)} \pi_j \frac{1}{\delta^+(j)}.$$

So $\mathbf{z}$ is a stationary distribution of a random walk on G.

[4] https://en.wikipedia.org/wiki/PageRank

7.5 Application: Random Walks on Graphs and PageRank

If the graph G is strongly connected, we know that there is a unique stationary distribution by the *Existence of a Stationary Distribution Theorem*. In many real-world digraphs, however, that assumption is not satisfied. To ensure that a meaningful solution can still be found, we modify the walk slightly.

To make the walk irreducible, we add a small probability at each step of landing at a uniformly chosen node. This is sometimes referred to as *teleporting*. That is, we define the transition matrix

$$Q = \alpha P + (1 - \alpha) \frac{1}{n} \mathbf{1}\mathbf{1}^T,$$

for some $\alpha \in (0, 1)$ known as the damping factor (or teleporting parameter). A typical choice is $\alpha = 0.85$.

Note that $\frac{1}{n}\mathbf{1}\mathbf{1}^T$ is a stochastic matrix. Indeed,

$$\frac{1}{n}\mathbf{1}^T\mathbf{1} = \frac{1}{n}\mathbf{1}n = \mathbf{1}.$$

Hence, Q is a stochastic matrix (as a convex combination of stochastic matrices).

Moreover, Q is clearly irreducible since it is strictly positive. That is, for any $x, y \in [n]$, one can reach y from x in a single step:

$$Q_{x,y} = \alpha P_{x,y} + (1 - \alpha)\frac{1}{n} > 0.$$

This also holds for $x = y$ so the chain is lazy.

Finally, we define **PR** as the unique stationary distribution of $Q = (q_{i,j})_{i,j=1}^{n}$; that is, the solution to

$$\text{PR}_i = \sum_{j=1}^{n} \text{PR}_j\, q_{j,i},$$

with **PR** ≥ 0 and

$$\sum_{i=1}^{n} \text{PR}_i = 1.$$

Quoting Wikipedia[5] again:

> The formula uses a model of a random surfer who reaches their target site after several clicks, then switches to a random page. The PageRank value of a page reflects the chance that the random surfer will land on that page by clicking on a link. It can be understood as a Markov chain in which the states are pages, and the transitions are the links between pages – all of which are all equally probable.

Here is an implementation of the PageRank algorithm. We will need a function that takes as input an adjacency matrix A and returns the corresponding transition matrix P. Some vertices have no outgoing links. To avoid dividing by 0, we add a self-loop to *all vertices with out-degree* 0. We use `numpy.fill_diagonal` for this purpose.

Also, because the adjacency matrix and the vector of out-degrees have different shapes, we turn `out_deg` into a column vector using `numpy.newaxis` to ensure that the division is done one column at a time. (There are many ways of doing this, but some are slower than others.)

---

[5] https://en.wikipedia.org/wiki/PageRank

```
def transition_from_adjacency(A):

    n = A.shape[0]
    sinks = (A @ np.ones(n)) == 0.
    P = A.copy()
    np.fill_diagonal(P, sinks)
    out_deg = P @ np.ones(n)
    P = P / out_deg[:, np.newaxis]

    return P
```

The following function adds the damping factor. Here mu will be the uniform distribution. It gets added (after scaling by `1-alpha`) one row at a time to P (again after scaling by `alpha`). This time we do not need to reshape mu.

```
def add_damping(P, alpha, mu):
    Q = alpha * P + (1-alpha) * mu
    return Q
```

When computing PageRank, we take the transpose of Q to turn multiplication from the left into multiplication from the right.

```
def pagerank(A, alpha=0.85, max_iter=100):

    n = A.shape[0]
    mu = np.ones(n)/n
    P = transition_from_adjacency(A)
    Q = add_damping(P, alpha, mu)
    v = mu
    for _ in range(max_iter):
        v = Q.T @ v

    return v
```

NUMERICAL CORNER Let's try a star with edges pointing out. Along the way, we check that our functions work as we expect them to.

```
n = 8
G_outstar = nx.DiGraph()
for i in range(1,n):
    G_outstar.add_edge(0,i)

nx.draw_networkx(G_outstar, labels={i: i+1 for i in range(n)},
                 node_color='black', font_color='white')
plt.axis('off')
plt.show()
```

7.5 Application: Random Walks on Graphs and PageRank

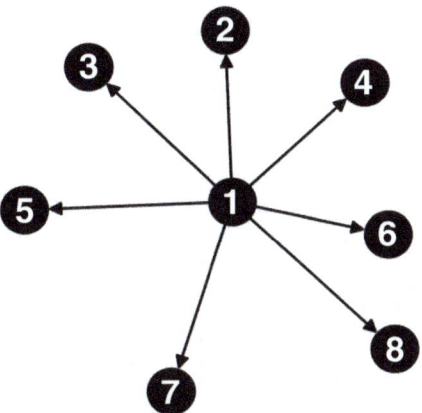

Figure 7.3 Graphical output of code.

```
A_outstar = nx.adjacency_matrix(G_outstar).toarray()
print(A_outstar)
```

```
[[0 1 1 1 1 1 1 1]
 [0 0 0 0 0 0 0 0]
 [0 0 0 0 0 0 0 0]
 [0 0 0 0 0 0 0 0]
 [0 0 0 0 0 0 0 0]
 [0 0 0 0 0 0 0 0]
 [0 0 0 0 0 0 0 0]
 [0 0 0 0 0 0 0 0]]
```

We compute the matrices P and Q. We use numpy.set_printoptions to condense the output.

```
P_outstar = transition_from_adjacency(A_outstar)
np.set_printoptions(formatter={'float': '{: 0.3f}'.format})
print(P_outstar)
```

```
[[ 0.000  0.143  0.143  0.143  0.143  0.143  0.143  0.143]
 [ 0.000  1.000  0.000  0.000  0.000  0.000  0.000  0.000]
 [ 0.000  0.000  1.000  0.000  0.000  0.000  0.000  0.000]
 [ 0.000  0.000  0.000  1.000  0.000  0.000  0.000  0.000]
 [ 0.000  0.000  0.000  0.000  1.000  0.000  0.000  0.000]
 [ 0.000  0.000  0.000  0.000  0.000  1.000  0.000  0.000]
 [ 0.000  0.000  0.000  0.000  0.000  0.000  1.000  0.000]
 [ 0.000  0.000  0.000  0.000  0.000  0.000  0.000  1.000]]
```

```
alpha = 0.85
mu = np.ones(n)/n
```

```
Q_outstar = add_damping(P_outstar, alpha, mu)
print(Q_outstar)
```

```
[[ 0.019  0.140  0.140  0.140  0.140  0.140  0.140  0.140]
 [ 0.019  0.869  0.019  0.019  0.019  0.019  0.019  0.019]
 [ 0.019  0.019  0.869  0.019  0.019  0.019  0.019  0.019]
 [ 0.019  0.019  0.019  0.869  0.019  0.019  0.019  0.019]
 [ 0.019  0.019  0.019  0.019  0.869  0.019  0.019  0.019]
 [ 0.019  0.019  0.019  0.019  0.019  0.869  0.019  0.019]
 [ 0.019  0.019  0.019  0.019  0.019  0.019  0.869  0.019]
 [ 0.019  0.019  0.019  0.019  0.019  0.019  0.019  0.869]]
```

While it is tempting to guess that 1 is the most central node of the network, no edge actually points to it. In this case, the center of the star has a low PageRank value.

```
print(pagerank(A_outstar))
```

```
[ 0.019  0.140  0.140  0.140  0.140  0.140  0.140  0.140]
```

We then try a star with edges pointing in.

```
n = 8
G_instar = nx.DiGraph()
G_instar.add_node(0)
for i in range(1,n):
    G_instar.add_edge(i,0)

nx.draw_networkx(G_instar, labels={i: i+1 for i in range(n)},
                 node_color='black', font_color='white')
plt.axis('off')
plt.show()
```

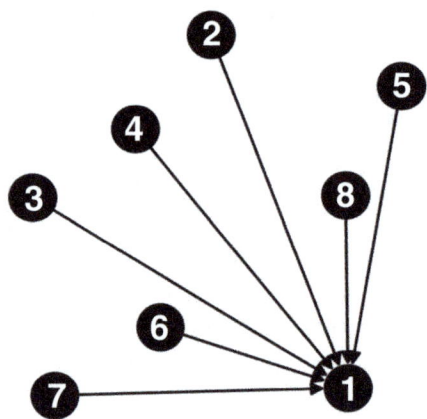

Figure 7.4 Graphical output of code.

```
A_instar = nx.adjacency_matrix(G_instar).toarray()
print(A_instar)
```

```
[[0 0 0 0 0 0 0 0]
 [1 0 0 0 0 0 0 0]
 [1 0 0 0 0 0 0 0]
 [1 0 0 0 0 0 0 0]
 [1 0 0 0 0 0 0 0]
 [1 0 0 0 0 0 0 0]
 [1 0 0 0 0 0 0 0]
 [1 0 0 0 0 0 0 0]]
```

```
P_instar = transition_from_adjacency(A_instar)
print(P_instar)
```

```
[[ 1.000   0.000   0.000   0.000   0.000   0.000   0.000   0.000]
 [ 1.000   0.000   0.000   0.000   0.000   0.000   0.000   0.000]
 [ 1.000   0.000   0.000   0.000   0.000   0.000   0.000   0.000]
 [ 1.000   0.000   0.000   0.000   0.000   0.000   0.000   0.000]
 [ 1.000   0.000   0.000   0.000   0.000   0.000   0.000   0.000]
 [ 1.000   0.000   0.000   0.000   0.000   0.000   0.000   0.000]
 [ 1.000   0.000   0.000   0.000   0.000   0.000   0.000   0.000]
 [ 1.000   0.000   0.000   0.000   0.000   0.000   0.000   0.000]]
```

```
Q_instar = add_damping(P_instar, alpha, mu)
print(Q_instar)
```

```
[[ 0.869   0.019   0.019   0.019   0.019   0.019   0.019   0.019]
 [ 0.869   0.019   0.019   0.019   0.019   0.019   0.019   0.019]
 [ 0.869   0.019   0.019   0.019   0.019   0.019   0.019   0.019]
 [ 0.869   0.019   0.019   0.019   0.019   0.019   0.019   0.019]
 [ 0.869   0.019   0.019   0.019   0.019   0.019   0.019   0.019]
 [ 0.869   0.019   0.019   0.019   0.019   0.019   0.019   0.019]
 [ 0.869   0.019   0.019   0.019   0.019   0.019   0.019   0.019]
 [ 0.869   0.019   0.019   0.019   0.019   0.019   0.019   0.019]]
```

In this case, the center of the star does indeed have a high PageRank value.

```
print(pagerank(A_instar))
```

```
[ 0.869   0.019   0.019   0.019   0.019   0.019   0.019   0.019]
```

◁ **NC**

7.5.2.2 A Notion of Centrality for Undirected Graphs

We can apply PageRank in the undirected case as well.

Consider a random walk on the undirected graph G. That is, at every step, we pick a neighbor of the current state uniformly at random. If needed, add a self-loop to any isolated vertex. Then the transition matrix is

$$P = D^{-1}A,$$

where D is the degree matrix and A is the adjacency matrix. A stationary distribution $\pi = (\pi_1, \ldots, \pi_n)^T$ is a row vector satisfying in this case

$$\pi_i = \sum_{j=1}^n \pi_j p_{j,i} = \sum_{j \in N(i)} \pi_j \frac{1}{\delta(j)}.$$

We already know the solution to this system of equations. In the connected case without damping, the unique stationary distribution of a random walk on G is given by

$$\pi_i = \frac{\delta(i)}{\sum_{i \in V} \delta(i)}, \quad \forall i \in V.$$

In words, the centrality of a node is directly proportional to its degree, namely how many neighbors it has. Up to the scaling factor, this is known as degree centrality.

For a general undirected graph that may not be connected, we can use a damping factor to enforce irreducibility. We add a small probability at each step of landing at a uniformly chosen node. That is, we define the transition matrix

$$Q = \alpha P + (1 - \alpha) \frac{1}{n} \mathbf{1}\mathbf{1}^T,$$

for some $\alpha \in (0, 1)$ known as the damping factor. We define the PageRank vector **PR** as the unique stationary distribution of $Q = (q_{i,j})_{i,j=1}^n$; that is, the solution to

$$\text{PR}_i = \sum_{j=1}^n \text{PR}_j \, q_{j,i},$$

with $\mathbf{PR} \geq 0$ and

$$\sum_{i=1}^n \text{PR}_i = 1.$$

NUMERICAL CORNER We revisit the star example in the undirected case.

```
n = 8
G_star = nx.Graph()
for i in range(1,n):
    G_star.add_edge(0,i)

nx.draw_networkx(G_star, labels={i: i+1 for i in range(n)},
                 node_color='black', font_color='white')
plt.axis('off')
plt.show()
```

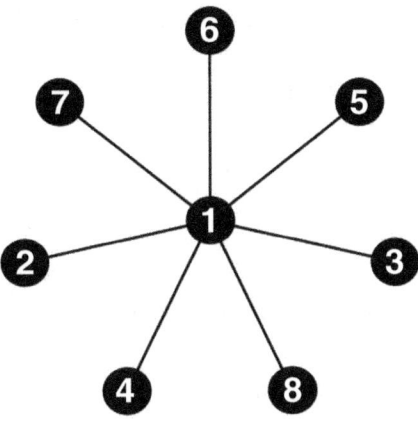

Figure 7.5 Graphical output of code.

We first compute the PageRank vector without damping. Here the random walk is periodic (why?) so power iteration may fail (try it!). Instead, we use a small amount of damping and increase the number of iterations.

```
A_star = nx.adjacency_matrix(G_star).toarray()
print(A_star)
```

```
[[0 1 1 1 1 1 1 1]
 [1 0 0 0 0 0 0 0]
 [1 0 0 0 0 0 0 0]
 [1 0 0 0 0 0 0 0]
 [1 0 0 0 0 0 0 0]
 [1 0 0 0 0 0 0 0]
 [1 0 0 0 0 0 0 0]
 [1 0 0 0 0 0 0 0]]
```

```
print(pagerank(A_star, max_iter=10000, alpha=0.999))
```

```
[ 0.500  0.071  0.071  0.071  0.071  0.071  0.071  0.071]
```

The PageRank value for the center node is indeed roughly seven times larger than the other ones, as can be expected from the ratio of their degrees.

We try again with more damping. This time the ratio of PageRank values is not quite the same as the ratio of degrees, but the center node continues to have a higher value than the other nodes.

```
print(pagerank(A_star))
```

```
[ 0.470  0.076  0.076  0.076  0.076  0.076  0.076  0.076]
```

◁ **NC**

CHAT & LEARN There are many other centrality measures besides PageRank, such as betweenness centrality, closeness centrality, and eigenvector centrality. Ask your favorite AI chatbot to explain these measures and discuss their similarities and differences with PageRank.

7.5.3 Personalized PageRank

We return to the MathWorld dataset. Recall that each page of MathWorld concerns a particular mathematical concept. In a section entitled "SEE ALSO," other related mathematical concepts are listed with a link to their MathWorld page. Our goal is to identify "central" vertices in the resulting graph.

NUMERICAL CORNER We load the dataset again.

```
data_edges = pd.read_csv('mathworld-adjacency.csv')
data_edges.head()
```

```
   from    to
0     0     2
1     1    47
2     1   404
3     1  2721
4     2     0
```

The second file contains the titles of the pages.

```
data_titles = pd.read_csv('mathworld-titles.csv')
data_titles.head()
```

```
                       title
0   Alexander's Horned Sphere
1              Exotic Sphere
2    Antoine's Horned Sphere
3                       Flat
4           Poincaré Manifold
```

We construct the graph by adding the edges one by one. We first convert df_edges into a NumPy array.

```
edgelist = data_edges[['from','to']].to_numpy()
print(edgelist)
```

```
[[    0     2]
 [    1    47]
 [    1   404]
 ...
 [12361 12306]
 [12361 12310]
 [12361 12360]]
```

7.5 Application: Random Walks on Graphs and PageRank

```
n = 12362
G_mw = nx.empty_graph(n, create_using=nx.DiGraph)
for i in range(edgelist.shape[0]):
    G_mw.add_edge(edgelist[i,0], edgelist[i,1])
```

To apply PageRank, we construct the adjacency matrix of the graph. We also define a vector of title pages.

```
A_mw = nx.adjacency_matrix(G_mw).toarray()
titles_mw = data_titles['title'].to_numpy()
pr_mw = pagerank(A_mw)
```

We use `numpy.argsort` to identify the pages with highest scores. We apply it to `-pr_mw` to sort from the highest to lowest value.

```
top_pages = np.argsort(-pr_mw)
```

The top 25 topics are:

```
print(titles_mw[top_pages[:25]])
```

```
['Sphere' 'Circle' 'Prime Number' 'Aleksandrov-Čech Cohomology'
 'Centroid Hexagon' 'Group' 'Fourier Transform' 'Tree' 'Splitting
 Field' 'Archimedean Solid' 'Normal Distribution' 'Integer Sequence
 Primes' 'Perimeter Polynomial' 'Polygon' 'Finite Group' 'Large
 Number' 'Riemann Zeta Function' 'Chebyshev Approximation Formula'
 'Vector' 'Ring' 'Fibonacci Number' 'Conic Section' 'Fourier Series'
 'Derivative' 'Gamma Function']
```

We indeed get a list of central concepts in mathematics – including several we have encountered previously such as `Normal Distribution`, `Tree`, `Vector`, and `Derivative`.

◁ **NC**

There is a variant of PageRank, referred to as Personalized PageRank (PPR), that aims to tailor the outcome to specific interests. This is accomplished from a simple change to the algorithm. When teleporting, rather than jumping to a uniformly random page, we instead jump to an arbitrary distribution which is meant to capture some specific interests. In the context of the Web for instance, this distribution might be uniform over someone's bookmarks.

We adapt `pagerank` as follows:

```
def ppr(A, mu, alpha=0.85, max_iter=100):
    n = A.shape[0]
    P = transition_from_adjacency(A)
    Q = add_damping(P, alpha, mu)
    v = mu
```

```
    for _ in range(max_iter):
        v = Q.T @ v
    return v
```

NUMERICAL CORNER To test PPR, consider the distribution concentrated on a single topic, `Normal Distribution`. This is topic number 1270.

```
print(np.argwhere(titles_mw == 'Normal Distribution')[0][0])
```

1270

```
mu = np.zeros(n)
mu[1270] = 1
```

We now run PPR and list the top 25 pages.

```
ppr_mw = ppr(A_mw, mu)
```

```
top_pers_pages = np.argsort(-ppr_mw)
```

The top 25 topics are:

```
print(titles_mw[top_pers_pages[:25]])
```

```
['Normal Distribution' 'Pearson System' 'Logit Transformation'
 'z-Score' 'Erf' 'Central Limit Theorem' 'Bivariate Normal
 Distribution' 'Normal Ratio Distribution' 'Normal Sum Distribution'
 'Normal Distribution Function' 'Gaussian Function'
 'Standard Normal Distribution' 'Normal Product Distribution'
 'Binomial Distribution' 'Tetrachoric Function' 'Ratio Distribution'
 'Kolmogorov-Smirnov Test' 'Box-Muller Transformation' 'Galton Board'
 'Fisher-Behrens Problem' 'Erfc' 'Normal Difference Distribution'
 'Half-Normal Distribution' 'Inverse Gaussian Distribution'
 'Error Function Distribution']
```

This indeed returns various statistical concepts, particularly related to the normal distribution.

◁ **NC**

CHAT & LEARN The PageRank algorithm has been adapted for various applications beyond web search, such as ranking scientific papers, analyzing social networks, and even ranking sports teams. Ask your favorite AI chatbot to discuss some of these applications and how the PageRank algorithm is modified for each case.

7.5 Application: Random Walks on Graphs and PageRank

Self-assessment quiz (with help from Claude, Gemini, and ChatGPT)

1. Consider a random walk on the following graph:

   ```
   G = nx.Graph()
   G.add_edges_from([(0, 1), (1, 2), (2, 0)])
   ```

   What is the transition matrix for this random walk?

   a) $\begin{bmatrix} 1/3 & 1/3 & 1/3 \\ 1/3 & 1/3 & 1/3 \\ 1/3 & 1/3 & 1/3 \end{bmatrix}$

   b) $\begin{bmatrix} 0 & 1/2 & 1/2 \\ 1/2 & 0 & 1/2 \\ 1/2 & 1/2 & 0 \end{bmatrix}$

   c) $\begin{bmatrix} 1 & 0 & 0 \\ 0 & 1 & 0 \\ 0 & 0 & 1 \end{bmatrix}$

   d) $\begin{bmatrix} 0 & 1 & 0 \\ 0 & 0 & 1 \\ 1 & 0 & 0 \end{bmatrix}$

2. In a random walk on a directed graph, the transition probability from vertex i to vertex j is given by:
   a) $p_{i,j} = \frac{1}{\delta^-(j)}$ for all $j \in N^-(i)$
   b) $p_{i,j} = \frac{1}{\delta^+(j)}$ for all $j \in N^+(i)$
   c) $p_{i,j} = \frac{1}{\delta^-(i)}$ for all $j \in N^-(i)$
   d) $p_{i,j} = \frac{1}{\delta^+(i)}$ for all $j \in N^+(i)$

3. The transition matrix P of a random walk on a directed graph can be expressed in terms of the adjacency matrix A as:
   a) $P = AD^{-1}$
   b) $P = A^T D^{-1}$
   c) $P = D^{-1} A$
   d) $P = D^{-1} A^T$

4. In a random walk on an undirected graph, the stationary distribution π satisfies:
   a) $\pi_i = \frac{\delta^+(i)}{\sum_{j \in V} \delta^+(j)}$ for all $i \in V$
   b) $\pi_i = \frac{1}{\delta(i)}$ for all $i \in V$
   c) $\pi_i = \frac{1}{|V|}$ for all $i \in V$
   d) $\pi_i = \frac{\delta(i)}{\sum_{j \in V} \delta(j)}$ for all $i \in V$

5. Personalized PageRank differs from standard PageRank in that:
   a) It considers the user's browsing history.
   b) It jumps to a nonuniform distribution when teleporting.

c) It uses a different damping factor.
  d) It only considers a subset of the graph.

Answer for 1: b. Justification: Each node has a degree of 2, and the probability of transitioning to each neighbor is 1/2.

Answer for 2: d. Justification: The text states, "In words, at each step, we choose an outgoing edge from the current state uniformly at random," which corresponds to the transition probability $p_{i,j} = \frac{1}{\delta^+(i)}$ for all $j \in N^+(i)$, where $\delta^+(i)$ is the out-degree of vertex i and $N^+(i)$ is the set of vertices with an edge from i.

Answer for 3: c. Justification: The text states, "The transition matrix of a random walk on G satisfying the conditions of the definition above is $P = D^{-1}A$, where D is the out-degree matrix."

Answer for 4: d. Justification: The text states, "In the connected case without damping, the unique stationary distribution of a random walk on G is given by $\pi_i = \frac{\delta(i)}{\sum_{i \in V} \delta(i)}$, $\forall i \in V$."

Answer for 5: b. Justification: The text states, "When teleporting, rather than jumping to a uniformly random page, we instead jump to an arbitrary distribution μ which is meant to capture some specific interests."

7.6 Further Applications: Gibbs Sampling and Generating Images

In this section, we derive an important application of Markov chains known as Markov chain Monte Carlo (MCMC). We specialize it to Gibbs sampling and apply it to the generation of handwritten digits using a restricted Boltzmann machine (RBM).

7.6.1 Markov Chain Monte Carlo (MCMC)

Suppose we are interested in generating samples from a target distribution $\pi = (\pi_i)_{i \in \mathcal{S}}$ over a set $\mathcal{S}$. We have done this before. For instance, we generated samples from a mixture of Gaussians to test k-means clustering in different dimensions. There are many more applications. A canonical one is to estimate the mean of a function f under π: Generate n independent samples $Z_1, \ldots, Z_n$, all distributed according to π, then compute

$$\frac{1}{n} \sum_{i=1}^{n} f(Z_i),$$

which is approximately $\mathbb{E}[f(Z_1)]$ by the law of large numbers, provided n is sufficiently large. Furthermore, this type of problem plays an important role in Bayesian inference.

7.6.1.1 Sampling from Simple Distributions

When π is a standard distribution or $\mathcal{S}$ is relatively small, this can be done efficiently by using a random number generator, as we have done previously.

NUMERICAL CORNER Recall how this works. We first initialize the random number generator and use a seed for reproducibility.

7.6 Further Applications: Gibbs Sampling and Generating Images

```
seed = 535
rng = np.random.default_rng(seed)
```

To generate, say, 1,000 samples from a multivariate normal, say with mean $(0,0)$ and covariance $\begin{pmatrix} 5 & 0 \\ 0 & 1 \end{pmatrix}$, we use `numpy.random.Generator.multivariate_normal` as follows.

```
mean = np.array([0., 0.])
cov = np.array([[5., 0.], [0., 1.]])
x, y = rng.multivariate_normal(mean, cov, 1000).T
```

Computing the mean of each component we get:

```
print(np.mean(x))
```

-0.035322561120667575

```
print(np.mean(y))
```

-0.009499619370100139

This is somewhat close to the expected answer: $(0,0)$.

Using a larger number of samples, say 10,000, gives a better result.

```
x, y = rng.multivariate_normal(mean, cov, 10000).T
print(np.mean(x))
print(np.mean(y))
```

-0.0076273930440971215
-0.008874190869155479

◁ **NC**

Sampling from an arbitrary distribution on a finite set is also straightforward – as long as the set is not too big. This can be done using `numpy.random.Generator.choice`. Borrowing the example from the documentation, the following:

```
aa_milne_arr = ['pooh', 'rabbit', 'piglet', 'christopher']
print(rng.choice(aa_milne_arr, 5, p=[0.5, 0.1, 0.1, 0.3]))
```

['pooh' 'pooh' 'piglet' 'christopher' 'piglet']

generates five samples from the set $\mathcal{S} = \{\text{pooh}, \text{rabbit}, \text{piglet}, \text{christopher}\}$ with respective probabilities $0.5, 0.1, 0.1, 0.3$.

But this may not be practical when the state space $\mathcal{S}$ is very large. As an example, later in this section, we will learn a "realistic" distribution of handwritten digits. We will do so using the MNIST dataset.

```
from torchvision import datasets, transforms
from torch.utils.data import DataLoader

mnist = datasets.MNIST(root='./data', train=True,
                       download=True, transform=transforms.
                       ToTensor())
train_loader = DataLoader(mnist, batch_size=len(mnist),
                          shuffle=False)

imgs, labels = next(iter(train_loader))
imgs = imgs.squeeze().numpy()
labels = labels.numpy()
imgs = np.round(imgs)
```

Each image is 28 × 28, so the total number of (black and white) pixels is 784.

```
nx_pixels, ny_pixels = imgs[0].shape
nx_pixels, ny_pixels
```

(28, 28)

```
n_pixels = nx_pixels * ny_pixels
n_pixels
```

784

To specify a distribution over all possible black and white images of this size, we need in principle to assign a probability to a very large number of states. Our space here is $\mathcal{S} = \{0, 1\}^{784}$, imagining that 0 encodes white and 1 encodes black and that we have ordered the pixels in some arbitrary way. How big is this space?

Answer: 2^{784}.

Or in base 10, we compute $\log_{10}(2^{784})$, which is:

```
784 * np.log(2) / np.log(10)
```

236.00751660056122

So a little more than 10^{236}.

This is much too large to naively plug into rng.choice!

So how to proceed? Instead we'll use a Markov chain, as detailed next.

7.6.1.2 General Setting

The idea behind MCMC is simple. To generate samples from π, use a Markov chain $(X_t)_{t \geq 0}$ for which *it is the stationary distribution*. Indeed, we know from the *Convergence to Equilibrium Theorem* that if the chain is irreducible and aperiodic, then the distribution at time t is close to π when t is large enough; and this holds for any initial dsitribution. Repeating this multiple times produces many independent, approximate samples from π.

The question is now:

1. How to construct a transition matrix P whose stationary distribution is the given target distribution π?

2. How to ensure that this Markov chain is relatively easy to simulate?

Regarding the first question, we have seen how to compute the stationary distribution of a transition matrix (provided it exists and is unique). How do we invert the process? Note one difficulty: Many transition matrices can have the same stationary distribution. This is in fact a blessing, as it gives room for designing a "good" Markov chain.

Regarding the second question, note that an obvious chain answering the first question is one that ignores the current state and chooses the next state according to π. We have already seen that this can be a problematic choice.

7.6.1.3 Metropolis–Hastings

We develop one standard technique that helps answer these two questions. It is known as the Metropolis–Hastings algorithm. It consists of two steps. We assume that $\pi > 0$; that is, $\pi_i > 0, \forall i \in \mathcal{S}$.

Proposal distribution: We first define a proposal chain, namely a transition matrix Q on the space $\mathcal{S}$. This chain *does not* need to have stationary distribution π. But it is typically a chain that is easy to simulate. A different way to think of this chain is that, for each state $x \in \mathcal{S}$, we have a proposal distribution $Q(x, \cdot)$ for the next state.

For instance, on the space of 28×28 black-and-white images, we might pick a pixel uniformly at random and flip its value with probability $1/2$.

Hastings correction: At each step, we first pick a state according to Q, given the current state. Then we accept or reject this move according to a specially defined probability that depends on Q as well as π. This is where the target distribution π enters the picture, and the rejection probability is chosen to ensure that the new chain has the right stationary distribution, as we will see later. But first we define the full algorithm.

Formally, the algorithm goes as follows. Let $x_0 \in \mathcal{S}$ be an arbitrary starting point and set $X_0 := x_0$. At each time $t \geq 1$:

- Pick a state Y according to the distribution $Q(X_{t-1}, \cdot)$; that is, row X_{t-1} of Q.
- With probability

$$\min\left\{1, \frac{\pi_Y}{\pi_{X_{t-1}}} \frac{Q(Y, X_{t-1})}{Q(X_{t-1}, Y)}\right\}$$

we set $X_t := Y$ (i.e., we accept the move), and otherwise we set $X_t := X_{t-1}$ (i.e., we reject the move).

We make three observations:

1. Taking a minimum with 1 ensures the acceptance probability is indeed between 0 and 1.
2. We only need to know π up to a scaling factor since the chain depends only on the ratio $\frac{\pi_Y}{\pi_{X_{t-1}}}$. The scaling factor cancels out. This turns out to be critical in many applications of MCMC. We will see an example in the next subsection.

3. If Q is symmetric, so that $Q(x, y) = Q(y, x)$ for all $x, y \in S$, then the ratio $\frac{Q(Y, X_{t-1})}{Q(X_{t-1}, Y)}$ is just 1, leading to a simpler formula for the acceptance probability. In particular, in that case, moving to a state with a larger probability under π is *always* accepted.

NUMERICAL CORNER Suppose $S = \{1, \cdots, n\} = [n]$ for some positive integer n and π is proportional to a Poisson distribution with mean $\lambda > 0$. That is,

$$\pi_i = Ce^{-\lambda} \frac{\lambda^i}{i!}, \quad \forall i \in S$$

for some constant C chosen so that $\sum_{i=1}^{n} \pi_i = 1$. Recall that we do not need to determine C as it is enough to know the target distribution up to a scaling factor by the second preceding remark.

To apply Metropolis–Hastings, we need a proposal chain. Consider the following choice. For each $1 < i < n$, move to $i + 1$ or $i - 1$ with probability $1/2$ each. For $i = 1$ (respectively $i = n$), move to 2 (respectively $n - 1$) with probability $1/2$, otherwise stay where you are. For instance, if $n = 4$, then

$$Q = \begin{pmatrix} 1/2 & 1/2 & 0 & 0 \\ 1/2 & 0 & 1/2 & 0 \\ 0 & 1/2 & 0 & 1/2 \\ 0 & 0 & 1/2 & 1/2 \end{pmatrix},$$

which is indeed a stochastic matrix. It is also symmetric, so it does not enter into the acceptance probability by the third preceding remark.

To compute the acceptance probability, we only need to consider pairs of adjacent integers as they are the only ones that have nonzero probability under Q. Consider state $1 < i < n$. Observe that

$$\frac{\pi_{i+1}}{\pi_i} = \frac{Ce^{-\lambda}\lambda^{i+1}/(i+1)!}{Ce^{-\lambda}\lambda^i/i!} = \frac{\lambda}{i+1}$$

so a move to $i + 1$ happens with probability

$$\frac{1}{2} \min\left\{1, \frac{\lambda}{i+1}\right\},$$

where the $1/2$ factor comes from the proposal distribution. Similarly, it can be checked (try it!) that a move to $i - 1$ occurs with probability

$$\frac{1}{2} \min\left\{1, \frac{i}{\lambda}\right\}.$$

And we stay at i with probability $1 - \frac{1}{2}\min\left\{1, \frac{\lambda}{i+1}\right\} - \frac{1}{2}\min\left\{1, \frac{i}{\lambda}\right\}$. (Why is this guaranteed to be a probability?)

A similar formula applies to $i = 1, n$. (Try it!)

We are ready to apply Metropolis–Hastings.

```
def mh_transition_poisson(lmbd, n):
    P = np.zeros((n,n))
    for idx in range(n):
        i = idx + 1 # index starts at 0 rather than 1
        if (i > 1 and i < n):
            P[idx, idx+1] = (1/2) * np.min(np.array([1, lmbd/(i+1)]))
```

7.6 Further Applications: Gibbs Sampling and Generating Images

```
            P[idx, idx-1] = (1/2) * np.min(np.array([1, i/lmbd]))
            P[idx, idx] = 1 - P[idx, idx+1] - P[idx, idx-1]
        elif i == 1:
            P[idx, idx+1] = (1/2) * np.min(np.array([1, lmbd/(i+1)]))
            P[idx, idx] = 1 - P[idx, idx+1]
        elif i == n:
            P[idx, idx-1] = (1/2) * np.min(np.array([1, i/lmbd]))
            P[idx, idx] = 1 - P[idx, idx-1]
    return P
```

Take $\lambda = 1$ and $n = 6$. We get the following transition matrix.

```
lmbd = 1
n = 6
```

```
P = mh_transition_poisson(lmbd, n)
print(P)
```

```
[[0.75       0.25       0.         0.         0.         0.        ]
 [0.5        0.33333333 0.16666667 0.         0.         0.        ]
 [0.         0.5        0.375      0.125      0.         0.        ]
 [0.         0.         0.5        0.4        0.1        0.        ]
 [0.         0.         0.         0.5        0.41666667 0.08333333]
 [0.         0.         0.         0.         0.5        0.5       ]]
```

TRY IT! *Rewrite* the function mh_transition_poisson without an explicit loop by using broadcasting and vectorization.

We use our simulator from Section 7.2.2. We start from the uniform distribution and take 100 steps.

```
seed = 535
rng = np.random.default_rng(seed)

mu = np.ones(n) / n
T = 100
X = mmids.SamplePath(rng, mu, P, T)
```

Our sample is the final state of the trajectory.

```
X[T]
```

2.0

We repeat 1,000 times.

```
N_samples = 1000 # number of repetitions
```

```
freq_z = np.zeros(n) # init of frequencies sampled
for i in range(N_samples):
    X = mmids.SamplePath(rng, mu, P, T)
    freq_z[int(X[T])-1] += 1 # adjust for index starting at 0

freq_z = freq_z/N_samples
```

We plot the frequencies.

```
plt.bar(range(1,n+1),freq_z, color='lightblue', edgecolor='black')
plt.show()
```

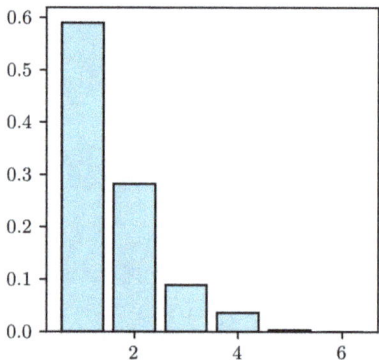

Figure 7.6 Graphical output of code.

If we increase the parameter λ (which is not quite the mean; why?), what would you expect will happen to the sampled distribution?

TRY IT! *Redo* the simulations, but this time implement a general Metropolis–Hastings algorithm rather than specifying the transition matrix directly. That is, implement the algorithm for an arbitrary π and Q. Assume the state space is $[n]$.

◁ NC

It remains to prove that π is the needed stationary distribution of the Metropolis–Hastings algorithm. We restrict ourselves to the symmetric case; that is, $Q(x,y) = Q(y,x)$ for all x,y.

Theorem 7.6.1 *(Correctness of Metropolis–Hastings) Consider the Metropolis–Hastings algorithm with target distribution π over finite state space S and symmetric proposal chain Q. Assume further that π is strictly positive and Q is irreducible over S. The resulting Markov chain is irreducible and reversible with respect to π.*

Proof idea: It is just a matter of writing down the resulting transition matrix P and checking the detailed balance conditions. Because of the minimum in the acceptance probability, one has to consider two cases each time.

Proof Let P denote the transition matrix of the resulting Markov chain. Our first task is to compute P.

Let $x, y \in \mathcal{S}$ be a pair of distinct states such that $Q(x, y) = Q(y, x) = 0$. Then, from x (respectively y), the proposal chain never picks y (respectively x) as the possible next state. Hence $P(x, y) = P(y, x) = 0$ in that case.

So let $x, y \in \mathcal{S}$ be a pair of distinct states such that $Q(x, y) = Q(y, x) > 0$. Applying the Hastings correction, we get that the overall probability of moving to y from the current state x is

$$P(x, y) = Q(x, y)\left(1 \wedge \frac{\pi_y}{\pi_x}\right) > 0,$$

where we used the symmetry of Q and the notation $a \wedge b = \min\{a, b\}$. Similarly,

$$P(y, x) = Q(y, x)\left(1 \wedge \frac{\pi_x}{\pi_y}\right) > 0.$$

Since $P(x, y)$ is strictly positive exactly when $Q(x, y)$ is strictly positive (for distinct x, y), the chain P has the same transition graph as the chain Q. Hence, because Q is irreducible, so is P.

It remains to check the detailed balance conditions. There are two cases. Without loss of generality, say $\pi_x \leq \pi_y$. Then the previous formulas for P simplify to

$$P(x, y) = Q(x, y) \quad \text{and} \quad P(y, x) = Q(y, x)\frac{\pi_x}{\pi_y}.$$

Hence,

$$\pi_x P(x, y) = \pi_x Q(x, y) = \pi_x Q(y, x) = \pi_x \frac{\pi_y}{\pi_y} Q(y, x) = \pi_y P(y, x),$$

where we used the symmetry of Q to obtain the second equality. That establishes the reversibility of P and concludes the proof. □

CHAT & LEARN The Metropolis–Hastings algorithm can be used for Bayesian inference. Ask your favorite AI chatbot to explain how MCMC methods are used in Bayesian inference and to provide an example of using the Metropolis–Hastings algorithm for parameter estimation in a simple Bayesian model.

7.6.2 Gibbs Sampling

We have seen that one challenge of the Metropolis–Hastings approach is to choose a good proposal chain. Gibbs sampling is a canonical way of addressing this issue that has many applications. It applies in cases where the states are vectors, typically with a large number of coordinates, and where the target distribution has the kind of conditional independence properties we have encountered previously in Chapter 6.

7.6.2.1 General Setting

Here we will assume that $\mathcal{S} = \mathcal{Z}^d$ where $\mathcal{Z}$ is a finite set and d is the dimension. To emphasize that states are vectors, we use boldface letters, $\mathbf{x} = (x_i)_{i=1}^d$, $\mathbf{y} = (y_i)_{i=1}^d$, and so on, to denote them.

We will need the following special notation. For a vector $\mathbf{x} \in \mathcal{Z}^d$ and an index $i \in [d]$, we write

$$\mathbf{x}_{-i} = (x_1, \ldots, x_{i-1}, x_{i+1}, \ldots, x_d)$$

for the vector resulting when **x** when the coordinate x_i is dropped.

If π is the target distribution, we let $\pi_i(x_i|\mathbf{x}_{-i})$ be the conditional probability that $X_i = x_i$ given that $\mathbf{X}_{-i} = \mathbf{x}_{-i}$ under the distribution π, so that $\mathbf{X} = (X_1, \ldots, X_d) \sim \pi$. We assume that $\pi_\mathbf{x} > 0$ for all $\mathbf{x} \in \mathcal{Z}^d$. As a result, $\pi_i(x_i|\mathbf{x}_{-i}) > 0$ as well (prove it!).

A basic version of the Gibbs sampler generates a sequence of vectors $\mathbf{X}_0, \mathbf{X}_1, \ldots, \mathbf{X}_t, \ldots$ in $\mathcal{Z}^d$ as follows. We denote the coordinates of $\mathbf{X}_t$ by $(X_{t,1}, \ldots, X_{t,d})$. We denote the vector of all coordinates of $\mathbf{X}_t$ except i by $\mathbf{X}_{t,-i}$.

Pick $\mathbf{X}_0$ according to an arbitrary initial distribution μ over $\mathcal{Z}^d$. At each time $t \geq 1$:

- Pick a coordinate i uniformly at random in $[d]$.
- Update coordinate $X_{t,i}$ according to $\pi_i(\,\cdot\,|\mathbf{X}_{t-1,-i})$ while leaving all other coordinates unchanged.

We will implement this in a special case in the next subsection. But first we argue that it has the desired stationary distribution.

It suffices to establish that the Gibbs sampler is a special case of the Metropolis–Hastings algorithm. For this, we must identify the appropriate proposal chain Q.

We claim that the following choice works: for $\mathbf{x} \neq \mathbf{y}$,

$$Q(\mathbf{x}, \mathbf{y}) = \begin{cases} \frac{1}{d}\pi_i(y_i|\mathbf{x}_{-i}) & \text{if } \mathbf{y}_{-i} = \mathbf{x}_{-i} \text{ for some } i \in [d] \\ 0 & \text{otherwise.} \end{cases}$$

The condition "$\mathbf{y}_{-i} = \mathbf{x}_{-i}$ for some $i \in [d]$" ensures that we only consider moves that affect a single coordinate i. The factor $1/d$ means that we pick that coordinate uniformly at random among all coordinates. For each $\mathbf{x}$, we stay put with the remaining probability.

In general, this Q is not symmetric. For $\mathbf{x} \neq \mathbf{y}$ with $Q(\mathbf{x}, \mathbf{y}) > 0$ where i is the non-matching coordinate, the acceptance probability is

$$\min\left\{1, \frac{\pi_\mathbf{y}}{\pi_\mathbf{x}} \frac{Q(\mathbf{y}, \mathbf{x})}{Q(\mathbf{x}, \mathbf{y})}\right\} = \min\left\{1, \frac{\pi_\mathbf{y}}{\pi_\mathbf{x}} \frac{\frac{1}{d}\pi_i(x_i|\mathbf{y}_{-i})}{\frac{1}{d}\pi_i(y_i|\mathbf{x}_{-i})}\right\}$$

$$= \min\left\{1, \frac{\pi_\mathbf{y}}{\pi_\mathbf{x}} \frac{\pi_i(x_i|\mathbf{x}_{-i})}{\pi_i(y_i|\mathbf{x}_{-i})}\right\},$$

where we used that $\mathbf{x}_{-i} = \mathbf{y}_{-i}$ in the second equality.

Recall the definition of the conditional probability as a ratio: $\mathbb{P}[A|B] = \mathbb{P}[A \cap B]/\mathbb{P}[B]$. Applying that definition, both conditional probabilities $\pi_i(x_i|\mathbf{x}_{-i})$ and $\pi_i(y_i|\mathbf{x}_{-i})$ have the *same denominator*. Their respective numerators on the other hand are $\pi_\mathbf{x}$ and $\pi_\mathbf{y}$. Hence,

$$\min\left\{1, \frac{\pi_\mathbf{y}}{\pi_\mathbf{x}} \frac{\pi_i(x_i|\mathbf{x}_{-i})}{\pi_i(y_i|\mathbf{x}_{-i})}\right\} = \min\left\{1, \frac{\pi_\mathbf{y}}{\pi_\mathbf{x}} \frac{\pi_\mathbf{x}}{\pi_\mathbf{y}}\right\} = 1.$$

In other words, the proposed move is always accepted! Therefore $P = Q$, which is indeed the Gibbs sampler. It also establishes by *Correctness of Metropolis–Hastings Theorem* that P is reversible with respect to π. It is also irreducible (why?).

Here we picked a coordinate at random. It turns out that other choices are possible. For example, one could update each coordinate in some deterministic order; or one could update blocks of coordinates at a time. Under some conditions, these schemes can still produce an algorithm simulating the desired distribution. We will not detail this here, but our implementation below does use a block scheme.

7.6 Further Applications: Gibbs Sampling and Generating Images

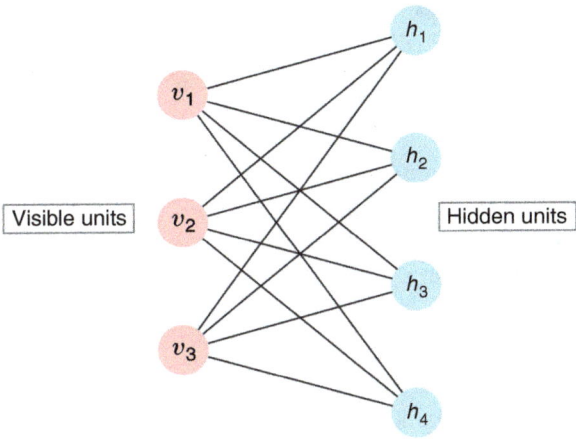

Figure 7.7 A restricted Boltzmann machine or RBM.

7.6.2.2 An Example: Restricted Boltzmann Machines

We implement the Gibbs sampler on a specific probabilistic model, a so-called restricted Boltzmann machine (RBM), and apply it to the generation of random images from a "realistic" distribution. We will not describe them in great details here, but only use them as an example of a complex distribution.

Probabilistic model: An RBM has m visible units (i.e., observed variables) and n hidden units (i.e., hidden variables). It is represented by a complete bipartite graph between the two. See Figure 7.7. Visible unit i is associated a variable v_i and hidden unit j is associated a variable h_j. We define the corresponding vectors $\mathbf{v} = (v_1, \ldots, v_m)$ and $\mathbf{h} = (h_1, \ldots, h_n)$. For our purposes, it will suffice to assume that $\mathbf{v} \in \{0,1\}^m$ and $\mathbf{h} \in \{0,1\}^n$. These are referred to as binary units.

The probabilistic model has a number of parameters. Each visible unit i has an offset $b_i \in \mathbb{R}$ and each hidden unit j has an offset $c_j \in \mathbb{R}$. We write $\mathbf{b} = (b_1, \ldots, b_m)$ and $\mathbf{c} = (c_1, \ldots, c_n)$ for the offset vectors. For each pair (i, j) of visible and hidden units (or, put differently, for each edge in the complete bipartite graph), there is a weight $w_{i,j} \in \mathbb{R}$. We write $W = (w_{i,j})_{i,j=1}^{m,n}$ for the weight matrix.

To define the probability distribution, we need the so-called energy (as you may have guessed, this terminology comes from related models in physics): For $\mathbf{v} \in \{0,1\}^m$ and $\mathbf{h} \in \{0,1\}^n$,

$$\mathcal{E}(\mathbf{v}, \mathbf{h}) = -\mathbf{v}^T W \mathbf{h} - \mathbf{b}^T \mathbf{v} - \mathbf{c}^T \mathbf{h}$$
$$= -\sum_{i=1}^{m} \sum_{j=1}^{n} w_{i,j} v_i h_j - \sum_{i=1}^{m} b_i v_i - \sum_{j=1}^{n} c_j h_j.$$

The joint distribution of $\mathbf{v}$ and $\mathbf{h}$ is

$$\pi(\mathbf{v}, \mathbf{h}) = \frac{1}{Z} \exp\left(-\mathcal{E}(\mathbf{v}, \mathbf{h})\right),$$

where Z, the partition function (a function of $W, \mathbf{b}, \mathbf{c}$), ensures that π indeed sums to 1.

We will be interested in sampling from the marginal over visible units; that is,

$$\rho(\mathbf{v}) = \sum_{\mathbf{h} \in \{0,1\}^n} \pi(\mathbf{v}, \mathbf{h}).$$

When m and/or n are large, computing ρ or π explicitly – or even numerically – is impractical. We develop the Gibbs sampler for this model next.

Gibbs sampling: We sample from the joint distribution π and observe only $\mathbf{v}$.

We need to compute the conditional probabilities given every other variable. The sigmoid function, $\sigma(x)$, will once again make an appearance.

```
def sigmoid(x):
    return 1/(1 + np.exp(-x))
```

Fix a visible unit $i \in [m]$. For a pair $(\mathbf{v}, \mathbf{h})$, we denote by $(\mathbf{v}_{[i]}, \mathbf{h})$ the same pair but with coordinate i of $\mathbf{v}$ flipped. Given every other variable, namely $(\mathbf{v}_{-i}, \mathbf{h})$, and using a superscript v to indicate the probability of a visible unit, the conditional probability of v_i is

$$\pi_i^v(v_i | \mathbf{v}_{-i}, \mathbf{h}) = \frac{\pi(\mathbf{v}, \mathbf{h})}{\pi(\mathbf{v}, \mathbf{h}) + \pi(\mathbf{v}_{[i]}, \mathbf{h})}$$

$$= \frac{\frac{1}{Z} \exp(-\mathcal{E}(\mathbf{v}, \mathbf{h}))}{\frac{1}{Z} \exp(-\mathcal{E}(\mathbf{v}, \mathbf{h})) + \frac{1}{Z} \exp(-\mathcal{E}(\mathbf{v}_{[i]}, \mathbf{h}))}.$$

In this last ratio, the partition functions (the Z's) cancel out. Moreover, all the terms in the exponentials *not depending* on the i-th visible unit actually factor out and cancel out as well – they are identical in all three exponentials. Similarly, the terms in the exponentials *depending only on* $\mathbf{h}$ also factor out and cancel out.

What we are left with is:

$$\pi_i^v(v_i | \mathbf{v}_{-i}, \mathbf{h})$$

$$= \frac{\exp\left(\sum_{j=1}^n w_{i,j} v_i h_j + b_i v_i\right)}{\exp\left(\sum_{j=1}^n w_{i,j} v_i h_j + b_i v_i\right) + \exp\left(\sum_{j=1}^n w_{i,j}(1 - v_i) h_j + b_i(1 - v_i)\right)},$$

where we used the fact that flipping $v_i \in \{0, 1\}$ is the same as setting it to $1 - v_i$, a transformation that indeed sends 0 to 1 and 1 to 0.

This expression does not depend on $\mathbf{v}_{-i}$. In other words, the i-th visible unit is conditionally independent of all other visible units given the hidden units.

We simplify the expression:

$$\pi_i^v(v_i | \mathbf{v}_{-i}, \mathbf{h})$$

$$= \frac{1}{1 + \exp\left(\sum_{j=1}^n w_{i,j}(1 - 2v_i) h_j + b_i(1 - 2v_i)\right)}$$

$$= \sigma\left(\sum_{j=1}^n w_{i,j}(2v_i - 1) h_j + b_i(2v_i - 1)\right).$$

7.6 Further Applications: Gibbs Sampling and Generating Images

In particular, the conditional mean of the i-th visible unit given everything else is

$$0 \cdot \pi_i^v(0|\mathbf{v}_{-i}, \mathbf{h}) + 1 \cdot \pi_i^v(1|\mathbf{v}_{-i}, \mathbf{h}) = \pi_i^v(1|\mathbf{v}_{-i}, \mathbf{h})$$
$$= \sigma\left(\sum_{j=1}^n w_{i,j} h_j + b_i\right)$$
$$= \sigma\left((W\mathbf{h} + \mathbf{b})_i\right).$$

Similarly for the conditional probability of the j-th hidden unit given everything else, we have

$$\pi_j^h(h_j|\mathbf{v}, \mathbf{h}_{-j})$$
$$= \sigma\left(\sum_{i=1}^m w_{i,j} v_i (2h_j - 1) + c_j(2h_j - 1)\right).$$

The conditional mean given everything else is

$$0 \cdot \pi_j^h(0|\mathbf{v}, \mathbf{h}_{-j}) + 1 \cdot \pi_j^h(1|\mathbf{v}, \mathbf{h}_{-j}) = \pi_j^h(1|\mathbf{v}, \mathbf{h}_{-j}) = \sigma\left((W^T\mathbf{v} + \mathbf{c})_j\right).$$

And the j-th hidden unit is conditionally independent of all other hidden units given the visible units.

We implement the Gibbs sampler for an RBM. Rather than updating the units at random, we use a block approach. Specifically, we update all hidden units independently, given the visible units; then we update all visible units independently, given the hidden units. In each case, this is warranted by the conditional independence structure revealed above.

We first implement the conditional means using the formulas previously derived.

```
def rbm_mean_hidden(v, W, c):
    return sigmoid(W.T @ v + c)

def rbm_mean_visible(h, W, b):
    return sigmoid(W @ h + b)
```

We next implement one step of the sampler, which consists of updating all hidden units, followed by updating all visible units.

```
def rbm_gibbs_update(rng, v, W, b, c):
    p_hidden = rbm_mean_hidden(v, W, c)
    h = rng.binomial(1, p_hidden, p_hidden.shape)
    p_visible = rbm_mean_visible(h, W, b)
    v = rng.binomial(1, p_visible, p_visible.shape)
    return v
```

Finally, we repeat these steps k times. We only return the visible units v.

```
def rbm_gibbs_sampling(rng, k, v_0, W, b, c):
    counter = 0
    v = v_0
    while counter < k:
        v = rbm_gibbs_update(rng, v, W, b, c)
```

```
        counter += 1
    return v
```

Here v_0 comprises the initial visible unit states. We do not need to initialize the hidden ones as this is done automatically in the first update step. In what follows, we will take the initial distribution of **v** to be independent Bernoullis with success probability 1/2.

NUMERICAL CORNER We apply our Gibbs sampler to generating images. As mentioned previously, we use the MNIST dataset to learn a "realistic" distribution of handwritten digit images. Here the images are encoded by the visible units of an RBM. Then we sample from this model.

We first need to train the model on the data. We will not show how this is done here, but instead use `sklearn.neural_network.BernoulliRBM`.

```
from sklearn.neural_network import BernoulliRBM

rbm = BernoulliRBM(random_state=seed, verbose=0)
```

To simplify the analysis and speed up the training, we only keep digits 0, 1, and 5.

```
mask = (labels == 0) | (labels == 1) | (labels == 5)
imgs = imgs[mask]
labels = labels[mask]
```

We flatten the images (which have already been "rounded" to black-and-white; see Section 7.6.1).

```
X = imgs.reshape(len(imgs), -1)
```

We now fit the model. Choosing the hyperparameters of the training algorithm is tricky. The following seem to work reasonably well.

```
rbm.n_components = 100
rbm.learning_rate = 0.02
rbm.batch_size = 50
rbm.n_iter = 20
rbm.fit(X)
```

BernoulliRBM(batch_size=50, learning_rate=0.02, n_components=100,
             n_iter=20, random_state=535)

We are ready to sample from the trained RBM. We extract the learned parameters from `rbm`.

```
W = rbm.components_.T
W.shape
```

(100, 784)

7.6 Further Applications: Gibbs Sampling and Generating Images

```
b = rbm.intercept_visible_
b.shape
```

(784,)

```
c = rbm.intercept_hidden_
c.shape
```

(100,)

To generate 25 samples, we first generate 25 independent initial states. We stack them into a matrix, where each row is a different flattened random noise image.

```
n_samples = 25
z = rng.binomial(1, 0.5, (n_samples, n_pixels))
```

To process all samples simultaneously, we make a small change to the code. We use numpy.newaxis to make the offsets into column vectors, which are then automatically added to all columns of the resulting weighted sum.

```
def rbm_mean_hidden(v, W, c):
    return sigmoid(W.T @ v + c[:,np.newaxis])

def rbm_mean_visible(h, W, b):
    return sigmoid(W @ h + b[:,np.newaxis])
```

For plotting, we use the following script.[6]

```
def plot_imgs(z, n_imgs, nx_pixels, ny_pixels):
    nx_imgs = np.floor(np.sqrt(n_imgs))
    ny_imgs = np.ceil(np.sqrt(n_imgs))
    plt.figure(figsize=(8, 8))
    for i, comp in enumerate(z):
        plt.subplot(int(nx_imgs), int(ny_imgs), i + 1)
        plt.imshow(comp.reshape((nx_pixels,ny_pixels)),
                   cmap='gray_r')
        plt.xticks([]), plt.yticks([])
    plt.show()
```

We are now ready to run our Gibbs sampler. The outcome depends on the number of steps we take. After 100 steps, the outcome is somewhat realistic.

---

[6] Adapted by ChatGPT from https://scikit-learn.org/stable/auto_examples/neural_networks/plot_rbm_logistic_classification.html

```
v_0 = z.T
gen_v = rbm_gibbs_sampling(rng, 100, v_0, W, b, c)

plot_imgs(gen_v.T, n_samples, nx_pixels, ny_pixels)
```

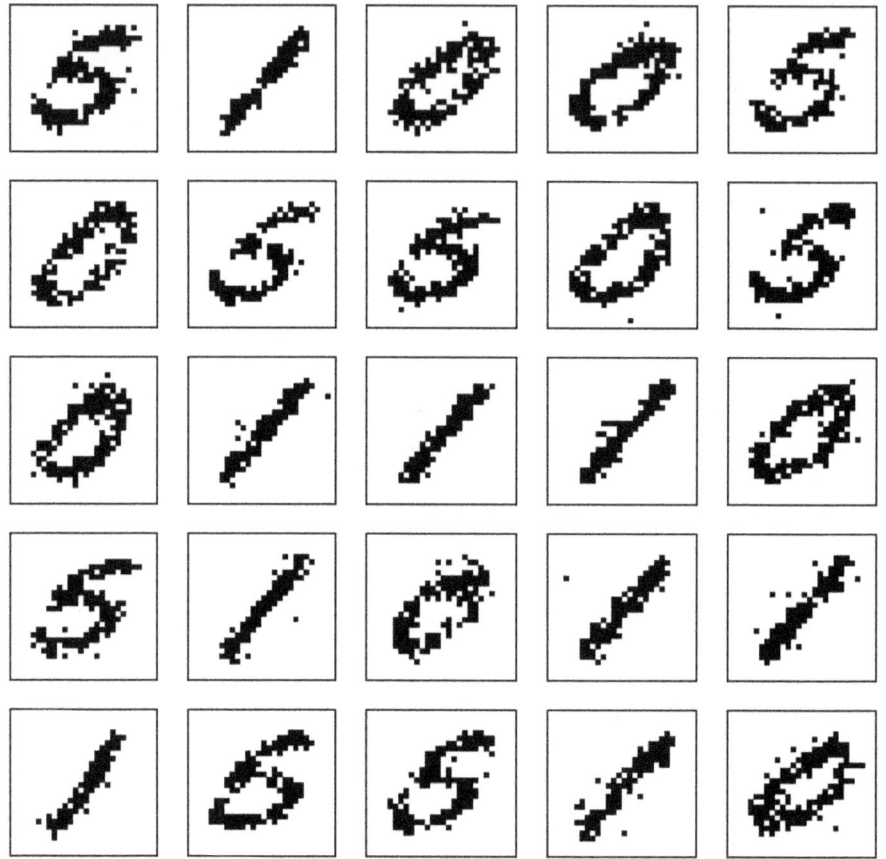

Figure 7.8 Graphical output of code.

◁ **NC**

CHAT & LEARN The RBM can be stacked to form a deep belief network (DBN). Ask your favorite AI chatbot about the process of greedy layer-wise pretraining of a DBN using RBMs. Discuss how this can be used for initializing the weights of a deep neural network and compare the performance with random initialization.

Self-assessment quiz (with help from Claude, Gemini, and ChatGPT)

1 In the context of Markov chain Monte Carlo (MCMC), what is the primary goal?
   a) To find the maximum likelihood estimate of a parameter.

7.6 Further Applications: Gibbs Sampling and Generating Images

b) To generate samples from a complex target distribution.

c) To optimize a loss function using gradient descent.

d) To cluster data points based on similarity.

2. In the Metropolis–Hastings algorithm, what is the role of the proposal chain Q?

   a) It determines the stationary distribution of the resulting Markov chain.

   b) It is used to compute the acceptance probability for the proposed moves.

   c) It generates the candidate states for the next move in the Markov chain.

   d) It ensures that the resulting Markov chain is irreducible and aperiodic.

3. What is the purpose of the Hastings correction in the Metropolis–Hastings algorithm?

   a) To ensure that the proposal chain is symmetric.

   b) To make the resulting Markov chain irreducible and aperiodic.

   c) To ensure that the resulting Markov chain has the desired stationary distribution.

   d) To improve the mixing time of the resulting Markov chain.

4. What is the role of the energy function $\mathcal{E}(\mathbf{v}, \mathbf{h})$ in a restricted Boltzmann machine (RBM)?

   a) It determines the acceptance probability in the Metropolis–Hastings algorithm.

   b) It defines the joint probability distribution of the visible and hidden units.

   c) It represents the cost function to be minimized during training.

   d) It controls the learning rate of the RBM.

5. What is the partition function Z used for in the RBM's joint probability distribution $\pi(\mathbf{v}, \mathbf{h})$?

   a) It normalizes the energy function.

   b) It scales the weights matrix W.

   c) It ensures that the probability distribution sums to one.

   d) It adjusts the biases $\mathbf{b}$ and $\mathbf{c}$.

Answer for 1: b. Justification: The text states that "The idea behind MCMC is simple. To generate samples from π, use a Markov chain for which it is the stationary distribution."

Answer for 2: c. Justification: The text describes the proposal chain as follows: "We first define a proposal chain, that is, a transition matrix Q on the space $\mathcal{S}$. This chain does not need to have stationary distribution π. But it is typically a chain that is easy to simulate."

Answer for 3: c. Justification: The text states that the Hastings correction is "where the target distribution π enters the picture, and the rejection probability is chosen to ensure that the new chain has the right stationary distribution, as we will see later."

Answer for 4: b. Justification: The text defines the joint distribution of $\mathbf{v}$ and $\mathbf{h}$ as $\pi(\mathbf{v}, \mathbf{h}) = \frac{1}{Z} \exp(-\mathcal{E}(\mathbf{v}, \mathbf{h}))$.

Answer for 5: c. Justification: The text explains that Z, the partition function, "ensures that π indeed sums to 1."

7.7 Exercises

7.7.1 Warm-Up Worksheets
(with help from Claude, Gemini, and ChatGPT)

Section 7.2

E7.2.1 Given a Markov chain with state space $S = \{1, 2, 3\}$ and transition matrix
$$P = \begin{pmatrix} 0.2 & 0.5 & 0.3 \\ 0.4 & 0.1 & 0.5 \\ 0.6 & 0.3 & 0.1 \end{pmatrix},$$
verify that P is a stochastic matrix.

E7.2.2 For the Markov chain in E7.2.1, compute P^2.

E7.2.3 For the Markov chain in E7.2.1, if the initial distribution is $\mu = (0.2, 0.3, 0.5)^T$, compute $\mathbb{P}[X_2 = 2]$.

E7.2.4 Consider a Markov chain with states $S = \{1, 2\}$ and transition matrix
$$P = \begin{pmatrix} 0.5 & 0.5 \\ 0.2 & 0.8 \end{pmatrix}.$$
If the initial distribution is $\mu = (0.3, 0.7)^T$, compute the distribution after one step.

E7.2.5 Given a Markov chain with state space $S = \{1, 2, 3, 4\}$ and transition matrix
$$P = \begin{pmatrix} 0 & 1/2 & 0 & 1/2 \\ 1/3 & 0 & 2/3 & 0 \\ 0 & 1/4 & 0 & 3/4 \\ 1/2 & 0 & 1/2 & 0 \end{pmatrix},$$
draw the transition graph.

E7.2.6 Given a Markov chain with state space $S = \{1, 2, 3\}$ and transition matrix
$$P = \begin{pmatrix} 0.1 & 0.4 & 0.5 \\ 0.2 & 0.6 & 0.2 \\ 0.3 & 0.3 & 0.4 \end{pmatrix},$$
and initial distribution $\mu = (0.1, 0.2, 0.7)^T$, compute $\mathbb{P}[X_0 = 1, X_1 = 2, X_2 = 3]$.

E7.2.7 For the Markov chain in E7.2.6, compute $\mathbb{P}[X_2 = 2 | X_0 = 3]$.

E7.2.8 Given a Markov chain with state space $S = \{1, 2, 3, 4\}$ and transition matrix
$$P = \begin{pmatrix} 0.2 & 0.3 & 0.4 & 0.1 \\ 0.1 & 0.4 & 0.2 & 0.3 \\ 0.3 & 0.1 & 0.5 & 0.1 \\ 0.2 & 0.2 & 0.1 & 0.5 \end{pmatrix},$$
verify that P is a stochastic matrix.

E7.2.9 Consider a two-state Markov chain with state space $S = \{0, 1\}$ and transition matrix
$$P = \begin{pmatrix} 1/3 & 2/3 \\ 1/2 & 1/2 \end{pmatrix}.$$
If the chain starts in state 0, what is the probability that it will be in state 1 after two steps?

7.7 Exercises

E7.2.10 A Markov chain on states $\{1, 2, 3\}$ has the transition matrix
$$P = \begin{pmatrix} 0 & 1/2 & 1/2 \\ 1/3 & 0 & 2/3 \\ 1/4 & 3/4 & 0 \end{pmatrix}.$$
Draw its transition graph.

E7.2.11 Consider a Markov chain with state space $S = \{1, 2, 3\}$ and transition matrix
$$P = \begin{pmatrix} 1/2 & 0 & 1/2 \\ 0 & 1 & 0 \\ 1/3 & 1/3 & 1/3 \end{pmatrix}.$$
If the initial distribution is $\mu = (1/4, 1/2, 1/4)^T$, find the marginal distribution of the chain at time 2.

E7.2.12 A three-state Markov chain has transition matrix
$$P = \begin{pmatrix} 1/4 & 1/2 & 1/4 \\ 1/3 & 1/3 & 1/3 \\ 0 & 0 & 1 \end{pmatrix}.$$
Identify any absorbing state; that is, a state from which the chain cannot leave.

E7.2.13 A two-state Markov chain has the transition matrix
$$P = \begin{pmatrix} 1/2 & 1/2 \\ 1 & 0 \end{pmatrix}.$$
If the initial distribution is $\mu = (1/3, 2/3)^T$, find the distribution of the chain at time 1.

E7.2.14 A Markov chain has the transition matrix
$$P = \begin{pmatrix} 0.2 & 0.8 & 0 \\ 0.5 & 0 & 0.5 \\ 0 & 0.4 & 0.6 \end{pmatrix}.$$
If the chain is currently in state 2, what is the probability it will be in state 3 after two steps?

E7.2.15 Consider a Markov chain with state space $S = \{1, 2\}$ and transition matrix
$$P = \begin{pmatrix} 0 & 1 \\ 1 & 0 \end{pmatrix}.$$
If the chain starts in state 1, what is the expected number of steps until it returns to state 1?

Section 7.3

E7.3.1 Determine if the following transition matrix is irreducible:
$$P = \begin{pmatrix} 0 & 1 & 0 \\ 0 & 0 & 1 \\ 1 & 0 & 0 \end{pmatrix}.$$

E7.3.2 Give an example of a 2×2 transition matrix that is not irreducible.

E7.3.3 Given the transition matrix $P = \begin{pmatrix} 0.4 & 0.6 \\ 0.7 & 0.3 \end{pmatrix}$, check whether the probability distribution $\pi = (0.6, 0.4)^T$ is a stationary distribution of the Markov chain.

E7.3.4 Let $P = \begin{pmatrix} 0 & 1 \\ 1/2 & 1/2 \end{pmatrix}$ be the transition matrix of a Markov chain. Verify whether $\pi = (1/3, 2/3)^T$ is a stationary distribution.

E7.3.5 Find a stationary distribution for the Markov chain with transition matrix $P = \begin{pmatrix} 0.5 & 0.5 \\ 0.5 & 0.5 \end{pmatrix}$.

E7.3.6 Determine whether the following Markov chain is irreducible:

```
P = np.array([[0.5, 0.5, 0], [0.4, 0.6, 0], [0, 0, 1]])
```

E7.3.7 Verify that the uniform distribution $\pi = \left(\frac{1}{3}, \frac{1}{3}, \frac{1}{3}\right)^T$ is a stationary distribution for the transition matrix $P = \begin{pmatrix} 0.4 & 0.3 & 0.3 \\ 0.2 & 0.5 & 0.3 \\ 0.4 & 0.2 & 0.4 \end{pmatrix}$.

E7.3.8 A Markov chain has transition matrix $P = \begin{pmatrix} 1/2 & 1/2 & 0 \\ 0 & 1/3 & 2/3 \\ 1/4 & 1/4 & 1/2 \end{pmatrix}$. Is this matrix doubly stochastic?

E7.3.9 Verify that for any stochastic matrix P, the vector $(1, 1, \ldots, 1)$ is a right eigenvector of P with eigenvalue 1.

E7.3.10 Find the left eigenvector of the transition matrix $P = \begin{pmatrix} 0.6 & 0.4 \\ 0.3 & 0.7 \end{pmatrix}$ corresponding to eigenvalue 1.

E7.3.11 For the transition matrix $P = \begin{pmatrix} 0.7 & 0.2 & 0.1 \\ 0.4 & 0.4 & 0.2 \\ 0.6 & 0.1 & 0.3 \end{pmatrix}$, find the stationary distribution by solving the linear system $\pi P = \pi$ after replacing the last equation with $\sum_{i=1}^{3} \pi_i = 1$.

Section 7.4

E7.4.1 Given the transition matrix of a Markov chain:

$$P = \begin{pmatrix} 0.2 & 0.8 \\ 0.6 & 0.4 \end{pmatrix},$$

determine if the chain is lazy.

E7.4.2 Prove that a finite-state Markov chain with a transition matrix containing only positive entries is aperiodic.

E7.4.3 Given a Markov chain with transition matrix

$$P = \begin{pmatrix} 0.4 & 0.6 \\ 0.7 & 0.3 \end{pmatrix}$$

and initial distribution $\mu = (0.2, 0.8)^T$, compute $\lim_{t \to \infty} \mu P^t$.

E7.4.4 For the transition matrix $P = \begin{pmatrix} 0.4 & 0.3 & 0.3 \\ 0.2 & 0.5 & 0.3 \\ 0.4 & 0.2 & 0.4 \end{pmatrix}$ and initial distribution $\mu = (1/3, 1/3, 1/3)^T$, compute μP^t for $t = 1,000$.

Section 7.5

E7.5.1 Consider the undirected graph G with adjacency matrix
$$A = \begin{pmatrix} 0 & 1 & 1 & 0 \\ 1 & 0 & 1 & 1 \\ 1 & 1 & 0 & 1 \\ 0 & 1 & 1 & 0 \end{pmatrix}.$$
Compute the degree matrix D for the graph.

E7.5.2 Given the same graph as in E7.5.1, compute the transition matrix P for the random walk on the graph.

E7.5.3 For the same graph as in E7.5.1, verify that the transition matrix P is stochastic.

E7.5.4 Given the graph in E7.5.1, compute the stationary distribution π of the random walk.

E7.5.5 Given the following adjacency matrix of a directed graph:
$$A = \begin{pmatrix} 0 & 1 & 0 & 0 \\ 0 & 0 & 1 & 0 \\ 1 & 0 & 0 & 1 \\ 0 & 0 & 1 & 0 \end{pmatrix},$$
compute the transition matrix P of the random walk on this graph.

E7.5.6 Consider the undirected graph in Figure 7.9.

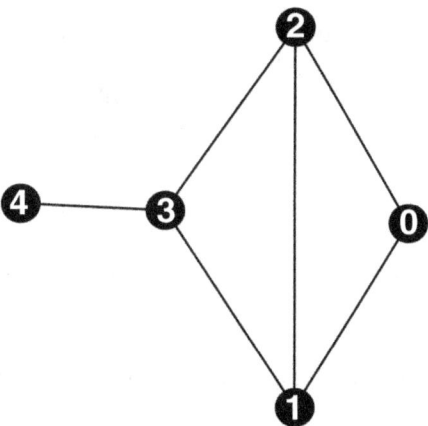

Figure 7.9 Graph for E7.5.6.

Compute the stationary distribution π of the random walk on this graph.

E7.5.7 Given the following adjacency matrix of a directed graph:
$$A = \begin{pmatrix} 0 & 1 & 0 & 0 \\ 1 & 0 & 1 & 0 \\ 0 & 1 & 0 & 1 \\ 0 & 0 & 1 & 0 \end{pmatrix},$$
compute the modified transition matrix using a damping factor of $\alpha = 0.8$.

E7.5.8 For the graph in E7.5.7, compute the modified transition matrix focused on node 1 using a damping factor of $\alpha = 0.8$.

E7.5.9 Consider the directed graph in Figure 7.10.

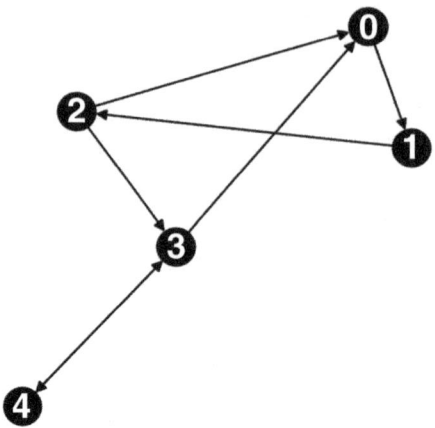

Figure 7.10 Graph for E7.5.9.

Compute the modified transition matrix using a damping factor of $\alpha = 0.9$.

E7.5.10 For the graph in E7.5.9, compute the modified transition matrix focused on node 2 using a damping factor of $\alpha = 0.9$.

E7.5.11 Consider the directed graph G with adjacency matrix

$$A = \begin{pmatrix} 0 & 1 & 0 & 0 \\ 0 & 0 & 1 & 0 \\ 1 & 0 & 0 & 1 \\ 0 & 0 & 0 & 0 \end{pmatrix}.$$

Add self-loops to any vertex without outgoing edges and then compute the new adjacency matrix A'.

E7.5.12 For the graph in E7.5.11, compute the transition matrix P for the random walk.

E7.5.13 For the graph in E7.5.11 with damping factor $\alpha = 0.85$, compute the modified transition matrix Q.

Section 7.6

E7.6.1 Given a target distribution $\pi = (0.1, 0.2, 0.3, 0.4)^T$ and a proposal chain Q with transition matrix

$$Q = \begin{pmatrix} 0.5 & 0.5 & 0 & 0 \\ 0.5 & 0 & 0.5 & 0 \\ 0 & 0.5 & 0 & 0.5 \\ 0 & 0 & 0.5 & 0.5 \end{pmatrix},$$

compute the acceptance probability for a proposed move from state 2 to state 1.

E7.6.2 For the same target distribution and proposal chain as in E7.6.1, compute the acceptance probability for a proposed move from state 2 to state 3.

E7.6.3 Given a target distribution $\pi = (0.1, 0.2, 0.3, 0.4)^T$ and a symmetric proposal chain Q with transition matrix

$$Q = \begin{pmatrix} 0.5 & 0.25 & 0.25 & 0 \\ 0.25 & 0.5 & 0 & 0.25 \\ 0.25 & 0 & 0.5 & 0.25 \\ 0 & 0.25 & 0.25 & 0.5 \end{pmatrix},$$

compute the acceptance probability for a proposed move from state 1 to state 2.

E7.6.4 For the same target distribution and symmetric proposal chain as in E7.6.3, compute the acceptance probability for a proposed move from state 2 to state 1.

E7.6.5 Consider a Metropolis–Hastings algorithm with target distribution $\pi(x) = \frac{1}{Z}e^{-x^2/2}$ on the state space $S = \mathbb{Z}$ (the integers), and proposal distribution $Q(x, y) = \frac{1}{2}$ if $|x - y| = 1$ and $Q(x, y) = 0$ otherwise. If the current state is $x = 2$, what is the probability of accepting a proposal to move to $y = 3$?

E7.6.6 In a Gibbs sampler with state space $S = \mathbb{Z}^2$, suppose the current state is $(x_1, x_2) = (3, -1)$. If the first coordinate is updated according to the conditional distribution $\pi_1(x_1|x_2 = -1)$, and the new value is $x_1' = 2$, what is the new state of the Gibbs sampler?

E7.6.7 Given a restricted Boltzmann machine (RBM) with visible units $\mathbf{v} = (v_1, v_2, v_3)$, hidden units $\mathbf{h} = (h_1, h_2)$, weight matrix

$$W = \begin{pmatrix} 1 & -1 \\ 2 & 1 \\ -1 & 2 \end{pmatrix},$$

visible biases $\mathbf{b} = (1, -1, 2)$, and hidden biases $\mathbf{c} = (-1, 1)$, compute the conditional probability $\pi_1^v(1|\mathbf{v}_{-1}, \mathbf{h})$ for $\mathbf{v} = (0, 1, 0)$ and $\mathbf{h} = (1, 0)$.

E7.6.8 For the same RBM as in E7.6.7, compute the conditional probability $\pi_2^h(1|\mathbf{v}, \mathbf{h}_{-2})$ for $\mathbf{v} = (0, 1, 0)$ and $\mathbf{h} = (1, 0)$.

E7.6.9 Consider an RBM with two visible units and two hidden units. The weight matrix is

$$W = \begin{pmatrix} 1 & -2 \\ 3 & 0 \end{pmatrix}.$$

If the offset vectors are the zero vectors, the visible units are in state $\mathbf{v} = (1, 0)$, and the hidden units are in state $\mathbf{h} = (1, 1)$, compute the energy $\mathcal{E}(\mathbf{v}, \mathbf{h})$.

E7.6.10 Given the visible units $\mathbf{v} = (1, 0)$ and hidden units $\mathbf{h} = (0, 1)$ with weights $W = \begin{pmatrix} 0.4 & -0.2 \\ 0.3 & 0.5 \end{pmatrix}$ and biases $\mathbf{b} = (0.1, -0.3)$ and $\mathbf{c} = (0.2, -0.1)$, compute the energy $\mathcal{E}(\mathbf{v}, \mathbf{h})$ in an RBM.

E7.6.11 Given a binary vector $\mathbf{v} = (1, 0, 1)$ and weight matrix $W = \begin{pmatrix} 0.5 & -0.2 \\ 0.3 & 0.8 \\ -0.6 & 0.1 \end{pmatrix}$, and bias vector $\mathbf{c} = (0.1, -0.3)$, compute the conditional mean $\mathbb{E}[\mathbf{h}|\mathbf{v}]$ for the hidden units in an RBM.

E7.6.12 For a vector $\mathbf{v} = (1, 0, 1)$, a weight matrix $W = \begin{pmatrix} 0.5 & -0.2 \\ 0.3 & 0.8 \\ -0.6 & 0.1 \end{pmatrix}$, and a bias vector $\mathbf{b} = (0.2, -0.1, 0.3)$, compute the conditional mean $\mathbb{E}[v_i|\mathbf{h}]$ for the visible units in an RBM, assuming $\mathbf{h} = (0, 1)$.

7.7.2 Problems

7.1 Let $A_1, \ldots, A_m$ be disjoint events and let B be such that $\mathbb{P}[B] > 0$. Show that

$$\mathbb{P}[A_1 \cup \cdots \cup A_m | B] = \mathbb{P}[A_1|B] + \cdots + \mathbb{P}[A_m|B].$$

7.2 (Adapted from [Nor]) Suppose $(X_n)_{n \geq 0}$ is a Markov chain. Show that, for any positive integer $k \geq 2$, the stochastic process $(Y_n)_{n \geq 0}$ with $Y_n = X_{nk}$ is also a Markov chain and derive its transition matrix in terms of the transition matrix P of $(X_n)_{n \geq 0}$.

7.3 Let $G = (V, E)$ be the Petersen graph. Consider the following random walk on G. We start at $X_0 = v_0$. Then, for each $t \geq 0$, we let X_{t+1} be a uniformly chosen neighbor of X_t, independently of the previous history. Formally, fix $X_0 = v_0$ and let $(Z_t)_{t \geq 0}$ be an i.i.d. sequence of random variables taking values in $\{1, 2, 3\}$ and satisfying

$$\mathbb{P}[Z_t = 1] = \mathbb{P}[Z_t = 2] = \mathbb{P}[Z_t = 3] = 1/3.$$

Then define, for all $t \geq 0$,

$$X_{t+1} = f(X_t, Z_t) = v_{i, Z_t}$$

if $X_t = v_i$.

a) Under what conditions on $x_0, \ldots, x_t$ does

$$\mathbb{P}[X_t = x_t, X_{t-1} = x_{t-1}, \ldots, X_0 = x_0] > 0?$$

b) Prove that $(X_t)_{t \geq 0}$ is a Markov chain by following the argument used for the *Weather Model*.

7.4 Let (X_t) be as in Problem 7.3. Compute

$$\mathbb{P}[X_T = x_T, X_{T-1} = x_{T-1}, \ldots, X_0 = x_0].$$

Justify your answer carefully.

7.5 Consider a random walk on the graph in Figure 7.11, where at each step a uniformly random neighbor is chosen. Write down the transition matrix of the chain.

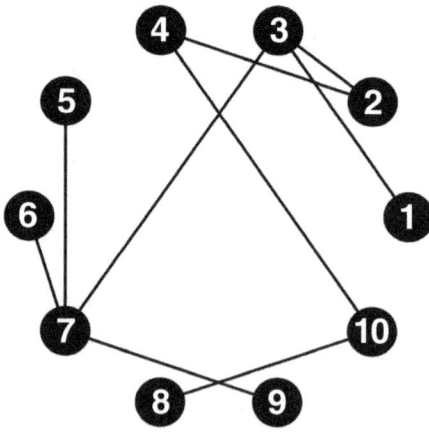

Figure 7.11 Graph for Problem 7.5.

7.6 Let $a, b \in \mathbb{R}$ with $a < 0$ and $b > 0$. Show that
$$|a + b| < |a| + |b|.$$
[*Hint:* Consider the cases $a + b \geq 0$ and $a + b < 0$.]

7.7 Let $P = (p_{i,j})_{i,j=1}^{n}$ be a transition matrix reversible with respect to a probability distribution $\boldsymbol{\pi} = (\pi_i)_{i=1}^{n}$. Assume that the initial distribution is $\boldsymbol{\pi}$. Show that for any sample path $z_0, \ldots, z_T$, the reversed path has the same probability; that is,
$$\mathbb{P}[X_T = z_0, \ldots, X_0 = z_T] = \mathbb{P}[X_T = z_T, \ldots, X_0 = z_0].$$

7.8 Let $\mathbf{x} = (x_1, \ldots, x_n)^T$ be a row vector with n components. Its ℓ_1-norm is defined as
$$\|\mathbf{x}\|_1 = \sum_{i=1}^{n} |x_i|.$$
Let P be a stochastic matrix. Show that, if $\mathbf{x} \geq 0$ (i.e., all entries of $\mathbf{x}$ are nonnegative), then for any positive integer k,
$$\|\mathbf{x}P^k\|_1 = \|\mathbf{x}\|_1.$$

7.9 Let $A_1, \ldots, A_r$ be any collection of events.

a) Prove the product rule
$$\mathbb{P}\left[\cap_{i=1}^{r} A_i\right] = \prod_{i=1}^{r} \mathbb{P}\left[A_i \,\Big|\, \cap_{j=1}^{i-1} A_j\right],$$
provided all conditional probabilities above are well-defined. [*Hint:* Apply the definition of conditional probability and simplify. You may want to try $r = 2, 3$ first.]

b) Prove that the product rule also holds for conditional probabilities: Let D be an additional event and show that
$$\mathbb{P}\left[\cap_{i=1}^{r} A_i \,\Big|\, D\right] = \prod_{i=1}^{r} \mathbb{P}\left[A_i \,\Big|\, D \cap \left(\cap_{j=1}^{i-1} A_j\right)\right],$$
provided all conditional probabilities above are well-defined.

7.10 Let $A_1, \ldots, A_r$ be a partition of Ω and let B be an event. Prove the law of total probability
$$\mathbb{P}[B] = \sum_{i=1}^{r} \mathbb{P}[B|A_i]\mathbb{P}[A_i],$$
provided all conditional probabilities above are well-defined. [*Hint:* Use the definition of conditional probabilities and the probability of a disjoint union.]

7.11 Let A and B be events with positive probability. Prove *Bayes' Rule*
$$\mathbb{P}[A|B] = \frac{\mathbb{P}[B|A]\mathbb{P}[A]}{\mathbb{P}[B]}.$$
[*Hint:* Use the definition of conditional probabilities.]

7.12 Let $(X_t)_{t \geq 0}$ be a Markov chain on the state space $\mathcal{S}$. For any $x_{t-1}, x_t \in \mathcal{S}$ and subset $\mathcal{P} \subseteq \mathcal{S}^{t-1}$ of state sequences of length $t - 1$, show directly from the definition of a Markov chain that
$$\mathbb{P}[X_t = x_t \,|\, X_{t-1} = x_{t-1}, (X_0, \ldots, X_{t-2}) \in \mathcal{P}] = \mathbb{P}[X_t = x_t \,|\, X_{t-1} = x_{t-1}].$$

[*Hint:* Use the definition of the conditional probability, sum over all paths in $\mathcal{P}$, then use the definition of a Markov chain and simplify.]

7.13 Let $(X_t)_{t\geq 0}$ be a Markov chain on the state space $\mathcal{S}$. For any nonnegative integer $s < t$, $x_t \in \mathcal{S}$, and $(x_0, \ldots, x_s) \in \mathcal{S}^{s+1}$, show directly from the definition of a Markov chain that

$$\mathbb{P}[X_t = x_t \mid X_s = x_s, \ldots, X_0 = x_0] = \mathbb{P}[X_t = x_t \mid X_s = x_s].$$

[*Hint:* Sum over all possible trajectories from time $s+1$ to time $t-1$, then use the multiplication rule and the definition of a Markov chain. Do Problem 7.9b first].

7.14 Let $(X_t)_{t\geq 0}$ be a Markov chain on the state space $\mathcal{S}$. For any nonnegative integer $s < t$, $x_s, x_t \in \mathcal{S}$, and subset $\mathcal{P} \subseteq \mathcal{S}^s$ of state sequences of length s, show directly from the definition of a Markov chain that

$$\mathbb{P}[X_t = x_t \mid X_s = x_s, (X_0, \ldots, X_{s-1}) \in \mathcal{P}] = \mathbb{P}[X_t = x_t \mid X_s = x_s].$$

[*Hint:* Argue as in Problem 7.13 and use Problem 7.12.]

7.15 Let $(X_t)_{t\geq 0}$ be a Markov chain on the state space $\mathcal{S}$. For any integer $h \geq 0$, $x_{t-1} \in \mathcal{S}$ and subsets $\mathcal{P} \subseteq \mathcal{S}^{t-1}$, $\mathcal{F} \subseteq \mathcal{S}^{h+1}$ of state sequences of length $t-1$ and $h+1$ respectively, show directly from the definition of a Markov chain that

$$\mathbb{P}[(X_t, \ldots, X_{t+h}) \in \mathcal{F} \mid X_{t-1} = x_{t-1}, (X_0, \ldots, X_{t-2}) \in \mathcal{P}]$$
$$= \mathbb{P}[(X_t, \ldots, X_{t+h}) \in \mathcal{F} \mid X_{t-1} = x_{t-1}].$$

A different way of saying this is: $(X_0, \ldots, X_{t-2})$ (i.e., the past) and $(X_t, \ldots, X_{t+h})$ (i.e., the future) are independent given X_{t-1} (i.e., the present). [*Hint:* Sum over all paths in $\mathcal{F}$ and argue as in Problem 7.14.]

7.16 Let A, B, C be three events. Assume that C is independent of A, B, and $A \cap B$. Show that

$$\mathbb{P}[B \mid A \cap C] = \mathbb{P}[B \mid A].$$

7.17 Let $(X_t)_{t\geq 0}$ be a Markov chain on the state space $\mathcal{S}$. Prove that for any $s < T$ and any $x_s, \ldots, x_T \in \mathcal{S}$,

$$\mathbb{P}[X_{s+1} = x_{s+1}, X_{s+2} = x_{s+2}, \ldots, X_T = x_T \mid X_s = x_s] = \prod_{t=s+1}^{T} \mathbb{P}[X_t = x_t \mid X_{t-1} = x_{t-1}].$$

7.18 Let $P, Q \in \mathbb{R}^{n \times n}$ be stochastic matrices. Show that PQ is stochastic.

7.19 Let $(X_t)_{t\geq 0}$ be a Markov chain on the state space $\mathcal{S}$. Prove that for any $s < t$ and any $x_s, x_t \in \mathcal{S}$,

$$\mathbb{P}[X_t = x_t \mid X_s = x_s] = (P^{t-s})_{x_s, x_t}.$$

7.20 Let $(X_t)_{t\geq 0}$ be a Markov chain over $[n]$ with transition matrix $P = (p_{i,j})_{i,j=1}^n$. Let $\boldsymbol{\pi}^{(0)}$ and $\boldsymbol{\pi}^{(1)}$ be distinct stationary distributions of P (as row vectors). Show that, for any $\alpha \in (0, 1)$,

$$\boldsymbol{\pi}^{(\alpha)} = (1-\alpha)\boldsymbol{\pi}^{(0)} + \alpha \boldsymbol{\pi}^{(1)},$$

is yet another stationary distribution.

7.21 Let $P = (p_{i,j})_{i,j=1}^n$ be a transition matrix over $[n]$. Recall that a stationary distribution satisfies
$$\sum_{i=1}^n \pi_i p_{i,j} = \pi_j, \qquad \forall j \in \mathcal{S}.$$
Show that the equation for $j = n$ is a linear combination of the equations for $j = 1, \ldots, n-1$. [*Hint:* Sum over j above.]

7.22 Let $P = (p_{i,j})_{i,j=1}^n$ be a transition matrix over $[n]$. Recall that a stationary distribution satisfies
$$\sum_{i=1}^n \pi_i p_{i,j} = \pi_j, \qquad \forall j \in \mathcal{S}.$$
In Problem 7.21, it was shown that the equation for $j = n$ is a linear combination of the equations for $j = 1, \ldots, n-1$. But a stationary distribution must also satisfy $\sum_{i=1}^n \pi_i = 1$. Show that replacing the equation for $j = n$ with this latter equation leads to the system
$$\begin{pmatrix} ((P - I_{n \times n})_{[:,1:n-1]})^T \\ \mathbf{1}_{1 \times n} \end{pmatrix} \pi^T = \begin{pmatrix} \mathbf{0}_{(n-1) \times 1} \\ 1 \end{pmatrix}.$$

7.23 Let $P \in \mathbb{R}^{n \times n}$ be a lazy, irreducible transition matrix. Show that P^2 is irreducible.

7.24 Prove the *Law of Total Expectation* for discrete random variables.

7.25 Let $P^{(1)}, P^{(2)}, \ldots, P^{(r)} \in \mathbb{R}^{n \times n}$ be stochastic matrices. Show that for any $\alpha_1, \ldots, \alpha_r \in [0, 1]$ with $\sum_{i=1}^r \alpha_i = 1$,
$$\sum_{i=1}^r \alpha_i P^{(i)}$$
is stochastic. That is, a convex combination of stochastic matrices is a stochastic matrix.

7.26 Consider the graph G in Figure 7.12.

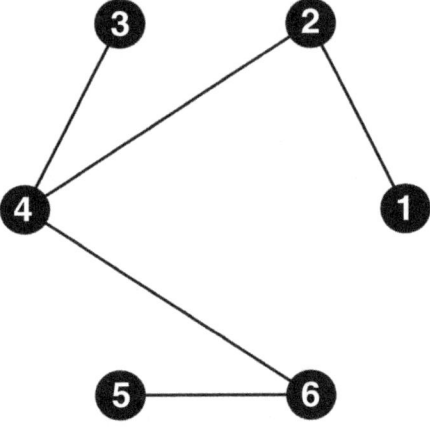

Figure 7.12 Graph for Problem 7.26.

Let $(X_t)_{t \geq 0}$ be a random walk on the graph G; that is, at each step pick a uniform neighbor of the current vertex.

a) Compute the transition matrix P of $(X_t)_{t \geq 0}$.

b) Suppose we start at state 3 at time 0, so that $X_0 = 3$. Compute the distribution of X_2.

7.27 Let $Q \in \mathbb{R}^{n \times n}$ be a matrix with nonnegative entries (whose rows do not necessarily sum to 1).

a) Show that any eigenvalue λ of Q satisfies
$$|\lambda| \leq \max_i \|Q_{i,\cdot}\|_1.$$
[*Hint:* Mimic the proof of the stochastic case.]

b) Use the argument in (a) to show that a left eigenvector $\mathbf{z} = (z_1, \ldots, z_n)^T$ (as row vector) corresponding to eigenvalue λ with $|\lambda| = \max_i \|Q_{i,\cdot}\|_1$ satisfies
$$\|Q_{j,\cdot}\|_1 < \max_i \|Q_{i,\cdot}\|_1 \implies z_j = 0.$$

7.28 Let $P \in \mathbb{R}^{n \times n}$ be a stochastic matrix and consider the block form
$$P = \begin{pmatrix} Q & \mathbf{a} \\ \mathbf{b}^T & c \end{pmatrix}$$
where $Q \in \mathbb{R}^{(n-1) \times (n-1)}$, $\mathbf{a}, \mathbf{b} \in \mathbb{R}^{n-1}$, and $c \in \mathbb{R}$.

a) Show that, if P is irreducible, then $\mathbf{a} \neq \mathbf{0}$.

b) Show that, if P is irreducible, then $\mathbf{b} \neq \mathbf{0}$.

7.29 Let $P \in \mathbb{R}^{n \times n}$ be an irreducible stochastic matrix and consider the block form
$$P = \begin{pmatrix} Q & \mathbf{a} \\ \mathbf{b}^T & c \end{pmatrix}$$
where $Q \in \mathbb{R}^{(n-1) \times (n-1)}$, $\mathbf{a}, \mathbf{b} \in \mathbb{R}^{n-1}$, and $c \in \mathbb{R}$.

a) Show that $Q - I_{(n-1) \times (n-1)}$ is nonsingular. [*Hint:* Argue by contradiction that, if there is a nonzero (row) vector $\mathbf{x}$ such that $\mathbf{x}(Q - I_{(n-1) \times (n-1)}) = \mathbf{0}$, then $\mathbf{y}(P - I_{n \times n}) = \mathbf{0}$ for $\mathbf{y} = (\mathbf{x} 0)$. Use Problems 7.27 and 7.28.]

b) Use (a) to find the unique stationary distribution of P from the solution of $\mathbf{x}(Q - I) = -\mathbf{b}^T$. This is known as the "remove an equation" approach.

7.30 Recall that, for a vector $\mathbf{x} = (x_1, \ldots, x_n)$, we let $\|\mathbf{x}\|_\infty = \max_{i \in [n]} |x_i|$. Show that, if Q is a stochastic matrix, then
$$\|Q\mathbf{x}\|_\infty \leq \|\mathbf{x}\|_\infty.$$

7.31 Let $P = (p_{i,j})_{i,j=1}^n \in \mathbb{R}^n$ be a transition matrix.

a) Let $\alpha_1, \ldots, \alpha_m > 0$ such that $\sum_{i=1}^m \alpha_i = 1$. Let $\mathbf{x} = (x_1, \ldots, x_m) \in \mathbb{R}^n$. Show that
$$\sum_{i=1}^m \alpha_i x_i \leq \max_i x_i,$$
and that equality holds if and only if $x_1 = x_2 = \cdots = x_m$.

b) Let $\mathbf{0} \neq \mathbf{y} \in \mathbb{R}^n$ be a right eigenvector of P with eigenvalue 1, that is, $P\mathbf{y} = \mathbf{y}$. Assume that $\mathbf{y}$ is not a constant vector, that is, there is $i \neq j$ such that $y_i \neq y_j$. Let

$k \in [n]$ be such that $y_k = \max_{i \in [n]} y_i$. Show that for any $\ell \in [n]$ such that $p_{k,\ell} > 0$ we necessarily have

$$y_\ell = y_k.$$

[*Hint:* Use that $y_k = \sum_{i=1}^n p_{k,i} y_i$ and apply (a).]

c) Assume that P is irreducible. Let $\mathbf{0} \neq \mathbf{y} \in \mathbb{R}^n$ again be a right eigenvector of P with eigenvalue 1. Use (b) to show that $\mathbf{y}$ is necessarily a constant vector.

d) Use c) to conclude that $\dim(\text{null}(P^T - I)) = 1$ when P is irreducible.

7.32 Prove the *Correctness of Metropolis–Hastings* for general (i.e., possibly asymmetric) Q.

7.33 On the space of 28×28 black-and-white images, consider the following Markov chain: At each step, we pick a pixel uniformly at random and flip its value with probability $1/2$.

a) Is the chain irreducible? Explain.

b) What is the stationary distribution?

7.34 Construct two distinct transition matrices on three states whose stationary distribution is uniform.

7.35 Consider the "independent sampler" over the finite state space $\mathcal{S}$: at each step, ignore the current state and choose the next state according to the target distribution π. Show that this Markov chain has stationary distribution π.

7.36 In the example on Metropolis–Hastings for the Poisson distribution truncated to support $[n]$, derive the acceptance probabilities for the states $i = 1$ and $i = n$.

7.37 For the general Gibbs sampler, write down explicitly the staying probability $Q(\mathbf{x}, \mathbf{x})$ and check it is indeed in $[0, 1]$.

7.38 Suppose π is a strictly positive probability distribution over $\mathcal{Z}^d$, where $\mathcal{Z}$ is finite.

a) For $i \in [d]$ and $\mathbf{x} \in \mathcal{Z}^d$, give an explicit expression for $\pi_i(x_i|\mathbf{x}_{-i})$ by applying the definition of the conditional probability.

b) Show that, for all $i \in [d]$ and all $\mathbf{x} \in \mathcal{Z}^d$, $\pi_i(x_i|\mathbf{x}_{-i}) > 0$.

7.39 Show that the Gibbs sampler is irreducible when π is strictly positive.

8 Neural Networks, Backpropagation, and Stochastic Gradient Descent

We end the book with an introduction to the basic mathematical building blocks of modern artificial intelligence (AI). We first derive a generalization of the *Chain Rule* and give a brief overview of automatic differentiation. We then describe backpropagation in the context of progressive functions, implement stochastic gradient descent (SGD), and apply these methods to deep neural networks (specifically, multilayer perceptrons). Here is a more detailed overview of the main sections of the chapter.

Background: Jacobian, chain rule, and a brief introduction to automatic differentiation: Section 8.2 introduces the Jacobian matrix, which generalizes the concept of the derivative to vector-valued functions of several variables, as well as the generalized *Chain Rule* for composing differentiable functions in this setting. It also covers some useful matrix algebra, specifically the Hadamard and Kronecker products. Finally, the section gives a brief introduction to automatic differentiation, a powerful technique for efficiently computing derivatives that is central to modern machine learning, and illustrates its use with the PyTorch library.

Building blocks of AI 1: Backpropagation: Section 8.3 develops the mathematical foundations for automatic differentiation in the context of multilayer progressive functions, which are sequences of compositions with layer-specific parameters. It explains how to systematically apply the *Chain Rule* to compute gradients of these functions. The section contrasts two methods for computing gradients: the forward mode and the reverse mode (also known as backpropagation). While the forward mode computes the function and its gradient simultaneously in a recursive manner, the reverse mode is often more efficient, especially for functions with many parameters but a small number of outputs. The reverse mode achieves this efficiency by in essence computing matrix–vector products instead of matrix–matrix products, making it particularly well-suited for machine learning applications.

Building blocks of AI 2: Stochastic gradient descent: Section 8.4 discusses stochastic gradient descent (SGD), a popular optimization algorithm used to train machine learning models, particularly in scenarios with large datasets. It is a variation of gradient descent where, instead of computing the gradient over the entire dataset, it estimates the gradient using a randomly selected subset of data points (either a single sample or a mini-batch). The key idea behind SGD is that, while each update may not be perfectly aligned with the true gradient, the expected direction of the update is still in the direction of the steepest descent, leading to convergence over time. This approach offers computational advantages, especially when dealing with massive datasets, as it avoids the expensive calculation of the full gradient at each iteration. The section provides detailed examples of applying SGD together with backpropagation. Additionally, it covers the use of PyTorch, demonstrating how to handle datasets, construct models, and perform optimization tasks using mini-batch SGD.

Building blocks of AI 3: Neural networks: Section 8.5 introduces neural networks, specifically focusing on the multilayer perceptron (MLP) architecture. It explains how each layer of an MLP consists of an affine map followed by a nonlinear activation function. In the setting of a classification task, the output layer uses the softmax function to produce a probability distribution over the possible classes; the loss function used to train the MLP is the cross-entropy loss. The section then walks through a detailed example of computing the gradient of the loss function with respect to the weights in a small MLP, using the *Chain Rule* and properties of Kronecker products. This gradient computation is generalized to MLPs with an arbitrary number of layers. Finally, the section demonstrates how to implement the training of a neural network in PyTorch, using the Fashion-MNIST dataset.

8.1 Motivating Example: Classifying Natural Images

In this chapter, we return to the classification problem. This time we consider more complex datasets involving natural images. We have seen an example previously, the MNIST dataset. We use a related dataset known as Fashion-MNIST developed by Zalando Research. Quoting from their GitHub repository[1]:

> Fashion-MNIST is a dataset of Zalando's article images – consisting of a training set of 60,000 examples and a test set of 10,000 examples. Each example is a 28x28 grayscale image, associated with a label from 10 classes. We intend Fashion-MNIST to serve as a direct drop-in replacement for the original MNIST dataset for benchmarking machine learning algorithms. It shares the same image size and structure of training and testing splits.

We first load the data and convert it to an appropriate matrix representation. The data can be accessed via `torchvision.datasets.FashionMNIST`.[2]

```
import torch
from torchvision import datasets, transforms
from torch.utils.data import DataLoader, TensorDataset

fashion_mnist = datasets.FashionMNIST(root='./data', train=True,
                                      download=True,
                                      transform=transforms.
                                      ToTensor())
```

For example, the first image and its label are the following. The `squeeze` below removes the color dimension in the image, which is grayscale.

```
img, label = fashion_mnist[0]
plt.figure()
plt.imshow(img.squeeze(), cmap='gray')
plt.show()
```

---

[1] https://github.com/zalandoresearch/fashion-mnist
[2] https://pytorch.org/vision/stable/generated/torchvision.datasets.FashionMNIST.html

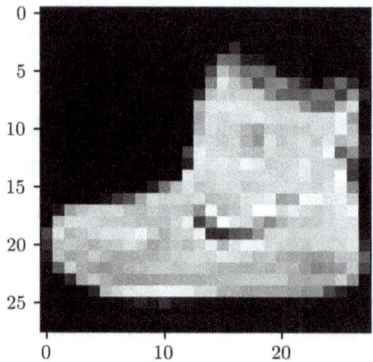

Figure 8.1 Graphical output of code.

```
label
```

9

This label is not particularly meaningful. One can get the actual names of the classes as follows.

```
def FashionMNIST_get_class_name(label):

    class_names = ["T-shirt/top", "Trouser", "Pullover", "Dress",
    "Coat", "Sandal", "Shirt", "Sneaker", "Bag", "Ankle boot"]

    return class_names[label]

print(f"{label}: '{FashionMNIST_get_class_name(label)}'")
```

9: 'Ankle boot'

The purpose of this chapter is to develop some of the mathematical tools used to solve this kind of classification problem:

- neural networks,
- backpropagation,
- stochastic gradient descent.

8.2 Background: Jacobian, Chain Rule, and a Brief Introduction to Automatic Differentiation

We introduce the Jacobian of a vector-valued function of several variables as well as the *Chain Rule* for this more general setting. We also give a brief introduction to automatic differentiation. We begin with some additional matrix algebra.

8.2.1 More Matrix Algebra: Hadamard and Kronecker Products

First, we introduce the Hadamard product and division. The Hadamard product of two matrices (or vectors) of the same dimension, $A = (a_{i,j})_{i \in [n], j \in [m]}, B = (b_{i,j})_{i \in [n], j \in [m]} \in \mathbb{R}^{n \times m}$, is defined as the element-wise product

$$A \odot B = (a_{i,j} b_{i,j})_{i \in [n], j \in [m]}.$$

Similarly the Hadamard division is defined as the element-wise division

$$A \oslash B = (a_{i,j}/b_{i,j})_{i \in [n], j \in [m]}$$

where we assume that $b_{i,j} \neq 0$ for all i, j.

Example 8.2.1 *As an illustrative example,*

$$\begin{bmatrix} 1 & 2 \\ 3 & 4 \end{bmatrix} \odot \begin{bmatrix} 0 & 5 \\ 6 & 7 \end{bmatrix} = \begin{bmatrix} 1 \times 0 & 2 \times 5 \\ 3 \times 6 & 4 \times 7 \end{bmatrix} = \begin{bmatrix} 0 & 10 \\ 18 & 28 \end{bmatrix}.$$

Recall that $\mathbf{1}$ is the all-one vector and that, for $\mathbf{x} = (x_1, \ldots, x_n) \in \mathbb{R}^n$, $\mathrm{diag}(\mathbf{x}) \in \mathbb{R}^{n \times n}$ is the diagonal matrix with diagonal entries $x_1, \ldots, x_n$.

Lemma 8.2.2 *(Properties of the Hadamard Product) Let* $\mathbf{a} = (a_1, \ldots, a_n), \mathbf{b} = (b_1, \ldots, b_n), \mathbf{c} = (c_1, \ldots, c_n) \in \mathbb{R}^n$. *Then the following hold:*

a) $\mathrm{diag}(\mathbf{a}) \, \mathbf{b} = \mathrm{diag}(\mathbf{a} \odot \mathbf{b})$;

b) $\mathbf{a}^T (\mathbf{b} \odot \mathbf{c}) = \mathbf{1}^T (\mathbf{a} \odot \mathbf{b} \odot \mathbf{c})$

and, provided $a_i \neq 0$ for all i, the following hold as well:

c) $\mathrm{diag}(\mathbf{a}) (\mathbf{b} \oslash \mathbf{a}) = \mathrm{diag}(\mathbf{b})$;

d) $\mathbf{a}^T (\mathbf{b} \oslash \mathbf{a}) = \mathbf{1}^T \mathbf{b}$.

Proof a) The product of a diagonal matrix and a vector produces a new vector whose original coordinates are multiplied by the corresponding diagonal entry. This proves the first claim.

b) We have

$$\mathbf{a}^T (\mathbf{b} \odot \mathbf{c}) = \sum_{i=1}^n a_i (b_i c_i) = \mathbf{1}^T (\mathbf{a} \odot \mathbf{b} \odot \mathbf{c}).$$

c) and d) follow respectively from a) and b). □

Second, we introduce the Kronecker product. Let $A = (a_{i,j})_{i \in [n], j \in [m]} \in \mathbb{R}^{n \times m}$ and $B = (b_{i,j})_{i \in [p], j \in [q]} \in \mathbb{R}^{p \times q}$ be arbitrary matrices. Their Kronecker product, denoted $A \otimes B \in \mathbb{R}^{np \times mq}$, is the following matrix in block form:

$$A \otimes B = \begin{pmatrix} a_{1,1} B & \cdots & a_{1,m} B \\ \vdots & \ddots & \vdots \\ a_{n,1} B & \cdots & a_{n,m} B \end{pmatrix}.$$

Example 8.2.3 *Here is a simple illustrative example from Wikipedia[3]:*

$$\begin{bmatrix} 1 & 2 \\ 3 & 4 \end{bmatrix} \otimes \begin{bmatrix} 0 & 5 \\ 6 & 7 \end{bmatrix} = \begin{bmatrix} 1\begin{bmatrix} 0 & 5 \\ 6 & 7 \end{bmatrix} & 2\begin{bmatrix} 0 & 5 \\ 6 & 7 \end{bmatrix} \\ 3\begin{bmatrix} 0 & 5 \\ 6 & 7 \end{bmatrix} & 4\begin{bmatrix} 0 & 5 \\ 6 & 7 \end{bmatrix} \end{bmatrix} = \begin{bmatrix} 0 & 5 & 0 & 10 \\ 6 & 7 & 12 & 14 \\ 0 & 15 & 0 & 20 \\ 18 & 21 & 24 & 28 \end{bmatrix}.$$

Example 8.2.4 *(Outer Product) Here is another example we have encountered previously, the outer product of two vectors* $\mathbf{u} = (u_1, \ldots, u_n) \in \mathbb{R}^n$ *and* $\mathbf{v} = (v_1, \ldots, v_m) \in \mathbb{R}^m$. *Recall that the outer product is defined in block form as the $n \times m$ matrix*

$$\mathbf{u}\mathbf{v}^T = \begin{pmatrix} v_1 \mathbf{u} & \cdots & v_m \mathbf{u} \end{pmatrix} = \mathbf{v}^T \otimes \mathbf{u}.$$

Equivalently,

$$\mathbf{u}\mathbf{v}^T = \begin{pmatrix} u_1 \mathbf{v}^T \\ \vdots \\ u_n \mathbf{v}^T \end{pmatrix} = \mathbf{u} \otimes \mathbf{v}^T.$$

Example 8.2.5 *(continued from Example 8.2.3) In the previous example the Kronecker product turned out to be commutative (i.e., we had* $\mathbf{v}^T \otimes \mathbf{u} = \mathbf{u} \otimes \mathbf{v}^T$*). This is not the case in general. Going back to the first example above, note that*

$$\begin{bmatrix} 0 & 5 \\ 6 & 7 \end{bmatrix} \otimes \begin{bmatrix} 1 & 2 \\ 3 & 4 \end{bmatrix} = \begin{bmatrix} 0\begin{bmatrix} 1 & 2 \\ 3 & 4 \end{bmatrix} & 5\begin{bmatrix} 1 & 2 \\ 3 & 4 \end{bmatrix} \\ 6\begin{bmatrix} 1 & 2 \\ 3 & 4 \end{bmatrix} & 7\begin{bmatrix} 1 & 2 \\ 3 & 4 \end{bmatrix} \end{bmatrix} = \begin{bmatrix} 0 & 0 & 5 & 10 \\ 0 & 0 & 15 & 20 \\ 6 & 12 & 7 & 14 \\ 18 & 24 & 21 & 28 \end{bmatrix}.$$

You can check that this is different from what we obtained in the opposite order.

The proof of the following lemma is left as an exercise (see Problems 8.7-8.10 and 8.16).

Lemma 8.2.6 *(Properties of the Kronecker Product) The Kronecker product has the following properties:*

a) *If B, C are matrices of the same dimension,*

$$A \otimes (B + C) = A \otimes B + A \otimes C \quad \text{and} \quad (B + C) \otimes A = B \otimes A + C \otimes A.$$

b) *If A, B, C, D are matrices of such size that one can form the matrix products AC and BD, then*

$$(A \otimes B)(C \otimes D) = (AC) \otimes (BD).$$

c) *If A, C are matrices of the same dimension and B, D are matrices of the same dimension, then*

$$(A \otimes B) \odot (C \otimes D) = (A \odot C) \otimes (B \odot D).$$

---

[3] https://en.wikipedia.org/wiki/Kronecker_product

d) If A, B are invertible, then

$$(A \otimes B)^{-1} = A^{-1} \otimes B^{-1}.$$

e) The transpose of $A \otimes B$ is

$$(A \otimes B)^T = A^T \otimes B^T.$$

f) If $\mathbf{u}$ is a column vector and A, B are matrices of such size that one can form the matrix product AB, then

$$(\mathbf{u} \otimes A)B = \mathbf{u} \otimes (AB) \quad \text{and} \quad (A \otimes \mathbf{u})B = (AB) \otimes \mathbf{u}.$$

Similarly,

$$A(\mathbf{u}^T \otimes B) = \mathbf{u}^T \otimes (AB) \quad \text{and} \quad A(B \otimes \mathbf{u}^T) = (AB) \otimes \mathbf{u}^T.$$

8.2.2 Jacobian

Recall that the derivative of a function of a real variable is the rate of change of the function with respect to the change in the variable. A different way to put this is that $f'(x)$ is the slope of the tangent line to f at x. Formally, one can approximate $f(x)$ by a linear function in the neighborhood of x as follows

$$f(x+h) = f(x) + f'(x)h + r(h),$$

where $r(h)$ is negligible compared to h in the sense that

$$\lim_{h \to 0} \frac{r(h)}{h} = 0.$$

Indeed, define

$$r(h) = f(x+h) - f(x) - f'(x)h.$$

Then by definition of the derivative

$$\lim_{h \to 0} \frac{r(h)}{h} = \lim_{h \to 0} \frac{f(x+h) - f(x) - f'(x)h}{h} = \lim_{h \to 0} \left[\frac{f(x+h) - f(x)}{h} - f'(x) \right] = 0.$$

For vector-valued functions, we have the following generalization. Let $\mathbf{f} = (f_1, \ldots, f_m) \colon D \to \mathbb{R}^m$ where $D \subseteq \mathbb{R}^d$ and let $\mathbf{x} \in D$ be an interior point of D. We say that $\mathbf{f}$ is diffentiable at $\mathbf{x}$ if there exists a matrix $A \in \mathbb{R}^{m \times d}$ such that

$$\mathbf{f}(\mathbf{x} + \mathbf{h}) = \mathbf{f}(\mathbf{x}) + A\mathbf{h} + \mathbf{r}(\mathbf{h})$$

where

$$\lim_{h \to 0} \frac{\|\mathbf{r}(\mathbf{h})\|_2}{\|\mathbf{h}\|_2} = 0.$$

The matrix $\mathbf{f}'(\mathbf{x}) = A$ is called the differential of $\mathbf{f}$ at $\mathbf{x}$, and we see that the affine map $\mathbf{f}(\mathbf{x}) + A\mathbf{h}$ provides an approximation of $\mathbf{f}$ in the neighborhood of $\mathbf{x}$.

We will not derive the full theory here. In the case where each component of $\mathbf{f}$ has continuous partial derivatives in a neighborhood of $\mathbf{x}$, then the differential exists and is equal to the Jacobian, as defined next.

Definition 8.2.7 (Jacobian) Let $\mathbf{f} = (f_1, \ldots, f_m): D \to \mathbb{R}^m$ where $D \subseteq \mathbb{R}^d$ and let $\mathbf{x}_0 \in D$ be an interior point of D where $\frac{\partial f_j(\mathbf{x}_0)}{\partial x_i}$ exists for all i, j. The Jacobian of $\mathbf{f}$ at $\mathbf{x}_0$ is the $m \times d$ matrix

$$J_{\mathbf{f}}(\mathbf{x}_0) = \begin{pmatrix} \frac{\partial f_1(\mathbf{x}_0)}{\partial x_1} & \cdots & \frac{\partial f_1(\mathbf{x}_0)}{\partial x_d} \\ \vdots & \ddots & \vdots \\ \frac{\partial f_m(\mathbf{x}_0)}{\partial x_1} & \cdots & \frac{\partial f_m(\mathbf{x}_0)}{\partial x_d} \end{pmatrix}.$$

Theorem 8.2.8 (Differential and Jacobian) Let $\mathbf{f} = (f_1, \ldots, f_m): D \to \mathbb{R}^m$ where $D \subseteq \mathbb{R}^d$ and let $\mathbf{x}_0 \in D$ be an interior point of D. Assume that $\frac{\partial f_j(\mathbf{x}_0)}{\partial x_i}$ exists and is continous is an open ball around $\mathbf{x}_0$ for all i, j. Then the differential at $\mathbf{x}_0$ is equal to the Jacobian of $\mathbf{f}$ at $\mathbf{x}_0$.

Recall that for any A, B for which AB is well-defined it holds that $\|AB\|_F \leq \|A\|_F \|B\|_F$. This applies in particular when B is a column vector, in which case $\|B\|_F$ is its Euclidean norm.

Proof By the *Mean Value Theorem*, for each i, there is $\xi_{\mathbf{h},i} \in (0, 1)$ such that

$$f_i(\mathbf{x}_0 + \mathbf{h}) = f_i(\mathbf{x}_0) + \nabla f_i(\mathbf{x}_0 + \xi_{\mathbf{h},i} \mathbf{h})^T \mathbf{h}.$$

Define

$$\tilde{J}(\mathbf{h}) = \begin{pmatrix} \frac{\partial f_1(\mathbf{x}_0 + \xi_{\mathbf{h},1} \mathbf{h})}{\partial x_1} & \cdots & \frac{\partial f_1(\mathbf{x}_0 + \xi_{\mathbf{h},1} \mathbf{h})}{\partial x_d} \\ \vdots & \ddots & \vdots \\ \frac{\partial f_m(\mathbf{x}_0 + \xi_{\mathbf{h},m} \mathbf{h})}{\partial x_1} & \cdots & \frac{\partial f_m(\mathbf{x}_0 + \xi_{\mathbf{h},m} \mathbf{h})}{\partial x_d} \end{pmatrix}.$$

Hence we have

$$\mathbf{f}(\mathbf{x}_0 + \mathbf{h}) - \mathbf{f}(\mathbf{x}_0) - J_{\mathbf{f}}(\mathbf{x}_0)\,\mathbf{h} = \tilde{J}(\mathbf{h})\,\mathbf{h} - J_{\mathbf{f}}(\mathbf{x}_0)\,\mathbf{h} = \left(\tilde{J}(\mathbf{h}) - J_{\mathbf{f}}(\mathbf{x}_0)\right)\mathbf{h}.$$

Taking a limit as $\mathbf{h}$ goes to 0, we get

$$\lim_{\mathbf{h} \to 0} \frac{\|\mathbf{f}(\mathbf{x}_0 + \mathbf{h}) - \mathbf{f}(\mathbf{x}_0) - J_{\mathbf{f}}(\mathbf{x}_0)\mathbf{h}\|_2}{\|\mathbf{h}\|_2} = \lim_{\mathbf{h} \to 0} \frac{\|\left(\tilde{J}(\mathbf{h}) - J_{\mathbf{f}}(\mathbf{x}_0)\right)\mathbf{h}\|_2}{\|\mathbf{h}\|_2}$$
$$\leq \lim_{\mathbf{h} \to 0} \frac{\|\tilde{J}(\mathbf{h}) - J_{\mathbf{f}}(\mathbf{x}_0)\|_F \|\mathbf{h}\|_2}{\|\mathbf{h}\|_2}$$
$$= 0,$$

by continuity of the partial derivatives. □

Example 8.2.9 *An example of a vector-valued function is*

$$\mathbf{g}(x_1, x_2) = \begin{pmatrix} g_1(x_1, x_2) \\ g_2(x_1, x_2) \\ g_3(x_1, x_2) \end{pmatrix} = \begin{pmatrix} 3x_1^2 \\ x_2 \\ x_1 x_2 \end{pmatrix}.$$

Its Jacobian is

$$J_{\mathbf{g}}(x_1, x_2) = \begin{pmatrix} \frac{\partial g_1(x_1, x_2)}{\partial x_1} & \frac{\partial g_1(x_1, x_2)}{\partial x_2} \\ \frac{\partial g_2(x_1, x_2)}{\partial x_1} & \frac{\partial g_2(x_1, x_2)}{\partial x_2} \\ \frac{\partial g_3(x_1, x_2)}{\partial x_1} & \frac{\partial g_3(x_1, x_2)}{\partial x_2} \end{pmatrix} = \begin{pmatrix} 6x_1 & 0 \\ 0 & 1 \\ x_2 & x_1 \end{pmatrix}.$$

Example 8.2.10 *(Gradient and Jacobian)* *For a continuously differentiable real-valued function $f: D \to \mathbb{R}$, the Jacobian reduces to the row vector*

$$J_f(\mathbf{x}_0) = \left(\frac{\partial f(\mathbf{x}_0)}{\partial x_1}, \ldots, \frac{\partial f(\mathbf{x}_0)}{\partial x_d}\right)^T = \nabla f(\mathbf{x}_0)^T$$

where $\nabla f(\mathbf{x}_0)$ is the gradient of f at $\mathbf{x}_0$.

Example 8.2.11 *(Hessian and Jacobian)* *For a twice continuously differentiable real-valued function $f: D \to \mathbb{R}$, the Jacobian of its gradient is*

$$J_{\nabla f}(\mathbf{x}_0) = \begin{pmatrix} \frac{\partial^2 f(\mathbf{x}_0)}{\partial x_1^2} & \cdots & \frac{\partial^2 f(\mathbf{x}_0)}{\partial x_d \partial x_1} \\ \vdots & \ddots & \vdots \\ \frac{\partial^2 f(\mathbf{x}_0)}{\partial x_1 \partial x_d} & \cdots & \frac{\partial^2 f(\mathbf{x}_0)}{\partial x_d^2} \end{pmatrix},$$

that is, the Hessian of f at $\mathbf{x}_0$.

Example 8.2.12 *(Parametric Curve and Jacobian)* *Consider the parametric curve $\mathbf{g}(t) = (g_1(t), \ldots, g_d(t)) \in \mathbb{R}^d$ for t in some closed interval of $\mathbb{R}$. Assume that $\mathbf{g}(t)$ is continuously differentiable at t; that is, each of its components is.*
Then

$$J_{\mathbf{g}}(t) = \begin{pmatrix} g_1'(t) \\ \vdots \\ g_m'(t) \end{pmatrix} = \mathbf{g}'(t).$$

Example 8.2.13 *(Affine Map)* *Let $A = (a_{i,j})_{i,j} \in \mathbb{R}^{m \times d}$ and $\mathbf{b} = (b_1, \ldots, b_m) \in \mathbb{R}^m$. Define the vector-valued function $\mathbf{f} = (f_1, \ldots, f_m) : \mathbb{R}^d \to \mathbb{R}^m$ as*

$$\mathbf{f}(\mathbf{x}) = A\mathbf{x} + \mathbf{b}.$$

This is an affine map. Note in particular that, in the case $\mathbf{b} = \mathbf{0}$ of a linear map,

$$\mathbf{f}(\mathbf{x} + \mathbf{y}) = A(\mathbf{x} + \mathbf{y}) = A\mathbf{x} + A\mathbf{y} = \mathbf{f}(\mathbf{x}) + \mathbf{f}(\mathbf{y}).$$

Denote the rows of A by $\boldsymbol{\alpha}_1^T, \ldots, \boldsymbol{\alpha}_m^T$.
We compute the Jacobian of $\mathbf{f}$ at $\mathbf{x}$. Note that

$$\frac{\partial f_i(\mathbf{x})}{\partial x_j} = \frac{\partial}{\partial x_j}[\boldsymbol{\alpha}_i^T \mathbf{x} + b_i]$$

$$= \frac{\partial}{\partial x_j}\left[\sum_{\ell=1}^{m} a_{i,\ell} x_\ell + b_i\right]$$

$$= a_{i,j}$$

so that

$$J_{\mathbf{f}}(\mathbf{x}) = A.$$

The following important example is a less straightforward application of the Jacobian.

It will be useful to introduce the vectorization $\text{vec}(A) \in \mathbb{R}^{nm}$ of a matrix $A = (a_{i,j})_{i,j} \in \mathbb{R}^{n \times m}$ as the vector

$$\text{vec}(A) = (a_{1,1}, \ldots, a_{n,1}, a_{1,2}, \ldots, a_{n,2}, \ldots, a_{1,m}, \ldots, a_{n,m}).$$

That is, it is obtained by stacking the columns of A on top of each other.

Example 8.2.14 *(Jacobian of a Linear Map with Respect to its Matrix)* We take a different tack on the previous example. In data science applications, it will be useful to compute the Jacobian of a linear map $X\mathbf{z}$ – with respect to the matrix $X \in \mathbb{R}^{n \times m}$. Specifically, for a fixed $\mathbf{z} \in \mathbb{R}^m$, letting $(\mathbf{x}^{(i)})^T$ be the i-th row of X we define the function

$$\mathbf{f}(\mathbf{x}) = X\mathbf{z} = \begin{pmatrix} (\mathbf{x}^{(1)})^T \\ \vdots \\ (\mathbf{x}^{(n)})^T \end{pmatrix} \mathbf{z} = \begin{pmatrix} (\mathbf{x}^{(1)})^T \mathbf{z} \\ \vdots \\ (\mathbf{x}^{(n)})^T \mathbf{z} \end{pmatrix}$$

where $\mathbf{x} = \text{vec}(X^T) = (\mathbf{x}^{(1)}, \ldots, \mathbf{x}^{(n)})$.

To compute the Jacobian, let us look at its columns that correspond to the variables in $\mathbf{x}^{(k)}$, namely columns $\alpha_k = (k-1)m + 1$ to $\beta_k = km$. Note that only the k-th component of $\mathbf{f}$ depends on $\mathbf{x}^{(k)}$, so the rows $\neq k$ of $J_\mathbf{f}(\mathbf{x})$ are 0 for the corresponding columns.

Row k on the other hand is $\mathbf{z}^T$ from our previous formula for the gradient of an affine map (see Example 3.2.2). Hence one way to write the columns α_k to β_k of $J_\mathbf{f}(\mathbf{x})$ is $\mathbf{e}_k \mathbf{z}^T$, where here $\mathbf{e}_k \in \mathbb{R}^n$ is the k-th standard basis vector of $\mathbb{R}^n$.

So $J_\mathbf{f}(\mathbf{x})$ can be written in block form as

$$J_\mathbf{f}(\mathbf{x}) = \begin{pmatrix} \mathbf{e}_1 \mathbf{z}^T & \cdots & \mathbf{e}_n \mathbf{z}^T \end{pmatrix} = I_{n \times n} \otimes \mathbf{z}^T =: \mathbb{B}_n[\mathbf{z}],$$

where the last equality is a definition.

We will need one more wrinkle.

Example 8.2.15 *(Jacobian of a Linear Map with Respect to its Input and Matrix)* Consider again the linear map $X\mathbf{z}$ – this time as a function of both the matrix $X \in \mathbb{R}^{n \times m}$ and the vector $\mathbf{z} \in \mathbb{R}^m$. That is, letting again $(\mathbf{x}^{(i)})^T$ be the i-th row of X, we define the function

$$\mathbf{g}(\mathbf{z}, \mathbf{x}) = X\mathbf{z} = \begin{pmatrix} (\mathbf{x}^{(1)})^T \\ \vdots \\ (\mathbf{x}^{(n)})^T \end{pmatrix} \mathbf{z} = \begin{pmatrix} (\mathbf{x}^{(1)})^T \mathbf{z} \\ \vdots \\ (\mathbf{x}^{(n)})^T \mathbf{z} \end{pmatrix}$$

where as before $\mathbf{x} = \text{vec}(X^T) = (\mathbf{x}^{(1)}, \ldots, \mathbf{x}^{(n)})$.

To compute the Jacobian, we think of it as a block matrix and use the two previous examples. The columns of $J_\mathbf{f}(\mathbf{z}, \mathbf{x})$ corresponding to the variables in $\mathbf{z}$, namely columns 1 to m, are

$$X = \begin{pmatrix} (\mathbf{x}^{(1)})^T \\ \vdots \\ (\mathbf{x}^{(n)})^T \end{pmatrix} =: \mathbb{A}_n[\mathbf{x}].$$

The columns of $J_\mathbf{f}(\mathbf{z}, \mathbf{x})$ corresponding to the variables in $\mathbf{x}$, that is, columns $m + 1$ to $m + nm$, are the matrix $\mathbb{B}_n[\mathbf{z}]$. Note that, in both $\mathbb{A}_n[\mathbf{x}]$ and $\mathbb{B}_n[\mathbf{z}]$, the subscript n indicates the number of rows of the matrix. The number of columns is determined by n and the size of the input vector:

- the length of $\mathbf{x}$ divided by n for $\mathbb{A}_n[\mathbf{x}]$;
- the length of $\mathbf{z}$ multiplied by n for $\mathbb{B}_n[\mathbf{z}]$.

So $J_\mathbf{f}(\mathbf{z}, \mathbf{x})$ can be written in block form as

$$J_\mathbf{f}(\mathbf{z}, \mathbf{x}) = \begin{pmatrix} \mathbb{A}_n[\mathbf{x}] & \mathbb{B}_n[\mathbf{z}] \end{pmatrix}.$$

Example 8.2.16 *(Elementwise Function)* Let $f: D \to \mathbb{R}$, with $D \subseteq \mathbb{R}$, be a continuously differentiable real-valued function of a single variable. For $n \geq 2$, consider applying f to each entry of a vector $\mathbf{x} \in \mathbb{R}^n$; that is, let $\mathbf{f}: D^n \to \mathbb{R}^n$ with

$$\mathbf{f}(\mathbf{x}) = (f_1(\mathbf{x}), \ldots, f_n(\mathbf{x})) = (f(x_1), \ldots, f(x_n)).$$

The Jacobian of $\mathbf{f}$ can be computed from f', the derivative of the single-variable case. Indeed, letting $\mathbf{x} = (x_1, \ldots, x_n)$ be such that x_i is an interior point of D for all i,

$$\frac{\partial f_j(\mathbf{x})}{\partial x_j} = f'(x_j),$$

while for $\ell \neq j$

$$\frac{\partial f_\ell(\mathbf{x})}{\partial x_j} = 0,$$

as $f_\ell(\mathbf{x})$ does not in fact depend on x_j. In other words, the j-th column of the Jacobian is $f'(x_j)\,\mathbf{e}_j$, where again $\mathbf{e}_j$ is the j-th standard basis vector in $\mathbb{R}^n$.

So $J_\mathbf{f}(\mathbf{x})$ is the diagonal matrix with diagonal entries $f'(x_j)$, $j = 1, \ldots, n$, which we denote by

$$J_\mathbf{f}(\mathbf{x}) = \mathrm{diag}(f'(x_1), \ldots, f'(x_n)).$$

8.2.3 Generalization of the Chain Rule

As we have seen, functions are often obtained from the composition of simpler ones. We will use the vector notation $\mathbf{h} = \mathbf{g} \circ \mathbf{f}$ for the function $\mathbf{h}(\mathbf{x}) = \mathbf{g}(\mathbf{f}(\mathbf{x}))$.

Lemma 8.2.17 *(Composition of Continuous Functions)* Let $\mathbf{f}: D_1 \to \mathbb{R}^m$, where $D_1 \subseteq \mathbb{R}^d$, and let $\mathbf{g}: D_2 \to \mathbb{R}^p$, where $D_2 \subseteq \mathbb{R}^m$. Assume that $\mathbf{f}$ is continuous at $\mathbf{x}_0$ and that $\mathbf{g}$ is continuous at $\mathbf{f}(\mathbf{x}_0)$. Then $\mathbf{g} \circ \mathbf{f}$ is continuous at $\mathbf{x}_0$.

The *Chain Rule* gives a formula for the Jacobian of a composition.

Theorem 8.2.18 *(Chain Rule)* Let $\mathbf{f}: D_1 \to \mathbb{R}^m$, where $D_1 \subseteq \mathbb{R}^d$, and let $\mathbf{g}: D_2 \to \mathbb{R}^p$, where $D_2 \subseteq \mathbb{R}^m$. Assume that $\mathbf{f}$ is continuously differentiable at $\mathbf{x}_0$, an interior point of D_1, and that $\mathbf{g}$ is continuously differentiable at $\mathbf{f}(\mathbf{x}_0)$, an interior point of D_2. Then

$$J_{\mathbf{g} \circ \mathbf{f}}(\mathbf{x}_0) = J_\mathbf{g}(\mathbf{f}(\mathbf{x}_0))\, J_\mathbf{f}(\mathbf{x}_0)$$

as a product of matrices.

Intuitively, the Jacobian provides a linear approximation of the function in the neighborhood of a point. The composition of linear maps corresponds to the product of the associated matrices. Similarly, the Jacobian of a composition is the product of the Jacobians.

Proof To avoid confusion, we think of $\mathbf{f}$ and $\mathbf{g}$ as being functions of variables with different names, specifically,

$$\mathbf{f}(\mathbf{x}) = (f_1(x_1, \ldots, x_d), \ldots, f_m(x_1, \ldots, x_d))$$

and

$$\mathbf{g}(\mathbf{y}) = (g_1(y_1, \ldots, y_m), \ldots, g_p(y_1, \ldots, y_m)).$$

We apply the *Chain Rule* for a real-valued function over a parametric vector curve. That is, we think of

$$h_i(\mathbf{x}) = g_i(\mathbf{f}(\mathbf{x})) = g_i(f_1(x_1,\ldots,x_j,\ldots,x_d),\ldots,f_m(x_1,\ldots,x_j,\ldots,x_d))$$

as *a function of x_j only* with all other x_ℓ's fixed.

We get that

$$\frac{\partial h_i(\mathbf{x}_0)}{\partial x_j} = \sum_{k=1}^{m} \frac{\partial g_i(\mathbf{f}(\mathbf{x}_0))}{\partial y_k} \frac{\partial f_k(\mathbf{x}_0)}{\partial x_j}$$

where, as before, the notation $\frac{\partial g_i}{\partial y_k}$ indicates the partial derivative of g_i with respect to its k-th component. In matrix form, the claim follows. $\square$

Example 8.2.19 *(continued from Example 8.2.13)* Let $A \in \mathbb{R}^{m \times d}$ and $\mathbf{b} \in \mathbb{R}^m$. *Define again the vector-valued function* $\mathbf{f}: \mathbb{R}^d \to \mathbb{R}^m$ *as* $\mathbf{f}(\mathbf{x}) = A\mathbf{x} + \mathbf{b}$. *In addition, for* $C \in \mathbb{R}^{p \times m}$ *and* $\mathbf{d} \in \mathbb{R}^p$, *define* $\mathbf{g}: \mathbb{R}^m \to \mathbb{R}^p$ *as* $\mathbf{g}(\mathbf{y}) = C\mathbf{y} + \mathbf{d}$.

Then

$$J_{\mathbf{g} \circ \mathbf{f}}(\mathbf{x}) = J_{\mathbf{g}}(\mathbf{f}(\mathbf{x}))\, J_{\mathbf{f}}(\mathbf{x}) = CA,$$

for all $\mathbf{x} \in \mathbb{R}^d$.

This is consistent with the observation that

$$\mathbf{g} \circ \mathbf{f}(\mathbf{x}) = \mathbf{g}(\mathbf{f}(\mathbf{x})) = C(A\mathbf{x} + \mathbf{b}) + \mathbf{d} = CA\mathbf{x} + (C\mathbf{b} + \mathbf{d}).$$

Example 8.2.20 *Suppose we want to compute the gradient of the function*

$$f(x_1, x_2) = 3x_1^2 + x_2 + \exp(x_1 x_2).$$

We could apply the **Chain Rule** directly, but to illustrate the perspective that is coming up, we think of f as a composition of "simpler" vector-valued functions. Specifically, let

$$\mathbf{g}(x_1, x_2) = \begin{pmatrix} 3x_1^2 \\ x_2 \\ x_1 x_2 \end{pmatrix}, \qquad h(y_1, y_2, y_3) = y_1 + y_2 + \exp(y_3).$$

Then $f(x_1, x_2) = h(\mathbf{g}(x_1, x_2)) = h \circ \mathbf{g}(x_1, x_2)$.

By the **Chain Rule**, we can compute the gradient of f by first computing the Jacobians of $\mathbf{g}$ and h. We have already computed the Jacobian of $\mathbf{g}$ in Example 8.2.9,

$$J_{\mathbf{g}}(x_1, x_2) = \begin{pmatrix} 6x_1 & 0 \\ 0 & 1 \\ x_2 & x_1 \end{pmatrix}.$$

The Jacobian of h is

$$J_h(y_1, y_2, y_3) = \begin{pmatrix} \frac{\partial h(y_1, y_2, y_3)}{\partial y_1} & \frac{\partial h(y_1, y_2, y_3)}{\partial y_2} & \frac{\partial h(y_1, y_2, y_3)}{\partial y_3} \end{pmatrix} = \begin{pmatrix} 1 & 1 & \exp(y_3) \end{pmatrix}.$$

The Chain Rule *stipulates that*

$$\nabla f(x_1, x_2)^T = J_f(x_1, x_2)$$
$$= J_h(\mathbf{g}(x_1, x_2)) J_\mathbf{g}(x_1, x_2)$$
$$= \begin{pmatrix} 1 & 1 & \exp(g_3(x_1, x_2)) \end{pmatrix} \begin{pmatrix} 6x_1 & 0 \\ 0 & 1 \\ x_2 & x_1 \end{pmatrix}$$
$$= \begin{pmatrix} 1 & 1 & \exp(x_1 x_2) \end{pmatrix} \begin{pmatrix} 6x_1 & 0 \\ 0 & 1 \\ x_2 & x_1 \end{pmatrix}$$
$$= \begin{pmatrix} 6x_1 + x_2 \exp(x_1 x_2) & 1 + x_1 \exp(x_1 x_2) \end{pmatrix}.$$

You can check directly (i.e., without the composition) that this is indeed the correct gradient (transposed).

Alternatively, it is instructive to "expand" the Chain Rule as we did in its proof. Specifically,

$$\frac{\partial f(x_1, x_2)}{\partial x_1} = \sum_{i=1}^{3} \frac{\partial h(\mathbf{g}(x_1, x_2))}{\partial y_i} \frac{\partial g_i(x_1, x_2)}{\partial x_1}$$
$$= \frac{\partial h(\mathbf{g}(x_1, x_2))}{\partial y_1} \frac{\partial g_1(x_1, x_2)}{\partial x_1} + \frac{\partial h(\mathbf{g}(x_1, x_2))}{\partial y_2} \frac{\partial g_2(x_1, x_2)}{\partial x_1}$$
$$+ \frac{\partial h(\mathbf{g}(x_1, x_2))}{\partial y_3} \frac{\partial g_3(x_1, x_2)}{\partial x_1}$$
$$= 1 \cdot 6x_1 + 1 \cdot 0 + \exp(g_3(x_1, x_2)) \cdot x_2$$
$$= 6x_1 + x_2 \exp(x_1 x_2).$$

Note that this corresponds to multiplying $J_h(\mathbf{g}(x_1, x_2))$ by the first column of $J_\mathbf{g}(x_1, x_2)$.

Similarly

$$\frac{\partial f(x_1, x_2)}{\partial x_2} = \sum_{i=1}^{3} \frac{\partial h(\mathbf{g}(x_1, x_2))}{\partial y_i} \frac{\partial g_i(x_1, x_2)}{\partial x_2}$$
$$= \frac{\partial h(\mathbf{g}(x_1, x_2))}{\partial y_1} \frac{\partial g_1(x_1, x_2)}{\partial x_2} + \frac{\partial h(\mathbf{g}(x_1, x_2))}{\partial y_2} \frac{\partial g_2(x_1, x_2)}{\partial x_2}$$
$$+ \frac{\partial h(\mathbf{g}(x_1, x_2))}{\partial y_3} \frac{\partial g_3(x_1, x_2)}{\partial x_2}$$
$$= 1 \cdot 0 + 1 \cdot 1 + \exp(g_3(x_1, x_2)) \cdot x_1$$
$$= 1 + x_1 \exp(x_1 x_2).$$

This corresponds to multiplying $J_h(\mathbf{g}(x_1, x_2))$ by the second column of $J_\mathbf{g}(x_1, x_2)$.

CHAT & LEARN The Jacobian determinant has important applications in change of variables for multivariable integrals. Ask your favorite AI chatbot to explain this application and provide an example of using the Jacobian determinant in a change of variables for a double integral.

8.2.4 Brief Introduction to Automatic Differentiation in PyTorch

We illustrate the use of automatic differentiation to compute gradients in PyTorch.

Quoting Wikipedia[4]:

> In mathematics and computer algebra, automatic differentiation (AD), also called algorithmic differentiation or computational differentiation, is a set of techniques to numerically evaluate the derivative of a function specified by a computer program. AD exploits the fact that every computer program, no matter how complicated, executes a sequence of elementary arithmetic operations (addition, subtraction, multiplication, division, etc.) and elementary functions (exp, log, sin, cos, etc.). By applying the chain rule repeatedly to these operations, derivatives of arbitrary order can be computed automatically, accurately to working precision, and using at most a small constant factor more arithmetic operations than the original program. Automatic differentiation is distinct from symbolic differentiation and numerical differentiation (the method of finite differences). Symbolic differentiation can lead to inefficient code and faces the difficulty of converting a computer program into a single expression, while numerical differentiation can introduce round-off errors in the discretization process and cancellation.

8.2.4.1 Automatic Differentiation in PyTorch

We will use PyTorch. It uses tensors, which in many ways behave similarly to NumPy arrays. We first initialize the tensors. Here each tensor corresponds to a single real variable. With the option requires_grad=True, we indicate that these are variables with respect to which a gradient will be taken later. We initialize the tensors at the values where the derivatives will be computed. If derivatives need to be computed at different values, we need to repeat this process. The function .backward computes the gradient using backpropagation, to which we will return later. The partial derivatives are accessed with .grad.

NUMERICAL CORNER This is better understood through an example.

```
x1 = torch.tensor(1.0, requires_grad=True)
x2 = torch.tensor(2.0, requires_grad=True)
```

We define the function. Note that we use torch.exp, the PyTorch implementation of the (element-wise) exponential function. Moreover, as in NumPy, PyTorch allows the use of ** for taking a power.

```
f = 3 * (x1 ** 2) + x2 + torch.exp(x1 * x2)

f.backward()

print(x1.grad)   # df/dx1
print(x2.grad)   # df/dx2
```

tensor(20.7781)
tensor(8.3891)

---

[4] https://en.wikipedia.org/wiki/Automatic_differentiation

The input parameters can also be vectors, which allows to consider functions of large numbers of variables. Here we use `torch.sum` for taking a sum of the arguments.

```
z = torch.tensor([1., 2., 3.], requires_grad=True)

g = torch.sum(z ** 2)
g.backward()

print(z.grad)   # gradient is (2 z_1, 2 z_2, 2 z_3)
```

```
tensor([2., 4., 6.])
```

Here is another typical example in a data science context.

```
X = torch.randn(3, 2)     # Random dataset (features)
y = torch.tensor([[1., 0., 1.]])   # Dataset (labels)
theta = torch.ones(2, 1, requires_grad=True)   # Parameter assignment

predict = X @ theta     # Classifier with parameter vector theta
loss = torch.sum((predict - y)**2)   # Loss function
loss.backward()   # Compute gradients

print(theta.grad)   # gradient of loss
```

```
tensor([[-2.1107],
        [27.7279]])
```

CHAT & LEARN Ask your favorite AI chatbot to explain how to compute a second derivative using PyTorch (it's a bit tricky). Ask for code that *you can apply* to the previous examples.

◁ NC

8.2.4.2 Implementing Gradient Descent in PyTorch

Rather than explicitly specifying the gradient function, we could use PyTorch to compute it automatically. This is done next. Note that the descent update is done within `with torch.no_grad`, which ensures that the update operation itself is not tracked for gradient computation. Here the input x0 as well as the output xk.numpy(force=True) are NumPy arrays. The function `torch.Tensor.numpy` converts a PyTorch tensor to a NumPy array (see the documentation for an explanation of the `force=True` option). Also, quoting ChatGPT:

> In the given code, `.item` is used to extract the scalar value from a tensor. In PyTorch, when you perform operations on tensors, you get back tensors as results, even if the result is a single scalar value. `.item` is used to extract this scalar value from the tensor.

```
def gd_with_ad(f, x0, alpha=1e-3, niters=int(1e6)):
    xk = torch.tensor(x0, requires_grad=True, dtype=torch.float)

    for _ in range(niters):
        value = f(xk)
        value.backward()

        with torch.no_grad():
            xk -= alpha * xk.grad

        xk.grad.zero_()

    return xk.numpy(force=True), f(xk).item()
```

NUMERICAL CORNER We revisit a previous example.

```
def f(x):
    return x**3
```

```
print(gd_with_ad(f, 2, niters=int(1e4)))
```

(array(0.03277362, dtype=float32), 3.5202472645323724e-05)

```
print(gd_with_ad(f, -2, niters=100))
```

(array(-4.9335055, dtype=float32), -120.07894897460938)

◁ **NC**

CHAT & LEARN The section briefly mentions that automatic differentiation is distinct from symbolic differentiation and numerical differentiation. Ask your favorite AI chatbot to explain in more detail the differences between these three methods of computing derivatives.

Self-Assessment Quiz (with help from Claude, Gemini, and ChatGPT)

1. Let $A \in \mathbb{R}^{n \times m}$ and $B \in \mathbb{R}^{p \times q}$. What are the dimensions of the Kronecker product $A \otimes B$?
   a) $n \times m$
   b) $p \times q$
   c) $np \times mq$
   d) $nq \times mp$

2. If $\mathbf{f}: \mathbb{R}^d \to \mathbb{R}^m$ is a continuously differentiable function, what is its Jacobian $J_{\mathbf{f}}(\mathbf{x}_0)$ at an interior point $\mathbf{x}_0$ of its domain?
   a) A scalar representing the rate of change of $\mathbf{f}$ at $\mathbf{x}_0$

8.2 Jacobian, Chain Rule, and a Brief Introduction to Automatic Differentiation

b) A vector in $\mathbb{R}^m$ representing the direction of steepest ascent of **f** at $\mathbf{x}_0$
c) An $m \times d$ matrix of partial derivatives of the component functions of **f** at $\mathbf{x}_0$
d) The Hessian matrix of **f** at $\mathbf{x}_0$

3. In the context of the **Chain Rule**, if $\mathbf{f}\colon \mathbb{R}^2 \to \mathbb{R}^3$ and $\mathbf{g}\colon \mathbb{R}^3 \to \mathbb{R}$, what is the dimension of the Jacobian matrix $J_{\mathbf{g}\circ\mathbf{f}}(\mathbf{x})$?
    a) 3×2
    b) 1×3
    c) 2×3
    d) 1×2

4. Let $\mathbf{f}\colon D_1 \to \mathbb{R}^m$, where $D_1 \subseteq \mathbb{R}^d$, and let $\mathbf{g}\colon D_2 \to \mathbb{R}^p$, where $D_2 \subseteq \mathbb{R}^m$. Assume that **f** is continuously differentiable at $\mathbf{x}_0$, an interior point of D_1, and that **g** is continuously differentiable at $\mathbf{f}(\mathbf{x}_0)$, an interior point of D_2. Which of the following is correct according to the *Chain Rule*?
    a) $J_{\mathbf{g}\circ\mathbf{f}}(\mathbf{x}_0) = J_{\mathbf{f}}(\mathbf{x}_0) J_{\mathbf{g}}(\mathbf{f}(\mathbf{x}_0))$
    b) $J_{\mathbf{g}\circ\mathbf{f}}(\mathbf{x}_0) = J_{\mathbf{g}}(\mathbf{f}(\mathbf{x}_0)) J_{\mathbf{f}}(\mathbf{x}_0)$
    c) $J_{\mathbf{g}\circ\mathbf{f}}(\mathbf{x}_0) = J_{\mathbf{f}}(\mathbf{g}(\mathbf{x}_0)) J_{\mathbf{g}}(\mathbf{x}_0)$
    d) $J_{\mathbf{g}\circ\mathbf{f}}(\mathbf{x}_0) = J_{\mathbf{g}}(\mathbf{x}_0) J_{\mathbf{f}}(\mathbf{g}(\mathbf{x}_0))$

5. Let $A = (a_{i,j})_{i,j} \in \mathbb{R}^{m \times d}$ and $\mathbf{b} \in \mathbb{R}^m$. Define the vector-valued function $\mathbf{f}\colon \mathbb{R}^d \to \mathbb{R}^m$ as $\mathbf{f}(\mathbf{x}) = A\mathbf{x} + \mathbf{b}$. What is the Jacobian of **f** at $\mathbf{x}_0$?
    a) $J_{\mathbf{f}}(\mathbf{x}_0) = A^T$
    b) $J_{\mathbf{f}}(\mathbf{x}_0) = A\mathbf{x}_0 + \mathbf{b}$
    c) $J_{\mathbf{f}}(\mathbf{x}_0) = A$
    d) $J_{\mathbf{f}}(\mathbf{x}_0) = \mathbf{b}$

Answer for 1: c. Justification: The text defines the Kronecker product as a matrix in block form with dimensions $np \times mq$.

Answer for 2: c. Justification: The text defines the Jacobian of a vector-valued function as a matrix of partial derivatives.

Answer for 3: d. Justification: The composition $\mathbf{g} \circ \mathbf{f}$ maps $\mathbb{R}^2 \to \mathbb{R}$, hence the Jacobian matrix $J_{\mathbf{g}\circ\mathbf{f}}(x)$ is 1×2.

Answer for 4: b. Justification: The text states: "The *Chain Rule* gives a formula for the Jacobian of a composition. [...] Assume that **f** is continuously differentiable at $\mathbf{x}_0$, an interior point of D_1, and that **g** is continuously differentiable at $\mathbf{f}(\mathbf{x}_0)$, an interior point of D_2. Then
$$J_{\mathbf{g}\circ\mathbf{f}}(\mathbf{x}_0) = J_{\mathbf{g}}(\mathbf{f}(\mathbf{x}_0)) J_{\mathbf{f}}(\mathbf{x}_0)$$
as a product of matrices."

Answer for 5: c. Justification: The text states: "Let $A \in \mathbb{R}^{m \times d}$ and $\mathbf{b} = (b_1, \ldots, b_m) \in \mathbb{R}^m$. Define the vector-valued function $\mathbf{f} = (f_1, \ldots, f_m)\colon \mathbb{R}^d \to \mathbb{R}^m$ as $\mathbf{f}(\mathbf{x}) = A\mathbf{x} + \mathbf{b}$. [...] So $J_{\mathbf{f}}(\mathbf{x}) = A$."

8.3 Building Blocks of AI 1: Backpropagation

We develop the basic mathematical foundations of automatic differentiation. We restrict ourselves to a special setting: multilayer progressive functions. Many important classifiers take the form of a sequence of compositions where parameters are specific to each layer of composition. We show how to systematically apply the *Chain Rule* to such functions. We also give a few examples.

8.3.1 Forward vs. Backward

We begin with a fixed-parameter example to illustrate the issues. Suppose $f\colon \mathbb{R}^d \to \mathbb{R}$ can be expressed as a composition of $L+1$ vector-valued functions $\mathbf{g}_i\colon \mathbb{R}^{n_i} \to \mathbb{R}^{n_{i+1}}$ and a real-valued function $\ell\colon \mathbb{R}^{n_{L+1}} \to \mathbb{R}$ as follows:

$$f(\mathbf{x}) = \ell \circ \mathbf{g}_L \circ \mathbf{g}_{L-1} \circ \cdots \circ \mathbf{g}_1 \circ \mathbf{g}_0(\mathbf{x}) = \ell(\mathbf{g}_L(\mathbf{g}_{L-1}(\cdots \mathbf{g}_1(\mathbf{g}_0(\mathbf{x}))\cdots))).$$

Here $n_0 = d$ is the input dimension. We also let $n_{L+1} = K$ be the output dimension. Think of

$$h(\mathbf{x}) = \mathbf{g}_L(\mathbf{g}_{L-1}(\cdots \mathbf{g}_1(\mathbf{g}_0(\mathbf{x}))\cdots))$$

as a prediction function (i.e., a regression or classification function) and think of ℓ as a loss function.

Observe first that the function f itself is straightforward to compute recursively *starting from the inside* as follows:

$$\mathbf{z}_0 := \mathbf{x}$$
$$\mathbf{z}_1 := \mathbf{g}_0(\mathbf{z}_0)$$
$$\mathbf{z}_2 := \mathbf{g}_1(\mathbf{z}_1)$$
$$\vdots$$
$$\mathbf{z}_L := \mathbf{g}_{L-1}(\mathbf{z}_{L-1})$$
$$\hat{\mathbf{y}} := \mathbf{z}_{L+1} := \mathbf{g}_L(\mathbf{z}_L)$$
$$f(\mathbf{x}) := \ell(\hat{\mathbf{y}}).$$

Anticipating the setting of neural networks, our main application of interest, we refer to $\mathbf{z}_0 = \mathbf{x}$ as the "input layer," $\hat{\mathbf{y}} = \mathbf{z}_{L+1} = \mathbf{g}_L(\mathbf{z}_L)$ as the "output layer," and $\mathbf{z}_1 = \mathbf{g}_0(\mathbf{z}_0), \ldots, \mathbf{z}_L = \mathbf{g}_{L-1}(\mathbf{z}_{L-1})$ as the "hidden layers." In particular, L is the number of hidden layers.

Example 8.3.1 *We will use the following running example throughout this subsection. We assume that each $\mathbf{g}_i$ is a linear map; that is, $\mathbf{g}_i(\mathbf{z}_i) = \mathcal{W}_i \mathbf{z}_i$ where $\mathcal{W}_i \in \mathbb{R}^{n_{i+1} \times n_i}$ is a fixed, known matrix. Assume also that $\ell\colon \mathbb{R}^K \to \mathbb{R}$ is defined as*

$$\ell(\hat{\mathbf{y}}) = \frac{1}{2}\|\mathbf{y} - \hat{\mathbf{y}}\|^2,$$

for a fixed, known vector $\mathbf{y} \in \mathbb{R}^K$.

Computing f recursively starting from the inside *as above gives here*

$$\mathbf{z}_0 := \mathbf{x}$$
$$\mathbf{z}_1 := \mathcal{W}_0 \mathbf{z}_0 = \mathcal{W}_0 \mathbf{x}$$

8.3 Building Blocks of AI 1: Backpropagation

$$\mathbf{z}_2 := \mathcal{W}_1 \mathbf{z}_1 = \mathcal{W}_1 \mathcal{W}_0 \mathbf{x}$$

$$\vdots$$

$$\mathbf{z}_L := \mathcal{W}_{L-1} \mathbf{z}_{L-1} = \mathcal{W}_{L-1} \cdots \mathcal{W}_1 \mathcal{W}_0 \mathbf{x}$$

$$\hat{\mathbf{y}} := \mathbf{z}_{L+1} := \mathcal{W}_L \mathbf{z}_L = \mathcal{W}_L \mathcal{W}_{L-1} \cdots \mathcal{W}_1 \mathcal{W}_0 \mathbf{x}$$

$$f(\mathbf{x}) := \ell(\hat{\mathbf{y}}) = \frac{1}{2} \|\mathbf{y} - \hat{\mathbf{y}}\|^2 = \frac{1}{2} \|\mathbf{y} - \mathcal{W}_L \mathcal{W}_{L-1} \cdots \mathcal{W}_1 \mathcal{W}_0 \mathbf{x}\|^2.$$

In essence, we are comparing an observed outcome $\mathbf{y}$ *to a prediction* $\mathcal{W}_L \mathcal{W}_{L-1} \cdots \mathcal{W}_1 \mathcal{W}_0 \mathbf{x}$ *based on input* $\mathbf{x}$.

In this section, we look into computing the gradient with respect to $\mathbf{x}$. *(In reality, we will be more interested in taking the gradient with respect to the parameters, i.e., the entries of the matrices* $\mathcal{W}_0, \ldots, \mathcal{W}_L$, *a task to which we will come back later in this section. We will also be interested in more complex – in particular, nonlinear – prediction functions.)*

NUMERICAL CORNER To make things more concrete, we consider a specific example. We will use torch.linalg.vector_norm to compute the Euclidean norm in PyTorch. Suppose $d = 3$, $L = 1$, $n_1 = 2$, and $K = 2$ with the following choices:

```
x = torch.tensor([1.,0.,-1.], requires_grad=True)
y = torch.tensor([0.,1.])
W0 = torch.tensor([[0.,1.,-1.],[2.,0.,1.]])
W1 = torch.tensor([[-1.,0.],[2.,-1.]])

z0 = x
z1 = W0 @ z0
z2 = W1 @ z1
f = 0.5 * (torch.linalg.vector_norm(y-z2) ** 2)

print(z0)
```

tensor([1., 0., -1.], requires_grad=True)

```
print(z1)
```

tensor([1., 1.], grad_fn=<MvBackward0>)

```
print(z2)
```

tensor([-1., 1.], grad_fn=<MvBackward0>)

```
print(f)
```

tensor(0.5000, grad_fn=<MulBackward0>)

◁ **NC**

8.3.1.1 Forward Mode

We are ready to apply the *Chain Rule*:

$$\nabla f(\mathbf{x})^T = J_f(\mathbf{x}) = J_\ell(\mathbf{z}_{L+1}) J_{\mathbf{g}_L}(\mathbf{z}_L) J_{\mathbf{g}_{L-1}}(\mathbf{z}_{L-1}) \cdots J_{\mathbf{g}_1}(\mathbf{z}_1) J_{\mathbf{g}_0}(\mathbf{x})$$

where the $\mathbf{z}_i$'s are as above and we used the fact that $\mathbf{z}_0 = \mathbf{x}$. The matrix product here is well-defined. Indeed, the size of $J_{\mathbf{g}_i}(\mathbf{z}_i)$ is $n_{i+1} \times n_i$ (i.e., number of outputs by number of inputs) while the size of $J_{\mathbf{g}_{i-1}}(\mathbf{z}_{i-1})$ is $n_i \times n_{i-1}$ – so the dimensions are compatible.

So it is straightforward to compute $\nabla f(\mathbf{x})^T$ recursively as we did for f itself. In fact, we can compute both simultaneously. This is called the forward mode:

$$\begin{aligned}
\mathbf{z}_0 &:= \mathbf{x} \\
\mathbf{z}_1 &:= \mathbf{g}_0(\mathbf{z}_0), \quad F_0 := J_{\mathbf{g}_0}(\mathbf{z}_0) \\
\mathbf{z}_2 &:= \mathbf{g}_1(\mathbf{z}_1), \quad F_1 := J_{\mathbf{g}_1}(\mathbf{z}_1) F_0 \\
&\vdots \\
\mathbf{z}_L &:= \mathbf{g}_{L-1}(\mathbf{z}_{L-1}), \quad F_{L-1} := J_{\mathbf{g}_{L-1}}(\mathbf{z}_{L-1}) F_{L-2} \\
\hat{\mathbf{y}} := \mathbf{z}_{L+1} &:= \mathbf{g}_L(\mathbf{z}_L), \quad F_L := J_{\mathbf{g}_L}(\mathbf{z}_L) F_{L-1} \\
f(\mathbf{x}) &:= \ell(\hat{\mathbf{y}}), \quad \nabla f(\mathbf{x})^T := J_\ell(\hat{\mathbf{y}}) F_L.
\end{aligned}$$

Example 8.3.2 *(continued)* *We apply this procedure to the running example. The Jacobian of the linear map* $\mathbf{g}_i(\mathbf{z}_i) = \mathcal{W}_i \mathbf{z}_i$ *is the matrix* $\mathcal{W}_i$, *as we have seen in Example 8.2.13. That is,* $J_{\mathbf{g}_i}(\mathbf{z}_i) = \mathcal{W}_i$ *for any* $\mathbf{z}_i$. *To compute the Jacobian of* ℓ, *we rewrite it as a quadratic function,*

$$\begin{aligned}
\ell(\hat{\mathbf{y}}) &= \frac{1}{2} \|\mathbf{y} - \hat{\mathbf{y}}\|^2 \\
&= \frac{1}{2} \mathbf{y}^T \mathbf{y} - \frac{1}{2} 2 \mathbf{y}^T \hat{\mathbf{y}} + \frac{1}{2} \hat{\mathbf{y}}^T \hat{\mathbf{y}} \\
&= \frac{1}{2} \hat{\mathbf{y}}^T I_{n_{L+1} \times n_{L+1}} \hat{\mathbf{y}} + (-\mathbf{y})^T \hat{\mathbf{y}} + \frac{1}{2} \mathbf{y}^T \mathbf{y}.
\end{aligned}$$

From Example 3.2.3,

$$J_\ell(\hat{\mathbf{y}})^T = \nabla \ell(\hat{\mathbf{y}}) = \frac{1}{2} \left[I_{n_{L+1} \times n_{L+1}} + I_{n_{L+1} \times n_{L+1}}^T \right] \hat{\mathbf{y}} + (-\mathbf{y}) = \hat{\mathbf{y}} - \mathbf{y}.$$

Putting it all together, we get

$$\begin{aligned}
F_0 &:= J_{\mathbf{g}_0}(\mathbf{z}_0) = \mathcal{W}_0 \\
F_1 &:= J_{\mathbf{g}_1}(\mathbf{z}_1) F_0 = \mathcal{W}_1 F_0 = \mathcal{W}_1 \mathcal{W}_0 \\
&\vdots \\
F_{L-1} &:= J_{\mathbf{g}_{L-1}}(\mathbf{z}_{L-1}) F_{L-2} = \mathcal{W}_{L-1} F_{L-2} = \mathcal{W}_{L-1} \cdots \mathcal{W}_1 \mathcal{W}_0 \\
F_L &:= J_{\mathbf{g}_L}(\mathbf{z}_L) F_{L-1} = \mathcal{W}_L F_{L-1} = \mathcal{W}_L \mathcal{W}_{L-1} \cdots \mathcal{W}_1 \mathcal{W}_0 \\
\nabla f(\mathbf{x})^T &:= J_\ell(\hat{\mathbf{y}}) F_L = (\hat{\mathbf{y}} - \mathbf{y})^T F_L = (\hat{\mathbf{y}} - \mathbf{y})^T \mathcal{W}_L \mathcal{W}_{L-1} \cdots \mathcal{W}_1 \mathcal{W}_0 \\
&= (\mathcal{W}_L \mathcal{W}_{L-1} \cdots \mathcal{W}_1 \mathcal{W}_0 \mathbf{x} - \mathbf{y})^T \mathcal{W}_L \mathcal{W}_{L-1} \cdots \mathcal{W}_1 \mathcal{W}_0.
\end{aligned}$$

NUMERICAL CORNER We return to our concrete example.

```
with torch.no_grad():
    F0 = W0
```

```
    F1 = W1 @ F0
    grad_f = (z2 - y).T @ F1
```

```
print(F0)
```

```
tensor([[ 0.,  1., -1.],
        [ 2.,  0.,  1.]])
```

```
print(F1)
```

```
tensor([[ 0., -1.,  1.],
        [-2.,  2., -3.]])
```

```
print(grad_f)
```

```
tensor([ 0.,  1., -1.])
```

We can check that we get the same outcome using AD.

```
f.backward()
print(x.grad)
```

```
tensor([ 0.,  1., -1.])
```

◁ **NC**

8.3.1.2 Reverse Mode

What we just described corresponds to performing the matrix products in the *Chain Rule* formula,

$$\nabla f(\mathbf{x})^T = J_f(\mathbf{x}) = J_\ell(\hat{\mathbf{y}}) J_{\mathbf{g}_L}(\mathbf{z}_L) J_{\mathbf{g}_{L-1}}(\mathbf{z}_{L-1}) \cdots J_{\mathbf{g}_1}(\mathbf{z}_1) J_{\mathbf{g}_0}(\mathbf{x}),$$

from right to left. But there is another way to do this – from left to right! This is called reverse mode. First we compute f recursively as we did previously, in particular we compute the $\mathbf{z}_i$'s, then going backward we compute

$$G_{L+1} := J_\ell(\hat{\mathbf{y}})$$
$$G_L := G_{L+1} J_{\mathbf{g}_L}(\mathbf{z}_L)$$
$$\vdots$$
$$G_1 := G_2 J_{\mathbf{g}_1}(\mathbf{z}_1)$$
$$\nabla f(\mathbf{x})^T := G_1 J_{\mathbf{g}_0}(\mathbf{z}_0)$$

This may seem like a rather minor modification to our previous algorithm. It is not – it is much faster! To see this, we need to count the number of elementary operations involved in implementing each mode.

First a simple calcultion: How many elementary operations (i.e., additions and multiplications) does it take to multiply an $n \times m$ matrix $A = (a_{ij})_{i,j}$ and an $m \times \ell$ matrix $B = (b_{ij})_{i,j}$? Let's ask ChatGPT. Here's the answer:

"To calculate the number of elementary operations required to multiply an $n \times m$ matrix by an $m \times \ell$ matrix, consider the computation involved for each element of the resulting $n \times \ell$ matrix.

Each element of the resulting matrix is the dot product of a row from the first matrix and a column from the second matrix. If the first matrix is denoted as A and the second matrix as B, then the element at position i, j in the resulting matrix C is calculated as

$$c_{ij} = a_{i1}b_{1j} + a_{i2}b_{2j} + \ldots + a_{im}b_{mj}.$$

This computation involves m multiplications and $m-1$ additions, making a total of $m+(m-1) = 2m - 1$ elementary operations for each element.

Since matrix C has $n \times \ell$ elements, the total number of elementary operations required for the entire matrix C is

$$(n\ell)(2m - 1) = 2nm\ell - n\ell.$$

Thus, multiplying an $n \times m$ matrix by an $m \times \ell$ matrix takes $2nm\ell - n\ell$ elementary operations."

Returning to computing the gradient, we count the number of elementary operations needed for each mode. To simplify the calculation, we assume that $n_0 = d$, $n_1 = n_2 = \cdots = n_L = m$, and $n_{L+1} = K$.

Forward: The matrix $F_0 = J_{\mathbf{g}_0}(\mathbf{z}_0)$ has dimensions $m \times d$. The matrix F_1, as a product of $J_{\mathbf{g}_1}(\mathbf{z}_1) \in \mathbb{R}^{m \times m}$ and $F_0 \in \mathbb{R}^{m \times d}$, has dimensions $m \times d$; it therefore takes $m(2m - 1)d$ operations to compute. The same holds for $F_2, \ldots, F_{L-1}$ (check it!). By similar considerations, the matrix F_L has dimensions $K \times d$ and takes $K(2m - 1)d$ operations to compute. Finally, $\nabla f(\mathbf{x})^T = J_\ell(\mathbf{z}_{L+1})F_L \in \mathbb{R}^{1 \times d}$ and takes $(2K - 1)d$ operations to compute. Overall the number of operations is

$$(L - 1)m(2m - 1)d + K(2m - 1)d + (2K - 1)d.$$

This is approximately $2Lm^2 d$ if we think of K as a small constant and ignore the smaller-order terms.

Reverse: The matrix $G_{L+1} = J_\ell(\mathbf{z}_{L+1})$ has dimensions $1 \times K$. The matrix G_L, as a product of $G_{L+1} \in \mathbb{R}^{1 \times K}$ and $J_{\mathbf{g}_L}(\mathbf{z}_L) \in \mathbb{R}^{K \times m}$, has dimensions $1 \times m$; it therefore takes $(2K - 1)m$ operations to compute. The matrix G_{L-1}, as a product of $G_L \in \mathbb{R}^{1 \times m}$ and $J_{\mathbf{g}_{L-1}}(\mathbf{z}_{L-1}) \in \mathbb{R}^{m \times m}$, has dimensions $1 \times m$; it therefore takes $(2m - 1)m$ operations to compute. The same holds for $G_{L-2}, \ldots, G_1$ (check it!). By similar considerations, $\nabla f(\mathbf{x})^T = G_1 J_{\mathbf{g}_0}(\mathbf{z}_0) \in \mathbb{R}^{1 \times d}$ and takes $(2m - 1)d$ operations to compute. Overall the number of operations is

$$(2K - 1)m + (L - 1)(2m - 1)m + (2m - 1)d.$$

This is approximately $2Lm^2 + 2md$ – which can be much smaller than $2Lm^2 d$! In other words, the reverse mode approach can be much faster. Note in particular that all computations in the reverse mode are matrix–vector products (or more precisely row vector–matrix products) rather than matrix–matrix products.

Example 8.3.3 *(continued) We apply the reverse mode approach to our previous example. We get*

$$G_{L+1} := J_\ell(\hat{\mathbf{y}}) = (\hat{\mathbf{y}} - \mathbf{y})^T$$
$$G_L := G_{L+1} J_{g_L}(\mathbf{z}_L) = G_{L+1} \mathcal{W}_L = (\hat{\mathbf{y}} - \mathbf{y})^T \mathcal{W}_L$$
$$\vdots$$
$$G_1 := G_2 J_{\mathbf{g}_1}(\mathbf{z}_1) = G_2 \mathcal{W}_1 = [(\hat{\mathbf{y}} - \mathbf{y})^T \mathcal{W}_L \cdots \mathcal{W}_2] \mathcal{W}_1$$
$$\nabla f(\mathbf{x})^T := G_1 J_{\mathbf{g}_0}(\mathbf{z}_0) = [(\hat{\mathbf{y}} - \mathbf{y})^T \mathcal{W}_L \cdots \mathcal{W}_2 \mathcal{W}_1] \mathcal{W}_0$$
$$= (\mathcal{W}_L \mathcal{W}_{L-1} \cdots \mathcal{W}_1 \mathcal{W}_0 \mathbf{x} - \mathbf{y})^T \mathcal{W}_L \mathcal{W}_{L-1} \cdots \mathcal{W}_1 \mathcal{W}_0,$$

which matches our previous calculation. Note that all computations involve multiplying a row vector by a matrix.

NUMERICAL CORNER We try our specific example.

```
with torch.no_grad():
    G2 = (z2 - y).T
    G1 = G2 @ W1
    grad_f = G1 @ W0

print(G2)
```

```
tensor([-1., 0.])
```

```
print(G1)
```

```
tensor([1., 0.])
```

```
print(grad_f)
```

```
tensor([ 0., 1., -1.])
```

We indeed obtain the same answer yet again.

◁ **NC**

To provide a little more insight in the savings obtained through the reverse mode, consider the following simple calculations. Let $A, B \in \mathbb{R}^{n \times n}$ and $\mathbf{v} \in \mathbb{R}^n$. Suppose we seek to compute $\mathbf{v}^T B A$. By associativity of matrix multiplication, there are two ways of doing this: Compute $\mathbf{v}^T(BA)$ (i.e., first compute BA then multiply by $\mathbf{v}^T$) or compute $(\mathbf{v}^T B) A$. The first approach requires $n^2(2n - 1) + n(2n - 1)$ operations, while the second only requires $2n(2n - 1)$. The latter is much smaller since $2n^3$ (the leading term in the first approach) grows much faster than $4n^2$ (the leading term in the second approach) when n is large.

Why is this happening? One way to understand this is to think of the output $\mathbf{v}^T B A$ as a *linear combination of the rows of A* – a very specific linear combination, in fact. In the first approach, we compute BA which gives us n different linear combinations of the rows of A – none being the one we want – and then we compute the desired linear combination by multiplying by $\mathbf{v}^T$. This is wasteful. In the second approach, we immediately compute the coefficients of the specific linear combination we seek – $\mathbf{v}^T B$ – and then we compute that linear combination by multiplying to the right by A.

While the setting we examined in this subsection is illuminating, it is not exactly what we want. In the machine learning context, each "layer" $\mathbf{g}_i$ has parameters (in our running example, these were the entries of $\mathcal{W}_i$) and we seek to optimize with respect to those parameters. For this, we need the gradient with respect to the parameters, not the input $\mathbf{x}$. In the next subsection, we consider a generalization of the current setting, progressive functions, which will allow us to do this. The notation gets more complicated, but the basic idea remains the same.

8.3.2 Progressive Functions

As mentioned previously, while it may seem natural to define a prediction function h (e.g., a classifier) as a function of the input data $\mathbf{x} \in \mathbb{R}^d$, when fitting data we are ultimately interested in thinking of h as a function of the parameters $\mathbf{w} \in \mathbb{R}^r$ that need to be adjusted – over a fixed dataset. Hence, in this section, the input $\mathbf{x}$ is fixed while the vector of parameters $\mathbf{w}$ is now variable.

8.3.2.1 A First Example

We use the example from the previous subsection to illustrate the main ideas. That is, suppose $d = 3, L = 1, n_1 = 2$, and $K = 2$. Fix a data sample $\mathbf{x} = (x_1, x_2, x_3) \in \mathbb{R}^3, \mathbf{y} = (y_1, y_2) \in \mathbb{R}^2$. For $i = 0, 1$, we use the notation

$$\mathcal{W}_0 = \begin{pmatrix} w_0 & w_1 & w_2 \\ w_3 & w_4 & w_5 \end{pmatrix} \quad \text{and} \quad \mathcal{W}_1 = \begin{pmatrix} w_6 & w_7 \\ w_8 & w_9 \end{pmatrix}.$$

and let

$$\ell(\hat{\mathbf{y}}) = \frac{1}{2}\|\mathbf{y} - \hat{\mathbf{y}}\|^2 = \frac{1}{2}(y_1 - \hat{y}_1)^2 + \frac{1}{2}(y_2 - \hat{y}_2)^2.$$

We change the notation for the "layer" function $\mathbf{g}_i$ to reflect the fact that it is now a function of two (concatenated) vectors: the input $\mathbf{z}_i = (z_{i,1}, \ldots, z_{i,n_i})$ from the previous layer and a layer-specific set of parameters $\mathbf{w}_i$. That is,

$$\mathbf{g}_i(\mathbf{z}_i, \mathbf{w}_i) = \mathcal{W}_i \mathbf{z}_i = \begin{pmatrix} (\mathbf{w}_i^{(1)})^T \\ (\mathbf{w}_i^{(2)})^T \end{pmatrix} \mathbf{z}_i$$

with $\mathbf{w}_i = (\mathbf{w}_i^{(1)}, \mathbf{w}_i^{(2)})$, the concatenation of the rows of $\mathcal{W}_i$ (as column vectors). A different way to put this is that

$$\mathbf{w}_i = \text{vec}(\mathcal{W}_i^T),$$

where we took the transpose to turn the rows into columns. More specifically,

$$\mathbf{g}_0(\mathbf{z}_0, \mathbf{w}_0) = \mathcal{W}_0 \mathbf{z}_0 \quad \text{with} \quad \mathbf{w}_0 = (w_0, w_1, w_2, w_3, w_4, w_5)$$

(i.e., $\mathbf{w}_0^{(1)} = (w_0, w_1, w_2)$ and $\mathbf{w}_0^{(2)} = (w_3, w_4, w_5)$) and

$$\mathbf{g}_1(\mathbf{z}_1, \mathbf{w}_1) = \mathcal{W}_1 \mathbf{z}_1 \quad \text{with} \quad \mathbf{w}_1 = (w_6, w_7, w_8, w_9)$$

(i.e., $\mathbf{w}_1^{(1)} = (w_6, w_7)$ and $\mathbf{w}_1^{(2)} = (w_8, w_9)$).

8.3 Building Blocks of AI 1: Backpropagation

We seek to compute the gradient of

$$f(\mathbf{w}) = \ell(\mathbf{g}_1(\mathbf{g}_0(\mathbf{x}, \mathbf{w}_0), \mathbf{w}_1))$$
$$= \frac{1}{2}\|\mathbf{y} - \mathcal{W}_1\mathcal{W}_0\mathbf{x}\|^2$$
$$= \frac{1}{2}(y_1 - w_6(w_0x_1 + w_1x_2 + w_2x_3) - w_7(w_3x_1 + w_4x_2 + w_5x_3))^2$$
$$+ \frac{1}{2}(y_2 - w_8(w_0x_1 + w_1x_2 + w_2x_3) - w_9(w_3x_1 + w_4x_2 + w_5x_3))^2$$

by applying the *Chain Rule* backward, as we justified in the previous subsection – but this time we take the gradient with respect to the parameters

$$\mathbf{w} := (\mathbf{w}_0, \mathbf{w}_1) = (w_0, w_1, \ldots, w_9).$$

Notice a key change in the notation: We now accordingly think of f *as a function of* $\mathbf{w}$; the role of $\mathbf{x}$ is implicit.

On the other hand, it may seem counterintuitive that we now think of $\mathbf{g}_i$ as a function of *both* its own parameters and its inputs from the previous layer when we just stated that we only care about the gradient with respect to the former. But, as we will see, it turns out that we need the Jacobians with respect to both, as the input from the previous layer *actually depends on the parameters of the previous layers*. For instance, $\mathbf{g}_1(\mathbf{z}_1, \mathbf{w}_1) = \mathcal{W}_1\mathbf{z}_1$ where $\mathbf{z}_1 = \mathbf{g}_0(\mathbf{z}_0, \mathbf{w}_0) = \mathcal{W}_0\mathbf{z}_0$.

Recall that we have already computed the requisite Jacobians $J_{\mathbf{g}_0}$ and $J_{\mathbf{g}_1}$ in a previous example. We have also computed the Jacobian J_ℓ of ℓ. At this point, it is tempting to apply the *Chain Rule* and deduce that the gradient of f is

$$J_\ell(\mathbf{g}_1(\mathbf{g}_0(\mathbf{x}, \mathbf{w}_0), \mathbf{w}_1)) J_{\mathbf{g}_1}(\mathbf{g}_0(\mathbf{x}, \mathbf{w}_0), \mathbf{w}_1) J_{\mathbf{g}_0}(\mathbf{x}, \mathbf{w}_0).$$

But this is not correct. For one, the dimensions do not match! For instance, $J_{\mathbf{g}_0} \in \mathbb{R}^{2\times 9}$ since $\mathbf{g}_0$ has 2 outputs and 9 inputs (i.e., $z_{0,1}, z_{0,2}, z_{0,3}, w_0, w_1, w_2, w_3, w_4, w_5$) while $J_{\mathbf{g}_1} \in \mathbb{R}^{2\times 6}$ since $\mathbf{g}_1$ has 2 outputs and 6 inputs (i.e., $z_{1,1}, z_{1,2}, w_6, w_7, w_8, w_9$). So what went wrong?

The function f is *not* in fact a straight composition of the functions ℓ, $\mathbf{g}_1$, and $\mathbf{g}_0$. Indeed the parameters to differentiate by are introduced progressively, each layer injecting its own additional parameters, which are not obtained from the previous layers. Hence we cannot write the gradient of f as a simple product the Jacobians, unlike what happened in Subsection 8.3.1.

But not all is lost. We show below that we can still apply the *Chain Rule* step-by-step in a way that accounts for the additional parameters on each layer. Taking a hint from Subsection 8.3.1, we proceed forward first to compute f and the Jacobians, and then go backward to compute the gradient ∇f. We use the notation $\mathbb{A}_n[\mathbf{x}]$ and $\mathbb{B}_n[\mathbf{z}]$ from Section 8.2.

In the forward phase, we compute f itself and the requisite Jacobians:

$$\mathbf{z}_0 := \mathbf{x}$$
$$= (x_1, x_2, x_3)$$
$$\mathbf{z}_1 := \mathbf{g}_0(\mathbf{z}_0, \mathbf{w}_0) = \mathcal{W}_0\mathbf{z}_0$$
$$= \begin{pmatrix}(\mathbf{w}_0^{(1)})^T\mathbf{x} \\ (\mathbf{w}_0^{(2)})^T\mathbf{x}\end{pmatrix} = \begin{pmatrix}w_0x_1 + w_1x_2 + w_2x_3 \\ w_3x_1 + w_4x_2 + w_5x_3\end{pmatrix}$$

$$J_{\mathbf{g}_0}(\mathbf{z}_0, \mathbf{w}_0) := \begin{pmatrix} \mathbb{A}_2[\mathbf{w}_0] & \mathbb{B}_2[\mathbf{z}_0] \end{pmatrix} = \begin{pmatrix} \mathcal{W}_0 & I_{2\times 2} \otimes \mathbf{z}_0^T \end{pmatrix}$$

$$= \begin{pmatrix} w_0 & w_1 & w_2 & x_1 & x_2 & x_3 & 0 & 0 & 0 \\ w_3 & w_4 & w_5 & 0 & 0 & 0 & x_1 & x_2 & x_3 \end{pmatrix}$$

$$\hat{\mathbf{y}} := \mathbf{z}_2 := \mathbf{g}_1(\mathbf{z}_1, \mathbf{w}_1) = \mathcal{W}_1 \mathbf{z}_1$$

$$= \begin{pmatrix} w_6 z_{1,1} + w_7 z_{1,2} \\ w_8 z_{1,1} + w_9 z_{1,2} \end{pmatrix}$$

$$= \begin{pmatrix} w_6 (\mathbf{w}_0^{(1)})^T \mathbf{x} + w_7 (\mathbf{w}_0^{(2)})^T \mathbf{x} \\ w_8 (\mathbf{w}_0^{(1)})^T \mathbf{x} + w_9 (\mathbf{w}_0^{(2)})^T \mathbf{x} \end{pmatrix}$$

$$= \begin{pmatrix} w_6(w_0 x_1 + w_1 x_2 + w_2 x_3) + w_7(w_3 x_1 + w_4 x_2 + w_5 x_3) \\ w_8(w_0 x_1 + w_1 x_2 + w_2 x_3) + w_9(w_3 x_1 + w_4 x_2 + w_5 x_3) \end{pmatrix}$$

$$J_{\mathbf{g}_1}(\mathbf{z}_1, \mathbf{w}_1) := \begin{pmatrix} \mathbb{A}_2[\mathbf{w}_1] & \mathbb{B}_2[\mathbf{z}_1] \end{pmatrix} = \begin{pmatrix} \mathcal{W}_1 & I_{2\times 2} \otimes \mathbf{z}_1^T \end{pmatrix}$$

$$= \begin{pmatrix} w_6 & w_7 & z_{1,1} & z_{1,2} & 0 & 0 \\ w_8 & w_9 & 0 & 0 & z_{1,1} & z_{1,2} \end{pmatrix}$$

$$= \begin{pmatrix} w_6 & w_7 & (\mathbf{w}_0^{(1)})^T \mathbf{x} & (\mathbf{w}_0^{(2)})^T \mathbf{x} & 0 & 0 \\ w_8 & w_9 & 0 & 0 & (\mathbf{w}_0^{(1)})^T \mathbf{x} & (\mathbf{w}_0^{(2)})^T \mathbf{x} \end{pmatrix}$$

$$f(\mathbf{x}) := \ell(\hat{\mathbf{y}}) = \frac{1}{2} \|\mathbf{y} - \hat{\mathbf{y}}\|^2$$

$$= \frac{1}{2} (y_1 - w_6(w_0 x_1 + w_1 x_2 + w_2 x_3) - w_7(w_3 x_1 + w_4 x_2 + w_5 x_3))^2$$

$$+ \frac{1}{2} (y_2 - w_8(w_0 x_1 + w_1 x_2 + w_2 x_3) - w_9(w_3 x_1 + w_4 x_2 + w_5 x_3))^2$$

$$J_\ell(\hat{\mathbf{y}}) = (\hat{\mathbf{y}} - \mathbf{y})^T$$

$$= \begin{pmatrix} w_6(\mathbf{w}_0^{(1)})^T \mathbf{x} + w_7(\mathbf{w}_0^{(2)})^T \mathbf{x} - y_1 & w_8(\mathbf{w}_0^{(1)})^T \mathbf{x} + w_9(\mathbf{w}_0^{(2)})^T \mathbf{x} - y_2 \end{pmatrix}.$$

We now compute the gradient of f with respect to $\mathbf{w}$. We start with $\mathbf{w}_1 = (w_6, w_7, w_8, w_9)$. For this step, we think of f as the composition $\ell(\mathbf{g}_1(\mathbf{z}_1, \mathbf{w}_1))$. Here $\mathbf{z}_1$ does not depend on $\mathbf{w}_1$ and therefore can be considered fixed for this calculation. By the *Chain Rule*

$$\frac{\partial f(\mathbf{w})}{\partial w_6} = \frac{\partial \ell(\mathbf{g}_1(\mathbf{z}_1, \mathbf{w}_1))}{\partial w_6} = \frac{\partial \ell(\hat{\mathbf{y}})}{\partial \hat{y}_1} \frac{\partial g_{1,1}(\mathbf{z}_1, \mathbf{w}_1)}{\partial w_6} + \frac{\partial \ell(\hat{\mathbf{y}})}{\partial \hat{y}_2} \frac{\partial g_{1,2}(\mathbf{z}_1, \mathbf{w}_1)}{\partial w_6} = (\hat{y}_1 - y_1) z_{1,1}$$

where we used the fact that $g_{1,2}(\mathbf{z}_1, \mathbf{w}_1) = w_8 z_{1,1} + w_9 z_{1,2}$ does not depend on w_6 and therefore $\frac{\partial g_{1,2}(\mathbf{z}_1, \mathbf{w}_1)}{\partial w_6} = 0$. Similarly

$$\frac{\partial f(\mathbf{w})}{\partial w_7} = \frac{\partial \ell(\mathbf{g}_1(\mathbf{z}_1, \mathbf{w}_1))}{\partial w_7} = \frac{\partial \ell(\hat{\mathbf{y}})}{\partial \hat{y}_1} \frac{\partial g_{1,1}(\mathbf{z}_1, \mathbf{w}_1)}{\partial w_7} + \frac{\partial \ell(\hat{\mathbf{y}})}{\partial \hat{y}_2} \frac{\partial g_{1,2}(\mathbf{z}_1, \mathbf{w}_1)}{\partial w_7} = (\hat{y}_1 - y_1) z_{1,2}$$

$$\frac{\partial f(\mathbf{w})}{\partial w_8} = \frac{\partial \ell(\mathbf{g}_1(\mathbf{z}_1, \mathbf{w}_1))}{\partial w_8} = \frac{\partial \ell(\hat{\mathbf{y}})}{\partial \hat{y}_1} \frac{\partial g_{1,1}(\mathbf{z}_1, \mathbf{w}_1)}{\partial w_8} + \frac{\partial \ell(\hat{\mathbf{y}})}{\partial \hat{y}_2} \frac{\partial g_{1,2}(\mathbf{z}_1, \mathbf{w}_1)}{\partial w_8} = (\hat{y}_2 - y_2) z_{1,1}$$

$$\frac{\partial f(\mathbf{w})}{\partial w_9} = \frac{\partial \ell(\mathbf{g}_1(\mathbf{z}_1, \mathbf{w}_1))}{\partial w_9} = \frac{\partial \ell(\hat{\mathbf{y}})}{\partial \hat{y}_1} \frac{\partial g_{1,1}(\mathbf{z}_1, \mathbf{w}_1)}{\partial w_9} + \frac{\partial \ell(\hat{\mathbf{y}})}{\partial \hat{y}_2} \frac{\partial g_{1,2}(\mathbf{z}_1, \mathbf{w}_1)}{\partial w_9} = (\hat{y}_2 - y_2) z_{1,2}.$$

In matrix form, this is

$$\begin{pmatrix} \frac{\partial f(\mathbf{w})}{\partial w_6} & \frac{\partial f(\mathbf{w})}{\partial w_7} & \frac{\partial f(\mathbf{w})}{\partial w_8} & \frac{\partial f(\mathbf{w})}{\partial w_9} \end{pmatrix}$$

$$= J_\ell(\hat{\mathbf{y}}) \, \mathbb{B}_2[\mathbf{z}_1]$$

$$= (\hat{\mathbf{y}} - \mathbf{y})^T (I_{2\times 2} \otimes \mathbf{z}_1^T)$$
$$= (\hat{\mathbf{y}} - \mathbf{y})^T \otimes \mathbf{z}_1^T$$
$$= \begin{pmatrix} (\hat{y}_1 - y_1)z_{1,1} & (\hat{y}_1 - y_1)z_{1,2} & (\hat{y}_2 - y_2)z_{1,1} & (\hat{y}_2 - y_2)z_{1,2} \end{pmatrix}$$

where we used *Properties of the Kronecker Product Lemma (f)* in the second to last line.

To compute the partial derivatives with respect to $\mathbf{w}_0 = (w_0, w_1, \ldots, w_5)$, we first need to compute partial derivatives with respect to $\mathbf{z}_1 = (z_{1,1}, z_{1,2})$ since f depends on $\mathbf{w}_0$ through it. For this calculation, we think again of f as the composition $\ell(\mathbf{g}_1(\mathbf{z}_1, \mathbf{w}_1))$, but this time our focus is on the variables $\mathbf{z}_1$. We obtain

$$\frac{\partial f(\mathbf{w})}{\partial z_{1,1}} = \frac{\partial \ell(\mathbf{g}_1(\mathbf{z}_1, \mathbf{w}_1))}{\partial z_{1,1}}$$
$$= \frac{\partial \ell(\hat{\mathbf{y}})}{\partial \hat{y}_1} \frac{\partial g_{1,1}(\mathbf{z}_1, \mathbf{w}_1)}{\partial z_{1,1}} + \frac{\partial \ell(\hat{\mathbf{y}})}{\partial \hat{y}_2} \frac{\partial g_{1,2}(\mathbf{z}_1, \mathbf{w}_1)}{\partial z_{1,1}}$$
$$= (\hat{y}_1 - y_1)w_6 + (\hat{y}_2 - y_2)w_8$$

and

$$\frac{\partial f(\mathbf{w})}{\partial z_{1,2}} = \frac{\partial \ell(\mathbf{g}_1(\mathbf{z}_1, \mathbf{w}_1))}{\partial z_{1,2}}$$
$$= \frac{\partial \ell(\hat{\mathbf{y}})}{\partial \hat{y}_1} \frac{\partial g_{1,1}(\mathbf{z}_1, \mathbf{w}_1)}{\partial z_{1,2}} + \frac{\partial \ell(\hat{\mathbf{y}})}{\partial \hat{y}_2} \frac{\partial g_{1,2}(\mathbf{z}_1, \mathbf{w}_1)}{\partial z_{1,2}}$$
$$= (\hat{y}_1 - y_1)w_7 + (\hat{y}_2 - y_2)w_9.$$

In matrix form, this is

$$\begin{pmatrix} \frac{\partial f(\mathbf{w})}{\partial z_{1,1}} & \frac{\partial f(\mathbf{w})}{\partial z_{1,2}} \end{pmatrix}$$
$$= J_\ell(\hat{\mathbf{y}}) \mathbb{A}_2[\mathbf{w}_1]$$
$$= (\hat{\mathbf{y}} - \mathbf{y})^T \mathcal{W}_1$$
$$= \begin{pmatrix} (\hat{y}_1 - y_1)w_6 + (\hat{y}_2 - y_2)w_8 & (\hat{y}_1 - y_1)w_7 + (\hat{y}_2 - y_2)w_9 \end{pmatrix}.$$

The vector $\left(\frac{\partial f(\mathbf{w})}{\partial z_{1,1}}, \frac{\partial f(\mathbf{w})}{\partial z_{1,2}} \right)$ is called an adjoint.

We now compute the gradient of f with respect to $\mathbf{w}_0 = (w_0, w_1, \ldots, w_5)$. For this step, we think of f as the composition of $\ell(\mathbf{g}_1(\mathbf{z}_1, \mathbf{w}_1))$ as a function of $\mathbf{z}_1$ and $\mathbf{g}_0(\mathbf{z}_0, \mathbf{w}_0)$ as a function of $\mathbf{w}_0$. Here $\mathbf{z}_0$ does not depend on $\mathbf{w}_0$ and therefore can be considered fixed for this calculation. By the *Chain Rule*

$$\frac{\partial f(\mathbf{w})}{\partial w_0} = \frac{\partial \ell(\mathbf{g}_1(\mathbf{g}_0(\mathbf{z}_0, \mathbf{w}_0), \mathbf{w}_1))}{\partial w_0}$$
$$= \frac{\partial \ell(\mathbf{g}_1(\mathbf{z}_1, \mathbf{w}_1))}{\partial z_{1,1}} \frac{\partial g_{0,1}(\mathbf{z}_0, \mathbf{w}_0)}{\partial w_0} + \frac{\partial \ell(\mathbf{g}_1(\mathbf{z}_1, \mathbf{w}_1))}{\partial z_{1,2}} \frac{\partial g_{0,2}(\mathbf{z}_0, \mathbf{w}_0)}{\partial w_0}$$
$$= ((\hat{y}_1 - y_1)w_6 + (\hat{y}_2 - y_2)w_8)z_{0,1}$$
$$= ((\hat{y}_1 - y_1)w_6 + (\hat{y}_2 - y_2)w_8)x_1,$$

where we used the fact that $g_{0,2}(\mathbf{z}_0, \mathbf{w}_0) = w_3 z_{0,1} + w_4 z_{0,2} + w_5 z_{0,3}$ does not depend on w_0 and therefore $\frac{\partial g_{0,2}(\mathbf{z}_0, \mathbf{w}_0)}{\partial w_0} = 0$.

Similarly (check it!)

$$\frac{\partial f(\mathbf{w})}{\partial w_1} = ((\hat{y}_1 - y_1)w_6 + (\hat{y}_2 - y_2)w_8)x_2$$

$$\frac{\partial f(\mathbf{w})}{\partial w_2} = ((\hat{y}_1 - y_1)w_6 + (\hat{y}_2 - y_2)w_8)x_3$$

$$\frac{\partial f(\mathbf{w})}{\partial w_3} = ((\hat{y}_1 - y_1)w_7 + (\hat{y}_2 - y_2)w_9)x_1$$

$$\frac{\partial f(\mathbf{w})}{\partial w_4} = ((\hat{y}_1 - y_1)w_7 + (\hat{y}_2 - y_2)w_9)x_2$$

$$\frac{\partial f(\mathbf{w})}{\partial w_5} = ((\hat{y}_1 - y_1)w_7 + (\hat{y}_2 - y_2)w_9)x_3.$$

In matrix form, this is

$$\begin{pmatrix} \frac{\partial f(\mathbf{w})}{\partial w_0} & \frac{\partial f(\mathbf{w})}{\partial w_1} & \frac{\partial f(\mathbf{w})}{\partial w_2} & \frac{\partial f(\mathbf{w})}{\partial w_3} & \frac{\partial f(\mathbf{w})}{\partial w_4} & \frac{\partial f(\mathbf{w})}{\partial w_5} \end{pmatrix}$$
$$= J_\ell(\hat{\mathbf{y}}) \, \mathbb{A}_2[\mathbf{w}_1] \, \mathbb{B}_2[\mathbf{z}_0]$$
$$= (\hat{\mathbf{y}} - \mathbf{y})^T \mathcal{W}_1 (I_{2 \times 2} \otimes \mathbf{z}_0^T)$$
$$= ((\hat{\mathbf{y}} - \mathbf{y})^T \mathcal{W}_1) \otimes \mathbf{x}^T$$
$$= \Big(((\hat{y}_1 - y_1)w_6 + (\hat{y}_2 - y_2)w_8)x_1 \quad \cdots \quad ((\hat{y}_1 - y_1)w_7 + (\hat{y}_2 - y_2)w_9)x_3 \Big)$$

where we used *Properties of the Kronecker Product Lemma (f)* in the second to last line.

To sum up,

$$\nabla f(\mathbf{w})^T = \Big((\hat{\mathbf{y}} - \mathbf{y})^T \otimes (\mathcal{W}_0 \mathbf{x})^T \quad ((\hat{\mathbf{y}} - \mathbf{y})^T \mathcal{W}_1) \otimes \mathbf{x}^T \Big).$$

NUMERICAL CORNER We return to the concrete example from the previous subsection. This time the matrices W0 and W1 require partial derivatives.

```
x = torch.tensor([1.,0.,-1.])
y = torch.tensor([0.,1.])
W0 = torch.tensor([[0.,1.,-1.],[2.,0.,1.]], requires_grad=True)
W1 = torch.tensor([[-1.,0.],[2.,-1.]], requires_grad=True)

z0 = x
z1 = W0 @ z0
z2 = W1 @ z1
f = 0.5 * (torch.linalg.vector_norm(y-z2) ** 2)

print(z0)
```

```
tensor([ 1.,  0., -1.])
```

```
print(z1)
```

```
tensor([1., 1.], grad_fn=<MvBackward0>)
```

```
print(z2)
```

```
tensor([-1.,  1.], grad_fn=<MvBackward0>)
```

```
print(f)
```

```
tensor(0.5000, grad_fn=<MulBackward0>)
```

We compute the gradient $\nabla f(\mathbf{w})$ using AD.

```
f.backward()
```

```
print(W0.grad)
```

```
tensor([[ 1.,  0., -1.],
        [ 0.,  0., -0.]])
```

```
print(W1.grad)
```

```
tensor([[-1., -1.],
        [-0., -0.]])
```

These are written in the form of matrix derivatives

$$\frac{\partial f}{\partial \mathcal{W}_0} = \begin{pmatrix} \frac{\partial f}{\partial w_0} & \frac{\partial f}{\partial w_1} & \frac{\partial f}{\partial w_2} \\ \frac{\partial f}{\partial w_3} & \frac{\partial f}{\partial w_4} & \frac{\partial f}{\partial w_5} \end{pmatrix} \quad \text{and} \quad \frac{\partial f}{\partial \mathcal{W}_1} = \begin{pmatrix} \frac{\partial f}{\partial w_6} & \frac{\partial f}{\partial w_7} \\ \frac{\partial f}{\partial w_8} & \frac{\partial f}{\partial w_9} \end{pmatrix}.$$

We use our formulas to confirm that they match these results. We need the Kronecker product, which in PyTorch is implemented as `torch.kron`.

```
with torch.no_grad():
    grad_W0 = torch.kron((z2 - y).T @ W1, z0.T)
    grad_W1 = torch.kron((z2 - y).T, z1.T)
```

```
print(grad_W0)
```

```
tensor([ 1.,  0., -1.,  0.,  0., -0.])
```

```
print(grad_W1)
```

```
tensor([-1., -1.,  0.,  0.])
```

Observe that this time these results are expressed in vectorized form (i.e., obtained by concatenating the rows). But they do match with the AD output.

◁ **NC**

8.3.2.2 General Setting

More generally, we have $L + 2$ layers. The input layer is $\mathbf{z}_0 := \mathbf{x}$, which we refer to as layer 0. Hidden layer i, $i = 1, \ldots, L$, is defined by a continuously differentiable function $\mathbf{z}_i := \mathbf{g}_{i-1}(\mathbf{z}_{i-1}, \mathbf{w}_{i-1})$ which this time takes *two vector-valued inputs*: a vector $\mathbf{z}_{i-1} \in \mathbb{R}^{n_{i-1}}$ fed from the $(i-1)$-st layer and a vector $\mathbf{w}_{i-1} \in \mathbb{R}^{r_{i-1}}$ of parameters specific to the i-th layer, so that

$$\mathbf{g}_{i-1} = (g_{i-1,1}, \ldots, g_{i-1,n_i}) \colon \mathbb{R}^{n_{i-1}+r_{i-1}} \to \mathbb{R}^{n_i}.$$

The output $\mathbf{z}_i$ of $\mathbf{g}_{i-1}$ is a vector in $\mathbb{R}^{n_i}$ which is passed to the $(i+1)$-st layer as input. The output layer is $\mathbf{z}_{L+1} := \mathbf{g}_L(\mathbf{z}_L, \mathbf{w}_L)$, which we also refer to as layer $L + 1$.

For $i = 1, \ldots, L + 1$, let

$$\overline{\mathbf{w}}^{i-1} = (\mathbf{w}_0, \mathbf{w}_1, \ldots, \mathbf{w}_{i-1}) \in \mathbb{R}^{r_0 + r_1 + \cdots + r_{i-1}}$$

be the concatenation of the parameters from the first i layers (not including the input layer, which does not have parameters) as a vector in $\mathbb{R}^{r_0+r_1+\cdots+r_{i-1}}$. Then the output of layer i as a *function of the parameters* is the composition

$$\begin{aligned}\mathcal{O}_{i-1}(\overline{\mathbf{w}}^{i-1}) &= \mathbf{g}_{i-1}(\mathcal{O}_{i-2}(\overline{\mathbf{w}}^{i-2}), \mathbf{w}_{i-1}) \\ &= \mathbf{g}_{i-1}(\mathbf{g}_{i-2}(\cdots \mathbf{g}_1(\mathbf{g}_0(\mathbf{x}, \mathbf{w}_0), \mathbf{w}_1), \cdots, \mathbf{w}_{i-2}), \mathbf{w}_{i-1}) \in \mathbb{R}^{n_i},\end{aligned}$$

for $i = 2, \ldots, L + 1$. When $i = 1$, we have simply

$$\mathcal{O}_0(\overline{\mathbf{w}}^0) = \mathbf{g}_0(\mathbf{x}, \mathbf{w}_0).$$

Observe that the function $\mathcal{O}_{i-1}$ depends implicitly on the input $\mathbf{x}$ – which we do *not* think of as a variable in this setting. To simplify the notation, we do not make the dependence on $\mathbf{x}$ explicit.

Letting $\mathbf{w} := \overline{\mathbf{w}}^L$, the final output is

$$\mathbf{h}(\mathbf{w}) = \mathcal{O}_L(\overline{\mathbf{w}}^L).$$

Expanding out the composition, this can be written alternatively as

$$\mathbf{h}(\mathbf{w}) = \mathbf{g}_L(\mathbf{g}_{L-1}(\cdots \mathbf{g}_1(\mathbf{g}_0(\mathbf{x}, \mathbf{w}_0), \mathbf{w}_1), \cdots, \mathbf{w}_{L-1}), \mathbf{w}_L).$$

Again, we do not make the dependence on $\mathbf{x}$ explicit.

As a final step, we have a loss function $\ell \colon \mathbb{R}^{n_{L+1}} \to \mathbb{R}$ which takes as input the output of the last layer and measures the fit to the given label $\mathbf{y} \in \Delta_K$. We will see some example below. The final function is then

$$f(\mathbf{w}) = \ell(\mathbf{h}(\mathbf{w})) \in \mathbb{R}.$$

We seek to compute the gradient of $f(\mathbf{w})$ with respect to the parameters $\mathbf{w}$ in order to apply a gradient descent method.

Example 8.3.4 *(continued)* *We return to the running example from Subsection 8.3.1. That is,* $\mathbf{g}_i(\mathbf{z}_i, \mathbf{w}_i) = \mathcal{W}_i \mathbf{z}_i$ *where the entries of* $\mathcal{W}_i \in \mathbb{R}^{n_{i+1} \times n_i}$ *are considered parameters and we let* $\mathbf{w}_i = \text{vec}(\mathcal{W}_i^T)$. *Assume also that* $\ell \colon \mathbb{R}^K \to \mathbb{R}$ *is defined as*

$$\ell(\hat{\mathbf{y}}) = \frac{1}{2}\|\mathbf{y} - \hat{\mathbf{y}}\|^2,$$

for a fixed, known vector $\mathbf{y} \in \mathbb{R}^K$.

Computing f recursively gives

$$\mathbf{z}_0 := \mathbf{x}$$
$$\mathbf{z}_1 := \mathcal{O}_0(\overline{\mathbf{w}}^0) = \mathbf{g}_0(\mathbf{z}_0, \mathbf{w}_0) = \mathcal{W}_0 \mathbf{z}_0 = \mathcal{W}_0 \mathbf{x}$$
$$\mathbf{z}_2 := \mathcal{O}_1(\overline{\mathbf{w}}^1) = \mathbf{g}_1(\mathbf{z}_1, \mathbf{w}_1) = \mathcal{W}_1 \mathbf{z}_1 = \mathcal{W}_1 \mathcal{W}_0 \mathbf{x}$$
$$\vdots$$
$$\mathbf{z}_L := \mathcal{O}_{L-1}(\overline{\mathbf{w}}^{L-1}) = \mathbf{g}_{L-1}(\mathbf{z}_{L-1}, \mathbf{w}_{L-1}) = \mathcal{W}_{L-1} \mathbf{z}_{L-1} = \mathcal{W}_{L-1} \cdots \mathcal{W}_1 \mathcal{W}_0 \mathbf{x}$$
$$\hat{\mathbf{y}} := \mathbf{z}_{L+1} := \mathcal{O}_L(\overline{\mathbf{w}}^L) = \mathbf{g}_L(\mathbf{z}_L, \mathbf{w}_L) = \mathcal{W}_L \mathbf{z}_L = \mathcal{W}_L \mathcal{W}_{L-1} \cdots \mathcal{W}_1 \mathcal{W}_0 \mathbf{x}$$
$$f(\mathbf{x}) := \ell(\hat{\mathbf{y}}) = \frac{1}{2}\|\mathbf{y} - \hat{\mathbf{y}}\|^2 = \frac{1}{2}\|\mathbf{y} - \mathcal{W}_L \mathcal{W}_{L-1} \cdots \mathcal{W}_1 \mathcal{W}_0 \mathbf{x}\|^2.$$

8.3.2.3 Applying the Chain Rule

Recall that the key insight from the *Chain Rule* is that to compute the gradient of a composition such as $\mathbf{h}(\mathbf{w})$ – no matter how complex – it suffices to *separately* compute the Jacobians of the intervening functions and then take *matrix products*. In this section, we compute the necessary Jacobians in the progressive case.

It will be convenient to rewrite the basic composition step as

$$\mathcal{O}_i(\overline{\mathbf{w}}^i) = \mathbf{g}_i(\mathcal{O}_{i-1}(\overline{\mathbf{w}}^{i-1}), \mathbf{w}_i) = \mathbf{g}_i(\mathcal{I}_i(\overline{\mathbf{w}}^i)) \in \mathbb{R}^{n_{i+1}},$$

where the input to layer $i + 1$ (both layer-specific parameters and the output of the previous layer) is

$$\mathcal{I}_i(\overline{\mathbf{w}}^i) = \left(\mathcal{O}_{i-1}(\overline{\mathbf{w}}^{i-1}), \mathbf{w}_i\right) \in \mathbb{R}^{n_i + r_i},$$

for $i = 1, \ldots, L$. When $i = 0$, we have simply

$$\mathcal{I}_0(\overline{\mathbf{w}}^0) = (\mathbf{z}_0, \mathbf{w}_0) = (\mathbf{x}, \mathbf{w}_0).$$

Applying the *Chain Rule* we get

$$J_{\mathcal{O}_i}(\overline{\mathbf{w}}^i) = J_{\mathbf{g}_i}(\mathcal{I}_i(\overline{\mathbf{w}}^i)) J_{\mathcal{I}_i}(\overline{\mathbf{w}}^i).$$

First, the Jacobian of

$$\mathcal{I}_i(\overline{\mathbf{w}}^i) = \left(\mathcal{O}_{i-1}(\overline{\mathbf{w}}^{i-1}), \mathbf{w}_i\right)$$

has a simple block diagonal structure

$$J_{\mathcal{I}_i}(\overline{\mathbf{w}}^i) = \begin{pmatrix} J_{\mathcal{O}_{i-1}}(\overline{\mathbf{w}}^{i-1}) & 0 \\ 0 & I_{r_i \times r_i} \end{pmatrix} \in \mathbb{R}^{(n_i + r_i) \times (r_0 + \cdots + r_i)}$$

since the first block component of $\mathcal{I}_i$, $\mathcal{O}_{i-1}(\overline{\mathbf{w}}^{i-1})$, does not depend on $\mathbf{w}_i$ whereas the second block component of $\mathcal{I}_i$, $\mathbf{w}_i$, does not depend on $\overline{\mathbf{w}}^{i-1}$. Observe that this is a fairly large matrix whose number of columns in particular grows with i. That last formula is for $i \geq 1$. When $i = 0$ we have $\mathcal{I}_0(\overline{\mathbf{w}}^0) = (\mathbf{x}, \mathbf{w}_0)$, so that

$$J_{\mathcal{I}_0}(\overline{\mathbf{w}}^0) = \begin{pmatrix} \mathbf{0}_{d \times r_0} \\ I_{r_0 \times r_0} \end{pmatrix} \in \mathbb{R}^{(d + r_0) \times r_0}.$$

We partition the Jacobian of $\mathbf{g}_i(\mathbf{z}_i, \mathbf{w}_i)$ likewise; that is, we divide it into those columns corresponding to partial derivatives with respect to $\mathbf{z}_i$ (the corresponding block being denoted by A_i) and with respect to $\mathbf{w}_i$ (the corresponding block being denoted by B_i):

$$J_{\mathbf{g}_i}(\mathbf{z}_i, \mathbf{w}_i) = \begin{pmatrix} A_i & B_i \end{pmatrix} \in \mathbb{R}^{n_{i+1} \times (n_i + r_i)},$$

evaluated at $(\mathbf{z}_i, \mathbf{w}_i) = \mathcal{I}_i(\overline{\mathbf{w}}^i) = (\mathcal{O}_{i-1}(\overline{\mathbf{w}}^{i-1}), \mathbf{w}_i)$. Note that A_i and B_i depend on the details of the function $\mathbf{g}_i$, which typically is fairly simple. We give examples in the next subsection.

Plugging back above we get

$$J_{\mathcal{O}_i}(\overline{\mathbf{w}}^i) = \begin{pmatrix} A_i & B_i \end{pmatrix} \begin{pmatrix} J_{\mathcal{O}_{i-1}}(\overline{\mathbf{w}}^{i-1}) & 0 \\ 0 & I_{r_i \times r_i} \end{pmatrix}.$$

This leads to the recursion

$$J_{\mathcal{O}_i}(\overline{\mathbf{w}}^i) = \begin{pmatrix} A_i J_{\mathcal{O}_{i-1}}(\overline{\mathbf{w}}^{i-1}) & B_i \end{pmatrix} \in \mathbb{R}^{n_{i+1} \times (r_0 + \cdots + r_i)}$$

from which the Jacobian of $\mathbf{h}(\mathbf{w})$ can be computed. Like $J_{\mathcal{I}_i}$, $J_{\mathcal{O}_i}$ is a large matrix. We refer to this matrix equation as the *fundamental recursion*.

The base case $i = 0$ is

$$J_{\mathcal{O}_0}(\overline{\mathbf{w}}^0) = \begin{pmatrix} A_0 & B_0 \end{pmatrix} \begin{pmatrix} \mathbf{0}_{d \times r_0} \\ I_{r_0 \times r_0} \end{pmatrix} = B_0.$$

Finally, using the *Chain Rule* again,

$$\nabla f(\mathbf{w}) = J_f(\mathbf{w})^T$$
$$= [J_\ell(\mathbf{h}(\mathbf{w})) J_\mathbf{h}(\mathbf{w})]^T$$
$$= J_\mathbf{h}(\mathbf{w})^T \nabla \ell(\mathbf{h}(\mathbf{w}))$$
$$= J_{\mathcal{O}_L}(\overline{\mathbf{w}}^L)^T \nabla \ell(\mathcal{O}_L(\overline{\mathbf{w}}^L)).$$

The matrix $J_{\mathcal{O}_L}(\overline{\mathbf{w}}^L)$ is computed using the recursion above, while $\nabla \ell$ depends on the function ℓ.

8.3.2.4 Backpropagation

We take advantage of the fundamental recursion to compute the gradient of $\mathbf{h}$. As we have seen, there are two ways of doing this. Applying the recursion directly is one of them, but it requires many matrix–matrix products. The first few steps are

$$J_{\mathcal{O}_0}(\overline{\mathbf{w}}^0) = B_0,$$
$$J_{\mathcal{O}_1}(\overline{\mathbf{w}}^1) = \begin{pmatrix} A_1 J_{\mathcal{O}_0}(\overline{\mathbf{w}}^0) & B_1 \end{pmatrix},$$
$$J_{\mathcal{O}_2}(\overline{\mathbf{w}}^2) = \begin{pmatrix} A_2 J_{\mathcal{O}_1}(\overline{\mathbf{w}}^1) & B_2 \end{pmatrix},$$

and so on.

Instead, as in the case of differentiating with respect to the input $\mathbf{x}$, one can also run the recursion backward. The latter approach can be much faster because, as we detail next, it involves only matrix–vector products. Start from the end, with the equation

$$\nabla f(\mathbf{w}) = J_\mathbf{h}(\mathbf{w})^T \nabla \ell(\mathbf{h}(\mathbf{w})).$$

8.3 Building Blocks of AI 1: Backpropagation

Note that $\nabla \ell(\mathbf{h}(\mathbf{w}))$ is a vector – not a matrix. Then expand the matrix $J_\mathbf{h}(\mathbf{w})$ using the recursion above:

$$\begin{aligned}
\nabla f(\mathbf{w}) &= J_\mathbf{h}(\mathbf{w})^T \nabla \ell(\mathbf{h}(\mathbf{w})) \\
&= J_{\mathcal{O}_L}(\overline{\mathbf{w}}^L)^T \nabla \ell(\mathbf{h}(\mathbf{w})) \\
&= \begin{pmatrix} A_L J_{\mathcal{O}_{L-1}}(\overline{\mathbf{w}}^{L-1}) & B_L \end{pmatrix}^T \nabla \ell(\mathbf{h}(\mathbf{w})) \\
&= \begin{pmatrix} J_{\mathcal{O}_{L-1}}(\overline{\mathbf{w}}^{L-1})^T A_L^T \\ B_L^T \end{pmatrix} \nabla \ell(\mathbf{h}(\mathbf{w})) \\
&= \begin{pmatrix} J_{\mathcal{O}_{L-1}}(\overline{\mathbf{w}}^{L-1})^T \{A_L^T \nabla \ell(\mathbf{h}(\mathbf{w}))\} \\ B_L^T \nabla \ell(\mathbf{h}(\mathbf{w})) \end{pmatrix}.
\end{aligned}$$

The key is that both expressions $A_L^T \nabla \ell(\mathbf{h}(\mathbf{w}))$ and $B_L^T \nabla \ell(\mathbf{h}(\mathbf{w}))$ are *matrix–vector products*. That pattern persists at the next level of recursion. Note that this supposes that we have precomputed $\mathbf{h}(\mathbf{w})$ first.

At the next level, we expand the matrix $J_{\mathcal{O}_{L-1}}(\overline{\mathbf{w}}^{L-1})^T$ using the fundamental recursion:

$$\begin{aligned}
\nabla f(\mathbf{w}) &= \begin{pmatrix} J_{\mathcal{O}_{L-1}}(\overline{\mathbf{w}}^{L-1})^T \{A_L^T \nabla \ell(\mathbf{h}(\mathbf{w}))\} \\ B_L^T \nabla \ell(\mathbf{h}(\mathbf{w})) \end{pmatrix} \\
&= \begin{pmatrix} \begin{pmatrix} A_{L-1} J_{\mathcal{O}_{L-2}}(\overline{\mathbf{w}}^{L-2}) & B_{L-1} \end{pmatrix}^T \{A_L^T \nabla \ell(\mathbf{h}(\mathbf{w}))\} \\ B_L^T \nabla \ell(\mathbf{h}(\mathbf{w})) \end{pmatrix} \\
&= \begin{pmatrix} \begin{pmatrix} J_{\mathcal{O}_{L-2}}(\overline{\mathbf{w}}^{L-2}) A_{L-1}^T \\ B_{L-1}^T \end{pmatrix} \{A_L^T \nabla \ell(\mathbf{h}(\mathbf{w}))\} \\ B_L^T \nabla \ell(\mathbf{h}(\mathbf{w})) \end{pmatrix} \\
&= \begin{pmatrix} J_{\mathcal{O}_{L-2}}(\overline{\mathbf{w}}^{L-2}) \{A_{L-1}^T \{A_L^T \nabla \ell(\mathbf{h}(\mathbf{w}))\}\} \\ B_{L-1}^T \{A_L^T \nabla \ell(\mathbf{h}(\mathbf{w}))\} \\ B_L^T \nabla \ell(\mathbf{h}(\mathbf{w})) \end{pmatrix}.
\end{aligned}$$

Continuing by induction gives an alternative formula for the gradient of f. Indeed, the next level gives

$$\nabla f(\mathbf{w}) = \begin{pmatrix} J_{\mathcal{O}_{L-3}}(\overline{\mathbf{w}}^{L-3}) \{A_{L-2}^T \{A_{L-1}^T \{A_L^T \nabla \ell(\mathbf{h}(\mathbf{w}))\}\}\} \\ B_{L-2}^T \{A_{L-1}^T \{A_L^T \nabla \ell(\mathbf{h}(\mathbf{w}))\}\} \\ B_{L-1}^T \{A_L^T \nabla \ell(\mathbf{h}(\mathbf{w}))\} \\ B_L^T \nabla \ell(\mathbf{h}(\mathbf{w})) \end{pmatrix}.$$

and so on. Observe that we do not in fact need to compute the large matrices $J_{\mathcal{O}_i}$ – only the sequence of vectors $B_L^T \nabla \ell(\mathbf{h}(\mathbf{w}))$, $B_{L-1}^T \{A_L^T \nabla \ell(\mathbf{h}(\mathbf{w}))\}$, $B_{L-2}^T \{A_{L-1}^T \{A_L^T \nabla \ell(\mathbf{h}(\mathbf{w}))\}\}$, and so on.

These formulas may seem cumbersome, but they take an intuitive form. Matrix A_i is the submatrix of the Jacobian $J_{\mathbf{g}_i}$ corresponding only to the partial derivatives with respect to $\mathbf{z}_i$, which are the input from the previous layer. Matrix B_i is the submatrix of the Jacobian $J_{\mathbf{g}_i}$ corresponding only to the partial derivatives with respect to $\mathbf{w}_i$, the layer-specific parameters. To compute the subvector of ∇f corresponding to the parameters $\mathbf{w}_i$ of the $(i + 1)$-th layer, we repeatedly differentiate with respect to the inputs of the previous layer (by multiplying by the corresponding A_j^T) starting from the last one, until we reach layer $i + 1$ at which point we take partial derivatives with respect to the layer-specific parameters (by multiplying by B_i^T).

The process stops there since the layers preceding it do not depend on $\mathbf{w}_i$ and therefore its full effect on f has been accounted for.

In other words, we need to compute

$$\mathbf{p}_L := A_L^T \nabla \ell(\mathbf{h}(\mathbf{w}))$$

and

$$\mathbf{q}_L := B_L^T \nabla \ell(\mathbf{h}(\mathbf{w})),$$

then

$$\mathbf{p}_{L-1} := A_{L-1}^T \mathbf{p}_L = A_{L-1}^T \left\{ A_L^T \nabla \ell(\mathbf{h}(\mathbf{w})) \right\}$$

and

$$\mathbf{q}_{L-1} := B_{L-1}^T \mathbf{p}_L = B_{L-1}^T \left\{ A_L^T \nabla \ell(\mathbf{h}(\mathbf{w})) \right\},$$

then

$$\mathbf{p}_{L-2} := A_{L-2}^T \mathbf{p}_{L-1} = A_{L-2}^T \left\{ A_{L-1}^T \left\{ A_L^T \nabla \ell(\mathbf{h}(\mathbf{w})) \right\} \right\}$$

and

$$\mathbf{q}_{L-2} := B_{L-2}^T \mathbf{p}_{L-1} = B_{L-2}^T \left\{ A_{L-1}^T \left\{ A_L^T \nabla \ell(\mathbf{h}(\mathbf{w})) \right\} \right\},$$

and so on. The $\mathbf{p}_i$'s are referred to as adjoints; they correspond to the vectors of partial derivatives of f with respect to the $\mathbf{z}_i$'s.

There is one more detail to note. The matrices A_i, B_i depend on the output of layer $i-1$. To compute them, we first proceed forward: we let $\mathbf{z}_0 = \mathbf{x}$, then

$$\mathbf{z}_1 = \mathcal{O}_0(\overline{\mathbf{w}}^0) = \mathbf{g}_0(\mathbf{z}_0, \mathbf{w}_0),$$

$$\mathbf{z}_2 = \mathcal{O}_1(\overline{\mathbf{w}}^1) = \mathbf{g}_1(\mathcal{O}_0(\overline{\mathbf{w}}^0), \mathbf{w}_1) = \mathbf{g}_1(\mathbf{z}_1, \mathbf{w}_1),$$

and so on. In that forward pass, we also compute A_i, B_i along the way.

We give the full algorithm now, which involves two passes. In the forward pass, or forward propagation step, we compute the following.

Initialization:

$$\mathbf{z}_0 := \mathbf{x}$$

Forward layer loop: For $i = 0, 1, \ldots, L$,

$$\mathbf{z}_{i+1} := \mathbf{g}_i(\mathbf{z}_i, \mathbf{w}_i)$$

$$\begin{pmatrix} A_i & B_i \end{pmatrix} := J_{\mathbf{g}_i}(\mathbf{z}_i, \mathbf{w}_i)$$

Loss:

$$z_{L+2} := \ell(\mathbf{z}_{L+1})$$

$$\mathbf{p}_{L+1} := \nabla \ell(\mathbf{z}_{L+1}).$$

In the backward pass, or backpropagation step, we compute the following.

Backward layer loop: For $i = L, \ldots, 1, 0$,

$$\mathbf{p}_i := A_i^T \mathbf{p}_{i+1}$$

$$\mathbf{q}_i := B_i^T \mathbf{p}_{i+1}$$

Output:
$$\nabla f(\mathbf{w}) = (\mathbf{q}_0, \mathbf{q}_1, \ldots, \mathbf{q}_L).$$

Note that we do not in fact need to compute A_0 and $\mathbf{p}_0$.

Example 8.3.5 *(continued)* We apply the algorithm to our running example. From previous calculations, for $i = 0, 1, \ldots, L$, the Jacobians are

$$J_{\mathbf{g}_i}(\mathbf{z}_i, \mathbf{w}_i) = \begin{pmatrix} \mathbb{A}_{n_{i+1}}[\mathbf{w}_i] & \mathbb{B}_{n_{i+1}}[\mathbf{z}_i] \end{pmatrix}$$
$$= \begin{pmatrix} \mathcal{W}_i & I_{n_{i+1} \times n_{i+1}} \otimes \mathbf{z}_i^T \end{pmatrix}$$
$$=: \begin{pmatrix} A_i & B_i \end{pmatrix}$$

and

$$J_\ell(\hat{\mathbf{y}}) = (\hat{\mathbf{y}} - \mathbf{y})^T.$$

Using the Properties of the Kronecker Product Lemma, *we obtain*

$$\mathbf{p}_L := A_L^T \nabla \ell(\mathbf{h}(\mathbf{w})) = \mathcal{W}_L^T(\hat{\mathbf{y}} - \mathbf{y})$$

$$\mathbf{q}_L := B_L^T \nabla \ell(\mathbf{h}(\mathbf{w})) = (I_{n_{L+1} \times n_{L+1}} \otimes \mathbf{z}_L^T)^T (\hat{\mathbf{y}} - \mathbf{y}) = (\hat{\mathbf{y}} - \mathbf{y}) \otimes \mathbf{z}_L$$
$$= (\hat{\mathbf{y}} - \mathbf{y}) \otimes \mathcal{W}_{L-1} \cdots \mathcal{W}_1 \mathcal{W}_0 \mathbf{x}$$

$$\mathbf{p}_{L-1} := A_{L-1}^T \mathbf{p}_L = \mathcal{W}_{L-1}^T \mathcal{W}_L^T (\hat{\mathbf{y}} - \mathbf{y})$$

$$\mathbf{q}_{L-1} := B_{L-1}^T \mathbf{p}_L = (I_{n_L \times n_L} \otimes \mathbf{z}_{L-1}^T)^T \mathcal{W}_L^T(\hat{\mathbf{y}} - \mathbf{y}) = \mathcal{W}_L^T (\hat{\mathbf{y}} - \mathbf{y}) \otimes \mathbf{z}_{L-1}$$
$$= \mathcal{W}_L^T (\hat{\mathbf{y}} - \mathbf{y}) \otimes \mathcal{W}_{L-2} \cdots \mathcal{W}_1 \mathcal{W}_0 \mathbf{x}$$

$$\mathbf{p}_{L-2} := A_{L-2}^T \mathbf{p}_{L-1} = \mathcal{W}_{L-2}^T \mathcal{W}_{L-1}^T \mathcal{W}_L^T (\hat{\mathbf{y}} - \mathbf{y})$$

$$\mathbf{q}_{L-2} := B_{L-2}^T \mathbf{p}_{L-1} = (I_{n_{L-1} \times n_{L-1}} \otimes \mathbf{z}_{L-2}^T)^T \mathcal{W}_{L-1}^T \mathcal{W}_L^T (\hat{\mathbf{y}} - \mathbf{y})$$
$$= \mathcal{W}_{L-1}^T \mathcal{W}_L^T (\hat{\mathbf{y}} - \mathbf{y}) \otimes \mathbf{z}_{L-2} = \mathcal{W}_{L-1}^T \mathcal{W}_L^T (\hat{\mathbf{y}} - \mathbf{y}) \otimes \mathcal{W}_{L-3} \cdots \mathcal{W}_1 \mathcal{W}_0 \mathbf{x}$$

and so on. Following the pattern, the last step is

$$\mathbf{p}_1 := \mathcal{W}_1^T \cdots \mathcal{W}_{L-1}^T \mathcal{W}_L^T (\hat{\mathbf{y}} - \mathbf{y})$$

$$\mathbf{q}_0 := B_0^T \mathbf{p}_1 = \mathcal{W}_1^T \cdots \mathcal{W}_{L-1}^T \mathcal{W}_L^T (\hat{\mathbf{y}} - \mathbf{y}) \otimes \mathbf{x}.$$

These calculations are consistent with the case $L = 1$ that we derived previously (check it!).

CHAT & LEARN The efficiency of backpropagation has been key to the success of deep learning. Ask your favorite AI chatbot about the history of backpropagation and its role in the development of modern deep learning.

Self-Assessment Quiz (with help from Claude, Gemini, and ChatGPT)

1 In the backpropagation algorithm, what does the "forward pass" compute?

   a) The adjoints $\mathbf{p}_i$ for each layer i.

b) The gradients $\mathbf{q}_i$ for the parameters of each layer i.
c) The function values $\mathbf{z}_i$ and the Jacobians A_i, B_i for each layer i.
d) The final gradient $\nabla f(\mathbf{w})$ with respect to all parameters.

2. What is the purpose of the "backward pass" in the backpropagation algorithm?
   a) To compute the function values $\mathbf{z}_i$ for each layer i from the input $\mathbf{x}$.
   b) To compute the Jacobians A_i, B_i for each layer i using the fundamental recursion.
   c) To compute the adjoints $\mathbf{p}_i$ and the gradients $\mathbf{q}_i$ for each layer i using the fundamental recursion.
   d) To compute the final output $\ell(\mathbf{z}_{L+1})$ of the progressive function.

3. What is the computational complexity of the backpropagation algorithm in terms of the number of layers L and the matrix dimensions m?
   a) $\approx Lm$
   b) $\approx Lm^2$
   c) $\approx Lm^2 d$
   d) $\approx Lm^3 d$

4. In the context of progressive functions, what is the significance of the matrices A_i and B_i?
   a) They represent the Jacobians of the layer functions with respect to the inputs and parameters, respectively.
   b) They are the intermediate values computed during the forward pass.
   c) They are the adjoints used in the backpropagation algorithm.
   d) They are the matrices of parameters for each layer.

5. In the context of progressive functions, which of the following best describes the role of the vector $\mathbf{w}_i$?
   a) The input to the i-th layer.
   b) The output of the i-th layer.
   c) The parameters specific to the i-th layer.
   d) The concatenation of parameters from all layers up to i.

Answer for 1: c. Justification: The section presents the forward propagation step which computes "the following: Initialization: $\mathbf{z}_0 := \mathbf{x}$ Forward layer loop: For $i = 0, 1, \ldots, L$, $\mathbf{z}_{i+1} := \mathbf{g}_i(\mathbf{z}_i, \mathbf{w}_i)$ $(A_i, B_i) := J_{\mathbf{g}_i}(\mathbf{z}_i, \mathbf{w}_i)$ Loss: $\mathbf{z}_{L+2} := \ell(\mathbf{z}_{L+1})$."

Answer for 2: c. Justification: The backward pass is described as follows: "Backward layer loop: For $i = L, \ldots, 1, 0$, $\mathbf{p}_i := A_i^T \mathbf{p}_{i+1}$ $\mathbf{q}_i := B_i^T \mathbf{p}_{i+1}$ Output: $\nabla f(\mathbf{w}) = (\mathbf{q}_0, \mathbf{q}_1, \ldots, \mathbf{q}_L)$."

Answer for 3: b. Justification: The text derives that the number of operations in the reverse mode is approximately $2Lm^2$, stating "This is approximately $2Lm^2$ – which can be much smaller than $2Lm^2 d$!"

> Answer for 4: a. Justification: The text defines A_i and B_i as the blocks of the Jacobian $J_{\mathbf{g}_i}(\mathbf{z}_i, \mathbf{w}_i)$ corresponding to the partial derivatives with respect to $\mathbf{z}_i$ and $\mathbf{w}_i$, respectively.
>
> Answer for 5: c. Justification: The text explains: "In the machine learning context, each 'layer' $\mathbf{g}_i$ has parameters (in our running example, these were the entries of $\mathcal{W}_i$) and we seek to optimize with respect to those parameters."

8.4 Building Blocks of AI 2: Stochastic Gradient Descent

Having shown how to compute the gradient, we can now apply gradient descent to fit the data.

To get the full gradient, we consider n samples $(\mathbf{x}_i, y_i)$, $i = 1, \ldots, n$. At this point, we make the dependence on $(\mathbf{x}_i, y_i)$ explicit. The loss function can be taken as the average of the individual sample contributions, so the gradient is obtained by linearity,

$$\nabla\left(\frac{1}{n}\sum_{i=1}^{n} f_{\mathbf{x}_i, y_i}(\mathbf{w})\right) = \frac{1}{n}\sum_{i=1}^{n} \nabla f_{\mathbf{x}_i, y_i}(\mathbf{w}),$$

where each term can be computed separately by the procedure above.

We can then apply gradient descent. We start from an arbitrary $\mathbf{w}^0$ and update as follows:

$$\mathbf{w}^{t+1} = \mathbf{w}^t - \alpha_t \left(\frac{1}{n}\sum_{i=1}^{n} \nabla f_{\mathbf{x}_i, y_i}(\mathbf{w}^t)\right).$$

In a large dataset, computing the sum over all samples may be prohibitively expensive. We present a popular alternative.

8.4.1 Algorithm

In stochastic gradient descent (SGD), a variant of gradient descent, we pick a sample I_t uniformly at random in $\{1, \ldots, n\}$ and update as follows:

$$\mathbf{w}^{t+1} = \mathbf{w}^t - \alpha_t \nabla f_{\mathbf{x}_{I_t}, y_{I_t}}(\mathbf{w}^t).$$

More generally, in the so-called mini-batch version of SGD, we pick instead a uniformly random subsample $\mathcal{B}_t \subseteq \{1, \ldots, n\}$ of size b without replacement (i.e., all subsamples of that size have the same probability of being picked):

$$\mathbf{w}^{t+1} = \mathbf{w}^t - \alpha_t \frac{1}{b} \sum_{i \in \mathcal{B}_t} \nabla f_{\mathbf{x}_i, y_i}(\mathbf{w}^t).$$

The key observation about the two stochastic updates above is that, in expectation, they perform a step of gradient descent. That turns out to be enough and it has computational advantages.

Lemma 8.4.1 *Fix a batch size $1 \leq b \leq n$ and and an arbitrary vector of parameters $\mathbf{w}$. Let $\mathcal{B} \subseteq \{1, \ldots, n\}$ be a uniformly random subsample of size b. Then*

$$\mathbb{E}\left[\frac{1}{b}\sum_{i \in \mathcal{B}} \nabla f_{\mathbf{x}_i, y_i}(\mathbf{w})\right] = \frac{1}{n}\sum_{i=1}^{n} \nabla f_{\mathbf{x}_i, y_i}(\mathbf{w}).$$

Proof Because $\mathcal{B}$ is picked uniformly at random (without replacement), for any subsample $B \subseteq \{1, \ldots, n\}$ of size b without repeats

$$\mathbb{P}[\mathcal{B} = B] = \frac{1}{\binom{n}{b}}.$$

So, summing over all such subsamples, we obtain

$$\mathbb{E}\left[\frac{1}{b} \sum_{i \in \mathcal{B}} \nabla f_{\mathbf{x}_i, y_i}(\mathbf{w})\right] = \frac{1}{b} \sum_{B \subseteq \{1,\ldots,n\}} \mathbb{P}[\mathcal{B} = B] \sum_{i \in B} \nabla f_{\mathbf{x}_i, y_i}(\mathbf{w})$$

$$= \frac{1}{b} \sum_{B \subseteq \{1,\ldots,n\}} \frac{1}{\binom{n}{b}} \sum_{i=1}^{n} \mathbf{1}\{i \in B\} \nabla f_{\mathbf{x}_i, y_i}(\mathbf{w})$$

$$= \sum_{i=1}^{n} \nabla f_{\mathbf{x}_i, y_i}(\mathbf{w}) \frac{1}{b\binom{n}{b}} \sum_{B \subseteq \{1,\ldots,n\}} \mathbf{1}\{i \in B\}.$$

Computing the internal sum requires a combinatorial argument. Indeed, $\sum_{B \subseteq \{1,\ldots,n\}} \mathbf{1}\{i \in B\}$ counts the number of ways that i can be picked in a subsample of size b without repeats. This is $\binom{n-1}{b-1}$, which is the number of ways of picking the remaining $b-1$ elements of B from the other $n-1$ possible elements. By definition of the binomial coefficient and the properties of factorials,

$$\frac{\binom{n-1}{b-1}}{b\binom{n}{b}} = \frac{\frac{(n-1)!}{(b-1)!(n-b)!}}{b\frac{n!}{b!(n-b)!}} = \frac{(n-1)!}{n!} \frac{b!}{b(b-1)!} = \frac{1}{n}.$$

Plugging back gives the claim. □

As a first illustration, we return to logistic regression. Recall that the input data is of the form $\{(\alpha_i, b_i) : i = 1, \ldots, n\}$ where $\alpha_i = (\alpha_{i,1}, \ldots, \alpha_{i,d}) \in \mathbb{R}^d$ are the features and $b_i \in \{0, 1\}$ is the label. As before we use a matrix representation: $A \in \mathbb{R}^{n \times d}$ has rows α_i^T, $i = 1, \ldots, n$ and $\mathbf{b} = (b_1, \ldots, b_n) \in \{0, 1\}^n$. We want to solve the minimization problem

$$\min_{\mathbf{x} \in \mathbb{R}^d} \ell(\mathbf{x}; A, \mathbf{b})$$

where the loss is

$$\ell(\mathbf{x}; A, \mathbf{b}) = \frac{1}{n} \sum_{i=1}^{n} \{-b_i \log(\sigma(\alpha_i^T \mathbf{x})) - (1 - b_i) \log(1 - \sigma(\alpha_i^T \mathbf{x}))\}$$

$$= \text{mean}\left(-\mathbf{b} \odot \log(\sigma(A\mathbf{x})) - (1 - \mathbf{b}) \odot \log(1 - \sigma(A\mathbf{x}))\right).$$

The gradient was previously computed as (see Section 3.6.1)

$$\nabla \ell(\mathbf{x}; A, \mathbf{b}) = -\frac{1}{n} \sum_{i=1}^{n} (b_i - \sigma(\alpha_i^T \mathbf{x})) \alpha_i$$

$$= -\frac{1}{n} A^T [\mathbf{b} - \sigma(A\mathbf{x})].$$

For the mini-batch version of SGD, we pick a random subsample $\mathcal{B}_t \subseteq \{1, \ldots, n\}$ of size B and take the step

$$\mathbf{x}^{t+1} = \mathbf{x}^t + \beta \frac{1}{B} \sum_{i \in \mathcal{B}_t} (b_i - \sigma(\alpha_i^T \mathbf{x}^t)) \alpha_i.$$

We modify our previous code for logistic regression. The only change is to pick a random mini-batch which can be fed to the descent update subroutine as dataset.

```
def sigmoid(z):
    return 1/(1+np.exp(-z))

def pred_fn(x, A):
    return sigmoid(A @ x)

def loss_fn(x, A, b):
    return np.mean(-b*np.log(pred_fn(x, A))
                   - (1 - b)*np.log(1 - pred_fn(x, A)))

def grad_fn(x, A, b):
    return -A.T @ (b - pred_fn(x, A))/len(b)

def desc_update_for_logreg(grad_fn, A, b, curr_x, beta):
    gradient = grad_fn(curr_x, A, b)
    return curr_x - beta*gradient

def sgd_for_logreg(rng, loss_fn, grad_fn, A, b,
                   init_x, beta=1e-3, niters=int(1e5), batch=40):

    curr_x = init_x
    nsamples = len(b)
    for _ in range(niters):
        I = rng.integers(nsamples, size=batch)
        curr_x = desc_update_for_logreg(
            grad_fn, A[I,:], b[I], curr_x, beta)

    return curr_x
```

NUMERICAL CORNER We analyze a dataset from [HTF].[5] Quoting [HTF, Section 4.4.2],

> The data [...] are a subset of the Coronary Risk-Factor Study (CORIS) baseline survey, carried out in three rural areas of the Western Cape, South Africa (Rousseauw et al., 1983). The aim of the study was to establish the intensity of ischemic heart disease risk factors in that high-incidence region. The data represent white males between 15 and 64, and the response variable is the presence or absence of myocardial infarction (MI) at the time of the survey (the overall prevalence of MI was 5.1% in this region). There are 160 cases in our data set, and a sample of 302 controls. These data are described in more detail in Hastie and Tibshirani (1987).

We load the data, which we have slightly reformatted, and look at a summary.

---

[5] https://web.stanford.edu/~hastie/ElemStatLearn/data.html

```
data = pd.read_csv('SAHeart.csv')
data.head()
```

```
     sbp  tobacco   ldl  adiposity  typea  obesity  alcohol   age  chd
0  160.0    12.00  5.73      23.11   49.0    25.30    97.20  52.0  1.0
1  144.0     0.01  4.41      28.61   55.0    28.87     2.06  63.0  1.0
2  118.0     0.08  3.48      32.28   52.0    29.14     3.81  46.0  0.0
3  170.0     7.50  6.41      38.03   51.0    31.99    24.26  58.0  1.0
4  134.0    13.60  3.50      27.78   60.0    25.99    57.34  49.0  1.0
```

Our goal is to predict chd, which stands for coronary heart disease, based on the other variables. We use logistic regression again.

We first construct the data matrices. We only use three of the predictors.

```
feature = data[['tobacco', 'ldl', 'age']].to_numpy()
print(feature)
```

```
[[1.200e+01 5.730e+00 5.200e+01]
 [1.000e-02 4.410e+00 6.300e+01]
 [8.000e-02 3.480e+00 4.600e+01]
 ...
 [3.000e+00 1.590e+00 5.500e+01]
 [5.400e+00 1.161e+01 4.000e+01]
 [0.000e+00 4.820e+00 4.600e+01]]
```

```
label = data['chd'].to_numpy()
A = np.concatenate((np.ones((len(label),1)),feature),axis=1)
b = label
```

We try mini-batch SGD.

```
seed = 535
rng = np.random.default_rng(seed)
init_x = np.zeros(A.shape[1])
best_x = sgd_for_logreg(rng, loss_fn, grad_fn, A, b, init_x,
                        beta=1e-3, niters=int(1e6))
print(best_x)
```

```
[-4.06558071  0.07990955  0.18813635  0.04693118]
```

The outcome is harder to vizualize. To get a sense of how accurate the result is, we compare our predictions to the true labels. By prediction, let us say that we mean that we predict label 1 whenever $\sigma(\alpha^T \mathbf{x}) > 1/2$. We try this on the training set. (A better approach would be to split the data into training and testing sets, but we will not do this here.)

```
def logis_acc(x, A, b):
    return np.sum((pred_fn(x, A) > 0.5) == b)/len(b)
```

```
logis_acc(best_x, A, b)
```

0.7207792207792207

◁ **NC**

8.4.2 Example: Multinomial Logistic Regression

We give a concrete example of progressive functions and of the application of backpropagation and SGD.

Recall that a classifier h takes an input in $\mathbb{R}^d$ and predicts one of K possible labels. It will be convenient for reasons that will become clear below to use one-hot encoding of the labels. That is, we encode label i as the K-dimensional vector $\mathbf{e}_i$. Here, as usual, $\mathbf{e}_i$ is the i-th standard basis vector of $\mathbb{R}^K$, namely the vector with a 1 in entry i and a 0 elsewhere. Furthermore, we allow the output of the classifier to be a probability distribution over the labels $\{1, \ldots, K\}$; that is, a vector in

$$\Delta_K = \left\{ (p_1, \ldots, p_K) \in [0,1]^K : \sum_{k=1}^{K} p_k = 1 \right\}.$$

Observe that $\mathbf{e}_i$ can itself be thought of as a probability distribution, one that assigns probability one to i.

8.4.2.1 Background on Multinomial Logistic Regression

We use multinomial logistic regression to learn a classifier over K labels. In multinomial logistic regression, we once again use an affine function of the input data.

This time, we have K functions that output a score associated with each label. We then transform these scores into a probability distribution over the K labels. There are many ways of doing this. A standard approach is the softmax function $\boldsymbol{\gamma} = (\gamma_1, \ldots, \gamma_K)$: for $\mathbf{z} \in \mathbb{R}^K$

$$\gamma_i(\mathbf{z}) = \frac{e^{z_i}}{\sum_{j=1}^{K} e^{z_j}}, \quad i = 1, \ldots, K.$$

To explain the name, observe that the larger inputs are mapped to larger probabilities.

In fact, since a probability distribution must sum to 1, it is determined by the probabilities assigned to the first $K-1$ labels. In other words, we could drop the score associated with the last label. But to keep the notation simple, we will not do this here.

For each k, we have a regression function

$$\sum_{j=1}^{d} w_j^{(k)} x_j = \mathbf{x}_1^T \mathbf{w}^{(k)}, \quad k = 1, \ldots, K$$

where $\mathbf{w} = (\mathbf{w}^{(1)}, \ldots, \mathbf{w}^{(K)})$ are the parameters with $\mathbf{w}^{(k)} \in \mathbb{R}^d$ and $\mathbf{x} \in \mathbb{R}^d$ is the input. A constant term can be included by adding an additional entry 1 to $\mathbf{x}$. As we did in the linear regression case, we assume that this preprocessing has been performed previously. To simplify the notation, we let $\mathcal{W} \in \mathbb{R}^{K \times d}$ be the matrix with rows $(\mathbf{w}^{(1)})^T, \ldots, (\mathbf{w}^{(K)})^T$.

The output of the classifier is

$$\mathbf{h}(\mathbf{w}) = \boldsymbol{\gamma}(\mathcal{W}\mathbf{x}),$$

for $i = 1, \ldots, K$, where γ is the softmax function. Note that the latter has no associated parameter.

It remains to define a loss function. To quantify the fit, it is natural to use a notion of distance between probability measures, here between the output $\mathbf{h}(\mathbf{w}) \in \Delta_K$ and the correct label $\mathbf{y} \in \{\mathbf{e}_1, \ldots, \mathbf{e}_K\} \subseteq \Delta_K$. There are many such measures. In multinomial logistic regression, we use the Kullback–Leibler divergence, which we have encountered in the context of maximum likelihood estimation. Recall that, for two probability distributions $\mathbf{p}, \mathbf{q} \in \Delta_K$, it is defined as

$$\mathrm{KL}(\mathbf{p} \| \mathbf{q}) = \sum_{i=1}^{K} p_i \log \frac{p_i}{q_i}$$

where it will suffice to restrict ourselves to the case $\mathbf{q} > \mathbf{0}$ and where we use the convention $0 \log 0 = 0$ (so that terms with $p_i = 0$ contribute 0 to the sum). Notice that $\mathbf{p} = \mathbf{q}$ implies $\mathrm{KL}(\mathbf{p} \| \mathbf{q}) = 0$. We proved previously that $\mathrm{KL}(\mathbf{p} \| \mathbf{q}) \geq 0$, a result known as *Gibbs' Inequality*.

Going back to the loss function, we use the identity $\log \frac{\alpha}{\beta} = \log \alpha - \log \beta$ to rewrite

$$\begin{aligned} \mathrm{KL}(\mathbf{y} \| \mathbf{h}(\mathbf{w})) &= \sum_{i=1}^{K} y_i \log \frac{y_i}{h_i(\mathbf{w})} \\ &= \sum_{i=1}^{K} y_i \log y_i - \sum_{i=1}^{K} y_i \log h_i(\mathbf{w}), \end{aligned}$$

where $\mathbf{h} = (h_1, \ldots, h_K)$. Notice that the first term on the right-hand side does not depend on $\mathbf{w}$. Hence we can ignore it when optimizing $\mathrm{KL}(\mathbf{y} \| \mathbf{h}(\mathbf{w}))$. The remaining term is

$$H(\mathbf{y}, \mathbf{h}(\mathbf{w})) = -\sum_{i=1}^{K} y_i \log h_i(\mathbf{w}).$$

We use it to define our loss function. That is, we set

$$\ell(\hat{\mathbf{y}}) = H(\mathbf{y}, \hat{\mathbf{y}}) = -\sum_{i=1}^{K} y_i \log \hat{y}_i.$$

Finally,

$$\begin{aligned} f(\mathbf{w}) &= \ell(\mathbf{h}(\mathbf{w})) \\ &= H(\mathbf{y}, \mathbf{h}(\mathbf{w})) \\ &= H(\mathbf{y}, \gamma(\mathcal{W}\mathbf{x})) \\ &= -\sum_{i=1}^{K} y_i \log \gamma_i(\mathcal{W}\mathbf{x}). \end{aligned}$$

8.4.2.2 Computing the Gradient

We apply the forward and backpropagation steps from Section 8.3.2. We then use the resulting recursions to derive an analytical formula for the gradient.

The forward pass starts with the initialization $\mathbf{z}_0 := \mathbf{x}$. The forward layer loop has two steps. Set $\mathbf{w}_0 = (\mathbf{w}_0^{(1)}, \ldots, \mathbf{w}_0^{(K)})$ equal to $\mathbf{w} = (\mathbf{w}^{(1)}, \ldots, \mathbf{w}^{(K)})$. First we compute

$$\mathbf{z}_1 := \mathbf{g}_0(\mathbf{z}_0, \mathbf{w}_0) = \mathcal{W}_0 \mathbf{z}_0$$

$$J_{\mathbf{g}_0}(\mathbf{z}_0, \mathbf{w}_0) := \begin{pmatrix} A_0 & B_0 \end{pmatrix}$$

where we defined $\mathcal{W}_0 \in \mathbb{R}^{K \times d}$ as the matrix with rows $(\mathbf{w}_0^{(1)})^T, \ldots, (\mathbf{w}_0^{(K-1)})^T$. We have previously computed the Jacobian (see Example 8.2.15):

$$A_0 = \mathbb{A}_K[\mathbf{w}_0] = \mathcal{W}_0 = \begin{pmatrix} (\mathbf{w}_0^{(1)})^T \\ \vdots \\ (\mathbf{w}_0^{(K)})^T \end{pmatrix}$$

and

$$B_0 = \mathbb{B}_K[\mathbf{z}_0] = I_{K \times K} \otimes \mathbf{z}_0^T = \begin{pmatrix} \mathbf{e}_1 \mathbf{z}_0^T & \cdots & \mathbf{e}_K \mathbf{z}_0^T \end{pmatrix}.$$

In the second step of the forward layer loop, we compute

$$\hat{\mathbf{y}} := \mathbf{z}_2 := \mathbf{g}_1(\mathbf{z}_1) = \boldsymbol{\gamma}(\mathbf{z}_1)$$
$$A_1 := J_{\mathbf{g}_1}(\mathbf{z}_1) = J_{\boldsymbol{\gamma}}(\mathbf{z}_1).$$

So we need to compute the Jacobian of $\boldsymbol{\gamma}$. We divide this computation into two cases. When $1 \leq i = j \leq K$,

$$\begin{aligned}(A_1)_{ii} &= \frac{\partial}{\partial z_{1,i}} \left[\gamma_i(\mathbf{z}_1) \right] \\ &= \frac{\partial}{\partial z_{1,i}} \left[\frac{e^{z_{1,i}}}{\sum_{k=1}^K e^{z_{1,k}}} \right] \\ &= \frac{e^{z_{1,i}} \left(\sum_{k=1}^K e^{z_{1,k}} \right) - e^{z_{1,i}} \left(e^{z_{1,i}} \right)}{\left(\sum_{k=1}^K e^{z_{1,k}} \right)^2} \\ &= \gamma_i(\mathbf{z}_1) - \gamma_i(\mathbf{z}_1)^2,\end{aligned}$$

by the quotient rule.

When $1 \leq i, j \leq K$ with $i \neq j$,

$$\begin{aligned}(A_1)_{ij} &= \frac{\partial}{\partial z_{1,j}} \left[\gamma_i(\mathbf{z}_1) \right] \\ &= \frac{\partial}{\partial z_{1,j}} \left[\frac{e^{z_{1,i}}}{\sum_{k=1}^K e^{z_{1,k}}} \right] \\ &= \frac{-e^{z_{1,i}} \left(e^{z_{1,j}} \right)}{\left(\sum_{k=1}^K e^{z_{1,k}} \right)^2} \\ &= -\gamma_i(\mathbf{z}_1) \gamma_j(\mathbf{z}_1).\end{aligned}$$

In matrix form,

$$A_1 = \mathrm{diag}(\boldsymbol{\gamma}(\mathbf{z}_1)) - \boldsymbol{\gamma}(\mathbf{z}_1) \boldsymbol{\gamma}(\mathbf{z}_1)^T.$$

The Jacobian of the loss function is

$$J_\ell(\hat{\mathbf{y}}) = \nabla \left[-\sum_{i=1}^K y_i \log \hat{y}_i \right]^T = -\left(\frac{y_1}{\hat{y}_1}, \ldots, \frac{y_K}{\hat{y}_K} \right)^T = -(\mathbf{y} \oslash \hat{\mathbf{y}})^T,$$

where recall that $\oslash$ is the Hadamard division (i.e., element-wise division).

We summarize the whole procedure next.

Initialization:

$$\mathbf{z}_0 := \mathbf{x}$$

Forward layer loop:

$$\mathbf{z}_1 := \mathbf{g}_0(\mathbf{z}_0, \mathbf{w}_0) = \mathcal{W}_0 \mathbf{z}_0$$

$$\begin{pmatrix} A_0 & B_0 \end{pmatrix} := J_{\mathbf{g}_0}(\mathbf{z}_0, \mathbf{w}_0) = \begin{pmatrix} \mathbb{A}_K[\mathbf{w}_0] & \mathbb{B}_K[\mathbf{z}_0] \end{pmatrix}$$

$$\hat{\mathbf{y}} := \mathbf{z}_2 := \mathbf{g}_1(\mathbf{z}_1) = \boldsymbol{\gamma}(\mathbf{z}_1)$$

$$A_1 := J_{\mathbf{g}_1}(\mathbf{z}_1) = \text{diag}(\boldsymbol{\gamma}(\mathbf{z}_1)) - \boldsymbol{\gamma}(\mathbf{z}_1) \boldsymbol{\gamma}(\mathbf{z}_1)^T$$

Loss:

$$z_3 := \ell(\mathbf{z}_2) = -\sum_{i=1}^{K} y_i \log z_{2,i}$$

$$\mathbf{p}_2 := \nabla \ell_{\mathbf{y}}(\mathbf{z}_2) = -\left(\frac{y_1}{z_{2,1}}, \ldots, \frac{y_K}{z_{2,K}}\right) = -\mathbf{y} \oslash \mathbf{z}_2.$$

Backward layer loop:

$$\mathbf{p}_1 := A_1^T \mathbf{p}_2$$

$$\mathbf{q}_0 := B_0^T \mathbf{p}_1$$

Output:

$$\nabla f(\mathbf{w}) = \mathbf{q}_0,$$

where recall that $\mathbf{w} := \mathbf{w}_0$.

Explicit formulas can be derived from the previous recursion.

We first compute $\mathbf{p}_1$. We use the *Properties of the Hadamard Product Lemma*. We get

$$\begin{aligned}
\mathbf{p}_1 &= A_1^T \mathbf{p}_2 \\
&= [\text{diag}(\boldsymbol{\gamma}(\mathbf{z}_1)) - \boldsymbol{\gamma}(\mathbf{z}_1)\boldsymbol{\gamma}(\mathbf{z}_1)^T]^T [-\mathbf{y} \oslash \boldsymbol{\gamma}(\mathbf{z}_1)] \\
&= -\text{diag}(\boldsymbol{\gamma}(\mathbf{z}_1))(\mathbf{y} \oslash \boldsymbol{\gamma}(\mathbf{z}_1)) + \boldsymbol{\gamma}(\mathbf{z}_1)\boldsymbol{\gamma}(\mathbf{z}_1)^T (\mathbf{y} \oslash \boldsymbol{\gamma}(\mathbf{z}_1)) \\
&= -\mathbf{y} + \boldsymbol{\gamma}(\mathbf{z}_1) \mathbf{1}^T \mathbf{y} \\
&= \boldsymbol{\gamma}(\mathbf{z}_1) - \mathbf{y},
\end{aligned}$$

where we used the fact that $\sum_{k=1}^{K} y_k = 1$.

It remains to compute $\mathbf{q}_0$. We have by parts (e) and (f) of the *Properties of the Kronecker Product Lemma*

$$\begin{aligned}
\mathbf{q}_0 = B_0^T \mathbf{p}_1 &= (I_{K \times K} \otimes \mathbf{z}_0^T)^T (\boldsymbol{\gamma}(\mathbf{z}_1) - \mathbf{y}) \\
&= (I_{K \times K} \otimes \mathbf{z}_0)(\boldsymbol{\gamma}(\mathbf{z}_1) - \mathbf{y}) \\
&= (\boldsymbol{\gamma}(\mathbf{z}_1) - \mathbf{y}) \otimes \mathbf{z}_0.
\end{aligned}$$

Finally, replacing $\mathbf{z}_0 = \mathbf{x}$ and $\mathbf{z}_1 = \mathcal{W}\mathbf{x}$, the gradient is

$$\nabla f(\mathbf{w}) = \mathbf{q}_0 = (\boldsymbol{\gamma}(\mathcal{W}\mathbf{x}) - \mathbf{y}) \otimes \mathbf{x}.$$

8.4 Building Blocks of AI 2: Stochastic Gradient Descent

It can be shown that the objective function $f(\mathbf{w})$ is convex in $\mathbf{w}$.

NUMERICAL CORNER We will use the Fashion-MNIST dataset.[6] We first check for the availability of GPUs and load the data.

```
device = torch.device("cuda" if torch.cuda.is_available()
                     else ("mps" if torch.backends.mps.
                     is_available()
                     else "cpu"))
print("Using device:", device)
```

Using device: mps

```
from torchvision import datasets, transforms
from torch.utils.data import DataLoader
import torch.nn as nn
import torch.optim as optim

seed = 42
torch.manual_seed(seed)

if device.type == 'cuda': # device-specific seeding and settings
    torch.cuda.manual_seed(seed)
    torch.cuda.manual_seed_all(seed)   # for multi-GPU
    torch.backends.cudnn.deterministic = True
    torch.backends.cudnn.benchmark = False
elif device.type == 'mps':
    torch.mps.manual_seed(seed)   # MPS-specific seeding

g = torch.Generator()
g.manual_seed(seed)

train_dataset = datasets.FashionMNIST(root='./data', train=True,
                     download=True, transform=transforms.
                     ToTensor())
test_dataset = datasets.FashionMNIST(root='./data', train=False,
                     download=True, transform=transforms.
                     ToTensor())

BATCH_SIZE = 32
train_loader = DataLoader(train_dataset, batch_size=BATCH_SIZE,
                     shuffle=True, generator=g)
test_loader = DataLoader(test_dataset, batch_size=BATCH_SIZE,
                     shuffle=False)
```

---

[6] This example is inspired by https://pytorch.org/tutorials/beginner/basics/quickstart_tutorial.html and https://www.tensorflow.org/tutorials/keras/classification

We used `torch.utils.data.DataLoader`, which provides utilities to load the data in batches for training. Taking mini-batches of size `BATCH_SIZE = 32`, we apply a random permutation of the samples on every pass over the training data (with the option `shuffle=True`). The function `torch.manual_seed` is used to set the global seed for PyTorch operations (e.g., weight initialization). The shuffling in `DataLoader` uses its own separate random number generator, which we initialize with `torch.Generator` and `manual_seed`. (You can tell from the fact that `seed=42` that Claude explained that one to me...)

CHAT & LEARN Ask your favorite AI chatbot to explain the lines:

```
if device.type == 'cuda':  # device-specific seeding and settings
    torch.cuda.manual_seed(seed)
    torch.cuda.manual_seed_all(seed)   # for multi-GPU
    torch.backends.cudnn.deterministic = True
    torch.backends.cudnn.benchmark = False
elif device.type == 'mps':
    torch.mps.manual_seed(seed)   # MPS-specific seeding
```

We implement multinomial logistic regression to learn a classifier for the Fashion-MNIST data. In PyTorch, composition of functions can be achieved with `torch.nn.Sequential`. Our model is:

```
model = nn.Sequential(
    nn.Flatten(),
    nn.Linear(28 * 28, 10)
).to(device)
```

The `torch.nn.Flatten` layer turns each input image into a vector of size 784 (where 784 = 28^2 is the number of pixels in each image). After the flattening, we have an affine map from $\mathbb{R}^{784}$ to $\mathbb{R}^{10}$. Note that there is no need to preprocess the inputs by adding 1s. A constant term (or "bias variable") is automatically added by PyTorch (unless one chooses the option `bias=False`). The final output is 10-dimensional.

Finally, we are ready to run an optimization method of our choice on the loss function, which are specified next. There are many optimizers available. Here we use SGD as the optimizer. The loss function is the cross-entropy, as implemented by `torch.nn.CrossEntropyLoss`, which first takes the softmax and expects the labels to be the actual class labels rather than their one-hot encoding.

```
loss_fn = nn.CrossEntropyLoss()
optimizer = optim.SGD(model.parameters(), lr=1e-3)
```

We implement special functions for training.

```
def train(dataloader, model, loss_fn, optimizer, device):
    size = len(dataloader.dataset)
    model.train()
    for batch, (X, y) in enumerate(dataloader):
        X, y = X.to(device), y.to(device)
```

```
        pred = model(X)
        loss = loss_fn(pred, y)
        optimizer.zero_grad()
        loss.backward()
        optimizer.step()

def training_loop(train_loader, model, loss_fn, optimizer, device,
                  epochs=3):
    for epoch in range(epochs):
        train(train_loader, model, loss_fn, optimizer, device)
        print(f"Epoch {epoch+1}/{epochs}")
```

An epoch is one training iteration where all samples are iterated once (in a randomly shuffled order). In the interest of time, we train for 10 epochs only. But it does better if you train it longer (try it!). On each pass, we compute the output of the current model, use `backward` to obtain the gradient, and then perform a descent update with `step`. We also have to reset the gradients first (otherwise they add up by default).

```
training_loop(train_loader, model, loss_fn, optimizer, device,
              epochs=10)
```

Epoch 1/10
Epoch 2/10
Epoch 3/10
Epoch 4/10
Epoch 5/10
Epoch 6/10
Epoch 7/10
Epoch 8/10
Epoch 9/10
Epoch 10/10

Because of the issue of overfitting, we use the *test* images to assess the performance of the final classifier.

```
def test(dataloader, model, loss_fn, device):
    size = len(dataloader.dataset)
    correct = 0
    model.eval()
    with torch.no_grad():
        for X, y in dataloader:
            X, y = X.to(device), y.to(device)
            pred = model(X)
            correct += (pred.argmax(dim=1) == y).type(torch.float).
                sum().item()
```

```
print(f"Test error: {(100*(correct / size)):>0.1f}% accuracy")
```

```
test(test_loader, model, loss_fn, device)
```

Test error: 78.7% accuracy

To make a prediction, we take a `torch.nn.functional.softmax` of the output of our model. Recall that it is implicitly included in `torch.nn.CrossEntropyLoss`, but is not actually part of `model`. (Note that the softmax itself has no parameter.)

As an illustration, we do this for each test image. We use `torch.cat` to concatenate a sequence of tensors into a single tensor.

```
import torch.nn.functional as F

def predict_softmax(dataloader, model, device):
    size = len(dataloader.dataset)
    num_batches = len(dataloader)
    model.eval()
    predictions = []
    with torch.no_grad():
        for X, y in dataloader:
            X, y = X.to(device), y.to(device)
            pred = model(X)
            probabilities = F.softmax(pred, dim=1)
            predictions.append(probabilities.cpu())

    return torch.cat(predictions, dim=0)

predictions = predict_softmax(test_loader, model, device).numpy()
```

The result for the first test image is shown below. To make a prediction, we choose the label with the highest probability.

```
print(predictions[0])
```

[4.4307165e-04 3.8354204e-04 2.0886613e-03 8.8066678e-04 3.6079765e-03
 1.7791630e-01 1.4651606e-03 2.2466542e-01 4.8245404e-02 5.4030383e-01]

```
predictions[0].argmax(0)
```

9

The truth is:

```
images, labels = next(iter(test_loader))
images = images.squeeze().numpy()
labels = labels.numpy()
```

```
print(f"{labels[0]}: '{mmids.FashionMNIST_get_class_name
    (labels[0])}'")
```

```
9: 'Ankle boot'
```

Above, `next(iter(test_loader))` loads the first batch of test images.

◁ NC

Self-Assessment Quiz (with help from Claude, Gemini, and ChatGPT)

1. In stochastic gradient descent (SGD), how is the gradient estimated at each iteration?
   a) By computing the gradient over the entire dataset.
   b) By using the gradient from the previous iteration.
   c) By randomly selecting a subsample and computing its gradient.
   d) By averaging the gradients of all samples in the dataset.

2. What is the key advantage of using mini-batch SGD over standard SGD?
   a) It guarantees faster convergence to the optimal solution.
   b) It reduces the variance of the gradient estimate at each iteration.
   c) It eliminates the need for computing gradients altogether.
   d) It increases the computational cost per iteration.

3. Which of the following statements is true about the update step in stochastic gradient descent?
   a) It is always equal to the full gradient descent update.
   b) It is always in the opposite direction to the full gradient descent update.
   c) It is, on average, equal to the full gradient descent update.
   d) It has no relationship to the full gradient descent update.

4. In multinomial logistic regression, what is the role of the softmax function γ?
   a) To compute the gradient of the loss function.
   b) To normalize the input features.
   c) To transform scores into a probability distribution over labels.
   d) To update the model parameters during gradient descent.

5. What is the Kullback–Leibler (KL) divergence used for in multinomial logistic regression?
   a) To measure the distance between the predicted probabilities and the true labels.
   b) To normalize the input features.
   c) To update the model parameters during gradient descent.
   d) To compute the gradient of the loss function.

Answer for 1: c. Justification: The text states that in SGD, "we pick a sample uniformly at random in $\{1, \ldots, n\}$ and update as follows: $\mathbf{w}^{t+1} = \mathbf{w}^t - \alpha_t \nabla f_{\mathbf{x}_{I_t}, y_{I_t}}(\mathbf{w}^t)$."

Answer for 2: b. Justification: The text implies that mini-batch SGD reduces the variance of the gradient estimate compared to standard SGD, which only uses a single sample.

Answer for 3: c. Justification: The text proves a lemma stating that "in expectation, they [stochastic updates] perform a step of gradient descent."

Answer for 4: c. Justification: The text defines the softmax function and states that it is used to "transform these scores into a probability distribution over the labels."

Answer for 5: a. Justification: The text introduces the KL divergence as a "notion of distance between probability measures" and uses it to define the loss function in multinomial logistic regression.

8.5 Building Blocks of AI 3: Neural Networks

In this section, we introduce neural networks. Unlike the previous examples we encountered, this one is not convex. Based on the theory we developed in Chapter 3, finding a local minimizer is the best we can hope for in general from descent methods. Yet, in many application settings, stochastic gradient descent (and some variants) have proven very effective at computing a good model to fit the data. Why that is remains an open question.

We describe the basic setup and apply it to classification on the Fashion-MNIST dataset. As we will see, we will get an improvement over multinomial logistic regression. We use a particular architecture referred to as a multilayer perceptron (MLP). These are a special class of progressive functions.

8.5.1 Multilayer Perceptron

Each of the main layers of a feedforward neural network has two components, an affine map and a nonlinear activation function. For the latter, we restrict ourselves here to the sigmoid function (although there are many other choices of activation functions).

The Jacobian of the elementwise version of the sigmoid function (which we will need later on)

$$\boldsymbol{\sigma}(\mathbf{t}) = (\sigma_1(\mathbf{t}), \ldots, \sigma_n(\mathbf{t})) := (\sigma(t_1), \ldots, \sigma(t_n))$$

as a function of several variables can be computed from σ', the derivative of the single-variable case. Indeed, we have seen in a previous example (see Example 8.2.16) that $J_{\boldsymbol{\sigma}}(\mathbf{t})$ is the diagonal matrix with diagonal entries

$$\sigma'(t_j) = \frac{e^{-t_j}}{(1 + e^{-t_j})^2} = \sigma(t_j)(1 - \sigma(t_j)), \qquad j = 1, \ldots, n,$$

which we denote

$$J_{\boldsymbol{\sigma}}(\mathbf{t}) = \mathrm{diag}(\boldsymbol{\sigma}'(\mathbf{t})) = \mathrm{diag}(\boldsymbol{\sigma}(\mathbf{t}) \odot (\mathbf{1} - \boldsymbol{\sigma}(\mathbf{t}))),$$

where $\boldsymbol{\sigma}'(\mathbf{t}) = (\sigma'(t_1), \ldots, \sigma'(t_n))$ and $\mathbf{1}$ is the all-one vector.

We consider an arbitrary number of layers $L + 2$. As a special case of progressive functions, hidden layer, i, $i = 1, \ldots, L$, is defined by a continuously differentiable function

8.5 Building Blocks of AI 3: Neural Networks

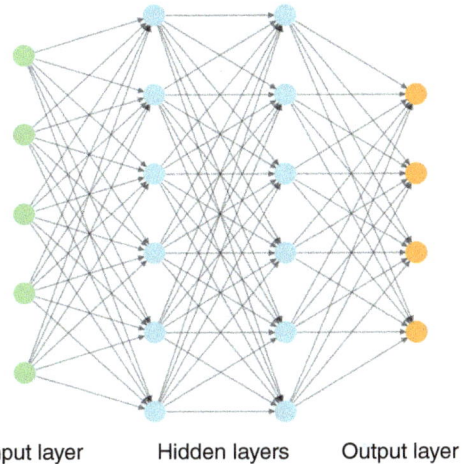

Input layer   Hidden layers   Output layer

Figure 8.2 Feedforward neural network.

$z_i := g_{i-1}(z_{i-1}, w_{i-1})$ which takes two vector-valued inputs: a vector $z_{i-1} \in \mathbb{R}^{n_{i-1}}$ fed from the $(i-1)$-st layer and a vector $w_{i-1} \in \mathbb{R}^{r_{i-1}}$ of parameters specific to the i-th layer,

$$g_{i-1} = (g_{i-1,1}, \ldots, g_{i-1,n_i}) : \mathbb{R}^{n_{i-1}+r_{i-1}} \to \mathbb{R}^{n_i}.$$

The output z_i of g_{i-1} is a vector in $\mathbb{R}^{n_i}$ which is passed to the $(i+1)$-st layer as input. Each component of g_{i-1} is referred to as a neuron. Here $r_{i-1} = n_i n_{i-1}$ and $w_j = (w_{i-1}^{(1)}, \ldots, w_{i-1}^{(n_i)})$ are the parameters with $w_{i-1}^{(k)} \in \mathbb{R}^{n_{i-1}}$ for all k. Specifically, g_{i-1} is given by

$$g_{i-1}(z_{i-1}, w_{i-1}) = \sigma(\mathcal{W}_{i-1} z_{i-1}) = \left(\sigma\left(\sum_{j=1}^{n_{i-1}} w_{i-1,j}^{(1)} z_{i-1,j}\right), \ldots, \sigma\left(\sum_{j=1}^{n_{i-1}} w_{i-1,j}^{(n_i)} z_{i-1,j}\right) \right)$$

where we define $\mathcal{W}_{i-1} \in \mathbb{R}^{n_i \times n_{i-1}}$ as the matrix with rows $(w_{i-1}^{(1)})^T, \ldots, (w_{i-1}^{(n_i)})^T$. As we have done previously, to keep the notation simple, we ignore the constant term (or "bias variable") in the linear combinations of z_{i-1}. It can be incorporated by adding a 1 input to each neuron. We will not detail this complication here.

The input layer is $z_0 := x$, which we refer to as layer 0, so that $n_0 = d$.

Similarly to multinomial logistic regression, layer $L+1$ (i.e., the output layer) is the softmax function

$$\hat{y} := z_{L+1} := g_L(z_L, w_L) = \gamma(\mathcal{W}_L z_L),$$

but this time we compose it with a linear transformation. We implicitly assume that γ has K outputs and, in particular, we have that $n_{L+1} = K$.

So the output of the classifier with parameters $w = (w_0, \ldots, w_L)$ on input x is

$$h(w) = g_L(g_{L-1}(\cdots g_1(g_0(x, w_0), w_1), \cdots, w_{L-1}), w_L).$$

What makes this an MLP is that, on each layer, all outputs feed into the input of the next layer. In graphical terms, the edges between consecutive layers form a complete bipartite graph. See Figure 8.2.

We again use cross-entropy as the loss function (although there are many other choices of loss functions). That is, we set

$$\ell(\hat{\mathbf{y}}) = H(\mathbf{y}, \hat{\mathbf{y}}) = -\sum_{i=1}^{K} y_i \log \hat{y}_i.$$

Finally,

$$f(\mathbf{w}) = \ell(\mathbf{h}(\mathbf{w})).$$

8.5.2 A First Example

Before detailing a general algorithm for computing the gradient, we adapt our first progressive example to this setting to illustrate the main ideas. Suppose $d = 3$, $L = 1$, $n_1 = n_2 = 2$, and $K = 2$; that is, we have one hidden layer and our output is two-dimensional. Fix a data sample $\mathbf{x} = (x_1, x_2, x_3) \in \mathbb{R}^3$, $\mathbf{y} = (y_1, y_2) \in \mathbb{R}^2$. For $i = 0, 1$, we use the notation

$$\mathcal{W}_0 = \begin{pmatrix} w_0 & w_1 & w_2 \\ w_3 & w_4 & w_5 \end{pmatrix} \quad \text{and} \quad \mathcal{W}_1 = \begin{pmatrix} w_6 & w_7 \\ w_8 & w_9 \end{pmatrix}$$

and let

$$\ell(\hat{\mathbf{y}}) = H(\mathbf{y}, \hat{\mathbf{y}}) = -y_1 \log \hat{y}_1 - y_2 \log \hat{y}_2.$$

The layer functions are as follows:

$$\mathbf{g}_0(\mathbf{z}_0, \mathbf{w}_0) = \sigma(\mathcal{W}_0 \mathbf{z}_0) \quad \text{with} \quad \mathbf{w}_0 = (w_0, w_1, w_2, w_3, w_4, w_5)$$
$$\mathbf{g}_1(\mathbf{z}_1, \mathbf{w}_1) = \boldsymbol{\gamma}(\mathcal{W}_1 \mathbf{z}_1) \quad \text{with} \quad \mathbf{w}_1 = (w_6, w_7, w_8, w_9).$$

We seek to compute the gradient of

$$\begin{aligned} f(\mathbf{w}) &= \ell(\mathbf{g}_1(\mathbf{g}_0(\mathbf{x}, \mathbf{w}_0), \mathbf{w}_1)) \\ &= H(\mathbf{y}, \boldsymbol{\gamma}(\mathcal{W}_1 \sigma(\mathcal{W}_0 \mathbf{x}))) \\ &= -y_1 \log \left[Z^{-1} \exp(w_6 \sigma(w_0 x_1 + w_1 x_2 + w_2 x_3) + w_7 \sigma(w_3 x_1 + w_4 x_2 + w_5 x_3)) \right] \\ &\quad - y_2 \log \left[Z^{-1} \exp(w_8 \sigma(w_0 x_1 + w_1 x_2 + w_2 x_3) + w_9 \sigma(w_3 x_1 + w_4 x_2 + w_5 x_3)) \right] \end{aligned}$$

where

$$\begin{aligned} Z &= \exp(w_6 \sigma(w_0 x_1 + w_1 x_2 + w_2 x_3) + w_7 \sigma(w_3 x_1 + w_4 x_2 + w_5 x_3)) \\ &\quad + \exp(w_8 \sigma(w_0 x_1 + w_1 x_2 + w_2 x_3) + w_9 \sigma(w_3 x_1 + w_4 x_2 + w_5 x_3)). \end{aligned}$$

In the forward phase, we compute f itself and the requisite Jacobians:

$$\begin{aligned} \mathbf{z}_0 &:= \mathbf{x} \\ &= (x_1, x_2, x_3) \\ \mathbf{z}_1 &:= \mathbf{g}_0(\mathbf{z}_0, \mathbf{w}_0) = \sigma(\mathcal{W}_0 \mathbf{z}_0) \\ &= \begin{pmatrix} \sigma(w_0 x_1 + w_1 x_2 + w_2 x_3) \\ \sigma(w_3 x_1 + w_4 x_2 + w_5 x_3) \end{pmatrix} \\ J_{\mathbf{g}_0}(\mathbf{z}_0, \mathbf{w}_0) &:= J_\sigma(\mathcal{W}_0 \mathbf{z}_0) \begin{pmatrix} \mathbb{A}_2[\mathbf{w}_0] & \mathbb{B}_2[\mathbf{z}_0] \end{pmatrix} \\ &= \operatorname{diag}(\sigma'(\mathcal{W}_0 \mathbf{z}_0)) \begin{pmatrix} \mathcal{W}_0 & I_{2 \times 2} \otimes \mathbf{z}_0^T \end{pmatrix} \\ &= \begin{pmatrix} \operatorname{diag}(\sigma'(\mathcal{W}_0 \mathbf{z}_0)) \mathcal{W}_0 & \operatorname{diag}(\sigma'(\mathcal{W}_0 \mathbf{z}_0)) \otimes \mathbf{z}_0^T \end{pmatrix}, \end{aligned}$$

8.5 Building Blocks of AI 3: Neural Networks

where we used the *Chain Rule* to compute the Jacobian J_{g_0}.

Then

$$\hat{y} := z_2 := g_1(z_1, w_1) = \gamma(\mathcal{W}_1 z_1)$$
$$= \begin{pmatrix} Z^{-1} \exp(w_6 \sigma(w_0 x_1 + w_1 x_2 + w_2 x_3) + w_7 \sigma(w_3 x_1 + w_4 x_2 + w_5 x_3)) \\ Z^{-1} \exp(w_8 \sigma(w_0 x_1 + w_1 x_2 + w_2 x_3) + w_9 \sigma(w_3 x_1 + w_4 x_2 + w_5 x_3)) \end{pmatrix}$$

$$J_{g_1}(z_1, w_1) := J_\gamma(\mathcal{W}_1 z_1) \begin{pmatrix} \mathbb{A}_2[w_1] & \mathbb{B}_2[z_1] \end{pmatrix}$$
$$= [\text{diag}(\gamma(\mathcal{W}_1 z_1)) - \gamma(\mathcal{W}_1 z_1)\gamma(\mathcal{W}_1 z_1)^T] \begin{pmatrix} \mathcal{W}_1 & I_{2 \times 2} \otimes z_1^T \end{pmatrix}$$
$$= \Big([\text{diag}(\gamma(\mathcal{W}_1 z_1)) - \gamma(\mathcal{W}_1 z_1)\gamma(\mathcal{W}_1 z_1)^T]\mathcal{W}_1$$
$$[\text{diag}(\gamma(\mathcal{W}_1 z_1)) - \gamma(\mathcal{W}_1 z_1)\gamma(\mathcal{W}_1 z_1)^T] \otimes z_1^T\Big),$$

where Z was introduced previously and we used the expression for J_γ from Section 8.4.2.

Finally

$$f(w) := \ell(\hat{y}) = H(y, \hat{y})$$
$$= -y_1 \log \left[Z^{-1} \exp(w_6 \sigma(w_0 x_1 + w_1 x_2 + w_2 x_3) + w_7 \sigma(w_3 x_1 + w_4 x_2 + w_5 x_3)) \right]$$
$$- y_2 \log \left[Z^{-1} \exp(w_8 \sigma(w_0 x_1 + w_1 x_2 + w_2 x_3) + w_9 \sigma(w_3 x_1 + w_4 x_2 + w_5 x_3)) \right]$$
$$J_\ell(\hat{y}) = -(y \oslash \hat{y})^T.$$

We first compute the partial derivatives with respect to $w_1 = (w_6, w_7, w_8, w_9)$. For this step, we think of f as the composition of $\ell(z_2)$ as a function of z_2 and $g_1(z_1, w_1) = \gamma(\mathcal{W}_1 z_1)$ as a function of w_1. Here z_1 does not depend on w_1 and therefore can be considered fixed for this calculation. By the *Chain Rule* and the *Properties of the Kronecker Product Lemma (f)*, we get

$$\left(\frac{\partial f(w)}{\partial w_6} \quad \frac{\partial f(w)}{\partial w_7} \quad \frac{\partial f(w)}{\partial w_8} \quad \frac{\partial f(w)}{\partial w_9} \right)$$
$$= -(y \oslash \hat{y})^T \left\{ [\text{diag}(\gamma(\mathcal{W}_1 z_1)) - \gamma(\mathcal{W}_1 z_1)\gamma(\mathcal{W}_1 z_1)^T] \otimes z_1^T \right\}$$
$$= \left\{ -(y \oslash \gamma(\mathcal{W}_1 z_1))^T [\text{diag}(\gamma(\mathcal{W}_1 z_1)) - \gamma(\mathcal{W}_1 z_1)\gamma(\mathcal{W}_1 z_1)^T] \right\} \otimes z_1^T$$
$$= (\gamma(\mathcal{W}_1 z_1) - y)^T \otimes z_1^T$$
$$= (\hat{y} - y)^T \otimes \sigma(\mathcal{W}_0 x)^T,$$

where we used the *Properties of the Hadamard Product Lemma* and the fact that $\hat{y} = \gamma(\mathcal{W}_1 z_1)$ similarly to a calculation we did in the multinomial logistic regression setting.

To compute the partial derivatives with respect to $w_0 = (w_0, w_1, \ldots, w_5)$, we first need to compute partial derivatives with respect to $z_1 = (z_{1,1}, z_{1,2})$ since f depends on w_0 through it. For this calculation, we think again of f as the composition $\ell(g_1(z_1, w_1))$, but this time our focus is on the variables z_1. This is almost identical to the previous calculation, except that we use the block of $J_{g_1}(z_1, w_1)$ corresponding to the partial derivatives with respect to z_1 (i.e., the "$\mathbb{A}$" block). We obtain

$$\left(\frac{\partial f(w)}{\partial z_{1,1}} \quad \frac{\partial f(w)}{\partial z_{1,2}} \right)$$
$$= -(y \oslash \hat{y})^T \left\{ [\text{diag}(\gamma(\mathcal{W}_1 z_1)) - \gamma(\mathcal{W}_1 z_1)\gamma(\mathcal{W}_1 z_1)^T]\mathcal{W}_1 \right\}$$
$$= -(y \oslash \gamma(\mathcal{W}_1 z_1))^T [\text{diag}(\gamma(\mathcal{W}_1 z_1)) - \gamma(\mathcal{W}_1 z_1)\gamma(\mathcal{W}_1 z_1)^T]\mathcal{W}_1$$
$$= (\gamma(\mathcal{W}_1 z_1) - y)^T \mathcal{W}_1$$

The vector $\left(\frac{\partial f(\mathbf{w})}{\partial z_{1,1}}, \frac{\partial f(\mathbf{w})}{\partial z_{1,2}}\right)$ is called an adjoint.

We now compute the gradient of f with respect to $\mathbf{w}_0 = (w_0, w_1, \ldots, w_5)$. For this step, we think of f as the composition of $\ell(\mathbf{g}_1(\mathbf{z}_1, \mathbf{w}_1))$ as a function of $\mathbf{z}_1$ and $\mathbf{g}_0(\mathbf{z}_0, \mathbf{w}_0)$ as a function of $\mathbf{w}_0$. Here $\mathbf{w}_1$ and $\mathbf{z}_0$ do not depend on $\mathbf{w}_0$ and therefore can be considered fixed for this calculation. By the *Chain Rule*

$$\left(\frac{\partial f(\mathbf{w})}{\partial w_0} \quad \frac{\partial f(\mathbf{w})}{\partial w_1} \quad \frac{\partial f(\mathbf{w})}{\partial w_2} \quad \frac{\partial f(\mathbf{w})}{\partial w_3} \quad \frac{\partial f(\mathbf{w})}{\partial w_4} \quad \frac{\partial f(\mathbf{w})}{\partial w_5}\right)$$
$$= (\gamma(\mathcal{W}_1 \mathbf{z}_1) - \mathbf{y})^T \mathcal{W}_1 \left[\text{diag}(\sigma'(\mathcal{W}_0 \mathbf{z}_0)) \otimes \mathbf{z}_0^T\right]$$
$$= [(\gamma(\mathcal{W}_1 \mathbf{z}_1) - \mathbf{y})^T \mathcal{W}_1 \text{diag}(\sigma'(\mathcal{W}_0 \mathbf{z}_0))] \otimes \mathbf{z}_0^T$$
$$= [(\hat{\mathbf{y}} - \mathbf{y})^T \mathcal{W}_1 \text{diag}(\sigma'(\mathcal{W}_0 \mathbf{x}))] \otimes \mathbf{x}^T$$
$$= [(\hat{\mathbf{y}} - \mathbf{y})^T \mathcal{W}_1 \text{diag}(\sigma(\mathcal{W}_0 \mathbf{x}) \odot (\mathbf{1} - \sigma(\mathcal{W}_0 \mathbf{x})))] \otimes \mathbf{x}^T$$

where we used *Properties of the Kronecker Product Lemma (f)* in the second to last line and our expression for the derivative of the sigmoid function in the last line.

To sum up,

$$\nabla f(\mathbf{w})^T = \left([(\hat{\mathbf{y}} - \mathbf{y})^T \mathcal{W}_1 \text{diag}(\sigma(\mathcal{W}_0 \mathbf{x}) \odot (\mathbf{1} - \sigma(\mathcal{W}_0 \mathbf{x})))] \otimes \mathbf{x}^T \quad (\hat{\mathbf{y}} - \mathbf{y})^T \otimes \sigma(\mathcal{W}_0 \mathbf{x})^T\right)$$

NUMERICAL CORNER We return to the concrete example from the previous section. We rewrite the gradient as

$$\nabla f(\mathbf{w})^T = \left([(\mathbf{z}_2 - \mathbf{y})^T \mathcal{W}_1 \text{diag}(\mathbf{z}_1 \odot (\mathbf{1} - \mathbf{z}_1))] \otimes \mathbf{z}_0^T \quad (\mathbf{z}_2 - \mathbf{y})^T \otimes \mathbf{z}_1^T\right).$$

We will use `torch.nn.functional.sigmoid` and `torch.nn.functional.softmax` for the sigmoid and softmax functions respectively. We also use `torch.dot` for the inner product (i.e., dot product) of two vectors (as tensors) and `torch.diag` for the creation of a diagonal matrix with specified entries on its diagonal.

```
import torch.nn.functional as F

x = torch.tensor([1.,0.,-1.])
y = torch.tensor([0.,1.])
W0 = torch.tensor([[0.,1.,-1.],[2.,0.,1.]], requires_grad=True)
W1 = torch.tensor([[-1.,0.],[2.,-1.]], requires_grad=True)

z0 = x
z1 = F.sigmoid(W0 @ z0)
z2 = F.softmax(W1 @ z1, dim=0)
f = -torch.dot(torch.log(z2), y)

print(z0)
```

```
tensor([ 1.,  0., -1.])
```

```
print(z1)
```

```
tensor([0.7311, 0.7311], grad_fn=<SigmoidBackward0>)
```

```
print(z2)
```

```
tensor([0.1881, 0.8119], grad_fn=<SoftmaxBackward0>)
```

```
print(f)
```

```
tensor(0.2084, grad_fn=<NegBackward0>)
```

We compute the gradient $\nabla f(\mathbf{w})$ using AD.

```
f.backward()
print(W0.grad)
```

```
tensor([[-0.1110, -0.0000,  0.1110],
        [ 0.0370,  0.0000, -0.0370]])
```

```
print(W1.grad)
```

```
tensor([[ 0.1375,  0.1375],
        [-0.1375, -0.1375]])
```

We use our formulas to confirm that they match these results.

```
with torch.no_grad():
    grad_W0 = torch.kron((z2 - y).T @ W1 @ torch.diag(z1 * (1-z1)),
            z0.T)
    grad_W1 = torch.kron((z2 - y).T, z1.T)
```

```
print(grad_W0)
```

```
tensor([-0.1110, -0.0000,  0.1110,  0.0370,  0.0000, -0.0370])
```

```
print(grad_W1)
```

```
tensor([ 0.1375,  0.1375, -0.1375, -0.1375])
```

The results match with the AD output.

◁ **NC**

8.5.3 Computing the Gradient

We now detail how to compute the gradient of $f(\mathbf{w})$ for a general MLP. In the forward loop, we first set $\mathbf{z}_0 := \mathbf{x}$ and then we compute for $i = 0, 1, \ldots, L - 1$

$$\mathbf{z}_{i+1} := \mathbf{g}_i(\mathbf{z}_i, \mathbf{w}_i) = \sigma\left(\mathcal{W}_i \mathbf{z}_i\right)$$

$$\begin{pmatrix} A_i & B_i \end{pmatrix} := J_{\mathbf{g}_i}(\mathbf{z}_i, \mathbf{w}_i).$$

To compute the Jacobian of $\mathbf{g}_i$, we use the *Chain Rule* on the composition $\mathbf{g}_i(\mathbf{z}_i, \mathbf{w}_i) = \sigma(\mathbf{k}_i(\mathbf{z}_i, \mathbf{w}_i))$ where we define $\mathbf{k}_i(\mathbf{z}_i, \mathbf{w}_i) = \mathcal{W}_i \mathbf{z}_i$. That is,

$$J_{\mathbf{g}_i}(\mathbf{z}_i, \mathbf{w}_i) = J_\sigma(\mathcal{W}_i \mathbf{z}_i) J_{\mathbf{k}_i}(\mathbf{z}_i, \mathbf{w}_i).$$

In our analysis of multinomial logistic regression, we computed the Jacobian of $\mathbf{k}_i$. We obtained

$$J_{\mathbf{k}_i}(\mathbf{z}_i, \mathbf{w}_i) = \begin{pmatrix} \mathbb{A}_{n_{i+1}}[\mathbf{w}_i] & \mathbb{B}_{n_{i+1}}[\mathbf{z}_i] \end{pmatrix}.$$

Recall that

$$\mathbb{A}_{n_{i+1}}[\mathbf{w}_i] = \mathcal{W}_i.$$

and

$$\mathbb{B}_{n_{i+1}}[\mathbf{z}_i] = \begin{pmatrix} \mathbf{e}_1 \mathbf{z}_i^T & \cdots & \mathbf{e}_{n_{i+1}} \mathbf{z}_i^T \end{pmatrix} = I_{n_{i+1} \times n_{i+1}} \otimes \mathbf{z}_i^T,$$

where here $\mathbf{e}_j$ is the j-th standard basis vector in $\mathbb{R}^{n_{i+1}}$.

From a calculation in Section 8.5.1, the Jacobian of

$$\sigma(\mathbf{t}) = (\sigma_1(\mathbf{t}), \ldots, \sigma_{n_{i+1}}(\mathbf{t})) := (\sigma(t_1), \ldots, \sigma(t_{n_{i+1}}))$$

is

$$J_\sigma(\mathbf{t}) = \operatorname{diag}(\sigma(\mathbf{t}) \odot (\mathbf{1} - \sigma(\mathbf{t}))).$$

Combining the previous formulas, we get

$$J_{\mathbf{g}_i}(\mathbf{z}_i, \mathbf{w}_i) = J_\sigma(\mathcal{W}_i \mathbf{z}_i) J_{\mathbf{k}_i}(\mathbf{z}_i, \mathbf{w}_i)$$
$$= \operatorname{diag}\left(\sigma(\mathcal{W}_i \mathbf{z}_i) \odot (\mathbf{1} - \sigma(\mathcal{W}_i \mathbf{z}_i))\right) \begin{pmatrix} \mathbb{A}_{n_{i+1}}[\mathbf{w}_i] & \mathbb{B}_{n_{i+1}}[\mathbf{z}_i] \end{pmatrix}$$
$$= \begin{pmatrix} \widetilde{\mathbb{A}}_{n_{i+1}}[\mathbf{z}_i, \mathbf{w}_i] & \widetilde{\mathbb{B}}_{n_{i+1}}[\mathbf{z}_i, \mathbf{w}_i] \end{pmatrix}$$

where we define

$$\widetilde{\mathbb{A}}_{n_{i+1}}[\mathbf{z}_i, \mathbf{w}_i] = \operatorname{diag}\left(\sigma(\mathcal{W}_i \mathbf{z}_i) \odot (\mathbf{1} - \sigma(\mathcal{W}_i \mathbf{z}_i))\right) \mathcal{W}_i$$

and

$$\widetilde{\mathbb{B}}_{n_{i+1}}[\mathbf{z}_i, \mathbf{w}_i] = \operatorname{diag}\left(\sigma(\mathcal{W}_i \mathbf{z}_i) \odot (\mathbf{1} - \sigma(\mathcal{W}_i \mathbf{z}_i))\right) \left(I_{n_{i+1} \times n_{i+1}} \otimes \mathbf{z}_i^T \right)$$
$$= \operatorname{diag}\left(\sigma(\mathcal{W}_i \mathbf{z}_i) \odot (\mathbf{1} - \sigma(\mathcal{W}_i \mathbf{z}_i))\right) \otimes \mathbf{z}_i^T,$$

where we used the *Properties of the Kronecker Product Lemma (f)*.

For layer $L + 1$ (i.e., the output layer), we have previously computed the Jacobian of the softmax function composed with a linear transformation (see Section 8.5.2). We get

$$\mathbf{z}_{L+1} := \mathbf{g}_L(\mathbf{z}_L, \mathbf{w}_L)$$
$$= \gamma(\mathcal{W}_L \mathbf{z}_L) \begin{pmatrix} A_L & B_L \end{pmatrix} := J_{\mathbf{g}_L}(\mathbf{z}_L, \mathbf{w}_L)$$
$$= \Big([\operatorname{diag}(\gamma(\mathcal{W}_L \mathbf{z}_L)) - \gamma(\mathcal{W}_L \mathbf{z}_L) \gamma(\mathcal{W}_L \mathbf{z}_L)^T] \mathcal{W}_L$$
$$\quad [\operatorname{diag}(\gamma(\mathcal{W}_L \mathbf{z}_L)) - \gamma(\mathcal{W}_L \mathbf{z}_L) \gamma(\mathcal{W}_L \mathbf{z}_L)^T] \otimes \mathbf{z}_L^T \Big)$$
$$=: \begin{pmatrix} \widetilde{\mathbb{C}}_K[\mathbf{z}_L, \mathbf{w}_L] & \widetilde{\mathbb{D}}_K[\mathbf{z}_L, \mathbf{w}_L] \end{pmatrix}$$

Also, as in the multinomial logistic regression case, the loss and gradient of the loss are

$$\mathbf{z}_{L+2} := \ell(\mathbf{z}_{L+1}) = -\sum_{i=1}^{K} y_i \log z_{L+1,i}$$

$$\mathbf{q}_{L+1} := \nabla \ell(\mathbf{z}_{L+1}) = \left(-\frac{y_1}{z_{L+1,1}}, \ldots, -\frac{y_K}{z_{L+1,K}}\right).$$

Initialization: $\mathbf{z}_0 := \mathbf{x}$

Forward loop: For $i = 0, 1, \ldots, L-1$:

$$\mathbf{z}_{i+1} := g_i(\mathbf{z}_i, \mathbf{w}_i) = \sigma(\mathcal{W}_i \mathbf{z}_i)$$

$$\begin{pmatrix} A_i & B_i \end{pmatrix} := J_{\mathbf{g}_i}(\mathbf{z}_i, \mathbf{w}_i) = \begin{pmatrix} \widetilde{\mathbb{A}}_{n_{i+1}}[\mathbf{z}_i, \mathbf{w}_i] & \widetilde{\mathbb{B}}_{n_{i+1}}[\mathbf{z}_i, \mathbf{w}_i] \end{pmatrix}$$

and

$$\mathbf{z}_{L+1} := \mathbf{g}_L(\mathbf{z}_L, \mathbf{w}_L) = \gamma(\mathcal{W}_L \mathbf{z}_L)$$

$$\begin{pmatrix} A_L & B_L \end{pmatrix} := J_{\mathbf{g}_L}(\mathbf{z}_L, \mathbf{w}_L) = \begin{pmatrix} \widetilde{\mathbb{C}}_K[\mathbf{z}_L, \mathbf{w}_L] & \widetilde{\mathbb{D}}_K[\mathbf{z}_L, \mathbf{w}_L] \end{pmatrix}.$$

Loss:

$$\mathbf{z}_{L+2} := \ell(\mathbf{z}_{L+1})$$

$$\mathbf{p}_{L+1} := \nabla \ell(\mathbf{z}_{L+1}) = \left(-\frac{y_1}{z_{L+1,1}}, \ldots, -\frac{y_K}{z_{L+1,K}}\right).$$

Backward loop:

$$\mathbf{p}_L := A_L^T \mathbf{p}_{L+1} = \widetilde{\mathbb{C}}_K[\mathbf{z}_L]^T \mathbf{p}_{L+1}$$

$$\mathbf{q}_L := B_L^T \mathbf{p}_{L+1} = \widetilde{\mathbb{D}}_K[\mathbf{z}_L]^T \mathbf{p}_{L+1}$$

and for $i = L-1, L-2, \ldots, 1, 0$:

$$\mathbf{p}_i := A_i^T \mathbf{p}_{i+1} = \widetilde{\mathbb{A}}_{n_{i+1}}[\mathbf{z}_i, \mathbf{w}_i]^T \mathbf{p}_{i+1}$$

$$\mathbf{q}_i := B_i^T \mathbf{p}_{i+1} = \widetilde{\mathbb{B}}_{n_{i+1}}[\mathbf{z}_i, \mathbf{w}_i]^T \mathbf{p}_{i+1}$$

Output:

$$\nabla f(\mathbf{w}) = (\mathbf{q}_0, \mathbf{q}_1, \ldots, \mathbf{q}_L).$$

NUMERICAL CORNER We implement the training of a neural network in PyTorch. We use the Fashion-MNIST dataset again. We first load it again. We also check for the availability of GPUs.

```
device = torch.device('cuda' if torch.cuda.is_available()
                     else ('mps' if torch.backends.mps.
                     is_available()
                     else 'cpu'))
print('Using device:', device)
```

Using device: mps

```
from torchvision import datasets, transforms
from torch.utils.data import DataLoader
```

```python
import torch.nn as nn
import torch.optim as optim

seed = 42
torch.manual_seed(seed)

if device.type == 'cuda':  # device-specific seeding and settings
    torch.cuda.manual_seed(seed)
    torch.cuda.manual_seed_all(seed)   # for multi-GPU
    torch.backends.cudnn.deterministic = True
    torch.backends.cudnn.benchmark = False
elif device.type == 'mps':
    torch.mps.manual_seed(seed)   # MPS-specific seeding

g = torch.Generator()
g.manual_seed(seed)

train_dataset = datasets.FashionMNIST(root='./data', train=True,
                          download=True, transform=transforms.
                          ToTensor())
test_dataset = datasets.FashionMNIST(root='./data', train=False,
                          download=True, transform=transforms.
                          ToTensor())

BATCH_SIZE = 32
train_loader = DataLoader(train_dataset, batch_size=BATCH_SIZE,
                          shuffle=True, generator=g)
test_loader = DataLoader(test_dataset, batch_size=BATCH_SIZE,
                          shuffle=False)
```

We construct a two-layer model.

```python
model = nn.Sequential(
    nn.Flatten(),                   # Flatten the input
    nn.Linear(28 * 28, 32),         # First Linear layer with 32
                                    #   nodes
    nn.Sigmoid(),                   # Sigmoid activation function
    nn.Linear(32, 10)               # Second Linear layer with 10
                                    #   nodes (output layer)
).to(device)
```

As we did for multinomial logistic regression, we use the SGD optimizer and the cross-entropy loss (which in PyTorch includes the softmax function and expects labels to be actual class labels rather than one-hot encoding).

8.5 Building Blocks of AI 3: Neural Networks

```
loss_fn = nn.CrossEntropyLoss()
optimizer = optim.SGD(model.parameters(), lr=1e-3)
```

We train for 10 epochs.

```
mmids.training_loop(train_loader, model, loss_fn, optimizer, device,
                    epochs=10)
```

Epoch 1/10
Epoch 2/10
Epoch 3/10
Epoch 4/10
Epoch 5/10
Epoch 6/10
Epoch 7/10
Epoch 8/10
Epoch 9/10
Epoch 10/10

On the test data, we get:

```
mmids.test(test_loader, model, loss_fn, device)
```

Test error: 64.0% accuracy

Disappointingly, this is significantly less accurate than what we obtained using multinomial logistic regression. It turns out that using a different optimizer gives much better results.

```
loss_fn = nn.CrossEntropyLoss()
optimizer = optim.Adam(model.parameters())
```

```
mmids.training_loop(train_loader, model, loss_fn, optimizer, device)
```

Epoch 1/3
Epoch 2/3
Epoch 3/3

```
mmids.test(test_loader, model, loss_fn, device)
```

Test error: 85.0% accuracy

CHAT & LEARN We mentioned that there are many optimizers available in PyTorch besides SGD and Adam. Ask your favorite AI chatbot to explain and implement a different optimizer, such as Adagrad or RMSprop, for the MLP. *Compare the results* with those obtained using SGD and Adam.

◁ NC

CHAT & LEARN Regularization techniques are often used to prevent overfitting in neural networks. Ask your favorite AI chatbot about L_1 and L_2 regularization, dropout, and early stopping. Discuss how these techniques can be incorporated into the training process and their effects on the learned model.

Self-Assessment Quiz (with help from Claude, Gemini, and ChatGPT)

1. What is the role of the sigmoid function in a multilayer perceptron (MLP)?
   a) It is used as the loss function for training the MLP.
   b) It is used as the nonlinear activation function in each layer of the MLP.
   c) It is used to compute the gradient of the loss function with respect to the weights.
   d) It is used to initialize the weights of the MLP.

2. In an MLP, what is the purpose of the softmax function in the output layer?
   a) To introduce nonlinearity into the model.
   b) To normalize the outputs into a probability distribution.
   c) To compute the gradient of the loss function.
   d) To reduce the dimensionality of the output.

3. What is the Jacobian matrix of the elementwise sigmoid function $\sigma(\mathbf{t}) = (\sigma(\mathbf{t}_1), \ldots, \sigma(\mathbf{t}_n))$?
   a) $J_\sigma(\mathbf{t}) = \text{diag}(\sigma(\mathbf{t}))$
   b) $J_\sigma(\mathbf{t}) = \sigma(\mathbf{t}) \odot (1 - \sigma(\mathbf{t}))$
   c) $J_\sigma(\mathbf{t}) = \text{diag}(\sigma(\mathbf{t}) \odot (1 - \sigma(\mathbf{t})))$
   d) $J_\sigma(\mathbf{t}) = \sigma(\mathbf{t})(1 - \sigma(\mathbf{t}))^T$

4. In the forward phase of computing the gradient of the loss function in an MLP, what is the output of the i-th hidden layer?
   a) $\mathbf{z}_{i+1} := \mathbf{g}_i(\mathbf{z}_i, \mathbf{w}_i) = \sigma(\mathcal{W}_i \mathbf{z}_i)$
   b) $\mathbf{z}_{i+1} := \mathbf{g}_i(\mathbf{z}_i, \mathbf{w}_i) = \mathcal{W}_i \mathbf{z}_i$
   c) $\mathbf{z}_{i+1} := \mathbf{g}_i(\mathbf{z}_i, \mathbf{w}_i) = \gamma(\mathcal{W}_i \mathbf{z}_i)$
   d) $\mathbf{z}_{i+1} := \mathbf{g}_i(\mathbf{z}_i, \mathbf{w}_i) = \mathcal{W}_i \sigma(\mathbf{z}_i)$

5. What is the output of the backward loop in computing the gradient of the loss function in an MLP?
   a) The gradient of the loss function with respect to the activations of each layer.
   b) The gradient of the loss function with respect to the weights of each layer.
   c) The updated weights of the MLP.
   d) The loss function value.

Answer for 1: b. Justification: The text states that "Each of the main layers of a feedforward neural network has two components, an affine map and a nonlinear activation function. For the latter, we restrict ourselves here to the sigmoid function."

Answer for 2: b. Justification: The text states that the softmax function is used in the output layer to produce a probability distribution over the possible classes.

Answer for 3: c. Justification: The text states that the Jacobian of the elementwise sigmoid function is:

$$J_\sigma(\mathbf{t}) = \text{diag}(\sigma'(\mathbf{t})) = \text{diag}(\sigma(\mathbf{t}) \odot (1 - \sigma(\mathbf{t})))$$

where $\odot$ denotes the Hadamard (elementwise) product.

Answer for 4: a. Justification: The text defines the output of the i-th hidden layer as

$$\mathbf{z}_{i+1} := \mathbf{g}_i(\mathbf{z}_i, \mathbf{w}_i) = \sigma(\mathcal{W}_i \mathbf{z}_i)$$

where σ is the sigmoid activation function and $\mathcal{W}_i$ is the weight matrix for the i-th layer.

Answer for 5: b. Justification: The text states that the output of the backward loop is the gradient of the loss function with respect to the weights of each layer:

$$\nabla f(\mathbf{w}) = (\mathbf{q}_0, \mathbf{q}_1, \ldots, \mathbf{q}_L)$$

where $\mathbf{q}_i := B_i^T \mathbf{p}_{i+1} = \widetilde{\mathbb{B}}_{n_{i+1}}[\mathbf{z}_i, \mathbf{w}_i]^T \mathbf{p}_{i+1}$ is the gradient with respect to the weights of the i-th layer.

8.6 Exercises

8.6.1 Warm-Up Worksheets
(with help from Claude, Gemini, and ChatGPT)

Section 8.2

E8.2.1 Let $A = \begin{pmatrix} 2 & 1 \\ 0 & -1 \end{pmatrix}$. Compute the vectorization $\text{vec}(A)$.

E8.2.2 Let $\mathbf{a} = (2, -1, 3)$ and $\mathbf{b} = (1, 0, -2)$. Compute the Hadamard product $\mathbf{a} \odot \mathbf{b}$.

E8.2.3 Let $A = \begin{pmatrix} 1 & 2 \\ -1 & 0 \end{pmatrix}$ and $B = \begin{pmatrix} 3 & -1 \\ 2 & 1 \end{pmatrix}$. Compute the Kronecker product $A \otimes B$.

E8.2.4 Let $A = \begin{pmatrix} 1 & 2 \\ 3 & 4 \end{pmatrix}$ and $B = \begin{pmatrix} 5 & 6 \\ 7 & 8 \end{pmatrix}$. Compute the Hadamard product $A \odot B$.

E8.2.5 Let $A = \begin{pmatrix} 1 & 2 \\ 3 & 4 \end{pmatrix}$ and $B = \begin{pmatrix} 5 & 6 \\ 7 & 8 \end{pmatrix}$. Compute the Kronecker product $A \otimes B$.

E8.2.6 Let $\mathbf{f}(x, y) = (x^2 y, \sin(xy), e^{x+y})$. Compute the Jacobian matrix of $\mathbf{f}$ at the point $(1, \frac{\pi}{2})$.

E8.2.7 Let $\mathbf{f}(x, y) = (x^2 + y^2, xy)$ and $\mathbf{g}(u, v) = (uv, u + v)$. Compute the Jacobian matrix of the composition $\mathbf{g} \circ \mathbf{f}$ at the point $(1, 2)$.

E8.2.8 Let $\mathbf{a} = (1, 2, 3)$, $\mathbf{b} = (4, 5, 6)$, and $\mathbf{c} = (7, 8, 9)$. Compute $\mathbf{a}^T(\mathbf{b} \odot \mathbf{c})$ and $\mathbf{1}^T(\mathbf{a} \odot \mathbf{b} \odot \mathbf{c})$ and verify that they are equal.

E8.2.9 Let $A = \begin{pmatrix} 1 & 2 \\ 3 & 4 \end{pmatrix}$ and $B = \begin{pmatrix} 5 & 6 \\ 7 & 8 \end{pmatrix}$. Compute $(A \otimes B)^T$ and $A^T \otimes B^T$ and verify that they are equal.

E8.2.10 Let $\mathbf{g}(x, y) = (x^2 y, x + y)$. Compute the Jacobian matrix $J_\mathbf{g}(x, y)$.

E8.2.11 Let $f(x, y, z) = x^2 + y^2 + z^2$. Compute the gradient of f at the point $(1, 2, 3)$.

E8.2.12 Let $f(x) = 2x^3 - x$ and $g(y) = y^2 + 1$. Compute the Jacobian of the composite function $g \circ f$ at $x = 1$.

E8.2.13 Let $f(x, y) = xy$ and $\mathbf{g}(x, y) = (x^2, y^2)$. Compute the Jacobian matrix of $f \circ \mathbf{g}$ at the point $(1, 2)$.

E8.2.14 Let $A = \begin{pmatrix} 1 & 2 \\ 3 & 4 \end{pmatrix}$ and $\mathbf{b} = \begin{pmatrix} 5 \\ 6 \end{pmatrix}$. Define the function $\mathbf{f}(\mathbf{x}) = A\mathbf{x} + \mathbf{b}$. Compute the Jacobian matrix of $\mathbf{f}$ at any point $\mathbf{x} \in \mathbb{R}^2$.

E8.2.15 Let $f(x) = \sin(x)$. Define the function $\mathbf{g}(x, y, z) = (f(x), f(y), f(z))$. Compute the Jacobian matrix of $\mathbf{g}$ at the point $(\frac{\pi}{2}, \frac{\pi}{4}, \frac{\pi}{6})$.

E8.2.16 Use PyTorch to find the gradient of $f(x) = x^3 - 4x$ at $x = 2$. Provide the PyTorch code and the result.

Section 8.3

E8.3.1 Let $A = \begin{pmatrix} 1 & -1 \\ 0 & 2 \end{pmatrix}$ and $B = \begin{pmatrix} 2 & 1 \\ -1 & 3 \end{pmatrix}$. How many elementary operations (additions and multiplications) does it take to compute AB?

E8.3.2 Let $A = \begin{pmatrix} 1 & -1 \\ 0 & 2 \end{pmatrix}$ and $\mathbf{v} = (2, -1)$. How many elementary operations (additions and multiplications) does it take to compute $A\mathbf{v}$?

E8.3.3 Let $\ell(\hat{\mathbf{y}}) = \|\hat{\mathbf{y}}\|^2$ where $\hat{\mathbf{y}} = (\hat{y}_1, \hat{y}_2)$. Compute $J_\ell(\hat{\mathbf{y}})$.

E8.3.4 Let $\mathbf{g}_0(\mathbf{z}_0) = \begin{pmatrix} 1 & 2 \\ -1 & 0 \end{pmatrix} \mathbf{z}_0$ and $\ell(\hat{\mathbf{y}}) = \|\hat{\mathbf{y}}\|^2$. Compute $\nabla f(\mathbf{x})$ where $f(\mathbf{x}) = \ell(\mathbf{g}_0(\mathbf{x}))$ and $\mathbf{x} = (1, -1)$.

E8.3.5 Let $\mathbf{g}_0$ and ℓ be as in E8.3.4. Let $\mathbf{g}_1(\mathbf{z}_1) = \begin{pmatrix} -1 & 0 \\ 1 & 1 \end{pmatrix} \mathbf{z}_1$. Compute $\nabla f(\mathbf{x})$ where $f(\mathbf{x}) = \ell(\mathbf{g}_1(\mathbf{g}_0(\mathbf{x})))$ and $\mathbf{x} = (1, -1)$ using the reverse mode.

E8.3.6 Let $\mathbf{g}_0(\mathbf{x}, \mathbf{w}_0) = \mathcal{W}_0 \mathbf{x}$ where $\mathcal{W}_0 = \begin{pmatrix} w_0 & w_1 \\ w_2 & w_3 \end{pmatrix}$ and $\mathbf{w}_0 = (w_0, w_1, w_2, w_3)$. Let $\mathbf{x} = (-1, 1)$ be fixed. Compute the Jacobian $J_{\mathbf{g}_0}(\mathbf{x}, \mathbf{w}_0)$ with respect to $\mathbf{w}_0$ only by directly computing the necessary partial derivatives (i.e., without using the formulas in the text), and then compare to the formulas in the text.

E8.3.7 Let $g_1(\mathbf{z}_1, \mathbf{w}_1) = \mathcal{W}_1 \mathbf{z}_1$ where $\mathcal{W}_1 = \begin{pmatrix} w_4 & w_5 \end{pmatrix}$ and $\mathbf{w}_1 = (w_4, w_5)$. Compute $J_{g_1}(\mathbf{z}_1, \mathbf{w}_1)$ with respect to both $\mathbf{z}_1$ and $\mathbf{w}_1$ by directly computing the necessary partial derivatives (i.e., without using the formulas in the text), and then compare to the formulas in the text.

E8.3.8 Let $h(\mathbf{w}) = g_1(\mathbf{g}_0(\mathbf{x}, \mathbf{w}_0), \mathbf{w}_1)$ where $\mathbf{g}_0$ and g_1 are as in E8.3.6 and E8.3.7 and $\mathbf{w} = (\mathbf{w}_0, \mathbf{w}_1) = (w_0, w_1, w_2, w_3, w_4, w_5)$. Let $\mathbf{x} = (-1, 1)$ be fixed. Compute $J_h(\mathbf{w})$ by directly computing the necessary partial derivatives (i.e., without using the formulas in the text).

E8.3.9 Let $f(\mathbf{w}) = \ell(g_1(\mathbf{g}_0(\mathbf{x}, \mathbf{w}_0), \mathbf{w}_1))$ where $\ell(\hat{y}) = \hat{y}^2$, $\mathbf{g}_0$ and g_1 are as in E8.3.6 and E8.3.7, and $\mathbf{w} = (\mathbf{w}_0, \mathbf{w}_1) = (w_0, w_1, w_2, w_3, w_4, w_5)$. Let $\mathbf{x} = (-1, 1)$ be fixed. Compute $J_f(\mathbf{w})$ by directly computing the necessary partial derivatives (i.e., without using the formulas in the text), and then compare to the formulas in the text.

Section 8.4

E8.4.1 Given a dataset with five samples, compute the full gradient descent step and the expected SGD step with a batch size of 2. Assume that the individual sample gradients are: $\nabla f_{\mathbf{x}_1, y_1}(\mathbf{w}) = (1, 2)$, $\nabla f_{\mathbf{x}_2, y_2}(\mathbf{w}) = (-1, 1)$, $\nabla f_{\mathbf{x}_3, y_3}(\mathbf{w}) = (0, -1)$, $\nabla f_{\mathbf{x}_4, y_4}(\mathbf{w}) = (2, 0)$, and $\nabla f_{\mathbf{x}_5, y_5}(\mathbf{w}) = (1, 1)$.

E8.4.2 Compute the softmax function $\gamma(\mathbf{z})$ for $\mathbf{z} = (1, -2, 0, 3)$.

E8.4.3 Compute the Kullback–Leibler divergence between the probability distributions $\mathbf{p} = (0.2, 0.3, 0.5)$ and $\mathbf{q} = (0.1, 0.4, 0.5)$.

E8.4.4 In linear regression with a single feature, the loss function for a single sample (x, y) is given by

$$\ell(w, b; x, y) = (wx + b - y)^2.$$

Compute the gradients $\frac{\partial \ell}{\partial w}$ and $\frac{\partial \ell}{\partial b}$.

E8.4.5 Suppose we have a dataset with three samples: $(x_1, y_1) = (2, 3)$, $(x_2, y_2) = (-1, 0)$, and $(x_3, y_3) = (1, 2)$. We want to perform mini-batch SGD for linear regression with a batch size of 2. If the first mini-batch randomly selected is $B = \{1, 3\}$, compute the SGD update for the parameters w and b, assuming a learning rate of $\alpha = 0.1$. The model is initialized at $w = 1$ and $b = 0$.

E8.4.6 For the linear regression problem with a single sample $(\mathbf{x}, y) = ((1, 2), 3)$, compute the gradient of the loss function $f(\mathbf{w}) = (\mathbf{x}^T \mathbf{w} - y)^2$ at $\mathbf{w} = (0, 0)$.

E8.4.7 Consider the logistic regression loss function for a single sample (x, y) where $x \in \mathbb{R}$ and $y \in \{0, 1\}$:

$$\ell(w; x, y) = -y \log(\sigma(wx)) - (1 - y) \log(1 - \sigma(wx)),$$

where $\sigma(z) = \frac{1}{1+e^{-z}}$ is the sigmoid function. Compute the gradient $\nabla \ell(w; x, y)$ with respect to w.

E8.4.8 Consider a multinomial logistic regression problem with three classes ($K = 3$). Given an input vector $\mathbf{x} = (1, -1)$, and a weight matrix

$$W = \begin{pmatrix} 1 & 2 \\ -1 & 0 \\ 0 & 1 \end{pmatrix},$$

compute the softmax output $\gamma(W\mathbf{x})$.

E8.4.9 For the multinomial logistic regression problem with a single sample $(\mathbf{x}, \mathbf{y}) = ((1, 2), (0, 0, 1))$ and $K = 3$ classes, compute the gradient of the loss function $f(\mathbf{w}) = -\sum_{i=1}^{K} y_i \log \gamma_i(W\mathbf{x})$ at $W = \begin{pmatrix} 0 & 0 \\ 0 & 0 \\ 0 & 0 \end{pmatrix}$.

E8.4.10 For the linear regression problem with two samples $(\mathbf{x}_1, y_1) = ((1, 2), 3)$ and $(\mathbf{x}_2, y_2) = ((4, -1), 2)$, compute the full gradient at $\mathbf{w} = (0, 0)$.

E8.4.11 For the multinomial logistic regression problem with two samples $(\mathbf{x}_1, \mathbf{y}_1) = ((1, 2), (0, 0, 1))$ and $(\mathbf{x}_2, \mathbf{y}_2) = ((4, -1), (1, 0, 0))$, and $K = 3$ classes, compute the full gradient at $W = \begin{pmatrix} 0 & 0 \\ 0 & 0 \\ 0 & 0 \end{pmatrix}$.

E8.4.12 In a binary classification problem, the logistic regression model predicts probabilities of 0.8 and 0.3 for two samples. If the true labels for these samples are 1 and 0, respectively, compute the average cross-entropy loss.

E8.4.13 In a multiclass classification problem with four classes, a model predicts the following probability distribution for a sample: $(0.1, 0.2, 0.3, 0.4)$. If the true label is the third class, what is the cross-entropy loss for this sample?

Section 8.5

E8.5.1 Compute the sigmoid function $\sigma(t)$ for the following values of t: $1, -1, 2$.

E8.5.2 Compute the derivative of the sigmoid function $\sigma'(t)$ for the following values of t: $1, -1, 2$.

E8.5.3 Given the vector $\mathbf{z} = (1, -1, 2)$, compute $\sigma(\mathbf{z})$ and $\sigma'(\mathbf{z})$.

E8.5.4 Given the matrix $W = \begin{pmatrix} 1 & -1 \\ 2 & 0 \end{pmatrix}$ and the vector $\mathbf{x} = (1, 2)$, compute $\sigma(W\mathbf{x})$.

E8.5.5 Given the matrix $W = \begin{pmatrix} 1 & -1 \\ 2 & 0 \end{pmatrix}$ and the vector $\mathbf{x} = (1, 2)$, compute the Jacobian matrix of $\sigma(W\mathbf{x})$.

E8.5.6 Given the vectors $\mathbf{y} = (0, 1)$ and $\mathbf{z} = (0.3, 0.7)$, compute the cross-entropy loss $H(\mathbf{y}, \mathbf{z})$.

E8.5.7 Given the vectors $\mathbf{y} = (0, 1)$ and $\mathbf{z} = (0.3, 0.7)$, compute the gradient of the cross-entropy loss $\nabla H(\mathbf{y}, \mathbf{z})$.

E8.5.8 Given the vectors $\mathbf{w} = (1, 2, -1, 0)$ and $\mathbf{z} = (1, 2)$, compute $\mathbb{A}_2[\mathbf{w}]$ and $\mathbb{B}_2[\mathbf{z}]$.

8.6.2 Problems

8.1 Consider the affine map

$$\mathbf{f}(\mathbf{x}) = A\mathbf{x} + \mathbf{b},$$

where $A \in \mathbb{R}^{m \times d}$ and $\mathbf{b} = (b_1, \ldots, b_m) \in \mathbb{R}^m$. Let $S \subseteq \mathbb{R}^m$ be a convex set. Show that the following set is convex:

$$T = \{\mathbf{x} \in \mathbb{R}^d : \mathbf{f}(\mathbf{x}) \in S\}.$$

8.2 (Adapted from [Khu]) Consider the vector-valued function $\mathbf{f} = (f_1, \ldots, f_d) : \mathbb{R}^d \to \mathbb{R}^d$ defined as

$$f_i(\mathbf{x}) = x_i^3,$$

for all $\mathbf{x} \in \mathbb{R}^d$ and all $i = 1, \ldots, d$.

a) Compute the Jacobian $J_{\mathbf{f}}(\mathbf{x})$ for all $\mathbf{x}$.

b) When is $J_{\mathbf{f}}(\mathbf{x})$ invertible?

c) When is $J_{\mathbf{f}}(\mathbf{x})$ positive semidefinite?

8.3 Let $A = (a_{i,j})_{i,j=1}^n \in \mathbb{R}^{n \times n}$ be a symmetric matrix.

a) Let $\mathbf{v} = (v_1, \ldots, v_n) \in \mathbb{R}^n$ be an eigenvector of A with eigenvalue λ. Let v_i be the largest element of $\mathbf{v}$ in absolute value; that is, $i \in \arg\max_j |v_j|$. Define the vector $\mathbf{w} = (w_1, \ldots, w_n)$ as

$$w_j = \frac{v_j}{v_i}, \quad j = 1, \ldots, n.$$

Show that

$$\lambda - a_{i,i} = \sum_{j \neq i} a_{i,j} w_j.$$

b) Use a) to show that, for any eigenvalue λ of A, there is i such that
$$|\lambda - a_{i,i}| \leq \sum_{j \neq i} |a_{i,j}|.$$

8.4 A symmetric matrix $A = (a_{i,j})_{i,j=1}^{n} \in \mathbb{R}^{n \times n}$ with nonnegative elements on its diagonal is said to be diagonally dominant if for all i
$$a_{i,i} \geq \sum_{j \neq i} |a_{i,j}|,$$
that is, each diagonal element is greater than or equal to the sum of the absolute values of the other elements in its row. Use Problem 8.3 to prove that such a matrix is positive semidefinite.

8.5 Consider multinomial logistic regression. Let
$$R = I_{K \times K} \otimes \mathbf{x}^T,$$
and
$$S = \text{diag}(\boldsymbol{\gamma}(\mathbf{v})) - \boldsymbol{\gamma}(\mathbf{v})\boldsymbol{\gamma}(\mathbf{v})^T$$
where
$$\mathbf{v} = \boldsymbol{\gamma}(g_0(\mathbf{x}, \mathbf{w})).$$

a) Show that
$$\nabla f(\mathbf{w}) = \Gamma(\boldsymbol{\gamma}(g_0(\mathbf{x}, \mathbf{w})))$$
where
$$\Gamma(\mathbf{u}) = R(\mathbf{u} - \mathbf{y}).$$

b) Use the *Chain Rule* to show that
$$\mathbf{H}_f(\mathbf{w}) = R^T S R.$$

c) Use b) and the *Properties of the Kronecker Product Lemma* to show that
$$\mathbf{H}_f(\mathbf{w}) = \left(\text{diag}(\boldsymbol{\gamma}(\mathcal{W}\mathbf{x})) - \boldsymbol{\gamma}(\mathcal{W}\mathbf{x})\boldsymbol{\gamma}(\mathcal{W}\mathbf{x})^T \right) \otimes \mathbf{x}\mathbf{x}^T.$$

8.6 Consider multinomial logistic regression. Use Problems 8.4 and 8.5 to show that the objective function is convex. [*Hint:* It is enough to show that S (defined in Problem 8.5) is diagonally dominant. Why?]

8.7 Prove part (a) of the *Kronecker Product Properties Lemma*.

8.8 Prove part (b) of the *Kronecker Product Properties Lemma*.

8.9 Prove parts (c) and (d) of the *Kronecker Product Properties Lemma*.

8.10 Prove part (e) of the *Kronecker Product Properties Lemma*.

8.11 Let A and B be symmetric matrices of size $n \times n$ and $m \times m$ respectively.

a) Show that $A \otimes B$ is symmetric. [*Hint:* Use Problem 8.10.]

b) Compute the eigenvectors and eigenvalues of $A \otimes B$ in terms of the eigenvectors and eigenvalues of A and B. [*Hint:* Try the Kronecker products of eigenvectors of A and B.]

c) Recall that the determinant of a symmetric matrix is the product of its eigenvalues. Show that
$$\det(A \otimes B) = \det(A)^n \det(B)^m.$$

8.12 Compute $\text{tr}(A \otimes B)$ in terms of $\text{tr}(A)$ and $\text{tr}(B)$. Justify your answer.

8.13 a) Show that if D_1 and D_2 are square diagonal matrices, then so is $D_1 \otimes D_2$.

b) Show that if Q_1 and Q_2 have orthonormal columns, so does $Q_1 \otimes Q_2$.

8.14 Let $A_1 = U_1 \Sigma_1 V_1^T$ and $A_2 = U_2 \Sigma_2 V_2^T$ be full SVDs of $A_1, A_2 \in \mathbb{R}^{n \times n}$ respectively.

a) Compute a full SVD of $A_1 \otimes A_2$. [*Hint:* Use Problem 8.13.]

b) Show that the rank of $A_1 \otimes A_2$ is $\text{rk}(A_1) \text{rk}(A_2)$.

8.15 Let P_1 and P_2 be transition matrices.

a) Let π_1 and π_2 (as row vectors) be stationary distributions of P_1 and P_2 respectively. Show that $\pi_1 \otimes \pi_2$ is a stationary distribution of $P_1 \otimes P_2$.

b) Assume that P_1 and P_2 are both irreducible and lazy. Show that the same holds for $P_1 \otimes P_2$.

8.16 Let **u** be a column vector and A, B be matrices of dimensions such that one can form the matrix product AB.

a) Let $\mathbf{a}_1^T, \ldots, \mathbf{a}_n^T$ be the rows of A. Prove that

$$A \otimes \mathbf{u} = \begin{pmatrix} \mathbf{u}\mathbf{a}_1^T \\ \vdots \\ \mathbf{u}\mathbf{a}_n^T \end{pmatrix}.$$

b) Prove part (f) of the *Kronecker Product Properties Lemma*.

8.17 Prove the *Composition of Continuous Functions Lemma*.

8.18 Consider the map $X\mathbf{z}$ as a function of the entries of the matrix $X \in \mathbb{R}^{n \times m}$. Specifically, for a fixed $\mathbf{z} \in \mathbb{R}^m$, letting $(\mathbf{x}^{(i)})^T$ be the i-th row of X we define the function

$$\mathbf{f}(\mathbf{x}) = X\mathbf{z} = \begin{pmatrix} (\mathbf{x}^{(1)})^T \mathbf{z} \\ \vdots \\ (\mathbf{x}^{(n)})^T \mathbf{z} \end{pmatrix}$$

where $\mathbf{x} = \text{vec}(X^T) = (\mathbf{x}^{(1)}, \ldots, \mathbf{x}^{(n)})$. Show that $\mathbf{f}$ is linear in $\mathbf{x}$, that is, $\mathbf{f}(\mathbf{x} + \mathbf{x}') = \mathbf{f}(\mathbf{x}) + \mathbf{f}(\mathbf{x}')$.

8.19 Let $f(x_1, x_2) = \sin(x_1^2 + x_2) + \cos(x_1 x_2)$. Compute the gradient of f using the *Chain Rule* by defining appropriate functions **g** and h such that $f = h \circ \mathbf{g}$.

8.20 Consider the function $f(x_1, x_2, x_3) = \sqrt{x_1 + x_2^2 + \exp(x_3)}$. Find the gradient of f at the point $(1, 2, 0)$ using the *Chain Rule* by defining suitable functions **g** and h such that $f = h \circ \mathbf{g}$.

8.21 Consider the function $f(x_1, x_2, x_3) = (x_1 + x_2^2)^3 + \sin(x_2 x_3)$. Find the gradient of f using the *Chain Rule* by defining suitable functions **g** and h such that $f = h \circ \mathbf{g}$.

8.22 For $i = 1, \ldots, n$, let $f_i \colon D_i \to \mathbb{R}$, with $D_i \subseteq \mathbb{R}$, be a continuously differentiable real-valued function of a single variable. Consider the vector-valued function $\mathbf{f} \colon D_1 \times \cdots \times D_n \to \mathbb{R}^n$ defined as

$$\mathbf{f}(\mathbf{x}) = (f_1(\mathbf{x}), \ldots, f_n(\mathbf{x})) = (f_1(x_1), \ldots, f_n(x_n)).$$

For $\mathbf{x} = (x_1, \ldots, x_n)$ such that x_i is an interior point of D_i for all i, compute the Jacobian $J_{\mathbf{f}}(\mathbf{x})$.

8.23 Let f be a real-valued function taking a matrix $A = (a_{i,j})_{i,j} \in \mathbb{R}^{n \times n}$ as an input. Assume f is continuously differentiable in each entry of A. Consider the following matrix derivative

$$\frac{\partial f(A)}{\partial A} = \begin{pmatrix} \frac{\partial f(A)}{\partial a_{1,1}} & \cdots & \frac{\partial f(A)}{\partial a_{1,n}} \\ \vdots & \ddots & \vdots \\ \frac{\partial f(A)}{\partial a_{n,1}} & \cdots & \frac{\partial f(A)}{\partial a_{n,n}} \end{pmatrix}.$$

a) Show that, for any $B \in \mathbb{R}^{n \times n}$,

$$\frac{\partial \operatorname{tr}(B^T A)}{\partial A} = B.$$

b) Show that, for any $\mathbf{x}, \mathbf{y} \in \mathbb{R}^d$,

$$\frac{\partial \mathbf{x}^T A \mathbf{y}}{\partial A} = \mathbf{x} \mathbf{y}^T.$$

8.24 Let $A = (a_{i,j})_{i \in [n], j \in [m]} \in \mathbb{R}^{n \times m}$ and $B = (b_{i,j})_{i \in [p], j \in [q]} \in \mathbb{R}^{p \times q}$ be arbitrary matrices. Their Kronecker product, denoted $A \otimes B \in \mathbb{R}^{np \times mq}$, is the following matrix in block form:

$$A \otimes B = \begin{pmatrix} a_{1,1}B & \cdots & a_{1,m}B \\ \vdots & \ddots & \vdots \\ a_{n,1}B & \cdots & a_{n,m}B \end{pmatrix}.$$

The Kronecker product satisfies the following properties (which follow from block formulas, but which you do not have to prove): 1) if A, B, C, D are matrices of dimensions such that one can form the matrix products AC and BD, then $(A \otimes B)(C \otimes D) = (AC) \otimes (BD)$; 2) the transpose of $A \otimes B$ is $(A \otimes B)^T = A^T \otimes B^T$.

a) Show that if D_1 and D_2 are square diagonal matrices, then so is $D_1 \otimes D_2$.

b) Show that if Q_1 and Q_2 have orthonormal columns, so does $Q_1 \otimes Q_2$.

c) Let $A_1 = U_1 \Sigma_1 V_1^T$ and $A_2 = U_2 \Sigma_2 V_2^T$ be full SVDs of $A_1, A_2 \in \mathbb{R}^{n \times n}$ respectively. Compute a full SVD of $A_1 \otimes A_2$.

d) Let A_1 and A_2 be as in c). Show that the rank of $A_1 \otimes A_2$ is $\operatorname{rk}(A_1) \operatorname{rk}(A_2)$.

References

[ASV] David F. Anderson, Timo Seppäläinen, and Benedek Valkó. *Introduction to Probability*. Cambridge University Press, Cambridge, 2017.

[Axl] Sheldon Axler. *Linear Algebra Done Right*. Springer, New York, 3rd edition, 2015.

[BHK] Avrim Blum, John Hopcroft, and Ravindran Kannan. *Foundations of Data Science*. Cambridge University Press, Cambridge, 2020.

[Bis] Christopher M. Bishop. *Pattern Recognition and Machine Learning*. Springer, New York, 2006.

[BV1] Stephen Boyd and Lieven Vandenberghe. *Convex Optimization*. Cambridge University Press, Cambridge, 2004.

[BV2] Stephen Boyd and Lieven Vandenberghe. *Introduction to Applied Linear Algebra: Vectors, Matrices, and Least Squares*. Cambridge University Press, Cambridge, 2018.

[HTF] Trevor Hastie, Robert Tibshirani, and Jerome Friedman. *The Elements of Statistical Learning: Data Mining, Inference, and Prediction*. Springer, New York, 2nd edition, 2009.

[HH] Susan Holmes and Wolfgang Huber. *Modern Statistics for Modern Biology*. Cambridge University Press, Cambridge, 2019.

[JWH+] Gareth James, Daniela Witten, Trevor Hastie, Robert Tibshirani, and Maxwell Taylor. *An Introduction to Statistical Learning: With Applications in Python*. Springer, New York, 2nd edition, 2023.

[Khu] André I. Khuri. *Advanced Calculus with Applications in Statistics*. Wiley, Hoboken, NJ, 2nd edition, 2006.

[LGN] Stephanie Lau, Joey Gonzalez, and Deborah Nolan. *Learning Data Science: Modeling and Algorithms*. O'Reilly, Sebastopol, CA, 2023.

[Mur1] Kevin P. Murphy. *Machine Learning: A Probabilistic Perspective*. MIT Press, Cambridge, MA, 2012.

[Mur2] Kevin P. Murphy. *Probabilistic Machine Learning: An Introduction*. MIT Press, Cambridge, MA, 2022.

[Mur3] Kevin P. Murphy. *Probabilistic Machine Learning: Advanced Topics*. MIT Press, Cambridge, MA, 2023.

[Nor] James R. Norris. *Markov Chains*. Cambridge University Press, Cambridge, 1998.

[Rud] Walter Rudin. *Principles of Mathematical Analysis*. McGraw-Hill, New York, 1976.

[Sol] Jon Solomon. *Numerical Algorithms: Methods for Computer Vision, Machine Learning, and Graphics*. CRC Press, Boca Raton, FL, 2015.

[Ste] William J. Stewart. *Introduction to the Numerical Solution of Markov Chains*. Princeton University Press, Princeton, NJ, 1994.

[Str] Gilbert Strang. *Linear Algebra and Learning from Data*. Wellesley-Cambridge Press, Wellesley, MA, 2019.

[TB] Lloyd N. Trefethen and David Bau, III. *Numerical Linear Algebra*. Society for Industrial and Applied Mathematics, Philadelphia, 1997.

[WR] Stephen J. Wright and Benjamin Recht. *Optimization for Data Analysis*. Cambridge University Press, Cambridge, 2022.

Index

2-norm, 247

absolute homogeneity, 7
activation function, 542
adjacency matrix, 279, 281
adjacent, 270
"affine functions are convex" lemma, 159
algebraic connectivity, 296
aperiodic, 446
automatic differentiation, 505

back substitution, 102
backpropagation, 524
basis, 77
Bayes' rule, 362
Bernoulli, 343
best approximating subspace problem, 217
"best subspace as maximimization" lemma, 217
"best subspace in matrix form" lemma, 218
bias variable, 543
bivariate Gaussian, 345
bivariate normal, 345
block matrix, 12

categorical, 344
Cauchy–Schwarz inequality, 6, 85
centroid, 37
chain, 367
chain rule, 135, 503
characterization of positive semidefiniteness, 213
Chebyshev's inequality, 22, 23
Cheeger constant, 304
Cheeger's inequality, 305
classification, 129
clique, 272
closed set, 14
clustering, 34
collider, 368
column space, 74
communicate, 277
communication lemma, 436
"completing an independent list" lemma, 78, 80
"composing with a nondecreasing function" lemma, 37
"composition of continuous functions" lemma, 503
concave function, 159
conditional, 400
conditional expectation, 363
conditional independence, 364

conditional probability, 362
conditional probability mass function, 363
connected component, 271
constrained optimization, 150
continuous function, 15
convergence analysis, 173, 381
convergence of gradient descent in the smooth case, 175
convergence of gradient descent in the strongly convex case, 177
convergence of k-means cost theorem, 42
convergence to equilibrium theorem, 447
convex function, 159, 213
convex set, 157
convexity of logistic regression, 183
correctness of Metropolis–Hastings, 472
Courant–Fischer theorem, 291, 292, 299
covariance, 24
covariance of a linear transformation, 29
cross-entropy, 544
cross-entropy loss, 181
cumulative distribution function, 27
curse of dimensionality, 56, 70
cut, 304
cut ratio, 304
cutset, 304
cycle, 271

degree, 270
degree centrality, 460
degree matrix, 283
derivative, 15
descent direction, 21
"descent direction and directional derivative" lemma, 142
descent direction lemma, 15, 21, 142
descent guarantee in the smooth case, 175
determinant, 344
diagonal matrix, 10, 208
diffentiable, 499
differential, 499
differential and Jacobian theorem, 500
dimension theorem, 78, 80
directed acyclic graph, 277
directed cycle, 276
directed graph, 276
directed path, 276
directional derivative, 140
directional derivative and gradient theorem, 141

Dirichlet, 348
discriminative model, 369
distribution of a sample path, 427

Eckart–Young theorem, 251
eigenvalue, 207
eigenvector, 207
EM algorithm, 382
EM guarantee, 384
energy-based model, 475
entropy, 352
equivalent definition of linear independence, 76
Erdős–Rényi random graph, 316
ergodic theorem, 448
Euclidean distance, 7
Euclidean norm, 6
existence of an SVD, 223
existence of stationary distribution, 439
exponential family, 343
extreme value theorem, 15

Fiedler vector, 296
first-order convexity condition, 161
first-order feasible directions, 152
first-order necessary optimality condition, 20, 21, 143
first-order optimality condition for convex functions on convex sets, 164
first-order optimality condition for unconstrained convex functions, 164
forest, 272
fork, 367
forward mode, 512
forward substitution, 103
Frobenius norm, 13, 247
full column rank, 79
full QR decomposition, 101
full SVD, 226

Gaussian mixture model, 376
generalized linear model, 356
generative model, 369
Gibbs sampling, 473
Gibbs' inequality, 351
"global minimizer of a strongly convex function" theorem, 166
global minimizer or maximizer, 18, 151
"global minimizers of a convex function" theorem, 163
gradient, 21, 133
gradient descent, 171
Gram–Schmidt algorithm, 97
Gram–Schmidt theorem, 88
graph, 269
graph distance, 271
graph drawing, 294
greedy algorithm, 219
"greedy finds best subspace" theorem, 220

Hadamard division, 497
Hadamard product, 497
handshaking lemma, 270

Hastings correction, 469
Hessian, 137
hidden layer, 542
high-dimensional cube theorem, 54
Householder lemma, 107
Householder reflection, 105
hyperplane, 105

identity matrix, 10
incidence matrix, 280, 281
incident, 270
in-degree, 276
independence, 23
"independent is shorter than spanning" lemma, 78, 80
"infimum over a convex set" lemma, 160
inhomogeneous Erdős–Rényi random graph, 316
initial distribution, 427
inner product, 6
input layer, 543
inverse transform sampling method, 27
invertibility lemma, 81
invertibility of positive definite matrices, 398
invertible matrix, 81
"inverting a block matrix" lemma, 397
"inverting a nonsingular system" theorem, 81
"inverting the order of eigenvalues" lemma, 311
irreducibility, 438
irreducibility lemma, 452
isolated, 270
isoperimetric number, 304

Jacobian, 500

Kalman filter, 405
Kalman gain matrix, 407
Kronecker product, 497
Kullback–Liebler divergence, 351
k-means objective, 34
k-NN regression, 69

L2-regularization, 256
ℓ_p-norm, 7
Lagrange multipliers, 151
Lagrange multipliers theorem, 151
Laplace smoothing, 372
Laplacian and connectivity lemma, 296
Laplacian and incidence lemma, 284
Laplacian and maximum degree lemma, 296
Laplacian matrix, 283
Laplacian quadratic form lemma, 295
law of total expectation, 363
law of total probability, 362
layer, 542
lazy, 447
learning rate, 171
least-squares problem, 94, 169
least squares via QR, 104
linear dependence lemma, 79
linear independence, 75
linear regression, 112, 358

linear subspace, 71
linear-Gaussian system, 401
linear-Gaussian system lemma, 402
Lloyd's algorithm, 39, 382
local minimizer or maximizer, 20, 151
log-partition function, 343
log-sum-exp trick, 390
logistic regression, 180, 359, 530
low-rank approximation, 250
"low-rank approximation in the induced norm" theorem, 252

majorization-minimization, 380
majorization-minimization lemma, 381
Majorize-Minimization, 175
marginal, 400
Markov chain, 425
Markov chain Monte Carlo, 468
Markov property, 426
Markov's inequality, 22
matrix norm, 13
"matrix norms and singular values" lemma, 249
maximum likelihood, 349
maximum likelihood estimator for exponential families, 353
mean centering, 238
mean value theorem, 16, 136
Metropolis–Hastings, 469
minimum of a quadratic function, 35
mixture, 375
mixture of spherical Gaussians, 31
"MLE via KL" theorem, 351
multicollinearity, 256
multilayer perceptron, 542
multinomial, 344
multinomial logistic regression, 533
multiplication rule, 362
multivariate Gaussian, 345, 399
multivariate normal, 345, 399

naive Bayes, 369
negative log-likelihood, 349
neighborhood, 270
neural network, 542
node centrality, 454
nonsingular matrix, 80
norm, 7
normal equations, 95, 169
normal or Gaussian distribution, 30
NP-hardness, 35, 308
null space, 74
"number of eigenvalues" lemma, 207

one-hot encoding, 344, 533
open set, 14
operations that preserve convexity, 159
optimal clustering lemma, 38
optimal representatives lemma, 37
"optimizing a separable function" lemma, 36
oriented incidence matrix, 281

orthogonal complement, 93
orthogonal decomposition lemma, 93
orthogonal matrix, 93
orthogonal projection on an orthonormal list, 89
orthogonal projection theorem, 89
orthogonality, 85
orthonormal expansion theorem, 86
out-degree, 276
outer product, 206, 498
output layer, 543
overfitting, 117
overflow, 372

PageRank, 454, 459
parametric family, 343
partial derivative, 21
partition, 34, 362
partition function, 343, 475
path, 271
permutation, 308
Personalized PageRank, 463
Petersen graph, 270
point-separating property, 7
polynomial regression, 115
positive definite matrix, 213
positive semidefinite matrix, 14, 213
positive semidefiniteness of the covariance, 28
power iteration lemma, 231, 233
principal components analysis, 238
principal submatrices lemma, 398
probability density function, 21
probability mass function, 21
progressive function, 522, 542
projection and rank-k approximation lemma, 250
properties of orthonormal lists, 86
properties of the Hadamard product, 497
properties of the Kronecker Product, 498
properties of the Laplacian theorem, 283
pseudorandom number generator, 348
Pythagoras' theorem, 85

QR decomposition, 100
quadratic bound for smooth functions, 174
quadratic bound for strongly convex functions, 166
quadratic form, 14
quadratic form and Frobenius norm lemma, 149

random walk on a graph, 451, 452
rank, 79, 202
rank-nullity theorem, 205
Rayleigh quotient, 143, 289
"reducing a spanning list" lemma, 78
regular, 270
"relating a function and its gradient" lemma, 177
residual sum of squares, 113
residuals, 113
restricted Boltzmann machine, 475
reverse mode, 513
reversibility and stationarity theorem, 453
reversible, 453

ridge regression, 256
"role of independence" lemma, 365
Rolle's theorem, 16
"row rank equals column rank" theorem, 79, 202
row space, 79

scatter plot, 3
Schur complement, 396
Schur complement lemma, 399
second directional derivative, 146
second directional derivative and Hessian theorem, 146
second partial derivatives, 137
second-order convexity condition, 162, 163
second-order necessary optimality condition, 147
second-order sufficient optimality condition, 149
self-loop, 276, 447
sigmoid, 542
sigmoid function, 180
similar, 211
single-nucleotide polymorphism, 201
singular value, 223
singular value decomposition, 223
singular vector, 223
smooth function, 174
softmax, 533
span, 73
spanning subgraph, 272
spectral decomposition, 210
spectral theorem, 210, 286
spherical Gaussian, 30
stationarity lemma, 435
stationary distribution, 435
stationary distribution on a graph, 453
stationary point, 143
statistical consistency, 356
steepest descent lemma, 170
step size, 171
stochastic gradient descent, 529
stochastic matrix, 428
stochastic process, 401, 425

stricltly convex function, 159
strongly connected, 277
strongly connected component, 277
strongly convex function, 166
subgraph, 272
supervised learning, 132
SVD and rank lemma, 224
SVD relations, 226
SVD via spectral decomposition, 223
symmetric matrix, 9
symmetry of the Hessian, 137

Taylor's theorem, 17, 144, 145
tensor, 506
Tikhonov regularization, 256
time marginals theorem, 429
time-homogeneous process, 428
topological order, 366
total derivative, 136
trace, 344
transition graph, 431
transition matrix, 428
transition matrix in terms of adjacency, 452
"transition matrix is stochastic" theorem, 428
transition probability, 427
transpose, 9
tree, 272
triangle inequality, 7
triangular matrix, 101

underflow, 371
undirected graph, 269

variance, 22
variance of a sum, 24
variational characterization of the algebraic connectivity, 299

weak law of large numbers, 25
"why project" theorem, 254

For EU product safety concerns, contact us at Calle de José Abascal, 56–1°, 28003 Madrid, Spain or eugpsr@cambridge.org.